P9-DGZ-827

EX LIBRIS
SCIENTIA
HUMANITAS
RELIGIO
UNIVERSITATIS SANCTI JOANNIS

AMERICAN PICTUREBOOKS
from Noah's Ark to the Beast Within

AMERICAN from Noah's Ark

PICTUREBOOKS to the Beast Within

by BARBARA BADER

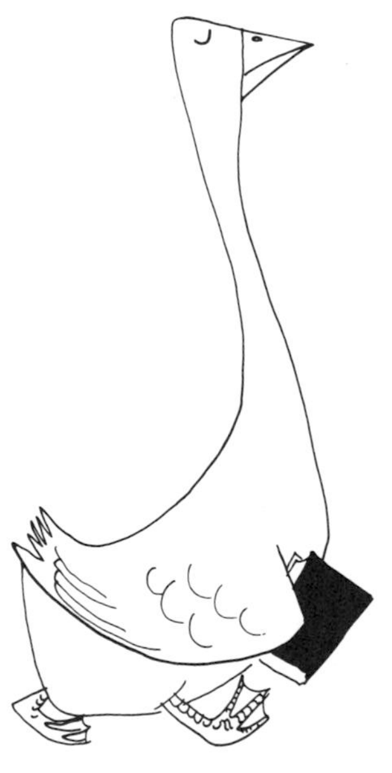

MACMILLAN PUBLISHING CO., INC.
New York
COLLIER MACMILLAN PUBLISHERS
London

The author would like to take special note of the invaluable contribution of Barbara Hall in designing the book.

Macmillan Publishing Co., Inc., 866 Third Avenue, New York, N.Y. 10022
Collier Macmillan Canada, Ltd.
Printed in the United States of America
10 9 8 7 6 5 4 3 2 1

Library of Congress Cataloging in Publication Data

Bader, Barbara. American picturebooks from Noah's ark to the beast within.
Bibliography: p. Includes index.
1. Illustrated books, Children's—History and criticism.
2. Illustrators, American. 3. Picture books for children.
4. Children's literature, American—History and criticism. I. Title.
NC965.B32 741.6'42 72–93304 ISBN 0–02–708080–3

The drawing on the title page is from *Petunia*, Roger Duvoisin (Knopf, 1950); the drawing on p. vi is from *Lion*, William Pène du Bois (Viking, 1956).

ACKNOWLEDGMENTS

The subject of this book is the development of picturebooks. It is not about prize winners or best-sellers, although books of both sorts are included. Rather it is based upon an attempt to identify all the picturebooks published; to examine as many as possible; and, in certain instances, to learn of the circumstances of their publication. Without the assistance of a great many persons, such an investigation could not have been carried through, and I would like to express my thanks to them.

To the editors, the promotion managers and their aides at the various publishing houses who provided access to the books and to information about them.

To the authors and artists and members of their families, the art directors, agents and publishers who answered specific queries and generously volunteered more than was asked: Peggy Bacon, H. M. Benstead, Eunice Blake, Dr. Mary Steichen Calderone, Ann Nolan Clark, Ingri and Edgar Parin d'Aulaire, Babette Deutsch, Sarah d'Harnoncourt, Annis Duff, Naomi Averill Elliot, Marie Hall Ets, Josette Frank, Don Freeman, Flavia Gág, Tibor Gergely, Milton Glick, Berta Hader, Clement Hurd, Edith Thacher Hurd, Vernon Ives, Abe Lerner, Dr. Robert Leslie, Albert Leventhal, Dorothy Markinko, Constance Morrow Morgan, Elizabeth Morton, Adele Gutman Nathan, Roberta Rauch, Esther Reno, Elizabeth Riley, Nina Rojankovsky, Richard Rostron, Hilda Scott, Evelyn Young Shaw, Donald Stevenson, Ellen Tarry, Dorothy Waugh, Matilda Welter, and the late Kurt Wiese.

To the libraries and other institutions that made special material available, and especially to the following individuals: Augusta Baker, Aileen Murphy and Naomi Noyes, of the New York Public Library; Angeline Moscatt, of the Central Children's Room, New York Public Library; Karen Nelson, of the Kerlan Collection, University of Minnesota; Anna Durovich, formerly of the Bureau of Indian Affairs, Department of the Interior; Harriet Morris, of the Department of Prints, Drawings and Photographs, Philadelphia Museum of Art; Jack Rau, formerly of the American Institute of Graphic Arts; Roberta Wong, formerly of the Department of Prints and Photographs, Metropolitan Museum of Art; Virginia Haviland, of the Library of Congress; and the staff of *The Horn Book*.

Special thanks for the loan of books not otherwise available are due to many of those cited elsewhere and also to the following: Margaret Bevans, Claire Huchet Bishop, Malcolm Collier, Caroline and Chester Rice, Justin Schiller, Millicent Selsam, and George Zaffo.

With respect to the book itself, I am indebted to Susan Hirschman and Ada Shearon for editorial assistance, and to the staff at Macmillan for their cooperation and good will.

Lastly, I am deeply grateful to those long concerned with the creation of picturebooks who shared their experience and their understanding with me: Esther Averill, Louise Seaman Bechtel, Morris Colman, Beatrice Creighton, Roger Duvoisin, John G. McCullough, Ursula Nordstrom, Lucille Ogle, and William R. Scott.

CONTENTS

STARTING POINTS 2

E. BOYD SMITH 13

THE ERRATIC, ECLECTIC TWENTIES 23

WANDA GÁG 32

FOREIGN BACKGROUNDS 38
The Petershams 38, the d'Aulaires 42, *The Painted Pig* and other Latin Americana 46, Bemelmans 47, Françoise 52, books out of Africa and Asia 56, Politi and the persistence of things foreign 58

THE DYNAMICS AND FUN OF THE FORM 60
Marjorie Flack 61, Kurt Wiese 65, *The Hole in the Wall* 68, Dorothy Kunhardt 71

THE SMALL CHILD'S WORLD 73

HELEN SEWELL 81

INFORMATION 88

PHOTOGRAPHIC BOOKS 100

IMPORTED FROM FRANCE 118
The Domino Press, the Artists and Writers Guild, the first of Rojankovsky

ROGER DUVOISIN 128

THE AMERICAN LINE 140
Ellis Credle 141, Robert Lawson 143, Glen Rounds 147, James Daugherty 151, Robert McCloskey 154

OF THE AMERICAN INDIAN 158

TWO MASTERS: MARIE HALL ETS AND WILLIAM PENE DU BOIS 167

SUI GENERIS: *SEVEN SIMEONS* AND *BUTTONS* 187

THE STORYTELLERS 199
Virginia Lee Burton 199, Hardie Gramatky 203, H. A. Rey 204, Don Freeman 206, Bill Peet 209

DESIGNED FOR CHILDREN 212
Holiday House 212, William R. Scott, Inc. 214, Cloth Books and Toy Books 235

THE EMOTIONAL ELEMENT 241
Harper and the most of Margaret Wise Brown

JEAN CHARLOT 265

GOLDEN BOOKS 277
and Rojankovsky concluded 295

DR. SEUSS 302

MARCIA BROWN 313

EXPANDING POSSIBILITIES: EASTER, FOR INSTANCE 323

NEW LOOKS 332
Nicolas Mordvinoff 333, Paul Rand 338, Antonio Frasconi 343, Joseph Low 346, Juliet Kepes 350

SOCIAL CHANGE 364

NEGRO IDENTIFICATION, BLACK IDENTITY 373

MORE INFORMATION 383

RUTH KRAUSS; RUTH KRAUSS AND MAURICE SENDAK 416

CROCKETT JOHNSON 434

THE JAPANESE ADVENT 443
and Blair Lent

FEELINGS EXTENDED 459
Charlotte Zolotow 464, Gene Zion and Margaret Bloy Graham 466, *A Tree Is Nice* 470, Russell Hoban and Lillian Hoban 472, *Rain Makes Applesauce* 478, Bernard Waber 480

. . . AND A FEW ENDEARMENTS 485
All Kinds of Time 485, Mary Chalmers 487, Palmer Brown 492

MAURICE SENDAK 495

AWAY FROM WORDS 525
Leo Lionni 525, Remy Charlip 530, *Nothing Ever Happens on My Block* 538, Wordless Books 539

THE FABULISTS 544
Tomi Ungerer 544, Edward Gorey 552, Harriet Pincus 559, William Steig 563, Margot Zemach 565

NOTES 573

BIBLIOGRAPHY 581

INDEX 592

The place of publication can be assumed to be New York unless another is given.
Statements enclosed in single quotes are paraphrased.

A picturebook is text, illustrations, total design; an item of manufacture and a commercial product; a social, cultural, historical document; and, foremost, an experience for a child.

As an art form it hinges on the interdependence of pictures and words, on the simultaneous display of two facing pages, and on the drama of the turning of the page.

On its own terms its possibilities are limitless.

Overleaf: The drawings are from *Selections from Feng Tse-kai's Drawings of Children* (Peking, Foreign Languages Press, 1956); *Dreams of Glory and Other Drawings*, William Steig (Knopf, 1952); and *The Thurber Carnival*, James Thurber (Harper, 1945).

STARTING POINTS

Why picturebooks for children? It is easy to say that children who haven't yet learned to read enjoy looking at pictures and learn from them, and it is true as far as it goes; so do adults who can't read or don't, so do we all on occasion.

Early on, a child's understanding outstrips his vocabulary. He recognizes things before he can name them but until he can name them he doesn't really *know* them, hence his satisfaction in pictures of the commonplace—a dog, a cup, a flower—that help him master words and so extend his power. We can also say that they confirm his existence: a cup is not only a cup, it's Janey's cup or Billy's cup. If the cup is on a table, and a family sits down to breakfast, a story begins—to Janey and Billy, the story of their day, a story of themselves that they can see for themselves, that with the fewest of words they can picture. Even as a child comes to learn words, he continues for some time to think in images: the object or action is embodied in the word.

His fantasies are composed of images also, whether he is play-acting

or daydreaming, fancying himself a conquering hero;

they are plainly composed of images when they involve a transformation

or some other sort of visual metaphor, the equivalent of poetry's silent woods, nightingales and frigates. Visual associations or schemes, not logical reasoning, govern the course of a fantasy too; put into pictures, the sequence is self-evident.

Fantasy, of course, proceeds from feeling, and feelings, whether turned inward or outward, are notoriously resistant to words. "Every feeling waits upon its gesture," Eudora Welty has written, and the more so for children who lack the exact word or phrase—if there is one—for each intention or response. Pictures supply the gestures, they define the person, and in diverse ways they draw the distinctions that writing for adults tries to draw in words.

Not the least, for a child limited in his experience of the world, they furnish a context—the circumstances are immediately apparent. In reverse, we have John Holt's observation: "Words are not only a clumsy and ambiguous means of communication, they are extraordinarily slow. To describe only a very small part of his understanding of the world, a man will write a book that takes us days to read." This, as much as impact, is the meaning of the old saw, one picture is worth a thousand words, and we will see it illustrated many times over, beginning with Walter Crane's *Bluebeard* (1).

1. *Bluebeard*, pictures by Walter Crane. London, Routledge, 1873? 7⅜ x 9¾.

Knowing the story, we can see what's afoot: *Aha, he's going off and giving her the keys, telling her not this one, now the trouble will start.* It is in his raised eyebrow, his admonishing forefinger, her apparent submission—but what of the groom looking over his shoulder, does he know? or suspect? And see how grandly they live; no wonder she married him!

A child lingers over pictures and returns to them not simply because through them he can reconstruct the story but because he takes pleasure in the 'what' and the 'how' (in the same way that we reread books whose plots we know for other pleasures). Narration, then, is only the beginning of communication and art, as such, is the least of it.

But a curious thing happened to picturebooks toward the end of the nineteenth century: they became artistic. In England, Edmund Evans printed the books of Walter Crane, Randolph Caldecott and Kate Greenaway in color from woodblocks and printed them beautifully, not only cutting into the market for cheap chromos but creating a new market for picturebooks altogether. Though color was the key, under Evans's guidance the books were designed as a unit from cover to cover and illustrated with an eye to the means of reproduction, simply and directly, in pure flat colors. Crane, an innate designer, set the standard with his first toy-books; Caldecott, the livelier illustrator (2), continued the toybooks and made them more pictorial, expanding a line of text into a sequence of action, a flat statement into high comedy; and Greenaway, with *Under the Window* (3), swept all of Europe, such was the charm of her demure, old-fashioned children, her tranquil lanes and cloudless skies. (What dark visions she had

2. *John Gilpin*, pictures by Randolph Caldecott. London, Routledge, 1878. 7⅞ x 9.

3. *Under the Window*, by Kate Greenaway. London, Routledge, 1878. 7⅜ x 9⅛.

were unwelcome, and disappeared after the first edition.)

Poor Dicky's dead!—The bell we toll,
And lay him in the deep, dark hole.
The sun may shine, the clouds may rain,
But Dick will never pipe again!
His quilt will be as sweet as ours,—
Bright buttercups and cuckoo flowers
KG
32

Hers are not new renderings of childhood classics like the *Bluebeard* of Crane or Caldecott's *John Gilpin* but books of her own devising, about children, and as such an example to others—most immediately to Maurice Boutet de Monvel. Putting their songs into pictures (*Vieilles Chansons et Rondes, Chansons de France*) or making light of their manners (*La Civilité Puérile et Honnête*), he takes them as they come, good and bad; but in the illustrations for Anatole France's *Nos Enfants* and *Filles et Garçons* they are individuals, preoccupied with the business of living, and while we smile at them in recognition we respect their seriousness (4).

Then came *Jeanne d'Arc*, simple and dramatic and majestic, so exactly observant that a crowd remains a congregation of persons, so astutely composed—stage-managed, really—that the eye is constantly drawn back to the still center (5). You are there, in the trite phrase, watching from a high doorstep, seen in turn (the woman at lower left), looking now at the flaming torches, the jostling figures, the gleaming helmets, now at the cause of the agitation, calm and grave, now and again at the horseman behind her, remote and, for all that he holds the standard, detached from the scene.

When he took up illustration, Boutet de Monvel testifies, "I was obliged always to study the difficulties of reproduction, to do something that would come out well when printed. Of course, I found out directly that I could not put in the mass of little things which I had elaborated on my canvases. Gradually, through a process of elimination and selection, I came to put in only what was necessary to give the character."[1] In his color work he allowed little shadow, and the resulting combination of unaccented outline and flat tone was called Japanese; but printing by lithography* yielded thin, soft colors—"the suggestion, the impression of color,"[2] the artist called it—and the effect was different from that produced by woodblocks, whether in Evans's work or the woodcuts of the Japanese.

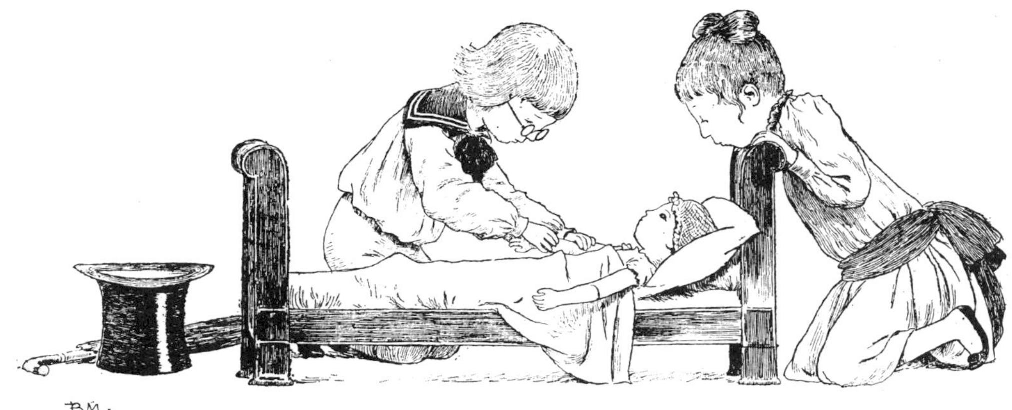

4. *Filles et Garçons,* text by Anatole France, pictures by Maurice Boutet de Monvel. Paris, Hachette, 1900. Detail.

5. *Jeanne d'Arc,* by Maurice Boutet de Monvel. Paris, Plon-Nourrit, 1896. 12½ x 9⅜.

Jeanne avait dit à Dunois, qui était venu au-devant d'elle : « Je vous amène le meilleur secours, le secours du Roi des cieux; il ne vient pas de moi, mais de Dieu même, qui, à la requête de saint Louis et de Charlemagne, a eu pitié de la ville d'Orléans. »

A huit heures du soir Jeanne entra dans Orléans. Le peuple se jeta au-devant d'elle. A la lueur des torches elle traversa la ville au milieu d'une foule si compacte qu'elle avait peine à se frayer passage. Tous, hommes, femmes, enfants, voulaient l'approcher ou au moins toucher son cheval, manifestant « si grande joie que s'ils eussent vu Dieu descendre parmi eux ». « Ils se sentaient, dit le journal du siège, réconfortés et comme désassiégés par la vertu divine de cette simple fille. » Jeanne leur parlait doucement, promettant de les délivrer.

15

While Crane, Caldecott and Greenaway had immediate and lasting success in the United States, Boutet de Monvel became the rage. Major articles about him appeared in *The Century, McClure's, Brush and Pencil, The Critic, Good Housekeeping, The Review of Reviews, Cosmopolitan*; he was commissioned to illustrate others and to write, for *The Century*, a separate longer history of Joan so that the pictures could be seen before the book's publication; exhibitions of his work toured widely in 1899, 1906–07 and 1921, and on the first occasion he accompanied the show, lecturing (in French) and painting children's portraits at the various stops. Meanwhile his books were appearing in translation: *Good Children and Bad* (Cassell) in 1890; La Fontaine's *Fables* (London, Society for Promoting Christian Knowledge, 1893), which was imported; *Joan of Arc* (Century) almost immediately, in 1897 (and again in 1907, 1912, 1916, 1918, 1923, 1926, 1931, sometimes from a different house and in a different form); and then in quick succession *Old Songs and Rounds* (Duffield, 1912), *Girls and Boys* (Duffield, 1913), *Our Children* (Duffield, 1917).[3]

6. *Johnny Crow's Garden*, by L. Leslie Brooke. London, Warne, 1903. 6¼ x 8.

7. *The Tale of Peter Rabbit*, by Beatrix Potter. London, Warne, 1903. 4 x 5¼.

No sudden spurt in American picturebooks resulted any more than it had from the smaller Crane-Caldecott-Greenaway conflagration. (The one consequential American in Boutet de Monvel's debt, E. Boyd Smith, lived long in France.) Rather, the opposite occurred: the artistic European book drove the homelier American product out of favor though not, immediately, out of the hands of children. Put another way, when the vivid McLoughlin Bros. toy-books—pamphlets, in paper, like Crane's—stood alone, they were little noted, but 'good' books made them look bad. And now there was someone to say officially what was good and bad, the children's librarian, spearhead of a movement to give children equal but separate treatment in libraries.

Why fuss—English prams, English picturebooks, French frocks, French picturebooks: what did it matter as long as children had the best? We were accustomed, in any case, to looking abroad for the best literature, the best music, the best art. Not until the close of

World War I, a time of national assertiveness, did the cry go up, why can't we have picture-books like theirs? By then it was too late; the Europeans had so far outdistanced us in color printing that, whatever the will, there was no way, not for another fifteen years.

Back to 1900 for a closer look. Though the McLoughlin books are doomed (to the disgust of one gentleman who vowed that 'had he the revenues of a multimillionaire, he would send the Messrs. McLoughlin each Christmas Day his personal cheque for ten thousand dollars'[4]), there is another threat in the form of the poster craze. "Such books as Denslow's Mother Goose . . . with a score of others of the comic poster order, should be banished from the sight of impressionable small children,"[5] wrote Anne Carroll Moore, then at the Pratt Institute Free Library, soon to organize children's work at the New York Public Library, and long to be "the yea or nay on all children's literature"[6] in America. On the other hand, Miss Moore greatly admired the work of Leslie Brooke which began to appear at this time, printed, as were the tales of his compatriot Beatrix Potter, by the new three- and four-color half-tone process, the ideal medium for watercolors (6, 7). Look at the Brooke and the Denslow (8), notice the similarity and the nature of the difference: Denslow's animals are no more caricatured than Brooke's, nothing about his interpretation is vulgar or malicious, where he differs from Brooke is in style.

Why then the aversion to his work which was almost universal among those professionally connected with children's books? The sway of the naturalistic aesthetic is the only possible explanation, the equation of artistic quality with the faithful representation of nature, and the consequent dismissal of anything else as 'primitive' or 'degenerate.' Denslow's figures prance about on the picture plane: there is no space, no 'atmosphere.' The contour lines are heavy, the interiors absolutely flat: the forms

8. *Animal Fair,* text adaptation and pictures by W. W. Denslow. G. W. Dillingham, 1904. 8½ x 11.

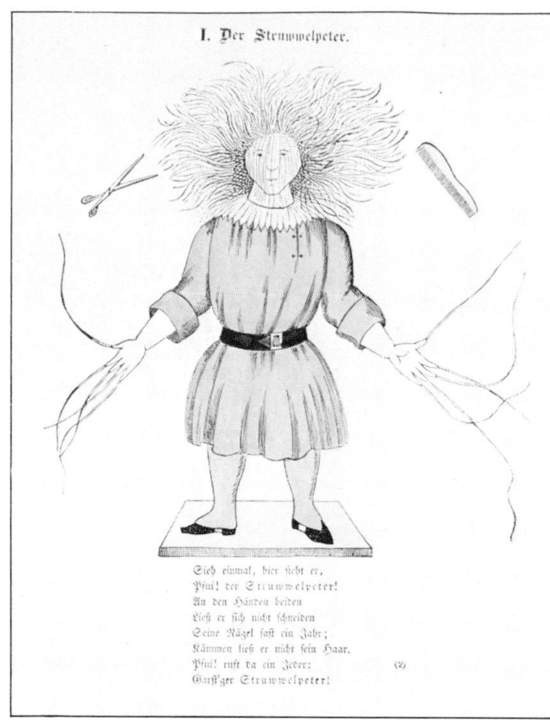

I. Der Struwwelpeter.
Sieh einmal, hier steht er,
Pfui! der Struwwelpeter!
An den Händen beiden
Ließ er sich nicht schneiden
Seine Nägel fast ein Jahr;
Kämmen ließ er nicht sein Haar.
Pfui! ruft da ein Jeder: (2)
Garst'ger Struwwelpeter!

9. *Struwwelpeter,* by Heinrich Hoffmann. Frankfurt am Main, J. Rütten, c. 1850. 7 x 9¼.

10. *Max and Moritz,* by Wilhelm Busch. Munich, Braun & Schneider, n.d. (first German edition, 1872). 5¼ x 8⅛.

are blatantly unshaded. The coloring is brash, arbitrary—in the sense of just so many inks—and abstracted, suggesting but not copying nature, and not aiming to. Thus the crux of Denslow's offense: in the face of five hundred years of Western painting, and of the Darwinian boost to belief in the progressive development of art, he and his fellows—Will Bradley was another—went their own way.

15
Hi! presto weedo! in a crack,
He hooks a chicken by the back;

Denslow reigns today as the first and best illustrator of *The Wizard of Oz,* and his picturebooks—toy-books in format, twelve in 1903, six in 1904—were not unappreciated in their time. But they failed "to preserve the traditions of perspective, color values, forms and proportions" (without which children would "gain false notions of things")[7] and librarians and educators scorned them.

Equally to be shunned was anything that smacked of 'the comics.' "With the awful warning before us of the Comic Supplement and its disheartening popularity if admitted by some mischance to the Children's Room, one would suppose [this] danger might be easily avoided." But it was not so: books were not free of the taint, a new Mother Goose was "hopelessly marred"[8] by such illustrations.

Struwwelpeter (9) was at the source of this, and if not always condemned, seldom recommended. Closer still to the comic strip, *Max and Moritz* (10) could not be condoned; one had only to look at its offspring, the Katzenjammer Kids, and shudder. (Americans were not alone; writes a German of Kate Greenaway: "What a gulf between these delightful works of art and the trashy caricatures of such stuff as our *Struwwelpeter.*"[9])

Cut off with the comics were the comic sequences that A. B. Frost and others had been contributing to American magazines—some of them complete in a few panels, some of them picture sheets much like those Busch made for *Fliegende Blätter* or that Steinlen made for *Chat Noir.* Not directed specifically at children,

11. "Our Cat Eats Rat Poison," by A. B. Frost. *Harper's Magazine* LXIII (July, 1881), 320. (Reprinted, extended and altered, in *Stuff and Nonsense,* Scribner, 1884.)

12. *Carlo,* by A. B. Frost. Doubleday, 1913. 9¼ x 7¾.

they became family favorites here, and when they appeared in *Stuff and Nonsense*, abroad: "the children were clean doubled up at the first start of the 'cat' episode—and I can honestly assert that I have never laughed so much at anything of that same kind,"[10] an English friend of Frost's recalled. The "cat episode" is Frost's masterwork of explosive articulation (11). "Watch the expression in its eyes, as shown here in number one, when it discovers the character of the food. Note the wondering look on its face and the slow movement of its paw across the stomach. Only a dot and a line, and yet there is a whole volume of anxiety, alarm, misery, and fright expressed in this same dot and line. . . ."[11]

Or hear Gleeson White in the premiere survey of children's book illustration: "A. B. Frost, by his cosmopolitan fun, 'understanded of all people,' has probably aroused more hearty laughs . . . than even Caldecott himself." ("It is needless to praise the literally inimitable humor of the tragic series 'Our Cat took Rat Poison.' ")[12]

Praising Frost's illustrations for *Uncle Remus*, Anne Carroll Moore quotes the compliment and omits the citation, regretting, again and again, "that Frost has done no series of picture books corresponding to the Caldecott picturebooks . . ."[13] None corresponding to Caldecott's perhaps, but his own. *Stuff and Nonsense* (Scribner, 1884), in which the separate pictures appear on successive pages, is one such, *The Bull Calf and Other Tales* (Scribner, 1892), another. The value of spacing out Frost's tricky humor came to be recognized. Many of his famous drawings, including those for "The Bull Calf," were strung among the ads in the back of *Scribner's Magazine*—according to Charles Dana Gibson, by Frank Doubleday, who was in charge of the pages. "In those days advertising wasn't what it is now," writes Gibson in 1928, "and people had to be tricked into looking at it."[14]

Frost put the experience to use in *Carlo*, conceived as a book in pictures. Carlo is an ordinary dog, pure plebeian—scruffy, gangling, awkward, often baffled, well-meaning (most of the time) but always in trouble, resigned to his lot however much baffled (12). In Frost's egalitarian view, cat and dog, man and child, master and servant are all fair game, and the rich and mighty, the hoity-toity, come off worst; if he is to be criticized for rough handling, it can't be on the basis of unkindness to animals. Carlo, in fact, makes

OUR CAT EATS RAT POISON—A TRAGEDY IN FIVE ACTS AND ONE TABLEAU.

Act 1.—SUSPICION.

Act 2.—THE PANG.

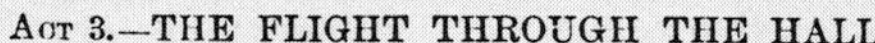

Act 3.—THE FLIGHT THROUGH THE HALL.

Act 4.—STARTLED ONES.

Act 5.—THE BEGINNING OF THE END.

CURTAIN—REQUIESCAT IN PACE.

"Gee! What a fourth!"

[63]

sense—how is he to know that the black animal he carries proudly into the house will cause a convulsion? "The pictures tell their own story, with no need of enlightenment from the sparing text,"[15] as a reviewer noted; and in that regard *Carlo* is the truest of picturebooks, a natural extension of the comic sheet into folio form, of serial into book.

As a children's book, it might as well have been nonexistent—unless it is one of those covered by the general denunciation of bad examples, the assumption being that whatever children saw, they would do. Whether proscription or protectiveness was the basis, "the great American tradition of A. B. Frost, Peter Newell, Kemble and the rest, whose comic sequences in the back pages of the magazines of the 'nineties' foretold the movie cartoon of today"[16]—this from James Daugherty in *The Horn Book* in 1940—found little favor among the monitors of children's reading. Was their humor broader, more given to acting out? So one hears, and to an extent, sees; but consider Steinlen's Bazouge, the counterpart in tragic comedy of Frost's cat (13). Or was it perhaps more offensive, as American, to a citizenry bent on refinement in behavior as in art?

Their books did not disappear the way Denslow's did—their audience was wider—but they were not recommended for children's reading or public purchase. The only American work to carry over, to win acceptance on the increasingly determinative lists, was Palmer Cox's *Brownies* and Gelett Burgess's *Goops*—merry imps (marvelous merry imps but not people) and cautionary creatures. Otherwise, from 1895–1900 to 1922, from the list Anne Carroll Moore drew up for the Iowa Library Commission to the fourth issued by the Bookshop for Boys and Girls, one finds little but a slow accretion of foreign names.

In this connection, a brief review. Caroline Hewins of the Hartford Public Library, the foremost advocate of separate quarters for children and special attention to what they read, issued her first list in 1882 and, beginning in 1897, compiled one that, in successive editions, was published by the American Library Association; John F. Sargent's broader, more inclusive list, the first of the classified and annotated catalogs, appeared under ALA auspices in 1890, subsuming and extending Miss Hewins's work; from 1905 the Carnegie Library in Pittsburgh, where Frances Jenkins Olcott directed children's work, put out a recommended list periodically, and in 1909 a

13. "The Sad Tale of Bazouge" from *Contes à Sara*, by T. A. Steinlen. Paris, Carteret, 1898. Details.

descriptive catalog of its holdings; drawing upon the initial Carnegie Library list, the first edition of the H. W. Wilson *Children's Catalog* appeared in 1909, to become and remain for many years the list of lists.

Two other developments have bearing. The Bookshop for Boys and Girls in Boston, Bertha Mahony's bailiwick, began issuing suggested lists its first year, 1916 (with help from the other "authoritative lists"); these evolved into *The Horn Book* (1924+), long the journal of record in the field, and into *Realms of Gold* (1929) which, with its sequel *Five Years of Children's Books* (1936), was properly called a Baedeker of children's books. Meanwhile Miss Moore had begun reviewing, first in *The Bookman* (1918–26), then in the New York *Herald Tribune* (1924–30); still later she would write for other journals, including *The Horn Book*: seldom if ever was she without an outlet for her views.

What we have then, for thirty or forty years, is Miss Moore endorsing (or tacitly damning) and, through New York Public Library programs, promoting; *The Horn Book* sorting and sifting and, through its selection of articles, sponsoring; the *Children's Catalog*—joined later by the school-oriented ALA Graded Lists—making permanent the evaluations of *The Horn Book*, Miss Moore, and a few of her colleagues, many of whom made their own lists.

There was considerable agreement, some shakedown and, from 1938 on, the ALA-administered Caldecott Medal for "the most distinguished American picture book" of each year, the ultimate accolade or the end of the road. For the most part, that was it: the books that got on the lists persisted, those that didn't faded away (until dissension led to open rebellion, late in our story). One outcome was the deliberate manufacture of books for the market, and its correlate, the avoidance of the foredoomed. This is not to suggest a dead hand or a raised club: much that was wanted was eminently worth having, and many editors, themselves former teachers or librarians, were quite in accord with their customers. How the process operated and what it yielded we can begin to see in the work of E. Boyd Smith.

E. BOYD SMITH

B. St. John, New Brunswick, 1860—raised in Boston—educated in France—illustrated many books—among which are:

So much and no more did Elmer Boyd Smith tell his interrogators, in just such clipped phrases, as if to be done with it, and quickly. (Once, asked his "Recreations, Amusements, Hobbies," he answered, "Work.")

Though he left few traces, there are some. Brought to Boston when he was six, he attended a local grammar school and art school, and for some years worked for The Riverside Press, the manufacturing arm of Houghton Mifflin, then preeminent among American printers. But it was in France, where he lived according to differing accounts for from twelve to twenty years, that Smith acquired what he considered his education. Winters he studied drawing and painting in Paris, summers he spent in Valombre, a hamlet to the north, "studying the life of the fields and general outdoor effects."[1] He exhibited paintings and drawings at the Paris Salon (a dubious distinction at that date) and is reputed to have done illustrations and caricatures for French newspapers and publishers.

His first book, *My Village*, the one thing he wrote entirely for adults, centers on Valombre —Valombre as a microcosm of the world, "the old, old story of life with all its good and bad, its lights and shadows." Carvol and Rosalie, next door, quarrel about his drinking, and their son Kaiser (b. 1870–71) now resists, now succumbs to the same disease; everyone turns out for a fire, buckets pass hand over hand until the blaze goes out, then water is shot promiscuously, "they can't give it up so soon"; old Désiré, dying, takes so long that his neighbors' sympathy gives way to irritation; with harvest comes a sense of well-being, and Smith watches the reaping and tying and stacking, grateful that the mowing machine has yet to invade Valombre (14). In word sketches and pen sketches (and monotints), a continuous history takes shape in which personal history and social history are indistinguishable. Cited equally as a study of character (*The Dial*, Chicago) and as rural sociology (*The Spectator*, London, where it was published the following year), it is, for its time, an individual, freshly thought work, which was to be true of whatever Smith did.

In January 1898 he was back in Boston, competing with A. B. Frost to illustrate Joel Chandler Harris's *Tales of the Home Folk in Peace and War*. That he won the commission

14. *My Village*, by E. Boyd Smith. Scribner, 1896. Detail.

on the heels of Frost's drawings for *Uncle Remus* was a plus for Smith, and with his pictures for a *Hiawatha Primer* that same year he became a Houghton Mifflin mainstay.

Married now, he returned to France briefly, but between 1900 and 1903 he found occasion to go West; reportedly he traveled on foot in the Rockies, sketching the landscape and the life of Indians and herders, and went up into Canada. From this trip came the illustrations for Andy Adams's *Log of a Cowboy* and Mary Austin's *Land of Little Rain*, Smith's reputation as a Western artist, and, it appears, his allegiance to American themes; for all that he had lived abroad, he was to undertake few foreign subjects.

15. *The Land of Little Rain*, by Mary Austin, illus. by E. Boyd Smith. Boston, Houghton Mifflin, 1903. Detail.

Out of print as of this writing, *The Land of Little Rain* is bound to reappear, and with it Smith's trenchant line drawings. Writes Mary Austin of her chosen land: "Desert is the name it wears upon the maps, but the Indians' is the better word. Desert is a loose term to indicate land that supports no man; whether the land can be bitted and broken to that purpose is not proven. Void of life it never is, however dry the air and villainous the soil." Void of human life it is not either, nor of small swift creatures and scavengers, and all this Smith distills into single steady images (15). The occasional full-page halftones are less felicitous; 'scenes' are not what was wanted.

The story of Noah's Ark, however, is a drama, and in Smith's hands a succession of skirmishes where everything is under control. At the start, according to one observer, "a little assemblage of the patriarch's neighbors [is listening] to his explanations of his mysterious conduct. One, with fingers tapping his upturned palm, scientifically demonstrates the impossibility of a flood; another, chin in air, evidently declares that it is all nonsense, and, besides, he has known it for years; an humble little woman prayerfully implores mercy; another obediently follows her lord, who bids her to come along and see what the old fellow is saying now; and a sly, merry-eyed humorist grins the grin of the augur at Noah, in enjoyment of this new scheme for advertising an excursion boat."[2]

Noah's Ark was announced as "The Humorous Book of the Year," sometimes "for children," sometimes "for adults"; accustomed to the crossover, reviewers refused to confine it to either. Anything further from *The Log of a Cowboy* or *The Land of Little Rain* or their successors, which had occupied Smith in the interim, is hard to imagine; for with *Noah* Smith showed himself to be a painter, a humorist, and insofar as children were concerned, an American with something of Leslie Brooke's wit, Boutet de Monvel's scale and way of working in color.

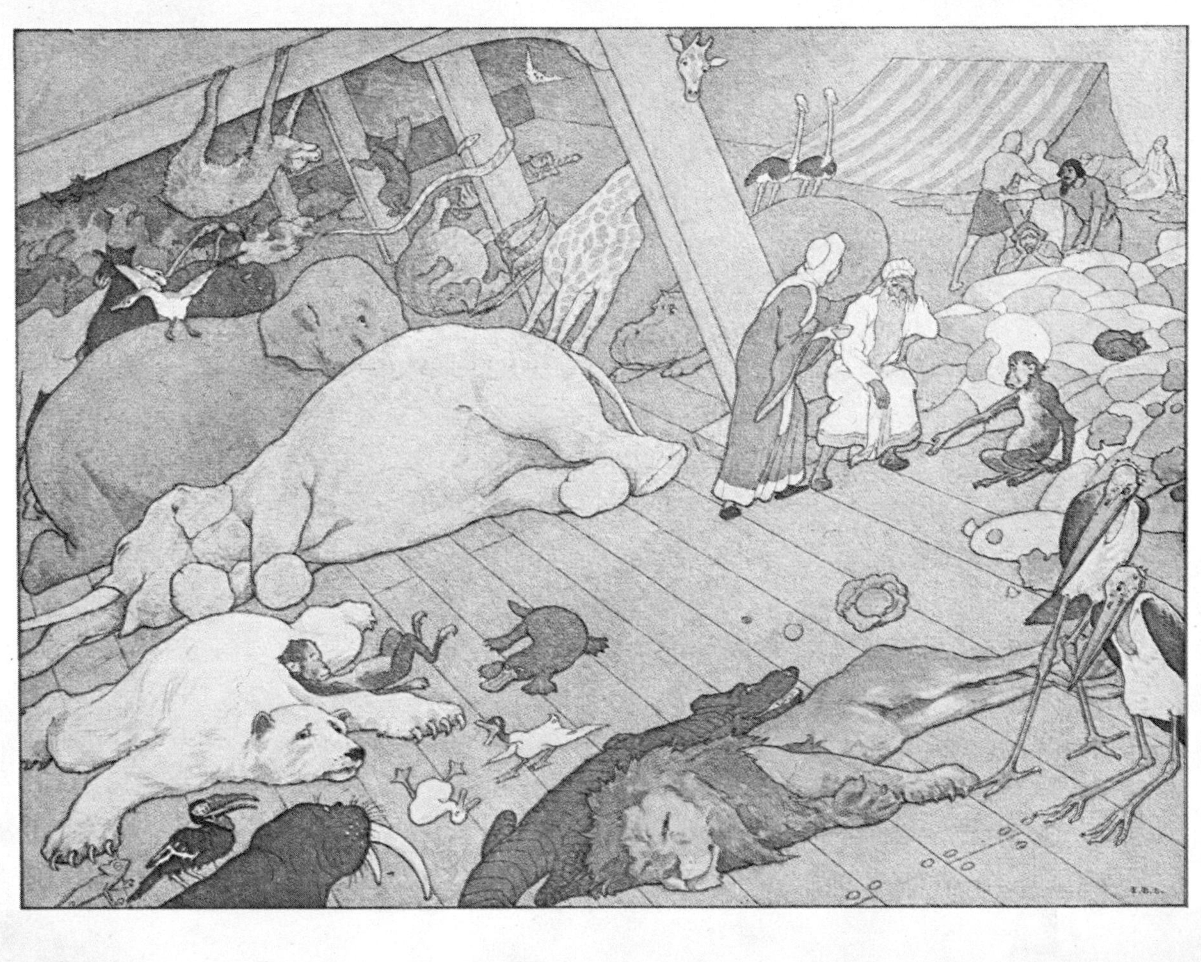

16. *The Story of Noah's Ark,* by E. Boyd Smith. Boston, Houghton Mifflin, 1905. 11 x 8¼.

Though making sport of Noah was not new, Smith is clever: his text is dry, even solemn, with Biblical phrasing and intonation, while in the pictures opposite Noah's neighbors titter; the workmen loll about, argue with one another, strike for higher wages; the dinosaurs try to squeeze aboard, the mammoths and mastodons sit on their haunches (all to become extinct); Mrs. Noah objects—"the domestic arrangements are impossible"; and when the rain, long delayed, finally comes (to the relief of those on the Ark), everyone is seasick (16).

It was Smith's way to make every detail carry a message, and with the general discomfiture he has a field day. Notice too the walrus's head looming up at bottom left, the toucan (?) and lizard beyond; Smith's corners, though not of his invention, were justifiably famous, and he had the Toulouse-Lautrec habit of cutting off a scene abruptly, which one senses as cutting into a scene, tightening and heightening it.

The Story of Pocahontas and Captain John Smith was apparently prompted by the three hundredth anniversary of the Jamestown settlement, which the ads featured; and as a historic epic in monumental tableaux, it is Smith's *Jeanne d'Arc.* But where Boutet de Monvel glorifies France in Joan, Smith sees in the meeting of Pocahontas and John Smith, of Indian and European, conflict and potential tragedy. Coming at a time when the romantic vision of Pocahontas had faded and young people were told that "untrained savage" though she was, "she was also the steadfast friend and helper of the feeble colony,"[3] it mediates between the two views and transcends them. Often with humor: old Uttamatomakkin, sent along with Pocahontas and her husband John Rolfe by Powhatan "to count the English, that he might learn their strength," has long since given up notching sticks ("Too many"), but at King James's court, not the least impressed, he pities the nobles their fancy dress (17).

Conceived much like Boutet de Monvel's coronation of Charles VII, Smith's presentation of Pocahontas at court has more activity, explicit and intrinsic, and less grandeur. Along the line of courtiers, heads turn to see Pocahontas, to catch the royal couple's reaction, to stare at Uttamatomakkin. Smith's sympathies

17. *The Story of Pocahontas and Captain John Smith,* by E. Boyd Smith. Boston, Houghton Mifflin, 1906. 12¼ x 9.

are evident: the easy dignity of Pocahontas, her supple gown and loose hair, accentuate the posturing and artifice around her (who is the savage now?) and Uttamatomakkin, the only fully modeled figure, looms dark and solid against a frieze of pale faces.

"Old and young" were the presumptive audience for *Pocahontas*, older children the more likely; *Santa Claus and All About Him*, however, is wholly for boys and girls—a friendlier term, once, than the categorical 'children.' A wise uncle might have contrived it to explain everything: how Santa knows when to get up and start working—the walrus and the polar bear wake him; how he learns what children are wanting each year—he goes from house to house eavesdropping; how he is able to get about without being seen—"he manages to make himself invisible to human eyes." ("The animals and birds can see him . . . but as they can't 'tell on him' he doesn't care.")

To fill in on the likes of little girls, he visits the fairies; to "refresh his memory as to how the great creatures look," he goes to the forests and jungles; and to make sure the toys work, he has his helpers test them (see the Little Men play baseball, fly an airship, run the trains): all to make Christmas the merrier.

And so much to see (18). Atmospheric and French from the haughty schoolgirls back,

comic and American from the fiendish motorists forward, the street scene is a delight as genre illustration, something of an accomplishment as painting—as painting for reproduction, properly, and just how carefully Smith calculated his results the originals attest.[4] It remains to be said about the four boys, one as patently Jewish as another is plainly black, that they represent to Smith "all sorts of children," and thus the breadth of Santa's sympathies.

The Circus and All About It (Stokes, 1909) followed—full of hurtling figures, foreshortening and dramatic perspective, ringing in Lautrec, Seurat—and then a change, "in response to a demand for a radical change in juveniles,"[5] *The Farm Book.*

Clara Hunt, head of children's work at the Brooklyn Public Library, is credited with making the demand of the president of Houghton Mifflin ("And I do not care to speak with a subordinate"[6]). What she wanted we can infer from the publisher's "honest and true" pitch and from Miss Hunt's own reception of the book. Calling it "nearer to satisfying our ideals of what a picture book should be than

18. *Santa Claus and All About Him,* by E. Boyd Smith. Stokes, 1908. 11 x 8¼.

SANTA WANDERS ABOUT THE STREETS SEEING EVERYTHING BUT NEVER SEEN

19. *The Farm Book,* by E. Boyd Smith. Boston, Houghton Mifflin, 1910. 11 x 8¼.

anything heretofore done by an American artist," she goes on to say: "The two little people from the city—who perhaps have known only of the farmer as the grotesque 'Hayseed' of the comic; who have missed the training of doing things for themselves because in the artificial life of the city the apparatus of living obscures the connection between the producer and the town dweller—are turned loose in the country where the best play is to help in the real work of raking hay and churning butter and carrying grain to the mill; where too they gain a new respect for the dignity and beauty of productive work . . . ."[7]

Miss Hunt was prolix and given to preachment; for his part, Smith takes Bob and Betty to Uncle John's farm where they are loath "to miss anything" and curbs his comments. But it is true that on a farm there is work for everyone, and for children satisfaction and fun in the doing, for city children fascination in seeing how, for instance, butter is made from cream "and finally stamped into 'pats' or pound 'bricks' all ready for the market. And how the cheeses were made in their odd-looking presses." With, for the boys in from the field, a pitcher of buttermilk as another end product (19).

Outdoors Smith is back in Valombre in spirit, observing the swing of the sower's arm, the brush harrow, the corn marker, and in the fall, the wheat 'cradled,' threshed with the heavy flail, ground at the gristmill. Anyone interested in New England farming around the turn of the century might well start his researches here.

Or, for a sense of what trains once meant to children, one could begin with *The Railroad Book. The Farm Book* had been successful, *The Seashore Book* (Houghton Mifflin, 1912) took in the construction, launching and fitting out of a square-rigger; but now a railroad spur runs behind Bob and Betty's house, and they have a new interest. They recognize the engine whistles, marvel at the freight cars, fall in love with the caboose—and oh, to be a brakeman, walking freely on top. Their friend the engineer treats them to a ride in the cab, a

20. *The Railroad Book,* by E. Boyd Smith. Boston, Houghton Mifflin, 1913. 10 x 7⅞.

great moment; and sometimes, just occasionally, they go on a day train to the city with their parents. Now it is the conductor they admire, "slowly working his way through, punching holes in their nice new tickets, politely answering many questions, explaining timetables and connections"—his knowledge seems uncanny.

One has also to admire the scene, surprisingly beautiful in orange-red (the coat on the seat), magenta and gray-green, the diagonals pulling us into the depths of the car, the horizontals recalling us to the passengers, Bob and Betty at once in and out, their parents preoccupied, everyone somehow occupied, in transit, everything transient. Except the conductor, who holds the keys to the trip and anchors the composition (20).

A cross-country trip, with meals in the dining car and, best of all, nights in the sleeping car, tops off train travel for children and concludes the three books which for a long time gave them their first pictures of American life, "the best pictures of American life available."[8]

There was no reason for *Chicken World*, no precedent, no occasion, no demand, and for a number of years, no prospects. Smith kept on with it, adding to the pictures and the story, in France and after he returned permanently to the United States, and in 1910 it came out, to remain in print for more than forty years.

Equally life cycle and social comedy, *Chicken World* is 'the old, old story' of coming-of-age among the barnyard fowl or, world that it is, a microcosm still smaller and sharper than Valombre. But then there is nothing sentimental about chickens for all our talk of mother hens.

"Now Spring has come," Smith begins bluntly, "the Old Black Hen decides to set." And hatches a mixed brood of chicks and ducks, all of whom she tries to bring up properly—though, to her disgust, the ducks will be ducks (21). As the garden changes with the passing months in the border, and, closer to, spears of asparagus push up and blossoms turn into berries, the fledglings learn to dig for worms, to keep themselves tidy, to crowd around the farmer for feed, until the hen decides and the old rooster agrees, "They are plenty big enough to look after themselves."

At first desolate, they soon insist on being turned into the big chicken yard. " 'Now,' says a spiteful hen, 'we must teach them their place, or they will become insupportable.' " Alas for their lost childhood—the young cock's advances are resented, the old rooster turns on him, words pass, tempers flare, and feathers fly (22). Then, order restored, the young hens lay their first round of eggs. . . . "And so the wheel of chicken life goes round" to THE END, a roast bird on a platter.

With oddments like that and every page a picture-page, *Chicken World* is more fully a picturebook than anything Smith had done before (or would do again), and the pictures are by far his boldest. The brilliant reds, the coal blacks, the cool, clear greens were surely printed from separate plates and there are also a pure yellow and a pure blue—which is to say that, whether or not the nine plates that Smith once stipulated were employed, the printing was not done (or not wholly done) by the three-color camera-separated process, making a difference that is discernible even in black and white.

A chapter could be written about *Chicken World*—about the Boutet de Monvel borders and their relation to the inset scenes; about

21. *Chicken World,* by E. Boyd Smith. Putnam, 1910. 11 x 8½.

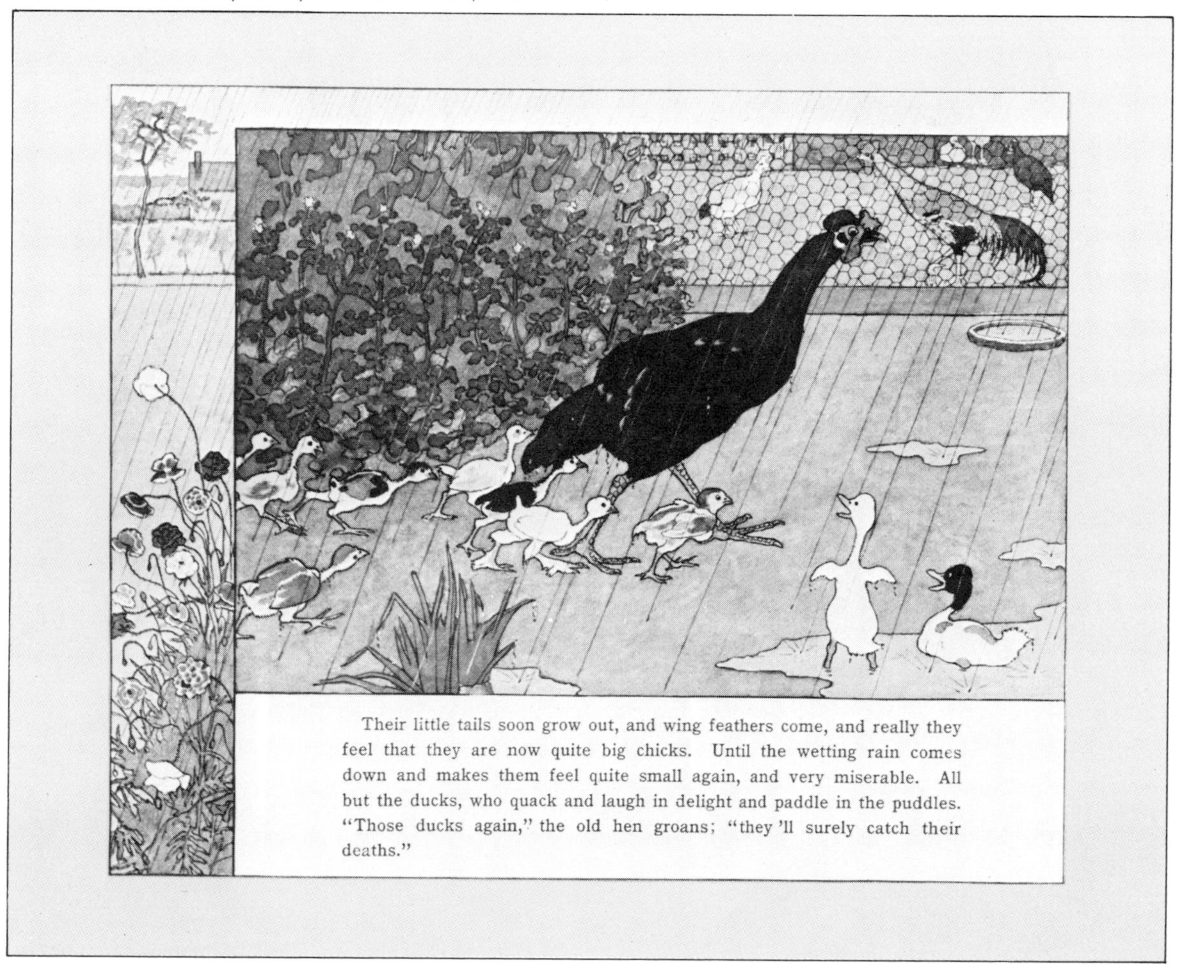

Their little tails soon grow out, and wing feathers come, and really they feel that they are now quite big chicks. Until the wetting rain comes down and makes them feel quite small again, and very miserable. All but the ducks, who quack and laugh in delight and paddle in the puddles. "Those ducks again," the old hen groans; "they 'll surely catch their deaths."

the occasional large-scale close-ups, a stratagem David Bland traces to the Dutchman Van Hoytema (*Het Leelijke Jonge Eendje*, 1893, etc.)[9] that in Smith's time begins to turn up from Chicago to Moscow; about the exact observation of animal behavior which Smith shares with Van Hoytema before, with the Père Castor series after (p. 123).

The last is what counted with children, that and the vitality and vividness of the illustrations: here was the life of the chicken in pictures that spoke for themselves.

The Story of Noah's Ark remained popular and spawned *The Early Life of Mr. Man Before Noah* (Houghton Mifflin, 1914) and *After They Came Out of the Ark* (Putnam, 1918); *The Story of Our Country* (Putnam, 1920) put schoolbook history (superior on slavery and the Civil War) into Smith's standard format; and there were curiosities like *Fun in the Radio World* (Stokes, 1923), a quiet man's view of what things were coming to.

Times had changed, the cost of full-color printing had soared, Smith had retired into himself (in a French house-and-garden in the backwoods of Wilton, Connecticut); but he was still intrigued by prehistoric life, and in 1944, the year after he died, *So Long Ago* (Houghton Mifflin) appeared, his last laugh at evolution.

Early in his career Smith had some imitators but he had no followers; when picture-book production would resume after a hiatus, styles, techniques, attitudes would be different.

22. *Chicken World,* by E. Boyd Smith. Putnam, 1910. 11 x 8½.

But in vain, for they come to blows and fight a furious battle, and feathers fly about. Of course the young cock is blamed. "He really is very impudent," says the Old Black hen; "none of my children ever behaved so before." He is soon forced to run for his life, and then keeps out of the way for a while.

THE ERRATIC, ECLECTIC TWENTIES

In 1918 Louise Seaman, after three years' teaching in a small progressive school in New Haven, was hired by Macmillan, on the recommendation of a friend, to write promotion material. Put to learn her new trade, she produced a sonnet on the catalog that, together with her teaching experience, persuaded George Brett, the president of Macmillan, to put her in charge of the firm's new juvenile department, in 1919 the first in the country and, as far as is known, the first anywhere.

Macmillan was by policy departmentalized, public libraries were growing, library work with children was growing fastest, Brett was a smart businessman: everything fit. So sensible was the move and so clearly successful that in 1922 Doubleday followed suit, naming May Massee as head—May Massee who, it was said, had only to go to an ALA conference to come back with a new job. She had taught (and liked only 'the reading and storytelling parts'), she had directed children's work at the Buffalo Public Library, she had edited the ALA reviewing organ, *The Booklist*: coming to Doubleday, she was already a personage.

The founding of the two departments brought new creativity and enterprise to children's book publishing, and the spur of competition. Other editors had specialized in children's books, but not exclusively and not with control over their own product from manufacturing to marketing; predominantly, publication consisted of new editions of proven classics. Louise Seaman inherited a strong list at Macmillan, half of British origin, put it in order and added to it in response to felt need, fresh discoveries, the tenor of the times; May Massee jettisoned most of the Doubleday backlist and built upon individual talents; both kept in close touch with librarians. In the nature of juvenile publishing, editors loom large, always on the lookout for new ideas and for artists and writers to execute them or, seeing promise in a new person, suggesting a direction, a subject, a specific project. At the outset, besides building a list, they were apt to do everything from designing the books to promoting them, or from choosing the type to visiting the bookstores.

It is easy to forget that, along with children's rooms in libraries, children's bookselling flourished in the period between the wars. Not only were there sizable children's sections in the book departments of emporiums like Halle Bros. and Marshall Field's, there were also, beginning in 1916 with Boston's Bookshop for Boys and Girls, independent bookstores catering to children. Tivolis for children some of them were, festooned with art and crammed with dolls and do-it-yourself toys and great big animals to clamber over, while others, concentrating on extensive stocks and expert guidance, amounted to libraries where everything could be bought. Meanwhile the big stores had begun to hold fairs, and the biggest names gave command performances: there was excitement in the selling and buying of children's books.

That a large retail market existed—that until the Second World War many people bought books for their children as a matter of course, books to be pored over, mulled over, kept forever—had an effect on the kinds of books published that was particularly marked in the case of picturebooks. For libraries it was enough to match home standards: all children

23. *The Square Book of Animals,* text by Arthur Waugh, pictures by William Nicholson. London, Heinemann, 1899. 10⅝ x 10⅝.

24. *ABC Book,* by C. B. Falls. Doubleday, 1923. 8⅞ x 11¾.

were to have, for a week or two, the splendid picturebooks that lucky children had for their own.

Neither May Massee nor Louise Seaman started out commissioning or soliciting picturebooks: there were still Crane and Caldecott and Greenaway, and now Beatrix Potter and Leslie Brooke, and from the Continent books whose color printing couldn't be touched. But C. B. Falls, taking a busman's holiday from designing posters, made a woodblock ABC for his daughter, and when it appeared on Miss Massee's first list, much of the doubting that a good picturebook could be made here subsided.

The Falls ABC, hailed as an American triumph, is an amalgam of William Nicholson's *Alphabet* of 1898 and his *Square Book of Animals,* done earlier but published later. *The Square Book of Animals* was intended for children; the *Alphabet,* a picture gallery of common types, aimed to amuse all ages: there were then ABCs of everything, it was a peg to hang pictures and rhymes on.

Nicholson was already known for the broad bold "Beggarstaff" posters he had done with his brother-in-law James Pryde, and the *Alphabet* and *Square Book of Animals,* with two other albums of the same period, widened his public and solidified his fame. Falls was only one of many influenced by Nicholson's handling of flat masses, his return to direct engraving and revival of squat block letters. Inescapably, Falls's work suffers by comparison (23, 24); he hasn't the skill (see the necks of the two swans and the way they join the bodies) and his statuesque silhouettes—many of them, unlike the swan, isolated from their immediate environment—stand forth as emblems rather than as flesh-and-blood animals. Children are said to have welcomed the Falls ABC as enthusiastically as their elders, a claim difficult to evaluate today when it has only limited appeal; if so, the explanation can be found in the oranges and greens, the russets and browns and blues, great dollops of bright color in a world of dainty to drab books.

The resemblance to Nicholson's work was not concealed or unknown (though over the years it tended to be forgotten). What counted was that it had been done here—"that an ABC book so admirable in design and in color printing has been produced on this side of the Atlantic."[1] No matter that its color printing was, in fact, in no way superior to that of the Denslow books nor that its horse was bright green, its wolf dull green—"color . . . had not played too many tricks with nature."[2] For Miss Moore, as for others zealous for domestic progress, that America could produce the equivalent of a British book was itself reason to rejoice.

The success of the Falls ABC did not bring artists flocking to the publishers nor, for that matter, send editors looking for them—not to do picturebooks. It was the heyday of the illustrated book, with glossy color plates by Rackham or black and white designs by Artzybasheff. But two books, hybrids, were prophetic. Margery Bianco's *The Velveteen Rabbit* (Heinemann, 1922; Doran, 1923) came with color lithographs by William Nicholson in his later sketchy style—illustrations drawn on stone, to be printed as lithographs—that made a nursery story into a nursery book. And in 1924 May Massee, who was notably color-prone (a bent she attributed to the brilliance of the Ballets-Russe), proved with the Petershams' illustrations for Margery Clark's *The Poppy Seed Cakes* that the public would accept those flat colors, 'that foreign look,' that buyers warned her against.

Picturebooks, however, remained something that came along when someone was inspired, usually by his or her own child.

Mary Liddell's *Little Machinery*, the first and virtually the last of its kind, is about a pixie, "a magic creature [who] grew up out of some pieces of a steam engine that was in a wreck, an old trolley car that couldn't run any more, and a broken automobile." A fellow of such parts is adaptable to steam, electricity or gas, and being magical, equally adept at sawing or digging or any number of other operations—in other words, an enchanted Erector set.

"He isn't making anything but noise in this picture" (25) but usually he's busy building rabbit hutches—while the rabbits vie with one another to hold his tools—or "all sorts of different shaped boxes for squirrels to keep nuts in." (For the rabbits, there are also shaving curls to hang on their ears.) He oversteps himself, though, when he starts a beaver dam—"the beaver didn't like it . . . he wanted to do it himself."

The mixture of practical mechanics and whimsy blossoms in the design. Little Machinery's carpenter tools hang from the frame of the text page, with their functions listed below. He saws furiously, electric sparks fly, "Do you think he knows he's sawing the border of the page?" He is industrious, and the drawings show just how he works; he is playful, and the pictures are part of the fun. The animals, whether in character or behaving like children, are his wards, so crucial that when he becomes chiefly a mechanism—a plow or loom, performing complex operations for no immediate purpose—the book loses much of its zest.

Little Machinery took shape, Mary Liddell relates, as the spontaneous creation of some children whose windows overlooked a construction site "through trees inhabited by a modern variety of squirrel and bird which likes the noise and bustle of machinery."[3] Similarly, Peggy Bacon was one evening telling "The Lion-Hearted Kitten" to her two-and-a-half-year-old, "making it up as I went along,"[4] when Ernestine Evans, talent scout supreme, happened by and suggested she write it down along with any others she had told him. Miss Evans took the manuscript to her friend Louise Seaman, and the result was the publication of Peggy Bacon's first book for children.

The Lion-Hearted Kitten (1927) was followed by *Mercy and the Mouse* (1928), another collection of stories illustrated by the author, and then a year later by *The Ballad of Tangle Street*, "told in most moving verses by the distinguished poet Peggy Bacon, with many extraordinary pictures from the same pen," as the blurb blazons abroad most becomingly. Peggy Bacon was known both as a writer and an artist; and whatever the medium she was inextricably humorist, parodist, satirist.

The Ballad of Tangle Street is heroic high-

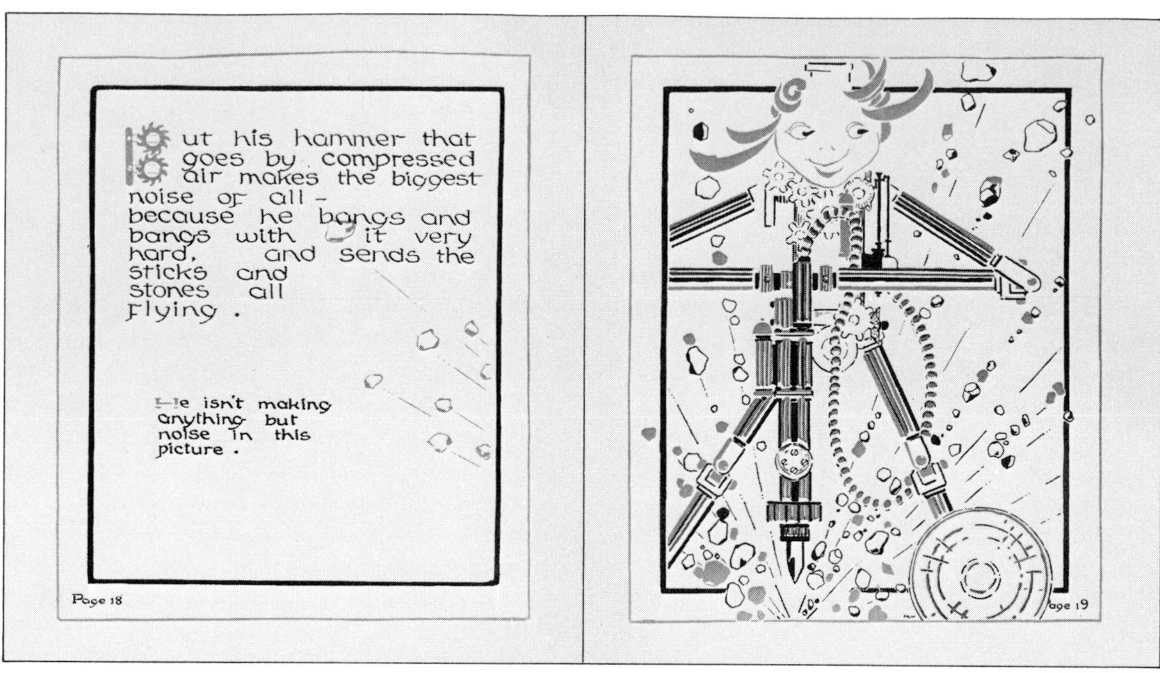

25. *Little Machinery,* by Mary Liddell. Doubleday, 1926. 7⅞ x 9.

class doggerel, solemnly served forth in five parts, with a lovely tatterdemalion pen drawing opposite each page of text (26). Listen my children and you shall hear . . . ?

No— "little children meek and mild,
who love your cream of wheat,
come hither, hark and be beguiled
by tale of Tangle Street.

All up and down this lovely street
you see each shop and dwelling,
with every kind of trade complete
for buying and for selling."

"And all the different people too," who know the cat—"Whose cat? Ah, whose!"—by different names . . .

"Miss Button calls the cat 'Elise,'
and feeds her fresh farina.
The ice man, Tony, gives her cheese
and calls her 'Concertina.' "

Which name, which dish, let puss decide . . . (and let those who fancy foot-loose cats take heart).

Like *Little Machinery, The Ballad of Tangle Street* is singular; and though late in date, as a maverick it is part of the irregular Twenties.

There was, however, one undertaking, the Happy Hour series, that looked jubilantly forward. "Here are a dozen of our favorite nonsense tales and rhymes, done up in little square books full of life and color," wrote Louise Seaman in the 1927 Macmillan catalog. "The artists were chosen by competition, for their special ability to interest and amuse small children. Each has a clear strong line, knowledge of color printing . . . and the right artistic feel about the whole of a book. So although they are both small and cheap, we feel that each volume is an achievement in bookmaking."

What had happened was that Charles Stringer, then head of the Jersey City Printing Company, had approached Louise Seaman with a proposal: his firm, a leader in commercial color lithography, was interested in extending the process to children's picturebooks and would do three- and four-color work at much less cost than anyone else if certain conditions were met. Given the possibilities, Miss Seaman developed the editorial program, recruited such newcomers as Berta and Elmer Hader, Kurt Wiese and Frank Dobias, and sent them off to the printer to learn how the books were to be made. The prescription called for a black key drawing, with tissue overlays for the additional colors, the colors to be flat, with no Ben Day tints and a minimum of overprinting, the books to be printed in groups of four using the same colors.

As a modus operandi, it was the wave of the future, and the results in terms of book design were little short of revolutionary. The cover design continues from front to back, and first Frank Dobias, then all of the others, exploited this feature to dramatic effect: his three Billy Goats Gruff trip-trip-trip over the bridge while around the bend—the spine—the wicked Troll awaits them. (For a later example of wraparound jacket design, see page 137.) Interspersed throughout the books are spot illustrations, some of them interacting across the two-page spread; filled-in framed drawings and some that are partially framed; and bleeds or quasi-bleeds, especially at the centerfolds: an armory of pictorial possibilities, thanks to lithography's capacity to combine diverse elements, allowing for unprecedented variety of layout and flexibility of interpretation.

The centerspreads are a story in themselves, but the Dobias onslaught from *The Bremen Band* will have to do. Center-sewn and consisting of only one signature, the books opened flat at the middle, and the artists made of that page a panorama. Going further, Dobias makes his the visual equivalent of a pop-up

26. *The Ballad of Tangle Street,* by Peggy Bacon. Macmillan, 1929. 11½ x 9.

27

28

27. *The Bremen Band,* pictures by Frank Dobias. Macmillan, 1927. 5¾ x 5½.

28. *The Three Little Kittens,* pictures by Kurt Wiese. Macmillan, 1928. 5¾ x 5½.

and puts the action in the lap of the onlooker (27).

For *The Three Little Kittens*, a rhyme consisting of a few words and a great deal of action, every phrase is dramatized and the whole spread is animated. Kurt Wiese scattered the naughty kittens all over the pages, seldom resorting to a groundline; and the type was hand-set around them, not only making the words part of the picture but also making them reinforce the action (28).

For the Haders, as for Kurt Wiese, the Happy Hour books were the first of many successes. One cannot look the Ugly Duckling in the eye and not pity his plight (30), such is their sympathetic grasp of a situation and the straightforward way they project it. In their other books too, whether it's Peter dropping off the train and Terry prudently hanging back in the long-lived *Wonderful Locomotive* (31) or the mournful clown and the laughing dog in the little-known *Two Funny Clowns* (29), the human appeal is instantaneous. Later, in watercolor, the Haders did more ambitious work (as in the Caldecott winner, *The Big Snow*) but nothing superior in terms of illustration or design to what they did in line and a few flat tones in the late Twenties and early Thirties.

Aesthetically, the star of the Happy Hour series is Mary Lott Seaman's *Golden Goose.*

29. *Two Funny Clowns,* by Berta and Elmer Hader. Coward-McCann, 1929. Detail.

30. *The Ugly Duckling,* text by Hans Christian Andersen, pictures by Berta and Elmer Hader. Macmillan, 1927. 5¾ x 5½.

31. *The Wonderful Locomotive,* text by Cornelia Meigs, pictures by Berta and Elmer Hader. Macmillan, 1928. Detail.

Here the flatness is absolute, and in the absence of modeling or shading a succession of planes is set up parallel (or diagonal) to the picture surface with space in between. So might a stage set be arranged, with the figures free to move, and the audience free to imagine them moving, almost at will. Here too the color limitation becomes a positive force. Bold, gloriously arbitrary, not flouting nature but breaking free of it, the colors are constituents of the design and expressive integers; intense as their Ballets-Russe counterparts, they appeal directly and unequivocally to the senses (32, 33, 34).

Reduced from fifty cents to twenty-five cents during the Thirties, the Happy Hour books were extinguished finally by a bigger bargain, the Little Golden Books, but they represent to this day the only effort by a major trade house not just to lower the price of picturebooks (other abortive attempts were made in that direction) but to produce something unique at low cost. They never became, nor were they intended to be, mass market items (the mass market for picturebooks was just developing, at five and ten cents); neither did they pretend to replace the classic renderings of Caldecott or his compeers. Indicatively, the 1929 Macmillan catalog touts them as "the gayest sort of well made cheap book one could possibly find to use for a birthday or Christmas card, for stockings, for prizes . . . ." For Christmas *presents*, for special occasions, one was expected to look elsewhere.

One looked still, in fact, largely to Europe. That same 1929 catalog boasts of four examples of "beautiful printing from Europe"—two from Germany, two from Czechoslovakia—and the rush to translate books and import them in sheets (less often, bound) embraced both the long-known (Elsa Beskow, Sibylle v. Olfers) and the quite new (Else Wenz-Vietor, André Hellé), with many firms participating. A story in itself is *The Red Horse*. The work of a Swedish artist living in Switzerland which was published in Germany, it was

32

33

spotted by Ernestine Evans in Oslo during a scouting trip for the new firm of Coward-McCann early in 1928. ("London, Copenhagen, Oslo, Stockholm, Berlin, Moscow, and home via Leipzig and Paris. Those were the days!"[5]) By arrangement with the German publisher who saw to the printing, it appeared on the first Coward-McCann list that fall.

Coward-McCann, starting out, was starting a juvenile list from scratch. Ernestine Evans, all-purpose editorial adviser, was a journalist by trade, an initiator by inclination. Variously a correspondent during the Russian Revolution, feature editor of the *Christian Science Monitor*, author of the first American study of Diego Rivera, she had a range of acquaintances as broad as her interests. Her reputation as an expert on children's books was based on the year-end roundups she edited for *The New Republic* in 1926 and 1927, where Bertrand Russell and Charles Beard led off and the top librarian-reviewers mopped up.

The 1928 and 1929 Coward-McCann lists, largely Ernestine Evans's doing, mark a turning point: of the twelve books published, all but four were picturebooks. They started not in the nursery, but in the studio; they didn't happen along, they were for the most part solicited. Their creators—Lois Lenski, the Haders, Kurt Wiese, Wanda Gág—were the new professionals. It was time for picturebooks to take hold in the United States.

It was time because 1929 also brought Maud and Miska Petersham's *Miki*, the first of the big colorful depictions of a foreign childhood and the first big colorful picture story to be printed here; because attention to the nature and needs of young children was extending the market downward in age and outward in interests; because Nicholson's *Clever Bill* and *Pirate Twins* supplied a new format and a new literary form that Americans adopted with alacrity.

All that was needed was a star performer and a big hit—Wanda Gág and *Millions of Cats.*

32-34. *The Golden Goose,* pictures by Mary Lott Seaman. Macmillan, 1928. 5¾ x 5½.

34

WANDA GÁG

Wanda Gág was as good as ready-made for the role of nursery celebrity. The daughter of Bohemian immigrants, hadn't she grown up in the Old World fastness of New Ulm, Minnesota; lost her father at fifteen and, to help support her mother, herself, and the six younger Gágs, sold place cards and post cards and, to the Minneapolis *Journal Junior*, picture stories for children; lost her ailing mother soon after and held the family together; drudged in New York, renounced commercial art, retired to the countryside, finally won acclaim for her drawings and prints? When *Millions of Cats* came out, didn't a local paper headline her triumph "NEW ULM'S CINDERELLA FINDS ART'S GOLDEN SLIPPER IN NEW YORK"? The fairy tale, however, was in the eye of the beholder.

"My father was too idealistic to face the fact that no artist could survive in a mediocre Middle Western village," she wrote anonymously in *The Nation* in 1927. "True, New Swabia had a rich European background and a sturdy pioneer past, but the vitiating spirit of Main Street was already becoming evident, and after all that was what my father had to combat." Continuing—her article was one of a series entitled "These Modern Women"—she observed that "My mother, who was a natural iconoclast, arranged our hair in unusual ways, refused to burden us with starched clothes, and considered shoes and stockings unnecessary in hot weather, Sundays included."[1]

If her father was a pariah and her mother a free spirit, Wanda Gág herself was a heretic. Social pressures notwithstanding, she refused to sacrifice her career for her family or, later, for marriage, and fond as she was of children, she weighed long and hard the question of having children vs. drawing for them. "This difficult debate with myself lasted for several years and ended with my conviction that if it came to a choice I was more interested in creating aesthetically than physically."[2] Reading her, one quickly decides that Wanda Gág is more interesting than her legend. Her thinking has a rigor that persists in her work, and she expresses herself with the same plain honesty.

35. "Farm Sale" by Wanda Gág from *New Masses,* August 1926.

It is simple enough, the account of how she began to do children's books. Ernestine Evans, seeing her work on exhibit, raised the possibility of her doing something for children; she already had, it turned out—there were some stories, polished in the telling, that she had been trying to sell for years, and for one, *Millions of Cats*, she had trial drawings. (Two of the others became *The Funny Thing* and *Snippy and Snappy.*)

Ernestine Evans suggested the long horizontal format of William Nicholson's *Clever Bill* "which was both small book and large one, a wide page and yet not 'big merchandise.' She agreed to that, for it suited her notion of the old man journeying home."[3] It also suited to perfection the tableaux she had stretched across two pages in *New Masses*, and one doesn't need her confirmation—"the drawings are done in the pen-and-ink style which I used in *New Masses* for the 'Farm Sale,' 'Circus,' etc."[4]—to recognize the relationship (35, 36).

Work for *New Masses*—where some of the signal graphic art of the period appeared—had to be forceful; it was printed on rough, porous stock, it was meant to strike home. In adopting the same style for her picturebooks, Gág produced drawings that, firmly contoured, tightly structured, distinctly black and white, have an immediate impact—an impact little diminished after forty-odd years by worn plates and some very indifferent printing.

The *New Masses* drawings were critical in another respect: they were friezes. Nicholson provided the size and the shape but he didn't break out of the picture frame or, more important, spread his illustrations across two pages to take advantage of the extra-wide opening. The innovation must be credited to Gág, who sometimes leaves a token margin, as in the beautiful opening sweep of the old man setting out over the hills (her favorite drawing in the book), and sometimes a more definite break, indicating a narrative lapse without disturbing the continuity—the last a variation on a very old device, the composite picture (36).

Equally extraordinary and, in terms of design and continuity, also prophetic is the Happiwork Story Box, one of five illustrating "The House That Jack Built" (37). This was the business that failed, that wiped out most of Wanda Gág's savings, that sent her to the country instead of to Europe, that started her telling stories to children again and doing the serious drawing that together culminated in *Millions of Cats*. It was an ingenious project: the boxes came flat, to be folded by the child, then stacked or nested; the story proceeded in continuous pictures and running text around each box and from the smallest to the largest. One notices first the dynamic design, then the way it cunningly fits each panel, then the way white is used, as a distinct third color and as a drawing element—and then of course there's

And so he went back over the sunny hills an
down through the cool valleys, to show all hi
pretty kittens to the very old woman.
It was very funny to see those hundreds an
thousands and millions and billions and trillio
of cats following him.

Snippy and Snappy and a crotchety stool. The Happiwork Story Box is a toy but it is not only clever and, yes, artistic, it has character.

If one had to sum up *Millions of Cats*, pictures and text, in a very few words, form and character would suffice. Form and character fused, yielding the folk quality much remarked in Gág's work. Was it based on an old tale, Anne Carroll Moore asked; Ernestine Evans, who knew the answer, astutely compared it to "The Three Bears," another story by a known author "that has a sort of patina."[5] Not only did words and pictures reinforce one another, both benefited by the hand-lettered text: that struck everyone. "A child will almost feel that he has made this book,"[6] Miss Moore observed, while Elizabeth Coatsworth put it in a poet's terms: "The text runs like a streamlet around the very old man and the very old woman and their house that had flowers, and through the hills where the old man walked hunting for a cat, and in and among the millions of cats which he finally found."[7] For there were—no one can forbear quoting, nor can I—

Cats here, cats there,
Cats and kittens everywhere
Hundreds of cats,
Thousands of cats,
Millions and billions and trillions of cats.

Words, and the very notion, are responsible for the success of *The Funny Thing*. Visually—graphically, pictorially—it doesn't hold a candle to *Millions of Cats*. The lengthy dialogue between kind old Bobo and the snickering, lip-smacking *aminal* is static by nature, forms are hardened into formula, there is neither fluidity nor flow. The exception is the Funny Thing himself, his funny faces, and the perfectly stupendous way his tail grows until it curls round and round the mountain.

But try telling it with or without the pictures and you have to pause repeatedly—to savor the word that isn't, *aminal*; to smack your lips too, over "And very good they are—dolls"; to relish with the Funny Thing the prospect of extra-beautiful blue points and a very long tail, and with Bobo the prospect of passing off balls of bird food as the miracle-working "jum-jills." "And very good they are—jum-jills" tops it off (38).

Notwithstanding the predominance of the text, *Snippy and Snappy* is a book that devolves on pictures, the most developed pictures-as-such of any of the early books. Here Gág works differently, more in the manner of her independent drawings and her lithographs, laying in close gradations of tone, employing plant forms as presences, animating the

36

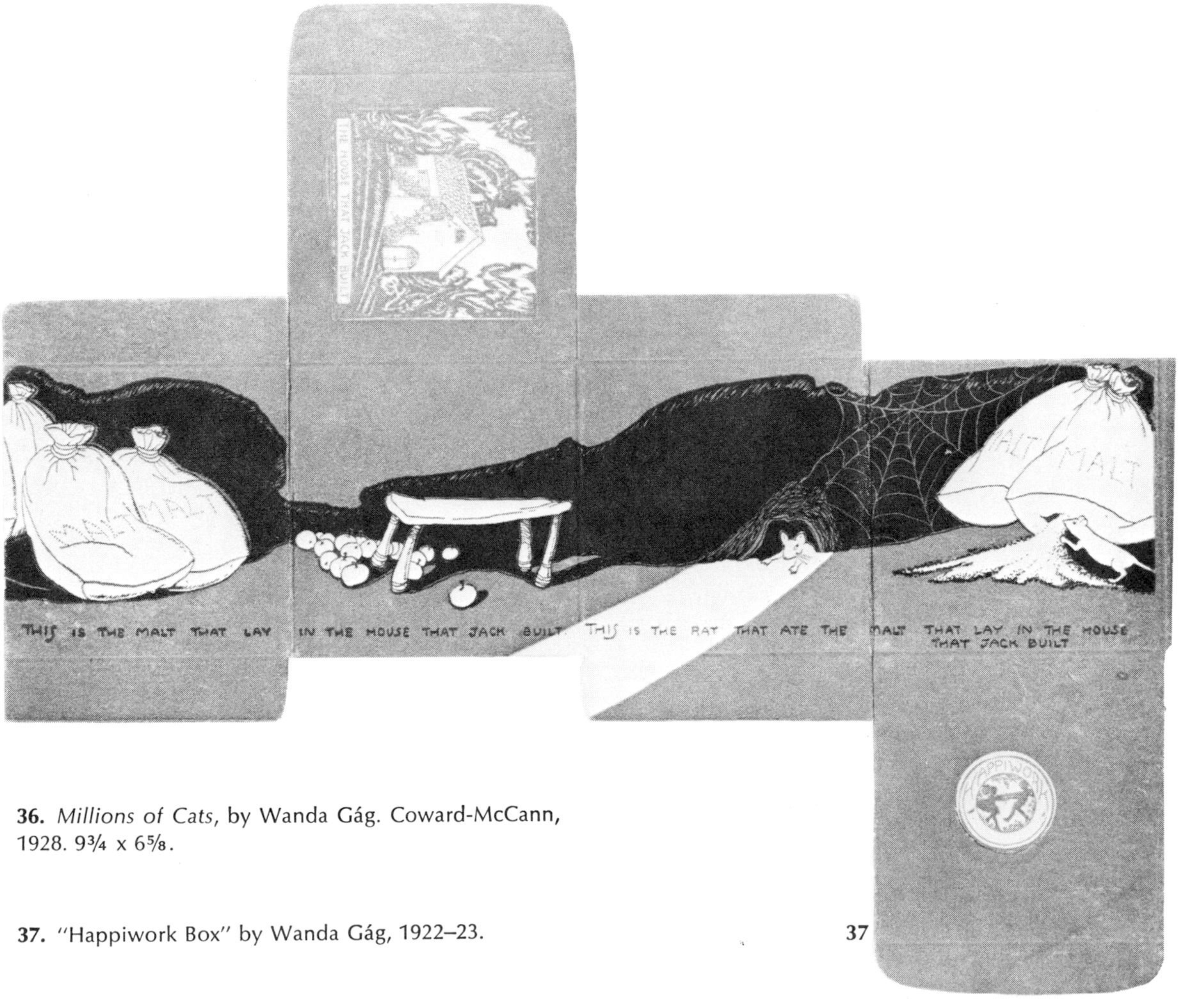

37

36. *Millions of Cats*, by Wanda Gág. Coward-McCann, 1928. 9¾ x 6⅝.

37. "Happiwork Box" by Wanda Gág, 1922–23.

And so on until he had eaten them all up.
"And *very* good they are—jum-jills," he said with a smack of his lips, after they were all gone.

38

Father Mouse read about the big wide world and the many big things in it.

39

Then Snappy found a footstool which had a green fringe around it.
"Look, Snippy," he cried, "here's a tree with funny leaves, and it's a tree with FOUR trunks."

40

38. *The Funny Thing,* by Wanda Gág. Coward-McCann, 1929.

39, 40. *Snippy and Snappy,* by Wanda Gág. Coward-McCann, 1931.

fringes of a mop, the legs of a lamp, giving a spooky cast to the night, a cozy glow to the mice's nook (39). One not only sees the mice, one feels with them. There is bliss in the glistening, gently rolling hay field, awe as Snippy and Snappy cross the dark threshold of their first house, and no end of curiosities inside (40). Scale is critical: outdoors and at home everything is in proportion, in the house they are dwarfed, diminutive, immediately at a disadvantage.

Still, any good illustrator might do as much; what is uniquely Wanda Gág's is the route from field to house, the trail of the blue knitting ball:

> They rolled it up, they rolled it down.
> They rolled it up and up and down.
> They rolled it up and DOWN and down,
> They rolled it UP AND DOWN.

And when they lose it to a little girl, the refrain recommences—"They followed it up, they followed it down"—as all the while Snippy and Snappy and the girl and the groundline and the lettering go up and down with the same easy sway. The climax is ordinary (Father Mouse warns them away from a trap) but the chant and its emphases stay on.

The first three stories, in a uniform format, were done in pen and ink; *The ABC Bunny*, the big book, was done in lithographs. It has been much admired for being real art, for the incorporation of a story line, for its action and suspense and endearing animal characters; and children do like it. To me it seems overlarge for its contents (even in its present reduced size), like a dollar birthday card, and overmannered—for Gág did have mannerisms and, unchecked, her naively drawn forms dramatically lit take on a theatrical quaintness (41). It is an effect she sometimes sought: "An old-fashioned parlor, arranged mainly for show rather than use, has something theatrical about it; and to portray this, I used a strong black and white design—an almost spotlight effect—to bring out the rococo pattern against the rich black shadows."[8] In *The ABC Bunny*, what cause?

Increasingly, in the Thirties, Gág concentrated on writing. She would do Grimm, that she decided early, and *Gone Is Gone*, an old tale of uncertain origin, can be regarded as a way station. An auspicious way station—as if, traveling from one metropolis to the next, one came upon a bright orderly village, the sort where flowers bloom on the station platform and sausages are sold inside and the inevitable lounger smiles a greeting. It is an experience, small, insignificant perhaps, but in its way perfect. The simile holds in another sense, for *Gone Is Gone*, the troubles of a husband who tries to do housework, patterned and precise and hilarious in the telling, no less controlled and comical in the drawing, stands between *Millions of Cats* and *Tales from Grimm*, and

42. *Gone Is Gone*, by Wanda Gág. Coward-McCann, 1935. Detail.

has none of the slackness or superfluities found in varying degrees in others of the books.

It is tempting to stop on the threshold of the two great Grimm collections, where a row of gingerbread figures has as much life as Lazy Heinz or Clever Elsie, for the remaining picturebooks are largely inert. *Snow White and the Seven Dwarfs* (Coward-McCann, 1938), done at the behest of Anne Carroll Moore to counter the Disney version, is hardly an improvement on it; Gág seems not to have found the more romantic Grimm tales particularly congenial. *Nothing at All* (Coward-McCann, 1941) has to its benefit the gradual transformation of blob into dog but again Gág was not at her best in color and the text—save for Nothing-at-all's incantatory "I'm busy/Getting dizzy"—is talky and not a little treacly.

The success of *Millions of Cats* is all the more impressive in that color, and the other standard allurements, played no part in it. Text, drawing and format together constitute its appeal and its lasting distinction.

41. *The ABC Bunny*, by Wanda Gág. Coward-McCann, 1933. 10¼ x 12.

43. *Tales from Grimm*, by Wanda Gág. Coward-McCann, 1936. Detail.

FOREIGN BACKGROUNDS

THE PETERSHAMS, THE D'AULAIRES, *THE PAINTED PIG* AND OTHER LATIN AMERICANA, BEMELMANS, FRANÇOISE, BOOKS OUT OF AFRICA AND ASIA POLITI AND THE PERSISTENCE OF THINGS FOREIGN

The world was making its way to America and, through picturebooks, American children were to see and know the world: it was almost an article of faith with May Massee, and she took it with her to Viking in 1933; it was natural to a cosmopolitan list like Knopf's; it crisscrossed publishers newly free to make bold with color and on the watch for colorful subjects. So quickly did the trend take hold, so concentrated was the production, that a visitor to the international exhibition of children's books in Hamburg in the summer of 1931 reported back: "In the case of our American books, the wealth of color seemed to be the outstanding feature for admiration, as well as the many-sidedness of our material. . . . It seemed quite natural that America, made up of many nationalities, should give her children books dealing with other countries and other sources . . . ."[1]

MAUD AND MISKA PETERSHAM

When the first systematic study of children's preferences in book illustration was made in 1922, it was 'discovered' that youngsters respond to storytelling quality, humor and action.[2] A 1929–30 investigation, confirming and extending these findings, identified realistic presentation and familiarity of subject matter as determinants.[3] Such studies, still being conducted, have to be viewed with a certain bemusement—one 'discovered' no interest among fourth-graders in a picture of toilet articles—and no uncertain skepticism (as testing the obvious by the available); but in the field of textbooks they make a limited kind of sense. If Tom, Dick and Harry take to a funny, lively picture of a bear making pancakes, in its own way realistic and familiar, they will want to read what goes with it (44). So went the reasoning, and such were the results that the Petershams were the leading illustrators of readers in the Twenties. *The Poppy Seed Cakes* aside and *Miki* as yet unseen, they are represented in the 1929 compilation *Realms of*

44. *In Animal Land*, by Mabel Guinnip La Rue, illus. by Maud and Miska Petersham. Macmillan, 1927. Detail.

Gold by more entries, all told, than any other illustrator(s) except Rackham.[4]

With *The Poppy Seed Cakes* and *Miki*, however, they came to be identified with the colorful treatment of highly flavored subjects, whether foreign, religious, patriotic or "things we use." But the nature of a book does not compel interest in it, and this the Petershams seem to have realized instinctively. Explaining the apparent disorder of their shelves, Maud Petersham wrote in 1925 that she and her husband collected books for their illustrations and classified them accordingly, by the qualities that attract and hold a child. "It may be that the illustration tells a story very obviously and clearly, or it may be bright clear color . . . or very decided action in the picture, or perhaps a certain kind of humor or fun . . . ."[5] They liked to put in little things that would please children—holes in the shape of hearts in the Three Bears' furniture—and "often we put a little unimportant story within a story." The last is from their Caldecott acceptance speech of 1946, so little did their approach change.

This is not to deny that *Miki* was 'the first of the international picture books,' as May Massee liked to say, and in fact it was roundly welcomed for its depiction of "everyday life in a picture book country."[6] That Hungary should, in a picturebook, become a "picture book country" is a curious inversion accounted for by the fact that the Petershams tacitly propelled their sneakered son Miki into the high-booted childhood of his father Miska. Many of their successors did likewise, and to a generation growing up on 'foreign dolls' and peasant party costumes it made no difference. Among their elders as well, thinking of the Old Country as old-fashioned was commonplace, while thinking of it as picturesque was encouraged by the relative plainness of American life.

Going abroad means, moreover, the disruption of routine, shucking responsibility, following impulse—for Miki, wanting to be in Hungary and, without a by-your-leave, being there; knocking at a strange door, sitting at a strange fire, sleeping in a strange bed; taking the family goose to find grass, staying over-

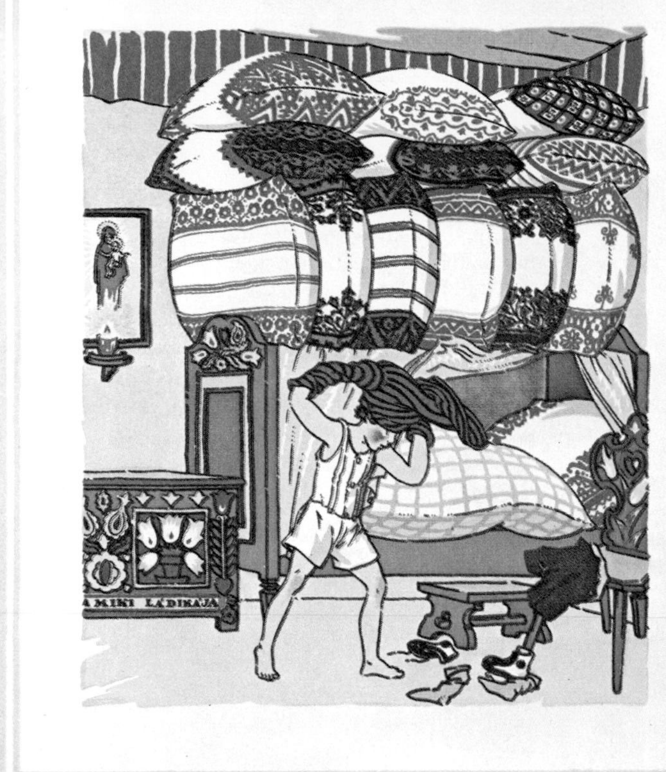

45. *Miki*, by Maud and Miska Petersham. Doubleday, 1929. 8½ x 10.

night at a shepherds' camp, going off with the goose and the shepherds' dog to Budapest: all highly irregular and at home unthinkable.

Far from being an everyday story of Hungary or anywhere, *Miki* is a cheerful flight of fancy colored by its setting. Boy and dog and goose sit around talking, that's how they decide to go to Budapest, and once there they have a high old time running back and forth across the bridges between Buda and Pest, comforting a tearful, tongue-less lion, riding and riding on the merry-go-round. Detail, incident and improvisation keep it going without a point or a plot, on the assurance that children would love to be in Miki's new boots—as who wouldn't?

The best of the pictures, the big curtained bed piled high with pillows, boxes in the flat color and surface patterns, and with them Miki's energy—his jersey half off, his sneakers askew (45). The color and design are organic to the material, the composition achieves a kinetic balance. But go outdoors and the color

46

46, 47. *Miki and Mary: Their Search for Treasures*, by Maud and Miska Petersham. Viking, 1934. 8¾ x 11.

becomes raw, its tints crude, the effect stagey: there is no less energy in the drawing—the three vagabonds dash across the bridges with a gusto that is contagious—only less finesse in the ensemble.

So many colors, the thinking went, what an asset—and for the Jersey City Printing Company, what an achievement. "In planographic printing," *Publishers' Weekly* reminded its readers, "each color is printed from a flat surface, and there has seemed to be no chance for the mixing of tones to obtain an effect like the four color process from half-tone plates. Mr. Stringer, however, has worked out a plan by which the effect of screening is obtained by pressing a Bendayed surface inked with lithographic ink on to the parts which are to be toned down, and when the plate is printed this screen effect reduces reds to pinks, blues to light blues, etc. By using this method and then overlaying colors a great variety of tones can be obtained, as, for instance, a deep brown is obtained by printing a solid yellow, then a screened red, and then a screened blue."[7]

47

Publishers' Weekly was not quite correct—the four-color process was even then being used in planographic printing abroad; but the excerpt, besides providing a clear description of a method that was to be widely adopted, is indicative of where American printing stood early in 1930.

In the fall of that year the first of the Petershams' Bible stories, *The Christ Child* (Doubleday), came out: soft and comparatively delicate, done in watercolors, printed in Germany. The illustrations are no less anecdotal, however, which accounts at least equally for the book's popular success.

Given the freedom to work as they would, in watercolors, and a subject that was eminently theirs, the Petershams produced in *Miki and Mary: Their Search for Treasures* a more perfect synthesis and a vicarious experience hard to top. *Miki and Mary* is all make-believe, the jaunt of two American children through a Europe composed unabashedly of picturebook places. Adventure is what they're after but children is what they are, and if their ocean liner isn't boarded by pirates, well, it does have a bang-up Punch and Judy show. At Mont-Saint-Michel they decide against dungeons and exchange their swords for an omelet pan, on the Grand Canal proud, haughty "Maria" gets dunked and comes out just plain Mary. Still, they stride about in wooden shoes (Brittany) and Turkish slippers (Rhodes) and bare feet (Jerusalem), and there's no end of treasures to fill their crossbone chest (46).

For those children, the great majority, to whom a trip is only as good as what can be brought back, there is no better picture in the book, and the Petershams, alert to children's interests, don't omit an item. In the suggestive rendering of the Piazza San Marco, however, they merge immediacy and movement with air and space and architectural splendor for a prime evocation of place (47). The wave border, ingeniously worked—see how the fishes come out of the white stripe, how one seems to grin, another to gasp—supplies a bond, a base, a rhythmic surge and, when there's no picture to look at, a bridging distraction.

Four years had passed since *The Christ Child*, and *Miki and Mary* was printed here, from plates made by a special method known as the Knudsen process. It is very much the product of its manufacture. Capitalizing on offset lithography's way with fade-ins and fade-outs, the Petershams eschewed their usual strong outlines and contrasts and designed instead for thin films of ink and graduated color tones, sometimes with real sensitivity.

Later, in the group of books picturing Early American stanzas and sayings which includes the Caldecott winner *The Rooster Crows* (Macmillan, 1945), the lithographic effects become a mannerism, essentially meaningless, and what would better have been broad and robust is finicky and fussy. As historic recreations, they have the slick quaintness of a wax-museum Williamsburg.

The Box with Red Wheels and *Circus Baby*, on the other hand, brought the Petershams back to where they began, portraying animals for the delight of small children. What can be inside the box with red wheels, the animals

48. *The Box with Red Wheels*, by Maud and Miska Petersham. Macmillan, 1949. 8 x 10.

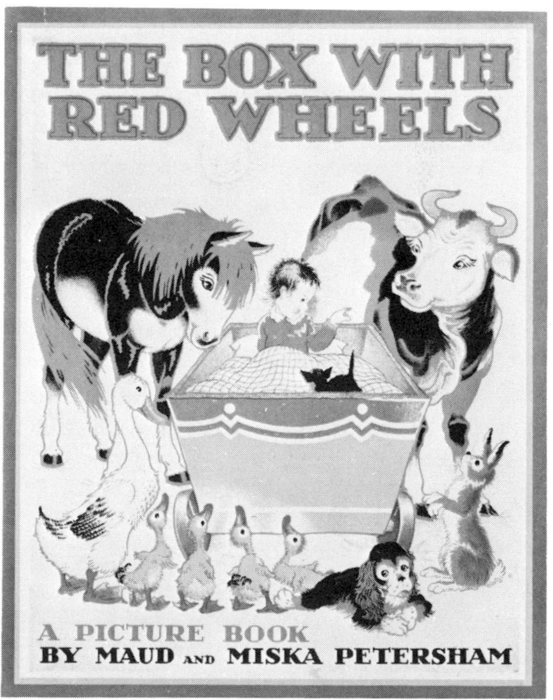

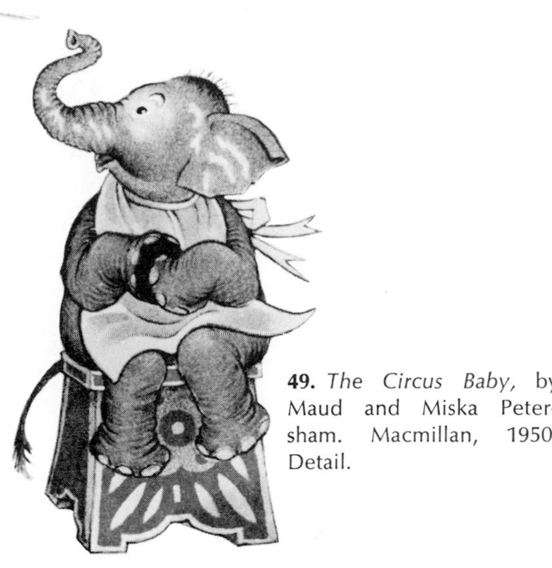

49. *The Circus Baby,* by Maud and Miska Petersham. Macmillan, 1950. Detail.

wonder, and one by one they look in, call out ("Moo-oo-oo-oo-oo-oo . . . Q-U-A-C-K"), shake their heads or flop in. The dog, looking wise, knows the answer; "It was a baby"—who pops up and won't be comforted until her mother lets the animals return. Repetition, suspense, surprise, satisfaction; barnyard animals, their sounds, their friendly presence; and a baby, wondering too, a fuzzy-haired fat baby: for a three-year-old, it is ideal. So is the look of the book, bright and solid and amply spaced, what is obvious about the drawing softened by the warm beige contours (48).

The Circus Baby is not without its lapses into the conveniently cute or comical but the spectacle of elephants playing house, of mother elephant trying to bring up baby after the fashion of the clown family, is inherently endearing and funny (49); and, "after all, *you* are an ELEPHANT" concludes the futile attempt with a nice plug for the natural order of things. When the Petershams addressed themselves to children and what they enjoy (or don't), their work has a sturdiness that sustains it irrespective of the subject.

INGRI AND EDGAR PARIN D'AULAIRE

It is not a judgment of either pair to say that in passing from the Petershams to the d'Aulaires one goes from illustration to art. More critical, where the Petershams strive to secure the interest of children, the d'Aulaires seek to express children's feelings, to develop a scene from within.

What at first seems a peculiar interpretation of the vivid abandon of *The Magic Rug* (Doubleday, 1931), the d'Aulaires' first picturebook, appears in an otherwise sensible 1932 article on "modern trends." "In the effort to get back to the simplicity of children's first conceptions of picture making," the author contends, "there has been a conscious imitation of their untrained handiwork with its fine disregard for perspective and proportion."[8] This of Edgar d'Aulaire, trained in Munich and Paris and Florence, illustrator of deluxe editions and proficient mural painter, of Ingri d'Aulaire, long a practicing portraitist?

And yet, even in the more finished drawings for *Ola*, there is a difference between the d'Aulaires' illustrations and those current in children's books. In disregarding, when it suited them, such conventions of post-Renaissance painting as perspective and proportion (part of what got the poster artists in trouble), the d'Aulaires had two alternative traditions to draw upon, one not long since revived, one still quite new—the decorative, often dramatic stylization of folk art and the willful, often expressive distortion of modernist art. In Ingri d'Aulaire's native Norway, which her husband adopted as his own, the folk strain had been renewed in the work, most notably, of Gerhard Munthe, while the modern idiom was theirs by training and prolonged contact. They made use of both, not so much in a formal, figurative sense as in reaching a rapprochement with children, extracting from folk art and modernist art the intensity and arbitrariness that cause them to be identified with the art of children.

"The arctic lights leap across the sky in cold, silent flames" as *Ola* opens, and a tawny sun, "afraid to show his pale face in winter," sits on the mountain tops (50). "In this country there is a forest [where] the trees turn into a crowd of solemn creatures. In the middle of the forest there was a small house. And in this house there lived a small boy. . . . The flaring arctic lights had awakened him and he decided to put on his clothes and go out . . . ." The mysterious vastness contracts to a frosted window, a carved bedstead, and then Ola is off on his skis and we are directly behind him, sharing the plunge (51).

Ola can't be told, it has to be experienced; one could have the whole text without half knowing the book. There is no proper label for this picture (52), it exists in the physical and psychological tug between flowered bank and endless sea, in Ola's wide-spaced, wide-open, unfocused eyes, his open and closed face. Read the caption and you know that he's going home, look at the picture and you read his thoughts.

50–52. *Ola,* by Ingri and Edgar Parin d'Aulaire. Doubleday, 1932. 8⅞ x 12.

50

But when he wanted to join their play they scampered, frightened, to all sides. A small hare was so stupid, it ran just in front of Ola's skis. "Run on, my seven-league boots," said Ola to his skis.

51

Ola decided that he would go home, too. He had heard that he could

52

Ola, Ola and Blakken (1933) and *Children of the Northlights* (1935) made the d'Aulaires' reputation as Norwegian emissaries to the United States. As spontaneous and almost as unstructured as *Miki* or *Miki and Mary*, they are ballasted more firmly by their background and forswear outright fantasy.

Beginning with *The Magic Rug*, the d'Aulaires' early books also established their medium, stone lithographs, as a brilliant new way of getting color into picturebooks; technically, they are as important in that respect as *Miki*. As the d'Aulaires explain, "It wasn't so much lithography in itself but color lithography which was the new idea, the complicated procedure of translating colors into infinite shades of blacks and grays and transferring the work to offset zincs to be printed in the right colors. This eliminates the photographic process, and gives the finished work a handdrawn look."[9]

Just how the artists worked up the black key drawing and, on separate stones, the drawings for each of the three or four additional colors, is too intricate to relate briefly; regardless, some general principles apply. Whether in monochrome or in several colors, a lithograph is in essence a drawing, and it need not be done directly on stone; anything executed with a lithographic pencil (or other greasy material) on paper can be transferred to stone, and the result may or may not be indistinguishable. In any case the printing of a book requires that a final transfer be made to zinc plates, which, in turn, can be done so as to bypass stone altogether. We shall see such variations and ignore many of them as immaterial; if we make much of the d'Aulaires' specific method, it is because of its importance as a precedent and the particularly effective use they made of it, not because it is *necessarily* superior.

In sum, when color was wanted, it was to be had, with—because lithographs retain the gradations of drawings—the semblance of tone. The elimination of the camera and the preservation of the hand-drawn look entailed also the elimination of the middleman: the artist did the color separations himself, which saved the publisher money as well as keeping the artist's work inviolate. So rich was the result that it commended the method further; as rich as it was, the procedure was arduous, the stones cumbersome and a nuisance to store. But a way had been shown, a touchstone—as it were—established, and lithographic drawing on zinc (p. 67) and acetate (p. 207) followed from lithographic drawing on stone.

Because of cost, color appeared in the d'Aulaire books only at alternate openings, and half the illustration fell to the black and white pages (a scheme that predominated, in one way or another, until quite recently). It is well known that monochromatic prints or drawings can have as much 'color' as those in several hues, and lithographs, capable of the most complete gamut of tone of any graphic medium, have uncommon potential in this regard. And as they can be any of many things from the barest sketch to the equivalent of a finished painting, the artist has uncommon

53. *The Conquest of the Atlantic*, by Ingri and Edgar Parin d'Aulaire. Viking, 1933. 9⅝ x 11⅞.

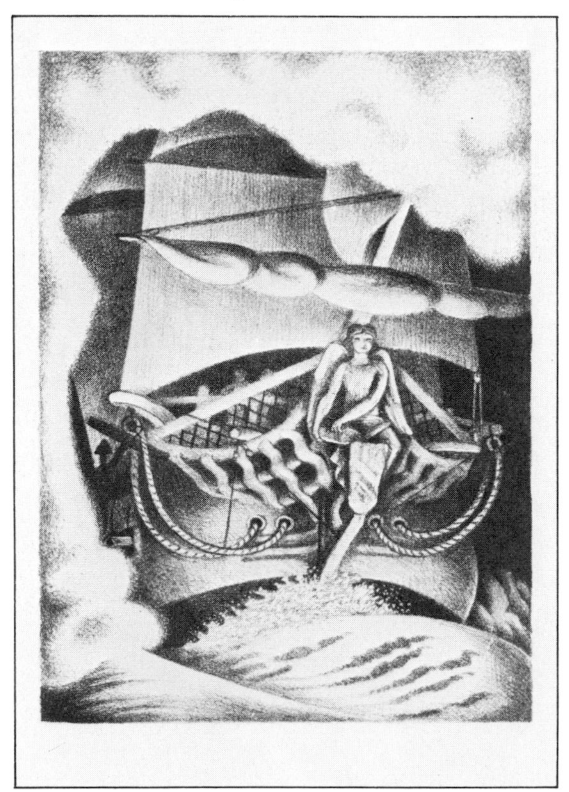

54. *Children of the Northlights*, by Ingri and Edgar Parin d'Aulaire. Viking, 1935. 8½ x 11¾.

latitude. For *Conquest of the Atlantic*, done largely in black and white (with sometimes a second color, seldom several), the d'Aulaires designed solidly, keeping a close harmony between tone applied in rhythmic strokes and modeling, and composing in the deep blacks and luminous white that are another glory of the medium (53). Altogether different, the reindeer design from *Children of the Northlights*, abstracted after the fashion of prehistoric rock images, is as beautiful as anything they have done and in its own way a consummate example of lithography (54).

There followed *George Washington* (1936), *Abraham Lincoln* (1939), *Leif the Lucky* (1941), *Pocahontas* (1949), *Benjamin Franklin* (1950), *Buffalo Bill* (1952), *Columbus* (1955, all Doubleday)—the pictorial gallery of American heroes that children took to happily and some adults received with reservations. Two of them, Bertha Mahony and Marguerite Mitchell, took the unprecedented step of criticizing the Caldecott winner, *Abraham Lincoln*, in the biographical paper written to accompany the d'Aulaires' acceptance speech. Just what they meant, however, in saying that 'there were qualities in the two *Olas* which some of us miss in the two American books,' that "perhaps the American scene and material needed a longer period of assimilation," is hard to fathom—unless it is what Lewis Gannett alluded to, neither as a shortcoming nor a virtue, when he remarked that their *George Washington* took on "something of the Franco-Norwegian charm of *Ola*."[10] If so, why cavil; in the acceptance speech Edgar d'Aulaire points out that he and his wife came to American themes "as children . . . not hampered by standard conceptions" though not entirely as strangers: the vast prairies, high with corn, cleft by sudden storms, comprised "the most perfect dreamland for a boy living in a European metropolis." "I don't think any American can appreciate this country as I do," Miska Petersham observed on the same occasion a few years later. His was a different American dream, of freedom and opportunity, but between the two men, d'Aulaire drawn here and Petersham in effect driven, much of the history of the United States is encompassed. It is not accidental that colonial and frontier America was put into picturebooks by 'foreigners'; for them it was as much a picturebook place as old Hungary or snowbound Norway was to Americans.

55. *George Washington*, by Ingri and Edgar Parin d'Aulaire. Doubleday, 1936. 8⅜ x 12.

The ingenuousness of *George Washington* accounts for much of its charm as a children's book, that combination of gravity and gentle raillery that aligns the horses of Washington and his companions-at-arms like Rockettes, that stands G. W. upright through an arctic blizzard crossing the Delaware, that thrusts frostbitten feet into the picture of the commander-in-chief wrapped in his cloak at Valley Forge (55). Nor has Washington any the less luster for the owl looking over his shoulder.

Abraham Lincoln is a more dimensional and therefore a more difficult hero, and neither the treatment of the subject nor the treatment of the illustrations is as successful—the latter because they lack the broad simplicity that is the d'Aulaires' strength. But with *Leif the Lucky* they are not only on home ground, they are immersed in Norse myth and Nordic fire-and-ice. "He shall eat till he bursts," growls King Olav when one of his men fails to stop on signal, while the others quaff from horns, rats and mice consort under the table, and a trough of flames licks at the line of feet. It is all larger than life, and full-up with grinning demons and dramatic invention.

Unfortunately some of the d'Aulaire books have lost in the printing over the years, a fate not uncommon to picturebooks. But to work such as theirs, where matter is inseparable from manner, the damage is particularly destructive, and reminds us that the more illustration relies on realization of a complex intention, the more it is likely to suffer from error, penury or just unconcern.

THE PAINTED PIG AND OTHER LATIN AMERICANA

Seldom, perhaps never, has a picturebook bowed as auspiciously as *The Painted Pig*. In October 1930 the first major exhibition of native Mexican arts opened at the Metropolitan Museum at the start of a twelve-month tour. Initiated by the American ambassador, Dwight Morrow (whose daughter Anne had recently married Charles Lindbergh), the show was organized by René d'Harnoncourt who, living in Mexico for some years, had studied and collected its indigenous art. Almost simultaneously *The Painted Pig* appeared, not only "the first Mexican picture book" but also the collaboration of Elizabeth Morrow, the ambassador's wife, and René d'Harnoncourt.

The book took shape around d'Harnoncourt's large collection of Mexican toys. At the suggestion of publishers, Mrs. Morrow, who tried to place it, wrote a new text. Though *The Painted Pig* is disjunct both in design—the framed pictures stand apart from the solid pages of type—and in structure, the disjuncture is not detrimental. As pictured, the story of a little girl with a pet pig bank and her brother who longs for one like it is equally the story of the clay pig—a hulking, scowling yellow pig with pink flowers, prevision of Churchill in coveralls—and of the toys Pedro won't take from the peddler in its place: a passing parade of straw horses, lions, rabbits (56), a blue crane made from a gourd, and jumping jacks of all descriptions, including a fierce bandit of a clown, his arms outstretched, pleading? threatening?

Discouraged—he has been put off time after time—Pedro sets out to make his own pig, while Pita waits loyally to be summoned. "Again there was quiet. Pita could hear the water running in the fountain and knew that Pedro must be wetting the clay. A little later he was slapping it between his hands and she heard him say: 'Now you be good.' Then he whistled a little, but finally that stopped. It was very stupid for Pita with nothing to do. She counted the leaves on the bush over her head—and then the thorns on each leaf. She tried to pick a red blossom, but she pricked her finger. . . . Finally she got up on her chair and looked over the wall" (57).

Mrs. Morrow tells her story with an easy grace, an awareness of what it's like to be a child, a sure sense of narrative structure. D'Harnoncourt's tight flat pictures, part primitive painting, part marionette theater, give a snap to her naturalism, and in their confines fancy expands. The big painted pig is no larger than he is to Pita and to Pedro (who finally gets, not his double, but his equal).

56 

 57

56, 57. *The Painted Pig,* text by Elizabeth Morrow, pictures by René d'Harnoncourt. Knopf, 1930. 8¼ x 10¾.

In that "Mexican year," as *Publishers' Weekly* called it, there appeared two other picturebooks, Jan and Zhenya Gay's *Pancho and His Burro* (Morrow) and *Tranquilina's Paradise* (Minton, Balch) by Susan Smith and Thomas Handforth. One can almost place them by their titles, the first a homely story emphatically colored, the second graceful and a little remote. Both pairs of collaborators had lived in Mexico, the new magnet for Americans. Here was a foreign country close at hand and ripe for picturing; there was no influx of Mexican books or talent, no importable *Red Horse* or immigrating Edgar d'Aulaire to supply the United States with local color.

This particular circumstance, true to an even greater extent of the rest of Latin America, influenced what American children saw and read over the years: they came to know Holland through Dutch-born Meindert DeJong and Hilda Van Stockum, Peru they knew through sojourners like Ann Nolan Clark and Helen Rand Parish. Of picturebooks on South American themes by South Americans, only two appeared: *The Legend of the Palm Tree* by Margarida Estrela Bandeira Duarte and Paulo Werneck (Grosset, 1940), a Brazilian book translated, and *Maria Rosa: Everyday Fun and Carnival Frolic with Children in Brazil* (Doubleday, 1942), for which Candido Portinari, newly known for his World's Fair murals, provided the pictures. (The war in Europe turned American attention briefly southward, a phenomenon reflected in children's books generally.)

With Mexico it was somewhat different; to offset the sleepy peons and plaster saints pictured by resident or transient Americans, there were the books of René d'Harnoncourt and Jean Charlot, both of whom, though they were Europeans who eventually became Americans, lived a Mexican life in Mexico and contributed to its artistic growth.

LUDWIG BEMELMANS

For Bemelmans, the bon vivant, picturebooks were an unlikely beginning. True, there is more to the Bemelmans story than May Massee's visit to his Eighth Street apartment, the Tyrolean landscape painted on the window shades to hide a bad view, and *Hansi*, the book that grew out of her visit and his Tyrolean boyhood. Before there was a *Hansi* there was a restaurant, the Hapsburg House, where Bemelmans painted trompe l'oeil murals and

58

58, 59. *Hansi,* by Ludwig Bemelmans. Viking, 1934. 9 x 12.

dispensed *gemütlichkeit* and generally impressed the publishing people who patronized it. But *Hansi,* his first book, was the kickoff.

As a picturebook, it's a monstrosity. Solid 9 x 12 pages of type confront similar pages with now a sketch at the top, now a colored panel part way down; for all its great size and its sixty-four pages, there are very few large-scale drawings: if Bemelmans gave any thought to the book he was making, there is no sign of it.

Still, *Hansi* is insidious. In Uncle Herman's house high in the mountains where Hansi goes for Christmas the smell of Lebkuchen spreads from cellar to roof (58). Earlier, the little mountain train, short and fat, shares the station with a sleek streamliner from Paris and Vienna; the stationmaster, glorious in red and gold, signals the start with his baton; snow piled high on either side whispers snowballs but no, Hansi isn't to open the window. And then, quickly, Post Seppl waits at the station with his mail sleigh, Aunt Amalie, Uncle Herman, cousin Lieserl and dachshund Waldl wait at the door, and here is Hansi, "like a little sack of potatoes," mumbling, his long message muffled as much by embarrassment (59). "If a dog is around that is a great help"—and Hansi pets Waldl, admires his tricks with Lieserl, follows her under the broad stomach of Romulus in the stable, proves to her that not even Uncle Herman can draw a pig without look-

59

ing; and so, circuitously, reaches safe harbor. "The house had welcomed Hansi. He had delivered the greeting and given out the three kisses—without any trouble."

It is true that Bemelmans's interjections are adult observations, that he is writing not so much about a little boy named Hansi as about a little boy like Hansi, and with nostalgic affection. But he is observant—a dog *is* a great help in making friends—and he remembers well. The pictures reinforce him: however haphazard the overall scheme, individual illustrations are attentive to detail, brisk and good-humored. Bemelmans, who took himself seriously as an artist, cannot have been comforted by Henry Pitz's observation that his drawings "seem to the average person the kind of thing that almost anyone could do and this is nearly true."[11] Acknowledging Bemelmans's charm, Pitz disparages his draftsmanship—but in what does his charm consist, when setting and circumstances are removed, if not in the perpendicular of a peruke, a Roman brow, a child's broad jowls (61)?

He was not a plodder: disinclined to do color separations, he left to Kurt Wiese the labor of translating his color drawings into their component hues on zinc plates, and the broad crayon strokes and mottled colors, lithography's own, suit the rustic simplicity of the high Tyrol.

The Golden Basket is something of an anomaly too, but a more harmonious one however much it appears to flout the canons of book design by inserting what amount to unframed paintings, deep compositions with strong chiaroscuro, in the two-dimensional text pages. Though not a picturebook in proportions, it is wholly pictorial in conception, the workings of an inn and the byways of Bruges as seen by two little English girls. Celeste and Melisande wake in a strange red room, rose to crimson

60. *The Golden Basket,* by Ludwig Bemelmans. Viking, 1936. 7⅛ x 9⅝.

61. *The Castle Number Nine*, by Ludwig Bemelmans. Viking, 1937. Detail.

to scarlet to tomato; it is still night, and the square outside is bathed in blue, the street lamps and the finials glisten (60). The scene is one to dream upon and back to bed they go; at breakfast, more wonders: two English ladies, look-alikes, with matching fur pieces—but one of the red foxes is cross-eyed, "and that is how they were told apart."

The pictures introduce another aspect of color printing, preseparated half-tones, and a name as inescapable as that of the Jersey City Printing Company, William Glaser. In the printing of watercolors, as here, preseparation was an expedient, used to circumvent first the imperfections, then the cost, of camera separation in four-color process. As tedious as it is for the artist, it has distinct advantages, enabling him to control his colors more closely, to have certain colors that are unattainable through process, to achieve effects—in *The Golden Basket*, what one connoisseur called "a fruitiness"—that process doesn't yield. As for Glaser, he was a printing broker who would take on a book for a publisher, contract for the platemaking and presswork, and deliver a finished product. Color work was his specialty, May Massee his best customer. He handled the d'Aulaires' first books, taking to the idea of color lithography because it promised new business for a plant he was connected with; he worked with Kurt Wiese on *Liang and Lo*, innovative in its own way, and *The Story about Ping*, with Bemelmans and his aides on *Hansi, The Golden Basket* and *Castle Number Nine*, with the young William Pène du Bois. In what has been termed "a medicine man period" in printing, Glaser, ingenious and secretive, was chief.

A more sophisticated affair than *Hansi, The Golden Basket* is otherwise notable for the debut of Madeline, exquisite Madeline, at the end of a staid double line of little girls. "Her hair is copper-red, she has blue eyes, and while she finishes her prayers she looks down at the toe of her shoe which follows the outline of the Knight's helmet." Shapes of things to come.

But first there was Baptiste—Baptiste the pensioner striding in his Saturday livery to the market (61), Baptiste the perplexed confiding to his cat: "Here we are alone. I am only sixty-five years old, I have been a good servant all of my life, and still I am not happy. Why?" A small ad in the newspaper and he is off with his seven pairs of pumps, his seven liveries and wigs, to the Tyrol. Now where is the Castle Number Nine? "Go over the bridge," gestures the innkeeper; "Past the church," points the guard; "Out of the city gate," says a little boy. And there on the second hill to the right, just as they said, is the Castle Number Nine, Count Hungerburg-Hungerburg standing on the bridge. But—Baptiste, take heed—today is not Friday, as the count proclaims; "When I'm [in] blue it's Monday, sir."

To cut it short, reluctantly, *Castle Number Nine* is Bemelmans's best story, and also his most interestingly illustrated book, a kind of running picture-story with everything in place—uniforms and pumps and wigs, innkeeper and courtyard, guard at his post, boy and gate and mountains beyond. Let the action narrow, and the picture cuts in—the count's poodle chases Baptiste's cat, followed by Baptiste's foot; let it spread, let dog pursue cat from cellar to tower, and we get a cross-section of the castle. It is an illustrated manuscript with the fluidity of a film.

With *Madeline* Bemelmans settled down to charm all and sundry and succeeded. Does anyone who knows it not know the story, not remember the verses, not summon up the two as one? The words are the story/ and phrase by phrase they are the images/ that Bemelmans paints page by page: there is hardly another book quite so compact and close-knit and self-reinforcing. For what occurs, we have an accident to thank; Bemelmans was in the hospital with a little girl who had had an appendix operation "and, standing up in bed, with great pride she showed her scar to me."[12] A tonsilectomy wouldn't have done at all.

One comes to think of *Madeline* in terms of color but actually there is full color at only four openings, where outdoor scenes occur, which should be a lesson of several sorts. Most of the illustration's are in black, or black and white, against a yellow ground, and they have the character of drawings as distinct from the Dufy-like paintings (62, 63). That the two don't conflict, that the abbreviated cartoon style of the former is for the most part not violated by overdevelopment in the latter, has much to do with making the book an artistic whole; when the reverse occurs in *Madeline's Rescue*, when the drawing becomes cruder and more cursory, the painting more dense and detailed, the illustration suffers as such and the total design falls apart.

In no respect do the later books have the integrity of *Madeline*, and one looks thereafter to his adult work for the best of Bemelmans.

62, 63. *Madeline,* by Ludwig Bemelmans. Simon & Schuster, 1939 (subsequently Viking). 8⅞ x 12.

and brushed their teeth

62

she loved winter, snow, and ice.

63

FRANÇOISE

France of the Paris boulevards in Bemelmans, France of the provinces in Françoise: the juxtaposition points up the contrast.

In America we saw first the coloring books she made for Tolmer, the catholic and creative French publisher (64). Listing *Images à Peinturler* and *Images à Colorier* in 1929, *The Horn Book* commended the field to young artists, observing that Françoise—full name, Françoise Seignobosc—had "set a stimulating new standard."[13] At least two more little paper books appeared here by 1931, *Les Paysans de France*, an introduction to children in five regions issued by Mitteldorfer Straus through The Peasant Village in New York, and *My Painting Book*, this one in translation, a Gordon Volland Publication of The Buzza Company in Minneapolis. From the latter and other sources the Saalfield Company, in Akron, took the Françoise pictures that Marion McNeil wrote a story around for *The Little Green Cart* (1931). Still others may turn up: just as Alice Dalgliesh snatched up the painting books at Woolworth's for her kindergartners, publishers of all stripes seized upon them for their own, sometimes unauthorized purposes. Indicatively, when *Fanchette and Jeannot* was brought out by Grosset in 1937, it carried the legend "Authorized American Edition." (On the other hand the many coloring books Françoise made for Platt & Munk, beginning in 1939, and for which she had contracted, failed to carry her name.)

For her coloring books and her story books, for ephemeral paper books and expensive trade books, she drew with the same lighthearted directness and gaiety, the very directness and gaiety of French provincial pottery; and like the artisans of the provinces, she has a definite sense of the space each composition is to fill. In *La Plus Vieille Histoire du Monde*, the story of the Creation, it is perhaps the strongest attribute (65).

This most improbable of cloth books—imagine the Unicorn Tapestries used as cushion covers—is illustrated here for your pleasure, because it is a minor work of art. The comparison holds in another sense (as it would not to the illusionist Gobelin tapestries, indistinguishable from paintings) for Françoise also respects the character of her material, its combination of flatness and roughness, its ability to absorb line and give it form. Another

64. *Images à Colorier* and *Images à Peinturler,* by Françoise. Paris, Tolmer, 1927. 9½ x 8⅝.

65. *La Plus Vieille Histoire du Monde,* by Françoise. Paris, Jardin des Modes, 1931. 9¾ x 8⅜.

reason for including a foreign item without further issue is to place it in Françoise's career, which, in the final accounting, was in the United States; though she continued to spend at least half the year in France, her major work was done expressly and exclusively for the American market.

French peasant life amused her—she is never tendentious about her Jeanne-Maries or Jean-Pierres—and so did American folkways. In the little-known *Mr. and Mrs. So and So* she tintypes the American tourist for all time. From bubbling departure (66) to humble return (67), it's a blithe, witty spoof of pretensions and improvidence—"they have to make presents, you know," Françoise remarks like a Frenchman. And this on pages all pink-and-blue innocence.

There was—there almost had to be—a *Gay Mother Goose* and a *Gay ABC*, even a *Thank-you Book* (1938, 1939, 1946, all Scribner), before Françoise found her own voice in *Jeanne-Marie Counts Her Sheep*, or rather the two voices, of frivolity (68) and common sense (69), that keep the book bouncing. In the pictures, the pattern holds: to count, there are toy sheep in a meadow, white forms on a green ground; to feast upon, there is Jeanne-Marie in full, festive color. Few counting books have a better reason for being, and seldom has the mandatory two-color, full-color scheme been put to better use.

It is the conclusion, however, that puts *Jeanne-Marie* among the elect:

> And do you know what
> happened?
> Patapon had one little
> lamb and a very small
> one!
> So Jeanne-Marie
> could not buy any shoes
> could not buy a red hat
> could not go to the fair
> could not buy a donkey
> could not have any
> house.
> There was just enough
> wool to knit a new pair
> of socks for Jeanne-
> Marie!
>
> But Jeanne-Marie tried to look
> very happy, anyway, for she
> did not want Patapon to feel sad.
> Patapon was so pleased
> with her one little
> Lamb!

Jean Charlot once wrote of a Mexican artist that her work was "compounded of contrarieties . . . innocent and ironical, infantile and wise." So it was with Françoise at her best.

THEY HAVE EVERYTHING
BUT STILL THEY ARE NOT
SATISFIED AND WANT BADLY
TO TRAVEL THEY DECIDE
TO GO ABROAD
AND ON A BEAUTIFUL
SPRING MORNING THEY
SAIL LEAVING HOUSE
AND DOG AND CAT AND
THE BABE, TOO ON THE
NORMANDIE
THEY SAIL BECAUSE Mrs
SO AND SO WANTS TO LEARN
FRENCH AS SOON AS POSSIBLE

NORMANDIE

66

66, 67. *Mr. and Mrs. So and So,* by Françoise. Oxford, 1939. 9 x 10½.

IT IS MARVELLOUS
TO SLEEP IN THE
OPEN AIR.
POMPON KEEPS
STILL ALL THE TIME
ON SUCH A SMALL
BOAT, EXERCISE
MAY BE DANGEROUS

67

"Patapon," says Jeanne-Marie, "maybe you will have four little lambs. Then we can go to the fair and ride on the merry-go-round. It is fun to ride on the merry-go-round, Patapon."

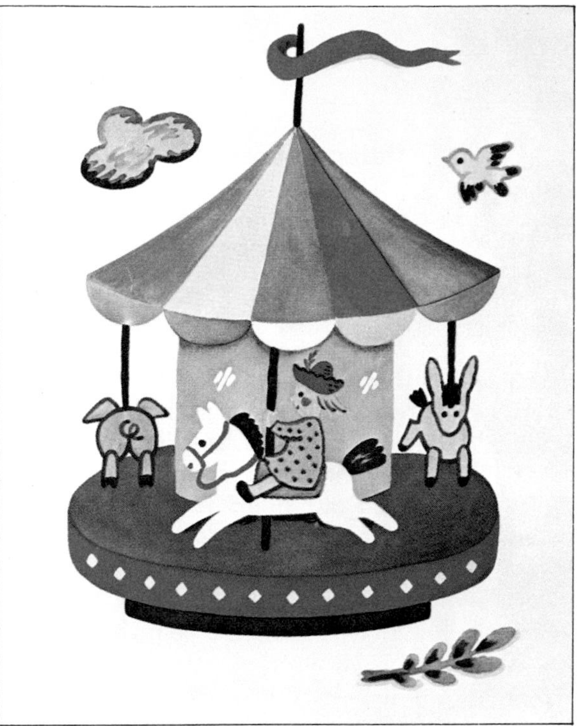

68

68, 69. *Jeanne-Marie Counts Her Sheep,* by Françoise. Scribner, 1951. 8 x 9¾.

Patapon answers:

"Yes, I will have four little lambs.

4

But we will stay in the green field where the daisies are white and the sun shines all day long. We do not need to ride on the merry-go-round, Jeanne-Marie."

69

70. *Penny-Whistle*, by Erick Berry. Macmillan, 1930. 7 x 8½.

BOOKS OUT OF AFRICA AND ASIA

Looking over the children's books set in Africa that appeared in the late Twenties and early Thirties one is struck first by their number, then by the fact that virtually all are illustrated—and a great many also written or edited—by Erick Berry. The wife of a British government officer stationed in Africa ('Erick Berry' is part nickname, part from an earlier marriage), she had firsthand knowledge of the West African interior at a time when few artists ventured below the Sahara. Rarer still, she was interested in the people, not the wildlife.

Her African books of those years, almost synonymous with *the* African books of those years, fall into four major groups: the jungle tales of Paul Du Chaillu, first published in the late nineteenth century, which she cut slightly for a new audience; the stories of African boys and girls that she and her husband Herbert Best both wrote (plus a few by other authors); two books of folklore, her own *Black Folk Tales* (far the better) and Logabola's *Folk Tales of a Savage*; and her small books —*Penny-Whistle* (Macmillan, 1930), *Mom du Jos: The Story of a Little Black Doll* (Doubleday, 1931), *Humbo the Hippo and Little-Boy-Bumpo* (Harper, 1932), and *Sojo: The Story of Little Lazy-Bones* (Harter, 1934).

Of the picturebooks, *Penny-Whistle* is the simplest and the most clever. Told to find a new note or else, Penny Whistle—so-called because he's never without it—puts on his pappy's tall shiny silk hat and sets out, "blowing on his penny whistle like this":

From everyone he meets—Big Bill the toucan, a parrot named Mary, an elephant who sends him spinning (in Pappy's big hat, 70), a cricket who just glares—he gets a new note, and Little-yalla-bird adds two more until, with a bit of help, he's got himself a tune:

And when he comes marching home—"can't that boy just play!"

Given a little help in turn, children could put together Penny Whistle's tune too ("Little David Play on Your Harp"), and with a little imagination, the different parts could be played by the members of a group. As nonsense to make music to, *Penny-Whistle* is one of a kind.

They are all dandy stories, even the most unassuming. Covered in paper over boards and printed on coarse stock (to sell for ten cents), *Sojo* tells in African trickster style of a lazy-bones who gets his chores done by 'letting' Elephant water the cabbages, 'letting' Hippo husk the corn, 'letting' little black Pig dig up the ground for a new garden—all in the name of a game, "but a sort of difficult one . . . I don't know if you could do it."

The round black figures with bright faces are part of the fun; lazy or not, they're lively, and one feels Erick Berry's affection for them.

Equally, in the granitic figure of King Opu Nui one feels Armstrong Sperry's respect—this although Opu Nui holds in one hand a big knife (the name Opu Nui means Big Stomach), in the other a very small pan of *poi* (signifying "that everyone in Bora Bora had to work harder than the King") (71). Accepting the Newbery Medal for *Call It Courage*, Sperry recounted the island's ups and downs—pastoral contentment, sudden prosperity, apathy and violence, prosperity's end, a crushing hurricane—and Opu Nui's steadfastness, his faith in the old self-reliant ways.

71. *One Day with Manu*, by Armstrong Sperry. Philadelphia, Winston, 1933. 8 x 10.

The book Sperry fashioned from his stay on Bora Bora, *One Day with Manu*, his first, is a long leisurely account of Polynesian life; in *One Day with Jambi* (Winston, 1934), set in Sumatra, Sperry made further use of his travels in the tropics. The last of the series, *One Day with Tuktu* (Winston, 1935), an Eskimo story, takes Sperry out of his own territory and into a separate subject area (p. 158).

From China and Japan less came forth than might have been expected, given the interest of the subject and the extent of the art, but Orientals were then barred from immigrating by law, and by tradition we looked to Europe for what was foreign in our background.

Kurt Wiese, who had been almost everywhere, had been in China the longest, and in his own *Liang and Lo* and *Fish in the Air*, in Marjorie Flack's *Story about Ping* and Claire Bishop's *Five Chinese Brothers* (as well as many that were not picturebooks), he put the stamp of his style on China for a generation; but his work is more important for what he did than for what he depicted, and we will take it up elsewhere. Thomas Handforth, typically the wandering artist, made in *Mei Li* (Doubleday, 1938) a book that has been much celebrated, the Caldecott Medal aside. I have always found it harsh and clumsy, with an obvious story line and more thuds in the telling—the whole no more Chinese than Hindustani.

Evelyn Young, the daughter of an English civil engineer and architect, was born and raised in China; she had already illustrated some Chinese nursery rhymes, published locally, when she did *Wu and Lu and Li* and *The Tale of Tai*. Unable to place them with a British publisher, she entrusted the manuscripts to a friend visiting the United States and, through Esther Reno, a prominent artists' agent, they reached the Oxford University Press, where Eunice Blake made entrancing little volumes of both of them. (Oxford was unusual in having, in Grace Allen and then Eunice Blake, two editors who were also accomplished designers.)

In their scale, in the economy of their line and the delicacy of their coloring, the illustrations are Chinese watercolors; but as entities freely disposed they range over the page in a way foreign to the Eastern idea of a continuous scene. *Wu and Lu and Li* unfolds in concise exposition, bits of dialogue, and images that one by one give substance to the words. Nothing and everything happens. Grandmother has come bringing presents and "some silver for you all to spend." In the village they meet some of their friends (72); Wu gives money to a blind beggar and can afford only a *little* red lantern; Lu gets a jar of ginger from her rich merchant uncle and is able to buy her mother another present, "a fan, most useful on such a hot day"; Li is so small he hardly understands what is happening (73).

Perhaps it is Chinese, or was—certainly it is not English or American—for Grandmother to be the catalyst and baby Li to bring each small episode to a climax. On the way home, lying in the grass, Wu and Lu make up poems —about blue cotton, blue sea, blue sky and

The twins who were too shy to speak,
two friends of Lu's, eating toffee-apples
on a stick.
And some others.

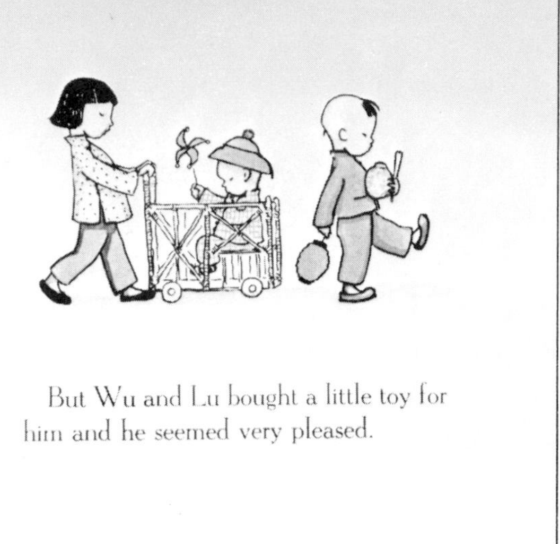

But Wu and Lu bought a little toy for
him and he seemed very pleased.

72, 73. *Wu and Lu and Li,* by Evelyn Young. Oxford, 1939. 5⅞ x 6½.

hills (Wu), about a little peach tree and a Bumble Bee (Lu)—when to their surprise Li says:

"Food
Is
Good."

Up to a point *The Tale of Tai* is more conventional. Padded and hooded against the New Year's cold (74), Tai goes to a fair in Peking, manages to lose all his relations—and, little daunted, to see the wonderful sights before a first and then a second attack of loneliness overtakes him. *Where is his mother*? "If you will give me a coin for charity, I will tell you," says an old priest. An American child would be —will be—nonplused but Tai, who has no money, sings a song, and the old man gives him a coin "which Tai gives to charity." The exchange made, Tai finds his mother at home, just as the priest tells him, and just as one expects, she is very glad to see him. Like *Wu and Lu and Li, The Tale of Tai* is unforced and understated, and both call to mind Eleanor Lattimore's stories of old China in *Little Pear.*

74. *The Tale of Tai,* by Evelyn Young. Oxford, 1940. 5⅞ x 6½.

Toward an aggressively militaristic Japan, conqueror of Manchuria and invader of China, there was little sympathy, residual or otherwise. Only Japanese art escaped the onus, and from it Lois Lingnell and Bentz Princehorn made the one major 'Japanese picturebook' of the prewar years, *Three Japanese Mice and Their Whiskers* (Farrar & Rinehart, 1934). The cover paper is Japanese in design, the lettering is done in the Japanese manner by brush, the illustrations are Japanese in technique and composition; and the story is insipid, with nothing of Japan in the conception or the telling: so much for empty emulation.

POLITI AND THE PERSISTENCE OF THINGS FOREIGN

From looking abroad for local color and exotic customs, Americans took to looking around. The impetus was partly socio-political—the specter of fascism in Europe compelled attention to the practice of democracy and appreciation of differences at home—and partly it stemmed from the schools and the displacement of history and geography by a broader, more people-oriented social studies.

In picturebooks the start was made at Scribner's where Alice Dalgliesh, late of

Teachers College, Columbia, and the Horace Mann School, became juvenile editor in 1934. She had begun to write young story-histories (*America Travels*, Macmillan, 1933) which became simpler, more factual and more pictorial (*America Begins* and *America Builds Homes*, both Scribner, 1938) and culminated in picturebook history (*The Thanksgiving Story, The Columbus Story, The Fourth of July Story*, all Scribner, 1954, 1955, 1956); the latter, 'first books for holidays,' enlisted recognized artists (p. 87) in the interpretation of what may be called the American heritage.

Katherine Milhous came to Miss Dalgliesh's attention through a series of Pennsylvania Dutch posters, and several books in this vein ensued, most happily *The Egg Tree* (p. 326) and *Appolonia's Valentine* (both Scribner, 1950 and 1954). The cheerful patterns, the plain dress, the odd ways of the diverse 'Pennsylvania Dutch' could have been made for picturebooks, and picturebooks, Katherine Milhous's leading, made them familiar to children around the country: many's the egg tree and many the valentine modeled after hers.

Though Leo Politi had done an earlier picturebook (*Little Pancho*, Viking, 1938) and his illustrations were prominent features of various books set in Mexico, it was a Los Angeles Mexican boy wearing angel's wings on a Christmas greeting that prompted Alice Dalgliesh to suggest what became *Pedro, the Angel of Olivera Street* (Scribner, 1946), the first of the books that were to make Politi's reputation.

Pedro is small and intimate and dear, with little of the obvious portent and pageantry that hobble the later books; but Politi as an interpreter of Mexican-American life has never the zest that he has in *Little Leo* remembering his own early life. Never mind that it's forty years since he went to his parents' native Italy in the garb of an Indian chief—there's fun on the transcontinental train where one little Indian, our little Leo, waves from the back platform; in New York where everyone looks at them (Mama's big hat? Papa's mustache? *my Indian costume*!); on the ship—except for Mama, who's seasick; in San Mateo, where nothing has changed, where Grandma has ravioli ready and makes cookies shaped like fruit and animals, and where the children tag behind Leo in his Indian suit, so absorbed that he is asked not to wear it to school (75).

They beg for Indian suits like his, and soon the quiet of San Mateo is no more; Mario and Gino, Ugo, Giovanni, Luigi and tiny Orlando are Indians too, whooping through the square and up and down the hill, bright specks against golden tints bleached by time and sun. One thinks back to Edgar d'Aulaire's vision of the prairies, to Bemelmans, nourished on Fenimore Cooper and Karl May, providing himself with pistols and ammunition before he leaves for America; and ahead, to village squares packed with cars and hung with Coca-Cola signs. With *Little Leo*, published in 1951, we have bridged World War II and the past has, in a sense, caught up with the future; among books to be taken seriously, there won't be any more *Mikis*.

75. *Little Leo*, by Leo Politi. Scribner, 1951. 8 x 10.

THE DYNAMICS AND FUN OF THE FORM

MARJORIE FLACK, KURT WIESE, *THE HOLE IN THE WALL*, DOROTHY KUNHARDT

Once again William Nicholson provides an example of a small body of work carrying a great deal of weight. Surrounded now by young children, grandchildren and the offspring of his second marriage, he made books for them—"made" not in the euphemistic sense of writing and illustrating but in the real sense, doing the words as well as the pictures in his own hand, putting the title on the cover (and letting it serve as the title page), drawing a child's train around it, a scroll for the child's name and the donor's inside; saying, in effect, this is something I made for you, not the product of printer and publisher (76). (A tiny "Printed in Great Britain" or "Printed in the U.S.A." is the only type, an inconspicuous notice on the back cover the only trademark.)

Like the illustrations for *The Velveteen Rabbit*, both *Clever Bill* and its successor *The Pirate Twins* were done in lithographs, to which they owe the handmade, all-of-a-piece quality, the very possibility of writing—handwriting—however and wherever one wants.

76. *Clever Bill,* by William Nicholson. London, Heinemann, 1926; New York, Doubleday, 1927. 9¾ x 6⅝.

77. *The Pirate Twins,* by William Nicholson. London, Faber, 1929; New York, Coward-McCann, 1929. 9¾ x 7.

76

77

How Nicholson settled on the long narrow horizontal format, for which there is no true precedent, we don't know; probably it appeared to him to be just what it is, the ideal way to illustrate a continuous story. Horizontality was not itself new; sometimes called the landscape format, it appears, for the obvious purpose of depicting a broadly extended scene, in Boutet de Monvel and E. Boyd Smith, and because it accommodated itself to picturebook-ness—that is, to the simultaneous presentation of text and pictures —it shows up often as picture on one side of the opening, text on the other. But a horizontal picture on every page, whatever the dimensions, was a rarity; in fact, a picture of equal weight on every page was uncommon regardless of the shape of the book.

Continuous lengthwise pictures—*Chicken World* (21), a continuous chronicle, has them, and so does *Carlo* (12), a form of continuous animation. (Think scroll—comic strip—motion picture.) But under the pictures in the Nicholson books is not a self-explanatory passage of text as in *Chicken World* or a caption as in *Carlo*, both instances of words to pause on, but a snippet of story, words to go on. Partly, it is true, *Carlo* is a running picture-story independent of words. Nicholson is not working in that tradition, his pictures are separate, self-contained images; but he deploys his words singly and in short phrases with lots of connectives and punctuates very sparingly—chiefly a dash here and there—so that he never comes to a stop even when he has to emphasize a point or explain this and that but contrives to keep the story moving along until it is time for the book to end. In this fashion *The Pirate Twins* logs twenty-eight pages in 108 words and, with a little cheating, two sentences (77).

For all intents and purposes, it is the debut of the running text, spare and suggestive, fluid, suspenseful, a form of writing unique to picturebooks. Two results were to follow: the fewer the words, the more each would count; the fewer the words, the more—meaning, not detail—would go into the pictures. But not necessarily immediately or simultaneously. First, in books of the same size and shape as

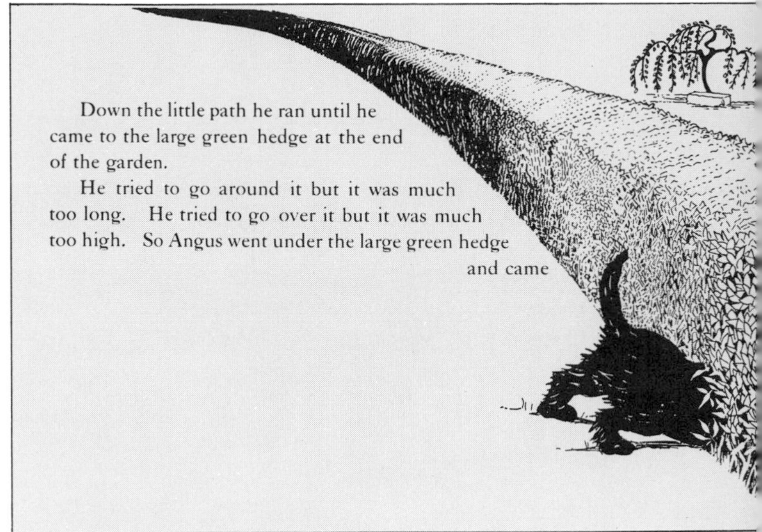

Down the little path he ran until he came to the large green hedge at the end of the garden.
He tried to go around it but it was much too long. He tried to go over it but it was much too high. So Angus went under the large green hedge
and came

78. *Angus and the Ducks,* by Marjorie Flack. Doubleday, 1930. 9¾ x 6½.

Clever Bill, Wanda Gág made more of the format, Marjorie Flack found a dozen uses for the run-on text, Kurt Wiese found as many ways to picture a story.

MARJORIE FLACK

Marjorie Flack drew, but not very well; she wrote, but she wasn't a writer; what she had was a feel for stories—situations, for the most part—that would tell well in words and pictures and a knack for dramatizing them: a true picturebook sense.

Angus is "a very young little dog"—the words are weighed—who is "curious about many places and many things." Most of all he is curious "about a NOISE which came from the OTHER SIDE of the large green hedge at the end of the garden," and one day, the door left open, no leash attached, NOBODY around, out he goes (78, 79). Angus is not wont to be silent, and having once barked and sent the ducks running, he watches them drink, and watches, and then says WOO-OO-OOF!! on the next page; but the ducks talk it over—*Quack*! *Quack*! *Quack*!—and then HISS-S-S-S-S-S-S, it is Angus who is running . . . under the green hedge, up the little path, into the house, under the sofa, where . . . (80, 81).

out on the OTHER SIDE.
There, directly in front of him,
were two white DUCKS.
They were marching forward,
one-foot-up and one-foot-
down.
Quack! Quack!
Quackety!
Quack!!!

79

The repetition, the emphasis, the repertoire of animal sounds are the stock in trade of oral storytelling but their delivery, like the timing, is controlled by the format and design. As a result it is virtually impossible to read *Angus and the Ducks* ineffectively. Other effects are inseparable from the format and design and are equally visual and aural: the anticipation and the pregnant pause as Angus goes under the large green hedge, the revelation and fluster when he emerges on the other side, just one instance of Flack's dramatic use of the page-turning; and the masterful conclusion, the same picture repeated on three successive pages, indicating the passage of time, while the words, perfectly paced, evenly spaced, tick out "exactly THREE minutes by the clock," minute by minute, page by page.

Angus and the Cat, which came along the next year, has a couple of comic incidents (Angus learning NOT to jump after a frog, learning that BALLOONS go—POP!) reminiscent of Frost, or before him Busch, and a heartwarming happy ending in dog and cat

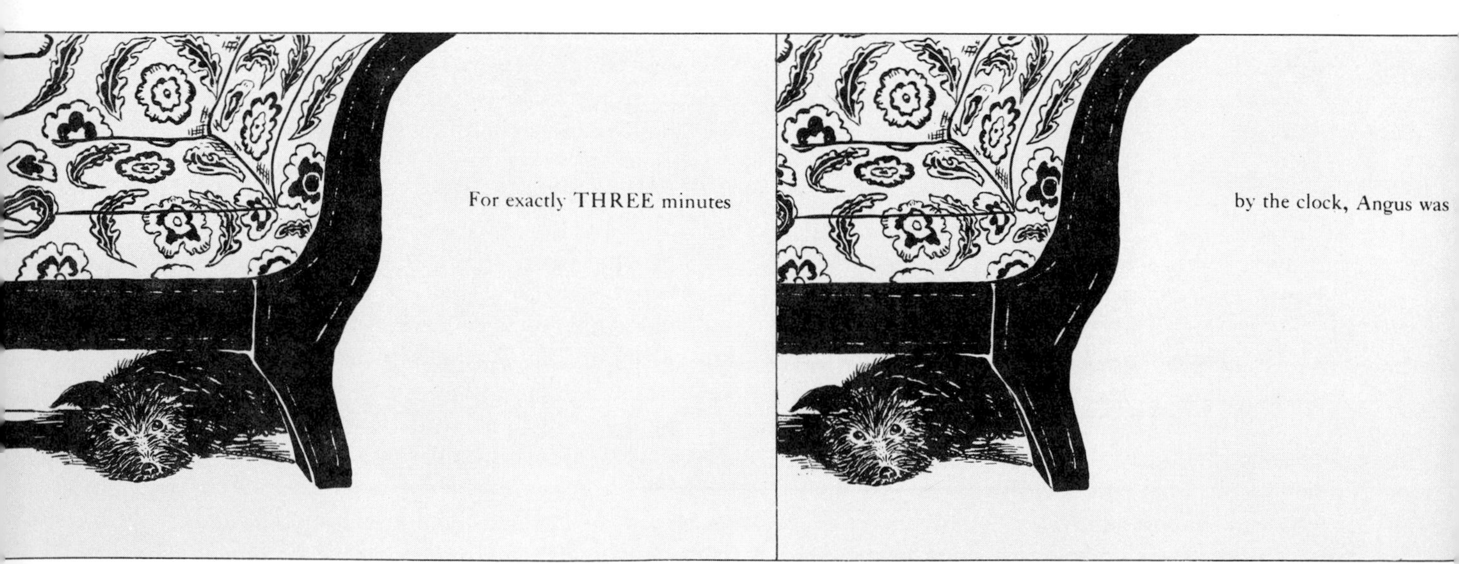

80

reconciled; but its centerpiece is the search of Angus for THAT CAT, that offensive cat he's been chasing futilely for three days. She runs into the bedroom, and then *pouf*! "Angus looked under the bed—no CAT was there. Angus looked out of the window" (82). While Angus keeps looking, more and more lonesome, children are one up on him—THAT CAT is never far off, ready to return when the time is ripe. In a rudimentary way, pictures are played against text, and the child is a co-conspirator.

Flack's strength as an illustrator, however mechanical her rendering, is that her meaning is always plain, even to a three-year-old. Looking at Angus, we can't miss the cat; looking out with him—over a vista that includes that hedge, those ducks, that watering trough from *Angus and the Ducks*—we can see clearly that "no CAT could he see ANYWHERE!" Moreover, as Dorothy White observes, "the sofa, the mantel, and the table," the places where Angus next looks, "have all been illustrated previously as haunts of the cat—the stage has been set, the background created in a substantial way before the main action takes place."[1]

There was a third Angus story, *Angus Lost* (Doubleday, 1932), and equally successful with small children were *Ask Mr. Bear* (Macmillan, 1932) and *Wait for William* (Houghton Mifflin, 1935). In the cumulative pattern of a Henny Penny, Danny, in *Ask Mr. Bear*, annexes one after another animal in his search for a birthday present for his mother before Mr. Bear whispers just what she'd like (shh, "a Big Birthday Bear Hug"). *Wait for William* is a before-and-after story (the 'youngest child successful' of folklore) with a resplendent middle—left-behind brother William riding down Main Street on the back of a circus elephant, the surprise of the parade.

Tim Tadpole is left behind too, and forlorn—he can't climb out to sit in the sun like Mr. Turtle, Miss Salamander and the Great Bullfrog until, after days of wiggly swimming, he finds himself kicking and he's on his way . . . (83). The transformation of Tim Tadpole into Tim Frog is natural science as a success story, wild life accommodated to child life (the climax: "TIM JUMPED!!"). Best is the spread pictured: the figure of Tim swinging, swimming, around the two pages, growing, changing shape, acquiring a new look, a new personality—another, different instance of Marjorie Flack's way of animating her material.

She not only begot scores of Scotties, Sealyhams and other small squat dogs, she opened up a new line of development, the almost-

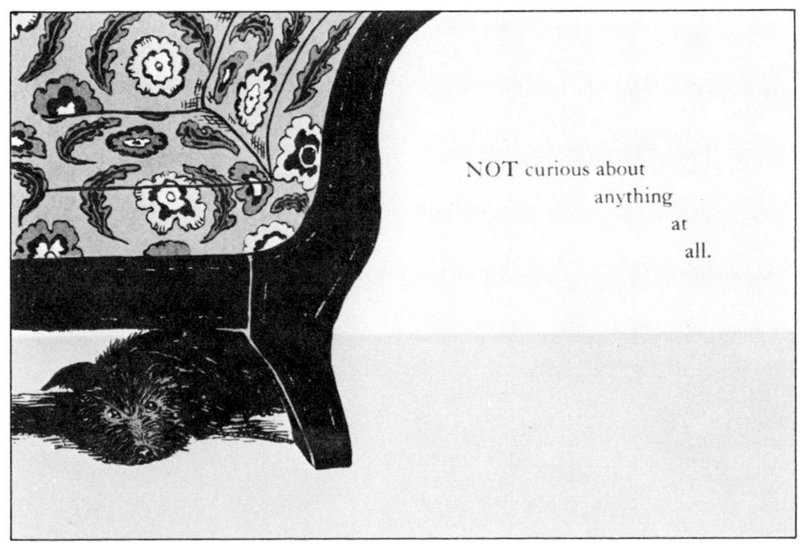
NOT curious about
anything
at
all.

81

79-81. *Angus and the Ducks,* by Marjorie Flack. Doubleday, 1930. 9¾ x 6½.

and then came a day
when out came a right arm!

Tim's tail was

shorter and
shorter and his
mouth was
growing wider
and wider.
"Now," said Tim,
"I will find the Sun!"

into his yard,
into the next yard—no CAT could he see ANYWHERE.

82. *Angus and the Cat,* by Marjorie Flack. Doubleday, 1931. 9¾ x 6½.

83. *Tim Tadpole and the Great Bullfrog,* by Marjorie Flack. Doubleday, 1934. 6¾ x 7½.

everyday story teased into a dramatic opus. And at the same time that she turned out others of her own, she wrote *The Story about Ping*, conceived and wrote the text for *Boats on the River*, and illustrated *The Country Bunny and the Little Gold Shoes*, each distinct and roundly satisfactory and atypical.

KURT WIESE

Born in Germany, Kurt Wiese had ranged the world before coming to the United States and he possessed, as May Massee remarked, an outstanding visual memory; he could work in a variety of mediums and styles, draw animals and people with equal sympathy, convey ideas and information effectively; and he became, almost immediately, the most versatile and productive artist in the field of children's books. He held the season's record, said *Publishers' Weekly* in the fall of 1930; and with thirteen books (for nine publishers), he was still the frontrunner in 1950.

Comparatively few were picturebooks, fewer as time passed, but those few included many types. *Karoo the Kangaroo* (Coward-McCann, 1929), the first of his own writing, initiated a long true-life series; *Joe Buys Nails* (Doubleday, 1931) just misses, by an injection of whimsy, being the first real-life boy's story; and for Lillian Rifkin's *Our Planet the Earth* (Lothrop, 1934) he pictured evolution in striking black and white.

More to the point of picturebooks is *Liang and Lo*. What Wiese could do to enliven a text he had shown in *The Three Little Kittens*; now the story is his and the pictures propel it —Liang and his tea-merchant father arriving in the country, to be ceremoniously greeted, and opposite, a field of buffaloes, just buffaloes, while overleaf awaits Lo, "a little boy his own age, who lived on a buffalo." ("Yes, he lived on the back of the animal, he ate there and he slept there . . .") In vignettes, in details, in full-page drawings, the elements of the plot take tangible, flexible shape: Liang and Lo decide to seek out a dragon and Lo's buffalo, urged along, stops at nothing (84); not even at the sight of the dragon (85).

Much of the excitement comes from the interaction between the two facing pages: the buffalo plunging ahead, the fish coming up to meet him; boys and buffalo stock-still on one rise, dragon gaping at them from the other. It looks simple and it is—the way anything pared to its essentials is simple.

The book was done in five colors and two colors and often, not always, Wiese uses the five-color opening for the large positioning scene, the two-color opening for the intermediate action (84). Thus, having seen the buffalo head into the river, all we need are his horns and a bit of his back, all we want is the splash-clang-swiftness of that wet crossing and that long, long sentence. And with the whole page the water, why not a surfacing school of fish—as long as the type-line rises too, loses its identification with the groundline, stops anchoring the scene? To appreciate what Wiese has done, it helps to think of what he might have done, or missed doing.

He might, for another thing, have closed the space between the two hills (85), it was not a technical impossibility. But had he made the scene continuous, he would have lost the sense of an abyss, reduced the isolation of the silhouetted figures, and altogether weakened the force of the confrontation.

Though the pictures are somewhat small for the page, the vigor of the drawing and the economy of the design more than compensate. Both gain from the free handling of color, in flat areas and accents that suggest contours, give way for highlights, build form rather than simply fill in space. Like *Miki* (and *Angus* and the majority of books of that time), *Liang and Lo* was printed in solid areas of flat color but for *Liang and Lo* Wiese worked directly on the plates, to which his black and white drawing had been transferred. No complete outline drawing was required, and to the spontaneity and vitality that result whenever the camera is circumvented was added, in 1930, the opportunity of working without constriction.

It all added up to a rouser, the sort of book "a ten-year-old loves to read aloud in a dramatic voice to a small brother, who literally

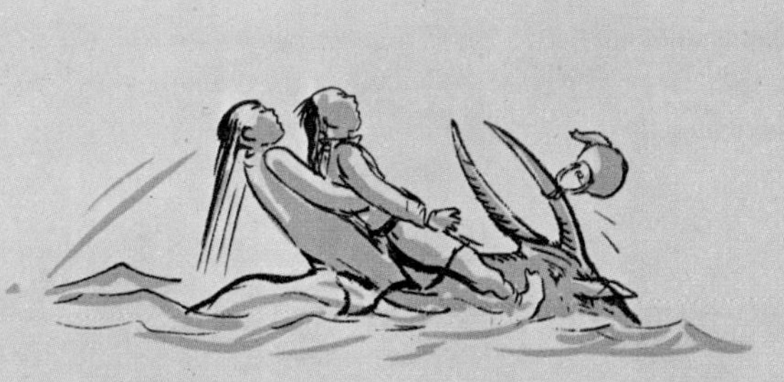
washed over his back and the boys were wet and the
rolls were wet and the salt was wet and only the teapot
remained dry and clattered against the horn while they
swam through the river.

And all the fish in the river
heard the noise and came up

shouts with glee when the snorting buffalo plunges into the dragon with such unexpected results."[2]

More shouts greeted the misadventures of Ping up to the final SPANK on his back, punishment for being the last duck to reach the houseboat in the evening. To avoid just that, the night before, Ping hides on shore, sees the houseboat sail away, and wakes to find that . . . (86).

In the course of the day's search he encounters captive fishing birds, strange dark birds with metal rings around their necks, and is himself captured—"down came a basket . . . and he could see no more of the Boy or the boat or the sky or the beautiful yellow water of the Yangtze river"—and, providentially, released; so that when next he hears the familiar "La-la-la-la-lei!" beckoning him to the wise-eyed boat, he hurries, and when he sees that, hurry or not, he's LATE again, up he marches over the little bridge and takes his spanking, glad to be home.

Ping is a real story, a full story, complete in words, but so full of images—the wise-eyed boat, the march of the many ducks, the assortment of boats on the Yangtze, the capture and imprisonment of Ping—that it seems made, as it was, for pictures. This was one of the first instances in picturebooks proper of a story being written by one person to be pictured by another, and as the first notable instance, the collaboration of an established author and illustrator, it was bound to be influential. Marjorie Flack didn't know China, Kurt Wiese did, that was the genesis; the ramifications were many. Artists would not necessarily have to provide material of their own, as they had been doing, and those with no particular talent for writing could contribute. So, independently, could writers, who might in time become writers of picturebooks. As books ceased to spring from pictorial impulses, they might change in nature—broaden, deepen, diversify.

(About Wiese's rich, luminous zinc lithographs for the original *Ping*—he redid them when the first set of plates wore out—little need be said except *look*; with his illustrations for Phil Stong's *Honk: the Moose* they represent probably his best work in color.)

Claire Huchet Bishop was a writer after, a storyteller before *The Five Chinese Brothers*—a natural storyteller, it appears, and once started, a natural writer. The story of the five Chinese brothers—identical in appearance, each possessed of a remarkable power—had been told and retold at the New York Public

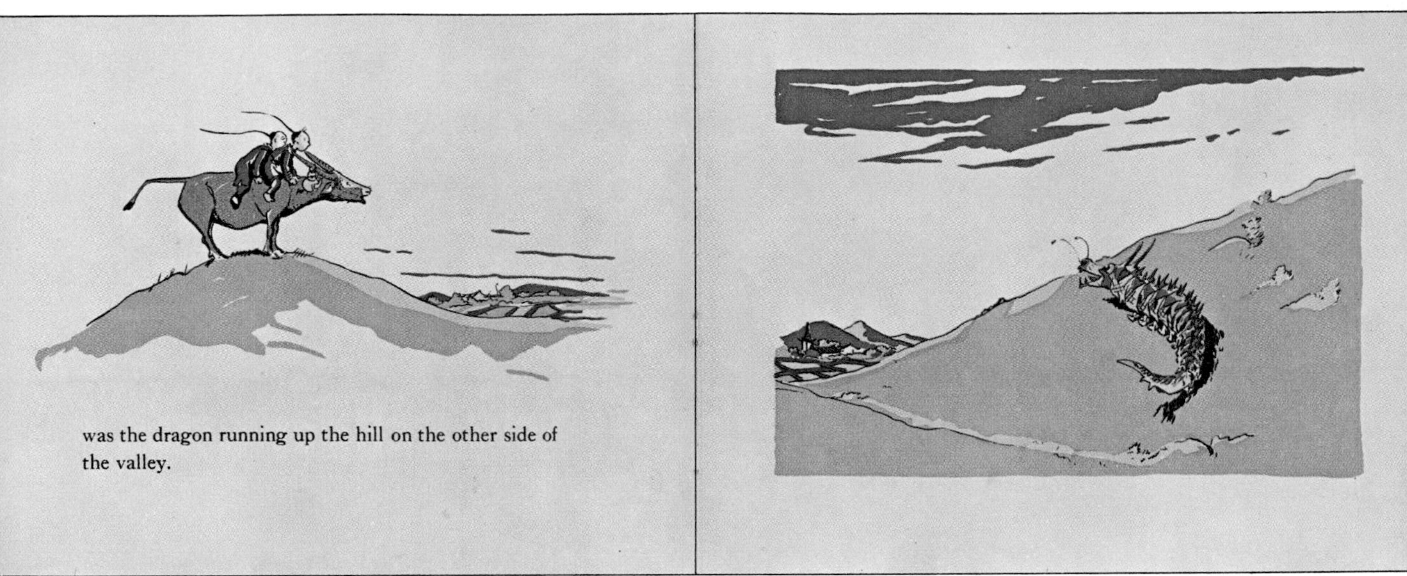

was the dragon running up the hill on the other side of

84, 85. *Liang and Lo,* by Kurt Wiese. Doubleday, 1930. 9¼ x 7.

86. *The Story about Ping,* text by Marjorie Flack, pictures by Kurt Wiese. Viking, 1933. 6¾ x 7⅞.

he was all alone on the Yangtze river.
There was no father or mother, no sisters or brothers, no aunts or uncles, and no forty-two cousins to go fishing with Ping, so Ping started out to find them, swimming down the yellow waters of the Yangtze river.
As the sun rose higher in the sky, boats came. Big boats and ittle boats, fishing boats and beggars' boats, house boa·s and raft boats, and all these boats had eyes to see with, but nowhere could Ping see the wise-eyed boat which was his home.

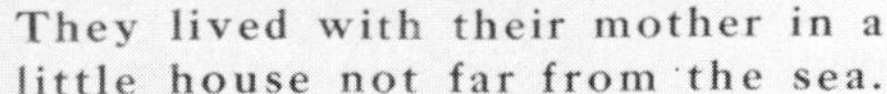
They lived with their mother in a little house not far from the sea.

87

Library, and like all such stories of supernatural prowess ("Six Servants," "The Fool of the World and the Flying Ship"), it not only requires no pictures, it resists picturization. More than that it has, like all patterned tales, a form of its own.

Working in two colors, drawing broadly, Wiese gives us not representations but strategic motifs; now spreading his picture across the wide opening, he sets the scene (87), now forswearing illustration, he lets the words speak for themselves as we take in just what each of the brothers can do. The first can swallow the sea; but a little boy gathering treasures offshore scorns his warning to come back, and the First Chinese Brother grows more and more uncomfortable (88–91) until he has no choice but to let it out, and the boy disappears—a boy that, wisely, Wiese never pictures, preventing the comic from being also tragic.

Condemned as a result to have his head cut off, the First Chinese Brother goes home on the pretext of saying good-by to his mother and sends the Second Chinese Brother back in his place—the one with the iron neck; drowning decreed instead, the Second Chinese Brother repeats the ruse, and the Third Chinese Brother comes back in his place (92). Development by development to the happy end (if he is impervious, he must be innocent), Wiese responds to the story, sometimes keeping pace via a facing picture, sometimes giving way to the words, sometimes preempting pages for pictures, sometimes parlaying the words into a whopping picture (sideways even)—playing with the book, the very form of a book, the way the story toys with fact.

THE HOLE IN THE WALL

The Hole in the Wall is, first and last, something to see—the story springs from the pictures and shapes up in the design of the book. (Not that René d'Harnoncourt, who's apparently heard a story or two, doesn't put a few twists in the telling.)

A dapper, debonair painter—d'Harnoncourt himself?—out for a walk with his pencils in his pocket sees a house that has no windows in its front wall "because the old man who owned the house did not want people from the street watching him eat." ("He always spilled coffee on his waistcoat—that is why he did not want anyone to watch him eat.")

"What a nice wall to draw on," and he does; but no sooner has he ambled on than the very thin figure of a man, roused by the smell of onion soup from next door, cocks his head and . . . (93). It can only end the way it began,

88

89

90

91

87–92. *The Five Chinese Brothers,* text by Claire Huchet Bishop, pictures by Kurt Wiese. Coward-McCann, 1938. 9¾ x 6½.

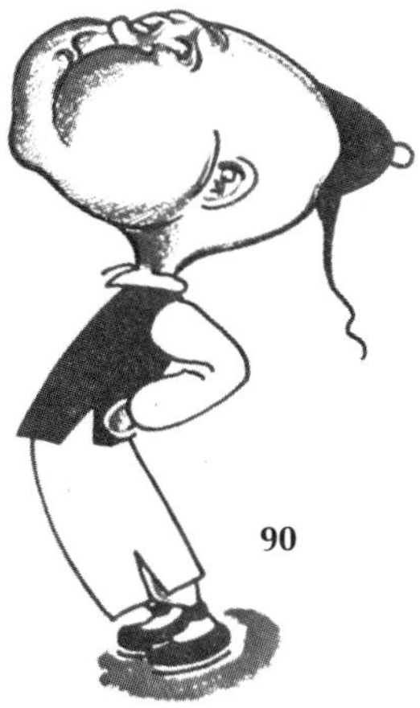

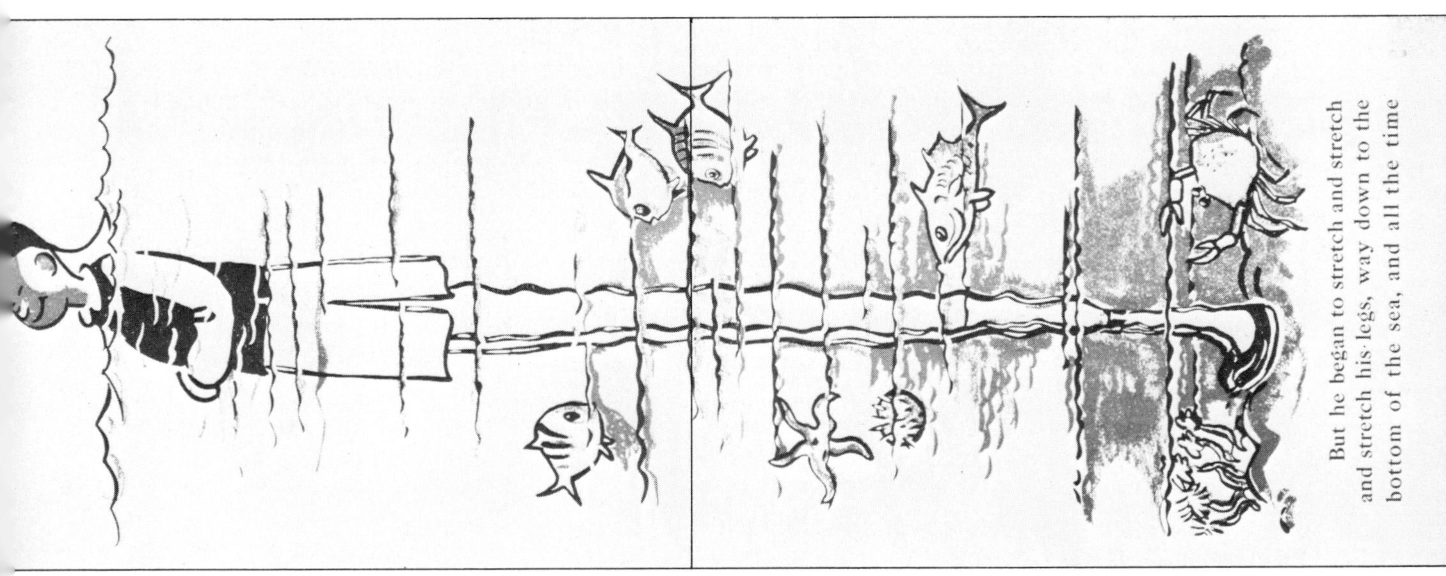

But he began to stretch and stretch
and stretch his legs, way down to the
bottom of the sea, and all the time

92

93. *The Hole in the Wall,* by René d'Harnoncourt. Knopf, 1931. 10¾ x 8¼.

with the artist's pencil first enlarging the hole so the newly fat man—who has no other home—can fit in, then erasing the figure so the old fellow inside—who raised a cry when he discovered the hole—can forever spill his coffee in privacy. Before Crockett Johnson's Harold took up his purple crayon, never was an artist so completely in command.

Taking over the pictorial devices of Busch and his comic-strip confederates (the sort-of speech balloons, the growing man, the buckling stool), d'Harnoncourt goes further and makes the whole page his field of action, laying it out in such a way—a different way in each case—that we take it in at once as design, in sequence as story. Murals work in a similar fashion, and also combine deep perspective with emphasis on the picture plane; and altogether these picture-filled white pages—only eight in number—might be walls that d'Harnoncourt, or his artist, painted on. (The eight appear on the right at each opening, and on the left hand page is a small figure drawing.) It is the specific sense of the story that he's serving, however, and its form, when he carries the action first into the distance (note also the painter vanishing at top right), then click-click-click down front to the turn of the page. The sense and the nonsense, with a Colorform flatness and broadness and clear brightness, and only the figure of the man and the hole he leaves behind in black.

Directly following *The Painted Pig, The Hole in the Wall* is a departure and, regrettably, a terminus; after an ABC with Elizabeth Morrow (*Beast, Bird and Fish*, Knopf, 1933), d'Harnoncourt went on to become director of the Museum of Modern Art and hesitated, as an amateur, to put forward his own casual work.

DOROTHY KUNHARDT

With Dorothy Kunhardt, words come to the fore, words running on and piling up and repeating themselves, stopping only to put a question—WRONG! then rushing on again until the listener, on tenterhooks, can stand it no longer. Wait: what is he thinking, that old man eating "more junket and more junket and more junket and more junket until at last people began to be very much surprised at how much junket he was eating and they began to tell their friends about him because he seemed to be such a very hungry old man"? While they're watching him eat, let them guess . . . (94).

That's easy—"We will just guess EVERYTHING except a walrus with an apple on his back and except a one year old lion blowing out the candle on his lovely birthday cake and except a cow with her head in a bag." So they start guessing, and page after page after page after page they continue, and everything they guess is equally outlandish. "WRONG!" says the old man, and he goes on eating his junket.

"Now all the time that all the people in the world were guessing and guessing [a] little boy on a tricycle was thinking and thinking and he was thinking that all the people . . . were very silly people to guess so many WRONG things"; and riding his tricycle up to the old man, he says, "Old man, I know what you are thinking about all the time you are eating your junket . . . you are thinking about"—can you guess?—"JUNKET." Right he is, and to the annoyance of all the people who pretend they were just pretending, he gets to lick the bowl, and so the old man won't be late for his supper, he gives him a lift on his tricycle; whereupon the two ride off to the tune of "Oh my Oh my Oh my Oh my Oh my but JUNKET IS NICE!" And how good, how wise of Dorothy Kunhardt to save the last licks all around for the little boy.

Junket Is Nice was the first of several rigmarole stories, noble nonsense that, like Lear's, could be at once ridiculous and poignant. *Now Open the Box* is about little Peewee, dear little Peewee the circus dog, who "doesn't know any tricks not a single one not even how to roll over not even how to shake hands but

94. *Junket Is Nice,* by Dorothy Kunhardt. Harcourt, 1933. 9⅝ x 6⅜.

smiling face and he said Now don't
uess yet because first I am going to
ive you a little help. I am going
tell you three things that I am
JOT thinking about .... and I
ally and truly am NOT.

I am NOT thinking about

There was the thin man. He
loved little Peewee.

95

95, 96. *Now Open the Box,* by Dorothy Kunhardt. Harcourt, 1934. 9¾ x 6¾.

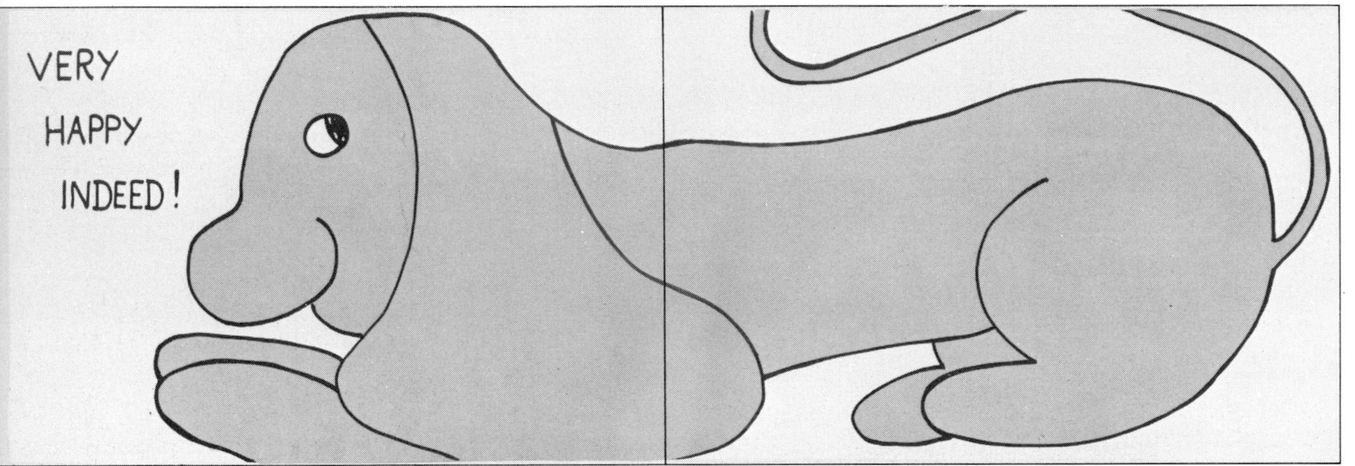

96

never mind he is so teeny weeny that everybody loves him" (95). The trouble is that teeny weeny Peewee begins to grow and gets to be an ordinary-size dog, and a commonplace dog who can't do tricks is no good to the circus; but just when everyone is crying copiously (and broken lines of tears stream down to the bottom of the page), poor little Peewee, about to depart forever, starts to grow again, and he keeps growing until his future as an attraction is assured (96).

Brave Mr. Buckingham (Harcourt, 1935), with its insistent "That doesn't hurt," *Lucky Mrs. Ticklefeather* (same), with her devoted puffin Paul—all together they became "an American institution."[3] (Without much help, as it happens, from the established institutions.) Lettered, when they were, in a schoolchild hand and illustrated with as little polish, they are just such books as a youngster might make himself, and children, laughing over them, sometimes crying a little, took them to their hearts—just as later they would yield to *Pat the Bunny* (p. 238) and smile knowingly at the child animals in *Tiny Nonsense Stories* (p. 292).

Drawing or not, Dorothy Kunhardt had the right ideas.

THE SMALL CHILD'S WORLD

The books we have seen thus far have been, in a traditional sense, storybooks, 'made-up' of imaginary characters and out-of-the-way experiences—experiences foreign in fact or foreign to a child. To a very small child more than foreign, nonexistent.

We know now that "the pre-school child lives in a world of his own; that it is a real world and not simply a crude or weak approximation to that of the adult."[1] We came to know it first in the 1920s, the decade of the preschool child as certainly as the twentieth century has been, as Swedish social critic Ellen Key anticipated, "the century of the child." Out of new research—first with problem children, in pediatrics and pedagogy—came the pioneering developmental studies: in 1921, Lucy Sprague Mitchell's essay-with-examples, *The Here and Now Story Book;* in 1925, Arnold Gesell's *The Mental Growth of the Preschool Child*, precursor of *The First Five Years of Life* (1940); in 1926 (after earlier publication abroad), Jean Piaget's *The Language and Thought of the Child*, followed in 1928 and 1929 by *Judgment and Reasoning in the Child* and *The Child's Conception of the World.* And these by no means exhaust the findings. Research was carried forward not only by Mrs. Mitchell and her colleagues at the City and Country School and the Bureau of Educational Experiments in New York and by Gesell and his associates at the Yale Psycho-Clinic—to say nothing of Piaget in Switzerland and his early critic Susan Isaacs in England—but also at the Iowa (University) Child Welfare Research Station under Bird T. Baldwin, at the Merrill-Palmer Nursery School in Detroit, at Teachers College, at the University of Minnesota, at the cooperative Washington (D.C.) Child Research Center. In 1923 Gesell decried the general ignorance about preschool children; in 1927 a survey uncovered 425 persons in more than 145 institutions working in the field.

The work had immediate application in the nursery schools that also sprang up all over the country (not to provide day-care for poor children, not then, but to provide enrichment for the offspring of the educated well-to-do). Concurrently, home economics departments, paced by the Merrill-Palmer School, developed child care curriculums, national organizations set up programs for parents, and the federal government, through the Children's Bureau, instituted other parent programs in conjunction with the states. "Thousands of young mothers have read entire volumes on the 'preschool age,'" was a 1929 observation.[2]

Picturebooks were bound to reflect the trend but they did not, for some time, advance it. Between the publication of Lucy Sprague Mitchell's prolegomena in 1921 and the debut of Margaret Wise Brown in 1937, of William R. Scott juveniles in 1938, her influence was indirect, her ideas only partially realized. The "here" and the "now," the familiar and the immediate, began to be heeded—became in fact a byword—while the attention to children's use of language that she espoused equally met with much less response. As for the here-and-now, it was more often than not taken to mean planes and trains and laundrymen, everyday matters-of-fact.

Fitting content and form to preschoolers was Mrs. Mitchell's chief concern, hence the mechanical stamp of some of her ideas; but if 'what happened to children during those years determined in large part their physical, mental and personality traits,'[3] as the specialists were saying, might there not be more to picturebooks than appropriateness?

Among 'consumer' groups, those who might be expected to take an interest in the books supplied to small children, the first to put theory into practice all around was the Child Study Association. At least as early as 1910, new publications were evaluated by a parent committee; in 1913 its first printed booklist appeared, a three-year compilation headed by books "For Children of Nursery Age"; and 1926 brought "The Child's First Books," featuring "over four hundred selected books for the preschool child," a list blessed by Gesell which invokes the names of Bird Baldwin and Lucy Sprague Mitchell as well. Quality and suitability are spotted in the annotations, norms of development in the introduction, with this proviso: "The important thing is to know the child to whom the story is told and the effect of the story upon his emotional life." The reference is to fairy tales and those who would banish them but the principle was to have wide application, to realistic stories as well as to fairy tales, and, in terms of feelings engendered, to children as a whole as well as to individuals.

That the parents of 'Child Study' were ahead of both teachers and librarians is hardly surprising. A small percentage of the eligible children were in kindergartens of any sort, far fewer in the private nursery schools, and there were, therefore, very few teachers directly concerned with youngsters under six. One who was, Alice Dalgliesh, produced in *First Experiences with Literature* (1932), one of the handful of books dealing exclusively with the interests of the very young as well as suitable choices for them. In the larger library world, picturebooks tended to remain picturebooks, regardless. At the day-care centers of the New York Kindergarten Association, Louise Seaman—now Louise Seaman Bechtel, writer, lecturer, interested party—learned differently, and the article with accompanying booklist she prepared for *The Horn Book* in 1941, "Books Before Five," was the first in a library periodical to single out young books, identify their strong points, and assign them to age groups. We must remember that the picturebook hours for five-to-sevens held in libraries since the beginning of the century were not supplemented (or replaced) by preschool story hours for three-to-fives until quite recently. Though a start was made late in the Thirties and activity increased in the Forties, it is not until the Fifties that preschool programs become standard fare, articles on conducting them proliferate, and attention is paid to books proper for the purpose. Only then do we find pressure put on publishers to furnish them similar to the pressure exerted much earlier for other material.

Dorothy Sherrill's *Little White Teddy Bear* "became very popular in days when less was available," Mrs. Bechtel noted, in extenuation, on her list; but however much had appeared by 1941, there are today a hundred times as many young books to choose among, and *A Little White Teddy Bear* remains in print, one of the record-setters. In full, it is *The Story of a Little White Teddy Bear Who Didn't Want to Go to Bed*, and that makes all the difference. Lettered in blue, outlined in black, touched up with local color, "Here he is," here is his house, his mamma, his daddy (who 'sometimes wears a hat to keep his head warm'), his big sister, his big brother; "See how little he is when he stands up with the other bears." A mother could be talking, or I telling you. "He is so little that he sleeps in a crib" and "eats his breakfast and dinner and supper at a little table of his own." But "He eats nicely; he doesn't spill. . . . And he is going to drink that big glass of milk all up." Good boy, as children still say.

Comes bedtime, one particular bedtime, and the adventure begins. Getting out of bed—he is "a bad little bear to do that," isn't he?—he dresses (97), walks quietly downstairs, and goes out, into the dark, the snow and the cold, all the colder because he forgot to put on his mittens. "Pretty soon" he's had enough but he has forgotten the way home, he is lost. . . . "And then do you know what happened?" You do, because you can see the automobile coming along the road, and here is his mamma "giving

He put on his cap
and his overshoes.

97. *The Story of a Little White Teddy Bear Who Didn't Want to Go to Bed*, by Dorothy Sherrill. Farrar & Rinehart, 1931. 4⅞ x 6¾.

him a big bear hug," his house with the lights "shining in the windows," his little table, cocoa and cookies ready, his crib, and no spanking—"because he said he would never do it again" when he was found. And, we're told, he never did.

Excise the warranty of good behavior, and *A Little White Teddy Bear* is cut to a toddler's measure. Even that might be allowed: little children *intend* to keep their promises. But the use of the present tense, the simple sentences and everlasting "and," the enumeration of particulars (breakfast and dinner and supper) and provision for recognition (mamma's apron, daddy's necktie, baby's blanket), the reiteration ("here he is," "here she is") and cumulation (here they are, "see how little he is")—all these accord with a three-year-old's thinking, his language, his likes; while the brevity of the little white teddy bear's defection, his mother's swift forgiveness, the return to a home where everything is waiting for him, this is independence and reassurance on the double, the way a three-year-old wants them. As for the miscreant's being a bear, even at two children are wont to put animals through just such forbidden and frightening paces.

The dedication tells us that Lois Lenski's *Little Family* "was made for S.C. and age 3," and it is not coincidence that it is also a small, hand-lettered book cast in the present tense. Where it differs from *A Little White Teddy Bear* is in having no plot. At age three and beyond, not only is a child's attention span short, he has little sense of sequence, of the order in which events occur; better then a string of incidents, as in the Angus books (among the few seen earlier that do suit small children), of related occurrences, as in *The Little Family*, or single, repeat-pattern items, as in the first half of *A Little White Teddy Bear*. If there is to be a plot, a beginning that leads to an end, reinforcement along the way is called for: the Gingerbread Boy's refrain (approximated in *Ask Mr. Bear*), the constant reminder that Goldilocks is just sitting in for the Three Bears (or, in *Circus Baby*, the elephants for the absent clowns).

To May Lamberton Becker, long the children's book critic of the New York *Herald Tribune* and an inveterate child-watcher, such diminutive books as the Sherrill and the Lenski were "little bits"—as distinct from those "two laps wide"—and she offers an interesting explanation of children's preferences, initially for the larger, soon after for the smaller: "It seems as if then they were making an unconscious effort to readjust the balance of nature, which is setting against them in surroundings where they are always the smaller, and prefer . . . something that will reassure them that they are really much bigger."[4] That little books can be held in small hands we know, and their intimacy we experience ourselves.

The other common denominator, hand-lettering, had for a time quite a vogue, as much for mechanical as aesthetic reasons. It had its detractors, those who claimed that the unfamiliar forms deterred beginning readers, and its defenders, who pointed out that children learned manuscript writing—that is, printing—before longhand in school. The argument reduces, I suspect, to one between the public school and private school forces, as per their differing practices at the time, and it soon evaporated; we can enjoy Howard Gág's incisive lettering for *Millions of Cats*, Dorothy Sherrill's gaucherie and Lois Lenski's trim forms for themselves and for what they add to the books' design—a harmony with the drawing that machine type lacks, an individual character and warmth, and in little books particularly, a concordant intimacy, the sense of a private communication. For the difference hand-lettering made to the Lenski books, one has only to look at the examples (98-102).

Before she came to picturebooks Lois Lenski had done much illustrating and some writing and, reversing the balance, she would do a great deal more; but for a brief period, roughly 1927 to 1937, she produced one after another picturebook of distinctive charm. As for instance: *Jack Horner's Pie* (Harper, 1927), nursery rhymes with funny quaint figures, and its successor *Alphabet People* (Harper, 1928); *The Wonder City* (Coward-McCann, 1929), a panorama of New York, part social science, a large part enjoyment; *Benny and His Penny* (Knopf, 1931), which has a coin set into its cover and delicate,

Mrs. Little washes
the clothes. She
rubs them on the
wash-board. The
water in the tap
is hot.

98

98, 99. *The Little Family*, by Lois Lenski. Doubleday, 1932. 4½ x 4½.

Mr. Little has a
lawn mower. He
cuts the grass.
Tommy is riding
his kiddie car

99

The little Auto goes
down the road. Mr.
Small toots the horn,
"Beep, beep!" He
scares the ducks
and chickens.

100. *The Little Auto,* by Lois Lenski. Oxford, 1934. 7 x 7.

fluttery cartoons that Mary Petty might almost have drawn. From this period, too, comes the snappy cloth book *Sing a Song of Sixpence* (p. 236).

Nonetheless it is the Littles and Mr. Small —little and small for no logical but every good reason—who delighted children and tried the patience of their parents; fixed a form of expression and a sign-off ("and that's all . . .") in young minds and old; and, setting the table, changing a tire, going to church, plowing with a tractor, roping a calf, piloting a plane, brought first the immediate and familiar, then the inaccessible and desirable, into what may well be every reading household.

The Littles are a model family saved from stuffiness by the prosaic sorts of things they do and the laconic matter-of-fact text. Similarly, what is chaste about the pictures is offset by their compact cheerfulness and certain small, light touches—the steam corkscrewing up from Mrs. Little's washbasin, Mr. Little's flapping shoelace, the flying grass-clippings (98, 99). As compositions, they have order, definition, above all equipoise; as illustrations, they come alive.

Mr. Small, going for an outing in the little Auto, is a cartoon figure, big of head and hat, always a little stiff, a little unreal—no-man, the better to be everyman (or, alternatively, a mannikin). The little Auto is disproportionately big too, most of the time, and for all the oiling and pumping and stopping for gas, it is his toy; he beats out a horse and buggy, plows UP HILL and speeds DOWN HILL, "scares the ducks and chickens" (100). This irresponsible delight in playing with a car, a car that is still a novelty and not a high-powered mechanism, is part of what children enjoy; had the little Auto been a later model, it might have been sooner for the scrap heap.

Of the Mr. Small books, *The Little Sail Boat*, blue and white, crisp and finished, is the beauty (101). The gray tones and modeled forms stand out against the flat ground, and there is little of the formula drawing or the slack design found elsewhere. Shipshape it is, but it is also less a toy-book and, perhaps on account of its subject too, has less attraction for small children. At four, boats are not to sail but to watch chugging and puffing and making waves.

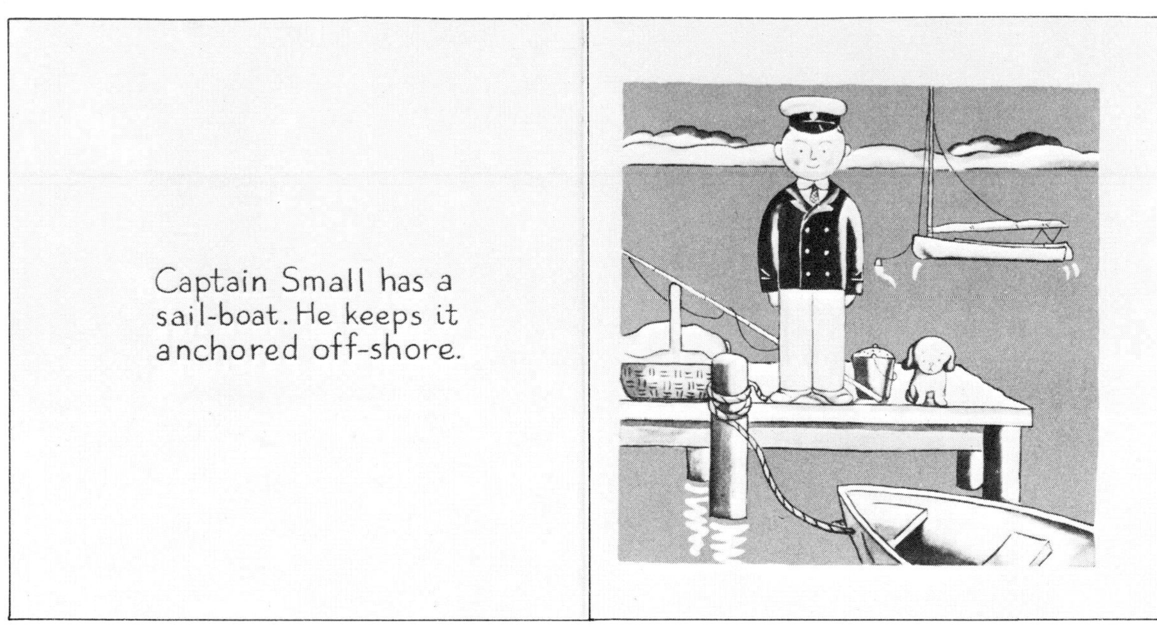

Captain Small has a
sail-boat. He keeps it
anchored off-shore.

101. *The Little Sail Boat,* by Lois Lenski. Oxford, 1937. 7 x 7.

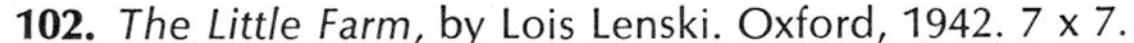

103. *Cowboy Small,* by Lois Lenski. Oxford, 1949. 7 x 7.

102. *The Little Farm,* by Lois Lenski. Oxford, 1942. 7 x 7.

He hauls them
in the trailer
behind the tractor.

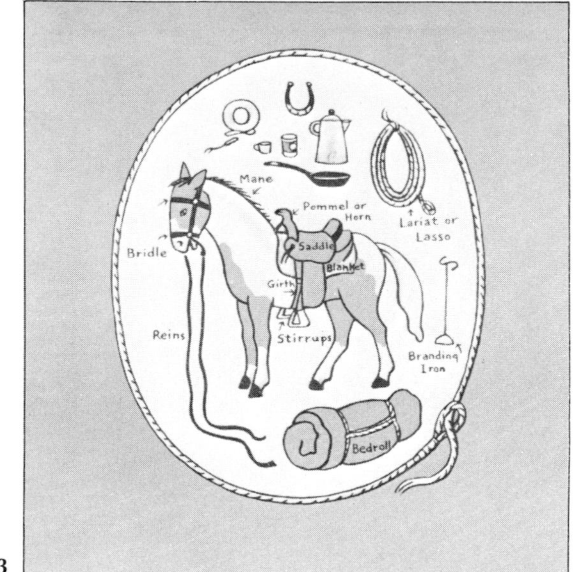

103

Tractors, however, are to ride and cowboys are to be, and the books to have, funny-looking or not, are *The Little Farm* and *Cowboy Small.* A day in the life of Farmer Small takes in the work of a year, with the tractor pulling a plow and a harrow in the spring, cutting hay in the summer, hauling apples in the fall (102). If he goes over a stone and loses a few, all the better—children will speak up and say so.

A dividend of a different sort is the paper-doll endpapers of *Cowboy Small*; indispensable as they (and the near-by glossary) may be to parents, children who have their own copy have been known to cut them up, the better to play cowboy with (103). In *Cowboy Small* they get not only directions, but also a script. Though it has no more plot than its predecessors, there is, in the windup, something of a story. "Next day, Cowboy Small rides a bucking bronco. '*Yip-pee!—Yip-pee! Ride 'em, cowboy!*'/ *Ker-plop*! Cowboy Small hits the dust!/ But—he's a pretty good cowboy, after all! Cactus is waiting, so—/ '*Giddap, Cactus!*' Cowboy Small rides again!"

Hi yo Silver it isn't, any more than Cactus is a proper name for a Wild West horse, and Cowboy Small hasn't any more business being as big as Cactus than Mr. Small has being as big as the little Auto; but any doubt as to who's in the saddle is dispelled by the endsheet, where he stands without his western togs on.

Two even more plainly to play out are *The Little Wooden Farmer* and *The Choosing Book*, both of them the product of Alice Dalgliesh's work with five-year-olds at the Horace Mann School. As originally published (it was reillustrated and, without a weaker second story, reissued in 1968), *The Little Wooden Farmer* was patently about wooden figures—the farm couple who lack livestock, the captain who obliges them, and the animals that are just what they ordered (104); and for preschool children the invitation to reenact the story was unmistakable. Either way, it has an easy-to-follow pattern and the pickup of a few surprises: no dog or cat does the captain find, but there they are, the farmer and his wife have found them for themselves.

One can't *not* participate in *The Choosing Book*; it puts hard questions like which of four nice houses Mother and Father and Ruth and Teddy select, which of four dogs Teddy favors (they all like him), which of four cats will be Ruth's . . . which dress for Ruth? which doll? (105, 106), which suit for Teddy? which toy? And then it is time to go home, to their new house in the country with their new possessions—the one still unidentified, the others

104. *The Little Wooden Farmer,* text by Alice Dalgliesh, pictures by Margaret Baumeister. Macmillan, 1930. 8⅜ x 7.

105, 106. *The Choosing Book,* by Alice Dalgliesh, pictures by Eloise Burns Wilkin. Macmillan, 1932. 3½ x 6.

now covered. Open-ended as it is, it forces a child to choose, which could prompt lively discussion in a group or occupy the solitary youngster endlessly as he reconsiders and revises his choices.

"The pictures are of the type one finds in department store advertising,"[5] a reviewer noted, and it was from a like source, the Sears-Roebuck catalog, that Mary Steichen Martin got the idea for one of the most characteristic of the preschool books, *The First Picture Book,* which, because it's also a first photographic book, we'll look at somewhat later. From knowing children at first hand, from seeing them *in situ,* a start was being made.

One doll had black hair, a red checked dress and a little red sunbonnet.

105

One had golden hair and a blue dress.

Another was a baby doll who said "Ma-ma."

106

HELEN SEWELL

With the pictures for Mary Britton Miller's book of poems, *Menagerie*, Helen Sewell was established as a serious illustrator; two commissions later she paused, took the words chosen by a young niece and her neighbor, and made a new sort of alphabet book, *ABC for Every Day*. She was not one to repeat herself or follow the beaten path.

Notice the wording, not "everyday," ordinary, but "every day," daily. Set in the pattern of a child's day, "awake" in the morning to "zip into bed" at night, are the doings of a boy and girl, and the words give added life to their activities: dressing means coping with "buttons," breakfast is a bowl of "cereal," the "dog" begs to go out, the girl, acceding, says "excuse us." Nouns, verbs, assorted phrases—whatever expresses the situation in a child's terms, Sewell uses (107, 108).

Visually, her masterstroke was eliminating black. The pictures—the pages—are peppermint-fresh configurations of pewter, cornflower blue, cherry red, and white, the white of the paper. As the broken-cylinder figures suggest, Sewell had studied with Archipenko, and in her hands the white of the paper is what light-filled space is to the modern sculptor: it penetrates, opens out, holds together. There is scope for imagination.

Suggestiveness, verbal and pictorial, is the substance of *A Head for Happy*, a lark that harks back to a childhood cruise. In a family of three girls, a stuffed boy doll is a fine idea —"But WHAT for a HEAD?" The youngest picks an apple, "TOO SMALL"; the next fetches a pumpkin, "TOO BIG"; and so they set out on Part II, The Journey to Find a Head. Here, at the heart of the book, each turn of the page takes us on another stage of the journey, posits the same question and answer,

107, 108. *ABC for Every Day,* by Helen Sewell. Macmillan, 1930. 8½ x 11.

109

109-112. *A Head for Happy*, by Helen Sewell. Macmillan, 1931. 8¼ x 7¾.

110

111

and snaps us along, stumped again (109, 110); then the sun winks, the pace quickens, and in close sequence come a solution and a setback (111, 112) and a reprieve that you can see coming too: the crab scuttles up the tree, throws down a cocoanut, Happy's new head gets a face, and the four strike up a dance—without another word.

The wordless picturebook was in the air. In Franz Masereel's *Passionate Journey* (originally *Mon Livre d'Heures*, 1919) and his other "novels in woodcuts," in Lynd Ward's *God's Man* (1929), it already existed in another form. Writing of *Passionate Journey* in 1926, Thomas Mann remarked upon its relation to movies, meaning of course such other "mute but eloquent creations"[1] as *The Cabinet of Dr. Caligari* and *The Last Laugh.* Hellmut Lehmann-Haupt has observed, rightly I think, that these picture-novels had no progeny among children's picturebooks, and they were soon to disappear almost entirely. But just as the "talkies" may have hastened if not caused the demise of picture-novels, the addition of sound to motion pictures may have checked the further development of wordless picturebooks. This is necessarily conjecture; the fact is that only one appeared (p. 539), the year following *A Head for Happy*, until more than three decades later.

If *A Head for Happy* is, in part, "told like a movie without words,"[2] its antecedents in graphic art are no less apparent. The paired pages during the trip represent pictographic art—which is equally the art of leaving out—keyed to the picturebook format; they tell two stories, of the vagaries of the journey and the frustration of not finding a head, which are separable and distinct but which, conjoined, give movement to the spreads and rhythm to the sequence. Cumulating, they pave the way for the roller-coaster climax, an example of pure if exalted comic-strip animation.

Withal, *A Head for Happy* does not so much do without words as make words do something vital, punctuate the story line and expel emotion. They are not essential to the continuity and, strictly speaking, one could do without them; but without "No head?" without "TOO HIGH!" the design would be less interesting, the drama would be weaker, the book just wouldn't be as funny.

Its rough edges are the turquoise green of a tropical sea, another nice touch; off San Francisco they encounter a whale with a curling

112

smile, boarding the train the persevering pekingese suddenly balks, home at last they throw a party for Happy—with one candle, a place for the doll, and a slice of cake, the first, for the dog; and for anyone who'd like to retrace the journey, there's a map of their round-the-world route. As much as it bears analysis, *A Head for Happy* is, most happily of all, full-up with the adventure of being a child.

In the next five years Helen Sewell did *Building a House in Sweden* with her sister Marjorie Cautley, a crisp, summery, genuinely Swedish sort of book all in the brown of new-cut pine; *The Dream Keeper and Other Poems* by Langston Hughes, for which she made strongly modeled, deeply shadowed drawings that are almost medallions; *Blue Barns*, a picture-story of a gluttonous goose, the gander she ignores, and the seven little ducks he adopts—given soft tones and sweeping contours; three handsome and interesting religious books; *Bluebonnets for Lucinda*, Frances Clarke Sayers's cameo of a Texas childhood, still bandbox-fresh in fine line, sharp flat color and rich crayon shading; and that's only a sampling. Came 1936, and Lewis Gannett wrote: "If I were giving prizes for illustrations in the season's children's books, I should give them all to Helen Sewell."[3]

The first of the books he had in mind, *Ming and Mehitable*, is a tiny, witty, quietly wise account of a pekingese—the constant companion of *A Head for Happy*—and his pigtailed mistress and her determination that he play 'baby' (113). Two confinements in doll clothes are enough for Ming, and he runs so far away that Mehitable can't find him. Nor does a chicken take to painted wings and tethering to a tree nor a brown bat to living in a house. Mehitable, it seems, cannot have her way or, for that matter, make another friend—a big dog growls at her, a monkey mocks her—so that when she finds Ming, gone native, she needs no prompting to promise him freedom from baby clothes forever.

The story has been done and redone (with increasingly severe overtones, as per the 1968 *Push Kitty*) but it hadn't then; indeed, *Ming and Mehitable* is the first picturebook—along with *Peggy and the Pony*, below—to turn on the turns of a child's mind. There is no 'plot' apart from Mehitable's adamancy, never mind Ming's disgust, her loneliness when he's gone, her recognition of his right to be himself too; the story is all in her face, and his. Because Sewell drew faces and figures that are in themselves expressive, she could tackle this kind of closet drama and carry it off. Looking at *Ming and Mehitable*, one would think there was nothing to it.

113. *Ming and Mehitable*, by Helen Sewell. Macmillan, 1936. 4⅜ x 5½.

Peggy and the Pony is a different quantity, a story not of a girl and a pony but of a little girl's yearning for a pony—too little a girl, her father would say. "She was also very fond of sweets." Thus, in two sentences, the book: strung on an individual preoccupation and blissfully unserious. Peggy's mother takes her to Europe. But neither a beautiful church nor fishing boats with red and blue sails (114) nor a peasant woman on a bicycle nor a castle in the sea has any charms for Peggy; she would rather have a horse. She does love French pastry and once when her mother isn't looking she eats eleven little cakes; she is *sick*, and after that she is careful—not even for sweets will she risk not being big and strong enough to ride a pony.

At this point the outcome is anyone's guess; except when Peggy eats the eleven cakes and you *know* she's going to be sick, *Peggy and the Pony* is no more predictable than the sweepstakes. Where other books drop clues, it tosses off non sequiturs. So it shouldn't be surprising that the visit to Aunt Daisy in England, so unpromising at the outset, produces at last a pony. "After she had looked at him for a long time, she climbed on his back and went for a lovely ride." A snapshot to prove to Daddy that she's big enough now, and the book closes.

Individual temperaments in conflict take *Jimmy and Jemima* a step further and make it a novel in embryo. Jimmy, the older, joins the Scouts and leaves Jemima to her dolls, or so he intends (115); but whatever he does, she does him one better. Let the whole family come to see Jimmy swim five strokes, Jemima jumps in and streaks to the end of the pond; let a horse throw him, and she rides it home; let him climb and climb a mountain, and she's perched at the top. When they're skating, he falls down, and this time Jemima is too proud and goes too far—and falls in. Lifesaving is nothing to a good Boy Scout and, safe in bed, Jemima is glad "to have a brother to pull her out when she fell into the water." For Jimmy, accepting his medal, "It was nice to have a sister to fall into the water so that he could pull her out."

The battle of the siblings or the battle of the sexes, the end couldn't be better, with a net gain on both sides and no backsliding. Put into pictures, it is independently funny—tarter too than the earlier books. Sewell was edging toward social comedy, and in *Belinda the Mouse* (Oxford, 1944), a spoof of teenage peccadilloes, she works herself almost out of picture-

114. *Peggy and the Pony*, by Helen Sewell. Oxford, 1936. 8 x 8½.

115. *Jimmy and Jemima*, by Helen Sewell. Macmillan, 1940. 5¾ x 8.

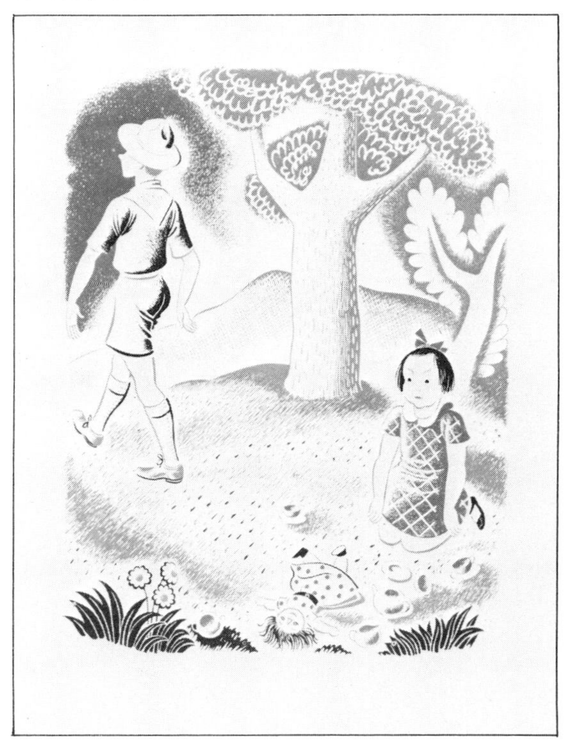

books, so much does it imply about family relations, feelings and responsibilities. Peggy is now the volatile big sister, one minute mooning over her diary, the next playing with her pet mouse; Helen Sewell's niece Pat was growing up; and with *Belinda*, the picturebooks come almost to a close. As a group, her youngsters have an interior life that powers the stories, and between the *ABC for Every Day* and *Belinda the Mouse* there arrived, without any fanfare, the psychological picturebook, funny because people are funny.

In 1947, as her contribution to the general counteroffensive against comics, she made *Three Tall Tales* (Macmillan) with Elena Eleska, clever if slight, and thereafter she illustrated what others had written: Maude Crowley's incomparable stories of Azor, the boy who listens, very sensibly, to what animals tell him; *The Bears on Hemlock Mountain*, Alice Dalgliesh's scary colonial adventure; and a book that deserves somewhere to be singled out for discussion, the *Grimm's Tales* that she and the very talented Madeleine Gekiere did jointly and antithetically, the first in broad masses and heavy line, the second in delicate, intricate tracery (116). Nor is this all.

As much as her style had already changed, it was changing still. Early on, she had done *A First Bible*, serene, sculptural, at once intimate and majestic—a classical concept of the Scriptures. For Alf Evers's *Three Kings of Saba*, one of her last undertakings, she added a scratchy line something like Gekiere's to her own strong masses and, with psychological acuity and bold design, produced three kings as different in mien as they are in mind and a journey that stretches across the text pages, dark and deep, to the obliteration of differences at Bethlehem. It is a stark and difficult book—much more so than the contemporaneous *Thanksgiving Story*—but to her credit Helen

Then poor Snow White wandered along through the wood in great fear; and the wild beasts roared about her, but none did her any harm. In the evening she came to a little cottage, and went in there to rest herself, for her little feet would carry her no further. Everything was

116

116. *Grimm's Tales,* illus. by Helen Sewell and Madeleine Gekiere. Oxford, 1954. Details.

117. *The Thanksgiving Story,* text by Alice Dalgliesh, pictures by Helen Sewell. Scribner, 1954. 8 x 10.

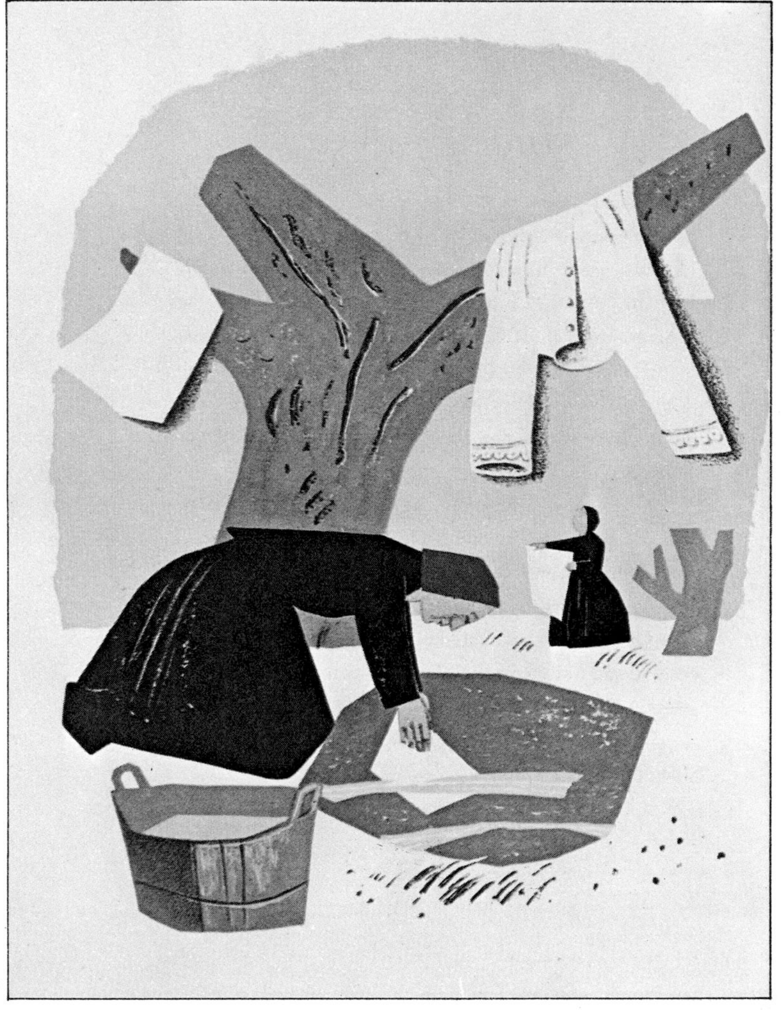

117

Sewell was always grown-up about children.

The Thanksgiving Story belongs to the group of simple personalized histories that Alice Dalgliesh wrote in the 1950s; as the jacket copy says, "This is a book to read aloud to children when they first want to know why we have Thanksgiving Day." No folderol about that; but assigned to creative artists, the products transcend the purpose.

Sewell is attentive to the birds, the gray gulls that sweep in at the start of the voyage and the bright flocks—feathered friends indeed—that turn up the first spring. The deck is a platform of planks in space, the first laundry a few stiff white garments hung on stubby branches (117); over and under the ground, left to right, a fish fertilizes the seeds, the corn sprouts, the plants grow, an ear is picked. Banished along with literalism are the stolid citizens of so many Plymouths; here is a pink cap, a soft cheek, and here are happy children—who eat their first Thanksgiving dinner on the ground.

Her last book was a wry *Sense and Sensibility* for the Limited Editions Club; she had illustrated Austen before, and Emily Dickinson, the *Little House* books on their first appearance and the Sally books of Elizabeth Coatsworth; and for Golden Books she designed a stand-up, punch-out *Christmas Manger*. Her work was a craft and a way of feeling: a life-work.

INFORMATION

Any consideration of informational books must begin with the Russians who, with a whole nation to educate after the Revolution, turned to the picturebook on an unprecedented scale. Many of the best artists were enlisted in the cause, men and women who elsewhere would have pursued 'pure' painting—or, as a Russian spokesman called it, 'mere' painting, for which there was little market in the Soviet Union. To advance the program, offset printing in two to five flat colors was perfected; books could be designed freely, with their pictures and text merged, and, eye-catching and unforbidding, they could be produced in large quantities at low cost. What technology facilitated, policy fostered: editions of fifty thousand are recorded in 1930, of a million or more in 1934, selling most commonly at ten cents (this when the average American printing was twenty-five hundred, the average price two dollars).

The Russian picturebooks of the period were paper, stapled, sometimes ingeniously folded—what we would consider pamphlets; there are a hundred in the stack pictured (118). Not conventional books, neither were they intended only for children; adults, as well, were learning to read, they too must be weaned to the changes in Soviet life. In the educative—informative, inspirational—books that were in the majority, two currents met. "Soviet Russia Abolishes the Fairies" chortled the *New York Times* in 1921,[1] and though the doctrinaire opponents of folklore and fancy were routed, the here and now and the actual, applicable past remained the dominant concern of pedagogues. (Interestingly, Lucy Sprague Mitchell's work was known and put to use.) At the same time, the prospective audience, child or adult, had a genuine interest in the Dnieprostroi Dam and the Gigant communal farm, in the making of a newspaper or the principles of a magnetic compass —an interest not very different, in fact, from American fascination with the products and technology of the machine age. "Work songs for the work gang," Ernestine Evans exulted;[2] "a textbook that reads like a fairy tale," Hellmut Lehmann-Haupt said in praise of Ilin's history of printing, *Black on White*.[3]

Their fresh good looks and their success in conveying information brought the books wide professional attention in the West. Visitors to the 1931 international book exhibition in Paris jammed the Russian booth, travelers in Russia mailed them home. Otto Neurath, of the Social and Economic Museum in Vienna, was struck by the graphic presentation of statistics, a practice he himself had been pursuing. When he and his wife and colleague Marie Neurath reached Britain early in World War II they joined forces with another exiled Neurath, publisher Walter, then, under the Adprint label, creating books —and series—for various firms. Out of this juncture came, in time, the Isotype books of Marie Neurath and Lancelot Hogben, bright and crisp encapsulations of fact issued in the United States (by the Chanticleer Press, through Lothrop) as "The How and Why Series" and "The Wonder World of Science." In Britain too, Penguin Books in general, Puffin Picture Books in particular, followed the Russian example in offering well-designed informative books at low cost, while in France the Père Castor series (p. 123), more distinctly pedagogical, owed much not only to Russian models but also to Russian émigré artists.

Between 1930 and 1932, in the first flush of

American interest, a few Russian picturebooks appeared here in translation but these were assorted items—a fable, a satire, a factual fancy—that had no identity or importance as a group. For fact or fiction, American publishers were still committed to traditional design and the bound book, and this is how information first appeared.

Wilfred Jones was best known for his edition of Firdausi's *Epic of Kings* when he devised, wrote and illustrated *How the Derrick Works*; like others at the time, he had as real a regard for modern machinery as for the tenth-century Persian epic, and he treated both as monumental. In *How the Derrick Works*, the formal power of the illustrations—done in black and white with the addition, at alternate openings, of a rich muted blue—is expressive of the force and rigor of the work under way, work in which men gain stature from their association with machines (119). The text is composed of brief, concrete explanations, and the very exactitude of observation is compelling. To an extent its virtues militated against it. It was too imposing, too stark to be the answer to a young boy's fancy, and it did not find its rightful audience among older children; but it remains an important 'first' and impressive in its own right.

Somewhat the same fate befell *What Makes the Wheels Go Round*, planned and begun by Boris Artzybasheff and carried through by his compatriot, engineer George Bock. Like its simpler Russian counterparts, *What Makes the Wheels Go Round* is not for children as children but as persons interested in the content, a thorough, detailed explanation of physical principles and their technical applications—e.g. water as a source of energy, the earliest waterwheel (120), the latest hydroelectric power plant. It has too much text to be a picturebook in the usual sense but its diagrams and cut-aways, in black and white and four colors, are integral and indispensable, just as Jones's drawings are, and in their way as considerable an achievement.

Simple mechanics to advanced technology, pictures are requisite to understanding (even

118. Russian picturebooks of the late Twenties and early Thirties.

RIGGING BEAMS FOR HOISTING

The drawing on the opposite page shows the simple method used to rig steel beams for hoisting.

Slings of wire rope are made in one piece so that they may be rigged as shown in the picture.

The steel beams rest on pieces of timber at each end. This makes it easy to slip the sling around and under them.

At each end of the sling is a loop. One of these loops is pulled through the other and lifted over the big hook. A type of sling easier to handle is one with two splices, forming loops at each end of a single line.

As the load line lifts the hook, a tremendous rumble and clatter comes from the steel beams as they settle themselves.

A guy rope is fastened to one end of the load to keep it from swinging wildly. Often one or two men ride the beams to the top of the building, hundreds of feet above the ground, although they are not supposed to do so nowadays.

Sometimes another type of sling is used, a simple line with a hook at either end. This is fastened to the beam by placing the hooks diagonally at opposite ends of the beam. The big hook of the boom catches the center of the line. As a rule this is used for single beams.

12

119. *How the Derrick Works,* by Wilfred Jones. Macmillan, 1930. 7¾ x 10.

as they were a prerequisite for scientific and industrial progress); and with construction booming and Lindbergh flying the Atlantic, picturebooks of the workings of a steam shovel and the operation of a plane followed almost perforce. But except for those that turned to photographs, few are notable for their illustrations or for elucidation, and indeed 1933 saw them taper off sharply, to resume on a different basis after the Second World War.

120. *What Makes the Wheels Go Round,* by George E. Bock and Boris Artzybasheff. Macmillan, 1931. Detail.

The only book in the early Thirties to give nature the weight of machines was Dorothy Waugh's introduction to insects, *Among the Leaves and Grasses.* As a young designer new to New York, Miss Waugh prepared it to demonstrate what she could do, drawing on a lifelong acquaintance with plants and animals —her father was head of the division of horticulture at Massachusetts State College— for her subject. Her dummy was at Holt when Larry June, of the ubiquitous Jersey City Printing Company, came to urge the use of offset for just such color printing. So *Among the Leaves and Grasses* became a showcase for offset as well as a showcase for Dorothy Waugh.

It is considerably more. Miss Waugh's determination to "put as much design as possible into the book"[4] accorded with the Art Deco propensity for designing the whole as a unit, an object of decorative art (which, in its Art Nouveau form, was characteristic of Walter Crane's work). Here the design has an editorial function as well, in identifying, enumerating and locating the topics (121); in relating them to one another and relating insects as a group to other members of the animal kingdom; and in displaying each topic, each type of insect, separately (122). The unified design accords further with the approach to the subject, the concept of insect-ness; not bees or spiders or crickets as such but bees and spiders and crickets as insects is what the book is about (though the individual portraits are appreciative and explicit).

So much for utility. The book is entitled, you'll notice, not 'Insects' or 'Introduction to Insects' but *Among the Leaves and Grasses*, a poetic metaphor, and Miss Waugh speaks, Homerically, of "crook-legged spiders" and "swift-winged dragon-flies." Or, with a quiet lyric drama, she tolls the crickets' passing:

> The apples that have fallen into the grass get too withered for food, and rot. The grasses themselves, where the Crickets loved to hide, turn brown and dry. The stones grow frosty and cold, with very little sun to warm them in the daytime, so the chinks that were cozy retreats are quite comfortless. Then the Crickets forget their worries about birds and mice, and their pleasure in music and the warm juice of fruit. For them, as for the Bumblebees and Wasps, when autumn grows late it is the end.

The uniform gaiety is perhaps inappropriate and the wide spacing of type lines impedes reading but the result of both, a book that is itself an attractive object, is in accordance with Miss Waugh's concept of the subject also as something to wonder at.

Among the Leaves and Grasses, a unit of design, sees nature whole; it is a view that Dorothy Waugh will pursue further to an even more successful resolution in *Warm Earth*. That the book did not make a more lasting impression than it did may be attributed to the incompatibility of the Art Deco—décoratif—aesthetic with concrete and specific illustration.

The Depression, breeding disenchantment with the machine, fostered interest in the mechanisms of human society and in the new social science that, in varying degrees, took

121

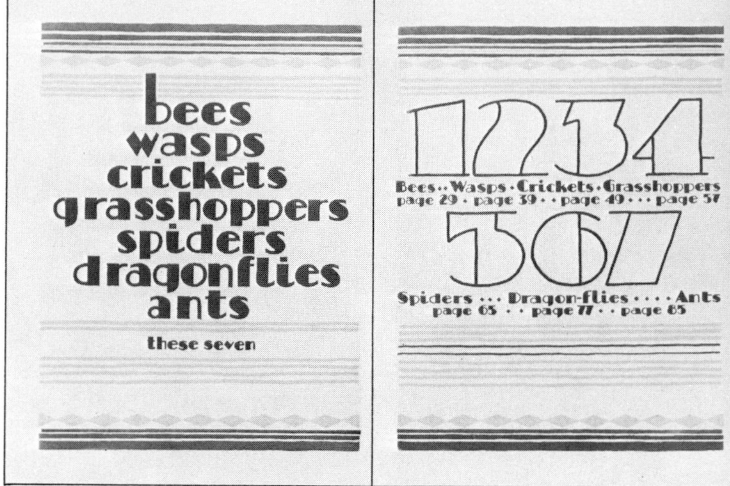
bees
wasps
crickets
grasshoppers
spiders
dragonflies
ants
these seven

1234
Bees.. Wasps · Crickets · Grasshoppers
page 29 · page 39 · · page 49 · · · page 57
567
Spiders ... Dragon-flies .... Ants
page 65 · · page 77 · · page 85

121, 122. *Among the Leaves and Grasses,* by Dorothy Waugh. Holt, 1931. 7½ x 10¼.

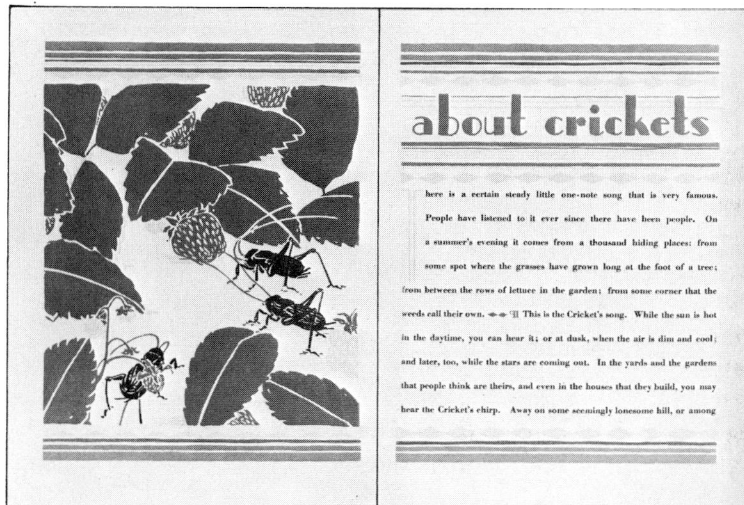
about crickets

here is a certain steady little one-note song that is very famous. People have listened to it ever since there have been people. On a summer's evening it comes from a thousand hiding places: from some spot where the grasses have grown long at the foot of a tree; from between the rows of lettuce in the garden; from some corner that the weeds call their own. ¶ This is the Cricket's song. While the sun is hot in the daytime, you can hear it; or at dusk, when the air is dim and cool; and later, too, while the stars are coming out. In the yards and the gardens that people think are theirs, and even in the houses that they build, you may hear the Cricket's chirp. Away on some seemingly lonesome hill, or among

122

both the past and present as its province. In this area as in so many others, the progressive schools pioneered in the 1920s and before. Under Katharine Taylor, the Shady Hill School in Cambridge devoted a year each to the study of salient civilizations; from its founding in 1917, the Lincoln School in New York sent classes down to the docks—to learn about ships, about trade, about lands and peoples. Direct results were *The Shady Hill Play Book* (1928), a collection of historic pageants performed by the students, and *Boats* (1927), by third grade children at

123. *The Delivery Men,* text by Charlotte Kuh, pictures by Kurt Wiese. Macmillan, 1929. 5¾ x 5½.

Lincoln and their teacher, Nell C. Curtis. (However different the approach, progressive schooling meant child participation.)

Also immediately productive was Lucy Sprague Mitchell's interest in the emerging field of 'human geography.' "In history programs with older children, could not . . . the study of ways of living that people developed be related to the lands they used?"[5] From her thinking came teaching, from her teaching, writing. *North America: The Land They Live In for the Children Who Live There* (1931) and *Manhattan, Now and Long Ago* (1934) combine poetry, exposition and illustrative stories and best domonstrate her method. Simultaneously, Gertrude Hartman, editor of *Progressive Education* magazine in its heroic youth, wrote first *The World We Live In* (1931), then *These United States* (1932), both subtitled "And How It (They) Came To Be." The direction was set. It was the Russian example, however, that would provide the impetus to pictorialize for the young child what was being set down in print for the older child.

Indicative of what was stirring was the appearance in 1929 of a new group of Happy Hour books featuring *The Fireman, The Policeman, The Postman, The Motorman, The Delivery Men*—what every child knows as community helpers. The author, Charlotte Kuh, had taught at the Francis Parker School

124. *How It All Began,* by Janet Smalley. Morrow, 1932. 6⅞ x 8⅛.

This is a furnace, down in the cellar. There is one in your house. It burns coal or oil or gas. It sends heat to every room by steam, hot water or hot air.
(The stove is smiling because it likes to make people comfortable.)
18
19

in Chicago, another progressive bastion. Her explanations are precise, thought-out, taking-in, as per her account of the fish peddler: "His wagon is almost half-filled with ice, and on the ice are lying fish. The push-cart man has no regular customers, as has the milkman or the grocery man. He must get people to notice him, if he wants to sell his wares. So he makes a great deal of noise and commotion. He shouts and almost sings all about his fish. He hopes that people will come to the back windows and call down to him, asking him to come up. . . ." In addressing the very young, one can hardly do better (nor in, unconsciously, documenting the life of a time). Kurt Wiese's genre illustrations are lively and equally observant and attest once again to his versatility (123).

Around the same time Janet Smalley, a commercial artist who found most children's books "a bit sugary for my taste,"[6] began a series that wasn't, though the first was called *Rice to Rice Pudding* (Morrow, 1928). With its successor *Plum to Plum Jam* (Morrow, 1929), it traces the process of turning natural substances into finished products—cotton bolls into clothing, elephant tusks into piano keys. Jingles in the pattern of "The House That Jack Built" comprise the text, jolly schematized drawings provide the pictures. Considerably more ambitious, *How It All Began* covers the history of Heat, Light, Houses, Clothing, Travel, Messages, Ships and Food in prose and diagrammatic as well as representational drawings (124). Personal and direct, it gives a quick light overview of a vast terrain.

But it was the Petershams' Russian-inspired Story Books whose vivid pictures of past and present life represented reality to a generation of American children. Indeed for many of us—I was of that generation—only *Life* magazine compared as a way of taking in the world. The Swiss lake houses on stilts, the piled-up pueblos of the Southwest, the thatched grass cones of Africa are all curious and inviting—in Petershamland remote past and remote present are indistinguishable—and almost always there are children, enviable children, to second the invitation. The bare-

125. *The Story Book of Things We Use,* by Maud and Miska Petersham. Winston, 1933. 8 x 8.

mats and baskets. They also learned how to make pots and jars out of the clay and mud of the lake.

Each family kept its animals in the house. The family lived in one part, and the goats and the cows lived in the other.

We know about these lake houses and how people lived in them because many ruins have been found. We find the ruins of these lake houses in Ireland and Switzerland and in some other places, but of course nobody is living in them now.

Long years ago these houses were all covered by the waters of the lake or the swamp in which they were built. Nobody dreamed that they were there. Then there came a very dry summer in Switzerland. There was no rain for weeks. The lake water became lower and lower, and pretty soon someone saw poles sticking up, and a rough platform. There were the lake dwellings of long ago.

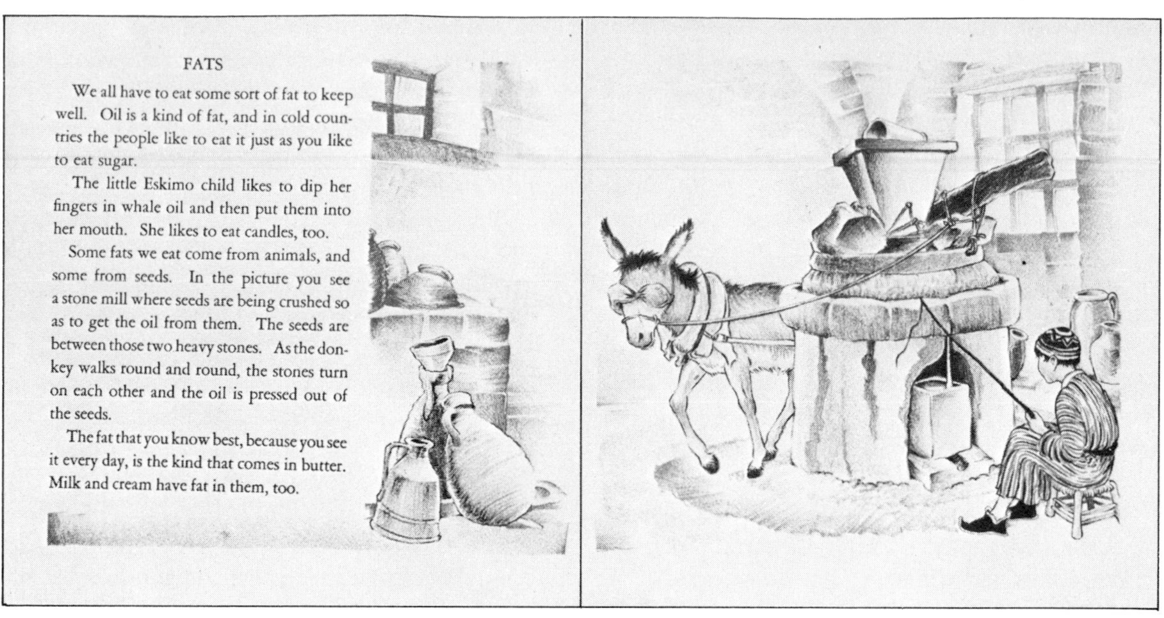

FATS

We all have to eat some sort of fat to keep well. Oil is a kind of fat, and in cold countries the people like to eat it just as you like to eat sugar.

The little Eskimo child likes to dip her fingers in whale oil and then put them into her mouth. She likes to eat candles, too.

Some fats we eat come from animals, and some from seeds. In the picture you see a stone mill where seeds are being crushed so as to get the oil from them. The seeds are between those two heavy stones. As the donkey walks round and round, the stones turn on each other and the oil is pressed out of the seeds.

The fat that you know best, because you see it every day, is the kind that comes in butter. Milk and cream have fat in them, too.

126. *The Story Book of Things We Use,* by Maud and Miska Petersham. Winston, 1933. 8 x 8.

armed, bare-legged boy peering down from the house platform, how close he is; and the story of how the ruins loomed up one dry summer, how intriguing (125). Back and forth one goes, between the pictures crytallizing a way of life and the text that fills in the background and points up certain details.

It is not always fully informative, as if the Petershams, having pictured a scene in toto, thought it self-explanatory. One wants to be told, however, why the donkey is blindfolded, what the little boy's task is (will he hit the donkey with that stick, that whip?), what kind of garb he is wearing, where this is taking place (126).

But consider: in the five Story Books of the series, each composed of four parts that were also published separately, the Petershams surveyed the history of houses, food, transportation (*Things We Use*, 1933); gold, coal, oil, iron and steel (*Earth's Treasures*, 1935); wheels, ships, trains, aircraft (so-titled, 1935); wheat, corn, rice, sugar (*Foods from the Field*, 1936); wool, cotton, silk, rayon (*Things We Wear*, 1939). A legendary Chinese empress watches a caterpillar spin a thread; Edward I, fearing poison, proscribes the burning of coal; American Indians dip a blanket into a pool to collect medicinal oil; fellow weavers smash Hargreaves's spinning jenny. Political history, ethnology, economics, technology, oddity—the range is enormous, hardly less than the story of man's works reconceived for children and reconstituted in pictures.

In preparing the pictures, moreover, the Petershams made extensive use of contemporary sources. The idea of emulating or adapting ancient models was not new to picturebooks; J. G. Francis's take-off *The Joyous Aztecs* (Century, 1929) and Frances Kent Gere's authentically handsome *Once Upon a Time in Egypt* (Longmans, 1937) are only two of the more interesting examples. But the Petershams' scope and purpose were novel. Chinese, Japanese, Egyptian, Assyrian, Greek, Mexican and medieval paintings, drawings, tapestries, etc. were copied as documentary evidence or approximated to give an aura of authenticity much as, photographed, they would be used subsequently in the Wonderful World series, American Heritage books and the like.

Of themselves, the illustrations in the first and simplest book are the best—stone lithographs in five colors (125) and monochrome (126), with definite outlines, solid forms and strong space-filling composition, just what many of the later Petersham books lack.

The only comparable project of the period was *A Child's Story of the World*, published in one volume by Simon and Schuster for the Junior Literary Guild and in six separate volumes—*The Story of the First Men, The Story of Ancient Civilization, The Story of the Middle Ages, The Story of the New Lands, The Story of America, The Story of the Modern Age*—by Grosset & Dunlap; the whole, however, was an undertaking of the Artists and Writers Guild (about which more later). This sweeping history was written by Donald Culross Peattie, then at the top of his fame for two thoughtful and substantive best sellers, *An Almanac for Moderns* (1935) and *Green Laurels* (1936); it was illustrated—with variety, imagination and much flair—by a newcomer, Naomi Averill.

But when we come to speak of the book, or books, it must be in terms of design. Those who maintain that flat color—or, alternatively, unshaded line—best suits the flatness of type, the plane that is the printed page, have strong support here. The illustrations, in three or four schematic colors alternating with two colors, score chiefly in terms of vigorous, expressive silhouette (127), symbolic design and pattern (128) and a combination of silhouette and patterned design (129); interior detailing is at a minimum, intimation at a premium. Though the placement of type remains constant, the form and disposition of the illustrations differ at every opening, and differ precisely in accordance with what's being conveyed. How to do much with little is the lesson.

Up to this point all of the informational books—and indeed almost all of the picture-books—have been what are known as regular trade books; that is, they were published by firms already identified with adult books and sold in the same manner, through bookstores and to libraries. Existing apart, selling usually for ten cents in chain stores, were the mass-

127. *The Story of the Modern Age,* text by Donald Culross Peattie, pictures by Naomi Averill. Grosset, 1937. 7⅞ x 8⅛.

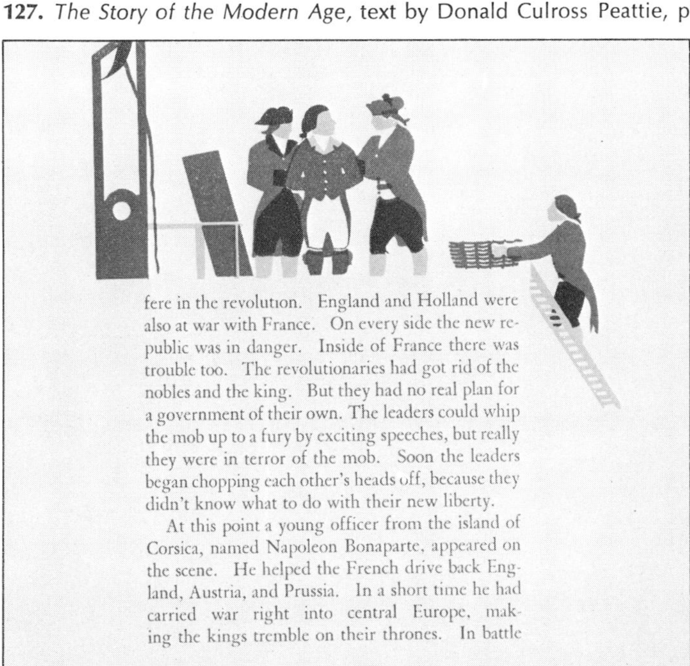

fere in the revolution. England and Holland were also at war with France. On every side the new republic was in danger. Inside of France there was trouble too. The revolutionaries had got rid of the nobles and the king. But they had no real plan for a government of their own. The leaders could whip the mob up to a fury by exciting speeches, but really they were in terror of the mob. Soon the leaders began chopping each other's heads off, because they didn't know what to do with their new liberty.

At this point a young officer from the island of Corsica, named Napoleon Bonaparte, appeared on the scene. He helped the French drive back England, Austria, and Prussia. In a short time he had carried war right into central Europe, making the kings tremble on their thrones. In battle

after battle he defeated the enemies of France. He conquered Belgium, Holland, Spain and most of Italy. He had proud Austria on her knees, and Germany too. Russia and England remained undefeated, but nervous.

Napoleon now made himself Emperor of France. He had discovered that winning glorious victories abroad kept people from noticing that the poor people were just as poor as ever. The bloodshed inside France stopped as soon as French soldiers shed the blood of other countries.

THE KNIGHTS OF CHRISTIAN EUROPE HAD THE CROSS FOR THEIR SYMBOL.

THE STORY OF THE MIDDLE AGES

Every child who has listened to fairy tales knows a good deal about the Middle Ages. Those were the times of brave knights, fair maidens with ropes of golden hair, wicked robber barons, and kings who really wore their crowns. The life of castle, walled town, and thatched cottage in the forest, that we read of in books, was then real, everyday life.

In those days Europe was far wilder than now. Great forests covered much of it, and the towns were small and farms farther apart than they are now. So there were far fewer people, and not many of those could read or write. In the woods were bands of robbers, like Robin Hood's band, and even in the great cities, danger lurked in the dark streets.

In order to be safe from roving bands of thieves

128. *The Story of the Middle Ages,* text by Donald Culross Peattie, pictures by Naomi Averill. Grosset, 1937. 7⅞ x 8⅛.

129. *The Story of Ancient Civilization,* text by Donald Culross Peattie, pictures by Naomi Averill. Grosset, 1937. 7⅞ x 8⅛.

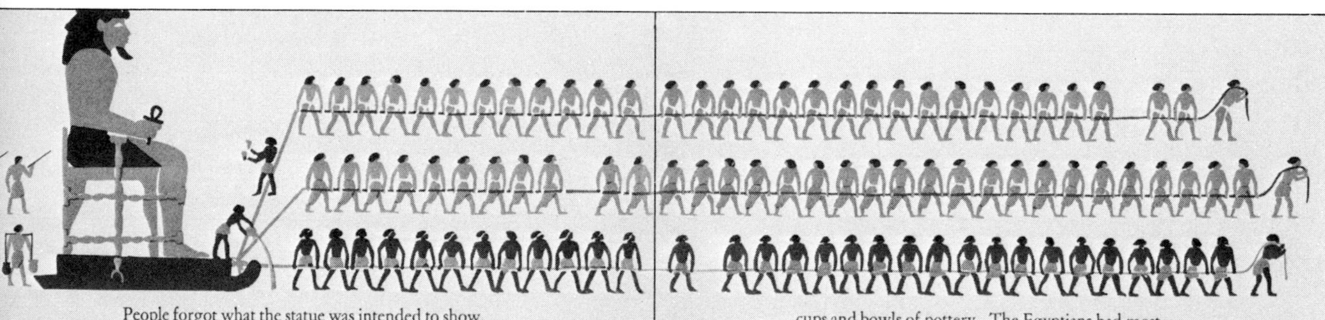

People forgot what the statue was intended to show. They called it the Sphynx, and they thought it was some queer sort of a goddess who was very ancient and knew everything and could answer riddles. But now we understand that the Sphynx was really a statue of a king or Pharaoh of ancient Egypt.

Beside making beautiful stone temples, carvings, and statues, the Egyptians were skillful workers in copper, iron, bronze, gold and silver. This put them far ahead of people like the Cave Men and all the barbarians who could only make things out of stone. Rich crops were grown by the Egyptian farmers. In Egypt were manufactured glass and fine dishes, and

cups and bowls of pottery. The Egyptians had most of our common farm animals such as horses, dogs, cows, and oxen, sheep, goats, and cats.

The government of Egypt was complicated. Policemen, tax-collectors, judges, messengers, and other officers and servants were needed to carry on the government of such a large and rich country. Perhaps it was all this government business that made the Egyptians invent a calendar of days, weeks, months, and years. They also invented the first clock, to mark the hours, but it was only a sort of sundial. They had to defend rich Egypt against neighbors who would have liked to break into it and so market books—which, however distinct their origin and distribution, were affected by the same developments as trade books.

One was the advent of progressive education. Shortly after Lucille Ogle, trained in art and briefly a teacher, went to work for the Harter Publishing Company (then the Harter School Supply Company), she was set to editing *Modern Education* (initially *Individual Instruction*), a quarterly that from 1928 through 1930 offered guidance in progressive methods and the use of materials to classroom teachers, serving as a practical Midwestern outlet for the theories advanced nationally, even internationally, by *Progressive Education.* Two leaders in combining individualized instruction with individual initiative, Carleton Washburne, Superintendent of the Winnetka Schools, and Helen Parkhurst, founder of the Dalton Plan, served as editorial advisers, and among the contributors were Katharine Gibson and Anne Horton of the Cleveland Museum, noted for involving children creatively with art.

In the wings was George Hubbard Judd, longtime head of the department of education at the University of Chicago and an advocate, contra Dewey, of information as a precondition for education. Judd proposed that the information be presented in capsules, small works on distinct periods of history or aspects of science, and he was instrumental in the publication of several such; but textbooks would not suffice—the information capsules must be universally available at low cost.

Out of this background came, in 1934 and 1935, *Talking Leaves* and *Seeing Stars,* two guides intended for children but not limited to children, that sold for ten cents and stand out still for clarity, efficiency and trim good looks. (Taken over by Rand McNally and revised, *Seeing Stars* exists today as *Neighbors in Space.*) Of the two, *Talking Leaves* excels as a graphic summation, concise and suggestive (130), while *Seeing Stars* adds photographs—recently taken at Yerkes Observatory—to the diagrams and drawings for balanced documentation (131). Edited and designed by Lucille Ogle, they were among the first of

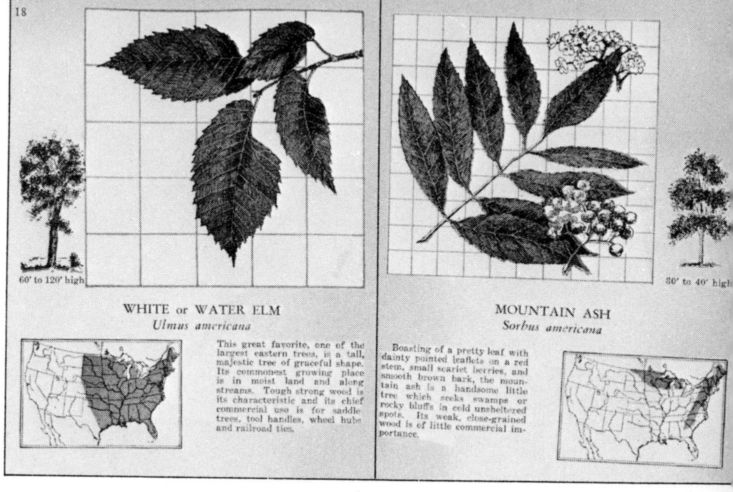

18

60′ to 120′ high

WHITE or WATER ELM
Ulmus americana

This great favorite, one of the largest eastern trees, is a tall, majestic tree of graceful shape. Its commonest growing place is in moist land and along streams. Tough strong wood is its characteristic and its chief commercial use is for saddle trees, tool handles, wheel hubs and railroad ties.

30′ to 40′ high

MOUNTAIN ASH
Sorbus americana

Boasting of a pretty leaf with dainty pointed leaflets on a red stem, small scarlet berries, and smooth brown bark, the mountain ash is a handsome little tree which seeks swamps or rocky bluffs in cold unsheltered spots. Its weak, close-grained wood is of little commercial importance.

130. *Talking Leaves,* text by Julius King, pictures by Evan Thurber. Cleveland, Harter, 1934. 5 x 6¼.

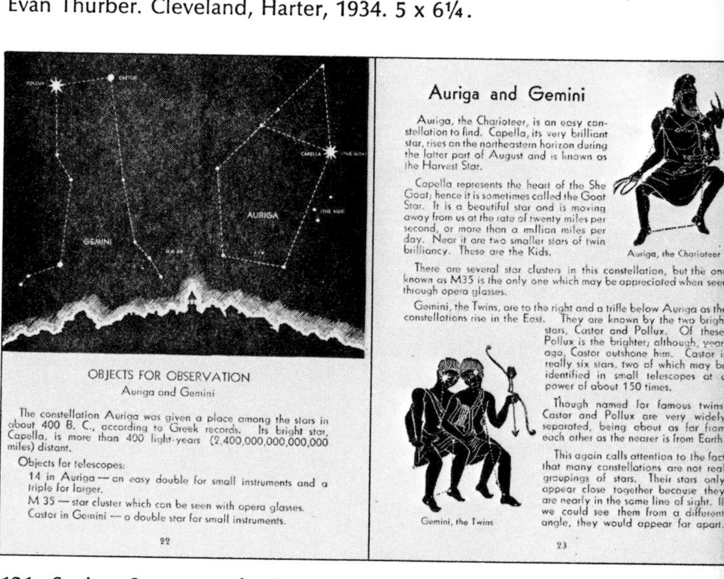

OBJECTS FOR OBSERVATION
Auriga and Gemini

The constellation Auriga was given a place among the stars in about 400 B. C., according to Greek records. Its bright star, Capella, is more than 400 light-years (2,400,000,000,000,000 miles) distant.

Objects for telescopes:
14 in Auriga — an easy double for small instruments and a triple for larger.
M 35 — star cluster which can be seen with opera glasses.
Castor in Gemini — a double star for small instruments.

22

Auriga and Gemini

Auriga, the Charioteer, is an easy constellation to find. Capella, its very brilliant star, rises on the northeastern horizon during the latter part of August and is known as the Harvest Star.

Capella represents the heart of the She Goat; hence it is sometimes called the Goat Star. It is a beautiful star and is moving away from us at the rate of twenty miles per second, or more than a million miles per day. Near it are two smaller stars of twin brilliancy. These are the Kids.

Auriga, the Charioteer

There are several star clusters in this constellation, but the one known as M35 is the only one which may be appreciated when seen through opera glasses.

Gemini, the Twins, are to the right and a trifle below Auriga as the constellations rise in the East. They are known by the two bright stars, Castor and Pollux. Of these, Pollux is the brighter; although, years ago, Castor outshone him. Castor is really six stars, two of which may be identified in small telescopes at a power of about 150 times.

Though named for famous twins, Castor and Pollux are very widely separated, being about as far from each other as the nearer is from Earth.

This again calls attention to the fact that many constellations are not real groupings of stars. Their stars only appear close together because they are nearly in the same line of sight. If we could see them from a different angle, they would appear far apart.

Gemini, the Twins

23

131. *Seeing Stars,* text by W. B. White, pictures by Ruth C. Williams. Cleveland, Harter, 1935. 5 x 6¼.

scores of instructive books she would have a hand in.

Photographs are themselves information; they have the ability, besides, of making the small large, of bringing the distant close, of making the unseen visible. The photographic book as such is the subject of the next section but the application of photography to fact is a development of the Thirties worth examining for its unique possibilities and the books that first realized them.

Nature is a topic dear to those who provide books for young children and the number of invitations to explore the out-of-doors is uncountable; but after more than thirty years Harriet Huntington's *Let's Go Outdoors* not only remains in print, it remains a book one

132

133

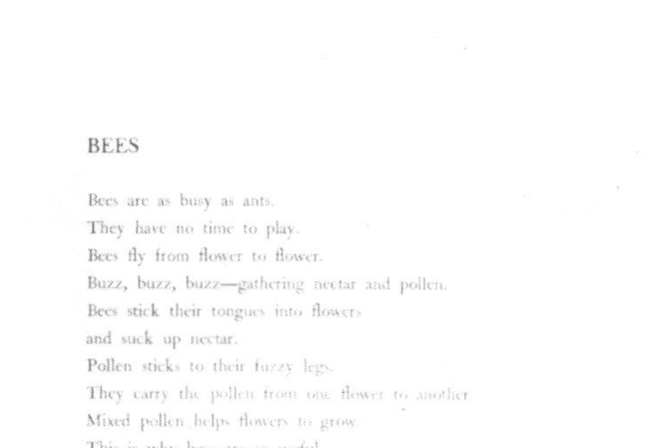

BEES

Bees are as busy as ants.
They have no time to play.
Bees fly from flower to flower.
Buzz, buzz, buzz—gathering nectar and pollen.
Bees stick their tongues into flowers
and suck up nectar.
Pollen sticks to their fuzzy legs.
They carry the pollen from one flower to another
Mixed pollen helps flowers to grow
This is why bees are so useful.
Because they mix the pollen of the flowers 38

134

132-134. *Let's Go Outdoors,* text by Harriet E. Huntington, photos by Preston Duncan. Doubleday, 1939. 8½ x 8⅛.

would pick out of a batch. There is first of all the design or scheme: the two children absorbed in a frog on the cover (132); a vista wide as all outdoors for the endpapers (133); and in the body of the book, the various creatures pictured and described in a neat, straightforward layout (134). Each of the insects or reptiles is immediately in a one-to-one relationship with the child observer, the kind of close relationship that, paradoxically, makes nature the more mysterious. To further isolate the object, backgrounds are blurred or entirely suppressed. It is a method common in graphic illustration and there is in the close cropping, too, both concentration and sensitivity to composition.

The book is not without flaws. In three separate photographs an insect may be three different sizes, none of them actual, with nowhere an object of known size as a standard. Now and again the text talks nonsense ("They have no time to play"—true, but why put it that way?) and makes sentences of what are not. (Because it wants to be easy to read.)

Let's Go Outdoors is a considerable achievement regardless—one which Harriet Huntington repeated with her own photographs in *Let's Go to the Seashore* and others—and something of a marvel in one respect: originally printed in gravure, a process that yields rich blacks and softly graded middle tones, it is still printed in gravure and hardly less effective in its twenty-fourth printing than it was in its first.

Such is not the case with Henry Kane's Wild World Tales, usable in their later coarse, washed-out offset printing only because of the excellence of the original photographs. Kane's first book, *The Alphabet of Birds, Bugs and Beasts* (Houghton Mifflin, 1938), was a mélange of light verse, informative exposition, cartoons, photographs and, finally, the letters of the alphabet, a confusion of purpose not unusual then (or entirely absent today). But with the Wild World Tales—*The Tale of the Whitefoot Mouse* (Knopf, 1940), *The Tale of the Bullfrog* and their successors—Kane presented his subjects plain, in life stories composed of photographs, drawings and text (135). The inclusion of the drawings was severely criticized without recognizing that they might enlarge the story and enliven the telling.

What Kane did, essentially, was to document with photographs what had hitherto been done in words and drawings. Photography, moreover, enabled him to deal with subjects that elude the artist—the mouse, the frog, the crow, the moth instead of Kurt Wiese's kangaroo, walrus, elephant, bear. It was also a move away from personalization and toward representative individualization: the animal less as a hero, more as one of a kind. The simpler the animal, too, the closer one comes to bedrock science—compare, in this respect, *Let's Go Outdoors* with the typical 'Day at the Zoo.'

Kane did the obvious so well that he set a standard. His explanations are meticulous yet colorful, and he has a fine sense of drama; he is telling a story, not precisely a true story but one that could be true. Though he does not capture every development on film, one is not aware of lapses: the close-up of the head of a Cooper's hawk, for instance, instantly conveys the danger to the bullfrog in the hawk's swooping attack, and the succeeding photo of the taut leaping bullfrog, spread over two pages, completes the incident without the two having once appeared together. It is legitimate trickery, the equivalent of the quick cut in films.

There is in fact much that is filmic in *The Tale of the Bullfrog*: the limpid underwater sequences, the violent movement, the shot of a snow blanket pierced with reeds—pure Stroheim or Welles—as "All through the long winter . . . he lay motionless, hardly seeming alive, as cold as the rest of his underwater world." (He, the bullfrog, we don't see.) But the book remains firmly a book, disdaining the devices—bleeding, imbalance, abutting of pictures—that, then and since, have sometimes achieved visual stimulation at the cost of communicating the content. In design, *The Tale of the Bullfrog* and its mates are solid, stately, serene, the better to display the pictures and text.

The Thirties was a beginning, and as always with beginnings, individual books and individual names stand out. Charting the further progress of informational books—some of it true progress as well as expansion—will be a matter of examining areas and trends.

135. *The Tale of the Bullfrog,* by Henry B. Kane. Knopf, 1941. 7⅛ x 9.

His mouth had grown from a little round opening until it reached from ear to ear—or, rather, from where his ears would be. Already there were signs that they would soon appear, just behind his eyes. His tail at last began to shrink.

During all the time when these changes in his body were taking place the tadpole had not eaten a thing. For nourishment he had drawn upon the stored-up energy in his big fat tail. Gradually it was being absorbed into his body, and now it had become very much smaller. Gone were the thin fleshy fins. Only the central part was left, and that was dark and shrunken and misshapen. The color too was being transferred to the body, and his skin was becoming rapidly darker.

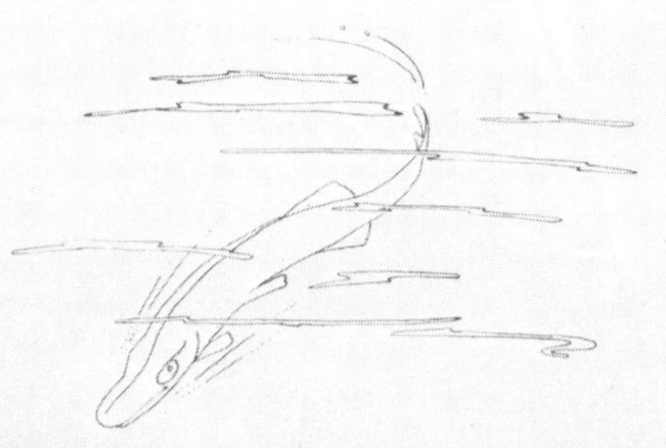

PHOTOGRAPHIC BOOKS

When the invention of the half-tone process made it possible to print photographs with type in books (rather than pasting them in or binding them in as separate plates), they began to turn up in books for children too—not, however, as photographs, images of the real, but as narrative illustrations, counterfeits of the unreal. Dolls and stuffed animals and other small toys were put into position and photographed playing themselves or a Peter Rabbit role, either way acting out a story. The misuse of photography and misconstruction of make-believe are well stated in a 1904 review of one such book, *The Life of a Wooden Doll*: "The advertiser of the day may demand a photograph to prove an assertion; he uses it to show that imagination has nothing to do with his claims. The child demands the imaginative element in all its joys. . . . It takes no very efficient pictorial suggestion to bring before the young and fervid fancy all manner of gallant actions, to enact fairy tales, to make the world of fiction all alive. But if you photograph the puppets, you set before the ardent auditor a lifeless record."[1] Even after books of the sort had been abandoned, the practice of picturing a toy model in place of the original persisted on the assumption, valid in a different context, that children invest their toys with the semblance of reality; thus, a 1932 French photographic alphabet, smartly up-to-date, featuring a live elephant and a dead herring, turns to a file of lead soldiers for *uniform*, a water-borne replica for *yacht*.[2]

In *The First Picture Book* there is no equivocation, no 'semblance of reality,' but reality itself, thrice over: the everyday world of the child under three, the objects of that world, straightforward photographs of those objects. Or, as the subtitle puts it with charming plainness, *Everyday Things for Babies* presented, in Mary Steichen Martin's words, "as 'objectively' as possible" by her father, photographer Edward Steichen.

It was an idea whose time had come. On the one hand, straight photography—the work of Stieglitz, Strand, Weston, Steichen—was making an impact in exhibitions and luxury magazines; development of the 35mm miniature camera, capable of shooting quickly with existing light, brought 'candid' shots of celebrities and casual, unposed pictures of ongoing life; and with appreciation of the authentic, unretouched photos of the past and the explosion in photojournalism came recognition of photography's documentary potential in the present. In 1930 there appeared *Fortune* magazine, with photographs of industrial leaders by Berenice Abbott, of industrial plants by Margaret Bourke-White; *Atget, Photographe de Paris*, arranged by Abbott in tribute to a great precursor; books bearing photographs by Ansel Adams (*Taos Pueblo*, text by Mary Austin) and Walker Evans (Hart Crane's *The Bridge*); and the first of the modern photographic books, *The First Picture Book*.

On the other hand, 1930 was the crest of the preschool movement and the heyday of the here and now. Militating against "imaginary flights into fairyland, heaven, or even such real though remote places as Japan or Holland or Ireland," scorning parents who "love to repeat the fairy-tales of their youth and see little eyes grow big," aunts and uncles who "dote on taking little ones to *Peter Pan* and the like," "old-school kindergartners [who] die hard on 'Little Red Riding Hood,'" Elisabeth Irwin, founder of The Little Red

Schoolhouse, concludes: "*The First Picture Book* is one that sentimental adults will hate."

"A cup of milk beside a plate with a slice of bread and butter, is the first picture. It has no artistic shadow or modernistic slant. It has no explanatory caption, no accompanying story. It is followed by a series of equally realistic photographs including in their range a teddy bear, a washbasin with faucets and toothbrush [136], a child's wagon, a chair, a brush and comb."[3] The objects are "very much alone, very much there, very much themselves,"[4] as another reviewer noted; they are also quite abstracted in many cases, objectified by their isolation (wooden blocks laid out on a black ground), their proportions (a looming alarm clock, its face filling the page), and their number (a scattering of balls like pebbles on a beach); and they are quite beautiful. In the sparkling soap bubbles, the sheen of enamel, the shine of metal; in the slow curve of the basin, the boldly formed faucet, the shadowed transparency of the glass is the exaltation of the ordinary. An aesthetic is operating here as certainly as an ethic.

In *The Second Picture Book* (Harcourt), appearing the following year, the objects are put to use by children—one drinks from the cup, another plays with the teddy bear, still others brush their teeth and wash their hands. This was for the next stage, when the child, "at first static, and observant of his surroundings . . . begins to run around and participate in his environment." Continuing her prefatory remarks, Mary Steichen Martin (later Dr. Mary Calderone) explains the absence of a text: "Children are extraordinarily able to provide their own, but so much is read *to* them . . . that this ability falls into disuse . . . and too many children never find it again." Finally she asks for "information concerning the actual responses of the babies to the pictures" ("which would be invaluable to makers of picture books").

A questionnaire was included but the reaction was not sufficient to warrant recording the answers. As an attempt to enlist the participation of parents it was unique, however, and no venture more fully exemplifies the thinking—or the purposefulness—of the

136. *The First Picture Book,* prepared by Mary Steichen Martin, photos by Edward Steichen. Harcourt, 1930. 7⅛ x 8¼.

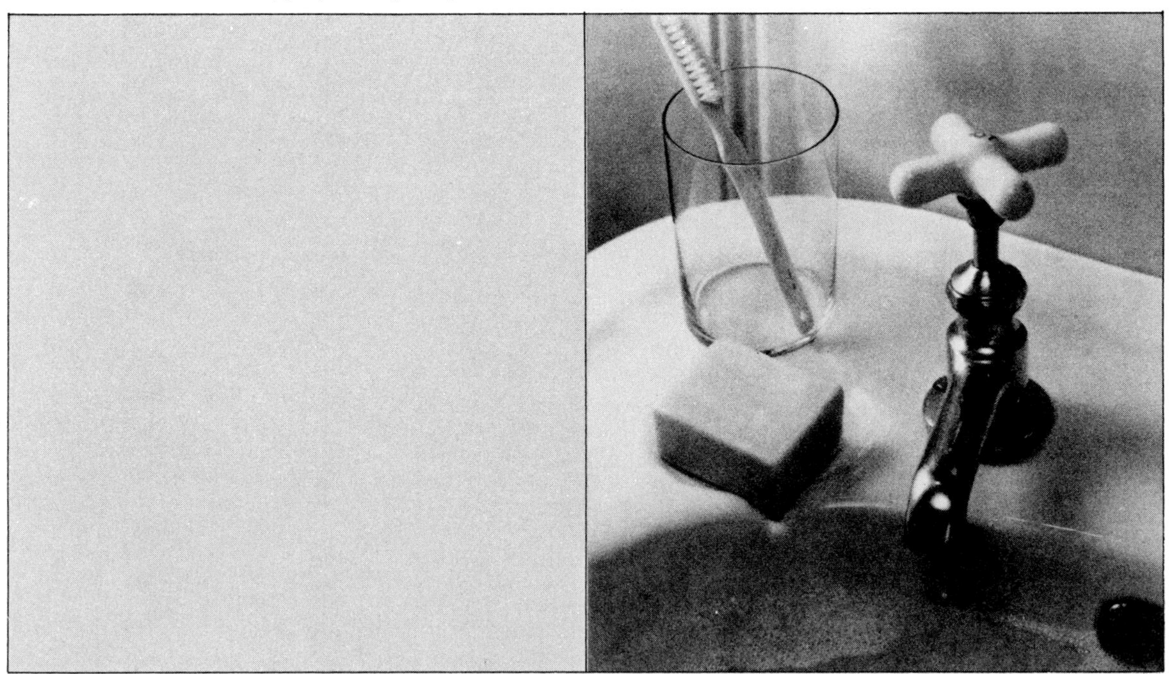

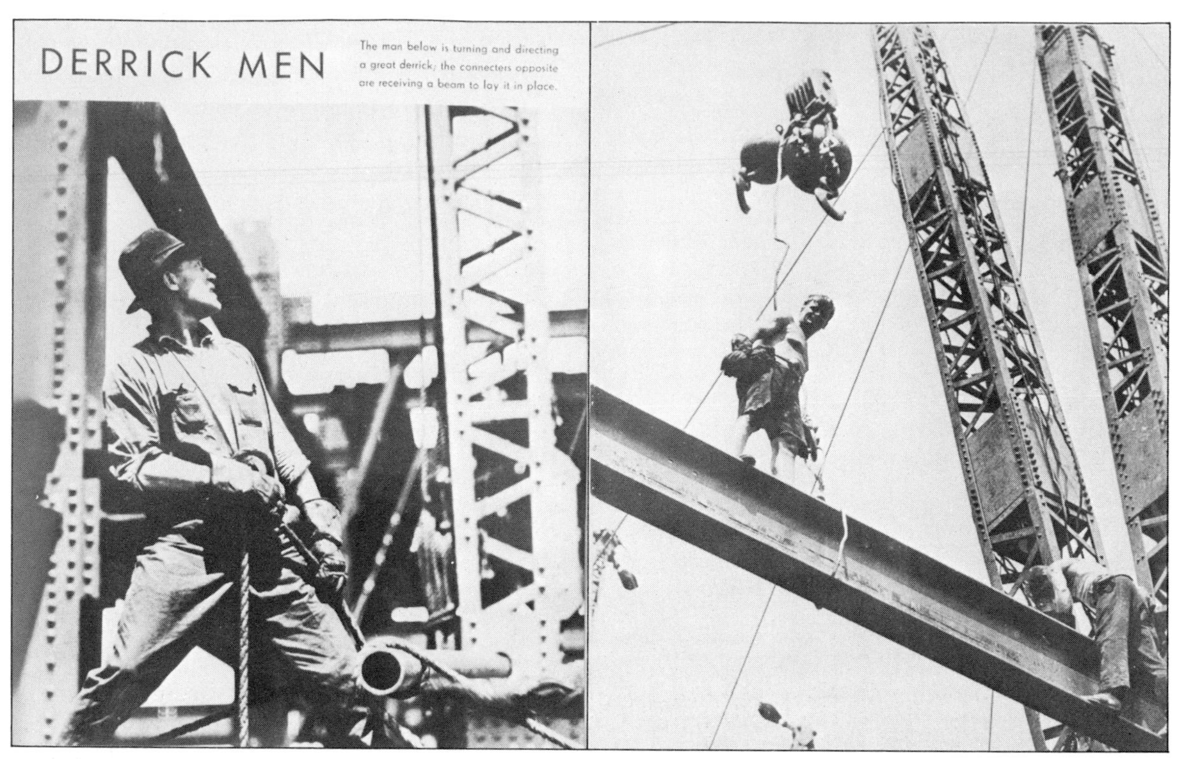

DERRICK MEN

The man below is turning and directing a great derrick; the connecters opposite are receiving a beam to lay it in place.

137, 138. *Men at Work,* by Lewis W. Hine. Macmillan, 1932. 7⅞ x 10. **137**

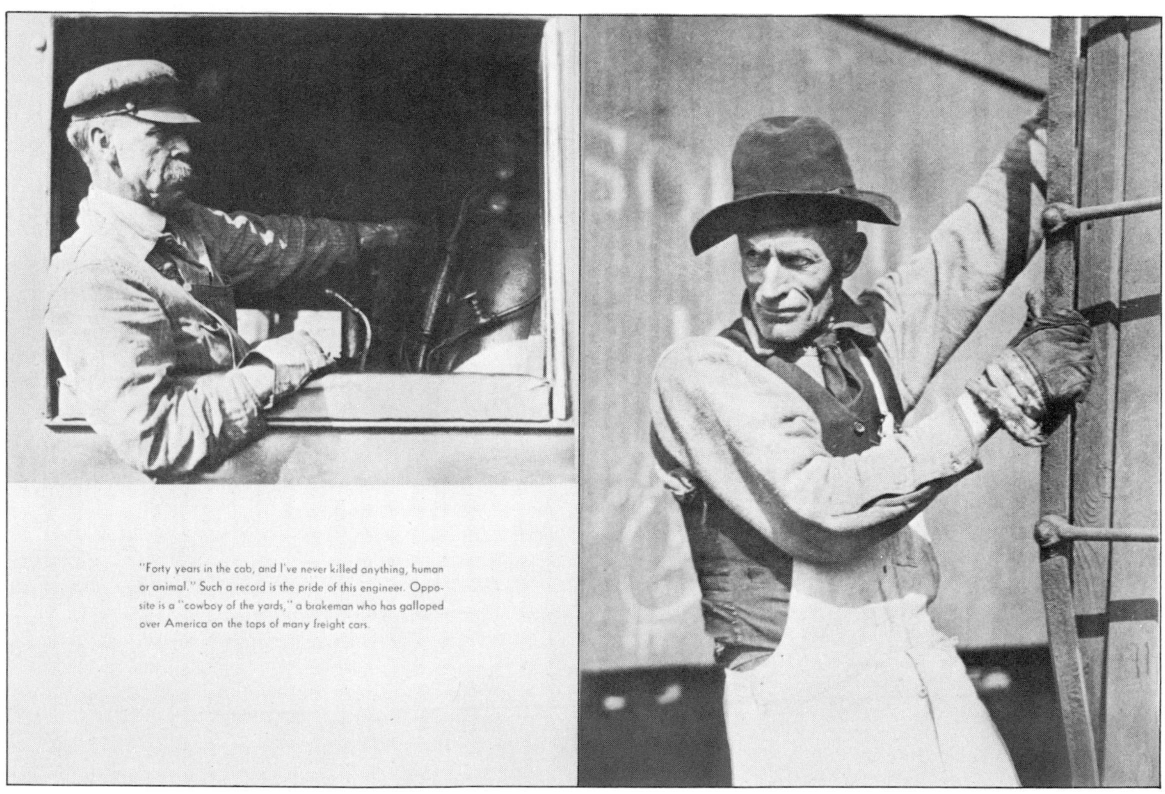

"Forty years in the cab, and I've never killed anything, human or animal." Such a record is the pride of this engineer. Opposite is a "cowboy of the yards," a brakeman who has galloped over America on the tops of many freight cars.

138

preschool movement than *The First* and *The Second Picture Book*.

Elisabeth Irwin's expectations were borne out: whether from sentimentality or obtuseness or both, opposition was immediate and lasting (neither made *Children's Catalog*). More open, more catholic (to Bertha Mahony's credit), *Five Years of Children's Books* listed both with a characteristic, even predictable reservation: "however fine the pictures, the photographic picture books have less space for the workings of a child's fancy and are sooner exhausted than imaginative pictures." Contrast Mary Steichen Martin's advocacy of the everyday—"It is unwise for a baby to get his *first* experiences of an object through the picturization of it. This may lead to a fantasy habit"[5]—and you have an extension of The Great Fairy Tale Debate that raged between 1929 and 1931.

Despite the cool to lukewarm response in library circles, *The First Picture Book* sparked a vogue for photographs in children's books. With its sequel appeared *Peggy and Peter* by Lena Towsley (Farrar & Rinehart), the idyllic day of two ideal children, a book similar in content to *The Second Picture Book* but what later pedagogese would call more structured; *The Picture Book of Animals* (Macmillan), a collection of photographs, with brief captions, culled from the files of a German nature magazine by Isabel Ely Lord; one of the very few photographic excursions into fantasy, *The Shadow's Holiday* (Farrar & Rinehart), the collaboration of Larry June and Joseph Alger; *The Iron Horse* (Knopf) by Adele Gutman Nathan and Margaret S. Ernst, based on photographs of historic vehicles from the B & O centennial exhibition; and others of a more conventional Sunday supplement sort.

There remained, distinct from the photograph-as-document, the deliberately persuasive documentary photograph. Jacob Riis took his camera to Hell's Kitchen and the Lower East Side to demonstrate *How the Other Half Lives* (1890), the condition of *The Children of the Poor* (1892), the results of *The Battle with the Slum* (1902), but his photographs, poorly printed, were little regarded at the time. Lewis Hine, a trained sociologist and a classroom teacher, used his camera as a research tool and a vehicle of interpretation and, benefiting from the rapid advance in printing, produced from 1908 onward the first 'photo stories' which led to his one book, a book for children, *Men at Work*.

Hine was teaching botany and nature studies at the Ethical Culture School in New York when the superintendent, Frank Manny, handed him a camera as an aid. Soon he had a camera club, a camera class (Paul Strand was a pupil) and, through his grounding in the social welfare movement, a new vocation. His photographs of immigrants at Ellis Island appeared in *The Charities and Commons*, which as *Survey* and its spin-off *Survey Graphic*, became the intellectual organ of social work and published much of Hine's output; for the National Child Labor Committee he photographed children in mills and mines, selling newspapers (at midnight) and tending stalls (at 10:00 P.M.), and his pictures, appearing everywhere, were instrumental in the passage of the first child labor laws; during World War I he photographed American Red Cross Relief in France and those in need of relief in Southeastern Europe; in the Twenties, increasingly, he photographed workers in industry, calling his pictures work portraits, considering them affirmative revelations, and in 1930 he recorded the construction of that supreme affirmation, the Empire State Building.

"I have toiled in many industries and associated with thousands of workers," Hine writes in the brief introduction to *Men at Work*. "Some of them are heroes; all of them persons it is a privilege to know. I will take you into the heart of modern industry where machines and skyscrapers are being made, where the character of the men is being put into the motors, the airplanes, the dynamos upon which the life and happiness of millions of us depend."

The bulk of the photographs, and the best, come from the Empire State series. Some of them had appeared elsewhere and the most spectacular would turn up again and again—the 'sky boy' swinging over the city a quarter-mile up; two workmen at the skeleton's edge, lesser skyscrapers huddled at their feet; two more going aloft by cable, "like spiders spinning a fabric of steel against the sky." In the book, however, they have a place in the construction process, and the daring is part of the doing. Below the connectors riding on the cable, the others poised on a beam, is the man directing the derrick (137), behind him the men responsible for drilling the foundation—a sensitive young face and, opposite, an intent figure holding the pneumatic drill by his index fingers.

Close as Hine is to Wilfred Jones in his respect for the workers and the work and in the contained force of his images, the two mediums, drawing and photography, impose different conditions and elicit a different response. From Jones we learn just how the beam is rigged and, in the background, precisely how a rigged beam looks (119); choosing what to see, he can choose what to show. With Hine, we are straining on the left, waiting confidently on the right, barely conscious of the web of girders in the first case, backed, supported, by the derrick in the second (137); from the given, he chooses the telling configuration.

The job finished with a shot of two men atop the mooring mast, Hine turns to other workers elsewhere, the railroad men and mechanics and miners he had photographed before. Close-ups, most of them, they make more of the individual, his skill and his accomplishment, more too of the look of his face (138). These are the work portraits, their individuality accentuated by their juxtaposition.

Men at Work fared poorly as a juvenile but not only is it singled out, without classification, in histories of photography, it is sometimes cited as having initiated the boom in picturebooks—photographic picturebooks—for the adult market. What the record reveals is a more general pattern of movement from the juvenile field to the adult with *Men at Work*, in 1932, as a likely intermediary. In October 1931, under the heading "Photographic Picture Books," *Publishers' Weekly* reports on "the vogue for the photograph in children's books"; in July 1933, per "The New Vogue for Picture Books," on the signs that, after a half-century hiatus (and more than a decade of success in Germany), "the picture book is coming again into its own"; in March 1934, on further "signs that the books of pictures for an adult audience are coming into their own." With Comenius's *Orbis Pictus* (1658), picturebooks had started as a vehicle of instruction for the young, and "Orbis Pictus" was the title chosen by *The Nation* for a 1935 editorial on "the rapid increase in the number of picture books for adults."

Most were pictorial records of the present or recent past; made by assembling photographs from various sources, they devolved not on photography per se but on photographs as used; and while photography buffs were looking to *Men at Work*, those interested in make-up were looking at *The Farmer Sows His Wheat* (1932) and *Skyscraper* (1933), which appeared, conspicuously, among the American Institute of Graphic Arts Fifty Books of the Year.

The Farmer Sows His Wheat (Minton, Balch), Adele Gutman Nathan's follow-up to *The Iron Horse*, was based on an International Harvester film, *The Romance of the Reaper*, augmented by photos from the company archives and commercial picture files. Across the endpapers, anticipating the tossing trees in *Let's Go Outdoors*, stretch acres of waving wheat; backing the title are sheaves of wheat, for a title page like the credits of a film. Inside, a cropped close-up and a cut-out silhouette show small, skillful gesture and large movement; to one side, filling the page, is the pattern a combine makes, an image of mechanical harvesting, to the other, close-up, the combine itself and its functioning. Fluidity coexists with clarity, order, logic—hence the AIGA accolade to designer Harrie Wood, who, by his handling of the material, 'made' the book.

Skyscraper, read the credits, "is the joint work of ELSA H. NAUMBURG, who did the research work and collected the photographs, CLARA LAMBERT, who wrote the verses, and LUCY SPRAGUE MITCHELL, who wrote the exposition." The skyscraper described is the Empire State Building and many of the photographs are Hine's but the book is about an archetypal building, at once a building type and an entity:

> It is time to summon the workers,
> it is time to summon the world
> For SKYSCRAPER is to be built!

The verses, saying and saying again like Lucy Sprague Mitchell's *Here and Now* stanzas, ringing out, recalling Ernestine Evans's 'work songs for the work gang,' surge on alongside the pictures, telling who and how, what it feels like, sounds like, looks like (139, 140); while Mrs. Mitchell, introducing each section, each stage of construction, explains the scheme and the relation of the parts to the whole.

If the bolter balanced on a beam looks familiar (140), he is (137); but cropping the picture at the top and isolating it opposite a web of cables instead of bleeding it to a base of control changes its aspect, bringing the man closer at the same time that it increases his peril. Reading the text after, one sees that it corresponds (140); taking in words and pictures together, the normal procedure, one gets in each case (137, 140) a different message.

The paean of praise that is *Skyscraper* is also the most thoroughly documented of books, with a page given over to detailed acknowledgments (to architects, contractors, suppliers), picture credits incorporated in the list of illustrations that serves as the table of

139. *Skyscraper,* text by Elsa H. Naumburg, Clara Lambert and Lucy Sprague Mitchell. John Day, 1933. 8⅜ x 10⅛.

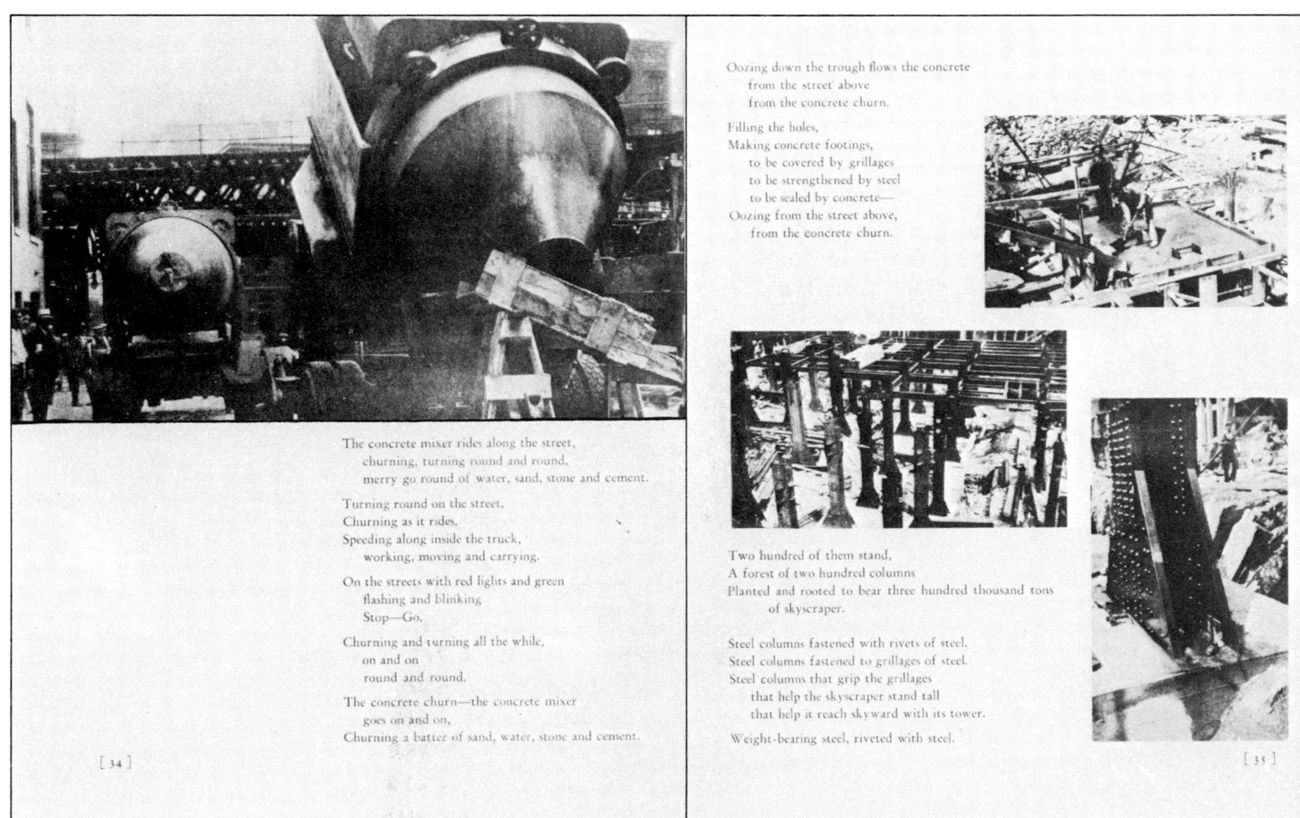
The concrete mixer rides along the street,
churning, turning round and round,
merry go round of water, sand, stone and cement.

Turning round on the street,
Churning as it rides.
Speeding along inside the truck,
working, moving and carrying.

On the streets with red lights and green
flashing and blinking
Stop—Go.

Churning and turning all the while,
on and on
round and round.

The concrete churn—the concrete mixer
goes on and on,
Churning a batter of sand, water, stone and cement.

[34]

Oozing down the trough flows the concrete
from the street above
from the concrete churn.

Filling the holes,
Making concrete footings,
to be covered by grillages
to be strengthened by steel
to be sealed by concrete—
Oozing from the street above,
from the concrete churn.

Two hundred of them stand,
A forest of two hundred columns
Planted and rooted to bear three hundred thousand tons
of skyscraper.

Steel columns fastened with rivets of steel.
Steel columns fastened to grillages of steel.
Steel columns that grip the grillages
that help the skyscraper stand tall
that help it reach skyward with its tower.

Weight-bearing steel, riveted with steel.

[35]

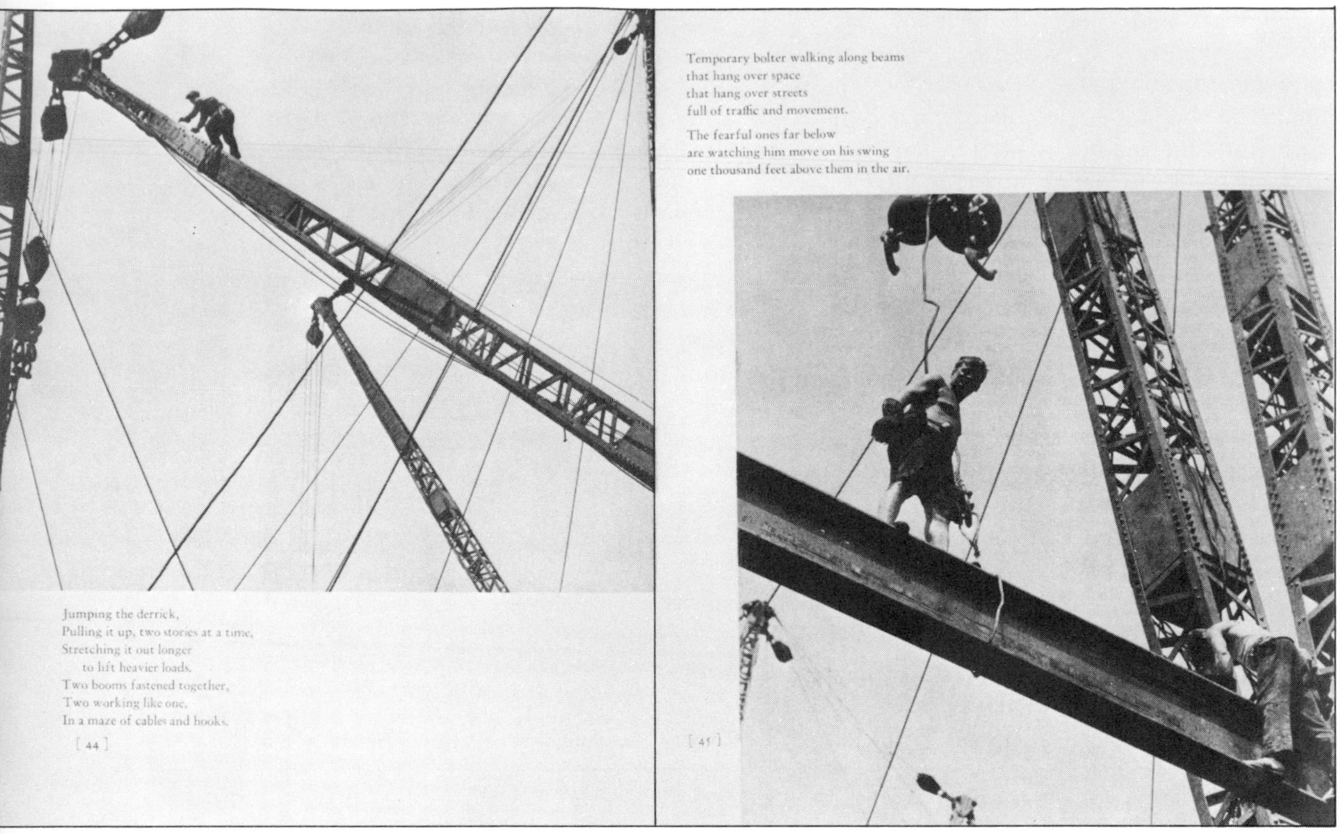

Jumping the derrick,
Pulling it up, two stories at a time,
Stretching it out longer
to lift heavier loads.
Two booms fastened together,
Two working like one,
In a maze of cables and hooks.

[44]

Temporary bolter walking along beams
that hang over space
that hang over streets
full of traffic and movement.

The fearful ones far below
are watching him move on his swing
one thousand feet above them in the air.

[45]

140. *Skyscraper*, text by Elsa H. Naumburg, Clara Lambert and Lucy Sprague Mitchell. John Day, 1933. 8⅜ x 10⅛.

contents, and, at the close, a remarkable bibliography. Could it have been reduced and remained legible, the bibliography would have been worth reproducing here, not merely for its entries—at random, "Daily Construction Record & Report of Starret Bros. & Eken. Unpublished"; "'Bamboo Hut the Model of the First Skyscraper!' *Popular Mechanics*, 57: 432, March 1932"; "'Progress and Poverty,' Edmund Wilson, *New Republic*, 67: 13–14, May 20, 1931"—but because it puts the innards of the book and the building and the background of both on display. Along with the acknowledgments and the credits it is saying in essence what the book is saying, that every given, whether photo or fact, concrete column or steel skeleton, is somehow begotten; that both say so graphically is *Skyscraper's* distinction.

It was, indeed, a product of its time that in its multimedia scope and its particularity was never repeated, for not only did enthusiasm for enterprises like the Empire State wane (as Mrs. Mitchell already recognizes), so did the experimental energy so marked at the start of the Thirties. In photography per se, there was to be nothing more done for children by anyone of the stature of Steichen and Hine until the E. D. Valens-Berenice Abbott science demonstrations of the 1960s. But a strain of innovative idealism persisted in mass-market books, and two key figures, Sam Lowe the erstwhile social worker at Whitman Publishing, then at its subsidiary the Artists and Writers Guild (p. 126), and Lucille Ogle, at Harter and later with Lowe at A & W, were alert to the uses of photography—as was Rand McNally when in 1934 it introduced "a new line of 10- and 15-cent juveniles."

The announcement leads off a *Publishers' Weekly* article on "The Ten-Cent Juvenile" that marks the advent of mass-market picture-books of trade caliber and, tacitly, indicates the place of the photographic book among them. So little of either development is recorded elsewhere that it is worth quoting at some length:

"For a number of years booksellers have noted . . . that much of their children's book business was being taken over by five-and-ten cent stores which were displaying picture books at ten cents. A few years ago these books were generally unhappy examples of bookmaking, patently cheap in writing, printing and illustration. But more recently, with the development of less expensive processes of color printing and with the economies accompanying mass distribution, these books have become definite competitors, in physical appearance as well as in sales, of higher priced juveniles.

"Booksellers have discovered, especially since the depression, that many parents are unwilling and often unable to spend money on books for their children. . . . Obviously [the five- and ten-cent books] will never take the place of the higher-priced books, which have, in the past few years, become notable examples of fine bookmaking. . . . But there is an additional market, as yet practically untouched by the bookstores, for the less expensive titles, and as such they should receive consideration."

Singled out among the Rand McNally books are *The Book of Dogs*, for its photographs of "100 leading breeds," and *Happy Hours*, which is, as the article notes, very much on the order of *Peggy and Peter*. "One of the Harter titles," it tells us, "is *Talking Leaves*. . . . Another striking title is *A Picture Book of Houses Around the World*, by Otta Taggart Johnston, a large sized, paper-bound book with excellent photographs."[6]

A Picture Book of Houses might have been put together by Lucy Sprague Mitchell: "The photographs in this book have been selected . . . to show children that people are dependent upon their environment for the materials of which their homes are built." Reference is made also to nomadic peoples who "build their homes very simply so that they may either abandon them . . . or pack and carry them to new locations"; to homes in warm countries "built to allow the cooling breezes to pass through" and "the house boats of China upon which many people live all their lives because the land is so crowded." "As children read this book," moreover, "they will see that the pictures have been arranged according to climatic conditions of the earth. . . ."

They will see, too, a Negro sharecropper's

141. *A Picture Book of Houses Around the World,* by Otta Taggart Johnston. Cleveland, Harter, 1934. 9 x 12.

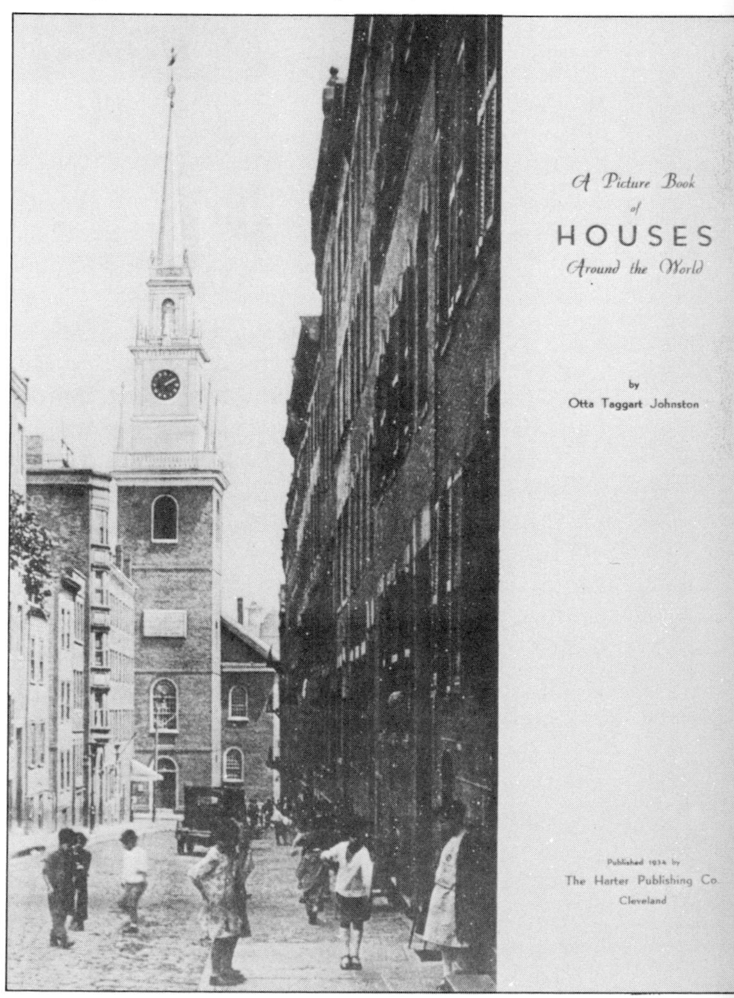

cabin in South Carolina (in verse that could hardly be worse: "Made of logs or stick of wood/ Our house to us is very good"); more reformist, a slum clearance project in Amsterdam (which, "like many a city,/ Upon the poor has taken pity"); and, most startling, a Revolutionary monument and its contemporary environs, a picture that makes its own comment (141). The representative illustrations, however, show tepees and desert tents, stone and clay huts—all manner of adaptations to the environment.

That children were meant to learn from the book—and from its mate, *A Picture Book of Children Around the World*—reflects not only their makers' orientation but also the expectation of sales to schools, directly (Harter, remember, sold school supplies) or through Woolworth's, then synonymous with the five-and-ten. A publicity release on the Woolworth letterhead announcing "to teachers" a new Artists and Writers Guild series is indicative; pointing out that the entire series "was written by teachers," it lists as "outstanding features" a wide interest range, the use of prominent illustrators and the selection of photographs from among "thousands" and "from many available sources."

The sources had expanded to include government agencies and, through Roy Stryker's Farm Security Administration program (1935–42), the work of such outstanding photographers as Dorothea Lange, Walker Evans, Carl Mydans, Russell Lee. In the Artists and Writers Guild books published under other imprints—notably *On Top of the World* (McKay, 1937) and *See How We Work* (Grosset, 1940)—such sources are in evidence. The former, "An Eskimo Picture Book" written by Lucille Ogle under the pseudonym Nadine Leigh, combines photographs, drawings and text much the way Henry Kane does and anticipates by fifteen years Anna Riwkin-Brick's *Elle Kari* et al and the photo-stories of foreign children by the Gidals and others that followed in their wake.

Trade book production, as distinct from mass-market and textbook production, concentrated oń animals and how-things-work and centered on books for which the author provided the pictures—instead of a kaleidoscope, one had a continuous sequence. Characteristic, and enormously successful, was the series initiated by *The Train Book* (Harcourt, 1933) in which William Clayton Pryor (joined later by his wife, Helen Sloman Pryor) sets forth in large photographs and a few words how Bill and Martha, a brother and sister much like E. Boyd Smith's Bob and Betty, learn about "how a railroad is run," "the ocean liner in port and at sea," "a city fire department and how it works," etc., etc. Not that people and their lives were totally ignored: photographs played a part in picturing the American Indian, a late Thirties' preoccupation, an even bigger and more critical part in representing the Negro realistically (p. 375).

Say 'photographic book' to many people, however, and they think first of Ylla and her animals. The United States cannot claim her exclusively: raised in Central Europe, she studied and started her career in Paris, only in 1940 coming here to live, and her work appeared simultaneously on both sides of the Atlantic. Rather, her photographs spoke an international language which, when interpreted by an American author, took on a distinctly American accent; there is in fact no parallel to the publication of a similar or identical group of her pictures in different countries with different texts.

The first of her books seen here, *Big and Little* (Scribner, 1938), does not fall into this category; an album of photographs of animals and their young, it was printed in France for issuance also in England and the United States and represents on the one hand what Bettina Hürlimann has said, too stringently I feel, about Ylla's books in general, an assemblage of attractive photographs akin to "picture books for adults,"[7] and on the other the kind of photo-album of mother and baby animals already available in more modest forms.

Beyond any technical mastery or affinity for animals, what Ylla did was to startle; singly or in sequence, she shows us animals as we see ourselves, and it is this quality that Margaret Wise Brown seized upon for the book that set off the Ylla boom here (and was not published abroad), *They All Saw It.* We will see, and read, much more of the work of Margaret Wise Brown, who by this time had written many picturebooks, but there is no clearer evidence of her creativity than what she did with an eleven-year assortment of Ylla photographs:

They all saw it!
The sea lion saw it first (142).

. . . .

What in the world was it?
The rooster rolled his yellow eye.

When the little cat saw it
he jumped in the air.

The polar bear was asleep
so he didn't see it (143).

But the hippopotamus
saw it all right.

And he bellowed.
The little dog wondered.

And all the baby animals
ran to find their mothers.
The little kitten jumped
in his mother's arms
and he watched from there.

The little calf
couldn't find his mother.
But he saw it.

. . . .

They all saw it!
The bunnies wiggled their noses.
What in the world was it?

THIS IS WHAT IT WAS!
It was a gray elephant
with golden wings.
Such things can happen.
A gray elephant with
golden wings comes
walking across the world.
Such things can happen.
So anything might happen.

The monkey had been expecting it (144).

142

142,143. *They All Saw It,* photos by Ylla, text by Margaret Wise Brown. Harper, 1944. 8¾ x 11½.

143

144. *They All Saw It,* photo by Ylla, text by Margaret Wise Brown. Harper, 1944. 8¾ x 11½.

They All Saw It is a big book that seems enormous, with the text printed—inscribed in capitals—on tomato red pages opposite each picture and the photographs given full play. And a remarkable lot they are—besides those shown, the great glaring profile of a rooster, the cavernous mouth of a hippo, two giraffes, necks and heads only, nuzzling: not photographs of animals but photographs of animals *being.*

The first of the picture-stories, *The Sleepy Little Lion,* capitalizes on his cunningness and the appeal of lion and foxterrier confiding, lion and rabbits snuggling (145), to iterate and reiterate that they "liked him very much"; on some stunning shots of lion on zebra rug and lion on mirror where, with little ado, he is "put"; and on the completely disarming pictures of his sleeping face and his stretchy yawn for a bedtime story that concludes "And YOU go to sleep too!" Published in France the same year as *Le Petit Lion*

145. *The Sleepy Little Lion,* photos by Ylla, text by Margaret Wise Brown. Harper, 1947. 9¼ x 11⅛.

146. *Le Petit Lion,* photos by Ylla, text by Jacques Prévert. Paris, Arts et Métiers Graphiques, 1947. 8¼ x 10⅜.

Then they brought some rabbits
to play with him.
The rabbits liked him very much.

145

Et voilà le petit lion avec des lapins blancs.

Il n'y a pas cinq minutes qu'ils se connaissent qu'ils sont déjà copains comme lapins.

Les lapins blancs n'ont pas beaucoup d'imagination, tout est très simple pour eux et ils prennent tout simplement le petit lion pour un bon gros lapin comme eux.

Evidemment, ils trouvent qu'il a les oreilles "un peu courtes", ce qui est plutôt ridicule pour un lapin, mais ils évitent de parler de cela, parce que, pour rien au monde, ils ne voudraient vexer leur nouvel ami.

146

with the pictures rearranged and a text by Jacques Prévert, it is an entirely different matter, not the search for friends of a lion too little to stay awake but the search for adventure of a lion cub filled with jungle lore; and not a gentle fancy strung on pictures but a full-blown anthropomorphic tale, both more literal and more artificial, where the animals think ahead and speak (146).

From one group of Ylla photographs, the basis of each book, to the next, the amount of variation between editions differs, depending on the nature of the material; when the pictures form a natural sequence, as in *Two Little Bears* (published in at least ten countries), there is considerable similarity; when they are more apparently set up, more detached and, often, most amazing, they give rise to books so unlike they can hardly be called editions—here *Tico-Tico*, with a text by Niccolo Tucci, in England *O Said the Squirrel*, "story by Margaret Wise Brown" (enlisted by the British publisher, who was unhappy with the American version). Comparing them is a lesson in cultural and/or stylistic differences and, once again, in the disparate uses to which the same pictures can be put—even when, as in *The Little Elephant/Le Petit Eléphant*, they appear in the identical order. From that book, a last look at Ylla alone, as she will be long remembered, all texts and treatments aside (147). For a good picture, she didn't need a performance.

Ylla gained attention as a zoo photographer. Lilo Hess, Ylla's closest successor, was photographing animal behavior before her pictures appeared in books (Dorothy Childs Hogner's *Odd Pets*, Crowell, 1951) and she began to do her own (*Rabbits in the Meadow*, Crowell, 1963). With *Foxes in the Woodshed* (Scribner, 1966), she hit her stride, forgoing domesticated animals for creatures of the wild. In their backgrounds is the difference in their work—portraiture in Ylla's case, documentation in Lilo Hess's. Their methods differed correspondingly. For *Two Little Bears*, her most 'natural' book, Ylla bought two cubs from a wild animal farm and raised them, then, having made pets of them, let them loose in the Connecticut woods "to play and be photographed." Hess, intent on picturing the life cycle of her subjects as it was in life, would accustom a wild pair to her presence so that when they mated she could begin her record of their young unobtrusively.

Every aspect of the story is pictured; there is no recourse to simulation like Kane's and, concomitantly, no attempt to work up a 'plot.' Not only is what is seen what occurs (and the reverse), what is shown is what should be known. Here Hess's background in zoology is critical: she can tell us categorically that raccoons do not dunk their food to cleanse it or even to wet it because, for one thing, in 1948 she photographed for *Life* magazine a raccoon wetting food "that is already wet" (as

147. *The Little Elephant*, photos by Ylla, text by Arthur Gregor. Harper, 1956. 9¼ x 11⅛.

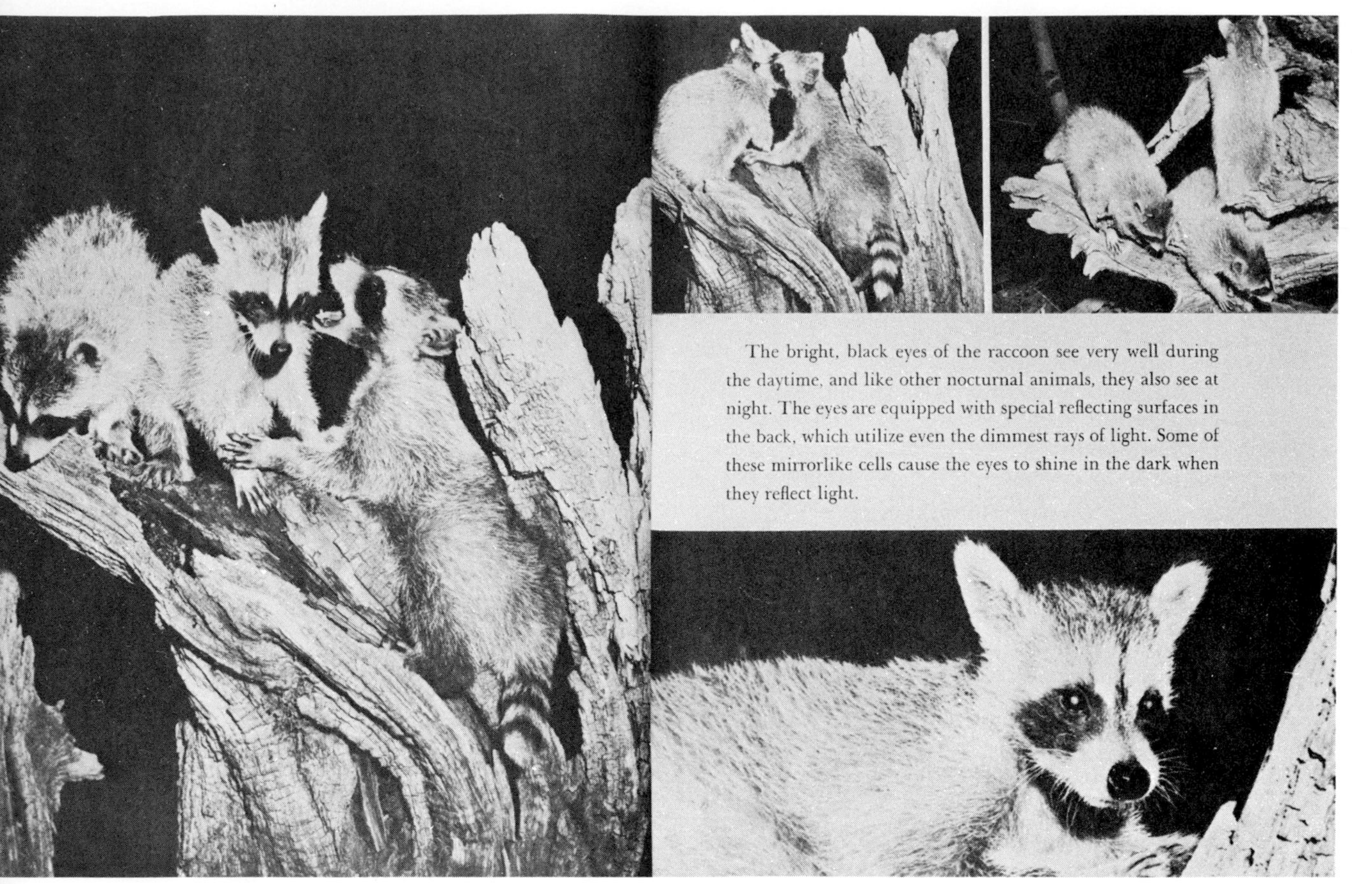

The bright, black eyes of the raccoon see very well during the daytime, and like other nocturnal animals, they also see at night. The eyes are equipped with special reflecting surfaces in the back, which utilize even the dimmest rays of light. Some of these mirrorlike cells cause the eyes to shine in the dark when they reflect light.

148. *The Curious Raccoons,* by Lilo Hess. Scribner, 1968. 7⅜ x 9.

part of a photo-essay, "How Smart Are Animals?"[8]) and she knows now that "they like to roll, prod, and pummel their food or any object between the palms of their hands in the water." Equally critical and evident also in *The Curious Raccoons* is her ability to photograph, without disturbing them, animals that are neither tame nor, on the other hand, unthinking, and this even in extreme circumstances (148). Thereby she shows us not only what should be known, that they can see at night, but what is better understood if seen, the shine of their special mirrorlike eye-cells. Thoroughly familiar with her subjects, she makes them familiar to us.

Otherwise photography was moribund in children's books—used as an adjunct, but not really utilized. *Life,* appearing in 1936, put a new pictorial method forward; documentary photographers and documentary films proliferated; the Erskine Caldwell-Margaret Bourke-White *You Have Seen Their Faces* (1937), the James Agee-Walker Evans *Let Us Now Praise Famous Men* (1941) and others pursued the documentary approach in books: all with little or no reflection in the juvenile field. Photography as an art-form engendered exhibitions and monographs, photography of all sorts yielded *The Family of Man* (1955), exhibit and book: the manifold possibilities were not explored.

William R. Scott, a lively firm with a graphic bent (p. 214), was an exception, now and again publishing, in the Fifties and early Sixties, something distinctive and distinctly photographic. *What's Inside?* was the first, "The Story of an Egg That Hatched" told in full-page photos with facing text as the egg begins to crack ("What can be breaking the egg and making it crack?"), feathers, feet and beak appear, the wet, weary bird rests and drys his feathers, and standing on his webbed feet, shows himself to be a baby gosling (149). While the text, querying, plays a little game, the camera, clicking, puts before us an egg on a page sized to fit, and in his first hours a little goose "who has taken . . . a whole day and a whole night to break through the shell and be born." A whole day and a whole night and a vast mystery in eighteen picture-pages.

"But," the last of them informs us, "a goose isn't born in a day. Lots of things happened before. . . ." What happened of course is that a mother goose built a nest, laid her eggs, sat on them, turned them, covered them when she left to get food and take a quick swim, and wet them afterward—all to make it easier for her babies to break through (150). The second of the pictures, the slightly cracked egg, begins the reprise in which the same photographs appear reduced in size with an explanation of what is occurring, to be followed by what comes after—the family out for a walk, the goslings doing as their mother does, picking at the grass, the start of the process of growing into "big, white, fluffy geese just like their parents" (151). Incidentally, "This story never ends. It goes on and on." The time of E. Boyd Smith's roasted bird and skewed irony is past, and author and photographer keep level with children.

The photographs, indeed, seem taken for children in a way that Steichen's sleek pictures, for instance, don't—for young children, that is, which those of a Hine or a Lilo Hess weren't. Partly it has to do with perspective, with shooting low, from a child's angle; partly it derives from scale and compactness, partly from modulation, so that one sees not the forms but the image; and partly it is a matter of sensibility, of a feeling for smallness and weakness (149) and for smallness secure under parental protection (151). On photographer Rena Jakobsen's part, as on Ylla's, a way of seeing underlying a way of doing.

At Scott, where the proprietors handled their own design and production and could put their know-how to work to please themselves, few books were ever *done* in the sense that they couldn't be redone—altered at a later printing, revised for a new edition, or remade completely. Mary McBurney Green's

149. *What's Inside?* text by May Garelick, photos by Rena Jakobsen. Scott, 1955. 8¼ x 7.

Can it be a robin?

No.
Robins' eggs are much smaller.
And besides, they are blue.
It's not a robin.

Then what kind of a bird is it?

For a whole month she did these same things every day.
Every day she sat on the eggs.
Once each day, she turned them.
After each swim, she wet them.
All this she did to help her babies—to make it easier for them to break through the shell and get born.
Then, one day, from inside one of the shells, she hears a little tapping noise—*tap, tap, tap.*
The mother goose knows that at last one of her babies is stirring inside the egg.

150

151

150, 151. *What's Inside?* text by May Garelick, photos by Rena Jackobson. Scott, 1955. 8¼ x 7.

152, 153. *Is It Hard? Is It Easy?* text by Mary McBurney Green, photos by Len Gittleman. Scott, 1960. 8⅛ x 9⅞.

Is It Hard? Is It Easy? came out in 1958 as the account of two children who have, to be stuffy, complementary capacities: what one finds easy, the other finds hard, the moral being "Some things are easy and some are hard for Ann and Tim and you and me and everyone else I know." Bright, broadly simplified drawings by Lucienne Bloch put Tim and Ann through the indicated paces. In 1960 it reappeared with the text completely rewritten and photographs—high-contrast photographs, close to silhouettes—substituted for the drawings. Now it is "four friends, Bill, Ann, Tim, and Sue" who show what they can do and can't, which brings it closer to John and Mary and me and you, and further from the matching of skills. The photographs give us four children—real persons, individuals—but, casting them in shadow, leave us with four persons whose identity doesn't assert itself. (To *draw* four small children of the same size so that they are distinguishable is difficult without recourse to exaggeration, and to escape from their identity thereafter is virtually impossible.)

The conjunction of authenticity and abstraction is the crux, and the design promotes it—design meaning, to start with, what is done with the photographs. As rewritten, the text concentrates on *active* activities, and we have Sue hopping in stop-motion sequence much like Muybridge's famous galloping horse, with the fence (in the brown of the lettering) drawn in behind her as a measure or gauge, a connective band, an offsetting design (152). Another page, another pursuit; another situation, another solution. Sue, tying her shoe, sits on the floor and concentrates, her whole figure bespeaking her purpose, while standing in for Ann, who can't, are her legs and her untied shoes (153). The text, abbreviated too, is an operative element in the design, consonant with both the purport and the form of the pictures.

Catch a Cricket, text by Carla Stevens, photos by Martin Iger, followed the next year, combining the active design of *Is It Hard?* with the intimate nature study of *What's Inside?*, and each of the collaborators

But Ann's friend, Sue, can't skip.
She hops instead. Skipping is hard for Sue.

152

But Sue can tie
her own shoes.
"Easy for me," says Sue.
When Ann tries to tie
her own shoelace,
it comes undone
and drags on the floor.
"It's hard for me," says Ann.

153

154

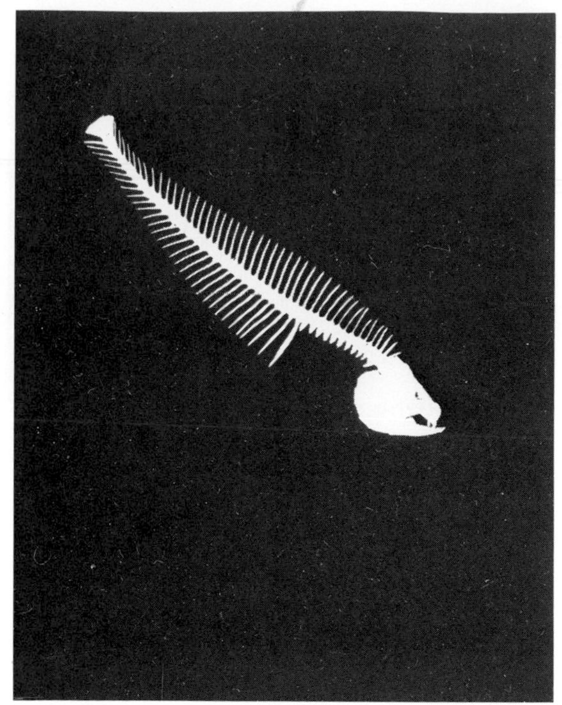

155

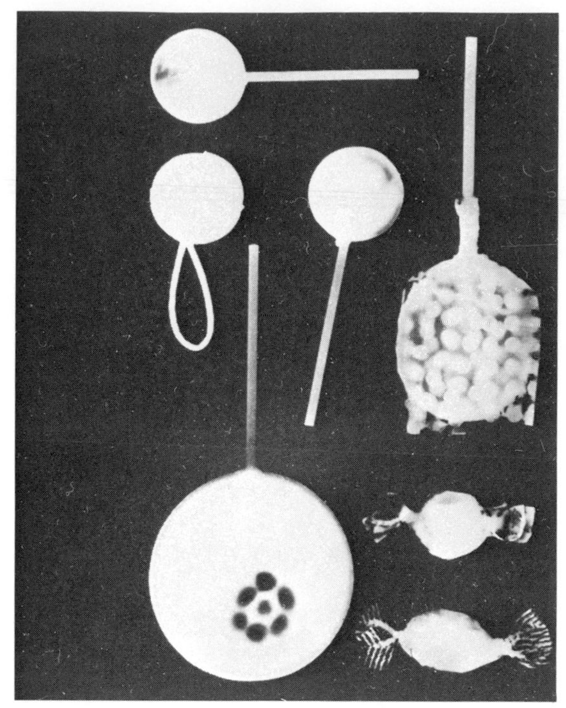

154, 155. *Shapes and Things,* by Tana Hoban. Macmillan, 1970. 7⅞ x 9⅞.

156-159. *Look Again!* by Tana Hoban. Macmillan, 1971. 8 x 9.

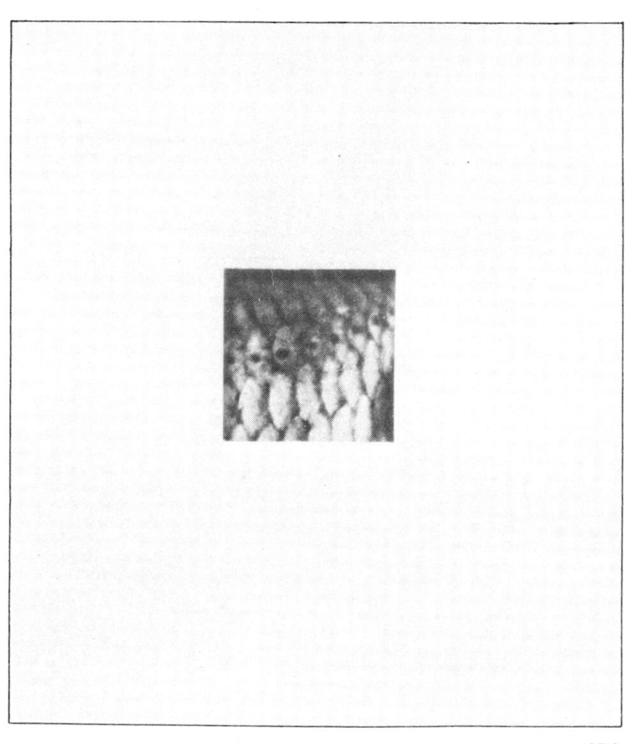

156

branched out successfully, albeit in old directions—Carla Stevens (with her husband Leonard) in *The Birth of Sunset's Kittens* (1969) and Martin Iger (with his wife Eve Marie) in *Building a Skyscraper* (1967); while in *Window into an Egg* (Geraldine Lux Flanagan, 1969) we see just what goes on inside before the bird cracks the shell, a double return to beginnings.

Shapes and Things, photograms of familiar objects presented plain, without captions, was new, young, uniquely photographic—forty years later, a counterpart to Steichen's *First Picture Book*. The objects are at once recognizable and miraculous, tangible and illusory (154), things and essences and pure form (155). Tana Hoban followed it with *Look Again!*, and the photographic book took on fresh life.

Look Again! is a four-part perspective, magnifying pattern, texture, formal design, inviting a guess, assuring an answer (156); taking in the whole subject, its identity and its nature (157); turning over to its rear, its surroundings or its child-life (158); looking back on another fragment of its existence, now through the other end of the telescope (159). One after another aspect of photography (and optics) is engaged, and one after another response to reality. The endpapers are a brilliant yellow, the title page has white block letters on black, the jacket puts the title letters in orange, an alert, and gives us, in a circle, the semblance of a peephole to the interior. A total concept and total, vital design.

The most interesting and apt use of color photography—by and large mired at the technicolor travelogue level—has also been as a foil to black and white, in the Millicent Selsam-Jerome Wexler plant series where, after pages of sober germination and growth, a flower suddenly bursts forth in full color, and, following fertilization, "The ovary grows bigger and bigger" until "The green tomatoes turn red" before your eyes, yielding a seed-catalog specimen all the more ablaze for the grayness before.

But next year, any next year, is a new season.

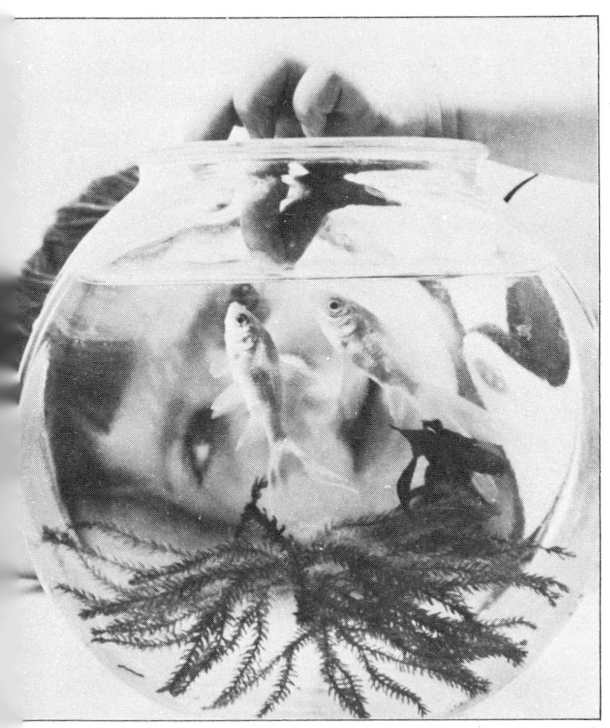

158

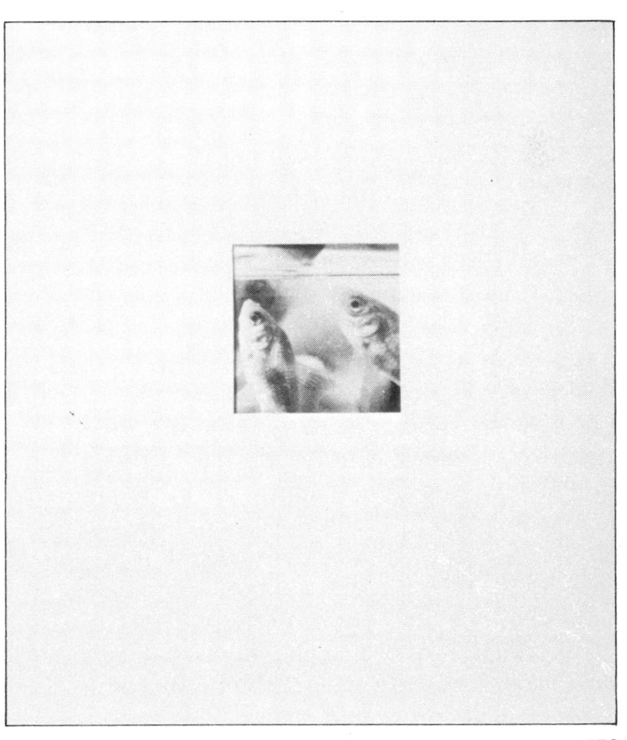

159

IMPORTED FROM FRANCE

THE DOMINO PRESS, THE ARTISTS AND WRITERS GUILD, THE FIRST OF ROJANKOVSKY

From England came the aesthetic book, domestic intimacy, good humor; from Russia, vivid instruction. From France, after Boutet de Monvel, came Edy Legrand and color, freedom, verve.

E. M. Forster wrote a paean to *Macao et Cosmage* (1919) and titled it "Happiness!"[1] Douglas Bliss, the English critic, found the book "incomparably larger, gayer and more high-spirited than anything English of its kind," and from the vantage point of 1929, 'in every way an innovation.'[2] John Lewis speaks of it in the same vein as making "a lively contrast to insipid watercolors, printed in three- or four-colour half-tone,"[3] and remarks, as of 1967, that *Macao* and its successor *Voyages et Glorieuses Découvertes* "are far more inventive in their sweeping use of colour than almost anything that has appeared since."[4]

In the United States it was the second, *Voyages et Glorieuses Découvertes des Grands Navigateurs et Explorateurs Français*, that was the landmark—"although intended for children . . . quickly snapped up by artists and book-lovers."[5] Published by Tolmer, the enterprising printer-typophile-publicist, it was done by the stencil process known as 'pochoir' on vast 11″ × 15″ pages in any number of colors. Such is the illustrative range—from violent dislocation to monumental calm, from near-monochrome to multicolored cacophony, from suave court scenes to spreading panoramas of the New World—that no single page or even a spread represents more than a sample (160). But almost any one demonstrates, in Esther Averill's words, Legrand's "ability to lift a scene of this world, by strength of his imagination, into a higher, more vibrant stratum."[6]

The one book that approaches it in brilliance and breadth—and for children, is simpler and more cheerful—is Rojankovsky's *Daniel Boone* as Miss Averill originally published it, in French and English, in Paris in 1931. This was the first venture, the founding venture, of the Domino Press, both of them products of the time and place. Esther Averill and her partner Lila Stanley were Americans-in-Paris, just then buying French designs for an American stationery manufacturer; Feodor Rojankovsky, a valued source, was a Russian émigré—erstwhile officer of the Czar, set designer and illustrator in Poland, peripatetic commercial artist. He pressed upon them a Polish ABC for American publication, they preferred that an example of his new work be well produced in France; and the Domino Press came into being when no American firm would back the projected *Daniel Boone*, no French firm distribute the finished book. Faber & Faber took on a small quantity in England, where it became *The Observer*'s "choice among all the children's books of the season";[7] the French-language edition they marketed themselves—to kudos for Rojankovsky from *Gebrauchsgraphik*; and ultimately it was distributed in the United States by the Bookshop for Boys and Girls, featured in the *Horn Book*, and touted by Anne Carroll Moore as "a unique first book in American history."[8]

It was a uniquely daring book of American—or any other—history. As much as Edy Legrand had departed from the realistic picture-histories of Boutet de Monvel or Job, Rojankovsky is still less descriptive, still less literal. Speaking of his "boldness in juxtaposition of colors," *Gebrauchsgraphik* says, "Who but a Russian would ever venture to beset a grass-green meadow with violet trees, heighten the effect by introducing a chrome-yellow tree, and crown the whole by perching a red squirrel in the branches."[9] The allusion is to a specific illustration but all exhibit the same chromatic scheme, set by Rojankovsky's vision regardless of local color or its variations (161).

The choice of Daniel Boone as a subject had been determined in part by his enthusiasm for the American frontier, 'le Pays Sauvage,' in part by his penchant for draw-

160. *Voyages et Glorieuses Découvertes des Grands Navigateurs et Explorateurs Français,* pictures by Edy Legrand. Paris, Tolmer, 1921. 10⅞ x 14¾.

Que devint-il ? Suivant les uns, il vécut retiré à Saint-Malo, suivant les autres, dans un village nommé Limollan. Les dernières années de sa vie furent celles d'un homme qui, ne cherche ni les honneurs ni la gloire, mais la mémoire pleine de souvenirs de ses lointains voyages, termine ses jours dans la sérénité des grands esprits et des sages. On ignore l'année de sa mort.

Des siècles plus tard, en 1848, des marins retrouvèrent, au Canada, enlisée dans la vase la "Petite Hermine", que Cartier avait dû abandonner au retour de son deuxième voyage. Le temps et l'eau avaient fait leur œuvre : de la glorieuse "Hermine", il ne restait que des débris. Ils sont pieusement conservés dans un musée, à Saint-Malo.

Telle est, en résumé, la vie de Cartier. Sa fin fut obscure; son œuvre n'en reste pas moins éclatante. Tout le premier, avec des moyens précaires, il s'établit dans des contrées que les neiges et les glaces défendaient contre la curiosité humaine. Au nom de son pays, il prit possession de territoires où l'activité de ses compatriotes s'épanouit pendant des siècles. C'est grâce à lui que, maintenant encore, dans les maisons et dans les fermes, sous le ciel septentrional du Canada, chante le doux parler de France.

... Et depuis, de nombreux vaisseaux quittent les ports de France, vers les terres découvertes par Cartier.

Voyez cet homme ! Ce n'est pas un damoiseau; ce n'est pas un de ces courtisans à perruque frisée, que l'on voit papillonner autour d'un Roi. Des muscles puissants. Sous le front, une volonté de fer. L'œil doux cependant. Avec un tel homme, on le sent, on vivra de grandes aventures. Si le danger arrive, on n'aura pas peur.

Tel est *Robert Cavelier, sieur de la Salle,* dont nous allons vous entretenir à présent.

Il était né à Rouen en 1640, vers le début du règne de Louis XIV. Dès sa jeunesse, il rêve de découvertes et de voyages; au collège de Rouen, son pupitre est bourré de livres, où navigateurs et explorateurs racontent leur histoire. Il voudrait faire comme eux. A 23 ans, ayant perdu son père, maître d'une rente de 400 livres, il s'embarque pour le Canada, que l'on appelle à cette époque la Nouvelle France.

Le pays où nous entrons avec Cavelier, ne ressemble plus à celui que nous a révélé Cartier. Des colons se sont établis; ils cultivent la terre, font la chasse aux ours, aux castors, aux renards, dont les fourrures constituent une marchandise précieuse pour l'Europe. Malheureusement, les peuplades indiennes voient d'un très mauvais œil les étrangers s'installer chez ing animals and trees. The design had still another basis, Rojankovsky's experience in modern advertising layout and illustration. When he started on the book he was engaged in the making of deluxe catalogs, and "Kentucky—the Paradise of Hunters" that Boone strides toward with his companions is a veritable catalog of big and small game. ("In the beginning," Miss Averill has written, "there were animals and Indians everywhere, and happy enough hunting grounds for all."[10]) The trees stretch upward, the wilderness stretches out, taking over the space that is properly theirs; and each in its own place, a doe regards the resting Boone, a carved tree marks the spot where he "killed a. bar." Begun as a book without words, *Daniel Boone* remains a collection of tableaux vivants—one does not so much enter into its narrative as into its spirit.

"Much of the spirit would have been lost," as Miss Averill puts it, "if Rojankovsky himself had not reproduced the designs on the lithographic stones from which they are printed." Thus he achieved a marked crispness and depth, "the true lithographic values in gradations of the blacks, blues and reds, to relieve the pure, flat tones of the greens and yellows."[11] The first of the designs, she notes, were "in the smart, graphic manner" of the concluding map; "But as the artist drew and redrew the birds and animals, the trees of the forest and the figure of Boone, he was compelled to give them a more rounded life. . . ."[12]

The Domino Press, Paris, persisted with *Powder: The Story of a Colt, a Duchess and the Circus* (text by Esther Averill and Lila Stanley, pictures by Rojankovsky, 1933) which was issued simultaneously in England (by Faber), in the United States (by Smith & Haas, soon to be Random House) and France (under the D. P. imprint), a first for a French-made children's book; its sequel, *Flash*, appeared the following year in the same fashion. But with trouble brewing in Europe and the currency unstable, "the brief period during which people had had a tendency to think in international terms was drawing to a close."[13] After bringing out *The Fable of a Proud Poppy* (hand-colored woodcuts by Emile Lahner, text by 'John Domino,' 1934), the firm—Esther Averill, a small stock of books, an abiding idea—removed to New York.

Already in work, long in work, was *The Voyages of Jacques Cartier*, which Miss Averill derived—"retold"—from the explorer's journals and contemporary documents, and Rojankovsky illustrated eloquently and vibrantly in black and white. The Père Castor natural histories and the Golden Books, Little, Big and Tall, that followed from them were to make his name synonymous with fuzzy animals, blooming children and fountains of color; in *Cartier*, conceived for an older audience even than *Daniel Boone*, he is a draftsman and a classicist.

Cartier is not a picturebook, a pictorial history, but larger of page and designed as a unit, it brings to a longer text a battery of illustrations as diverse as those in *Grands Navigateurs*: the full-length, full-page figure of Cartier at the helm, "a man admirably suited to head this voyage of exploration"; clear-cut delineations of place, be it an Indian village or a quay-side scene; a single auk, a pair of peering foxes—or Indians done up as demons, masked specters gliding by in a canoe. There is drama and action in the dispatch of a spy, the planting of the French cross, and for following the course of the journey and the course of events, for grasping just what manner of land this new world was, the picture maps, miniatures on a grand scale (162). Here Rojankovsky re-creates the wilderness and inserts the Indian village, complete to tilled fields, without distorting geographic proportions; and without color makes the forms of trees and animals and topographic features distinct. The closer one looks, the more one enters into this living world of antlered buck, black on speckled clearing, doe in white on shadowed bank, pointed firs and foliage and naked branches, black and white penetrating; with an armed Indian running along the lower border, turning the real back to make-believe. It is at once fine design

Depuis douze ans, Boone rêvait de voir le Kentucky. Un jour, il remplit sa poire à poudre, appela son chien et s'aventura seul dans le Pays Sauvage. Mais les difficultés auxquelles il se heurta l'obligèrent à revenir.

Enfin, il réalisa son rêve. Avec son vieil ami Finley et quatre autres compagnons, il avança péniblement vers l'ouest, en suivant les traces des bisons jusqu'aux régions inexplorées.

161. *Daniel Boone,* text by Esther Averill and Lila Stanley, pictures by Feodor Rojankovsky. Paris, Domino Press, 1931. 11¼ x 14⅜.

and a feat of representation—just what kind of feat comparison with the color projections of Covarrubias or Cornelius DeWitt makes plain (p. 413).

Design is preeminent in the section headings where Rojankovsky's habit of constructing scenes in flat planes and giving rounded form to figures becomes a method of demarcation and a dramatic device (163). The astute use of positive and negative silhouetting, of patterning and free drawing, distinguishes the top vignette, while below, the crouching Indian, his blowgun at the ready, is sliced off to accentuate his profile and also cast into relief, a warning to temper the welcome. *Cartier*, spare and factual in the telling, "leaned heavily upon Rojankovsky's illustrations for dramatic interest," Miss Averill observes[14]—to the extent that what might have been a decorative motif serves as an epigraph.

Closest to pure drawing, to self-existent, self-willed illustration, is the serene and spacious waterfront view, a composition Rojankovsky referred to as his 'Prix de Rome' (164). The sweep of the near boat from bow to stern and, in a different tempo, the taut curves of ship's skeleton; the tracery of mast and yards and rigging; the white solidity of wall and, abutting, the dappled see-through tree, evince absolute command of the pen for line reproduction and yield an abstract beauty.

In black and white Rojankovsky did, thereafter, Jean Mariotti's South Pacific legend, *Tales of Poindi/Contes de Poindi*, the last Domino Press publication (New York, 1939), and *Cortez the Conqueror* (text by Covelle Newcomb, Random House, 1947), an oversize book with some of the attributes of *Cartier* but not its integrated design. What he might have done had circumstances been different *Cartier* continues to attest.

The original edition, the *Voyages*, was distributed by Viking from 1941 on; reduced in size, slightly revised and—with some new illustrations—redesigned, it appeared on the Harper list in 1956 as *Cartier Sails the Saint Lawrence*, a volume more closely attuned to the needs and perhaps the interests of young people but one which hasn't the stylistic consistency or, in the new illustrations, the fineness of execution of its predecessor. (Compare the fussy details of the headpiece on p. 36 and the coarseness of the one on p. 40 with the subtle economy of their counterparts on pp. 55 and 72, or the rendering of waves and foam on p. 13, old, and p. 14, new.) Also redone, drastically, was *Daniel Boone* (Harper, 1945), which for practical reasons was transformed from a picture album with captions into a story with pictures; to fit the new longer text, the pictures were separated and spaced out. As printed, they are crude compared to the originals, but the story

162-164. *The Voyages of Jacques Cartier*, by Esther Averill, illus. by Feodor Rojankovsky. New York, Domino Press, 1937. 8½ x 11.

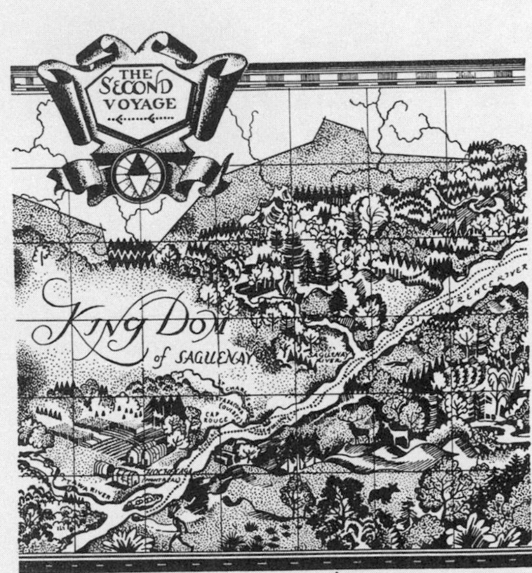

fins, and are made about the body and head like a greyhound, as white as snow and without a spot. There are many of them living in the River between the salt and fresh water. The natives call them *adothuys* and say that they are very good to eat."

The Captain left the Saguenay behind him and pursued his way up the tapering Saint Lawrence. The fresh waters of the River were filled with quantities of fish such as salmon, lampreys and eels. Game, too, abounded in the giant forests which hemmed the River in on both its shores. Beyond the forest to the north

40

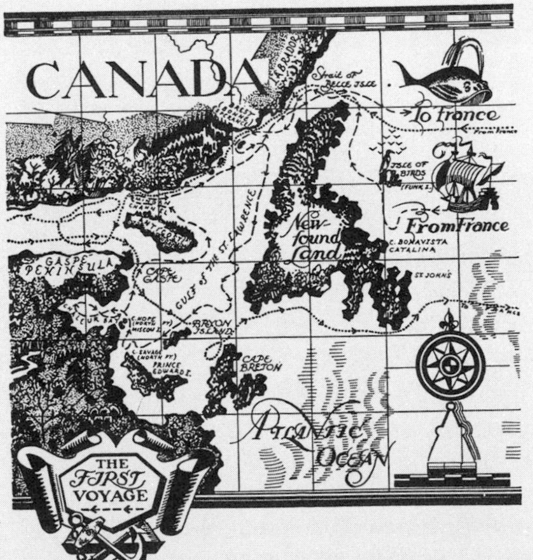

rose the purple peaks of the Laurentian Mountains.

He passed the little river isle now called Hare Island, and the verdant isle which he named Isle aux Coudres, meaning Isle of Hazel Trees. Finally he came to another, larger island where the grapes were so plentiful that his sailors called it the Isle of Bacchus, in honor of the Greek God of Wine. The Captain named it officially the Isle of Orleans, after the young Duke of Orleans, son of King Francis.

41

162

163

164

THE ROYAL COMMISSION FOR THE SECOND VOYAGE

Jacques Cartier had not found gold on any of the shores or islands of the Gulf of the Saint Lawrence and the Indians whom he had met there seemed to be poor, wandering tribes possessing nothing more valuable than birch bark canoes. The King was disappointed in this. But the "unknown sea" which Cartier had discovered beyond Anticosti Island gave such promise of leading westward to the Orient that King Francis agreed to send the Captain on a second voyage to North America. On the 31st of October, 1534, the Captain's "friend at Court,"

as expanded is stronger, a gain offsetting a loss.

Esther Averill wrote again about Indians (*King Philip*, 1950) and, in an entirely different vein, created in Jenny Linsky and the other members of the Cat Club a world entire with its creatures of privilege, its outcasts, its rebels—and so extended a history that, she comments, "Sometimes I feel that fate has made me a kind of Balzac of the Cat Club."[15] One quotes Miss Averill readily: she has written extensively about the Domino Press, extensively and acutely about picturebooks, and with particular understanding about French picturebooks. Her several articles on Steinlen, Job, Hellé and their contemporaries constitute, in fact, the only substantial body of writing in English on the subject.

Rojankovsky we must take up again where, after *Daniel Boone*, he began his second career—with 'Père Castor' or 'Father Beaver,' the French educator Paul Faucher who, in Isabelle Jan's words, set out to create "anti-bookish books." As she relates, "his first albums were 'book-games,' of unusual appearance and easy to handle, whose use of graphic devices and color, freedom of layout, and flexibility of typography stimulated the child to creative manipulation."[16] Recognizable in the description (besides the precepts of progressivism) is the mass-produced Russian book, a direct inspiration, and Russian émigrés—Nathalie Parain, Hélène Guertik, Rojankovsky—headed the roster of artists during the first decade.

From Russia Rojankovsky brought not only a flair for color but also a particular way of drawing animals that was at once warmly sympathetic and unsentimental (qq.v. 118). It was a manner suited to the Père Castor program of instruction by personal involvement and with Rojankovsky on hand, skilled at natural history, the program developed in that direction. Two large albums of animal portraits appeared, *Les Petits et Les Grands* and *En Famille* (1933 and 1934, text by Rose Celli), and with *Panache l'Écureuil* there began the small oblong life stories—together

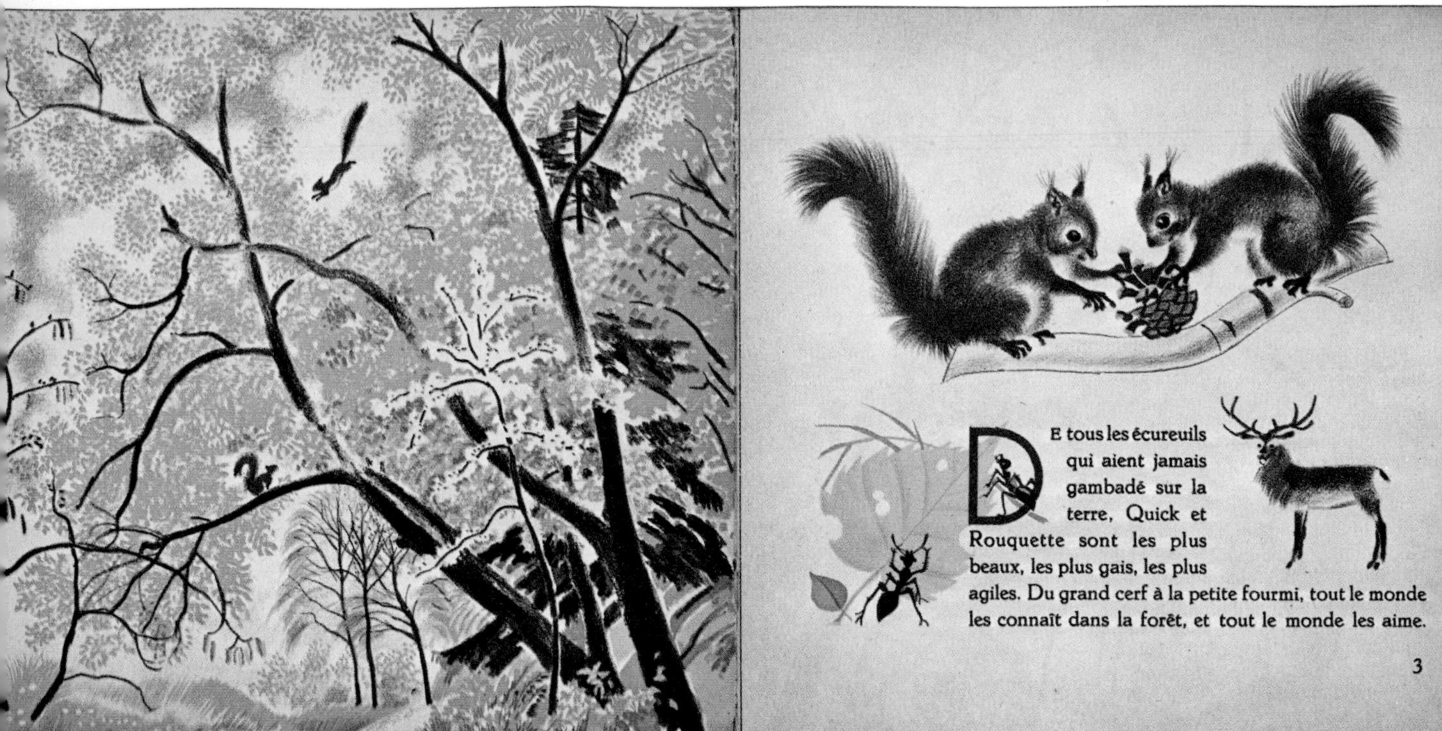

E tous les écureuils
qui aient jamais
gambadé sur la
terre, Quick et
Rouquette sont les plus
beaux, les plus gais, les plus
agiles. Du grand cerf à la petite fourmi, tout le monde
les connaît dans la forêt, et tout le monde les aime.
3

165

prompting Alexander Benois, the great connoisseur and Diaghilev collaborator, to observe that "Rojankovsky, from the educational point of view, deserved the palm for persuading and encouraging children to observe nature in all phases of its creation."[17]

In *Panache* we see the large and small world of the red squirrel, lightness and air and minute observation mingling, and in the detail of ants, leaves and initial letter, something of the nicety of design that runs through the series (165). *Quipic le Hérisson*, coming three years later and more various, more developed, has in its hedgehog hero a quizzical charmer and, again and again, a layout that's a knockout (167). In the former the feathery crayon effect, in the latter the softly graded and flecked fur, the waxy Cézanne apples, the hearty greens, attest to the books' being done, like *Daniel Boone*, by direct lithography. (More recently they have been printed by photo-offset, with distinctly inferior results.) The series went to eight books, eight fresh views of wild life.

There are children gazing solemnly from the pages of *Quipic*, dreamily contemplating the birds in *Coucou*, but in *Calendrier des Enfants* they come into their own, ski and skate (January), toss a crêpe (February, 166), fly their kites (June), play at the beach (August)—wondering children for the most part still, in a book designed, handsomely, to set off their gestures and moods. Among the last things Rojankovsky did before leaving France was *Cigalou*, and at Cigalou's coming to the mountain the dogs set up a chorus of rejoicing, the very rocks and glaciers sigh: they love him because he loves them all. When we incline, by habit, to regard Rojankovsky's later work as more exuberant than his Père Castor books as well as more involved with children, we would do well to remember *Cigalou* (168).

On a trip abroad in the early Thirties Sam Lowe acquired the American rights to the Père Castor output, which accorded with his own interest in publishing well-designed,

165. *Panache l'Écureuil,* text by Lida, pictures by Feodor Rojankovsky. Paris, Flammarion, 1934. 9 x 8¼.

166. *Calendrier des Enfants,* text by Y. Lacôte, pictures by Feodor Rojankovsky. Paris, Flammarion, 1936. 7⅜ x 6½.

166

167. *Quipic le Hérisson,* text by Lida, pictures by Feodor Rojankovsky. Paris, Flammarion, 1937. 8¾ x 8.

168. *Cigalou,* text by Marie Colmont, pictures by Feodor Rojankovsky. Paris, Flammarion, 1939. 7⅜ x 6½.

Il y a bien un petit escalier pour descendre, mais ue voulez-vous qu'un hérisson fasse d'un escalier ? Quipic prend un chemin plus court. Roulé en boule, l se laisse tomber, et, une fois sur l'herbe, il se sauve toutes pattes dans le dos des bohémiens.

Quand Tara revient avec la terre laise, Quipic est déjà dans le bois, aché sous un as de feuilles, t les bohémiens, urieux, s'injurient entre eux.

LORSQUE, la nuit venue, Quipic regagna le jardin, il poussa un soupir de soulagement. Il se mit à chercher sa maman, ses frères et ses sœurs. Il avait peur d'être grondé.

Pas du tout. Mère Echarde était bien trop contente : elle venait d'attraper une souris ! Et les enfants couraient de tous côtés après les pommes et les poires tombées.

167 168

soundly conceived, roundly beneficial books at popular prices. Lowe, trained at the Henry Street Settlement, was working at a social agency in Racine when the local Western Printing Company fell heir to the assets of Hamming-Whitman, a Chicago publisher, and finding itself in the children's book business, tapped him for its new subsidiary, Whitman Publishing. (The Albert Whitman Company of Chicago was a somewhat later outgrowth of these events.) When the success of Whitman gave rise, in turn, to the Artists and Writers Guild, he became its editorial head.

The name has the ring of honest craftsmen toiling in happy seclusion, of a kind of MacDowell Colony populated by the seven dwarfs, but in fact it came from a line of playing cards acquired by Western and it designated, by affiliation, a new line of books —per *PW*, "a new line of inexpensive picture books for very young children, designed to sell through ten-cent stores."[18] Of the twenty-eight books on that first 1935–36 list, seven were Père Castor titles, and most of the remainder were of French or British origin also, "reprinted by arrangement with the [original] publishers from a high-priced edition." Equally indicative in its way, the one American work of consequence was the huge *Knave of Hearts* with four-color process illustrations by Maxfield Parrish throughout, "an exact reprint"—at twenty cents—"of a $10.00 book" published by Scribner in 1925. It might almost have been chosen to demonstrate the capability of the new Western plant in Poughkeepsie where, following the playing cards, the A & W books were printed.

The Knave of Hearts falls into the realm of social history, of 'putting a Maxfield Parrish into every home,' to paraphrase the catalog; more pertinent to the progress of picturebooks is *The Picture Play Book* from the Père Castor group. "My congratulations to you!" Dorothy Baruch, one of the pioneers of preschool progressivism, is quoted in the same catalog as writing. "I think you are doing a marvelous piece of work in bringing translations of popular and worthwhile books from other countries to us here and in putting [them] out at such moderate cost. . . . My joy was complete when I discovered you had translated Parain's 'Jeux' which has been one of my favorites with its modern and vivid pictures." Nathalie Parain's *Jeux en Images*, the original of *The Picture Play Book* (169), is not quite one of the 'book-games' but it is, as the title suggests, an inducement to active, imaginative play; it is also a direct successor to her *Mon Chat* of 1930, a book second only to *Daniel Boone* in the attention its looks attracted. Between *Mon Chat* (45 francs) and *Jeux en Images* (8 francs), between *Jeux en Images* (Fr.) and *The Picture Play Book* (U.S.) there is little difference in design or

169. *The Picture Play Book,* text by Rose Celli, pictures by Nathalie Parain. Poughkeepsie (N.Y.), Artists & Writers Guild, 1935. 9⅜ x 12.

TENNIS
Two little sisters,
Two little racquets,
A ball!
It's you
who will send it.
It's I
who will get it
and send it back to you.
And the ball
flies
from racquet
to racquet
from sister
to sister,
without stopping ever.

production; strong clear color, clean outlines and a counterpoint of interesting textures distinguish all three.

The two large Rojankovsky animal albums appeared in that same group, and other books illustrated by Nathalie Parain and Hélène Guertik; but A & W controlled the rights to the Rojankovsky natural histories also, and these, enlarged in size and hardbound, were issued through Harper as conventional trade books at a standard trade price. They did not do well then or when four of them were brought out again by Golden Books in the Sixties; to American ears there is a condescending sound to the squirrels, Quick and Reddie, chasing each other "like children," something stilted and cloying about Reddie's saying to Quick, "No more play, my love," and overmuch exclaiming, expostulating and outright moralizing—all at variance with the frank, spirited pictures.

Also brought out as Harper books were the *Calendrier* which, with a new text by Margaret Wise Brown, became *The Children's Year* (1937), and Hans Christian Andersen's *Ce Que Fait Le Vieux Est Bien Fait/The Old Man Is Always Right* (1940), as well as other Père Castor books not illustrated by Rojankovsky—none of which, whatever their merits, had much impact; nor did three unusual geographies of Russian descent, *Up the Mountain, Down the River, Along the Coast* (all 1940), which A & W adapted from a different French source.

Neither can it be claimed that that first auspicious A & W list took the five-and-tens by storm and brought fine modern design (or Maxfield Parrish) into every household. But many persons—young parents, artists, publishers and future publishers—saw and admired them and bought them; the Père Castor principles of active participation—set forth at the front of each—were propagated; and through the Harper books too, Rojankovsky became known to a more general public. Though the next A & W list for Woolworth's was quite different in nature (it is the strongly photographic list referred to earlier), A & W had, under its own imprint and those of other publishers, served as the conduit not only for French methods and design but, back of them, for the Russian mass-publishing push; and with Rojankovsky and a new improved set of presses it would be in a position to respond in kind with Little Golden Books and their satellites.

When all is said there was, however inadvertently, something to the name 'Artists and Writers Guild,' something perhaps better expressed when the organization became, for extraneous reasons, Artists and Writers Press. What it came to represent, in furtherance of Western's printing business—a purpose it shared with Whitman—was a wholesale marshaling of talents for the creation and manufacture of picturebooks. There was precedent at Western in the production by Whitman of Disney books—to which the firm held exclusive rights from 1932 on—in different versions for different publishers. *Snow White*, for instance, whether marketed as a big two-dollar folio by Harper, in a one-dollar version by McKay, as a fifty-cent book by Grosset & Dunlap, or at ten cents by Whitman itself, was basically a Whitman product. Similar arrangements had been made earlier with the proprietors of comic-strip characters, and in a sense the Père Castor books, advertised as such, constituted another licensed property; had the Rojankovsky natural histories done well at a dollar, a cheaper version was in the offing.

What distinguished A & W, however, was the development of original material for a like array of publishers. Between 1935 and 1947 more than three hundred books were done for or in concert with major trade houses—a figure that does not include licensed material (other than the Père Castors) and specifically excludes all school-related pamphlets and books, a large part of the production (and after 1947, predominant). Though they came to be recognizable by the lushness of their color printing—done in full color, Western's specialty—they stand forth in a larger sense as a signal instance of practical vision.

ROGER DUVOISIN

170

At four, Roger Duvoisin's elder son drew himself into a story of a little boy whose drawings come to life. When he had trouble resolving it, Duvoisin père took it over and, drawing in the manner of a child, made what was to be his first book, *A Little Boy Was Drawing* (170). Says the Postman to Tom when he first gets up from his paper: "Oh yes, I look a little queer, but it's all your fault. Why did you make my mouth so large, one eye so much higher than the other, one leg so short? Well, you will get used to me. And anyway, I like the gray of my uniform very much." A just reproof, a sign of approval, and the ultimate compliment: he takes Tom seriously.

Duvoisin's background in art was extensive and varied. He had designed stage scenery and done posters and illustrations in Geneva, his birthplace; moved on to France to manage an old pottery; designed textiles in Lyons and Paris. It was as a fabric designer under contract to Mallinson's, a leading silk manufacturer, that he came to New York in 1927, hoping, he avows, to go on to Hollywood to

170. *A Little Boy Was Drawing,* by Roger Duvoisin. Scribner, 1932. Detail.
171, 172. *Donkey-Donkey,* by Roger Duvoisin. Whitman, 1933. 6½ x 8½.

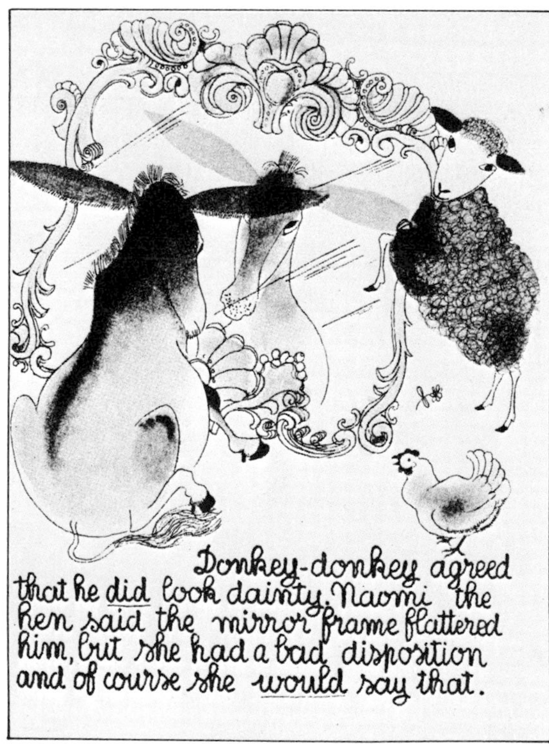

Donkey-donkey agreed that he did look dainty. Naomi the hen said the mirror frame flattered him, but she had a bad disposition and of course she would say that.

171

"See how funny I would look with my ears up!"

172

design scenery. In writing, on the other hand, he was a novice working in a foreign language. Nonetheless the 1932 Scribner catalog introduces him as a talented newcomer "to the ranks of writers for children," a statement not so misguided as it may seem.

The following year artists wandering in Woolworth's lighted on a little book selling for ten cents—Duvoisin's *Donkey-Donkey* in the original Whitman edition published by Sam Lowe, the first of its several embodiments. With sad-eyed good humor, *Donkey-Donkey* exemplifies the futility of trying to be what one is not. Discontented with the look of his ears, Donkey-donkey tries to hold them down like Hector the dog's; straight out like Fuzzy-fuzzy the lamb's, Phoebe the goat's, Fanny the cow's ("So many people *cannot* be wrong, Donkey-donkey"); and in front like Rosa the pig's. Expectably, ridicule and worse await him, but always with an extra fillip like the ornate Louis XV mirror that frames his foolishness (171).

If Donkey-donkey is foolish he is, to start with, "a nice little donkey"—an individual with feelings, as fallible as the next person. So too the others. Fatuously, as if posing for the photographer, Phoebe and Fanny and the farmer's brother (whose ears also stick out) show off their superiority; and Donkey-donkey, his ears now extended too, goes away again, "again happy although somewhat doubtful, as you can see by his expression." An endearing aside, that last, but unnecessary: expressing feelings is Duvoisin's forte, and *Donkey-Donkey* is the book that said so.

Also evident already is that Duvoisin writes as slyly as he draws—"I suspect in fact that she just went to sleep," he remarks with Beatrix Potter punctiliousness when Rosa the pig, supposedly ruminating, fails to twitch an ear or flick an eyelid for two pages; and that, regardless, he composes not in words *or* in pictures but in images. During Rosa's doze, an inchworm traverses the top of the fence and Donkey-donkey, at first alert and expectant, rests his nose on it in baleful resignation, the one marking actual, the other psychological time. Best of all, most graphic, is Hector's demonstration of how *he*'d look with his ears up (172); faced with such a ridiculous sight, what can Donkey-donkey do but lay his down straightaway?

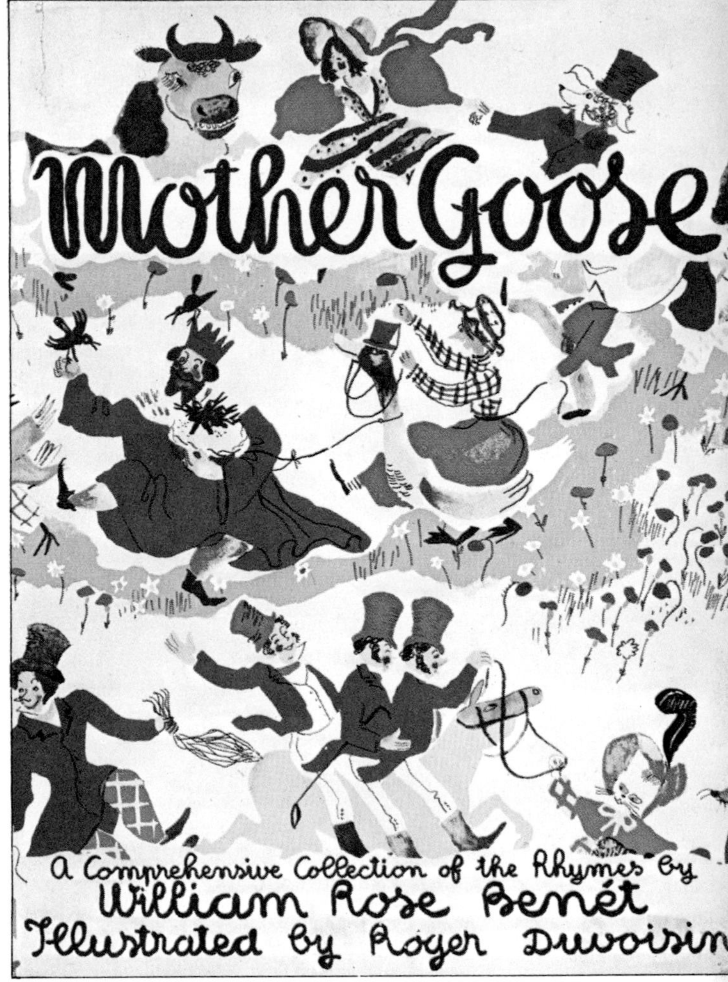

173. *Mother Goose,* ed. by William Rose Benét, illus. by Roger Duvoisin. Heritage, 1936. 9⅝ x 13.

Craftiness in line and tone and then splash! an explosion of color: the Heritage *Mother Goose* (173). Printers and production people cheered—"the book might have stepped out of an Italian or Soviet book shop";[1] buyers for big chains spoke darkly of 'sophistication'; reviewers divided, some regarding the break from tradition as a sacrilege; librarians were cautious—were Duvoisin's "hectic tempo" and brilliant color "suitable fare for the nurs-

174. Cover, *The New Yorker,* February 10, 1945.

175. Lord & Taylor ad, New York *Herald Tribune,* December 23, 1945.

ery"?[2] Meanwhile, parents bought—fifteen thousand copies were sold at the then considerable price of $3.75, ten thousand more as quickly at $2.50.[3]

Actually, only forty of the 160 pages are in color, and a more valid criticism would be that some of the designs are crowded and chaotic. At worst, the Old Woman Tossed Up in a Basket bears down on Peter, Peter, Pumpkin-Eater, the Three Wise Men of Gotham risk being crushed by the Barber Who Shaved the Mason, and the type gives ground to all four. But all is not anarchy and the excitement is infectious: not only has every rhyme a picture, but every picture has a point, be it only the cat's wary watchfulness in "I Love Little Pussy."

Duvoisin's signature is everywhere—in the inky upright script, the field-flower palette, the piquant pen notations—and everywhere is gaiety and vivacity. A Gallic Mother Goose.

During these same years and into the Forties, Duvoisin did advertising and editorial illustration, magazine covers, display design and murals, bringing to this so-called commercial work the very qualities that distinguish his books, and no less individuality.

To many persons, in fact, he was the M. Duvoisin who did *New Yorker* covers. In 1935, when he undertook his first, the usual *New Yorker* cover was a cartoon in color, and for a long time colored cartoons were relieved only by decoratively stylized scenes, masses of color and pattern. Duvoisin, instead, painted the feel of a place, the gist of a situation. His produce market is row upon row of tiny tender-green lettuces and drifts of strolling shoppers, each distinct; his Caribbean isle approached by a cruise ship reads from vignette to vignette as the natives go about their business unawares.

Moreover, of the handful of serious covers that the magazine carried during the several years of the Second World War, two are his. In 1939 he had illustrated W. H. Hudson's *Tales of the Pampas,* and Dorothy Waugh's appreciation of one of the drawings suits the image of a soldier in the South Pacific writing home (174). Calling it a "beautiful composition," she notes "the cohesion, the interplay of all movements to one nucleus of effect and attention, the oneness and the completeness of the whole; and also the use of form solely to create a mood."[4] At the same time it can be taken in at a glance, a prerequisite for a magazine cover in its function as a poster.

Totally different but equally distinctive were Duvoisin's Lord & Taylor ads, especially the celebrated spoof of perfume names that appeared, as it happens, also in 1945 (175).

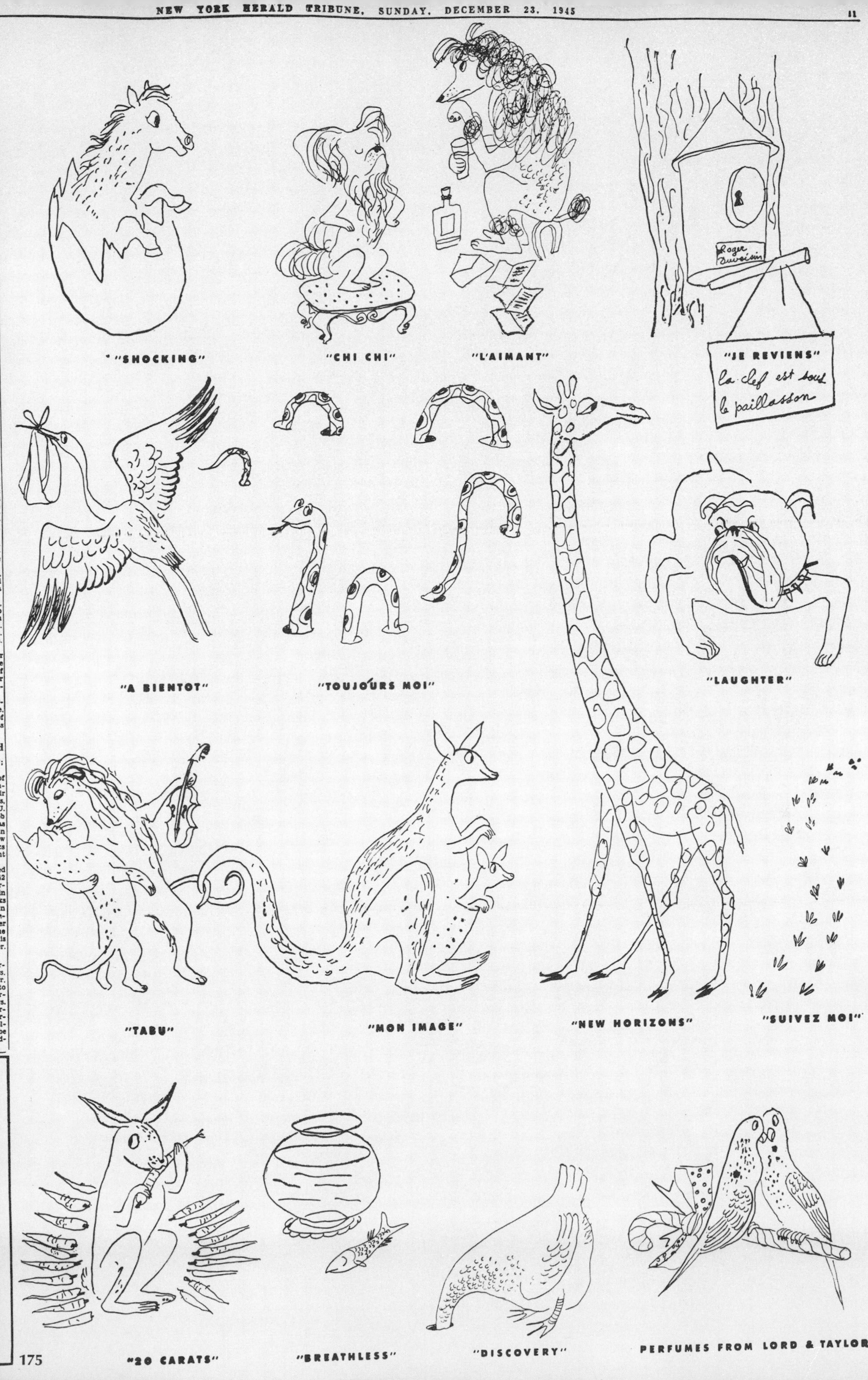
"SHOCKING"
"CHI CHI"
"L'AIMANT"
Roger Duvoisin
"JE REVIENS"
la clef est sous le paillasson
"A BIENTOT"
"TOUJOURS MOI"
"LAUGHTER"
"TABU"
"MON IMAGE"
"NEW HORIZONS"
"SUIVEZ MOI"
"20 CARATS"
"BREATHLESS"
"DISCOVERY"
PERFUMES FROM LORD & TAYLOR

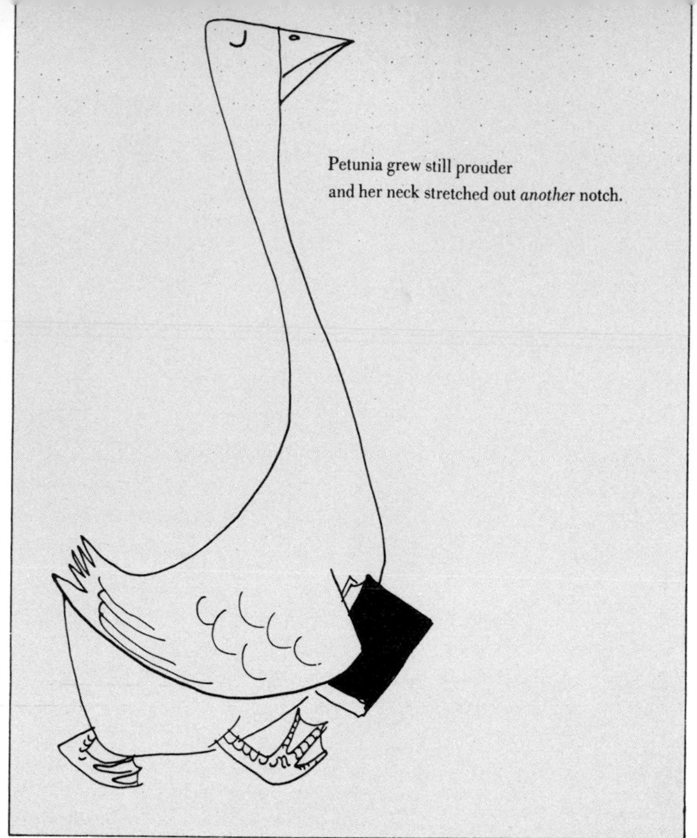

Petunia grew still prouder
and her neck stretched out *another* notch.

176

. . then, suddenly, she saw something she had never seen before in the meadow. What was it?

Petunia stole closer and closer, and sniffed at it from all sides.

"By Goosey Gander," she said, "it does not smell like food for a goose. But I believe I have seen such a thing before . . . ."

177

Here, in essence (no pun intended), is his great wit and his talent for conveying nuances of expression and implication. That it should have appeared under the aegis of a fashionable store is a double-edged delight.

Gradually Duvoisin gave up other work to concentrate on picturebooks—on picturebooks per se, not illustration, the only exceptions being works of the interest of Natalie Savage Carlson's *The Talking Cat* (Harper, 1952) and Robert Louis Stevenson's *Travels with a Donkey* (Limited Editions Club, 1957). (Only those who don't know *The Talking Cat* will question the pairing.) His doing so is obviously indicative of Duvoisin's bent; his being able to do so is symptomatic of a phenomenon we will encounter later, the enormous expansion in the picturebook field that followed the war.

Of his work of the later Forties, the nature books Duvoisin did in collaboration with Alvin Tresselt for Lothrop are the most important, and in his oeuvre generally they hold a special place. The first, *White Snow, Bright Snow* (1947), won him the Caldecott; almost any one might have been in the mind of the child who identified Duvoisin as "the man who knows how to draw the weather";[5] and together they have sold more than a million copies at trade prices, an impressive showing for books that have neither characters nor plot (and no didactic purpose).

Children like them. They are not equally good, and a few, by either artistic or literary standards, are not very good at all, but children like them. They have a realness about them, compounded of integrity and immediacy, that overrides any momentary failure of

176-178. *Petunia*, by Roger Duvoisin. Knopf, 1950. 8 x 10.

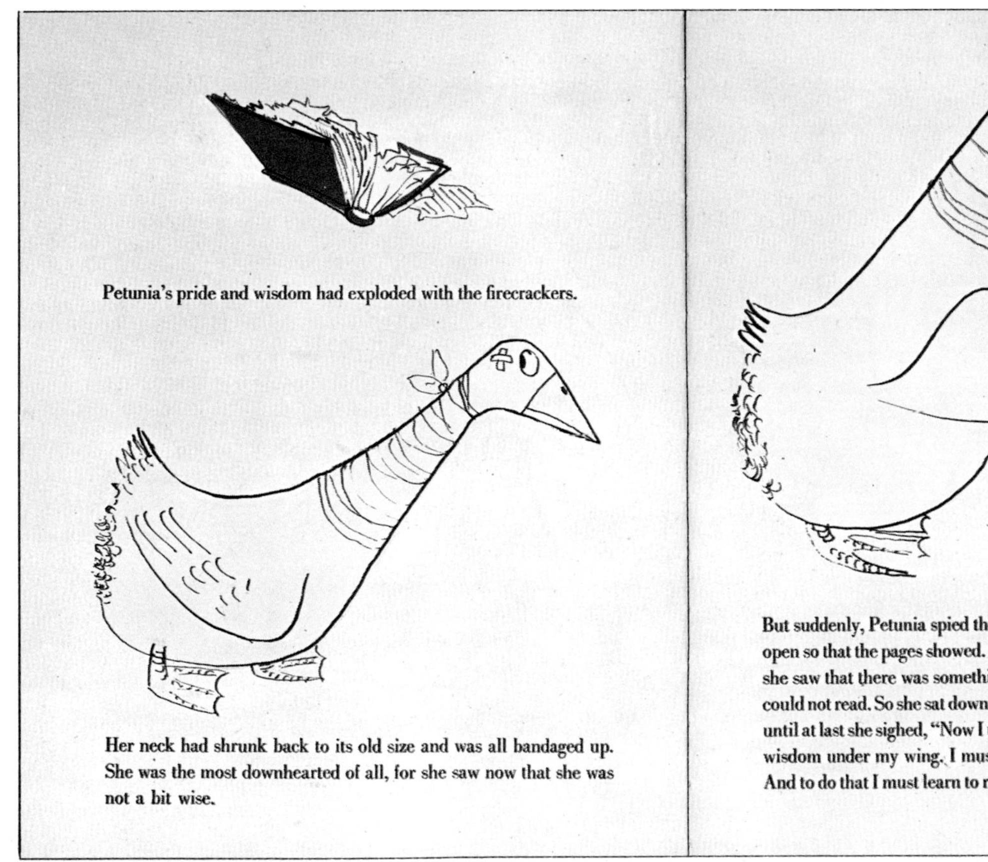

Petunia's pride and wisdom had exploded with the firecrackers.
Her neck had shrunk back to its old size and was all bandaged up. She was the most downhearted of all, for she saw now that she was not a bit wise.
But suddenly, Petunia spied the Book. The firecrackers had blown it open so that the pages showed. She had never seen them before. Now she saw that there was something written inside the Book which she could not read. So she sat down and thought and thought and thought, until at last she sighed, "Now I understand. It was not enough to carry wisdom under my wing. I must put it in my mind and in my heart. And to do that I must learn to read."

178

execution. And it pays not always to strive for easy attractiveness: the colors in *Sun Up* (1949), an evocation of a hot summer day, are indeed muggy, and one perfectly understands the chickens taking shelter in the shadow of the barn, the cows in the shade of a tree; one senses why "everything hid from the burning sun." And yet they are the same three, red, yellow and dark blue, that Duvoisin uses in *White Snow, Bright Snow* to very different purpose. The same and not the same, for the colors—especially the red and the yellow—that are clear and at full strength in *White Snow, Bright Snow* are mixed by overprinting or muted by Ben Day tints in *Sun Up*, and in place of chill excitement comes torpor. (En masse, Duvoisin's books comprise an anthology of the possibilities of pre-separation, tints and other extra-studio techniques.)

Besides the four on the seasons, there were, through the Fifties and beyond, several others, among them *Wake-Up, Farm!* (1955) and *Wake-Up, City!* (1957), ideal springboards for small children, and a book that does almost the same thing for the beach, *I Saw the Sea Come In* (1954). But the one that has always been my favorite—it was a family favorite too—is *Follow the Road.*

Follow the Road opens on a spread rendered in black line and green wash, the green so deep that it blends with the black and gives the appearance of monochrome. What we see is a shadowed green world full of sharp details, a microcosm at once vast and intimate (179). Pulling it together is the meandering road, like no road and every road—or, like the scene itself, an abstraction.

Does such a lackadaisical dirt track have direction, extension? Is it really going somewhere? The little boy thinks so before he stops to play marbles; but turn the page and close to is the clay surface rimmed with wildflowers, a frog catching flies in the middle. Then a final curve and the road straightens out, heads through the trees toward the horizon, emerges black-topped and strung with telephone poles: "the road didn't stay, couldn't stay, not today."

The surface smoothens, widens, sports a center stripe, carries school bus and trailer truck, surges into the center of a big city . . . "The policeman raised his hand—stop! He blew his whistle—stop! The bell clanged and the light turned red—STOP!" Traffic comes to a halt . . . "But on went the road, under the wheels of the cars and trucks. And under the feet of all the people crossing to the other side. Past the city, across railroad tracks and under railroad tracks, over a river and through twisty pretzel clover-leaf roads onto a SUPERHIGHWAY THROUGHWAY TURNPIKE."

As the day draws to a close it slows down again, ambles past bandstand and fresh egg stand, carries the farmer on his tractor chugging home, whistling, the little boy pulling his wagon up the hill, puffing—his silhouette black against the red-streaked sky, the windows of his house beacons in the coming darkness.

But the road didn't stay, couldn't stay, not today.
On it ran, past the little boy,
over the hills and through the valleys.
All over the world.

The text speaks for itself; lyrical and urgent, swinging from a shout to a whisper, always a voice, a presence, it is as fine as any of the many Tresselt has done. And Duvoisin fills it out, now in soft waves of country clover, now in the blank stares of tall buildings—grayed to highlight the bright street bustle and the cars in a child's red, yellow and blue.

In forty-one years, 1932–1972, Duvoisin illustrated by his own accounting 146 books, thirty-one of which he also wrote. Not all of the latter are picturebooks: *The Three Sneezes* (Knopf, 1941) is a collection of Swiss tales, *And There Was America, They Put Out to Sea* and *The Four Corners of the World* (all Knopf, 1938, 1943 and 1948) are story-histories, kaleidoscopic and withal, personal.

Unquestionably the best of the picturebooks are his, not necessarily because they are the best illustrated but because they are the best books. Consider *Petunia,* the story of a silly goose who equates the possession of a book with the acquisition of wisdom. She is the philosopher who can't see beyond his own stone, the expert who interprets his figures as facts, anyone who takes symbol for substance. Petunia not only can't read, she doesn't know she needs to; but armed with a book she is all-knowing.

Duvoisin's masterly line drawing of Petunia, eyes lowered, head high, book tucked under her arm, is justly famous (176). Such clear bold line was, as Louise Seaman Bechtel observed, comparatively rare in the artist's earlier work; here it wiggles furiously for King the rooster's comb, thickens and thins as the animals stoop and stretch, and shoots off the top of the page as Petunia becomes still prouder and her neck grows still longer.

But single images don't tell the tale, their disposition in sequence does. In cartoon sequence, albeit around the double-page (177), across top or bottom, incorporating telling objects (178)—in any of a variety of ways. The design is fluid and dramatic, the action is continuous: it is a picture-*story* par excellence.

As befits the strong line, the color is flat, sometimes clear and flat (178), sometimes extended by a full-strength mixture, a tint or a combination of the two—the deep green, the pink and the yellow-green respectively (177). And whether Petunia, all white except for her beak, is silhouetted against the colored back-

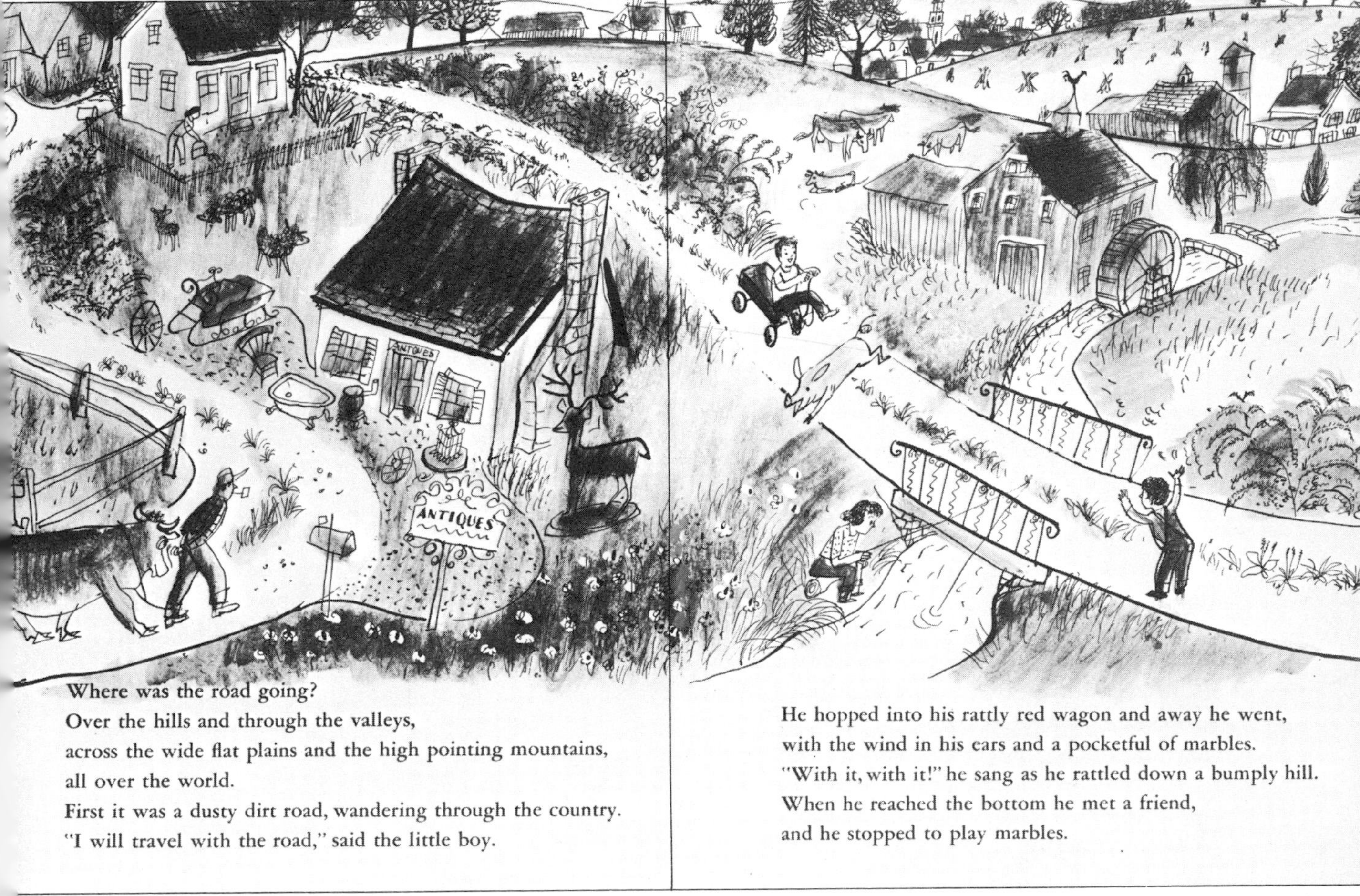

ANTIQUES
ANTIQUES
Where was the road going?
Over the hills and through the valleys,
across the wide flat plains and the high pointing mountains,
all over the world.
First it was a dusty dirt road, wandering through the country.
"I will travel with the road," said the little boy.
He hopped into his rattly red wagon and away he went,
with the wind in his ears and a pocketful of marbles.
"With it, with it!" he sang as he rattled down a bumply hill.
When he reached the bottom he met a friend,
and he stopped to play marbles.

179. *Follow the Road,* text by Alvin Tresselt, pictures by Roger Duvoisin. Lothrop, 1953. $8\frac{1}{8}$ x $9\frac{3}{4}$.

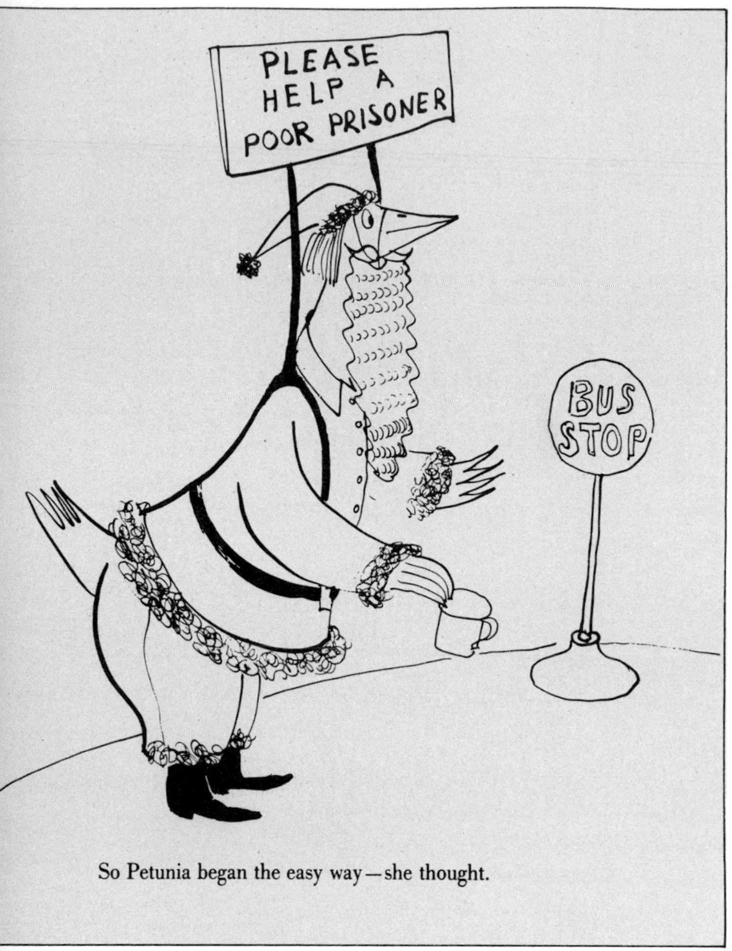

180. *Petunia's Christmas,* by Roger Duvoisin. Knopf, 1952. 8 x 10.

ground (178) or the white itself forms the ground (177), white is the matrix—the wellspring and the cement—on the four-color as well as the one-color spreads, showing the drawings to advantage and unifying the design.

Drawing and design and dramatic action: follow Petunia's head as it makes a shallow sweep around the double-page and watch her expression change (177); see the tattered book, the bandaged neck, the doleful look—and the Rodin-thinker recovery (178).

It is all there in the pictures, the text could be a string of captions; but at its least it is something more. Petunia has just acquired the marvelous book:

She slept with it she swam with it.

And knowing that she was so wise,

Petunia also became proud.
and prouder and prouder so proud

that her neck stretched out several notches.

The words are parallel pictures in print and, keyed to the five pictures of Petunia, the rhythm, the stress, the pacing are dictated by the arrangement and spacing.

For the most part, though, Petunia's silliness takes shape in exchanges with the other animals. Poor sad King the rooster stops shaking his comb for fear it might fall off ("Plastic comb, I'd say," says Petunia); poor worried Ida the hen can't account for the extra chicks Petunia's addition assigns her ('Six less than nine?' "That's *more* than nine. . . . *Lots* more, my dear!"). Poor put-upon animals, the refrain is as constant as Petunia's comebacks are surprising, and the book reads as well as it looks.

Petunia, wised up, went on to new adventures. They follow no set pattern for with Petunia established as a personality almost anything could happen. But she is most felicitously cast, in *Petunia's Christmas*, as the underdog's best friend. Specifically, Charles the handsome gander is set to be Christmas dinner, prompting Petunia to devise truly devious means—like war paint—to free him from captivity, and when that fails, of raising money to buy his freedom (180). But contributions lag and time is short, so Petunia the streetcorner Santa becomes "the gayest Christmas goose you ever saw," ringed with wreaths and strung, wing to wing, with ornaments. In one guise after another, Petunia is the funniest sight Duvoisin ever conjured up. And, daft and deft, *Petunia's Christmas* adds to economical line a sparing, calculated use of color, breaking into bright hues only for the outlandish goings on and for the joyous all-join-in wedding of the two geese on Christmas day.

Nobody celebrates Christmas like Duvoisin —except children. Lives there a child who hasn't at some time wondered about those surplus Santas on the streets and in the shops at Christmastime? Worse, they turn up tired on subways, sipping coffee in cafeterias, and—of all things—having their shoes shined. Simple enough, decides Duvoisin's one-and-only Santa Claus, he'll unmask them. But when he shows Mrs. Santa his trophies, a sleighful of Christmas beards, she reproaches him: he can be in only one place at a time—"Then how do you think people can have true Christmas cheer in their homes when they see you for only a moment or not at all?" Back go the beards, with a conciliatory box of candy and, for children, their questions answered, their doubts eased.

The crux of the story is imprinted on the jacket (181). Wraparound jacket designs (and now, identically printed covers) provide a hinged stage for Duvoisin, a setting for interplay between front and back. Here the action is aptly, and hilariously, broken at the spine, with a thrust that insists that the book be turned over.

Need it be said that he always has an idea? In the case of *A for the Ark*, a web of ideas. The alphabet lends itself to the animals of the Ark; their entrance into the Ark suggests Noah's difficulties in keeping them in order, alphabetically and otherwise (182, 183); the approaching storm brings darkening skies, haste, a final recapitulation before the Flood; and then the story takes over as it should, in three pages predominantly of text. But when the waters recede the animals must leave the Ark, and because Noah is acting in God's stead, the last shall be first. It becomes a game: "Can you tell now the names of the animals pictured with each letter . . . ?" ("If not, you will find them on the last page.") Majestically, the Roman capitals descend, each with an animal profiled in sinuous line (184).

The scheme of printing, in full-color process and two colors at alternate openings, plus the way Duvoisin uses it—modeling in full color (183), outlining and filling in with a flat wash otherwise (182)—results in two distinct modes of illustration, as different as painting and drawing, which is in fact what they are. It is not the best design, perhaps, but it is a good, changing show. There is pith

181. *One Thousand Christmas Beards,* by Roger Duvoisin. Knopf, 1955. 7½ x 10.

B
"B follows A" called Noah.
"B is for the Bears;
B is for the Beavers.
All Aboard! All the animals
who begin with a B."
"AB—Now come the C's,"
called Noah.
"C for the Camels;
C for the Cows;
C for the Crows;
C for the Chickadees.
But not for you," said Noah to the
Kangaroos. "You begin with a K not
a C. Wait for your turn."
C

182

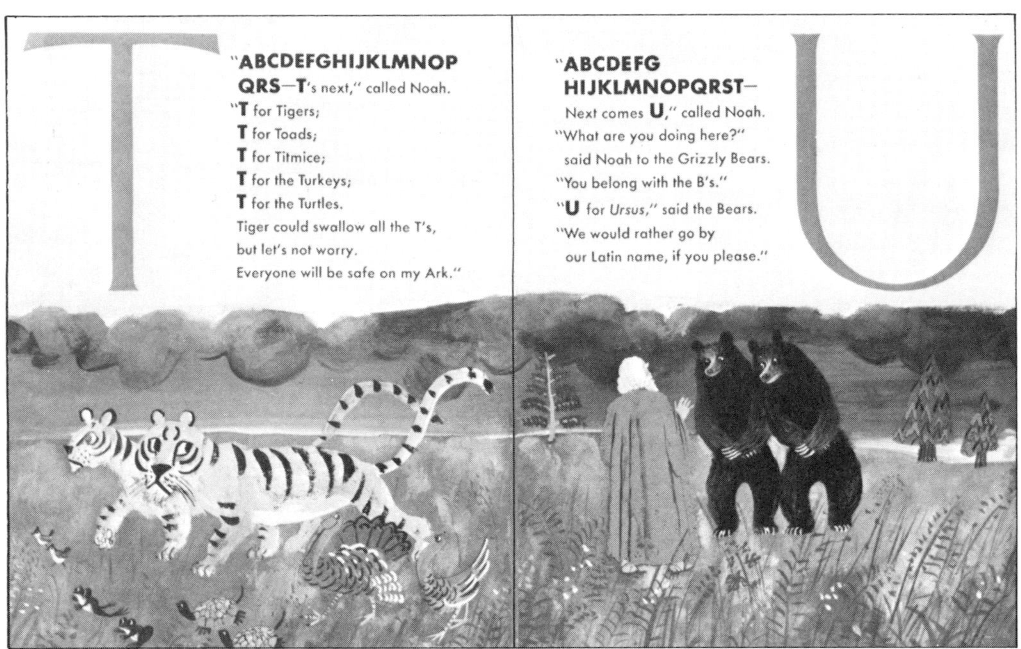
T
"ABCDEFGHIJKLMNOP
QRS—T's next," called Noah.
"T for Tigers;
T for Toads;
T for Titmice;
T for the Turkeys;
T for the Turtles.
Tiger could swallow all the T's,
but let's not worry.
Everyone will be safe on my Ark."
"ABCDEFG
HIJKLMNOPQRST—
Next comes U," called Noah.
"What are you doing here?"
said Noah to the Grizzly Bears.
"You belong with the B's."
"U for *Ursus*," said the Bears.
"We would rather go by
our Latin name, if you please."
U

183

184

I
H
G
F
E
D

in the drawn pages, and even without the rich red of Noah's robe or the blue-black of the lowering clouds, there is drama in the painted ones.

Humor and affection shoulder each other throughout. The letter S brings the sheep into safe company; the wolves eye the weasels, "Both night thieves, but you cannot steal anyone from my Ark." If there is a recurrent motif, it is that the Lion and the Lamb shall lie down together alliteratively. But for sheer artistry, the back pages are the book's triumph (184). Here, svelter, are Veronica the hippopotamus and a dromedary with no less aplomb than The Camel Who Took a Walk (other Duvoisin troupers); and, blocked in clear, vivid hues, the capitals offsetting them, with a strip of color balancing, bordering, at the middle.

Of all the characters Duvoisin has drawn into being, probably the favorite of children is the Happy Lion, the joint creation of the artist and his wife, Louise Fatio. Petunia has dash, sang-froid, even a certain sex appeal; the happy lion has friendliness and a friend, François (185). There is nothing new in the idea of an importunate bear, a reluctant dragon or a sociable lion being mistaken for fierce; what matter? its very persistence as a theme attests to its durability. Besides, children, we know, are always new.

On the face of it, the happy lion is a lucky fellow. He has his own red-tiled house and rock garden in the zoo of a snug, sparkling French town—a playhouse in a toy town, to American youngsters—and he considers himself a universal pet: doesn't everyone stop to say "*Bonjour*"? But let him once leave his domain—let the keeper neglect to close his door—and Monsieur Dupont faints, Madam Pinson pelts him with vegetables, the town band and the crowd take flight. "I suppose," he muses, "this must be the way people behave when they are not at the zoo." Not François the keeper's son: François says "*Bonjour*" comme toujours; they will always be friends.

A gentle parable told and drawn with spirit, *The Happy Lion* is a minor classic. Others in

185. *The Happy Lion,* text by Louise Fatio, pictures by Roger Duvoisin. McGraw-Hill, 1954. 7¾ x 9½.

182-184. *A for the Ark,* by Roger Duvoisin. Lothrop, 1952. 8¼ x 10⅜.

the series have more plot and less to say—though, so persuasive is the star of the little zoo, no less appeal to children.

Over the years art changed, printing practices changed, and Duvoisin's work changed—as one can see in the successive appearances of Petunia and the Happy Lion. What one cannot do is date a book by any single factor: different material continued to elicit different treatment. In 1965 there appeared, among others, *Hide and Seek Fog* (text by Alvin Tresselt, Lothrop), pure mood in watercolors printed by full-color process, and *The Rain Puddle* (text by Adelaide Holl, Lothrop), of which Duvoisin said: "What attracts me to this story is that it has the charming ingenuousness of a little folk tale, and I have tried to keep my illustrations just as simple."[6] Composed of a few flat cut-out forms accented with line, they appear throughout on the right-hand page opposite the text, one of the simplest possible arrangements too. Speaking of Duvoisin, editors invariably praise his craftsmanship; the sensibility is there for anyone to see.

THE AMERICAN LINE

ELLIS CREDLE, ROBERT LAWSON, GLEN ROUNDS, JAMES DAUGHERTY, ROBERT McCLOSKEY

When we come to Americans picturing American life, we come to drawing—chiefly drawing in line, with pen or dry brush or crayon, as distinct from wash drawing or painting. Drawing in black and white. To identify as American a bent for black and white in apposition to the Continental penchant for strong color, the English preference for pastels, is almost too pat a formulation. But drawing is the idiom of reportage whether the artist has a comment to make or a story to tell or both; and drawing in crayon for lithographic reproduction, in pen and ink for mechanical engraving, came into their own in the newspapers and magazines, popular and radical, that burgeoned everywhere in the late 1800s–early 1900s, as well as in the books that appeared in one after another differently illustrated edition. Nowhere did the illustrated magazine flourish more than in the United States—to the extent that David Bland speaks of its having "usurped some of the functions of the American illustrated book";[1] and nowhere did the photo-mechanical processes take quicker hold, producing, as Joseph Pennell noted, pen draftsmen where there had been none before.

The American artists who began doing distinctly American picturebooks in the Thirties are not only heirs to the *Harper's-Scribner's-St. Nicholas* comic tradition, they also follow from the realism of the 'Ash Can School' of John Sloan and his circle, erstwhile newspapermen all. Fanned into social protest in the pages of the *Masses, Liberator* and *New Masses*, it was subsequently turned upon the American Scene, writ large, by the triumvirate of Thomas Hart Benton, Grant Wood and John Steuart Curry, and upon the diversity—and divergences—of American life by participants in the Federal Art Projects, both phenomena of the Thirties.

Committed to 'art for everyone,' the Federal Art Projects explored the possibilities of —in Oliver Larkin's words—"the cheap and easily distributed print,"[2] the etching, lithograph, woodcut (and now serigraph) that, original and yet reproducible, was potentially the most democratic of mediums. Less cheap, the preserve of collectors, prints had retained interest from the time of Whistler, and where one might expect to find in the journals of the Twenties reviews of avant-garde exhibitions, there is word—earnest, extended discussion—of show upon show of drawings and prints by artists who did just that.

Natural as it was for Americans to draw and, in the mid-Thirties, to want to draw the American scene, it was also convenient for publishers faced with a rising demand for books based on American life—particularly for those presenting "the activities of American children"[3]—and, simultaneously, with the high costs and uncertain results of color printing. But it would not do to regard the books as simply equations of supply and demand.

Drawing is itself a good, a line has its own personality, a drawing in line makes its own statement.

These artists wrote also, and not only—except in Ellis Credle's case—as a means of making picturebooks. The work of two of them, Lawson and Daugherty, won the Newbery Medal, predecessor of the Caldecott, awarded through the ALA annually since 1922 for "the most distinguished contribution to American literature for children"; and the writings of Rounds and McCloskey are distinctive by any standard: they were as successful as authors as they were as illustrators. Why, as professional artists, they should have undertaken to write is more easily explained—by the encouragement juvenile publishing gives to every creative urge—than their marked talent or skill at writing. They are not alone: that "one-man movement" Howard Pyle—the term, interestingly, is Lawson's[4]—wrote, in *Pepper and Salt, The Wonder Clock, Otto of the Silver Hand*, not only his own best material but stories that live independently; and in our time William Pène du Bois and Maurice Sendak, in a different vein Wanda Gág and Jean Charlot, have written seriously and well.

The 'Americans' as a group were narrative artists; they had, in America past and present, a ready-made subject; the making of picturebooks was a natural entrée to writing; their work showed them to have an individual approach to their subject-matter; and the result, added up however one likes, was a body of writing and drawing that together embodied the America of each.

ELLIS CREDLE

Like many another starting out, Ellis Credle concocted fairy tales and garnered rejection slips before finding in her own background the basis of lifelike books.

Down Down the Mountain, set in the Blue Ridge country where Credle taught for four years, is the story of two children "who raise turnips on their tilted farm to buy some squeaky shoes"—as a reporter, catching the key details, put it.[5] Now and again she had told stories to children too, and from the telling—the "creaky-squeaky-creaky" song of the shoes that Hetty and Hank covet, their need to "wait and wait and wait" before the turnips poke up—comes much of the folk flavor remarked upon. The turnips picked and bagged, "down, down, down" the mountain the two go, meeting, like all good-hearted folk heroes, one after another supplicant until, reaching the store that holds the precious shoes, they discover that they have only one turnip left. But they won't return bare-footed: that one turnip is the biggest turnip at the County Fair (in modern stories, the Lord provides prizes), netting them a five-dollar gold piece and, besides the shoes, presents all around.

It was good for American children to know, "in the ready-made life of cities, how much there still is left of bright adventure in the mountains," wrote the New York *Herald Tribune* reviewer, echoing Clara Hunt's tribute to *The Farm Book* many years earlier; they would benefit too from learning that 'the purchase of a pair of shoes is not everywhere taken for granted.'[6]

In the illustrations the lesson is plain. Hetty and Hank's mother, tall, stooped, intent on her work, washes clothes by the side of the stream (like Helen Sewell's Pilgrims, laying them on the branches to dry) and their father busies himself feeding corncobs to the pigs, neither of them pausing as they explain to the expectant children why shoes aren't to be had for the asking (186). The undulating line, the surface agitation, has something of Thomas Benton's restless energy, here harnessed to the story, and the rough-hewn, deep-cleft, unfinished quality suits the log cabin locale.

In the book, the presence of color—a warm brown used also for the text, a brisk blue—gives the pages a cheerful, less strained aspect. Designing in two colors other than black was not totally new to picturebooks nor was the choice of brown as a base color; but any decision to print the text in the color of the pictures—or to print both in a color other than black—is noteworthy, tempering the

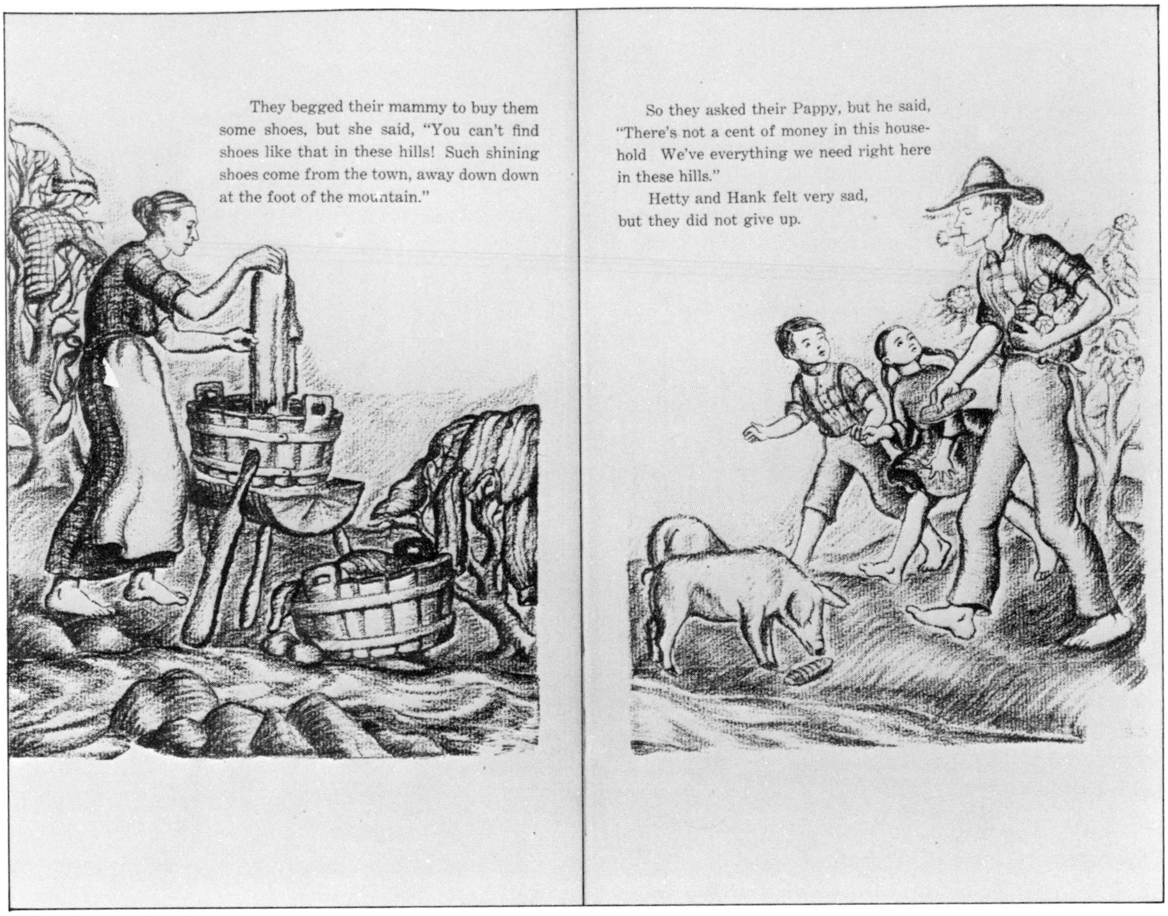

They begged their mammy to buy them some shoes, but she said, "You can't find shoes like that in these hills! Such shining shoes come from the town, away down down at the foot of the mountain."

So they asked their Pappy, but he said, "There's not a cent of money in this household We've everything we need right here in these hills."

Hetty and Hank felt very sad, but they did not give up.

186. *Down Down the Mountain,* by Ellis Credle. Nelson, 1934. 8¾ x 11⅝.

187. *Across the Cotton Patch,* by Ellis Credle. Nelson, 1935. 10¾ x 8⅝.

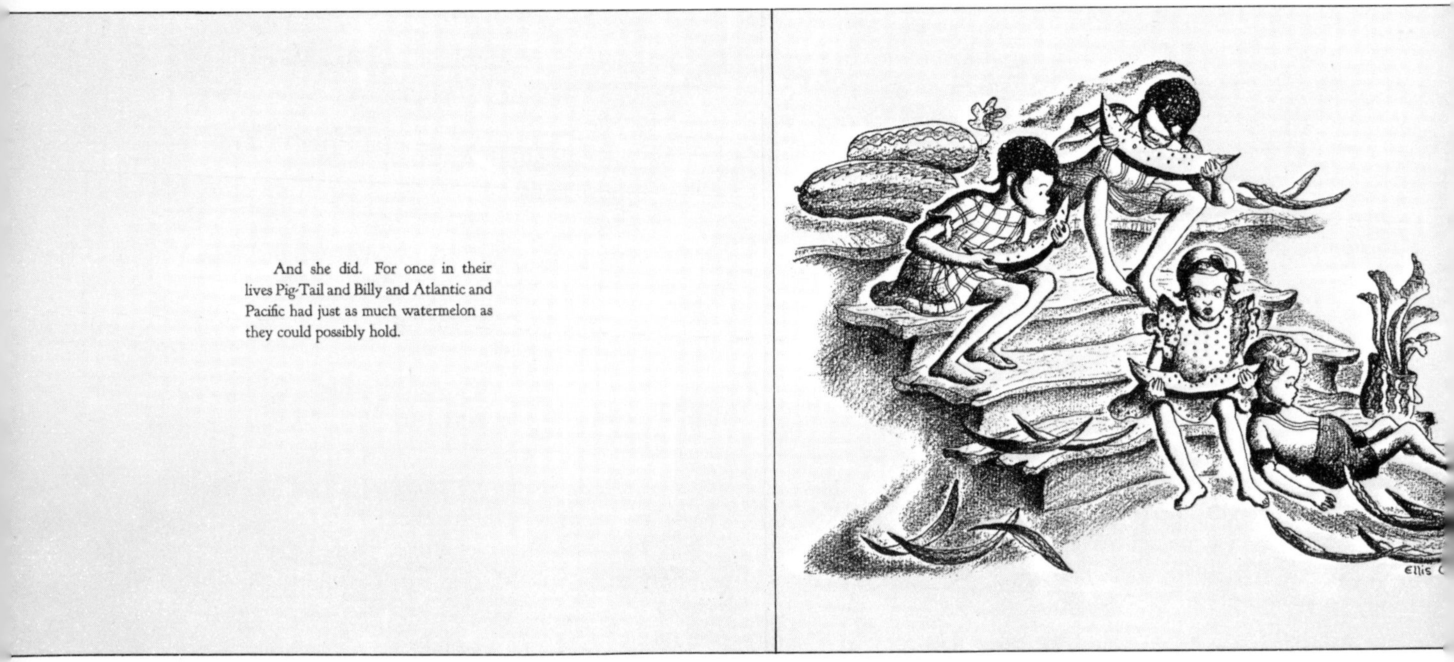

And she did. For once in their lives Pig-Tail and Billy and Atlantic and Pacific had just as much watermelon as they could possibly hold.

severity of black and white to a rich monochrome and yielding a more individual, less mechanical look.

Ellis Credle returned to the plantation world of her childhood for *Across the Cotton Patch*, wrote a fuller story, a breezy account of the mischief four children get into, and drew lively, larkish pictures of the youngsters riding off on old Dan, the big boar; chewing tobacco and suffering; chasing crows, vagrant sheep, a marauding cow—this in the course of "taking care of the plantation." Good care too, if excessive (to spot new trouble, Pig-Tail stations herself on top of the house with spyglasses), and when Mama and Papa, Mammy Sara and Pappy return home from the store, they get their reward (187).

Across the Cotton Patch is open about the differences between black and white, and erases them with good humor. Pig-Tail, who gets around her brother Billy by appealing to his manly pride, has a harder time with the black twin Atlantic. She herself can't stay in the cornfield to scare off the crows, Pig-Tail points out to Atlantic, because she'd get freckles. "Mama told me if I get freckled I can't get a husband when I get grown." But Atlantic "wants a husband as bad as you does," and, black or not, "Ah can get mo' blacker"; it will have to be Pacific, "all time talkin' 'bout you ain't never gwine git married." If there's a moral here under the horseplay, it's the common possession of wiliness and foolishness, the individuality of persons. The store-bought names and the dialect embarrass us today but for Ellis Credle, looking back in 1935, this is the way it was; and listening to Pig-Tail and Billy speak their own variant of standard English, we have to recognize, with its reviewers, that *Across the Cotton Patch* comes alive as a picture of American children in a way that its bland and stilted—and indeterminate—contemporaries don't.

Received warmly, it ran afoul of the emerging demand for positive portrayals of Negro life, portrayals that would, in the first instance, omit old differences of station and speech; but that is another story, more appropriate to Ellis Credle's next book (p. 375).

ROBERT LAWSON

An apprenticeship in advertising design and magazine illustration taught Robert Lawson what could be done and how to do it, experience in etching increased his technical and expressive range. Besides acclaim as a draftsman, he brought to children's books a traditional style and, harking back too, a flat refusal to regard them as something distinct and apart. "The question of whether, strictly speaking, A. B. Frost was a 'children's illustrator,' " he wrote, "must be decided by those more interested in strictly speaking."[7]

Strictly speaking, *The Hurdy-Gurdy Man* is not a picturebook or anything else one can put a name to. Margery Bianco wrote a story of music's power to charm, a new-old tale of dour townsfolk willy-nilly set to dancing, and Lawson made pictures of whatever took his fancy however he envisioned it. It might be the delicatessen keeper who bars the hurdy-gurdy man's monkey, a classical portrait bust and all the funnier for it (188) or the baker, no more hospitable, whose hat balloons out of the frame, a conceit, like her overtowering curls, favored in book design from the miniaturists forward (189). Or, romantically pic-

188

189

188, 189. *The Hurdy-Gurdy Man*, text by Margery Bianco, pictures by Robert Lawson. Oxford, 1933. 7 x 7.

their door-yards, instead of being neat and tidy like all the other door-yards round about, were just a tangle of roses and

14

lilacs and snow-berry bush, growing any way at all that they chose. And in one yard there were yellow day-lilies crowding

15

190

190, 191. *The Hurdy-Gurdy Man,* text by Margery Bianco, pictures by Robert Lawson. Oxford, 1933. 7 x 7 .

191

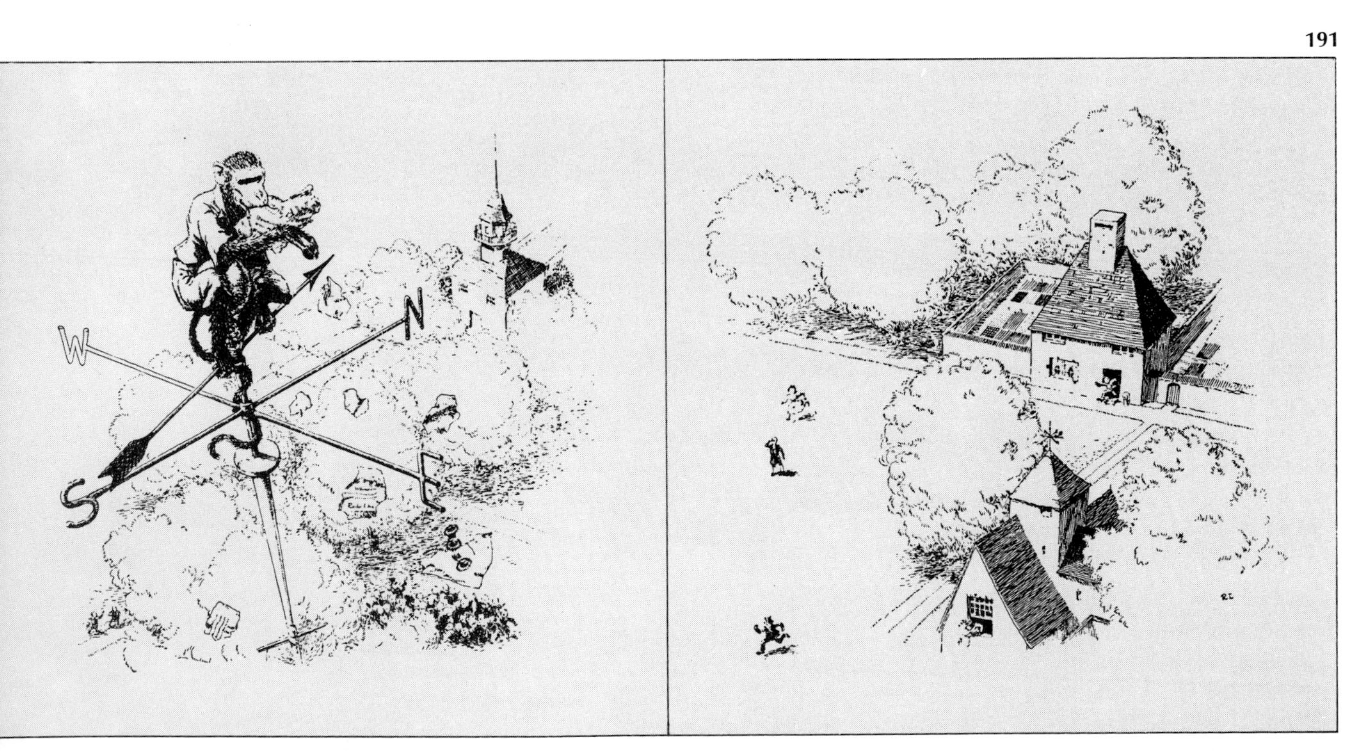

turesque, the cottages of two kindly souls, deviants from the sterile norm (190); appropriating a double-page spread, a dramatic, very current aerial view of the monkey demolishing the local law against street music (191).

Lawson knew a good subject for drawing when he saw it but he was after something else too, something bound up with the sense of the story. The hurdy-gurdy man we see only once, at the start, and thereafter we get, in effect, his reactions to the town and the town's reaction to him. Come from nowhere, he is the archetypal vagrant, vanishing good spirit; at the close, the town's first picnic in full swing, he is gone—"Where, indeed?" It is a gingery, sentimental work, illustrated in the fine-etched manner that, in Arthur Mason's *Wee Men of Ballywooden* (1930), first made Lawson's name; and a book that, giving free rein to both, is unafraid of words or pictures.

In *Ferdinand* the technique has altered, Lawson is dealing in stark black and white rather than in line and the suggestion of tone, and the dynamics are fitted to a standard picturebook format. But it is a dynamic text and a no less vital picturization, with a clear-cut image for each development, each emotional shift. *Ferdinand*, like *Peter and the Wolf*, proceeds by motifs—ethereal timbres for "Once upon a time in Spain," tinkling for "there was a little bull and his name was Ferdinand," hollow bombast for the parade of the Picadores (192), a single echoing twang for the entrance of FERDINAND (193). In the picture of the Picadores there is a coarseness, a certain tattiness, almost vulgarity—Lawson had an informed respect for the vigor of comic strips; in the other, the artful play of tiny tentative head against yawning blackness, framed by the massive doors and topped, over-topped by the cartouche, lightly etched, the ineffable weight of authority.

At the last is the silhouette of Ferdinand "under his favorite cork tree, smelling the flowers just quietly," a scene suggestive of sunset, an eternal sunset, and of those films that fade similarly, drawing back, disengaging. But *Ferdinand* is only one of many picture-

192

193

192, 193. *The Story of Ferdinand,* text by Munro Leaf, pictures by Robert Lawson. Viking, 1936. 6⅞ x 8⅛.

books that, in its choice of vantage points, its quick cuts, its total flexibility, would have been unthinkable before motion pictures.

Ferdinand—the unbelligerent bull, the fable, the book—was headed for world fame. Not without demurrers: letters objected that it was propaganda, communist or fascist or pacifist propaganda indiscriminately; and author Leaf, much miffed, shot back that it was innocent fun, that Ferdinand, if anything, was "just a superior soul, a philosopher, [whose] refusal to fight in the bull-ring at Madrid when there was a lovely bouquet to smell was a proof of good taste, and strength of character as well."[8] But there was a war on in Spain, the incendiary Civil War; pacifists were shifting position; everyone had a position: in the world at large, it was the age of ideology. No wonder, then, that Ferdinand fell afoul of the cross-currents; if he was the first of his picturebook kind to be called 'subversive,' it was a testimony as well to his prominence: his was also the first original story that Disney bought for films.

194. *They Were Strong and Good,* by Robert Lawson. Viking, 1940. 8¼ x 10.

The succeeding Leaf-Lawson collaboration, *Wee Gillis* (1938), is a comic Scots' version of stage Irish hijinks with highly elaborated, very dramatic pictures. It comes across but like the bagpipes Gillis gets to play (sitting contentedly in his own dooryard, a second Ferdinand), the noise it makes is disproportionate to what it's tooting about.

Lawson was continuously active in those years, with varying results. Nineteen-thirty-seven brought *Four and Twenty Blackbirds,* the nursery rhyme book edited by Helen Dean Fish, where the illustrations are rigid and heavy and calculated to a T. In Richard and Florence Atwater's 1938 farce *Mr. Popper's Penguins* the pictures have just the right mock-seriousness to make the goings-on wildly funny, in the 1939 *Pilgrim's Progress* they have the fluorescent glow and the fervor of oleo Madonnas. Lawson could not invest ordinary people with individuality, he required oddities, and though he was least successful with women, his youths are young Galahads or nothing.

But 1939 also brought *Ben and Me,* the first book of Lawson's writing and the best of a picaresque series—stretching into *I Discover Columbus* (1941), *Mr. Revere and I* (1953), *Capt. Kidd's Cat* (1956)—that is both juvenile and adult, fantasy and history. Whatever its charm *Rabbit Hill* (1944), Lawson's Newbery winner, is a type where *Ben and Me,* "A New and Astonishing LIFE of BENJAMIN FRANKLIN. As written by his Good Mouse AMOS," is a creation.

So is *They Were Strong and Good.* If it is easier to admire *They Were Strong and Good* than to like it, it evokes genuine admiration and not dutiful respect. Lawson presents to us his forebears: the sea captain whose parrot, a present for one friend, eats up the Panama hat intended for another ("So one friend didn't get his hat, and the other friend *almost* didn't get a parrot"); the captain's wife, his mother's mother, who "liked the monkeys and the sugar cane and the parrots, but . . . did *not* like"—bent over the railing—"sailing on the sea"; and on the other side, his father's father who "was always fighting

195. *Ben and Me,* by Robert Lawson. Boston, Little, Brown, 1939. Detail.

something," be it Indians or Yankees or the Powers of Evil (194), and *his* wife, "my father's mother," who thought he had a fine loud voice.

Lawson is proud, amused, grateful—for himself, the ME they begot, and for "the country that they helped to build." In 1940 it was still possible to be patriotic in this simple, open fashion without being smug. He reminds children that, as recently as his grandmother's time, Paterson, New Jersey, looked not "like this"—a wasteland of smokestacks and mills—but "like this"—a thriving, woodsy village; that at least one little girl, his mother, was afraid of stubborn Indians and rowdy lumberjacks and welcomed the calm of a convent school: that America was made quickly and all kinds of experiences went into the making.

The rendering is harsh and the women are prettified, and to an extent the one grates against the other; but what rankles chiefly is the repeated casting of blacks as physical and visual accessories. Admittedly, this is family history and, in its way, American history. We are left, however, not only with slaves bearing burdens cheerfully but with slaves weeping when their master goes off to fight the Yankees, a lopsided view at the very least.

They Were Strong and Good won the Caldecott, and on receipt of the Newbery for *Rabbit Hill* Lawson became the first to take both prizes; it would be more accurate, nonetheless, to say that he scored in both fields than that he excelled in either.

At an exhibition of illustrations, a child reputedly said of Lawson's: "I like *his* best. He draws them up neat, and you can tell what they mean."[9] But over the years clarity became fixity as Lawson's line hardened, his strokes stiffened, and his drawings lost all semblance of spontaneity. Only his animals escaped, and when Amos the vestry mouse confronts bumbling Ben Franklin, it is Franklin, not Amos, who is the fabrication. He was inventive, and he could be very funny. He was, after all, the father of the brain behind the father of electricity (195). What Amos is sailing down, in good weather, is the string of *that kite.*

GLEN ROUNDS

In 1936 Glen Rounds's *Ol' Paul, the Mighty Logger* made its appearance on the second Holiday House list, wrapped in stout rough paper and bringing a fresh wind out of the West. For youngsters it was the first version of Paul Bunyan in the vernacular—a simple, vigorous vernacular, at once easy to read and grown-up—and it paved the way for Pecos Bill and Stormalong and the other wonder-workers of America. Close on the heels of ol' Paul came Whitey the young cowboy, Rounds's own prototype figure and the perpetual hero of his fiction.

Rounds had turned up at Holiday House the year before looking for something to illustrate and, it seems, literally talked himself into a book, he was that good at spinning yarns. He was a natural, too, for *Story Parade* magazine which started up the same year and,

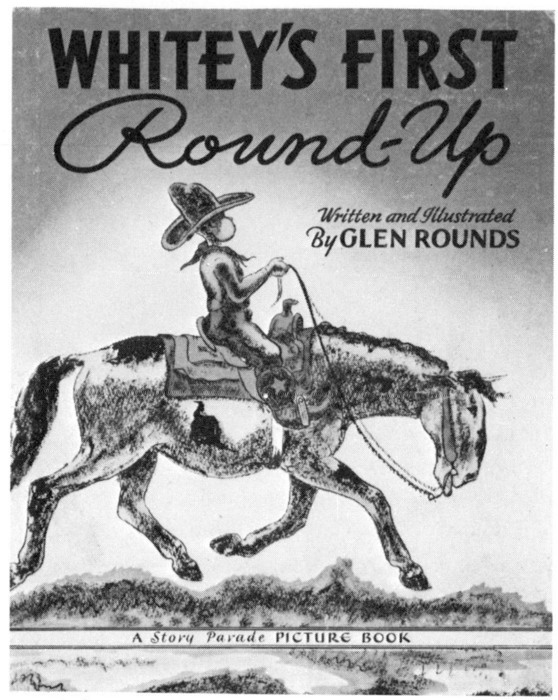

196. *Whitey's First Round-Up,* by Glen Rounds. Grosset, 1942. 7⅞ x 9¼.

197. *Whitey's First Roundup,* by Glen Rounds. Holiday House, 1960. 5½ x 7⅞.

in 1937, published the first of the Whitey stories.

Story Parade—stories by Elizabeth Coatsworth, Alice Dalgliesh, Walter de la Mare, Cornelia Meigs, illustrations by Lois Lenski, Fritz Eichenberg, Helen Sewell, Kurt Wiese—aimed to fill the void left by the decline of the old *St. Nicholas.* It printed old tales retold, new books serialized, poems, contributions by children, an occasional article, but its forte was regional Americana, and many of the stories, through a hook-up with the Artists and Writers Guild, found their way into books. Published by Grosset & Dunlap and dubbed Story Parade Picture Books (a second, slightly older series was called Story Parade Adventure Books), they were equally picturebooks and story books. Thin and flat, they were not tall or oblong, large or small, the marks—stigmata—of a picturebook; designed, like picturebooks, so that the whole page was illustrated and plentifully provided with color, they retained from story books consecutive paragraphs of type. They were slender and inviting but they didn't look 'babyish,' they had lots of reading but they didn't look 'hard.'

The four Whitey books in the group, beginning with *Whitey's First Round-Up* (1942), are Rounds's nearest approach to picturebooks for many years and his only fling with full color. Whitey himself turns up as an accessory in *Pay Dirt* (1938), an account of prospecting during the Depression, and as a prime mover in the enduring *Blind Colt* (1941), two Holiday House books with collateral illustrations. On his own again, first in adaptations from *Story Parade* stories, then in *Whitey Takes a Trip* (1954), the first of the characteristic little novels, he is the same plugger who, at the outset, "was getting along towards nine years old, a man grown, practically. . . . too old for homemade haircuts"; but the books are longer, the pictures—in black and white—fewer. If anything, however, they have more force; as time passed Rounds thickened and quickened his line, and his drawings have a new crackle, a new spring (196, 197).

"As he wrote different kinds of books," the

flap copy for one points out, "he developed suitable drawing styles: for the young Whitey cowboy stories, easy flowing strokes; for the horse books, spare dramatic lines set in endless space; for the writing about wild animals in their haunts, strongly contrasted shadings and patternings." None of these are picturebooks but so fully do the pictures convey the intent that the books seem almost to emanate from them.

In the Western frontier life series initiated with *The Treeless Plains*, they can properly be called partners with the text—illustrations, certainly, of sod houses inside and out, of social doings and natural disasters, but also, appearing in the wide margins of every page, the inflection, the intonation withheld from the matter-of-fact narrative. "Brush and poles, when they could be found, usually had to be hauled considerable distances . . . but the tough sod blocks were always available close by and at no cost beyond the labor of plowing and hauling them into place. So in time the plains settlers came to use this peculiar material almost as freely and expertly as the Eastern frontiersmen had used their logs" (198).

It is a needling, twitchy line—Rounds's lines are plainly gestures—and there is hardly a drawing without some humor, whether it's a sly detail—the cock lording it over the hens—or, tersely sketched, the slope of the shoulders, the snap of the brim, the turn of the head that speak volumes (199). "What with one thing and another, it wasn't without reason that the people of the towns and the cattlemen living in their log houses . . . began to speak of these lean people with their heavy plow shoes and clothes faded by sun and constant wind as Sodbusters."

199

Setting verse to pictures, animating American folk ballads, launched Rounds into picturebooks good and proper, and in *The Boll Weevil* he met his match (200). That is one mean misbegotten critter, a monster riding on top of the Memphis train, a devilish dwarf standing up in the farmer's coat "like a natural man," always "looking for a home, just looking for a home." Pictures are not always a plus, the words may be funnier plain, but the Boll Weevil that Rounds calls up to wipe out one of his typically lean and hungry farm families is a varmint beyond our power to imagine; and as a group the ballad books—*Billy Boy* (1966), *The Strawberry Roan* (1970), etc.—are just such an undertaking as Anne Carroll Moore might have wished for A. B. Frost.

198, 199. *The Treeless Plains,* by Glen Rounds. Holiday House, 1967. Details.

200. *The Boll Weevil,* pictures by Glen Rounds. San Carlos (Calif.), Golden Gate, 1967. Detail.

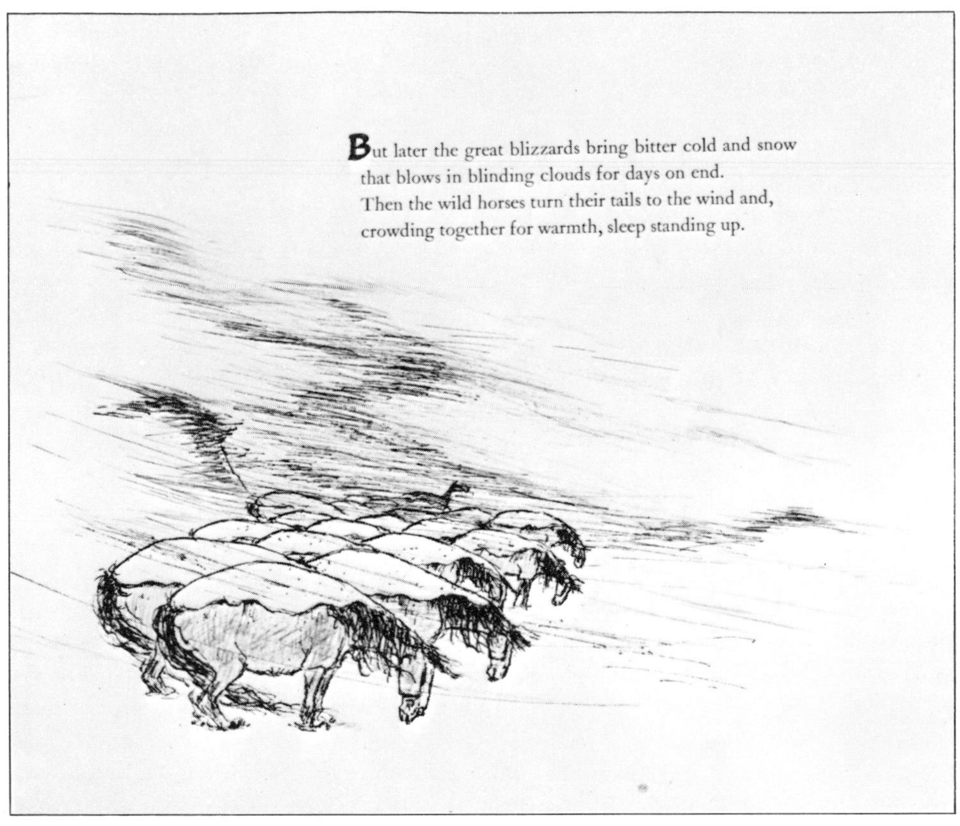

But later the great blizzards bring bitter cold and snow
that blows in blinding clouds for days on end.
Then the wild horses turn their tails to the wind and,
crowding together for warmth, sleep standing up.

201. *Wild Horses of the Red Desert,* by Glen Rounds. Holiday House, 1969. 10¾ x 8⅞.

202. *Once We Had a Horse,* by Glen Rounds. Holiday House, 1971. 5½ x 6¼.

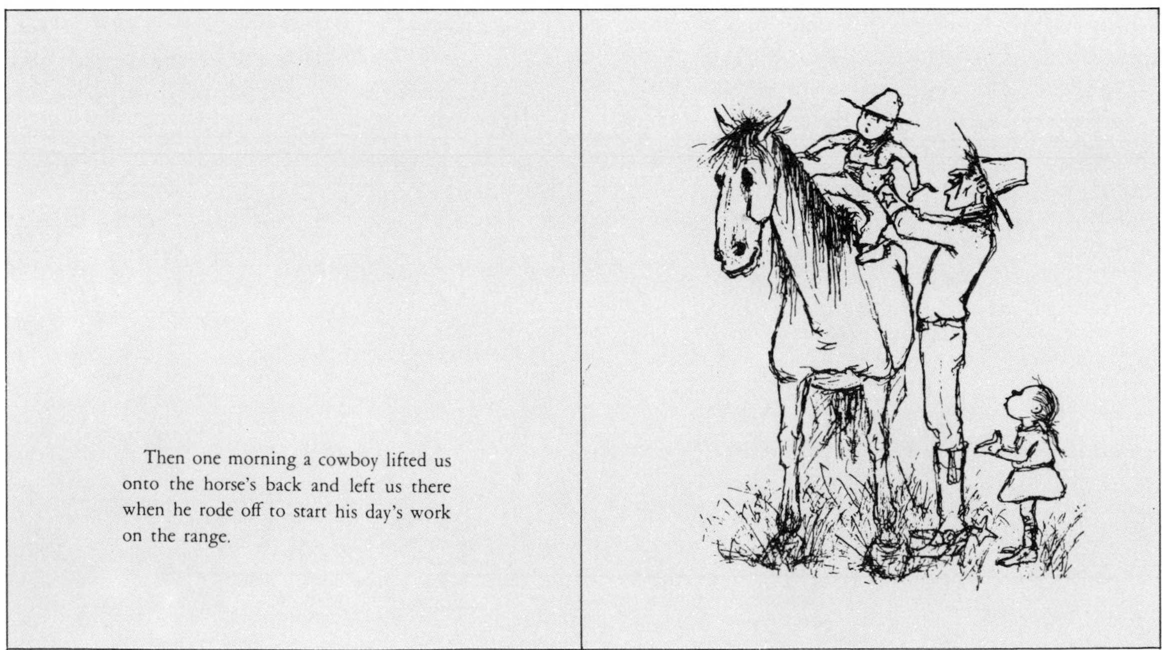

Then one morning a cowboy lifted us
onto the horse's back and left us there
when he rode off to start his day's work
on the range.

Wild Horses of the Desert is a different quantity, a kind of pictorial summation of themes and motifs that run through the horse books from *The Blind Colt* on; indeed, the image of the horses huddled against the snow (201) appears almost exactly as it does in *Stolen Pony* (1948), sequel to *The Blind Colt*. *Wild Horses* is a big book, loose and spiky for the most part, the visual equivalent of the horses' wary, wide-ranging existence.

Its antithesis and its complement, a 'baby Whitey' one might say, is *Once We Had a Horse*, the summer's tale of two youngsters who find out that "learning to ride a horse is much more difficult than it looks." Staying on, once put, is one thing, getting back on without help is another, and roping the old horse to get him to the fence to get on sensibly never does come right. "However, we had plenty of time, and sooner or later we always found a way to get on his back. As the summer went on we became better riders and often carried switches to hurry the old horse along." Then of course he'd stop short and they'd slide over his head; but one way or another they played with him all summer, "and he seemed to enjoy it as much as we did." The book is a confidence, casual and unhurried, compact, open and at the same time enclosed (202). Nice.

One thinks again of Frost, of the brother and sister and dog united in disaster (12). Without claiming for Rounds Frost's virtuosity, it is hard not to see in their keen, frank delineation of character, their way with movement and gesture, their unspoken humor, two artists who are kindred in spirit.

JAMES DAUGHERTY

When James Daugherty came to the attention of the book world, juvenile and adult, as the illustrator of Stewart Edward White's *Daniel Boone* (1926), he was known elsewhere as a painter of 'synchronist' abstractions derived from Delaunay, Matisse, Cézanne—a reminder that "James Daugherty, Buckskin Illustrator,"[10] "as thoroughly American as Faneuil Hall,"[11] had drunk at other waters besides the Wabash. ("An advance-guard wolf in square sheep's clothing," Hilton Kramer called him years later.[12])

The frontier of Boone and Davy Crockett was a childhood legacy, Europe and especially its Baroque art he absorbed as a young man; World War I found him working for the Navy, camouflaging ships (in cubist shapes) and designing posters; the Twenties brought exhibitions at the Société Anonyme, the radical showcase founded by Katherine Dreier and Marcel Duchamp, and commissions for murals at those 'palaces of the people,' Loew's movie theaters. Out of all this came, somehow, the massive figures, the swirling forms and fluid rhythms that are Daugherty's signature, and a long and immensely busy career as a book illustrator.

One link Daugherty himself indicates. In illustrating for children, he wrote, the artist draws not only from the model but above all without the model, "for mere human anatomy cannot endure the strains, pantomimes, posturings, or sublime acrobatics of the inhabitants of a lively imagination in full pictorial flight and frenzy."[13]

Sometimes the compositions appear cramped, the frame has trouble containing the picture, sometimes the forms are difficult to distinguish, often one wants to step back; but in the American books—*Abe Lincoln Grows Up, Knickerbocker's History of New York, Uncle Tom's Cabin* just in 1928–29—the gusto *feels* right and one doesn't look to find fault.

On the big pages, in the open spreads of *Andy and the Lion*, his first picturebook, it *is* right; and Daugherty, mindful that he is drawing now for young children, eliminates and simplifies and enlarges, concentrating the action, the physical and emotional force, in the figures of the two protagonists, a scheme as bold as the draftsmanship.

Wholly of Daugherty's doing, the first thing he wrote himself, *Andy and the Lion* is the Androcles legend become an American boy's dream-come-true. A lion fancier to begin with, Andy gets a book from the library about lions, dreams lions, thinks lions, and on the

AT LAST THEY BOTH STOPPED FOR BREATH. THE LION HELD OUT HIS PAW TO SHOW ANDY WHAT WAS THE MATTER. IT WAS A BIG THORN STUCK IN HIS PAW. BUT

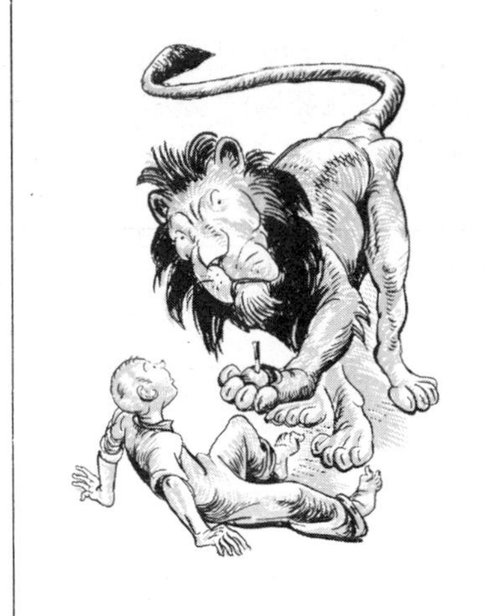

203

ANDY HAD AN IDEA. HE TOLD THE LION TO JUST BE PATIENT AND THEY'D HAVE THAT THORN OUT IN NO TIME. FORTUNATELY

204

ANDY ALWAYS CARRIED HIS PLIERS IN THE BACK POCKET OF HIS OVERALLS. HE TOOK THEM OUT AND GOT A TIGHT GRIP. THEN

205

way to school next morning meets a lion—who is as upset by Andy as Andy is by him. Off they go, round and round a rock, until . . . (203–208). This of course is "a tale of kindness remembered"; and comes the circus, the biggest lion breaks away, Andy finds himself in its path, thinking his last moment has come . . . "But then who should it be but Andy's own lion." They recognize each other joyfully and, all made aright (Andy gets a medal for bravery, the lion wears a bow and a big smile), "the next day Andy took the book back to the library."

Generically *Andy and the Lion* may be a tall tale but there's hardly a child who, in the wide-open way of the young, doesn't take it at its word. Isn't Andy, heading to the library in overalls and bare feet, any ordinary boy back when? Isn't the lion with him to THE END? Moreover, Daugherty is smart enough to get the book out of the library but, as it were, leave the story in the book: we don't know, unless we're wised-up adults, just what it is about lions that Andy's been reading. A child isn't faced with a walking legend or, on the other hand, a clear case of autosuggestion. In 1960, looking back on fifty years' changes in children's books, Louise Seaman Bechtel spoke of "the advent of the American folk hero [who] fitted both the comic-book aspects of heroism and a changing concept of the fairy tale."[14] Scaled down, so does Andy.

"Any who are interested in the picturebook technique as a form will do well to study the subtle nuances that have been worked out on these pages," said Lynd Ward, whose own *Stop Tim!* (Farrar & Rinehart, 1930), written by his wife May McNeer, was one of the first of the headlong, hair's-breadth picture tales; and he calls attention to "the interlocking relationship between word and picture that is of the essence of this technique."[15]

In the pivotal episode (and elsewhere) one sees immediately that the pictures form a self-contained, self-explanatory sequence—a comic sequence, in effect, harking back to Frost and the *Fliegende Blätter* tradition. It is also, in the fullest sense, animated drawing. But while Andy and the lion pantomime their thoughts—Andy, you'll notice, points to himself and there is no pretense that they speak—the text, a kind of voice-over narration, gives pause ("Andy had an idea"), raises expectations ("Fortunately"), tenses up ("Then"), takes a breath ("until the thorn") and breaks the tension with the words "came . . . out."

The dangling, luring-on adverb (then, fortunately), a device we saw in Marjorie Flack, is used not only as an enticement, an automatic page-turner, but as an integral part of the story—because, fortunately, Andy always carried his pliers in the back pocket of his overalls. Indeed, if Andy didn't have those pliers there'd be no story, and if he didn't know he had them he wouldn't have "an idea" of what to do. What is complete in the pictures is what occurs; how it comes about, as well as the pitch and the tempo, is the contribution of the text.

The design of the book enhances the pictures by giving them the appropriate breathing space; in serving them up singly and keeping the text separate (when, brief as it is, it might have been run underneath), it assures undivided attention to each and a full measure of curiosity about the next—at the same time reserving the occasional double-page spread as a dramatic alternative; and by using a cartoon typeface—all in capitals, with a wide-spaced, hand-lettered look—and setting the text in short lines, it harmonizes the words with the pictures in weight and dash, in openness and placement on the page.

Writers and especially coiners of titles who want to suggest uncommon fullness are apt to invoke Isaak Walton's 'compleat,' and in the same spirit it might be bestowed on *Andy and the Lion.* On the jacket is a dashing new drawing of Andy, his dog and the lion stepping out; on the endpapers—like the jacket, in the tawny yellow second color—a long view of the lion piled with children and pulling more on roller skates; and among the front matter, a sketch of Andy deep in a book, the lion serving as a footstool, another of the two stone lions of the New York Public Library, their tails entwined, a third of the lion and a kitten sharing a saucer of milk: a

203–208. *Andy and the Lion,* by James Daugherty. Viking, 1938. $7\frac{7}{8} \times 10\frac{1}{2}$.

bounty of illustration, relish, association.

It started Daugherty on writing, and his first full-length work, another *Daniel Boone* (1939), won the Newbery. More biographies and histories followed, all abundantly illustrated, but no more of his own picturebooks. In private, he continued to paint color abstractions. For his young public, *Andy and the Lion* stands alone.

ROBERT McCLOSKEY

Whitey is a cowboy, a Westerner, Hetty and Hank are mountaineers, but Lentil, the tow-headed harmonica player of Alto, Ohio, is the all-American small-town boy, not only natural but, in the popular imagination, typical—another Skeezix or Tom Sawyer. And like *Miki* and *Ola, Hansi* and *Little Leo,* the book goes by his name, a real story about a real boy not very different from Bob McCloskey, whose first book it was.

Lentil can't sing (at school he's not even trusted with a songbook), he can't pucker his lips to whistle, "but he did want to make music" so he saves up for a harmonica, practices in the tub, plays along the street, sets out to become an expert. Now, as they say when the plot thickens, the town of Alto has not only its leading citizen, Colonel Carter—donor of the library, the park, the Soldiers and Sailors Monument—but also its local grouch, Old Sneep, who knew the Colonel as a boy and, like an old hand at melodrama, confides to the audience: "He ain't a mite better'n you or me and he needs takin' down a peg or two."

The occasion for this aside is the Colonel's imminent return after two years away; and as the townspeople plan it, it will be a bang-up affair, with flags and banners and speeches and, foremost, the band playing as the Colonel steps from his private railroad car. The train is in, the crowd is holding its breath . . .

209. *Lentil,* by Robert McCloskey. Viking, 1940. 8⅞ x 11⅞.

People would smile and wave hello to Lentil as he walked down the street, because everyone in Alto liked Lentil's music; that is, everybody but Old Sneep. Old Sneep didn't like much of anything or anybody. He just sat on a park bench and whittled and grumbled.
JONES
BANK

He planted himself in the center of the road, raised one hand to stop the traffic, and then beckoned with the other, the way policemen do, for Mrs. Mallard to cross over.

210. *Make Way for Ducklings,* by Robert McCloskey. Viking, 1941. 8⅞ x 11⅞.

"Then there was a wet sound from above. SLURP! SHLURP!" There sits Old Sneep on top of the station, sucking a lemon, making the musicians' mouths pucker so they can't play a note, making the mayor wring his hands, making Colonel Carter, stepping forth, frown . . . until Lentil takes his trusty harmonica, strikes up "Comin' 'round the Mountain When She Comes," and saves the day. The Colonel sings, he takes a turn at playing, and when he promises the town a new hospital, "everybody was happy, even Old Sneep!" "So," concludes McCloskey, "you never can tell what will happen when you learn to play the harmonica."

Easy does it, thanks to the pictures—the drawings. More than most, *Lentil* is a book of drawings, a book of big drawings, double-page spreads every one, filling the pages or seeming to, which is also to say that it is less than most a book of separable illustrations (209). The library, the park, the monument are all there along Lentil's route, and the jaunty comic flavor is always there, whether in the look of the storekeeper who has taken out harmonica after harmonica or in the pose—arms out, chin up—of the well-fed Columbia who crowns the monument. McCloskey has his fun too with the dogs and cats who flee when Lentil opens his mouth to sing; with the townspeople who read of the Colonel's return with the rapt attention due a great event; with the musicians miserably puckered up, the mayor unable to get out a word of welcome, the bald, corpulent umbrella-carrying colonel.

In part this is cartooning of the old sort, kidding everybody, but Alto, Ohio—otherwise Hamilton, where McCloskey grew up—is also the recognizable small town we soar toward on the endpapers, and it too is omnipresent, sketched in with McCloskey's litho crayon. The quick sureness of the drawing and the fullness of the scene, together with the familiar figure of Lentil, give us the feeling that we have in a novel, of stepping into an ongoing life. It is a life that McCloskey has drawn into existence.

In *Make Way for Ducklings*, however, each opening is a story in itself. There is always something interesting going on, the drawing of the ducks, particularly, is lively and lifelike, the views of the Boston Public Garden, the State House et al are, cliché or not, breath-

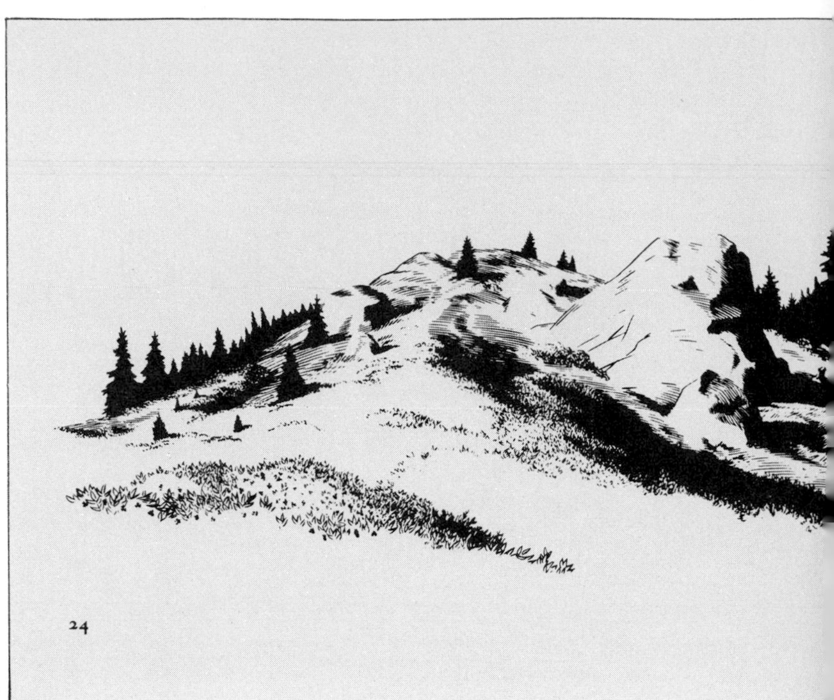

211

taking; but there is no basis for every drawing's being the same size or for everything's being so big, for a soft-focus panorama of the park and a realistically detailed depiction of the ducks and a caricature of a frantic policeman each to spread over two pages. There is also the question of whether the three manners are not themselves incompatible.

For children, however, interesting is better than perfect, and children love the scenic flights and the baby ducks and the tubby policeman equally and uncritically. Perhaps not quite equally: the long march of Mrs. Mallard and her brood from the Charles River, where for safety's sake the mallards build their nest, to the Public Garden with its swan boats and promise of peanuts—that perky single-file procession, startling passers-by on the sidewalk, holding up traffic at the intersections—is a high point in picturebook drama (210).

Blueberries for Sal is so much of a piece artistically that, contrariwise, one takes what happens for a natural occurrence. Little Sal and her mother are out picking blueberries on Blueberry Hill—her mother dropping them in a pail for canning, Sal dropping hers in her mouth—and Little Bear and his mother are come to eat blueberries, storing up food "for the long, cold winter," on the other side of the hill; and somehow, because Little Sal and Little Bear both sit down and fall behind, they get mixed up, Little Sal trailing behind Little Bear's mother, Little Bear following behind Little Sal's.

The two mothers are equally absorbed in thoughts of next winter, Little Sal and Little Bear are both scrambling, bright-eyed children, and the lay and look of the land are everywhere an active part of the story. The hill sweeps up and over, spiky evergreens stand dark against the sky, tree trunks measure the distance as Little Sal sets out, all-awkward, all-alert, to find her mother (211). The expanse is boundless but, crisply defined, the setting has character and she has personality (212).

Together, the immediately real and the immeasurable carry us to the climax, Little Bear's mother gulping at the sight of Little

Over on the other side of the hill, Little Sal ate all of the berries she could reach from where she was sitting, then she started out to find her mother.
25

211, 212. *Blueberries for Sal,* by Robert McCloskey. Viking, 1948. 10⅞ x 8½.

Sal ("She was old enough to be shy of people, even a very small person like Little Sal"), Little Sal's mother gasping at the sight of Little Bear ("She was old enough to be shy of bears, even very small bears like Little Bear"). Meanwhile the two children look up in trustful friendliness and the blueberries grow all around. An island in the sky is *Blueberries for Sal*—printed, appropriately, in deep blueberry blue.

One Morning in Maine (1952), its successor, is more in the nature of a home movie. Sal, a tooth gone, scoots around being endearing and the morning's occurrences, strung out, constitute the story; and *Time of Wonder* (1957), McCloskey's first in color (and, like *Make Way for Ducklings*, a Caldecott winner), is all rapt description and shimmery pictures. Neither expresses a child's feelings so much as an adult's feelings about children, the good life and, in *Time of Wonder,* the wonderfulness of words. A throng of children are playing off the tip of the island: "They dive off the rock and swim, then stretch out, dripping, in the sun, making salty young silhouettes on the old scars made by the glacier."

But *Lentil* led also to *Homer Price* (1943) —"Half-a-dozen episodes in the life of a small-town boy who mended radios, caught burglars with the aid of his pet skunk Aroma, made an incredible number of doughnuts in his uncle's automatic doughnut-maker, and engaged in other adventures that delight boys and girls,"[16] as one assessment put it. Here indeed was Mark Twain reconstituted—"solemn and devastating humor"[17] was another comment—and with the further doings of Homer, *Centerburg Tales* (1951), it demonstrated, if anything more was required, McCloskey's mastery of the comic anecdote. Of the little he illustrated of the work of others, Anne Malcolmson's American hero tales, *Yankee Doodle's Cousins,* and Keith Robertson's books about Henry Reed, a snappy suburban Homer, stand out for the same reason. Moreover, in *Make Way for Ducklings,* known wherever picturebooks are known, he can be said to have created a modern young counterpart of the old-time whopper or, embellishing a real incident, a new American legend.

OF THE AMERICAN INDIAN

Eskimos and Indians, Indians and Eskimos. They were close by and strange, linked to us geographically and historically but separate, 'natives,' doing for themselves, following their own ways, meeting danger. To everyday American children, theirs was a life in which a child too faced trials and might triumph or, helping, be of real aid. A life, moreover, that took concrete, visible form, perfect for picturing.

In the first flush of process reproduction, the Demings' *Indian Child Life* (Stokes, 1899) and *Red Folk and Wild Folk* (Stokes, 1902) appeared, comprising stories and, in the second instance, folk tales by Therese O. Deming and full-page color plates after paintings by her husband E. W. Deming, who specialized in Indian subjects. Though they were not really picturebooks (both in fact were compilations of two volumes), they were the closest thing to it, and nothing perhaps is more indicative of the lag in picturebook publication than that they held sway for more than thirty years. Equally indicative—of developments in and out of publishing—was the resurgence of the Demings in the early Thirties in a number of colorful inexpensive readers.

Then there were the Hollings. In the Twenties, when the cost of process soared and its reputation plummeted and the Eastern trade publishers used it sparingly, the P. F. Volland Company, a commercial printer based in Joliet, brought out series after series for the popular market ($.50 to $2.00) printed in full color—on sized paper—throughout. If it was not fastidious publishing (Raggedy Ann was the house star), neither is it entirely to be despised: Padraic Colum's *The Six Who Were Left in a Shoe*, illustrated by Dugald Stewart Walker, was a "Sunny Book" as well as *Peeps, Really Truly Sunshine Fairy*. So was the first of Holling C. Holling's Indian books, *Little Big Bye and Bye* (1926), while for two other series his wife Lucille Holling illustrated *Kimo, the Whistling Boy* (1928), a Hawaiian story (for which "the artist obtained her material by a visit to Hawaii") and he produced, in *Claws of the Thunderbird* (also 1928), a fuller book with some of the illustrative detail—the parts of an arrow, the process of fashioning them—that was to become a Holling trademark. In those years too they began the collaboration on research and illustration that eventuated in *The Book of Indians* (1935); but the Hollings' later work, from *The Book of Indians* forward, is a story in itself (p. 410).

Meanwhile the rapid advance in aviation was opening up the Arctic, and for the first time since Peary's explorations early in the century Eskimos began to turn up in force. Marjorie Flack's first book, *Taktuk, an Arctic Boy*, written with Helen Lomen, appeared in 1928, as did one of the initial Holling collaborations, *Choo-Me-Shoo the Eskimo*. In picturebooks proper, the Haders' *Tooky* (Longmans, 1931) tells of a seal taken away to the circus and the boy who cries with him when he departs; Armstrong Sperry's *One Day with Tuktu* (Winston, 1935) merges fiction and fact in the manner of its South Pacific predecessors; and, completing the spectrum, the photo-documentary *On Top of the World* (p. 108) depicts Eskimo life as a whole, as a way of life. (It had as its mate, not surprisingly, *Navajo Boy*.)

From the same source, the Artists and Writers Guild, came *Choochee*, the first book by Naomi Averill, illustrator—scenarist, decorator — of *A Child's Story of the World* (p. 95). Choochee—"small bright brown eyes" and "small flat nose," "two suits of reindeer skin" and "sealskin boots"—is an Eskimo boy in a universal adventurer's plight: setting out alone to catch sight of whales at sea, he gets lost and, lonely already, watches his mitten float away too (213). "If only Pup-pup had come with me," he cries. "He would know which way to go."

If Tooky the seal removed to the circus could as well be an uprooted elephant or bear, Pup-pup the pet seal who finds Choochee—by way of his floating mitten—could be any good dog Tray. In the one a new setting is grafted onto a perennial plot, in the other, the emphasis changing, the plot is fitted into the setting. Why not, after all, a faithful searching seal, who was to know the difference? Didn't it bring Choochee closer, create a bond between him and the children at home? Plainly not enough was known to write, no less to recognize, an Eskimo story, and the stories about Eskimo children that passed as such were—along with the doings of little African Ojo or little Arabian Ahmed—sympathetic projections of familiar situations for the most part, on the principle of brotherhood-under-the-skin.

But *Choochee* is authentic as to particulars and, in its modernism, peculiarly suited to presenting them. That there is an affinity between so-called primitive art and modern design has long been apparent. Thus, the fine lines of tatooing across the cheeks of Choochee's father, "one for each whale he had captured," and his hunting hat "trimmed with blue beads and sea lion bristles," objects of admiration to Choochee, are in a different way objects of admiration to the artist too (214); and her abbreviated style permits us to see them plain. Extending deeper, to a congruence, even a confluence of styles, are the fine flowing lines of the waves, akin to the delicate line-engraving that the Eskimos did on ivory (213). As far as children are concerned, however, the suppression of facial features is a deficiency, and overall the abstract rendering of the sea doesn't spell

213

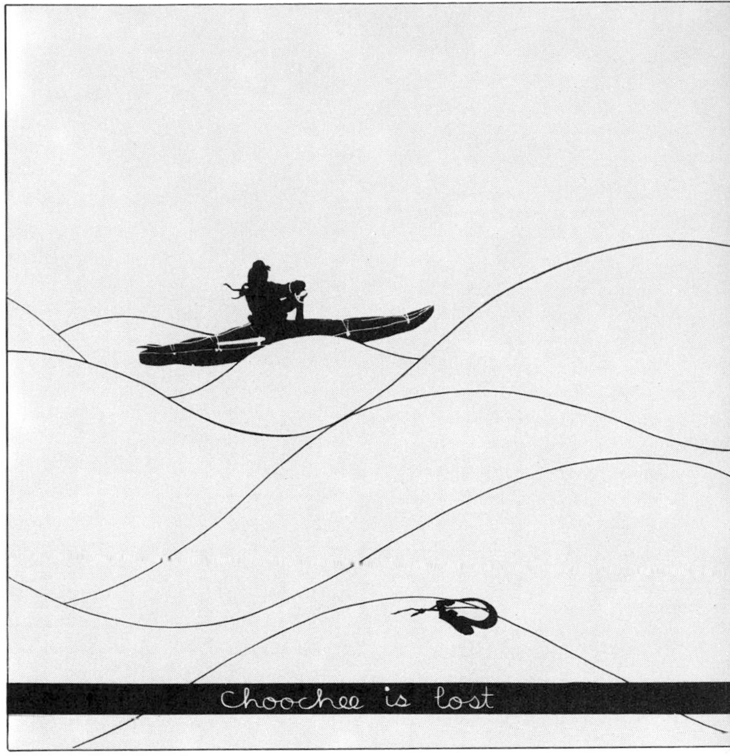
Choochee is lost

213, 214. *Choochee,* by Naomi Averill. Grosset, 1937. 9¼ x 9¼.

Choochee's father in his hunting hat

214

Each hunter singled out a running buffalo
and sent an arrow straight into its

215. *Whistling-Two-Teeth,* by Naomi Averill. Grosset, 1939. 9⅜ x 9¼.

danger; what is admirable, inventive design falls short as picturebook illustration.

Whistling-Two-Teeth doesn't entirely resolve the conflict—he himself is a pudgy would-do-well—but it comes closer. It is also more nearly natural as an Indian story. The problem is to find buffaloes for the tribe, and Whistling-Two-Teeth, following the Medicine Man's advice to stay out alone and take no food or drink, dreams the prophetic dream—forty-nine buffaloes with snow on their backs—that sends the tribe northward to a herd and a hunt. This is child-sized heroism with the heroics left to the hunters, vividly pictured (215). In solid flat color they sweep over the double-page spreads as they did over the Plains Indians' own skin paintings, parallel, in profile, filling the picture space, active from edge to edge, exuberantly two-dimensional. Among the tribes, the Plains Indians alone filled a flat surface with painted figures, they alone represented events; their art was as good as made for a Plains Indians picturebook and for an artist who, whatever the work, uses flat color not as if it were prescribed but proper, and for her, second nature.

Even as whites began to draw upon Indian art of the past, a new school of Indian painting arose, a school of easel painting in watercolor (both transparent and opaque) that, however, "takes its subject matter almost exclusively from Indian life and retains much of tribal tradition in concept and execution."[1] Its hub was Santa Fe, site of a cosmopolitan art colony and of one of the big Indian Service boarding schools. Practicing artists and an art-minded populace, modernists for the most part, encouraged Indian aspirants—in John Sloan's community, Mary Austin wrote in 1926, "there was bound to be a place for Awa Tsireh and Fred Kabotie";[2] and, equipped with copies of Sioux paintings and Pueblo designs, Dorothy Dunn began in 1933 the determined revival of Indian art at the Government Indian School.

Indian affairs were at a turning point. A 1932 issue of *Progressive Education* devoted to Indian education carried a report that "Today, instead of teaching that 'everything Indian is bad,' we try to help the children . . . understand something of the precious nature of the heritage they have as Indians";[3] and articles by the two foremost champions of the Indians, John Collier and Oliver La Farge, pointed the way to further progress. In 1933 Collier, hitherto the strongest critic of government policy and practice, took office in the new administration as Commissioner of Indian Affairs. The following year the Indian Reorganization Act was passed, writing into law a 'New Deal for Indians' of tribal self-rule and cultural rebirth; and 1936 saw the establishment of the Indian Arts and Crafts Board, soon to be headed by René d'Harnoncourt, and the appointment of Willard Beatty —one-time aide of Carleton Washburne at Winnetka, lately superintendent of the Bronxville (New York) schools, long the president of the Progressive Education Association—as Director of Indian Education.

Time, identifying Beatty as "the titular head of U.S. Progressive Education," captioned his picture "Pottery and blankets are in his curriculum,"[4] and sneered. If pottery and blankets and other native arts were indeed in the offing, so on the same basis were books, Indian books. Rose Brandt, in charge of elementary education, had for some years been collecting the writings of Indian children—a selection appears in the special issue of *Progressive Education*—and using them in a beginner's reader; now she was commissioned to compile and edit a series of these writings to be printed at the school shops for general distribution.

At about the same time "a field supervisor of the Indian Service's Education Division dropped a small hectographed booklet on the desk of the Director of Education. The booklet was hand bound in a red and white cloth, and on the cover bore the title 'Home Geography.' Inside was a simple, yet delightful account of life in Tesuque Pueblo as it is influenced by environmental factors. Its author was the day school teacher in the Tesuque Pueblo, Mrs. Ann Nolan Clark. She had prepared the booklet to help her children learn to read and to aid them in understanding and appreciating the life about them. It had been hectographed and then illustrated by the children themselves."[5]

The "Home Geography" ultimately became *In My Mother's House* (p. 166); more immediately, it alerted Beatty and the Division to Ann Nolan Clark's capability, and she was "freed of regular teaching and encouraged to write about the lives of Indian children and Indian people in various parts of the country."[6] The books were to be illustrated, moreover, by Indian artists—a Who's Who, just about, of Indian artists.

The first to appear, early in 1940, were *Little Boy with Three Names*, the adventures, and uncertainties, of Little Joe/Tse/u/ José la Cruz home at Taos Pueblo from the Santa Fe School for the summer, illustrated by Tonita Lujan, a Taos Indian student of Dorothy Dunn's; and two Navajo stories—illustrated by Navajo artists—*Little Herder in Spring*, one of four taking Little Herder and her flock through the seasons, and a fairy tale that's a caution (in either sense), *Who Wants To Be a Prairie Dog*. Sioux adventures and fairy tales were scheduled too, and stories of other pueblos—more than a dozen small books by 1943.

And they were to be bilingual; in the case of the Navajo books, to appear in the new written Navajo. Where the average white child was born into a world of books, the Education Division newsletter pointed out in 1940, the Navajo, the largest Indian tribe in the country and the one with the largest proportion of non-English speaking members (almost nine out of ten), had no system of recorded language.[7] The simple practical alphabet devised for the government by Oliver La Farge and a Smithsonian scholar, John P. Harrington, would permit the teaching of reading in Navajo, the introduction of writing in Navajo and, as its use spread, "the accurate transfer of new ideas in the native tongue."[8] To facilitate its use the Mergenthaler Linotype Company, with the help of La Farge and Harrington, developed a special type with additional characters, and this is how the bilingual readers were printed—"the first publication in Navajo of anything save the Bible, religious tracts, and scientific monographs."[9]

Looking at the books, one forgets all that.

The land
  around my mother's hogan
  is big.
It is still.
It has walls of red rocks.
And way, far off
  the sky comes down
  to touch the sands.

So begins *Little Herder in Autumn*, the start of Little Herder's story. It is incantatory, an Indian chant; it is direct, a child's talk; it speaks precisely and allusively, poet-fashion. Harry Behn, who lived among the Yavapais in Arizona as a child, recalls: "They were our instructors in good manners, in careful observation of natural signs, in being responsive to the spirit of everything that lived and grew on the earth."[10] Observant and responsive. Here, in part, is "Weaving":

The warp threads
  are the drum beats,
  strong sounds
  underneath.
The colored yarns
  are the singing words
  weaving through
  the drum beats.
When the blanket is finished
  it is like a finished song.
The warp
  and the drum beats,
  the colored wools
  and the singing words
  are forgotten.
Only the pattern
  of color
  and of sound
  is left.

In the drawings is the same precision and clarity, a sense of form, of steady, ordered activity (216). They represent, too, an individual solution of the problem of working in black and white, neither the flat stylized drawing of many Pueblo artists, nor the minutely shaded drawing of the White man as the Indian knew it. For Hoke Denetsosie, who was twenty at the time, the book was something entirely new.

"So not knowing the first thing about the fundamentals and principles of illustration the work really launched several months of extensive experimentation, the result of which was the black and white technique finally achieved. The use of simple black and white technique was employed because it is more readily understandable for a child.

"The nature of the series, being concerned with Navajo life, called for illustration genuine in every sense of the word. I had to observe and incorporate in pictures those characteristics which serve to distinguish the Navajo from other tribes. Further, the setting of the pictures had to change to express local changes as the family moved from place to place. The domestic animals raised by the Navajo had to be shown in a proper setting just as one sees them on the reservation. The sheep could not be shown grazing in a pasture, nor the horses in a stable, because such things are not Navajo.

"In other words the ideas were represented in an earnest attempt to express as far as possible the author's feelings, but without hindering the illustrator's freedom."

The last could of course be the credo of any illustrator, and the statement as a whole is as interesting for its general applicability as for what it tells about Denetsosie and the Little Herder books. It appears in the profile of the artist that was a regular feature of the Indian Life Readers—one of their many merits. That they did not, as it was hoped, "find a permanent place in the libraries of white schools throughout the country,"[11] or in public libraries, can only be wondered at. The great number written by Ann Nolan Clark particularly, and illustrated by Van Tsihnahjinnie, Oscar Howe, Velino Herrera, Andrew Stand-

SPINNING

My mother's spindle
is a slender stick
on a hardwood whorl.

Under her fingers
it spins like a dancer,
winding itself
in twisted yarn.

'ADIZGI

Shimá bibee'adizí tsin
ts'óósí 'át'é, dóó bąąh si'ánígíí
tsin ntł'izígíí bee 'ályaa.

Bíla' yee náyiiłtasgo
'alzhishí nahalingo náábał
náhoodiłgo
hahaasdiz nihileeh.

55

216. *Little Herder in Autumn,* text by Ann Nolan Clark, pictures by Hoke Denetsosie. Washington, U.S. Office of Indian Affairs, 1940. 9⅞ x 6⅞.

MY FATHER

My father is tall.
He is strong.
He is brave.
He hunts
and he rides
and he sings.

He coaxes the corn
and the squash plants
to grow
out of the sand-dry earth.

SHIZHÉ'É

Shizhé'é nineez.
'Ayóígo bidziil.
Dóó doo náldzid da.
Naalzheeh, dóó
łį́į́' nabighé,
dóó ni't'i'a'

Bizaadk'ehgo naadą́ą́'
dóó na'aghízí bit'ąą'
t'áá hóółtsaiigi
hadahiniséh.

15

ing Soldier, and others illustrated by Fred Kabotie and Gerald Nailor, are easy, lively reading and good-looking; and the Little Herder series is outstanding in any company. They continue to be issued by the Bureau of Indian Affairs—now only in paper, smaller in some cases, and not as well printed—and to be used in Indian schools. The *Little Boy with Three Names,* one for school, one for home, one for church, has, however, become history; as the current foreword explains, "Day schools have been built in each of the pueblos now, and the boys and girls attend [elementary] school . . . in their own home town, just as non-Indian children do."

Beginning in the mid-Thirties, some of the cultural ferment was reflected in commercial publishing. *Komoki of the Cliffs,* written by Isis L. Harrington, a former teacher in the

217. *I Am a Pueblo Indian Girl,* text by E-Yeh-Shure' (Louise Abeita), pictures by Allan Houser, Tony Martinez, Gerald Nailor and Quincy Tahoma. Morrow, 1939. 12 x 9.

Indian Service, and illustrated from drawings by Indian children, was brought out by Scribner in 1934 (and chosen by the AIGA as one of the fifty best-illustrated books of the year); *Ebird,* written and illustrated by a thirteen-year-old, Charles Cleek, came from Morrow in 1938; a reading text, *Moonlight and Rainbow,* illustrated by a Navajo, Narcisco Abeyta, was issued by McKnight & McKnight in 1939; and there may well be others. But what Indian art and the Indian spirit could make of a picturebook, given the best in design and color printing, was shown by *I Am a Pueblo Indian Girl* and *In My Mother's House.*

"The art of painting in our mode, but with an Indian technique, has spread from tribe to tribe," Oliver La Farge writes in the introduction to *I Am a Pueblo Indian Girl,* and lyric poems, made spontaneously, constitute "a living literature" handed down from past to present. "Now the new and the ancient art have been brought together, and not by a white man, but by my friend, E-Yeh-Shure's father. . . . When his daughter turned her natural gift as a poet to work in English, he saw its promise, and had the inspiration to bring together Indian artists, Navajo, Apache, Pueblo, in a cooperative endeavor to make a truly Indian book."

There are eleven subjects—The Earth, My Country, My Home, The Corn Plant, Making Bread, and the like—and for each, a picture. Only two are put into verse, the rest being descriptive passages—a dossier on the corn plant, for instance. It is compact and informative but not so compact as the picture; or, to put it differently, the picture stands still while the text elaborates and expands. But the static arrangement invites us to look upon the pictures as paintings, each for itself, and the one difficulty was deciding which to reproduce (217).

Oddly, the artists' names do not appear in the book but we know from their signatures that Allan Houser and Gerald Nailor are responsible for the great majority. Houser, an Apache, the great-grandson of Geronimo, and Nailor, a Navajo, both studied at the Santa Fe School and at the time that the pictures for the book were done they shared a studio in Santa Fe. Their work is very similar, done in the flat Pueblo watercolor style; they are both sure draftsmen with a pronounced sense of design, and their work has at once great calm and a zest for life. What is in fact surprising is that two such strong artists should be working so much alike—surprising, that is, to anyone accustomed to individuality as a criterion of artistic stature.

I Am a Pueblo Indian Girl was beautifully —and expensively—printed, the cost partly underwritten by a special edition of five hundred copies sponsored by the National Gallery of the American Indian, despite its name a private group. But it is not solely a museum piece. "When we are through making our bread and the oven cools our dog uses the oven for his house—when grandmother isn't looking." Though the pictures and the text don't mesh, they are one at heart.

The accomplishment of *In My Mother's House*, on the other hand, is its *being* as a book, the integration of pictures and text in a spacious articulated design—a consonant design. The short lines called for two columns of text, ordinarily taboo in picturebooks; the pictures are done in several styles, sometimes modeled, in full perspective, sometimes with a suggestion of shading, sometimes absolutely flat, either as motifs or as figures. In the layout each element is distinct and related— 'Our Fathers make the ditches' that help the water to feed the plants, that help the rain to fill the pots (218). Even if one does not 'read' the traditional designs, they have meaning; in them a way of thinking is made visible.

Elsewhere the flat roofs of the pueblo stretch across the two pages in bare outline with here and there, coming and going, a single small figure:

> My Mother's house,
> It does not stand alone.
> Its sister houses are around it;
> Its sister houses are close to it.
>
> Like holding hands,
> The houses stand close together
> Around the plaza.
>
> Houses are the stay-in places,
> But the plaza
> Is the live-in place
> For all the people.

Herrera habitually worked in several styles, it was natural for him to vary his treatment, and while there is, to the critical eye, a certain discord—especially when the treatment varies within a single composition—one has to recognize the intent, demarcation. Demarcation in the parts, and in the whole, harmony. Here is a book composed, as well, of twenty-nine subjects—there is even a table of contents—expressed in prose poems that follow no set pattern, have no standard length, no consistent four-line or six-line stanza; where the ideas dictate the form and extent, and the breaks come irregularly, naturally, "the way thoughts come."[12] In the finished book, correspondingly, no two openings are alike—a stimulus, as it happens, to the child who might otherwise be lulled into inattention; but Mrs. Clark's quiet rhythms have their counterpart too, in the delicate adjustment of typographic constants, and one senses the volume first and last as a whole.

Velino Herrera was, with Awa Tsireh and Fred Kabotie, the most widely recognized of the Indian artists (and also self-taught, a product of the pre-New Deal period); and it was fitting that he should illustrate the most celebrated of Indian picturebooks. But while *In My Mother's House* established Ann

Nolan Clark as a writer for children, and some of her subsequent books—like *Blue Canyon Horse* and *The Desert People*, both illustrated by Allan Houser—are similar in nature, neither it nor the great 1940 exhibition of Indian art organized by René d'Harnoncourt had the effect of establishing a place for the Indian artist, or Indian art, in the contemporary scene or, specifically, in children's books. Houser did some further illustrating, Denetsosie illustrated Jonreed Lauritzen's *The Ordeal of the Young Hunter*, helping to make it "the best Indian book of the year, or of several years,"[13] and that was about it; there were no more picturebooks. Not until one comes, quite recently, to such Indian-inspired work as Tom Bahti's illustrations for *Before You Came This Way* (Dutton, 1969) and *When Clay Sings* (Scribner, 1972).

What did bear seed was the mode of expression that Mrs. Clark learned from the Indians, adults and children, and not only a mode of expression but a way of feeling. Little Herder looking upon the land around her mother's hogan, her Pueblo counterpart saying of "Home," "This is my Mother's house . . . I live in it," is saying this is mine and I am me, it is part of me and I am part of it: for a child, any child, a wonderful thing. To bolster them, teachers of Indian children encouraged them to express what was theirs, and Mrs. Clark put what was theirs into words that were, in effect, their own; but beyond the value of her work in teaching Indian children or, in the case of *In My Mother's House*, in teaching white children about Indians, was its value as an example of children speaking in their own voice, naturally, about what was closest to them.

218. *In My Mother's House*, text by Ann Nolan Clark, pictures by Velino Herrera. Viking, 1941. 8½ x 10½.

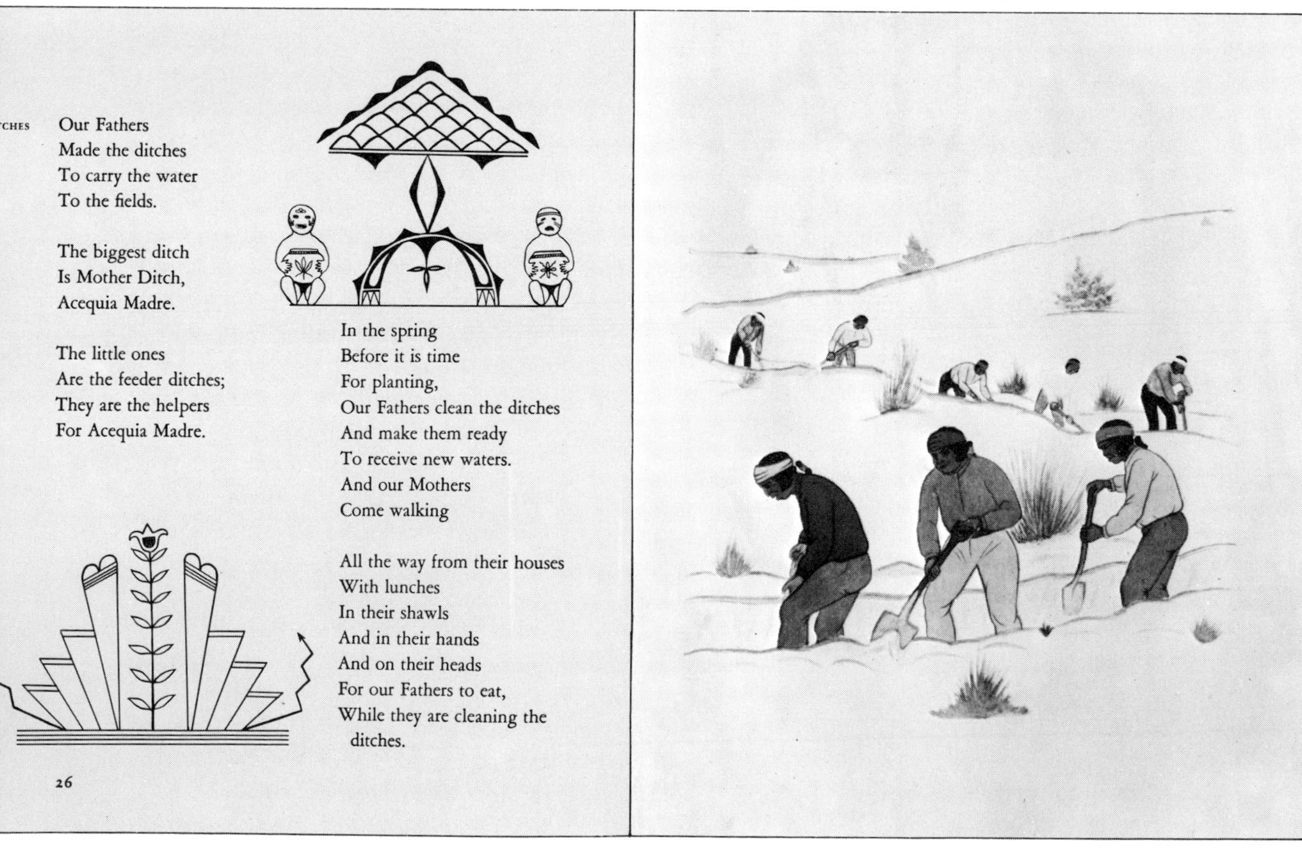

DITCHES
Our Fathers
Made the ditches
To carry the water
To the fields.

The biggest ditch
Is Mother Ditch,
Acequia Madre.

The little ones
Are the feeder ditches;
They are the helpers
For Acequia Madre.

In the spring
Before it is time
For planting,
Our Fathers clean the ditches
And make them ready
To receive new waters.
And our Mothers
Come walking

All the way from their houses
With lunches
In their shawls
And in their hands
And on their heads
For our Fathers to eat,
While they are cleaning the
ditches.

26

TWO MASTERS, MARIE HALL ETS AND WILLIAM PÈNE DU BOIS

By the mid-Thirties, many artists were doing an occasional picturebook, either writing their own texts or, more rarely, illustrating someone else's story, and a few individuals with a flair for the form and some ability to draw were turning out others. The one group were illustrators attracted to a new field, the other part-time practitioners; in neither case had picturebooks become something that one undertook as a career, a creative expression, a fulfillment of purpose—a métier.

With Marie Hall Ets and William Pène du Bois picturebooks were an occupation and a preoccupation. Creating their own material, working in a style that grew from it—however it might differ from book to book in the case of Ets or evolve with time in the case of Pène du Bois—and writing well enough to have done only that, both produced a succession of books that, over the years, bear the individual stamp of their creators' talent and of their approach to children.

MARIE HALL ETS

Marie Ets was trained as an artist and schooled as a social worker; her work with children and—after further study in child psychology—her interest in their response to drawings led to the making of her first book.

Mister Penny is, in effect, Doctor Dolittle as a poor old man. His jacket closed with a giant safety pin, his home "a tumbledown shed on a stony field by a path to the village of Wuddle," he is the willing victim of kindness to animals—to an old horse, Limpy, who feigns injury because a bandaged foreleg makes him feel like a race horse; Mooloo, a cow too lazy to chew her cud; Splop, an inquisitive goat; a lamb and a pig and a fat hen and, most trouble of all, Doody the cocky rooster.

When Mister Penny is off earning money to feed them, they raid the cranky neighbor's garden (219); and bring down upon Mister Penny the demand that in recompense he plow and weed and mow for the neighbor—stay home and lose his job—or, alternatively, give over the animals: "I suppose the hog would do for bacon, and the lamb for stew." Limpy overhears, and in the dark of the night—a solid black picture—the animals bestir themselves and do the work. Work, they discover, has its rewards, and when last seen Mister Penny and his ménage have the sprucest, most comfortable home in Wuddle as well as the happiest.

Droll, loose-limbed, a little ragged at the edges, the illustrations set the tone. As pictures they have the merit—and the appeal to children—of being at once filled to the frame, uncluttered and distinct. The forceful blend of positive and negative images is achieved by a batik process whereby, as Marie Ets describes it, the original drawing is transferred to linen paper and the white parts are painted out with gum arabic. "When the gum has hardened, but before it begins to crack, I brush the whole drawing with ink." Then,

219. *Mister Penny*, by Marie Hall Ets. Viking, 1935. 10½ x 8.

"When the ink has dried—usually overnight—the solid black drawing goes under a shower of warm water," washing away the gum arabic and, "as if by magic," revealing the picture.[1] It is a method that admits of surprises and unexpected effects, and gives to the results a happy spontaneity; one whereby, furthermore, forms stand out against a contrasting ground with few details and almost no shading—except in the night scenes which, almost totally in black, achieve a striking chiaroscuro.

Other stories about Mister Penny appeared after a long interval, *Mister Penny's Race Horse*—who but Limpy?—in 1956 and *Mister Penny's Circus* in 1961, while the separate *Mr. T. W. Anthony Woo* (1951, all Viking) is very much in the same spirit. But far from exploiting the success of *Mister Penny*, Marie Ets came forth in 1939 with an entirely different kind of book, the sensitive and realistic—thoroughly real—*Story of a Baby*.

The previous year *Life* magazine had published photographs of the birth of a baby. Anticipating some objections from subscribers, the editors alerted them in advance; parents who didn't want their children to see the pictures could remove them (and mine did). Nonetheless that particular issue was banned in parts of the United States and in all of Canada, and newsdealers excised the offending section in other places.

In this climate of opinion, Marie Ets's description and drawings of embryo and fetus from fertilization of the egg to birth of the baby appeared and, so delicate was the handling, met no opposition. It is an instructive and, equally, a dramatic book. Large originally, then small, now large again, it starts with a speck in a shadowed uterus—"a house with no windows or doors—a house smaller than a grain of salt from the shaker, or a grain of sand from the beach. But this was a house that could grow, and a house that was going to have roots."

In a uniform frame, the house grows—Ets retains the image without forgoing the scientific terms—and the baby-to-be grows faster, so fast that at three months he has to fold his legs beneath him, "like a Buddha in a shrine" (220); at six months "curl up like a monkey when it sleeps, and move here and there to

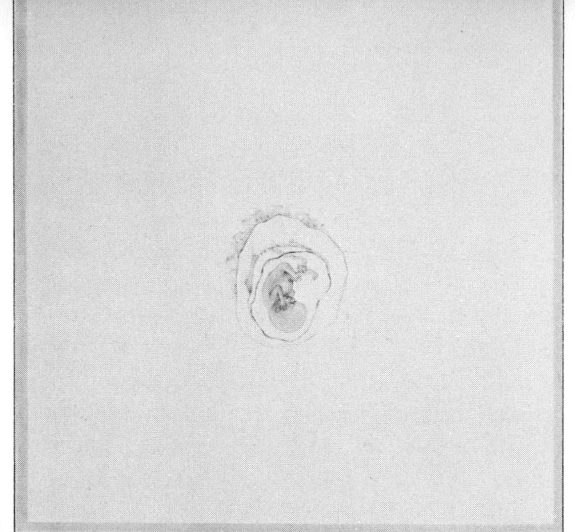

220

220-223. *The Story of a Baby*, by Marie Hall Ets. Viking, 1939. 9 x 12.

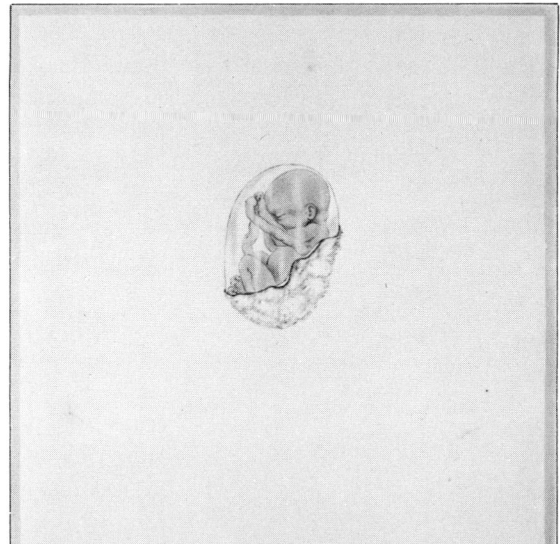

221

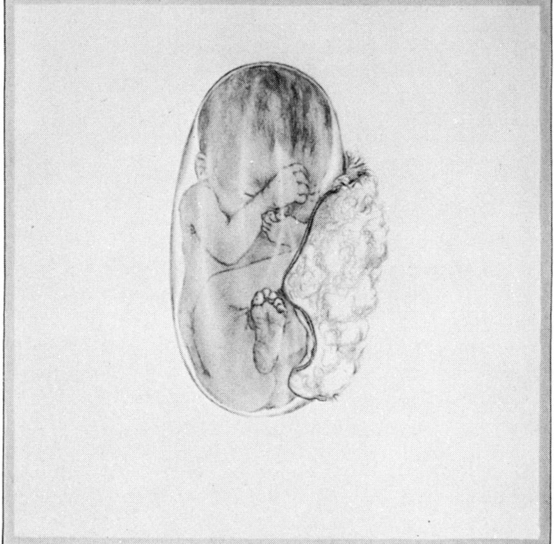

222

find room for his head" (221). Hair appears on his body, "as if he were going to have down like a baby bird or beast. But he was not going to be a baby bird or beast, and the hair would stop growing and fall off . . . before he was ready to be born." (Earlier, parallel pictures suggest the first stages of phylogenetic recapitulation.) "And the eighth month passed. And the ninth," until "he was so squeezed that he scarcely could move" (222).

With the tenth month, "the time had come, and the walls in the mother started pushing. . . . It was the middle of the night. But she told the baby's father it was time for him to take her to the hospital near by, where everything was waiting for a baby to be born." And at last "there he was—a baby newborn—a baby with all of his fingers and all of his toes, with two ears, and two eyes, and a mouth, and a nose. The nurse quickly covered him with warm towels—all but his face—for he was wet and must not get cold. Then she looked at the clock, for most people want to know what time their baby came. But the

223

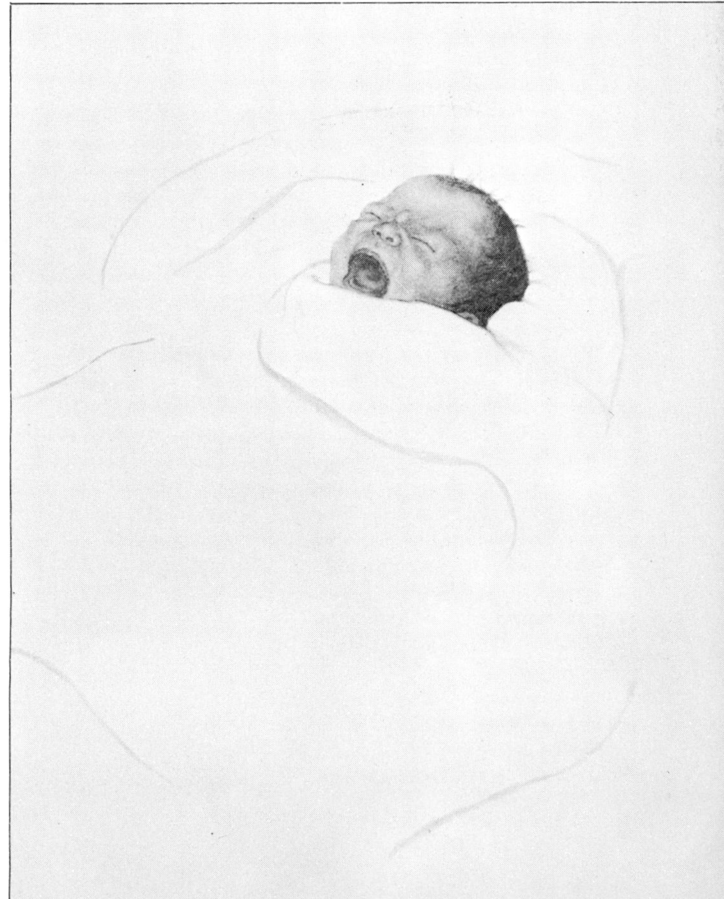

doctor was watching the baby. It was time for him to breathe. Why didn't he breathe?

"We can't wait for him much longer, thought the doctor. We must try to *make* him breathe. And he slapped the newborn baby on the bottoms of his feet" (223).

The baby's first cry is not the end of the book; there is much about his care those early weeks that is, like the rest, informative and reassuring. The book was conceived for young children and it is addressed to them; there is firmness in its delicacy and, in both pictures and text, the sweet quick beauty of confrontation with new life.

What came next, in 1944, was *In the Forest*, timeless, placeless, a child's own dream of dominion as if he were speaking it:

> I had a new horn and a paper hat
> And I went for a walk in the forest.

A "big wild lion," hearing the horn, wakes up, combs his hair, and comes too; two elephant babies stop their splashing and put on sweaters and shoes, two big brown bears bring their peanuts and jam; and one by one or two by two, the animals forsake ponds and trees and fall in line . . . "When I went for a walk in the forest" (224). He is the piper, the host at the party; they are themselves and children, animal children. The lion is unmistakably king of the beasts, he wears his crown; but the rabbit too shy to speak leads the parade with the little boy.

The dream ends in a game of hide-and-seek; the little boy, eyes closed, is *It*, the animals vanish, and his father appears in their stead. "*He* was hunting for *me*." Riding piggy-back, he is borne homeward, dependent again and secure; he'll hunt for his animals another day "when I come for a walk in the forest." (Later, in 1953, there was to be *Another Day*.)

The simple rhythmic telling with its refrain has the ring of a child's chanting, the pattern

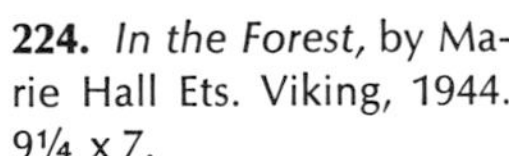

224. *In the Forest,* by Marie Hall Ets. Viking, 1944. 9¼ x 7.

I blew my horn. The lion roared. The elephants trumpeted through their trunks.
The big bears growled. The kangaroos drummed. The stork clapped his bill.

and cumulation represent a folktale-type ordering of what children practice naturally, with or without logic. The speech is to-the-point, sensory, first-hand, sharing with *In My Mother's House* the first-person mode of address but less reflective, more immediate—a cultural difference, perhaps. It is not, however, the flat assertion that attention to children's utterances and, more particularly, the wish to make the story *theirs*, were just then bringing into use; not a communication—"I take Daddy's hand and we go" (*Saturday Walk*, 1941)—but a reverie, self-communion. (And often discomfiting to adults reading aloud, who take refuge in declamation.)

The pictures, for their part, approximate a mime drama, with movement and character conveyed chiefly by the silhouetted figures. Yet there is a visual richness in the semblance of texture and tone achieved by the use of a grainy paper that corresponds to the richness of the story and sets the book apart from a surface narrative like *Mister Penny*. "Complete integrity of conception and execution" was Marcia Brown's summation.[2]

During the furor over comic books, Ets produced, in *Oley the Sea Monster* (Viking, 1947), one of the few books in strip form to stand up independently, and the only one in true strip form—several frames to a page—that has endured. A baby seal had turned up on the Chicago waterfront, to the consternation of the populace, and Ets mocks the wholesale panic (and the benefit to businessmen of a new tourist attraction) at the same time that she engages our sympathy with poor friendly, friendless Oley.

The book that explodes, though, demolishing conventional virtue and flouting safety first, is *Little Old Automobile* (225). He's a willful demon on wheels (otherwise an average four-year-old) as he barrels down the country road, throwing over animals and people, scorning pleas that he stop, chanting,

The monkeys shouted and clapped their hands. But the rabbit made no noise at all—when I went for a walk in the forest.

"I don't want to! I don't want to AND I WON'T!" His comeuppance is equally drastic: totally demolished when he challenges an oncoming train, his parts are divided among his victims, human and animal, the front seat falling to the farmer, odd parts to the rabbits "for their hide-and-seek" (226). A fine bit of bluster it is, drawn on handkerchief linen for a right, raggedy look; and a reminder of what we've always known from "The Gingerbread Boy," that nothing is as satisfying as a complete catharsis.

Play with Me is as serene and tentative as *Little Old Automobile* is violent and definite. Unlike *In the Forest*, its solitary child finds the animals she encounters to be diffident, wary, and it is not until she sits quietly, not

225, 226. *Little Old Automobile,* by Marie Hall Ets. Viking, 1948. 8⅜ x 10½.

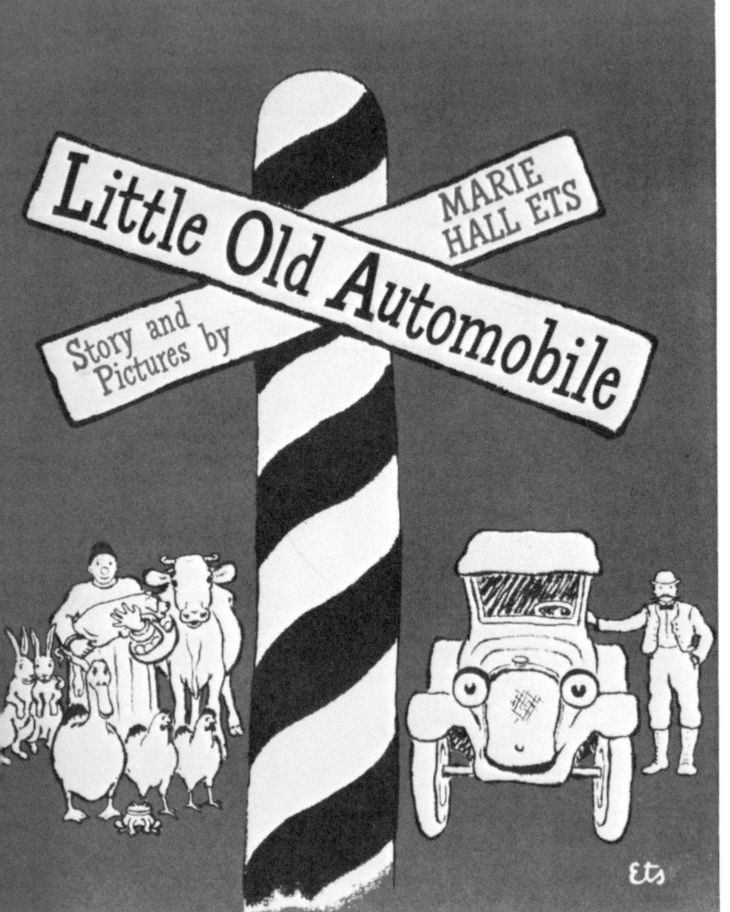

225

226

trying to touch them or catch them, just watching "a bug making trails in the water," waiting "without making a sound," that they return and gather round her (227). She tells it in her own words but there is this difference too, that it is an experience she relates, a could-be-true revelation, and what makes it a child's is her way of seeing—the bug "making trails," the snake "sneaking . . . zigzagging and sliding," or the need to be still "So they wouldn't get scared and run away." One could cast it into the third person, substitute 'she' for the occasional 'I,' with little loss of feeling; but then one would have to give her a name or ostentatiously *not* name her, use the awkward and remote 'the little girl.' If an experience is to be universal, better that it not be Susan's or Mark's; and if it's to be anybody's, better that it be somebody's. So we have, handy, the first person; but it is the child's perception of the experience that validates it, not the choice of pronoun.

Tending to reinforce the universality is the sketchy, scattered drawing. The child is neither an individual nor a type, she embodies eager, clumsy, unpretty little-girlness. It was Marie Ets's first book in color—in nominal color, that is, for in her earlier books she achieves what has been called "that curious richness of color which seems possible only in black and white."[3] Nor is this color for the sake of being colorful, of giving form to objects or atmosphere to the scene. The dominant color, in fact, is once again white, the white of the paper, now chastened by the faun background as earlier, in *Mister Penny*, it was emboldened by the black. And because the sun and its rays are white too, the little girl's golden cap of hair comes to be the cynosure, the true sun.

The whole outdoors and no green. How paradoxical, then, that Marie Ets won the Caldecott for her one book done in local color, the Mexican story *Nine Days to Christmas* (written with Aurora Labastida, Viking, 1959). But the use is such that the artist's term 'local color,' meaning correspondence with objects, becomes also the writer's term, projection of the setting; and that, specifically, is what the color is for.

Corollary to the picture stories is *Beasts and Nonsense*, a collection of rhymes with pictures —or pictures with rhymes—that is equally about the peccadilloes of people and the peculiarities of animals, and often about both (228). Which comes off better (or worse) is a moot question; what is certain is that, man and beast, we're all in this together —in a word, absurd. It's Belloc without the uppishness, Thurber devoid of gloom— with a special dispensation for children, who also suffer indignities at the hands of adults (229).

227. *Play with Me*, by Marie Hall Ets. Viking, 1955. 7½ x 10.

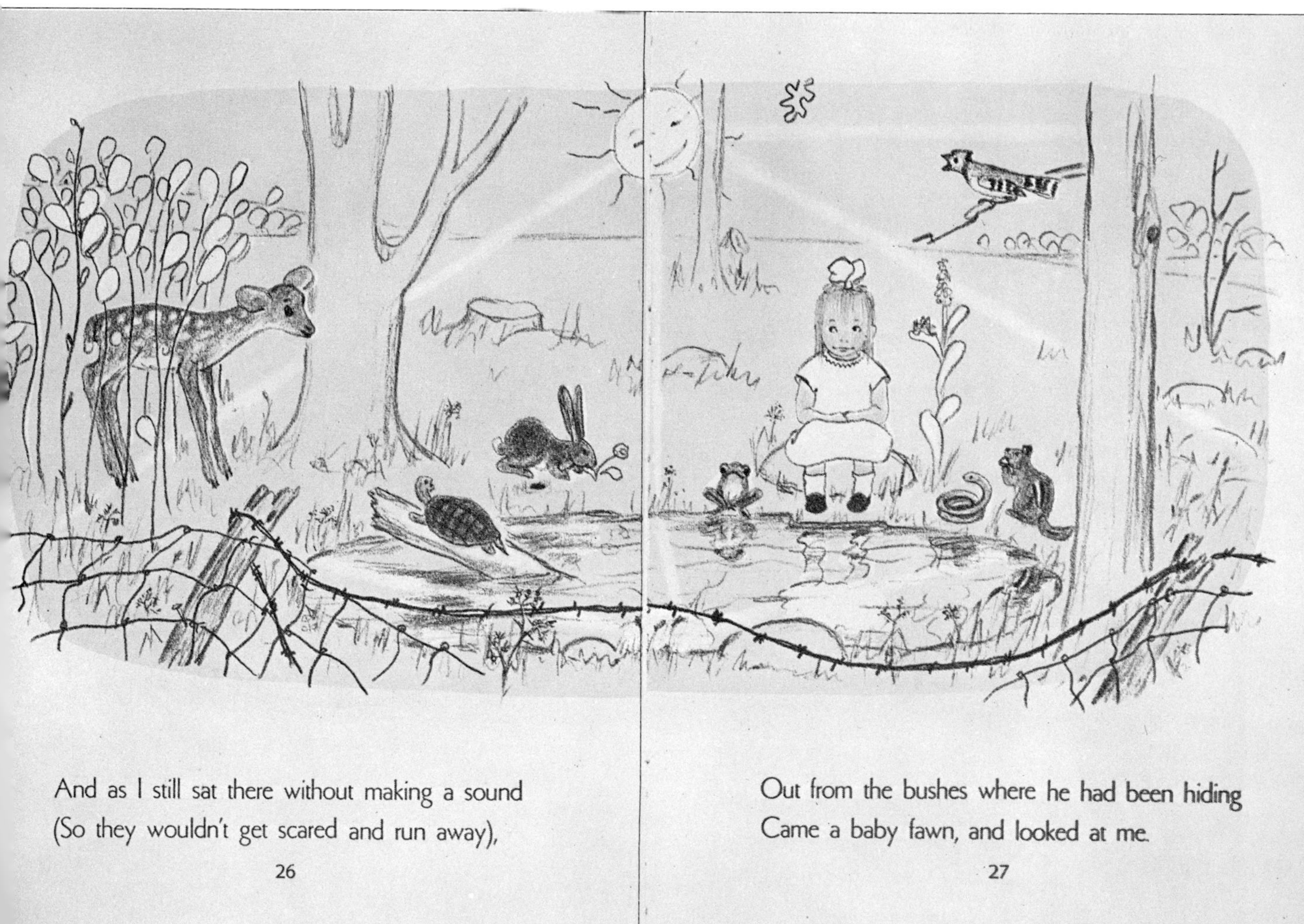
And as I still sat there without making a sound
(So they wouldn't get scared and run away),

26

Out from the bushes where he had been hiding
Came a baby fawn, and looked at me.

27

MISS WINNIFRED OZON

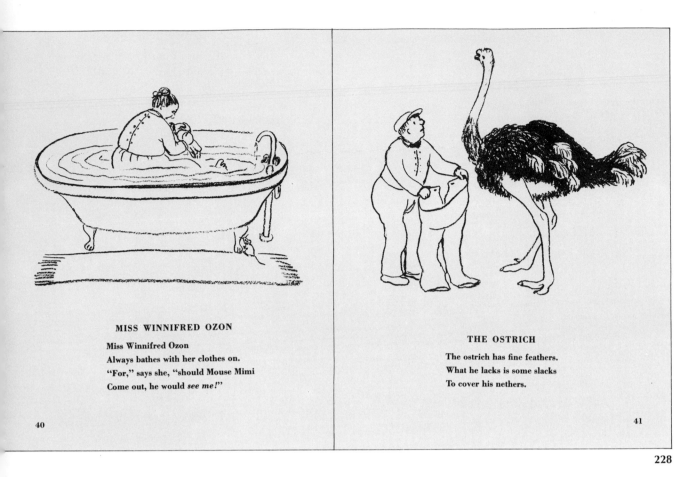

Miss Winnifred Ozon
Always bathes with her clothes on.
"For," says she, "should Mouse Mimi
Come out, he would *see me!*"

40

THE OSTRICH

The ostrich has fine feathers.
What he lacks is some slacks
To cover his nethers.

41

228

In one way or another the commonality of man and animal, raised to communion in *In the Forest* and *Play with Me*, runs through the best of Marie Ets's books without exception; it appears as faithfulness among friends in *Mister Penny* and as jointly bearing the blows, jointly sharing the spoils in *Little Old Automobile*. Visually, too, all things are one: a sort of stylization that holds down details and dispenses with descriptive color, concentrating on contour, on expressive form, has the effect of conveying life as a continuum and, it might be added, making of the real and the unreal a single realm.

229

228, 229. *Beasts and Nonsense,* by Marie Hall Ets. Viking, 1952. 7 x 9⅛.

WILLIAM PÈNE DU BOIS

William Pène du Bois is the boy fascinated with the circus, mechanical conveyances and islands who, grown up, wrote and illustrated books for the child he had been. About the circus and mechanical conveyances and islands, and a huge dog and a gentle cow—two gentle cows—and a shrewd black boy; and good food and uniforms and medals; and marvels of detection. A world of wonders.

He was twenty, 'discovered' by both Eunice Blake and May Massee, when his first three books appeared, and he had a story, "The Fish-Net Mystery," germ of a fourth, in *Story Parade*. *Elisabeth the Cow Ghost*, *Giant Otto*, *Otto at Sea*, *The Three Policemen*: had he stopped there, the four in their original forms would do him honor.

In its initial small square shape, *Elisabeth the Cow Ghost* is butter and milk and plaintive mischief—a neat tight little book and, like Nicholson's two, pure storytelling. Elisabeth lives in a town in Switzerland and belongs to a man named Paul, and when she is a cream-colored calf everyone who sees her says, "What a gentle calf! What dreamy eyes!" And when she grows older, "Such a gentle cow . . ."; older still, aged, "What a gentle old cow . . . ."

> UNTIL
>
> Elisabeth grew tired of being called so gentle and became quite angry.
>
> After a while she grew awfully old and was ready to die but just before she died, she heard Paul say:
>
> "Isn't it a shame? She is such a gentle cow with such dreamy eyes." This made Elisabeth so mad that she decided to come back in the form of a ghost . . . to show everybody how fierce she really was.

On her first try, her gentle look shows her to be "the ghost of poor Elisabeth, the most gentle cow that ever lived." On her second, head hooded, her cream-colored body gives her away (230); on her next, Paul recognizes her, wrapped in sheets, by her dreamy eyes. Finally, at Paul's birthday party, an extraordinary-looking ghost appears, "all covered with sheets, with a hood over its eyes and a spear on its tail," and it snorts: "I am the ghost of a cow famous for fierceness and cruelty. I shall haunt you and scare you all every moment of your lives." Scare them it does, and thereafter, satisfied, Elisabeth apologizes; she'll "never do it again, never never again."

How did he think them up, people asked Pène du Bois, and he'd have an answer; but the originality of *Elisabeth the Cow Ghost* lies less in its imaginativeness—construed as fancy—than its fresh clear vision. Elisabeth, "ready to die," anticipates her death and plots her revenge; Paul, once she has died, plans a party "to forget Elisabeth who made him feel so sad"; and at the last, while Paul waves, Elisabeth floats out the window, "really a very gentle cow with very dreamy eyes." It is a sweet-spirited book, embracing love and death with equanimity.

We are illustrating it in color, little color as there is, because Elisabeth's cream-colored self is so much a part of the story, as cow and even more as cow ghost; and because, in design terms, it represents an especially adroit use of a second color. Chiefly, a second color, discernible in black and white as a different tone, was used to pick up the picture—articulate form, suggest contour, supply contrast (31, 101, 203): to provide some color at low cost throughout. In such cases it is more or less neutral, part of the aesthetic scheme, though if it's the color of something, a local or characteristic color (the blue sky and water in *The Little Sail Boat*, the tawny hue of *Andy and the Lion*), it may add verisimilitude also. But for the second color to function actively along with the drawing, to be by its very presence or absence a clue to the state of affairs, is rare—as rare as it is simple. In the sprightly *Travels of Ching* (Scott, 1943), for instance, Robert Bright gives the little Chinese doll a red robe that, through the proverbial thick and thin, stands out against the black and white pages: in a ricksha, a U.S. mail pouch, falling from a skyscraper, sunk in snow, Ching is where red is. Just so, Elisabeth is where yellow is, and where it isn't—a terrible ghost.

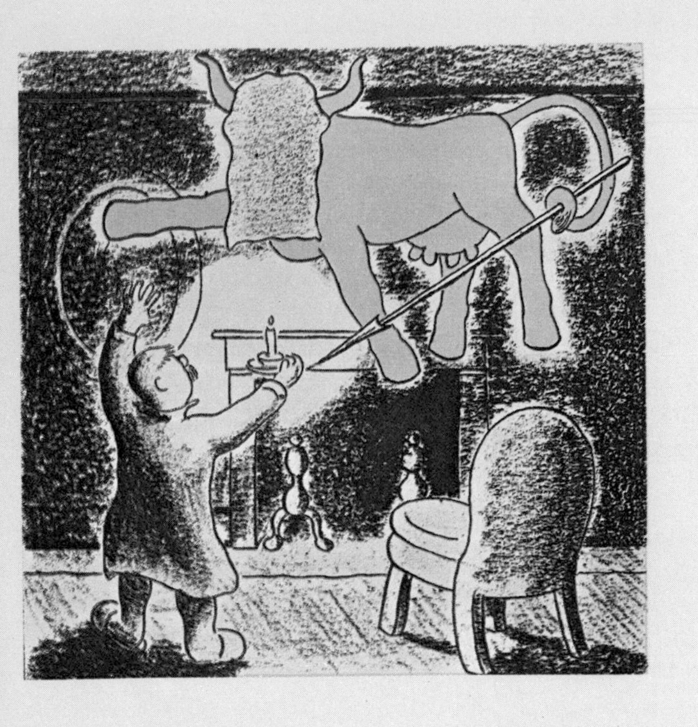

230. *Elisabeth the Cow Ghost,* by William Pène du Bois. Nelson, 1936. 5⅞ x 5⅞.

Enter the giant otterhound Otto, in two small square books (the match of *Elisabeth*) in a gay striped French-holiday box (231). In the first, *Giant Otto,* his master Duke decides that Otto is too big for a little French town and they embark for Africa—by tugboat and behind, a barge for Otto—where they whirl 852 attacking Arabs (and their eight camels) into a helpless heap, Sambo-and-tiger fashion, and collect Otto's first medal. The second, *Otto at Sea,* takes Otto and Duke on a good will trip to America at the behest of the President of France. Aboard a steamer whose captain carries along his garden table, whose first mate is deaf and poor-sighted (the captain 'signs' orders in big gloves), whose other passengers are two Tyrolean mountain-climbing champions. All of which serves as a sideshow as Otto gets on with the business of keeping the ship steady in a storm and, when it capsizes, carrying—and towing—the survivors to New York where he gets a ticker tape welcome and, naturally, another medal.

Obviously, *Otto at Sea* is a more garnished affair than *Giant Otto* but both are simple cheerful books about a big lovable dog who has only to be himself. When Pène du Bois redid them twenty and more years later, the difference in manner, apparent at a glance (236), is the difference between a custard and a soufflé. But more of that later.

Detective stories, that was the next thing, long stories with, still, lots and lots of pictures.

If one had to select a single Pène du Bois book for a Presidential library or a time capsule, the one that is Pène du Bois *complet et parfait,* it would be *The Three Policemen*—set on an obscure island, Farbe (n. lat. 58°, w. long. 16°); featuring three buffoons, officers Peter, Paul and Joseph, and a wizard at devising and detecting, young black Bottsford; and from the start—the officers rise and dress to recorded bells—propelled by a host of mechanical devices.

To catch the sea serpent making off with the Farbons' nets, Peter, Paul and Joseph, at Bottsford's instigation, encase themselves in oxygen-supplied fish suits, only to be hauled in by their better, a boat gotten up as a sea monster. But it is all a masquerade; in Pène du Bois's books, as his sister remarked, "There are no villains."[4] (Not then.) Who is the master of the sea monster but the returning mayor, testing the three policemen; and what is it to be but a floating hotel, uniquely fitted, for the whole of Farbe (232). And, yes, there are medals for Peter, Paul and Joseph, and for young Bottsford, henceforward Emperor Bottsford the First, a dazzling ermine-caped epauletted uniform.

The Great Geppy, a circus detective story, is also in its way an island story, says Pène du Bois, because "circuses are surely little self-contained governments which can be considered islands."[5] It has the most remarkable of his heroes, without doubt, in the umbrella-striped horse Geppy who fills the Bott Circus's order for a detective who can get into all the acts—walk a tightrope, train lions, be shot from a cannon—and besides, be a freak.

"Are you sure you want to become a freak?" the Lion Man asks Geppy when he reports for work at the Freak House. "What a foolish question," Geppy counters. "I am a freak already." But Captain Bolivar, the freak manager, is an artist: "no freak is really a worthwhile freak unless he is awfully hard to explain." So the Lion Man now sports a cow's tail and Geppy, "just a striped horse," becomes a striped sea-horse, "the largest sea-horse in captivity"—and has to endure aspersions on his stripes: "He's a sea-horse all right . . . but those stripes are obviously fake." (The world is a circus, is it not?)

Matching the sharp play of ideas, and the tenderness underneath, is the fine pen technique, a shift in Pène du Bois's style toward the meticulous outlines and infinite gradations of his mature work (233).

The Flying Locomotive (Viking, 1941), a longish small story in the shape of a long small

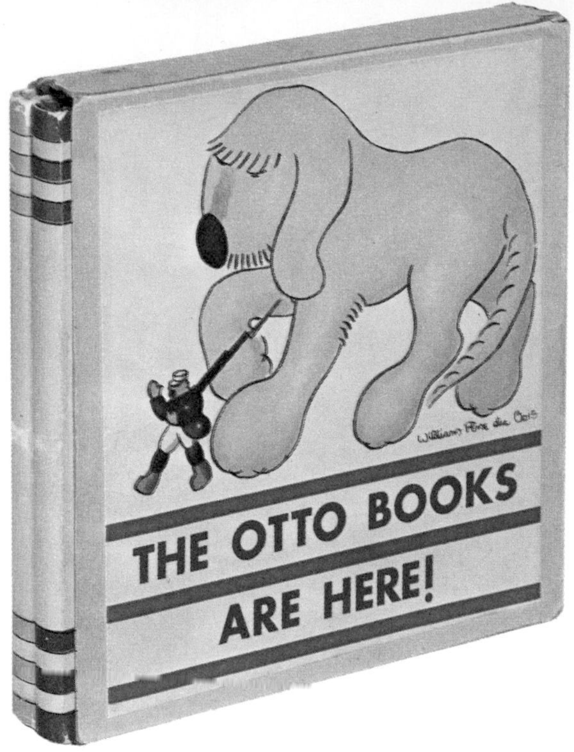

231. *Giant Otto & Otto at Sea,* by William Pène du Bois. Viking, 1936. 6½ x 6½.

232. *The Three Policemen,* by William Pène du Bois. Viking, 1938. 7⅛ x 9¾.

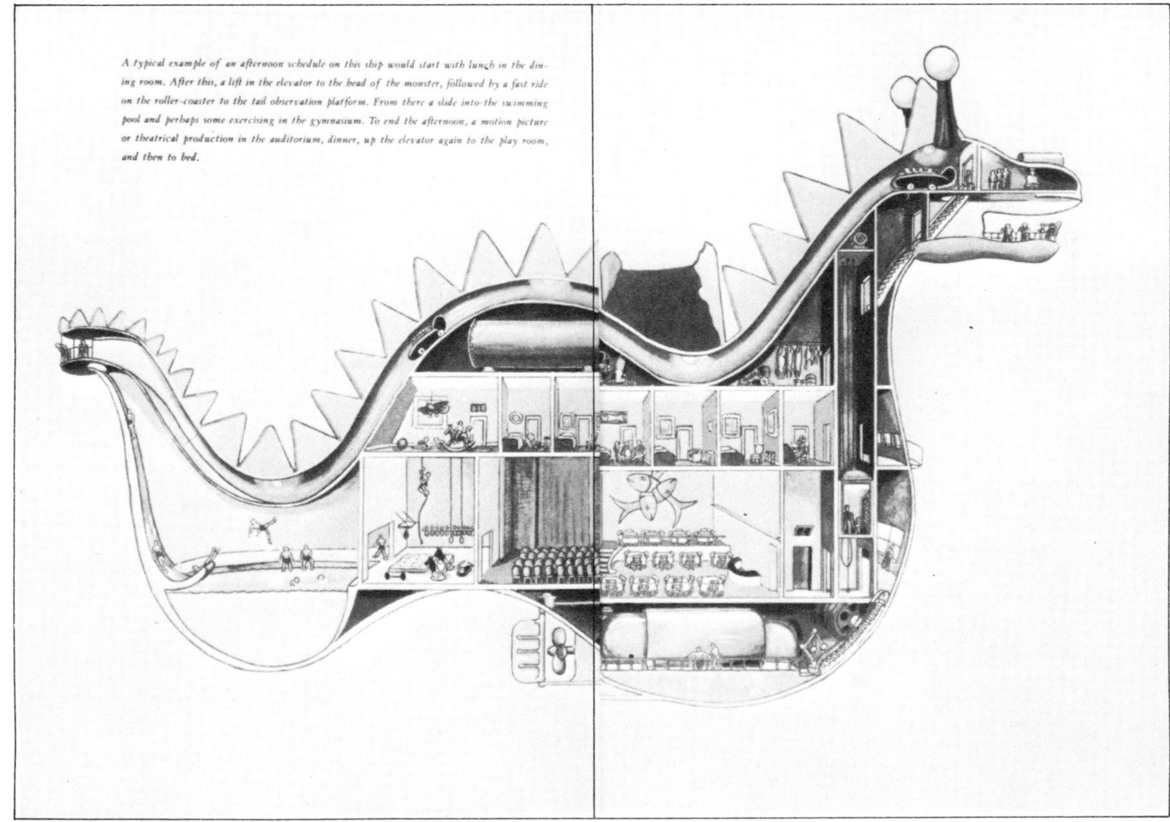

233. *The Great Geppy,* by William Pène du Bois. Viking, 1940. 7⅛ x 9⅝.

picturebook (a locomotive shape), has drawings in the same delicate, discerning line and for a plot the friendship between a boastful locomotive of modest attainments and a modest prize cow. A nice conceit, but in its devolution slight, a fairy tale.

With the war came a break, and when Pène du Bois left the service he had ready a long novel, *The Twenty-One Balloons* (Viking, 1947), which took the Newbery. This, even more than its predecessors, is an 'adult' children's book: Professor Sherman, retiring after forty years of teaching arithmetic to restive boys, takes off from San Francisco in a balloon outfitted for long peaceful drifting—and turns up in the Atlantic three weeks later with the wreckage of twenty balloons. He has, it seems, run into the biggest explosion of all time, the 1883 eruption of the Pacific island of Krakatoa; and the destruction of its extraordinary civilization—a story, as Pène du Bois indicates, much like Fitzgerald's "The Diamond as Big as the Ritz"—is the core of the book, an insidious mix of reality, irony and fantastic invention.

To an unusual degree they are all linked, and to omit one is, as it were, to leave a hole in a jigsaw puzzle. *Peter Graves* (1950), the story of the fabulous antigravity substance Furloy, elaborates on the perils and rewards of earth-defying invention; and another long book, *The Giant* (1954), is a moving demonstration of the problems of being larger-than-life size. El Muchacho, The Boy—a normal young boy magnified—is first glimpsed, horrifically, as "an eye the size of a clock face on a skyscraper." In both—in all three—so fantastic are the circumstances, so resounding their human implications, that the power of words to evoke exceeds the ability of pictures to portray; and in fact the pictures are ancillary.

Narrating *The Giant* is 'Señor Bill,' who is otherwise engaged in writing and illustrating *A* [Teddy] *Bear's Guide to the World's Pleasure Spots*—otherwise William Pène du Bois, recently author-illustrator of *Bear Party* (Viking, 1951), the account of a costume ball that brings peace to Koala Park "where real teddy bears live in trees" and the prelude to *Bear Circus* (p. 183).

Coming some years later, after *The Giant, Lion* marks a return to pictorial works and a surge of pictorial invention. *Lion*, indeed, is a pictorial invention.

As Pène du Bois put it, How did he ever think of such a crazy idea?

"The plot of *Lion* is extremely simple. The foreman of an Animal Factory in Heaven where animals are being designed . . . thinks of a name for an animal and that name is LION.

"The name LION seems so good to him that he decides to design the animal to go with it himself. He hasn't done any actual designing since he was a very young boy and drew a wiggly line with a brown crayon which he named WORM. For designing WORM, a highly functional multi-purpose animal, he received a medal, and was made foreman of the factory. (He wasn't literally made 'foreman,' he was put in charge—his name was Foreman and the job as we've come to know it was named after him.)

"Well, not having designed an animal in years, centuries perhaps, he is a bit out of practice and unsure of himself. His first design

palace. It was called THE ANIMAL FACTORY.
It had three rooms. There was a white fur room for cold days, and a white feather room for hot days. It had a roof made of silver fish scales.
9

234. *Lion,* by William Pène du Bois. Viking, 1956. 7½ x 10.

for LION is a small multi-colored bug with a fur body, a head trimmed with feathers and the tail of a fish. Not feeling too sure of this design, he puts the same question to six of his assistants, and this question is, 'TELL ME IN ONE WORD WHAT IS WRONG WITH THE LION.' As boss, he doesn't feel like hearing a more lengthy criticism from his underlings.

"The answers come back in one word each: 'SIZE,' 'FEATHERS,' 'COLOR,' 'LEGS,' 'HAIRCUT,' and finally that one marvelous answer he's been waiting for, '*NOTHING!*' and the KING OF BEASTS has been designed!

"That's all there is to the story."

The year before, Pène du Bois had gotten a Christmas card from his cousin, artist Margot Tomes, showing a lion with the thin legs of a poodle, his cousin's poodle, and he'd written her, unsolicited, that if he were asked to tell in one word what was wrong with the lion, he'd answer 'LEGS.' So much for immediate inspiration; but there is much more to the book than the story.

"What does an Animal Factory in Heaven look like? That took a bit of soaking [in the tub, where ideas come]. I first decided that it should be off by itself, a unit apart, in the suburbs of Heaven. Then came the question of gravity—is there gravity in Heaven? Of course not! God invented gravity to keep things put as he placed them on other planets. There is no need for gravity in Heaven. Angels have wings so they can keep their hands free as they go up, down, sideways, across, playing lutes, flutes and oboes. But for sitting at a drawing table, and I'm thinking with partiality based on my own experience, I reasoned that there should be a slight force of gravity to hold things in place such as pots of paint and boxes of crayons. So I placed the Animal Factory on a magnetic platform. This created a danger to the younger, smaller, angels with little wings . . . so I placed a raised platform high above the factory, a platform on which to land which was connected to the factory by a very long slide. Up there the gravitational pull would be quite mild—just enough to slide an angel gently into the factory itself.

"What kind of power should be used to make animals? I suppose atomic power would be truest, but I thought steam power would be warmer so I borrowed a magnificent steam engine from F.A.O. Schwarz Toy Store and used that familiar machine to make the Animal Factory look like a factory. Actually if one is creative no mechanical power is needed at all.

"The buildings themselves were made from materials on hand such as fur, feathers, and fish scales. There were two badminton courts for exercise during lunch hour. Badminton was invented at the Animal Factory, the rackets being strung with leftover cat gut, and the birds made with bits of leftover leather and feathers."

Thus, in part before the story proper begins,

235. *Lion,* by William Pène du Bois. Viking, 1956. 7½ x 10.

and then full scale at the second opening, the Animal Factory (234): a different kind of island and, run by its own laws, another small world. If one wouldn't necessarily assume the magnetic platform, it seems altogether fitting for angels to arrive at work via a spin down a long winding slide.

"Just one more thing. It says in the book that there were one hundred and four artists who sat on silver stools behind one hundred and four white wooden tables. The studio was actually quite like a classroom.

"They sat in twenty-six rows of four angels each, alphabetically: four A's in the first row, four B's in the second, four C's in the third and so forth; and like a classroom, the bright angels sat in the front rows and the dunces in the back rows. . . .

"The first angel is designing that most delicate, industrious and well organized of all animals, the wondrous ant; while sitting next to him, a brilliant and witty angel is designing the clever and imaginative aardvark to eat the ants his meticulous comrade is creating. . . .

"Now walk back to the rear of the room and consult the dunces. In row Y some waggish dolt is working on the Yak which he obviously cribbed from the Ox in row O—while in row Z an even lazier angel is leaning over his shoulder and copying the Yak and calling it a Zebu, while next to him an uninspired angel is putting black and white stripes on a rejected drawing of a horse . . . and calling it the Zebra.

"Those are some of the ideas," Pène du Bois concludes, "which went into *Lion*."[6] In the sport they make of the animal alphabet, they call to mind Duvoisin's *A for the Ark*; but here, internalized, they hang in the air. As Artist Foreman walks about the studio seeking inspiration, he sees in the first row a drawing of an ALLIGATOR, in the second a BEAR, in the third a CHICKEN, in the last a ZEBRA—from which the alert observer will infer A to Z but not, I think, an order of rank, a graded classroom. In creating his heavenly atelier, Pène du Bois sees it as a complete equivalent world, and the totality amplifies and underpins the story without its dimensions being readily apparent.

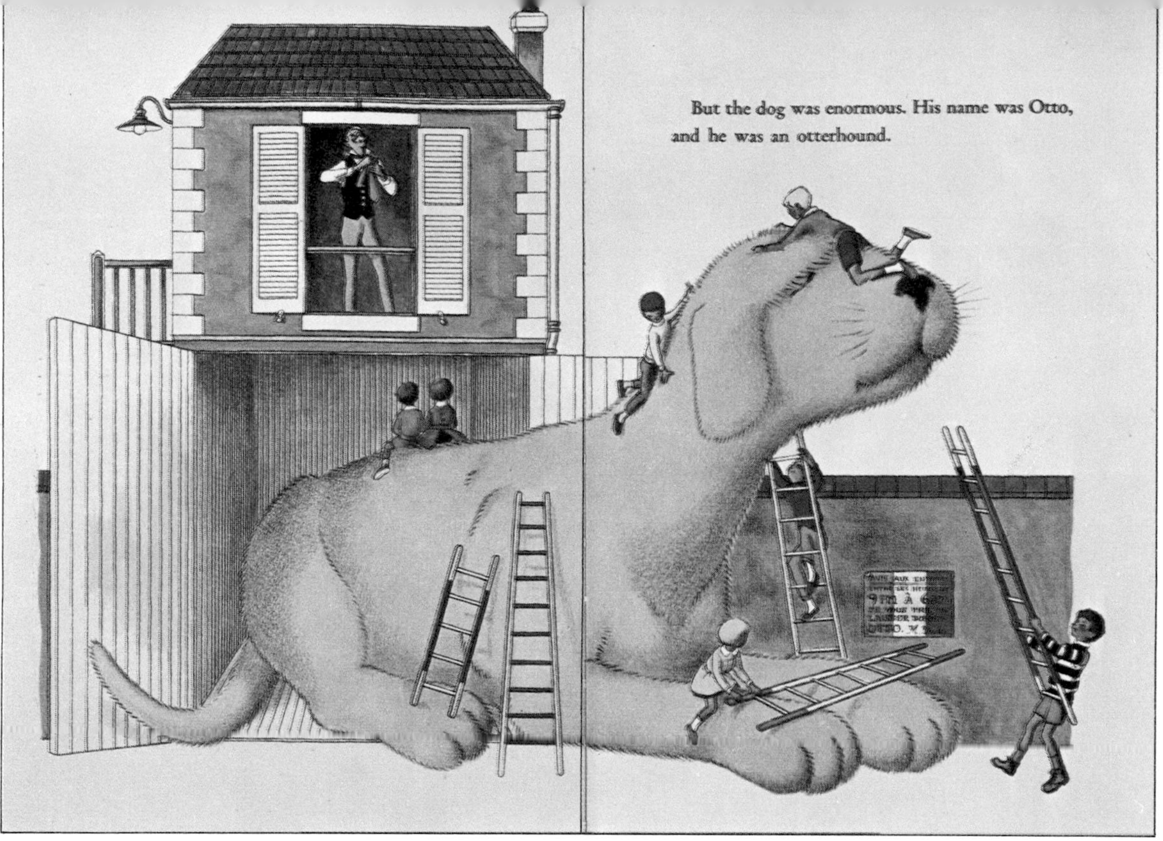

But the dog was enormous. His name was Otto,
and he was an otterhound.

236. *Otto in Africa,* by William Pène du Bois. Viking, 1961. 6⅝ x 9¾.

236

237

237. *The Three Policemen,* by William Pène du Bois. Viking, 1960. 6¼ x 9¼.

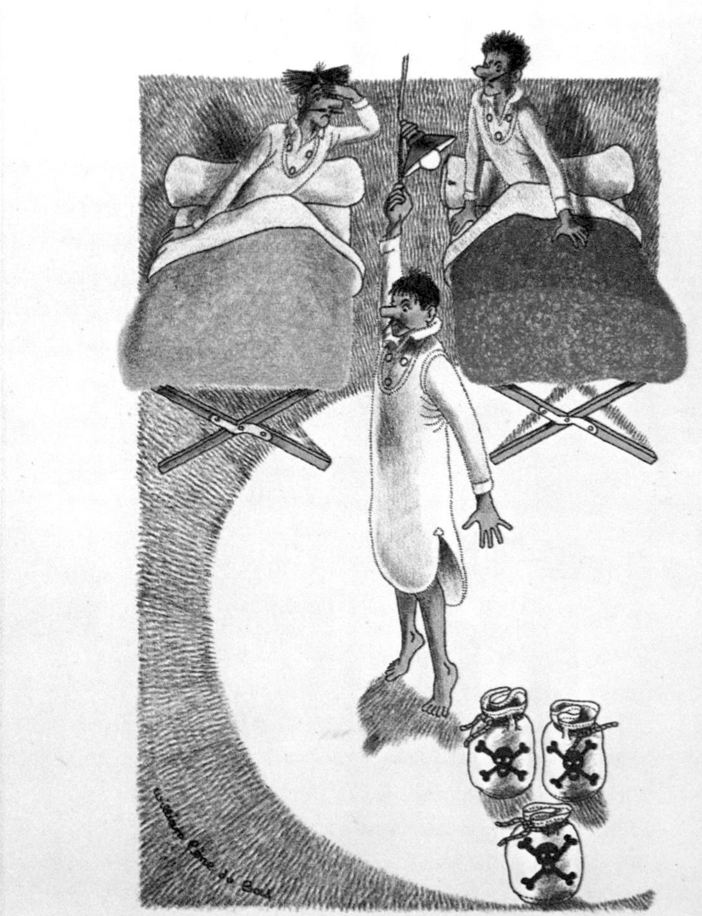

For this reason, among others, *Lion,* along with most of the later books, best suits older than picturebook children. Better too that they be able to read for themselves the label LION on the drawing of the small, multicolored, furred, feathered, fish-tailed bug (235); and the painful words, broadcast in red, SIZE, FEATHERS, COLOR, LEGS, HAIRCUT, and finally the welcome NOTHING! NOTHING! NOTHING! Whereupon Artist Foreman flies off to his boss the Chief Designer, he and all of Heaven in black and white, with color—"a frivolous device for the amusement and camouflage of lesser planets"—confined to his creation, LION. That color, and noncolor, make their own comment is part of a design scheme—key words in red, labels in old apothecary lettering; black and white open line, color modeling and shading—which in turn binds together pictures and text, content and realization, looking and reading.

There began now the redoing of early books that, along with illustrating the writings of others, was to occupy Pène du Bois for many years. The style and tenor of his work had changed radically, if not his subject matter; and so had printing technology. *Bear Party*, done in full color, was printed in Belgium—prettily would be the word; *Lion* was done brilliantly by pre-separation. Both were first condensed in *Life*, and the *Life* version of *Lion* can only be called, by comparison, drab. But by comparison with *Lion*—especially with the gorgeous double-page picture of LION set to rights—the brightest of full-color reproduction pales. Nonetheless, pre-separation is toilsome and restricting to an illustrator, and Pène du Bois, quit of it in the picturebooks after *Lion*, spread himself with new freedom.

His compositions had become more elaborate and what is not always the same thing, more loaded; there was not only more to the pictures, there was more going on in them, implicitly and explicitly. *Otto at Sea*, the first redone (in 1958), is very little changed as to text, but the illustrations are filled with activity and implication, and it is a quite different, more complex book. *Otto in Africa*, the *Giant Otto* that was, gives us a new version of Otto's first appearance (236), and a good basis for comparing the new with the old look (231). Duke has become debonair, Otto is well groomed, plush where before he was shag; and there is a precision and polish that one finds in all of Pène du Bois's later work. Though the original *Ottos* will always hold first place for many (me among them), the new pictures are a potent come-on.

More serious—drastic, dubious—than the change in the looks of the books is the change in their nature that began with a new Otto story, *Otto in Texas* (1959), spilled over into *Otto in Africa*, and flooded *Otto and the Magic Potatoes* (1970). *Otto in Texas* has Otto, dog detective, flushing out three picture-painting grandmas who are tapping oilman Sam Hill's best well—three imposters really, Duke concludes, since Otto would not mistreat old ladies "the way he did THESE BAD MEN!" Partly it's a spoof of Texas, land of liveried footmen and rope-twirling ladies-of-the-house, partly it's a cat's cradle of surprises; and entertaining as it is, it is miscast as a picturebook.

Of the remaining remakes, *The Three Policemen* is the same story with new and better pictures—pictures that put Pène du Bois's new spiffy manner to splendid use. In pure singing (pre-separated) color and trim, toned black and white—tricolor red, white and blue overall—is a fusillade of fresh, enormously funny images (237). Funnier the longer you look at them, when you realize that Peter whose mustache turns up (he's the optimist), Paul whose mustache sticks straight out (maybe yes, maybe no), and Joseph whose mustache turns down (disaster!) have, on sudden awakening, hair to match—just as, on the jacket, the fish suits that the three spring from are, in turn, smiling, noncommittal and frowning. Pène du Bois remarks that, as a child, he would turn quickly from a thrilling frontispiece, "Bill Ballantine slipped from his trapeze and fell into the lion cage below (see page 178)," to the indicated page "to find out whether or not he was chewed up."[7] Throughout *The Three Policemen* the pictures have that tantalizing quality; you can no more not read the story, not know what's afoot or what will happen next, than you can not laugh. (This version is, obviously, the one that would go into the time capsule.)

Elisabeth the Cow Ghost Pène du Bois rewrote, reconceived, and torpedoed—this from the point of view of the small stone-in-a-pond original. But if one is justified, usually, in expecting an adapter to be faithful to his source, one cannot fault an author for altering his own material. By itself, however, the second *Elisabeth* (1964) is interesting graphically and otherwise numbing, arcane. It opens like a film with pictures flowing behind the titles, and climaxes, also cinematically, in a violent wordless sequence and a blackout; and the continuous tone technique, a matter of close hatching and crosshatching, along with the startling perspectives and sudden shifts, gives to the whole the aspect of a brooding, eruptive black and white movie. Of all of Pène du Bois's books, it is the one which seems most nearly oblivious of children.

The next year he began, with *The Alligator Case* (Harper), a new line of small-town-uproar detective stories and in the year following, a curious series on the seven deadly sins. To crib from the jacket copy, *Lazy Tommy Pumpkinhead* (Harper, 1966) lingers over laziness, *Pretty Pretty Peggy Moffitt* (Harper, 1968) is all vanity; and a good deal more bracing, *Porko von Popbutton* (Harper, 1969)—the ins and outs of ice hockey at a boys' boarding school—expands upon gluttony, while *Call Me Bandicoot* (Harper, 1970) turns stinginess to profit in a story of the world's most remarkable storyteller. In neither group, indicatively, are the pictures of great importance.

On then to *Bear Circus*. If *The Three Policemen* has competition as the quintessence of Pène du Bois, it is *Bear Circus*. The show begins on the cover where "*The BEARS of Koala Park and* WILLIAM PÈNE DU BOIS *present* BEAR CIRCUS *for our friends the KANGAROOS*." On the half-title page, before the opening of the circus tent, are "The kangaroo and the real teddy bear . . . ." (238); on the title spread, "The kangaroo is good at hopping across the land," and, per the picture, curious about what's in the tent; comes the copyright and, inside the tent, "The real teddy bear climbs well, straight up and down" a circus pole. "The kangaroo is special, and the real teddy bear is special. This is a story about true friendship."

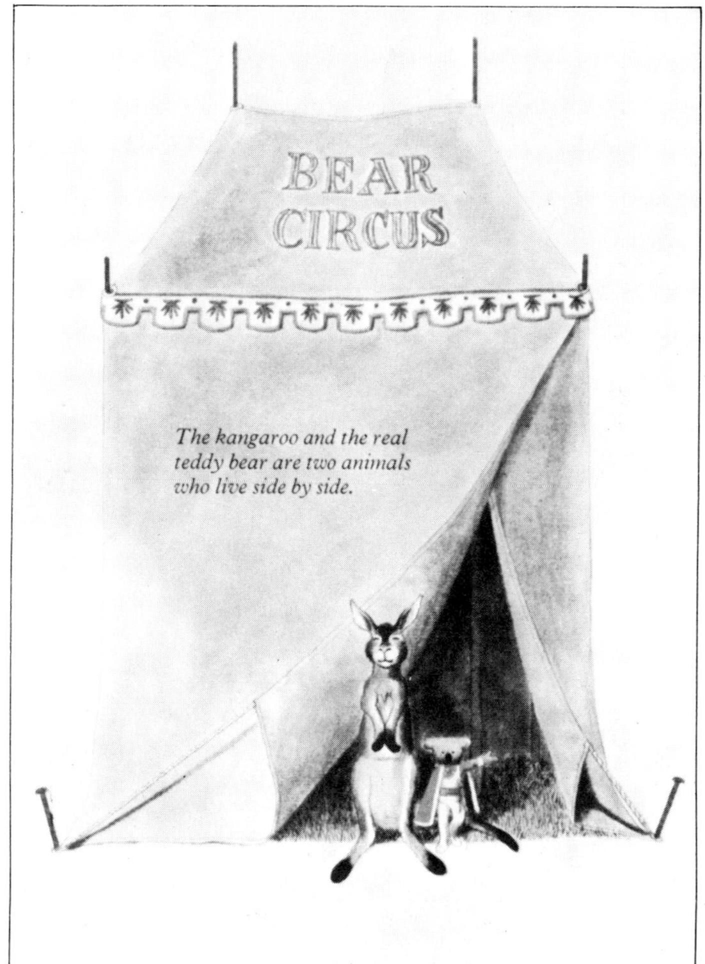
BEAR
CIRCUS
The kangaroo and the real
teddy bear are two animals
who live side by side.

238. *Bear Circus,* by William Pène du Bois. Viking, 1971. 7⅞ x 10⅞.

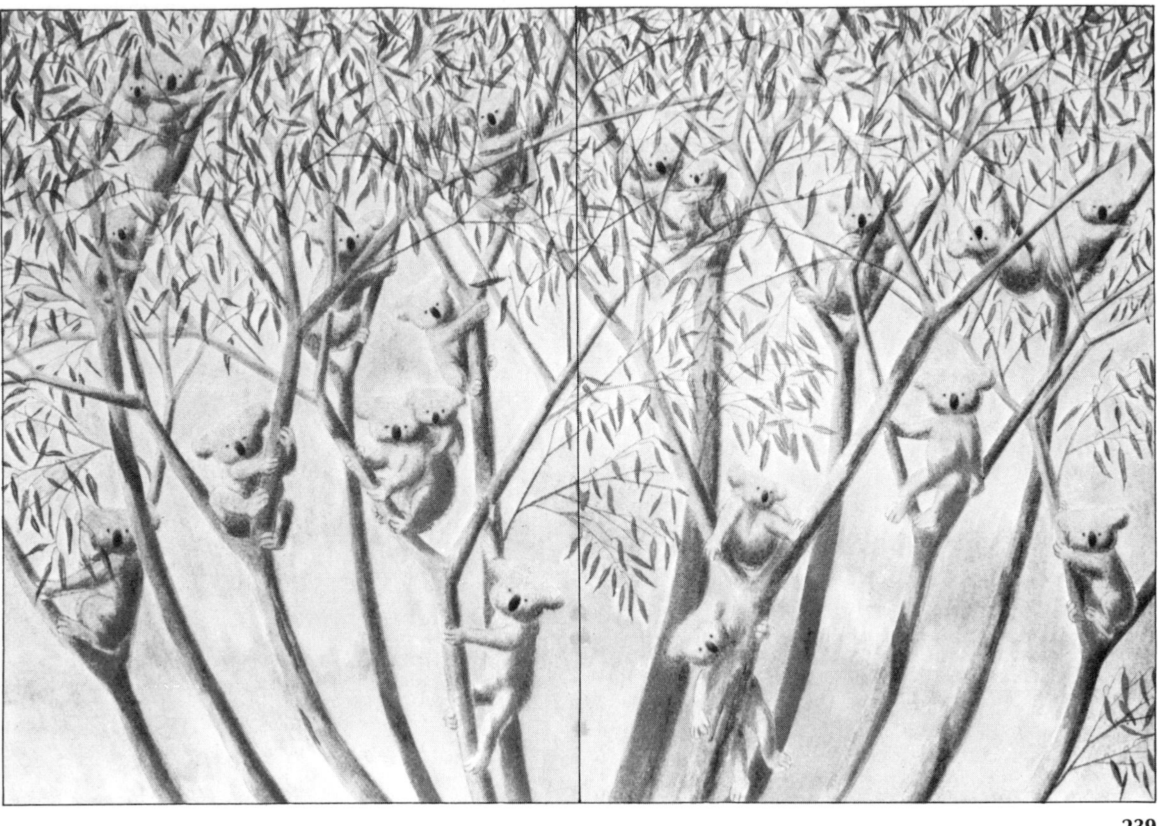

239

ACT I
The fanfare concluded, we are at Koala Park (where the bear sentry flourishes a boomerang), ready for action. And immediately the bears, who live in gum trees and eat only their leaves (239), are overrun by grasshoppers after the same food (240, 241).

ACT II
"What will we do now?" But the kangaroos are approaching, hopping over the hill, even as the bears lament. They tuck the bears in their pouches, hoist them to their heads, and the friends are off to search for food.

ACT III
'Now just about this time' an airplane, a circus airplane, carrying midgets and dwarfs to entertain children, runs into a cloud of grasshoppers and, its engines clogged, starts to crash. Everybody jumps, performing acrobatics from the parachutes—"a fine show of landing safely"—while the plane chugs on.

ACT IV
The bears and the kangaroos have just discovered a grove of gum trees when the plane crashes . . . (242). The circus things, too small for the kangaroos, are a little too big for the bears, but in time, out of gratitude, they'll put on a circus for their friends. Seven years later—"real teddy bears are slow," it takes them five years just to learn to put up the tent—Bear Circus is ready to begin.

ACT V
Scene I: "A CHILD'S GARDEN OF BEARS," wherein the youngest bears, the girls in pink sashes, the boys in blue, do stunts—tumbling, balancing, juggling.
Scene II: "THE THREE FUR BROTHERS," starring a Milkman bear clown, a Farmer bear clown, a Banker bear clown and a HOT-WATER BOTTLE, 'the first act all clowns learn when they go to clown school.'
Scene III: "THE GREAT MYSTY BEAR" and his magic top hat.

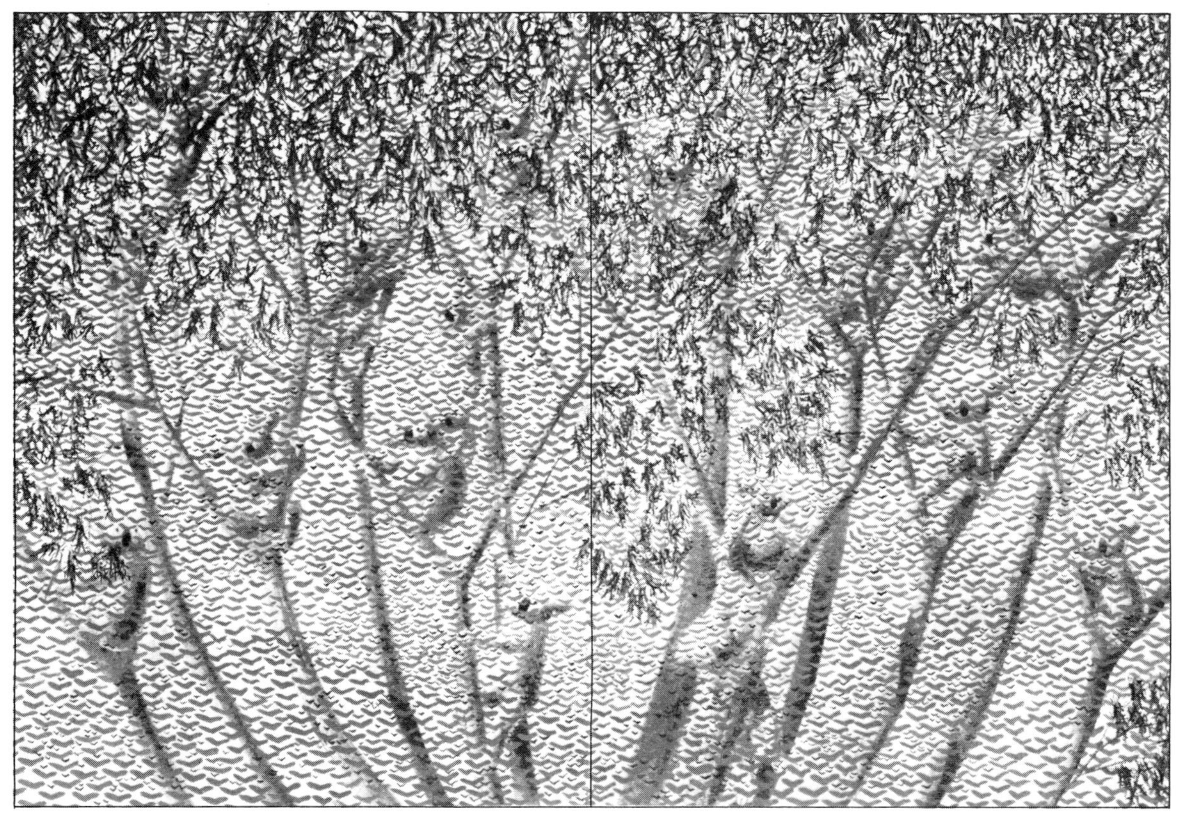

240

239-241. *Bear Circus*, by William Pène du Bois. Viking, 1971. 7⅞ x 10⅞.

241

The pink airplane crashed into a million tiny bits, scattering pretty circus things all over the bears' new home.

"It must have been a Christmas present which opens itself," said the baby bear.

"I think you are right," said his friend.

26

27

242

242, 243. *Bear Circus,* by William Pène du Bois. Viking, 1971. 7⅞ x 10⅞.

243

Scene IV: A tower of strength, "THE ALI BABAS."
Scene V: The incredible "SPLASHO!," feature act of the evening. Shot up from a teeterboard . . . through a hole in the top of the tent . . . while the clowns wait with a bathtub on wheels . . . the great SPLASHO, yellow-suited from head to foot, comes down a cloud of GREEN . . . "THE GRASSHOPPERS ARE BACK!"

The ACTs are of course an addition, a device to demonstrate how, sequence by sequence, usually in two openings, *Bear Circus* reveals its wonders, putting a new foot forward in each instance. But that once again is only the beginning; however one interprets the saying, each picture, each spread, is worth those eternal thousand words. Moreover, this time they are drawn, detail by detail, for the enchantment of small children (243).

Pène du Bois dedicates the book to the Fratellinis, favorites of his own childhood, and like their clowning it surpasses showmanship.

SUI GENERIS:
SEVEN SIMEONS AND *BUTTONS*

A Russian folktale adapted and illustrated by Artzybasheff, the story of an alley cat told in short lines by Tom Robinson and big pictures by Peggy Bacon: variously singular, each a culmination, both exceptional.

SEVEN SIMEONS

In the comparatively few years before *Time* and *Life* and *Fortune* claimed him, Boris Artzybasheff brought to the making of books for children a special wit and polish and a total sense of style; *making*, indeed, is the operative word.

As a young Russian émigré he found it expedient, at the start, to produce Russian art. The murals for a restaurant that brought him attention and his first book commission, Mamin Siberiak's *Verotchka's Tales* (1922), and the illustrations themselves are done in the bold heavy manner of the renowned Bilibin, painter, stage designer and picture-book-maker (1902–07) to the Czar. The next step was to essay other foreign settings and, as reviewers regularly observed, he seemed able to make the most diverse countries and cultures his. In quick succession came Harriet Martineau's Norwegian *Feats on the Fiord* (1924), Ella Young's Celtic *Wonder Smith and His Son* (1927), Mukerji's Indian *Gay Neck* (1927) and *Ghond the Hunter* (1928)—after *Feats*, books not so much illustrated and ornamented as integrally designed and decorated, and that in a manner reflective of their origin.

The book that introduced Artzybasheff as a designer-decorator, however, the first he had the opportunity to plan in its entirety—"from the bright jacket through every detail of heading and initials"[1]—was Padraic Colum's assemblage of legends of Fire, Water, Earth and Air, *The Forge in the Forest* (1925). Noteworthy as a revival of the Art Nouveau concept of the book as a harmonious and expressive whole, it has the further distinction of giving to color the same character as black and white. This was the period, before offset lithography came into general use, when an illustrated book, one of Rackham's or Dulac's or Willy Pogany's, would have line drawings printed with the text and color half-tones on glossy paper laid in separately, the one integral, the other an accessory—albeit, in many cases, the excuse for the book. Varicolored, shaded, dense and deep, they are in effect oil paintings (because of the coated stock) in a field of clear-cut even black and white. What Artzybasheff did was to employ clear-cut even color also, in line and en masse, so that his are not 'colored' pictures but pictures composed of several colors, black among them.

So important was lithography to picture-books both as a method of illustration and a means of reproduction that we have dwelt upon it; as a means of reproduction, however, line engraving—photomechanical line engraving, as introduced late in the nineteenth century—has its own attributes, yielding until quite recently the cleanest, sharpest image (as well as the cheapest). This is an asset, obviously, only if one wants a clean, sharp image; and to be had, concomitantly, only by planning for it. We have referred to Joseph Pennell's assertion, made in the 1890s, that photo-

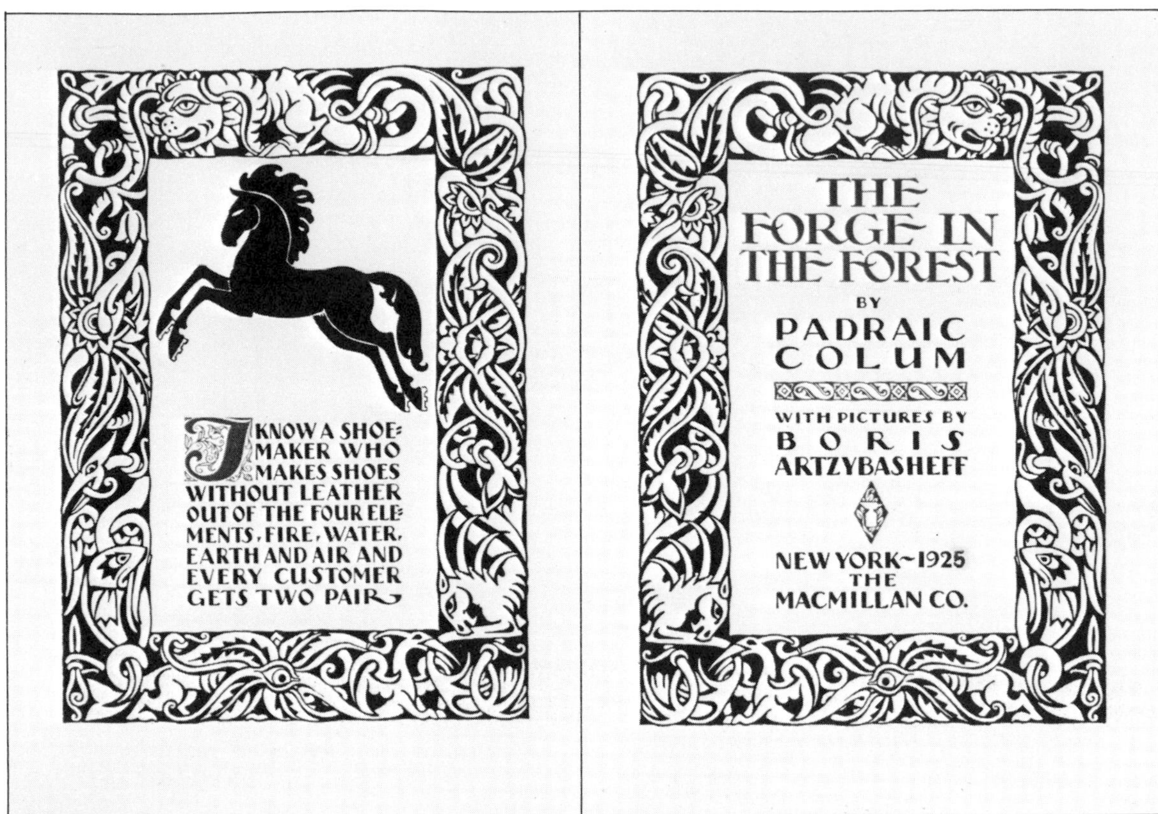

244

244, 245. *The Forge in the Forest,* by Padraic Colum, illus. by Boris Artzybasheff. Macmillan, 1925. 5¼ x 7⅜.

engraving was responsible for the emergence of pen draftsmen in America, and spoken of Rojankovsky's *Cartier* as evincing command of the pen for line reproduction. Those pen draftsmen who emerged, in America as elsewhere, responded to the new process in different ways: some, rid of the reproductive wood engraver, felt free to draw as they liked, counting on the photomechanical process for faithful reproduction while others, a few at least, began to draw with the method of reproduction in mind.

Séan Jennett provides an instructive comparison: "The lines [of the freely done drawing] are not even in colour. The artist's hand varies the pressure of the pen, and this is most easily seen at the commencement and end of each line, especially if it is fine. The line begins and develops almost out of nothing, deepens in colour, and again diminishes and fades away. In the lightest parts there is scarcely any ink at all, and what there is is thin and grey and only on the surface of the paper. . . . There is, in short, tone to the line as well as disjunction. Such a drawing cannot be satisfactorily reproduced by line block. Tone is impossible and the line must be an even black. The fine particles either tend to vanish, or from the effort to preserve them become much coarser . . . and the reproduction, however well done, is bound to be unsatisfactory . . . ."

On the other hand, the drawing made for reproduction will, ideally, "look as though it were itself printed, with every line fully black and clear. A print derived from such an original may be almost indistinguishable from it, and is then a true reproduction. If, as often happens, a reduction in scale is to take place, it must be allowed for in the thickness of the lines and in the closeness of their spacing. This does not mean that fine line is impossible

. . . what is necessary is that the line be distinct and defined."[2] In Rojankovsky's illustrations for *Cartier* (162–164), in Artzybasheff's for *The Forge in the Forest*, the conditions are met and attendant possibilities are pursued.

The advent of photoengraving was timely; much of what it encouraged was in accordance with the aesthetic impulses of Art Nouveau, and it is well known that Beardsley was quick to adapt his work to the medium. In the books, his and others', that (along with posters) were central to Art Nouveau, solid even line became solid even mass, precisely outlined—silhouette or partial silhouette—or stippled pattern; white space, bounded by line, took on shape, and black and white shape became equivalent, interchangeable, equivocal; not only was the flatness of the picture plane asserted, but the surface became a part of the design or composition. *The Forge in the Forest* is not in fact the harmonious whole that its successors were but both the close-set, chunky title spread (244) and the illustration composed of space and waving tendrils (245) are in their way the outcome of this development.

The use of black on white, white on black, a marked feature of Artzybasheff's work—as of Beardsley's—is to the fore in *The Fairy Shoemaker* and *Poor Shaydullah*, but there are other reasons to look at both. *The Fairy Shoemaker* consists of five poems of magic set off by occasional pictures—a handful of familiar poems and some black and white pictures turned into what Lynd Ward greeted as an 'enchanting and perfectly made picture book.'[3] The wonderful wasteful audacity of setting a stanza in the center of a square page, facing it with a picture or, as often, another stanza, has a charm of its own and the pictures so favorably displayed are, for the first time, high-spirited childlike fun (246). "How would you like to roll in your carriage,/Look for a duchess's daughter in marriage?" pre-

245

Little Cowboy, what have you heard,
 Up on the lonely rath's green
  mound?
Only the plaintive yellow bird
 Sighing in sultry fields around,
Chary, chary, chary, chee-ee!—
Only the grasshopper and the bee?—

8

246

247

246. *The Fairy Shoemaker,* illus. by Boris Artzybasheff. Macmillan, 1928. 7⅜ x 8½.

247. *Poor Shaydullah,* by Boris Artzybasheff. Macmillan, 1931. 7⅜ x 8½.

ceded in the picture by a prancing dog and chewing on a pretzel; or see the King "so old and gray/He's nigh lost his wits"—a party snapper and an apple his scepter and orb.

Poor Shaydullah is funny on the face of it, without props (247). Born of a trip to Morocco, this is the first book of Artzybasheff's writing and his only original story, the sly, perverse fable of a proud beggar who gets his due from Allah—or does he? Intoned as if Artzybasheff had listened with one ear to the Koran, with the other to the blandishments of Scheherezade, it is, all told, about as reverential as Bernard Shaw—a thought easy to come by since GBS, by God, is Allah.

Shaydullah and the Lion lolling on their elbows, sharing their misfortunes; Shaydullah listening to the plaint of the barren Banana

Tree, a glum female figure—an African carving—with a great arching headdress of banana leaves; God/GBS/Allah appearing to Shaydullah in a fiery ball of buxom busybody angels: each will have its champions. But there remains, indomitable, the frontispiece image of Shaydullah, lids lowered, shoulders drooping, hands clasped, a ragged, tattered vision of complacent misery; "Poor Shaydullah," says the title, and underneath, a finger points

248. *Three and the Moon,* by Jacques Dorey, illus. by Boris Artzybasheff. Knopf, 1929.

Both *The Fairy Shoemaker* and *Poor Shaydullah* were done in a variation of scratchboard. What Barbara Cooney has to say about the medium, which she uses with particular skill, is interesting in itself and broadly pertinent:

"Scratchboard is a drawing board, one surface of which is coated with a smooth, white, chalklike surface, which takes ink readily. You can draw with black ink on the white surface, and by scraping (scratchboard is called 'scraperboard' in England) or scratching through a black-inked surface with a sharp instrument, you can draw in white line on a black surface."

Noting that "Like wood engraving, which it resembles in appearance, scratchboard has an affinity for the printed page," marrying well "with the clean letters of type" and preserving "the flat surface of the page," Cooney observes further:

"For the artist, the medium is a good disciplinarian. It allows no subterfuge, no sketchy representations, no incomplete statements . . . . [The artist] must draw with precision, for there is a finality too in drawing on scratchboard . . . . [He] must think in terms of a limited palette, in bold black and white with perhaps five in-between grays, obtained by parallel lines, crosshatching, or stippling. These grays can be either black on white or white on black."[4]

The application to *The Fairy Shoemaker* and *Poor Shaydullah* is obvious. Hardly less apparent, however, is the difference between them and, greater still, the difference between either of them and Barbara Cooney's work, close in its effect to wood engraving (p. 264). Artzybasheff did not use a prepared scratchboard, he devised a way to use celluloid sprayed with black that could be lifted with engravers' tools "to obtain a sharpness of contour and extreme precision of line, and"—sometimes—"to more closely simulate woodcut."[5] We see him simulating woodcut (and wood engraving) in details of the Cowboy drawing but for the most part he is, in *The Fairy Shoemaker*, working with a breadth and dash alien to wood, and in *Poor Shaydullah*, working in ways peculiar to what we will call, for convenience sake, scratchboard. "There is plenty of scope for freedom and invention in this medium," writes John Farleigh who, as an engraver, turned to scratchboard with forethought. "Black lines, and white equally, can be drawn easily and fluently, a thing not possible in wood; while a combination of specially prepared tints gives the designer a range of tones that will work well into any design."[6]

Elsewhere in *Poor Shaydullah* Artzybasheff uses the mechanical tints—embossed patterns, not unlike Ben Day tints in appearance—that Farleigh refers to, but he is just as apt to use "rags, pieces of wood, fingers or any odd means" to get textural and tonal effects. "A rough turkish towel, for example, may be employed for a certain stipple-like tone"[7]—as it may have been for the grainy wall behind Shaydullah. Indeed, the book is a study in suggestive contrasts, in small—parallel patch and squiggly tear, tattered sleeve and raveled shawl, as in large—light against dark, smooth against rough, solid against pattern. Beyond drawing for the medium, meeting its conditions, beyond designing in terms of its black-and-whiteness, Artzybasheff enlarges it, developing new techniques and discovering new qualities.

We could be speaking equally of the means of reproduction. As a medium, scratchboard exists for mechanical reproduction, initially for photoengraving; its end product, its purpose, is the printed picture, uniquely so in the case of Artzybasheff's work on celluloid. In that sense it is a vehicle, the means of reproduction the medium; and we can say that instead of a reproductive medium being just that, it becomes with Artzybasheff (as later, in offset, with Duvoisin and others) a means of creating something new for the printed page.

Like *The Forge in the Forest*, *Three and the Moon* is designed in color for line engraving and the flat surface of the page. But Jacques Dorey's French legends elicit no elaborate decoration, no period setting or special aura: this is a modern treatment of medieval motifs, at once vibrant and reserved, done in a pale lilac and black with strange stinging colors for the few full-page pictures (248). Where before they were part of a decorative scheme, moreover, now the colors have a structural and symbolic function; they are as basic to the design and as important to the picture as the drawing.

We can only approximate them here (as we can only approximate, in a book done in full-color offset, an odd hue differently achieved); four, sometimes five per picture, they were produced separately, according to the artist's dictates, in a manner fundamentally the same as for *Seven Simeons*, of which we have a detailed description:

"Mr. Artzybasheff first made a rough pencil sketch, then drew a finished preliminary sketch in the correct colors. The next step was to make an exact-size drawing, a replica all in black of the preliminary sketch. From this black drawing the photo-engraver made a line plate, which was proofed in light blue ink [which does not photograph] on drawing board. Mr Artzybasheff then made his finished drawings, using a different engraver's proof for each color: that is, what was eventually to be reproduced in red was drawn in black ink on one of the blue proofs; what was to be green was drawn in black on a second proof; and the drawings for the yellow and black were similarly done on separate sheets. A line engraving was made from each of these new drawings, and the plates were proofed in their correct colors. The first all-black drawing and the plate made from it was discarded, their use being to give the artist a key on which to base the correct register of the final four colors."

"It was a laborious process," concludes the description, "but the only means by which such intricacies of color separation and register . . . could have been accomplished"; and in 1937 when *Seven Simeons* came out *PW* deemed it worthy of "special mention."[8] 'Such intricacies' are not present in *Three and the Moon* but the principles are the same (and remain the same whether engraving or lithography is the method of reproduction). The colors of course were not the same nor, another wrinkle, were precisely the same ones used for every picture.

The technique too varies sometimes, expressively, within a picture. The dark tumbling figure is a character out of a Russian wood-

249. *Volga,* illus. by I. Y. Bilibin. Petrograd, Bilibin, 1904. Detail.

250. *Seven Simeons,* by Boris Artzybasheff. Viking, 1937. Detail.

engraving, deep-scored and solid; the demons are a mass of movement—a pit of fire, a bed of snakes; and the green sprouts that spring up among them, a sweep and a curl of the brush, are as free as the magenta aureole is regular and fixed.

Is this children's illustration? One would have to say, first, what the artist would have said, that it is not illustration: "There is no situation suspended in the caption of a drawing," as one of his interviewers put it. In avoiding the literal, the all too real, his intention was to preserve the author's dream world; in toto, "to add to, not subtract from, the aesthetic values of a book."[9] Those illustrations by Rackham et al that had nothing to do with the physical book had exactly to do with the contents, and on both grounds they were anathema to others besides Artzybasheff—"an intrusion upon the author's domain and an offense against good taste," according to the 1928 AIGA catalog of American Book illustration. To children, nonetheless, the despised half-tone plates were the raisins in the cookie, the prize in the Crackerjack box.

Excepting *The Fairy Shoemaker*, the question is not whether the illustration was for children but whether the books were; whether they were not, rather, imaginative publishing for young people as an imaginative audience. The Depression, accentuated by certain developments in the trade—a fallow period at Knopf and, most particularly, the retirement of Louise Seaman from Macmillan—brought a virtual halt to that kind of inspired, unpragmatic (and expensive) publishing. For his part Artzybasheff was determined not to do illustration as such or, for that matter, to be typed as a children's illustrator; and in 1933 he began the long association with Time, Inc. that led to the celebrated portrait covers of *Time* and, during the war, to the grotesque humanoid machines that appeared in both *Time* and *Life*.

His *Aesop's Fables*, the last in the preceding line, came out in 1933 and when next he did a book for children it was something out of his own childhood and wholly a children's book. *Seven Simeons* is not, however, Bilibin-come-to-America, whatever was said. Bilibin's books were grand and they were partially printed in gold, and *Seven Simeons* is grand and partially printed in golden yellow, but *Seven Simeons* is to Bilibin's work as filigree is to inlay (249, 250). The very impossibility of reproducing the crisp, delicate line in color (by camera-separated process) is the reason for the black and white illustrations here; the jester, for instance, should be imagined in green and gold, the horsemen in red and black.

For all the splendor, the drawing is economical, detail being reserved for brocaded costumes and rococo carvings, and the scheme is simple. "Each left-hand page is filled with some drawing, text appearing only on the facing pages, simply set in English Monotype Baskerville. Across one pair of pages spreads an array of soldiers, and their oblique formation actually usurps part of the right-hand text page. Yet this very irregularity is made to seem perfectly natural. Indeed, the mounted king is seen stopping an execution, holding up a monitory hand while the text just ahead of him cries out in the genteelest Baskerville accents: 'Stop! Do not chop!' "[10] (251) Similarly, the jester springs forward at the foot of the right-hand margin, ready to speak his piece at the turn of the page, just when the text calls for him. Artzybasheff is truly illustrating but in a larger sense, for the book as a whole—text, large and small pictures, layout and typography—is put to the purpose of conveying the story.

Seven Simeons won every possible honor for design, hence the ease of quoting enthusiasts who know genteel Baskerville from plain-spoken Times Roman. To illumine, once, just what such a book entails, here is its curriculum vitae from *PW*:

> "Seven Simeons" (*Viking Press*, $2) was designed by Milton B. Glick and Boris Artzybasheff. It was set in 12 point English Monotype Baskerville 4 points leaded. The text was composed by the Press of A. Colish; the title page was set by the Spiral Press. Photoengravings were made by the Chromatic Engraving Co. The text press work in 4 colors was done by Quinn &

251–253. *Seven Simeons,* by Boris Artzybasheff. Viking, 1937. 8½ x 11⅛.

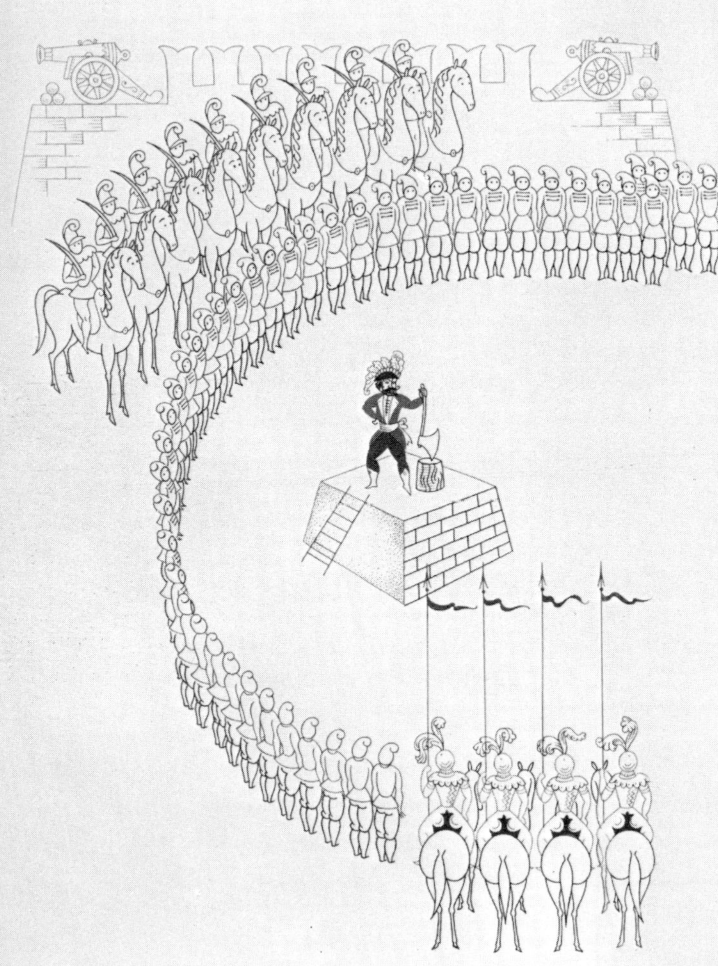

wrote, "Our King and my dear Father: I have found the man worthy of my hand and I shall marry him so soon as we have your blessing. The High and Mighty King Douda, my future husband and your son-in-law, sends to you his envoys with greetings and best wishes. And we both hope that you will come to our wedding."

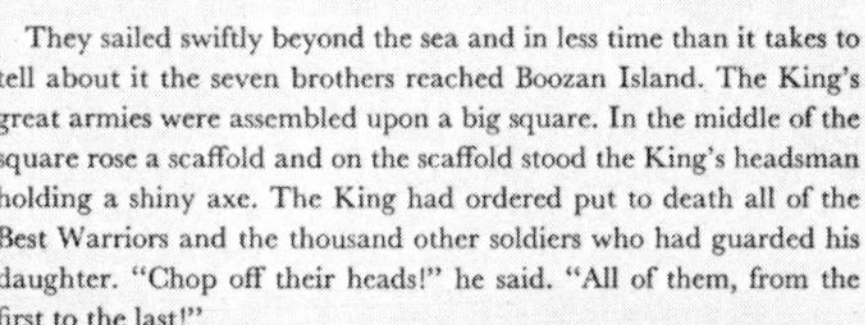

They sailed swiftly beyond the sea and in less time than it takes to tell about it the seven brothers reached Boozan Island. The King's great armies were assembled upon a big square. In the middle of the square rose a scaffold and on the scaffold stood the King's headsman holding a shiny axe. The King had ordered put to death all of the Best Warriors and the thousand other soldiers who had guarded his daughter. "Chop off their heads!" he said. "All of them, from the first to the last!"

"Stop! Do not chop!" cried the seventh Simeon from the ship's poop. "We have brought you a letter from your daughter."

So delighted was the Boozan King when he read the letter that he said, "Let the fools go. I forgive them. It must have been God's own will that my dear daughter should marry King Douda."

The brothers were given a great feast and sent back with the King's blessing for the wedding. He himself could not go because of important matters of state which required his direct attention, such as training his army and seeing that his spare army was well groomed.

Faster than before, the brothers sailed back towards their own home. In no time, in the distant blue, King Douda's kingdom appeared in their view.

"Our thanks to you, my good fellows," said King Douda cheerfully, when the Simeons stood before him and the Princess. "It was

251

Boden. The Country Life Press did the press work on the jacket. Russell Rutter Co. bound the book in Bancroft natural finish, tyrol green. The paper used was Warren's No. 1854, medium finish; the surface and color were made to match special samples.[11] [To which should be added blind-stamping on the sides and stamping in gold on the backbone by Durget & Forbes.]

It makes one think, not without admiration, of the Empire State Building.

The story, we know, is Russian, the tale of seven brothers of the same name born on the same day each of whom has mastered a different trade, the seventh Simeon being, to his chagrin, a master thief; and it relates their success in stealing a bride for—in this version—the vain king. (In Jeremiah Curtin's old and homelier one, which I prefer, he is lovelorn, and the story starts not with his foibles but with the birth of the brothers to an old peasant couple.) Is the book then "Russian from start to finish," as proclaimed? The question is perhaps as immaterial as whether, earlier, the illustrations were for children. Is the intricate, opulent Fabergé ware 'Russian'? Is its antithesis, the constructivism of Lissitzky? As it happens, with a change of dress the foppish king and his chichi bride might be the first-nighters that another cosmopolitan Russian, Alajalov, immortalized on the cover of *The New Yorker*. They, and the scenes they appear in, are bedizened, aflutter, bedazzling (252); the seven Simeons sharing their simple loaf have a casual grace, a purity of line and mien and, one feels, of motive (253); the ranked soldiers reflect, in their massing and mathematical precision, the pictographs Artzybasheff was doing at the time for *Fortune* (251). If *Seven Simeons* is any single thing from start to finish, it is the varied talents of its maker turned upon the material.

In any case, it is too lighthearted to be wholly Russian. But on this occasion Artzybasheff does not jest: no soldier breaks ranks to blow his nose, no horse flicks its tail, no standard droops—it is a serious business, beheading, and nothing distracts from the execu-

252

253

tioner and the little king. The vast seriousness is the very source of the fun. Playing it straight—playing fair even with foolish Douda and his bride—Artzybasheff skirts comic opera and produces, purely for children, a frank and generous fairy tale. On the wedding day, "they were both so good-looking that all the people cheered and cried 'Hurrah!' "

It is a delicately beautiful big book and a narrative spectacle and there is nothing really like it. Using only open line and solids, no one has dared quite so much nor, in color, employed line engraving to such effect. New plates were made in 1961 and *Seven Simeons* is now printed by offset, an indication of advancing technology; but it remains the work of a linear artist beguiled by Beardsley in his youth and a culmination—a terminus, perhaps —of that tradition.

BUTTONS

Buttons, by contrast, is straight lithography and real life. Gavarni and Daumier, wrote Baudelaire, completed Balzac, each in his way rounding out "La Comédie Humaine"; and from Géricault to Bellows to Kaethe Kollwitz lithography has lent itself to the rough and ready and everyday.

In *Buttons*, nonetheless, Tom Robinson's text is printed in its entirety first, set like poetry, so that it may be read and absorbed independently, the only time to my knowledge that this was done (254). It is an insinuating text, low key but continuously compelling; a story of survival through sheer grit in which pity has no place and "our hero" blunders into a happy ending. Chasing a rival, he is treed, and the sight of a fire ladder sends him through the window of a house where he takes refuge in the basement. Kidneys—"nice fresh kidneys"—and a barred door and gentle attention have their effect and "After a while he didn't want to [run away]. He stopped scratching and began to purr." He forgets he was an alley cat, begins to look like a gentleman, act like a gentleman, *be* a gentleman—and, hero that he is, lives "happily ever after."

Peggy Bacon's pictures preserve his dignity

254

Because the ash can was home.
When he grew bigger and stronger
He looked at his home and didn't care much about it,
So he started up the alley.
He was working toward the daylight at the end of it.
In these days he spent the night where he was when it came.
Sometimes he met other cats.
At first these cats looked at him and let him alone
Because he didn't have anything they wanted.
When he got farther up the alley, he began to find things that other cats wanted.
They tried to take them away from him.
Sometimes they did.
Sometimes they didn't.
When he got bigger and stronger
Nobody took anything away from him.
But they tried;
You could tell that by looking at him.
His ears were torn,
His face was scratched,
His tail was broken,
His fur coat looked ragged and moth eaten,
His legs were bent and twisted till he walked pigeon-toed and bow-legged.

254, 255. *Buttons,* text by Tom Robinson, pictures by Peggy Bacon. Viking, 1938. 9 x 12.

(255). Reading those same lines, considering how they might have been pictured, one appreciates her battered, unbowed fighter and his demi-world of roofs and siding and brick wall, clotheslines and fire escapes.

She had, to start with, a dummy—blank pages with the text pasted in as it was to appear, the stage upon which the artist pictures the story. How the text should divide, which lines should fall on each page, had been decided by the author and editor, as per the brackets added here; that they should appear at the foot of the page—a decision involving the designer also—roughly determined the layout. The script (a term some, indeed, use for picturebook text) calls for an alley at the start, a house at the close, but there are few explicit 'stage directions' or specified stage properties, and the description, in the largest sense, devolves on the pictures.

"When he got further up the alley, he began to find things that other cats wanted. They tried to take them away from him." The cat's progress up the alley—he is not, even at birth, a 'kitten'—is psychological as much as physical, a metaphor for maturing, so once having shown the light at the end of the tunnel (per "He was working toward the daylight"), Bacon has no need to position him precisely; from one page to the next he advances in terms of his encounters with other cats. He finds "things"—the right word for the sense of the story, leaving it to the artist to furnish something plausible, a chop, for the other cats to snatch at. But neither the finding nor the fighting—by a literal interpretation two separate steps—is the subject of the picture; rather, we see the cat at bay, a paw on the chop, snarling: 'He began to find *things that they wanted*, they *tried* to take them away from him.' (Turn-of-page.)

Did they succeed, or didn't they? "Sometimes they did. Sometimes they didn't." Now, in the picture, do they or don't they? A big bristling black cat stands over the tabby but you won't find Bacon deciding, tipping Robinson's seesaw one way or the other, not when he wants to get on to "When he got bigger and stronger/Nobody took anything away from him" on the facing page; not when she can give us, opposite the tabby cowering, the tabby drawn up and glaring, daring anyone to touch his quarry.

In a narrow sense, this is not illustration either; if Artzybasheff, in *Shaydullah* and *Moon* especially, extracts images symbolic of the story, Bacon telescopes, synthesizes, strikes a balance, putting its essence into pictures that tell their own tale and leave the text intact. "When he woke up," the text says of the cat in the basement ashcan, "he was not alone." Instead of showing, redundantly, a waking cat and watching people, the pictures project his feelings at being found—a small head, suddenly alert, an arched figure and a furious, frightened snarl. What the author relates as a development, the artist visualizes as drama.

For all that the text is printed separately, giving it extra weight, *Buttons* is also the first of the big books of drawings, the predecessor of *Lentil* as "one of a projected series of picture books in black and white of the American scene."[12] (The series apparently got no further than McCloskey.) One would not, unprompted, think of the scene as 'American' but of the setting as realistic—newly realistic, in 1938, for picturebooks; but to sponsors of the trend the two were synonymous. " 'Look, Mummy, that's *our* alley!' " a child is quoted as saying in extenuation.[13]

It was nothing new for Peggy Bacon to draw cats (viz. *The Ballad of Tangle Street*) or to make lithographs, sometimes lithographs of cat life; in that respect *Buttons* is a healthy union of commerce and art, an extension of one of the things she did best. It had issue too in paintings—pastels—of "the very toughest cats that ever ruled the backyards and alleys of Manhattan," as *Times* critic Edward

His ears were torn,
His face was scratched,
His tail was broken,

Alden Jewell remarked when they went on exhibit the following spring[14] (and, with illustrations from *Buttons*, were featured in *Life*).

As lithography, her work is distinct from both the filled-in, roundly modeled, high-contrast illustrations of the d'Aulaires (53) and the brisk sketches McCloskey did for *Lentil* —"litho crayon drawings" transferred from paper to the plate (209). The difference extends beyond technique: the d'Aulaire, framed four-square, and the McCloskey, bounded by the page, are composed in relation to a definite space, while the Bacon, even this fuller than usual example, floats free, its axis the tension between the two cats. Elsewhere background is suppressed entirely, everywhere detail is roughed in or grayed over; light and air suffuse the pictures, and the figures, by the power of their drawing, dominate them. The description reaches back, once again, to Daumier.

Assigning a lineage to *Seven Simeons* and *Buttons* is not to exalt them. Different in every respect, they appeared a year apart and within ten years of *Millions of Cats* and the boom in American picturebooks. Two completely realized examples, representing antipodes of graphic art, intent and sensibility—it is point enough.

Seven Simeons and *Buttons* were both published by Viking, they are both what her associates still refer to as 'May Massee's books.' So are the stories of a foreign childhood by the Petershams, the d'Aulaires, Bemelmans, Kurt Wiese and, later, Taro Yashima; the stories of American life, expanding into studies of American life or native fiction, by Lawson, Daugherty and McCloskey, and Ann Nolan Clark's *In My Mother's House*, along with the other accounts of the American Indian that it led to; Marjorie Flack's Angus books, her small *Ping*, her big *Boats on the River*; the run of great books by Marie Hall Ets and William Pène du Bois; such popular favorites as *Ferdinand* and, still to come, the first of Don Freeman, plus the quite special, also upcoming, *My Dog Rinty*.

The majority of her picturebooks, the large majority of her Viking picturebooks (1933–c.1958), were still in print in 1973 and the remainder had, with very few exceptions, long healthy lives on the recommended lists. She had a particular affinity with librarians, publishing the sort of book that was admired or that, once out, seemed what one should admire—books with a kind of moral and artistic authority. It can almost be said that she aspired to produce important books, and succeeded.

At Viking she had the assistance of top designers and production men: Milton Glick, overall head of design and production from 1929 to 1960, directly involved not only with *Seven Simeons* but also, notably, with *In My Mother's House* (and later the designer, with such illustrators as Daugherty and Valenti Angelo, of one after another handsome book for older children); Abe Lerner, who worked on children's books between 1937 and 1942, the period of *Andy and the Lion, The Great Geppy* and *Make Way for Ducklings*; and Morris Colman, his successor and subsequently the designer of both adult books and juveniles, whose list of credits came to be a list of books published—indicatively, in 1955–56, *Crow Boy* (p. 446), *Lion* and *Play with Me*.

If May Massee's books have one thing in common (besides, usually, size), they are the work of individuals—of author-illustrators with a strong personal style; and for such work, spectacular design, even distinctly original design, is counter-productive, drawing to itself attention that belongs to the word-and-picture content or, more exactly, competing with it for attention. The men at Viking were not designers of this sort; unless one fixes on it, one notices not the make-up but the book. As an inspired comment puts it: "The illustrations to be found in *Lentil* seem to me to make that book a much more desirable collector's item than the Doves Press Bible.[15] It can be said with reason that *Lentil* has no great typographic distinction; on the other hand, the design is entirely adequate and the book serves its purpose—the entertainment of readers—with complete effectiveness. That is the best criterion of any book, is it not?"[16]

THE STORYTELLERS

VIRGINIA LEE BURTON, HARDIE GRAMATKY, H. A. REY, DON FREEMAN, BILL PEET

Their natural heroes are animals or machines; their styles are integral, individual, identifiable. Independent of tastes in art or trends in thinking, their work is timeless and consequently slow to date. They are humorists and romancers, moralists and entertainers. Their books sell.

VIRGINIA LEE BURTON

When fathers talk about reading picturebooks to their children, the palm is likely to go to Virginia Lee Burton. 'Gusto' was Felix Ranlett's good word. "By gusto we"—he and his two small sons—"mean speed, action, a leaning forward into the breeze. We mean savor and relish in the telling. We mean vigor of line and movement in the illustrations. Gusto is the twinkle in the storyteller's eye infused into his printed words. It is the carryover into type of a tongue racing to keep pace with a swift story."[1]

Virginia Lee Burton also had two boys for whom she made her first books—not only for them but with them, gauging her success by their reactions and listening to their suggestions. Overmuch is made of the home-lives of juvenile authors and illustrators—of their cooking, their pets, their Early Colonial houses—but surely those two boys account for Burton's being the one woman among the assembled storytellers. Like its one-shot relation cartooning, narrative illustration seems to be a male bent even when, as in the picturebook field, all things are equal.

As Ranlett might have guessed, Burton waited to write the text until she had told the story fully in pictures. "I pin the sketched pages in sequence on the walls of my studio so I can *see* the book as a whole."[2] (Disney cartoons were made the same way, without a script, by pinning sketches on story-boards for review; and, much earlier, Busch too pictured his story first.) Then came the rough dummy, the finished drawings, the final dummy, the pasted-in words. "Whenever I can substitute picture for word I do."[3] She also juggled words to make the text fit the design.

Burton knew exactly what she wanted in a picturebook, hers or another's, and she wanted a good deal—information and significant detail as well as the accustomed clarity, humor and imagination. The wonder is that she achieved what she wanted without losing the spontaneity that Ranlett, among many, praises in her work. One can open *Mike Mulligan and His Steam Shovel* almost at random and find a spread that fits the bill, but read it, look into it, and you are carried off posthaste with the heroes.

Or rather with all deliberate speed:

Mike Mulligan had a steam shovel,
a beautiful red steam shovel.
Her name was Mary Anne.
Mike Mulligan was very proud of Mary Anne.
He always said she could dig as much in a day
as a hundred men could dig in a week,
but he had never been quite sure
that this was true.

Sympathetic, succinct, provocative, it is the best of beginnings, prompting reflection, promising action. In the accompanying picture, Mike introduces Mary Anne; they are not still again until the last page, and the words are never again so important.

When Mary Anne and Mike come rolling over the hills (Wanda Gág-child-peasant hills), leaving dark downtown towers and dark dormitory houses for the sunny world of Popperville, the progression is a story in itself (256). In Popperville, meanwhile, so much is going on that one could play the old child's game of committing items to memory and still overlook, perhaps, the two women gesticulating over the fence or that characteristic Burton touch, the posts, hedges, tree-rows and fences that border the backyards and enclose the scene. Elsewhere no detail distracts and Mary Anne and Mike themselves succumb to the smoke and steam and flying dirt (257). Swirls and sweeps of smoke and steam

256, 257. *Mike Mulligan and His Steam Shovel,* by Virginia Lee Burton. Boston, Houghton Mifflin, 1939. 9¼ x 8½.

They left the canals
and the railroads
and the highways
and the airports
and the big cities
where no one wanted them any more
and went away out in the country.
They crawled along slowly
up the hills and down the hills
till they came to the little town
of Popperville.

256

257

and dirt, orchestrated with sound—"BING! BANG! CRASH! SLAM! LOUDER AND LOUDER, FASTER AND FASTER"—and timed by the spreading setting sun.

Furiously dug, the cellar of the new town hall is finished in a day, but the final triumph is not all Mike Mulligan's and Mary Anne's; they have in fact dug themselves into a hole. Says mean, cantankerous Henry B. Swap: "The job isn't finished because Mary Anne isn't out of the cellar, so Mike Mulligan won't get paid." But the little boy who cheered Mike and Mary Anne along has an out (which Burton, with an asterisk, credited to one Dickie Birkenbush): let Mary Anne be the furnace and Mike Mulligan be the janitor of the new town hall. Even Henry B. Swap

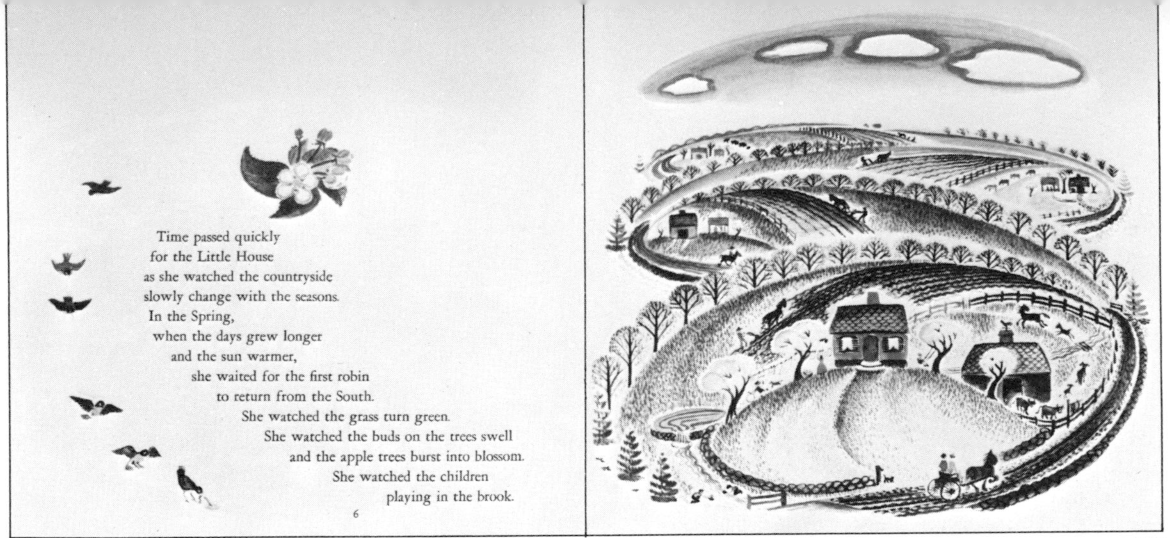

Time passed quickly
for the Little House
as she watched the countryside
slowly change with the seasons.
In the Spring,
when the days grew longer
and the sun warmer,
she waited for the first robin
to return from the South.
She watched the grass turn green.
She watched the buds on the trees swell
and the apple trees burst into blossom.
She watched the children
playing in the brook.
6

258

Pretty soon there was an elevated train
going back and forth above the Little House.
The air was filled with dust and smoke,
and the noise was so loud
that it shook the Little House.
Now she couldn't tell when Spring came,
or Summer or Fall, or Winter.
It all seemed about the same.
24

259

258, 259. *The Little House,* by Virginia Lee Burton. Boston, Houghton Mifflin, 1942. 9½ x 8⅞.

smiles—just as, when last seen, Old Sneep is savoring an ice cream cone. Like *Lentil, Mike Mulligan and His Steam Shovel* is cracker-barrel Americana, tow-headed lad subduing local grouch.

The pastoral strain comes to the fore in *The Little House*, a record of urban decay and a brief for rural blessedness that, appearing in 1942, bridges Model T mistrust of cities and low octane flight from them. As Burton observes, she had a problem: the Little House remained in one place while change occurred around her. At the outset the sun crosses the sky, marking the passage of bright days, and the moon waxes and wanes, the darkness revealing the lights of the city on the horizon. The seasons change, and the lines of trees that sweep across the hills come into leaf, turn red, go bare (258); until "one day" a horseless carriage comes down the country road, then steam shovels and trucks and a steam roller—from the advent of the first car, transportation is the index of 'progress.' Small houses, tall houses, tenement houses encroach upon the Little House: "Everyone and everything moved much faster than before." Trolley cars and then elevated trains cross in front, skyscrapers close in from the back, the seasons vanish in the infernal smoke and din (259). Crushed between skyscrapers and boarded up, the Little House—sound as ever underneath—is at last delivered . . . by the great-great-granddaughter of its builder, who sees in it her grandmother's house "way out in the country on a hill covered with daisies and apple trees growing around." And so, moved on rollers, she will be again.

Never had riverboat melodrama a maiden more grievously abandoned, a more precipitate rescue, a more sanguine end. But easy as it is to mock *The Little House*, the book provides a magic-lantern look at modern city development before wholesale leveling blurred its lineaments. Thirty years later it is history become historical truth, what happened become the nub of what happened. For children it had and has the dimensions of legend, and every left-behind rundown frame structure on a city street is the Little House.

Between *Mike Mulligan* and the Caldecott-winning *Little House*, Burton did *Calico, the Wonder Horse* (Houghton Mifflin, 1941) "for both Aris and Mike in an attempt to wean them away from comic books."[4] "A symphony in comics" Burton's family dubbed *Calico* as she carefully calculated the circles, spirals, right angles and diagonals to get just the feeling of movement or repose she wanted; the figures, silhouetted, are secondary to the evolving design. Originally printed in eight different colors, a deliberate rainbow that dominated the story, the book was redone in

260

he name of a coward," quoth Robin, "I scorn.
Therefore my long-bow I'll lay by.
And now for thy sake a staff I will take,
Thy courage and manhood to try."

hen Robin Hood stepped to a thicket of trees,
And chose him a staff of ground-oak.
Now this being done, away he did run
To the stranger, and merrily spoke:

o! See my staff! It is lusty and tough.
Now here on the bridge we will play.
Whoever falls in, the other shall win
The battle and so we'll away."

ith all my whole heart," the stranger replied,
"I scorn in the least to give out."
This said, they fell to it without more dispute,
And their staffs they did flourish about.

irst Robin Hood gave the stranger a bang,
So hard that it made his bones ring.
The stranger he said, "This must be repaid.
I'll give you as good as you bring."

he stranger gave Robin a crack on the crown,
Which caused the blood to appear.
Then Robin, enraged, more fiercely engaged,
And followed his blows more severe.

, then into fury the stranger he flew,
And gave him a terrible look,
And with it a blow that laid him full low
And tumbled him into the brook.

prithee, good fellow, O, where art thou now?"
The stranger, in laughter, he cried.
Quoth bold Robin Hood, "Good faith, in the floo
And floating along with the tide.

needs must acknowledge thou art a brave soul;
With thee I'll no longer contend.
For needs must I say, thou hast won the day.
Our battle shall be at an end."

261

260. "From Madrid to Moscow," by Caran d'Ache (Emmanuel Poiré). Detail.

261. *Song of Robin Hood,* ed. by Anne Malcolmson, music arranged by Grace Castagnetta, illus. by Virginia Lee Burton. Boston, Houghton Mifflin, 1947. 9 x 11.

1950 in black and white with a colored border —redone and redrawn, with more modeling and less dynamism. In either version, however, *Calico* is not a comic book but a take-off on comic books, and the illustrations have more in common with the strip silhouettes of Caran d'Ache, the nineteenth-century French comic illustrator, than with the crypto-naturalism of contemporary comics (260).

What came of this is more important: the *Song of Robin Hood,* in which the ballads are bordered by a decorative strip recapitulating the story line (261). In essence Burton was always a pictographic artist, at one with the prehistoric men who painted and engraved in caves, the Egyptians whose profiled figures fill band upon band on the walls of tombs, the Romans who carved the events of Trajan's campaigns in a ribbon round his column: like theirs, hers are picture-stories, a sequence of interlinked images.

In *Song of Robin Hood* they are pure picture-stories lovingly embellished, cartoon strips secured by ivy and oak and thistles. Because of their decorative framework they have been traced to the great fifteenth-century Books of Hours, but where Fouquet's is a courtly art of framed paintings, Burton's is a popular art of stop-motion pictures. What is medieval—earlier medieval—stems from another facet of Burton's career, the fabric patterns she made from linoleum blocks; artisan-artist, she uses her inventory of forms to adorn her narrative much as did the carvers at Chartres who edged their figures of saint and sinner with grape vines.

HARDIE GRAMATKY

Draw and tell stories for children, and the shadow of Walt Disney hovers near. Long before the name Disney meant Disneyland and children's classics emasculated, it meant Mickey House and Minnie and their cohorts Pluto the Pup, the Goof, Donald Duck (1928+); the Silly Symphonies (1929+) making fun with sound; and the best of them, *The Three Little Pigs* (1933), thumbing its nose at the Depression to the tune of "Who's Afraid of the Big Bad Wolf?" Nineteen thirty-seven brought *Snow White and the Seven Dwarfs,* the first of the feature-length films, followed by *Fantasia, Pinocchio, Dumbo*—ergo Dopey, Jiminy Cricket and a fresh cast of characters. What Disney wrought is immeasurable; how he did it, that alone, is reflected in scores of picturebooks.

Hardie Gramatky was a Disney animator become watercolorist and illustrator. When he watched the tugboats from his New York studio window, they took on personality, and in *Little Toot* they become people. Other animated machines have push or drive in a single direction, they want to break away (*Stop Tim!, Little Old Automobile*), prove that they have power (the redoubtable *Little Engine That Could,* 1930) or that they haven't lost their power (Mary Anne); Little Toot, like any other person, just wants to be taken seriously.

He is growing up. No more fun and games (262); no more sulks because the other tugs laugh at his little toot-toot-toot (263); he'll work, make father Big Toot proud. But he's afraid of rough water—a machine, a tugboat, he's afraid—and out in the ocean rescuing a liner he's terrified (264). The ship comes free from the rocks and Little Toot, now the harbor hero, escorts it in; withal, his conquest of the Atlantic is a conquest of fear.

As a book, *Little Toot* was a hands-down winner: it was fresh and lively and children would love it, was the consensus. They did and more than thirty years later they still do, with a devotion that makes teenagers refuse to give it up and men marrying take it along with their transistors and records.

Like a Disney character going through his paces, Little Toot is personality in constant motion. When his spirits soar, his bow sweeps up, his visor perks, his flag whips smartly behind; morose, even his smokestack sags; aghast, everything tenses. In animating the inanimate—a leaf, a chair—as in working with animals, a Disney animator, wrote Robert Feild in 1942, "must be able to feel exactly how the particular character would behave under all circumstances."[5] This after remark-

262

262-264. *Little Toot,* by Hardie Gramatky. Putnam, 1939. 7 x 7¾.

263

264

ing that "action is demanded every fraction of a second."[6] *Little Toot* catches the action on the wing, the feelings at their apogee, leaving the onlooker to fill in the intervals.

It is also one of the airiest books ever, all white space and transparent washes and sweeps of brush (where Disney is controlled, tight, ultra-finished). The full-color pages have the clear gaiety of sun after rain but the two-color pages that predominate have much of the freest, most limpid drawing (263). Regardless, one is never far from the artist's hand and his pleasure in the doing, a pleasure sometimes free of purpose: the sparkling frontispiece could be a gallery watercolor were it not for the familiar look of that little tug in the middle.

In subsequent books Gramatky applied the same formula with less success, probably because it was a formula—the likes of Hercules the superannuated fire engine and Loopy the irresponsible airplane are not to be seen from any window.

H. A. REY

In the picturebook world, Curious George is a naturalized American. H. A. Rey brought him, in manuscript, by boat from Lisbon via Rio in 1940 and immediately found a publisher; had the book first appeared in Germany, the Reys' birthplace, or in France, where they lived before the war, doubtless Georg or Georges would have become George in short order just as, fanning out from America, he became familiar to children in a dozen languages. Rey's "jolly bright pictures" were admired here for their European manner—a central European manner, actually, that he shares with Bemelmans—but like Duvoisin and Rojankovsky (and unlike Bemelmans), his work is universal in outlook. Universal and uniquely versatile, for the same artistic shorthand—flexible outline figures, flat washes, a modicum of shadowing—serves him equally well in telling his own stories and in dramatizing the quite different texts of his wife and others (pp. 247, 248).

Curious George, who made his debut in a

prior French edition of *Cecily G. and the Nine Monkeys* (Houghton, 1942), is one of those creations that come to seem inevitable, so completely is he the-small-boy-who-gets-into-scrapes. Everyone knows that monkeys look like people. Disney avoided them as looking too much like people to caricature—that is, they were caricatures of people to start with. In Rey's work the problem doesn't come up. George doesn't feed himself bananas with his feet or swing by his tail (like many African monkeys, he has no tail). He does what any youngster can do or could, given sufficient agility; he is Tarzan, not one of the apes. Add a measure of deviltry and, presto, 'that boy is a little monkey.'

Rey has great fun with him, letting him scamper around the edges of the story, pantomiming relish, contentment, stupefaction to the workaday words, "After a good meal and a good pipe, George felt very tired" (265). But tomorrow is another day, a day for discovering the telephone, alarming the fire department, escaping from jail, walking the high (telephone) wires, surveying the city by balloon (266), before settling down—momentarily—in the zoo. With balloons for all his new zoo friends, a buoyant end.

Rey is as flexible as his hero—or heroes: Cecily G. (for Giraffe), Elizabite the Carnivorous Plant and Pretzel the dachshund are all long benders. When George is just monkeying around, Rey closes in on him; when he has a bird's-eye view, the artist 'takes' him from a high angle and the scene expands to fill the frame. The choice of movie terminology is deliberate. What film technique (live, before cartoon) did to expand the possibilities of picturebook illustration can be seen with exceptional clarity in *Curious George* and in Rey's work generally.

In successive stories George became a fixture, a guy who could be trusted to get out of whatever trouble he got into, so it was good news—for fearful kids, concerned parents, ministering librarians and booksellers—when word came that *Curious George Goes to the Hospital* (Houghton, 1966). If George could do it, so could Dick or Jane.

265

265, 266. *Curious George,* by H. A. Rey. Boston, Houghton Mifflin, 1941. 8½ x 10⅛.

266

267. *Newsstand,* by Don Freeman. (Special Theatre Number, Vol. II, No. 3, January 1940) 9 x 7.

DON FREEMAN

A determined steam shovel, a brave tugboat, a curious monkey anyone can understand; but a mouse who turns the pages for the prompter at the Metropolitan Opera House and, for kicks, plays Papageno in *The Magic Flute*—who would conceive of such a story? what child would put up with it?

Lydia and Don Freeman's *Pet of the Met*, a perennial favorite, bears out the unconventional wisdom that there are no good or bad subjects, only good or bad treatments. Freeman, who describes himself as "backstage struck," sketched the Broadway scene for newspapers and magazines for many years; on his own, he put out a very irregular periodical, *Newsstand*, consisting of lithographs and short write-ups of New York life on all fronts. The tribute to Heywood Broun, theater critic and people's champion, typifies Freeman's manner and point of view, his combination of theatrics and social criticism (267). A fine bit of bravura John Sloan, it shows the same eye for incident, a like skill in handling light and dark. Even closer in spirit to Sloan, with whom he studied at the Art Students League, are Freeman's side-street vignettes of battered lives, their pathos offset by signs of pride.

From drawing on stone for small editions (per *Newsstand*), Freeman proceeded to drawing on zinc for offset reproduction and, for *Pet of the Met*, to drawing on Dynabase, the thin plastic medium whose use Morris Colman advanced at Viking. 'Its slightly grained surface takes a pencil, prismacolor, the way litho pencil takes to stone (almost),' Freeman writes;[7] and, as Colman explains, "the drawing is exposed by direct contact with the film in a vacuum base," bypassing the camera (and the half-tone screen) and retaining "every minute element of each stroke of the artist" (almost).[8] The autographic quality of *Pet of the Met*—the illusion that one could run one's fingers over the paper and feel the crayon, the sense that the artist has just stroked in those streaked layers of color, that he has just dashed off those broken black outlines—has much to do with its visual impact. That and the color itself, the four colors used throughout becoming, to the average eye, full color.

Not gratuitous color, which is why even today, when full-color printing has become commonplace, the scene during the perform-

And when the Prince played upon his flute, one by one the stage animals came out and danced to the magic music.

268

ance of *The Magic Flute* dazzles (268): it is preceded (in reverse order) by a spreading glow as the Opera House fills, by the pink-accented black and white elegance of the Petrinis (269), by the shadowed depths of their attic home. Color is used with calculation, for a colorful story.

During his stint in the prompter's box, Maestro Petrini forgets himself and springs on stage, only to be interrupted during his dance by Mefisto the cat, terrible from his red cape to his outstretched claws. But even Mefisto is not immune to music's charms (by now the Freemans can get away with anything), and

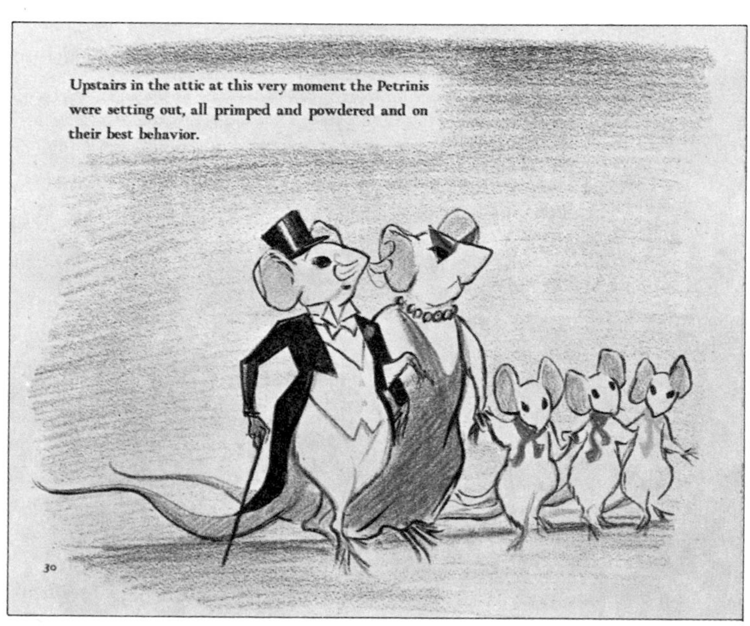

Upstairs in the attic at this very moment the Petrinis were setting out, all primped and powdered and on their best behavior.
30

269

268, 269. *Pet of the Met,* text by Lydia and Don Freeman, pictures by Don Freeman. Viking, 1953. 9¾ x 7⅞.

the two pirouette together "until the curtain had to be brought down."

That wasn't the last of the Petrinis. In *Norman the Doorman* (Viking, 1959) they venture into the thinly veiled 'Majestic' Museum where cousin Norman's mouse-trap sculpture, entered in a contest anonymously, takes first prize—a spoof of both the pretensions of the cognoscenti and the pretentiousness of modern art. *The Guard Mouse* (Viking, 1967) takes them around London, of all places, in the company of cousin Clyde who, stiff-backed and fur-hatted, guards the cracks in the walls of Buckingham Palace, a natural role for an upstanding mouse.

What more natural, too, than for a toy bear to want a pillow when he resettles in a cave (270)? Besides the picaresque/picturesque adventures of the mouse clan, Freeman did many other books—single books and sorts of books in a variety of mediums. *Beady Bear*, a slip of a story for small children done in scratchboard drawings, is a neat conjunction of ends and means. Left behind by his boy, Beady reads that "B is for Bear, an animal brave who lives in a cave," and takes off. He can't seem to get settled and, worse, he muffs his chance to be brave—becoming unwound, he topples over on the ground. He needs his boy with a key, and his boy . . . ? "I need Beady!" The kickoff and the comeback are devices (that work) but the sight of that desolate little bear trudging back and forth—for a pillow, a flashlight, the newspapers—and discovering that the comforts don't make home, that's the simple truth in black and white.

Among storytellers, Freeman is unusual in his involvement with the vagaries of life. A boy dispatched to the barber drags his feet; by a kind of crazy logic that Freeman sets up, he takes everything floppy and fuzzy, in need of shearing or clipping, as an okay for his own unruly mop. Then, the kill—a woman shopping mistakes his crouching head for a real mop, and he's off with a bound to the barber chair. It couldn't happen, hardly, but it touches a common chord and sheer graphic energy—some of Freeman's best on-the-spot drawing (271)—puts it over the top.

And what should he bring back but his very own little pillow!
6

270. *Beady Bear,* by Don Freeman. Viking, 1954. 9⅜ x 7.

271. *Mop Top,* by Don Freeman. Viking, 1955. 7 x 10.

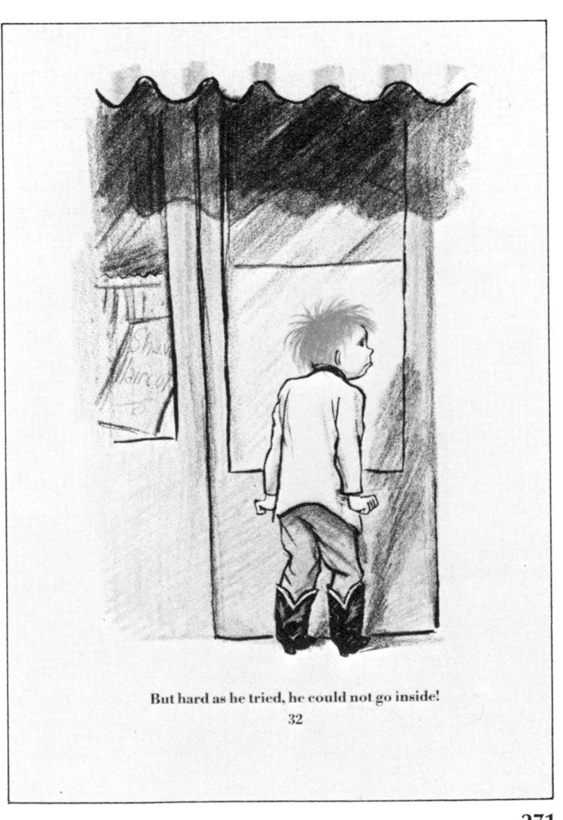

But hard as he tried, he could not go inside!
32

271

272 273

Dandelion thought he should have a manicure too.
13

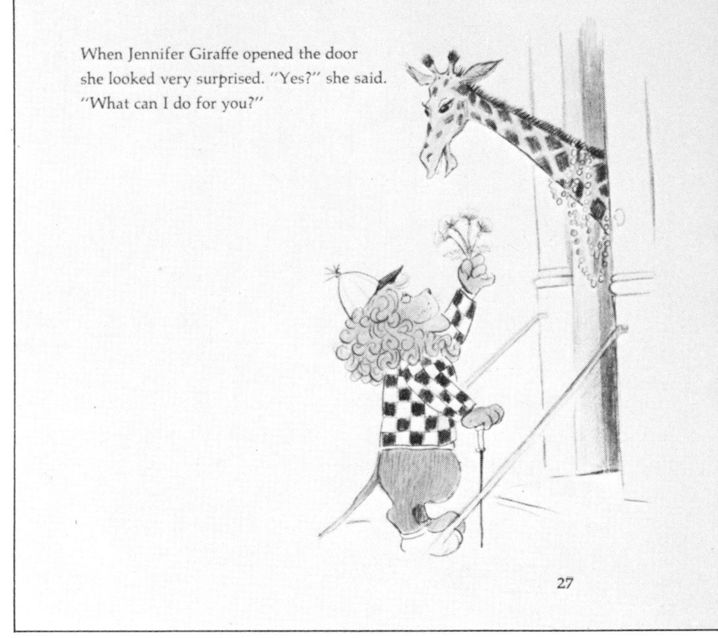

When Jennifer Giraffe opened the door
she looked very surprised. "Yes?" she said.
"What can I do for you?"
27

272, 273. *Dandelion,* by Don Freeman. Viking, 1964. 10 x 8⅛.

Nothing that Freeman has done, though, is more deft than *Dandelion*—in the spirit of the title, Mop Top as a fop. Between the two pictures (272, 273), little remains to be told except that, drenched in a downpour, curls and cap gone, divested of his jacket, Dandelion is welcomed to the party by Jennifer Giraffe. That silly-looking lion who came to the door earlier was he, he confesses to his friends, but "from now on I'll always be just plain me."

Appropriately plain-spoken and free of rinkydink rhyme, held to two colors and spared extraneous background, *Dandelion* is all Dandelion's show, and all the funnier because it's played straight.

BILL PEET

While others invented different plots for a stock character, Bill Peet invented different characters for a stock plot, and succeeded so well that his publisher periodically issues a new poster incorporating the latest additions to the Bill Peet Menagerie. To meet Chester the Worldly Pig, Huge Harold the overgrown rabbit, Ella the egotistical elephant, Kermit the Hermit crab is to know them always: each is a personality.

"Until a character becomes a personality, it cannot be believed." Not a novel observation but particularly apt coming from the old maestro Walt Disney, Peet's long-time employer.[9] Built into it is the distinction between a character with a gimmick and a repertoire of gags, and the one with a rounded, independent reality.

Peet started at the Disney studio as a sketch artist, laying out stories in a continuity of drawings, and in time (and with practice as a parent) became a screenwriter, still illustrating the continuity. ("Screenwriters as such have never been much use to us. Nearly all of our story men started as artists years ago. They think in terms of pictures. That's how we tell our stories, not with words." W. D.[10]) His feature credits include *Fantasia, Dumbo, The Three Caballeros, Cinderella* and several from later years, and he came up with the ideas for many short cartoons.

274. *Chester the Worldly Pig,* by Bill Peet. Boston, Houghton Mifflin, 1965. Detail.

275. *Kermit the Hermit,* by Bill Peet. Boston, Houghton Mifflin, 1965. Detail.

Peet's books are different, most of them. He is the most humane of cartoonists. His heroes are sometimes blamelessly odd, sometimes ornery, but always victims; whether we are born with big ears or get swelled heads, we suffer. There is first hope, then disaster, then discovery of some peculiar advantage in being different. (Not, be it noted, miracle surgery or renunciation.) The funniness starts with the incongruity of a pig balancing on its nose or a crab of a crab—but the incongruity is not itself made fun of: we don't laugh at Chester for wanting to be an acrobat, we laugh at the figure he cuts (274), nor at Kermit for making a face, but at the face he makes (275).

Buford is a runt of a mountain sheep all of whose growth goes into his horns until he's hopeless, and helpless, as a mountain climber (276). He might be another Dumbo, but where Dumbo is taunted for tripping over his big ears . . . "The rest of the sheep were greatly alarmed by Buford's close call. From then on they pitched in to help." (In Disney land cruelty evokes pity; in Peet country misfortune elicits sympathy.) Buford, of course, refuses to be a burden and heads for the lowlands and the security of flat ground.

Enter Peet the master of spatial composition, the peer of McCloskey in this respect. The particular landscape is always part of the action, and exploited for dramatic effect. Buford, standing on a ledge "gazing into the valley far below," is a tiny figure against a sky rimmed with mountains that descend to a boundless plain; safely down, the sun too going down, he trots through a straggly pine forest, respite but not shelter, leaving behind among the last rocks the ravens and buzzards that, black silhouettes against the crimson sky, signify danger averted. One has to read the scene.

The scene may take in real people doing real things, like the man who comes to fix the windmill (277). All is placid, the cattle go about their bovine business, but Buford, recognizing a new danger, conceals himself. Here the exaggerated flatness and the dispersal of the cattle throw into relief the intentness of the man and the woefulness of Buford in hiding, a detail that is prime Peet. However large the scene, the leading character is always distinct, always individuated; played against the broad sun-lit rump of the steer, Buford, standing in its shadow, has the poignance of the shut-out who has only to make his presence known to become prey.

How Buford overcomes his handicap is typical of Peet's ingenuity (278), just as each of the stories demonstrates his inventiveness. Or, as a justly quoted review of *Kermit the Hermit* put it, "This is Peet's best since *Chester the Worldly Pig*, which was his best since *Randy's Dandy Lions*, which was his best since *Ella*, etc, etc. etc."[11]

276 278

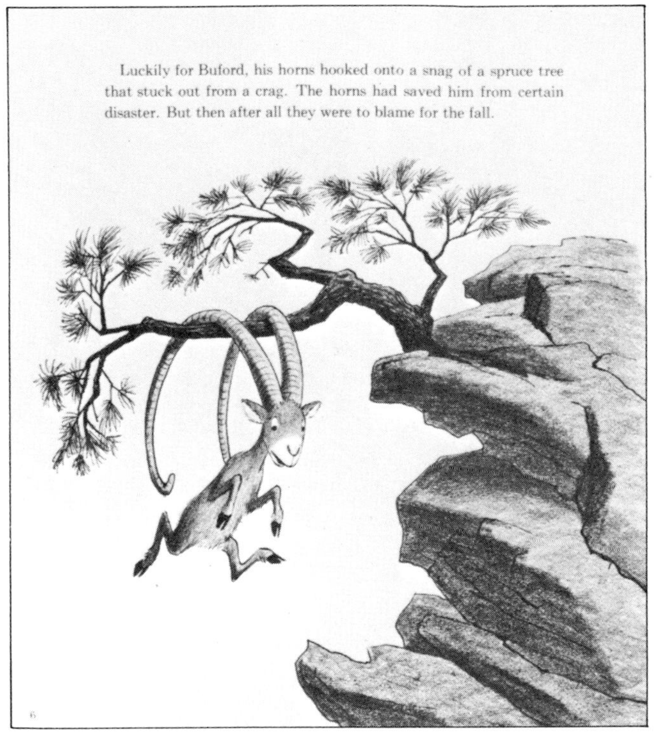

Luckily for Buford, his horns hooked onto a snag of a spruce tree that stuck out from a crag. The horns had saved him from certain disaster. But then after all they were to blame for the fall.

As suddenly as that Buford became the star attraction at the Little Big Pine winter resort. A special ski lift was rigged up for the remarkable ram, so there was no more struggling up steep slopes. It was all downhill from then on.

276-278. *Buford the Little Bighorn*, by Bill Peet. Boston, Houghton Mifflin, 1967. 8⅝ x 9¾.

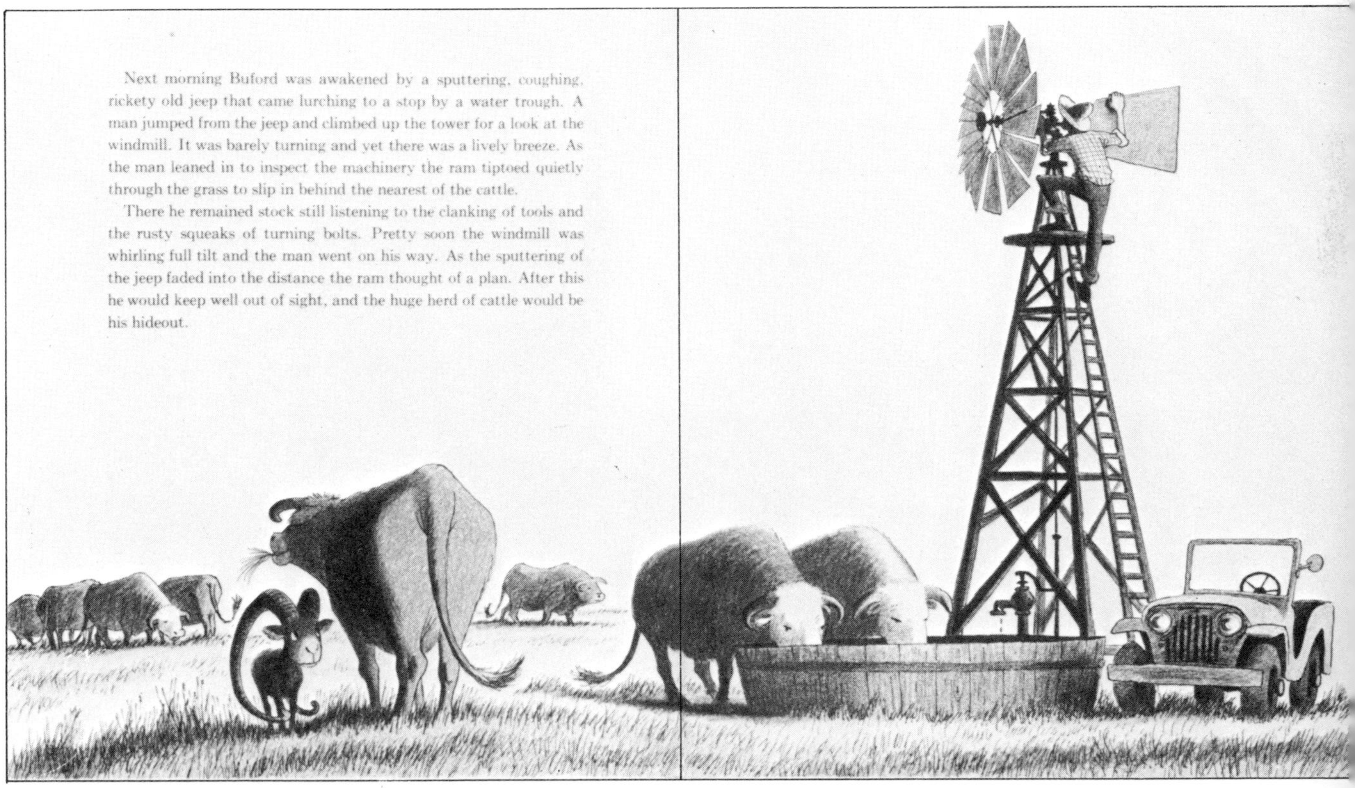

Next morning Buford was awakened by a sputtering, coughing, rickety old jeep that came lurching to a stop by a water trough. A man jumped from the jeep and climbed up the tower for a look at the windmill. It was barely turning and yet there was a lively breeze. As the man leaned in to inspect the machinery the ram tiptoed quietly through the grass to slip in behind the nearest of the cattle.

There he remained stock still listening to the clanking of tools and the rusty squeaks of turning bolts. Pretty soon the windmill was whirling full tilt and the man went on his way. As the sputtering of the jeep faded into the distance the ram thought of a plan. After this he would keep well out of sight, and the huge herd of cattle would be his hideout.

277

DESIGNED FOR CHILDREN

HOLIDAY HOUSE, WILLIAM R. SCOTT, INC., CLOTH BOOKS AND TOY BOOKS

The years 1935–1940, which brought to a climax the first period in modern picturebook publishing, also brought into the field new blood and new ideas—new blood and not simply new talent because the moving spirits were editors, designers and publishers, and some were all three.

Juvenile publishing now commanded serious attention and, having weathered the Depression, benefited from the existence of both a healthy retail market and an alert and active institutional market, each with its own potential. In book design and production generally, wrote Evelyn Harter in January 1935, "a new vigor is abroad";[1] and in relation to young children there was, after years of study, a new sophistication. "We are not dangerously new," said Lucy Sprague Mitchell in the foreword to *Another Here and Now Story Book* in 1937, nor, being progressive, "dangerously traditional." They were less orthodox, more open; and to the urban and informational type of story predominant in the first *Here and Now Story Book* (1921) were added "stories relating to country experiences . . . stories centered in emotional situations . . . and frankly humorous yarns."[2] When the two streams merged—the one relating to the make-up of the book, the other to the interests of the child—we had, from firms founded for the purpose, books designed for children, the first of the new ongoing forces.

HOLIDAY HOUSE

At the same time that she wrote of "new vigor," Evelyn Harter—an astute commentator, herself designer-production manager at Smith & Haas and the wife of Milton Glick—singled out as a book "no one should miss," "Helen Gentry's little *Tom Thumb*,"[3] one of three for children that Miss Gentry printed privately in California in 1934. The others, small but not minuscule, were editions of Andersen's *Nightingale* and Irving's *Rip Van Winkle*, both AIGA choices for the 'fifty best.'

Helen Gentry was an alumnus of the Grabhorn Press, California's finest; at its East Coast counterpart, The Printing House of William Edwin Rudge, Vernon Ives, seeing the books, confided to Miss Gentry his own interest in publishing for children; and when she came East the two, with a college friend of Ives's, Theodore Johnson, set up Holiday House—to bring out books "worthy of inclusion in a child's permanent library," as the first catalog grandly announces ("blithely announces," Ives says in retrospect[4]).

Holiday House was never, in a big way, a picturebook house. It is important to us because it went into business to produce "what printers call fine books" (the words are Helen Gentry's[5]) exclusively for children; because it made a stir in design circles and among children's book specialists; and for two internal reasons—it brought out unusual items with an eye to pleasing children and its products gave to the printed page, illustration aside, something of the character of a picture.

It was the unusual items, indeed, that most particularly had the character of a picture, and nothing better typifies the early Holiday House bent than the nursery rhyme broadsides and the 'stocking books,' examples of which appeared on the first, 1935, list. The broad-

279. "A Was an Archer," pictured by Valenti Angelo. Holiday House, 1935. 9 x 12.

sides—three initially, two each in 1936 and 1937—were mostly the work of Valenti Angelo, his first work for children and an ideal vehicle for an artist with a lean, clean, inherently typographic style. Hung on the walls "of any nursery or school room" as they were meant to be, they were of themselves fine design, a picture of fine design; and none more so than "A Was an Archer" of sturdy wit (279). Selling for fifty cents, they represent a revival of the old English illustrated poem or ballad, printed on a single sheet for posting, but "A Was an Archer" itself has roots in the decorated initial letters and borders of illuminated manuscripts, and it would not be inappropriate to call it, in printed form, just that. An illuminated manuscript for the modern nursery at a price of fifty cents: a bold thought, that, and as it turned out, rash; there was no practical way to market them.

The stocking books too had their drawbacks in the marketplace; easy to hold, they were also easy to pocket. On the positive side, they spread the idea of stocking books per se, "tiny volumes in chapbook form [to] delight small souls, particularly when found in the top of Christmas stockings," and the 1937 *Night Before Christmas* sparked a special vogue for tiny Christmas books. Pluses and minuses

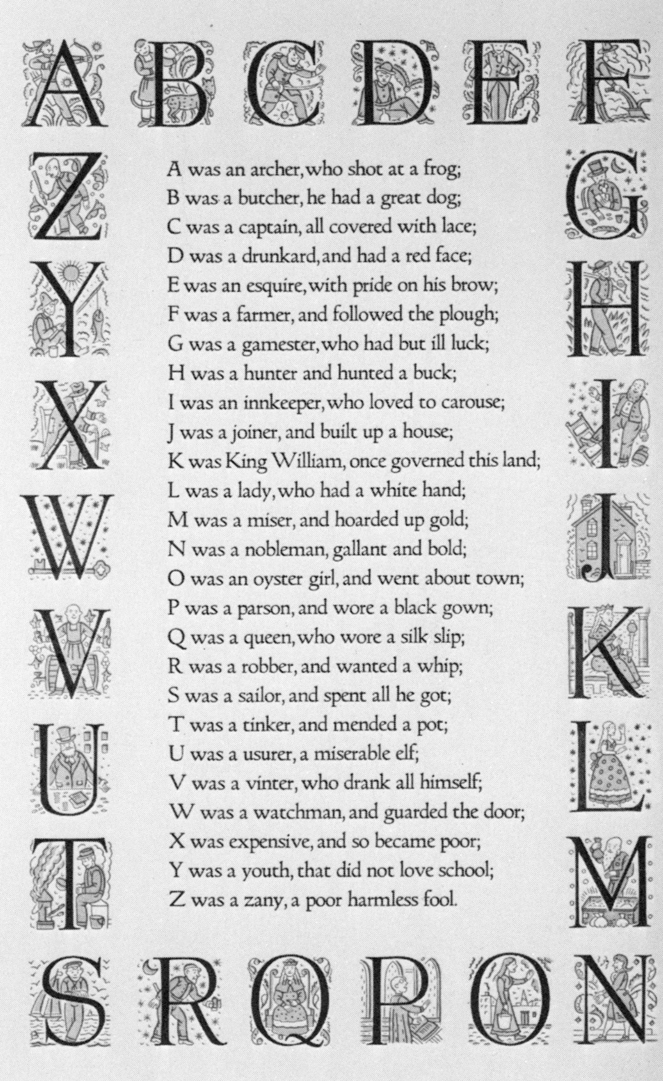

A was an archer, who shot at a frog;
B was a butcher, he had a great dog;
C was a captain, all covered with lace;
D was a drunkard, and had a red face;
E was an esquire, with pride on his brow;
F was a farmer, and followed the plough;
G was a gamester, who had but ill luck;
H was a hunter and hunted a buck;
I was an innkeeper, who loved to carouse;
J was a joiner, and built up a house;
K was King William, once governed this land;
L was a lady, who had a white hand;
M was a miser, and hoarded up gold;
N was a nobleman, gallant and bold;
O was an oyster girl, and went about town;
P was a parson, and wore a black gown;
Q was a queen, who wore a silk slip;
R was a robber, and wanted a whip;
S was a sailor, and spent all he got;
T was a tinker, and mended a pot;
U was a usurer, a miserable elf;
V was a vinter, who drank all himself;
W was a watchman, and guarded the door;
X was expensive, and so became poor;
Y was a youth, that did not love school;
Z was a zany, a poor harmless fool.

apart, they are revolutionary little revivals—`at least as much so as the broadsides—with cut-flush uncovered board sides (or covers) stamped in red; and a red cloth backbone; a petite allover-pattern endpaper—dollhouse wallpaper—with a blank area not, as usual, for the owner's name but for his thumbprint; and inside, instead of the minuscule letters of modern miniature books, good-sized readable type. Type in keeping with the character of the story, set in accordance with its own char-

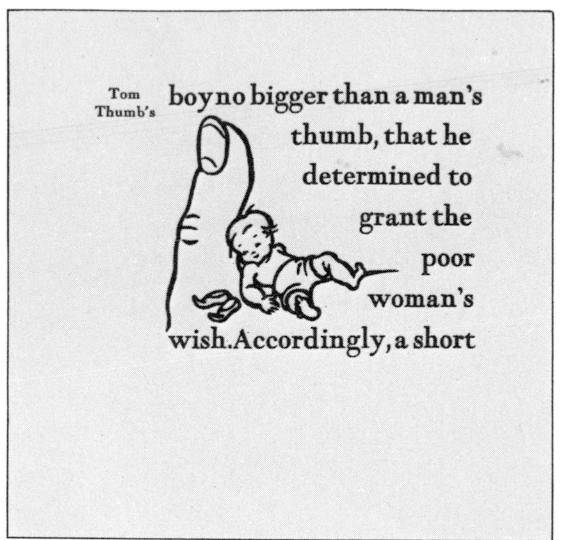
Tom Thumb's boy no bigger than a man's thumb, that he determined to grant the poor woman's wish. Accordingly, a short

280. *The History of Tom Thumb,* illus. by Hilda Scott. Holiday House, 1939. 3⅜ x 3¼.

leaving Thumbelina crying, for she didn't want to live with the horrid toad, nor have her ugly son for a husband. But the little fish under the water had heard the old toad, and now thrust their heads out to see for themselves. No, Thumbelina was much too beautiful for a toad to carry off. So they all gathered

281. *Thumbelina,* by Hans Christian Andersen, illus. by Hilda Scott. Holiday House, 1939. 3⅜ x 3¼.

acter, and set around drawings that have the same feel (280, 281).

Except that the pictures are colored, *Tom Thumb* is as Helen Gentry originally brought it out in 1934, to become the model for the series; now it appeared, boxed, with *Thumbelina*—Tom large against the small, a stalwart little fellow, Thumbelina, who is tinier still ("no bigger than the woman's thumb joint") and dainty, small against the large, a relationship that in its way the text of each bears to the page. They are two variations on the theme of size, with distinct personalities, and at a glance stories of different sorts; design talks. (The artist, Hilda Scott, who had set type at The Helen Gentry Press, became a prominent designer-art director.)

There were eight stocking books when the series came to an end in 1939; in the meantime Holiday House had shifted from fine editions—four out of five on the first list—to original books, thoughtfully made, in a few selected areas. But the founding spirit brought forth also, beginning in 1939, cloth books artfully silk-screened, the cloth itself "strong and safely chewable" (p. 237).

Once, apropos of the children's books in that year's AIGA show, Ives wrote in *Story Parade* ("Making Books Is Fun"): "See how nicely they open and hold in your hand. Notice that the type is not muddy-looking but clear and sharp, pleasantly arranged on the page, and surrounded by plenty of white space. And feel of the paper. It is not thick and fluffy, but turns nicely, with a little crackle, and lies flat as it should. And when you have done these things, you will have found for yourself the pleasure that only a well-made book can give you."[6] You just might, even at eight or nine, and how good to know that someone thinks so.

WILLIAM R. SCOTT, INC.

"In spite of the number of juveniles published every year," says the Publisher to the Reader in the first Scott catalog, "there still exist fields but sparsely covered. For example, there is little published for the very young child. . . ."

Scott—William R. Scott, his wife Ethel McC. Scott, her brother John C. McCullough—started by publishing not books for children but literary fare—reprints, essays, poetry, some art books. But the Scotts had small children who were at the Bank Street Schools and the City and Country School; Ethel Scott talked with Jessie Stanton, a colleague of Lucy

Sprague Mitchell's at Bank Street (successor to the Bureau of Educational Experiments); and Mrs. Mitchell talked to all of them. What was needed, she affirmed, really *needed*, were books that would have significance to young children, and she had the very editor for them, a member of her Writers' Laboratory just beginning to publish, Margaret Wise Brown.

Other needs, according to that initial 1938 catalog, are a "perennial" one for intermediate-age stories written from the child's world out "where adults are not perpetually and eternally right"; and, for older children, "vivid and pictorial source material . . . [with] the immediacy and flavor of eye-witness account." The latter, represented on the first list by *The Log of Columbus' First Voyage to America*, was a sound idea that foundered; the former was more an attitude than a program one could implement.

But one could take a promising text, try it out with children, revise it until it had their full, enthusiastic attention, select an artist, test pictures and text . . . and given talent, wisdom and work, have a book that preschoolers would like and their parents would not find a trial.

The testing process was important—and methodical. As William Scott explained: "We have secured the co-operation of six progressive schools in New York . . . [which] have allowed their classrooms to be used as try-out laboratories. Manuscripts to be tried out are read to groups of ten or a dozen children by the group teacher at regular 'story' times. The children are not told they are being used as guinea pigs, but they are closely watched. Young children are brutally frank. If they do not like a story, they make that fact very clear . . . . If the manuscript interests four-year-olds, it is tried out on twos, threes, fives, sixes, and sevens to establish the area of its age range. Thus the preliminary series of try-outs becomes an objective means of selecting material of compelling interest to young children of a specific age range.

The revised text and the pictures ready, "another series of 'try-outs' is scheduled with new groups of children; the author and illustrator are encouraged to attend.

"We consider this stage of the process of the greatest value, as it puts author, artist, and publisher into direct contact with children during the final shaping of the manuscript into a book. Pictures and statements that are confusing to a child are cleared up; humor that isn't funny is revised or dropped; the all-important matter of timing is checked; the book is custom-made for its eventual users."[7]

As important, however, was the concept of collaboration. In Scott history, 1938–1972, only a handful of persons steadily wrote and illustrated their own books, the great majority being the joint undertaking of author, artist and, in a real sense, publisher. For many years, moreover, the author was likely to be someone who had worked with children, the artist a painter who had done little illustration—two kinds of expertise combining to create something new, different, individual. A ballet, perhaps.

Or the original edition of *The Little Fireman* which, come upon unawares, seemed to me the most breathtaking picturebook I'd ever seen (283-286).

> FIRE! FIRE! FIRE! This is no false alarm but a dashing story about the little fireman who saves fifteen fat ladies, splashes out the blaze, and returns triumphantly to his pink ice cream.
>
> Hosefuls of color by a brilliant new Russian illustrator, Esphyr Slobodkina, an abstract painter. The originals for these illustrations were made of cut-out colored papers, for, according to Miss Slobodkina, scissors enforce a simplicity of line which cannot be achieved by a pen. The amusing story is by Margaret Wise Brown.
>
> *Ages: 4–6, 40 pages, printed on substantial paper, $1.50*

We are going to quote Scott catalogs wholesale because there is no better introduction to the books. What needs be said about the story will wait insofar as it relates to another book on the first list. The spreads are a show in themselves, the typography, fitted to the layout, telling how the story should be told and, of itself, comprising part of the picture, changing color, size, direction; the pictures being, by proportions and placement and perspective, what they are about—the big vs. the little fireman snapped in action (283), the streets, mapped, a segment of the town (286). Everything is simple, clear-cut, straight-on. But look at the two firemen sleeping above, the Dalmatian puppy dogs below (284); the two firemen are on yellow, a yellow floor, in the light, the dogs on blue, in the dark except for the pool of light that shines through —and the pole passes from one floor to another by passing through a smaller blue pool. An artistic deception but as illustration plain as plain.

If *The Little Fireman* is the star of the group, its virtuoso performer, *Bumble Bugs and Elephants: A Big and Little Book* is its standard-bearer.

> A SIMPLE RHYTHMIC PATTERN of pictures and words is built around the very big and the very little. The child grasps the 'plot' in the first few pages, so that he can 'read' the story through the pictures. This makes it uniquely his own—a book that no one has to help him read. To quote Lucy Sprague Mitchell, *This is the youngest book I have ever seen.*
>
> In bringing this book to its final form, Clement Hurd, the artist, discarded many finished pictures, keeping only those that won the complete approval of a group of two and three-year-olds to whom they were submitted. Mr. Hurd was a student of Fernand Leger, is a painter, and has done three theater murals as well as private commissions.
>
> *Ages: 2 and 3, 16 pages, printed on extremely tough cardboard, ring binding, $1.00*

The words are by Margaret Wise Brown, and they begin, in traditional story fashion, "Once upon a time/there was a great big bumble bug/and a tiny little bumble bug/And there was a great big butterfly/and a little tiny butterfly"—only to continue "There was a great big frog/and a very little frog/And there was a big red squirrel/and two little red squirrels" . . . at which point you too will have grasped the 'plot,' or rather the point that, in the usual sense, there isn't one, only a word pattern, as indeed the title page puts it. A pattern of big and little coexisting once upon a time and for all time.

Bumble bugs first—a child's coinage, struck from bumblebee but distinct, the image of a buzzing creature; and naturally small. Elephants last, "a great big elephant" and, balanced on its curled trunk, "a little tiny elephant." A little tiny black elephant, a double incongruity and so twice as funny. (For they are funny, these opposing pairs.) But whether naturally large or naturally small or naturally large and small, like dogs (282), the animals are not big/older, little/younger, not adult and child, but large and small specimens of the same thing—elsewhere big person and little person. To a child, of course, he is the little person.

It was an idea that Margaret Wise Brown was to develop not only in *The Little Fireman* but also in *The Little Fisherman* (pictures by Dahlov Ipcar, Scott, 1945), *The Little Cowboy* and *The Little Farmer* (both Esphyr Slobodkina, Scott, 1948). In all of them big and little are mates, equal to the end. But at the end of *The Little Fireman*, after supping on big and little mutton chops, big and little dishes of pink ice cream, ***the great big fireman dreams*** *a very little dream* and *the little fireman dreams* ***a great big dream***; while at the close of *The Little Farmer*, plainer still, ***the big farmer dreams of a great green land where he is very*** *little* and *the little farmer dreams of a land where everything is little and he is very* ***big***.

May Lamberton Becker, speaking of the swing in children's preferences from large to small books, reflected, you'll recall, on their yearning for "something that will reassure them that they are really much bigger," and the jacket copy for *The Little Farmer* points out the persistence of bigness and littleness in nursery literature, "perhaps because children

There were two little
dogs and a great big dog

282. *Bumble Bugs and Elephants*, text by Margaret Wise Brown, pictures by Clement Hurd. Scott, 1938. 8¾ x 8¾.

themselves are small persons living in a big world." The big and little books aside—*Big Dog Little Dog* (Leonard Weisgard, Doubleday, 1943) is tangential, a father and son story—Margaret Wise Brown wrote again and again about little big people, creatures, things: *The Bad Little Duckhunter* (Clement Hurd, Scott, 1947) who learns better; *Two Little Miners, Five Little Firemen, Seven Little Postmen* (p. 285); *Two Little Trains* (p. 270); *Little Fur Family* and from it, *Three Little Animals* (p. 261).

She had once, she recounted, "tried out a story about a little rowboat that floated away and was found by a little boy and a little girl on the other side of an ocean. 'Why do little boys and girls always have to find it?' asked one five-year-old boy. 'Why can't a fisherman find it and tie it to his big boat and use it?' He was right. All this planned plot where little children figure gets a little forced after the tenth story. But more important than that, I think his remark showed the five-year-old's real interest in real people like fishermen and sailors and captains who really do something on the sea, and not in other little children planted conveniently on the shore."[8] Her response, an answer to both the sense of being small and the inclination to think big, was a big and little fisherman and, with Lois Lenski, real little firemen. (Margaret Wise Brown, in fact, almost never wrote about children.)

But the pattern in *Bumble Bugs and Elephants* is a word pattern also, rhythmic and reiterative in the way of children just learning to talk. "They sort of half-chant their ideas—like 'red light, green light, red light, green light'—over and over," is Brown's observation (the year before her book *Red Light Green Light* came out). "If they like the sounds of the words at all, they repeat them, and make a pattern of them. 'The House That Jack Built' is loved by them because it has this type of rhythmic pattern. So have all the Mother Goose rhymes."[9] With this difference, that "The House That Jack Built" adds to what went before, lengthens and comes to a logical end while *Bumble Bugs*, born anew at every step, in effect makes itself up as it goes along, in couplets, another two- to three-year-old passion; and any number of items—of any sort—may be added to it, in any number of stanzas.

283

283-286. *The Little Fireman,* text by Margaret Wise Brown, pictures by Esphyr Slobodkina. Scott, 1938. 6⅜ x 7¾.

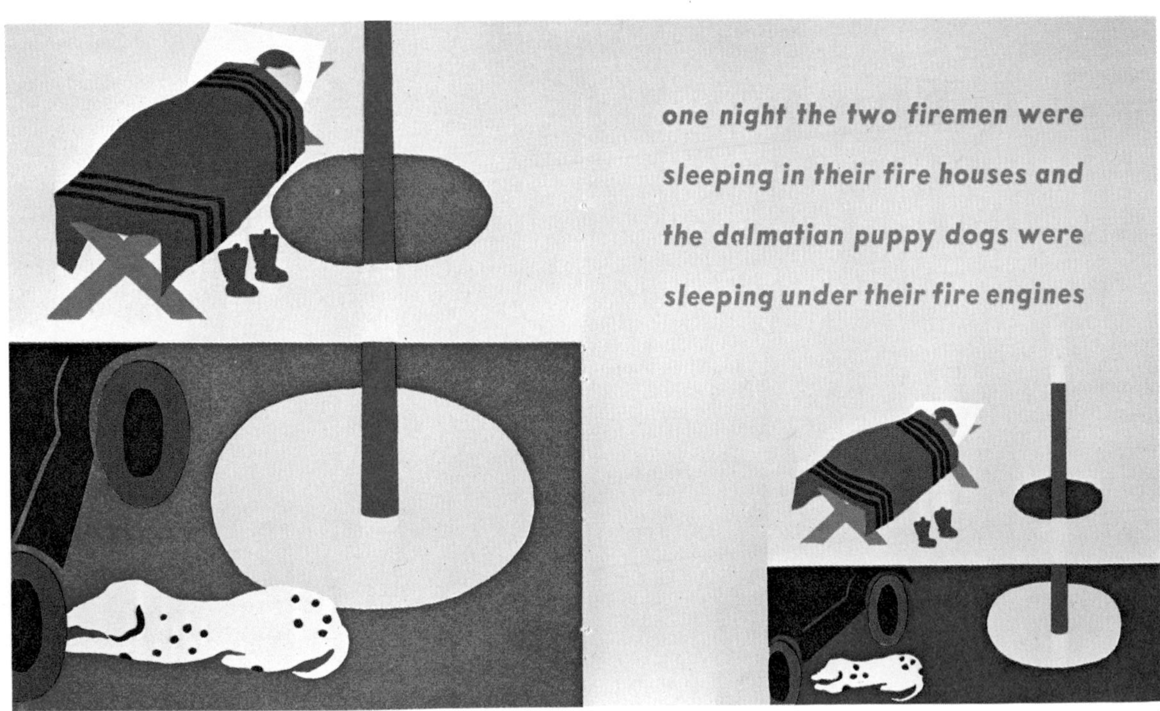

284

"fire! fire! fire!"
called the people in the streets

285

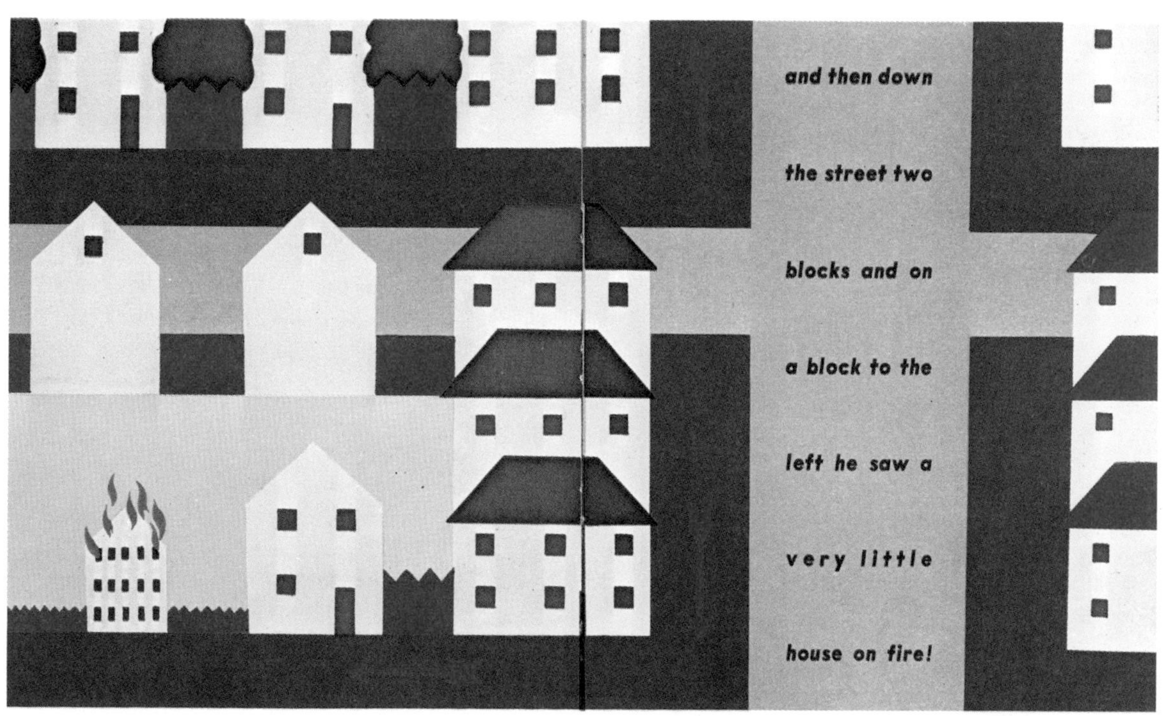
and then down
the street two
blocks and on
a block to the
left he saw a
very little
house on fire!

286

Listing among gaps to be filled older stories "where adults are not perpetually and eternally right," Scott could have been describing *Hurry Hurry* (and quite possibly was).

Hurry Hurry,
A Tale of Calamity and Woe,
OR:
A Lesson in Leisure,

RELATING *the dire mishaps which befell a certain* NURSE *who went* TOO FAST, *together with a faithful account of her* REFORM; *the whole comprising a powerful* LESSON.

A ROLLICKING MORAL TALE in a streamlined Victorian setting. Easy-reading story by Edith Thacher with elegant designs by Mary Pepperell Dana.

Ages: 5–9, 48 pages, easy reading, $1.50

This is turnabout for fair, a child who knows better than Nurse—and for all children, revenge for everlastingly being told to hurry. In too much of a hurry to get Suzie to school to read a DANGER sign, Nurse takes a tumble (287). "You'd better look out, Lady," everyone calls after her, "and not be in such a hurry next time, or something worse may happen." But she persists, and it does; until worst of all, she takes over the wheel of Uncle George's touring car, tears along so fast that Uncle George and Suzie fly out, and runs it *smash*! into a *GLUE FACTORY*. Then, covered from her shoulders to her feet, she has to walk slowly.

Help her? Hurry and help her scrape the glue off? "No," says Suzie, "I won't help you, Nurse, unless you make me a promise." Nurse drags her feet—literally, figuratively. "Stuff and Nonsense! This is no time for promises." But she can't stay gluey all the rest of her life. "What do I have to promise, Suzie?" "You have to promise to walk just like that and never, never hurry anyone, anywhere, ever again."

To bring a hurrier to a halt, what could be handier than pots of glue; and what better retribution than Nurse repeating after Suzie and Uncle George: *"I, Nurse, promise . . . ."* But this is a merciful modern story, and at the end of a week Nurse, much nicer, decides she likes to go slow.

287. *Hurry Hurry,* text by Edith Thacher, pictures by Mary Pepperell Dana. Scott, 1938. 5½ x 8⅝.

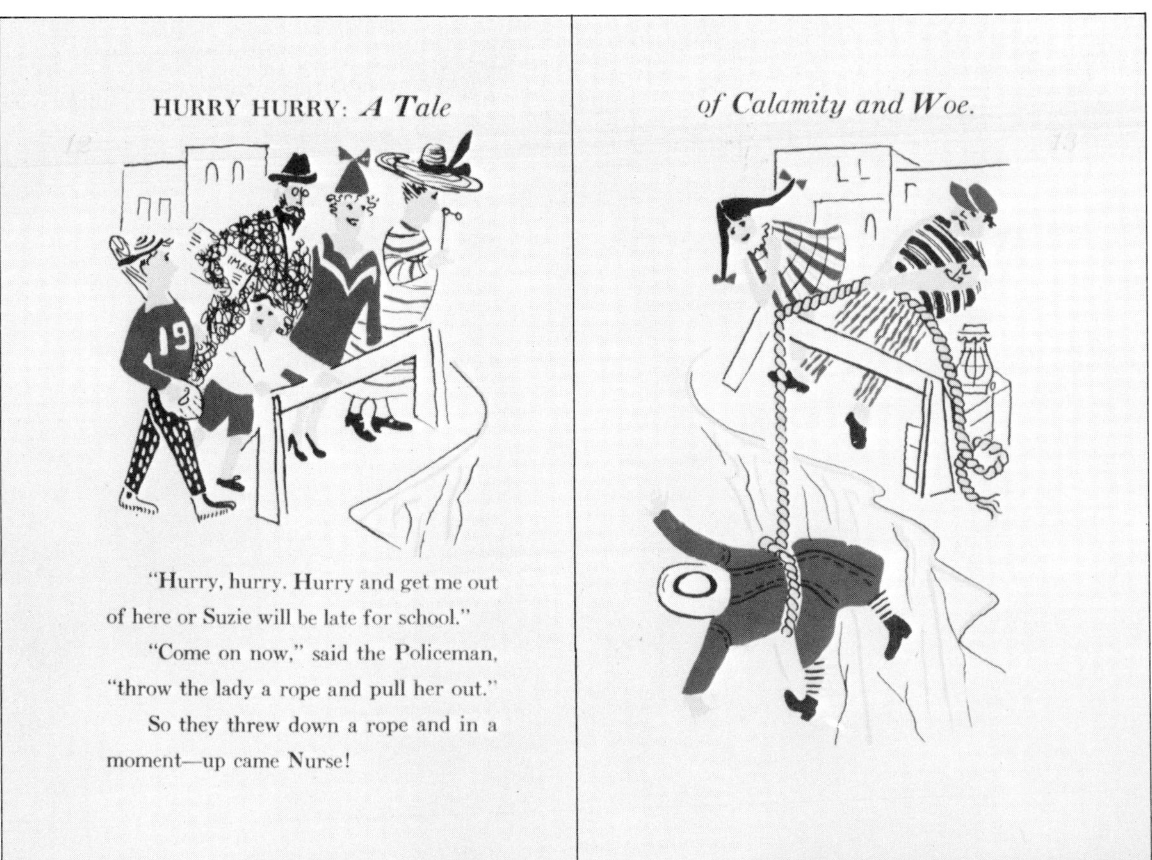

HURRY HURRY: *A Tale*
of Calamity and Woe.
"Hurry, hurry. Hurry and get me out of here or Suzie will be late for school."
"Come on now," said the Policeman, "throw the lady a rope and pull her out."
So they threw down a rope and in a moment—up came Nurse!

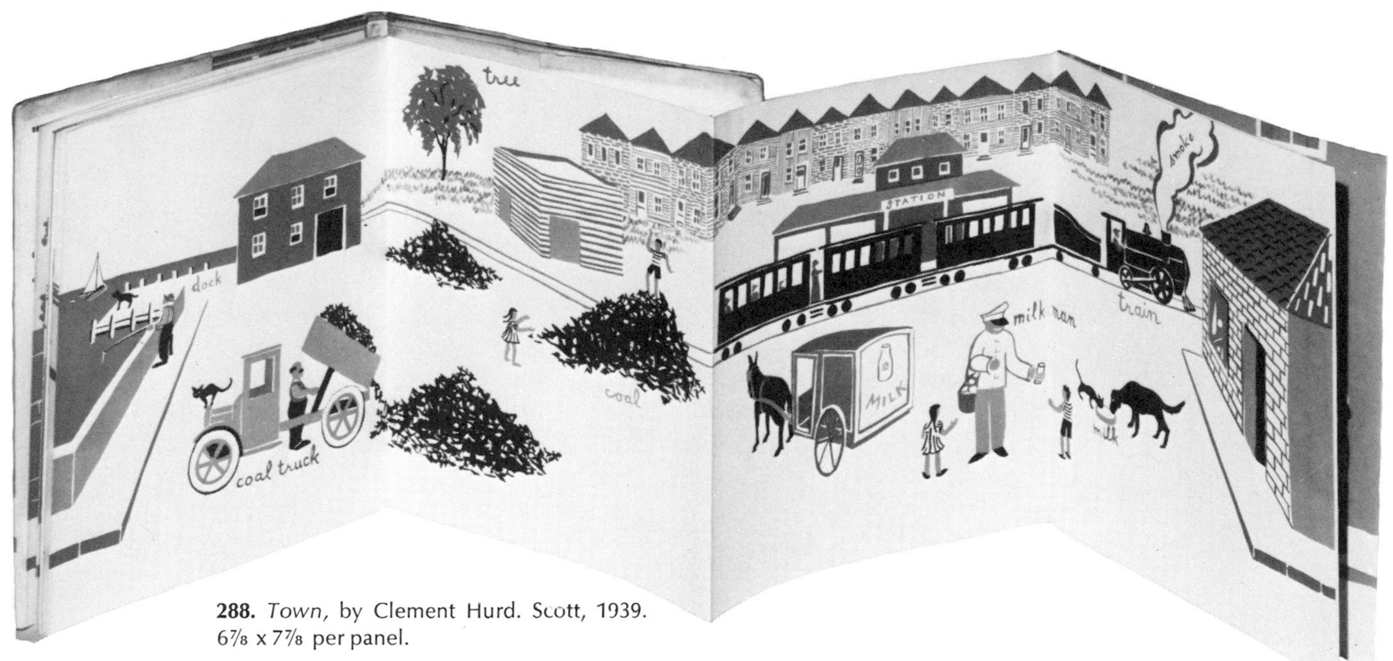

288. *Town,* by Clement Hurd. Scott, 1939. 6⅞ x 7⅞ per panel.

Hurry Hurry has peppery pictures by Mary Dana—another who, like Duvoisin, is funny in the fewest of lines—and a disarming mock-Victorian title page (the catalog announcement is modeled after it) and an open inviting interior; but the contents proved more durable than the package. Scott tried it again in 1947 with Nurse as plain Miss Smith and a plainer, no-elegant-nonsense look; and, alas, *A Tale of Calamity and Woe* as *A Story of What Happened to a Hurrier*. But the strategy, *if you can't beat 'em, join 'em*, didn't work, and *Hurry Hurry* never did well for Scott; reborn in 1960, however, as a Harper "I Can Read" with illustrations by Clement Hurd and a tighter text, it is good sport still.

Completing the first Scott list were *Cottontails*, "a tactile book on cloth" (p. 236) and *Columbus' Log*. This was 1938, when Norman Rockwell nostalgia reigned on the *Saturday Evening Post*, Al Parker's glamour girls brought Hollywood to the *Ladies' Home Journal*, and commercial art in general cultivated cultural backwardness. On the fine art front, modernist art was under fire from Right and Left—from champions of the American Scene and proponents of Social Realism. In picturebooks, it was the year of *Andy and the Lion*, *Buttons*, the first *Three Policemen*—a typical good Thirties' year. But as against these, even against *The Three Policemen*, the Scott list looked like the October Revolution.

William Scott and Margaret Wise Brown dutifully took the books to Anne Carroll Moore for approval, and she pronounced them "Truck"; the *Horn Book*, where omission was synonymous with disapproval, took notice only of *Columbus*. The preschool books had, however, a nursery school and home market independent of the library structure, and they were not without friends in high places. May Lamberton Becker, on the *Herald Tribune*, was a steady supporter, and Louise Seaman Bechtel, who had herself worked with the Writers' Laboratory and contributed to *Another Here and Now Story Book*, helped open the door at *Horn Book* as a reviewer and member of the editorial board. But across the country acceptance was slow in coming—for any of the early lists.

On the second was *The Noisy Book* and Gertrude Stein's *The World Is Round*: a book encouraging children to make noise and a children's book by the writer most baffling to adults.

There were also, born of *Bumble Bugs*, the panorama books *Town* and *Country*. Panoramas—on cardboard or heavy paper, unfolding like screens—were nothing new as such. Originally they were just what the name implies, panoramic views of celebrated places or historic scenes, and the Soviets adapted them, cleverly, to public works and the five-year plan. In the twentieth century, too, they descended to the nursery, and the Czechs in particular contrived simple close-up panoramas of barnyard animals and active children, panoramas that a child could set up around him and play in, like stage sets. (As conceived in 1940, the d'Aulaires' *Animals Everywhere* [Doubleday] was a panorama book somewhat of this sort, in color on the side showing the animals from the front, in monochrome on the side showing them from the rear; reissued in 1954 as a conventional picturebook, its front-back scheme makes less sense.)

Town and *Country*, however, have something in common also with those Oriental screens which, like handscrolls, tell a continuous story—in *Country*, the story of two children who arrive by train, ride in a wagon via mountains and waterfall to the farm where animals, a pond and field-work await them and the beach is not far off. In *Town*, expectably, more goes on and the boy and girl, town-dwellers to start with, are in their element. (In its simpler way, this is Boyd Smith's Bob and Betty anew, with town—or city—become an intriguing habitat too.) Boy and dog head outdoors past an organ grinder and a friendly policeman to meet girl and cat, and the two go on to the park (where boy and cat climb an apple tree), to the waterfront, the coalyard and railroad station (288)—and then head for home.

"These ingenious books," says the flap, can be "opened out as play backdrops for toys, hung up as murals on the nursery wall, or read," either as picturebooks or early readers. 'Read,' that is, by following the suggested story on the back page or utilizing the labels on the pictures or, easy enough, keeping your eyes open. Better the last two, for the story as outlined—"A little boy and his black dog came out of their house one morning"—reduces the excitement of discovery to a flat recital of fact and the verve of the pictures to verification.

Bumble Bugs, *Town* and *Country* and, upcoming, *The World Is Round* were for Clement Hurd a springboard—the proper word for an artist who, among other things, is a master of locomotion. *The Race* (Random, 1940) between a monkey and a duck, by land, sea and airplane, continued as a Wonder Book (1946) and resumed, rewritten, as an I Can Read (*Last One Home Is a Green Pig*, 1959); *The Merry Chase* (Random, 1941) of a dog and a cat went on too, in the guise of *Run, Run, Run* (Harper, 1951); and *Catfish* (Viking, 1970) is the wildest thing on wheels since Marie Ets's *Little Old Automobile*.

Using flat forms and broad generalized outline, composing over a large area, hanging loose, Hurd worked then the way children think of working, setting down how things seem, the idea of things. Those who thought to discredit much modernist art by noting its resemblance to the work of children were right in their perception if wrong in their conclusion: the expressionists and fauves, particularly, borrowed the techniques of children's art deliberately, to recapture their spontaneity and oneness with the world. "Art does not render the visible, it renders visible," said Klee. But such work is analogous rather than imitative; and this is true of Hurd although, later, it will not always be true of others.

In 1939 he and Edith Thacher were married, a conjunction of complementary talents and the start of the most durable and productive partnership in picturebooks. They did some books together (*Last One Home* and *Catfish* among them) and some separately, and both collaborated with Margaret Wise Brown—Edith Hurd, then teaching, was also a member of the Writers' Laboratory and a contributor to *Another Here and Now*. Hers, indeed, is one of the few authentically funny stories—one of the few, too, that dispenses with a didactic introduction; "The Elephant's Delicate Taste," it's called, and it is told Just So.

Of several literary lights asked to consider writing for children, Gertrude Stein was the only one who responded. (One of the others,

Bill Scott thinks, was Hemingway.) And so "Rose is a rose is a rose" (*Geography and Plays*, 1922), spread abroad as "a rose is a rose is a rose is a rose" (*The Autobiography of Alice B. Toklas*, 1933), became *The World Is Round*, Chapter I, "Rose Is a Rose"—printed, at Gertrude Stein's insistence, on rose-colored paper in blue (289).

"Rose was her name and would she have been Rose if her name had not been Rose. She used to think and then she used to think again." She has a big white dog named Love and a little black one called Pépé, only the little black dog isn't hers, it won't even say how do you do to Rose because once when she was young (she is nine now and nine is not young) Rose shut Pépé up in a room and he was so nervous he did what he had been taught never to do in a room. And when he was let out he went up to Rose and bit her and nobody could blame him, it was the only time he ever bit anyone. "And all this time the world just continued to be round."

Rose sings songs and her songs make her cry.

Why am I a little girl
Where am I a little girl
When am I a little girl
Which little girl am I

Rose has a cousin named Willie and he sings too, it is in the family to sing, and his songs make him excited. (Willie is an exciting boy, once he was almost drowned. Twice he was almost drowned.)

My name is Willie and I am not like Rose
I would be Willie whatever arose,
I would be Willie if Henry was my name
I would be Willie always Willie all the same.

The question, is it a book for children, is better put as the rhetorical, how could it not be? Not only is "the playfulness with sounding words" equally a child's pleasure, as Margaret Wise Brown observes—adding that "a two-year-old's song, 'cereal cereal cereal, lay me lay me lay me,' echoes Miss Stein's 'Let Lucy Lilly Lilly Lucy' "[10]—but the rhymes, the rhythms, the monosyllabic beat, the running on, the simplicity, the exactness (this from William Gass's stock-taking of Stein[11]) can be called childlike too and, in censure, were. No matter: "I sing," she said in *A Long Gay Book*, "and I sing and the tunes I sing are what are tunes if they come and I sing."

So there is the writing; but there is also what is written—Rose and Pépé and Rose and Willie and Rose and Billie the lion that Willie gives her who is "neither there nor here, Billie the lion never was anywhere. The end of Billie the lion." And there is Rose and the world and all creation going round and round. "What could she do but try and remember

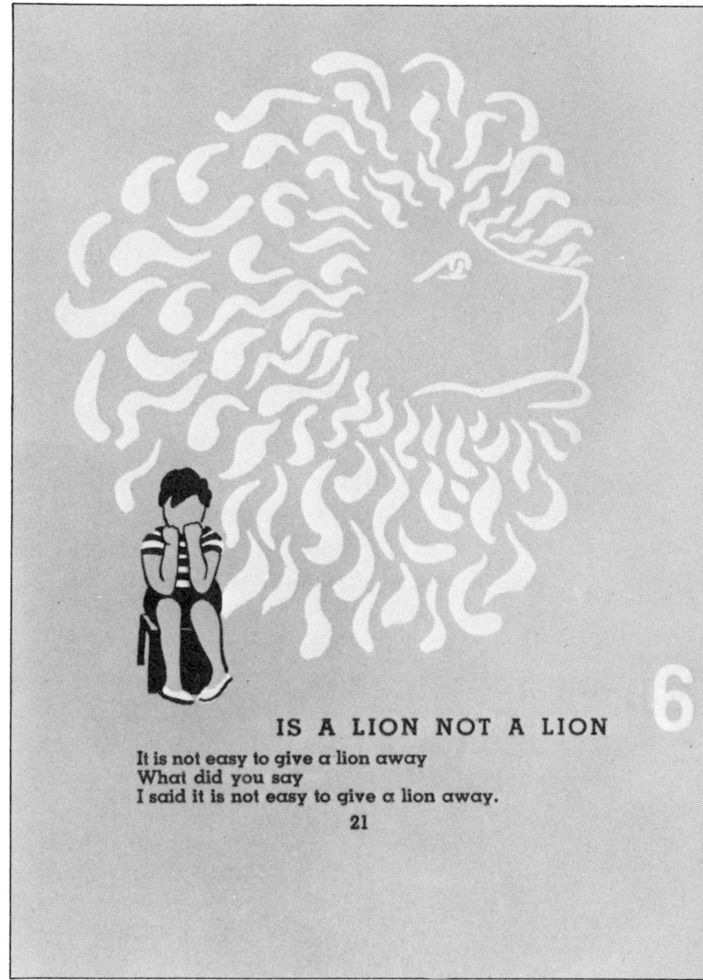

6
IS A LION NOT A LION
It is not easy to give a lion away
What did you say
I said it is not easy to give a lion away.
21

289. *The World Is Round,* by Gertrude Stein, illus. by Clement Hurd. Scott, 1939. 7¾ x 10.

the mountains were so high they could stop anything."

Louise Bechtel states it well: " 'The World Is Round,' says the title, yes, that is another appalling fact, the refrain of this book. Also the sun, the moon, and alas, even the stars we once thought five-pointed, are round, and keep going round and round. Where do *I* come in? Please make someone stop it all and listen to *me*."[12]

In time Rose climbs a mountain, taking along only, for comfort, a blue chair. "And there is a night of fear"—this is Mrs. Bechtel again—"but not half so fearsome as the woods in the Snow White movie. And was she lost? 'She never had been lost and so how could she be found even if everything did go around and around.' "[13] And on a tree trunk, yes, all around, she carves "Rose is a Rose is a Rose." (And on another discovers *Rose* and underneath it *Willie* and under *Willie, Billie.*)

So it goes round and round, "ridiculously simple" and subtle, introspective and aware, to a last little chapter, "The End."

> Willie and Rose turned out not to be cousins, just how nobody knows, and so they married and had children and sang with them and sometimes singing made Rose cry and sometimes it made Willie get more and more excited and they lived happily ever after and the world just went on being round.

Reading it now, one is reminded of how quickly Beckett, another mystifier, has come plain; but in 1939 such were the uncertainties that the opinions of children were much sought and cited. One called it "more relaxing than anything I have ever heard of," another "simple and dreamy" ("You can forget yourself and live in a separate world while you are reading it"). "It is much more *human* than most books," was a further comment.[14] These were the remarks of children eleven to thirteen, there was appreciative comment at nine, and fives were reportedly attentive; but "the new style writing" that a nine-year-old liked "because it is the way I, or any other child, would think and write," made little headway in books for older children while in the picturebook field it thrived. Margaret Wise Brown, reinforced, wrote like Gertrude Stein writing like a child—whether more like Gertrude Stein or like a child is immaterial; and through her the stream of consciousness, as it were, entered the mainstream.

When three-year-olds heard *The World Is Round*, discussion quickly reverted "to a story they had just listened to about sounds"[15]—inescapably, *The Noisy Book*. At lunch a young artist, Leonard Weisgard, had told Margaret Wise Brown about his father taking him around London and recording the street noises and cries, "at which we both agreed that shapes could suggest sounds, and that maybe a book of sounds could be done for children—the two, three and four year olds who were hearing these sounds for the first time—in which the shapes behind the objects making the noise could suggest the sound."[16]

The next day, armed with a first draft, she went through the various groups at the Bank Street nursery school "to see what this book written in the form of questions would mean to the children of different ages and what questions they might ask which could be included in the book. I listened carefully to the sounds the children made in answer to the questions, listened to the timing to judge the length of the book, revised my original sketch and that same afternoon handed Leonard the manuscript. Four days later he came back with the pictures and he had so well demonstrated his premise . . . that no one to this day has ever consciously noticed what he was up to"[17]—"which [her typescript of the article adds] I consider the ultimate success of an applied somewhat surrealist idea used in children's books, where it belongs."

He had accomplished also the introduction of cubist planes, he had made a picturebook in the McKnight Kauffer-Stuart Davis idiom of the Thirties—"a simplified, formalized and more expressive symbol of the things represented" (Aldous Huxley on Kauffer[18]) employing "broad generalizations of form and non-imitative use of color" and "a conceptual instead of an optical perspective" (Davis on

Davis[19]). Like Davis too, he is caught up in the dynamics of the city, the tempo and fragmentation of modern urban life (290).

What Weisgard did was in the air and Kauffer and Davis are handy correlates only, Kauffer in applied art (poster and jacket design and illustration), Davis in 'pure' painting. And it is less important that the cover design for Kauffer's 1937 Museum of Modern Art exhibition catalog is echoed in *The Noisy Book* than that the design was, in Kauffer's words, "an endeavor to dramatize shapes in space"; just as it is more to the point that Davis, a devotee of jazz, perceived that qualities of music—like Weisgard's sounds—have their counterpart in painting, than that there exist certain formal correspondences between their work. What was in the air was a new non-imitative way of working generally, a way of expressing intangibles, communicating emotion, sensation—one which invited the viewer, too, to see things in a new way. To picturebooks, it brought an alternative to story-telling illustration; and it is not too much to say that, beginning with the early Scott books, modern art—or as we now style it, modernist art—enabled picturebooks to cease being primarily stories.

The Noisy Book is indeed about Muffin, a little dog who gets a cinder in his eye, goes to the doctor, has a bandage put over his eyes, and can't see: "Everything looked as dark to him as when you close your eyes . . . BUT MUFFIN COULD HEAR"—and the book is really about the noises that Muffin hears. What are they, what is making them? In the first half of the book we see (291); and we see, as well, the shapes by which Weisgard suggests their sounds. Then the real questions begin: "It began to snow But could Muffin hear that?" *No*, chorus children confronted with snowflakes falling in a vacant surrealist cityscape. But the big question is a little noise . . . "squeak squeak squeak It was not a mouse What could it be?" A big horse going squeak squeak squeak? Titters, and if the reader pauses, a hearty *NO* to meet Margaret Wise Brown's. A policeman going squeak squeak squeak? More giggles, and *NO* again. A garbage can? a big fierce lion? an empty house? The *NO*s rise to a contemptuous clamor before the book takes a breath, quiet now, "What do YOU think it was?" And out of lots of guesses nobody will be right but that's fine, because everybody loves a surprise. "It was a BABY DOLL And they gave the baby doll to Muffin for his very own."

The question form is familiar from *They All Saw It* where Margaret Wise Brown, some years later, would wring suspense from an assortment of Ylla photographs; and it is the form in which the many succeeding Noisy Books are cast. It engages children point-blank, with queries that are real questions; it expects them to make noise, and guides it; and it sets them thinking about the many sounds they know. Children don't so much learn from a book like *The Noisy Book*, Margaret Wise Brown and William Scott agreed in a radio interview, as they have a chance to exhibit their knowledge; and Brown liked to tell about the youngsters who corrected her description of a car as going honk-honk. "They told me an automobile went awurra-awurra. I realized for the first time that I was 'dated.' I'd gone back to my *own* childhood for the sound of a horn."[20] Yet *honk* persists still, a signal substituting for a sound (and a word easier to say than *awurra*).

The Country Noisy Book keeps Muffin in a box for the journey, as good as blindfolded, and once loose in the country everything is new to him; let listeners then look at the pictures and tell him what goes Quack quack Quack quack, let them listen—clever, this—to Whip poor Will Whip poor Will Whip poor Will and tell him what was that. *The Seashore Noisy Book*, going further afield, puts Muffin on a sailboat in a fog . . . DONG DONG ding DONG DONG; and overboard, making a BIG SPLASH. *The Indoor Noisy Book* afflicts him with a cold, and in his bed upstairs he hears the sounds of the household and then, happily, footsteps coming up . . . If one includes the off-key *Noisy Bird Book*, there are eight in all, including—what else?—*The Quiet Noisy Book*. Only one, *The Winter*

Noisy Book, was not illustrated by Weisgard, and that by Charles Shaw in a fashion particularly attentive to the shape and color of sounds.

The Noisy Book was not Leonard Weisgard's first; he had written and illustrated a smart little nothing, *Suki, the Siamese Pussy*, for Nelson in 1937 and done a sophisticated *Cinderella* for Doubleday in 1938—both in the suave and airy French manner of *The Picture Play Book* (169). He and the guiding spirits at Scott knew and admired the French and Russian product, and "though they might err according to our American standards in being oversophisticated for children," wrote Margaret Wise Brown in 1947, "that seemed at the time, in 1936, preferable to the timid and oversentimentalized American approach then so prevalent, an approach which seemed more designed for librarians than to record the lusty first impressions of very young children."[21] *The Noisy Book* is modern, alive and *American*—bold playful cacophonous American.

Weisgard & Brown followed it with *Punch & Judy*.

> Right this way, ladies and gentlemen, for the greatest little show on earth. That notorious, gay, witty and wicked rogue, Mr. Punch, has at last been captured and put into pictures and print. A classic of the puppet stage for over three centuries, now for the first time in book form for children.
>
> . . . .
>
> The heavy paper jacket turns into a stage with cut-out puppets, so that you can put on your own show—admission three pins, a skate-key or what have you. Step right up, ladies and gentlemen . . . .

What the catalog doesn't tell us is that we can sing along too, straight through, to the tune of "For He's a Jolly Good Fellow"—and who but MWB would have thought it? Nor was there ever a snazzier mix of pictures and typography or, on the part of Leonard Weisgard, a handsomer performance (292). An

290, 291. *The Noisy Book*, text by Margaret Wise Brown, pictures by Leonard Weisgard. Scott, 1939. 7 x 8½.

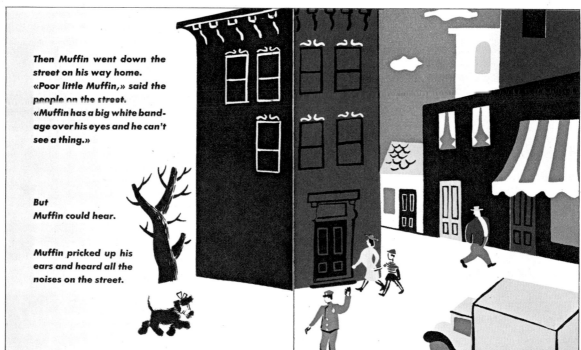

Then Muffin went down the street on his way home.
«Poor little Muffin,» said the people on the street.
«Muffin has a big white bandage over his eyes and he can't see a thing.»
But
Muffin could hear.
Muffin pricked up his ears and heard all the noises on the street.

290

291

inspired book but not, WHANGO! a commercial success. (Prematurely anti-fusty? Or does it lack that elusive common touch?)

Weisgard collaborated with Brown also on *The Poodle and the Sheep* (1941) for Dutton, on *Night and Day* (1942), *Little Chicken* (1943) and others for Harper (which also took over the Noisy Books in 1950), on the luscious big *Golden Egg Book* and its successors for Golden Books (p. 290); and he decorated a posthumous collection of her verse, *Nibble Nibble* (1959), for Scott: numerically he is the leading Brown illustrator. But by no books are they better known together than by the books they did for Doubleday, she under the name of Golden MacDonald.

We have spoken of *Big Dog Little Dog* (1943) and alluded, apropos of children's word play, to *Red Light Green Light* (1944). For all that in MWB's view Golden MacDonald was a distinct persona, *Red Light Green Light* and the similar subsequent *Whistle for the Train* (1956) are a direct extension of the thinking that produced *The Noisy Book*; that is, they are immediate everyday experiences set up in word patterns. Word patter, one might almost say, and that is the difference—poetic word patter, the idiom that Brown was to carry further in books like *Goodnight Moon* (1947).

RED LIGHT	Goodnight stars
GREEN LIGHT	Goodnight air
GOOD MORNING	Goodnight noises everywhere.

A truck comes out of a truck's house, *a garage*; a car comes out of a car's house, *another garage*; a jeep out of a jeep's house, *a tent*; a horse out of . . . *a barn*; a boy out of . . . *a home* (surprised?); a dog out of . . . *a kennel*; a cat down from . . . *a tree*; and a mouse . . . ? "The mouse came out of the house of the mouse *a hole*." (Sound that out aloud and it sings.) Through the day they go down "Dog roads Cat roads And mouse roads through the grass . . . Green light they can go. Red light they can't" (293); until at last it is night and they all go home, each one into its

PUNCH AND JUDY

Judy came running back into the room.

Hello, Judy. Back so soon?

Where is our child, Mr. Punch?

Gone, Judy dear. Gone to sleep.

What have you done with our child, Mr. Punch? I heard it crying just a minute ago. Where is it?

Gone to sleep, I tell you.

Judy grabbed Punch by the nose.

Tell me where the child is, Mr. Punch, or I'll pull off your nose.

Ouch! Let go of my nose! Gone to sleep, I say. Gonnnnn— How should I know where it is? I dropped it out the window.

Then out you go after it.

And Judy threw Punch out the window.

292. *Punch & Judy,* adaptation by Margaret Wise Brown, pictures by Leonard Weisgard. Scott, 1940. 8⅝ x 9⅝.

293. *Red Light Green Light,* text by Margaret Wise Brown, pictures by Leonard Weisgard. Doubleday, 1944. 10⅛ x 7⅞.

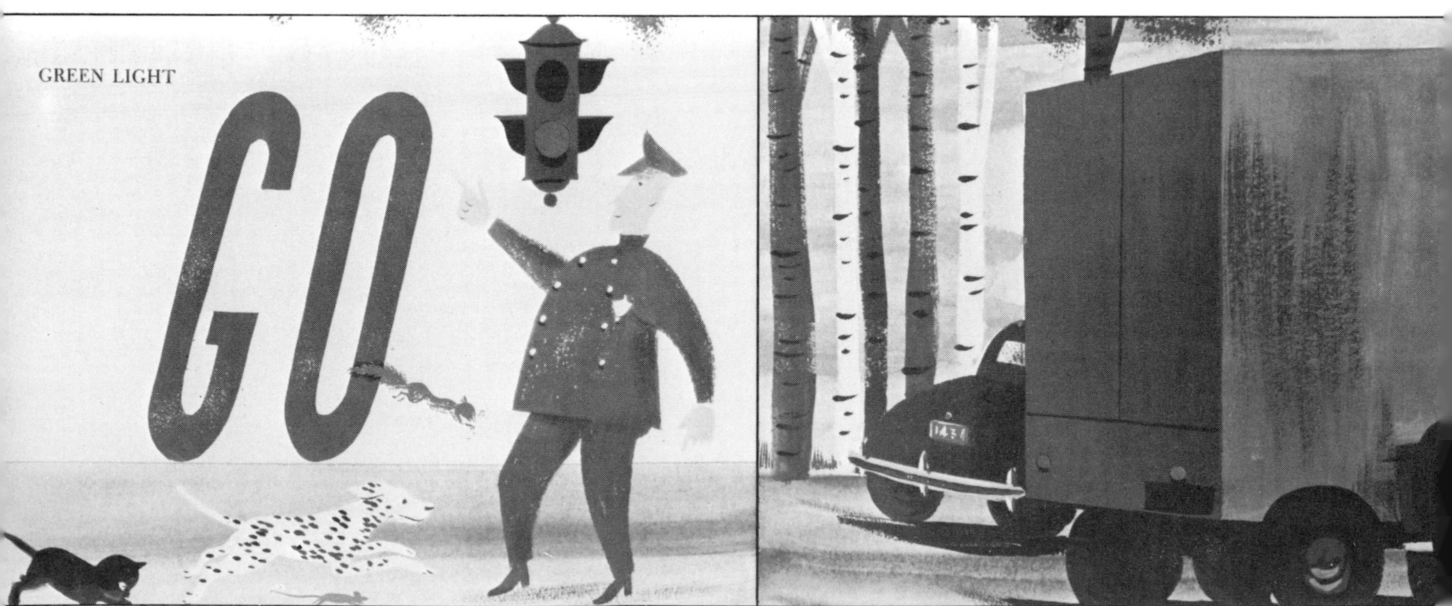
GREEN LIGHT
GO

own house to sleep, and the traffic light stands sentinel.

In *Red Light Green Light* there is new scope for the illustrator, spreads that are wholly his when words cease (a pause in the saying/singing), and the world of hither and yon, stop and go extends to page-edge in a montage, really, of myriad details; and other spreads in which the words are part of the picture, symbolic as they are in modern life, and as they were becoming in advertising design, expressive forms in themselves. *GO* of course is green, and only red and green punctuate the sepia-toned whole—most eloquently at the last where, outside the dusky dreaming house, a lone traffic light blinks red and green and, overleaf in the darkness, RED LIGHT/ GREEN LIGHT/GOOD NIGHT shines forth in red, green and white type.

The Doubleday books proceeded with *Little Lost Lamb* (1945) and the Caldecott winner *The Little Island* (1946), the former, I think, soppy, the latter bordering on the precious too in its conversations between fish and kitten, and rendered all too literally, calendar art where an imaginative concept—a Douanier Rousseau—was wanted.

But in the same year Weisgard did *Rain Drop Splash* with Alvin Tresselt, the first of the nature series that Duvoisin was to take over, a book that shares with *Red Light Green Light* limited coloration—yellow and rust tones, this time, on sepia—and a free adaptation of the modern mode to a world in motion, now a world of water in motion. There is no plot, no cast, but there is activity aplenty, accelerating as brook tumbles into lake, lake overflows into river, river runs on to city (294); and slowing as river flows into sea and at last the rain stops. A very satisfactory ensemble it is, with its big brown Lydian type balancing the broad simple masses, the one

294. *Rain Drop Splash,* text by Alvin Tresselt, pictures by Leonard Weisgard. Lothrop, 1946. 8⅜ x 9¾.

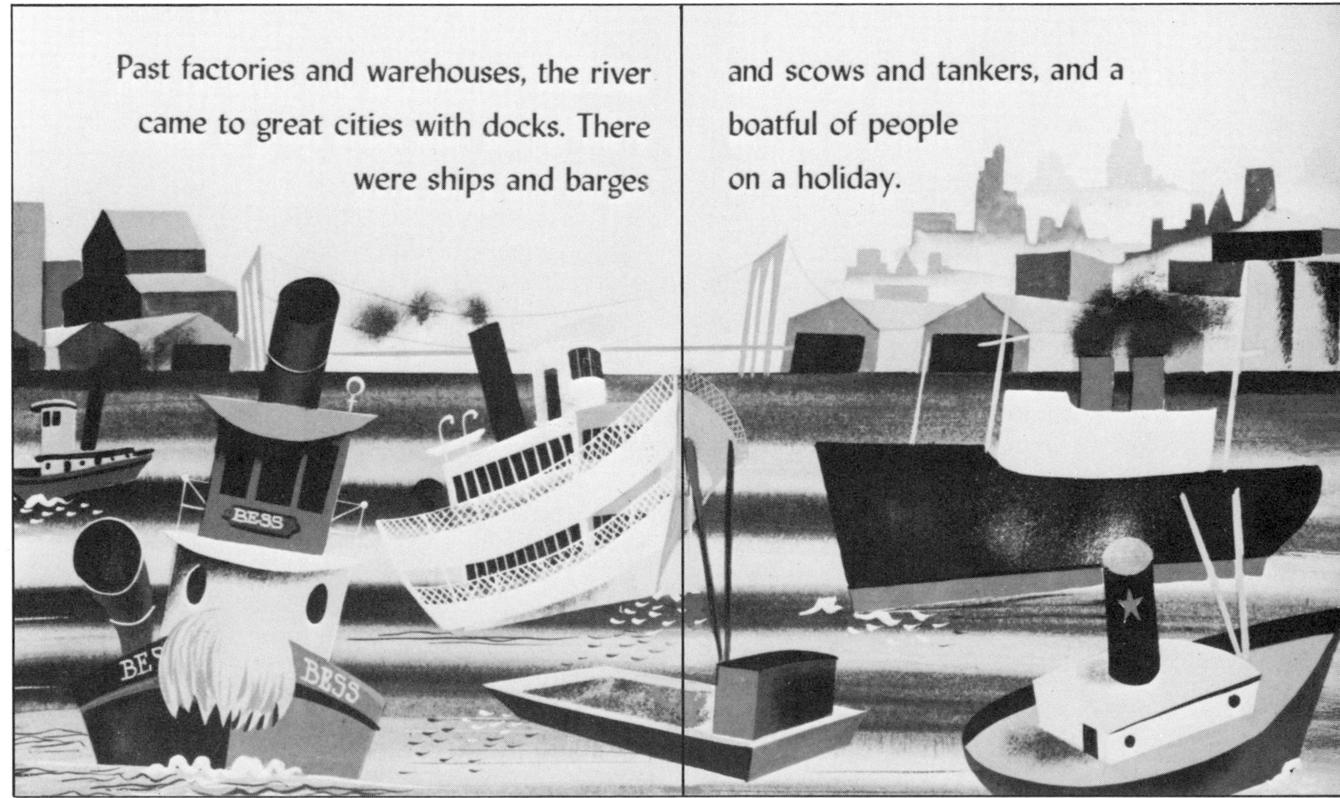

Past factories and warehouses, the river
came to great cities with docks. There
were ships and barges
and scows and tankers, and a
boatful of people
on a holiday.
BESS
BESS

architectonic, an inscription, the other a medley of shapes. By comparison, most of Weisgard's later picturebook work is showier and less substantial.

Meanwhile Scott went on developing the distinctive Scott book, the very young book of few words, big pictures and close contact with child life. There were such books as *Saturday Walk* which started in 1941 as a spiral-bound cardboard book like *Bumble Bugs* and goes on still in its 1954 version, older and more developed; and a *Saturday Ride* (1942) on a train and a *Saturday Flight* (1944)—these, like the cloth books (p. 236), designed for "Independence and Indestructibility."

Above the cardboard-cloth book level, as well, books should not be a passive experience: ergo 'participation.' "If indestructible books help the young child be independent of the adult in book enjoyment, then picture books should help continue that independence. . . . If, in addition"—to contents of immediate interest, simple easy-to-remember language, and clear 'readable' pictures—"the book gives him a part in the storytelling, lets him make noises, guess what is coming, or participate in any one of a number of ways, he will enjoy it more than the 'sit-quiet' books and will come to feel that reading isn't something that adults have to do for you."[22]

So, for one, *The Guess Book*, a picture-quiz with separate clues for each 'What-Am-I' (295); at the close of each series, a recap (296); and then the answer (for 295, a birthday cake, for 296, a mitten). "Three year olds got immense pleasure out of identifying the objects . . . but didn't begin to piece them together logically until they were three and one-half or four. Having worked out the answers . . . the joy of re-reading the book over and over with the reassurance of knowing the answers was tremendous . . . and the fun of stumping new people with it, especially the 'know-it-all' adult, was a wonderful, bolstering and exciting experience."[23] It is not irrelevant that *The Guess Book* is the work of an abstract artist—that "I am always, always red" is an all-red page, "I go on wheels" just wheels, a scattering of emblematic shapes; in the sense that *abstract* means *to draw out of* or *away from*, it is basic to isolating each attribute.

Participation might take other forms, and provide other boons. *This Is the Way the Animals Walk* (1946), writes Louise Woodcock, and Johnnie, trotting and waddling and hopping in turn, walks the same way too; "BUT LOOK—Here's Johnnie's daddy! How does a *daddy* walk?" Like a little trotting dog? a hopping white bunny? a waddling old duck? Of course not—"THIS is the way a DADDY walks!" "When you are three or four," the catalog reminds us, "it is a tremendous joke to pretend you are a crowing rooster . . . . Miss [Ida] Binney's spirited pictures point up the humor of attitude that is half the fun. But the other half of the fun is valuable, too; for observation, comparison, and imitation are pillars of the learning process."[24]

Observation, comparison, imitation—and from these, identification.

Thus, *Everybody Has a House* (1944) encourages children "to compare their own house with all the different kinds of houses that familiar animals have";[25] *Everybody Eats* (1946) "offers the comforting reassurance that he"—the reluctant eater—"has this common ground of eating with the rest of the animal world";[26] and *Just Like You—All Babies* [animal babies] *Have Mummies and Daddies* (1946).

If poor eating seems a doubtful prospect for bibliotherapy, other problems present themselves. *Timid Timothy* (1944) is a 'fraidy cat, literally, who is coached by his mother to present a brave front to the world. "Outbluffing bullies is one thing, but becoming a bully yourself is something else again," and "Timothy learns that 'the better part of valor is discretion.' "[27] Getting along is the theme, too, of *The Smart Little Boy and His Smart Little Kitty* (1947). "The kitty can do things Peter can't but Peter wishes he could. Peter can do things the kitty can't. But that little kitty doesn't even care! Louise Woodcock has done the impossible—she has stated the

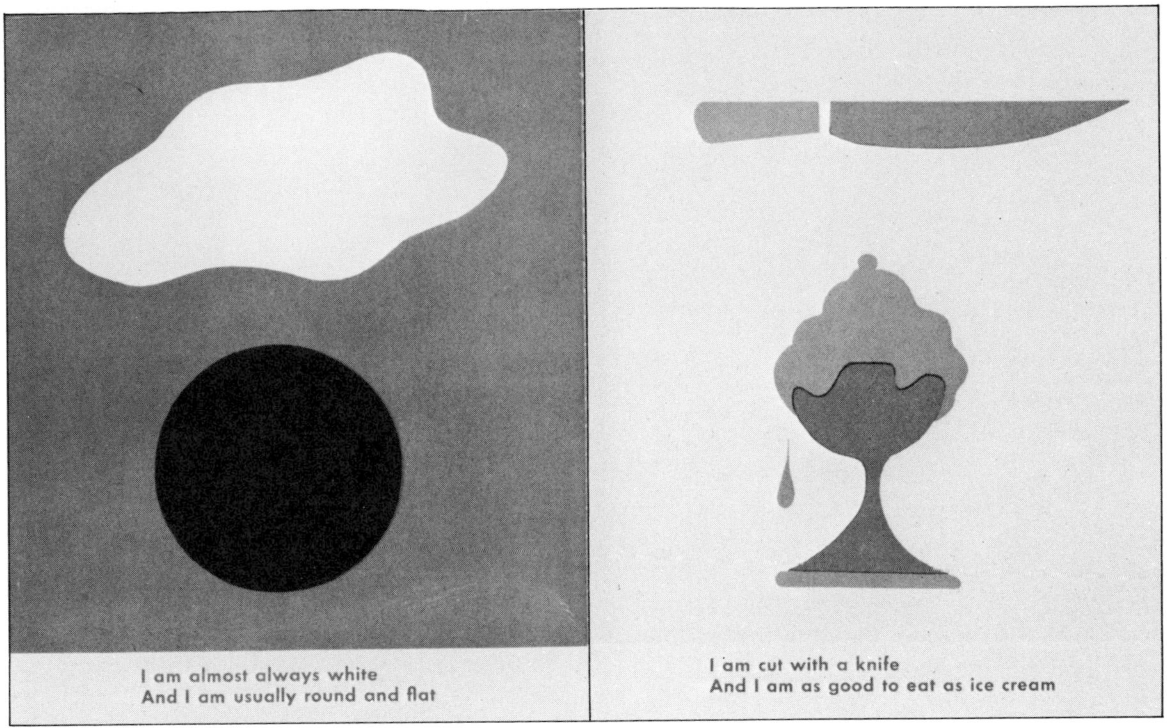

I am almost always white
And I am usually round and flat
I am cut with a knife
And I am as good to eat as ice cream

295

295, 296. *The Guess Book,* by Charles Shaw. Scott, 1941. 7 x 8.

296

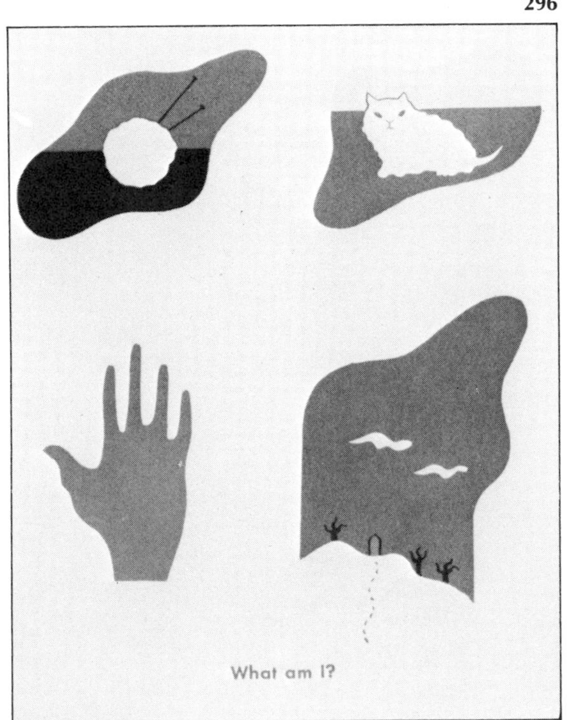

philosophy of tolerance on a two-year-old level and put it across."[28]

For certain problems the answer, whether simple or profound, is reassurance. *At Our House* (1943) "might be called a security chart for young children. We find out where Daddy goes all day long when he leaves Our House in the morning. Every hour of the day we know where everyone is"—thanks to the cut-away drawings—"and have a share in the activities of the whole family."[29] But to youngsters day is day and dark is dark, and different; exactly, says *Dark Is Dark* (1947), each has its own life. And knowing what goes on *While Susie Sleeps* (1948), other children can rest easy too.

The Scott list had evolved; in becoming therapeutic, it had become emotionally sensitive and poetic. *Just Like You* is billed as "a love story—the love of parent and child," and *Dark Is Dark,* we hardly need be told, is "For the poetic child." The radiant Margaret Wise Brown-Jean Charlot *A Child's Good*

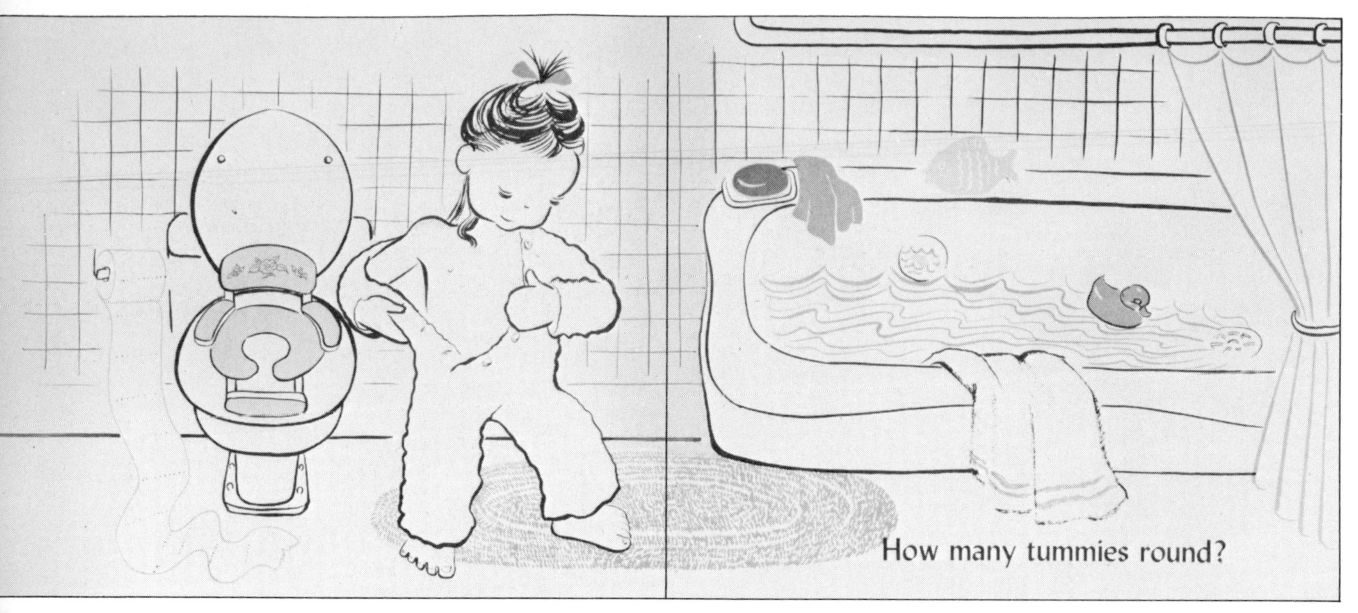

297. *How Many Kisses Good Night,* text by Jean Monrad, pictures by Lucienne Bloch. Scott, 1949. 9 x 8.

Night Book of 1943 (p. 269) may have been the impetus; and with others of her books it must have been instrumental in making the 'good-night book'—the true bedtime story—a flourishing new genre.

One such is *How Many Kisses Good Night.* "How many eyes? How many noses? How many fingers? How many toeses?" it asks, mother undressing toddler; "How many ears, like roses curled?" in the tub, "And"—wrapped in a towel—"lips for the merriest smile in the world?" "How many tummies round?" (297); "How many teeth? How many pink tongues hiding underneath?" Finally, "How many blankets tucked round just right? How many kisses to say . . . GOOD NIGHT!" It is here-and-now tangible down to the audacious potty seat and no less a lullaby, a tried-and-true invitation to count fingers and toes and enlightened about a child's interest in all of his body. A sweet-looking book too, in pewter, pink and blue, one of several that Lucienne Bloch illustrated in a simple and open fashion for Scott.

No one, however, has quite achieved the simplicity of Grace Skaar—a simplicity not only of words and pictures but also of concept. Here, as William Scott remarked, was the new nursery literature—a real literature, sometimes—"at the youngest possible level."[30]

"Let's take a very young book that has proved successful with many two-year-olds, *Nothing But Cats* . . . . Here is the entire text of the book. You must imagine each word image with a big clear picture all by itself on a two-page spread [298].

"'Big cats and/little cats and/fat cats and/thin cats and/spotted cats and/tall cats and/short cats./All kinds of cats, and they all say,/"MEOW." '[31]

"You may well say that it can't be so very hard to write a book with only seventeen different words in it, but from actual experience these are the hardest books of all to write."

At any level, "Writers must subordinate their own interest in their material to an interest in the reader and an awareness of what meanings and feelings their material can have for him"; and at the two-year-old level the need is even more evident. "Significant communication *is* possible, but it must be stated in terms the child can understand—no mean feat for an adult who moves freely in a wider range of experience.

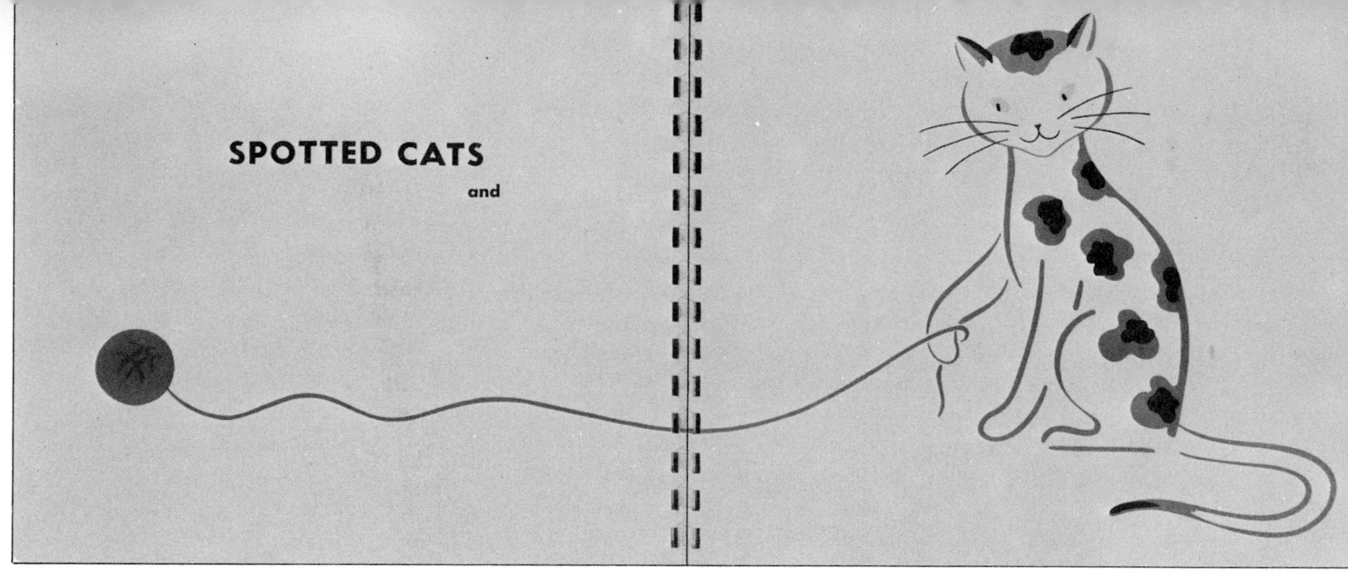

298. *Nothing But Cats, Cats, Cats,* by Grace Skaar. Scott, 1947. 9½ x 8.

"Now let's look into what is being communicated with these seventeen words about cats. The story is about simple, familiar things that a two-year-old knows (cats of different kinds). There is a real sense of suspense, of wanting to know what comes next. There is a generalization at the end, a satisfactory conclusion that covers all cats (no matter how different they look, they all say the same thing).

"Underlying this simple generalization is a basic mathematical concept: you can generalize about similarities but not about differences."[32]

Nothing But Cats—originally *Nothing But Cats, Cats, Cats*—had a companion volume, *All About Dogs* (sad and happy, hungry and full, they all say BOW-WOW), and, combined, they go on still. So does *The Very Little Dog,* in tandem now with *The Smart Little Boy.* (For the child, each stands foursquare by itself and in some respects is better thus; but the purchaser who equates words or pages with content is mollified by getting two for the price of one.)

Another thing about dogs, says *The Very Little Dog* to a slightly older audience, is that

299. *The Very Little Dog,* by Grace Skaar. Scott, 1949. 8⅞ x 7⅞.

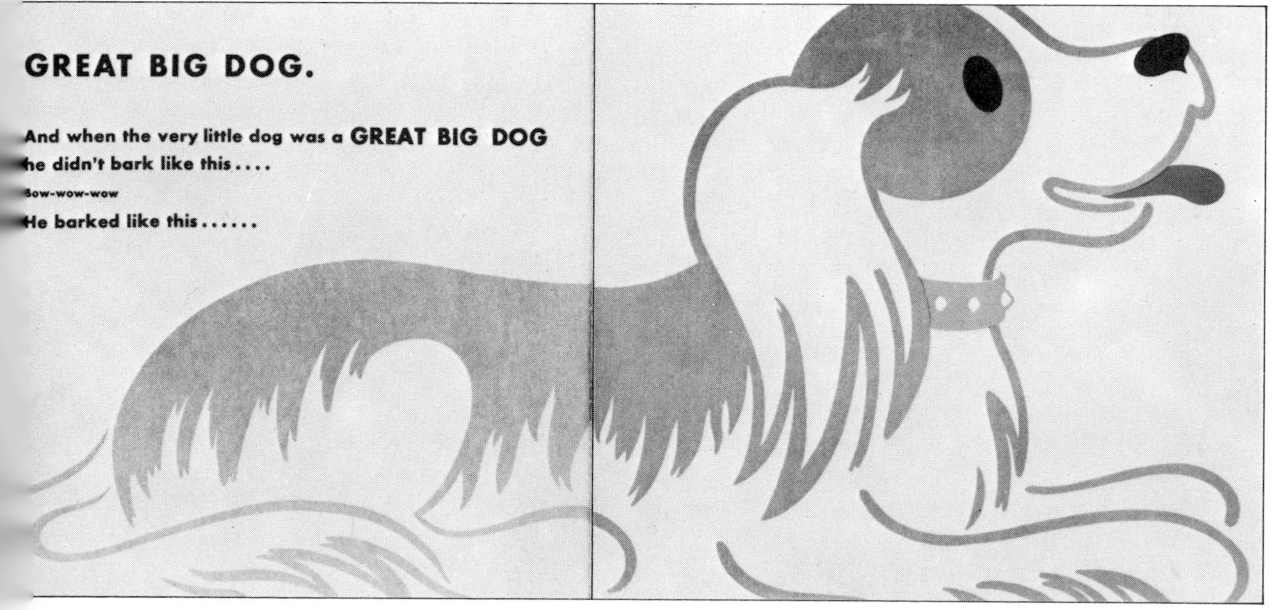

regardless of what they do, they grow. "Once there was a dog, a VERY little dog. And when he barked, he barked a little bark—a VERY little bark, like this . . . . Bow-wow-wow./ Every day the very little dog ate all his food and he drank all of his milk, too. And so he grew bigger./ . . . And when it was cold and the wind blew, he wore his warm, red coat. And he grew bigger and BIGGER and BIGGER until he was a . . . ." (299)

Usually he is a good dog and does what he should, but even when he is not so good he grows bigger. "This book," we're alerted, "doesn't make the usual moralizing connection between being good and growing up. Instead, it tells in very few words, and illustrates in pictures that practically bark the experience of growing bigger."[33] And for the very little child, what more vital experience?

For all the seriousness of purpose, there was a light touch; and for all the purposiveness, a book like *Caps for Sale*—"A Tale of a Peddler, Some Monkeys & Their Monkey Business." The peddler, wearing/bearing "his own checked cap, then a bunch of gray caps, then a bunch of brown caps, then a bunch of blue caps, and on the very top a bunch of red caps," goes along calling out his wares: "Caps! Caps for sale! Fifty cents a cap!" and when he can't sell any caps in town, takes a walk in the country—"slowly, slowly, so as not to upset his caps"—until he comes to a great big tree (300).

He sleeps for a long time; awakes fresh and rested; feels to make sure the caps are in place; and finds only his own checked cap!

> He looked to the right of him.
> No caps.
> He looked to the left of him.
> No caps.
> He looked in back of him.
> No caps.
> He looked behind the tree.
> No caps.
> Then he looked up into the tree.
> And what do you think he saw?

300. *Caps for Sale,* by Esphyr Slobodkina. Scott, 1957. 6¾ x 8⅝.

He walked for a long time until he came to a great big tree.

"That's a nice place for a rest," thought he.

And he sat down very slowly, under the tree and leaned back little by little against the tree-trunk so as not to disturb the caps on his head.

Then he put up his hand to feel if they were straight — first his own checked cap, then the gray caps, then the brown caps, then the blue caps, then the red caps on the very top.

They were all there.

So he went to sleep.

No need to tell the librarian or teacher who knows that *Caps for Sale* will rivet the most restless audience or the child who, once hearing it, mimics in turn the peddler's furious "You monkeys, you, you give me back my caps," and the monkeys' infuriating "Tsz, tsz, tsz." At last the peddler, beside himself, throws down his own cap and starts to walk off; whereupon each monkey pulls off his cap "and all the gray caps, and all the brown caps, and all the blue caps, and all the red caps came flying down out of the tree." And the peddler, his stack intact, walks slowly back to town calling out....

It was an old tale stripped to plot-scheme, suspense, patterned language and repetition, a great comic situation broadcast; and if it were possible to construct the ideal picture-story by rote, this would be a model to follow. The pictures are important, partly because they are extraordinarily good—meticulous in the manner of the modern primitives, colored an odd memorable mustard, red and robin's-egg blue; and partly because the text and the layout play to them. One need only look at the peddler napping, note his checked trousers, tight collar, mustache, tie; the different solid trees in the back to right and left, the gnarled outspread branches above, studded with single leaves, each in its way genus *tree*; the red tulip-form flowers, genus *flower*; and capping all, the pillar of caps—to appreciate the difference between simplicity and inspired simplification. And one has only to turn the page, to the sun smiling down on a single flower on a curve of the world, a corner of the globe, while the text reads "He slept for a long time," to understand contrast and harmony.

It was not always so; as first done by Slobodkina in 1940, the pictures lacked definition, they were by comparison limp. On the other hand, when *The Little Fireman* was redone in successive stages to reach its present red and green state, it lost its initial brilliance though not its good looks.[34] It lost some of its pizazz, too, as, with the addition of punctuation and capitalization and the restriction of type to a single color, it became more utilitarian. (*The World Is Round* is another reissued—in 1966—in a new and more practical form, in rose and black on white.)

Apart from her Scott books, Esphyr Slobodkina did a deep-hued *Sleepy ABC* with Margaret Wise Brown (Lothrop, 1953) and others of her own, in *The Wonderful Feast* (Lothrop, 1955) particularly, reverting to the Ballets-Russe colorations so pronounced in the first *Little Fireman.*

We have already spoken of the Scott photographic books as a distinct phenomenon, and we will be seeing where the firm's interest in basic science and the mechanics of living led. Jean Charlot, both with and without Margaret Wise Brown, did the bulk of his children's book work for Scott, and Crockett Johnson, also upcoming, did a few dandies; Remy Charlip started there and Edward Gorey had a go at Edward Lear. But the firm's impact is not to be measured by careers started or continued nor, wholly, by new types of books developed, important as they were; the ideas had ramifications, and these took root.

But there did not arise a new literature for twos and threes on the foundation of the early books, and Scott itself shifted to a somewhat more complex book for a somewhat older child. The spiral-bound cardboard books so perfect for toddlers to handle alone were regarded as a nuisance both in retail outlets and in libraries; the tape-backed cardboard books that succeeded them did not suit libraries either; and overall—in regard to content too—the home market shrank while the library market for preschool books had not yet burgeoned. Nor has it fostered work on quite that young and intimate a level.

But while the new spirit persisted there were, for the babies, an array of cloth books, and while the war lasted there were toy-books.

CLOTH BOOKS AND TOY BOOKS

When it first began to occur to adults that, as Darton puts it, "*The* Child was *a* child, and . . . different at ages five and fifteen,"[35] there came into being what were long called rag

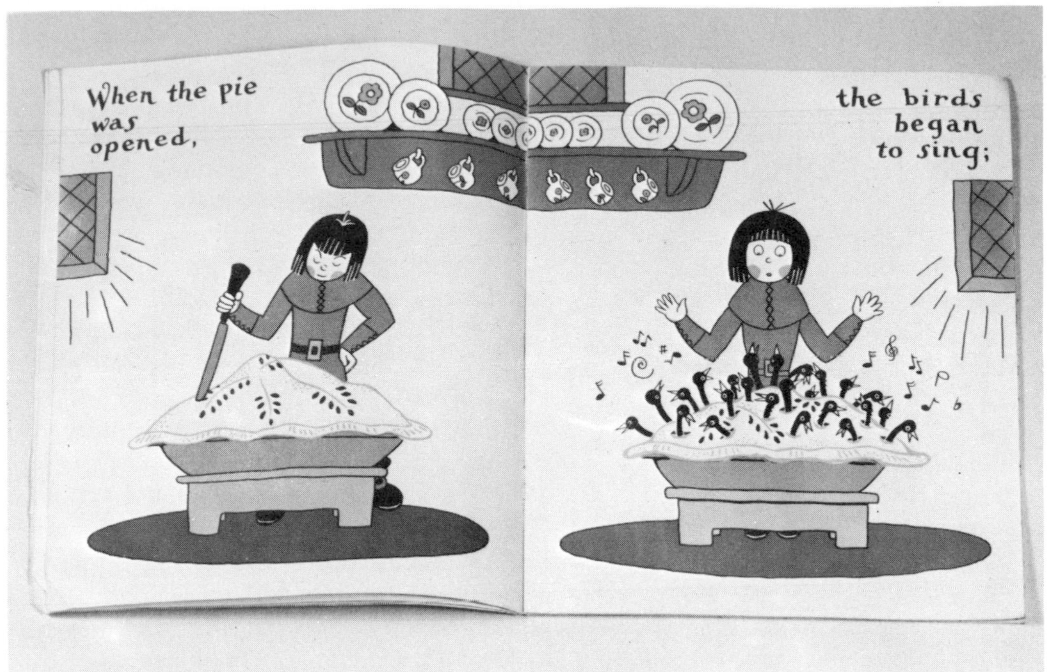
When the pie
was
opened,
the birds
began
to sing;

301. *Sing a Song of Sixpence,* pictures by Lois Lenski. Harper, 1930. 7 x 8¼.

books, printed first on paper pasted to cloth, then on the linen itself, their purpose no more or less than to be indestructible. In England, in the nineteenth century at least, they were part of the stock of regular trade publishers, but here they remained specialty items, the province of such firms as Gabriel and Saalfield, until in 1930, when nursery-consciousness crystallized, Harper had the idea of having established illustrators undertake them; and, said *PW*, "Rag books with excellent illustrations have been needed for some time."[36]

For *Sing a Song of Sixpence*, Lois Lenski drew big flat simple pictures, well suited to printing on the coated linen and, bright and animated, with lettering that fairly dances, well suited too to the young audience (301). But improvement or not, *Sing a Song of Sixpence* and its mate, Jimmy Garthwaite's *Chicken Little*, had no successors and the project died aborning.

Cottontails, on the initial Scott list, was not an improvement, it was something new—"A Tactile Book." Perhaps the first; certainly the first intended as other than a novelty.

> Don't touch! According to John Dewey, when you tell a child to keep his hands off you are really saying keep your mind off. The purpose of this book is to satisfy the small child's insatiable desire to learn through touch. There are pictures of familiar things printed on brightly-colored cloth to which various tactile objects are hand sewn with shoemaker's thread: a tree with red bead apples; rabbits with ball fringe tails [302]; a lamb with a bell on his neck; a train with button wheels; etc. The illustrator is a portrait painter and ecclesiastical artist.

The idea was Ethel McCullough Scott's, the printing was done by the Scotts on their own press, other family members pitched in with needle and thread and, as *PW* reported, "keeping up with orders was a laborious business."[37]

Cottontails didn't last beyond the second Scott season but by then there were two more easily managed cloth books, both by Mary Dana, *Our Day* (303) and, for singing, *The Jingle Book*. By then too the Holiday House cloth books were in their second year (304); and the first of Elena Eleska's cloth books was in the offing (305): a veritable blaze of cloth books, all stemming from the same reforming, child-serving impulse, all simply and gaily designed, all silk-screened onto good cloth, all washable, pressable, chewable—in toto, handsome and functional, every one.

Leonard Weisgard had a particular flair for the medium, and besides *Cloth Book No. 1* (Familiar Objects), he did *Nos. 3, 4* and 5—Vehicles (1940), Food (1940) and one that might be titled 'Familiar Activities' (1941); while Glen Rounds was responsible for *No. 2,* Zoo Animals (1939) and Kurt Wiese for *No. 6,* Farm Animals (1942). "By

302

302. *Cottontails,* conceived by Ethel McCullough, pictured by Sister Mary Veronica. Scott, 1938. 6¾ x 8. **303.** *Our Day,* by Mary Dana. Scott, 1940. 7¾ x 8. **304.** *Cloth Book No. 1,* by Leonard Weisgard. Holiday House, 1939. 7 x 7½. **305.** *I See,* by Elena Eleska. Eleska, 1941. 8⅛ x 9⅛. **306.** *Our Neighbors,* by Elena Eleska. Eleska, 1944. 10 x 12.

303

304

305

306

then," Vernon Ives writes, "wartime austerity prevented us from getting cloth of the proper quality. That was the end of the cloth books, for when the war came to a close we were shifting our emphasis from the declining trade (bookstore) market to the expanding school library market."[38]

Eleska held on the longest; the making of cloth books was her own and her only business, and she developed it further than it had been before. The next three, very like *I See*, were *I Count*, *I Play* and *Papa, Mama, Baby*—very like but not identical for *Papa, Mama, Baby*, later issued as *I Love*, came to be more elaborately printed after wartime restrictions were lifted. But the Eleska masterwork, intended to be the first of a series under the common title "Our Neighbors," was a book of costume dolls of the Americas—or rather twelve double-page imprinted cloth models of costumed figures for children to cut out, sew and stuff as regular dolls (306). Paper dolls become cloth dolls, a costume book become "A Creative Play Book"; either way ingenious and, moreover—as the Japanese say of plain, practical elegance—*shibui*. Eleska was a widely traveled artist and avocational anthropologist whose hope was to cultivate "an international spirit in children";[39] but her plan to do further books on Europe, Asia and Africa did not materialize, and she herself withdrew from the field in 1952.

Meanwhile *Pat the Bunny* came out, took off and goes on, a novelty that children never tire of (307). With her characteristic delight, May Lamberton Becker tells why:

"Here is a fat box-shaped book for babies and very small youngsters, pink as tooth-paste, with a trick at every turn. Paul and Judy can pat the bunny: now 'you' pat the bunny, and here he is, pure cotton wool. 'You' can play peekaboo, look in a mirror, feel Daddy's scratchy face, read Judy's book, and actually put your finger through Mummy's ring. Midway of these thrills, if a tiny finger is poked at a red ball it really squeaks. It is a little darling, this pink book for a pre-reader, the find of the season."[40]

Pat the Bunny and its successor *The Telephone Book* (1942)—"You can say hello," "You can bathe the baby and make him swim," "You can find a letter and post it"[41]—give the child a chance to do things he wants to do, real things that are part of his everyday life; and packaging them is another instance of Dorothy Kunhardt's mother wit. But the im-

307. *Pat the Bunny*, by Dorothy Kunhardt. Simon & Schuster, 1940. 4 x 5¼.

What is the little kitten looking for?
Pick the tomato from the vine and you will see.

308. *Pick the Vegetables,* text by Esther Reno, pictures by Leonard Weisgard. Lothrop, 1944. 8 x 10⅜.

mediate success of *Pat the Bunny* gave rise, in the trade field, to the likes of *The Fuzzy Kitten* and *The Wooly Lamb* and Pinky the embossed pink elephant—gimmick books, that is to say, with touching added to seeing but nothing intrinsic gained.

The 'feelies' were not alone, however. Manual participation was in the air and various die-cut marvels were on the boards, making of books if not always toys at least instructive playthings, just when American entry into World War II and the impending shortage of metal and plastic and other materials created a new market for them. "More Children's Books in the Toy Department," headlined *PW* in August 1942,[42] and the spring of 1943 found trade publishers exhibiting at the annual Toy Fair for the first time. All sorts of books were selling—"Because toys are scarce and dollars are plentiful," said *Life* that December, "more children are getting books for Christmas than ever before";[43] but activity books and animated books—the novelty books of various kinds—sold best. A little novelty sufficed: *Don't Frighten the Lion* (1942), Margaret Wise Brown's and H. A. Rey's disarming idea of a dog's day at the zoo, came with doll cutouts inside the cover which, Harper editor Ursula Nordstrom attested, "largely explain [its] popularity."[44]

Not that *Don't Frighten the Lion* isn't extra fun with a paper-doll dog to dress up like a little girl ("No Dogs Allowed" in the zoo)—or that *Anybody at Home?*, Rey's second open-the-flap book which appeared that same year, isn't fun still. 'I know a secret,' *Anybody at Home?* seems to say, 'and you know it too . . . peekaboo.' *Where's My Baby* (1943) has a similar appeal, and *Feed the Animals* (1944) and *See the Circus* (1956, all Houghton Mifflin), though inherently more mechanical, share their success. As small inexpensive paper books still profitable for a trade house to market, they are virtually unique.

Other interesting novelties came and went (including a group of punch-out playbooks by Rey in the guise of 'Uncle Gus'), some of them books that aspired to more than diversion. "PICK THEM YOURSELF!" says *Pick the Vegetables*: "Here is a book full of vegetables that you can pick yourself. Some of them grow down in the ground, and some grow up above the ground. After you pick the vegetables you can put them in the basket on the last page." Pick the vegetables, in other words, like a gardener; and like a child on a treasure hunt, you'll find other booty—behind the tomato (308), a white house. 'As toothsome looking a crop as was ever promised by a seed catalog, and prettier,' was the gist of the *New York Times* review,[45] which *Parents' Magazine* underscored by calling *Pick the Vegetables* the only one of its sort "to demonstrate that books can be both 'trick' and artistic in appearance."[46]

Loris Corcos's *Size One* is another. *Size One* was among the first of the lace-a-shoe books, and one that, to begin with, makes sense—a baby shoe enclosing a baby's fascinations ("Granny's glasses/Daddy's tie/Mustn't touch"—scissors and pins—"I wonder why") and a baby being dressed, with encouragement to finish alone (309). A cheerful little doodad and a ready-made self-helper but, as produced, fragile and consequently ephemeral.

In the mass market, lacing books and tell-time books and the like have been more durable—in part because they are more sturdily made but also because they are distributed, with other mass-market books, like toys. For trade books, the retail boom was over by 1947; "Toy Buyers Show Little Interest in Books Except Toy Books, Cheap Lines," was the *PW* banner in March of that year,[47] and in April, more ominously still, "Booksellers are Overstocked in Juvenile Department," particularly, *PW* notes, in picturebooks.[48] There was more to this than the end of wartime shortages: there was the overwhelming allure of Golden Books.

And what happened, it is hardly an exaggeration to say, is that Golden Books took over the retail market and libraries took over trade picturebooks, demanding—and getting—library editions that very year. But more of this later; the immediate effect was an end to cloth books on a par with picturebooks, to playbooks as Creative Playthings and, where 'babies' were concerned, to the innovative impulse altogether.

309. *Size One,* by Loris Corcos. Lothrop, 1945. Approx. 6 x 6.

THE EMOTIONAL ELEMENT

HARPER AND THE MOST OF MARGARET WISE BROWN

Just before sailing for France in 1930, the story goes, Clare Newberry wrote *Herbert the Lion*, and to earn her return passage she illustrated it. The book was brought out in 1931 by the small, decidedly modern firm of Brewer, Warren & Putnam, publishers also of Ozenfant and Le Corbusier and (as Payson & Clarke) of Blaise Cendrars's *Little Black Stories for Little White Children*, illustrated—per the auspicious French edition—by Pierre Pinsard. For its part, *Herbert the Lion* was deemed "the most charming and frivolous of the year's crop of picture books" by the *Horn Book*;[1] and it has proved to be no passing fancy. Considerably altered, it was reissued by Harper in 1939, and, as redesigned once more in 1956, goes on still—one of those occasional books that, like Nicholson's pair, pass imperceptibly through the looking glass.

"There was once a little girl named Sally who wanted a baby lion," it begins offhandedly. "She already had a dolls' house, two dolls, a tea set, and a toy zebra on wheels, but she did not like any of them." (No mama's girl, she.) "All she wanted was a lion, a real live lion. So"—at the turn of a page—"one day her mother brought her one from downtown. Then Sally was very happy."

She names the lion Herbert and they are together all day, eating hot cereal for breakfast (310), for luncheon spinach and a poached egg, for supper "baked potato and applesauce and a round cookie with raisins in it." "Of course" Herbert has sunbaths at the seaside, "And the way he took his cod-liver oil was simply beautiful." Herbert grows and Grows and GROWS (311) and he is friendly, friendlier than Sally's grandmother fancies (312) or her Aunt Barbara—or for that matter the milkman or the postman or even the cook; until no one will come to the house and Sally's father decrees the zoo for Herbert. Sally cries and Herbert cries but then Sally's mother remembers "our ranch." "And now every summer vacation Sally and Herbert play together in the mountains. And in the winter Herbert stays on the ranch by himself. He doesn't really mind, for he is a lion, and lions are never lonely so long as they have plenty of room. And to keep Sally from getting too lonely . . . her parents have given her *a very small kitten.*"

That's the way it was to start with, a close-knit, concise, nicely rounded story that retains an air of improvisation and parts Sally and Herbert without playing false to its initial premise. As rewritten in 1939, it continues—begins again, really—with Herbert on the ranch trying to make friends with newborn chicks, frightening the resident cat, and startling Walter the hired man. Though he wins them over he is still lonesome for Sally so—in the third episode—he sets off to see her, arriving just when Grandmother is having tea with Aunt Barbara. Sally, however, is delighted, they have ice cream and cake to celebrate, Herbert—who ate en route—gets a stomach ache, and Sally's parents decide they must move to the ranch, the lot of them, to keep Sally and Herbert together. Some palaver about fresh air and scenery and quiet—and "As for Sally and Herbert, they have each other to play with, and Timmie

310

310–312. *Herbert the Lion*, by Clare Newberry. Brewer, Warren & Putnam, 1931. 10⅞ x 9¼.

311

312

[the cat] and Walter and the kitten and all the chickens besides. What more could anyone wish?"

One could easily wish for less, and the third (1956) version does excise Timmie and Walter and the chickens but it retains the artificial 'happily ever after' ending and, circumstantiating it, certifies it real. What has been added is chiefly the sight of Herbert lolling on a drug store counter ("He hadn't any money but that was all right, for no one thought of asking him to pay"); what is diminished, because less central, is the "absurdly plaintive" picture, as *Horn Book* called it, of Herbert growing in friendliness as he grows in size—basic still, I suspect, to the book's appeal.

Clare Newberry, meanwhile, turned to cat portraiture. A series of cat beauties came out in *House Beautiful.* Famous New York cats 'sat' for her ('No, they don't sit still and pose'[2]), and she added to the roll a fat tabby kitten, *Mittens* (1936). And after him the Siamese kitten *Babette* (1937), *April's Kittens* (1940), *Pandora*, a Persian cat (1944), *Smudge* (1948), *T-Bone, the Baby Sitter* (1950), *Percy, Polly and Pete* (1952), Pounce in *Ice Cream for Two* (1953), *Widget* (1958); along with *Barkis* (1938) the cocker spaniel puppy and *Marshmallow* (1942) the little white rabbit—each of whom, be it known, has a rival in a cat.

But she didn't only draw "some of the very best cat pictures that have ever been made,"[3] she also drew her own children; and the stories themselves portray youngsters and cats with equal acuity, and have not a little to say about the vagaries of people in general. Mittens, bought to satisfy Richard's longing for a kitten (he's almost six, he wears size seven suits . . . "Surely I'm big enough now"), takes flight after Richard's pesky little cousin pulls his tail (313), and isn't to be found. But an ad in the paper—"Lost: black-and-gray tabby kitten. Child's pet. REWARD"—brings a boy with a big yellow tomcat ("Hello, kid! . . . How about that reward?"), a phone call peddling Persian kittens, two little girls with a surplus litter

—assorted offers of "little cats, big cats, fat cats, and thin cats . . . black cats, white cats, red cats, yellow cats, gray cats, and brown cats . . . But not one of them was Mittens." Pictured are two pages of "Cats That Weren't Mittens," a pause before, overleaf, the lost Mittens is found.

Babette is also the story of Chatty, short for Charity, the first of the Newberry youngsters left alone because their mothers have to work. (In *Ice Cream for Two*, the bond between mother and son in a fatherless household is focal.) Chatty's lonely Saturdays end when Babette and her mother are left in her care but then, just before Christmas, she learns that their owner is leaving for a job in California. Her mother can't afford a Siamese, "much as I'd like to. But I will get you a nice plain kitten. . . . There are some darling ones at the A & P—black with white noses." These of course won't do any more than 'the cats that weren't Mittens' (we see a page of them too); and you may have guessed, with Christmas coming and

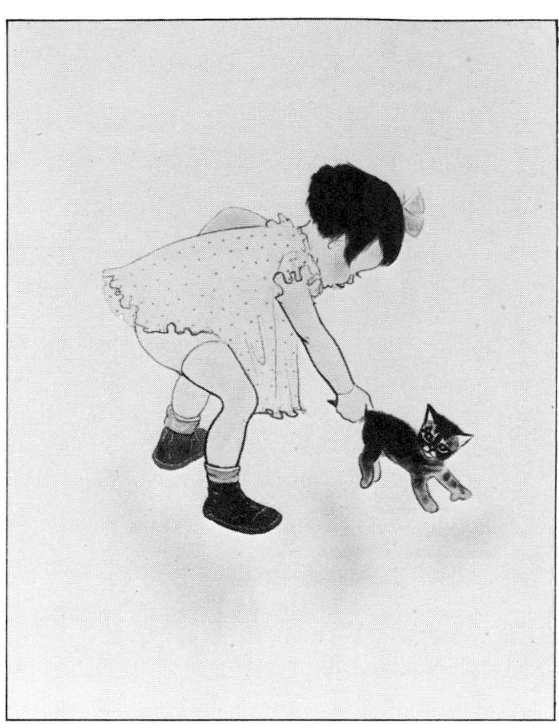

313. *Mittens,* by Clare Turlay Newberry. Harper, 1936. 7¼ x 9¼.

314. *Babette,* by Clare Turlay Newberry. Harper, 1937. 7¼ x 9¼.

All you had to do was turn the knob underneath it and the wires inside became a lovely bright red. But Chatty was not allowed to turn on the plate unless her mother was right there and said she might.

"Oh dear!" said Chatty, aloud. "What shall I do?"

And her question was answered in a very strange way.

The radiator in the corner suddenly gave a long-drawn-out *whooooooooosh!* For a moment Chatty stared at it. Then she giggled. Once more she ran to the cupboard, got a tin pan, poured the milk from the saucer into it, and set it on the hot radiator.

In a few minutes the milk was warm. And this time when it was put before Babette she drank it hungrily, her tiny tongue going *slap, slap, slap,* until the dish was empty.

While Babette washed herself beside the radiator Chatty fixed her own lunch, a fat peanut-butter sandwich and a glass of milk. When she had finished eating she washed the dishes, dried them nicely, and put them back in the cupboard, just as her mother liked her to do.

Babette felt playful now. She began to scamper about the room, patting things with her little brown paws and jumping sideways stiff legged. She seemed to think everything in the room was alive, from the table legs to Chatty's bedroom slippers. And when she found a rubber ball on the floor she pounced upon it and fought it, with such a fierce look on her baby face that Chatty could not help laughing.

« 16 »

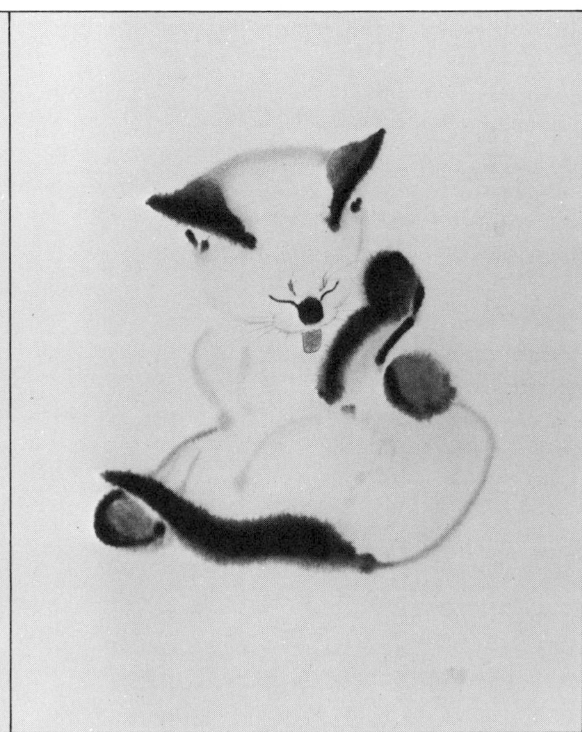

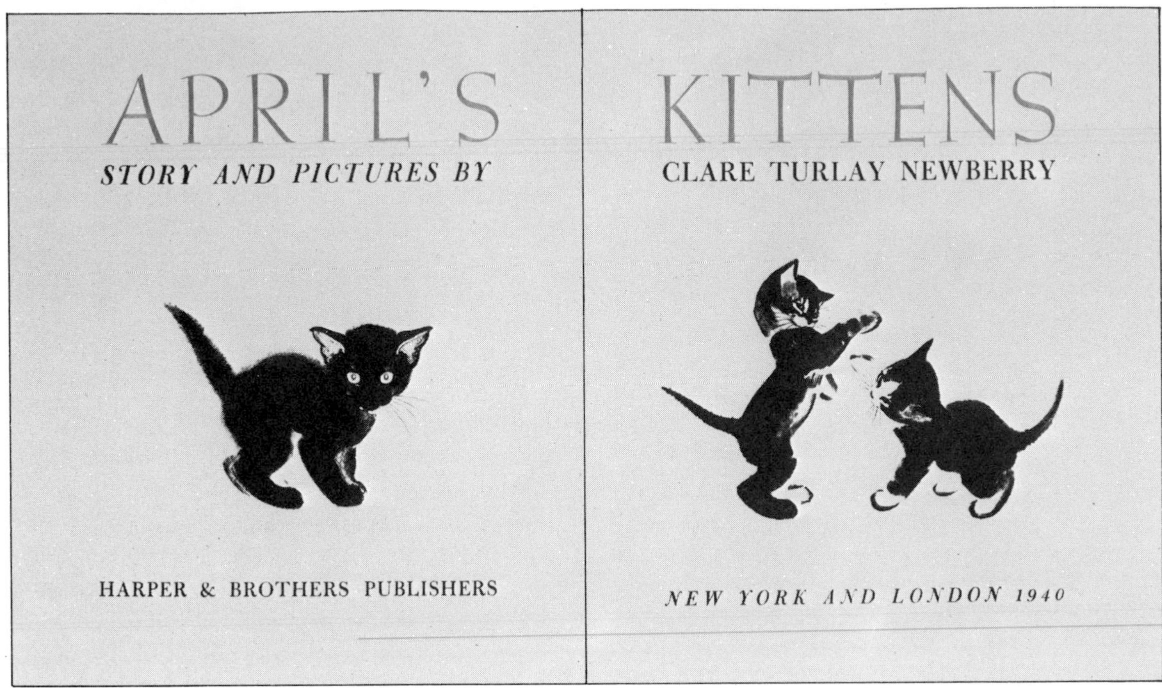

315. *April's Kittens,* by Clare Turlay Newberry. Harper, 1940. 8¾ x 10½.

Babette being cat number two, and tiny—too tiny to travel—what's in the offing. Sometimes happiness is a soft kitten (314), and if the story hasn't the muscle of *Mittens,* who is to say it nay?

April's Kittens—Sheba's, actually—have the misfortune to be born in a very small New York apartment; a 'one-cat apartment,' April's father calls it, and he's adamant that the three kittens or—if April wants to keep Brenda, her favorite—their mother, Sheba, be given away. Brenda is irresistible . . . but poor Sheba will think April no longer loves her, and so she is April's choice. The moral nut cracked, the rest is simple arithmetic: April is too big for her crib, the apartment is too small for a bed, they'll move to a roomier one—a two-cat apartment, besides.

In *Barkis,* the cocker spaniel puppy arrives belatedly on James's birthday just when he is feeling a little sad, "the way you cannot help feeling when you have had all your gifts and it is nearly bedtime and you know you won't have another birthday for a whole long year." You couldn't help feeling resentful, either, of a sister who never shared her kitten wanting half your new puppy, and James rebuffs Nell Jean outright. The upshot is that Nell Jean doesn't stop Barkis from scampering away, only to start up when he disappears and rush to rescue him from the creek. But he has been in the cold water a month before he should even have been bathed . . . and "If Barkis dies it will all be my fault," she thinks wretchedly. Needless to say, Barkis recovers, and needfully, when James offers to share him, Nell Jean confesses her dereliction.

They are real stories. Real stories longer and more material, for the most part, than the usual picturebook story; and yet they come with pictures, on a separate page generally, whose appeal is independent of them. (Early on, a duplicate of one of the best was apt to be tipped in at the back.) The attraction that the combination has for children suggests that a hybrid needn't be a misfit. That the books aren't, in turn, patchworks—that they are, in fact, lovely books—is the doing of Arthur Rushmore.

"Early in the history of the publication of the Newberry kitten books," Evelyn Harter writes, "Arthur Rushmore [art director] of Harper's reached the conclusion that gravure was the best possible process for printing these wash pictures. It is more expensive than other processes, but by this process very tiny little piles of ink are actually deposited on the page. This is because the paper pulls the ink out of the little dots in the plate in the same way that an engraved calling card does. The result is that you can actually feel a certain roughness if you run your fingers across the page . . . and the visual effect is highly suggestive of kitten's fur."[4]

Another Rushmore contribution was setting the type by hand at the family Golden Hind Press, as the Rushmores did for all the Harper picturebooks at one time; but whereas elsewhere flexibility and comeliness are joint gains (319), in the case of the Newberrys, where a page of unrelieved type faces a single large 'floating' image, the benefit is quite particularly commodiousness—a page that is even and airy and easily read (314). However, it is the title spreads, combining typographic and pictorial elements, that are Rushmore's crowning glory as designer; and Valenti Angelo was not hyperbolizing when he said that the one for *April's Kittens* would be 'long remembered among children's books.'[5] (315). The title letters are blazoned across the wide opening, in red, like a marquee, and their brilliance makes the black blacker, their chiseled contours make the kittens softer and sootier. Imposing and spirited, it is both fanfare and foretaste.

Even as the kitten books were becoming a category Clare Newberry complained to Ursula Nordstrom, newly in charge at Harper's, that 'she was so sick of cats that she'd like to write a story about a hyena.' "Why don't you?" was the rejoinder;[6] and the result was the snappy tongue-in-cheek "truly original"[7] *Lambert's Bargain* (316–318)—dedicated, naturally, "To Ursula."

We are showing selected scenes first, like a movie or TV trailer, because they are the ideal advertisement for the book; and between them the drawings and the dialogue—or cartoons and repartee—leave little to be

316–318. *Lambert's Bargain,* by Clare Turlay Newberry. Harper, 1941. 7⅞ x 10.

"I don't know if my sister wants a hyena," he said, edging ard the door.

'Did she ever say she didn't?" demanded the pet shop man.

d Lambert had to admit that she had not.

'Tell you what I'll do," said the pet shop man. "I like to a kid nice to his sister. And I hate to see you pass up an ortunity like this one. So what would you say if I *gave* you beautiful pet, absolutely free of charge? You couldn't ask better than that, could you?"

[10]

316

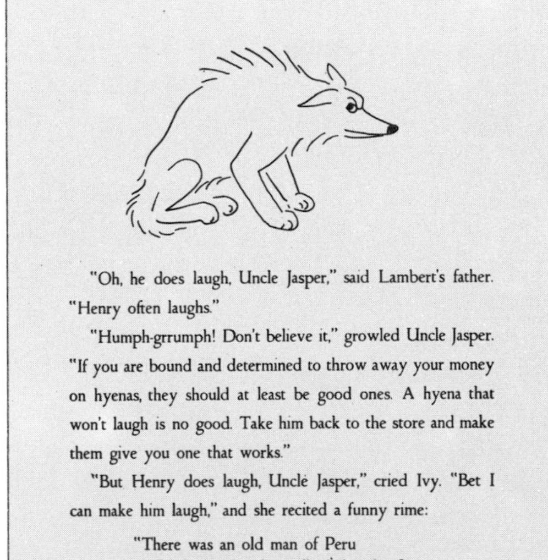

"Oh, he does laugh, Uncle Jasper," said Lambert's father. "Henry often laughs."

"Humph-grrumph! Don't believe it," growled Uncle Jasper. "If you are bound and determined to throw away your money on hyenas, they should at least be good ones. A hyena that won't laugh is no good. Take him back to the store and make them give you one that works."

"But Henry does laugh, Uncle Jasper," cried Ivy. "Bet I can make him laugh," and she recited a funny rime:

"There was an old man of Peru
Who had rather he walked than he flew;
He liked to go round

[24]

317

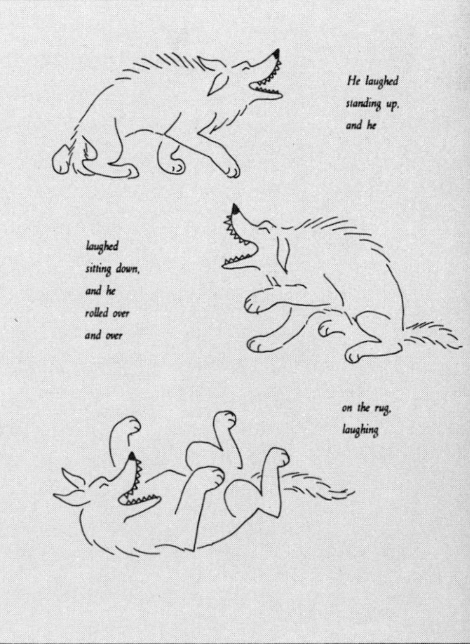

He laughed standing up, and he

laughed sitting down, and he rolled over and over

on the rug, laughing

318

added. Henry the hyena, whom little sister Ivy very definitely does not want ("what she had really wanted was a little red handbag with a mirror in it"), has not only been laughing before Uncle Jasper arrives, he has been laughing at everyone in the family; and, horrors, what if he laughs at stuffy Uncle Jasper too? But even after Henry proves himself a real hyena by laughing at Lambert's father taking a spill, and once more at anyone who happens by, he never seems to find Uncle Jasper silly; "And as that was exactly the way Uncle Jasper felt about it they soon became the best of friends." At the last he is taking Henry home to comfort him in his declining years—he had always wanted a pet hyena "but my father wouldn't hear of it"—and Ivy, recompensed, has a little red handbag with a mirror in it, "after all."

The flavor, the wit, the pace, the pratfalls too, are reminiscent of a Katharine Hepburn-Cary Grant film of that period; but as an unsentimental kids' contretemps it is a first —the first of many on the newly invigorated Harper list.

Legend has it that Charlotte Zolotow, then Ursula Nordstrom's secretary, suggested a park book as an antidote to visions of rural bliss; that she was told to "write it"; that she sat down and turned it out in a lunch hour. And indeed it looks, at a glance, like nothing much—a few casual observations and some easygoing sketches.

"What is the park like?" asks a little boy who lives in the country, an express reversal of the usual setup; and the 'story' is his mother's account of dawn to dusk in a particular park (Washington Square Park to habitués) that could be almost any. First to arrive is the cleaner with his long pointed pole who spears "the things of yesterday"—ice cream wrappers, cigarette butts, peanut shells—and on his heels the dressed-up people hurrying to work heedless of him. The shoeshine man calls out "Shinnemmmm-mmup?" hopefully but "no one stops so early." Nurses and grandmothers and young mothers come with babies and toddlers, the "sunlight dances in the branches of the trees," and the park assumes its morning aspect (319)—easily, inevitably, with never a "then" or a "soon."

The shoeshine man has found a customer, the cleaner is busy filling his cart, a baby peers into another carriage, a second beguiles a little girl, two birds are, each in its way, taking in the scene; and while the mothers knit and talk, across the wide sidewalk that is the picture space two children are absorbed in their play—"a little boy who had pancakes for breakfast and a little girl who ate bread and jam."

They might have been 'a little boy and a little girl,' which would tell us nothing that we can't see for ourselves and, moreover, do nothing to interest us in them; they might have been Billy and Nancy, hardly more interesting and, under the circumstances, pointless, since they are not characters in a continuing story or even necessarily known to one another. In identifying them by what they had for breakfast—as elsewhere she tags other children by their bedtimes or their assortment of brothers and sisters—Charlotte Zolotow preserves their anonymity and gives us as a handle on them just what a child himself thinks of as important. But Mr. Humphrey Gillingwater and Selma Daley, rushing to work in the morning, strolling home at sundown, have names: grown-ups are known by their names.

Morning gives way to high noon and the lunchtime exodus, when "the park belongs to the birds for a little while"; afternoon brings the carriages back and, with school out, bikes and baseball and sailboats, "The park is loud with light and sound. You can hardly hear the birds." With the sun's setting the carriages and the big and small children head for home; "Even the shoeshine man picks up his box and goes home."

"As the lights in the children's rooms go out, the park begins another life." On the benches sit the "grown-up boys and girls," whispering; leaving hand in hand, they pass the city dogs out for their evening run, racing and barking and rolling in the grass; and at the last there remains only an old

A little boy who had pancakes for breakfast
and a little girl who ate bread and jam
play together in the sand pile.
The mothers settle on the benches
and begin knitting. The sun is warmer now.

319. *The Park Book,* text by Charlotte Zolotow, pictures by H. A. Rey. Harper, 1944. 9⅜ x 7⅞.

man covered with newspapers asleep on a bench.

"Here," says the catalog, "is the noise and the quiet, the light and the darkness, the loneliness as well as the friendliness of every park." *The Park Book* may be the counterpart of *The Farm Book* and *The Seashore Book* et al but it is leagues away from the story of "how Bob and Betty spend the summer at the seashore with an old sea captain." And while it exists in the wake of Margaret Wise Brown, whom Charlotte Zolotow originally had in mind to do it, it is not the book that Margaret Wise Brown would have done. Personal and individual, informal, particularized, it is a sheaf of snapshots sharpened by insight, a stone cupped in the hand vs. the shimmer of pebbles in a stream.

The sun high, "a shiny black cocker spaniel dozes under a bench," the old man feeding the pigeons "uses up his crumbs, crumples his brown paper bag and gets up. Leaning ahead of each step he shuffles away." Later, in the still heat that ushers in *The Storm Book* (p. 465), "the white fox terrier [crawls] under the latticework of the porch," "a little caterpiller climbs carefully up a dusty blade of grass and then climbs down again." The small precise details, the multiplicity of images, coalesce as felt experience. The end —the aim, the result—is awareness, emotional and sensory awareness both.

Thus, the one false note is the reappearance of the country boy at the close, and his acquiescent "It doesn't have all the things a meadow has, but I like the park." No more than Good Times in the Park is the book a sales pitch, a catalog of attractions; it assumes an openness and empathy and says not 'I like the park' but, as it were, 'I like life.'

Rey, whose every figure is animated, fills out the scene, park-like, with incidental activity, and indeed makes a scene of what is hardly more than a border, graphically and, one might say, topographically (319). To take a few words, or many, and design a double-spread around them, different in each instance, reflecting in their layout the lay of the land, is an accomplishment all the more considerable for being inconspicuous. It is as if Zolotow and Rey were accomplices where, by contrast, Brown and Slobodkina in *The Little Fireman*, or Brown and Weisgard in *Red Light Green Light*, are performing a pas de deux.

The year of *The Park Book* was also the year of *Pretzel*, Rey's first collaboration with his wife Margret and the beginning of the Harper picturebooks about the difficulties of being different. Not that there is anything glum about *Pretzel*, the story of an extra-long dachshund admired by everyone but the light of his life (320); but alongside the Munro Leaf-Ludwig Bemelmans dolors of a dachshund, *Noodle* (Stokes, 1937), it is a book of a different and tougher breed. The premise of *Noodle* is that just to be a dachshund is to be overlong—freakish and comical—and, when it comes to digging, an inconvenience; and Noodle, granted a wish by the dog fairy, scouts around among the animals for the most desirable size and shape before settling, wisely, for his own. Pretzel, on the other hand, is the rejected suitor who proves the value of his difference: "I'll get you out of there," he shouts after Greta falls into a deep hole, and when he grabs her by the scruff of the neck—"How good that Pretzel was so long!"

More troublesome—even tragic—are Spotty's spots (321); and when Aunt Eliza's needling results in his being left at home and spot remover fails him ("And he had thought he was pretty!"), he runs away, in the words of the jacket, "broken-hearted." But lo and behold, the kindly rabbits who give him shelter—brown-spotted rabbits like himself—shun the little white bunny in *their* midst; and he wants to know why. "To everybody's surprise"—this is the jacket—"it turned out that nobody *had* any reason. In the best rabbit tradition, everybody had just acted like everybody else." Carrots all around are in order.

320. *Pretzel*, text by Margret Rey, pictures by H. A. Rey. Harper, 1944. 7¾ x 10.

"Look what I can do!
Nobody except me can do THAT!"
said Pretzel when they met again.
And this is what he did:
"Not bad," said Greta. "Your name
certainly fits you. But I like the pretzels at
the baker's better, and I still don't care
for long dogs." Pretzel was very unhappy.

Concludes the jacket, sotto voce: "(*You will think, perhaps, that this is a story with a moral; but how could human beings be supposed to learn a lesson from creatures such as bunnies, and imaginary bunnies at that?*)" Unmistakable as Aunt Eliza's hypocrisy is, or the identity of the spotted Browns (averse, in turn, to Whities), *Spotty* scores with youngsters because of the injustice to one bunny who is a brother under any skin. He has, besides, a sister who stands up for him, a mother who won't rest until he's found and—for safekeeping—the thought, before he leaves home, to "take my breakfast along."

But why, a reviewer grumbled, did they have to be bunnies? Why dissimulate? And indeed, in the era of absolute realism just ending, it was customary for animals to be animals and people to be people. Angus the inquisitive Scottie, Ping the lag-behind duck, even Ferdinand the peaceable bull (no pacifist, remember) are each species-perfect—or imperfect. Janet Adam Smith has observed that before Beatrix Potter, animal books were "more in the tradition of fables—human situations described in animal terms—whereas Beatrix Potter is interested in animal nature. Under the petticoats and aprons, there are real pigs and hedgehogs."[8] In the subsequent turn to realism they lost their finery, and often their voices as well.

It wouldn't do. From Reynard the fox to Anansi the spider and Brer Rabbit, animal tricksters had provided popular amusement; from the earliest origin tales to Kipling's *Just So Stories*, explanations for their peculiar habits or looks proliferated. They took a hand in human affairs too, like Puss in Boots; and like the Three Bears, lived as proper people. In short, if fables were to be in eclipse, fancy would take other forms. With Babar there appeared thoroughly humanized animals in highly civilized circumstances, and from the comic strip tradition came Mickey Mouse and his harum-scarum crew. (Both perhaps traceable, paradoxically, to the way Potter clothed animal nature.) In either case, the only purpose was to entertain, and what better than an animal as a

They were getting ready for the party when Aunt Eliza came and took Mother Bunny aside. "How about Spotty?" she asked. "My advice is to leave him home."

"Why—I could not possibly!" Mother Bunny exclaimed.

"You know how upset Grandpa would be if he saw Spotty," Aunt Eliza said. "Do you want to spoil his birthday party?"

"I don't know what to do," Mother Bunny said weakly. "I don't want to hurt Spotty . . ."

"But you certainly don't intend to spoil the day for Grandpa and all the family," Aunt Eliza said firmly. Mother Bunny finally gave in. So

321. *Spotty,* text by Margret Rey, pictures by H. A. Rey. Harper, 1945. 8¼ x 9¾.

fellow-creature and, easily enough, a friend?

To a small child, an animal is a natural alter-ego, that we know; and for some years—witness Winnie-the-Pooh—part plaything, part friend. In straits, he is us at a safe remove and a loved one, himself; when he is bad, he is the other, when he is good, ourselves; we can love him and love ourselves. That animals are also very much as we are as small children, Margaret Wise Brown was to recognize and put to use. Relevant, too, is the presence of pictures: the fact that animals, pictured, are of themselves interesting or amusing; that, seen, they needn't be described as animals; that we accept them as Petunia or Curious George or Spotty, and enjoy them. (But a story that fails on a human basis isn't saved by the substitution of animals for people, regardless.)

Yet *Spotty* is a fable—or mock-fable; and the jacket's laconic "In the best rabbit tradition, everybody had just acted like everybody else," reminds us that there was something

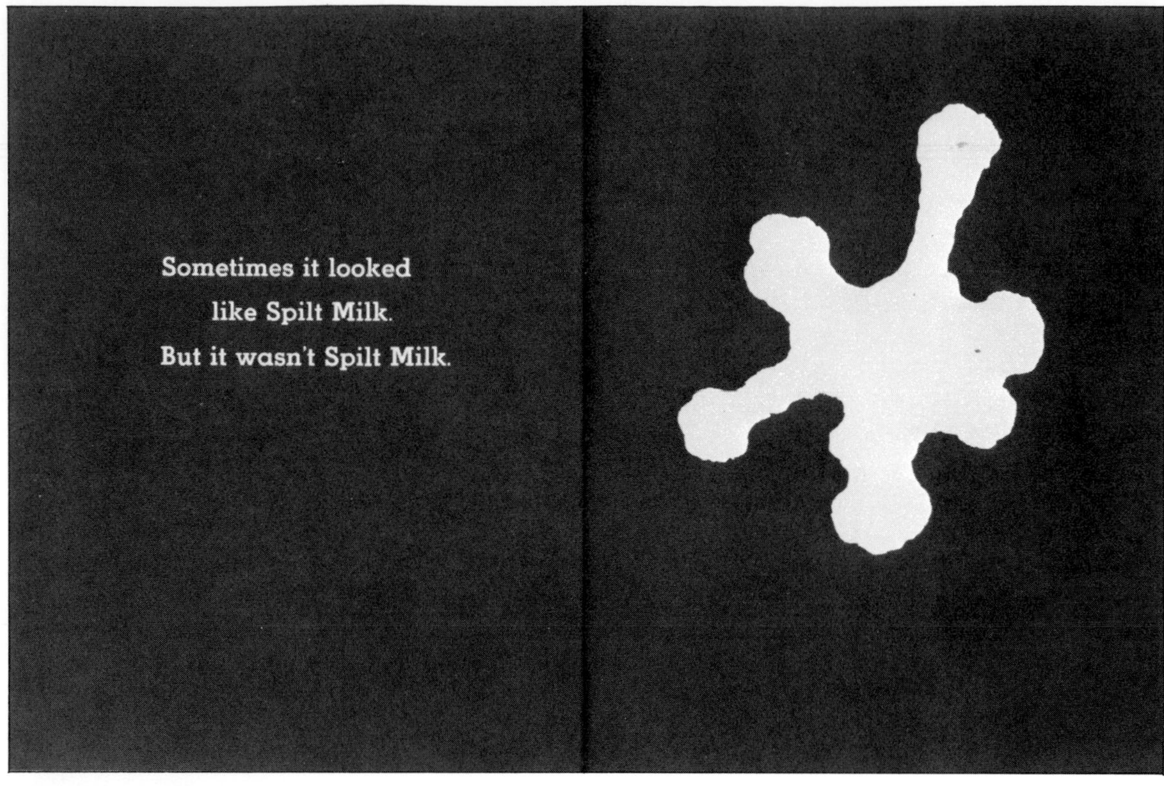

322, 323. *It Looked like Spilt Milk,* by Charles G. Shaw. Harper, 1947. 8 x 10.

322

about the ant and the grasshopper, too, that suggested them to Aesop (whoever he was) as provider and idler respectively. In the same context, 'don't be a rabbit' goes down far more readily than 'don't discriminate,' not because it evades the issue but because it puts it humorously, colorfully, persuasively—for children, as a sad bit of silliness not a moral blight.

So the reason for why rabbits is manifold, obvious as it must have seemed to the Reys; and, wittingly or not, the book represents, with certain others, a break with literal realism in search of a larger imaginative reality. "Mrs. Frederick C. Little's second son," you may recall, "looked very much like a mouse in every way." *Stuart Little* appeared on the same Harper list.

What is real need not be actual, in Walter de la Mare's words.

"Sometimes it looked like Spilt Milk. But it wasn't Spilt Milk" (322). To some, then, it looked like a Rorschach test—a way of judging personality by the image found in an ink blot; but it wasn't a Rorschach test or any device to bare the psyche. "Sometimes it looked like a Tree . . . a Great Horned Owl . . . a Mitten . . . a Birthday Cake" (323); and then you might guess it was Charles Shaw's. "Sometimes it looked like Spilt Milk. But it wasn't. . . . It was just a Cloud in the Sky." A cloud that might assume any shape, white on deep blue, in a book composed solely of such images.

"Sometimes it looked like a . . ." asks for an answer, but the series of riddles constitutes not a quiz, as in *The Guess Book,* but a game; and sure as children are to spot a Tree and a Mitten, the Birthday Cake gives pause—and with recognition, pleasure—while the Great Horned Owl is new and strange and tantalizing, like first meeting 'soporific' in Beatrix Potter. Part of the fun of the game is that you're right only to be wrong ("But it wasn't . . ."), and you know it; nor can you solve the mystery by any number of correct answers or any amount of logic—it isn't a game that you play to win. But you can, if you're young enough, turn the pages again and again and see the lovely cottony wiggly forms a cloud can take. "Sometimes"—the last time—"it looked like an Angel."

What is extraordinary is that this book which is not a participation book in any of the obvious ways—there isn't so much as a question mark in it—takes its life from the response of children. An artist's reverie, it becomes a colloquy between artist and child; touched off, I think, by the equivocal nature of 'sometimes' and the tentative quality of the cloud images.

These several, from *Lambert's Bargain* forward, form no coherent group but as Harper picturebooks of the Forties they have certain things in common. None are strikingly illustrated, although two—*Lambert* and *Spilt Milk*—were written by artists; and nowhere has the illustration an existence independent of the idea conveyed. Ursula Nordstrom differed from most of her colleagues—at this period, probably all—in being interested in the writing rather than in the artwork, which is also to say initially in the content. But neither are the books meant to broaden horizons or instill values—to improve children in some way. Asked by Anne Carroll Moore what qualifications she, not a teacher or a librarian, had for her position, she is said to have retorted, "I was a child." The content, whatever the subject, is emotional reality, a child's reality. Others—Ets, Pène du Bois, Duvoisin in particular—qualify too.

"How can you have the here and now without an emotion," Margaret Wise Brown once protested.[9] Little wonder, all told, that the Forties at Harper's was preeminently the period of Margaret Wise Brown.

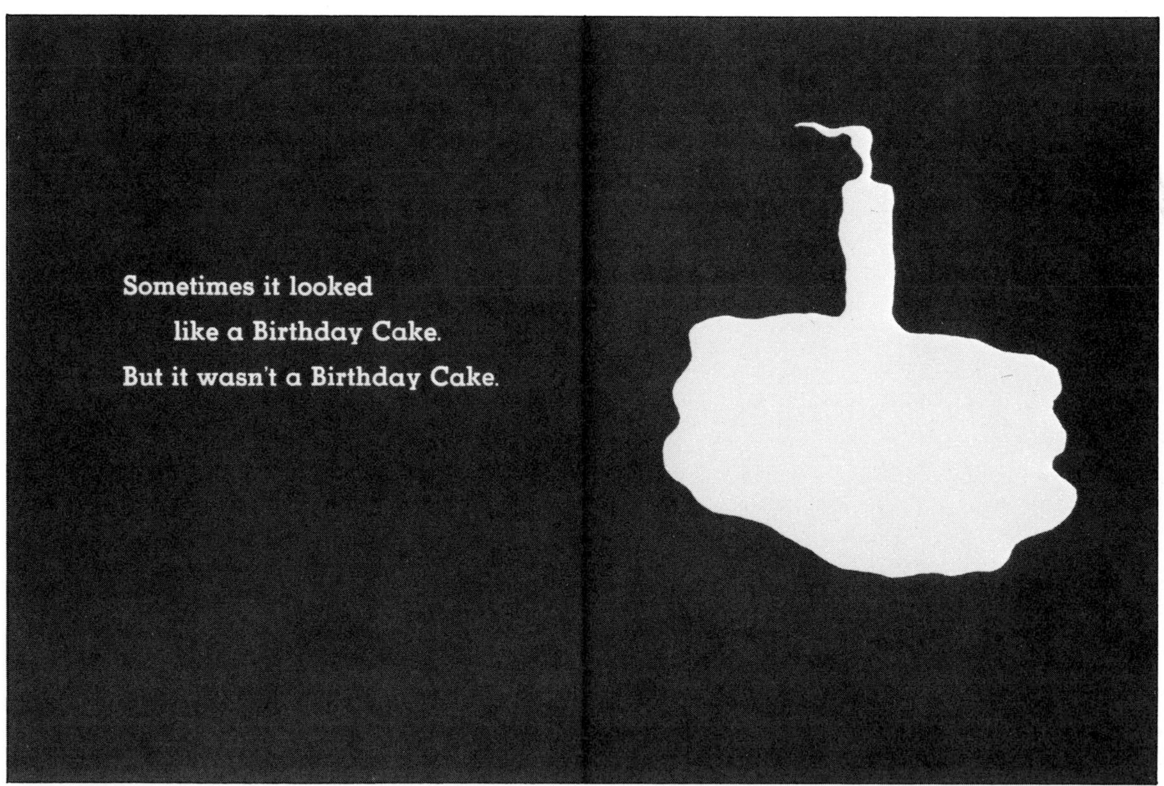

Sometimes it looked
like a Birthday Cake.
But it wasn't a Birthday Cake.

323

MARGARET WISE BROWN

In the short span between the publication of her first work in 1937 and her early death in 1952, Margaret Wise Brown wrote more than ninety picturebooks (some of which appeared posthumously). A few, issued both before and after her death, utilized stories previously published, for she also wrote herself (or adapted or translated) a half-dozen story collections—a judiciously simplified Uncle Remus, for one—and, beginning with the ubiquitous *Another Here and Now Story Book*, contributed to others. She wrote stories too for *Good Housekeeping*, and for *Story Parade* and other children's magazines; and as her interest in children's records grew, she wrote songs for her stories and stories in song; right along she wrote poetry.

She thought once of asking James Thurber to do a series of cartoons characterizing attitudes or states of mind, with questions for children to answer by 'reading' facial expressions.

She had a tiny old frame house tucked away in a Manhattan courtyard—with a brick-floored living room deep in fur and a fireplace for heat—and another, on a Maine island, where washbowls (the only washbowls) were set out under the apple trees. Her regular companion was a Kerry blue terrier on a kelly green leash; she hung a potted green bay tree with fruits in season (to the confoundment of the unknowing); and Clement Hurd remembers her as "the best polisher of brass that I ever knew and the easiest . . . We could only attribute it to her creative touch."[10]

Four, five, seven of her books appeared a year, of several sorts at various prices from assorted publishers; a long extravagant profile ran in *Life*; and Margaret Wise Brown became famous, the first author of picturebooks to be recognized in her own right. The first, too, to make the writing of picturebooks an art.

Maybe *When the Wind Blew* (1937) was submitted to Harper by a friend unbeknownst to her, as reported in *Life*, and maybe it wasn't; Ursula Nordstrom simply remembers taking it on—one of her first selections as an apprentice editor—because "children like sad stories."[11] And, wrote its author: "In *When the Wind Blew* I took a plot of Chekhov, about a very sad and bitter man trying to drown a fly in an ink blob and then suddenly deciding to save its life and by that one small gesture feeling better; and I tried to make a sad story for children, believing that many of the graver cadences of life are there at any age."[12]

An old, old lady is "all by herself in the world because she was so old everyone had forgotten her, and the children and the new people in the world didn't even know . . . she was alive." But she is not alone, she has seventeen cats and one little blue grey kitten who follow behind her when she goes to bathe in the ocean and mew for breakfast when they get home. She milks the cow and fills seventeen purple saucers for the cats, a little blue saucer for the kitten, and a big glass mug for herself. After, the cats clean their paws, the kitten cleans one paw—"and then his mother came and rolled him over and gave him a good scrubbing with her tongue"; and the little old lady does the dishes. Out in the sun to dry go dishes, cats, kitten, with the old lady along to watch.

"But one day" the wind begins to blow, and blows the sunlight cold, and the cats' fur all over their backs, and the kitten almost off his feet. The old lady brings them in one by one out of the wind—adding, for the kitten, a saucer of warm milk—and they curl up by the fire to sleep. Then she gets a toothache, and it aches and it aches. "The poor old lady, she sat there by her fire with a terrible toothache; and she didn't have any medicine to take, and she didn't have any dentist to come to her, and she didn't have anyone to make her hot broth and tell her it would soon be over. She just had seventeen cats and one little blue grey kitten. She didn't even have a hot water bottle, which is the very best thing in the world for old ladies to put on their toothaches. Poor old lady."

To be sick with no one to tend you, to lie in

bed shivering with the wind howling outside and whistling through the cracks ("and her toothache was all that there seemed to be in the world"): to a child it is sadder than starvation, which is unimaginable—as any suffering is closer and sadder than death—and sad rather than frightening, the way extreme danger is. If only "she had a hot water bottle to put against her jaw to soothe the ache that was there." And then she hears a click click purr, purr, click purr near her ear, and feels something warm along the side of her face ("What could it be?") and finds the little blue grey kitten—"Just as good as a fur-covered hot water bottle."

In a picturebook that would be the last line, or the next-to-last; but *When the Wind Blew* has the ampler form of a short story—"and the fire shadows danced on the old lady's ceiling, and the toothache went away. The cabin grew warmer, and the little blue grey kitten purred on . . . and it almost seemed as though the old lady were purring, too, as she fell sound asleep in the little house by the edge of the ocean with her seventeen cats and the little blue grey kitten."

Made up, it is a story with pictures—two facing pages of centered text, a small line drawing on each, and then a double-page illustration (by Rosalie Slocum, of *Another Here and Now*), a full solid bleed in strong color, separate and in turn all-absorbing. It was a novel form for a picturebook (though not distant in time from color inserts), a way of preserving the flow of the story, of setting off a text not composed image by image, opening by opening.

A similar alternation of words and pictures occurs in *The Dead Bird* which, with illustrations by Remy Charlip, was published by Scott in 1958 but utilizes, only slightly adjusted, a story from the 1938 collection *The Fish with the Deep Sea Smile*—a story, that is, conceived and complete in words. (*The Runaway Bunny*, so designed too, is also complete in words, as we'll see, although the text was meant for a picturebook from the start.) This circumstance aside, *The Dead Bird*—or "The Dead Bird"—is and is not like *When the Wind Blew*; for one thing, it is and is not a sad story.

"The bird was dead when the children found it," it begins; "But it had not been dead for long—it was still warm and its eyes were closed." The children feel for the beat of the bird's heart, and find none; the body grows cold and stiffens—"That was the way animals got when they had been dead for some time—cold dead and stone still with no heart beating." They are sorry it's dead and can't fly again, and glad they found it "because now they could dig a grave in the woods and bury it. They could have a funeral and sing to it the way grown-up people did when someone died."

The funeral follows, with a song to the little dead bird, and some crying "because their singing was so beautiful and the ferns smelled so sweetly and the bird was dead." A stone is placed on the spot and flowers planted round; "And every day, until they forgot, they went and sang to their little dead bird and put fresh flowers on his grave."

That children are naturally sympathetic and naturally egocentric, eager to emulate adults and fond of ceremony, ardent and quick to forget, was not Margaret Wise Brown's discovery; but understanding it well—recognizing too that the first dead thing encountered by most children is a bird—she is able to deal with death directly and, for them, honestly and immediately. Sorrow is expressed without embarrassment, joyfulness without shame; and a small child cannot but be comforted.

It is likely, too, that the clinical signs of death are meant to be a practical help to him, just as in "The Tickly Spider" in *Another Here and Now*, the child is "also" introduced to "the common-sense knowledge that animals and insects seldom attack anything perfectly still." *The Fish with the Deep Sea Smile* stemmed from a request for a book of stories especially for five-year-olds by John Macrae whose firm, Dutton, had just published *Another Here and Now*, where the stories are for twos, threes, fours, fives and sixes in turn—or rather, with their explanatory mat-

324, 325. *The Runaway Bunny,* text by Margaret Wise Brown, pictures by Clement Hurd. Harper, 1942; new edition, 1972. 8 x 6¾.

ter, for people working with them. For its part, *The Fish with the Deep Sea Smile* (deepest when he's smiled himself off a hook) is dedicated to Lucy Sprague Mitchell and it too has its purposes; but it has also several stories about "Sneakers, That Rapscallion Cat" that later turned up in a book of their own, another large group—some of them poems actually—designated as "Sleepy Stories," and, throughout, what Margaret Wise Brown was to refer to shortly as "interludes."

"There is another form I wonder about for five-year-olds. I call it an interlude, it is not a story with a plot, it isn't very long. It is somewhere between a story and a poem, a dwelling on some theme in words, a recreation of some experience. It is the thing some five-year-olds do in their own writings. I have tried to do it in 'The Wonderful Day,' 'The Dead Bird,' 'The Pale Blue Flower'; and perhaps 'The Children's Clock' and 'Christmas Eve' are only long interludes or incidents rather than real stories. Whether this is a good form for children's writings I am not sure. I think, because it is a quiet and simple form it might be, if it is read to a child at the right time."[13]

What she is describing tentatively and exploratively is of course the form she was to make uniquely her own in picturebooks.

In the offing too, anent 'themes' and 'experiences,' was attention to those "graver cadences of life" which—Brown had intended to say apropos of *When the Wind Blew*—"escape the scientific labeling and age leveling of the materialistic psychologist." (Edited out of the published article as inappropriate, the words were reinstated in a Harper biography.) Though she would always stress her indebtedness to her Bank Street training and to Mrs. Mitchell, *When the Wind Blew* represented for her "a protest against Bank Street doctrine"[14]—an impertinence of a sort, and then by extension a declaration of independence from all strictures.

As of 1944 she had turned out for Harper —all the while doing *Bumble Bugs*, the Noisy Books, *The Little Fireman—The Streamlined Pig* (sheer silliness), *The Polite Pen-*

guin ("Manners seem unreasonable and no use evading it"—MWB[15]), *Night and Day* (with Leonard Weisgard—to be "the most beautiful book we had ever done"[16]), *Don't Frighten the Lion* (the Rey zoo caper), *Little Chicken* (who discovers that "some wanted to play with him, and some didn't"), *SHHhhhh . . . BANG: a whispering book* ("She liked the idea of children going into a library and asking for *SHHhhhh . . . BANG*"—UN[17]), *Black and White* (an allegorical conflict), *The Big Fur Secret* (unbeknownst to adults, "animals don't talk"), *They All Saw It* (the Ylla album), *Horses* (by "Timothy Hay"); and in their midst, fresh and melodious and sure, *The Runaway Bunny*.

> Once there was a little bunny who wanted to run away.
> So he said to his mother, "I am running away."
> "If you run away," said his mother, "I will run after you.
> For you are my little bunny."
>
> "If you run after me," said the little bunny,
> "I will become a fish in a trout stream
> and I will swim away from you."
>
> "If you become a fish in a trout stream," said his mother,
> "I will become a fisherman and I will fish for you."
>
> "If you become a fisherman," said the little bunny,
> "I will become a rock on the mountain, high above you."
> "If you become a rock on the mountain high above me,"
> said his mother, "I will be a mountain climber,
> and I will climb to where you are."
>
> "If you become a mountain climber,"
> said the little bunny,"
> "I will be a crocus in a hidden garden."
> "If you become a crocus in a hidden garden,"
> said his mother, "I will be a gardener. And I will find you."
>
> "If you are a gardener and find me,"
> said the little bunny, "I will be a bird
> and fly away from you."
> "If you become a bird and fly away from me,"
> said his mother, "I will be a tree that you come home to."

"If you become a tree," said the little bunny,
"I will become a little sailboat,
and I will sail away from you."
"If you become a sailboat and sail away
from me,"
said his mother, "I will become the wind
and blow you where I want you to go." [324]

"If you become the wind and blow me," said
the little bunny,
"I will join the circus and fly away on a
flying trapeeze."
"If you go flying on a flying trapeeze," said
his mother,
"I will be a tightrope walker,
and I will walk across the air to you."

"If you become a tightrope walker and walk
across the air,"
said the bunny, "I will become a little boy
and run into a house."
"If you become a little boy and run into a
house,"
said the mother bunny, "I will become your
mother
and catch you in my arms and hug you."

"Shucks," said the little bunny, "I might just
as well
stay where I am and be your little bunny."
And so he did.
"Have a carrot," said the mother bunny. [325]

It is a game of hide-and-seek, with the child taking the lead; a fledgling's challenge and a mother's response in kind; rebellion and unfailingly, reassurance. Or, to Margaret Wise Brown, "an attempt to put the bold, tender, repeated cadence of an ancient French love song into the loving world of a child."[18] The cadence and the constancy: the song itself ends "If you become a corpse, I shall become the earth and I will embrace you."

The carrot was an afterthought, flashed from Maine—a fillip after the measured rhythm back and forth, and an anchor, the daily bill of fare. But if an afterthought, not an accident: knowing that food and bed stand for security to small children, Brown regularly led her firemen and bunnies to one or the other or both. For all its eloquence, nothing becomes *The Runaway Bunny* more than that last snap of carrot.

When Clement Hurd first did the illustrations in 1942, he was not accustomed to working in separations in shades of gray and the results fell short of his expectations; in 1972, prevailing upon Ursula Nordstrom to let him redo the book (a steady seller regardless), he prepared new drawings for the black-and-white text pages, remade some of the color spreads, and conceived an entirely new one for the last opening—a picture that one former child (a carrot-lover too) pronounced simply, "Heaven" (325).

Old or new, flat and bright like the pictures for *Goodnight Moon* (p. 259), or more atmospheric, more lyrical, the illustrations are one in that they dare the impossible, even the absurd—a bunny bird flying to a bunny tree, a bunny wind blowing a bunny boat—and because of Hurd's gentle, grave honesty, make it utterly natural. He imagines himself into the child/bunny world wholely, turns the runaway bunny into a sailboat by simply extending his ears, and has credit left, as it were, for a pennant waving on top (where a bunny-*shaped* boat all togged out would have been an affront). There is no cleverness, nothing to marvel at; the magic is in the image, not in the making.

This brings us, in time and tenor, to *Little Fur Family*, a very little book (with later, a standard-size edition). A very little book about little furry animals, species indeterminate, bound in rabbit fur and boxed, with a hole to show the little fur child's furry stomach. A little fur book for small hands to hold (cheeks to rub, arms to cuddle) with the smallest of stories, about being, just being, a little fur child. He goes out to play in the wild wild woods and wild grass tickles his nose and makes him sneeze . . . *kerchoo*; and his grandpa comes *thump thump thump* and says "Bless you," and sneezes too. "Bless you," says the little fur child. He catches a fish and throws it back in the river, catches a bug and throws it back in the air, catches "a little tiny tiny fur animal, the littlest fur animal in the world"—like the littlest last best babushka in a Russian nesting egg—and puts it back gently in the grass. The sun

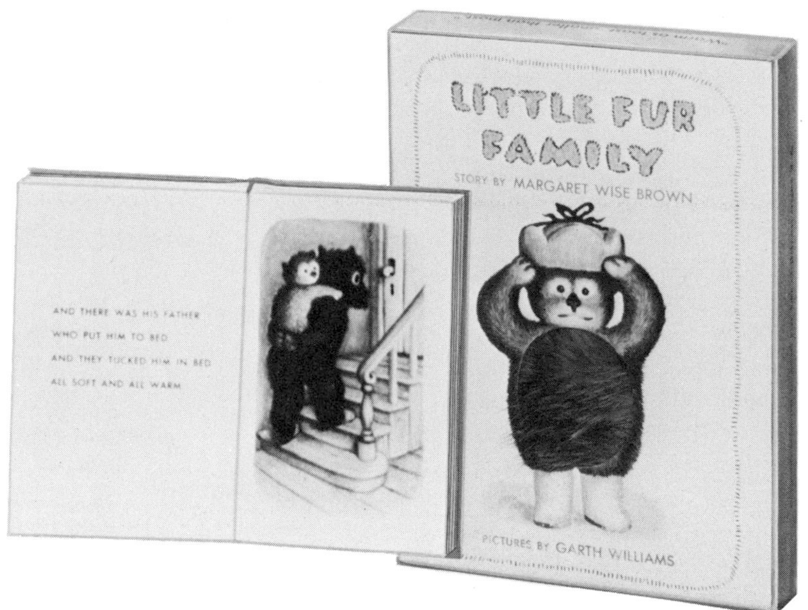

326. *Little Fur Family,* text by Margaret Wise Brown, pictures by Garth Williams. Harper, 1946. 2⅛ x 3¼.

goes down, the sky grows wild and red, and the little fur child runs home—to his mother and his father (326) and a snug sleepy song. In *Little Fur Family,* Margaret Wise Brown wrote, she only dared to be very simple; and as an entity it is as inevitable in its way as a wooden totem pole or a marble fish.

It is also a dear little funny book—funny because "a little tiny tiny fur animal, the smallest fur animal in the world," is funny, especially skedaddling to a hole in the ground; and a little tickly-nose sneeze is, and a grandpa sneeze, and his big red hanky; and a "warm wooden tree" with green shuttered windows and a red wooden door. The pictures take up where the words leave off, and what is funny in them too is just what would be funny to a very small child—chuckle-funny, the way Beatrix Potter is, not absurd or ludicrous.

Garth Williams also shared with Margaret Wise Brown (and with Beatrix Potter) a softness and warmth free of sentimental haze, at least in the books they did together. A *New Yorker* artist when E. B. White tapped him for *Stuart Little,* he could draw animals that look like real animals and, doleful or puzzled or grim, have the expressiveness of people. Concurrent with *Little Fur Family* he did his own first picturebook (reissued in 1970 in a new edition), *The Chicken Book,* a go-round of expressive drawing (327) capped by a down-to-earth admonition—that little chicken had better stop wishing for his breakfast, says his mother, and "Just come here and SCRATCH!"

His fuzzy animals, like Rojankovsky's, have spirit and substance, and it is not accidental that he followed Rojankovsky as Golden Books' top animal illustrator; but he makes individuals of them as Rojankovsky doesn't, and as few artists have been able to

327. *The Chicken Book,* a traditional story, pictures by Garth Williams. Howell, Soskin, 1946. Detail.

—Potter, of course, and Ernest Shepard, and in our time Sendak. With Clement Hurd, he was to give shape to Margaret Wise Brown's tenderest, most private work for children, her look-alike animal world.

She would start thinking, she wrote early on, "of the small animal dignity that children and puppies and shy little horses struggle so hard to maintain," of "the wonder and surprise at the world" of a kitten by itself for the first time;[19] and stories would come. She took to likening the mechanics of writing for small children—"the sudden starts and stops, the sounds and silences in the words"[20]—to writing for a puppy or a kitten. ("Dogs," she attested, "will also be interested in the Noisy Books the first time they hear them read with any convincing suddenness and variety of whistles, squeaks, hisses, thuds and sudden silences following an unexpected 'BANG!' "[21]) And *My World*, the child/bunny book very like our next, *Goodnight Moon*, had its origin, she said in a talk, in the life of her own dog.

". . . My dog has a world that I am a part of and more often no part of—a very certain world in which he has his home, in which he has himself, in which he has night and day, and hot and cold, and his poor little dinner that only comes once a day—his own dear door, and his own dear dish and his own dear rugs—his own dear me and his own dear cat that he chases across the fence whenever he gets sight of it.

"So every child has his own world. His dear day, his dear shoe, his dear self, his own dear sun that he sees every day, his own dear stars that he sometimes sees at night; his own dear pillow, his own dear bed, his own dear everything in the world that he knows. . . ."[22]

In *Goodnight Moon*, it is the close of day, and a room first brilliant with light darkens at each color opening as, outside, the moon rises and brightens the sky (328).

In the great green room
There was a telephone
And a red balloon
And a picture of—

Here, as Dorothy White remarks, "one should turn the page," but her daughter wasn't ready. " 'You haven't said about the rabbit on the bed.' She held the page down and went round the room pointing out all the things I hadn't said."[23] Then on to a picture of "The cow jumping over the moon" and "three little bears sitting on chairs" . . .

And two little kittens
And a pair of mittens
And a little toyhouse
And a young mouse

And a comb and a brush and a bowl full of mush
And a quiet old lady who was whispering "hush"

To interrupt the text is to do violence to it, and Mrs. White correctly points out that the intervals between page turnings are apt to be long when the pictures offer much to look at and a child has much to say. To give primacy to delivering the text, on the other hand, is to do violence to the child. Margaret Wise Brown, one suspects, would say to let the specific rhymes go and rely on the rhythm and reiteration to carry over, as they do.

Goodnight room

Goodnight moon
Goodnight cow jumping over the moon

Goodnight light
And the red balloon
Goodnight bears
Goodnight chairs

Goodnight to clocks and socks . . . to comb and brush; good night to nobody, goodnight mush; "And goodnight to the old lady whispering 'hush.' "

Goodnight stars
Goodnight air

Goodnight noises everywhere.

The old lady is gone, the cats are curled on her chair; the room is dim, in a deep shadowless shade save for the lights blazing in the toyhouse and the fire blazing on the hearth; the rabbit is asleep. Through the windows the sky is bright, the moon and the stars shine; the mouse sits on the sill.

Quietly, from picture to picture, the mouse has moved about, the only significant action in the course of the book. Hardly noticeable, he is never unnoticed. Turning the pages alone, a youngster will retrace his route; looking on—for the umpteenth time—point him out as soon as the page turns. (Some books children should *own*, and this is one of them.) Like the questions in the Noisy Books that have to be answered, he has to be accounted for; he brings the audience into the story.

Praising the pictures, Dorothy White speaks of the text as "inferior . . . the barest commentary"; and notes that her daughter "has very much more to say about the book than the author has."[24] Exactly. In saying less, the author allows the artist to say more, and the child to find more—to find the old lady knitting (the author doesn't say that), the cats playing with the yarn (or that), the extra blanket, the slippers, the fire. But why are we looking so hard? Because "In the great green room/There was a telephone/ And a red balloon. . . ." And would we be listening so intently were it not a 'great green room,' a 'telephone,' and a 'red balloon' —a real telephone, mind you, beside the child bunny's bed.

Of all of Margaret Wise Brown's writings, *Goodnight Moon* is probably the most abstract in form and concrete in substance; the closest to Gertrude Stein and to the utterances of children; the most circumscribed and, as put into pictures, the most difficult to exhaust. What about that mouse, for instance, inhabiting a room in a house? accepted by the family, untouched by the cats? (But they are rabbits, we remind ourselves, wavering.) For all the dear mittens and socks, the great green room is at the last—a mystery.

It is risky to interpret any variation in the course of Margaret Wise Brown's work as a change, to decide that she did—or meant—

328. *Goodnight Moon,* text by Margaret Wise Brown, pictures by Clement Hurd. Harper, 1947. 7⅞ x 6⅝.

first this, then that. She liked to say that she wrote her stories down in twenty minutes and polished them for two years or more; writing constantly, she had numerous manuscripts out on approval; and as we have noted, earlier work was apt to turn up at any time, either in a new form or newly published. Moreover—and this we've seen too, and will see again—she had by 1937–38, when she was just beginning, so many definite interests and ideas that the comparatively few years of her writing career could not absorb them. It is just because she followed different leads simultaneously that her work shapes up, as it were, in parallel columns.

But in the books closest to the lives of children, the ones about child animals, there is in the late Forties a noticeable shift, intentional or not, from security as a theme, and toward one form or another of independence—whether the freedom to go out after dark or, finally, the freedom to be oneself.

A little raccoon is impatient to see and know the things of the night. "Wait," his mother tells him, *Wait Till the Moon Is Full.* Wondering and questioning, growing "quietly fat," graduating from pull toy to rubber ball to sailboat, he waits as the moon grows bigger too; and then, baseball and bat at the ready, a new cockiness in his talk (329), he gets the answer to all his wants:

"If you want to go out in the woods
and see the night
and know an owl
and how dark is the dark
and see the moon
and how big is the night
and listen to the Whip poor Will
and stay up all night
and sleep all day
and see that the moon isn't a rabbit
and what color is the night
and see a bird fall out of his nest
and fly away in the moonlight
and find another little raccoon to play with,
off you go, for—"

"the moon is full." And in full color—like the frontispiece glimpse of a new-moon night—the raccoons and rabbits play baseball and skip rope under a big, pale yellow moon.

Songs are interlarded, songs that are part nonsense, part nature-lyric—where before, as in *Little Fur Family*, a lullaby might be sung at the close (or, elsewhere, a song appended). It was more and more important to Brown, this writing of songs, of poems to be sung; but alongside some of her picturebook texts the poems meant as such are weak tea. She wrote poetry, it could be said, except when she tried to; when she was writing naturally, the way a child does, not in standard forms (fatal to child poetry too). Or when—call it poetry or lighthearted verse—she was just rhyming or alliterating, relishing the sound and swing of words (p. 264).

Wait Till the Moon Is Full succeeds, then, in spite of the poems—because wanting to go out at night is as deep-seated as wanting to be safe in bed, and the exchanges between mother and child raccoon have a sweet and comic ring of truth. The extent of the dramatic realism was new; the extent of the resemblance, that is, to the familiar thrusts and feints of family life. Peter Rabbit (even as a rabbit) is warned by his mother not to go into Mr. McGregor's garden, disobeys, almost gets caught, loses his jacket and shoes, gets lost and can't get out, returns home sick—and has to have camomile tea while "Flopsy, Mopsy and Cottontail had bread and milk and blackberries for supper"; a mighty novel in miniature, a nursery Crime and Punishment. But from Lois Lenski's spic-and-span *Little Family* to the daily round *At Our House* to the loving warmth of *Little Fur Family*, there is no conflict; in *The Runaway Bunny*, the conflict is formalized and allegorical. In a sense—Margaret Wise Brown's chief sense—*Wait Till the Moon Is Full* is about the night and "all things that love the night" (a carryover from her earlier *Night and Day*) but implicit in the little raccoon's assertive "I want," his mother's restraining, assuring "Wait," is the conflict of wills inherent in growing up.

It could be a story in itself, and in *Bedtime for Frances* (p. 472) and its successors it

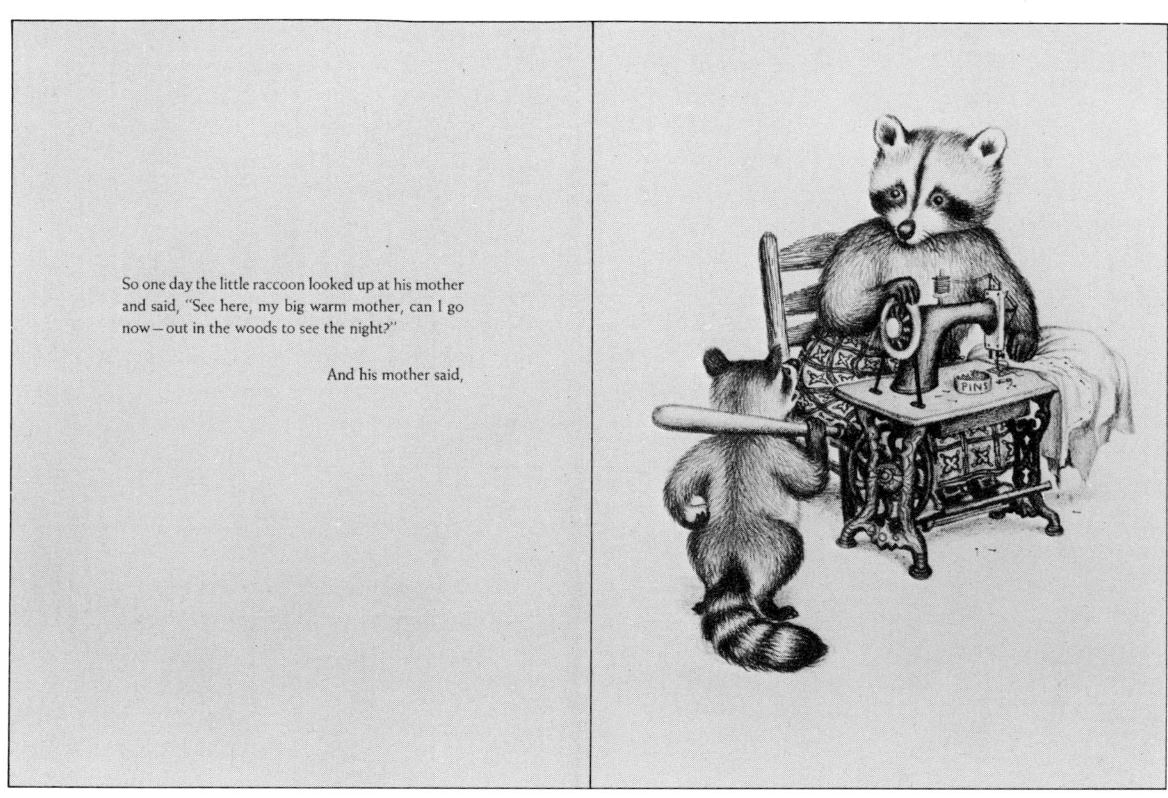

So one day the little raccoon looked up at his mother and said, "See here, my big warm mother, can I go now—out in the woods to see the night?"
And his mother said,
PINS

329. *Wait Till the Moon Is Full,* text by Margaret Wise Brown, pictures by Garth Williams. Harper, 1948. 7¾ x 9⅞.

would be. Here the characterization is less in the text than in the pictures, though there are clues, subtle clues that a listener might not catch, for the artist to expand on. The little raccoon whispers his first wish for a look at the dark; steps up his questions and raises his sights; and finally confronts his mother boldly—baby toys left behind (in the pictures), ball and bat in hand (ditto), ready to go out and play baseball when, simply, "the moon is full." In effect, the pictures put the story into words. But there is more to them than content, just as there is more to the story than plot; and in the faces of the two raccoons are the tremors of home.

Three Little Animals is a big book but otherwise a successor, of a sort, to *Little Fur Family*. Three little fur animals live together happily "in their own little warm animal world in their warm way. But the world of people was over the hill and the little animals naturally wondered what that world was like." Donning the garb of a proper gentleman, the first sets out, and then the second, dressed like a lady (yes, like). The little one has no clothes so he has to stay behind until, lonesome, he makes himself some things to wear: "Little plants planted on a saucer for a hat, hollow logs for shoes, and a coat of big green leaves." But, as the first two have already discovered, out in the world clothes are a cover-up ("everyone thought they were people") and the little one, too, is lost in the crowd (330).

Comes a big wind, blowing everyone's hat off, "And the three little animals saw each other's fur ears and they knew they were not like other people. So did the people." Off they run, throwing their togs to the wind, until they reach their home in the woods where they belong—"For they were little animals!"

The state of nature vs. the republic of man,

or, in Fifties' terms, individuality vs. conformity, *Three Little Animals* cannot be read other than as a parable of some sort; c. 1970, as an example of dropping out and doing your own thing. But whatever one finds in it, there's no escaping the pox on people—while animals ("in their warm way") are simple, happy, affectionate: wouldn't it be better to be one?

Brown didn't usually juxtapose the two worlds. Seeing the child world and the animal world as one, she ignored adults—the larger human world—except as parent-figures. In *Little Fur Family* there is no world of people over the hill, seen or unseen; as far as they and we are concerned, they are the people, and their way is the natural way. But turn Arcady into a suburb of Chicago and their simplicity becomes innocence, and they in turn become gallant or pathetic—Three Little Animals and the Great Grim World, it could be called.

Still, one little animal wears a flowerpot hat and log shoes; and who can deny him? In the animals' house is a grandfather clock and a log bed and here and there a clump of grass; a big bunny looks in at the door. On the street are short paunchy men and tall skinny men, men with briefcases, bundles, newspapers, tools—a city in motion. The wind sends hats flying like autumn leaves, and the people scatter in frantic disarray; the little animals doff their clothing, and into the distance sail shoes, laces flapping, and gloves, fingers curled. Given a large format and a big chewy subject, Garth Williams fills the spreads with lightly washed line drawings, precise and delicate, that bridge his two worlds as an illustrator, that of *Little Fur Family* and, in the same year, a Damon Runyon roadshow. In a coupling of Old Master draftsmanship and caricature, the animals and the natural landscape are fully and sensitively formed, the people and streetfronts tersely outlined. But regardless it is the images that carry, and especially the picture of the three little animals who, when all is said, are disarmingly themselves.

Introducing her Kerry blue to an interviewer early in 1952, Margaret Wise Brown remarked that "Crispin has a book of his own, called 'The Dog Who Belonged to Him-

330. *Three Little Animals,* text by Margaret Wise Brown, pictures by Garth Williams. Harper, 1956. 9⅛ x 12.

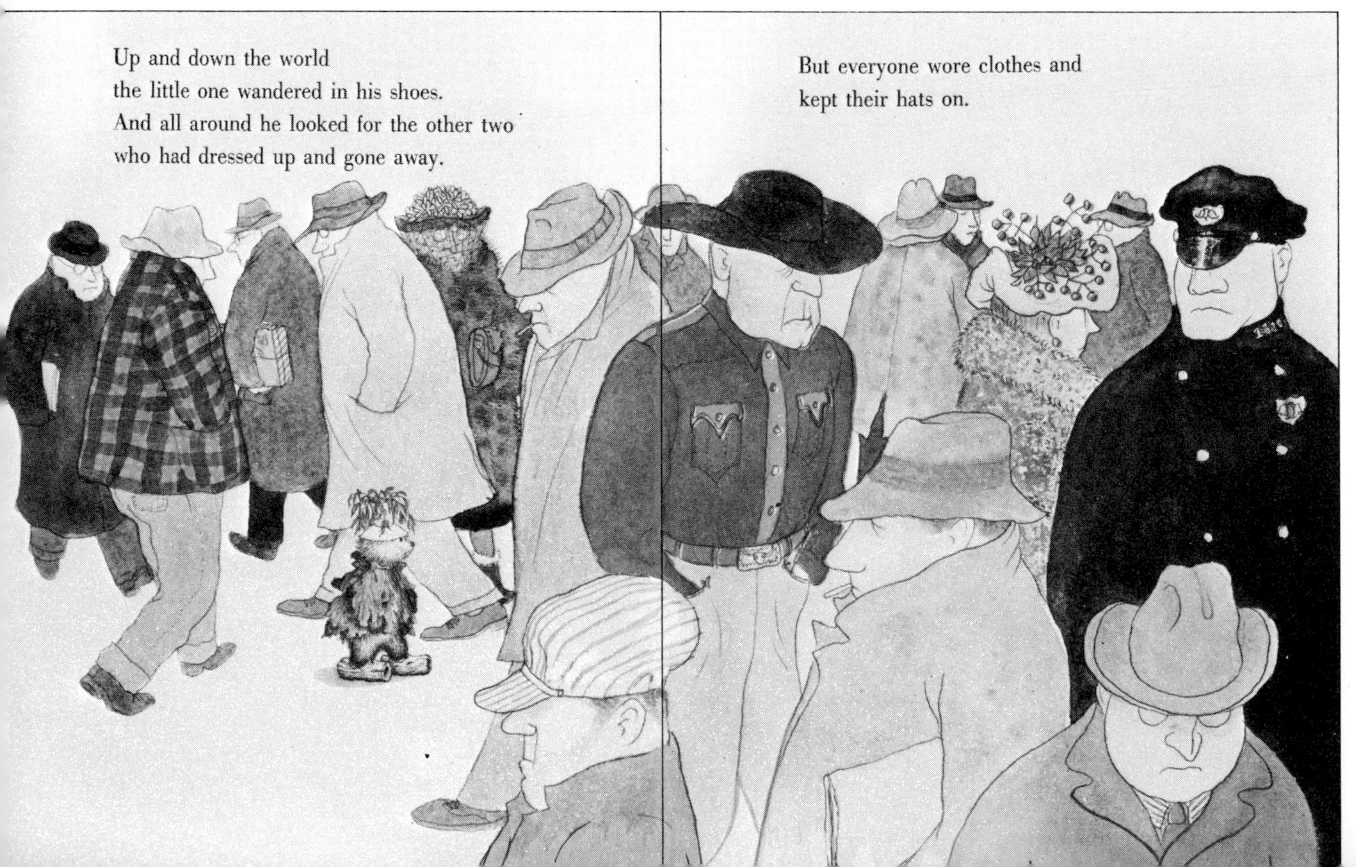

Up and down the world
the little one wandered in his shoes.
And all around he looked for the other two
who had dressed up and gone away.
But everyone wore clothes and
kept their hats on.

he belonged to himself.
In the mornings he woke himself up and he went to the icebox and gave himself some bread and milk. He was a funny old dog. He liked strawberries.
COOKIES

331. *Mister Dog,* text by Margaret Wise Brown, pictures by Garth Williams. Simon & Schuster, 1952. 6¼ x 7⅞.

self,' which will come out in October."[25] A Little Golden Book titled instead *Mister Dog*, it was one of the last things to appear before her death. Crispin's Crispian he is in full, because he belongs to himself (331); and when he has had his breakfast and taken himself for a walk ("wherever he wanted to go"), played with some other dogs, and some cats and rabbits, he finds a boy—in the book's stray, string-along fashion—who's hungry too; so Crispin's Crispian and the boy's boy go to the butcher ("to get his poor dog a bone," says Crispian, and gives it to himself) and then home to Crispian's two-story dog-house, where there is plenty of room for both of them. They have dinner, tidy up—"Crispin's Crispian was a *conservative* . . . he liked everything in its own place"—and go to bed; and Crispin's Crispian "curled in a warm little heap and went to sleep. And he dreamed his own dreams. That was what the dog who belonged to himself did." And, expectably, "The boy who belonged to himself curled in a warm little heap and went to sleep. And he dreamed his own dreams. That was what the boy who belonged to himself did." In other familiar words, *plus ça change.*

Meanwhile she had ideas about incorporating art—the art of the museums—in picture-books, and so *The House of a Hundred Windows* (1945) appeared, with paintings by Ryder and Audubon, Henri Rousseau, Ernst, Chirico, Tanguy—a mix of modern and near-modern masters—showing through the windows. She was still interested in giving young children 'a form to put their own observations into,'[26] per the Noisy Books, and the result, another collaboration with Leonard Weisgard, was *The Important Book* (1949): "The important thing about the wind is that it blows. You can't see it, but you can feel it on your cheek, and see it bend trees, and blow hats away, and sailboats. BUT THE IMPORTANT THING ABOUT THE WIND IS THAT IT BLOWS."

Little Old Mole
Little Old Mole
Where have you been?
Down a long dark hole
Said the Little Old Mole
That's where I've been.

332. *Where Have You Been?* text by Margaret Wise Brown, pictures by Barbara Cooney. Crowell, 1952. 5¼ x 4¾.

She was writing verse—after "I like bugs./ Black bugs,/Green bugs,/Bad bugs,/Mean bugs,/Any kind of bug . . ." (*The Fish with the Deep Sea Smile*), the group of riddling rhymes that comprise *Where Have You Been?* (332). Best reply: the mouse's "To see if the tick/Comes after the tock/I run down the clock." For these, Barbara Cooney's neat no-nonsense scratchboard illustrations (qq. v., p. 191) are a perfect foil; and teamed also on two Christmas books for Crowell, *Christmas in the Barn* (1952) and *The Little Fir Tree* (1954), Brown and Cooney manage a trim, snug simplicity appropriate to the audience and the occasion.

She was launched on the songs and musical stories; and the best of the musical stories, *The Little Brass Band*, was performed publicly as well as recorded, and later became a book. There were other records derived from books or published poems: *Wait Till the Moon Is Full*, two about Mittens, and a dozen or so more.

The First Story started as a musical story, turned into a story without music ("but maybe there will be music set to it some day"[27]), waited for 'the right artist,' was announced for 1945 with paintings by Rousseau, and finally appeared two years later illustrated by Marc Simont; a new version of Eden (first girl finds first boy), it meant a great deal to her. So did *The Dark Wood of the Golden Birds*, another allegory, in the form of a prose poem, *about* enchantment and *about* devotion; and consequently bloodless.

> Then one day the two children who didn't have a home
> came to the old man's house.
> They didn't have a home and they were all alone
> Because their mother and father were dead.
> The old man was sorry for them;
> and when he heard their happy laughter
> and saw how they ran with the bees from flower to flower
> he loved them.
> And he took them to live with him
> and gave them a home.

Once, explaining what she wanted in her work, Brown recalled a story she'd heard about a little boy who used to walk around murmuring to himself, "Miss Nancy Owl walked down the street with her eyes full of tears." Enough said then, it suffices now. The mouse still sits on the window sill.

JEAN CHARLOT

Paul Sachs, the Fogg Museum's great connoisseur of modern (and old) prints, wrote of Jean Charlot in 1954 as "the leader of color lithography in the Western World."[1] In *Current Biography 1945*, as in the press, he was "master muralist" Charlot. He is easily the most prominent artist to have come into the picturebook field not for an odd book, a command performance, but to *work*; and that said, the explanation is close at hand, for he was doing picturebooks, in fact and in name, before he was doing books for children, and work imbued with an understanding of childhood before he was doing children's books. A 1933 volume entitled *Picture Book* has original color lithographs by Charlot and "inscriptions"—interpretive captions, in French and English—by Paul Claudel. "Heralded by his sad begetter, triumphant enters Mr. Goodface," reads one, apropos of a mother and child. Close in spirit is the 1934 "Mother and Child" that Sachs particularly admired—the mother a bulwark, indrawn, immutable, the child, head thrust forward, feet planted wide, staring out; in "First Steps," the mother supports and guides the child with the rebozo she once carried him in.

Earlier, Charlot illustrated for Claudel *The Book of Christopher Columbus*, a "lyrical drama" or free-form pageant, patently unstageable (a dove on the screen, live doves on stage), that Charlot, in 'decorating,' dramatizes. Nereids and sea gods enter on cue, followed by St. Brandan singing matins in his floating cathedral, a Plateresque fantasy atop a sea monster; fourteen Spanish wag-mouths are fourteen small caricature heads, discreetly numbered (Aztec dialogues, in turn, pit God-head against God-head); and raised on the palm of a great recumbent nude, America, is Columbus holding his standard—opposite a towering two-headed Indian effigy, a snake coiled round its base with jaws open to admit a file of fleeing Aztec warriors. Put into words, it is dizzying—and incomplete, the merest suggestion. But Charlot's visualization, whatever the text, is explicitly and profoundly visual. Organically visual, much as Mexican art is, ancient to modern, in contradistinction to European.

"My rattles and hornbooks were the idols and Mexican manuscripts from my uncle Eugène Goupil's collection,"[2] he has written of his childhood in Paris. Grandfather Louis Goupil, Mexican-born—"a *charro* of note, a fine rider and able *coleador*"[3]—lived in an apartment crammed with mementos, among them "an army of wax figures, rehearsing the same simple plots that delighted me as a child and later recurred in my paintings: *tlachiqueros* sucking the sap out of magueys, *petate* weavers, trotting burden-bearers, and . . . females kneading dough, patting tortillas, fanning coal fires."[4] Grandfather's neighbor and friend, archaeologist Desiré Charnay, "would re-enact for me his jungle adventures,"[5] and on Charlot's first communion presented him with a coyote clay whistle—just such a whistle as Charnay had found, buried with a clay dog on wheels (the first evidence of the wheel in a generally wheelless civilization), next to a child mummy on the side of Popocatepetl.

The Mexico that Charlot found in turn was just beginning, in 1921, to resurrect its Indian culture and to value the popular arts still practiced. Social revolution was the spur, artistic revolution—the School of Paris—the seal: what the modernists were searching for existed in pre-Hispanic Mexico, said Rivera on his return from a decade in Europe. But there was to be no antiquarianism and no recourse to the picturesque; the new art was to be an art of and for the people. In what came to be known quickly as the Mexican mural renaissance, the Syndicate of Technical Workers, Painters and Sculptors—Rivera, Orozco, Siqueiros, Charlot, Mérida and others—painted bold, blunt frescoes on the walls of the Prepatoria (only to have them defaced by some offended people). "Off the scaffold those same painters . . . explored the marketplaces, the villages and churches, and all the other national art museums," Anita Brenner relates.[6] And when, with a change of government, support was withdrawn and the syndicate disbanded, there remained, in her words, "a living style, and a positive creed."[7]

Charlot, the scholar and critic of the group—rediscoverer of the printmaker-provocateur Posada, reviver of colonial woodcutting—became art director of the new *Mexican Folkways* (1925–26) and, from there, staff artist with the Carnegie Archaeological Expedition at Chichén Itzá, Yucatan (1926–29). Engaged to make copies of the bas-reliefs, he also helped Ann Axtell Morris copy and reconstruct crumbled frescoes, and contributed analysis as well as illustrations to the expedition's published report (and decorations to Mrs. Morris's juvenile, *Digging in Yucatan*, which describes their work together). From that three years' involvement with Maya art came impressions that, along with his affinity for Aztec forms, for the Indian aesthetic in all its permutations, were to shape his work and keep it Mexican long after his move to the United States in 1929.

The Maya profile—"with hanging lower lip, beak nose and receding forehead"[8]—is easy to spot (334–337); but it is no simple, easily sortable thing, this Mexican heritage. Introducing an appraisal of the Museum of Modern Art exhibition "Twenty Years of Mexican Art" (in *Art-Making from Mexico to China*, a collection of his acute critiques), Charlot confronts a detail from a Rivera lithograph with a detail from a pre-Hispanic Aztec codex (333). Elsewhere he writes of Carlos Mé-

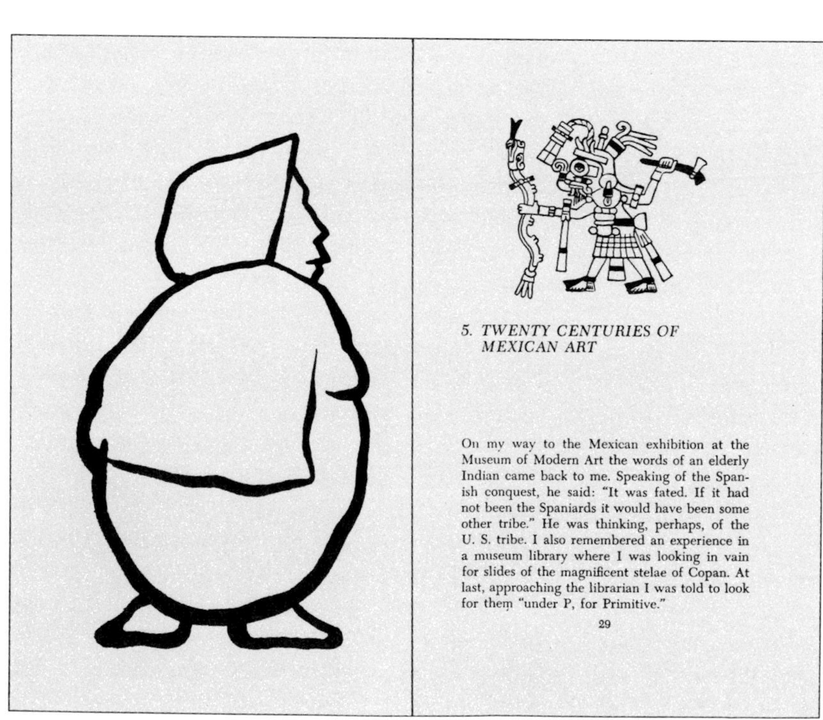

5. *TWENTY CENTURIES OF MEXICAN ART*

On my way to the Mexican exhibition at the Museum of Modern Art the words of an elderly Indian came back to me. Speaking of the Spanish conquest, he said: "It was fated. If it had not been the Spaniards it would have been some other tribe." He was thinking, perhaps, of the U. S. tribe. I also remembered an experience in a museum library where I was looking in vain for slides of the magnificent stelae of Copan. At last, approaching the librarian I was told to look for them "under P, for Primitive."

29

333. *Art-Making from Mexico to China*, by Jean Charlot. Sheed & Ward, 1950. 4³⁄₈ x 6³⁄₄.

334

334, 335. *The Sun, the Moon and a Rabbit,* by Amelia Martinez del Rio, illus. by Jean Charlot. Sheed & Ward, 1935. 9¾ x 7.

335

rida's paintings, c. 1919: "They put the heraldic colors and unbroken outlines found in codices to new creative uses. Then," he continues, "came Rivera, who showed great understanding in his 1923 kneeling figures, often women seen from the back, where legs and arms press close to the ovaloid of the torso, with an economy of shape that suggests a carving out of a glacier-smoothed matrix."[9] Or Charlot's description of Aztec sculpture folded into itself, "self-contained and self-sufficient,"[10] of the Aztec himself hugging the earth "throughout life and in death."[11]

Then, one might say, came Charlot and the two modes, open and linear, enclosed and sculptural, that distinguish his book work for children—admixtures both, and articulated in book terms.

The Sun, the Moon and a Rabbit is a collection of short, simply told stories—Toltec, Aztec and Spanish legends—for each of which Charlot drew a picture coequal to the story, its complement, not, any more than Artzybasheff's (248), an illustration. In an even, exact line he incises images that, sometimes on color, sometimes in color, seem to take on life in the very movement of the pen. They fill the page, in actuality or in effect, monumental in scale, terse and impassioned: pen-and-paper murals, as it were, for marriage with the type-page and for close steady viewing (334, 335).

There is nothing cursory in Charlot's simplifications—the four diggers are as identical, and different, as four gulls at the shore—and never a drawing, hardly a figure, without humor: an inherent humor, devoid of associations. The book is alive, too, with color, unabashed Mexican color: brilliant turquoise and emerald and magenta; some vivid red, some peach, some topaz; strong positive black and gray. But not more than two, black and one other, and usually one—one and white, as vibrant and distinct as any.

Tito's Hats is uniquely, tellingly two-colored—straw-hat colored and reddish brown, the color of the earth (used for the type and throughout). Tito needs a new hat, that's the point, and his father takes him to the market to buy one. Some are too big, some too small; he loses his father (336) and finds a hat "just the smallest bit too small" (337). But a haircut, Tito's first, makes the difference; and, well pleased, he goes shopping with his father for presents and then home, to show off his hat and, at bedtime, put it over his toes—where "as he went to sleep he could feel it . . . through the covers."

It's a middling sort of story, pleasantly real but somewhat flat (by the actor Mel Ferrer as a very young man). The pictures, though, couldn't be better—not for Charlot or for a young comfortable slice-of-life. As strong as the design is, it doesn't dominate the drawing, and as strong as the drawing is, it attends closely to the business of the story. The design—which includes the color scheme—assures that we see the hats as emblematic, the drawing gives us the persons; and the stocky earnestness that says small boy projects Tito above and beyond the pronounced features of the adults. We see everything from his point of view.

With *The Boy Who Could Do Anything* (1942) began the books of Mexican folk tales written by Anita Brenner, illustrated by Charlot and published—one of the firm's happy events—by Scott. Anita Brenner was a native of Mexico, a specialist in things Mexican and, whether writing socio-cultural history (the heady *Idols Behind Altars*, which we've quoted) or a tourist guide, a natural storyteller. Even the tales she retells of "things that happened long ago" have a modern ring—good, unoffending Jose (in "The Princess and Jose") is arrested because "we need prisoners to build the roads," Satan (in "The Devil and the Railroad") turns up in the big shiny car and the diamond stickpin of a banker; and, ironic, unfooled, they speak in the voice of the people, a voice usually blunted in books of folklore for children.

Despite its many line drawings (some originally in color, others edged with color), *The Boy Who Could Do Anything* is a collection of stories foremost; the books that ensued were single stories, however, integrally illustrated, and we will be looking at two of them. But first there came, out of Charlot's new association with Scott, and Scott's old association with Margaret Wise Brown, *A Child's Good Night Book.*

A Child's Good Night Book as it originally was (338). Overleaf, "All the little birds stop singing and flying and eating. And they tuck their heads under their wings and go to sleep. Sleepy birds." "The little fish in the darkened sea sleep with their eyes wide open. Sleepy fish." And so to sheep, to monkeys and lions and mice ("Sleepy wild things"); to little sailboats tied up at their docks ("Quiet sailboats"), cars, trucks and planes put away ("Quiet engines"); and, resuming, kangaroos and pussy cats and bunnies (339). "The children stop thinking and whistling and talking. They say their prayers, get under their covers and go to sleep. Sleepy children." In another double-spread are child, bunny, fish, bird, sheep cradled in a white cloth held like a hammock by two ministering angels, and overleaf is a simple prayer.

'My sleepy book' children spontaneously call it; and Margaret Wise Brown was mindful of "the sleep-inducing qualities of words and poetry that could be brought very quietly into a children's book," adding that "So many books are read at bedtime."[12] We have already nominated it as the first of the true bedtime stories and it is perhaps the purest: sleepy words, sleepy world; a hymn to sleep.

The pictures are of course lithographs, in manner and in mood—monumental, intimate, intense—like "Mother and Child" and others of that strain; but softer. The big little house, the prowling cat, the birds winging home, the single five-pointed star—all enlargements, distortions—are a child's way of itemizing and possessing his world; and the bunnies are enclosed by the page much as a child puts small things in a basket or box to protect them. In the first instance the items can be read serially and comprise, together, a world that he holds in his hands; in the second a knot of sleepy bunnies is held in a single fixed gaze.

Then, all at once, just as they left a store, a crowd of men came toward them. When they had passed Tito could not see his father. All the faces around him were strange, and he could not see his father anywhere.

336

336, 337. *Tito's Hats,* text by Melchor G. Ferrer, pictures by Jean Charlot. Garden City (Doubleday), 1940. 9 x 9.

337

As he stood holding it and looking at it, his father came walking out of the crowd.
Tito showed him the hat. The old man smiled. But they all saw that the hat was just the smallest bit too small.
Without saying a word Tito's father took him by the hand and led him off through the crowd.

The smallness, the closeness, the encompassability are, it seems to me, critical, both in an optical and psychological sense. The book is by nature small, small and concentrated, for very young children; or put as the jacket flap did, "This is a little book—and purposely so—for it is just the right size to take to bed." But there was library buyer resistance to the size—shelving was fixed and, in the Forties, librarians were inflexible—with the result that *A Child's Good Night Book* was redone in 1950 in a standard large vertical format. The compositions are similar in the main (there are two added items) but so large, and so severed by a strong dark outline, that one needs to hold them at a distance to see them whole. There are other, more subtle losses—of the opening, positioning double-spread, the fineness of drawing and coloring; and the change of type-face, to the emphatic Bodoni appropriate, by contrast, for *Two Little Trains*, is a loss too. Generally, it is beside the point to wish that one or another book might be brought back; there are good (i.e. valid) as well as bad reasons for their demise, and no assurance of belated or renewed success. But *A Child's Good Night Book* has lived on, handicapped as it is, and if the time were to come that a faithful copy of the original version could be made (photographically, of necessity, in the absence of the original plates), it would be a *mitzvah*—a good work and a blessing.

Margaret Wise Brown, who talked much about her books, said little about those done by Charlot; the credit, she felt, was largely his.

Two Little Trains is a ballad, an American ballad, MWB brand, of "a stream-lined train" and "a little old train"—two little trains—heading down the track to the West.

> Look down, look down
> That long steel track,
> That long steel track
> To the West.

It has a lovely roll and a familiar right heroic ring, and a pert, checking "Puff, Puff,

338, 339. *A Child's Good Night Book,* text by Margaret Wise Brown, pictures by Jean Charlot. Scott, 1943. 5 3/8 x 6 3/8.

Night is coming. Everything is going
other side of the world. Lights turn
to sleep. The sun goes over to the
on in all the houses. It is dark.

338

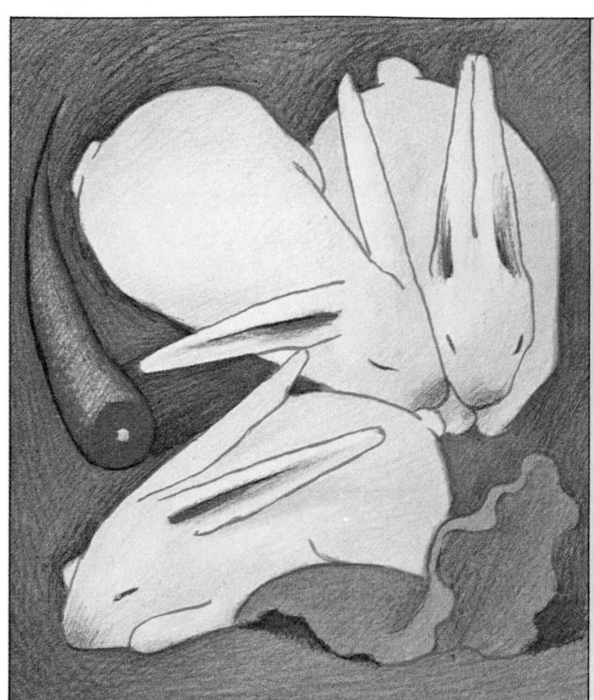

The bunnies close their bright red eyes.

Sleepy bunnies.

339

Puff" (the streamliner) and "Chug, Chug, Chug" (the old-timer); and Charlot, adding children, drawing a child's toy trains in a child's wiry line, their trains with them aloft —free-riders, little giants, not passengers— has turned it into a triumphant adventure (342–345). This can't be overstressed: the two little trains, taken plain, wend their rhythmic, descriptive way across the country and one could sing it against a film backdrop, something on the order of Pare Lorentz's *The River.* Charlot makes a child's story of the saga, a child's fantasy, and fills it with visual incident.

"What I love most," Maurice Sendak has written, "is the humor with which Charlot draws his sturdy little children completely undaunted by the severities of the trip. It rains and out come the umbrellas and wrap-around blankets. No fear is written on the children's faces. They sleep in undisturbed innocence under the fat half moon while the trains hurry on. On reaching the edge of the West, the children promptly climb out of their clothes and jump into the ocean that is big and that is blue.

"I relish, too, the bobbing heads of the cattle and geese aboard the two little trains . . . The marvelous black-and-white snow scene, with the cattle ducking their heads down so that only their horns show and the passive geese with snow dripping from their bills, is perhaps my favorite. [342] Yet, really, I have no favorite in the whole book."[13]

We have chosen four spreads, equally divided between color and black-and-white as the book is, to try to do it justice. This is, indeed, another of those occasions when economic necessity became artistic opportunity. Black and white also is the picture of the "deep dark river" filled with an eerie chain of fish devouring one another; the long dark tunnel—"Look through, look through"–ending in a distant archway of light (a picture almost identical with one Duvoisin did, in the early *All Aboard!*, when he too was drawing like a child). The colors, in turn, say color. It is a glory for the little old train to be very pink, for the streamliner to be inky blue (and heraldic? the girl on the one, the boy on the other); for the world at night to be deepest magenta—or deep purple—under the gold-

340

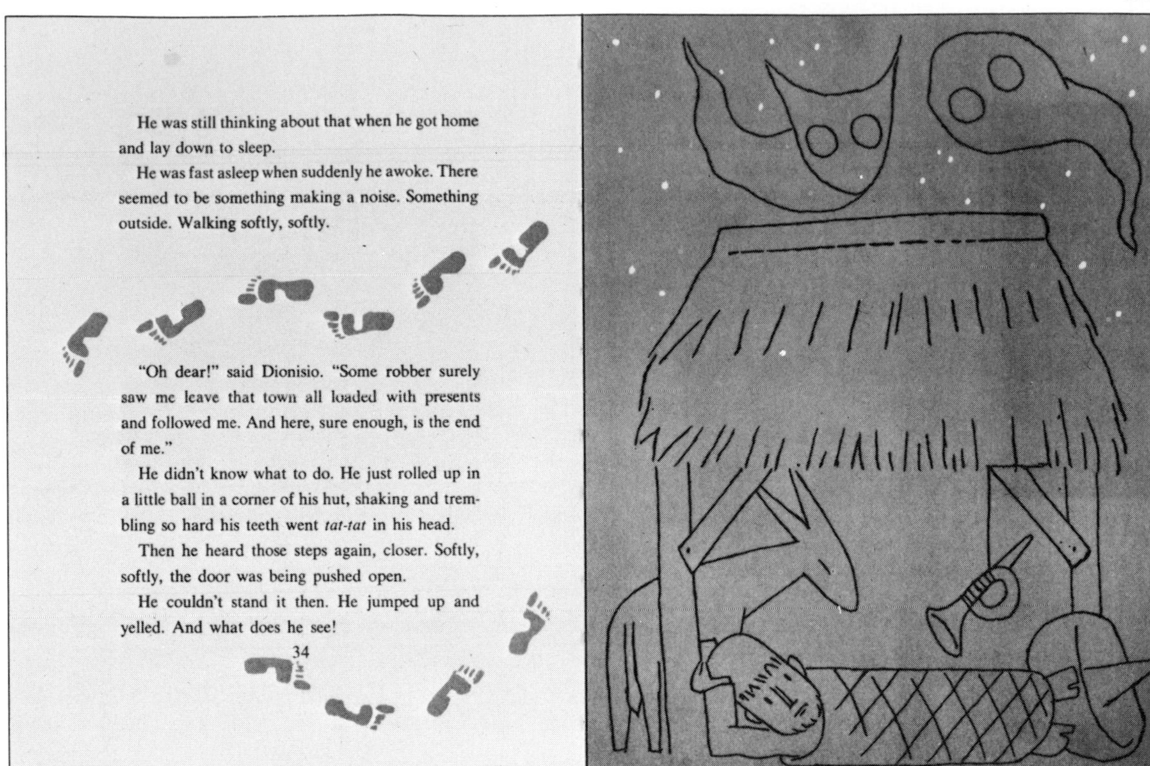

He was still thinking about that when he got home and lay down to sleep.

He was fast asleep when suddenly he awoke. There seemed to be something making a noise. Something outside. Walking softly, softly.

"Oh dear!" said Dionisio. "Some robber surely saw me leave that town all loaded with presents and followed me. And here, sure enough, is the end of me."

He didn't know what to do. He just rolled up in a little ball in a corner of his hut, shaking and trembling so hard his teeth went *tat-tat* in his head.

Then he heard those steps again, closer. Softly, softly, the door was being pushed open.

He couldn't stand it then. He jumped up and yelled. And what does he see!

34

340, 341. *A Hero by Mistake,* by Anita Brenner, illus. by Jean Charlot. Scott, 1953. $6\frac{3}{8}$ x $8\frac{1}{2}$.

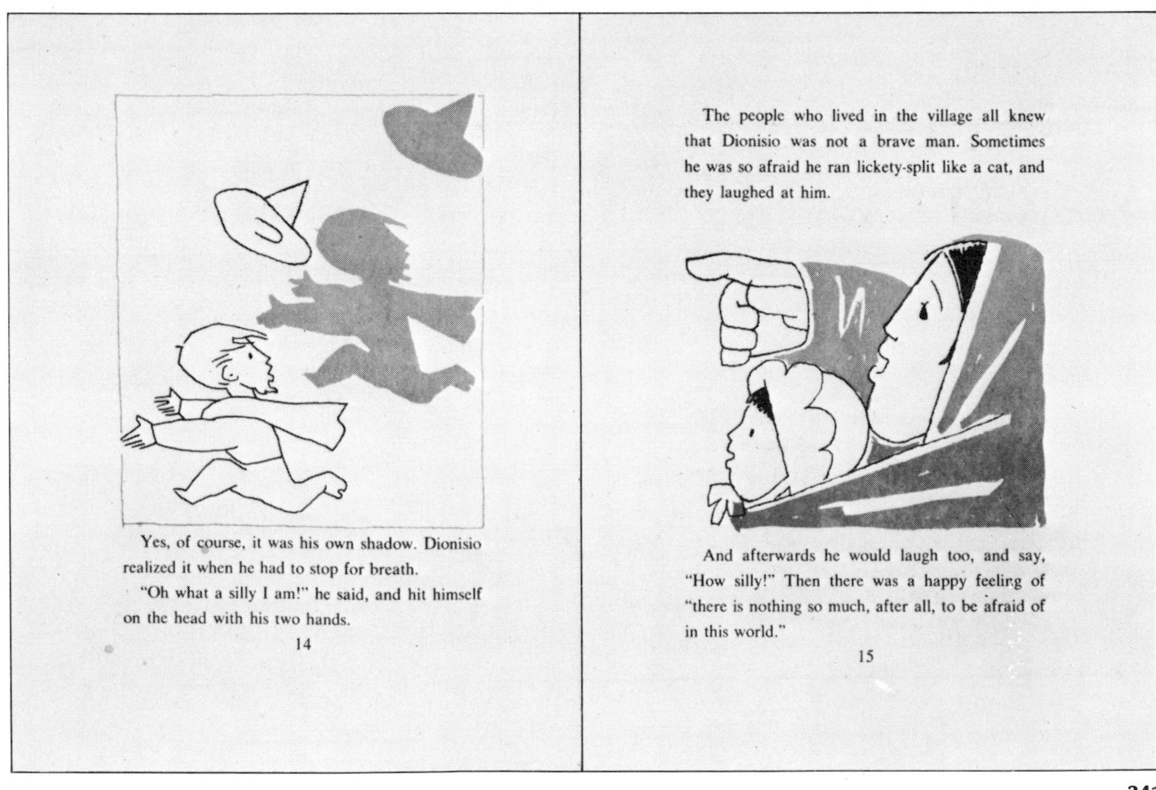

Yes, of course, it was his own shadow. Dionisio realized it when he had to stop for breath.

"Oh what a silly I am!" he said, and hit himself on the head with his two hands.

14

The people who lived in the village all knew that Dionisio was not a brave man. Sometimes he was so afraid he ran lickety-split like a cat, and they laughed at him.

And afterwards he would laugh too, and say, "How silly!" Then there was a happy feeling of "there is nothing so much, after all, to be afraid of in this world."

15

341

flecked moon. The windstorm is a tangle of confetti and streamers, the rain—this we couldn't reproduce—comes down in jagged blue streaks against two now-black trains ("it made them darker, and wet and shiny"), and the children and animals are as clay.

It comes back to visualization, to a story existing consummately in pictures.

A Hero by Mistake is very much a story to start with, "The Story of a Frightened Indian." "Grown men of course are not supposed to be afraid, and especially not Indians. Who ever heard of a frightened Indian?" But Dionisio is afraid of the shape following him—his own shadow; the far-away voice that answers in the mountains (*an echo*); the explosions that greet him when he goes to the market—firecrackers! "Oh," when he learns, "But . . . what a silly I am!" Happy to be safe, he buys a bugle, and when next he hears explosions, blows it. Five masked riders race past him, and after them come the townspeople; the robbers mistook Dionisio for an army bugler, and fled: "What a brave man you are!" How then, the celebration over, the presents loaded, can he say that he is afraid to be out alone at night? So Dionisio makes his way home, past a big glowing-eyed monster (a truck) and two small lights "that looked like eyes, again"—that he resolves to ignore, that turn out to be a wildcat that flees. ("A wildcat afraid of *me*!") Asleep finally, he hears footsteps, imagines robbers, finds his burro; hears more footsteps, goes to punish the burro, strikes down a robber, a famous one with a price on his head—and comes up a hero (and rich).

"And did Don Dionisio get over being afraid? The truth is, he didn't. Only, since people said he was brave, he acted brave, and somehow or other that made him feel so." What Dionisio didn't know was that he really *was* brave. "If you do what you are afraid to do, that is brave. That is the bravest thing there is, as a matter of fact. And so Dionisio, the frightened Indian, really became what people believed him to be: a very, very brave man."

Tonic for young Dionisios, it's a crackling good story that tells—aloud—as well as it reads; and, as a book, one of those deft ensembles of words and pictures that make a book, too, a performance (340, 341). Charlot draws with a vivid, imaginative economy that harmonizes with the telling; he dramatizes the distinctly double-take action across the double-spreads; and, pictures and design, he depicts the separate developments with a fluidity more often found in true picturebooks. But the ultimate artistry is the book's special presence, funny and simple and kind; gracious, really, in a French blue in partnership with white and black, "an item for any age of book collector to treasure."[14]

The Timid Ghost is as good a story: done in by a surfeit, a veritable avalanche of gold, he haunts the highways and byways seeking someone to fulfill his modest dream of a little house by the side of the road, the girl he loves, two cows and six rosebushes. "He was a ghost with a question: 'What would you do if you had a sackful of gold?' " As good a story but not perhaps for children, certainly not for young children; nor is the illustration, although Charlot, illuminating the whole page, the two pages as a unit, in gold and turquoise and the strong deep brown of the text, gives to the book a homely splendor, part manuscript, part mural (346). That it is architectonic, even more so than usual with Charlot, is not at the expense of the individual images, however; and Gumersindo and his bride, particularly, backed by the church bell, are humility and tenderness in silent compact. (Not that we love those fat toy cows the less.)

Charlot illustrated another Anita Brenner story, *Dumb Juan and the Bandits* (Scott, 1957) from *The Boy Who Could Do Anything*, in a more brusque assertive fashion. He did two more books with Margaret Wise Brown, *Fox Eyes* (Pantheon, 1951), an oddity for both, and *A Child's Good Morning* (Scott, 1952), which has the disadvantages of the second *Child's Good Night* without its sound reason for being; and two further picturebooks, Miriam Schlein's *When Will the*

The snow came down
And covered the ground,
And the two little trains going West.

And they got white and furry,
And still in a hurry
They puffed and chugged to the West.

342–345. *Two Little Trains*, text by Margaret Wise Brown, pictures by Jean Charlot. Scott, 1949. 7⅞ x 9½. **342**

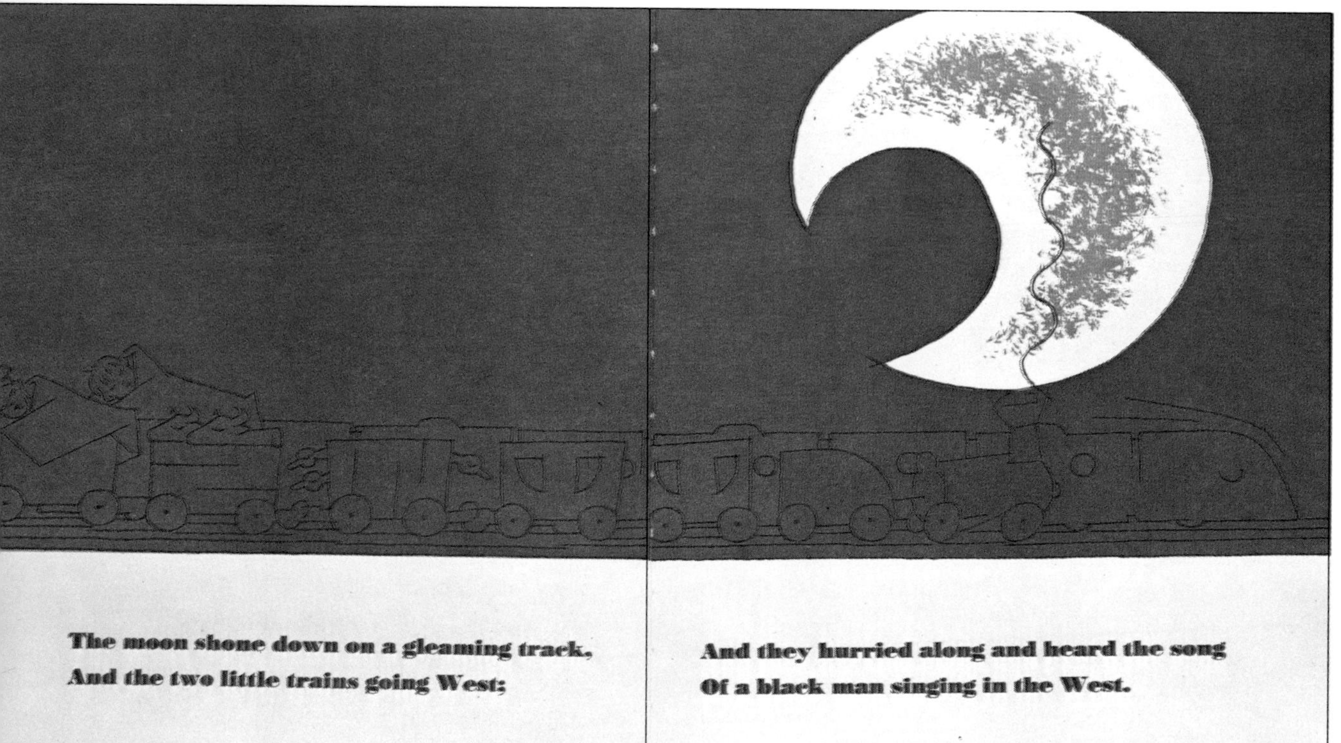

The moon shone down on a gleaming track,
And the two little trains going West;
And they hurried along and heard the song
Of a black man singing in the West.

343

The wind it blew, and the dust it flew
Around the two little trains going West.

But the dust storm drew not a toot or a whoo
Or a whistle from the trains going West.

344

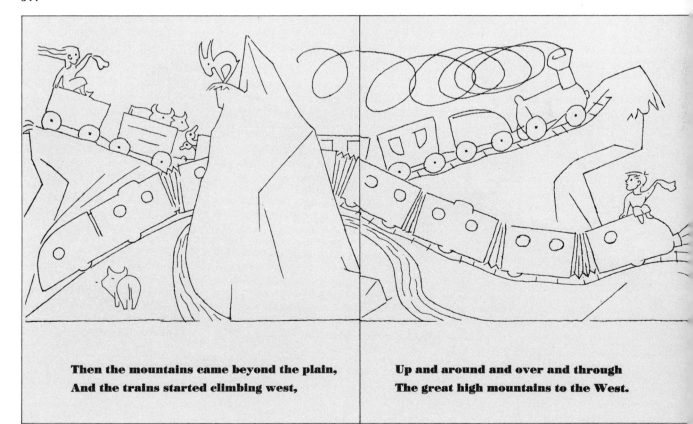

Then the mountains came beyond the plain,
And the trains started climbing west,

Up and around and over and through
The great high mountains to the West.

345

World Be Mine? (Scott, 1953) and *Kittens, Cubs and Babies* (Scott, 1959), with the same massive accentuated forms. (In its extreme stylization, an earlier picturebook, Dorothy Rhoads's *The Story of Chan Yuc* [Doubleday, 1941], anticipates this development.) There was besides, *Seven Stories About a Cat Named Sneakers* (Scott, 1955), a collection of early MWB material.

Chiefly, however, he became in the Fifties the illustrator of choice for Latin American themes (a development anticipated, too, by Monica Shannon's historical adventure of Baja California, *Tawnymore* [Doubleday, 1931]). Together the books constitute a roll call of austere, reverent Latin Americana, better suited than picturebooks to Charlot's heavy manner of the period.

There is one picturebook, however, not for children, that bears directly on his work for the very young. In Charlot's *Dance of Death*, the figure of Death, visiting King and Politician and Invalid (Death: "You look all right to me"), Housewife and Artist ("Your prices will skyrocket"), Businessman and Dentist ("It may hurt a little") and Poet, comes at last to a Child . . . a small child who sees in Death an angel. Death: ". . . a child is not easily fooled." He believed, too, in art's return to storytelling; in the graphic arts as the arts of reproduction; in what he saw in the United States as "a heartening revival in the use of handdrawn prints pulled in unlimited editions. . . . They are illustrations for trade books, more often for children's books."[15] To this revival he contributed work of a complex purity that is, I think, without parallel.

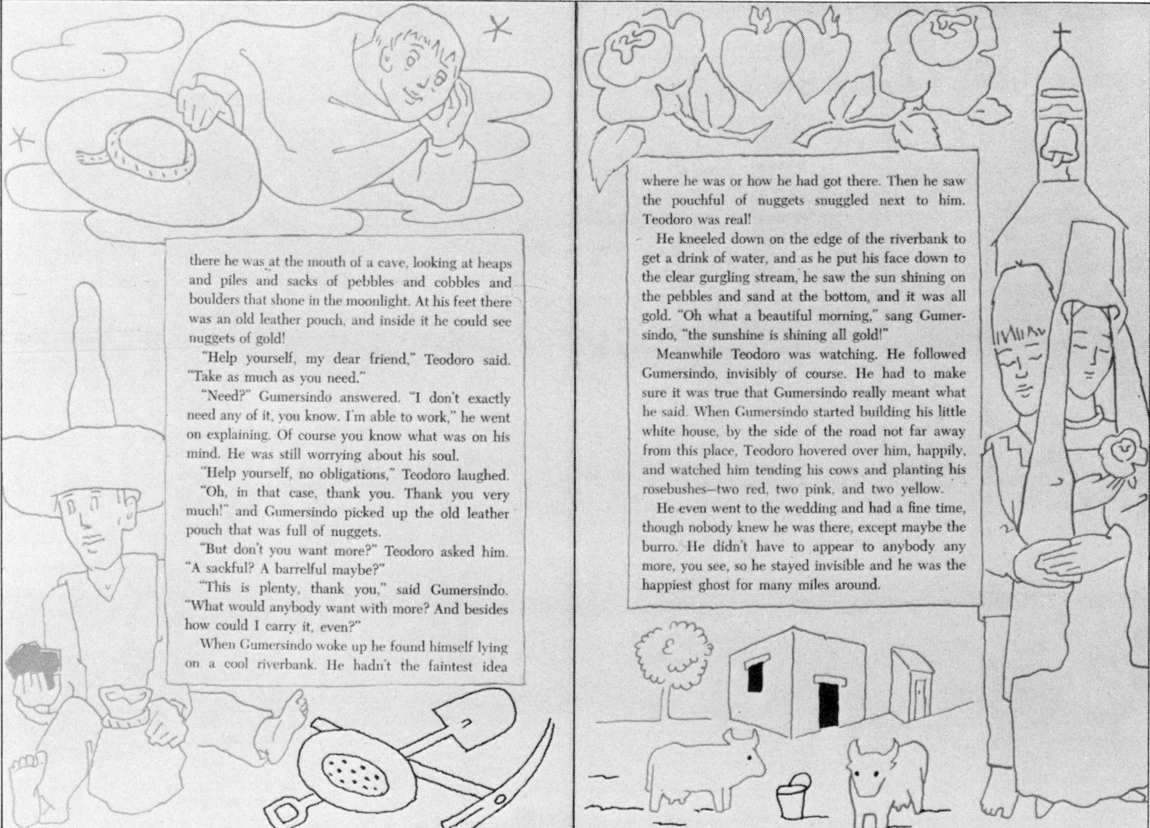

there he was at the mouth of a cave, looking at heaps and piles and sacks of pebbles and cobbles and boulders that shone in the moonlight. At his feet there was an old leather pouch, and inside it he could see nuggets of gold!

"Help yourself, my dear friend," Teodoro said. "Take as much as you need."

"Need?" Gumersindo answered. "I don't exactly need any of it, you know. I'm able to work," he went on explaining. Of course you know what was on his mind. He was still worrying about his soul.

"Help yourself, no obligations," Teodoro laughed.

"Oh, in that case, thank you. Thank you very much!" and Gumersindo picked up the old leather pouch that was full of nuggets.

"But don't you want more?" Teodoro asked him. "A sackful? A barrelful maybe?"

"This is plenty, thank you," said Gumersindo. "What would anybody want with more? And besides how could I carry it, even?"

When Gumersindo woke up he found himself lying on a cool riverbank. He hadn't the faintest idea where he was or how he had got there. Then he saw the pouchful of nuggets snuggled next to him. Teodoro was real!

He kneeled down on the edge of the riverbank to get a drink of water, and as he put his face down to the clear gurgling stream, he saw the sun shining on the pebbles and sand at the bottom, and it was all gold. "Oh what a beautiful morning," sang Gumersindo, "the sunshine is shining all gold!"

Meanwhile Teodoro was watching. He followed Gumersindo, invisibly of course. He had to make sure it was true that Gumersindo really meant what he said. When Gumersindo started building his little white house, by the side of the road not far away from this place, Teodoro hovered over him, happily, and watched him tending his cows and planting his rosebushes—two red, two pink, and two yellow.

He even went to the wedding and had a fine time, though nobody knew he was there, except maybe the burro. He didn't have to appear to anybody any more, you see, so he stayed invisible and he was the happiest ghost for many miles around.

346. *The Timid Ghost,* by Anita Brenner, illus. by Jean Charlot. Scott, 1966. 7¾ x 10⅞.

GOLDEN BOOKS

AND ROJANKOVSKY CONCLUDED

In the fall of 1942, with wartime shortages looming, Simon & Schuster introduced twelve Little Golden Books, light, sturdy board-covered volumes of 42 pages, 14 of them in full color, selling for 25 cents—the first quarter picturebook series on the modern market; an experiment, *PW* called it. "During the first 5 months the firm printed and sold 3 editions of each of the 12 titles, that is 1,500,000 books, or 125,000 of each title," and orders were on hand that, due to the growing shortages, would probably "never be filled." Plainly, 1942's experiment was 1943's "phenomenal success."[1] The next year, with Little Golden Books still rationed, Giant Golden Books were launched (initially at $1.50), "predicated on the idea that a group of juveniles larger in size and giving more value in color reproduction and text would parallel the success"[2] of their predecessors. In 1945 came *Pictures from Mother Goose*, by Rojankovsky, "the first in a series of portfolios containing large-sized full-color pictures for nursery walls";[3] and by 1953 there were also Big Golden Books (initially $1.00), Tiny Golden Books (boxed), Golden Story Books, Golden Play Books, Little Golden Records—and Little Golden Writing Paper besides.

As of 1953, too, nearly 300 million Little Golden Books had been sold; of the first two hundred titles published, over half had sold more than one million each, a dozen over two million, a favored four over three million; the number of outlets had expanded—and broadened—from the original eight hundred book and department stores to 120,000 points of sale, supermarkets leading in volume; the books had been published "with equally startling success" in England, France, Australia, Germany, Norway, Sweden, Mexico, Argentina, Saudi-Arabia — virtually everywhere, the same article notes, except the Soviet Union.[4]

But, says the 1955 catalog (tally: 500 million+), "We are . . . even prouder of the continued qualitative excellence of Golden Books than we are of their stupendous sales record. A glance through the pages that follow should, we feel, highlight once again the reasons why Golden Books continue preeminent in the field of juvenile literature."

The 'field of juvenile literature' did not think so; but more to the point is the proposition that Golden Books were like other books —only a better buy—whereas in fact Little Golden Books, and to a considerable extent the Big ones and the Giants, owed their success also to being different.

Going into the 1940s, Simon & Schuster was the one large general trade house without a children's books department or a regular juvenile list; and designedly—Leon Shimkin, Essandess president, was after something unique, something that the other publishers weren't doing. One of the things they were doing was producing expensive books—from experience, $2.50 books that three-year-olds took into the tub for company.

The Artists and Writers Guild (qq.v. p. 126) specialized in books at all prices; and with Sam Lowe's departure in 1940, Georges Duplaix, in charge of production, and Lucille Ogle were exploring the possibility of a uniform 25-cent series, either for Grosset & Dunlap, a regular customer, or under Western Printing auspices themselves. The multitalented Duplaix, who like Miss Ogle had joined A & W in 1936, first came to American attention three years earlier as the author-illustrator of *Gaston and Josephine* (Oxford, 1933), about a pair of French pigs at home and at sea, a book with the look of *Babar* in the year of *The Three Little Pigs. Gaston and Josephine in America* (Oxford, 1934), in turn, takes in a brush with three badmen out west, a picturemaking stint in Hollywood (Charlie Chaplin directing), and a stay at an Arizona ranch, where the pigs prove themselves all-around cowhands.

Duplaix didn't only have a popular touch, he had a feel for the incongruities that kids find funny—like circus animals revolting and locking their keepers in a cage or a bargeful of animals, cut loose, heading out to sea; and *Topsy Turvey Circus* and *The Merry Shipwreck*, both originally done by A & W for release by Harper (in 1940 and 1942), have had long later lives as Little (and larger) Golden Books. (*Gaston and Josephine*, newly illustrated by Rojankovsky, made a similar reappearance.) *The Big Brown Bear* (p. 282) is his too, and there were other Golden Books, Big and Little, by Duplaix as himself and—for, let us say, tenderer stories—as 'Nicole' (*The Happy Family*) and 'Ariane' (*Lively Little Rabbit*). He was also the translator of the first of the Père Castor animal histories to appear here, while his wife Lily Duplaix (who wrote picturebooks of her own) translated the remainder.

His assets included, moreover, considerable first-hand experience in production (he had made plates and done separations for A & W in his own shop); and as the one responsible for bringing Rojankovsky to America in late 1941, he had the exclusive use of Rojankovsky's services for ten years. Without delay, and with characteristic ingenuity, he contrived—for the newcomer and also for the new Nordstrom regime at Harper's—the perfect product/package/kick-off, *The Tall Book of Mother Goose* (p. 295).

When Duplaix, representing A & W, was working with Albert Leventhal, Simon & Schuster sales manager, on a Disney *Bambi* for Essandess distribution, the discussion of a popular-priced series of 'color books' arose, and Lucille Ogle prepared twelve pilots, to sell for a prospective price of 50 cents. Leventhal and Shimkin were impressed but Western, citing the Story Parade books and others for Grosset, was averse to A & W's doing another, competitive 50-cent line. Suppose the series were to sell for a quarter, Shimkin asked, what could A & W offer? The answer was that for a guaranteed order of 50,000 copies each, instead of the 25,000 originally projected, Essandess could have the same twelve books at a cost that would permit a 25-cent selling price. A switch of figures, and Little Golden Books were under way.

Simon & Schuster and Western were joint owners, with A & W doing the editorial work and design until, at the beginning of 1944, a new Graphics Division—soon formalized as the Sandpiper Press—was set up at Essandess with Duplaix at its head and Dorothy Bennett, formerly assistant curator of visual education at the American Museum of Natural History, as general editor. The A & W presence continued, however, and a Golden Book list of credits reads like the report of a present-day conglomerate: Copyright by Simon & Schuster, Inc. and Artists and Writers Guild, Inc. Designed and Produced by The Sandpiper Press and Artists and Writers Guild, Inc. Printed in the U. S. A. by Western Printing and Lithographic Company. Published by Simon & Schuster, Inc.

For a 1942 perspective on the initial Little Golden Library, here is Anne Eaton's *New York Times* review in its entirety:

"Parents and teachers of pre-school children will be grateful for these twelve attractive little books at a price within the reach of even the most limited pocketbook.

"Illustrators of widely different styles have given individual flavor to the volumes. Bob Smith in 'Baby's Book,' provides large, brightly colored pictures of toys and household objects; the soap for Tommy's bath, the orange for his breakfast, his shoes and blocks and bed, and on the last page we find Baby Tommy himself. The pictures drawn by Masha for 'The Three Little Kittens Who Lost Their Mittens' are as gay and mischievous as any ever made for that popular favorite; Rudolf's illustrations for 'The History of the Little Red Hen', who had to do all the work, have caught the zest and humor of the tale. The pictures by Miss Elliott for the selection of Mother Goose rhymes made by Phyllis Foster have a quaint and charming old-world flavor. 'The Alphabet from A to Z' (Apple to Zebra) has rhymes and animated drawings in color of familiar objects. Leah Cates has made very simple arrangements of twenty-three 'Nursery Songs' and in 'The Animals of Farmer Jones' large colored pictures by Rudolf Freund show the hungry animals (one to a page) waiting for the farmer to feed them. 'Bedtime Stories,' with pictures by Tenggren, contains Chicken Little, The Three Bears, The Three Little Pigs, Red Riding Hood and The Gingerbread Man.

"The editing and illustration of this series is uneven. The pictures in 'Prayers for Children' are over-sweet. Winifred Hoskins has illustrated 'The Golden Book of Fairy Tales' with more vigor than imagination and the books themselves are too lightly put together to be more than ephemeral. Nevertheless, the Little Golden Library will provide a pleasant book experience for the young child who later on, if his library grows as it should, will possess Mother Goose, the folktales and other classics of childhood in more durable form, to last him through his childish years."[5]

Miss Eaton was librarian of the Lincoln School from its founding in 1917 as a progressive experiment until her retirement in 1946, and from 1930 to 1946 she reviewed children's books for the *Times* (1935–1946 with Ellen Lewis Buell). She had a traditional belief in the benefits of good literature and art, and with it a conventional distaste for the comics; but *Topsy Turvy Circus,* she ventured in 1940, might well prove "a satisfactory substitute for the 'funnies.' "[6] When Little Golden Books appeared, she was a respected elder still in touch with children, and as against the views of librarians (and others) who saw in the series only crudity and commercialism, hers is a sensible balanced judgment.

Of the first twelve, ten are standard nursery fare—either traditional nursery literature (Mother Goose, simple folk and fairy tales, songs, prayers) or first aids to learning (*The Alphabet, My First Book, Counting Rhymes*): a readymade home library new in two respects, the concentration on preschool children and the abundance of color. The books were meant to be read aloud for the most part (we are speaking now not only of the first group); and Lucille Ogle recalls that as they shrank from 42 pages to 28 to 24 (the early ones were condensed), their popularity increased: the shorter book better suited short attention spans (and, perhaps, parental inclinations). They were also, as each certified, "prepared under the direction of Mary Reed, Ph.D., Assistant Professor of Education, Teachers College," an attempt to ensure that they would be professionally sound. Lucy Sprague Mitchell's services were enlisted, too, for a group of Bank Street Books.

On the commercial side, however, they were color books (the designation is Albert Leventhal's), made possible by the recent progress in full-color printing and Western's position as a leading commercial printer; and they came just as color was changing the aspect of mass-circulation magazines and technicolor was taking over the screen. That children respond to color is a truism; what is truer is that parents, by and large, will select a book with more color over one with less regardless of their respective merits. More color meaning, with increasing frequency, brighter color, in a world made over by modern color chemistry—inks, paints, dyes; courtesy of DuPont and competitors, a bright new world.

Parents had been impressed with the importance of reading to preschoolers, the books were cheap and colorful and, as we'll see, they worked; they appeared, moreover, just when wartime austerity was causing toys to disappear. In the sense in which the books of Crane and Caldecott and the McLoughlins were toy-books, the Little Golden Books are toy-books too—lightly constructed, easily handled playthings, all paper and pictures, as distinct from formal bound volumes. Miss Eaton was mistaken as to their durability, for the cover board is sufficiently heavy and the binding—side-stapled, after Swedish models—sufficiently strong to withstand a great deal of hard use; Little Golden Books may tear, or be torn, but they don't come apart. Otherwise, everything that made for economy, in the 1940s as in the nineteenth century, also made for an easy compatibility with small children—and I would include the flush-cut sides and the absence of a flyleaf (features found, incidentally, in some of the early Scott books). With picturebooks booming as a substitute for toys, here were books—available in quantity, thanks to Western's huge paper allocation—that were like toys to start with.

When all is said, however, two were original stories, and stories with the staying power to become all-time best sellers. In *The Animals of Farmer Jones*, says Miss Eaton, "large colored pictures . . . show the hungry animals . . . waiting for the farmer to feed them," and the jacket (the first group had jackets) promises similarly that "while the hungry animals . . . wait to be fed," children "will be making new farm friends through the delightful illustrations." The illustrations are splendid indeed, clear and vigorous and vivid, expert renderings with individuality (347); and the hold of hungry animals is undeniable. But it is the simple scheme, as Dorothy White sets it forth, that assures the book's success:

"'It is supper time on the farm. The ani-

347. *The Animals of Farmer Jones,* text by Leah Gale, pictures by Rudolf Freund. Simon & Schuster, 1942. 6¼ x 7⅞.

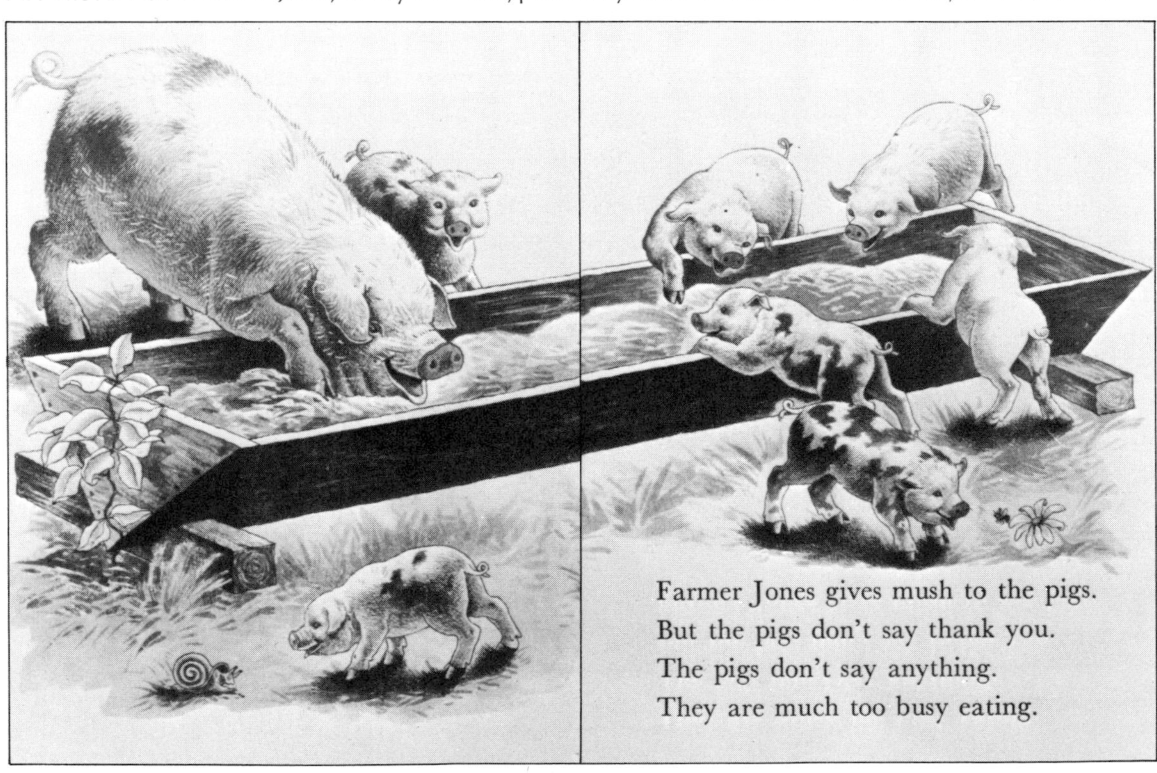

Farmer Jones gives mush to the pigs.
But the pigs don't say thank you.
The pigs don't say anything.
They are much too busy eating.

mals are very hungry. But where is Farmer Jones?' The story follows each animal to his place on the farm and each animal with his own particular grunt or gobble exclaims he is hungry and asks 'Where is Farmer Jones?' Supper time is six o'clock. Farmer Jones looks at his watch and collects the fodder—'oats for the horse, grain for the cows, . . . bones for the dog, milk for the cat and mush for the pigs.' The story then goes back over its tracks as each animal gets his food and grunts in gratitude. That is all—the everyday life on an ordinary American farm [she was writing in New Zealand] shaped into a narrative for a three- and four-year-old—yet it is precisely this form and shaping which is as rare in contemporary stories as it is common in traditional nursery tales."[7]

In 1956 *The Animals of Farmer Jones* was redone by Richard Scarry with less distinction, but the basis of its appeal remains.

The other new work is unmentioned by Miss Eaton and one can safely assume, given the polite evasiveness of juvenile reviewing at the time, that she had no use for it. The book is *The Poky Little Puppy*, the most popular original story Golden Books ever published and the start of a sub-genre of animal hanky-panky that is one of the bulwarks of the list—vide *The Saggy Baggy Elephant*, *The Tawny Scrawny Lion* on the one hand (cartoon Kipling), and on the other *The Lively Little Rabbit, The Shy Little Kitten* (powder-puff Potter).

The Poky Little Puppy has a pattern too, a regular merry-go-round of repetition. Five little puppies dig a hole under a fence, go "through the meadow . . . down the road, over the bridge, across the green grass, and up the hill"; stop to count themselves—"*one, two, three, four*"—and discover that one little puppy isn't there. "Now where in the world is that poky little puppy?" "He wasn't going down the other side. The only thing they could see going down was a fuzzy caterpillar. He wasn't coming up this side. The only thing they could see coming up was a quick green lizard." No, he has his nose to the ground, sniffing—"Rice pudding!" And home go the

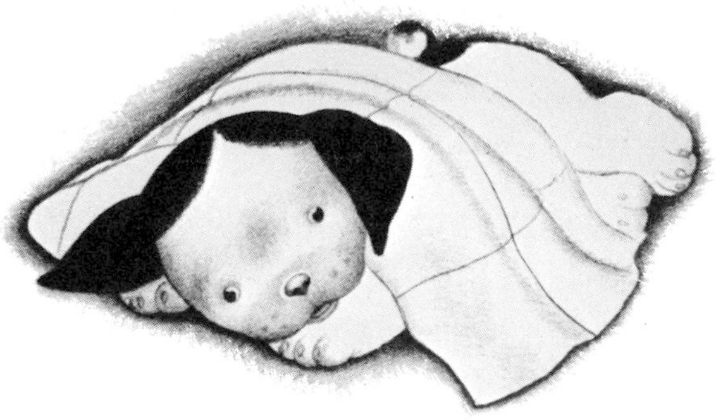

348. *The Poky Little Puppy,* by Janette Sebring Lowrey, pictures by Gustaf Tenggren. Simon & Schuster, 1942. 6¼ x 7⅞.

four little puppies, over the bridge, up the road, etc.; but their mother chides them for digging a hole under the fence and sends them to bed: "No rice pudding tonight!" Comes little poky, after everyone is asleep, and eats up all the rice pudding and crawls into bed (348), "happy as a lark."

The logic of these events, especially of the mother's not giving a thought to the poky little puppy (not so much poky as fancy-free), has always escaped me—to the point of doubting the logic of some children. Howsoever, after digging a second hole and being denied chocolate custard the next night (which the poky little puppy eats up with impunity), the four little puppies, faced with the loss of strawberry shortcake on the third, wait until they think their mother is asleep and . . . pounce on the poky little puppy? No, they fill up the hole, whereupon their mother, who's been watching, rewards them; and when the poky little puppy turns up—"Dear me! What a pity you're so poky! Now the strawberry shortcake is all gone!"

It may seem like pettifoggery to call *The Poky Little Puppy* to account, and it is; but we have looked at books about bunnies and Scotties and little bighorn sheep with perfectly appropriate seriousness: however slight the material, however light the treatment, the book hasn't to be flimsy. We can try to explain its popularity, assign a part to the repetitive pattern (with such good bits as one after another frog or grasshopper going down or coming up), another to the pudding and custard and shortcake lost and found; and give credit, too, to the appeal of small puppies, the pictures, the title, the title and picture on the cover. And as we do we come up against something peculiar to Little Golden Books, point of sale purchase.

If instead of singling out *The Poky Little Puppy* and wondering at its success, we consider which of the Little Golden Books have been more successful still—*The Night Before Christmas, Snow White, Prayers for Children, Three Little Kittens*, just to start with —it becomes obvious that parents (usually mothers) not children make the choice; that they select the familiar and 'suitable'; that they are buying the title, or the cover, not the book. Without recourse to reviews, reputations or examination, it can hardly be otherwise. My guess is that people who buy cunning decals to stick on cribs and toy cabinets find *The Poky Little Puppy* adorable and spoonfeed it to their young (a thesis that has the merit, besides, of preserving respect for children's stricter judgment).

Standard nursery fare sold, and such fare —material in the public domain or, like an ABC, ready at hand—was to be had for little or nothing; it sold on its looks, moreover, so it behooved the publisher to put money into the illustration. For some years what manuscripts were bought were purchased outright, for a small lump sum, the royalty going in its entirety to the illustrator—a reversal, or near-reversal, of prevailing practices. On that basis was talent recruited and held. Some of it came from trade books—Rojankovsky, Garth Williams, Leonard Weisgard; some from scientific or technical illustration—Rudolf Freund, who had been with the American Museum of Natural History, is a notable example. Others were A & W or Golden Book finds—Cornelius De Witt, Gertrude Elliott, Richard Scarry; artists who had attracted little notice—Eloise Wilkin; or were as yet little known—Tibor Gergely. With the exception of the first three and of Freund, later a leader in natural history illustration, they were to be in the main Golden Book artists, a career and a discipline in itself.

349. *The Big Brown Bear,* text by Georges Duplaix, pictures by Gustaf Tenggren. Simon & Schuster, 1947. 6¼ x 7⅞.

The Disney connection accounted for others and variously, incalculably, for what eventuated. A & W was still producing Disney books and it was natural that there be, beginning in 1944, a Walt Disney Little Library within the Little Golden Library. Just as naturally, Disney artists stopped in when they were in New York or otherwise established contact, and three of them—Gustaf Tenggren, Martin Provensen (with his wife Alice) and J. P. Miller—became Golden Book mainstays.

Tenggren, perpetrator of *The Poky Little Puppy,* had illustrated trade books in the Twenties but it was not until he worked for Disney (for one thing, as art director for *Snow White*) that he developed the cute quizzical winsomeness—or impudence—that made his name a byword for popular hokum. His animals have saucer eyes and bulging heads and Silly-Putty bodies, and his rabbits have the chronic Disney buck teeth—all the antic animals are his, and his work may well have inspired them; but his figures are mobile and always on the move, and their faces broadcast their feeling: however unlifelike, it's live-action art. Nor was it always overdrawn. His big brown bear assaulted by bees is a funny sympathetic figure without being a clown (349); and the book, a slip of a story about a bear whose wife warned him to keep away from those bees, is a simple unforced pleasure altogether.

Many things went on at Golden Books at once, and a particularly interesting case—a celebrated case—is that of *Tootle*, the little train who learned to stay on the track (350). A phrase sums it up, a look at the spread tells how Tootle was tricked into submission —convinced, too, that he 'couldn't have any fun' running wild; and David Reisman took the occasion, in *The Lonely Crowd* (1950), for a lengthy explication to the end that the story was "an appropriate one for bringing up children in an other-directed mode of conformity." Comparison is made with Little Red Riding Hood, a more realistic cautionary tale—which "does not present the rewards of virtue in any unambiguous form or show the adult world in any wholly benevolent light"—and we are left with *Tootle* as an object lesson in adult manipulation, by inference typical and supportive of Reisman's general thesis. Reprinted and frequently cited, the discussion has been incorporated into juvenile criticism—more accurately, into the ongoing criticism of juveniles.

There's no arguing about Tootle, he's a patsy. But in the same year there appeared that all-time rule-breaker, *The Taxi That Hurried*, and who is prodding the driver, objecting when he stops for a light, telling him that "We're terribly late and the train won't wait"—but a *mother*. (There were complaints.) A reckless mother of Lucy Sprague Mitchell's devising in a taxi that makes a

350. *Tootle*, text by Gertrude Crampton, pictures by Tibor Gergely. Simon & Schuster, 1946. Spread from subsequent 28-page edition. 6¼ x 7⅞.

He turned to the left, and up came another waving red flag, this time from the middle of the buttercups.

When he went to the right, there was another red flag waving.

There were red flags waving from the buttercups, in the daisies, under the trees, near the bluebirds' nest, and even one behind the rain barrel. And, of course, Tootle had to stop for each one, for a locomotive must always Stop for a Red Flag Waving.

"Red flags," muttered Tootle. "This meadow is full of red flags.

"Oh, how can I have any fun? Whenever I start, I have to stop. Why did I think this meadow was such a fine place? Why don't I ever see a green flag?"

Just as the tears were ready to slide out of his boiler, Tootle happened to look back over his coal car. On the tracks stood Bill, and in his hand was a big green flag. "Oh!" said Tootle.

He puffed up to Bill and stopped.

"This is the place for me," said Tootle. "There is nothing but red flags for locomotives that get off their tracks."

"Hurray!" shouted the people of lower Trainswitch, and jumped up from their hiding places. "Hurray for Tootle the Flyer!"

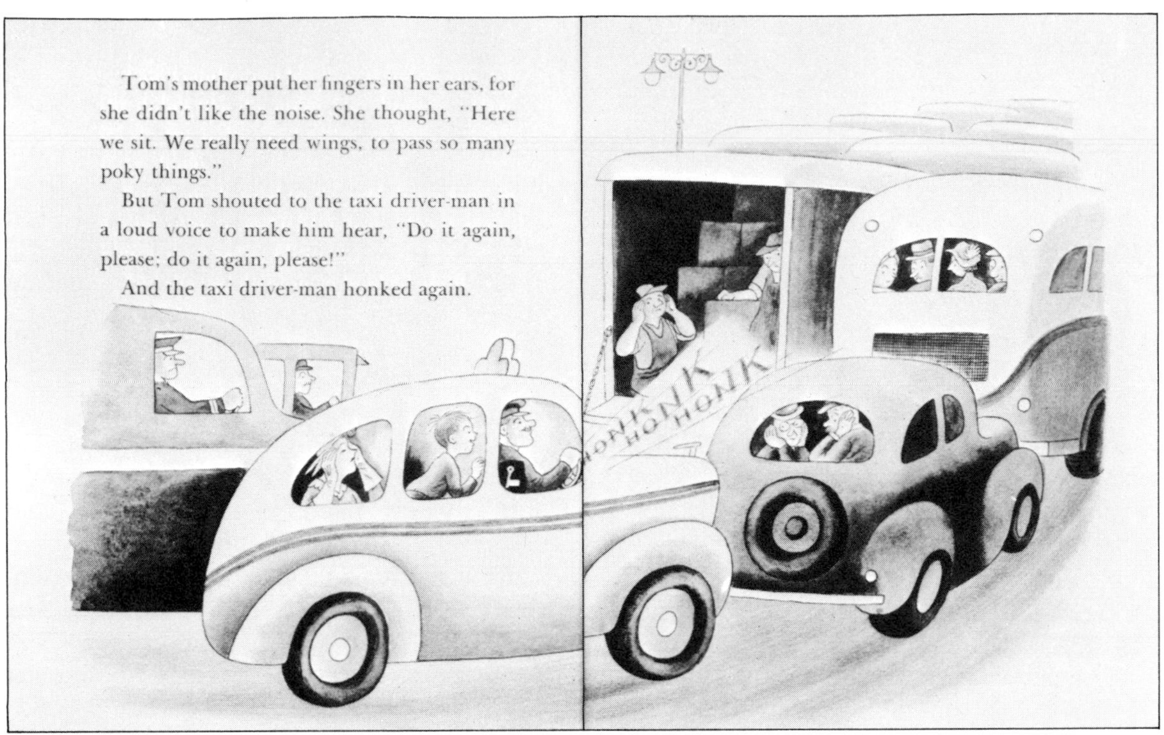

Tom's mother put her fingers in her ears, for she didn't like the noise. She thought, "Here we sit. We really need wings, to pass so many poky things."
But Tom shouted to the taxi driver-man in a loud voice to make him hear, "Do it again, please; do it again, please!"
And the taxi driver-man honked again.
HONK
HONK
HONK

351. *The Taxi That Hurried*, text by Lucy Sprague Mitchell, Irma Simonton Black & Jessie Stanton, pictures by Tibor Gergely. Simon & Schuster, 1946. 6¼ x 7⅞.

352. *Tommy's Wonderful Rides*, text by Helen Palmer, pictures by J. P. Miller. Simon & Schuster, 1948. 6¼ x 7⅞.

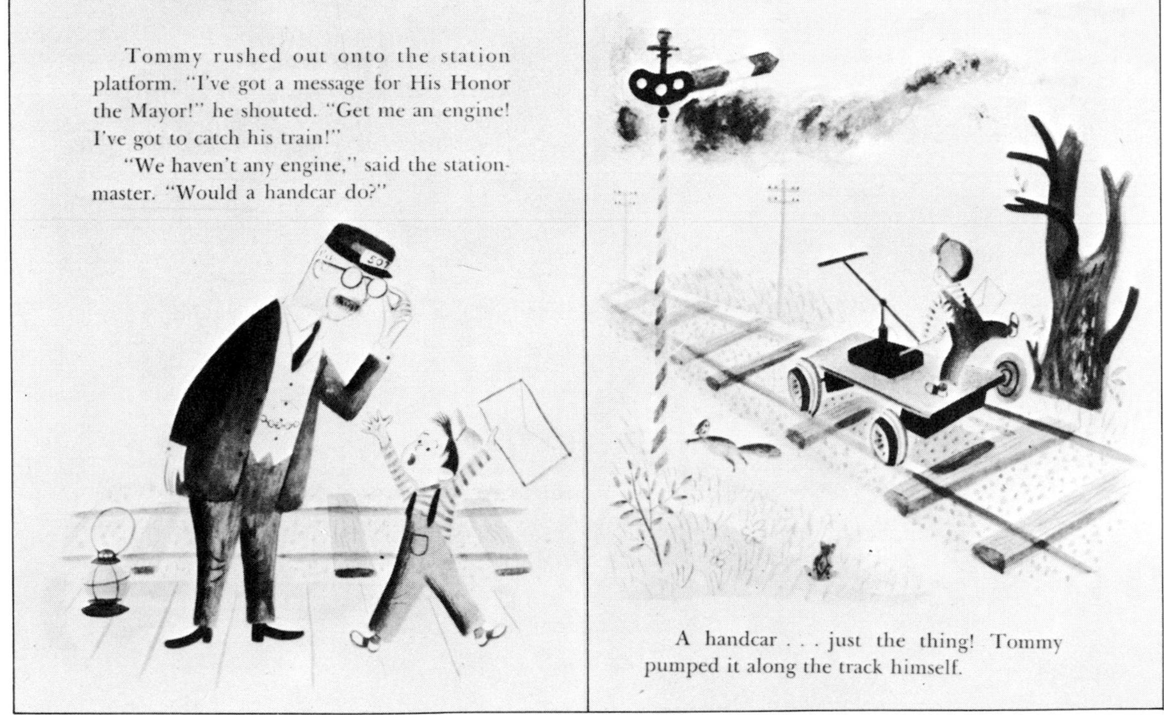

Tommy rushed out onto the station platform. "I've got a message for His Honor the Mayor!" he shouted. "Get me an engine! I've got to catch his train!"
"We haven't any engine," said the station-master. "Would a handcar do?"
A handcar . . . just the thing! Tommy pumped it along the track himself.

nuisance of itself (351) and winds up a hero: they catch the train.

That good bad taxi was followed by *Tommy's Wonderful Rides*—on a bus, a milk truck, a moving van, by taxi and hook-and-ladder and ambulance (a case of mistaken injury), on a police motorcycle and a railroad handcar (352) and lastly by aerial basket, all in order to deliver a message to the mayor. Nobody puts the brakes on this boy either, and nothing stops him: he's promised to deliver the message, and *"I always do what I promise to!"* (If that line doesn't sound familiar, it will; the author, Helen Palmer, is Mrs. Dr. Seuss.)

This might be the time, too, for *I Can Fly*. Another of the Bank Street Books—there were eight between 1946 and 1951—*I Can Fly* is a little girl's make-believe, the sort of thing Louise Woodcock did in *This Is the Way the Animals Walk* and everyone did imitating sounds but less literal, less set, more in a spirit of free-ranging spontaneous play. She can squirm like a worm, grab like a crab (353), and "Crunch crunch crunch/I'm a goat out to lunch." "Haw haw haw" she's a donkey in the straw, "Howl howl howl," an old screech owl; and—pure Ruth Krauss (p. 416 *et seq.*)—Gubble gubble gubble/I'm a mubble in a pubble." For "I can play/I'm anything that's anything./That's MY way." Blithe and spanking-bright, *I Can Fly* was an Honor Book in the 1951 New York *Herald Tribune* Spring Book Festival, "the first 25¢ juvenile ever to be [so] named," as the publishers proudly announced.

Louise Woodcock wrote a Bank Street Book too, and two other Little Golden Books—all illustrated by Eloise Wilkin—which hew to the here and now; and Eloise Wilkin's snub-nosed round-cheeked children, as spring-fed as Kate Greenaway's and dewier, turn up in scores of others: *We Help Mommy*, *The New Baby*, *My Kitten*, etc., etc.

Successfully established and past the war, Golden Books was looking for new material as well, and in a postion to secure it. As early as 1939, Margaret Wise Brown had done a Disney reader, *The Little Pig's Picnic*, for A & W (and D. C. Heath), but it was as a famous author that she made her Golden Books debut in 1947 with *The Golden Egg Book* (p. 290), followed by a book that was under way earlier, *Margaret Wise Brown's Wonderful Story Book*, and her first Little Golden Book, *The Little Golden Sleepy Book*. In the next few years there were fifteen more Little Golden Books (including *Mister Dog*), some cut to a standard MWB pattern—*The Train to Timbuktoo*—and others, like *The Color Kittens*, tailored to Little Golden Book circumstances. The kittens Brush and Hush have "buckets and buckets and buckets and buckets of color to splash around with," as did LGB artists; and on the way to discovering that green is made by mixing blue and yellow, they have a full-color field day.

Best, however, 'rightest,' were the jolly little workman ballads on which Edith Thacher Hurd collaborated—ballads because, prose or verse, they are celebrations, hero narratives running along on repetition and rhythmic sounds and phrases. Say *The Man in the Manhole* (p. 391) plus *The Little Fireman*, but homelier, livelier; to be formal, less archetypal and more anecdotal. A little house catches on fire, a policeman calls in the alarm, and the *Five Little Firemen* snap to.

" 'Sparks!' shouts the First Little Fireman. He puts on his white helmet, twirls his black mustache, and jumps into the little red Chief's car with its shiny brass bell. Cling, clang!"

With those words, I can feel again my children's excitement and recall our fondness for those little firemen: for the Second, "round as a pumpkin," who drives the hook-and-ladder, "the biggest fire engine of all"; the Third, who "has muscles as big as baseballs, he is that strong" ("He runs up the ladders and carries people down the ladders—that Third Little Fireman"); the Fourth, ready to "squirt lots of water"; and the Fifth, only human—"I sneeze in the smoke."

Then "Clang, clang, whoo, whee" . . . (354), and we're at the house of the Hurricane Jones family where the commotion climaxes in the cook's last-minute escape. "She is too fat to

353. *I Can Fly,* text by Ruth Krauss, pictures by Mary Blair. Simon & Schuster, 1950. 6¼ x 7⅞.

carry and too big to jump into a net and too jolly to stay and burn up in the flames. So they shoot up the life-line for the Hurricane Jones's jolly fat cook to slide down. 'Jewallopers!' says she. 'It was getting warm up there.'"

There would be no excuse for repeating all this good-natured horseplay, whatever my affection for it, were it not so rare in small children's books, where a void exists between burlesque or buffoonery, on the one hand, and drollery on the other. Here is honest, concerned humor—with a special citation for the cook "too fat to carry and too big to jump into a net and too jolly to stay and burn up in the flames."

Seven Little Postmen does as well, because it has a letter with a secret, a surprise, and lippety-lap rhyme that bounces it along from one little postman to the next—"Stamp stamp, clickety click,/The machinery ran with a quick sharp tick./The letter with the secret is stamped at last/And the round black circle tells that it passed/Through the cancelling machine/Whizz whizz fast!" The pictures are Tibor Gergely's again too, and they have the robust humor that the Hungarian-born Gergely (gâr-gā′) shares with H. A. Rey, and a punch and a zip the match of the most rambunctious text.

Quieter and gentler, but not torpid, is *Two Little Gardeners*, an eager, intimate processional from planting to harvest which has some of the loveliest long-looking pictures of any of the Little Golden Books (355). Comes spring . . . "And the worm turned in the ground. The groundhog cast his shadow, and the two little gardeners"—a boy and a girl—"came out of their house to plant their garden." There are weeds and drought to contend with, and unwelcome animals and bugs; but there are animal friends and allies too, and together they populate the pictures: the setting is all outdoors. The floppy-eared dog is

354

354. *Five Little Firemen,* text by Margaret Wise Brown & Edith Thacher Hurd, pictures by Tibor Gergely. Simon & Schuster, 1949. 6¼ x 7⅞. **355.** *Two Little Gardeners,* text by Margaret Wise Brown & Edith Thacher Hurd, pictures by Gertrude Elliott. Simon & Schuster, 1951. 6¼ x 7⅞.

355

always there too, taking shelter under the gardeners' umbrella and, the next morning, peering at the "little green sprouts sprouting out of the ground." He has his share of the harvest, we assume, seeing him stretched out under the table where "they ate and they ate and they ate"; and when the remaining food is stored away—the peas, beans and beets canned, the onions "dried and hung in big bunches," the potatoes and pumpkins put into bins—and the little gardeners sing a little song, he gives what looks to be a little howl.

So varied are the Little Golden Books that it is easier to define them by what they are not than by what they are; but in any respect *Two Little Gardeners* is atypical. It packs no wallop, it is not an enlargement or simplification of experience: it is not something anyone can immediately understand, to use a general criterion. It yields itself up to careful reading—unto "round little radish seeds, thin black lettuce seeds, round wrinkled pea seeds" ("And tiny parsley seeds and tomato plants and potato eyes"). It is inflected and gradual—no strong contrasts, no suddenness. And it has pictures to dwell on.

As diverse as the illustrators were in style and technique, they tend to adopt a common approach, emphasizing, even exaggerating, the crucial action or emotion, minimizing or eliminating incidental detail, flattening the picture space—all in the service of compression, of a compact, clear-cut, forceful statement. In *Mister Dog*, Garth Williams enlarges Crispin's Crispian until he all but fills the page and seems to fill the room; and his dominance is buttressed by the broad, simplified treatment of his surroundings (331). The pots are pots, the stove a funny old stove, where the raccoon mother's sewing machine is a specimen, a Smithsonian exhibit (329); nor is the bed he left behind, bedclothes awry, a real bed the way Frances's father's is, however lightly penciled in (p. 473). There is not the keenly observant drawing that elsewhere fleshes out the scene, and no attempt to invoke reality.

Broad simplification and suppression of background are evident too in Gergely's illustration for *The Taxi That Hurried* (351) though, when he needs to, he gives us the buildings along the street—as a stage-drop or backstop. And that is another thing: the space is either shallow or, in effect, nonexistent—identified with the picture-plane—and except where space and distance are requisite, enclosed on the sides too, either by the edge of the page pressing in on the image, as in *Mister Dog*, or by the image itself being cut off, as in *The Taxi That Hurried*, or both. Partly it is a matter of conservation of space, or paper, of getting the most out of every inch of the book, and partly, again, of focus.

Furthermore, heads are overlarge, even if not for the purpose of caricature—the perfectly valid purpose of caricature, the exaggeration of distinctive features; the essence of an individual not, as in 'straight' art, the individual himself. Crispin's Crispian is something of a caricature while the three little animals—or Stuart Little or Frances the badger—are not; and Gergely's beefy truck drivers and pudgy, balding postmen are caricatures too, of types. In a broad sense, this is the cartoon tradition.

On the other hand, we have Mary Blair's little girl (353) and J. P. Miller's little boy (352), also big of head but almost featureless, prototype figures not personages or, in either sense of the word, characters. This is what advertising art was after, a kind of universal recognition/identification devoid of individual associations, and advertising art was, as we'll see, beginning to make itself widely felt in picturebooks. But, apropos of picturebooks, it is well to remember that children themselves draw heads large—or, more precisely, faces—because in a child's consciousness faces loom large; and for the same reason they find big-headed people perfectly natural. (By adult standards, children's heads are large for their bodies, which may or may not have bearing.)

Common to all the foregoing is the intent—to put across an idea or a piece of information rather than to call forth real people, a particular moment, the world of these people at any moment. It is the difference, too, be-

356. *Poor Cock Robin.* McLoughlin Bros., c. 1872–1875.

tween the pictorial milieu of the McLoughlin books (356), akin to that of *Mister Dog*, and the milieu of Crane, Caldecott and Greenaway; and generally what is meant, justly or not, by the distinction between illustration-as-communication and illustration-as-art.

The McLoughlin series that *Cock Robin* came in, which sold for 25 cents (worth 50 per cent more in 1880 than in 1942), comprised such titles as *Three Bears, Visit of St. Nicholas, Humpty Dumpty, Three Little Kittens; Baby, Home Games for Boys* (and *Girls*), *My Mother, Wild Animals, Four-Footed Friends*—little or nothing (except 'darkie' stories) that was not to be found in some form on the Little Golden Books list. "These Toy Books," prospective purchasers were assured, "are produced at a very large outlay, on paper especially prepared, and are printed in colors, in the very best style, with the determination of having them better than any yet published." The resemblance, I think, is not accidental.

In terms of sales, Little Golden Books peaked in the late Forties and continued strong into the Fifties, and in those years they commanded the kind of serious attention ordinarily reserved for trade books, a recognition of the general interest in them—of the fact that they were being purchased not only in lieu of expensive books or of no books at all, but in addition to other books, for themselves. It is not just that Golden Books flooded the market with cheap books, as was often said; the books had caught the public fancy.

Hardly had Little Golden Books been launched than Giant Golden Books and Big Golden Books followed, a diversification of product that was also the founding of a dynasty. The first were compendiums or large-scale reference works: *Tenggren's Story Book* (Rip van Winkle, Doctor Dolittle, Uncle Remus of sorts) and *Walt Disney's Surprise Package* (surprise: Peter Pan, Alice in Wonderland, Chicken Little); Duplaix's *Animal Stories*, the first of several showcases for Rojankovsky; and, more substantial, *The Golden Dictionary, The Golden Bible, The Golden Encyclopedia.* The Tenggren and Disney books, whatever their demerits (they were roundly scored for violating the original texts), represent an established type of publishing, the favorite-story collection, smartened up with lavish color illustration. The *Dictionary* and the *Encyclopedia*, on the other hand, while hardly inventions, are genuine innovations, a picture-dictionary and a picture-encyclopedia, structurally sound, in a large attractive format for small children.

In either case, however, these are books that are big by nature, books you'd expect to be big. Margaret Wise Brown was preparing a collection of her own for publication, the *Wonderful Story Book*, when it occurred to her that a Big Golden Book might be something else, something original:

". . . I have enjoyed working on the Golden Story Book enormously and am constantly tempted to write new stories for the double page picture format that such a large and colorful book offers. And as spring goes into summer I remember more and more how little there really is that dwells on the actual rooted love of every child brought up on this land for the flowers they know and the birds they hear. . . . That is my idea in several sections of the book—to fill it with very accurate pictures of wild flowers and weeds and bugs that we are all brought up with. . . ."[8]

The large colorful book born of the obsession—the word is hers—"that there were not enough wild flowers in children's books"[9] was *The Golden Egg Book*, which appeared in 1947 along with another labeled "a new kind of Golden Book," *The Big Brown Bear. The Big Brown Bear*, which we looked at as the Little Golden Book it became in 1950, takes advantage of the large format for large, freely drawn pictures—sketches for frescoes by comparison with the tight, smooth illustration Tenggren did ordinarily—and for a simple, simultaneously running story: it is the epitome of the great big book—vs. the very little book—that small children take pleasure in. (But just because of its simplicity, it adapts successfully to LGB size.)

The Golden Egg Book is the orchid, or better perhaps the Easter bonnet—the sudden splurge of beauty-for-beauty's sake. Esther Averill recalls seeing it in a store window on a drab small-city street as an occasion (357);

357

357, 358. *The Golden Egg Book*, text by Margaret Wise Brown, pictures by Leonard Weisgard. Simon & Schuster, 1947. 9¼ x 13.

and so it was, like her *Daniel Boone* or Duvoisin's *Mother Goose*. Inside, the egg becomes the setting for the story and the wildflowers, different at each opening, border it, making the book a unique combination of big and little (358). What occurs, too, is a little thing enlarged—just as the flowers are a multiplicity of small things.

A bunny wonders what's inside an egg, pushes it, jumps on it, throws nuts at it, even a rock—"But because he was only a little bunny, it was a very little rock and he didn't throw it very hard and the egg didn't break." Sleepy, he falls asleep (just so: "He went to sleep because he was so sleepy") and out comes a little duck and wonders what he is; and pushes him, throws a rock at him, rolls him down a hill. "And the bunny woke up. 'Where is my egg?' said the bunny. 'And where did you come from?' 'Never mind that,' said the duck. 'Here I am.' So the bunny and the duck were friends. And," adds Margaret Wise Brown, "no one was ever lonely again."

It's a weighty conclusion for a sequence as tenuous as the animal encounters in the Ylla books, and rather too adult and abstract a formulation for three-year-olds who are satisfied that 'the bunny and the duck were

Who could tell what he would find?
And how would a little bunny know?
But there was something
inside that egg.
He could hear
something moving.
He shook it.

358

359

360

friends' and more concerned with their efforts to rouse one another. The book is otherwise vulnerable to criticism—the pictures are pretty-pretty; the bunny is a cuddle-bunny, not a rabbit; and the illustration doesn't so much illustrate—without a caption, he'd be guarding instead of shaking that egg—as look decorative, a stricture that, whatever their general accuracy, applies to the flowers too. But even at its least, as a greeting card superimposed on wallpaper, *The Golden Egg Book* has the legitimate appeal of—why not? —sweet greeting cards and pretty wallpaper. Children collect the one, gaze long at the other, and they're happy.

"If more paper and more new presses make their bow during the year," said the 1947 Golden Books catalog too, "a number of other Golden Books of all sizes and shapes" would be published; and 1948 brought *Tiny Animal Stories*, followed in 1949 by *Tiny Nonsense Stories*—twelve to a box ("a tiny permanent bookshelf"), written by Dorothy Kunhardt and illustrated by Garth Williams. They were tiny; tinier even than *Little Fur Family*. The feasibility was in the figuring: a column of Tiny Golden books, uncut, equals one-fourth of a Big Golden Book (359).

The stories are tiny too, but fully formed (361). In descending order, Theodore's grandfather, interceding after a day of can'ts and don'ts, sends Theodore to the store for lollypops, the storekeeper takes proper notice of his gun ("I'm a cowboy," says Theodore) and Granny, at Theodore's urging, unbends and has a lollypop too; "There's something about a lollypop," says old Mr. Pussycat, "that's very pleasant." Alfred Squirrel, in turn, sees "something exactly the shape of Santa Claus standing in the doorway" late at night, and "a Santa Claus voice" thanks him for the milk and the graham cracker and tells him that he's left "a Santa Claus cap for my special present"; the next morning—"Why Alfred!" says Mrs. Squirrel. "What can that

359–361. *Tiny Nonsense Stories*, text by Dorothy Kunhardt, pictures by Garth Williams. Simon & Schuster, 1949. 2⅛ x 3⅛.

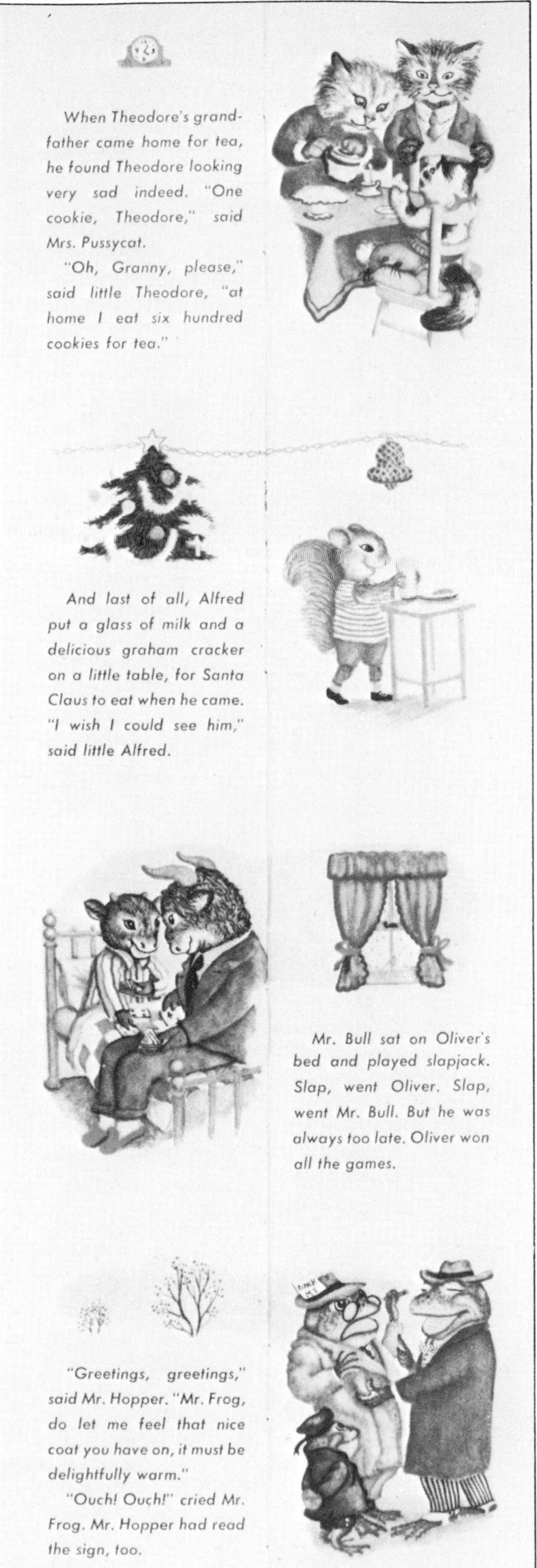

be! Open it quickly so we can see." But Alfred needn't hurry, he already knows: "It's my Santa Claus cap from Santa Claus." ("And" —overleaf—"it was.")

When Theodore's grandfather came home for tea, he found Theodore looking very sad indeed. "One cookie, Theodore," said Mrs. Pussycat.
"Oh, Granny, please," said little Theodore, "at home I eat six hundred cookies for tea."
And last of all, Alfred put a glass of milk and a delicious graham cracker on a little table, for Santa Claus to eat when he came. "I wish I could see him," said little Alfred.
Mr. Bull sat on Oliver's bed and played slapjack. Slap, went Oliver. Slap, went Mr. Bull. But he was always too late. Oliver won all the games.
"Greetings, greetings," said Mr. Hopper. "Mr. Frog, do let me feel that nice coat you have on, it must be delightfully warm."
"Ouch! Ouch!" cried Mr. Frog. Mr. Hopper had read the sign, too.
361

At three or four, nothing is worse than being babied, and better than going to the store alone for lollypops; or better altogether than getting ready for Christmas, having Santa come and, best of all, bring a present that's a surprise to your parents. They are quiet little stories, and yet everything that happens matters immensely; they have plenty of plot, but as much again is unstated.

The Two Snowbulls is more in the nature of a diversion—appropriately, with Oliver sick in bed and the snow just beginning to fall (as you can see, and he soon will). He can't go out to make a snowbull but Mr. Bull will make one for him outside his window. And "There he is" . . . with the snow falling down, down, down, until he's all covered himself. Mrs. Bull gets a broom "for that snowbull to hold," and puts it in his hand but "Quick! Quick! Look out the window! The snowbull is moving. He's sweeping with the broom!" Could it be . . . ? "Is that really Oliver's Daddy?"

April Fool! you can put together from the cover and the discomfiture of Raymond Frog's father. But would you guess that, the joke discovered, he gets on his train and calls back, "Oh, Raymond, pick up your mittens." And when Raymond leans over . . . it's his father's turn for "April Fool!" ("Ha, ha, ha!"), turning the tables on Raymond—and his mother—and joining the whole family in the day's joking.

One and all, they are family stories—with, fittingly, Theodore and Alfred and Oliver and Raymond on the front cover (359) and the elder Pussycats, Squirrels, Bulls and Frogs on the back (360). Family stories for an age at which the family bounds the world and 'nonsense stories' that devolve from the funny things that happen at home. Theodore pleading that ordinarily he eats "six hundred cookies for tea," Oliver regularly beating his father at blackjack, are recognized by children for what they are, childhood perquisites,

362

and appreciated for not being undermined. It is truth humorously turned out, and far from being threatening, reinforcing; and when one considers that the stories are complete in sixteen pages, that there are twelve to a set, the project looms not only as a best-ever buy (288 pages "all in full color" for $1.00) but, for once, as a mountain in the guise of a molehill.

Following *Pat the Bunny*, which followed *Junket Is Nice*, *Now Open the Box* et al (two of which became Little Golden Books themselves), *Tiny Animal Stories* and *Tiny Nonsense Stories* put Dorothy Kunhardt among the creative elect—in a special niche labeled Living Fun.

As themselves, Golden Books became a popular institution, and then like many another they split to become more and less. Leading off the 1956 catalog is *The Iliad and The Odyssey*, adapted by Jane Werner Watson, illustrated by the Provensens, a grandiose book presaged by *The Golden Bible: The Old Testament* (Rojankovsky) and *The New Testament* (the Provensens) but different in being not part of the common stock but Culture; the pictures, we're told, "re-create all the artistry, the power and the beauty of 'the glory that was Greece.'" At the close of the same catalog are listed the new Little Golden Books: six Disneys, two Captain Kangaroos, *Rin Tin Tin and the Lost Indian*, *The Lone Ranger* (and *Annie Oakley and the Six Gun Surprise* and *Gene Autry and Champion*), a Romper Room book; and on the original side, *My Little Golden Book About Travel*, *My LGB About the Sky*, *My LGB About God*, *The Little Golden Paper Dolls*, two photo-stories, two routine stories—a thirteen-to-eight preponderance of TV- or movie-derived material, the remainder cut and dried.

In taking the high road and the low road (not without some solid middle, like the Golden Nature Guides), Golden Books aban-

362,363. *The Tall Book of Mother Goose*, illus. by Feodor Rojankovsky. Harper, 1942. 4⅞ x 11⅞.

doned the common ground which the books had represented, both among themselves and vis-à-vis the general populace; and the list lost its individual character. But the operation was in the process of changing too, from mass-market publishing to the mass publishing of all kinds of books. In 1958 Simon & Schuster sold its half-ownership to Western, and Golden Books became the Golden Press, publisher by the mid-Sixties of illustrated books at all prices for all ages.

The significant picturebook was the Provensens' striking and witty rendering of *The Charge of the Light Brigade* (1964), a book which has a place in the annals of modern book design and illustration but, as art commenting on history, very little meaning for children.

Meanwhile, in one form or another, the original Golden Books go on. From an active backlist of about 250 Little Golden Books (now 39 cents), a balanced assortment of forty to fifty is issued at regular intervals (to make the most of less display space), a rotational scheme unknown—and unavailable—to conventional publishing. Some of the more successful titles turn up Big ($1.00) and Little, and there are many once Big and Giant that are now official Golden Book Favorites ($1.95–$5.95). The material is mined, but it stays alive; and much of it is alive, the product of an authentic popularizing impulse and auspicious circumstances.

ROJANKOVSKY CONCLUDED

It was "our own dear old Mother Goose, dressed in a brand new costume," said one enthusiast when the *Tall Book* appeared; but it wasn't (362). We knew Mother Goose as a genial old soul riding through the sky—per "Old Mother Goose when she wanted to wander,/Would ride through the air/On a very fine gander"—or seated with children around, and we had seen her as a barnyard goose in the self-same bonnet or tall pointed hat; sometimes, even, we had encountered her as story-lady and lady-goose at once, on facing or succeeding pages. Rojankovsky's

LITTLE MISS MUFFET
Little Miss Muffet
Sat on a tuffet,
Eating of curds and whey;
There came a big spider,
And sat down beside her,
And frightened Miss Muffet away.
11

363

LITTLE BIRD
Once I saw a little bird
Come hop, hop, hop;
So I cried, "Little bird,
Will you stop, stop, stop?"

I was going to the window
To say, "How do you do?"
But he shook his little tail,
And away he flew.
98

364. *The Tall Book of Mother Goose,* illus. by Feodor Rojankovsky. Harper, 1942. 4⅞ x 11⅞.

Mother Goose is none of these; rather, tawdry, tetchy, she *is* a goose (as in 'silly goose'), kindred in spirit if not in temper to Denslow's happily cackling Mother Goose. Both are heirs presumptive to one Elizabeth Goose (or Vergoose) whose incessant crooning of the rhymes, it was said, led her son-in-law in 1719 to style a collection 'Mother Goose's Melodies' and place "a goose-like creature with long neck and mouth wide open on the title-page."[10] The tale is discounted today (no firm record of the book has ever been found) and Perrault's 'la Mère Oye' is generally regarded as the grandmother of them all, but Rojankovsky's portrait has a cheerful asperity that Elizabeth Goose's son-in-law would have appreciated.

The practice of treating Mother Goose as a relic, a collection of quaint old-fashioned fancies, and peopling it with dainty shepherdesses and lanky simpletons, is a late nineteenth-century legacy. In the little chapbooks where the rhymes first appeared, there is simply the story pictured—and plain paddling of bare bottoms, where called for; in the popular toy-books of the mid-nineteenth century and after—markedly in the McLoughlin books—the story assumes dramatic proportions, with the Three Little Kittens finding their mittens by torchlight in the snow. But with the artistic book came idealization, with Greenaway a fashion for the old-fashioned set in, with Art Nouveau a decorative standard was established—all conspiring, along with sentimentality, to render the verses charmingly remote.

Duvoisin broke with the tradition, injecting gaiety and mischief; and Rojankovsky scuttles it and draws people, real children particularly. A serious little girl in heavy pants, sweater and hood examining a purse, one of his loveliest child portraits, is Kitty Fisher who found Lucy Locket's pocket ("There was not a penny in it,/But a ribbon round it"). A chubby tot trying to lift a watering can is Mistress Mary, a mother and son huddle under an umbrella in "Rain, Rain, Go Away." But best remembered probably, the picture of startled horror, is the pigtailed youngster popeyed at the sight of the spider that dangles beside her (363). They might be the boy or girl on the block, these earnest, active youngsters, or then again any child anywhere: it is not a modern Mother Goose so much as a human one.

The rhymes may be said, read, repeated for their sounds, but they're pictured as if they were stories (364). The Opies, in the introduction to *The Oxford Nursery Rhyme Book*, speak of a child's progession from listening without giving the words meaning to identifying the objects to understanding the stories, or seeking to. What they do not take up, and Rojankovsky does not resolve, is the problem of what is clearly Nonsense—the "silver bells and cockle shells and pretty maids all in a row." Nonsense, of course, means just what it says—no difficulty there; and no difficulty in picturing it if, like Lear, you are logically and consistently 'queer.' But when naturalism and oddity are mixed, as in Rojankovsky's "Mistress Mary," our common sense comes into play and tells us that it can't be so.

To be fair, that particular picture has been the undoing of many artists, and elsewhere Rojankovsky adopts a bright flat outline style for what can only be make-believe. Indeed, the different manners, coupled with the variety of layouts—the use of the long narrow page to different purpose for each rhyme—give the book a continuous element of surprise. The format, ideal for setting short lines of verse, also disposes of a problem endemic to Mother Goose books, that of presenting the rhymes separately, with a picture for each (for each verse, preferably) and still fitting a great many in. But quite apart from the practical—or impractical—aspects of the dimensions, a tall book as an entity is both a large book and a small one, a big deal and a bundle; and if you're small, eminently portable, something to tuck under your arm and carry close.

There followed *The Tall Book of Nursery Tales* (1944), with a meek and dowdy Country Mouse and a highfalutin City Mouse almost the equal, the two of them, of Mother Goose; and an Ugly Duckling who's beautiful

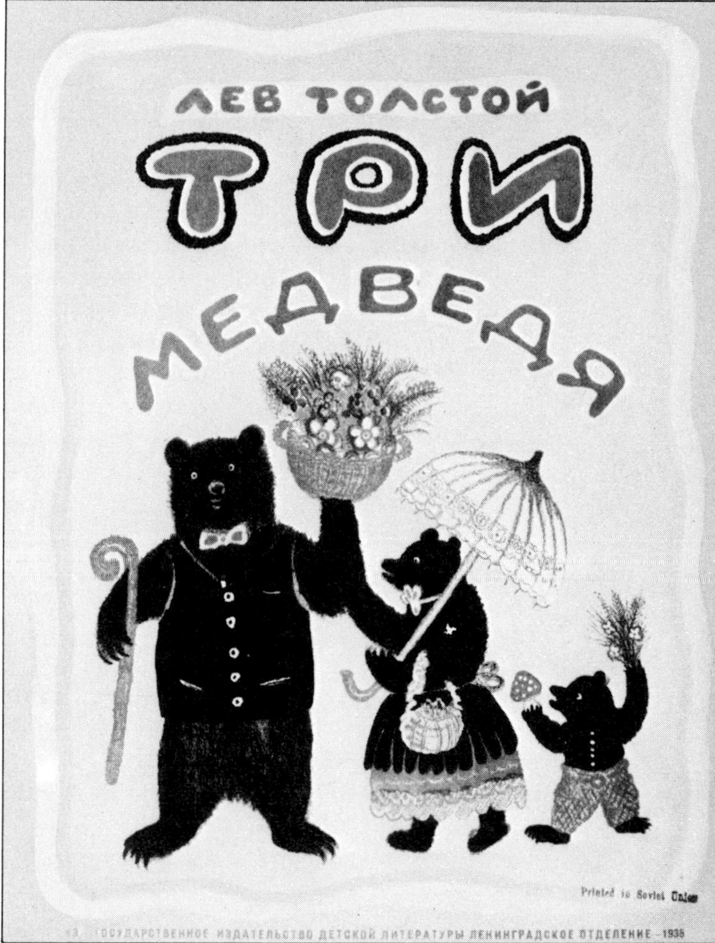

365. [The Three Bears], text by Lev Tolstoi, pictures by Yu. Vasnetzov. Leningrad, OGIZ, 1935.

too; and Three Little Pigs who are gross, an embarrassment. Mostly, however, when Rojankovsky missed in the thirty or so books he did for A & W and Golden Books, it was because the work is stale, what he did well done mechanically.

Not so *The Three Bears*, a story that might have been written for Rojankovsky to illustrate. His dark, hulking bears are distinctly Russian, and in fact the book is similar in spirit—in Russian peasant spirit—to an edition published in the Soviet Union in 1935 (365); displayed at the New York Public Library, it delighted children who, in the words of an observer, "seemed quite willing to accept Goldilocks, with short black braids flying over her shoulder, running through a dark Russian forest in place of the proverbial golden-haired child in an English wood."[11] Going his own way, Rojankovsky gives her red-gold braids and the look of a little heller and suggests, even, that she might have been waiting in the forest for the bears to depart.

Quite unlike the Russian version, which consists wholely of large complete scenes, exteriors or interiors with the appropriate figures (366 is a replica), Rojankovsky's unfolds in a fluid sequence of images. An impish Goldilocks, encircled by foliage, looks across from the copyright page to a log-framed picture of the three bears out for a walk; overleaf are a great ladder-back chair, a tufted Victorian armchair, and a nursery chair, brightly finished; opposite—a big planked bed with a camp blanket, a smaller painted bed with a patchwork quilt, and a tiny rounded bed with a pink coverlet. The mother bear is at the stove stirring a pot, three bowls of porridge sit steaming on the table, the bears go out (366), and Goldilocks knocks at the door. In each case the significant motif or action, and just that (367), the one related conceptually to the next.

As a picturebook, *The Three Bears* is Rojankovsky's dramatic opus. The other stories he illustrated for Golden Books are trivial, chiefly the occasion for additional soft-tex-

366, 367. *The Three Bears,* pictures by Feodor Rojankovsky. Simon & Schuster, 1948. 6¼ x 7⅞.

But the porridge was too hot to eat, so the
three bears went out for a walk in the forest.

366

big voice. "Someone has been tasting my
porridge."
"And someone has been tasting my
porridge," said the mama bear.

367

tured animals; and the texts he was given to illustrate by other publishers—from *Frog Went A-Courtin'* (1955) to *Cricket in a Thicket* (1963)—mostly draw on his ability to depict animals too, and landscape, rather than to dramatize a story.

Two that are not picturebooks but long stories with pictures are exceptions. Prishvin's *Treasure Trove of the Sun* (1952) is not only Russian and rural but it has, as the jacket attests, "the earthy quality of a folk tale"; one would expect Rojankovsky to do well with it, and he does. Claire Bishop's *All Alone* is set in the High Alps, the country, physically and spiritually, of *Cigalou* (168); and the cow staring out with frank interest, as if we were just passing by, brings back the bucolic bonhomie of the earlier book.

I Play at the Beach is a picturebook and apart, a child's observations, reflections—"little soliloquies," says the jacket aptly—in a crisp, radiant setting. The composite letterforms, a Rojankovsky signature, are properly playful and especially on the title page a kind of visual poetry, precise and abstract (368, 369). The little girl gazes out from the jacket in greeting, as direct as the title, and across her cap run the author's and illustrator's names. On the endpapers, shadowed, then running along the beach, are sister and brother (370); across the bottom front, in a jumble, the things of the beach, in the distance burning sun and the things of the sea. To take stock is to make an inventory—and to give credit, too, to Helen Gentry who designed the book.

The text is almost expendable. Going on from 'I play at the beach,' one could easily say 'I dig in the sand, I dive under the waves, I find seashells and coral, I watch the ants, the sandpipers and gulls'; or let a child say it, adding whatever Rojankovsky pictures—sand pail and shovel, inquisitive dog, lady reclining, reading (371). What Dorothy White had to say about *Goodnight Moon*, that the text was incidental to the illustrations, is true here as it wasn't there, partly because the text is literally what happens, the equivalent of a program, partly because the pictures are very much stronger.

To say that the pictures are stronger is to impute weakness, or weaknesses, to the text, and there are: "Along the sandy beach," as such, is excess verbiage, an obvious fact; the hole is properly a pool (or was it somehow 'made'?); to say that the tiny silver fish are "not lost," is an anthropomorphism and, moreover, without foundation, in that the child has no reason not to think that they belong in the pool, along with the coral. (And what of the coral, will the waves take that out too? if it didn't come from the sea, where then? what, after all, is it?) This is not cavilling; these are the very sorts of things that Margaret Wise Brown was openly alert to and avoided (and that, in the last instance, a proficient nature writer anticipates). When they occur, children either demand an explanation or, uncomprehending, tune out.

They tune out—lose interest—also because what is said is uninteresting, hence the objection to the redundant "along the sandy beach." But it is not only superfluous as a piece of information—something established and apparent—it is inert, unrevealing, a redundancy (sand + beach) in itself. In poetry it would be inadmissible as saying nothing about the child's feelings, about this particular beach, about the nature of beaches; in a brief picturebook text which, 'poetic' or not, shares the condition of poetry, there is as good reason to avoid any meaningless iteration. One does not find, in the similar work of Charlotte Zolotow and Alvin Tresselt, any 'sandy beaches' or 'tall mountains,' 'green grass' or 'blue sky.' In the Tresselt (and Duvoisin) *I Saw the Sea Come In*, "the broad white beach" is sometimes "the lonely white beach" (elsewhere "the beach") and as white more actual, more arresting, than if it were figuratively golden; the sand is in turn "slippery sand" or "wet sand" or "damp white sand."

The pictures in *I Play at the Beach* provide an analogy even as, by contrast, they prompt criticism of the text. An analogy, appropriately, from Melville Cane's credo in *Making a*

368

369

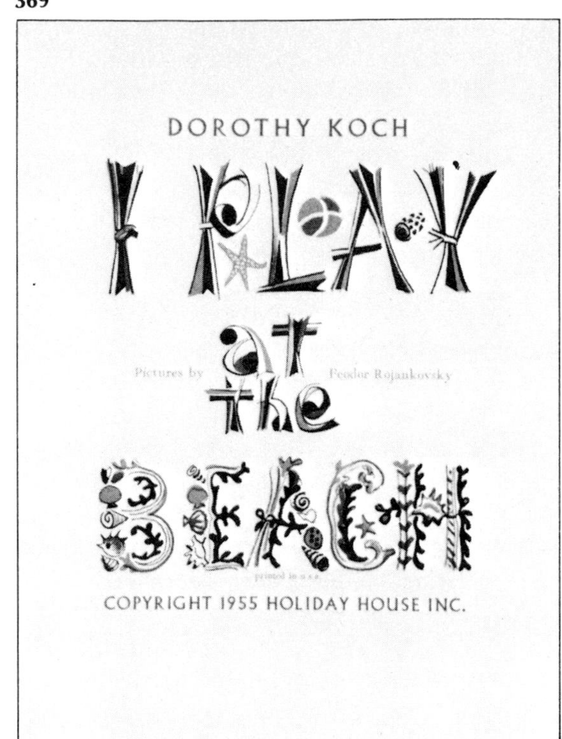

368-371. *I Play at the Beach*, text by Dorothy Koch, pictures by Feodor Rojankovsky. Holiday House, 1955. 7⅛ x 9.

370

Poem: "I strove as always for objective accuracy, tightness of statement, avoidance of useless decoration, in order to make the effect vivid in its graphic truthfulness."[12] If one were to add those other requisites of poetry, suggestability and a fresh, personal idiom, one would have Rojankovsky's accomplishment.

The idiom and the effect—the rain-washed clarity, the sparkle—are those of the *Calendrier des Enfants* (167). In his work for publishers other than Golden Books, Rojankovsky returned to the making of separations for direct, not photographic, reproduction, as he had done for the Père Castor books, and to working in lithographic crayon. The crayon, faithfully recorded, is the voice of *I Play at the Beach*, giving an underglow to sunlit arms and legs, a rich graininess to sand shadows, rounding contours, blending or tempering colors, stroking in a strand of hair, tracing the curve of calf and thigh; and the solid color areas are clean-cut, distinct.

I Play at the Beach appeared the same year as *Frog Went A-Courtin'*, the old ballad illustrated with funny, slightly frenetic animal capers and a crossfire of detail, which won the Caldecott. It is easy to believe that Rojankovsky was surprised.

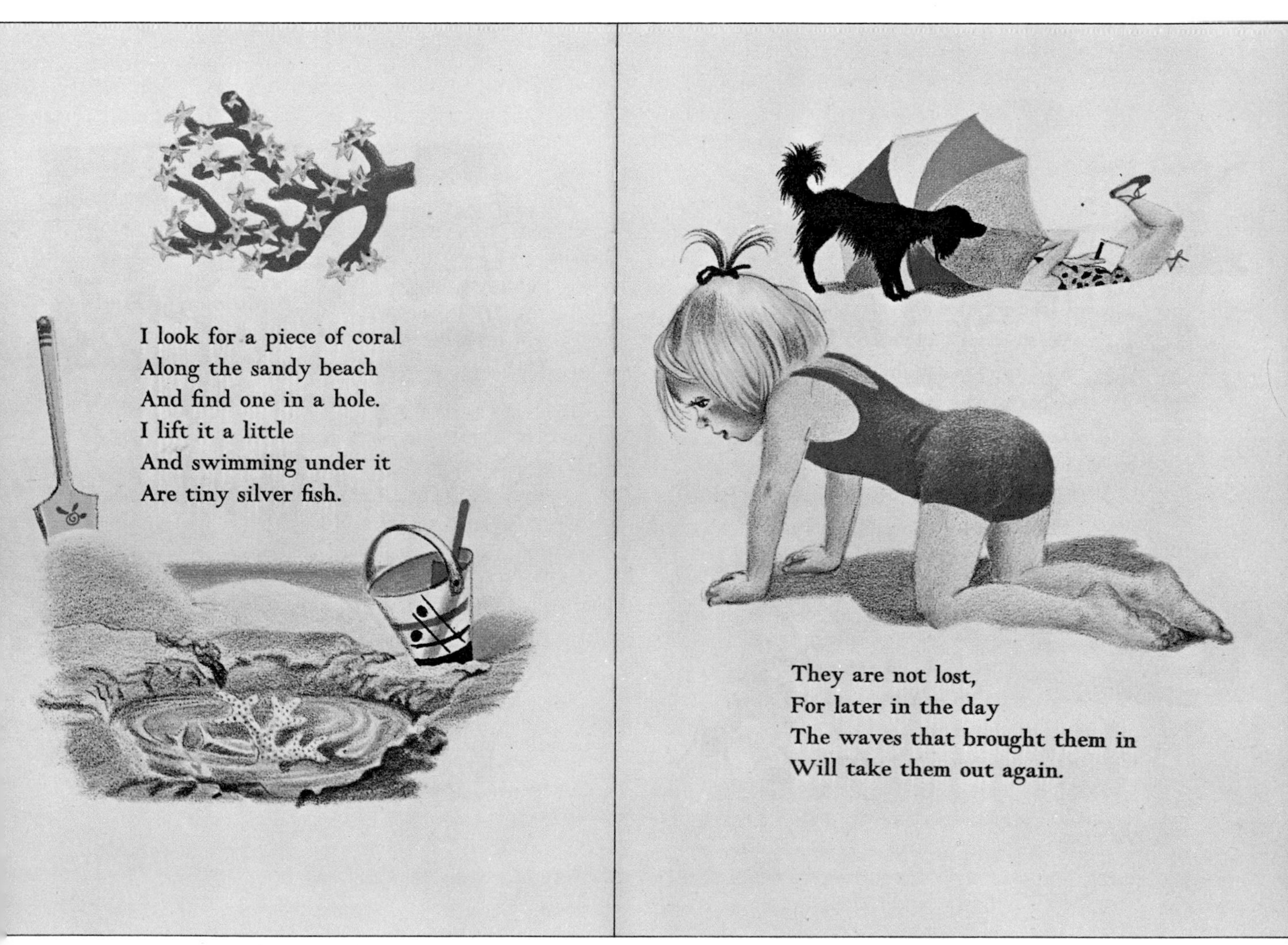
I look for a piece of coral
Along the sandy beach
And find one in a hole.
I lift it a little
And swimming under it
Are tiny silver fish.
They are not lost,
For later in the day
The waves that brought them in
Will take them out again.

371

DR. SEUSS

"There is no doubt that Dr. Seuss"—Theodor Seuss Geisel — "is the favorite author of American children today,"[1] a critic acknowledged in 1963. But however accurate the statement, the word 'author' sits poorly, and 'artist,' on the face of it, would seem an odder choice still. Piper, prophet, magician, priest —these are the words for Dr. Seuss; and for Geisel, entertainer-in-chief.

Self-portrayed as an upstart, an interloper, Geisel was, rather, a welcome recruit. On the one hand "the timid and oversentimentalized American approach"—Margaret Wise Brown's charge—was coming into question, on the other the popularity of the comics and especially, since their introduction in 1933, of comic books, drew attention to possible substitutes. *And to Think That I Saw It on Mulberry Street*, for all that it was reputedly turned down by twenty, twenty-five, twenty-six, twenty-seven or twenty-eight publishers, was endorsed immediately by Anne Carroll Moore and May Massee, among others; it had uniformly favorable, even enthusiastic reviews—Miss Moore seeing in the illustrations, for one thing, "the dynamic quality of the comic strip";[2] and the author was soon presiding at the first of his many autographing parties.

As the creator of "Quick, Henry! The Flit!" (372), "that polygon of artists" Dr. Seuss—Dr. for the Ph.D. he hadn't gotten, the pen name to save his own for Serious Writing—was already well known. His wacky animals were familiar too from cartoons in *Liberty* and *Judge* and a host of other magazines, and his wild inventiveness from *Boners* (February 1931) and *More Boners* (April 1931), two collections of schoolchild gaffes compiled by the impeccable 'Alexander Abingdon,' otherwise some editors at Viking. Geisel had illustrated the books for a flat fee, and their success stung him; the thing to do, obviously, was to write his own. And, by his accounting, children's books were the one sideline not specifically prohibited by his contract with Standard Oil, parent company of Flit.

A 1932 alphabet of odd animals found no takers, and exhibited at Geisel's alma mater, Dartmouth, scant encouragement: the idea was good, wrote an undergraduate critic, "but if juvenile impressions are as important as the child psychologists say they are, it is interesting to consider the strange new neuroses which such pictures could bring about."[3] But the "Da da *da* da de *dum* dum de *da* de de *da*" of a ship's engines became "And that is a story that no one can beat/And to think that I saw it on Mulberry Street," and held on; the book followed, Seuss history has it, to lay the lines to rest.

The "story that *no one* can beat" is young Marco's embellishment on the horse and wagon he sees on the way home from school (373), and it grows by leaps and bounds into a clamorous police-escorted caravan saluted by the mayor and showered with confetti . . . "But it still could be better. Suppose that I add . . . A Chinaman/Who eats with sticks . . . A big Magician/Doing tricks . . . A ten-foot beard/That needs a comb . . . No time for more,/I'm almost home." There, faced with his father's matter-of-fact calm, Marco is quashed; forewarned to "Stop turning minnows into whales," what can he say he's seen . . . "growing red as a beet,/'But a plain horse and wagon on Mulberry Street.' "

"Quick, Henry, the Flit!"
The human fly is a bit unbalanced for the moment, and small wonder! Henry has probably mislaid the familiar yellow can with the black band, and another good man is about to be sunk. It won't be the first time a mosquito has ruined a good day's work or a good night's sleep. Seriously (if you *can* be serious in Life) modern people aren't being bothered by flies, mosquitoes, and other insects this summer. They spray Flit, and let the insects do the worrying.
Clean-smelling Flit spray is stainless, and harmless to humans; but quick-death to all insects.
FLIT

372. *Life*, June 11, 1930.

Obviously, his father cannot be entrusted with Marco's latest tall tale, and so it remains a secret between Dr. Seuss and his audience "How"—to quote the jacket—"a plain horse and wagon on Mulberry Street/ Grows into a story that no one can beat." Call it a conspiracy against adulthood, maybe, but not a lesson "that although it's fun to imagine the outlandish, one should still tell the prosaic truth,"[4] or, conversely, an instance of being forced to lie "to keep the peace."[5] Geisel and his spokesmen have steadfastly disclaimed any moral or psychological 'message' ("nothing more than what meets the eye or ear," is friend Clifton Fadiman's dictum[6]) and, just as consistently, he

373. *And to Think That I Saw It on Mulberry Street,* by Dr. Seuss. Vanguard, 1937. 7⅞ x 10½.

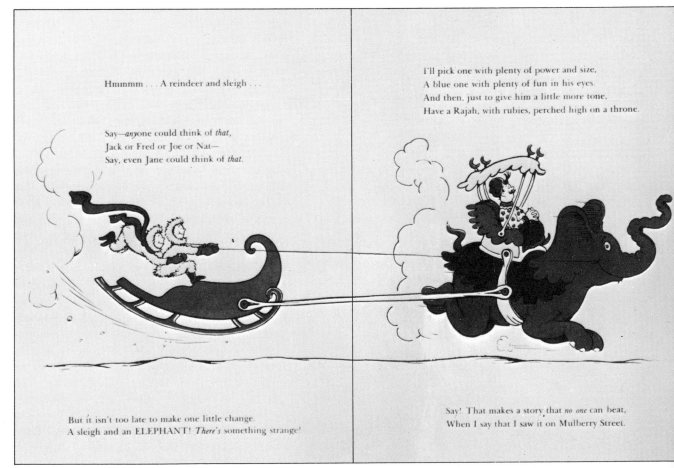

Hmmmm . . . A reindeer and sleigh . . .

Say—*anyone* could think of *that,*
Jack or Fred or Joe or Nat—
Say, even Jane could think of *that.*

But it isn't too late to make one little change.
A sleigh and an ELEPHANT! *There's* something strange!

I'll pick one with plenty of power and size,
A blue one with plenty of fun in his eyes.
And then, just to give him a little more tone,
Have a Rajah, with rubies, perched high on a throne.

Say! That makes a story that *no one* can beat,
When I say that I saw it on Mulberry Street.

has been interpreted and reinterpreted, accused of purveying candy-coated medicine or, alternatively, wormy apples. My hunch is that, in common with children, he is a natural moralizer; that it comes to him as unselfconsciously (and unambiguously) as rhyming lines from an engine's beat.

The 500 Hats of Bartholomew Cubbins is hors de combat—folkloric fantasy of a spoofing sort with a happy open end. Bartholomew, it seems, can't take off his hat to King Derwin of Didd for, as soon as he does, another appears in its place. For his impudence he's hauled off to the palace, hats flying; but to their chagrin no one—not Sir Snipps the royal maker of hats, the three wise men Nadd, the Father of Nadd, and the Father of the Father of Nadd, the Grand Duke Wilfred the King's twerp of a nephew, or the Yeoman of the Bowmen—can keep Bartholomew's head bare, however many hats they knock off. With the count at 150+, the King, at Wilfred's urging, dispatches Bartholomew to the dungeon to have his head chopped off; but, hat on, "It's against the rules." To the highest turret, then, where, says Wilfred, "I, in person, will push him off."

374. *The 500 Hats of Bartholomew Cubbins,* by Dr. Seuss. Vanguard, 1938. 9 x 11¾.

Frantically Bartholomew snatches off hats . . . 398 . . . 399 . . . until at 450, Sir Alaric, Keeper of the Records, notices that *the hats have begun to change* (374). As Bartholomew approaches the top, they become fancier and fancier, and number 500 surpasses even the King's Crown. Wilful Wilfred is stayed—spanked, too, for talking back; the King offers 500 pieces of gold for hat 500; and when Bartholomew takes it off, lo and behold, a breeze ruffles his hair. Bartholomew goes home newly rich, the King puts the 500 hats on exhibit . . . "But neither Bartholomew Cubbins, nor King Derwin himself, nor anyone else in the Kingdom of Didd could ever explain how the strange thing had happened. They could only say that it just 'happened to happen' and was not very likely to happen again."

To enumerate, appropriately, *The 500 Hats* had a plucky young hero who fancies his red hat for its upstanding feather and faces even the executioner with aplomb ("Well . . . the King says you have to, so please get it over with"); it has straight-faced ceremonial nonsense and, as a foil, a convincingly obnoxious brat; and it has a clipped, loaded text set precisely to pictures. Indeed, the very notion is visual and ideally suited to a two-color treatment—by all appearances, conceived in terms of it. Against the black, white and gray of the cartoons (done in tone, not line), the red hats have, rightly, a life of their own.

So, in *Bartholomew and the Oobleck* (Random, 1949), has the sticky green stuff, the oobleck, that King Derwin, bored with ordi-

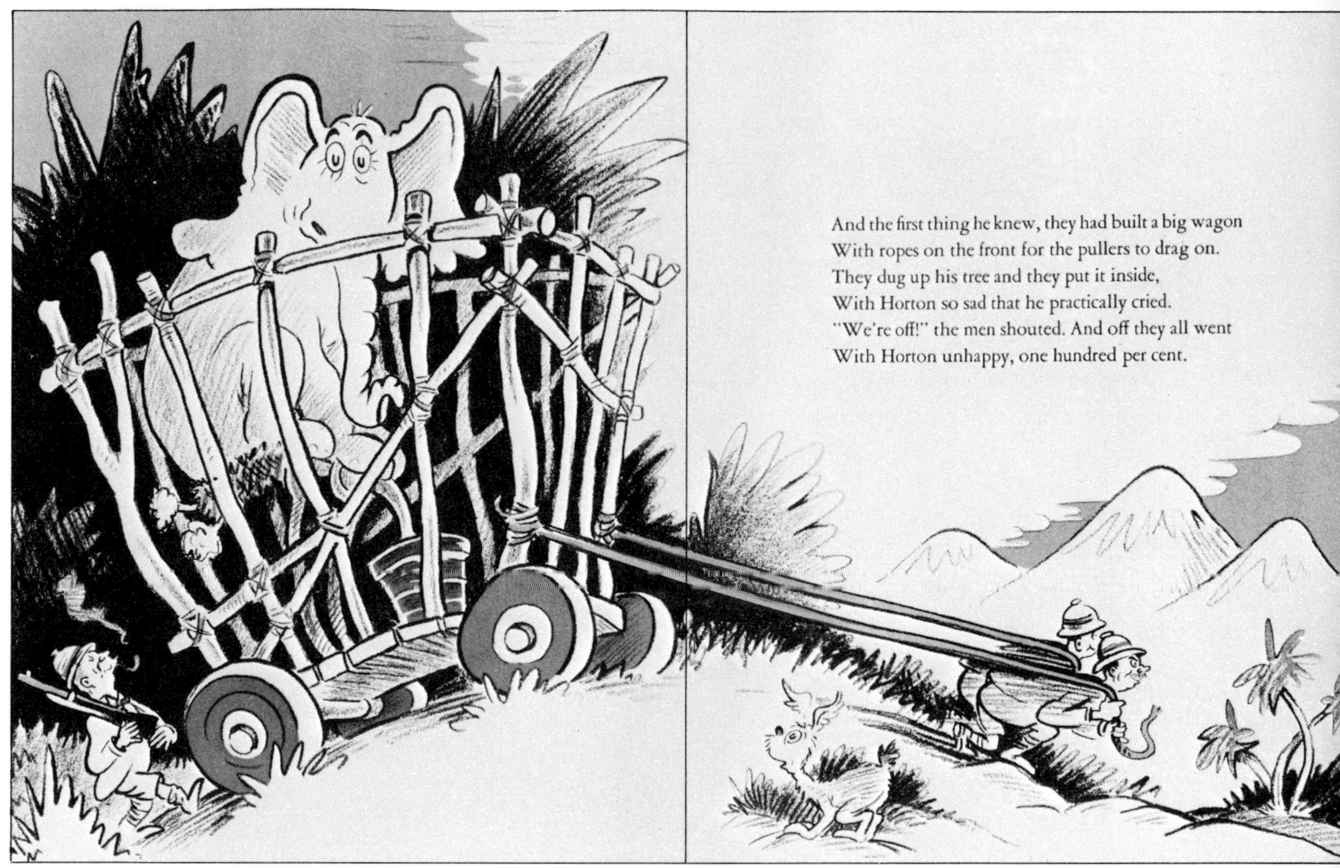

And the first thing he knew, they had built a big wagon
With ropes on the front for the pullers to drag on.
They dug up his tree and they put it inside,
With Horton so sad that he practically cried.
"We're off!" the men shouted. And off they all went
With Horton unhappy, one hundred per cent.

375. *Horton Hatches the Egg,* by Dr. Seuss. Random House, 1940. 8⅛ x 10¼.

nary rain, fog, sunshine and snow, prompts his magicians to bring down from the sky. First a vaporous cloud in the distance, it pelts against the palace like peanuts, then cupcakes, then footballs, glues birds to their nests and farmers to their plows, pours through windows, drips through ceilings, seeps through keyholes . . . and spreading over King Derwin, clings to his royal eyebrows, oozes into his royal ears. "Fetch my magicians," he orders Bartholomew, now the palace page. But they are buried in oobleck too, and the King has forgotten the magic words. "YOU ought to be saying some plain *simple* words!" blurts out Bartholomew, meaning it's all the King's fault and the least he can say is, "I'm sorry." And bellowing, then sobbing, the King complies. "And the moment the King spoke those words, something happened . . . Maybe there *was* something in those simple words 'I'm sorry.' Maybe there *was* something in those simple words, 'It's all my fault.' Maybe there was and maybe there wasn't." But as soon as the King speaks them, the sun begins to shine, the blobs grow smaller, and the oobleck starts to melt away.

No doubt about it, those simple words turned the trick. Geisel was deep into morality tales by this time, and *Bartholomew and the Oobleck* is similarly tinged—or, if you will, tainted. But if it is a lesser work than *The 500 Hats,* the cause is not so much the genial moralizing as the tidy disposition of untoward events. Besides, how can a gooey Midas touch compare with 500 irrepressible red feathered hats?

The book that kicked off the morality tales, *Horton Hatches the Egg,* is also—paradoxi-

"We win!" screamed the guests, "by a very large score!"
And poor, starving Thidwick climbed back on the shore.
Then, do you know what those pests did?
They asked in some more!

376. *Thidwick the Big-Hearted Moose,* by Dr. Seuss. Random House, 1948. 8 x 10⅞.

cally? characteristically?—the first truly wild thing Geisel did. *Mulberry Street*, for all its gusto and carnival colors, is conventional in design, and notwithstanding a certain loose energy in the drawing, *The 500 Hats* is as orderly a book as any. But *Horton*, along with many of its successors, looks like something funny that happened on the way to the printer (375). Geisel, in fact, recalls *Horton* as springing from one doodle superimposed upon another, and in his words, said to himself: "That's a hell of a situation. An elephant in a tree! What's he doing there?" Much cogitation and then—"Of course! He's hatching an egg!"[7]

He's hatching an egg, as almost everyone knows, for Mayzie the no-good lazy bird, and while she basks in Palm Beach Horton stays at his post through rain and hail and constant derision, repeating: "I meant what I said/And I said what I meant. . . ./An elephant's faithful/One hundred per cent!" Carted away, carried over mountain peaks and ocean swells (". . . But oh, am I seasick!/ One hundred per cent!") and sold, perch and all, to a circus, Horton at last has his reward: from the egg that Mayzie, chancing by, claims as her own, *"Horton the Elephant saw something whizz!/* IT HAD EARS AND A TAIL AND A TRUNK JUST LIKE HIS!" With the Elephant-Bird perched on his trunk—"And it should be, it *should* be, it SHOULD be like that!"—Horton heads home, "Happy,/ One hundred per cent!"

'And it should be, it *should* be, it SHOULD be like that': iced on a cake or written in the sky, it could be the official Seuss credo.

Thidwick the Big-Hearted Moose—who also started life as a doodle—is another lovable chump, put upon by pests he won't, he can't get rid of because, hold on, *"They're guests!"* More and more beaten down (376), harboring a bear and a swarm of bees besides, he is beset by hunters out to get his head for the Harvard Club wall. Guns to the front of him, a great drop behind, the ground giving way underneath . . . light dawns: "Today was the day,/Thidwick happened to know . . . */that OLD horns come off so that NEW ones can grow!"* Tossing his horns, pests and all, to the hunters, he's off; and, need it be said . . . "His *old* horns today are/Where *you* knew they would be./His guests are still on them,/ All stuffed, as they *should* be."

There isn't the satisfaction, though, in the mass retribution that there is in Mayzie's comeuppance, nor is Thidwick's loss of the pests a triumph on a par with Horton's gaining the Elephant-Bird. But then Horton has a mission—as against Thidwick's dubious obligation—and in sticking by the egg until it hatches he's as much a hero as a sap.

In *Horton Hears a Who!* he is a hero. No doodle is behind *Horton Hears a Who!* and, correspondingly, there was more to it than meets the eye. The intention was to encourage tolerance—in the first place, tolerance for the Japanese, whom Geisel had gotten to know on a post-World War II assignment. But Horton's dogged protection of the microscopic Whos, his firm "A person's a person, no matter how small," were taken rather as a plea for minority rights, and the book was faulted for its moralizing (where ten years earlier, before the McCarthy era, it would have been hailed). That children, always ready to champion the small against the large, ever took it as anything but that, is doubtful—the more so because it concludes by extolling the contribution of "the Smallest of All!"

The Whos are not only small, they're a world apart. How Horton hears them when there's "nothing there/But a small speck of dust blowing past through the air"; how, big as he is, he places the speck gently "on a very small clover"; how he guards the clover and, when it's stolen, tracks it down, "the three millionth flower" in a hundred-mile field; how, finally, besieged by scoffers, he exhorts the Whos to make themselves heard (377): all would be as nought if the Whos didn't have Whoville, Mayor and Town Hall and all appurtenances, for Geisel to picture as a kind of futurist flea circus terrarium (from

377. *Horton Hears a Who!* by Dr. Seuss. Random House, 1954. 8 x 10⅞.

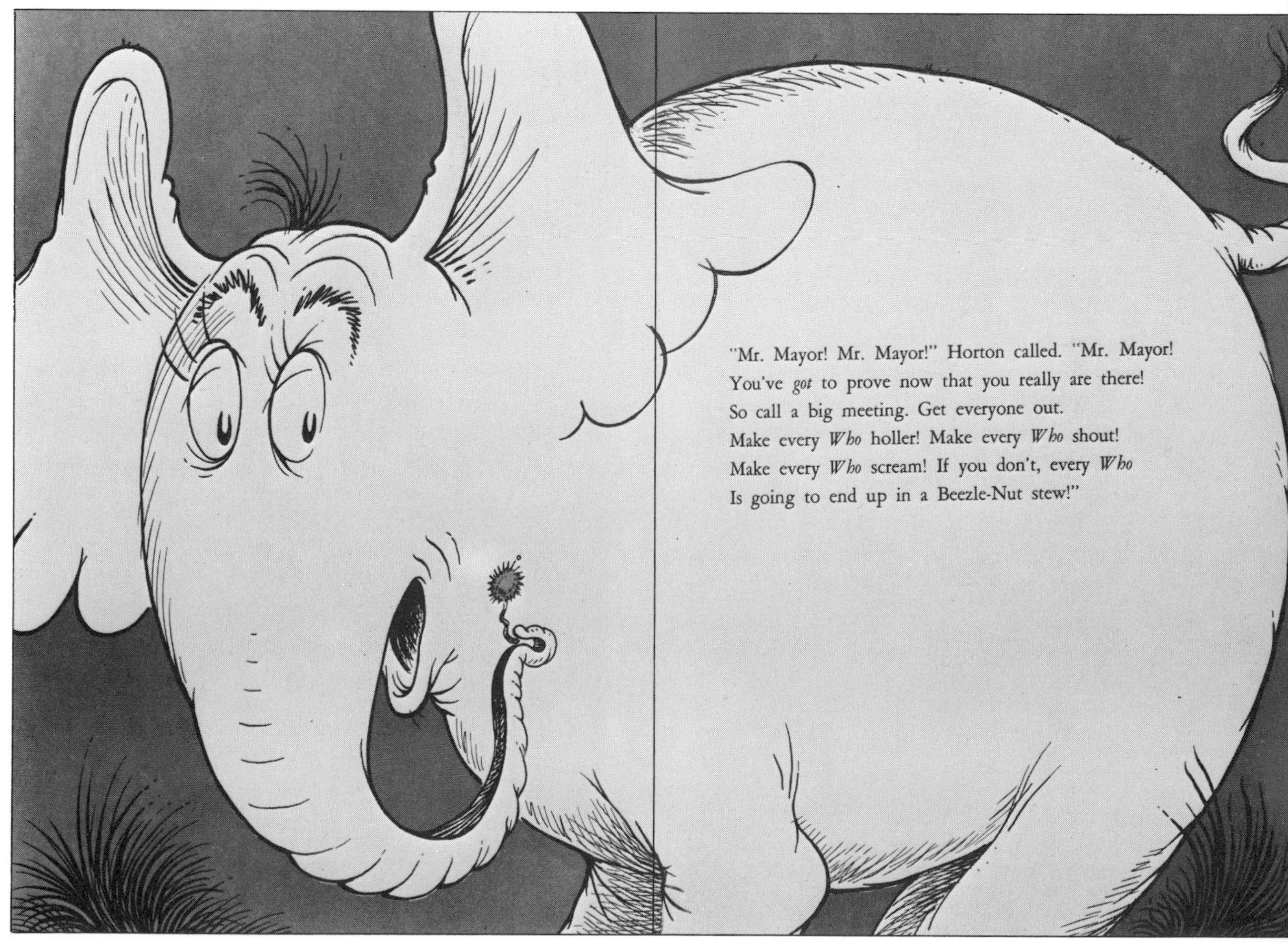

"Mr. Mayor! Mr. Mayor!" Horton called. "Mr. Mayor!
You've *got* to prove now that you really are there!
So call a big meeting. Get everyone out.
Make every *Who* holler! Make every *Who* shout!
Make every *Who* scream! If you don't, every *Who*
Is going to end up in a Beezle-Nut stew!"

which the last little malingering Who makes the necessary extra noise).

And why not? He'd done not only *McElligot's* (marvelous) *Pool*, but carrying on where *Mulberry Street's* Marco left off, *If I Ran the Zoo* (here's-what-I'd-do). Carrying on and going further, for while *Mulberry Street* is the story of a boy with big dreams, *If I Ran the Zoo* is about the dreams a boy has.

What young Gerald McGrew has in mind is to let the old animals go and capture some new—in out-of-the-way places "no others can get to." ("You have to get cold and you have to get wet, too.") The rhyme and the rhythm are hyper-contagious, the pace is somewhere between hightail and hurtle, and the content, at last, is pure Nonsense.

I'll go to the far-away Mountains of Tobsk
Near the River of Nobsk, and I'll bring back
an Obsk,
A sort of a kind of a Thing-a-ma-Bobsk
Who eats only rhubarb and corn-on-the-cobsk.
Then people will flock to my zoo in a mobsk.
"McGrew," they will say, "does a wonderful
jobsk!
He hunts with such vim and he hunts with
such vigor,
His New Zoo, McGrew Zoo, gets bigger
and bigger."

But dreams have to come to an end, and after his biggest haul (378), Gerald stands once more before the complacent keeper . . . a little boy with big ideas (still).

In *If I Ran the Circus* he's Morris McGurk, and old Sneelock whose vacant lot

378. *If I Ran the Zoo*, by Dr. Seuss. Random House, 1950. 9 x 12.

Stop . . . ?
Well, I should.
But I won't stop until
I've captured the Fizza-ma-Wizza-ma-Dill,
The world's biggest bird from the Island of Gwark
Who only eats pine trees and spits out the bark.
And boy! When I get *him* back home to my park,
The whole *world* will say, "Young McGrew's made his mark.
He's built a zoo better than Noah's whole Ark!
These wonderful, marvelous beasts that he chooses
Have made him the greatest of all the McGrewses!"

Morris means to turn into the Circus McGurkus is going to pitch in, know it or not.

After all, Mr. Sneelock is one of my friends.
He might even help out doing small odds
and ends.
Doing little old jobs, he could be of some aid . . .
Such as selling balloons and the pink lemonade.
I think five hundred gallons will be about right.
And THEN I'll be ready for Opening Night.

As it turns out, Sneelock—carpet slippers, small potbelly, Sherlock Holmes pipe, pince-nez—is the assistant every young ringmaster needs. Pipe puffing imperturbably, he plays William Tell's son for a Blindfolded Bowman; Colonel Sneelock the Spotted Atrocious Tamer; Kid Sneelock wrestling a Grizzly-Ghastly; Spout-Rider Sneelock, Drum Major Sneelock, and in a grand finale, Great Daredevil Sneelock "pulled through the air by three Soobrian Snipe/On a dingus contraption attached to his pipe!" But wait—"with his hair still combed neat," he plunges down, down . . . *"Four thousand, six hundred/And ninety-two feet!"*

Back outside the vacant lot, Morris says airily:

Why! He'll be a Hero!
Of *course* he won't mind
When he finds that he has
A big circus behind.

Where *Mulberry Street* silences Marco, at least momentarily, and the McGrew Zoo remains a pipe dream, *If I Ran the Circus* gives Morris his head and a grown-up helper besides. (Co-opted or conned or naturally cool, Sneelock is superb.)

But the Circus McGurkus isn't all Sneelock's show. On the side and entr'acte are a Drum-Tummied Snumm ("Doesn't hurt him a bit/Cause his Drum-Tummy's numb"); a Juggling Jott "Who can juggle some stuff/You might think he could not . . ." ("Such as twenty-two question marks,/Which is a lot./Also forty-four commas/And, *also,* one dot!"); the To-and-Fro Marchers who march in five layers ("The Fros march on Tos/And the Tos march on Fros"); and my favorite, a Hoodwink who winks in his wink-hood ("Without a good wink-hood/A Hoodwink can't wink good"). In sum, logical Nonsense, and as much found images, verbal and visual, as inventions.

And for recent graduates of alphabet books, what likelier, more logical, than a foray *On Beyond Zebra!* Brags a typical Seuss boy to a tyro who's just learned his letters: "My alphabet starts where your alphabet ends!" Drawing his new letters in forms that look vaguely Chinese and, at the same time, vaguely familiar, he fits each to an animal that somehow expresses a feeling you've had (379) or a perfectly reasonable notion (380). At the close, young Conrad (Cornelius o'Donald o'Dell), convinced that "the old alphabet ISN'T enough," has begun on his own brand-new letters; and for other "People who Don't stop at Z," there's a recap, *Yuzz*-a-matuzz to *Wum*bus (and *Um*bus) to *Hi*gh Gargelorum—and, overleaf, one to guess on.

Once, standing in as Mrs. Dr. Seuss, Helen Geisel explained to children that, "As a boy, Theodor Seuss Geisel was always drawing pictures. Whenever it was raining . . . he would be sketching funny animals all over the house. Scribbled on the telephone pad would be an elephant that was not at all like a regular elephant. Once his mother found something drawn on a roll of old wallpaper in the attic. This something, which had ears three yards long, he called a WYNNMPH." (As a graduate student at Oxford, he proposed illustrating *Paradise Lost* with the Archangel Uriel sliding down a sunbeam, oil can in hand to ease his passage.)

He was born an artist, she said, "He must have been born an artist because after he was born, he never went to art school or had any art training. What's more, his father and his mother, his uncles and his aunts, all said he couldn't—not even if his life depended upon it—draw a horse that looked like a horse, nor a dog that looked like a dog. And yet he *is* an artist!"[8] Agreed, for if he cannot draw from nature, he can and does draw expressively. And if he could draw a horse or a dog,

Q
When you go beyond Zebra,
Who knows . . ?
There's no telling
What wonderful things
You might find yourself spelling!
Like QUAN is for Quandary, who lives on a shelf
In a hole in the ocean alone by himself
And he worries, each day, from the dawn's early light
And he worries, just worries, far into the night.
He just stands there and worries. He simply can't stop . . .
Is his top-side his bottom? Or bottom-side top?

379, 380. *On Beyond Zebra!* by Dr. Seuss. Random House, 1955. 8 x 10⅞.

379

could he, would he draw his fantastic creatures?

Like Lear, with whom he is most often compared, his Nonsense is native to him, the expression of an angle of vision, a cast of mind, different from other people's. But quite apart from the fact that Lear could draw in the usual sense, it is not, like Lear's in the limericks and stories, an assemblage of incongruities, of the inherently irreconcilable. The Obsk from the far-away Mountains of Tobsk 'who eats only rhubarb and corn-on-the-cobsk' is a different order of Nonsense—nutsky—from the Blue-Bottle Fly who subsists "Mainly on Oyster-patties . . . and, when these are scarce, on Raspberry Vinegar and Russian leather boiled down to a jelly" ("The Story of Four Little Children . . ."). And the Quan, the Zatz-it, the Umbus (a cow with one head and tail and "ninety-nine faucets") are a far cry from The Bountiful Beetle ("who always carried a Green Umbrella when it didn't rain, and left it at home when it did") or The Absolutely Abstemious Ass.

If, however, one leaves Lear to his singularities and turns to the American scene, one finds an abundance of word play and doggerel ("For the Akhoond I mourn,/Who wouldn't?/He strove to disregard the message stern/But he Akhoodn't"), of bravado and, too, cockalorum, as a precedent, from "Yankee Doodle" to Mike Fink to the comic spurt at the turn of the century. The last embraces the work of George Thomas Lanigan ("The Akhoond of Swat"), John Kendrick Bangs, Oliver Herford, Carolyn Wells, Peter Newell . . . and the like of "The Brick Bat" and "The Round Robin" (Carolyn Wells's *Phenomenal Fauna*)—out of an accident of language, something new, whole, even operative.

Still more functional, however fantastic, are the inventions of Paul Bunyan natural history: the Gillygaloo, a hillside plover that laid square eggs so they wouldn't roll down the steep incline; the Hoop Snake, to be avoided only by jumping through its hoop as it approached; the Goofang, a fish that swam backward to keep the water out of its eyes; the Hangdown, the Hidebehind, the Sidehill Dodger (short legged on the uphill side).

Geisel too is a teller of tall tales and as such, thoroughly American. They're expansive, immoderate, uninhibited, preposterous—along the way they did diverge from what others were doing. But not until *The Cat in the Hat* does chaos take over, and a brash slapbang humor; there's almost nothing in the earlier books construable as violence, physical or emotional, except some of the miscreants' misdeeds.

The Cat in the Hat was designed to induce children to read. In 1954, John Hersey, writing in *Life* on 'why children bog down on the first R,' pointed one finger at "pallid primers" and their illustration: "Why should [children] not have pictures that widen rather than narrow the associative richness the children give to the words they illustrate—

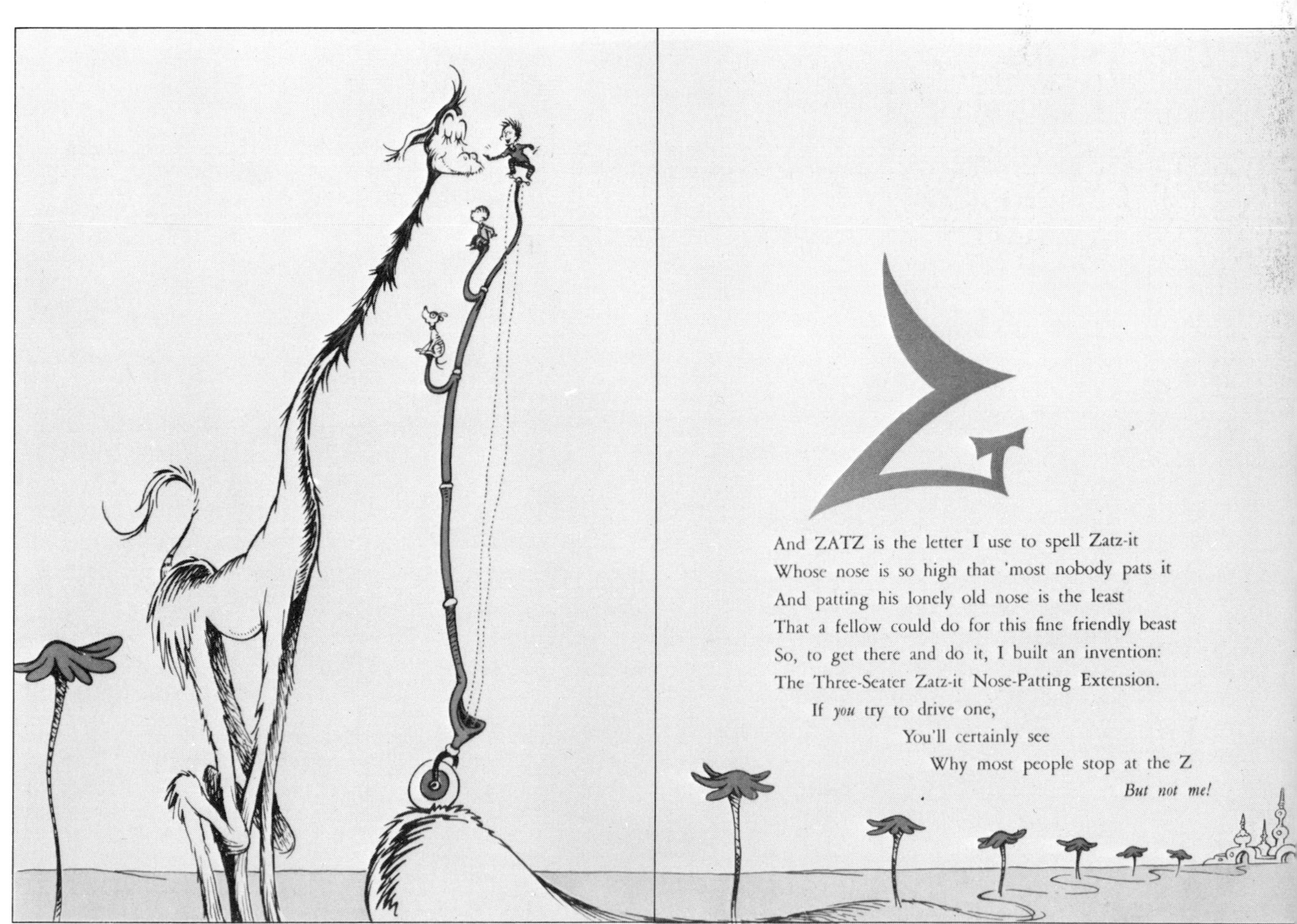

And ZATZ is the letter I use to spell Zatz-it
Whose nose is so high that 'most nobody pats it
And patting his lonely old nose is the least
That a fellow could do for this fine friendly beast
So, to get there and do it, I built an invention:
The Three-Seater Zatz-it Nose-Patting Extension.
If *you* try to drive one,
You'll certainly see
Why most people stop at the Z
But not me!

380

drawings like those of the wonderfully imaginative geniuses among children's illustrators, Tenniel, Howard Pyle, 'Dr. Seuss,' Walt Disney?"[9] Whatever might be said of the concatenation (of the rest more later), the significant fact is that Geisel and William Spaulding, textbook editor at Houghton Mifflin, acted upon the suggestion; the two had worked together on materials for functional illiterates during the war. The result, in 1957, was *The Cat in the Hat* (381), published in a trade edition by Random House, as a textbook by Houghton Mifflin; and with its runaway success, the beginning of Beginner Books, many of them written, all of them edited by Geisel, which we'll consider in connection with the contemporaneous Harper I Can Reads.

The Cat in the Hat made Geisel a celebrity and sent the sales of the earlier books soaring; by picturebook standards, however, they had always done well. That it also presaged—or caused—a decline in the subsequent picturebooks, as often alleged, is less demonstrable. On the whole they are more frantic, more forced, and it is fair to say that they add very little to what he had done before. But one need not deplore them to value more "the natural truthful simplicity of the untruthfulness"[10] that Beatrix Potter praised in *Mulberry Street* and the natural exuberance of the Horton books.

381. *The Cat in the Hat,* by Dr. Seuss. Random House, 1957. 6½ x 9.

"Look at me!
Look at me now!" said the cat.
"With a cup and a cake
On the top of my hat!
I can hold up TWO books!
I can hold up the fish!
And a little toy ship!
And some milk on a dish!
And look!
I can hop up and down on the ball!
But that is not all!
Oh, no.
That is not all . . .
16

MARCIA BROWN

For several years in the Forties Marcia Brown worked at the New York Public Library, in the Central Children's Room and, telling stories, outside (outdoors, often), all the while continuing to study art and ready herself for what she wanted to do, illustrate children's books, young children's books particularly.

She wasn't a librarian—she had a degree in education, not librarianship; but the Central Children's Room, then a part of the Reference Department, was hospitable to specially qualified individuals in its role of conservator and stimulus: books were circulated to children and adults but ideas and information constituted the basic stock in trade. "By the end of the second week after the opening," Anne Carroll Moore wrote in 1911, it was possible to group the clientele "as follows: Parents asking for help in the selection of books for their children's vacation reading or for purchase as gifts to children; teachers, social workers and persons connected with civic and charitable institutions seeking help in the selection of books for children and information concerning story telling and story literature; authors, illustrators, publishers, or their representatives, desiring to make a comparative study of various editions and to know what books have been written for children on a great variety of subjects; visitors from European countries attracted by what appeals to them as 'a new idea in education' and requesting detailed information concerning children's libraries and children's books."[1] So it continued—seconded for a time by the Bookshop for Boys and Girls in Boston—as a crossroads and a showcase, the American hub of children's books.

Exhibitions were an important part of the program—important to the participants as well as the public. Long famous, Artzybasheff continued to list as his first exhibitions the 1924 and 1925 display of his work at NYPL, presumably the original art for *Feats on the Fiord* and *The Forge in the Forest* which would have been shown in connection with the annual holiday exhibit of children's books. But it was in 1933 that exhibitions burgeoned: "Children's Books of Yesterday," a joint undertaking of the library and the Metropolitan Museum (with loans from other sources), touched off a series of national exhibitions of post-1903 work, in each case selected by a native of the country—the English by Jacqueline Overton of the exemplary Children's Library in Westbury, Long Island; the French by Claire Bishop, then on the staff, formerly with the first French children's library, *L'Heure Joyeuse*, in Paris; the German by Ernest Eisele of B. Westermann & Co., a leading importer; the Czech by Mrs. Jan Matulka, wife of the artist-illustrator and herself in charge of the extensive Czech collection at the Webster Branch. Paintings, drawings and prints set off the books; talks were given and stories told, and the stewards of the *Ile de France* brought grand guignol. Forty-second Street became a year-round festival.

Thenceforth Maria Cimino, who had arranged the displays, was responsible for exhibitions, and each of her annual reports is in essence a calendar of events. The birthdays of Kate Greenaway, Randolph Caldecott and Hans Christian Andersen occasioned special exhibits, and those of "Leslie Brooke, [storyteller] Marie Shedlock, Walter de la

Mare, Kenneth Grahame, William Shakespeare, Saint Patrick, Columbus, Abraham Lincoln and George Washington were celebrated with tables of particular interest."[2] February was given over to old valentines, many of them borrowed from public and private collections, and special storytelling; there was a Music Exhibition and a Circus Exhibition, one of Egyptian artifacts and one of Early American toys. And there was living art: in 1940, from early January to mid-March, Polish folk art; in February, the valentines; in March and April, local and then international children's art; during May, "watercolors and proof sheets for *The Great Geppy*"; all summer, a large Rackham exhibition; in the fall, a Mexican exhibition —"a children's miniature of the one that had just closed at the Modern Museum," as one artist remarked.[3]

During Marcia Brown's term at the library the exhibitions, some of which she organized herself, all of which she helped mount, reached a peak of ambitiousness and professionalism. "The exhibition of drawings and paintings lent by Mr. Daugherty and his publishers went up on the 16th of February," she wrote as part of the 1944 report, "presenting the problem of settling all that turbulent activity into an exhibition peaceful enough to stay on the walls. The studies of heads of Lincoln shown on the large table at the entrance to the reading room set a somber note, continued in the first proofs of the lithographs in soft brown and black. They presented in various scenes from his career, the growth of Lincoln as a personality and national figure. On the right wall were drawings of American folk heroes. . . ." And, she concluded, *Andy and the Lion* made new friends among youngsters "who were delighted to see the framed proofs shown with an amusing little statue over the picture books."

Still and all, when her own *Stone Soup* came out she confided to children, "Telling stories to boys and girls all over New York has been my greatest fun in library work" and "the old tale of the three soldiers" was one that they enjoyed.[4] *Stone Soup* is folklore, venerable but not celebrated, the sort of story librarians culled from collections rather than a Cinderella or Snow White or Three Bears, universally known and passed on. It was from the latter, the traditional nursery literature, that Walter Crane made his toy-books (and the McLoughlins made many of theirs) and an occasional book-beautiful was produced—Helen Sewell's *Cinderella* in 1934, Elizabeth MacKinstry's *Aladdin and the Wonderful Lamp* in 1935. But in the new era fairy tales were old hat or worse, bad medicine, poison, and save for an exceptional *Seven Simeons* creative energies turned elsewhere. In the Forties there did not exist single-volume picturizations of even the most famous of the traditional tales, a void that, like the toy-books before them, Little Golden Books helped to fill.

As a child "thinking that I would like one day to illustrate books for children," Marcia Brown testifies, "I always thought of the fairy tales that I loved";[5] and in the library she found them persistently popular: "Not for a moment did children who came of their own accord . . . and were free to choose their own books, desert their heroes, the personification of their dreams. The calls still came for Cinderella," but also "for stories about giants and princesses, for simple people raised to high station because of their gifts."[6] That is, for the gamut of folk and fairy tales, which she proceeded to put into picturebooks, in *Stone Soup* into a picturebook that was capable of being read aloud to a group, that could be presented to younger children as effectively as the story itself might be told to older children.

What is special about *Stone Soup*—special to it, almost—is the way the action moves across the pages from left to right, regardless of the relative position of the figures, and how much is accomplished on each occasion with a minimum of words and a single continuous or split picture (382). The three soldiers are wangling a meal from professedly destitute French peasants: " 'And now, if you please, three round, smooth

"And now, if you please, three round, smooth stones."
Those were easy enough to find.
The peasants' eyes grew round as they watched the soldiers drop the stones into the pot.

382. *Stone Soup,* by Marcia Brown. Scribner, 1947. 8⅛ x 10.

stones.'" Clearly in evidence—one, two, three. "Those were easy enough to find." Yes, the men come carrying them on the run. "The peasants' eyes grew round as they watched the soldiers drop the stones into the pot." The first, under surveillance, is about to go in. So we have, in one spread, the stones requisitioned ("three round, smooth stones"), fetched (they're "easy enough to find") and set cooking; and with the peasants we're wondering what can possibly come of it. (On the verso, "'Any soup needs salt and pepper'" . . . and, "'oh, if there were carrots, it would be much better.'") Not only is much accomplished but nothing is omitted; there is no hiatus, no waiting for words or pictures to catch up. The story is an anecdote, a mere incident, without any obvious pictorial attraction—just an exchange between three passing soldiers and the inhabitants of a village; a good story saved from oblivion and added to the common stock by tight, pungent scripting and nimble nonstop staging.

Marcia Brown had already done an original picturebook the year before, *The Little Carousel* (Scribner, 1946)—a book original also in the sense that the story takes place on a real sidewalks-of-New-York street (hers) and features a boy who might well be found there, looking longingly out the window: "Anthony was alone. His older brother had gone to play baseball. His father was away in the Navy. His mother was working." Done in the red, green and black of the Italian neighborhood, the book has authentic local color, and at a time when picturebooks tended toward archetypes and universals, it is personal and circumstantial. The cure for Anthony's complaint? A roving merry-go-round and a chance to earn a ride by turning the crank for the weary (wise and kind?) proprietor.

Henry could hardly wait until he was old enough to go out in the early morning with his father and the other men in the fishing boats. More than anything in the world Henry wanted to go to sea.

"Oh, you'll have to do plenty growing, mon, before you go," his father told him. "You is a good diver, but shark harass you plenty, you so little! He want you for his dinner."

383. *Henry-Fisherman: A Story of the Virgin Islands,* by Marcia Brown. Scribner, 1949. 9⅝ x 7⅞.

Two summers on the island of St. Thomas were behind *Henry-Fisherman*, as unusual then for its realistic portrayal of a black child as *The Little Carousel* was for entering into ordinary urban life. Henry's is the normal yearning to prove himself, which means, in the Caribbean, going to sea (383); and barely escaping a shark, prove himself he does. "But a boy like Henry could find many things to do on an island like St. Thomas, while he was waiting to grow up and go to sea." At one opening he's fetching water, balancing a can on his head; at another, searching for coral and shells; further on, helping with the family wash, going to the market place, tending the goats—all temptingly pictured in tropical coral and dark green, turquoise and gold and brown, or simply the coral and deep dark green. But handsomely put together as it is, complete to the neat solid sans serif and the interweaving palm-pattern endpapers, the story is for the most part static, the pictures more suggestive than involving. A pleasure to look at and, with its native lilt, to listen to, it hasn't a commensurate hold on children.

From later travels came other stories colored by a locality; but whether more successful (*Felice*, 1958) or less (*Tamarindo!*, 1960), they are a poor second to the folk and fairy tale 'singles' and, for that matter, to the illustrations for Philip Sherlock's collection of tales *Anansi, the Spider Man* (Crowell, 1954), product of a stay in Jamaica.

Stone Soup is done in line and wash, *Henry-Fisherman* in flat planes of color, gouache, the next, *Dick Whittington and His Cat*, in linoleum cuts: doing each book differently, in a manner suited to the matter at hand, was to be a hallmark of Marcia Brown's work. The legend of Dick Whittington, the poor orphan scullion deterred from running away by the prophetic ring of the Bow Bells—"Turn again, Whittington,/Lord Mayor of London"—while unbeknownst to him, his cat is making his fortune, is both a personal tale and historic pageantry; and the difficulty is to balance the two. The technique and the use of it give us the rough, vigorous setting; the composition draws our eye beyond the passers-by into the lane where Dick sits huddled (384); and the text, telling of his dismay, is also a tale of disenchantment. (When he hearkens to the Bow Bells—"I'll go back and I'll take the cuffings of the cook, if I'm to be Lord Mayor of London.") There's a good deal to the story, and a good deal to the pictures, and not a little humor in both.

With *Dick Whittington* Brown was pioneering to a degree too; the fashion for Olde English stories sedulously half-timbered hadn't yet set in. But Perrault's *Puss in Boots* was one of the favorites of her childhood, much illustrated, that, she attests, "it was some years before I felt ready or capable of attempting."[7] Elsewhere she speaks admiringly of the work of Edy Legrand, his later work in line and wash or pastel, and specifically of *La Nuit de la Saint Sylvain*, published here in 1947 as *The Enchanted Eve*. Printed on paper tinted a dusty rose and blue, the whole page illuminated (385), it is a big

But when Dick got to London, how sad he was to find the streets covered with dirt instead of gold! And there he was in a strange place, without food, without friends, and without money. Dick was soon so cold and hungry that he wished he were back sitting by a warm fire in a country kitchen. He sat down in a corner and cried himself to sleep.

384. *Dick Whittington and His Cat,* adaptation and pictures by Marcia Brown. Scribner, 1950. 7⅝ x 10.

385. *La Nuit de la Saint Sylvain,* by Madeleine Ley, illus. by Edy Legrand. Paris, Colmann-Lévy, 1935. 9⅜ x 12⅛.

Maintenant les hivers ne font plus tant de glace, et la terre tournera longtemps sans doute avant que reviennent ces saisons d'autrefois où les canaux restaient pris pendant dix semaines, entre deux bordures de roseaux étincelants de givre, quand les paysans remontaient les fleuves jusqu'aux villes dans des traîneaux verts et rouges, pour les fêtes nocturnes du mois de février.

« Quelle glace épaisse! » pensait Barbara en arrivant au bord du canal — « dure comme la pierre, et si noire et brillante ».

Où étaient les poissons et les nénuphars, et les belles grenouilles de l'été ?

Ce jour-là presque tous les gens de la ville se retrouvent sur la glace où les lampions se reflètent avec des halos de couleurs. Du centre lumineux de la fête, une rumeur arrivait, et partout alentour on entendait sonner les grelots des attelages et crier les fers des traîneaux sur la neige durcie. Parfois des jeunes gens déguisés et masqués s'approchaient du bord en lançant des appels joyeux.

Barbara attacha ses patins. Elle tremblait d'impatience et aussi de crainte. Pourrait-elle se tenir dessus comme toutes ces fillettes robustes ? Mais dès les premiers pas — ô bonheur — elle se sentit emportée sans effort sur la glace noire et lisse. Bientôt, elle fut entourée d'une troupe d'enfants costumés. « D'où viens-tu, criaient-ils, petite fille verte? Quel beau petit manteau vert avec de la fourrure d'oiseau! Comme tu patines bien! »

385

splendorous book harking back to the historical albums of Job but itself a thing of great dash; Marcia Brown refers to it as "one of the most beautiful books I have ever known."[8] In their simpler way her French books particularly, the *Puss in Boots* and *Cinderella*, continue in that illustrious tradition.

She domesticates it, tempers it to the story and the audience. Where Job and Edy Legrand are always imposing and illustrate around the text, Brown illustrates the text itself, scene by scene, now bringing us close to hear Puss's sly command (386), now carrying the results of his scheme swiftly past us (387), now—dropping the springy line for pure floating pastel—taking us with Puss to the object of his scheming, the ogre's great castle (388). Three openings—and at the fourth the ogre will be dispatched in an explosive arc. That one finds, in place of squared-off blocks of text, text-lines fitted to the design, is the least of the difference; but without such extreme flexibility in type-setting, just then coming to the fore (*Petunia*, for instance, is of the same period), the over-all treatment would be impossible, another example of craft intersecting with art.

Of the technique, Brown observed in 1955: "In the past few years we have seen more and more books using a crayon and line technique, with the drawings reproduced directly from the artist's own color separations by means of a contact method with no camera work [p.

The cat, delighted at the way his scheme was working out, marched on ahead. He came to some peasants who were mowing a meadow and said, "My good people, tell the king when he passes by that the field you are mowing belongs to the Marquis of Carabas. If you do not, you will be chopped into mincemeat!"
When the carriage rolled by, the king noticed the fine field. "To whom does this land belong?" he asked the mowers.
"To my lord the Marquis of Carabas," they said all together, for the cat's threat made them tremble.
"You have a splendid estate," said the king to the marquis.
"As you see, Sire, this field yields a rich harvest every year."

386

The master cat, still keeping well ahead of the carriage, met some reapers. He said to them, "My good people, tell the king that all this wheat belongs to the Marquis of Carabas. If you do not, you will be chopped into mincemeat!"
A moment later the king passed by, and of course he wanted to know, "To whom does this wheat belong?" "To my lord the Marquis of Carabas," called out the reapers. Again the king congratulated the young man.
And the cat, still trotting ahead of the carriage, gave the same warning to everyone he met.

387

386-388. *Puss in Boots,* 'free translation' from Perrault and pictures by Marcia Brown. Scribner, 1952. 8⅜ x 10½.

388

At last Master Slyboots came to a great castle, owned by the richest ogre ever known, for all the lands through which the king had passed belonged to him. The cat had taken care to find out who this ogre was and just what he could do. He demanded to speak to him, telling the guards, "I did not wish to pass so close to the castle without having the honor of paying my respects to your master."

389. *Cinderella,* 'free translation' from Perrault and pictures by Marcia Brown. Scribner, 1954. 7⅞ x 9⅞.

206] . . . By making their own plates, by exploring the variety of effects possible with hand-graphic techniques, illustrators can develop the freedom of fine artists in their print-making."[9] It is Charlot's observation turned round, and one has only to look at the mowers, never mind the figure Puss cuts, to appreciate the result (386). Nor can one fail to notice, throughout, the use of white space "in which the mind rests or fills in its own images."[10]

Despite their common origin, *Cinderella* is quite different, by turns tender and wry where *Puss* is all pomp and swagger. And if it is not to be mere plot, the Cinderella stereotype, the story cannot be similarly condensed or, to the same extent, told in pictures; we need the stepsisters' silly chatter and their taunting as much as we need the spectacle they make of themselves primping for the ball (389). *Cinderella,* in response, is a picture-story book, its illustrations separate from the text whether or not adjacent, and set into the page rather than bled; the considerable text is framed by white space and so are the pictures, and white space penetrates and binds the two. Line is the other link—quivering threads of line in the pictures and for the text type, a sharp and spirited Bembo. *Cinderella* is colored—chiefly in a rose and blue somewhat reminiscent of Edy Legrand's—but more than anything else it is a book of sparkling and witty drawings.

The Flying Carpet, which followed, takes

off again, into vivid varicolored patterns and a bold heavy line (390) and, for the most part, page-filling design. *The Three Billy Goats Gruff*, in turn, is an exuberant tease (391), pictured big as a billboard and as brash; "Now, I'm coming to gobble you up!" roars the troll at each trip-trapping billy goat gruff, and children in the back row squeal.

Such classics and demi-classics—*The Steadfast Tin Soldier* (Scribner, 1953) is another—are the common property of the Western world; but in the course of looking for a particular kind of story—"a big subject, with few words, that would say something to a little child"[11]—Marcia Brown lighted on an Indian fable, "The Hermit and the Mouse," and unwittingly began the combing of other cultures for picturebook material. It would have happened regardless: stories set in the 'emerging' countries were much in demand, folk tales traveled well (they always had), and folklore was felt to be a shortcut to understanding, the attitudes and expectations of a people externalized. That *Once a Mouse* was Marcia Brown's and won the Caldecott, her second (the first was for *Cinderella*), simply served to accelerate the process.

390. *The Flying Carpet,* adaptation and pictures by Marcia Brown. Scribner, 1956. Detail.

391. *The Three Billy Goats Gruff,* text by P. C. Asbjørnsen & J. E. Moe, pictures by Marcia Brown. Harcourt, 1957. Detail.

"A big subject, with few words, that would say something to a little child"—it almost had to be a fable, and *Once a Mouse* is important to us not because it is Indian in origin but because it is universal in application and, as a picturebook, equally a drama and a work of art. "One day a hermit sat thinking about big and little—Suddenly, he saw a mouse. . . ." (392). Turning the page, hurrying as he does, we find the mouse snatched from the crow's beak, soon to be comforted "with milk and grains of rice. But look!"—there is no respite—a cat is approaching, and the hermit, "mighty at magic as well as at prayer," turns his little pet into a fierce cat; the cat, cowering at the sound of a barking dog, into a big dog; the dog, attacked by a tiger, "into a handsome, royal tiger." A tiger who lords it over the other animals and, when the hermit rebukes him, sulks: "No one shall tell me that I was once a mouse. I will kill him." But the hermit, reading his mind, turns him back into "a frightened, humble, little mouse" —one last wordless act of magic, big to little

—"that ran off into the forest and was never seen again. And the hermit sat thinking about big— and little . . ."

Cut in wood, which "takes a certain amount of force"—this is Marcia Brown—"and a definite decision," it shows the wood plain ("Wood that lived can say something about life in a forest"). The colors are "the yellow-green of sun through leaves, the dark green of shadows, and the red that says India to me." Whether few or many, the pictorial elements are concentrated, emblematic ("Since the book is for very young children, the details are only those needed"[12]); and the design itself tells much of the story, be it the earth closing in on the mouse or the forest astir, forms blurred, become forces—as cat confronts cat. But the illustration is more than instrumental, it is rich in visual interest and contrast—consider the grove of trees, the stand of grass, the crow and, cutting across, the grain of the wood; in rhythm and movement and, withal, a sense of risk: however much the artist labored over the blocks, one feels them as a leap from mind to hand.

Marcia Brown continues to do books and, from her knowledge of children, of art and of publishing, to write and talk about picture-book illustration with a breadth that lights up the field. Almost alone she has spoken out publicly against the siren song of the cash register—that, in her recasting of *Once a Mouse*, turns the hermit publisher into a foraging conglomerate. "Can he ever stop thinking about big—to think once more about little?"[13]

In her own work she has given a new direction to that feeling for past works that is in the best library tradition. "From ancient India . . . a fable cut in wood" for four-year-olds—drawn and told with dignity and dispatch—is in fact no small thing.

392. *Once a Mouse,* by Marcia Brown. Scribner, 1961. 9 x 9⅜.

about to be snatched up by a crow.
He hurried

EXPANDING POSSIBILITIES: EASTER, FOR INSTANCE

By the early 1950s, picturebooks had assumed new importance to libraries, and libraries to picturebooks. In 1945, upon the establishment of the Children's Book Council ("for the year round promotion of reading"), Frederic Melcher wrote in *PW*: "The time to take this step is certainly now, when the tide of demand for children's books is at an all-time high . . . ."[1] A disinterested report in the Department of Commerce journal *Domestic Commerce* was quite specific:

"The greatest increase in book sales during the war was registered in children's publications, according to the best available trade estimates, but sales in these books were increasing even before the war. The shortage of games and toys in the stores was largely responsible for much of this gain. But a not unimportant factor was the increased interest of parents and publishers alike in providing colorful, entertaining books to help inculcate in the very young a love of reading and a desire to find out the why and how of things. Moreover, wartime developments in off-set printing and mass lithographing have virtually revolutionized children's books. In view of the record number of young children who have become accustomed to books, demands in this line should continue high."[2]

One firm that evidently thought so was the Regensteiner Corporation, a Chicago-based commercial printer (the Sears, Roebuck and Montgomery Ward catalogs), which in early 1946 established the Children's Press; contemplated were 10-cent books to be sold through chain stores, a 25-cent series, Star-Bright Books, of obvious inspiration, and a few dollar 'flats'—prospectively, another popular-market list. The next year, however, with pre-binding (vs. rebinding) a major topic of discussion among children's librarians, Children's Press became the first publisher to offer its books—indicatively, *You and the United Nations* (1947) plus *The Littlest Angel* (1946)—in a special library binding (the start of what was to be, in effect, a 'popular' library list). Doubleday went into dual editions later that same year.

Though the binding brouhaha prompted a correspondent to write drily to *PW* that "librarians would rather have good bindings than anything else,"[3] it had a realistic basis in the greatly increased demand for picturebooks in libraries and insufficient stock to meet the demand. Librarians, at first chary—"Are picture books and readers an asset or a liability?" was another 1947 question[4]—soon extended themselves to serve the new audience, and preschool story hours utilizing picturebooks became a regular part of the library program. Under the heading "Story hour and story telling," *Library Literature* lists almost nothing pertaining to preschoolers before 1943–45, two articles each from 1946 to 1948 and 1949 to 1951, seven from 1952 to 1954. Adding to the overall demand, the postwar babies were coming of picturebook age.

In 1948, opening an American Booksellers Association convention panel on "Children's Books, an Expanding Market," Margaret McElderry, juvenile editor at Harcourt, Brace, reminded her audience "of last year's birth statistics": "An average of 333,000 babies were born each month in this country. That certainly promises an expanding market."[5] It was not, however, to be a commensurately expanding retail market. The first drop in bookstore sales of juveniles had already taken place, with picturebooks particularly hard hit; "More than one bookseller pointed out that it is an inescapable fact that Simon and Schuster's *Golden Books*, big and little, have definitely affected the buying habits of people who are looking for picture books."[6] In the spring of 1942, you may recall, publishers exhibited at the Toy Fair for the first time; in the spring of 1952, on the same occasion, *PW* carried a "Toy Buying Guide for Booksellers" for the first time: "We Hate Toys and Games, But . . . ," a bookseller titled his piece of advice.

At the same time, production costs were way up—the cost of composition had risen 117 per cent since 1940, of plates 100 per cent, of printing 102 per cent Eunice Blake pointed out on the same ABA panel; the last figure meant that publishers would have to cut down on color, all the figures meant that, despite increased distribution, prices would have to rise—from $1.50 and $1.75 throughout the Forties to $2.00 and $2.50 for the equivalent picturebook by 1956.

But library book budgets were up too—in public libraries, 44 per cent between 1948 and 1950 alone; sales climbed (those of books of $1 or more almost doubled between 1952 and 1955) and, correspondingly, publication increased—from 929 new juveniles in 1948 to 1,245 in 1952 to 1,495 in 1956. The new series—Landmark, Signature, American Heritage—account for some of the increase but the expansion was pronounced in picturebooks as well; and with it—with the appearance, too, of new juvenile lists (Whittlesey House, Pantheon, World, Abelard, Parnassus, Obolensky, Atlantic Monthly Press, just in the Fifties), with new picturebook activity where there had been little or none—came diversification.

It is in the nature of libraries to be able to absorb not only a great many books—ten or fifteen copies of *Make Way for Ducklings* or *Curious George*—but also a great many titles. Parents are inclined to take home a pile (where a child might pick one or two); an assortment of books makes a more interesting and impressive showing; the diversity of the audience legitimizes, even mandates a range of choice; and books that are borrowed, read—once, twice, a few times—and then returned need not have the staying power of books bought to keep. At one time virtually every picturebook was meant to delight any child; in a library a successful picturebook is one that a substantial number of children like for some reason—or a number of adults seek out.

The nursery school movement, previously confined to special situations and a limited clientele, had expanded with the financing of day care centers for the children of defense workers during the war; and the postwar baby boom, the congregation of young couples in new child-centered communities, the conjunction of servantless households and economic prosperity, led to the widespread establishment of private and cooperative nursery schools. In a nursery school a *collection* of books is *used* with the children.

As librarians began to work directly with preschool children, they too needed books that could be rotated and read successfully to a group—a quite different situation, in both cases, from the favorite book read repeatedly to an individual child. One obvious result was a premium on large-scale, broadly defined illustration that showed well at a distance; but only one. The schools were making increased use of picturebooks in turn—not only stocking them in school and classroom libraries for beginning readers but reading them in class, in kindergarten (nearly universal now) and the primary grades, where introducing subject matter and building social attitudes were considered to be among the books' functions. If it was a far cry altogether from *Millions of Cats*, *Millions of Cats* was not eliminated: more children were seeing more books, and on the basis of the expanded market, many more kinds of books came to be made for them.

The first snowfall called for *White Snow*

Bright Snow; at Halloween, every ghost disappeared from the library; if a new baby was in the offing, or a visit from grandma, 'was there a book?' A snail in the playground? Harriet Huntington's *Let's Go Outdoors.* A trip to the firehouse? Lois Lenski or Margaret Wise Brown. This is not to suggest that such 'special' books could not be equally good any day of the year—those just cited were; it is rather that the nature of the demand encouraged their publication, and they multiplied.

Take Easter, for instance. In large measure, Easter in this country is a children's holiday, a small children's holiday. There are the Easter bunny and Easter eggs and Easter baskets; there are chicks and Easter bonnets too, but the bunny and the eggs are the chief things, and the eggs—colored or candied—are foremost.

In *The Country Bunny and the Little Gold Shoes*, DuBose Heyward, the author of *Porgy* and *Mamba's Daughters*, wrote as beguiling a story for young children as any I've ever read and read and read, at least for the first half.

> We hear of *the* Easter Bunny who comes each Easter Day before sunrise to bring eggs for boys and girls, so we think there is only one. But this is not so. There are really *five* Easter Bunnies, and they must be the five kindest, and swiftest, and wisest bunnies in the whole wide world, because between sunset on Easter Eve and dawn on Easter Morning they do more work than most rabbits do in a whole year.
>
> When one of the Easter Bunnies grows old and can no longer run fast, the old, wise, and kind Grandfather Bunny who lives at the Palace of Easter Eggs calls the bunnies together from the whole world to select the very best one to take the place.
>
> Often a mother bunny says to her child, "Now if you learn to be wise, and kind, and swift, some day you may grow up to be one of the Easter Bunnies." And all of the babies try their very best, so that they can grow up and go to work for the Grandfather Bunny at the Palace of Easter Eggs.
>
> One day a little country girl bunny with a brown skin and a little cottonball of a tail said, "Some day I shall grow up to be an Easter Bunny:—you wait and see!"

The big white bunnies who live in fine houses scoff, and so do the Jack Rabbits with long legs—the more so when, grown-up and married, she has twenty-one Cottontail babies to take care of. ("Only a country rabbit would go and have all those babies," is the disparaging, and pointed, comment.)

Thinking no more about being an Easter Bunny, Cottontail tends her babies and, when they're bigger, teaches two to sweep and two to make beds, two to cook and two to wash dishes . . . ; two to plant a garden, two to paint pictures. The last little boy bunny becomes the keeper of her chair, to seat her politely at table.

One day she hears that one of the five Easter Bunnies has grown too slow, and she takes her children to the Palace to see the contest, "sad because she thought that now she was nothing but an old mother bunny and could only look on." But the old, wise, and kind Grandfather is not satisfied with the contenders . . . (393). "What a large family you

393. *The Country Bunny and the Little Gold Shoes,* text by DuBose Heyward, pictures by Marjorie Flack. Boston, Houghton Mifflin, 1939. 8 x 9⅞.

But still he did not pick one. And he said to them, "You are pretty and you are fast, but you have not shown me that you are either kind or wise."
Then his kind old eyes looked everywhere and at last they rested on Little Cottontail Mother where she stood with her children around her. And he called her to come right up to the Palace steps. So she took her twenty-one children and went up
and stood before him.

"Let's go and find one—right away," said Carl.

Carl and Luke and Johnny went to the woods and they came back with a young white birch tree. It was so large that it had to stand on the floor. The children trimmed the tree with the eggs they had painted themselves and with many plain dyed ones. Susy and Appolonia hung small baskets from the branches. Under the tree Grandmom placed an enormous cookie rabbit which she had just taken from the oven.

Katy hung up the eggs she had found in the attic. If she had not found those eggs they would never have had an Egg Tree, Grandmom said. Katy felt very proud as she hung her egg with the lovely bird on the topmost branch.

"It is such a beautiful tree!" said Katy. "I wish that everyone in the world could see it."

"Yes," said Grandmom. "It makes a body feel as if Spring has come right into the house. We must give a party for it."

So Grandmom gave a party for the tree. All the children from all the farms about were invited.

"An Egg Tree!" they said. "We've never seen a tree that grows eggs on its branches!"

The children went home and told their fathers and mothers about it. The fathers and mothers all came to see the wonderful tree in the little red house.

394. *The Egg Tree,* by Katherine Milhous. Scribner, 1950. 7¾ x 9⅝.

have, my dear. I suppose they take all of your time?" *No, not any longer.* "Ah, you must be very *wise* to train so many children so well. But tell me, do they always look so happy, and do they always hold up their ears so prettily?" *Indeed they do.* "Then you must be very *kind* indeed to have such a happy home. It is too bad that you have had no time to run and grow swift, as I might then have made you my fifth Easter Bunny."

At a whisper, the little bunnies scatter and Cottontail rounds them up "in no time at all"; on the Grandfather's hesitation at her leaving them, the capable little sweepers, cooks, gardeners present themselves. Done—she is to "Come to the Palace tomorrow afternoon, for that is Easter Eve,

and you shall be
my fifth Easter Bunny."

That is the better half. Still to come is the great Palace, "piled high with eggs of gold and silver, and eggs that glittered like snow, chocolate eggs, eggs for rich children and eggs for poor children, for children who were sick and children who were well all over the world"; and for Cottontail, already tired, "the hardest trip of all," to the farthest, highest mountain to take the loveliest candy egg to a little boy who's been sick all year without complaining—which is where the little gold shoes come in.

Forgive it its excesses; allow it its inelegant pictures; grant it justice done, a pervading sense of vital importance and loving kindness.

The Egg Tree has no story to speak of, just a way of getting to the business of painting the eggs and trimming the tree; but the eggs and the tree and the Pennsylvania Dutch designs that accompany them are a pleasure to look at, and the custom has a natural appeal for children (394). A festive book, a Caldecott winner, acculturation plus holiday crafts.

In *Easter Treat* (Knopf, 1954), Duvoisin has Santa abroad incognito at Easter and, suspect, forced to prove his identity—a double celebration. For *The Easter Bunny That Overslept* the problem is that when he awakens and sets out with his basket, it's Mother's Day, "too late for Easter eggs." Still trying, he comes back as the Fourth-of-July Bunny (395); but the Fourth of July, he's admonished, is no time for Easter eggs either. On Halloween three little ghosts in brown shoes spurn the eggs as the proffered treat; and at last it's Christmas. Santa has no use for the eggs but he can use the Easter Bunny as a helper—dressed in a small Santa suit, he negotiates narrow chimneys—and when they've made the last delivery, Santa has a present specially for him: "A beautiful gold alarm clock."

As a conceit this has its charm, as a story its contrivances (a big wind drops the bunny at Santa's doorstep): as a passing-fancy picturebook it's just about ideal. There's that little Easter Bunny with the eggs no one wants (singing Happy Easter to You, to the tune of Happy Birthday); there's his manful try on the Fourth of July, his dismay on Halloween, his satisfaction as Santa's helper—and the amusing incongruity of his every reappearance, the contrasting picture of him back in his burrow (396). In sum, the dramatic passage of a year from holiday to holiday, as time does for children, with the changing seasons filling in between.

The opportunities for an artist are written into the book, and Adrienne Adams did some of her freshest, most suggestive work for it, never belaboring the whimsy, letting the story float on white paper in watercolor. This is four-color separation for a full-color effect, a difficult method and, in Adrienne Adams's words, "painfully tedious." It is a way of working in watercolor and keeping the con-

395. *The Easter Bunny That Overslept,* text by Priscilla and Otto Friedrich, pictures by Adrienne Adams. Lothrop, 1957. 7¾ x 9¾.

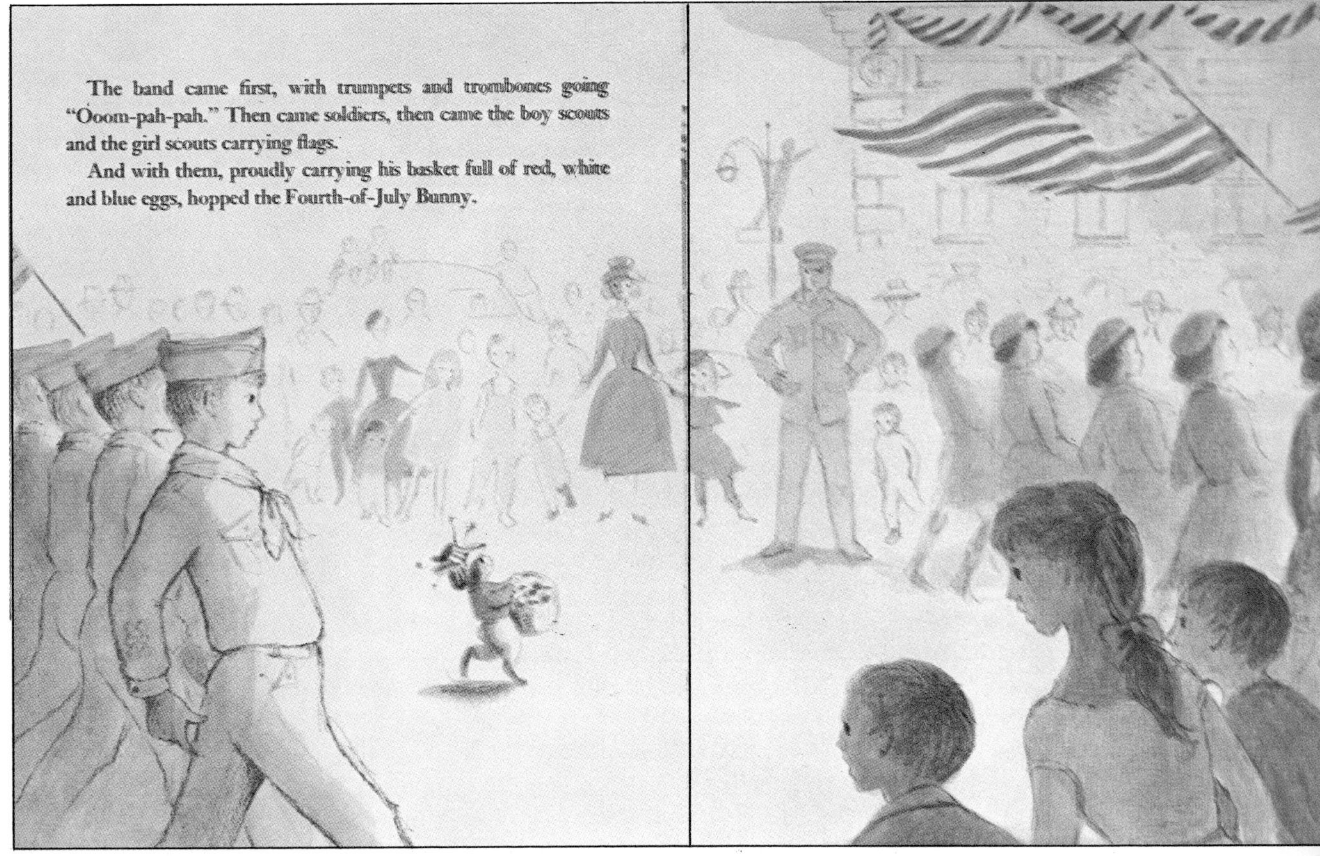

The band came first, with trumpets and trombones going "Ooom-pah-pah." Then came soldiers, then came the boy scouts and the girl scouts carrying flags.
And with them, proudly carrying his basket full of red, white and blue eggs, hopped the Fourth-of-July Bunny.

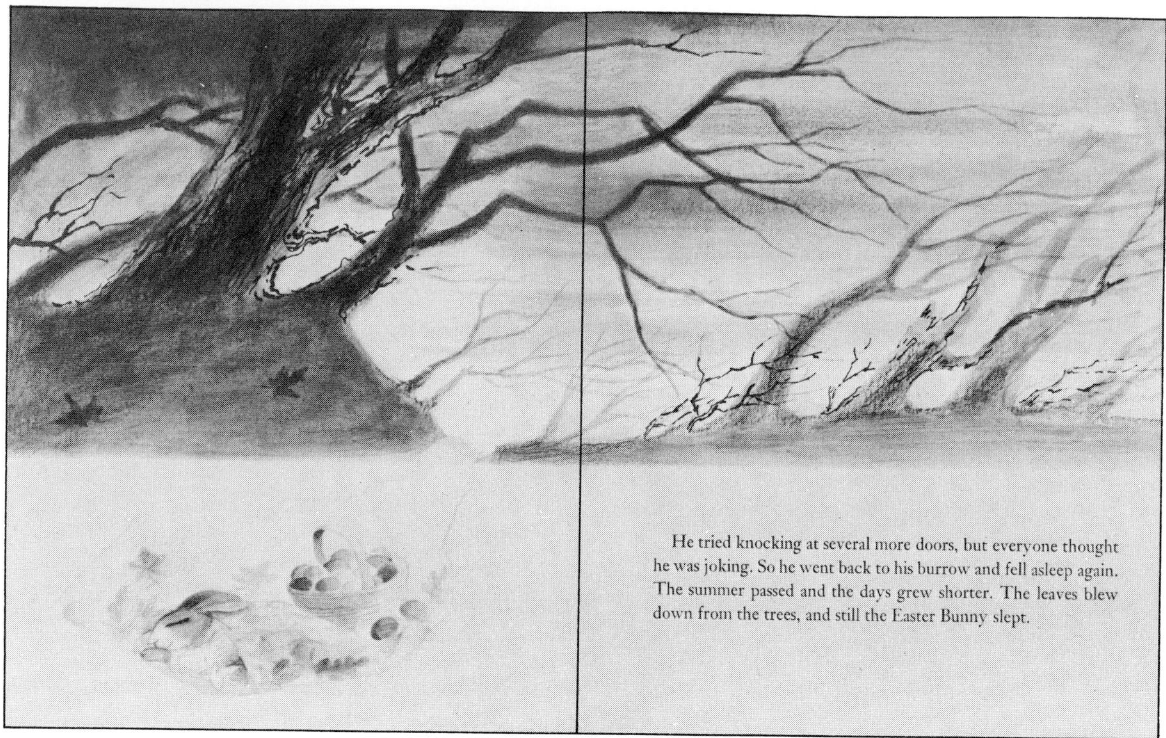

He tried knocking at several more doors, but everyone thought he was joking. So he went back to his burrow and fell asleep again. The summer passed and the days grew shorter. The leaves blew down from the trees, and still the Easter Bunny slept.

396. *The Easter Bunny That Overslept,* text by Priscilla and Otto Friedrich, pictures by Adrienne Adams. Lothrop, 1957. 7¾ x 9¾.

trol the artist foregoes with camera separation (as well as reducing the cost), and a way of working in watercolor when that seems more appropriate than crayon on acetate or line and flat color (which afford control too).

"In separating wash paintings for halftone reproduction," she writes, "I am dealing with overlapping gradations of the four different colors to achieve many other colors. I begin with the shades of black, my most important color, for it tells most of the story. I mentally select out all that is black in my painting and, calling this my key drawing, do it on illustration board. Then—on acetate, so that I can see through to the key drawing—I do a painting of only the red areas. With scotch tape I hinge the red drawing on the left of the key drawing so that I can fold it back out of the way when I do the blue drawing, which I hinge from the top. Then comes the yellow drawing, hinged on the right . . . .

"The real stumper, and the part that is difficult to explain without demonstrating, is this: each separated color-painting is done by me in tones of black so that it will photograph better and make a truer plate. Everyone knows that blue photographs weak, red photographs strong. If I do each painting in black, I can keep to true values. Of course, each plate will be printed in its intended color of ink."

After explaining how she finds the values of the colors and matches them in the same value of black, Adams concludes: "Such effort does not guarantee precise results. One must consciously design with the hazards in mind. Keep it casual, free. Let the color overlap carelessly; if a design is very carefully clean-cut and a flaw in the registration is made [i.e. the printing of one color over another], the error will stand out like a sore thumb. If many areas are loosely put together, one's eye accepts the looseness in its entirety."[7]

The method of proceeding, and the safeguards, produced a distinct style—airy, spacious, with room for the imagination to expand; unified, in that the colors are blends or gradations of a fixed few; allied to the picture-page, not superimposed on it. It is loose and casual, as Adrienne Adams indicates, and, as she implies, borne by the drawing. Duvoisin, working in flat colors (with Ben Day tints for tones), achieves a quite different appearance that, however, fits the same description (177); and whenever an artist puts down a drawing and lays color openly over it, he has the opportunity at least for a like loose expressiveness.

"The charming custom of giving brightly colored eggs to children at Easter is so old that no one quite knows how it began," reads the jacket copy for *The Whiskers of Ho Ho.* "Every country has its own legends and has passed them along from generation to generation. And all of them include eggs as a symbol of renewed life. Eggs are also one of the symbols of the Passover Feast, always associated with Easter. The Easter Bunny probably originated in Germany but his prototype, the hare, appears in the earliest Spring festivals in China as does the lovely tradition of dyeing eggs in bright colors to symbolize joy and good fortune."

In an old pagoda by the edge of a river live a very old man and a rabbit and a hen. "Ho Ho, the rabbit, was gray, with a short tail and long ears and very sensitive whiskers. Tsee Tsee, the hen, was white, with a long tail and small ears and no whiskers at all." (397)

"The old man's name was Kwang Fu. On his head he wore a skullcap. On his feet he wore straw sandals. And in between he wore a scarlet suit buttoned down the front with three pumpkin seeds. The pumpkin seeds came from Kwang Fu's garden, where he grew only two things—golden pumpkins in the fall and in the spring beautiful tall white lilies. Near the garden was a rice paddy, and on warm days Kwang Fu took off his sandals and waded in the water while he picked his rice. Every morning for breakfast, Kwang Fu ate an egg. Tsee Tsee laid the egg, but she and Ho Ho both ate rice pudding for breakfast. Kwang Fu would have liked rice pudding, too, but he ate the egg to please Tsee Tsee." (398)

397

397, 398. *The Whiskers of Ho Ho,* text by William Littlefield, pictures by Vladimir Bobri. Lothrop, 1958. 8⅞ x 9.

398

The above, put in conventional paragraph form, is the text facing the picture, where it runs in continuous unjustified lines of quite uneven length broken in accordance with the sentences and the phrasing. It is impossible to synopsize: nothing happens, no single piece of information is salient, and none is extraneous or unrelated to another. You learn for the first time that the old man's name is Kwang Fu, and you will need to have Tsee Tsee's eggs in mind; but the way to Kwang Fu's garden and the two things he grows there is via his scarlet suit "buttoned down the front with three pumpkin seeds," a piquant detail in itself; and the rice paddy leads to the rice pudding—anticipates it at least—and to Kwang Fu's consideration of Tsee Tsee's feelings which, though not critical to the plot, is fundamental to the story.

We need the river and the rice paddy and the garden too because they are already, naturally, "the color of honey," "deep green," "white with lilies in springtime and golden with pumpkins in the fall"; that is, they are colored their own colors and not to be painted by Kwang Fu, whose other prized possession is a tray of paints with which he has painted his pagoda "many times inside and out." With nothing left to paint, he is lost . . . until he takes notice of Tsee Tsee's daily egg.

But though the egg is "a lovely shape, and covered with blank space—just right for painting" (a lovely notion, consonant with Japanese and Chinese tales), Kwang Fu finds that his brushes are worn down to the handles. After a space of thinking—the landscape stretches to the horizon—Tsee Tsee removes "one of her exceptionally long tail feathers" and hands it to Kwang Fu. He paints swirls and squidges on the egg, and Ho Ho, "not quite satisfied," dips his sensitive whiskers into the paint and makes delicate patterns.

Working together every day, the three soon have "a great pile of eggs glowing in the garden with all the colors of the rainbow. They were too pretty to eat. In fact, they were pretty enough for presents." So Kwang Fu makes a raft of bamboo with a sail of rice paper, the eggs and the lilies are placed gently on board, Ho Ho takes the tiller, Tsee Tsee, at the prow, serves as lookout, and they sail east "for many days" to a strange land where people are preparing "for a holiday called Easter."

So, from China with love and lilies (Tsee Tsee carries those), the Easter bunny. *Horn Book* called it "fresh and charming . . . a delight for seasonal picture-book storytelling."[8]

There have been many, many others. For a start, *Miss Flora McFlimsey's Easter Bonnet* by Mariana (Lothrop, 1951), which came between *Miss Flora McFlimsey's Christmas Eve* and *Miss Flora McFlimsey and the Baby New Year*, the small distresses and gratifications of a timid Victorian doll; *The Golden Egg Book*, which was not conceived as an Easter book specifically but became *the* Easter book in popular sales; Palmer Brown's *Cheerful*, about a mouse who finds the world of his dreams in a candy egg (p. 492), and the Tresselt-Duvoisin *World in the Candy Egg* (Lothrop, 1967), which gives it life.

The point is not their number, nor even yet their variety except in what they make of the material at hand; and in that respect the four books that we've looked at are of particular interest. *The Country Bunny and the Little Gold Shoes*, presented "as told to Jenifer," is just such a story as a practiced storyteller might make up for a child, the story itself—the premise that there are several Easter bunnies, that the last and best of them is a brown country bunny with twenty-one children—Heyward's personal and particular version of a nebulous legend. *The Egg Tree*, as noted early on, takes material that is essentially pictorial and builds a picturebook around it.

"Priscilla and Otto Friedrich," the original jacket of *The Easter Bunny That Overslept* tells us, "are the parents of three daughters and a son: Liesel, 5, born in Germany; Molly, 4, in London; Nicholas, 3, in Paris; and Amelia, 2, in Long Island. Mrs. Friedrich, who was born in Peru and spent her childhood in Sumatra, says: 'The idea for this book came from one dreadful Easter which *ought* to have been put off until May . . . .' This is the Friedrichs' first book for children, although Mr. Friedrich, in addition to short fiction and criticism, has published a novel . . . ." (He was also a foreign correspondent, whence the children born here and there.)

Apart from the rampant cosmopolitanism, the item is not unusual; but it is news, and suggestive. A blustery Easter, a houseful of children, an idea; picturebooks in the house presumably. A manuscript, an editor, an illustrator: *The Easter Bunny That Overslept.* This is not to make it sound as easy as one, two, three, but as possible as one and one and one.

The medium had by the Fifties almost infinite possibilities. Consider that we started with classifications on the one hand and exceptional talents on the other, moved through guiding forces and increased collaboration to the exceptional, unclassifiable book—*Goodnight Moon* can stand as representative; that along the way fantasy and realism, the particular and the general, even the near and the far—in distance, in time—ceased to exist as categories.

Consider *The Whiskers of Ho Ho.* The others (including, to an extent, *The Egg Tree*) devolve upon the Easter bunny as a kind of Santa Claus figure, and concern his —or her—efforts to deliver the eggs, much as countless stories have dealt with the vagaries of Santa's reindeer. The decorating of the eggs in *The Egg Tree* is of course local lore. William Littlefield, starting with the givens of eggs and bunny, imagines an old man in China with a tray of paints, a white hen with a long tail, a rabbit with pliant whiskers—all highly pictorial—and out of them makes a story of friendship, common effort, artistic creation and, almost incidentally, Easter.

It was Littlefield's only picturebook. Vladimir Bobri was a successful advertising artist whose first picturebook, Blossom Budney's *A Kiss Is Round* (Lothrop, 1954), was also one of the first in the abstract-concept line; and the facility that a Bobri and a Paul Rand (p. 338) had for conceptualizing—as against delineating, individuating—had much to do not only with the books' effectiveness but with their very feasibility. Though Bobri had several manners at his command, his work for Blossom Budney's *N Is for Nursery School,* Inez Rice's *The March Wind,* Charlotte Zolotow's *Sleepy Book* (all Lothrop, 1956, 1957, 1958) has in common the bright impersonality of most advertising art. In *The Whiskers of Ho Ho,* given a text whose title is the measure of its difference, he has the wisdom to draw pictures—lightly, loosely—rather than to design pages. This too is working positively with overlays, and it is worth mentioning that "every color you could imagine"—attributed to Kwang Fu's tray of paints—is suggested by the massing and varying, in density and pattern, of another fixed few. Moreover, printed in brown ink on ivory paper, the book has a manuscript mellowness. (One and one and one and one and one.)

The Easter Bunny That Overslept and *The Whiskers of Ho Ho* are Lothrop books, as are several of the others just mentioned. Beatrice Creighton came to Lothrop as juvenile editor in 1940, to remain until her retirement in 1967. In 1944 she published *One God: The Ways We Worship Him* by Florence Mary Fitch, designed—in the words of a reviewer—"to help children understand and respect religions different from their own";[9] integral, and indispensable, are the photographs "selected by Beatrice Creighton" which comprise more than half the book. As new and as sensitively articulated is Marion Downer's *Discovering Design* which came in 1947—an introduction to the elements of design as found first in nature, then in art. These, with the nature series that began with *Rain Drop Splash* (1946) and *White Snow Bright Snow* (1947), became in effect the flagships of the Lothrop list.

That in their wake followed the modest *Whiskers of Ho Ho,* or the imposing *A for the Ark,* seems entirely in order—as natural as *Ho Ho* itself springing, as the editor put it, from "the lovely tradition of dyeing eggs in bright colors to symbolize joy and good fortune."

NEW LOOKS

NICOLAS MORDVINOFF, PAUL RAND, ANTONIO FRASCONI, JOSEPH LOW, JULIET KEPES

Introducing Gyorgy Kepes's *Language of Vision* in 1944, S. I. Hayakawa wrote: "Something of the quality of a child's delight in playing with colors and shapes has to be restored to us before we learn to see again, before we unlearn the terms in which we ordinarily see." That "restoration of vision," he avers, "is what Mr. Kepes's 'grammar' of vision would accomplish . . . ." In the body of the book Kepes repeatedly groups—and illustrates—children's art, the work of 'primitive' tribes, early European paintings and those of the Far East as having one or another trait in common with the new nonrepresentational art. And that art, as we've had occasion to observe, found in the art of children "a more vital expression of reality"[1] than that achievable by an exact and complete literal rendering.

The 'new looks' are not several, to be set side by side, but related aspects of a new way of visualizing, of realizing forms in space, color as form. When they appeared in picturebooks in strength around 1950 they brought back to children, in effect, what children had given to the art that produced them; and the picturebooks, in turn, embodied qualities native to children's art.

Kepes's book, written toward the end of World War II, carries within it a prescription for a different, better postwar world, one in which design will have an integral role. That modern art be recognized as an intrinsic part of modern living—to paraphrase a 1949 Museum of Modern Art pamphlet—was a pervasive sentiment; that the barriers between pure and applied art be destroyed was a corollary. The functional, organic aesthetic, equivalent to the Bauhaus aesthetic, had arrived in force just prior to the war with the establishment by Moholy-Nagy of the Institute of Design, originally the 'New Bauhaus,' in Chicago, where Kepes had charge of the Light (advertising arts) Workshop; with the beginning of Josef and Anni Albers's teaching at Black Mountain College; with the coming also of Herbert Bayer, of Gropius, Breuer, Mies van der Rohe.

For some years—beginning in 1937, continuing, even increasing during the war—the Container Corporation of America commissioned full-page advertisements akin to posters from an array of artists; and these—the work of Kepes and Bayer, of Cassandre, Covarrubias, de Kooning, Leger, Leo Lionni, Paul Rand, Ben Shahn—were widely exhibited and much discussed and admired. The war ending, activity proliferated. In 1946 the Walker Art Center in Minneapolis began publication of *Everyday Art Quarterly* (later *Design Quarterly*); in 1949 the Museum of Modern Art played host to—and helped select—the annual exhibition of advertising and editorial art of the New York Art Directors Club; in 1952 and 1953 the *covers* of record albums were reviewed in the *New York Times*; in 1956 the Library of Congress displayed "Modern Art Influences on Printing Design"—for a scattered sampling.

World War II in picturebooks is a story of

toy-books and gimmicks, an occasional misplaced *Now Daddy's in the Army*, and life as usual; except for a war-bred infusion of European talent (Rojankovsky, the Reys, Gergely), there is no break in the continuity between, say, 1938 and 1949, and except for economics, no prewar and postwar. The new looks in picturebooks, however, were a postwar phenomenon, reflecting both the assimilation of modern art by modern design and the movement of individuals identified with modern design into what they viewed as an allied field. That there had existed no distinction between pure and applied art in picturebooks, that modernist art had long since found its way into the field independently, does not controvert the reality of what occurred.

NICOLAS MORDVINOFF

As far as picturebooks are concerned, Nicolas Mordvinoff burst upon the scene in 1950 as half of Will and Nicolas, creators of *The Two Reds*—"unusual," "uncommon," "remarkable," read whom you will. ("It takes great courage, for reasons too numerous and obvious to mention, [even] to name a children's book *The Two Reds*," Fritz Eichenberg wrote.[2]) There followed the next year *Finders Keepers*, less tight and true, more arbitrarily, exaggeratedly pictured, which won the Caldecott; and then year by year others by 'Will and Nicolas' which for various reasons—of text and illustration—failed to click. In the mid-Sixties Mordvinoff ceased doing illustration entirely and resumed his own painting and sculpture.

One of the many talented Russians uprooted by the Revolution, he had studied in Paris, then took up a peripatetic residence in the South Pacific. In Tahiti he met a writer, William Stone, who asked him to illustrate first one, then another book for young people; and one of the three they did together, *Pépé Was the Saddest Bird*, is half pictures and altogether a joy (399).

Pépé's cross is his halo. He had started as an egg with a band around it; as his mother tells him, somewhat testily, goodness was thrust upon him. And indeed Pépé, a curiosity to all the other myna birds on the island, has no opportunity to be bad; Mimi, islander Tané's cat, won't even chase him. Papa advises travel—as sometimes changing people—but a tour of the neighboring plantations on the back of Fati the pig, an outing popular with the myna birds, leaves him, though bruised, with his halo intact; and a desperate try at stunt-flying to shake it off, climaxing with an unintended plunge into Tané's palm roof, finds him chagrined but otherwise unchanged.

399. *Pépé Was the Saddest Bird,* by William Stone, illus. by Nicolas Mordvinoff. Knopf, 1944. Detail.

Tané and his wife Vahiné are quarreling—like myna birds—over a piece of paper (*Give me that money, you will only go and waste it . . . No, I earned it and I intend to spend it*) and while Pépé watches, it flutters to the floor. Unthinking, he swoops down and snaps it up—at last "acting exactly like any myna that ever lived"—and with a little pop! his halo is gone. When he lands in a crowd of his fellows, they snatch at the paper and Pépé yanks it back: "Nobody knew him from any other myna bird. Pépé hardly knew himself!"

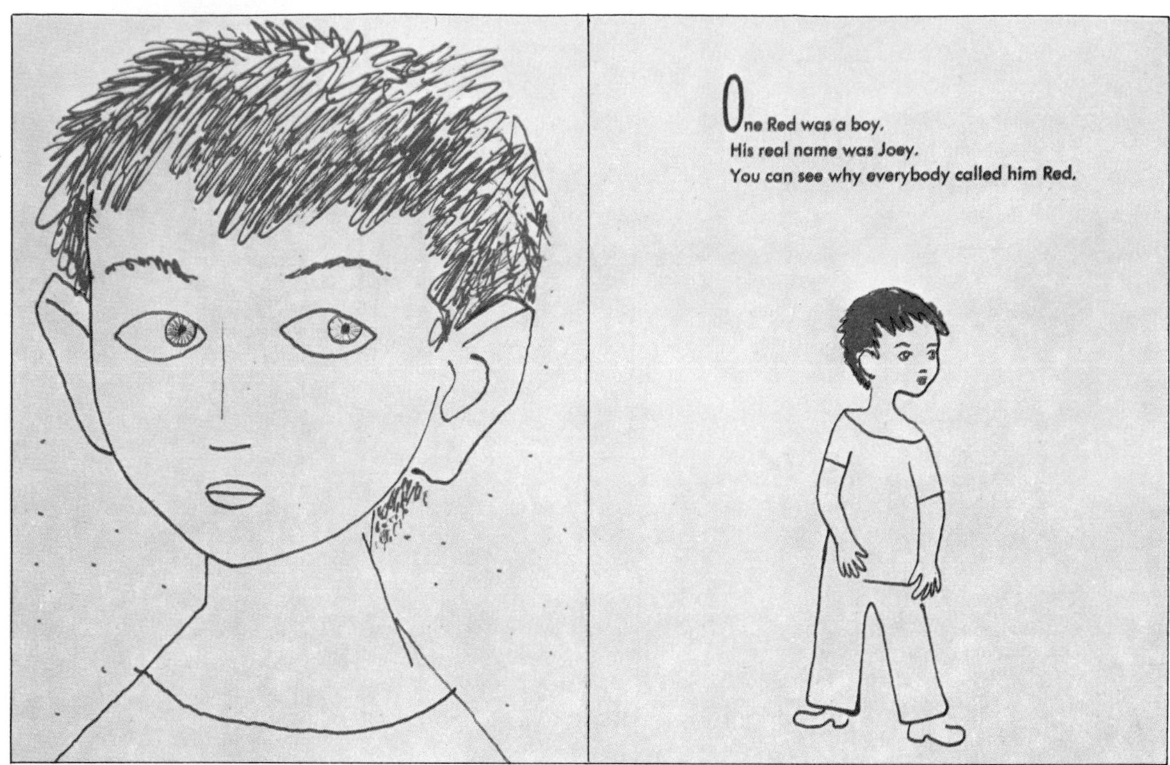

One Red was a boy.
His real name was Joey.
You can see why everybody called him Red.

400

400-403. *The Two Reds*, text by William Lipkind, pictures by Nicolas Mordvinoff. Harcourt, 1950. 8⅜ x 10¾.

The other Red was a cat.
His real name was known only to cats.
I think it was something like
Mr. Furpatto Purrcatto.

401

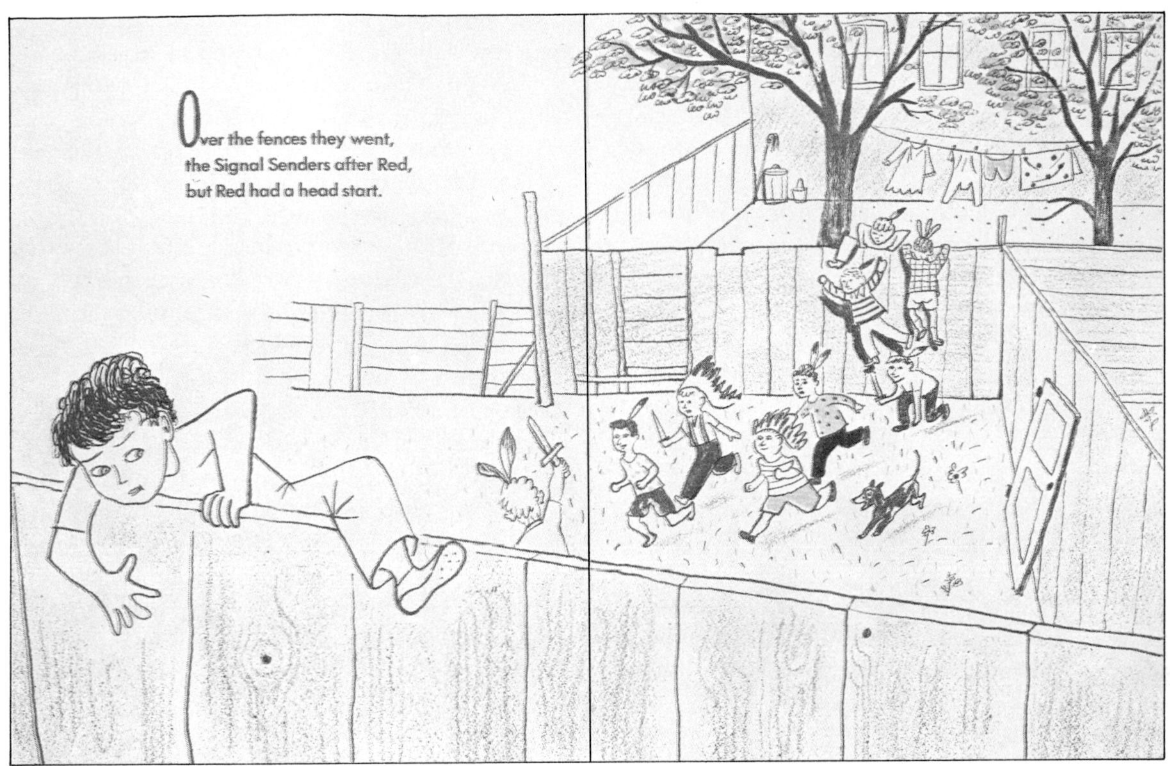
Over the fences they went,
the Signal Senders after Red,
but Red had a head start.

402

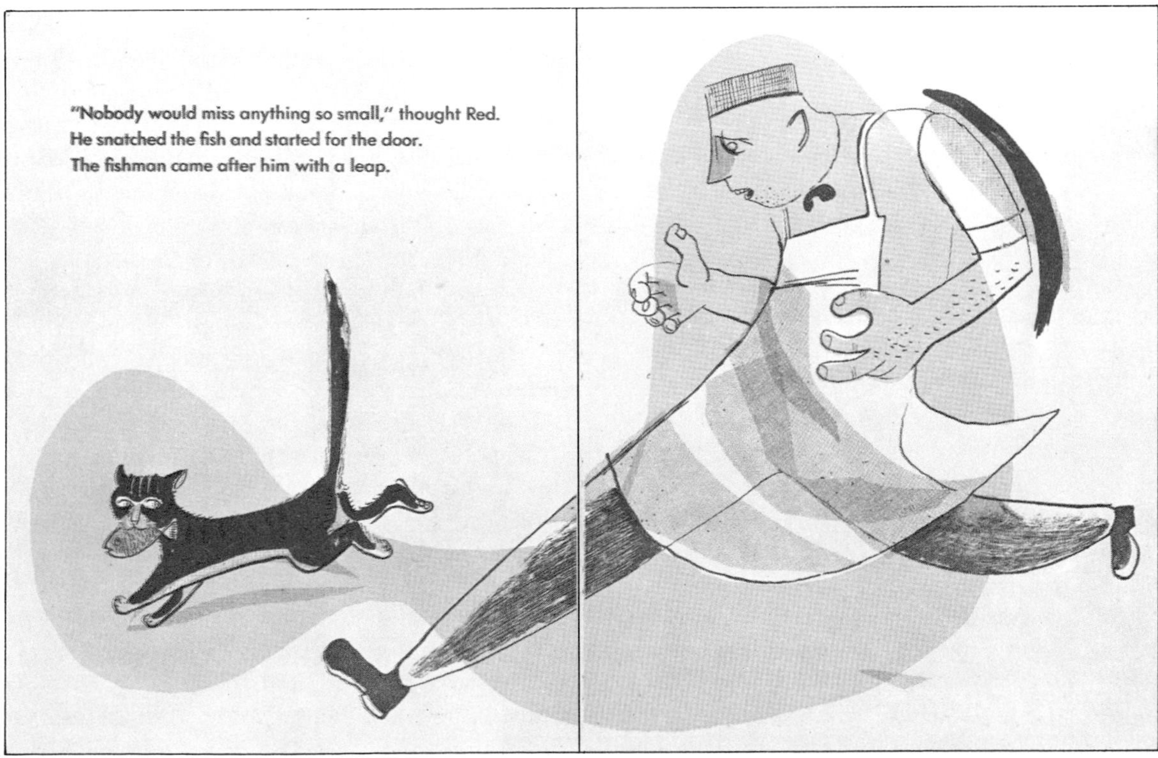
"Nobody would miss anything so small," thought Red.
He snatched the fish and started for the door.
The fishman came after him with a leap.

403

The story has an easy way about it, rather like Tané and Vahiné who, with the paper gone, kiss and make up ("it had not been very much money anyway"); and if it isn't necessarily for children, it isn't not. Mordvinoff illustrates it with a delicacy—of feeling as well as manner—that balances, blends amusement and sympathy; and his depictions of the island and the islanders, even, gloriously, of Fati the pig and his passengers, have a similar precise sensitivity. When he is not drawing with an open line, he is flecking in a sandhill, stroking in shadows, crisping a goat's curls like the etcher he was; the pictures are quite different one from another, and in telling a story that could easily have been reduced by pictures, they tell instead somewhat more.

On the basis of the books Mordvinoff came to the United States, exhibited in New York, took an apartment on St. Mark's Place—in the variegated, vivid, still pristine East Village—and took in William Lipkind, a writer friend, as a temporary boarder. Usually these stories add more color than light, but *The Two Reds*, which came of that particular residency, owes much of its uncommonness to being a projection of (what nobody called then) inner city life.

The two Reds are Red the boy (400) and Red the cat (401). They live on the same block but, we're told, they are not friends.

> They lived on St. Mark's Place, where three hundred different sounds of traffic might be rattling and rumbling in your ears at one time, making a tremendous roar like a waterfall.
> But in the backyards how quiet it was! Even the chirp of a single sparrow was a great noise.

On the street are pedestrians of all ages, shapes and conditions, vehicles ranging from pushcart and bike to bakery van and bus, buildings narrow and tall, curtained and shuttered, carved and plain; in the backyard, beginning the story that isn't in words, are Red the boy (plus a clothesline, garbage cans, bottles, a broken chair) and overhead in a tree, crouching, Red the cat. "The boy Red liked fish"—he has goldfish in a bowl on the window sill—"and the cat Red liked fish"—he is creeping down the fire escape—"but that's why they didn't like each other."

It's morning, a bright morning, when together but apart Red the boy goes out to play and Red the cat, hungry, sets out to look for food. A fruit wagon interests Red the boy, who'd like to ride the fruit wagon horse; "It all looks like food for horses," thinks the cat. Red calls to a pigeon to come, the cat tells the pigeon to just sit still, the pigeon flies to the top of a lamppost "without saying a word." They part when the cat smells fish, the boy smells fire, and each one follows his nose.

Peeping through the knothole in a fence, Red sees/"The Seventh Street Signal Senders," a gang of boys sporting Indian feathers, "getting ready to initiate a new member"/so up a ladder he goes to "a grandstand seat" on top of the fence;/but the Signal Senders spot him—"A spy, a spy!"/and the chase is on (402). At each of the five openings (the slashes mark the turn of the page) the excitement mounts—on a sudden red spread is "A spy, a spy!"—and then we switch to the fortunes of the cat who, "Meanwhile," has sniffed out a fish store/and in a flash, finds himself also pursued (403). Down one street races Red with the Signal Senders close behind, heading toward him around the corner comes the cat, Red tumbles over the cat, the fishman falls over Red, the Signal Senders come down in a heap on top of the fishman—"a melee . . . guaranteed to bring more laughs than the whacks in Punch & Judy."[3]

The two Reds get away quickly while the fishman chases the Signal Senders. They declare a truce—"Paws off my fish and friends?" "Prrk, prrk, goldfish are nothing but fins and scales anyhow"—and when last seen they are together, cat in lap, on the front steps.

The Two Reds is a small story, clearly plotted, that cannot be put in a nutshell; neither can it be told without reference to its own words or to what precisely is in its pictures. But it is not only a matter of story. "One Red was a boy. His real name was Joey.

You can see why everybody called him Red." "The other Red was a cat. His real name was known only to cats. I think it was something like Mr. Furpatto Purrcatto." The pairing, the parallels, the apposition in those two sets of short sentences; the good child-sense of Joey, given, and Mr. Furpatto Purrcatto, guessed; the direct address of "You can see," the also personal "I think"—simple as it is, inconsequential, immaterial, it is a crafty piece of business.

"It reaches out and pulls your eyes right to the page," said the AIGA jury,[4] which might have been speaking, to start with, of that pensive Picasso boy, that supercharged Klee cat (400, 401). Along with the inspired image making and smashing color, there is sheer illustration (402); and some spreads that artify (my coinage) the better to illustrate (403). If we dissect that last, there are as usual the gray of the text type and the outline drawing plus; the yellow that backs, that binds and divides cat and pursuer, and penetrates both; the red of the cat and the closing, advancing curve, and the Bendayed red, clearly visible as such, overlaid upon itself for shadow and pattern, on white for pink, on yellow for orange: a composition that has the force of a blow and a subtle, equivocal structure—a structure that the viewer assembles into a picture.

The picture, the composition is concentrated because there are only two visual units that the yellow, an abstract organic form, resolves into one; as an organic form it is free-flowing; here, liquid-like, it flows from larger into smaller area; in flowing it sets up movement. But as the various forms interpenetrate—the outline of the fishman is seen through his apron, the yellow overlays and underlies him—spatial relations fluctuate and another order of movement is set up, on the picture surface. And the two, the one in the flow of the lines, the other in the receding and advancing forms, exist in open space where the eye is encouraged, even required to move with them. The viewer experiences the picture—actively—by participating in it.

The Two Reds, done in two and three colors,

404. *Alphonse That Bearded One,* by Natalie Savage Carlson, illus. by Nicolas Mordvinoff. Harcourt, 1954. 6⅜ x 8⅛.

is a benchmark among books done by overlays, by acetate separations; and its particular attributes owe as much to the nature of the printing process as to the aesthetics and devices of modernist art. Indeed, the affinity between the two is fundamental to modern advertising art, as we shall see further. But it was not alone, *Petunia* appeared the same year; and in *Petunia* as well we see the brilliant flat printing inks, the positive use of Ben Day tints and in particular of transparency (177, 178). We have spoken of the loose casual liveliness that comes of letting contours and colors overlap; we might say more specifically that in their overlapping is set up, too, some of the surface movement so pronounced in Mordvinoff. And point out also that it is the movement of the eye following Petunia's head that creates the directional movement, spatial and temporal, of that one extraordinary spread.

Mordvinoff followed Duvoisin as the illustrator of the second of Natalie Savage Carlson's books of French Canadian tales, this one a single story, *Alphonse That Bearded One*. Alphonse, trained "to march to the beat of a drum, to shoulder a gun and to handle the sword well," is sent by his 'brother' (who himself pleads infirmity) as a soldier—though Corporal Pagot and his sidekick Genest have their doubts (404). But there is more to a trained bear than they can imagine, and Alphonse, performing an Indian war dance, is the saving of the day. It's a sly, hilariously funny story and Mordvinoff, whether looking like Duvoisin or quite like himself, makes light work of Alphonse (and some other bears), of the French and the Indians.

Something of the same spirit prevails in his treatment of the *Just So Stories* (Garden City, 1952); later books are less pointed, less buoyant. His was a brief ascendancy, but auspicious.

PAUL RAND

"In advertising, the contemporary approach to art is based on a simple concept, a concept of the advertisement as an organic and functional unit, each element of which is integrally related to the others, in harmony with the whole, and essential to the execution of the idea."

Paul Rand, *Thoughts on Design*, 1947

"On the surface they have appeared disarmingly simple, almost childlike, using easy, everyday selling phrases and puns, illustrated with gay, animated animals, birds, fish, abstracted in form so that every meaningless line is blanked out."

Eugene Ettenberg on the Rand Ohrbach ads, *American Artist*, October 1953

To put in evidence next *I Know a Lot of Things* (1956) and *Sparkle and Spin* (1957) would be akin to dropping the other shoe; but in fact *I Know a Lot of Things* is "For Catherine," age three, via Margaret McElderry at Harcourt. The correspondence existed, the books came about.

Paul Rand was the model of the modern designer/art director, one of the first of a new breed on the American scene. For students of graphic design there was Kauffer; from France Cassandre, from Germany Bayer; and then there was Paul Rand. Almost from his appearance as art director of *Esquire* in 1936 his work was reproduced and displayed, analyzed, imitated. Throughout the war he did covers for *Direction* magazine that are eloquent still (foremost: the barbed wire cross that says Merry Christmas, 1940); his patchwork steed for Stafford fabrics, his animated brandy snifter for Coronet —and snifter-headed waiter with the same sublime smile—stand forth as individual figures and identities; his book jackets, and especially in the Fifties his covers for the new 'quality' paperbacks, give pause even as they catch the eye. Humorously or trenchantly, Rand speaks in symbols.

It would be good, thus, to pass directly to *Sparkle and Spin: A Book About Words*, which more than the picturebooks per se is a natural extension, even an exemplification of Rand's way of working. But first there was, also with his wife Ann, *I Know a Lot of Things*, the sort of book that has more to do with how adults think about children than with what children think, or what they know.

"I know when I look in a mirror what I see is me," is fair enough, and "I know a cat goes meow"; but though "a dog goes bowwow and that is how they talk," the Dalmatian's spots dancing over the page are disconcerting, and it's just not so, today, that "Of course I know a horse can pull a wagon full of wood." Nor, without being told, would a youngster necessarily know that that green-blinkered, potato-bodied creature was a horse or that those white spheres ringed with black, log-ends, represent a load of wood. When a child devises formula figures (often identical for dog or cat or horse), when he schematizes generally, he is drawing for himself; if an artist, in emulation, adopts a scheme or a perspective that is not representative (however unrepresentational), he fails to communicate. A different failure of communication is the kerosene lamp with a happy new-moon grin—"the moon is a light for the night"—which, whatever its nostalgic charm, might as

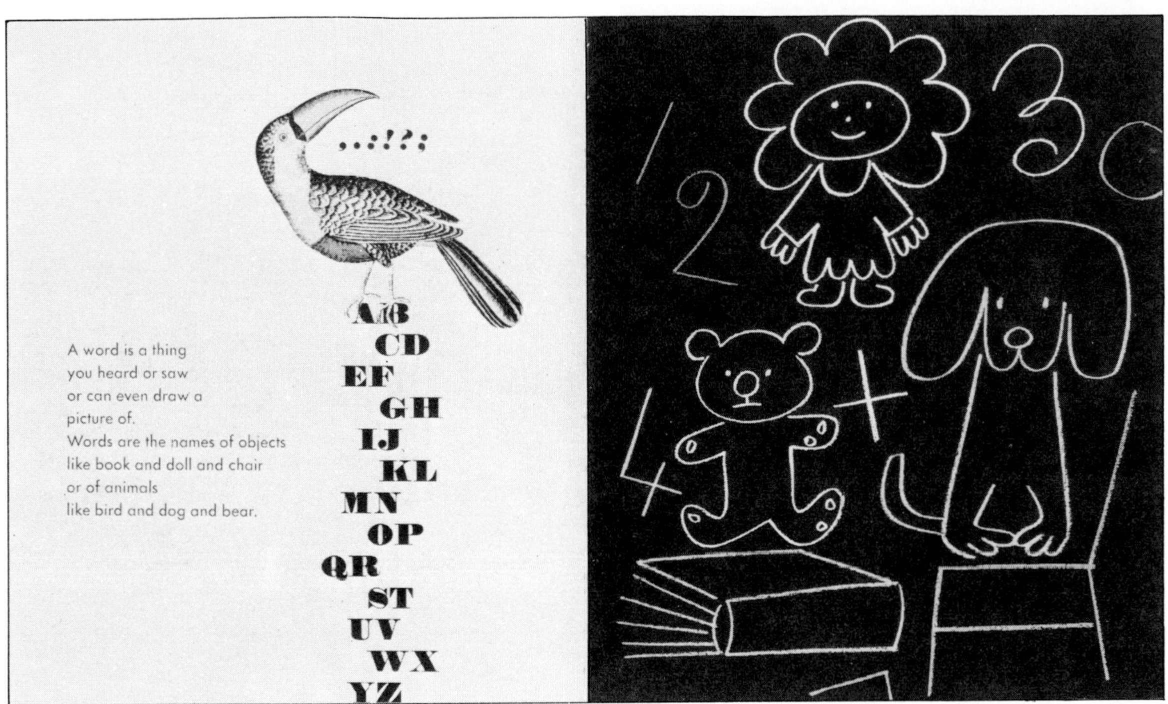

A word is a thing
you heard or saw
or can even draw a

Words are the names of objects
like book and doll and chair
or of animals
like bird and dog and bear.

405

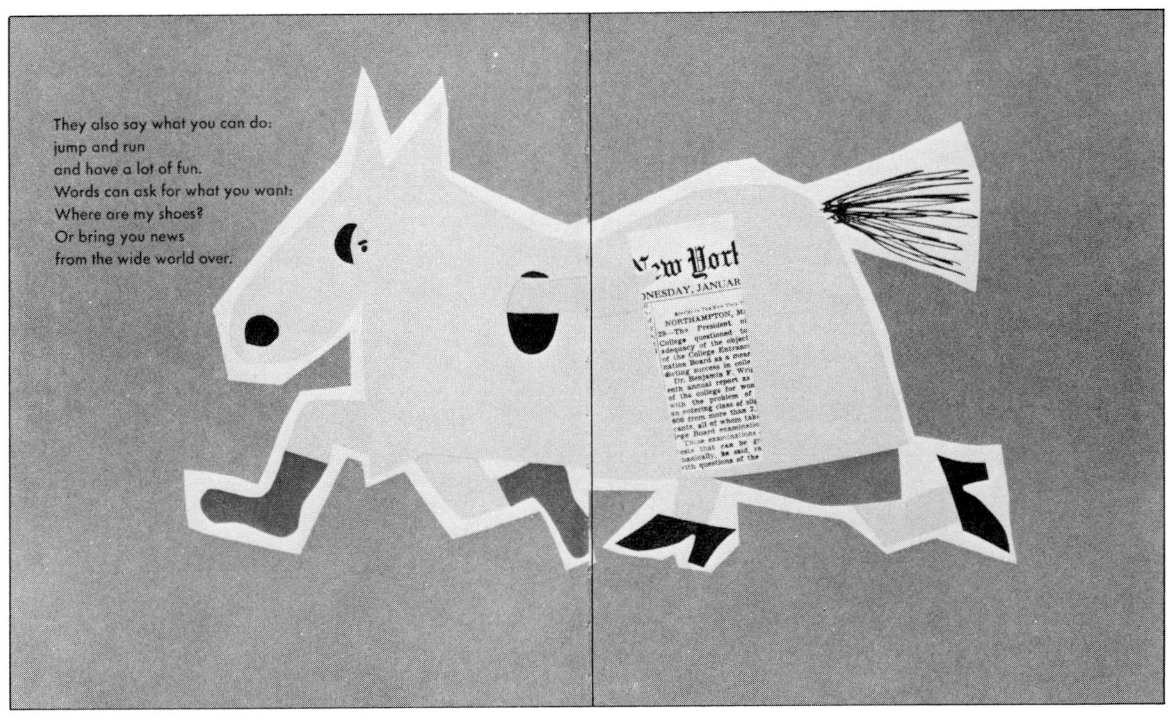

They also say what you can do:
jump and run
and have a lot of fun.
Words can ask for what you want:
Where are my shoes?
Or bring you news
from the wide world over.

406

405, 406. *Sparkle and Spin,* text by Ann Rand, pictures by Paul Rand. Harcourt, 1957. 8¼ x 10.

well be an incense burner for all that its silhouette says to most children.

As if Rand realized, *Sparkle and Spin* is free even of sophisticated off-shades: when it's bright, it's RED.

What the book is after, loosely, is to illustrate the capacities and qualities of words; what it conveys are the capacities and qualities of pictures. And that too is an adult formulation, for it is their playfulness that is the abiding pleasure, the way they can be different things at once. Not that a pair of pears are hares (before you can read, who cares?) but that drawing ears on a pear produces a rabbit, that the shape of a pear, reversed, is the body of a rabbit (408). Not onomatopoeia, spontaneously understood, but a train leaving a trail of TOOT TOOT TOOTS, the Os smoke rings in the sky (407).

The image of two children masquerading as a horse, running, jumping, wearing big shoes, bringing the news, is a clever integration of unrelated, uninteresting words (406); and because of that scrap of newspaper out of nowhere, crazy, the way kids like. So too the peculiar puzzled bird perched atop the alphabet and, one, two, three—the bird in the round, an old engraving, the extra-flat formal letters, the casual figures chalked on the blackboard (405). Everything is itself and, by its character, origin, identity, by the form it takes, something else besides; and because each 'something else' is different, we cannot merge objects into a uniform image: were all chalked, that is, or all cut-outs, we would see them as one.

This of course is the nature of collage or more properly construction (we will go into the distinction later), that it will not be neutral, stable, will not sit quietly on the page as a picture. In the most obvious instance (405), the solid black page filled with a child's drawings must remain a blackboard; the bird, thinking : ! ?, gripping the top letters, remains a palpable alien presence—animated taxidermy; and the letters cannot be only the alphabet or, alternatively, only a supporting column. The cut-out horse is as it were cut

407, 408. *Sparkle and Spin,* text by Ann Rand, pictures by Paul Rand. Harcourt, 1957. 8¼ x 10.

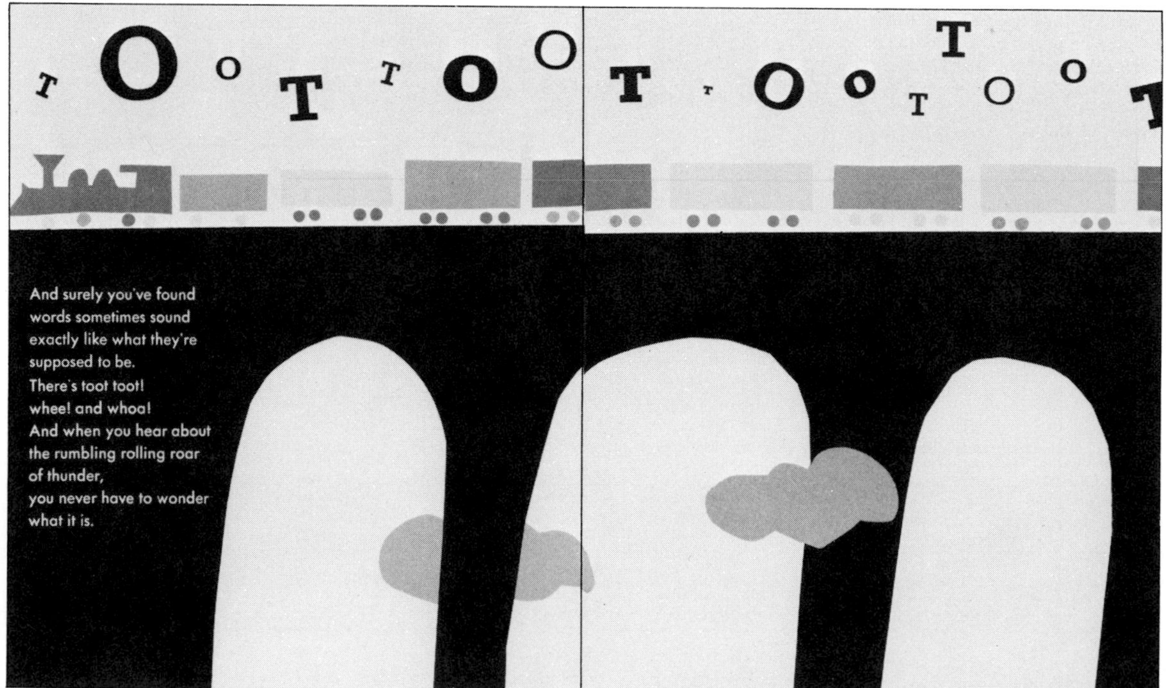

And surely you've found
words sometimes sound
exactly like what they're
supposed to be.
There's toot toot!
whee! and whoa!
And when you hear about
the rumbling rolling roar
of thunder,
you never have to wonder
what it is.

407

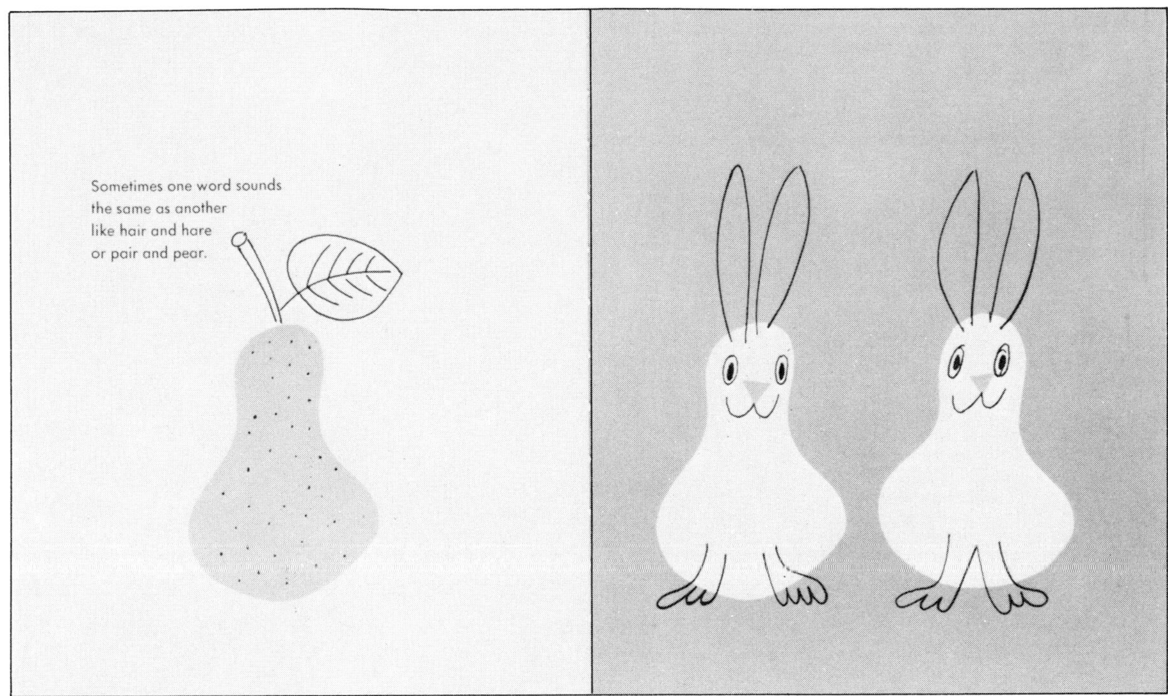

Sometimes one word sounds
the same as another
like hair and hare
or pair and pear.

408

out of—or escaped from—the page, his stringy tail (itself an improvisation) also a scribble; and we have, in addition, a question of what is level with what, of advancing and receding planes on a very flat surface (406). Emphatically flat too is the viaduct, and with the toy train—red, yellow and blue—openly unreal (407); but drifting behind, between, before are nonchalant clouds.

The clown/jester/juggler, my pick of the pack (409), exists more nearly on the picture surface but the composition remains taut, like the tops delicately balanced; and all-of-a-piece though it appears to be, the sparkle is in his eye, the spin an illusion of the stripes. When the wonder of a clown spinning a top on his nose wears off (a little), the tops continue to turn and to vibrate in space.

Rand provided surprises, and he kept them alive. He'd been inspired, he said of a blithe UN poster, by children's art "with its incomparable spontaneity." Much of his poster design, and most of his work for children, is done more or less in the manner of a child, and out of that manner he made a new style—a situation different from that of the artist who absorbs something of child art into his own, as outreach is from introspection. Out of that manner and out of construction, real or simulated—cut-paper, scribbles, patterns, cut pictures. He was not the only one in and out of picturebooks to do so, though what they may owe to his example is unassessable. It was a way of freely associating, freshly integrating diverse object-facts into a single simultaneous event; and it furthered the elucidation of concepts.

Drawing a face on a pear, moreover, is like putting a mustache on a subway poster, not just a transformation but a gesture; a scrap of newspaper or, elsewhere, a specimen shell, is a fragment of the real world. Braque (whose father was a house-painter) and then Picasso, Juan Gris, introduced such fragments into their abstract compositions to assert, paradoxically, the reality of the painted surface; in advertising—a bona fide bottle of brandy on the Coronet waiter's tray—they emphasize the real object that is the product; in a picturebook they have, with the hand-drawing, the magic of an actual presence—on the printed page. Smooth, even printing

Some words are gay and bri
and full of light
like tinsel and silver
and sparkle and spin,
while lurk and murk
or moan and groan
are just as dark as night.

409. *Sparkle and Spin,* text by Ann Rand, pictures by Paul Rand. Harcourt, 1957. 8¼ x 10.

and in contrast, a sweep of the hand, a scissor-cut, a tangible specimen.

As Cubism contributed the collage element, and Surrealism gave it meaning (exploited variously by advertising), the flat, even painting of de Stijl—Mondrian, Doesburg—and its adherence to a few pure colors entered in also. Where painters strove to efface any sign of brushwork and deliberately reduced the number of their colors, the one was natural in printing, the other an advantage, particularly in printing by other than full-color process; and in picturebooks, the results could be telling, viz. the brilliant orange and blue sheets that constitute the end papers of *I Know a Lot of Things.* But a mode that is mechanical can be all the more charged with life by evidence of handwork, of improvisation, as the designers discovered and, in books, photo-offset facilitated.

An original drawing is in its nature drawn, in conjunction with a flat rectilinear form it is assertively a drawing; printed thus, a thumbprint, in effect, on the page. And if it is a child's drawing or in keeping with a child's impulse, additionally spontaneous by association, additionally, essentially unbookish. The approach is susceptible of abuse; Rand, it is worth noting, uses it with extreme selectivity, for natural gestures, additions, improvisations. Shells are 'pasted' at random on a mound of sand; but this is Rand—a boy is buried underneath.

The Rands did two further picturebooks, *Little 1* and *Listen! Listen!* (both Harcourt, 1962 and 1970), neither as clear-cut, as forthright—as almost anything—as *Sparkle and Spin.* The texts are weak in all: *Sparkle and Spin* succeeds because the pictures have a life of their own.

ANTONIO FRASCONI

Concurrent with the new attention to graphic design was a revival of interest in the traditional graphic arts, in the print—no longer the small cabinet or portfolio print for a collector's perusal but the large color print to be mounted and hung. In this movement Antonio Frasconi had a role somewhat analogous to Paul Rand's: more than the experimental engravings spawned by Atelier 17, set up by Stanley William Hayter in New York in 1940, or, from 1945, the related work of Mauricio Lasansky and his group at Iowa, Frasconi's woodcuts were accessible, articulate, popular. Strong of design and strong of statement, they appeared everywhere in the Fifties, in exhibition and reproduction; and also on Christmas cards, on paperback, magazine and record album covers, in editorial matter; and in books of his own devising—Lorca, Whitman, Aesop, the unique *Book of Many Suns.*

If his work was consciously "in the tradition of Posada,"[5] his woodcuts, as such, harked back to Munch and Gauguin in strong direct cutting, in exposing to advantage the texture and pattern of the plank. The honest, rugged look, the surface that seems alive, had much to do with Frasconi's broad appeal (410); and countless artists and illustrators were seduced by the grain of the plank.

One can know him, if not fully, as well by his work for children as otherwise. Presenting *A Book of Many Suns* in *Graphis,* Manuel Gasser speculates that "the ubiquitous sun in Frasconi's art is to be interpreted as a mark of his attachment to childhood and the child's world. For the first thing any child draws when it sits down to project its inner world on to paper is the sun. And when it has reached the age of its first landscapes, the sun again is the one thing that will never be left out of the picture."[6] Be that as it may (Gasser goes on to infer the children's books), Frasconi is attached, as well, to the personified wind, the gesturing hand, a host of popular symbols; and sun, corn, cock, basilica,

410. *See and Say,* by Antonio Frasconi. Harcourt, 1955. 8⅜ x 10¼.

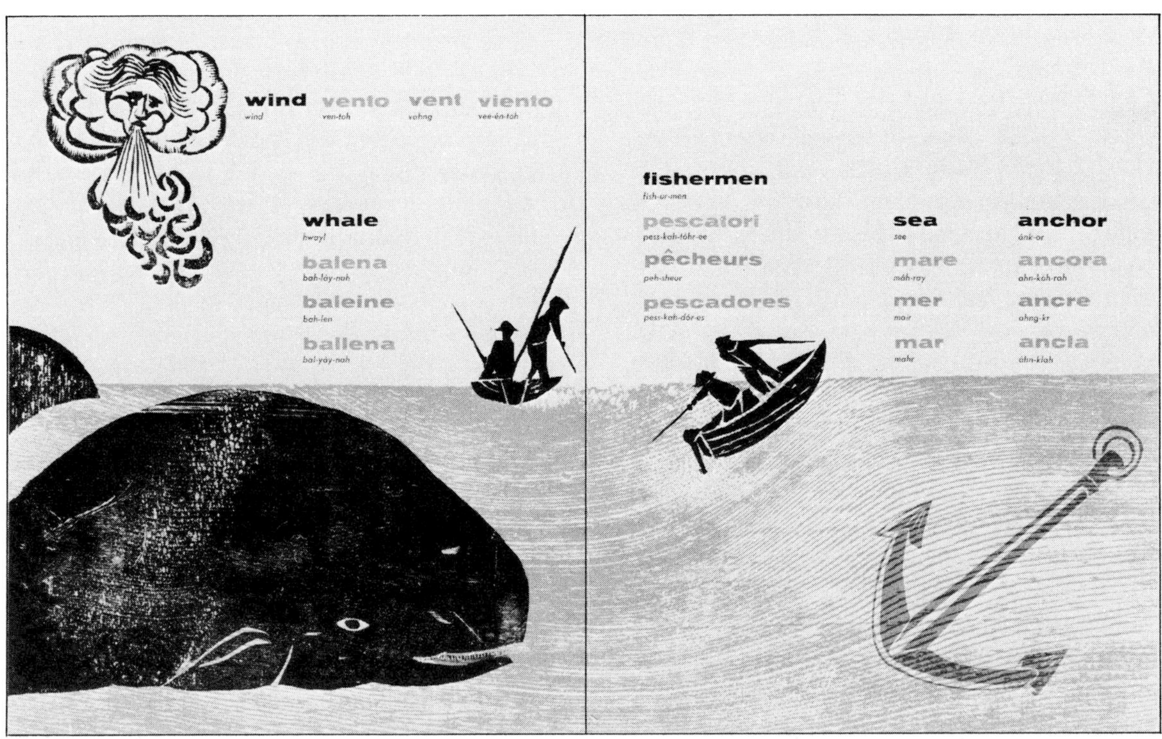

his work is never childlike, it is always his own.

No less to be counted in is what another critic called—before *See and Say* and the others appeared—"Frasconi's Brio With a Book": "Frasconi has cherished books and printing since his boyhood in Montevideo . . . where he took his first job, at twelve, as a printer's apprentice. A richly self-educated man, he has sought to pass on his feeling for books to his two young sons . . . . For Pablo [the elder, "named after the artist's idol, Picasso"], Frasconi has made by hand a series of unique books—there is but one copy of each—picturing for the boy the natural world which the artist observes so scrupulously and renders so freshly."[7] As illustrated, they range from a bestiary—whose images reappear in *See and Say*—to an assemblage of acrobats, both fold-outs, and a lacy page of Hydrox cookie imprints, part of a volume printed entirely from crackers.

The story of *See and Say* itself, "A Picture Book in Four Languages," was told by Margaret McElderry in *Print*:

"In retrospect, it seems inevitable that Antonio Frasconi's first book for children should be a picture book in four languages. But in the beginning, when we first discussed the possibilities, we had little idea of what might evolve. All we were certain of was that Antonio felt great enthusiasm and interest in doing something for children . . . . Naturally, Antonio's small son Pablo was uppermost in his father's thoughts, but also Antonio looked back into his own childhood and later experiences, searching for just the right idea. Since Antonio was brought up in an Italian-speaking family in Uruguay, where Spanish is the language used in the schools, and then later began to study English preparatory to coming to the United States, he is more aware than many of the importance of languages. Therefore, to give a small child a sense of other ways of speaking, the knowledge that there is more than one language in our world, seems of utmost importance to him . . . .

"That is—the idea for it. And then followed the hard work and the fun that are part of making a picture book. We made long lists of objects that interest children and with which they are generally familiar. From these Antonio made a selection, representing the greatest variety and offering him the most pictorial possibilities. Putting all his energies and time into the project, he then made his woodcuts. In turn, some of these were discarded or changed as we went over them together and substitutions were made.

"Meanwhile, we were working on the words in four languages and a simple pronunciation guide. A preliminary color proof of a double-spread had been run by the printer, Kellogg and Bulkeley, who by this time were greatly interested in the technical problems of preparing copy from wood blocks for offset printing. When the words were ready, we made a second color proof and included all the type. Since each language is printed in a different color—black for English, blue for Italian, red for French, and green for Spanish—the words are an important part of the over-all page design and layout, and it was essential for Antonio to have the type in color to dummy up the book.

"He prepared an exact—and most beautiful—dummy and when this was finally as he wanted it, he began the arduous work of making color separations for the printer. He pulled a proof of each block for each color on rice paper which was then mounted on acetate—four sheets for each book page, in exact register. Color proof for the entire book, which came next, showed Antonio just where certain changes were necessary. The decision was reached to lighten the colors a trifle and to apply the ink sparingly so that the quality of the woodcuts would be preserved. All of this was worked out closely with the printer—and when the final run was off press, we had a book which pleased the artist, the publisher, and now we hope the public."[8]

It definitely pleased *Print*, which procured four pages as an insert, and hardly a book on illustration has appeared since without something from it, usually the mighty murmurous whale (410).

One selects it because of its power as a

Christmas tree
Kris-mus tree
albero di Natale
áhl-bay-roh dee Nah-táh-lay
arbre de Noël
ahr-br duh Noh-el
árbol de Navidad
ahr-bóhl day nah-vee-dahd
tomato
to-máh-toh
pomodoro
poh-moh-doh-roh
tomate
toh-máht
tomate
toh-máh-tay
cake
kayk
torta
tohr-tah
gâteau
ga-toh
torta
tohr-tah

fly
fly
mosca
mos-kah
mouche
moo-sh
mosca
mos-kah
peas
peez
piselli
pee-zél-lee
pois
pwah
guisantes
ghee-sán-tays
dog
dawg
cane
káh-nay
chien
sh'eyng
perro
pér-oh

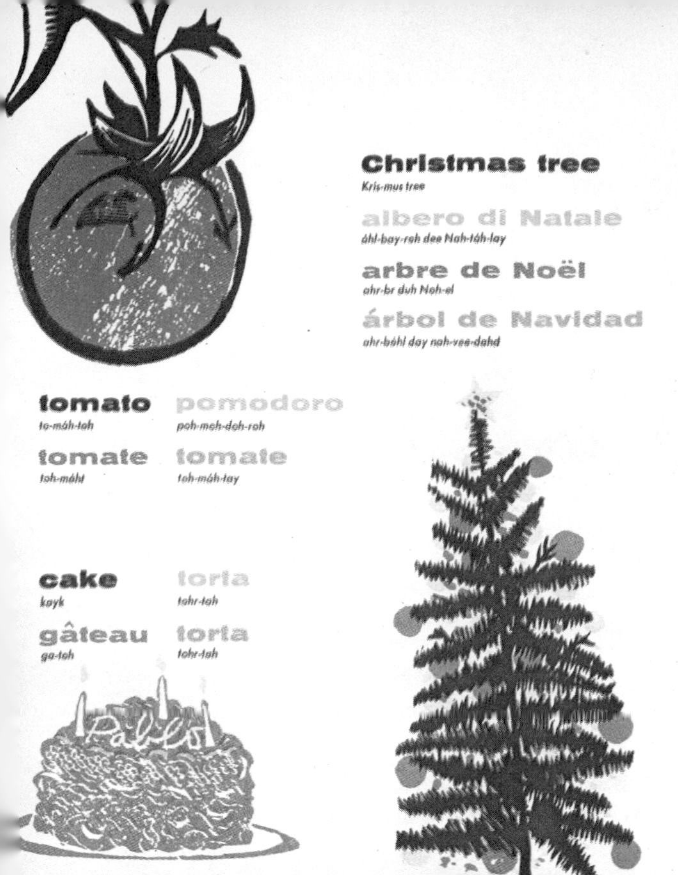

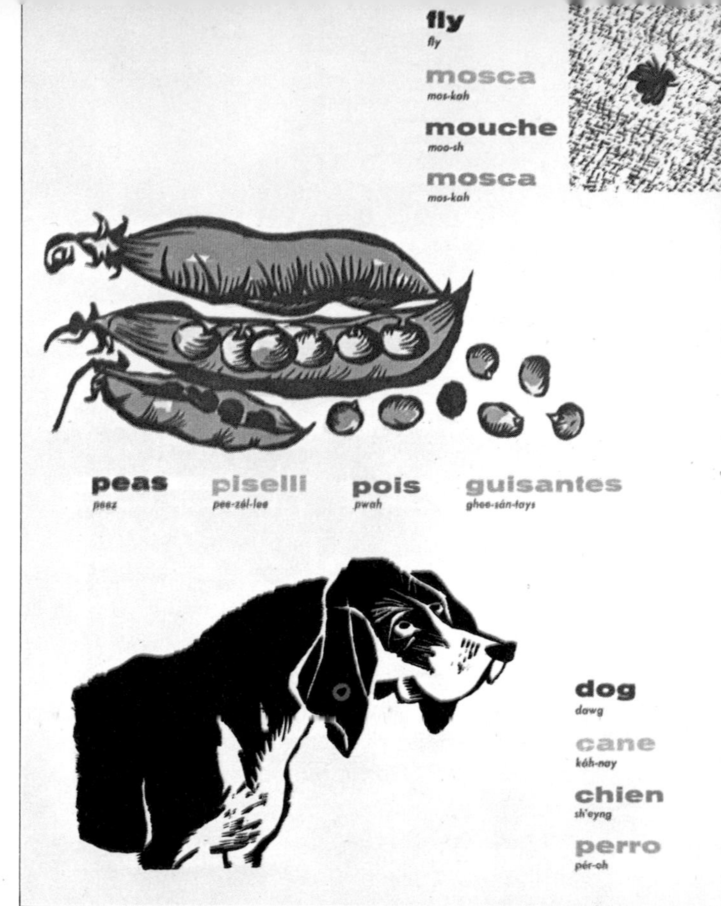

411

411, 412. *See and Say,* by Antonio Frasconi. Harcourt, 1955. 8⅜ x 10¼.

412

413. *The House That Jack Built,* pictures by Antonio Frasconi. Harcourt, 1958. 7⅞ x 10¼.

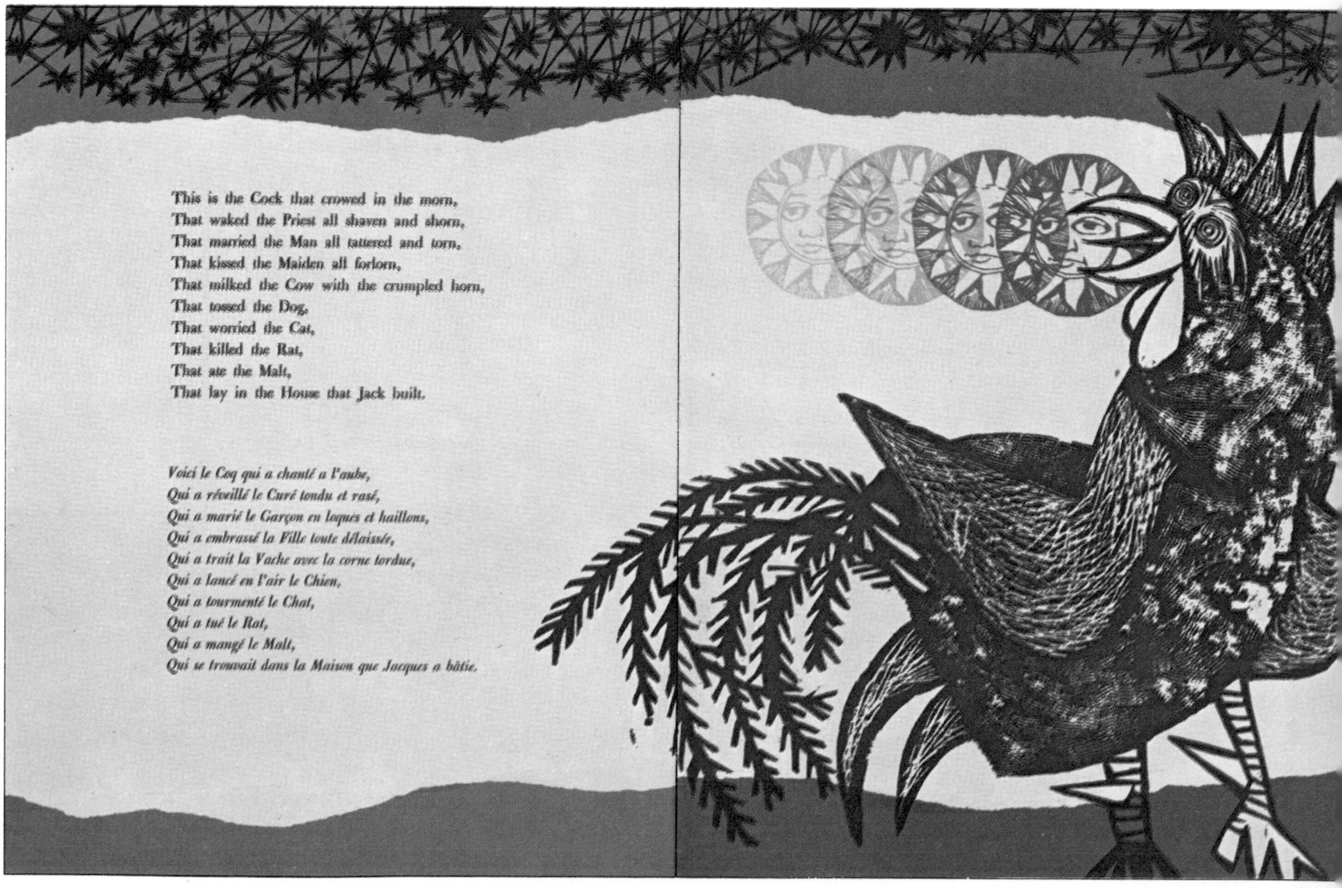

This is the Cock that crowed in the morn,
That waked the Priest all shaven and shorn,
That married the Man all tattered and torn,
That kissed the Maiden all forlorn,
That milked the Cow with the crumpled horn,
That tossed the Dog,
That worried the Cat,
That killed the Rat,
That ate the Malt,
That lay in the House that Jack built.
Voici le Coq qui a chanté a l'aube,
Qui a réveillé le Curé tondu et rasé,
Qui a marié le Garçon en loques et haillons,
Qui a embrassé la Fille toute délaissée,
Qui a trait la Vache avec la corne tordue,
Qui a lancé en l'air le Chien,
Qui a tourmenté le Chat,
Qui a tué le Rat,
Qui a mangé le Malt,
Qui se trouvait dans la Maison que Jacques a bâtie.

413

composition, because it is in fact the one double-spread designed as a unit; and it calls to mind the seductive fishermen-and-pier prints, crisscrossed with nets—printed from netting affixed to the block—of that same period. Otherwise the pages, the spreads, are composites, extraordinarily various and entirely simple (411, 412). To get a variety of effects, Frasconi was in the habit of cutting several blocks and printing them together as a single composition; and he has often dealt in separate motifs—a small accordion-fold volume, aptly called *Kaleidoscope*, is a collection of such motifs, not unlike an Eames "House of Cards," but meaningful. *See and Say*, one has to remember, is in essence a dictionary; for a very small child it is a book of pictures; and for each, for anyone, a collection of independently interesting, separately conceived *felt* images—rather as if Comenius's *Orbis Pictus*, that first pictured Latin vocabulary, had been illustrated (granting much) by a local Dürer. It is light, and at the same time intense; folk-print popular, and individual.

The House That Jack Built swings toward intensity and individuality (413). The chicken that is a chicken in *See and Say* is, as "the Cock that crowed in the morn," a specter; the coloring is highly schematized and though vivid, somehow cold—even in the spread pictured, the brightest in the book; there is a great, great deal of technique in evidence and often it overloads the simple image. Compelling as the pictures are, the book isn't something to be fond of, it isn't fun; and "The House That Jack Built" is after all a sort of game. Better a single sheet, broadside or book-page, with a small Frasconi emblem at the start of each new verse.

There have been others too—*The Snow and the Sun* (1961), *See Again, Say Again* (1964, both Harcourt)—without the graphic simplicity or frank joyousness of *See and Say*. Frasconi's resounding picturebook of more recent years is rather the suite of woodcuts that, set to poems and parts of poems by Melville, constitutes *On the Slain Collegians* (1971). In the life of an artist there may be a time for children, and a time that is not.

My father works in a store in this **block.**

What are you able to build with your
Castles and palaces, temples and docks.
Rain may keep raining and others go r
But I can be happy and building at h

We play with **blocks** like these.

414. *The Rainbow Dictionary*, by Wendell W. Wright, illus. by Joseph Low. Cleveland, World, 1947. Detail.

JOSEPH LOW

Joseph Low, artist, printer—artist-printer—was teaching at Indiana University; Wendell Wright, dean of the School of Education, compiled a dictionary for preschoolers; World, nearby in Cleveland, was to publish it; Abe Lerner, formerly of Viking, was art director; and *The Rainbow Dictionary*—"not only a picture book . . . but a series of gay little stories in which the word is given its various meanings"[9]—was illustrated by Joseph Low (414). Indeed, Low shared top billing with the compiler, and it is his little, and larger, four-color drawings, as neat and crisp, as 'meet,' as chapbook cuts, that give the massive book its vitality.

On the basis of the commission Low moved East, set up a hand-press, and announced his presence.

"Joseph Low came in the mail one morning in an unassuming envelope containing what used to be termed a 'plain brown wrapper,' and in that, the card shown below [415]. It was a dreary, gray March day, and my delight in that first mailing piece was enormous. At the time I was art director of the publishers, William Morrow & Co., and for more than a year one of my duties had been to see the artists who wished to make book-jackets or illustrations for the firm. While some of the work had been good, much of it had been mediocre. This one piece, though, gave promise of something too seldom seen—highly original creative commercial art of a strong individual character. So, following the advice of Low's charming poodle, I dropped him a card and, as advertised, he brought his portfolio in for me to see . . . .

"Aside from the general gaiety and wit of the work, two things immediately struck my eye. First, illustration and type were beautifully wed in work that clearly and primarily was designed for printing. Secondly, it was the work of a man on whom the folk-arts have had an enormous influence . . . . Equally obvious is the fact that Low has fused this material into the creation of work that has the quality of timelessness—that is paradoxically traditional yet modern, and also unmistakably his own. Through almost all of it there runs the feeling of the clear, crisp, wood-cut line. To a large degree, I think, this accounts for the vivid brilliance of his drawings. Color seems to play a secondary role. Line, almost incredibly crisp and sharp, comes first. Line—and mass—then color . . . ."[10]

Thus Frank Lieberman; now Henry Pitz:

"The key designs for these mailing pieces are cut on battleship linoleum (Low now likes this material better than wood). They are locked in with the type and usually printed in black on some fine paper stock. Then the colors (usually three or four) are stenciled by hand.

"The areas for each color are cut out of heavy cellophane which is mounted on a heavy cardboard mat. The mat, with its cellophane window, is then hinged with Scotch tape to a cardboard base and paper guides are pasted on the base so that when the paper is placed against them and the frame lowered, the stencil openings will be in exact register. Low uses watercolors, usually the more transparent hues, and brushes them on with a fine-haired Japanese stencil brush. Variations of color and brush textures are possible."[11]

The mailing pieces, as Pitz remarks, did their job; and Low was soon busy with work for advertisers, magazines, publishers—on his jackets and record album covers, using color prominently. "And splendid color it is, for Low has a very special color sense. He is able to put together unusual combinations of flat color and, by cunning overprinting and running a restless pattern of one color through another, is able to call up subtle overtones."[12] He illustrated, in black and white, Milton Rugoff's *Harvest of World Folk Tales* (Viking, 1949), a capital bedside-shipboard plus fireside collection, proof that folklore isn't only for babes nor, as David Bland noted, "light-hearted fantastic drawing";[13] and, for children specifically, *Mother Goose Riddle Rhymes* (Harcourt, 1953), in the manner of the mailing pieces too, but bright with color.

Mother Goose Riddle Rhymes, a rebus or hieroglyphic Mother Goose, has every virtue except an appeal to its intended audience. Quite possibly an idea whose time is past (few children know the rhymes well enough to pick up the pictorial clues), it has, as an entity, a witty sparkle—style, charm—but it

415. Mailing piece, by Joseph Low. c. 1948. 6½ x 8.

I am His Highness' Dog at Kew;
Pray tell me, sir, whose dog are you?

I am the dog of JOSEPH LOW who makes some of the nicest designs, illustrations, drawings, &c. you have ever seen. Or have you? He'll be glad to show you samples any time you drop him a card at Box 778, Morristown, N. J., or phone Morristown 4-4816J.

416

417 **416, 417.** *Smiling Duke*, by Joseph Low. Boston, Houghton Mifflin, 1963. 10⅝ x 8⅜.

exists in a near-vacuum, a quaint exercise in a strange idiom. Leo Lionni was to point out that the revival of old woodcuts and engravings was a danger, a crutch "in less skillful hands," a temptation to "less original talents."[14] Low himself did not rest there. But the key drawing remained an armature and the patches of chosen color here and there—originally stenciled, as in the chapbooks and broadsides whence they derived, subsequently printed from (tissue) separations—continued as a counterpoint, ever more independent of outline. While their carefully casual placement might be regarded, on sight, as a variant of the overlapping we have observed before, its basis was different and it resulted in a radical alteration, the color ranging freely about the form.

The change in Low's case was general: he began drawing more freely in the later Fifties, using a reed pen with brush tones, and applying his washes loosely. His work was fresh, off-the-cuff, pithy, much like André François's illustrations for John Symonds, which Low admired; and like François's work overall (excepting *Little Boy Brown*, p. 362), it didn't catch on. Two books that are his own are worth pausing on: *Adam's Book of Odd Creatures* (Atheneum, 1962) only momentarily—a diverting, incidental rhyming alphabet; and the Chaplinesque *Smiling Duke* (416).

Duke is a dog who, loving all, is loved by none. Smile as he will—didn't his father write "Smile and the world smiles with you" on a stone—he is rebuffed by elephants, by geese . . . . "Not tigers, no, nor butterflies,/ Nor apes [417], nor eagles met his tries/ With anything but frightened stares:/This went for chipmunks, too, and bears. . . . Might Dad be wrong? *Can* parents err?" Never: "Duke's problem lay, not in his heart, /But in his smile, which gave a start/To everyone on whom he turned it." ("Are you surprised that they all spurned it?") That is until the last when there comes into Duke's life a loving poodle—with a snaggle-tooth smile just like his.

Smiling Duke, a love of a book, is all Low: the nifty mock-serious verse, the uncouth expressive drawing, the transparent depths of the washes, no-color poppy and gray-green; the humor, the solemnity, the emotion. Though it is not 'right' for children (the verse is overelaborate, the irony is misplaced), unlike much that is right—i.e. suitable—it is not an anemic neuter. The subject is love, unobscured, imperative, and love, it says, is a trial; the climax is laughter through tears, the end total capitulation. There is something about Low (and François) that is keen and uncompromising; and to adults, particularly, it is disquieting. A prickly pear.

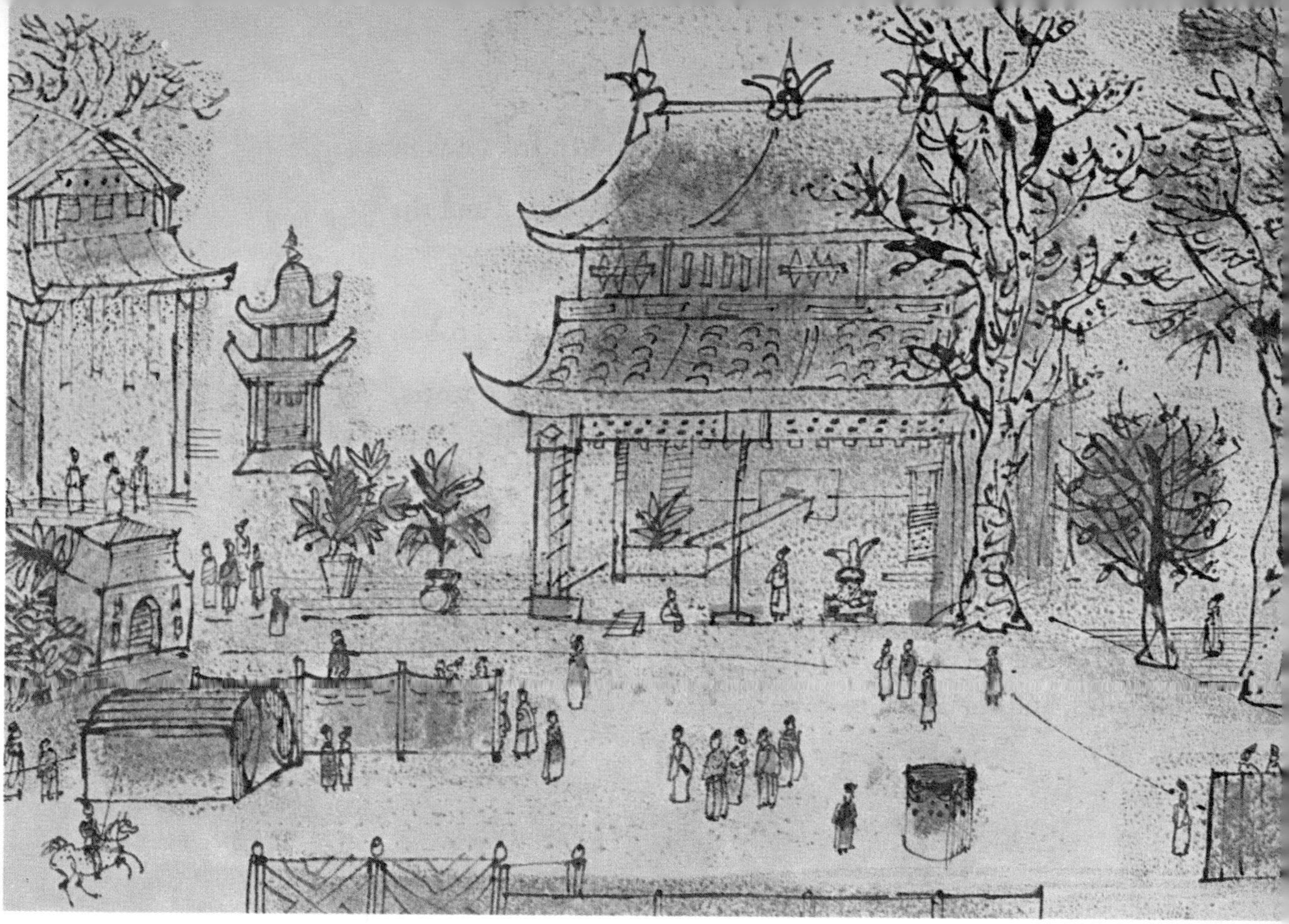

418

He was nonetheless the choice of Elizabeth Riley at Crowell to illustrate one of the first of the Let's-Read-and-Find-Outs, and his work for that series, depictions of nature and nature-concepts, is some of his best (p. 408). That he can impart information and demonstrate principles—particularize and generalize—without loss of personality would be praise in another instance; but in fact Low's artistic personality from the mailing pieces forward has been part artistic intelligence, and a set subject in a fixed, limited framework—such as *Shrimps* for seven-year-olds—is rather an opportunity than otherwise.

The penchant in recent years for putting folk tales, folkish tales—every sort of traditional material—into picturebooks has touched Low too; and he has had occasion to work in full color. Full color is a medium for him, as linocuts were, and half-tone separation; a graphic art, not painting (418, 419).

418, 419. *The Legend of the Willow Plate,* text by Alvin Tresselt and Nancy Cleaver, pictures by Joseph Low. Parents', 1968. 10 x 7$^{3}/_{8}$.

419

The Legend of the Willow Plate, the story attached to the familiar dinnerware pattern, is one of lovers parted, reunited, vanquished, transcendent as doves; of a beautiful high-born maiden, a handsome poetic clerk, a proud father, a rich and powerful suitor and, forsooth, a faithful nurse: romantic, Chinese by ascription, outwardly a stereotype, potentially a curio. But it has dramatic conviction, thanks to a reserved, not ungraceful text ('forsooth,' *enfin*, is not quite fair) and to Low's drawings; and it is not Chinoiserie. The blue and white willow plate pattern is re-created on the endpapers as a point of departure, and Low draws thereafter in his own way in blue ink; but his (accustomed) spatter washes are suggestive of Chinese mists, and the use of color to blend even as line delimits is common to both. They are jewel colors, however, for a fairy tale.

It is appropriate that we will be seeing more of Low somewhat later; he has not had, as yet, any one big successful book, there is no final judgment that can be passed, no place —except as stimulus, progenitor—that can be assigned him. He does beautiful intelligent sincere work.

The sentence is meant to sound unfinished, and expectant.

JULIET KEPES

English-born, Juliet Kepes is a graduate of the Institute of Design and the wife of Gyorgy Kepes; from childhood, she attests, she liked to draw "living, moving and acting things"[15]—animals in action, that is, not animal portraits; what she has done, befittingly, is to depict active animals in books of markedly individual design. There the simple addition ends.

Five Little Monkeys, the first, is lots of story, lots of old-fashioned story, really, and for a brief picturebook lots of text. It had to go into small type, which could have destroyed its looks, and there are a great many words on a page—a great many per picture—which could have destroyed it for children: if one were setting out to make a large (8⅝ x 9⅝) small (40 pp.) picturebook, this is not how one would go about it. Little matter: the story is about five mischievous monkeys (420), their pranks and, after a bad scare, their good deeds; and in Tiger the Terrible, who *seldom* leaves his cave, they have a worthy antagonist (421). He too is spared at the end, however, when the monkeys have him by the hair, tail, whiskers, by the intercession of Pecarry the wild pig, local conciliator, who earlier got the monkeys out of their hole. A real hole, a pit, baited with bananas: it's the kind of story where you want to know things like that.

Likewise the pictures, not cut to any standard measure or consistent pattern, fully alive and interesting. The monkeys, Japanese in their limberness, in the brushwork, and Ter-

420, 421. *Five Little Monkeys*, by Juliet Kepes. Boston, Houghton Mifflin, 1952. 8⅝ x 9⅝.

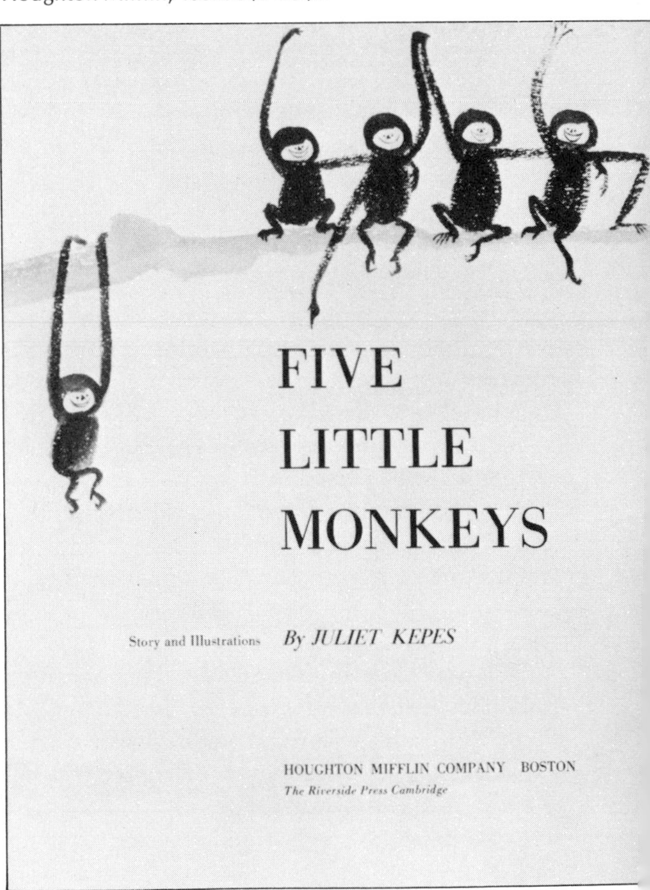

FIVE
LITTLE
MONKEYS
Story and Illustrations By JULIET KEPES
HOUGHTON MIFFLIN COMPANY BOSTON
The Riverside Press Cambridge

420

rible, a child's apparition, are as they are in the original, in black and white; at alternate openings is color, flat vivid turquoise for the sky, fire red for the sun, the jungle a tangle, a tissue of greens and at night a miasma pierced by the turquoise, red, yellow eyes of the animals. Those weird eyes, disembodied dots surmounted by a pair of ears, a set of horns, perhaps tell it best; yet no single novelty—not the feet stampeding off the page nor the pit as deep as the Grand Canyon—conveys what is new about the book, the freedom with which, opening after opening, it animates its contents.

From *Five Little Monkeys* to *Seven Remarkable Bears* sounds like Anaheim to Azusa, the next stop on the line; but more than the passage of two years and a difference in authorship separates them. Where *Five Little Monkeys*, in toto, is functional anarchy, *The Seven Remarkable Bears* is timed, staged, orchestrated impeccably—and bright, clear-cut, a sparkler.

Po is the only polar bear in the zoo; he has "a fine cage with seven deep, dark caves, seven large blue icebergs and even a diving tower"; but he is unhappy, he is lonesome. He grows careless—thin, scraggly, downright dirty; and "worst of all, he was always hungry." Mr. Fitz the keeper is too busy to notice him: "That is, not until one very special Sunday" when Mr. Fitz, in his best Sunday uniform, with his best booming Sunday voice, pitches him his daily allotment—"Nice fresh cod today"—and Po growls back, "Better make it two today." He has company, he tells Mr. Fitz, another polar bear has moved into the second cave. Nothing doing; but a little boy intervenes: "You heard what the bear said. He wants another fish for his friend."

So it goes day by day, fish by fish, and daily Po's appearance improves (422). On Saturday when he emerges from his swimming pool, "His fluffy tail stuck out behind, his ears stood straight and clean, his fur was smoothly combed and purest white, his toenails were clean and neatly clipped." He growls a pleasant "Good morning" to Mr. Fitz and refuses an eighth salmon. "Seven is

421

fine. Quite enough, thank you." Mr. Fitz is confused—he can't be Po, that's it, he's too fat and clean, he must be one of Po's friends, he has no business being there. But the only way to prove it, one way or the other, is to look in the caves.

"All the people were quiet. Mr. Fitz looked very brave and very white. The little boy looked very worried and very white. Po looked most worried of all. He stepped back toward his caves and watched very carefully. Then he smiled into his stiff, clean whiskers. He sneezed. It was a loud, long sneeze. And out from six of the seven caves came six more sneezes."

Out of the six caves come in turn six 'hellos' and, on suggestion, six 'thank yous.' His friends can't be seen, Po explains, because they are very REMARKABLE . . . *remarkable*; they are INVISIBLE . . . *invisible*. Mr. Fitz is impressed, the crowd is elated, only the little boy isn't fooled. But Po, safe, welcomes a conspirator: "It gets pretty lonesome around here with only invisible friends."

Po from skin and bones and grumbles to sleek well-being, striking one after another pose—disgruntled, adamant, insinuating, apprehensive—is an illustrator's prize. To his advantage, to its advantage, the illustration is exceedingly simple: the cat stalking the fish-cart; now and again the neighboring bears, a balloon man, youngsters on a donkey, a camel; when called for, the crowd-chorus

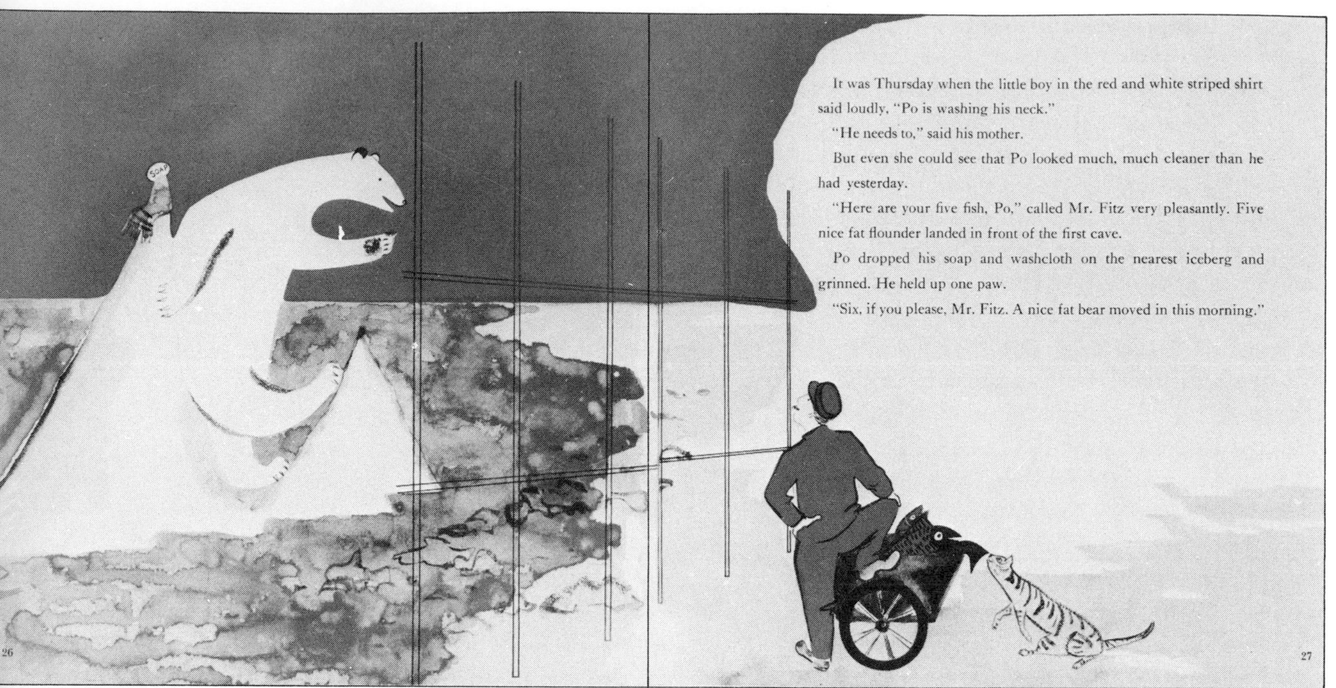

It was Thursday when the little boy in the red and white striped shirt said loudly, "Po is washing his neck."
"He needs to," said his mother.
But even she could see that Po looked much, much cleaner than he had yesterday.
"Here are your five fish, Po," called Mr. Fitz very pleasantly. Five nice fat flounder landed in front of the first cave.
Po dropped his soap and washcloth on the nearest iceberg and grinned. He held up one paw.
"Six, if you please, Mr. Fitz. A nice fat bear moved in this morning."
SOAP
26
27

422. *The Seven Remarkable Bears,* text by Emilie McLeod, pictures by Juliet Kepes. Boston, Houghton Mifflin, 1954. 9½ x 9.

—good details, lightly brushed in. Mostly it's a skit featuring the three principals and, not least, the seven impending caves; and it unfolds in broad rhythms and accents, the pictures abstracting the essence of the anecdotal, episodic narrative.

Individually, none carries a great deal of weight. The spread pictured, with its brilliant blue sky, its watery pool, its commanding silhouette of Po, its skeletal bars, is probably the most concentrated *and* developed (criteria for reduced reproduction, not art or illustration); usually, in reviews, the strong endpaper design was chosen. This is not to deprecate but to praise: there is nothing extraordinary about *The Seven Remarkable Bears* but its adroitness, the separate and combined abilities of author and illustrator. Horace Mann proposed to found a school with a teacher and a student on a bench; with three McLeod sentences and a Kepes bear (and a designer in the bushes), one might start a book.

Emily McLeod became the juvenile editor at Atlantic Monthly Press. Juliet Kepes, potentially another Duvoisin, turned away from storytelling illustration—from explicit characterization and dramatization—almost entirely. Besides drawings for books of light verse and the imaginative *Beasts from a Brush* (Pantheon, 1955), she did her own picturebooks, these composed of pictures strong in drawing and design, lacking in content, in expressive substance.

Frogs Merry is the antics of four frogs who at the outset escape being eaten as eggs, at the close sink into the mud for the winter; in the interim they make up games (423), elude two stalking herons, legs protruding from under lily pads ("Wherever can they be?"), escape a snapping turtle ("Where can they have vanished?") by climbing on her back; "All through the summer they frolic and play." They are ostensibly making sport of the "struggle for survival" in the "world of nature" (to telescope the catalog) but their capers don't qualify as natural history any more than they do as a story.

The frogs are marvelous: they're acrobats,

clowns, the essence of wicked glee; and frogs in their image have been turning up ever since. Count in too the dynamic, inventive design, the clever manipulation of the blue and green and the brilliant use of white, the wealth of visual and pictorial incident. *Frogs Merry* is good enough to look at to be good to look at, which is not a barbed compliment; had it a point, it would be a considerable book.

Lady Bird, Quickly (Atlantic-Little, Brown, 1964) has sequence, the passing of the message—"Lady Bird, Lady Bird, fly away home,/Your house is on fire, your children alone"—from fly to wasp, wasp to spider, spider to earwig . . . to grasshoppers, cicada, black ants, "three sturdy stag beetles," daddy-longlegs . . . until at the last lady bird flies to her 'burning' tree, alight with fireflies singing, with her children ("quite safe, not alone"), "Lady Bird, Lady Bird, fly away home." The warp is an old rhyme, the weft an assortment of insects, a cross of nursery tradition and nature study that could stand as a paradigm of thought-up picturebook fare. The insects are at once real and unreal (in *Frogs Merry* fashion), and in themselves lively, amusing; the occasional flowers and grasses and especially the backgrounds—a rainbow of lavenders, pinks, greens, yellows—are plainly lovely: to turn the pages is to revel in the color. Neither this nor that and ultimately nothing, the book is an object, a manufacture.

Ending on a bleak note was not deliberate. You will notice that a great number of the books in this section have been illustrated in color, extensively in some cases; what is shown in color throughout is predominantly work in which color is not descriptive, not coloring, but a structural and, often, an affective constituent; not applied, but organic to the material. *The Golden Goose, The Hole in the Wall, The Thanksgiving Story, Daniel Boone, Whistling Two-Teeth, The Little Fireman, The Noisy Book, Goodnight Moon,* Charlot, Charlot, Charlot—the list is by no means exhaustive but it is indicative: this is work that would be literally inconceivable except in its stipulated color. It is also, to a greater or less degree, modernist art.

When in the early Fifties color was more than ever in demand and costlier than ever, pre-separation itself advanced as an art; and pre-separation, while it may have as its end

423. *Frogs Merry,* by Juliet Kepes. Pantheon, 1961. 8⅞ x 6.

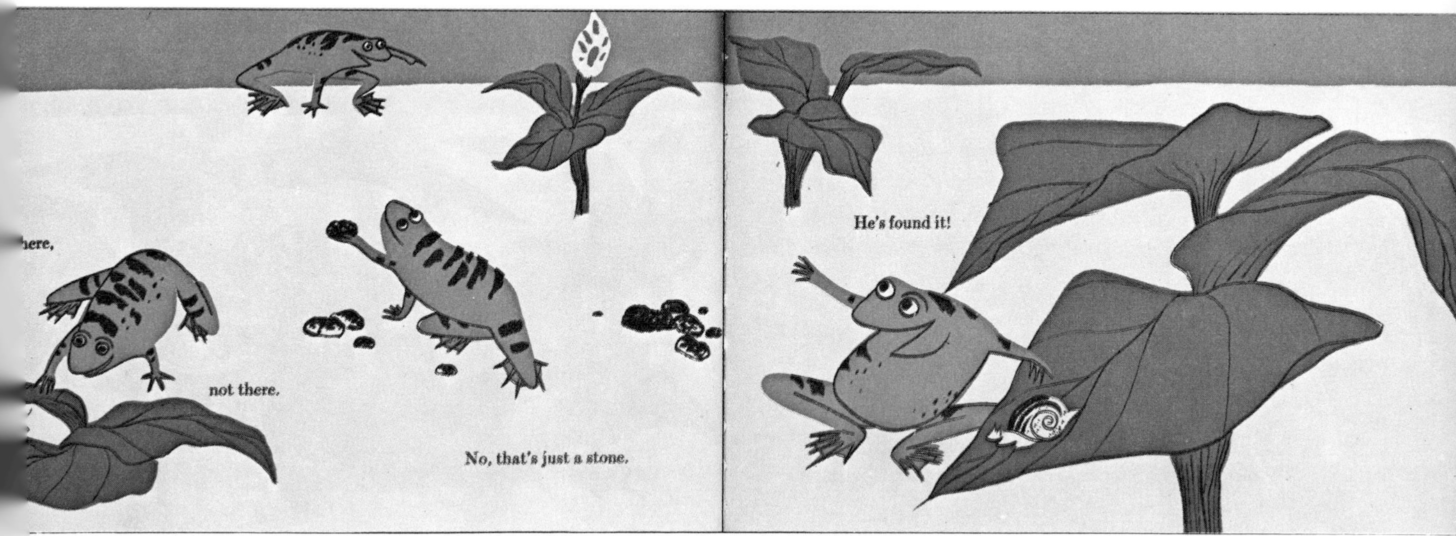

a picture indistinguishable in character from a multihued original, need not: a picture may be composed, as well, in terms of overlaid separations and pure color. In essence this is printing as opposed to reproduction, a tendency fostered in commercial art by artists' studies in designing for printing (the Constructivists, the Bauhaus), by the honest-expression-of-materials ethos (William Morris) extended into appreciation of old honest printing, incunabula to chapbooks; and fostered in the traditional graphic arts, in print-making, by an analogous reaction against the sham and second-hand, a comparable turn to direct cutting (or etching), to experimentation, to the practice of printing one's work oneself.

Low and Frasconi are of course exemplars in the first and second instance, and yet not mutually exclusive, for Low's mailing pieces and his personally printed books are 'original prints' and Frasconi's original prints translate readily into mass-printed design and illustration. Both streams immensely fructified picturebooks and it becomes a toss-up, later, whether in individual cases the press or the knife came first.

We have diverged from color, but not really; for what the nineteenth-century reproductive engravers accomplished in tone, in black and white, the nineteenth-century color printers and their heirs in three- and four-color process accomplished in regard to tints—that is, their exact graded reproduction; and the return to the press and the block and, native to them, line and mass, was also a turn to pure color. This, however, much reinforced by an aesthetic that gave to color a weight equal to line and mass, that made of color, form. One sees it, classically, in Mondrian and all that he inspired, one sees it—momentously toward the end—in Matisse.

It was in the Forties that Matisse undertook to work in cut-and-pasted paper extensively, the papers painted in brilliant colors of his choosing; and in 1947 the dazzling album *Jazz* appeared and, exhibited, reproduced, swept at least the looking world. His characteristic multilobed 'leaf' form was everywhere in evidence (*The Quiet Noisy Book*, 1950, is especially *Jazz*-y) and the scissors-cut became a standard line. As Alfred Barr observes, "Matisse, with that modest respect for the medium which characterizes his generation, never tries to conceal the stroke of his scissors."[16] Given the proclivity of children too for casual cut-outs, it had a natural place—per Rand—in picturebooks. Moreover, these were not *papiers collés*, collages, but *papiers découpés*, cut-papers, and they stimulated what I have chosen to call construction, the creation of images from paper and their assemblage, with or without ready-mades (Rand's newspaper scrap), into a composition; the two were to interbreed furiously later.

What one recalls first, however, about *Jazz* and the larger and smaller *papiers découpés* that accompanied it, is the vibrant, violent color—an abstract dance of hot (and cool) color. Color that follows no apparent 'scheme,' color such as hadn't been seen since the Ballets-Russe. Interestingly, the first of Matisse's true *papiers découpés*, "The Dancer," was made in 1938 for Léonide Massine; Matisse was designing the scenery and costumes for a new Massine ballet for the Ballets Russe de Monte Carlo, successor to the Diaghilev company, and "The Dancer" transposes to paper the flame-like strips on the dancers' tights. Whatever significance this may have (or not), for a sizable public *Jazz* and its companion pieces had an impact akin to that of Ballets-Russe decor thirty years earlier.

Observation has been made of "the extreme color restraints of the 1940's,"[17] manifest in terms of color conventions (the pastel nursery, the black cocktail dress), in references to 'tastefulness' and the distastefully 'loud.' I am not suggesting that Matisse was other than a catalyst; his own paintings, and others', had anticipated the change, the wedding of color to technology, economics, sociology—the tenor of the times—advanced it. Color came to stand on its own.

So, less obtrusively, did typography. Put at its simplest, typography is the choice and arrangement of type or the choosing of type and its arranging: "the use of type in design to a definite end,"[18] the work of the typographer. Once he was the printer; when consciousness of design demanded an aesthetically satisfying product, he became a new kind of professional, the specialist-typographer, designer of books. He might free-lance, he might work for an individual publisher or press, he might design new types as well. In this country Daniel Berkeley Updike and Bruce Rogers, in Britain Sir Francis Meynell, who fit the bill variously, wrought from Morris's revival of "the grandeur of printing" (Meynell) an agreeable, readable book—twentieth-century classic, *the* book to all purposes.

Updike, Rogers, Meynell proceeded traditionally, from printing, and from printing as traditionally practiced, i.e. type-setting. On the Continent were painters—Moholy-Nagy, Lissitzky, Bayer—designing posters, handbills, catalogs, books; also influenced by Morris to become artisans, committed socially to communication and to technology, they studied typography, and taught it—at the Bauhaus (1919–1928)—as a means to visual communication. Display artists in essence, they designed with type, with photographs, drawings, color, utilizing photo-engraving (later photo-offset); and from them came the modern graphic artist like Paul Rand who is also a typographer, and the modern typographer-book designer who, in practice, is also a graphic artist.

The New Typography, as such, aimed to be functional, organic; it "must start from the fulfillment of specific requirements," Bayer wrote in 1928.[19] This in contrast to what Jan Tschichold, who refined the work of the Bauhaus masters, designated 'decorative typography,' the fitting of the type-matter to a preconceived scheme or composition. Early, Bayer discarded what is known as justification, the setting of type in lines of a uniform measure, flush right as well as left, for a flush-left, variable-right arrangement, which permits even, natural spacing and avoids word-breaks. (This paragraph is not justified, the balance of the text is.) Tschichold, to whom decorative typography meant, then, centered or symmetrical typography, raised asymmetry to a principle of design as being more flexible, more individual, as allowing type-matter to be set and grouped "to express the sense of the words."[20] (How lines were to be aligned, whether or not they were to be justified, was to depend on the nature of the material too.) The difference, generally, is between Arthur Rushmore's title-spread for *April's Kittens* (315) and Walter Lorraine's design of the title-page for *Five Little Monkeys* (420)—a difference in appearance that is also a difference in tenor and in the way one gets the information. The one is a proclamation, in effect, the other a telegraphed announcement.

For picturebooks, the new typography was important not as a formula but as an impetus to devise new solutions, a freeing from formula. The basic forms of picturebook, with the text under the picture or on the facing page, gave way first to the dynamics of the medium; and so we find in *Angus and the Ducks* (78, 79) the page become the picture-space and the text set in it, strategically, but with a regard still for traditional paragraph form and, where more than a few words were involved, for filling the given space. (Where the space permitted, the paragraphs are squared off.) Another early divergence from formula, the rising type-line in *Liang and Lo* (84), we remarked upon; and, somewhat later, the shaped setting of the type in *Mike Mulligan* (256) and, more dramatically even, in *The Little House* (258–259), occasioned general comment. The latter, an effective graphic solution in that it unites the two pages visually, and true to the text insofar as the length of the lines is concerned (you may recall that Burton was not averse to adding or subtracting a word), has the weakness typographically of sacrificing articulation to the flow of the design. There is, nonetheless, something pleasantly naive about those type-pictures that is part and parcel of the Burton look; it is almost an embroidery look.

In the period with which we're concerned, the early and middle Fifties, the solutions are as diverse as the problems, the problems more diverse because of the multiplicity of available solutions. How the books might be designed, that is, influenced the way they were conceived, and the response to the manifold possibilities was a plethora of new approaches. The more so because even before the professional designer entered the field, artists with experience in advertising, like Duvoisin, made their mark; and with the recognition of graphic design as an art, artist-illustrators took it as their province too. Many designed their own books or collaborated on the design (as Burton had); but regardless, books came to be more *designed*, less *illustrated.*

Apropos of *Petunia* (177) and *Puss in Boots* (387), we have spoken of the flexibility of the narrative treatment: Duvoisin conceived of *Petunia* in continuous animation as it were; Marcia Brown, in the example cited, animated—and condensed—a segment of a given story. Elsewhere, the type-lines, appearing anywhere on the page, whether as legend—*See and Say*—or as running captions, continuous narration—*All Kinds of Time* (p. 486)—were part of the composition, coequal with the pictures; and in *See and Say*, a book of words, and *All Kinds of Time*, a book of word-images (and then some), the complement of the pictures, with the layout, the color, the design as a whole relating the different graphic elements and the very diverse motifs. "Inventive visual articulation" is Moholy-Nagy's phrase for the new typography.[21]

In *A Very Special House* (p. 428), what is the page, what is the picture? What—where—is the drawing on the wall, the words of the text, the SPECIAL labels, the little boy in the drawings, the drawings he's in, for that matter? Krauss and Sendak collaborated on the design, the text dictates its own setting, the assorted pictures and words are the picture that is the house, the story, the page; and, psychologically and materially, the fusion is complete.

But there is nothing wrong with the old picturebook forms, no intrinsic superiority in the composite, elastic ones. While 'form follows function,' Louis Sullivan's dictum, may no longer have absolute standing, it is still a good rule of thumb. For a simple evenly paced sequential story of few words and important pictures, there will never be anything wrong with the text-below-the-illustrations form of *Play with Me* (227) and *Harry the Dirty Dog* (p. 470). Nor, quite evidently, is there any need, within the form, for uniformity. In *Play with Me* the brief poetic text—which Margaret Wise Brown would have written more plainly as poetry, with fewer periods—is nonetheless set as poetry throughout; in *Harry the Dirty Dog* sentences break at natural pauses—in the story and for the voice—and the dialogue, a key constituent, has always a line to itself. We have emphasized this matter of flexibility in length of lines, of natural breaks, because it is integral to the development of picturebooks, to the style of writing for them. More and more they were continuous free-form narratives as in *Follow the Road* (179), also of this period—part poetry, part drama; or more poetry, more drama; and poetry and drama have regularly to be set as the lines fall, for comprehension and delivery.

The great difference between *Play with Me* and *Harry the Dirty Dog*, of course, is their appearance. Soft, tremulous, *Play with Me* is whisper-weight offset lithography, and the light even type-face is in accord. *Harry the Dirty Dog* represents, for one thing, the domestication of cartooning, and the broad simplified drawing, the bang, takes in turn a bold show-off type-face. "Good typography depends only secondarily on types, primarily on the way they are used" (Tschichold); but where the type is in prominent conjunction with a picture, and particularly with a *drawn* picture, that it have a character and weight in keeping with the draftsmanship is a distinct asset.

We spoke of *Play with Me* as the fruit of

offset lithography because of offset's ability to lay down a delicate film of color and to reproduce the most tenuous line; what offset could do, in fact, was to reproduce any kind of line and, in time—by this time—almost any kind of color treatment, from transparent watercolor to flat opaque gouache. The earliest offset picturebooks, of which the Angus books are typical, are drawn as they might have been for letterpress, for engraving, and the established text types or body types are not unsuited to them; those more freely drawn tended to be hand-lettered. We have seen what happened when the Lenski books went from hand-lettering to type (101, 102). Françoise, whose two-color work, especially, is not dissimilar, lettered her first books too; see then *Jeanne-Marie Counts Her Sheep*, a book of 1950 (68).

What had intervened was the typographic revolution. The new designers, designing display pieces, used display types actively; seeking clarity and emphasis, they used bold faces. (This book is printed in a body type; this is the **bold face** of the same body type.) In advertising, they used types variously, inventively, for immediate impact and legibility; they needed larger sizes of body type, and body types that would look well in larger sizes—quasi-display types; they could set short messages in type faces not suitable for books (as the 'Egyptian' type-face used in *Harry the Dirty Dog*, the 'Gothic' in *Jeanne-Marie*).

The seventy-nine books listed in the 1955–57 AIGA *Children's Books* catalog are set in eighty-two type-faces. (A different face might be used for the title page and for the text.) There are eighty-two type-faces chiefly because the great majority of the books are picturebooks (rather than books for older children): there was available to the designer of picturebooks a vast array of types including many that had to be specially set (practical when the text is brief) and, overlapping, many originally intended as display types in advertising. By this time, too, photo-composition—the setting of type not from the type proper, the type-metal, but from its image on film—had come into use; and photo-composition permits the letters to be enlarged—or otherwise modified—at will. It was ideally suited to children's books "in which we specialize," The Composing Room hardly needed remind its customers.

The history of The Composing Room, Inc. is a paraphrase of the foregoing—as, to a considerable extent, the divorcement of composition, the setting of type, from press work, the printing, parallels the rise of the graphic artist-typographer-designer. The Composing Room itself was founded in 1927 by Sol Cantor and Dr. Robert Leslie with the idea of producing "fine advertising composition with machine equipment."[22] New equipment was developed under its aegis, personnel was specially trained, large sizes of type and numerous display types were stocked; and once successful with advertising work, the firm was in a position to offer similar service to publishers, particularly, agressively, for young children's books. Part of selling typesetting was "showing in a variety of ways the uses and potential uses of type and of fresh trends in the graphic arts":[23] the journal *PM* (Production Manager), later *A-D* (Art Director) gave early and extended attention to Rand, Kepes, Bayer, to student work, new processes, the private presses alike; typographic and design clinics were held for production men, young artists, advertising people; the A-D Gallery, and later Gallery 303, displayed the new work.

In 1952, indicatively, The Composing Room issued *Young Faces*, a large booklet akin to a printer's keepsake, which—per the punning title—features type-faces particularly suitable for children's books in a setting (both meanings too) that shows them to advantage; each of the two-page spreads, with original illustrations, constitutes a pair of specimen pages, and their variety, the way that each is interesting both as graphic design and as young design, speaks equally for the state of the art and the state—or status—of The Composing Room. Of the many books cited in this section, more than half are Composing Room products; of the books of the Forties and Fifties illustrated herein, probably a larger percentage still, a hegemony that no single printer (or binder or supplier) approached.

Among publishers there was, as we've seen, a balance of interests and aptitudes; and at each house, a like succession. Elisabeth Hamilton published the Steichen-Martin *First* and *Second Picture Book* at Harcourt, and Dorothy Kunhardt's great nonsense, but not picturebooks as such on a regular basis; when she left for Morrow in 1945, she was succeeded by Margaret McElderry, and in 1950 Harcourt brought out *The Two Reds* and *All Kinds of Time*, the start of a stellar picturebook decade. Margaret McElderry had been assistant head of children's work at the New York Public Library; during the war she was with the Office of War Information in London, and afterward, briefly, in Belgium. It was all to stand her in good stead. If 'modern design' was premature on the Scott list in 1938–40, it was propitious—in a different context—a dozen years later; and with the most eminent of the new artist-designers—Rand, Frasconi, the first of Low—the Harcourt list made it at once desirable and reputable.

The other McElderry coup was publishing some of the best of the new European picturebooks, the work of Swiss artists Hans Fischer anf Felix Hoffmann. Apart from the Babar books—and the Père Castor phenomenon—almost nothing had come to the United States from the Continent since the great influx of 1929–31; there was less to be had, and little need for it. But with the end of the war the renaissance of the European picturebook, already begun in Switzerland, produced illustration that of itself claimed attention; and the appearance of the Selina Chönz-Alois Carigiet *A Bell for Ursli* (Oxford, 1950) began a period of highly selective re-publication—highly selective both in relation to what was available and by comparison with the period to follow. Fischer and Hoffmann were distinctive, Fischer superlatively so; and much of Fischer's work, and all of Hoffmann's, consists of renderings of old tales, still in short supply in the Fifties. That Fischer's books, done on five, six, seven stones, could not have been produced here from scratch was secondary (some were printed here, from proofs): they were felicitous additions, and on the Harcourt list they complemented the very different modern American work.

Meanwhile type marched on. Flexible, active typography is part of the picture in Leonard Kessler's *What's in a Line?* (p. 398), part of a design/demonstration—a demonstration of design—as mobile and vocal as a chalk talk: this is the first of the art-in-the-abstract-is books, the new young art appreciation (Helen Borten's *Do You See*

424. *Dress Up and Let's Have a Party,* by Remy Charlip. Scott, 1956. 8 x 5½.

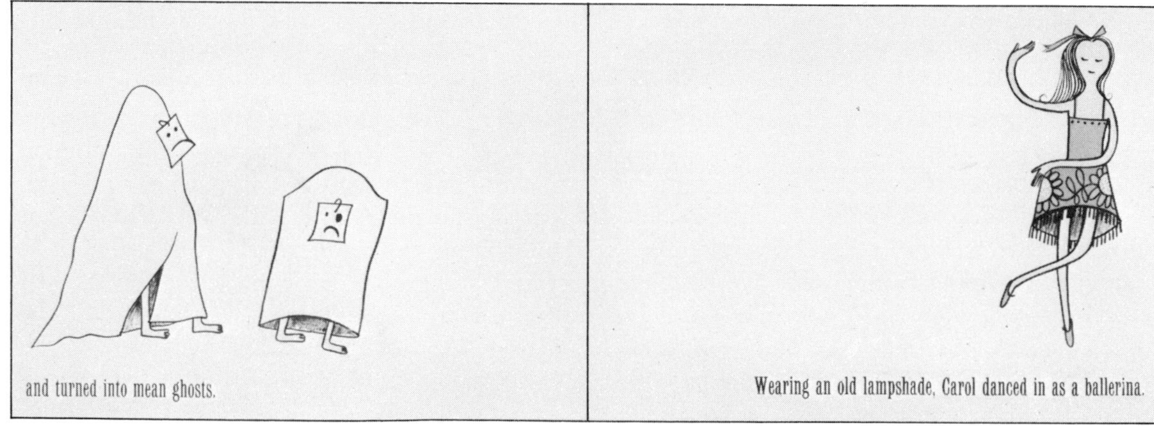

and turned into mean ghosts.
Wearing an old lampshade, Carol danced in as a ballerina.

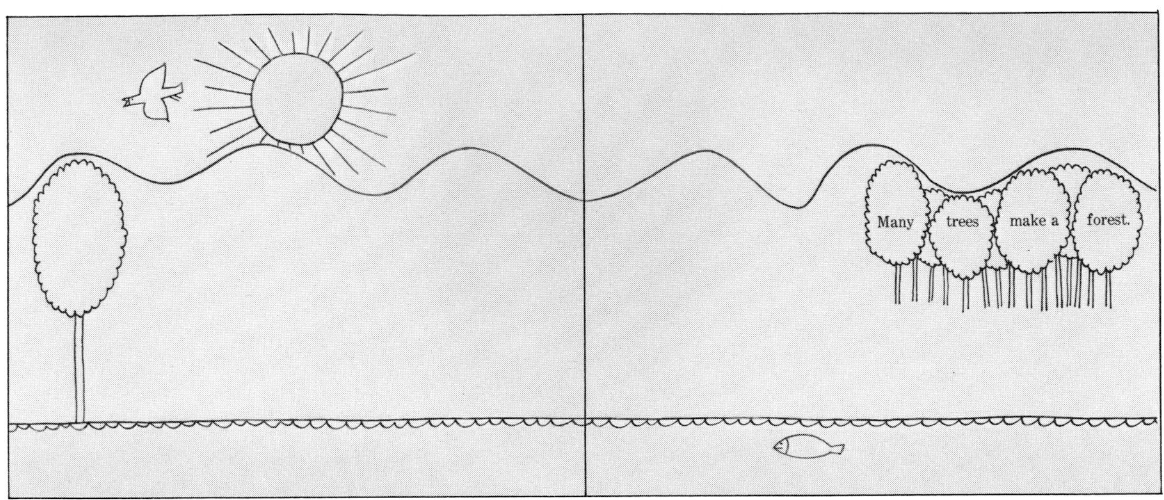

425. *Where Is Everybody?* by Remy Charlip. Scott, 1957. 9½ x 7¼.

What I See? et al). In Kessler's *Fast Is Not a Ladybug* (p. 396), the large type, widely spaced, tells "a slow story" in concert with the words; it is a picture of a slow story. Picture = design = scheme = concept.

Pictures, strategically cued, equal a continuous performance (424). This Remy Charlip, dancer and designer, recognized more clearly perhaps than anyone else; the phrase "the drama of the turning of the page" at the outset is his. The figures, bearing right, invite the turn of the page, and the text-line, in ticker tape fashion, leads us on—whether to the next comer or, as with the two ghosts, to what kind of get-up the guests will think up. (An aim was to stimulate children to do likewise; an outcome was the vaunted Paper Bag Players.) The text gets into the act, besides, by virtue of a typeface with an old-time theatrical flavor of its own.

Words wherever are the very basis of *Where Is Everybody?* (425). What they're about, that is to say, is where they are—as, in succession, bird, sun, hills, river make their appearance; and what they're about, where they are, determines just how—differently—they're set. (For what follows, see p. 531.) The purpose, to identify words with what they denote, yields a new kind of word-picture.

In *The Sound of Things* and *Roar and More,* it is the turn of letter combinations, patterns, configurations, whether or not words, to signify sounds (426–430). *The Sound of Things* is just that, the sound, pictured, of a boat dropping anchor, a truck's roar, a cannon's boom. *Roar and More* is more—the meaning of the title apart—for each sound-picture is introduced by a rhyme and a portrait that together key us to the coming sound. Indeed, it is their very great similarity that makes their differences noteworthy. As a demonstration of sound, or sounds, expressed as letters, expressed as design, *The Sound of Things* is tops: that advancing O, coming out of the word, becoming an open mouth, gives us the very shape of the sound as the mouth makes it. As graphic design itself it is distinctly the more interesting book; and, related, more dimensional, less literal. One could say, to accentuate the difference, that where *The Sound of Things* re-creates the sounds plastically, using type, *Roar and More* translates them typographically.

Still, *Roar and More* is the one that succeeded with children and, presumably, parents—because it is more than sounds, because the sounds can more easily be uttered, because it's for the presenting, the sharing, the reacting. It moves, things happen.

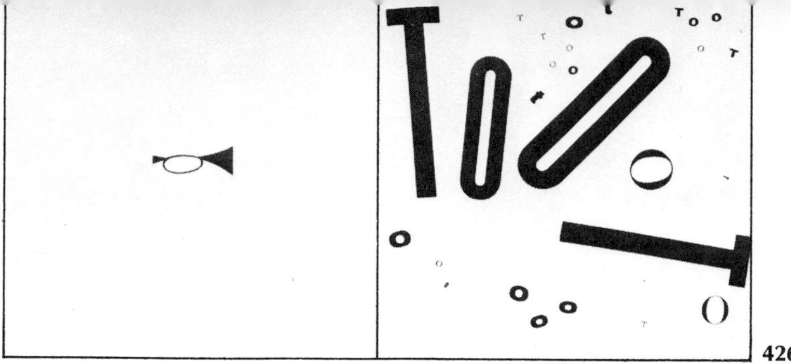

426

426, 427. *The Sound of Things,* by William Wondriska. Pantheon, 1958. 7 x 7.

427

If a lion comes to visit
Don't open your door
Just firmly ask "What is it?"
And listen to him roar.

428

428-430. *Roar and More,* by Karla Kuskin. Harper, 1956. 7¾ x 6⅝.

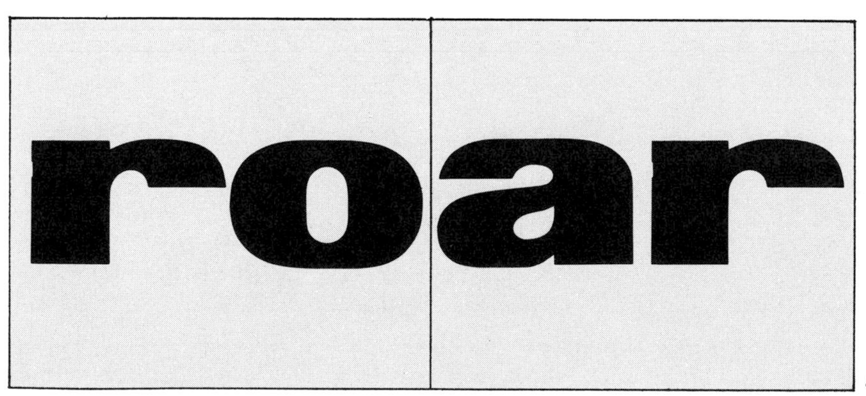

429

430

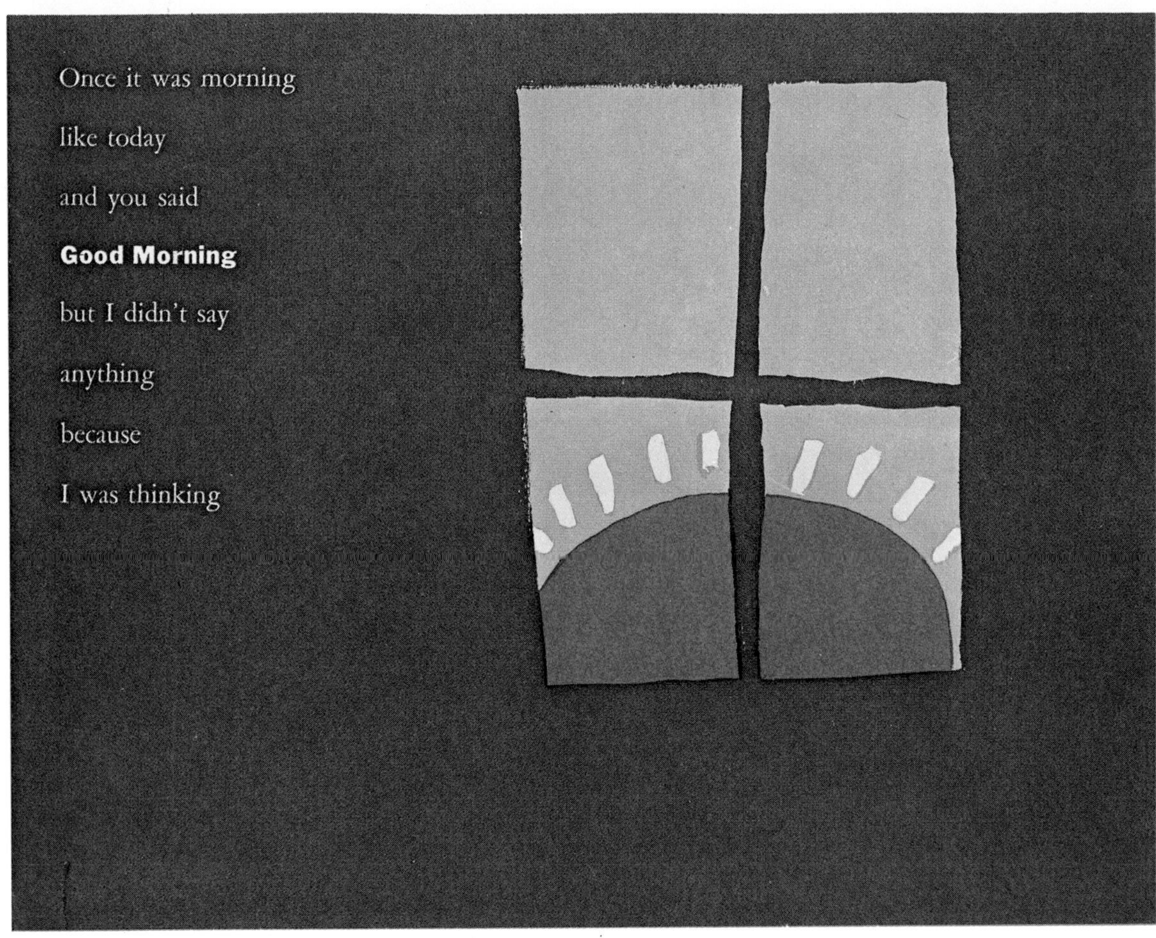
Once it was morning
like today
and you said
Good Morning
but I didn't say
anything
because
I was thinking

431. *The Thinking Book,* text by Sandol Stoddard Warburg, pictures by Ivan Chermayeff. Boston, Atlantic-Little, Brown, 1960. 9⅞ x 7¾.

Both books began as student projects at Yale in 1955 where Wondriska and Kuskin conceived, designed and printed them themselves. Josef Albers had become head of the School of Design in 1950, "new people were coming [Rand, in 1956]. . . . It was a very exciting time to have been there,"[24] Wondriska recounts. The choice of a specifically visual problem, one capable of solution in terms of type itself, and its execution by the artist himself are in the best Bauhaus tradition.

It was not a mold. Ivan Chermayeff—Institute of Design, Yale, honors and encomiums—illustrated, first, *The Thinking Book* (431). A youngster, unseen except on the jacket and title page, is thinking . . . thinking of pieces of dust floating in the sunshine, "of lemons and limes and oranges and yellows," while an urgent voice says **Put on** that shirt, the yellow one; "thinking of all the things under and over and all . . ." to **Overalls**—put on the overalls now; thinking, at the last, "That's why I couldn't put my socks on That's why I couldn't put my shoes on That's why I couldn't lace them up" ("I was thinking").

A dialogue between an inner voice and an outer voice, put as body type and bold face and, in pictures, the seen, present or envisioned: it is pure introspection and pure physical book, none more so. It is also somewhat as if we had *A Very Special House* without Sendak's little boy, and children, not seeing the child who's thinking, musing, didn't see themselves in it. Neither can one reading voice assume the two identities so apparent in print. To that extent it is too much a book; but to call it "primarily a designer's book" as the AIGA did—in a catalog (1958–60) dotted with high-style illustration—is to disregard not only the dreamy, discerning text but also the open joyousness of Chermayeff's very free drawing and his paint-box colors.

It is hard, at bottom, to accept the term 'designer's book' for *The Thinking Book* because it is so simply expressive, so little overtly 'designed.' But the term as it came into use in the Fifties is susceptible of two interpretations. Little of the designer work was illustration in the sense of rendering individuals, circumstances, events. Typically, it lacked emotional content; characteristically, it was a vehicle for the transmission of ideas. Given its origin, natural enough. And, not surprisingly, when some designers did attempt personal, individual illustration, it was found inexpressive. Or calculated, hermetic. Hence the construction of the term 'designer's book' as process not product, and antithetical, virtually, to 'children's book.'

Sparkle and Spin, however, is as much a designer's book as *Lentil*, for instance, is an illustrator's book; and *Red Light Green Light* and *Fast Is Not a Ladybug* are much 'designed.' They are conceptual books; and *The Thinking Book*, the pure product of a concept, is in that limited sense a designer's book. It was a period of conceptualizing (or, on the other hand, internalizing) and for that reason, as well as the cachet of the new design, hospitable to designers.

But all the new modes tended toward making art itself an experience, to borrow a phrase from John Dewey, and Josef Albers as well.

A last new look is, as it were, a non-look, in the traditional sense anti-art: André François. With Dubuffet, François might have said: "The idea that there are beautiful objects and ugly objects, people endowed with beauty and others who cannot claim it, has surely no other foundation than convention—old poppycock—and I declare that convention unhealthy."[25] Dubuffet was speaking of his graffiti-figures, François might have been speaking of *Little Boy Brown*.

Of *Little Boy Brown* altogether. Little boy Brown lives in the City, conveniently in a hotel; his father works in an office, his mother in a department store, both reached underground. "I am the only one who ever goes out of doors into the fresh air." One day, her day off, Hilda the chambermaid takes him to her home in the country, "the nicest time in all my life."

"Entering the spirit of the text completely, M. François has enriched it as he creates in pen and ink and warm brown wash the world that is so exciting to a child. So directly is he concerned with telling the story that artistic considerations seem to fall naturally into place. Each line is drawn with feeling and control of feeling. Little Boy Brown sometimes appears in different actions on the same page, the way a child draws. The drama of escaping from that fearsome fellow, Jack Frost, is apparent to anyone seeing him come down out of nowhere to nip the doorman's nose [432]. Tall buildings reach up the page, sliced to show details of structure and decoration, of the busy life going on in each cubicle, with wonderfully convenient subways and elevators . . . ."

Continues Marcia Brown: "Perhaps the most wonderful part of his day is something we feel and see in the drawings when Little Boy Brown reaches the house of Hilda's family. That is the marvelous beauty of space to one who has lived where the horizon and even the sky are crowded with shapes. To see the expanse of sky, broken only by one tree and one house, is a breathtaking experience.

"The details we notice now are not so much those that spell crowds and building materials but are much more personal, those of

432

433

432, 433. *Little Boy Brown,* text by Isobel Harris, pictures by André François. Lippincott, 1949. 6½ x 10.

patterns on wallpaper, the way a chair is made. We can feel the comfort and warmth of Hilda's house, shown in cross-section so that we can see the rapt child walking up and down the unfamiliar staircase. One can bloom in such a house. Even the animals lead their own lives. The mother at the tea table exudes hospitality."

One thinks story, hence intervention, reprieve; but at day's end they return on the bus.

"After the freedom of the country, we are almost smothered by the wealth of details of the city, the busyness of the adults. But Little Boy Brown can preserve his identity and his space, because he has the imagination of a child. The shape of Hilda's house, with the bird on the cake, the calm dog, the roses on the wall, is superimposed on the bricks of the hotel [433]. Above it the snow makes lace. The mind can provide space for the spirit. Author and artist are so successful in effacing themselves that it is Little Boy Brown who tells his story. To almost any small child this is a most personal book, because it is a book about himself."[26]

André François was not yet famous, the darling of *Graphis*, designer of ads, magazine covers, posters, cartoons; and he has never lost the power to insinuate and to move. In his honest rough directness, childlike in essence, is the art beyond art: so much for designers and categorical designers' books. *Little Boy Brown,* too, is a work that resists classification, that could be placed as fittingly in the emotional or social spectrum.

SOCIAL CHANGE

The charming photograph is the frontispiece of *The Horace Mann Kindergarten*, a curriculum study published by Teachers College in 1937 (when Horace Mann was the laboratory school of the college); one of its co-authors is Alice Dalgliesh. Exemplary use was made of books in an ideal setting; and in that ideal setting are pictured the ideal children who appeared, as well, in the books themselves. The little girl visiting a teeming pushcart market in *The Delivery Men* (123), the two an island and aloof, is the same sheltered—or privileged—child.

Her father, if he did any apparent work, worked in an office; her mother was home, with the cook. When they went to the store, they bought what they wanted; as a matter of course, they had a house and a car. The one variation was a conscious, intentionally edifying departure—calico and bare feet. We can deem it obtuseness, narrowness, smugness; but it was also adherence to an ideal of well-being that produced, in turn—as Ernestine Evans wrote of the Haders' *Big City*—'streets cleaner and traffic more orderly than my own impression of the city.'[1] That books might instead reflect ordinary life and the lives of ordinary children, to say nothing of the lives of poor children, was hardly thought of before the assertion that they should: that, in the 1940s, democracy demanded it. And then, as later, it was bound up with a concern for minority representation, initially in terms of intercultural or interracial understanding.

In fiction for children, where little contemporary realism existed altogether, the call was for books of 'social significance.' Among picturebooks, there were the attempts to counter prejudice that we've spoken of and others, related, to portray the Negro realistically (p. 376). Picturebooks, however, had long dealt with the immediate ostensible here and now—scooters and Scotties, as one skeptic put it;[2] the question remained of suitability, of the extent to which the small child needed "stories that will help him to see himself as part of the nation."[3] Below a certain age, the thinking was, "you can't feed social significance straight."[4]

We have always to distinguish between what the books reveal and what they intend; and with the realization beginning in the Forties that what they reveal is also what they convey, between the book that reflects reality and the one that makes a point of it. Thus, Clare Newberry's *Babette* and *April's Kittens*, involving in one case a limited income, in the other cramped quarters, are intrinsically realistic, for 1937 and 1940 uncommonly so. *The Little Carousel* (1946), Marcia Brown's account of a neighborhood-street youngster home alone without the price of a ride, is overt realism locally colored; *The Two Reds* (1950) takes the city —backyards, garbage cans—in full stride.

But it is an unpretentious book of the same year as *The Two Reds*, *Rosa-Too-Little*, that embodies what the early books lacked, the texture, intimate or public, of everyday life (434). Rosa, after a long summer spent learning to print her name, has just registered for her first library card, the beginning of the end of being "too little." Because Rosa lives on 110th Street in New York, there are scenes of the older girls skipping rope on the sidewalk, the boys flying pigeons from the roof, all the children playing under the fire-hydrant sprinkler; and because she lives on 110th Street—near where Sue Felt worked as a librarian—her name is Rosa Maldonado and the hydrant is *the Pompa.* Equally as real, however, is Mama, broad-browed, comfortably proportioned, resting for a moment in her apron while she examines the important paper—an order of realism evident again in Maurice Sendak's scenes of a Brooklyn childhood in, as it happens, *The Sign on Rosie's Door* (p. 509).

434. *Rosa-Too-Little,* by Sue Felt. Doubleday, 1950. 9¾ x 8. Detail.

Neither *Rosa* nor *Rosie*—still exceptional ten years later—makes a point of any difference, and one could say of *Rosa* in particular what was said approvingly of books about black children at the time, that no difference is mentioned. But as a story of real life, it is real inside and out, and being real for children—*simpatico*—it extinguishes the long-standing separation between 'us' and 'them.'

Rosa-Too-Little was presented and received as a book about the library, and we cannot call it a harbinger; but with the family identified as Puerto Rican, with some language difficulty and some economic difficulty indicated, it could be—in appearance, in tenor—a book of 1970. One reviewer speaks, without censure, of "the somber atmosphere . . . reflected in the sepia-and-black illustrations,"[5] which would not have occurred to me. The idea of a picturebook being other than gay and lively was itself new (a rare *Buttons* notwithstanding), and may well have been necessary—a concomitant of the coming psychological as well as social realism.

Where the Forties called for change, the Fifties, following up, was a period of elaborating on "the rich tapestry of American life," as a characteristic annotation put it.[6] If there was less reforming zeal, neither was there the apathy commonly associated with the Eisenhower years. Representative among older books were the Lenski regional stories, *And Now Miguel* (Mexican-American), *Plain Girl* (Amish), *Moccasin Trail* (to-be-or-not-to-be-Indian). In picturebooks, Politi and Milhous held forth, but the excitement, the advance was elsewhere, in graphic design and subjectivity.

Off to one side, of larger scope and intent, is William Gropper's *The Little Tailor*—per the jacket, "a story in pictures of America in the making." Gropper, best known for his sharp social criticism, had done some (benign) juvenile illustration; he had also, during the brief flowering of the novel-in-pictures, done *Alay-Oop* (1930), a romantic melodrama of the circus, fittingly fluid, florid and great fun. "The really original conception among this year's stories in pictures," is

Lewis Gannett's more sober assessment.[7]

"Many many years ago, in a sleepy little town called Nochi, which was hidden far away in the darkest end of Europe," our story begins, "there lived a little tailor who made the most beautiful clothes in the world." A fairy tale, yes; a modern fairy tale. People come to him from all over the province, the plain to look elegant, the meek to command respect; in his eyes, they are all the same (435). With his clothes, his fame spreads: in France he is *"le petit tailleur"*; in Italy *"il sarto piccolino"*; in Spain *"el sastre pequeño,"* in Germany *"der kleiner schneidermeister."* Cross-legged on his table, a poor man with many children, "mainly daughters," the little tailor knows nothing of this.

He has a letter from a friend in America urging him to come to the wonderful new country . . . "Where the buildings were so tall that they reached up into the sky. . . . Where fruit grew in baskets, apples in barrels, potatoes in sacks, and there were plates full of bread, already buttered." Not to mention the streets paved with gold. As he travels, he finds that his clothes, and his name, have gone before him . . . (436).

In New York are old friends and strangeness: the crowded East Side streets, people living on top of one another, a shop where tailors in one row make only sleeves, another group attach them to jackets, a line of women sew on buttons, pressers press; and when the season's work is done, work ceases (437). Walking the streets looking for a job, "He tried to recognize one of the thousands of sleeves he had made, so he might feel the same pride in his work that he had in the old country, but the coats and their sleeves were all strangers to him." Where is this dreamland of opportunity, he demands of the friend who wrote the glowing letters. All around you, he's told; and sure enough, the pushcart peddler is planning to open a little store, then a bigger one, the newsboy expects to be a reporter, the singing waiter is a composer, "they all have ambitions."

Returning home, the little tailor is greeted by his neighbor with tickets for a concert "her little boy was going to perform uptown" and an order for a dress and a suit. He has discovered America, he tells his wife; he is going to "create new designs for clothes starting right here in this room," clothes so beautiful that—

435-437. *The Little Tailor,* by William Gropper. Dodd, Mead, 1955. 6 x 8⅝.

435

When people were undressed, you could not tell the difference between the butcher and the soldier, the poet and the merchant, the fiddler and the lawyer, the baker and the teacher.
They were just sizes—tall, short, stout and thin.

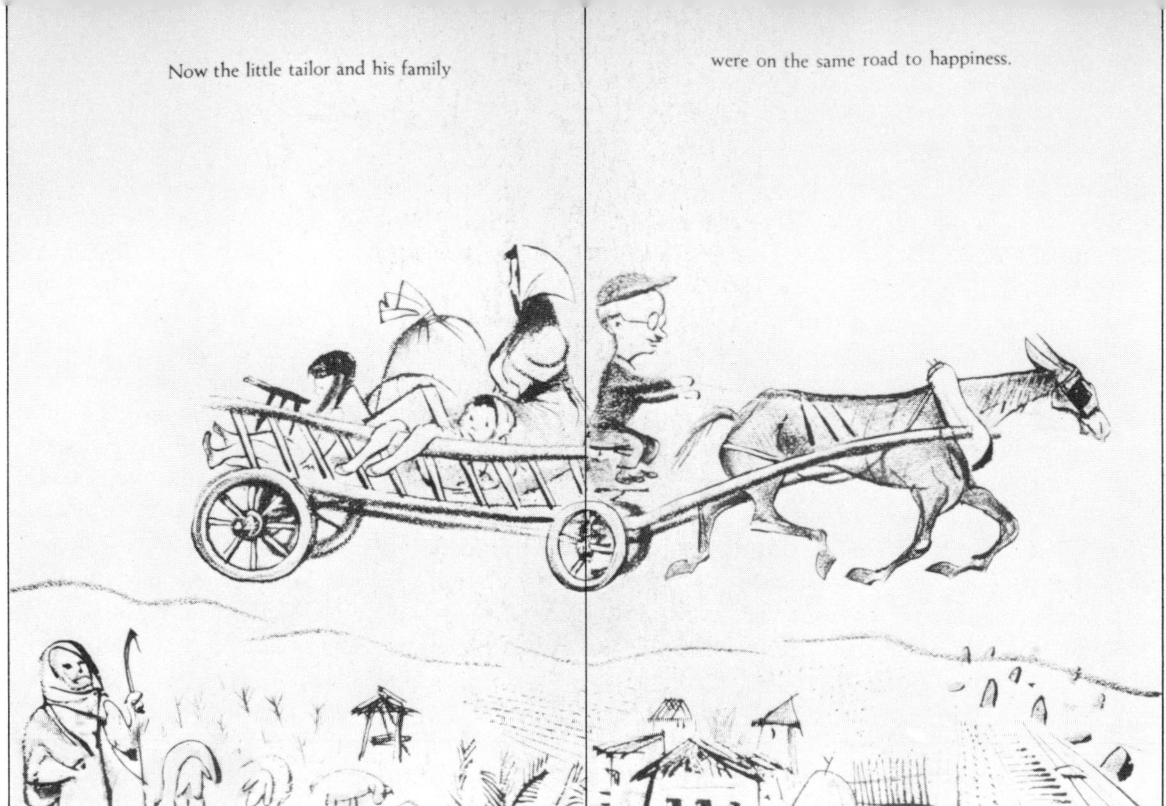
Now the little tailor and his family
were on the same road to happiness.

436

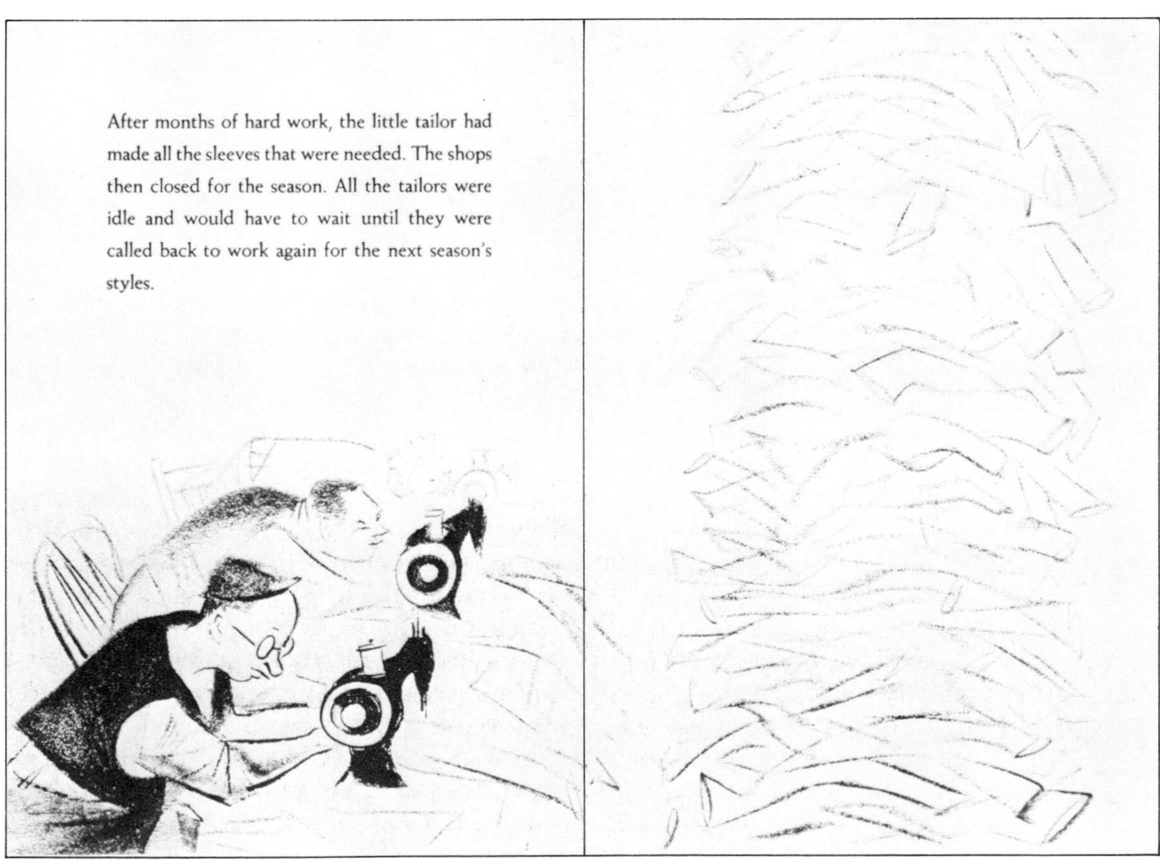
After months of hard work, the little tailor had made all the sleeves that were needed. The shops then closed for the season. All the tailors were idle and would have to wait until they were called back to work again for the next season's styles.

437

even before he has "a fine salon of his own on Fifth Avenue"—people from all walks of life will find their way to his door.

One can smile at the naivete, question the optimism, flinch at the rhetoric—"This is a country where everyone is free to say what he thinks, free to agree or disagree . . . where there are free elections, equal opportunity and fair play for every race, creed or color." But from the Sholom Aleichem beginnings to the Chagall-like flight to the exposé of piecework—a theme of Gropper prints—to the idealistic rhetoric itself, *The Little Tailor* is authentic Americana, as much a historical document as the immigrant biographies of Louis Adamic or Mary Antin. In 1955 it was the Promised Land revisited and, moreover, reaffirmed; and in 1955, ironically, Gropper's radical past and the wary present militated against it. That, and its being out of the ordinary, hard to classify. (Had picturebooks as such been subject to the Dewey decimal system, they could not have achieved their diversity.) For its good drawing and gusto too, it deserves somehow to be preserved.

What the Fifties arrived at, unnoticed, was democracy in action, represented nowhere better than by Stan the saving garbage man (p. 468). No mere neighborhood helper, Stan: he's an original, a dreamer—and after the junk he gives away one day is returned the next, a sadder but wiser garbage man, a real pro. He is also something of a cartoon character, like his pup predecessor *Harry the Dirty Dog*; and, whatever their iniquities, cartoons and comic strips did "keep abreast of contemporary life," as the Child Study Association's reading expert, Josette Frank, observed.[8] They weren't stuffy, and the acceptance of cartooning as one among many possible approaches was an additional if unintentional social leveler.

With the Sixties—Kennedy, the 'New Frontier'—the frontal attack resumed, ready to acknowledge differences, bent still on dispelling them. "Juanito was miserable. Only two days before, on his eighth birthday, he and his family had arrived in New York, all the way from Puerto Rico. Now he was in a new home, with no friends to talk to. For Juanito spoke only Spanish. And, to make him feel even lonelier . . . his dog was lost." How Juanito finds Pepito—who understands only Spanish too—is a tale of the city in cross-section, with Lily and Kim from Chinatown, Angelo from Little Italy, Sally and Susie from Park Avenue, Billy and Bud from Harlem all joining, Chicken-Little fashion, in the search (438). Ingenuous as it is, and unlikely, to call it contrived is to miss the point of its stylized naturalism, of a form designed for a function. Typography, color, layout have parts to play, and so, operatively, jubilantly, does the second language: when Pepito is found, riding behind a mounted policeman ("We've been looking for you, too"), his welcome to Juanito is *¡jau-jau!*

The next years brought an end to innocence and snap accommodation. The sit-ins had begun, the Freedom Rides followed in 1961; in 1962 James Meredith entered the University of Mississippi, in 1963 Martin Luther King marched on Birmingham; 1963 saw also the March on Washington, 1964 the Civil Rights Act and the 'War on Poverty,' 1965 disillusion—and in short order Watts, the cry for 'black power,' the emergence of the Black Panthers. That was the year, too, of the first large anti-war protests. In 1968 Dr. King was assassinated, and Robert Kennedy; the Kerner Commission reported that "our nation is moving towards two societies, one black, one white—separate and unequal"; the Chicago convention demonstrations erupted. The counterculture had come, and after black liberation, 'free schools,' 'open classrooms'; women's liberation; welfare rights, tenants' rights, student rights; community action and community control.

There appeared books—besides *The Autobiography of Malcolm X*, *Manchild in the Promised Land*, *Soul on Ice*, *Down These Mean Streets*, the testaments of teachers: Jonathan Kozol's *Death at an Early Age*, Herbert Kohl's *36 Children*, James Herndon's *The Way It Spozed To Be*. These last, with writer-researchers John Holt (*How Children Fail*) and Robert Coles (*Children of Crisis*),

They rode on a bus to Harlem,
where they met Billy and Bud.
"Have you seen a lost dog that's red,
shaggy, bowlegged, and big,
with little eyes?" they asked.
"No," said Billy.
He pointed to the name on his sweater.
Bud did the same, too.
"What is your dog's name?" Billy asked.
¡PEPITO!
As he said the name
Juanito could hold back
his tears no longer.
"Don't give up," said Billy.
"We're all with you.
We'll help you look."

438. *My Dog Is Lost!* text by Ezra Jack Keats and Pat Cherr, pictures by Ezra Jack Keats. Crowell, 1960. 6½ x 9¼.

formed, as it were, a new cadre, committed to preserving the spirits of ghetto children, of all children. "Some day, maybe, there will exist a well-informed, well-considered, and yet fervent conviction that the most deadly of all possible sins is the mutilation of a child's spirit . . . ." The words are Erik Erikson's, chosen by Kozol for his epigraph; Coles, Erikson's expounder, tells of discussing *Childhood and Society* with a black student jailed in Alabama in the early Sixties, of other copies in Southern freedom houses and Appalachian outposts. Within a few years of its publication in 1950 *Childhood and Society*, Erikson's first major work, had become "a classic . . . on the social significance of childhood."[9] The civil rights movement gave it new meaning.

This is important: picturebooks had tried to feed social significance to children, if not straight, obliquely, and some would continue to; but with recognition that childhood itself had social significance came books more concerned with reinforcing a child's identity, whatever his color or circumstance, than with acceptance—by him of others, by others of him. He was to have trust in himself and his world, and the joy of it, whatever it was.

So, *Linda* (439). Frank Asch was a young man who did, first, a very funny, funky book, *George's Store* (McGraw-Hill, 1969), the Marx Brothers at Alice's Restaurant as drawn for the *Berkeley Barb*. Linda wakes in a room that makes Edward Hopper's bleak interiors look cozy, and says her first GOOD MORNING to the mouse on her bed. Then it's GOOD MORNING street, dog, empty boxes (kids inside), junked mattress (bouncing) and car; and, surprise, GOOD MORNING DIME. The dime brings ICE CREAM, the ice cream FRIEND, and OH YES, another;—until LINDA and, arms outstretched, GOOD MORNING . . . NIGHTTIME.

Linda embraces Brownsville, Roxbury, every cruddy city neighborhood I can't name; and in the litter-landscapes are secrets to be found, as in any sylvan pool or field of grass. On the bare walls faces take shape, and fingers, running figures; a demon peers over a fence, a building front is a living signboard; the mouse grows into, at left, a little elephant. A bearded humpty-dumpty hefting a sack is

439. *Linda,* by Frank Asch. McGraw-Hill, 1969. 9¾ x 7¼.

SANTA CLAUS; between his lips hangs a cigarette, unlit, between his toes another, burning. Associative or absurd, imagery is abundant, even superabundant—the antithesis of impoverishment.

Linda is extreme, a culture shock; more squarely representative of the new social and emotional climate are Eleanor Schick's *City in the Summer* (1969) and *City in the Winter* (1970). *City in the Summer* tells of hot, restless days on the sidewalk and hot, placid days on the roof, and one particular day when Jerry's friend, his elderly neighbor, takes him on the subway to the beach—still in the morning, crowded and noisy, still again—and then on the subway, home. The constriction and release are almost palpable.

In *City in the Winter* (440), there are Jimmy and his young working mother and his grandmother who keeps house. Because of a blizzard, school is closed: "You and Grandma will have a good time today," says Jimmy's mother, "but there's no snow holiday for me." When she's gone, Jimmy has breakfast, pretending, with a toy cat, that the cats next door "were in the kitchen with him, eating hot breakfasts and staying warm beside the radiator." He helps his grandmother straighten up, she helps him find something to do: a carton becomes a barn for Jimmy's animals, "snowed in just like we are." At noon his lunch box, packed the night before, suggests a picnic on the floor.

The snow has stopped. Jimmy throws bits of bread on the near-by roof for the birds; in a few minutes it is gone, and he sees tiny footprints in the snow. Grandma knows he'd like to go out, so they head for the store to buy some milk, Jimmy walking behind, "stepping in her boot prints and holding on to her coat." It is very quiet and very cold, and the store is closed. But there is enough milk for tonight, Grandma says; "Let's go home and get warm!" Up the stairs, boots off, soup on, table set, they wait for his mother to come home (441). During dinner he tells about the day, before bed, about the bird footprints outside. "You can show them to me in the morning, before you go to school."

Without a story, it is a continuously eventful day; without a pattern or agenda (cf. *The Little Family*), the routine of a day. Without color—the same muted caramels and blues are used throughout—a convincing snowy day (cf.p.380). Without drama, close-felt. On the inside of the door where Jimmy's mother's keys hang are a snap lock, a bolt and a chain; when he stands listening to her leave in the morning, the chain is on. Everything is in place and accountable, each little thing that children put great stock in, in reality and in their books; and so no single scene is uninteresting, or unimportant. In the life of a city child, the chain on the door is important; to a child whose mother works, her leaving is important, her coming home most important of all. We spoke at the start about recognition as confirmation, validation; implicitly, it is self-recognition: *see me*. Security and a sense of worth grow from it.

Hence the value of visibility for blacks, unmarried mothers, plain folks alike; and the good of pans of water on the radiators, socks and slippers on Grandma, a chain on the door. There is of course another reason. Why is there a chain on the door? asks the child who's never seen one. Where is the little boy's father? comes quickly from the child whose own father is there every day. To enter into other, different lives as real as one's own is a means of understanding; and understanding, of caring. Jimmy is not unhappy or lonely,

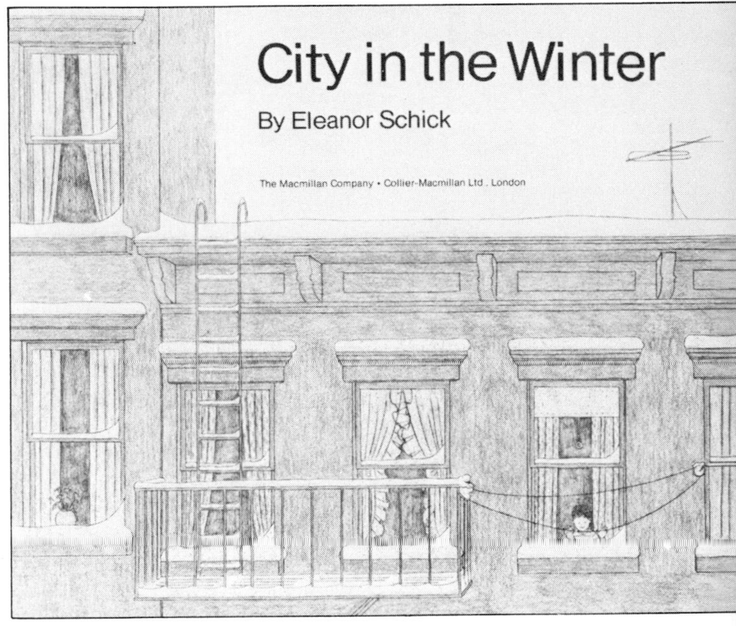

440

but the wait for his mother is long; waiting for a parent often seems long, how much longer, then, it must seem to Jimmy.

This is the emotional increment of the years between a *Little Family* (1932) and an *At*

440, 441. *City in the Winter*, by Eleanor Schick. Macmillan, 1970. 9¾ x 8.

Then he lined up his animals on the windowsill to watch
the sun go down. He waited as the sky turned orange,
then purple, and then dark. Grandma waited too.
But it was a long time before they heard the sound of boots
stamping in the hall and the key turning in the lock.
Jimmy ran to the door to hug his mother.
"I'm so glad you're home from the blizzard," he shouted.

441

Our House (1943) and such a book as *City in the Winter* (1970); we will see its development from the nascent conflict in *Wait Till the Moon Is Full* (1948) alluded to earlier. There is no overt conflict in *City in the Winter* nor is there the direct assertiveness of *Rosa-Too-Little*; both are internalized, however, not absent—once accepted, taken into consideration. The result is a socio-economic profile with psychological substance, to put it grandly; or Jimmy and his grandmother waiting to hear his mother mount the stairs. An extraordinary ordinary day: "I'm so glad you're home from the blizzard."

That *City in the Winter*, not 'Jimmy Stays Home' or 'The Day It Snowed,' followed *City in the Summer*—not 'Jerry Goes to the Beach' or 'One Hot Day'—is suggestive:

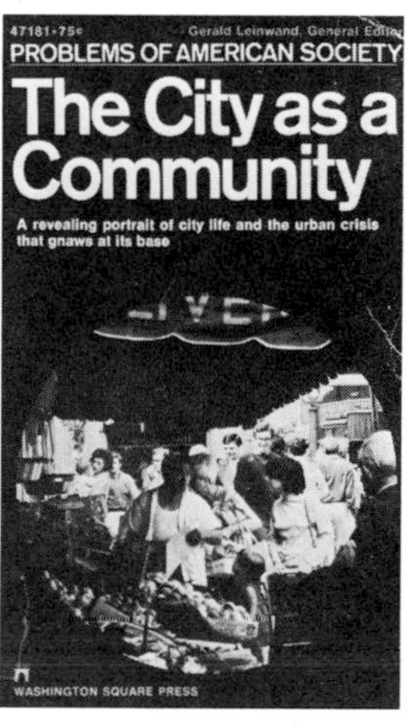

The City as a Community, published also in 1970, "is one of a series of volumes," we are told, "designed to become text materials for urban schools" and "partially funded under Title I, Elementary and Secondary Education Act, Public Law 89-10, 1965."

The Economic Opportunity Act of 1964, the instrument of the War on Poverty, which established Head Start (and the Community Action Program overall, Upward Bound, VISTA, the Job Corps); and, in its wake, the Elementary and Secondary Education Act of 1965, providing, most immediately, for grants to compensatory programs in low-income areas (Title I), were together largely responsible for the outpouring of 'minority' and 'disadvantaged' picturebooks in the later Sixties. Their publication was not subsidized, as was that of *The City as a Community*, but suddenly a huge market existed for them; in the words of one publisher's promotion head whose anonymity will be preserved, "That's when we began to get interested." By 1968 Head Start, the 'prep school' program for low-income preschoolers, extended to thirteen hundred summer and eleven hundred full-year projects, more book-minded than the usual nursery school: "Perhaps the most significant boost that Head Start children are given is their introduction to the world of words" is a contemporary estimate.[10] The manifold Title I programs, some of them for preschoolers also, had as many uses for 'supplementary materials,' and lists of appropriate books—those eligible for purchase—were drawn up at the administering state level. When *City in the Summer* appeared, *Booklist* duly noted: "Head Start and primary teachers will find this a nice addition to material on city life."[11]

The Library Services and Construction Act of 1964 was another contributory: under it was funded the Queens Borough Public Library preschool project, Operation Headstart, which gave its name to the national program; the making of the film, *The Pleasure Is Mutual: How To Conduct Effective Picture Book Programs*, used widely in Head Start training; and a spectrum of efforts to reach and serve the poor unthinkable before.

It would have been possible to approach the books thus, to demonstrate so many dollars, so many blacks, Indians, Chicanos, Appalachians, so many urban poor; but just as black liberation led to women's liberation, to gay liberation, and Community Action, upper case, to community activism, so new forces came into play, and persisted. This is not to follow in the footsteps of *The Little Tailor* and pronounce the coming of the best of all possible worlds, but to suggest, momentarily at least, a climate of broad social engagement, a striving to see people more nearly whole.

NEGRO IDENTIFICATION, BLACK IDENTITY

That certain books might, because of language, illustration or theme, "hurt and alienate" some children "while perpetuating stereotyped ideas in the minds of others" was an idea not itself advanced publicly until the 1940s. The particular formulation is from Augusta Baker's introduction to the 1957 edition of "Books About Negro Life for Children," where, all-embracing, it is coupled with a call for their elimination. In 1957 the future Coordinator of Children's Services at the New York Public Library was Storytelling Specialist; in 1946, when the first of the landmark lists appeared, she was children's librarian at the 135th Street Branch (later the Countee Cullen Branch). That first list came out under the auspices not of the library but of the Bureau for Intercultural Education, one of several agencies, public and private, just then issuing "children's book lists devoted to the democratic ideal."[1] In calling for the banishment of the bad old books and the publication of good new ones, Mrs. Baker invoked, in 1957 too, "the American heritage of freedom and equality," of belief in "the essential dignity and integrity of every human being."

Any history of the Negro in American children's books before this time, picturebooks or otherwise, would have to be concerned chiefly with the bad. The first widely circulated list of recommended titles, appended to an article on "Library Service for Negro Children" in the ALA *Children's Library Yearbook* of 1932, has seventeen entries altogether. Four are books by Erick Berry and Herbert Best set in Africa (qq. v. p. 56); Paul Laurence Dunbar's *Life and Works* is included, and Langston Hughes's *The Dream Keeper*, illustrated by Helen Sewell; three are wholly or in part the work of Mary White Ovington, one of the founders of the NAACP; there are three books of collective biography and three Uncle Remus collections; for younger children, besides one of the Berry books, we find only A. V. Weaver's *Frawg* (Stokes, 1930) and *Little Black Sambo*. Both, we're told, are popular with younger children "but may awaken self-consciousness in older ones because of the illustrations."

It was in the tangible areas of dialect and illustration that the first objections arose. The 1932 commentator remarks that "the most representative and most successful type of illustration has not yet been found for use in books about Negro children for Negro children," and she recommends "scientific investigation."[2] Her criterion is efficacy, her aim to encourage identification and so increase reading. It was a limited, pragmatic concern, without thought to the effect of a negative stereotype—in the common sense, caricature —on black children and children in general.

In 1938 Marjorie Hill Allee, who had just written one of the first of the teenage novels on integration, *The Great Tradition*, called it caricature ("Illustrations are a sore point with teachers and librarians who want good books about Negroes"[3]), and so did Eva Knox Evans in a 1941 *PW* article, "The Negro in Children's Fiction," that touched off an acerbic debate. Mrs. Evans, in *Araminta* and its successors, had written about children like those in her Atlanta (University) kindergarten, Erick Berry based the illustrations on photographs of those same children—and when the children saw the finished book, after having heard the stories and accepted the characters as familiars, they were dumbfounded: they had not realized that Araminta and Jerome Anthony were black because they didn't speak in dialect. Neither did they, Mrs. Evans reminded them, and she reminds the reader that Negro children "no longer affect, if they ever did, the halo of seventeen plaits with a different colored bow of ribbon on each braid."[4]

The response to the article—"one of the most discussed on children's books in recent numbers"[5]—centered on Mrs. Evans's objection to dialect. The defenders were rebuffed in turn by a group of black teachers and librarians: "We Negroes much prefer the sincere democratic feeling of Eva Knox Evans to the 'real affection' of [those] who wish to preserve the 'kindly quaintness' of the Negro," concluded Virginia Lacy Jones and Charlemae Rollins and five others.[6]

Distinctions are not always clear-cut, however, as *Little Black Sambo* demonstrates. Included on the 1932 list despite its potentially embarrassing illustrations, it remained in general esteem through the Thirties and, with new emphasis on the Indian setting, beyond. Dorothy Canfield Fisher, a practicing progressive, welcomed the publication of *Sambo and the Twins* in 1936. Anne Carroll Moore called it "the event of the year among children's books";[7] a 1940 New York Public Library report speaks in passing of "third grade Negro children clamoring for *Little Black Sambo*" on a class visit;[8] both appeared on the standard lists, *Sambo* itself into the Fifties (ALA *Basic Book Collection for Elementary Grades*) and Sixties (*Children's Catalog*). What Anne Eaton wrote in 1946, that it was "a classic of childhood no boy or girl should miss,"[9] expressed a common sentiment.

But the battle had been joined. "There is probably no library in the country that has not at some time been requested to take *Little Black Sambo* off its shelves because it is supposed to teach children that colored people are rather stupid, prefer fantastic colors, and are gluttonous. As a matter of fact most children regard Little Black Sambo as the hero of thrilling and enviable adventures whose appetite may be astonishing but is wholly admirable." So Clara Breed of the San Diego Public Library in *The Horn Book*, January 1945. In *Childhood Education* in November of that year Helen Trager, of the Bureau for Intercultural Education, sums up her opposition—based on "the distorted and ugly picture" imposed by the illustrations—as follows: "At the present time to dismiss these stories as harmless because they are liked by white children is to ignore the requirements for better intergroup relations."

Both *Sambo* and *Sambo and the Twins* appear as well on the 1946 list of "Books About Negro Life for Children," the first of the series (though not in subsequent editions): "Helen Bannerman's *Little Black Sambo* has been included because there is a lack of material for the pre-school and primary age groups. It is a book which, being out of copyright, has been mutilated in cheap editions and has thus been misinterpreted. The original small Stokes edition [the one everywhere listed] has no dialect and no condescension, and Little Black Sambo is clearly the hero. Unfortunately, there is an emotional attitude connected with the name *Black Sambo* because the words are now often used in derision and not as a term of affection . . . . It is a jungle story and should never be presented as a picture of Negro life, nor should it be the only book of Negro or jungle life given to a child." It was Mrs. Baker's hope that the list would stimulate the publication of others.

Overall, the library saw itself as responsible for preserving "the cultural heritage that literature hands on to succeeding generations";[10] the defender of *Little Black Sambo* spoke up also for *The Merchant of Venice* and for Kipling. That there might be a compelling reason to modify that position, that it might entail a 'clear and present danger,' was an idea that came hard to many—outside of libraries too.

Nor, any more than the larger civil liberties issue, will the question of suppression vs. judicious selection ever be put entirely to rest.

In the current arena, Ellis Credle had followed *Across the Cotton Patch* with a story entirely about a contemporary—1930s—Negro child, *Little Jeemes Henry.* Though his problem, how to get money to go to the circus, is universal, Jeemes Henry is distinctly the child of Southern sharecroppers in a world of fervent black preachers and cool, pleasant white folks. (In one of the funniest episodes, the cook at the big house turns away Jeemes Henry and his blackberries—"First thing you know dese white folks'll have me standin' over de hot stove cookin' blackberry jam"; and sure enough, 'Miss Mary' buys them.) A world, too, where the blacks have a mule wagon, the whites a big car—and a penny for Jeemes Henry when he opens the gate (442).

Jeemes Henry's father has set out for the city to "git myself a job and make a pocketful of money," and thereon hangs the tale; when Jeemes Henry, after the requisite mishaps, has at last earned his way to the circus, the caged, kicking Wild Man from Borneo is—happiness and horror—his Pappy. The first sight of Jeemes Henry, in his Sunday best, waiting in the cage while his grass-skirted father finishes "actin' wild" is as lacerating as anything in picturebooks. But Pappy, who has his 'pocketful o' money,' is jubilant at the hoax and a hero to the 'colored folk,' and Jeemes Henry, after a hoist to the clown's shoulder, is triumphant too. Similarly, one can elect to see only degradation in Pappy's pretense or one can, in the spirit of puttin' Massa on, of Zora Neale Hurston's tales, admire the man's wit and guts.

Publicly at least, *Little Jeemes Henry* was received with approbation untouched with disquiet (of any kind). Publisher and author were aware, however, of the growing objection to dialect and to drawings in general, and Credle's next book about a black child, *The Flop-Eared Hound* (Oxford, 1938), was written in standard English and illustrated with photographs by her husband Charles Townsend. An everyday story of a bothersome dog who proves his worth—with carefully composed, quite static pictures—*The Flop-Eared Hound* combines conventional appeal with evident realism: black children could at once like it and identify with it, white children like it and believe in it. With or without a plot, the photographic story became, for several years, the preferred way not merely to remedy a lack of acceptable material but to supply positive, credible models.

Around the time that Ellis Credle was producing *The Flop-Eared Hound* out of her Southern mountain experience, Stella Gentry Sharpe was asked by "a little colored boy" in

442. *Little Jeemes Henry,* by Ellis Credle. Nelson, 1936. 7¼ x 8⅝.

"Thank you, Jeemes Henry," said Mr. Moore, and he fished into his pocket and found a bright new penny for little Jeemes Henry.

Jeemes Henry bowed and scraped and showed all his white teeth. Then he ran back to the cotton patch and showed the penny to his Mammy.

"All Ah got to have now is foty-nine mo'!" cried Jeemes Henry joyfully.

"You just keep at it," urged Mammy. "You'll git 'em!"

443

443, 444. *Tobe,* text by Stella Gentry Sharpe, photographs by Charles Farrell. Chapel Hill, University of North Carolina Press, 1939. 7¼ x 10⅜.

444

her Chapel Hill neighborhood "why all his story books were about white children,"[11] and in response she wrote *Tobe*, an account of the doings of a black farm family. The University of North Carolina Press took it on in the same spirit, to meet a need, and apparently the need was felt: a second doubled printing followed six months after the first.

Tobe is an artless book written in primerese: "Daddy has a cart. He made it himself. Sometimes he lets us play with it." (443) But it is full of real work—bundling wheat and digging sweet potatoes, picking tomatoes and cotton (444)—and play; and the work that is really play—feeding the hens and the mules, trapping rabbits, gathering honey. Tired as the children are at times, and reluctant, there is (unrealistically?) no sense of drudgery; and the city or suburban child—shades of E. Boyd Smith—is bound to envy Tobe and his big brothers, they have so much more to *do* than he has, so many more grown-up responsibilities and opportunities. As a record of Southern rural life, unaffectedly photographed, *Tobe* merits its semipermanent place on preferred lists; but its durability is due, I suspect, to its old-fashioned simplicity—at each opening one topic, one photo and facing text—and its natural interest.

In contrast to *Tobe*'s modest portrayal of plain people, there appeared in 1944 *My Happy Days*, "a photographic representation of the real life of a happy boy in a home where he has the companionship of an intelligent sister and the comradeship of intelligent parents who, taking seriously the future of their children, endeavor to guide them properly in their studies, in their recreation, in their participation in the work of the home and in their contacts with persons and things." The words of the jacket precisely reflect the tone of the text and the gist of the book (445)—self-conscious, 'aspiring,' middle class. Idealistic. Eslanda Goode Robeson—Mrs. Paul Robeson—reviewed it for the *Hartford Courant*:

"At first struck by the warmth and charm of the boy and his family, the reader gradually becomes more and more impressed by

445. *My Happy Days,* text by Jane Dabney Shackelford, photographs by Cecil Vinson. Washington, Associated, 1944. 7¼ x 10⅜.

the underlying, fundamental importance of the story. For that story suggests the vital responsibility of American parents to their children, and how such responsibility can be, and is, fulfilled by parents of average intelligence and means. Such fulfillment brings real, constructive enjoyment and benefit to themselves, their children, and ultimately to the community and the Nation. . . .

"The fact that Rex Nelson is Negro is incidental, as I believe it should be. However, it may occur to some alert white folks that they are missing a great deal when they segregate themselves from the Nelsons and the many Negro families like them."[12]

Tobe can be considered a catalog, *My Happy Days* a catechism, but *My Dog Rinty* is a book—a piece of professional entertainment that has outlasted its purpose. Working with community groups on the South Side of Chicago, Marie Ets noticed the paucity of books about the black city child, and suggested the project; Ellen Tarry, an alumnus of the Bank Street Writers' Laboratory ("They wanted Claude McKay"—ET) and the author of two picturebooks, *Janie Belle* (Garden City, 1940) and *Hezekiah Horton* (Viking, 1942), was May Massee's natural choice as collaborator. A contest had been held in Harlem to choose the artist for *Hezekiah Horton* but this time ("Thank goodness") there was no need: Alexander Alland had just taken the photographs for *The Springfield Plan* (Viking, 1945), the record of a communitywide attack on racial and religious intolerance; he and his wife Alexandra were obviously qualified. (To Alexander Alland is due also the eventual recognition of Jacob Riis as a documentary photographer.)

Like many photographic books of the time, *The Springfield Plan* was conceived and constructed very like a documentary film—in this case knowingly: how wonderful it would be, says the jacket, if, inspired by one or another film, "we could take the pictures back with us, to study whenever we felt the need." ("Well, just that has been made possible in this book . . . .") Pare Lorentz's lyrical essays, the high-keyed March of Time reports, wartime evocations of bravery and sacrifice had all made their mark, and the semidocumentary —authenticity substantiating fiction—was in the offing. Louis de Rochemont's *House on 92nd Street* dates also from 1945.

It is not too much to call *My Dog Rinty*, similarly shot 'on location,' a semidocumentary. Rinty is, yes, a bad dog who makes good and the story is wholly fabricated but it involves real places, public and private, and real people in their real-life roles—including the man reading picturebooks at the library (Spencer Shaw) and the 'story-lady' upstairs (Augusta Baker).

The realities of life in Harlem are broached too. Forever getting away and causing damage, Rinty is sent to obedience school and cured of every bad habit except making holes in people's carpets and trying to tear up their floors. He's a born ratter and mouser, the trainer explains, "worth a fortune." Fame instead comes to David and Rinty: "They were wanted at the hotel where dogs are not allowed. They were wanted at the hospital. They were wanted at the ten-cent store. They were wanted at the flower shop." Their picture is in the papers, they're the "Pied Pipers of Harlem." "But best of all, the owner of a block of old buildings where the poor people live in Harlem said: 'David and Rinty have shown me that my old buildings are full of holes. I'm going to tear them down and build new ones.'" There will be a big yard in the center and a welcome for well-behaved children and dogs—David and Rinty first (446).

446. *My Dog Rinty,* by Ellen Tarry and Marie Hall Ets, photographs by Alexandra and Alexander Alland. Viking, 1946. 7¼ x 9⅜.

Showing the social range in a community, any community, from hardship to decency to comfort to luxury (in Harlem from tenements to David's walk-up to a project, River House, to Sugar Hill "where Joe Louis lives when he's in town"); indicating that the poor in old buildings live poorly; suggesting a concrete solution, that the buildings be replaced: all this was novel in a picturebook in 1946. Documenting life in a black community, intending that Harlem be seen like other places, the authors and photographers made it possible for other places to be seen like Harlem.

Of course *My Dog Rinty* lives for children for different reasons. A dog relinquished, then regained, everywhere shunned, then welcomed (the reiteration of "They were wanted . . .") is not to be denied. But without the brick-and-mortar development, authenticated by the photographs, one wouldn't hold to the thought that, honestly, there must be something to it, some boy and dog who caught rats and got their picture in the paper. See, they're right here, on the last page.

The space is a hiatus. Between the first of the Baker lists in 1946 and the fourth in 1961, intolerance was widely denounced, the Supreme Court acted on school segregation, the Montgomery bus boycott launched the civil rights movement; and the list of recommended 'Picture Books and Readers' gained four American entries and lost three, a net gain of one. If one adds *My Dog Rinty* and Ellen Tarry's later *Runaway Elephant* (Viking, 1950), classified among 'Stories for Younger Children,' the total is three. The significant increase was in fiction and nonfiction where 'problems' could be dealt with; if a single Negro child appeared in a picturebook —the little girl twice seen in *The Park Book*— it was cause for favorable comment.

The book that broke the jam was Ezra Jack Keats's 1962 *The Snowy Day*. The sight of Peter's head silhouetted against the snow-capped skyline, of his full-cheeked profile rounding out the curves of his hood, of his strikingly African skull as he sits in the tub 'thinking and thinking and thinking' about the day just gone—after this there was no question that a dark-skinned child could enhance a picturebook (447).

From the mottled snowflake endpapers (and matching flaps—a Keats trademark) to the crisp sunny forms in Peter's house, *The Snowy Day* is a beautiful book, and it won the Caldecott to general acclaim. Saying very little, following Peter through the snow—now he makes tracks, toes in, toes out, now he picks up a stick, smacks a tree and "Down fell the snow—plop!—on top of Peter's head" —it becomes every child's wintry day of discovery. The snowball put away in his pocket "for tomorrow" melts, or rather 'it isn't there': why explain when the loss is what saddens Peter, when the listening child knows? A wise book too, as well as beautiful; a popular success; something to cleave to: for a cause, a proper champion.

On the heels of the Lionni *Inch by Inch* (p. 528), it was also a big boost for collage; or specifically, in Keats's case, for the use of textured and patterned materials—the lineny bedclothes, the pajamas and wallpaper—for their associative and decorative properties. "Collage is a way of making art," Harold Rosenberg has written, "but it is not a specific art form, nor is it a style."[13] The lineny texture is a ready-made sheet, the flower pattern ready-made pajamas; and this is the way, imitatively, that collage has been used by children and homebodies right along. There is no introduction of the odd, the unexpected (Rand's quizzical bird), nor is there a stress on the reality of the object represented (the newspaper scrap, the pasted shells), major aspects of collage as a twentieth century art impulse. Yet Peter's pajamas and his mother's gingham check dress are pieces of everyday reality, and as such expressive, while the wallpaper, an unlikely choice, takes on the reality of any paper pattern.

At work too is the cut-paper stimulus. We do not see, often, the scissor-stroke that Matisse showed plain, but like Esphyr Slobodkina's cut-outs for *The Little Fireman*, Keats's work has a simplicity of line and a broadness of form foreign ordinarily to paint or pen. It seems likely, moreover, that Matisse is somewhere behind that wild wallpaper, the brilliant pink and orange and yellow buildings outside (under a violet sky); and that the very making of cut-outs, the play factor, frees the artist to play as well with color and pattern. Cut-outs, finally, are intrinsically flat —silhouetted form; and though Keats introduces a modicum of modeling and definition, essentially Peter, a dark child, is seen in silhouette. For young children it was the one wholly successful representation since the 1932 call for investigation of ways and means; and, like the book itself, an opening.

Keats did several more about Peter, increasingly anecdotal as Peter ostensibly grows older and increasingly given over to lush, extraneous visual effects—a direction heightened by his switch from painted and printed papers, and cut paper supplemented with paint, to paint itself—a heavy turbulent impasto.

In terms of books about Negro life, Keats's accomplishment was to make Peter the appealing counterpart of other children, and this was the course followed by others through most of the Sixties. Here and there a housing-project child appeared (Ann Herbert Scott's *Big Cowboy Western*, 1965) or a youngster living modestly with a grandmother (Joan Lexau's *Benjie*, 1964), but by

6

One winter morning Peter woke up and looked out the window. Snow had fallen during the night. It covered everything as far as he could see.

447. *The Snowy Day,* by Ezra Jack Keats. Viking, 1962. 9 x 8.

448. *Harriet and the Promised Land,* (text by Gwen Lawrence and Robert Kraus), pictures by Jacob Lawrence. Windmill-Simon & Schuster, 1968. 8⅞ x 11⅞.

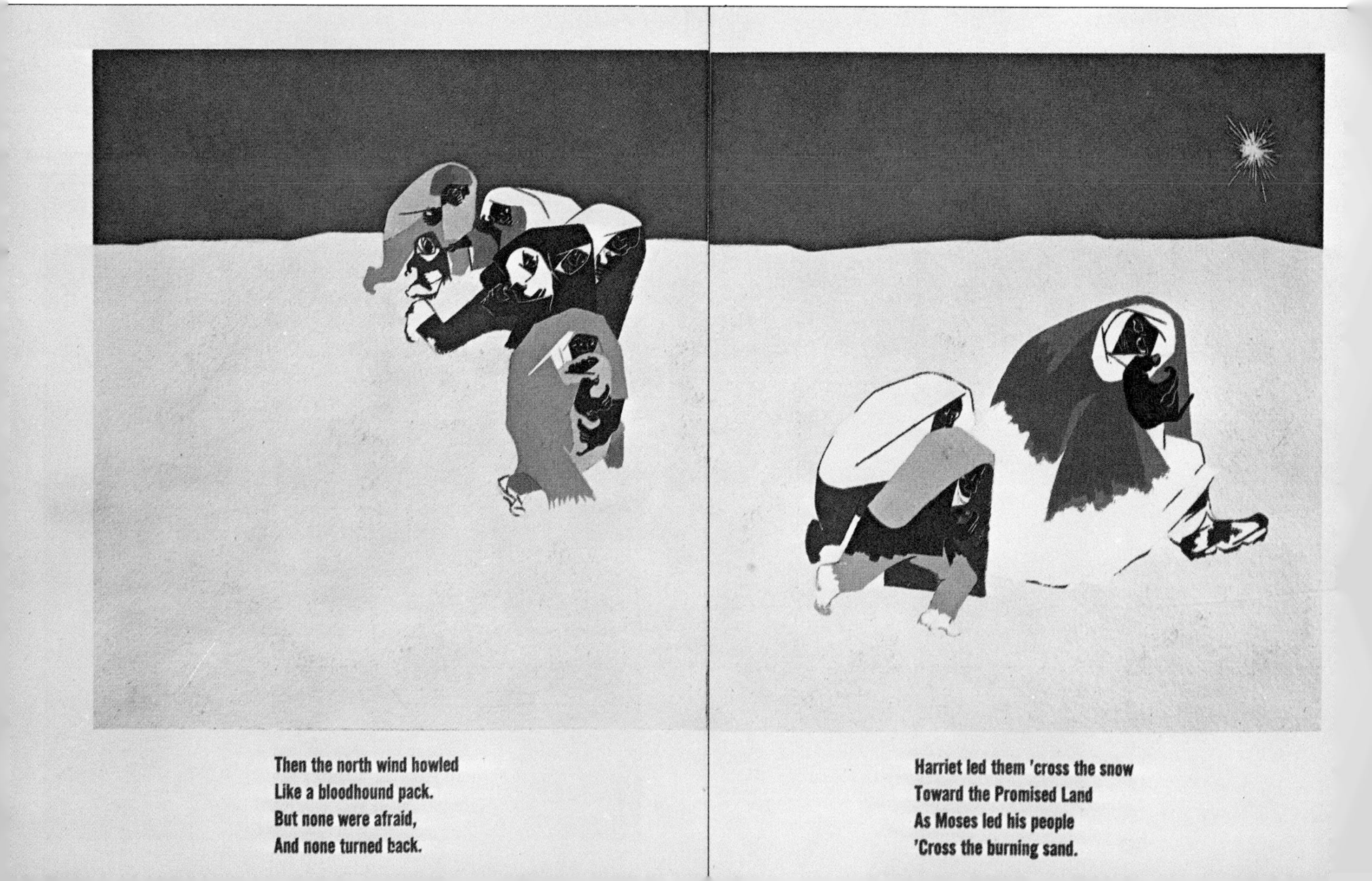

Then the north wind howled
Like a bloodhound pack.
But none were afraid,
And none turned back.

Harriet led them 'cross the snow
Toward the Promised Land
As Moses led his people
'Cross the burning sand.

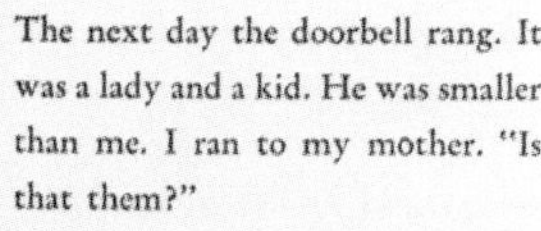
The next day the doorbell rang. It was a lady and a kid. He was smaller than me. I ran to my mother. "Is that them?"
They went in the kitchen but I stayed out in the hall to listen.

449. *Stevie,* by John Steptoe. Harper, 1969. 7 x 9.

and large Negro teachers and librarians actively opposed the identification of black life with deprivation, maintaining that a positive image was more beneficial to small children than a natural likeness. The change, when it came, came swiftly.

Banned along with latchkeys and loose plaster was the bandanna head—any reference to the toil and heartache of slavery and slavery's successor, sharecropping; and when *Oh Lord, I Wish I Was a Buzzard* came out of the Mississippi Head Start program early in 1967, it was a dubious prospect. Recalls an old woman of her childhood:

> My Daddy told us
> if we didn't pick a lot of cotton
> we were going to get a whipping.
>
> My Daddy told us
> if we did pick a lot of cotton
> we might get a sucker.

On the March through Mississippi in 1966 Stokely Carmichael raised the cry 'Black Power,' in 1967 the first Black Power Conference, at Newark, was held, in 1968 *Oh Lord, I Wish I Was a Buzzard* appeared: "As a little black girl picks cotton she wishes she could change places with more fortunate creatures. Striking illustrations capture the poignant mood of the story" (New York Public Library, *Children's Books 1968*). Black power, black pride, black identity.

Aliki's *A Weed Is a Flower: The Story of George Washington Carver* (Prentice-Hall, 1965), one of a group of picture-biographies that includes *The Story of Johnny Appleseed,* has a fearsome scene of night flight; but Carver's story on the whole is a happy one, and amenable to illustration. Not so Harriet Tubman's, not outwardly; and how does one picture a prophet?

It is not pretentious to say that it helps to be an artist, and, like Jacob Lawrence, "a phenomenon almost unique in our time: a narrative painter."[14] As a boy Lawrence came under the tutelage of Charles Alston at a Harlem settlement, continued his studies at the 135th Street Library art classes, then under the WPA; a stint with the CCC, a scholarship at the American Artists School, work with the Federal Art Project ("the experiences of his generation"[15]), the first of three Rosenwald Fellowships—and in 1941 Lawrence made his art world debut with a one-man show of *The Migration of the Negro During World War I* series at the Downtown Gallery. "A running narrative, with the cadences and simplicity of a spiritual, served as captions for the sixty panels which told the story in sparse symbols, harsh, poster-like colors and figures abstracted into silhouettes like those in an Egyptian wall painting."[16] The Museum of Modern Art and the Phillips Memorial Gallery in Washington vied for the sixty paintings, and finally divided them; *Fortune* published a portfolio of twenty-six.

Though the *Migration* series and the *Harlem* group that followed established Lawrence's reputation, he had already painted, also serially, the lives of Toussaint L'Ouverture, Frederick Douglass and Harriet Tubman herself. "I was always interested in Negro history,"[17] he told an interviewer in 1945; and, "My work is abstract in the sense of having been designed and composed, but it is not abstract in the sense of having no human content . . . I want the idea to strike right away."[18]

When cartoonist-illustrator Robert Kraus set up Windmill Books he asked Lawrence, among other artist friends, to consider what he might do for children, and Harriet was his choice of subject. Once again he did a series of paintings and, when a selection had been made, Kraus and Gwen Lawrence wrote the (unattributed) text; the result, *Harriet and the Promised Land*, is harsh and loving, rigorous, bold, exultant: a frenzied affirmation.

Harriet's hands, those famous calloused straining hands, grow big and bigger—guiding hands; the sheltering woods flicker, camouflaging fugitives and animals alike; the ground tilts up, levels out, deepens; only the North Star remains constant (448). There is suffering, fright, but no fear. The ballad rhythm rouses and binds:

> Harriet, grow bigger.
> Harriet, grow stronger.
> Harriet, work harder.
> Harriet, work longer.
>
> She said, "Believe in the Lord!"
> She said, "Believe in me!"
> She said, "Brothers! Sisters!
> We're going to be free!"

It is not a comfortable book to take in. At its calmest, there is a nervous energy about it; and in some compositions, a structural complexity such that forms are not quickly distinguishable. But it is a big work appropriate to a big idea, one whose personal and particular images have the quality of universal experience.

Lawrence was there, he had anticipated the new mood;. John Steptoe, at nineteen, emerged from it. *Stevie* is above all confident —a bold transposition of Rouault to the nursery (449). It is as if Steptoe, not knowing that there was a way to illustrate for young children, or being told, went his own way; and in his own way made something fresh of a child's perennial resentment of a newcomer—"his old crybaby self." That Stevie's mother leaves him at Robert's during the working week, that the two boys don't speak schoolbook English, is secondary, surely, to the strong bright intimacy. If *Stevie* is, circumstantially, a 'black' book, it is also, because of the substantiation, the more credible regardless; like *Rosa-Too-Little* it has character, like *My Dog Rinty* verisimilitude. The icon-like intensity is Steptoe's art.

In *Uptown* and especially in *Train Ride* (Harper, 1970 and 1971), the protagonists are older and the narrative—it is hardly a story—is diffuse, itself circumstantial, and topical, reflecting then-current attitudes. To the extent that *Train Ride* reflects chiefly attitudes rather than feelings, and has no 'beyond,' no larger frame of reference, it is limited and indeed exclusionary; but it is limited first.

MORE INFORMATION

More information, new information—not only what but, starting from World War II, how and why.

"Viewed as a cornerstone of democracy," says the 1943 Scott catalog, "education is something more than Reading, 'Riting and 'Rithmetic." Something more too than ingesting facts. "We have learned that if a mind is to apply and use knowledge creatively it must understand rather than memorize," and —John McCullough adds—"understanding comes in seeing the how and why of facts rather than in mechanically storing them."

PLANTS, ANIMALS AND PEOPLE

Dorothy Waugh's *Warm Earth* is the last of the old, the first of the new and withal, like her earlier *Among the Leaves and Grasses*, a vagrant bloom. Explaining how the nourishing earth is formed—"What makes the warm loam fruitful? What makes the cold stone barren? What changes rock to soil?"—and how it functions, it marvels still at "the magic of creation" of flowers; and from photographic studies, magnified, it makes delicate and lovely miniatures (450, 451). They are pencil drawings with a rich variety of shading and meticulous delineation, not imitations of photographs, and while they bring the distant close and make textures and patterns manifest, they take advantage of the artist's freedom to select and emphasize, to interpret and compose. "You're not drawing objects," Dorothy Waugh observes, "you're drawing feeling."[1] But at the end the objects are scrupulously indexed, iceland poppy (p. 4) to meadow mice (p. 41).

Irma Webber drew objects, none more plainly, but with a feeling for their form and for the design of the page that is spirited and individual (452–454). Billed as "A First Book About Plants," *Up Above and Down Below* tells, no more and no less, what makes plants

450. *Warm Earth,* by Dorothy Waugh. Oxford, 1943. 7⅛ x 6.

CAPILLARITY AND WATER'S UNDERGROUND TRAVELS

Water climbing by capillarity must pull itself up step by step, grain by grain, through the pores of the earth, resting on each particle until there is power enough to pull it up to the next. If the soil is fine-grained, as loam is, this climbing is not difficult. If the steps are higher and harder to ascend, as they are in coarse sand or gravel, there may never be enough pulling power for water to climb up by capillarity at all.

Fine-grained soils have good capillarity if they are not packed too tightly nor stirred too loosely. Few things help plants as much, for good capillarity makes it possible for water to travel through soil easily. In all this traveling water is able to reach and dissolve many substances which plants can use for food; and it washes over many roots as it seeps and climbs. Plant roots can't reach around for water; they must wait until it comes to them; so good capillarity in the soil is important.

Water climbing rapidly through fine pores and falling back to fill coarser pores (greatly enlarged)

33

CONTINUAL CHANGE

Again and again the cycle repeats. Animal and vegetable matter cease to live, and join the mineral matter of the soil. Micro-organisms help alter soil substances, especially humus, and cause them to change their forms. Water in the earth dissolves some of the substances and these serve as food for sun-seeking plants. The sun-fostered plants live and grow, perhaps to die at last and go directly back to the earth, or perhaps to be eaten first by animals, returning to the soil when time has been spent in the form of animal tissue.

Life carries richness from the soil to the light and death carries it back to the earth again. Slowly, century after century, the soil grows richer; the topsoil grows mellower; and plants flourish where the loam lies deep.

Out of the warm earth comes the substance of life to grow fruitful in a thousand forms

40

451. *Warm Earth,* by Dorothy Waugh. Oxford, 1943. 7⅛ x 6.

unique (454) and differentiates them from animals (who "depend on plants for food"); and it does it by presenting the evidence, specimen by specimen (452, 453), and in a conclusive round-up, all together (454). To an adult this is the deductive process at its simplest and most obvious, and we see from the start the lesson *similarity*—roots being roots, stems and leaves being stems and leaves, whatever their configuration; but to a young child it is "a story based on the simple but exciting observation that the roots of plants are surprisingly unlike the parts that grow above the ground,"[2] and, it might be added, different from one plant to another. The divided page is not merely a kind of cut-away; like the physically divided 'heads and tails' books, it isolates top and bottom forms and ensures that we see them as separate entities—separate and ultimately distinct: "Whatever a plant looks like, the part above ground has air all around it and the part below ground has earth all around it." Add the sunlight "they take into their leaves," "the mineral-filled water their roots take in from the earth," and we have, complete, the food-

452–454. *Up Above & Down Below,* by Irma E. Webber. Scott, 1943. 6¼ x 7⅝.

452

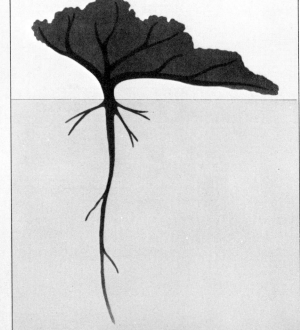

Sometimes it is the part above the ground that spreads way out, like a big shady oak tree

and the part below has a tap-root that grows down and down without branching much.

making plant, be it oak tree, potato or onion.

Travelers All (Scott, 1944) was a natural follow-up, the story of "How Plants Go Places," and it gave rise in turn to *Anywhere in the World*, styled—in a more scientific manner—"The Story of Plant and Animal Adaptation." We are advancing as it were, and the text is correspondingly more developed, the illustration more diverse. But in depicting living conditions in the four climatic zones and local adaptations to them, Dr. Webber is as orderly as always, and we need see very little of the book to grasp it as a whole (455, 456). That orderliness bespeaks faithfulness to fact and thorough understanding, but the botanist is an artist and a parent as well, and there is a relish in her pictures—the one crayoned in like a child's drawing, the

453

Up above there may be green stems and leaves
and below, a cluster of roots and swollen stems called tubers, or potatoes.

454

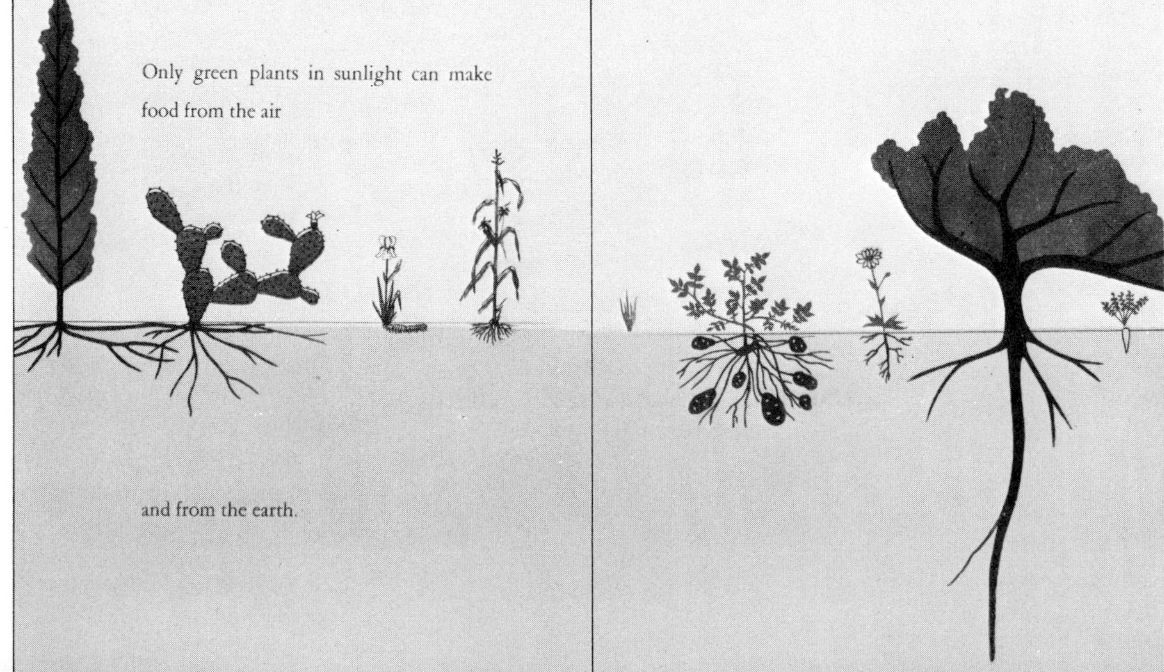

Only green plants in sunlight can make food from the air
and from the earth.

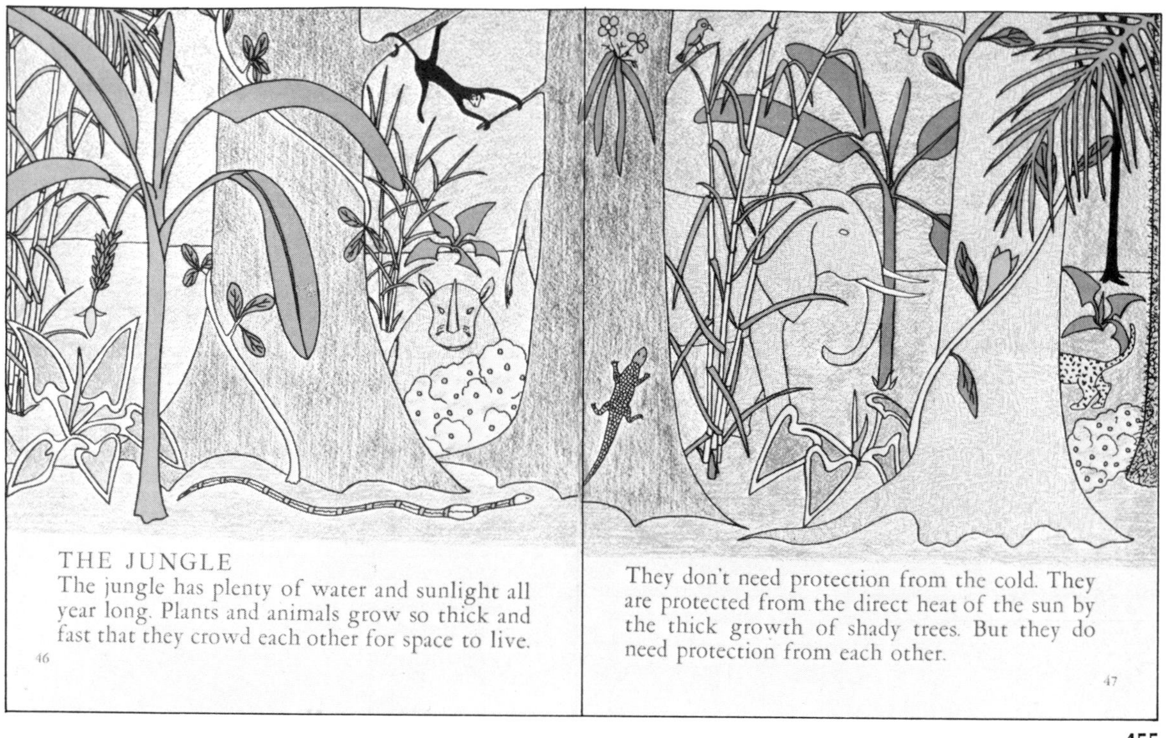

THE JUNGLE
The jungle has plenty of water and sunlight all year long. Plants and animals grow so thick and fast that they crowd each other for space to live.
46
They don't need protection from the cold. They are protected from the direct heat of the sun by the thick growth of shady trees. But they do need protection from each other.
47

455

455, 456. *Anywhere in the World,* by Irma E. Webber. Scott, 1947. 6½ x 7⅞.

456

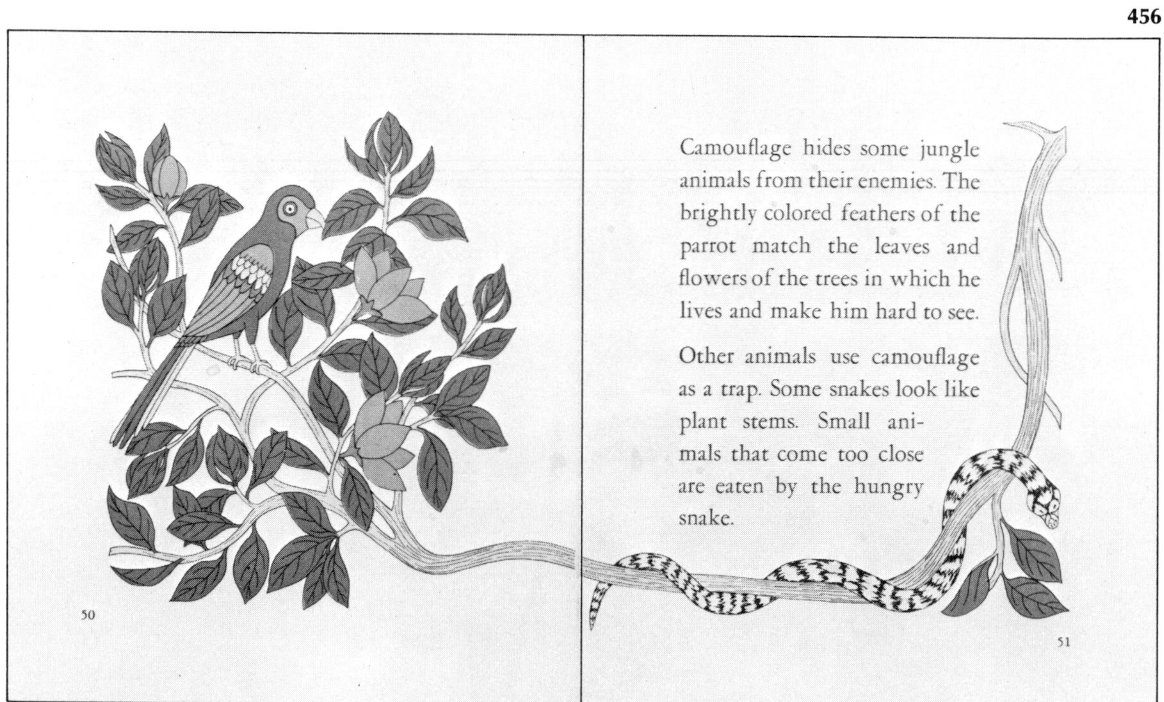

Camouflage hides some jungle animals from their enemies. The brightly colored feathers of the parrot match the leaves and flowers of the trees in which he lives and make him hard to see.
Other animals use camouflage as a trap. Some snakes look like plant stems. Small animals that come too close are eaten by the hungry snake.
50
51

other reminiscent of a botanical or zoological print—that gives them an independent life. The story of plant and animal adaptation ends, moreover, with people, adaptable to every clime, which—in terms of umbrellas and igloos, reservoirs and freighters—brings the lesson home.

These three books of Irma Webber's were the first to present basic laws of nature to young children—as James Newman noted, "ideas usually thought to be above this age group";[3] and systematic, graphic and good-looking, they haven't been bested.

The last in the series, *Bits That Grow Big* (Scott, 1949), is "The Story of Plant Reproduction with Many Easy-to-Do Experiments" —not a picturebook but a pictorial manual that allows a child to investigate for himself "What's Inside a Seed" and "Growing Spores"; the behavior of roots and bulbs; the principles of grafting and cutting and division: the "three ways in which plants grow new plants." With the upcoming *Let's Find Out* (1946) and *Now Try This* (1947), it was among the first of the basic experiment books, an extension to science of the Scott philosophy of proceeding from first-hand experience. The advent of the atomic bomb, wrote William Scott in the 1946 catalog one-year-after, and the efforts of the scientists responsible to alert laymen to its dangers, had spotlighted the gap between science and the humanities —what C. P. Snow was to call the 'two cultures'—and the only recourse was education: "immediate and urgent science education, starting not on the college or high school level, but with elementary school children," and not with the principles of advanced physics but with "the scientific attitude as a way of thinking." (No more talk of 'the magic of science,' was Ernestine Evans's way of putting it.[4]) Sputnik, and the big awakening, were still twelve years away.

Though Scott as a firm led in applying it to picturebooks, the idea of firsthand investigation was not unique with Scott. Coincident with *Bits That Grow Big* was Millicent Selsam's *Play with Plants*, an equally business-like book of experiments, the title notwithstanding. *Play with Trees* followed, and *Play with Vines* (all Morrow, 1949, 1951, 1952) and others for the middle age group, while for slightly older children there appeared *See Through the Sea* (written with Betty Morrow, Harper, 1955) and its successors—which is to say that in the field of natural science Millicent Selsam started early and held her own (qq. v. p. 117).

For young children she started earlier still, with the 1946 *Egg to Chick* (International), adjudged "nothing less than a tour de force" in the first survey of children's science books in *Scientific American*. "In 28 pages it recounts the changes that take place inside an egg from the time it is laid until the bedraggled chick cracks its way out and becomes, within a few hours, fully adept at managing its own life."[5] It was also, per the jacket, "an enthralling story": "Each stage is an event, an episode in a story that reaches a highly satisfactory climax when the chick at last begins to fend for itself in the outside world."

This is Scott language too, and reconstituted to embrace all the animals that grow from egg cells, people included, *Egg to Chick* led in 1952 to the first of the Millicent Selsam-Scott primers *All About Eggs (and How They Change into Animals)*, an "ABC of embryology"—that's *Scientific American*—which gives human birth "its natural place in the world of living things"—that's Scott-Selsam.

"Different kinds of eggs grow into different kinds of animals," it's as simple as that, some that you can guess (a nest in the crotch of a tree) and some that you mightn't ("a big lump of quivering jelly in the middle of a pond," tadpoles to be); and another big group that you don't ordinarily see: "A dog has babies, but where are the dog's eggs?" (457) And, likewise, the cow's, the whale's, the cat's eggs change into babies and grow until they are ready to be born . . . "just as you yourself were born one day." The standard how-you-were-born books, de Schweinitz (1928) to Levine (1949) to Gruenberg (1952), are beyond our purview, but it is interesting to see the birds and bees tack, natural and comfortable for children and

You don't see them but they are there just the same.
Hidden away inside the mother dog is a special sac—
a warm, safe place where the dog's eggs
change into little puppies.

457. *All About Eggs*, text by Millicent Selsam, pictures by Helen Ludwig. Scott, 1952. 6 x 7⅝.

their parents, become kindergarten science in *All About Eggs*. Tell only so much as is asked, experts advise; and what is asked first, Selsam answers.

All Kinds of Babies and How They Grow (Scott, 1953) followed almost perforce, to say that no matter what babies look like, "they all grow up to be the same kind of animals as their parents." (In other words, "Every kind of living thing in the world makes more of its own kind.") It is a truth awesome in its simplicity, and with *All About Eggs* an alternate route to the conclusion, first put forth by Scott as a reassurance, that *Just Like You—All Babies Have Mummies and Daddies* (1946). Indeed, one can hardly fail to see in the Scott books of the Fifties a biological approach to themes taken up in the Forties on a psychological basis—and thus to see in *A Time for Sleep: How the Animals Rest* (1953), the successor to *Eggs* and *Babies*, a counterpart to the good-night books or, in effect, 'Everybody Sleeps.'

Another early and long-time contributor to basic biology, Herbert Zim, worked downward—from *Mice, Men and Elephants* (1942) for teenagers to the 'monographs' *Elephants* (1946), *Snakes* et al for the middle age group to *What's Inside of Me?* and *What's Inside of Plants?* (both 1952), no less factual albeit for four-to-eights. It is his cold-turkey approach and his direct method that set Zim apart, and, related, his reliance on diagrammatic illustration. Not for him concepts or theories; "Modern Kids Want Facts,"[6] he felt, and endpapers included that's what he gave them. The books are indeed "unusual in format, with a simple text, printed in large type, appearing on every other left-hand page, and with additional information, in smaller type, appearing on the alternate left-hand pages"[7] —the latter, theoretically, for parents to read aloud while their children look at the pictures. In fact, as Louise Seaman Bechtel pointed out, all of the picture-pages "can be 'read' by those not yet able to read books."[8]

Both books have the usual Zim virtues of clarity, informativeness, pin-point accuracy and concision (a high norm), in large part because each component—text, illustrations, labels and captions—has its own role and none infringes upon the proper functions of the other. However, the more audacious book, *What's Inside of Me?*, leans particularly upon the pictures and might in turn have been defeated by the wrong ones. The very concept of 'what's inside' is of course pictorial, telling us that we're going to *see*; but here is a nice ordinary seven-year-old (or so) asking "What's inside of me?" and, overleaf, his innards (458). Nor is this all: we'll see inside the head, his brain, his heart, his stomach, his skin, and at the last, what his skeleton is like, little of which young children had been exposed to before. In Herschel Wartik's illustrations he is softly penciled in, an unassertive but not anonymous presence, and the interior of his body, colored plainly in red and yellow to set off the organs, is in perfect order and immediately impressive. Look, ma, I'm a biology book!

In the same format Zim did *What's Inside of Engines?*, *What's Inside the Earth?* and *What's Inside of Animals?* the next year, none of them as simple as the first two nor as inspired as *What's Inside of Me?* but rather the application of a formula. The last of the lot was *Things Around the House* (1954) but in this area he had, as we'll see, considerable competition.

If Herbert Zim was "the prolific Mr. Zim," as of the same date, 1949, Jeanne Bendick could be called 'the diversified Mrs. Bendick'; author-illustrator of books on electronics and weights and measures, for two, she was also sought out to illustrate almost anything even remotely technical. Little wonder then that she produced the first omnium gatherum of

458. *What's Inside of Me?* text by Herbert Zim, pictures by Herschel Wartik. Morrow, 1952. 6 x 8.

Beneath the skin and muscle that cover your body are many parts called organs. These fit and work together like parts of an auto or radio. Each organ does its own work and each helps the other. Some organs are large; some are small. Each is made of tiny parts called cells. Here are a few of the organs that are inside of you. Some of the others are behind this front layer.

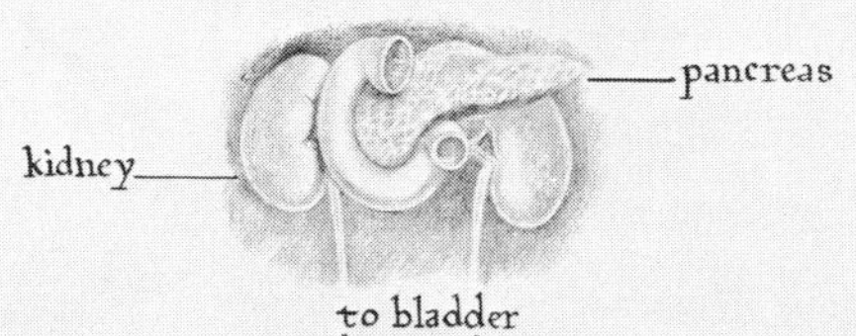

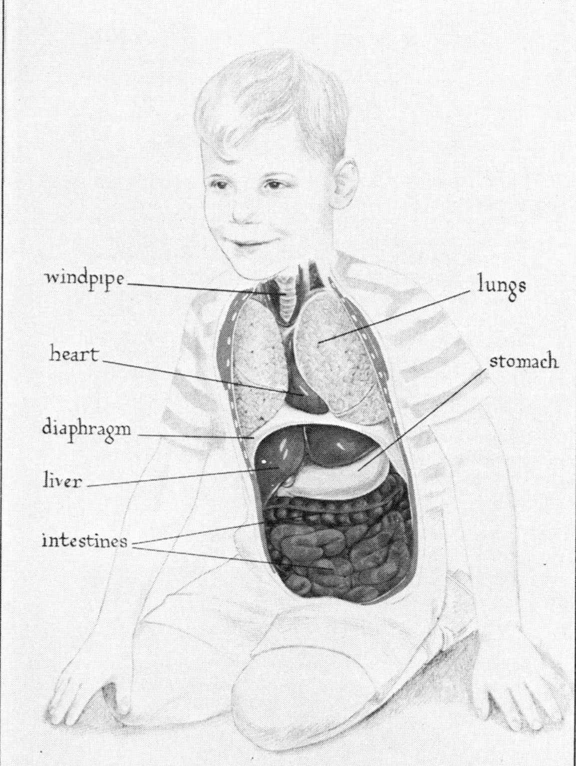

basic science, that hardy perennial *All Around You.*

How it happens that this unassuming—one could even say, unprepossessing—book, with none of the structural logic of a Webber or the factual exactitude of a Zim, has survived a revolution in science teaching and remains both popular and reputable does not so much defy understanding as analysis. Just taking note, then, there is in *All Around You* a sort of cozy clutter and, with it, a casual intermix of the sciences (459); there are pictures that look as if your favorite aunt drew them on the spur of the moment and the answers to lots and lots of questions—as excerpted from Glenn Blough's introduction, "Why the moon seems bright? How green plants grow? What makes rain and rainbows? How fish breathe under water? Why giraffes have long necks?" Herein, perhaps, lies an explanation, in that children, before they want to know anything in particular, want to know about everything—so we tell them that Washington won the Revolution, Eskimos live in igloos and giraffes eat the leaves of tall trees: we tell them *something*, knowing it is only a partial truth but one that will, for the moment, adequately fill their needs. On that basis *All Around You* can be considered a constructive ramble, a sort of *Farmer's Almanac* on home grounds.

The strain continued, more focused but hardly less informal, in *Wait for the Sunshine: The Story of Seasons and Growing Things* and *Not Only for Ducks: The Story of Rain* (both 1954) and the many others that Glenn Blough authored and Jeanne Bendick illustrated for McGraw-Hill, books that fall somewhere between Tresselt-Duvoisin intimations and out-and-out science.

459. *All Around You,* by Jeanne Bendick. McGraw-Hill, 1951. 7 x 10.

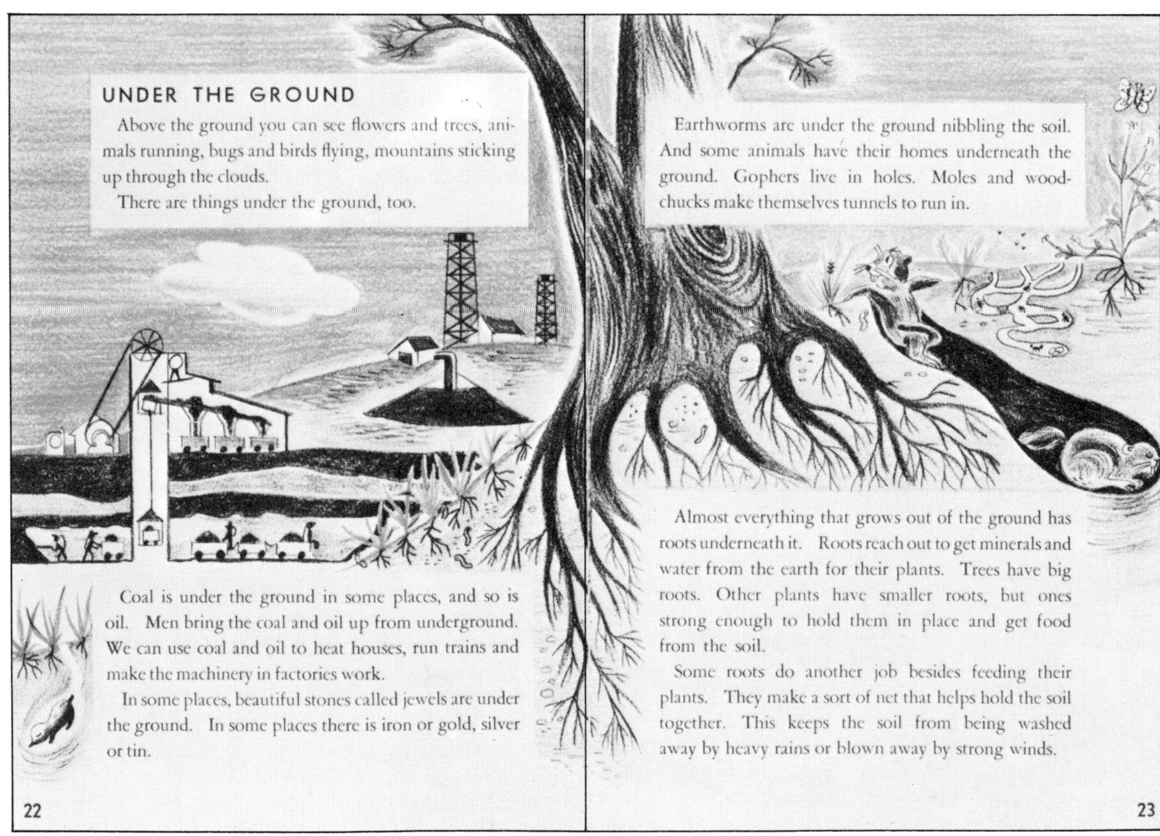

UNDER THE GROUND
Above the ground you can see flowers and trees, animals running, bugs and birds flying, mountains sticking up through the clouds.
There are things under the ground, too.
Earthworms are under the ground nibbling the soil. And some animals have their homes underneath the ground. Gophers live in holes. Moles and woodchucks make themselves tunnels to run in.
Coal is under the ground in some places, and so is oil. Men bring the coal and oil up from underground. We can use coal and oil to heat houses, run trains and make the machinery in factories work.
In some places, beautiful stones called jewels are under the ground. In some places there is iron or gold, silver or tin.
Almost everything that grows out of the ground has roots underneath it. Roots reach out to get minerals and water from the earth for their plants. Trees have big roots. Other plants have smaller roots, but ones strong enough to hold them in place and get food from the soil.
Some roots do another job besides feeding their plants. They make a sort of net that helps hold the soil together. This keeps the soil from being washed away by heavy rains or blown away by strong winds.
22
23

HOW THINGS WORK

Let's Find Out, says the first of the line—"Why does a teakettle sing? Why does it rain? Why do cold water pipes 'sweat'? Why are cracks left between squares in cement sidewalks?" etc. But the helter-skelter invitation to children on the jacket, similar to the teasers at the start of *All Around You*, is not indicative of the organization of the contents, a careful progression from heat and its properties to weather phenomena to air to—smart people, the Schneiders—airplanes. And though in both cases the questions are of real interest to youngsters, their very formulation—"What makes rain and rainbows?" vs. "Why does it rain?"—suggests a different level of interest and a different mode of response. According to Bendick, rain occurs when tiny drops of water join together and fall from the clouds; say the Schneiders, "You already know what happens when warm moist air is suddenly cooled," now "Let's find out . . . What happens when the cloud is cooled?" That done—via steam from a boiling kettle (the cloud) and a pan of ice-cold water—and 'rain' made, we can conclude "that when water is heated, it rises in the air as steam, or fog, or clouds. After it is cooled in the air, it comes back down again as water."

This is not only the experimental approach—the scientific method, so called—it is an attempt to get beyond mechanical explanations to first causes, in other words to the laws of physics; and making these accessible to young children was as much of a breakthrough as involving them in 'finding out.' The procedure—starting from the everyday, using common household materials, enlisting observation as well as demonstration, advancing step by step—enabled the child to learn for himself under expert guidance, and in that sense *Let's Find Out* and its successors can be likened to programmed instruction. In another sense, as books, they and their contemporaries in the biological sciences served to disseminate the aims and methods of the more innovative schools, public and private—Herman Schneider was affiliated with Bank Street, Herbert Zim taught at the Ethical

HEAT WORKS FOR YOU

The rain makes puddles so big that you can sail a boat in them.

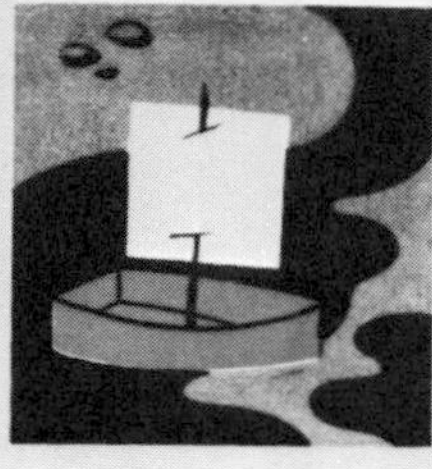

At noon, the puddle is smaller. The boat is almost grounded.

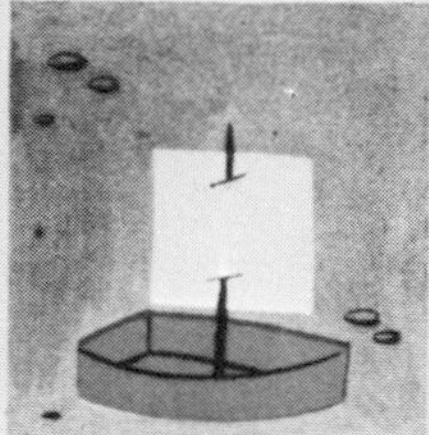

Later in the day, the water dries and the boat is high and dry.

WHAT makes the water dry out of the puddles?

You have seen other things that dry out. Grass that is wet early in the morning dries up in the warm sun.

After swimming you stand in the sun to dry.

Water dries out of a kettle that has been left heating on the stove.

Wet clothes in the sun dry faster than wet clothes in the shade.

Heat must have something to do with drying.
Does heat help water dry out of things?

17

460. *Let's Find Out,* text by Herman and Nina Schneider, pictures by Jeanne Bendick. Scott, 1946. 7¾ x 9½.

Culture Schools—much as the new social science had been spread abroad by the works of that period.

Of itself, *Let's Find Out: A First Picture Science Book*—now *Let's Find Out About Heat, Weather, and Air* but otherwise unaltered—continues as a model of its kind, like *All Around You* taking in more than current specialization permits and, again like *All Around You*, looking like a corpus of quick notations rather than a polished production (460). As a science illustrator, Jeanne Bendick combined plain drawing with making things plain, and it is as if the things as well as the drawings were easy to do.

On the same list as *Let's Find Out* there appeared *The Man in the Manhole, and the Fix-It Men*, story by Juniper Sage—code name for Margaret Wise Brown and Edith Thacher Hurd—and pictures by Bill Ballantine, a lark with a firm superstructure of fact. The Fix-It Men, besides big Tonio who stops

LIFT IT UP

Crowbars and See-saws

Very often people find that they have a big load to lift. A big stone has to be pried up out of the field. A heavy piece of old railroad track must be lifted to make way for a new piece A truck is stuck in the mud. There are all sorts of lifting and moving jobs.

Even in play, there are lifting jobs. Children who see-saw lift each other. Fat, thin, big, middle-sized, all children can see-saw and lift each other.

20

You can't see-saw by yourself. If you try you just stay at the bottom.

A heavy person at the other end isn't much use. Then you just stay at the top.

But people do see-saw even though they don't weigh the same.

It's easy to see how a heavy person can make his end of the see-saw go down and lift you up. But how can you make the heavier person go up?

Experiment Ten

LET'S FIND OUT how a light person can lift a heavy person.

YOU WILL NEED: a large and a small drinking glass, a ruler, and a pencil.

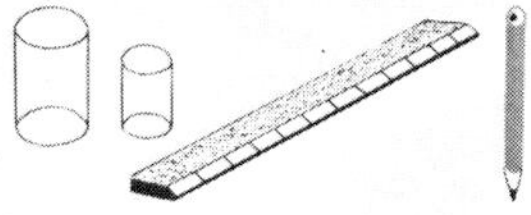

If you make a little see-saw of a ruler placed on a pencil, you can try to see-saw things with different weights.

TRY THIS. Place the pencil under the number 6 of the ruler to make a see-saw.

Place the large drinking glass on one end of the ruler. This is your heavy person. Put the small glass on the other end. That's you.

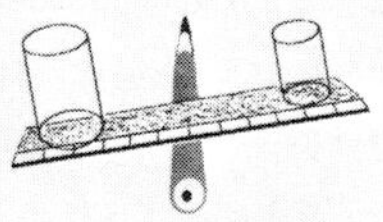

YOU WILL FIND that the heavier glass keeps the little see-saw tipped up. It's no good for see-sawing.

NOW TRY THIS. Move the larger, heavier glass, a little at a time, toward the number 6. You will come to a place where the small glass can lift the large one.

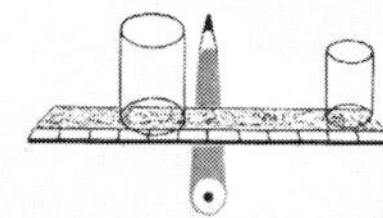

This shows that even though the small glass is lighter, it can lift the heavy one. The light thing farther away from the pencil can lift the heavy thing nearer the pencil.

A ruler, or a pencil, or any stick or bar used to lift something else is called a *lever.*

You have seen that a lever can help a light thing to lift a heavy one.

21

461

462

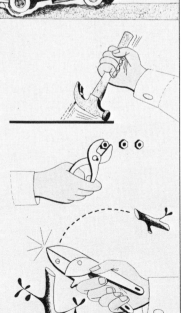

Levers at Work

Farmers, carpenters and roadmenders often use a lever called a crowbar. Perhaps you've seen workmen prying loose a curbstone, or moving a steel rail by using a crowbar.

A heavily loaded truck or a house can be lifted by one man using a very long lever.

When you use the claw of a hammer to pull out nails, you are using the hammer as a lever, with a curve in it.

A pump handle is a bent lever. You push down on the handle and you lift the heavy weight of water in the pump.

Big scales for weighing heavily loaded coal trucks are really long levers with the truck at the short end and a little two-pound weight at the long end. A two-pound weight can balance a truck weighing 20,000 pounds.

Scientists' scales are built so carefully and accurately that they can weigh the ink on this dot.

Pliers are two levers criss-crossed. Mechanics and electricians use them to hold or squeeze or twist bolts or wires with more force than they can with their bare hands.

Tin shears are two levers criss-crossed. Tinsmiths use them to cut heavy metal. Pruning shears are criss-crossed levers with long handles. They can cut a branch an inch thick with one snip.

461, 462. *Now Try This to Move a Heavy Load,* text by Herman and Nina Schneider, pictures by Bill Ballantine. Scott, 1954. 7¾ x 9½.

463. *Let's Look Under the City,* text by Herman and Nina Schneider, pictures by Bill Ballantine. Scott, 1954. 6¼ x 7½.

a leak in an underground pipe, are the Telephone Man who replaces a fallen wire, the truckman who tows away a smashed car, the road menders, the home repairers—MEN AT WORK all day, men asleep "in their own beds in their own houses" at night. For the Brown and Hurd partnership, it set the pace for *The Five Little Firemen, The Seven Little Postmen* and their sort; the real hero, though, was illustrator Ballantine who could bring a fat man down a manhole, turn a family of ducks loose in the flooded tunnel, cast a frog as kibitzer and, fun aside, make the underground plumbing and the repair job quickly intelligible.

Ballantine's cartoons are as clean-cut as they come—he is a comic but not a comedian—and teamed with the Schneiders the next year on *Now Try This*, the successor to *Let's Find Out*, and then on *Let's Look Under the City*, he gave to both books precision plus a happy snap (461–463). *Now Try This*—later styled *Push, Pull and Lift* or *Now Try This to Move a Heavy Load*—is about friction and the means of overcoming it (in case you skipped second grade); and more plainly methodical even than *Let's Find Out*, it proceeds from workaday problem to child equivalent to experimental solution (461) to —skipping a page—diverse applications (462). Basic mechanics, in short. *Let's Look Inside Your House* (pictures by Barbara Ivins, Scott, 1948) was the logical next, "A Picture-Science Book About Water, Heat and Electricity"—electricity meaning batteries and circuits to electric lights to the wiring of "your wonderful house." *Let's Look Under the City* (Scott, 1950), originally illustrated by the Halls and transformed in 1954 by Bill Ballantine's pictures, goes beyond the range of home experiments in going outside the house; but it also leaves behind the idea of the single-family house as a home to take in the support system—gas mains, water and sewage pipes, electric and telephone wires—for city living (463). In each case distinguished by a second color—unto the water that the construction man pours from his

All over the city, water from the clouds sprinkles and tinkles and swishes the dishes, because every faucet is joined to the city water system.

Winter and summer, night and day, there is water for the laundry, for the beauty shop, for the drug store, and for every faucet and hydrant in the city.

But who put all those pipes underground? How could anyone manage to pay for all that work?

The answer is that nobody could. Nobody could build or pay for a water system alone, but everybody can do it by getting together.

18

463

thermos. It's a long, long way, conceptually and graphically, from the benevolent furnace of *How It All Began* (124), though for the Schneiders a practical extension of *Let's Find Out* principles.

Only Julius Schwartz, in books illustrated by Marc Simont—particularly *Now I Know* and *I Know a Magic House* (1955 and 1956, both McGraw-Hill)—achieved nearly the same success in explaining everyday phenomena to young children, and that not experimentally (while from abroad there were Marie Neurath's contemporaneous *I'll Show You How It Happens* and *If You Could See Inside* in the Isotype series referred to earlier). And though there were to be many books of experiments, they can be called picturebooks only insofar as they employ pictures to demonstrate procedure. A pair that, coming early—before even the first of the Schneider books—should not be ignored are Mae and Ira Freeman's *Fun with Science* and *Fun with Chemistry* (1943 and 1944, both Random House) which present relatively simple experiments, illustrated photographically, as a foundation for the older beginner.

SIZE, SPEED, POINT OF VIEW → → → PROPORTION

How Big Is Big? At the same time, in 1946, that they undertook to make rain in the kitchen, the Schneiders offered "A Yardstick for the Universe—from Stars to Atoms," enlisting pictures to show what the unaided eye can't encompass; it is a lesson in relative size, a demonstration to the child—smaller than some things, bigger than others—that he is midway in the scheme of things ("just the right size"), and of itself a concept book. The first of the science concept books, mediating between pure instruction and bright ideas.

Revised in small but significant ways—to eliminate the "Terry" of the first instance, for one—and assigned to a different illustrator (the original pictures were by A. F. Arnold), *How Big Is Big?* reappeared in its now familiar format in 1950, feeling added to fact (464).

Penciled in at the front of Louise Bechtel's copy of *It Looks Like This* are the words "Is it Art? Nature?"—and certainly there's no pigeonholing this "Point-of-View Book." The work once more of Irma Webber, it is the story, the puzzle-story, of High Mouse and Back Mouse and Side Mouse and Front Mouse, each of whom lives in the indicated part of a barn, and to whom the same things —things that say MOO, things that say HEE HAW, things that say OINK OINK—look, as you'd expect, quite different. Then one day all of the mice hear a new noise, MEOW, and take shelter in the storeroom . . . (465). Naturally, disputation arises: who, then, will prove to be right?

"In our tryouts of the book, some children thought the front view of the animals was right, most of them thought the side views were right (after all that's how they usually see them in books) and the few back-view holders were shouted down."[9] What you'd expect, a child wouldn't. But the mice, when they have the opportunity to see the cat from all points of view, find out that none of them was wrong and SOMETHING ELSE, "that one thing can look . . . as many different ways as there are ways to look at it"; and children concluded in turn "that 'it all depends on how you look at things.'"[10] (Or, as Crockett Johnson was to put it, *Who's Upside Down?*)

Miriam Schlein was not out to teach science but to convey ideas when in 1952 she produced (among others) *Go with the Sun*, pictures by Symeon Shimin, "about a little boy who tries to do what the animals do when winter comes" and *Shapes*, pictures by Sam Berman, a novel look at 'round' and 'square' (which closes, "what *other* shapes are there?"); in 1953, *When Will the World Be Mine?*, pictures by Jean Charlot, a little snowshoe rabbit's yearning made "a symbol of all our yearning to possess," and for our particular purposes, *Fast Is Not a Ladybug: A Book About Fast and Slow Things*. She was "a full-time professional writer of young children's books," said Scott (publishers of the foregoing) with some pride; and as such she dealt in an assortment of concepts.

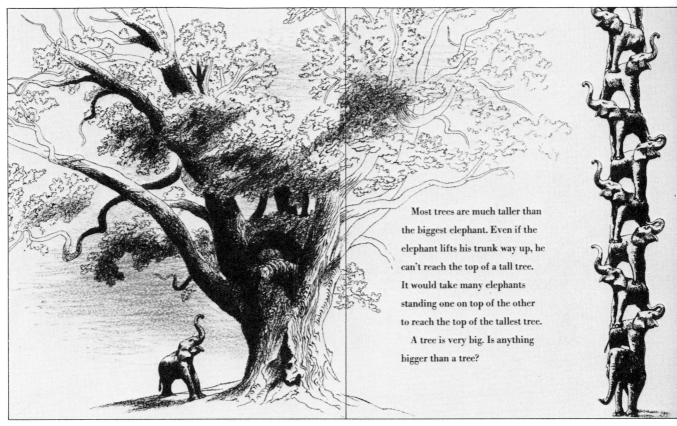

Most trees are much taller than the biggest elephant. Even if the elephant lifts his trunk way up, he can't reach the top of a tall tree. It would take many elephants standing one on top of the other to reach the top of the tallest tree.

A tree is very big. Is anything bigger than a tree?

464. *How Big Is Big?* text by Herman and Nina Schneider, pictures by Symeon Shimin. Scott, 1950. 7¾ x 9⅝.

465. *It Looks Like This,* by Irma E. Webber. Scott, 1949. 6¼ x 7⅝.

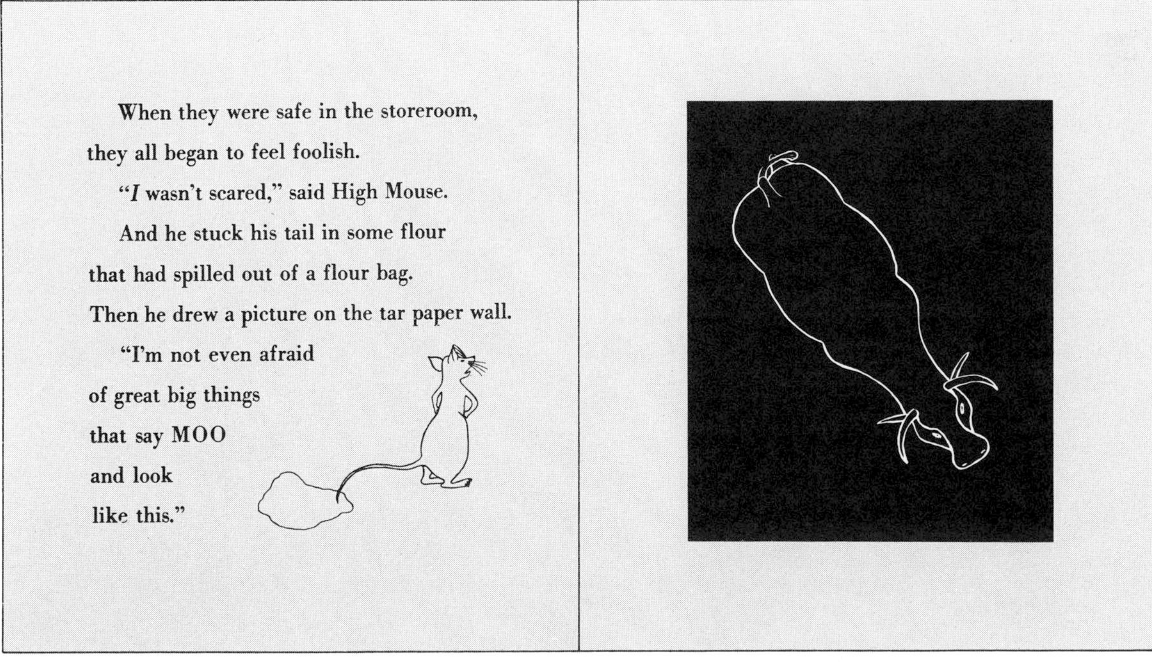

When they were safe in the storeroom,
they all began to feel foolish.
"*I* wasn't scared," said High Mouse.
And he stuck his tail in some flour
that had spilled out of a flour bag.
Then he drew a picture on the tar paper wall.
"I'm not even afraid
of great big things
that say MOO
and look
like this."

What does fast mean?
Fast means it takes
less time
to go from here to there.
Do *you* run fast?
But look, the dog runs faster than you.
And the horse runs faster than the dog.

466

Here is a slow story.

Once there was a seed, and a little girl buried the seed in the dirt. And slowly, very slowly, there came to be a rose bush that grew up from that little seed.

And a beautiful rose came to grow on that rose bush, slowly, very slowly. And the beautiful rose had petals that unfolded, slowly, one by one.

467

466, 467. *Fast Is Not a Ladybug,* text by Miriam Schlein, pictures by Leonard Kessler. Scott, 1953. 7⅝ x 8.

"What does fast mean?" (466) And the train on the track goes faster than the horse, and the plane in the sky faster than the train, and a rocket faster than a plane, and lightning faster still, "the fastest thing you can see in the whole world . . . ." BUT—"Just because all these things are faster than you, that doesn't mean you're slow." Oh no, "it is *easier* for a horse to run faster than you, and so, for *you,* you still run fast." Besides, "There are some things that never even *try* to be fast" (if the ladybug "felt like going fast, she would fly"), some things that are naturally, needfully slow (467). Growing—as shown also by the pictures in a family album—is always slow, must be slow. Thus the envoi: "It's fun to go fast, sometimes./But lots of times/I like to know/I can just go slow." Objective speed and subjective speed, and reconciliation.

So, "What does heavy mean?" The same thing? Well, "What is light for the elephant is heavy for you. What is light for you is heavy to the ant." (Remember, some things were easy and some were hard "for Ann and Tim and you and me," p. 114.) But whether things are *really* heavy or *really* light depends upon their WEIGHT, and weight is to be measured in ounces and pounds—Fast Is Not a Ladybug, maybe, but Heavy *Is* a Hippopotamus—and not, moreover, to be judged by appearances (468). Who cares? You should, because "Sometimes it is easier to figure things out by weight"; and sure enough, we rely on it—on an ounce weighing an ounce, a pound a pound, a ton 2,000 pounds, "no matter who in the great wide world is trying to pick it up!"

There followed *It's About Time* (Scott, 1955), about telling time and being on time, and shortly the Schlein-Kessler collaboration concluded. Her rackety-packety manner of writing for kids (one of the times 'children' won't do), the bounce, the sunshine the two together brought to a book, their blithe young way with ideas, ordinary ideas—these were picked up in turn by many others. *All My Shoes Come in Twos*, chimed Mary Ann and Len Hoberman in 1957, *How Do I Go?* in 1958 (both Little, Brown); and their work is just one obvious, better than average example.

It was unmistakable too that Leonard Kessler drew like a clever child. "He says he can actually draw like anybody else but likes to draw this way better. It speaks more directly than conventional drawing, he feels." ("It spoke out of the side of its mouth, however, to one library borrower"—this is all Scott, of course—"who wrote us to ask why we couldn't get someone who knew how to draw 'nice realistic' pictures.") It was the way that, earlier, Kessler had drawn *What's in a Line?* (469, 470), and the principles of graphic expression—the thick heavy lines for hippopotamus and log, the fast swings for speed, the squashed or spaced forms for slow growth—carry over; a way of visualizing induces a way of thinking, the drawing itself conveys ideas.

We've remarked before that children draw not appearances but ideas of things. Adds Miriam Lindstrom from close study: "Undaunted by subjects that professional artists would hesitate to attempt, they are prepared to picture every idea, whether or not it is one that adults are easily capable of visualizing. Lack of understanding does not keep them from symbolizing even some very abstract

468. *Heavy Is a Hippopotamus,* text by Miriam Schlein, pictures by Leonard Kessler. Scott, 1954. 7⅝ x 8.

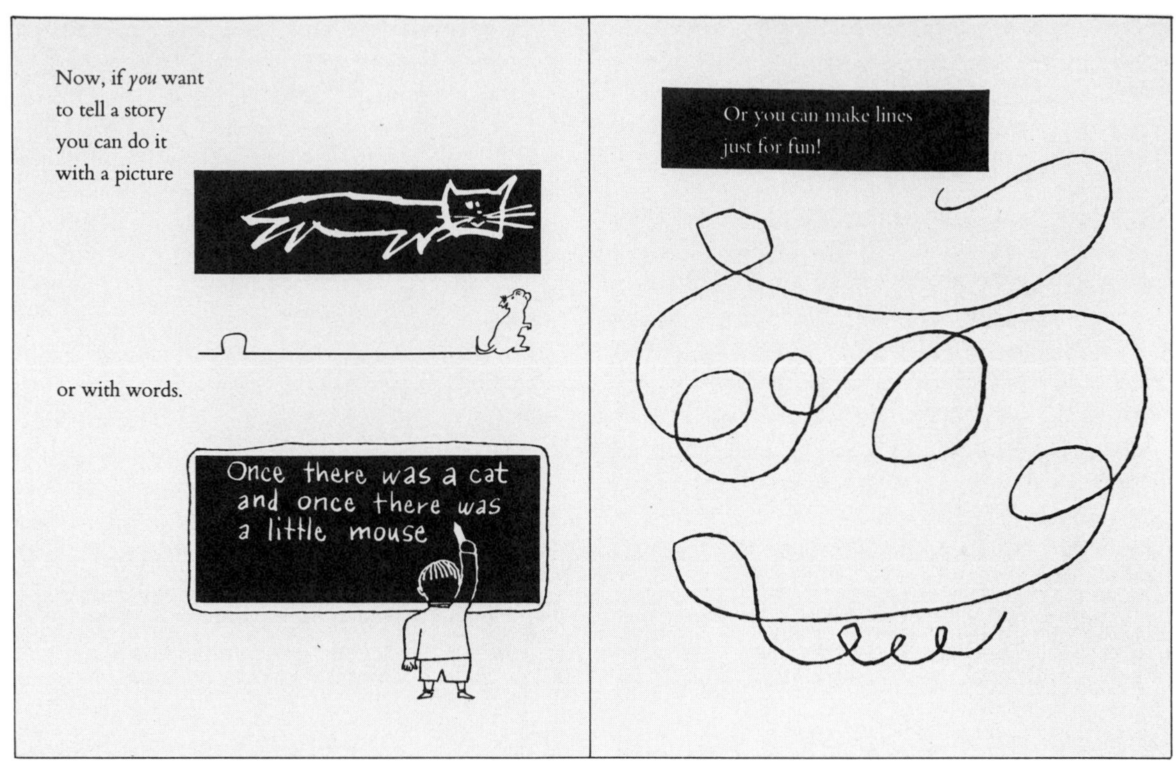

469

469, 470. *What's in a Line?* by Leonard Kessler. Scott, 1951. 7⅞ x 9½.

470

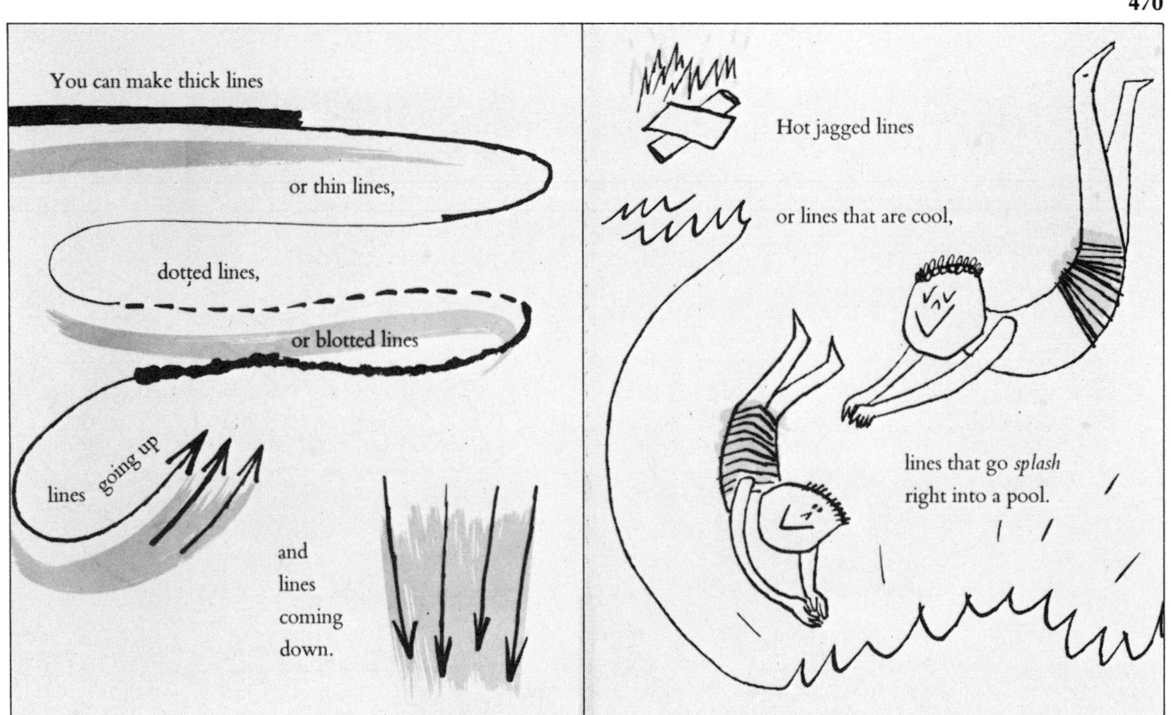

concepts in visual forms as their minds are able to associate very widely and loosely among slight similarities or analogies . . . ."[11]

Kessler draws like a child in the sense that his work is schematized and 'unfinished'; his children, with their big round heads and shorthand features, are a child's formula figures—and also as ideas of children, not individuals, easy to identify with; and he conceptualizes freely and imaginatively and as children needn't, intelligibly: he is an objective grown child. With his wife Ethel Kessler he did, among others, *Plink Plink*, "the thirsty book," and *Crunch Crunch*, "the hungry book" (1954 and 1955, both Doubleday); and though what was called the 'beep-beep, crunch-crunch' school of juvenile writing antedates them, they fall within it as examples of the mundane here-and-now. (Not that children objected; I still remember well "Plink plink goes the water in my sink.") But Kessler's particular ability to picture notions of things led also in other directions.

CROWELL AND SCIENCE, INC.: "LET'S-READ-AND-FIND-OUT"

In a 1951 interview Elizabeth Riley, the juvenile editor at Crowell, is quoted as touting *Lodestar: Rocket Ship to Mars*, Franklyn Branley's first solo (he had been doing experiment books with Nelson Beeler) and "Crowell's first excursion into space."[12] Branley followed with two others in 1955 and John Lewellen, joining the Crowell list, produced *Helicopters* (1954) and *Jet Transports* (1955). Branley was a teacher and a teacher of teachers who became director of educational services at the American Museum-Hayden Planetarium and ultimately its chairman; Lewellen was a flying enthusiast and a science writer. On the younger pictorial side John McCullough, a Scott partner (and author), and Leonard Kessler contributed *Farther and Faster* (1954): "a history of transportation . . . and something more . . . a book about ideas—how they pile up until someone synthesizes them into an invention";[13] and it had a familiar zip. There ensued:

1956 *Mickey's Magnet,*
by Franklyn Branley & Eleanor Vaughan,
illus. by Crockett Johnson

Tommy Learns to Fly,
by John Lewellen,
illus. by Leonard Kessler

1957 *Rusty Rings a Bell,*
by Branley & Vaughan,
illus. by Paul Galdone

1958 *Tommy Learns to Drive a Tractor*
by Lewellen, illus. by Kessler

1959 *A Book of Satellites for You,*
by Branley, illus. by Kessler

A Book of Moon Rockets for You,
by Branley, illus. by Kessler

1960 The "Let's-Read-and-Find-Out" series

Mickey's Magnet is the story—for it is that —of a small boy's discovery of what a magnet can do (471), and can't, and how to make another magnet (472). "All this he learned by himself, just as readers of the book will be able to do";[14] and with utmost satisfaction (473). Where in an ostensible science book a child is usually a puppet put through the requisite motions, or alternatively fancy takes over from fact, *Mickey's Magnet* is one and indivisible; it is a demonstration, a success story, and—thanks to Crockett Johnson's pictures—spontaneously funny: a complete pleasure.

Tommy, in turn, really learns to fly (474). This is no surrogate Pilot Small at the controls, no wishful thinking (*I Want to Fly*, Scott, 1943), but an eight-year-old boy: "It is not safe for children to drive cars. But it is safe for them to fly airplanes if their fathers are along. Airplanes have two steering wheels and two sets of rudder pedals. If Tommy made a mistake his father could take over." The presumption is not that, like the real Tommy Lewellen, children would immediately take to the air, but in learning with Tommy they learn that flying isn't all that

"Maybe a horseshoe magnet will help."
Mickey looks up. His father hands him something heavy.
This could *help?*
But how? Would it push the pins into a pile?
He'd try it and see.

471

He sits down to play with his collection. First he picks up the needle with a magnet. A pin is hanging from the needle.
The needle must be a magnet, too!

472

471-473. *Mickey's Magnet,* text by Franklyn M. Branley and Eleanor K. Vaughan, pictures by Crockett Johnson. Crowell, 1956. 5⅝ x 7⅞.

473

difficult or dangerous—whether or not there's a Beechcraft in their future—and at the same time, that a youngster can master a grown-up skill. Tommy's final test is to fly the plane home from Milwaukee to Chicago by himself, and no Indian stripling alone in the forest ever did better (though Tommy, a true eight, sometimes "gets so interested in looking at things on the ground that he forgets to fly").

It's tricky—that is, challenging; it's fun; and it's all quite plain (475). (Nor, until Edward Koren put a shaggy beast *Behind the Wheel* [Holt, 1972] was there such a nimble demonstration of how to do it.) In the same format with the same bright ease Kessler implemented Branley's simple but quite extensive explanations of rockets and satellites "for the very youngest reader." *A Book of Moon Rockets* and *A Book of Satellites* showed that it could be done; and for the first time too they brought to young children information unfamiliar to most adult laymen. Sputnik I had been launched in 1957, the ensuing furor over Russian scientific progress had brought the National Defense Education Act (1958), and scientific education was being revamped at all levels—at the youngest, newly introduced. For their particular audience, *Moon Rockets* and *Satellites,* without a wisp of a story or the least lyricizing, were the first entries of the space age.

From recognition of "the child's serious quest for science information"[15] came the Let's-Read-and-Find-Out series, by any standard—commercial, educational, creative—the most successful enterprise of its sort. Dr. Branley, whose idea it was, enlisted as co-editor his erstwhile mentor at Teachers College, Dr. Roma Gans, and himself wrote two of the first five. But Clyde Bulla, who simply wrote books children liked, was assigned another, and later authors have included picturebook pro Edith Thacher Hurd and busy artist Aliki and Dr. Gans as well; science writers as such had no edge. Even more diverse over the years was the roster of artists. Elizabeth Riley had made the outside choice of Crockett Johnson to illustrate *Mickey's Magnet* because of his artistic intel-

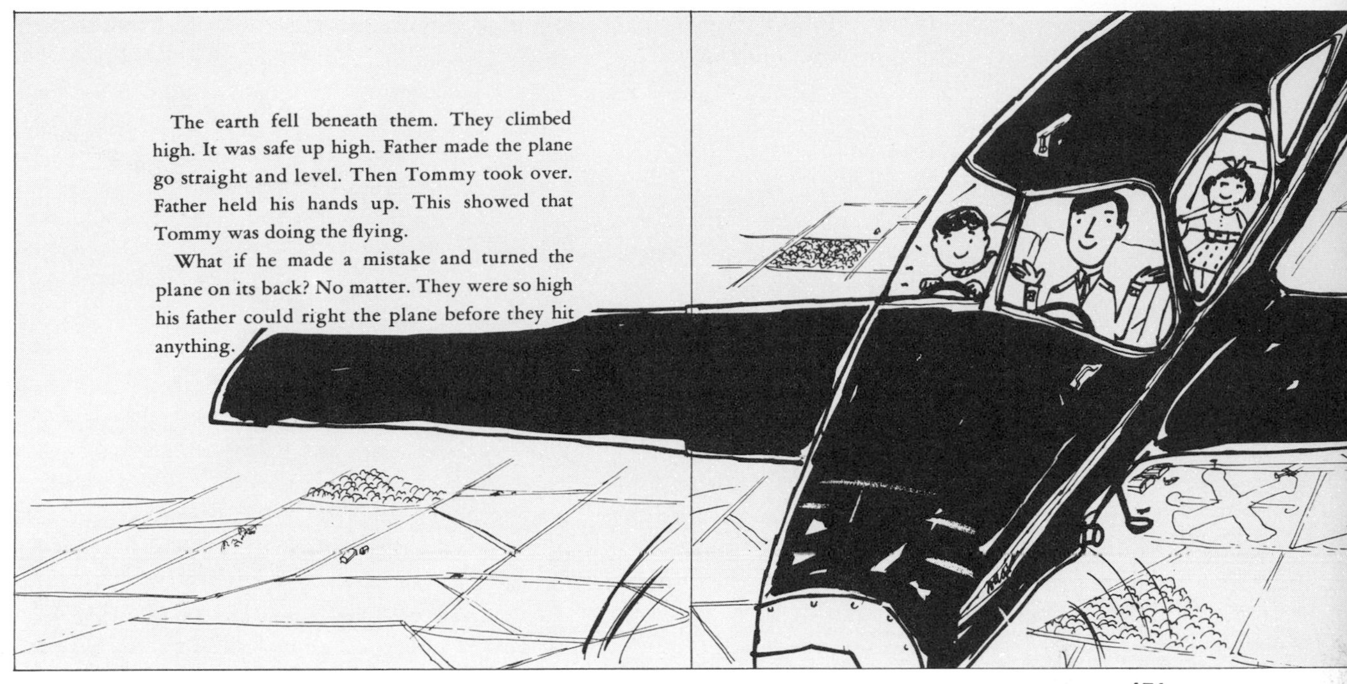

The earth fell beneath them. They climbed high. It was safe up high. Father made the plane go straight and level. Then Tommy took over. Father held his hands up. This showed that Tommy was doing the flying.
What if he made a mistake and turned the plane on its back? No matter. They were so high his father could right the plane before they hit anything.

474

ligence ("and because I wanted to work with him and see what he would bring to the book"[16]); and artistic intelligence was to be a prime consideration, sweeping in artists not ordinarily identified with books of fact to say nothing of science per se.

The overall format was preestablished (by Nonny Hogrogian, then on the design staff at Crowell); the pictures had to follow the text closely and they were checked on completion for scientific precision; and if one adds that many of the artists (besides Low) did some of their best work for the series, it would appear that constraint—and a clear purpose—are not to be disparaged.

Leonard Kessler, as one might expect, illustrated one of the initial Branleys, while Helen Borten, newly known for the art-concept book *Do You See What I See?* (Abelard, 1959), did the second; and the year after Ed Emberley made his bow with *The Wing on a Flea* (Little, Brown, 1961), "a book about shapes," he took his turn. Helen Stone, who had illustrated (chiefly) poet Phyllis McGinley, did a soft warm *Snow Is Falling*; Bill Sokol, a clever man with a line, handled

474, 475. *Tommy Learns to Fly,* text by John Lewellen, pictures by Leonard Kessler. Crowell, 1956. 8⅝ x 8.

475

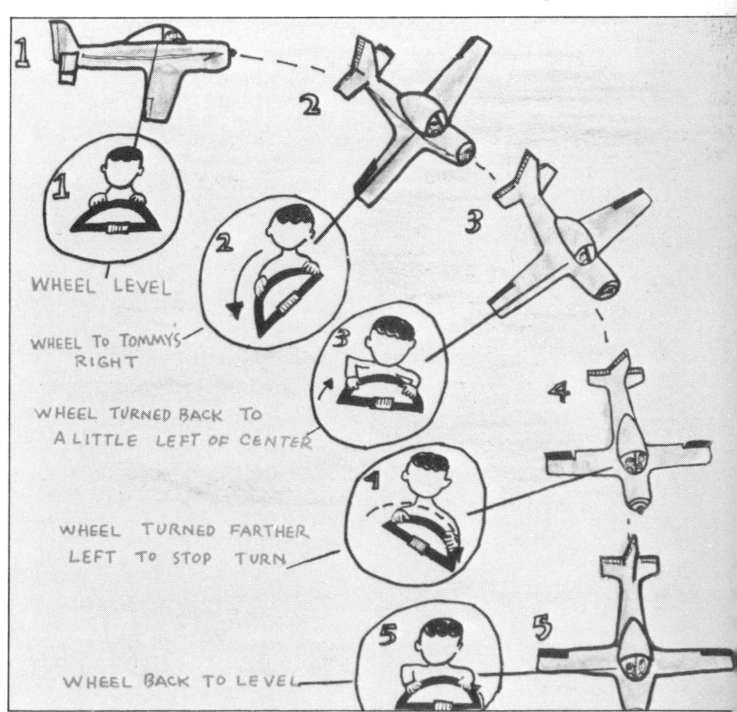

Rockets and Satellites; Aldren Watson, he of the immaculate outdoors, took on *The Clean Brook.* Ezra Jack Keats, Lucienne Bloch, Adrienne Adams and Bobri were other early recruits, and still others we'll see shortly.

The books spilled out in profusion—to the number of eight or nine in some of the early years (years of massive federal funds for their purchase)—and without demarcation; and they spread themselves in libraries throughout Mr. Dewey's 500s, the science classification, and made inroads on the 600s, Applied Science, in Health, Engineering and what have you. But if there was not a plan to publish specifically this and that, or to assign fields to individuals, certain strengths did emerge from the talent pool and with them, often, groups of books.

Branley continued to be the leading author, responsible for astronomy and space science and meteorology and physics, and it can only be said that as a group the nineteen titles he produced between 1960 and 1973 dominate the field or fields, especially in astronomy and space science. (Branley did more in the "A Book of . . ." line too, but what had once seemed "the very youngest reader" wasn't any longer. Jerome Bruner had recently written that "any subject can be taught effectively in some intellectually honest form to any child at any stage of development";[17] and these became the next step up.) Of themselves, they are almost as varied as the artists who did them.

Natural topics at the outset were the moon and the sun, or rather *The Moon Seems to Change* (1960) and *The Sun: our nearest star* (1961): not only were the books not categorized, they had odd sorts of titles—sometimes labels, as often statements of fact, injunctions, colloquial phrases—reflecting the circumstance that they didn't try to encompass a subject. In time *The Moon Seems to Change* had a helpmeet, *What the Moon Is Like*, and *What Makes Day and Night* was separate from both and from *The Sun: our nearest star*. In the field of straight nonfiction, where what wasn't a First Book of X, Y or Z was Allabout it, this was a distinct novelty.

476, 477. *The Moon Seems to Change,* text by Franklyn M. Branley, pictures by Helen Borten. Crowell, 1960. 8⅝ x 8.

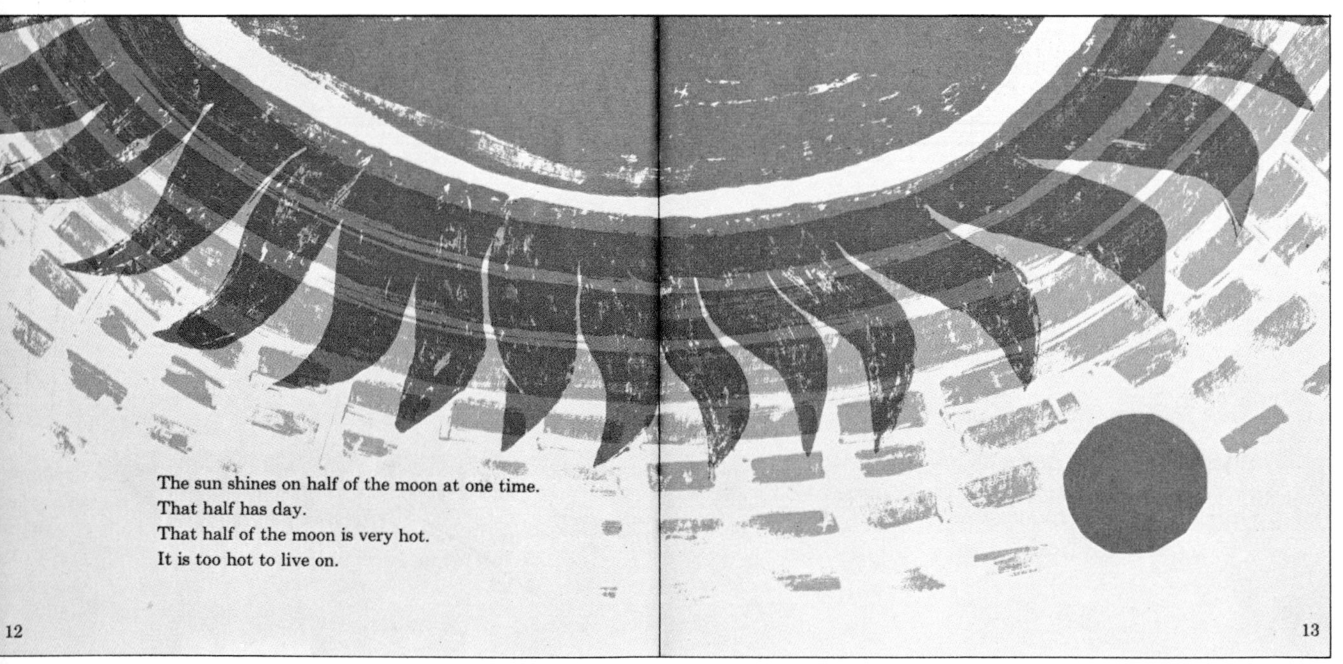

The sun shines on half of the moon at one time.
That half has day.
That half of the moon is very hot.
It is too hot to live on.
12
13

476

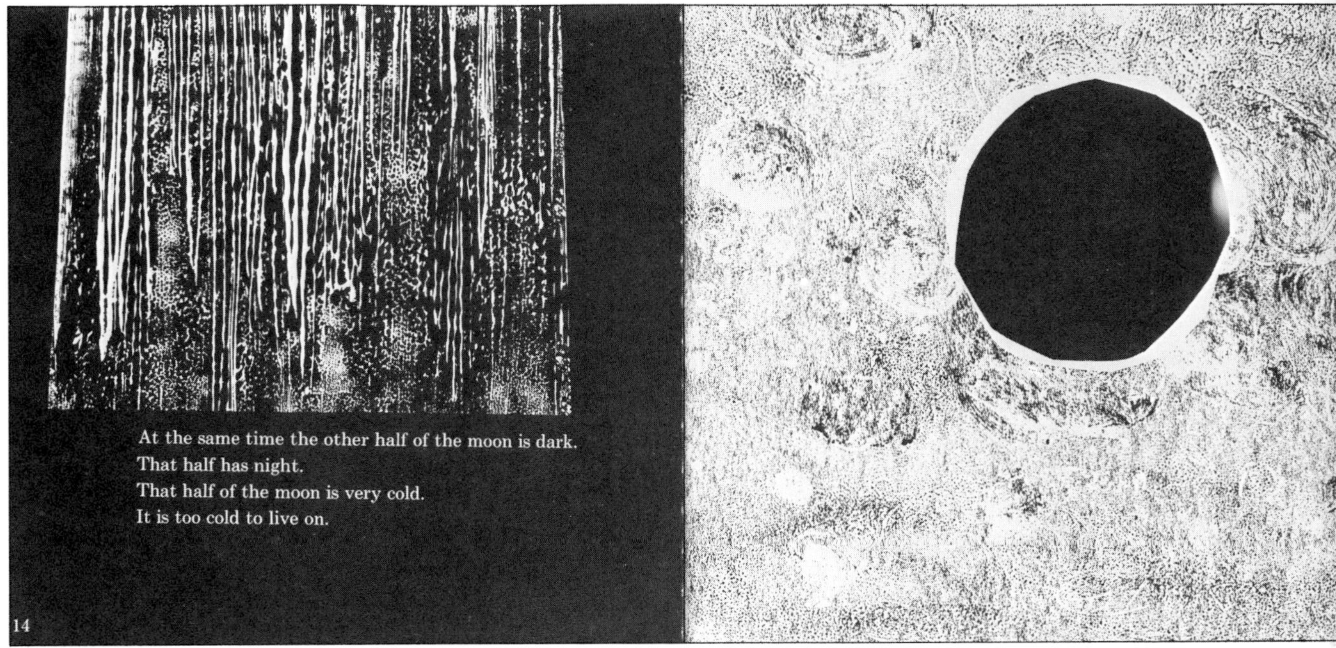

At the same time the other half of the moon is dark.
That half has night.
That half of the moon is very cold.
It is too cold to live on.
14

477

The Moon Seems to Change is an observation, probably the first that anyone makes. But the moon—the big, distant, rough, arid moon, turning on itself once a month ("You can turn around much faster!"), half lit and warmed by the sun (476) while the other half is dark and cold (477)—that moon that we now can conceive—"really does not change," however much it seems to; and why it seems to is what Branley explains. The pictures help, but their function is less to clarify than to conjure up, to present images of glaring heat and deepest cold, of size and distance and want of life. Concepts, in their magnitude abstract.

Paul Showers, a newspaperman with the *New York Times*, turned up on the second list with three books and took for himself eyes and nose and teeth, touching and talking—those parts of the body that first interest children and what are to them its most vital functions. (Only later did he extend himself to *Hear Your Heart* and, in the guise of *What Happens to a Hamburger*, the digestive process, keystones of orthodox biology.) They are friendly, offhand kids' books, and Paul Galdone, who had illustrated *Rusty Rings a Bell* and also for Branley, *Timmy and the Tin-Can Telephone* (1959), was just right for them; beginning in 1962, he was called on for several.

Characteristic, and then some, is *Your Skin and Mine.* The skin has layers, the epidermis and the dermis, and firmly but lightly we learn about them (478); we also learn that fingernails and toenails are parts of the skin, protection for "the tips of your fingers and toes," and like the hair "because they keep growing all the time." ("When you cut your hair you don't feel anything. When you cut your nails you don't feel anything either.") And we learn about fingerprints—look at them under a magnifying glass—and how to rub our fingers in fingerpaint and make them; and we can't help noticing, when we compare "Mark's" and "Henry's," that "Everybody's fingerprints are different."

But the first thing we see is that Henry's skin and Mark's and 'mine' are different colors —light brown (i.e. Oriental), dark brown and "white with freckles"; and before we're through we learn why (479). In the Forties, when tolerance became something to cultivate, anthropologically oriented books like *All*

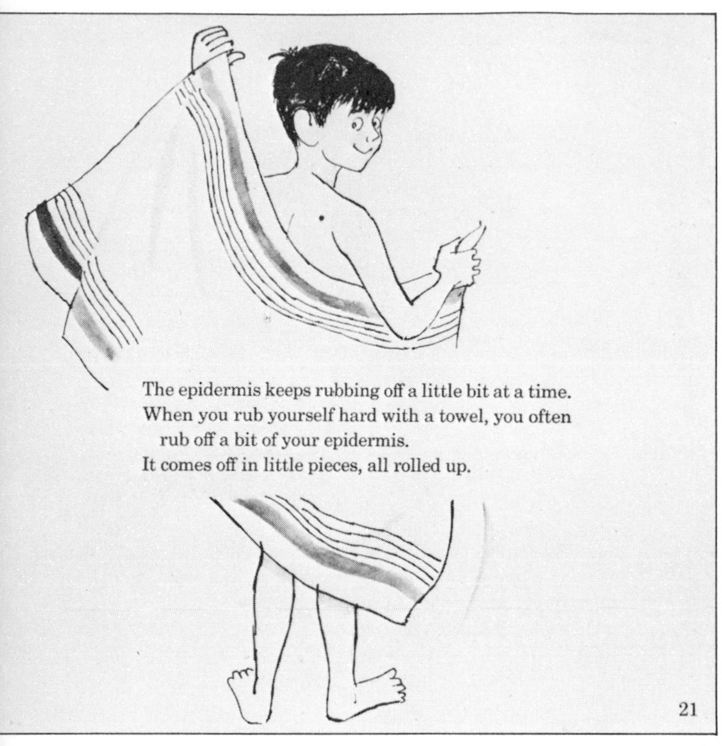

The epidermis keeps rubbing off a little bit at a time.
When you rub yourself hard with a towel, you often rub off a bit of your epidermis.
It comes off in little pieces, all rolled up.
21

478

478, 479. *Your Skin and Mine,* text by Paul Showers, pictures by Paul Galdone. Crowell, 1965. 8⅝ x 8.

About Us explained the origin of physical differences and stories like *Two Is a Team* made it their business to ignore them: that Negro Ted and white Paul quarrel and make up like any two boys is the point. In *Your Skin and Mine*, color is neither central nor is it extraneous, it is one more characteristic of skin.

(Naturally enough, *Straight Hair, Curly Hair*—the work of Augusta Goldin and Ed Emberley—appeared the following year.)

Another Let's-Read-and-Find-Out regular, Aliki, has done other picturebooks of a more imposing, even 'significant' sort, *A Weed Is a Flower* and *Oh Lord, I Wish I Was a Buzzard* among them; but she has also a genuine talent for light comedy and, whether writing or drawing, for quick and sure communication. Dinosaurs, in the children's book market, are like John Van Druten or, today, Neil Simon in summer stock: foolproof but also surprise-proof. Aliki has the wit to tell about *My Visit to the Dinosaurs*—that is, to the museum where children by the score first encounter them, big as life and hardly reassuring (480). This spread, as it happens,

479

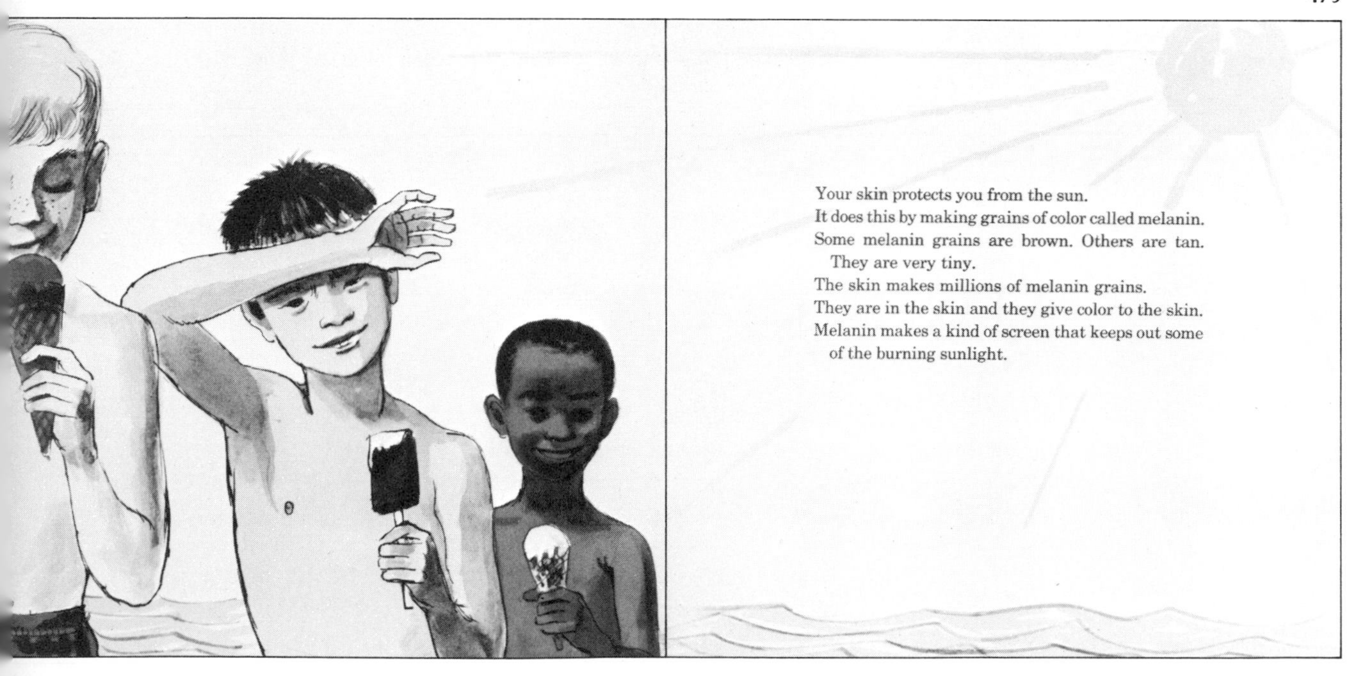

Your skin protects you from the sun.
It does this by making grains of color called melanin.
Some melanin grains are brown. Others are tan. They are very tiny.
The skin makes millions of melanin grains.
They are in the skin and they give color to the skin.
Melanin makes a kind of screen that keeps out some of the burning sunlight.

I had to stand far away from Tyrannosaurus to take its picture.
My father and my sister looked tiny next to it.
I was glad Tyrannosaurus Rex wasn't alive any more.
When you go to the museum, you will see what I mean.
32
33

480. *My Visit to the Dinosaurs,* by Aliki. Crowell, 1969. 8⅝ x 8.

comes at the close, after the young narrator has repeated his father's encouraging "No dinosaurs are alive today"; examined the skeleton and wondered "How could anyone know where all the pieces fit?"; and without breaking stride, launched into an account of fossils, paleontology (so called) and its dinosaur finds—Brontosaurus, Diclopodus, Triceratops and the rest. To paraphrase the last line, 'When you go to the museum, you'll know what you're seeing,' but like a visit, the book doesn't pretend to tell all. It's rather like a trip to the zoo, in fact, and why shouldn't it be?

If there was no urgent need for another book on dinosaurs, there was less need, given less clamor, for more books of natural history; but sometimes a need isn't apparent until it's met. What was wanted, the editors felt—much of the following is from Matilda Welter, in-house editor of the series—were not additional life-cycle stories, necessarily about individual animals and open to anthropomorphism, nor on the other hand encyclopedic treatments, tending as they do to diffusion and dryness and, one might add, superficiality. Hence the choice—in accord with the rest of the series—of a single trait or an aspect of the animal's life that would implicitly teach a concept; books in which, moreover, the author and artist, not the nature of the subject, control the material.

There are authors (and artists) who approach similar material similarly, and no discredit to them; but as time passed one noticed Judy Hawes's books only because they seemed always to be particularly good: she had no set approach, her work had no fixed pattern or persistent emphasis. And like her series-mates, she has a self-effacing, pliant style—perhaps a shade more pliant, and so potentially graceful, humorous, colloquial, poetic. Her books are all of them about small, literally cold-blooded creatures—insects, crustaceans, amphibians; and for one after another illustrator, they've been as Dante's visions or a view of the Alps. Somehow, something in those brief texts reverberates.

In the Let's-Read-and-Find-Out sequence, *Fireflies in the Night* is the book that brought everything together. Judy Hawes's first, it

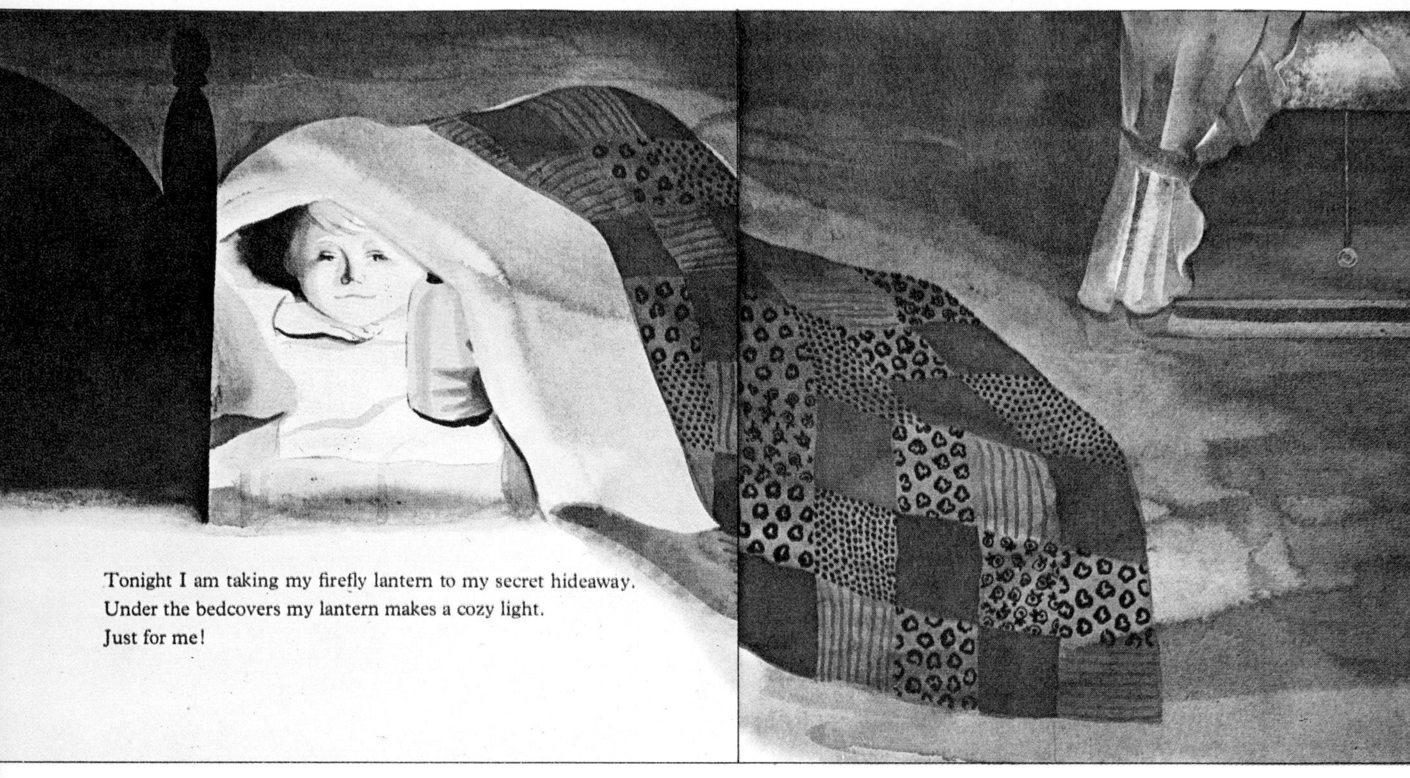
Tonight I am taking my firefly lantern to my secret hideaway.
Under the bedcovers my lantern makes a cozy light.
Just for me!

481. *Fireflies in the Night,* text by Judy Hawes, pictures by Kazue Mizumura. Crowell, 1963. 8⅝ x 8.

was also Kazue Mizumura's first go at anything other than Japanese material and at something other than a story (qq. v. p. 451). But there is a boy watching fireflies on a summer night (in LR&FOs, there is almost always a first-person voice if not, later, a physical presence)—a boy whose grandparents share his pleasure, whose grandfather helps him fix a glass jar to take on firefly hunts and, after each, "has something to tell me." Once it's how to make his firefly lantern brighter ("Just hold the jar upright in a bowl of warm water") and without saying so, why: "He knew it would work because fireflies always shine brighter in warm weather." So it follows that "People in hot countries use fireflies more than we do"—in net bags tied to their ankles as homemade flashlights ("Grandfather let me try this in the cornfield, because we have no jungle"); in the stone lanterns of Japan; and once, during a Cuban power failure, in an operating room.

"Fireflies," curiously, "make *cold* light"; and there's a not so simple explanation for it, leaving the youngster with more to learn. For the rest there are characteristic male and female firefly signals for him to try with a flashlight himself; but not yet . . . "Tonight I am taking my firefly lantern to my secret hideaway. Under the bedcovers my lantern makes a cozy light," and a lovely luminous picture (481). Soon his grandmother will come to say good night. " 'Lights out,' she will say. She will take my lantern outside and let my fireflies go . . . I'll catch some more tomorrow night." Or in the way of Ets's little boy going for a walk in the forest, another day.

The male and female firefly signals, though perhaps nothing else, prepare us for *Bees and Beelines.* 'How can bees, who fly more than a mile to find nectar, fly home in such a straight line?' the little girl ponders; and her uncle, "a scientist who studies bees," tells her about 'bee school' and 'flying-home lessons' (483) and how the bee's five eyes, two of them compound, enable her to see in all directions and get twelve thousand views of her hive at once. More impressive still, bee scouts communicate news of their finds—how far the nectar is and where—by 'dancing' in established patterns and at indicative speeds. As crisply as she charted the first flying lessons, Aliki maps out the dances, using sun, hive and flower as coordinates and making the message unmistakable (482). It may not be a coincidence that she too was experienced in commercial art.

Regardless of his varied experience, one would not think of Joseph Low to illustrate *How a Seed Grows*; yet there it was on the first LR&FO list, a sign, if there'd been no other, that something unusual was under way. But it is what he makes of *Shrimps* that shows scientific illustration as a creative art. So it is, variously, with Borten and Mizumura and others, but Low is not picturing concepts or evoking a mood, he is drawing the humble unpoetic shrimp. The strong-tailed, many-limbed shrimp, scooting away from a predatory fish or showing just what he's made of

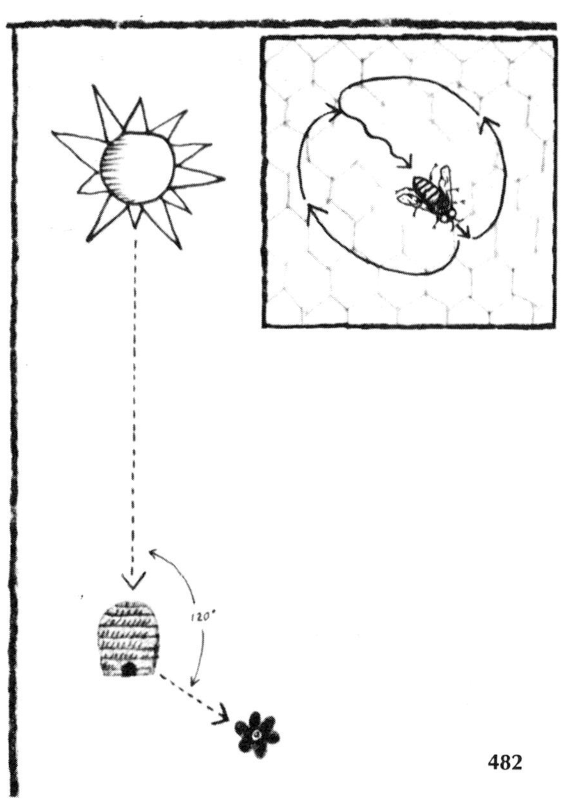

482

482, 483. *Bees and Beelines,* text by Judy Hawes, pictures by Aliki. Crowell, 1964. 8⅝ x 8.

483

(484). It is free and precise, expressive and instructive, and it needs no brilliant hues to give it color. When Low turns to color at alternate openings, shrimp-color and the aquamarine of the sea, it is in itself telling (485).

Why reproduce such a plain spread, pictures with so few pictorial elements, so little to catch and hold the eye? In fact, if one wants to find a highly developed spread in many of the best of the series, an artistically rich, arresting composition, one has to turn to derneath, and bears with it, in the form of arrows, the shrimp; the sun rises high in the sky, the band, lowered to the bottom of the page, denotes the tides running out, revealing the headland and hypothetically bearing away the shrimp; and a visual metaphor, delicately handled, becomes a quietly absorbing design.

So, elsewhere: it wasn't that science illustration was wangling to be art, it was that artists, dealing with scientific concepts and qualities, were finding fresh artistic means of expressing them.

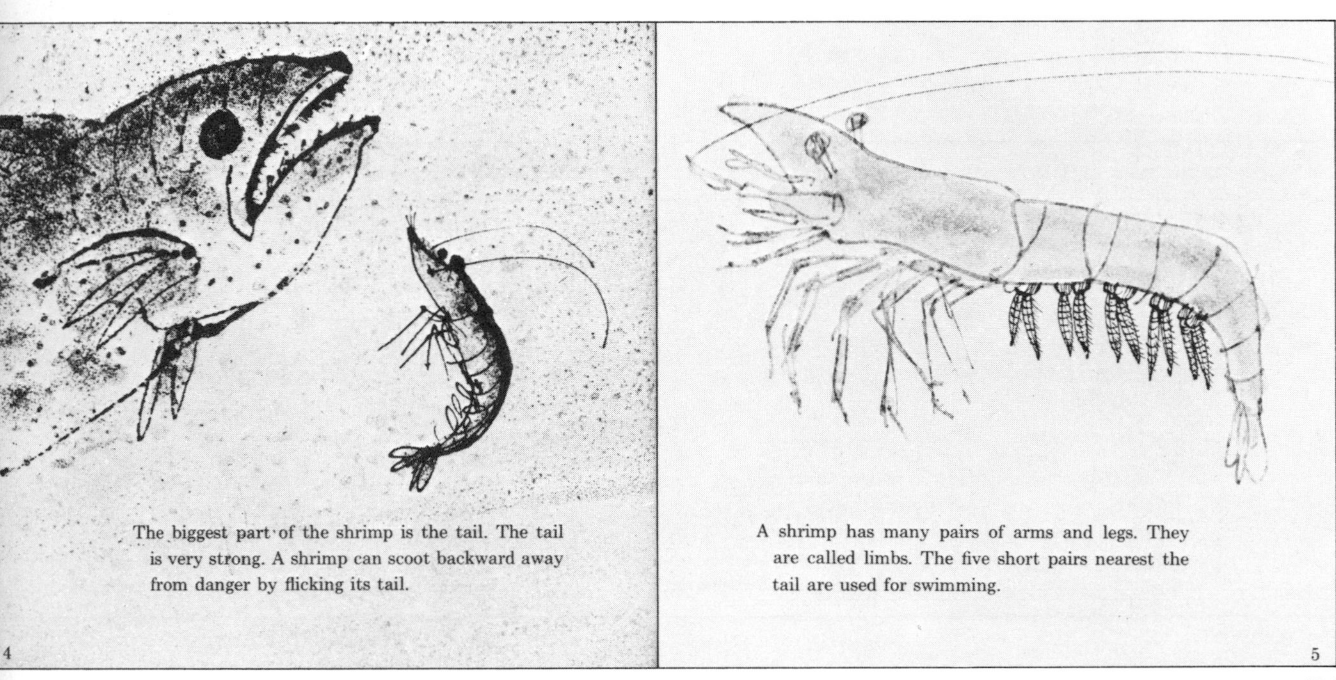

The biggest part of the shrimp is the tail. The tail is very strong. A shrimp can scoot backward away from danger by flicking its tail.

A shrimp has many pairs of arms and legs. They are called limbs. The five short pairs nearest the tail are used for swimming.

4 5

484

the title spread, the province solely of artist and designer (486). Otherwise simplicity and economy carry over from text to pictures, which add warmth, a touch of wit, a special grace; but in becoming a presence, a picture does not become a force. Being a presence, being personal to the artist, it can be plain without being empty, as Low's rendering of the tides is—an intelligent, not unaffecting presence. A translucent band of aquamarine, placed high on the page, sweeps over the headland whose outlines remain visible un-

The idea that young books in other subject areas, as well, be illustrated by artists of some note—that they be artistic books—was behind the Books to Begin On series at Holt, and Ezra Jack Keats did an exhilarating *Hawaii*, Ellen Raskin a very handsome *Books*; but the generalized and indicative illustrations—not precise, specific—and, it appears, the distinguished design itself tended to militate against them and limit their acceptance with children: they fail to suggest that *here are the facts*.

485

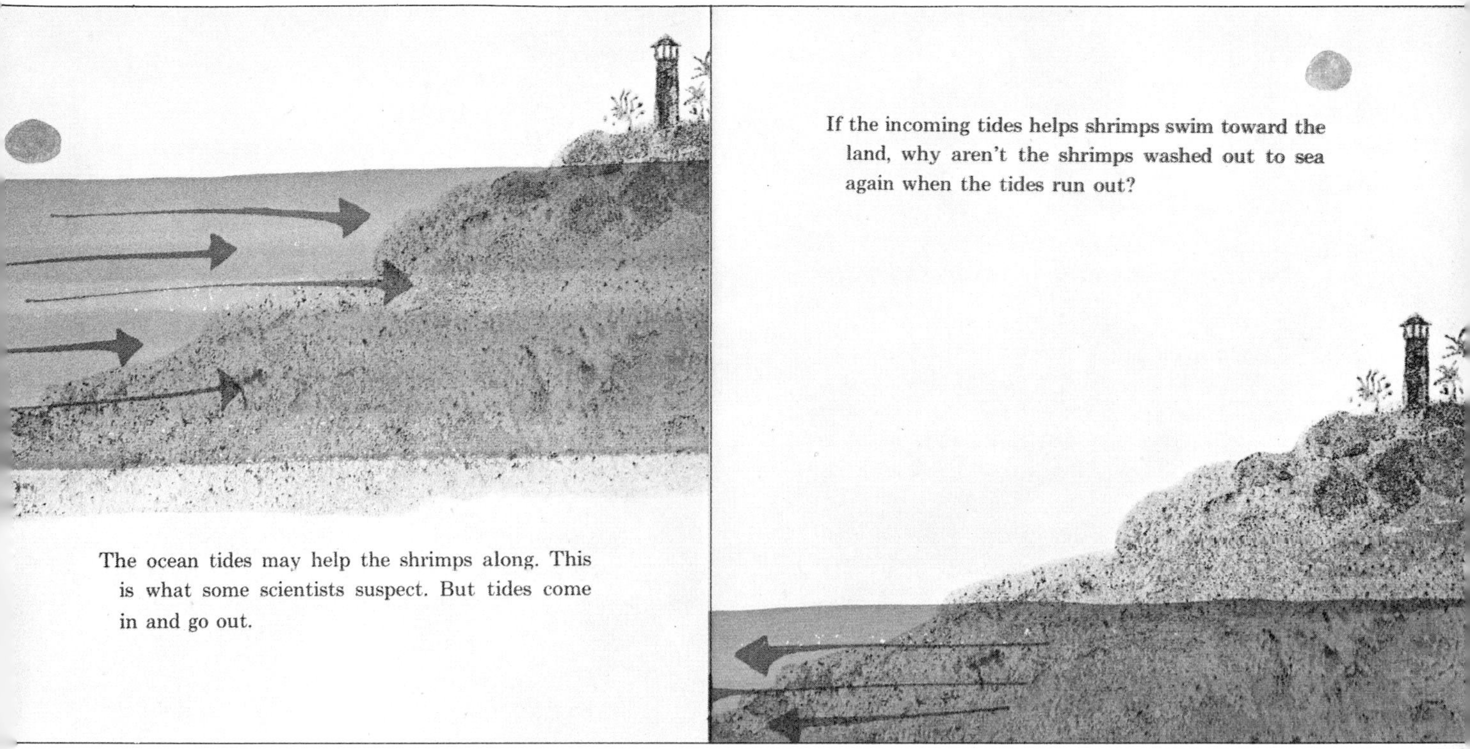

The ocean tides may help the shrimps along. This is what some scientists suspect. But tides come in and go out.

If the incoming tides helps shrimps swim toward the land, why aren't the shrimps washed out to sea again when the tides run out?

484–486. *Shrimps*, text by Judy Hawes, pictures by Joseph Low. Crowell, 1966. 8⅝ x 8.

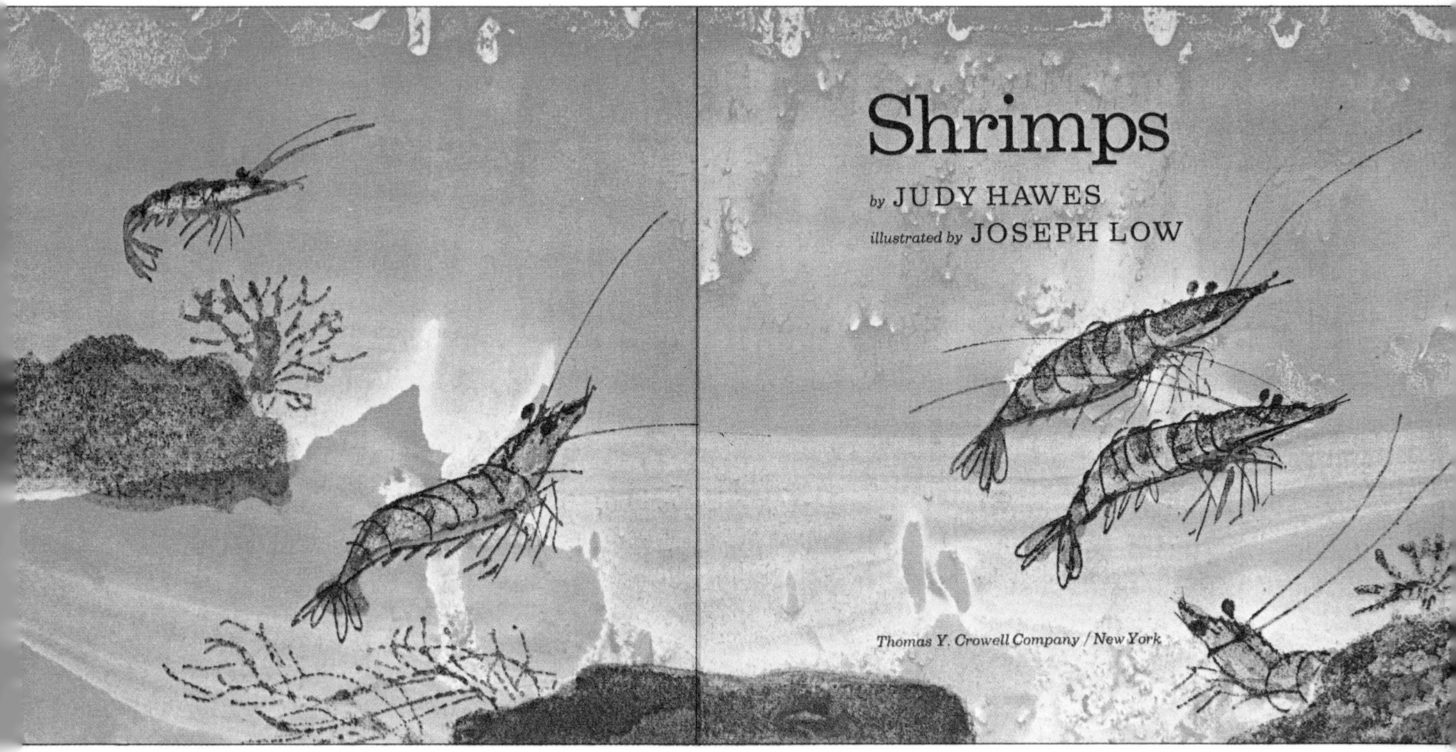

Shrimps

by JUDY HAWES

illustrated by JOSEPH LOW

Thomas Y. Crowell Company / New York

486

HISTORY AND GEOGRAPHY CONJOINED

It is time to take up the Hollings again, with *The Book of Indians*, and here indeed are the facts (487, 488). "As a boy," Holling begins, "I wanted to know all about Indians," and woven into the activities and adventures of his fictional children, a boy and a girl from each of the four major regions, are the relevant particulars and more; like a genre painter, Holling omits nothing from the scene. Under a platform attached to the wickiup, the family dogs—"of which there were many"—snooze: "There was always a scrap of meat to be hoped for, because the cooking fire was just a few feet away and a clay pot was forever simmering on the red coals." Far from being a distraction, the details are the very stuff of the story. Holling was an artist-illustrator before he was a writer—an artist-observer, storing up data aboard Great Lakes freighters or among the Southwest Indians, and, in the taxidermy department at the Field Museum, a transcriber of appearances. In writing as in drawing, he made a complete and meticulous record.

In *The Book of Indians*, the one balances the other, not in space but in weight—for the many words it takes to describe how, for

487, 488. *The Book of Indians,* text by Holling C. Holling, pictures by H. C. and Lucille Holling. Platt & Munk, 1935. 8 x 10⅝.

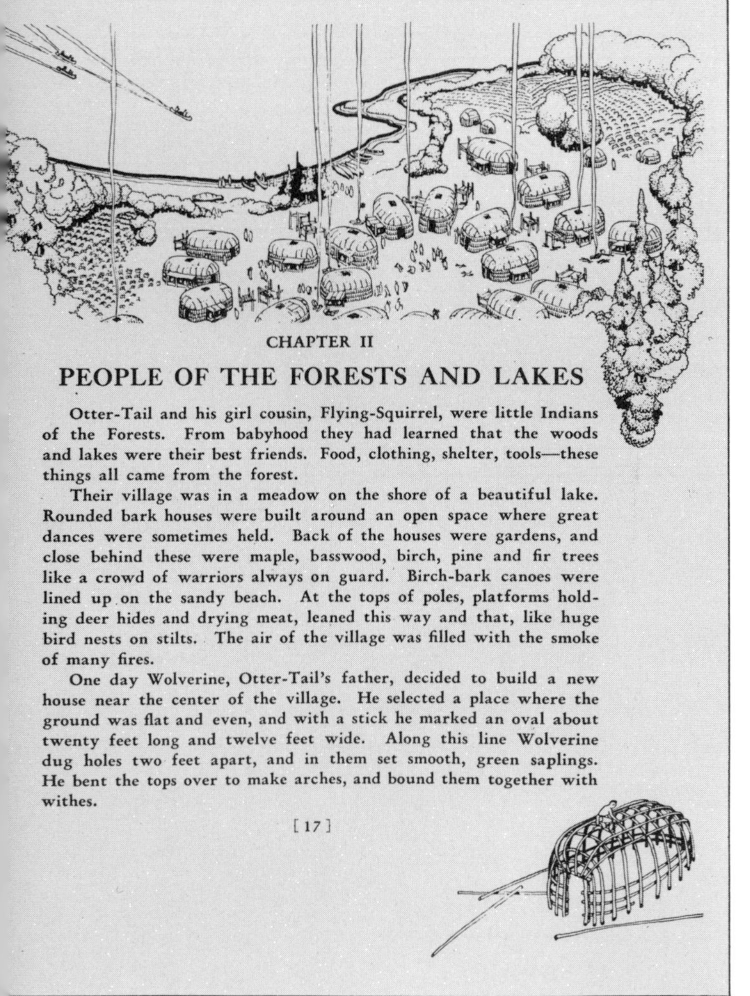

CHAPTER II

PEOPLE OF THE FORESTS AND LAKES

Otter-Tail and his girl cousin, Flying-Squirrel, were little Indians of the Forests. From babyhood they had learned that the woods and lakes were their best friends. Food, clothing, shelter, tools—these things all came from the forest.

Their village was in a meadow on the shore of a beautiful lake. Rounded bark houses were built around an open space where great dances were sometimes held. Back of the houses were gardens, and close behind these were maple, basswood, birch, pine and fir trees like a crowd of warriors always on guard. Birch-bark canoes were lined up on the sandy beach. At the tops of poles, platforms holding deer hides and drying meat, leaned this way and that, like huge bird nests on stilts. The air of the village was filled with the smoke of many fires.

One day Wolverine, Otter-Tail's father, decided to build a new house near the center of the village. He selected a place where the ground was flat and even, and with a stick he marked an oval about twenty feet long and twelve feet wide. Along this line Wolverine dug holes two feet apart, and in them set smooth, green saplings. He bent the tops over to make arches, and bound them together with withes.

[17]

487

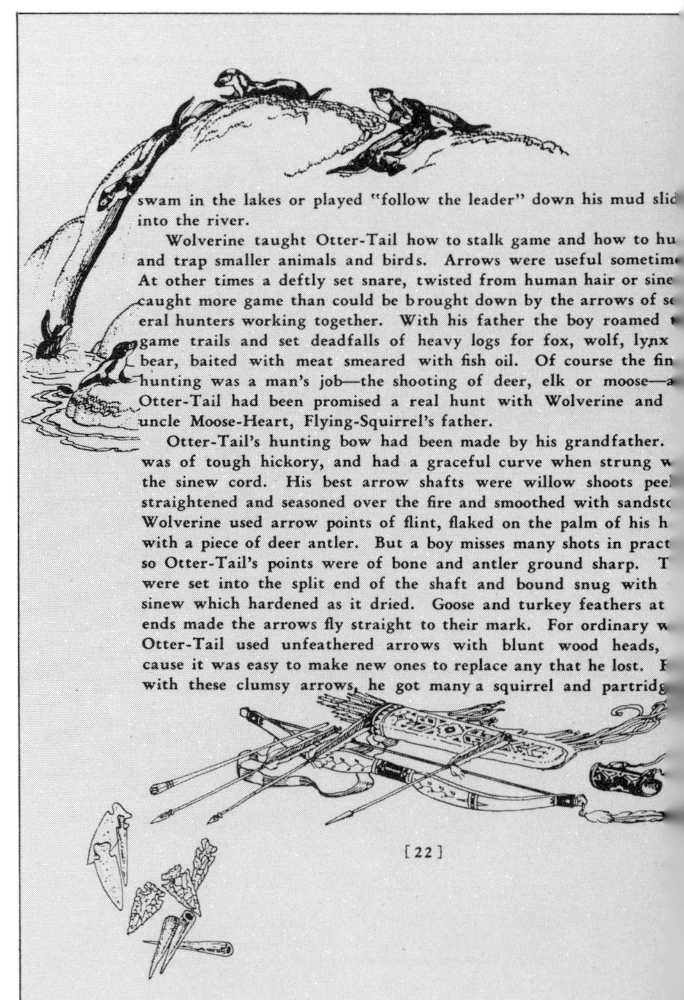

swam in the lakes or played "follow the leader" down his mud slid into the river.

Wolverine taught Otter-Tail how to stalk game and how to hu and trap smaller animals and birds. Arrows were useful sometim At other times a deftly set snare, twisted from human hair or sine caught more game than could be brought down by the arrows of s eral hunters working together. With his father the boy roamed game trails and set deadfalls of heavy logs for fox, wolf, lynx bear, baited with meat smeared with fish oil. Of course the fin hunting was a man's job—the shooting of deer, elk or moose—a Otter-Tail had been promised a real hunt with Wolverine and uncle Moose-Heart, Flying-Squirrel's father.

Otter-Tail's hunting bow had been made by his grandfather. was of tough hickory, and had a graceful curve when strung w the sinew cord. His best arrow shafts were willow shoots pee straightened and seasoned over the fire and smoothed with sandst Wolverine used arrow points of flint, flaked on the palm of his h with a piece of deer antler. But a boy misses many shots in pract so Otter-Tail's points were of bone and antler ground sharp. T were set into the split end of the shaft and bound snug with sinew which hardened as it dried. Goose and turkey feathers at ends made the arrows fly straight to their mark. For ordinary w Otter-Tail used unfeathered arrows with blunt wood heads, cause it was easy to make new ones to replace any that he lost. with these clumsy arrows, he got many a squirrel and partrid

[22]

488

instance, a wickiup was constructed would be incomprehensible without the marginal illustrations (beginning 487). On the other hand, the display of arrowheads, some of flaked flint, some of bone ground sharp (488), would be just so much decorative filler without the explanation of their differences.

Recognition of the Hollings' scrupulousness came from the most exacting quarters. The Indian Service's Education Division deemed *The Book of Indians* "one of the few books for children about Indians which we can wholeheartedly recommend" and "almost unique [in] having no misstatements, either in the text or in the pictures."[18]

The Book of Cowboys (Platt & Munk, 1936) followed in the same vein, and then there began the quartet of 'geo-histories' covering the United States from the Midwest eastward and westward—*Paddle-to-the-Sea* (1941) and *Tree in the Trail* (1942); from north to south—*Minn of the Mississippi* (1951); and around the circumference—*Seabird* (1948, all Houghton Mifflin): all big books bounteously illustrated, swathes of geography and history spiraling around a fixed center like a double helix around an atom.

In *Paddle-to-the-Sea* the focal point is the tiny wooden canoe-and-Indian set out by an Indian boy in the Canadian wilderness, carried by the melting snow into a stream which empties into Lake Superior and then transported, by lake currents and chance storms, by freighter and motorboat, through the Great Lakes and the St. Lawrence "and on at last to the sea," the Indian boy's very hope for him. It is a story very similar to an Iroquois legend, Holling learned later, and Paddle-to-the-Sea is one of those inanimate figures that, like the Steadfast Tin Soldier, quickly take on life; the words "Please put me back in the water" are carved on his bottom, and you find yourself hoping for him—hoping too that someone will save him from the sawmill's looming buzzsaw, that something will sweep him out from his prison under the dock (489), that somehow he'll survive fire and ice and Niagara Falls.

A great, great deal happens, the course of events carefully charted, the encroachments duly explained and incorporated into the story. At every opening is the big color picture putting Paddle into position for his next move and with it the marginal drawings that suggest how he got there. The big pictures themselves have a kind of magical realism, what is meant when art is taken as a lens on life. In reality, light is never so even, air so clear, colors so strong, contours so pronounced, everything so *present*: it is a thoroughly conventionalized rendering, realer than real, of a sort once common in commercial art and, in Photo-Realism, resurgent today. But it is not only what children at a certain age consider art to be, it is highly satisfactory as illustration.

Holling was to become smoother and slicker in *Tree in the Trail*, and in *Minn* more of a painter, immersed in light and shade, in both cases with a certain loss of integrity whatever the gain—in *Minn*—in terms of sheer dazzlement. At the same time, however, and not to be discounted, the marginal drawings sharpen and multiply until they approximate a pictorial encyclopedia.

They are all big and panoramic, the books of this period, a product of the new color presses, and so many of them are also panoramic visual resources that they appear to be a product equally of the era of world's fairs (Chicago, 1933–34; New York and San Francisco, 1939–40) just ending. Mabel Pyne's big *Little History* . . . and *Little Geography of the United States* (Houghton Mifflin, 1940 and 1941) are such, and so are those two whoppers, Arensa Sondergard's *My First Geography of the Americas* (1942) and *My First Geography of the Pacific* (1944), the earlier illustrated by Fritz Kredel, the second by Cornelius DeWitt (as "Cornelis"), both of them produced for Little, Brown by the Artists and Writers Guild.

The Americas represent a geographic unit become a unit of study, and conveniently taken, north to south, as the land lies and fame alights. Not so the Pacific with its proverbial 'far-flung islands' and remote peoples.

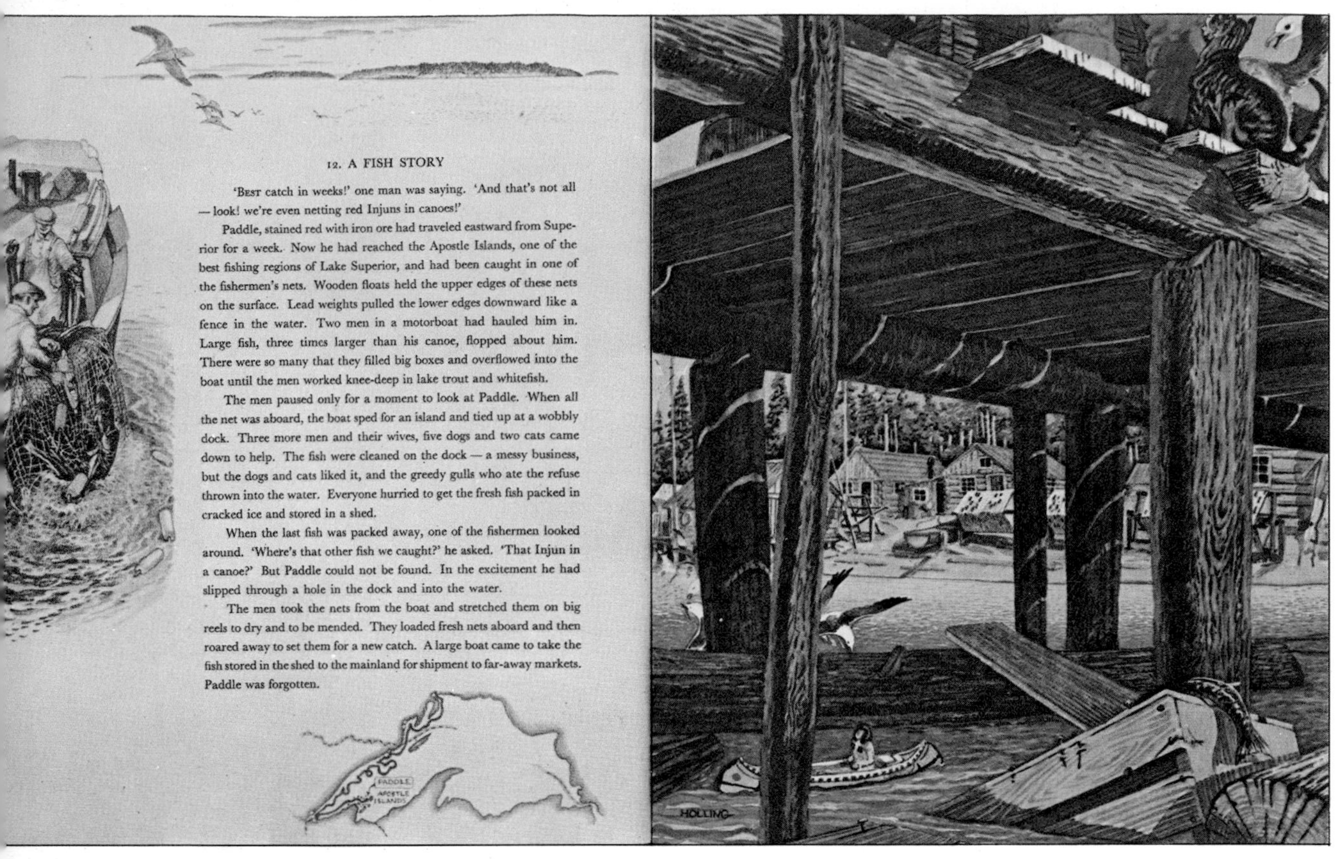

12. A FISH STORY

'Best catch in weeks!' one man was saying. 'And that's not all — look! we're even netting red Injuns in canoes!'

Paddle, stained red with iron ore had traveled eastward from Superior for a week. Now he had reached the Apostle Islands, one of the best fishing regions of Lake Superior, and had been caught in one of the fishermen's nets. Wooden floats held the upper edges of these nets on the surface. Lead weights pulled the lower edges downward like a fence in the water. Two men in a motorboat had hauled him in. Large fish, three times larger than his canoe, flopped about him. There were so many that they filled big boxes and overflowed into the boat until the men worked knee-deep in lake trout and whitefish.

The men paused only for a moment to look at Paddle. When all the net was aboard, the boat sped for an island and tied up at a wobbly dock. Three more men and their wives, five dogs and two cats came down to help. The fish were cleaned on the dock — a messy business, but the dogs and cats liked it, and the greedy gulls who ate the refuse thrown into the water. Everyone hurried to get the fresh fish packed in cracked ice and stored in a shed.

When the last fish was packed away, one of the fishermen looked around. 'Where's that other fish we caught?' he asked. 'That Injun in a canoe?' But Paddle could not be found. In the excitement he had slipped through a hole in the dock and into the water.

The men took the nets from the boat and stretched them on big reels to dry and to be mended. They loaded fresh nets aboard and then roared away to set them for a new catch. A large boat came to take the fish stored in the shed to the mainland for shipment to far-away markets. Paddle was forgotten.

489. *Paddle-to-the-Sea,* by Holling Clancy Holling. Boston, Houghton Mifflin, 1941. 9 x 11.

But even as World War II directed attention southward by default, it turned the Pacific into a battleground, our own particular battleground, and brought to our doorsteps New Guinea and Samoa and Guadalcanal. *My First Geography* presents the Pacific of war bulletins in a context of past discoveries, normal life and future prospects (e.g. the North Pacific as the link to Europe it has become) and that in a great imaginative sweep from Crusoe's island off Chile around to Alaska, "bought . . . for only $7,200,000." And notwithstanding the "treacherous Japanese air and naval attack" on Pearl Harbor, when we reach Japan tea leaves are being gathered and silk spun, and equally in evidence as being patterned after foreign models are steel mills and army platoons–this at the height of the Pacific War.

Were it not so well conceived, we would still want to look at it (490). Alaska is vast and variegated and this is not a typical spread; but it suggests the luxuriant physical maps—or schematized air views—that appear throughout and, accompanied by native elements, become the physical embodiment of each place. Each spread, in fact, tells its own story—Tahiti of volcanic ranges and towering palms, the Philippines of many thousand islands and many different peoples, Australia of emptiness and, overleaf, natural abundance. Reviewing it as (social) science, James Newman concluded—"Easily the most original and successful geography primer that has yet appeared."[19]

The statement might be amended to read, in the case of picturebooks, 'or has appeared yet.'

Even more dependent on DeWitt's illustration for their distinction were the regional histories he did with various authors between 1940—*The Story of Alaska* and *The Story of the Mississippi*—and 1948—*The Story of the Southwest*; ten in all, they were also produced by the Artists and Writers Guild, this time for Harper. As social science, the books vary between popular, topical history and a mix of historical lore, industries and crops, and local customs; but even were they more seriously intended, the pictures would still overshadow the text. As featured, they are lithographs (491), so intricately worked, in terms of separations and overprinting, as to be the equivalent of full-color illustrations; but they have the brilliance and subtlety of tones of work derived from artists' separations and the rich hand feel of lithography itself. Considering Western Printing's capability to do process work, to opt for autolithography was somewhat like deciding to bake your own bread—with the difference that the resulting product could be sold (for $1) at supermarket prices.

Lynd Ward once spoke of "DeWitt's great capacity for rendering a complex combination of human figures and landscapes"[20]—a capacity that combines the ability to work small and think big (492). Full-page pictures and

490. *My First Geography of the Pacific,* text by Arensa Sondergard, pictures by Cornelis (Cornelius DeWitt). Little, Brown, 1944. 11 x 12¾.

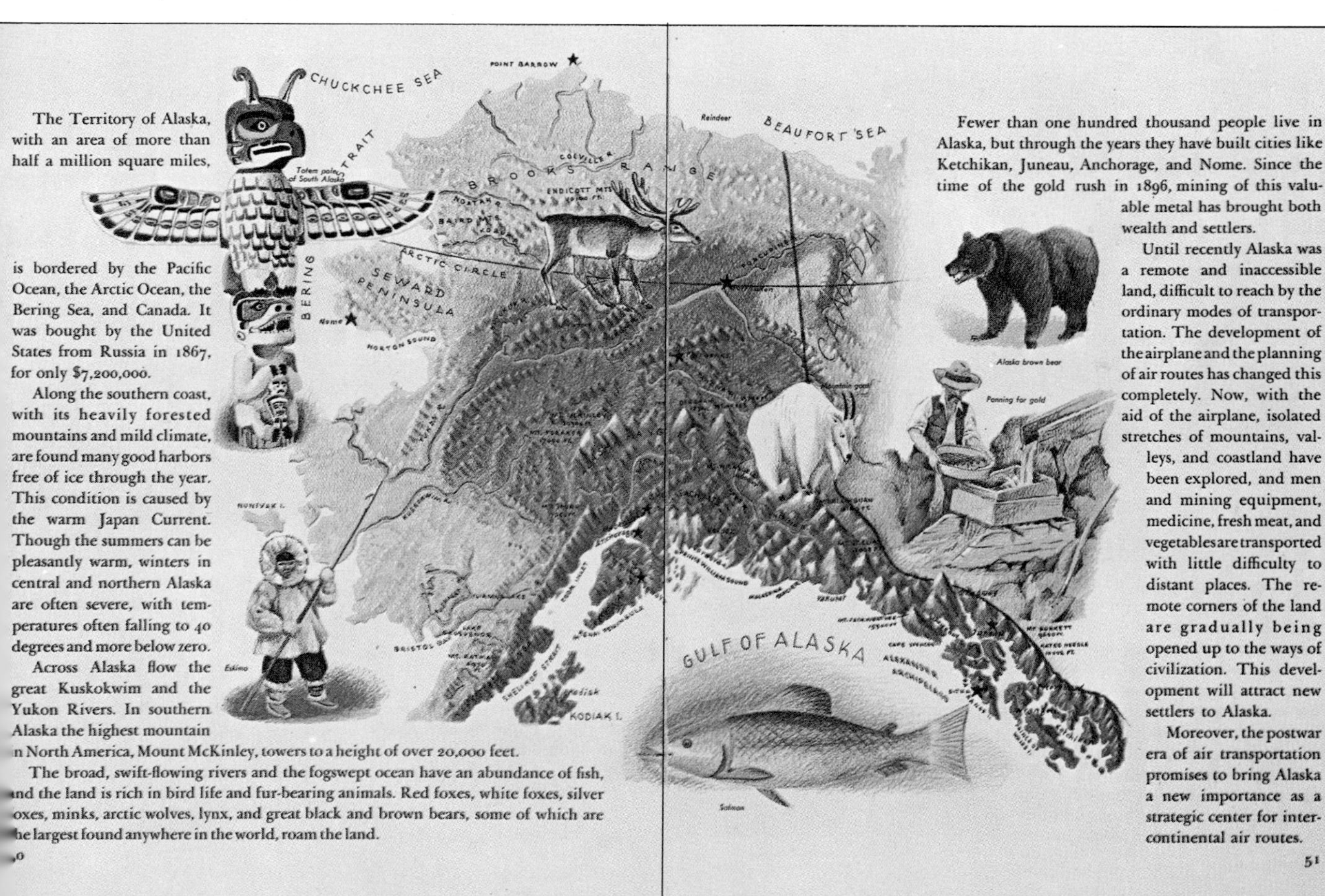

The Territory of Alaska, with an area of more than half a million square miles, is bordered by the Pacific Ocean, the Arctic Ocean, the Bering Sea, and Canada. It was bought by the United States from Russia in 1867, for only $7,200,000.

Along the southern coast, with its heavily forested mountains and mild climate, are found many good harbors free of ice through the year. This condition is caused by the warm Japan Current. Though the summers can be pleasantly warm, winters in central and northern Alaska are often severe, with temperatures often falling to 40 degrees and more below zero.

Across Alaska flow the great Kuskokwim and the Yukon Rivers. In southern Alaska the highest mountain in North America, Mount McKinley, towers to a height of over 20,000 feet.

The broad, swift-flowing rivers and the fogswept ocean have an abundance of fish, and the land is rich in bird life and fur-bearing animals. Red foxes, white foxes, silver foxes, minks, arctic wolves, lynx, and great black and brown bears, some of which are the largest found anywhere in the world, roam the land.

50

Fewer than one hundred thousand people live in Alaska, but through the years they have built cities like Ketchikan, Juneau, Anchorage, and Nome. Since the time of the gold rush in 1896, mining of this valuable metal has brought both wealth and settlers.

Until recently Alaska was a remote and inaccessible land, difficult to reach by the ordinary modes of transportation. The development of the airplane and the planning of air routes has changed this completely. Now, with the aid of the airplane, isolated stretches of mountains, valleys, and coastland have been explored, and men and mining equipment, medicine, fresh meat, and vegetables are transported with little difficulty to distant places. The remote corners of the land are gradually being opened up to the ways of civilization. This development will attract new settlers to Alaska.

Moreover, the postwar era of air transportation promises to bring Alaska a new importance as a strategic center for intercontinental air routes.

51

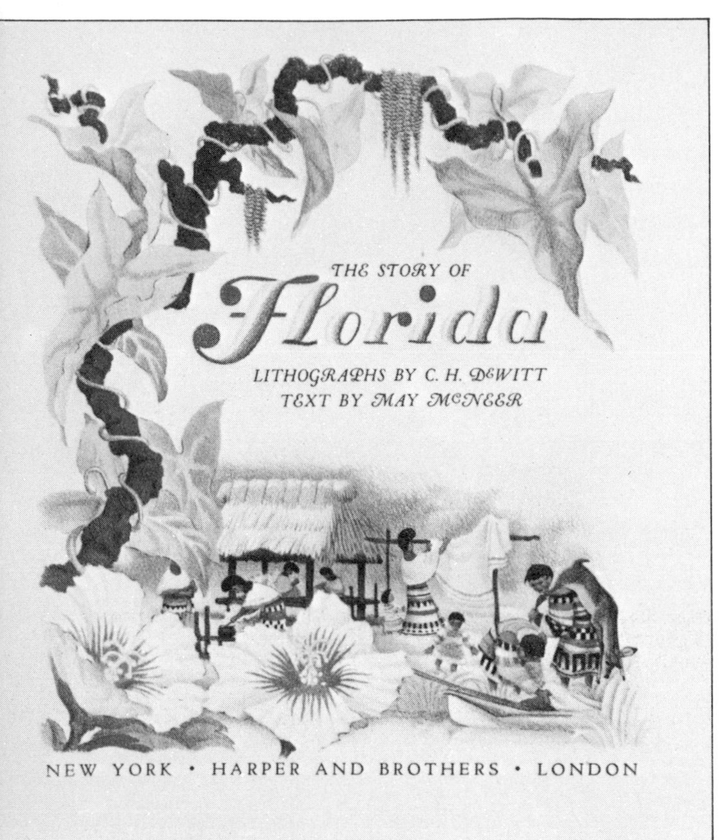

491. *The Story of Florida,* text by May McNeer, pictures by C. H. DeWitt. Harper, 1947. 9⅞ x 11.

marginal drawings are the norm in the regional histories, the former, in color, comprising a sequence of murals while the text tells the fuller story. But it is the pictures, vivid and vital, that make the events memorable.

THE REAL THING

Still and all, sometimes a youngster is solely and passionately concerned with particulars; he wants to know, as always, just what's what (493). *The Big Book of Real Trains*, published at $1.00 by Grosset, is another product of printing technology, mass production and distribution, this time applied to sheer elucidation. Wrote Louise Bechtel in the *Herald Tribune*:

"Here is an absolutely elegant train book, so big that all is very 'real.' The fine full-color pages show a Hudson Locomotive 4–6–4, its tender, an automobile car, a refrigerator car, a gondola, a flatcar, a tank car, the caboose. Clever little silhouettes across the bottom margin add each car until the whole freight train is complete.

"Now comes a grand double page on the parts of a locomotive, with thirty-five of them

492. *The Story of California,* text by May McNeer, pictures by C. H. DeWitt. Harper, 1944. 9⅞ x 11.

The Golden Spike

For years mountain passes echoed to the crack of whips and the shouts of mule skinners. Along the canyon trails creaked covered wagons bringing supplies to the westerners and taking gold back east. Stagecoaches creaked westward filled with daring travelers, dusty and shaken up but with guns ready for attacks by Indians and highwaymen. Ships filled with passengers and cargoes anchored in San Francisco Bay after long and perilous voyages.

But now speed was in demand. For more than a year riders of the Pony Express, with mail pouches swinging at their pommels, galloped ahead of Sioux and Comanches across the plains to California. Then the telegraph line reached the western shores, its crackling wires bringing news so swiftly that the Pony Express was abandoned. And now came rumors of a railroad!

Ships arriving in San Francisco began to unload rails and equipment, and Chinese coolies began the difficult construction of the railroad. The Transcontinental Railroad was built from two directions at once. Work trains started on the Union Pacific from Omaha, Nebraska, in 1864, and the Central Pacific built eastward from Sacramento, California, across mountain gorges. Builders advancing from Omaha had to bring ties, rails, spikes, and all the other equipment and supplies for their Irish laborers from Iowa. Most of the material used by the Central Pacific had been shipped around Cape Horn.

Construction trains on the plains were guarded by troops who fought off Indians as the engines pushed slowly westward. In the mountains Chinese workmen built bridges and miles of snow sheds to prevent avalanches from burying the trains. But neither snow nor Indians could stop the pounding of sledge hammers and shouts of men at work. After more than three years the two crews met at Promontory Point, Utah.

A crowd was there watching, and in cities all over the Union, from San Francisco to New York, people waited. A silver spike from Nevada was driven into the last tie, then a spike of silver, iron, and gold from Arizona. A prayer was offered, and then blows from a silver sledge drove in the last, the golden spike from California. The blows of the hammer were carried all over the country by electricity, to ring bells in cities throughout the nation. A great shout arose across the United States, for from east and west the country was united. A band of steel linked the forests of New England to the monarch redwoods of California.

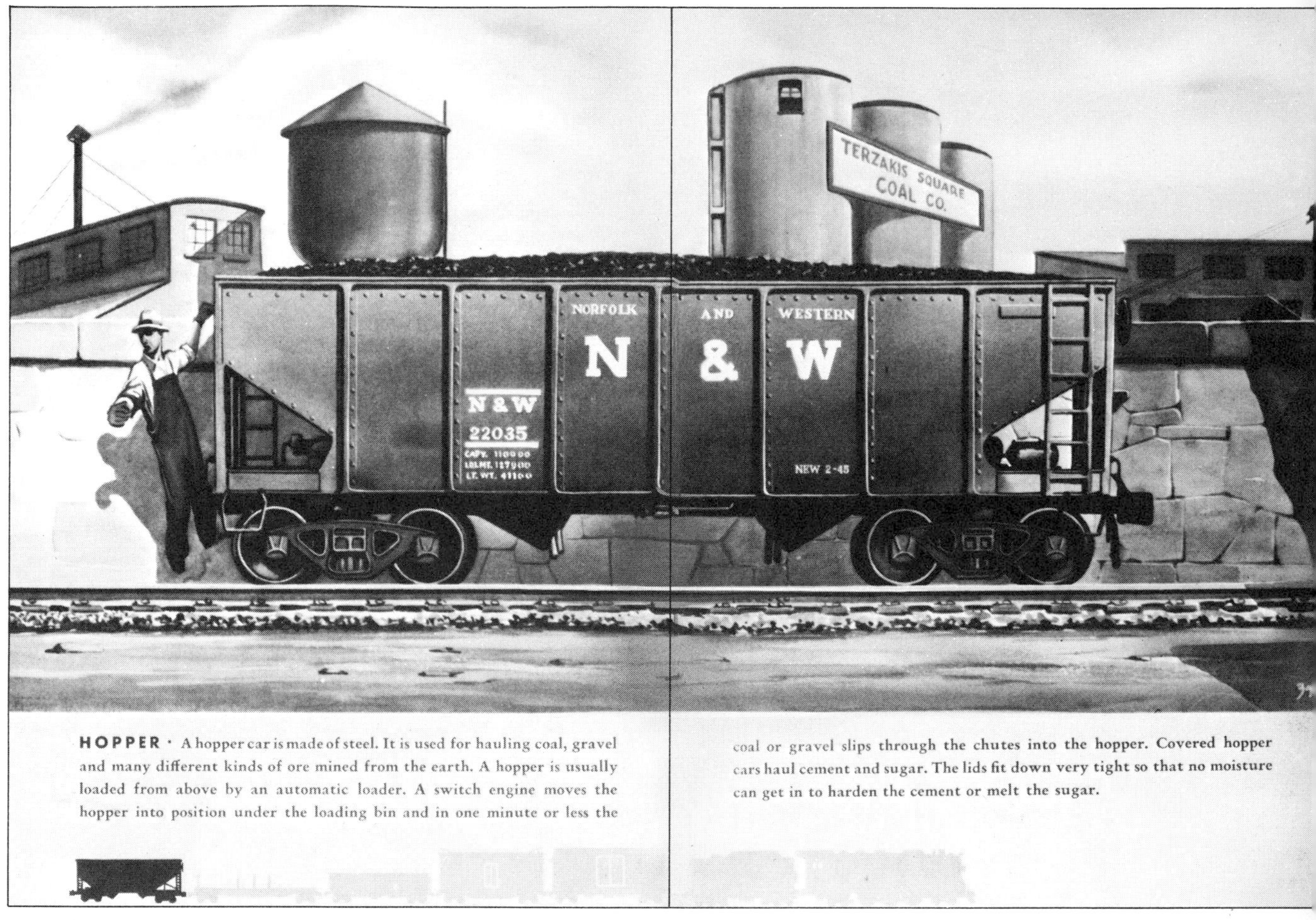

TERZAKIS SQUARE
COAL CO.
NORFOLK AND WESTERN
N & W
N & W
22035
NEW 2-45
HOPPER · A hopper car is made of steel. It is used for hauling coal, gravel and many different kinds of ore mined from the earth. A hopper is usually loaded from above by an automatic loader. A switch engine moves the hopper into position under the loading bin and in one minute or less the
coal or gravel slips through the chutes into the hopper. Covered hopper cars haul cement and sugar. The lids fit down very tight so that no moisture can get in to harden the cement or melt the sugar.

493. *The Big Book of Real Trains,* by George Zaffo. Grosset, 1949.

clearly labeled. Then two pages of train signals: whistles, air signal cord, lantern emergency stop. The bright blue endpapers give white line analyses of the Santa Fe 4–6–4, the New York Central 4–6–0 and the Baldwin Diesel Switcher.

"Small boys with a beginning interest in railroads are going to love this book. So are older boys who know lots already about trains, especially freight trains. What it lacks, already supplied by so many books, is anything about the engineer and what goes on in the cabin. . . ."[21]

The Zaffo books—also *The Big Book of Real Airplanes, Boats and Ships,* etc.—were novel in that they took the kind of precise representation featured in *Fortune,* blew it up to poster size, and provided pictures for small children to 'read' and older children to refer to no less, and study. It was straight pictorial information, in short, by nature 'ageless,' on a scale that itself suggests the original; and presented with more attention to fundamentals, greater economy and exactitude than heretofore. A small child could turn to it from *The Little Train* or *Pogo's Train Ride,* an older one would not find it childish. One of Mrs. Bechtel's confidants, a boy of eight, told her that his two favorite book people were Zaffo and Lucius Beebe. ("He is saving up to buy *Mixed Train Daily.*"[22])

The lack of embellishment, personal or romantic, is itself a sign of changing times; and, updated, the books satisfy still.

RUTH KRAUSS; RUTH KRAUSS AND MAURICE SENDAK

Ruth Krauss, who was taking courses in anthropology at Columbia, went to Harper's with the idea for a book on race relations, and the outcome was the sturdy nonsense of *A Good Man and His Good Wife*. She joined the Writers' Laboratory at Bank Street, and listened to children there and on her own; and out of their speech, formed poetry. With the merest prompting she seems to have grasped intuitively what the great Russian children's poet Kornei Chukovsky spent his life studying, "the whimsical and elusive laws of childhood thinking";[1] and there is no surer guide to her work, unbeknownst, than Chukovsky's summation *From Two to Five*.

"Once there was a good man and his good wife," the story begins, and it might be "The Husband Who Wanted to Do Housework" or any of the many old tales of married couples, folklore's domestic comedy. "The details of his awkwardness furnish the amusement for the story," writes Stith Thompson, "and these may be expanded at will."[2] Moreover, continues Thompson, writing on folktale types, "The fool is frequently so literal-minded that he follows instructions even in the most inappropriate situations,"[3] and he cites "the best-known tale of this type," "What Should I Have Done," otherwise known as "Lazy Jack" (Jacobs) or "Prudent Hans" (Grimm). It is what one sees in *A Good Man and His Good Wife*, but it is not nearly all.

The couple's cottage, Ruth Krauss writes, has "white walls and red curtains and lots of little cubbyholes and handyshelves"—construing 'handyshelves' as the twin, in sense and in

494

Then the good man had to learn things all over again.

But by the time he learned to find his fishing rod in the broom closet next to the pantry, and his tobacco box in the cubbyhole under the stairs, everything was changed again. Then he looked very stern and cried, "This is ridiculous!" again.

495

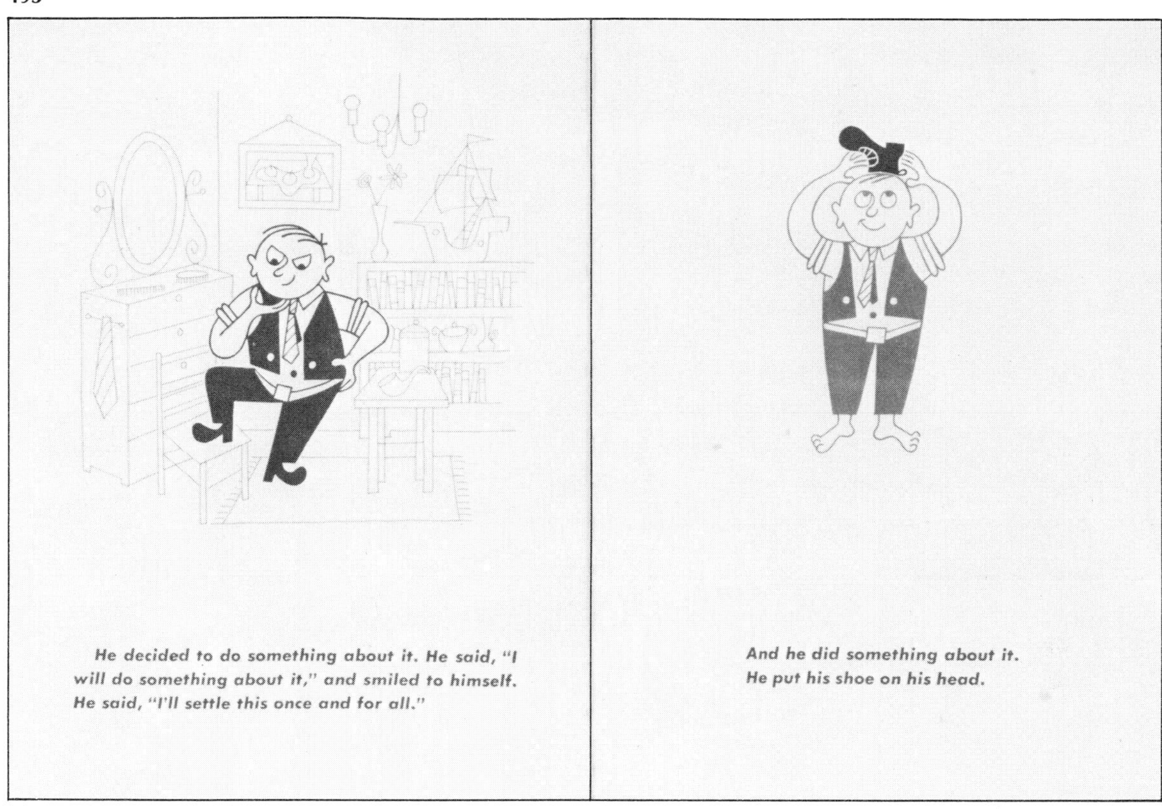

494–496. *A Good Man and His Good Wife*, text by Ruth Krauss, pictures by Ad Reinhardt. Harper, 1944. 6 x 8½.

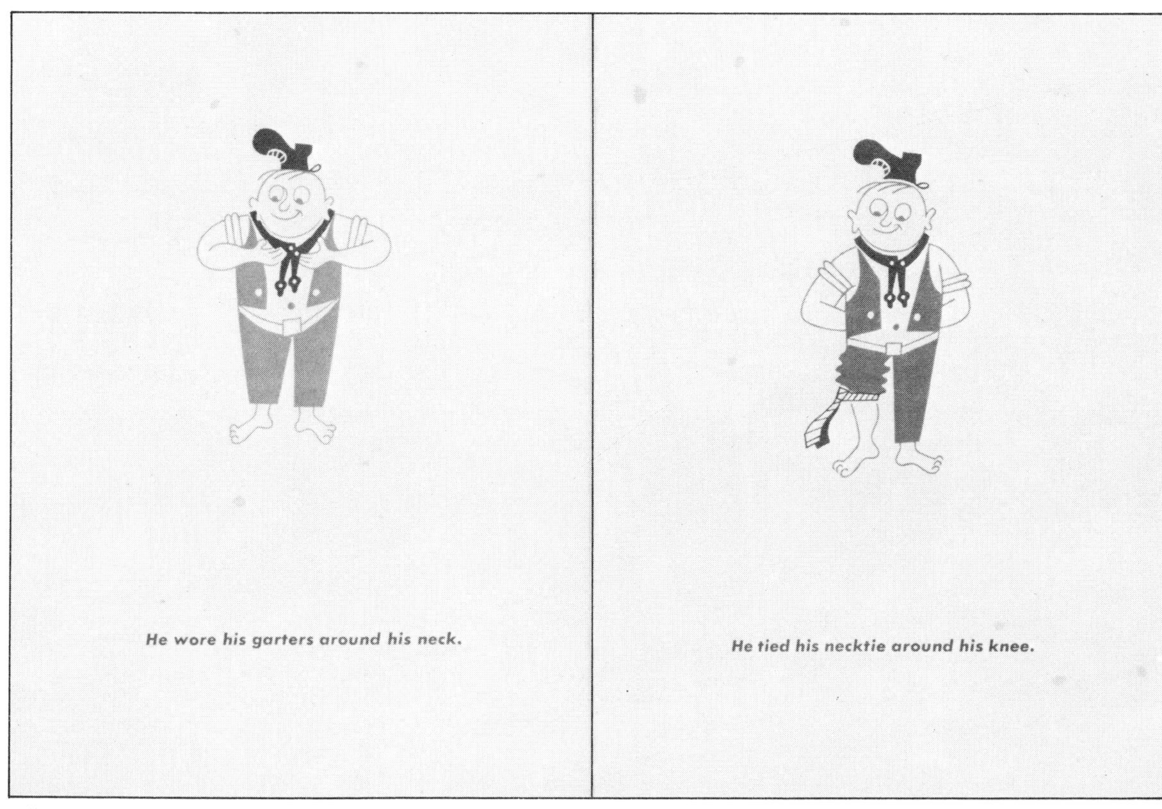

He wore his garters around his neck.
He tied his necktie around his knee.

496

sound, of 'cubbyholes,' the way children are wont to do. Comes the nonsense, and we're in on the game, for we can spot instantly—in Ad Reinhardt's two-color cartoons—just what it is that the poor husband is hunting for (494); and perceive that, no matter what it is, it's not where it should be. For—more nonsense—"I get so tired of the same things in the same place," says his wife. All right, he'll do something about it, he'll take her at her word (495, 496); "And that was how the good man cured his good wife of a bad habit." Not unlike the way kids confound their elders, sometimes innocently, sometimes not, by taking their words literally too.

Out of print for some time, *A Good Man and His Good Wife* was revived in 1962 with conventional illustrations by 'the 1956 Caldecott winner, Marc Simont' (*A Tree Is Nice*, p. 470), an ironic switch considering Ad

497

His mother said, "I'm afraid
it won't come up."

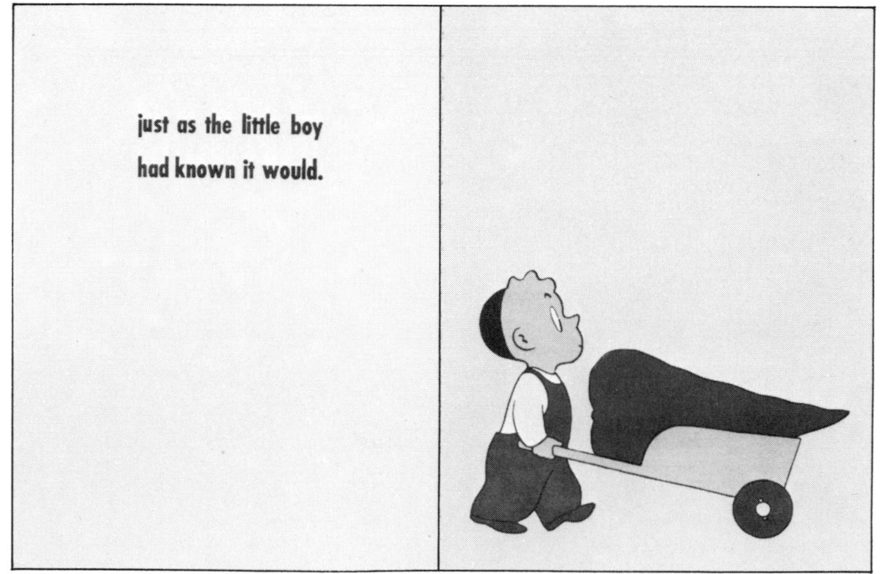
just as the little boy
had known it would.

498

497, 498. *The Carrot Seed,* text by Ruth Krauss, pictures by Crockett Johnson. Harper, 1945. 6 x 8.

Reinhardt's emergence, in the years following the original edition, as a leading abstract painter; and a loss for a book that remains nonetheless a wonderfully satisfying amalgam of folk-thought and child thinking.

There followed *The Carrot Seed*, child fable without peer. To tell it, tight and true as it is, one would have to have recourse to Ruth Krauss's words, so let us have Ruth Krauss's words as written and printed:

> A little boy planted
> a carrot seed.
>
> His mother said, "I'm afraid
> it won't come up." (497)
>
> His father said, "I'm afraid
> it won't come up."
>
> And his big brother said,
> "It won't come up."
>
> Every day the little boy pulled
> up the weeds around the seed
> and sprinkled the ground with
> water.
>
> But nothing came up.
>
> And nothing came up.
>
> Everyone kept saying it
> wouldn't come up.
>
> But he still pulled up the
> weeds around it every day
> and sprinkled the ground
> with water.
>
> And then, one day,
>
> a carrot came up
>
> just as the little boy
> had known it would. (498)

In the few nouns and verbs, the strategic 'ands' and 'buts,' is the essence of story; in the repetitions and rhythms, the essence of storytelling; in the interplay of silence and stress, storytelling and poetry, overlapping. And as it might in a poem, and should in a poem for young children, each sentence or line carries an image, a way of writing that perfectly suits picturebooks. But for a picturebook the image can be, as effectively, one of inaction—"But nothing came up./And nothing came up"—which, pictured and spaced out, marks time dramatically (remember Angus, "for exactly THREE minutes, by the clock" not curious about anything at all); or, to dramatic purpose too, one of gradual gathering action —"And then, one day," (the ground breaks) "a carrot came up" (towering green fronds) "just as the little boy had known it would" (giant red carrot).

From a monochromatic cream and brown, the book bursts into color with the appearance of no ordinary carrot; and that extraordinary carrot, the equivalent of Jack's miraculous beanstalk, is more than the vindication of the little boy's confidence, it is power. Besides knowing how, one has to know what to say, whether in words or in pictures; and in pictures, few if any said more—with less—than Crockett Johnson, "creator of Barnaby" and Ruth Krauss's husband.

As few words as there are in *The Carrot Seed*, there are fewer in *Bears*; and there were mutterings about a book that said nothing but *bears, bears, bears*. It came, as it happens, the year after a book called *Nothing But Cats, Cats, Cats*, which, you may recall, had a good bit to say; but I am reminded also of an ad that Eunice Blake ran at Nelson: "You Can Never Have Too Many ANIMAL STORIES," it read cheerily, "So We Have Published . . ." an entire list of them. Just bears too, a muchness of bears, is not to be belittled; or, as the flap copy puts it: "Here is a whole, solid, wonderful book of nothing *but* bears" (499).

> Bears, bears, bears, bears, bears.
> On the stairs
> Under chairs
> Washing hairs
> Giving stares
> Collecting fares
> Stepping in squares
> Millionaires
> Everywheres
> Bears, bears, bears, bears, bears.

It is the way children play with words, and with notions of things, rhyming them end-

499. *Bears,* text by Ruth Krauss, pictures by Phyllis Rowand. Harper, 1948. 7 x 9⅝.

lessly, ringing changes on the same sound, the same something; and the more nonsensical the result, the funnier it seems to them. But it begins in a correspondence they feel between sound and sense, or meaning: any old absurdities—bears laying bricks, shaking hands—wouldn't do. They wouldn't do as well, either, if they weren't things kids are close to—climaxing with that magic word 'millionaire.'

Not all, as some claimed, but much falls to the pictures, which cannot be real and ought not be whimsical—hence the value of Phyllis Rowand's natural artifice. Her bears are the funnier, and bearier, for being the same bear in assorted sizes and poses, and for their wide-eyed solemnity. Stepping in squares, they have purpose, aplomb; millionaires, they are debonair; and collecting fares—a neuter, a stumper—they are busy conductors and playful children both. But there's a sense in which they're children being bears collecting fares, stepping in squares—everywheres.

Rhyming is easy and insidious and popular, but Krauss uses rhyme only when she has a reason to; small and simple as her texts are—deceptively simple, in truth—each is shaped by the nature of the contents.

Chukovsky remarks on the child's "priceless urge to establish the causal connection between separate facts,"[4] so that he associates, willy-nilly, things that occur simultaneously or that bear a resemblance to one another. In tenor, in movement, *The Happy Day* is the most spontaneous of books, a natural that would appear to defy explanation; but behind it, comprising it, are simultaneous similar occurrences—what do they signify? what are they leading to?

> Snow is falling.
> The field mice are sleeping,
>
> the bears are sleeping,
>
> the little snails sleep in their shells;

500

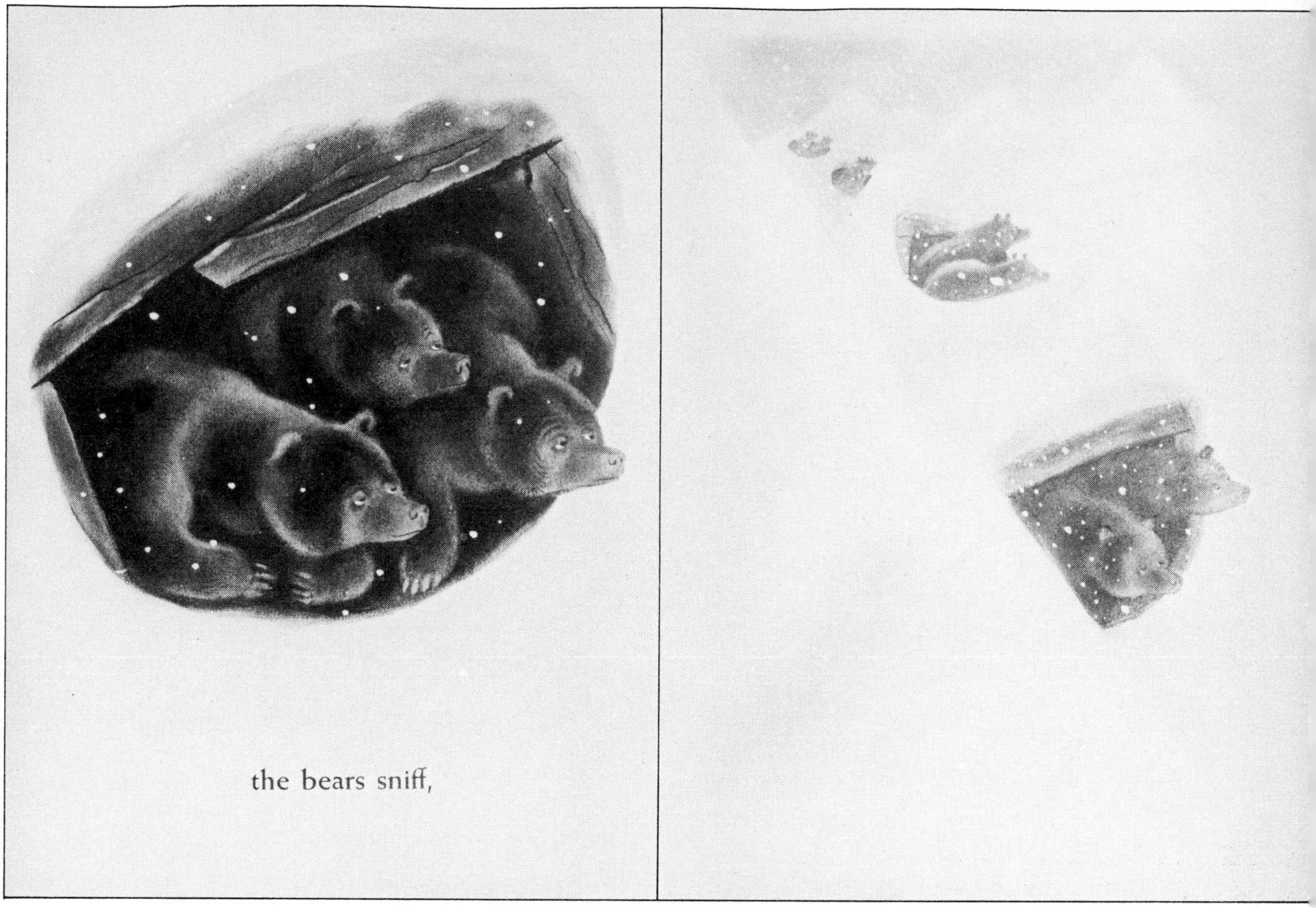

the bears sniff,

500, 501. *The Happy Day,* text by Ruth Krauss, pictures by Marc Simont. Harper, 1949. 8½ x 11⅝.

501

They sniff. They run. They stop.

They stop. They laugh.
They laugh. They dance.

and the squirrels sleep in the trees,
the ground hogs sleep in the ground.

Now, they open their eyes. They sniff.
The field mice sniff,

the bears sniff, (500)

the little snails sniff in their shells;

and the squirrels sniff in the trees,
the ground hogs sniff in the ground.

They sniff. They run.
The field mice run,
the bears run,

the little snails run with their shells,
and the squirrels run out of the trees,

the ground hogs run out of the ground.
They sniff. They run.

They run. They sniff.

They sniff. They run. They stop.
They stop. They laugh.
They laugh. They dance. (501)

They cry, "Oh!
A flower is growing in the snow."

In sum, various animals sleep, sniff, run, find the first flower growing in the snow; and it is yellow; a bright flat yellow flower against furry, fleecy black and gray and white, a child's flower-emblem bringing an end to winter.

It is a story contained, as it were, in five species, a string of verbs and an image; contained but not confined. 'Bears are sleeping' is a lullaby line, one of those phrases—envisionings—that have a special hold on children (later the basis of whole books); the 'snails in their shells'—sleeping, sniffing, running in their shells—are the unexpected, the amusing, the touch of nonsense. The animals' 'sniff' at the first whiff of spring is the spark, touching off action, curiosity; and a bit of onomatopoeia that, whether reading or listening, one imitates instinctively. So it goes to the last lines, in 'accidental' rhyme.

The pictures are prescribed: a set of the animals, in fixed order, sleeping, then sniffing, then running; or snug in their dens, popping out, taking to their heels—each of which is funny animal by animal as a sequence, and gathers force and momentum as bears and mice, snails, squirrels, ground hogs stream across the pages en masse, only to come to a halt, the lot of them, around a single small flower. A book pictured, one could say, in the writing too (Krauss had studied art), but written for such pictures as will fill it with life; as Marc Simont's quick and personable animal performers do.

Year by year the books appeared, marked by no special predilections, no particular manner or style, not then. They were—unusual praise—books children liked and adults appreciated.

The Backward Day takes us back to *A Good Man and His Good Wife*, but only so far. Getting up, a little boy says to himself, "Today is backward day"; and proceeds to put on his coat. Over his coat goes his suit, over his suit, his underwear: "Backward day is backward day." So backward goes he down the stairs (taking care to look over his shoulder), into the breakfast room, past his place and his chair; backward he turns his father's chair, and tucks his father's napkin at the back of his collar. "Goodnight, Pa," he greets his father, and "Goodnight," his father replies; and in a trice the whole household is turned around (502). The little boy is the one to right things. "Time to go to bed," and back up the stairs, backward, he goes—"backward oh backward oh backward oh backward oh backward and . . ." back into bed. Then it's time to get up again, to put on his underwear, suit, shoes, socks: "BACKWARD DAY IS DONE!"

The topsy-turvy nonsense that *A Good Man and His Good Wife* keeps at a distance, story-like, to laugh at, is transposed to the home as a reversal of the established order of things; or, as the jacket puts it more pointedly, "the conventional routine of the household is turned upside down." This we would label, not unreasonably, 'child psychology': the little boy, in control, upsets the applecart with impunity and then, of his own volition, rights it. Meanwhile we enjoy the incongruity with him.

Nursery rhymes, Chukovsky observed,

The little boy looked at his father. He looked at his mother. He looked at his baby sister. He said, "I'm so full I can't eat another thing."

502. *The Backward Day,* text by Ruth Krauss, pictures by Marc Simont. Harper, 1950. 6 x 8⅜.

abound in topsy-turvies—children ice-skating on a hot summer's day, a blind man gazing while a deaf man listens; and he searched for a reason for their persistent popularity, a psychological basis for the pleasure children take in any violation of the established order. As he tells it, his small daughter came to him one day, after she had mastered to her great satisfaction the fact that a dog goes bow-wow, a cat goes meow, and cried out—"looking mischievous and embarrassed at the same time" —"Daddy, 'oggie—meow!"

"That is," Chukovsky continues, "she reported to me the sensational and, to her, obviously incorrect news that a doggie, instead of barking, meows. And she burst into somewhat encouraging, somewhat artificial laughter, inviting me, too, to laugh at this invention.

"But I was inclined to realism.

" 'No,' said I, 'the doggie bow-wows.'

" 'Oggie—meow!' she repeated, laughing, and at the same time watched my facial expression which, she hoped, would show her how she should regard this erratic invention which seemed to scare her a little.

"I decided to join in her game and said:

" 'And the rooster meows!'

"Thus I sanctioned her intellectual effrontery. Never did even the most ingenious epigram of Piron evoke such appreciative laughter in knowledgeable adults as did this modest joke of mine, based on the interchange of two elementary notions. This was the first joke that my daughter became aware of—in the twenty-third month of her life. She realized that not only was it not dangerous to topsy-turvy the world according to one's whim, but, on the contrary, it was even amusing to do so, *provided that together with a false conception about reality there remained the correct one. . . .*"[5]

The emphasis is added, in accordance with the stress that Chukovsky himself places on verifying and self-examination, and additionally on self-appreciation, as explaining the value that the absurd, the incongruous—all manner of nonsense—has for a child. "*Others* do not seem to know that there is ice only in winter, that it is impossible to burn one's tongue with cold porridge . . . that mute people are incapable of crying 'Help.' *He*, however, has become so sure of these truths that he can even play with them."[6]

He knows, as surely, that a carrot does not grow to the size of a watermelon; but what a good joke on the doubters to pretend so.

The Backward Day, with another, younger 'make-believe,' *The Bundle Book* (Harper, 1951), brought to an end what one might call, *pace* Graham Greene, 'the entertainments,' for the next year there appeared the first of the inside-child books, *A Hole Is To Dig*.

RUTH KRAUSS AND MAURICE SENDAK

The year was 1952 and the dominant note was, collectively, color, size, design. Honors went, too, to the anecdotal: Lynd Ward's *The Biggest Bear* won the Caldecott, among the runners-up was *One Morning in Maine*.

In *Infant and Child in the Culture of Today* (1943), Gesell observes that at five or six, the child "is likely to define a word in terms of use. The wind is 'to make the clouds come,' it is 'to push the ships,' "[7] Gesell's interest is in the child's thought processes, his route to understanding cause and effect (at four, "Trees blow," they make the wind). Ruth Krauss, alerted, took notice of the definitions themselves and of what they said about how children felt. She asked children their meanings for words and tried out her own definitions on them; "A mother is to hug you" was vetoed—"A mother is to cook your food." The ones they approved she took to Harper's, jotted on 3 x 5 cards, as the basis for a book.

A first illustrator, Mordvinoff, could see nothing in them; but in Maurice Sendak's sketchbook were drawings of Brooklyn children that made Ursula Nordstrom think "he would be perfect for it,"[8] and Sendak, young and new—Marcel Aymé's *Wonderful Farm* (1951) was just behind him—took to the idea from the start. Author and editor sifted the definitions for those they liked best, some that they discarded ("Buttons are to keep people warm") Sendak championed, for what he could do with them; and from the three-way hook-up came *A Hole Is To Dig*, "A First Book of First Definitions" and a novelty all around.

"Here is a children's book without gaudy four-color pictures which can charm its more pretentious competitors right off the map," Marshall Lee wrote in that month's *PW* design review. "Wonderful little drawings printed in black on an India stock [buff] with type in rust brown on a small square page produce an enchanting effect."[9] (503-505)

Less apparent, perhaps, but no less noteworthy is what Ruth Krauss does with the definitions. Were one to set down the separate lines in some approximation of the way they appear in the book, one would have a kind of verse-drama for many voices, for there are sounds that repeat, words and phrases that recur, and thoughts that expand throughout—to say nothing of the exchanges, explicit and implicit, among the children as pictured. As two successive openings:

> Hands are to hold.
>   A hand is to hold up
>   when you want your turn.
>   A hole is to dig.
>
> The ground is to make a garden.
>   Grass is to have on the ground
>   with dirt under it
>   and clover in it.
>   Grass is to cut.
>   Maybe you could
>   hide things
>   in a hole.

Plainly to be seen in each instance are a theme or motif, and variations, with large type for the large-picture legend or dominant note, if there is one, and smaller sizes of type for parallel thoughts or offshoots or, sometimes, like-sounding nonsense—as "Hands are

503

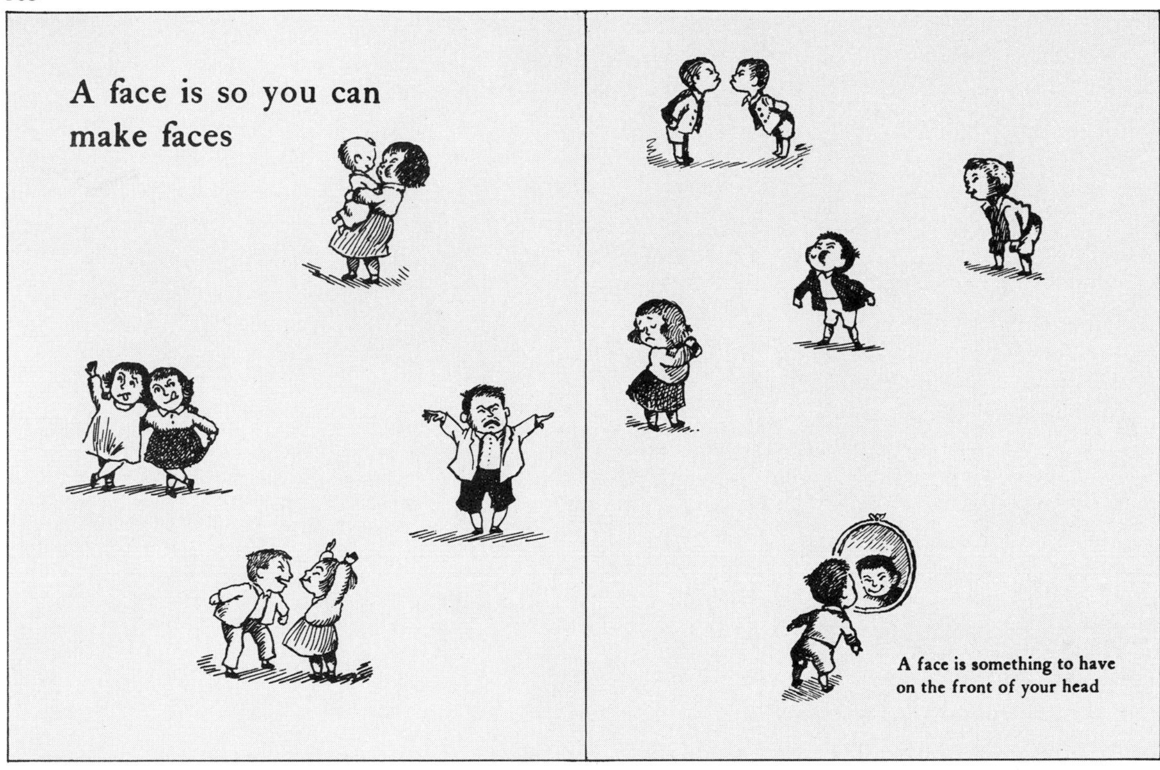

503, 504. *A Hole Is To Dig,* text by Ruth Krauss, pictures by Maurice Sendak. Harper, 1952. 5 x 6½.

504

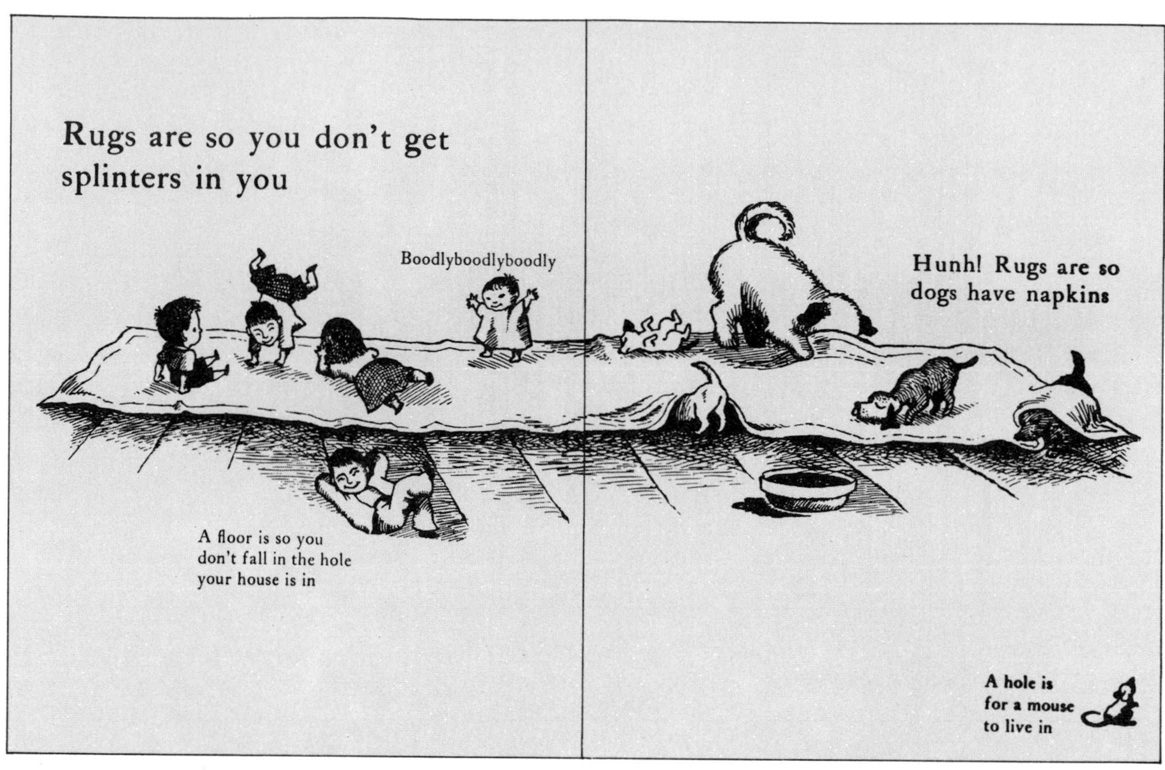

Rugs are so you don't get splinters in you
Boodlyboodlyboodly
Hunh! Rugs are so dogs have napkins
A floor is so you don't fall in the hole your house is in
A hole is for a mouse to live in

505. *A Hole Is To Dig,* text by Ruth Krauss, pictures by Maurice Sendak. Harper, 1952. 5 x 6½.

to eat with," mischief in itself, springs upon us "A tablespoon is to eat a table with." The patterns are many and unpredictable, no more to be anticipated than the sequence of motifs. But the book isn't *A Hole Is To Dig* for no reason: a hole is to hide things in, 'maybe,' besides, or "to sit in," "to plant a flower," "for a mouse to live in" (505), "to look through" (a knothole), and lastly, conclusively—"A hole is when you step in it you go down," and if you're a small Sendak child, bid fair to disappear. The finale is a parade winding across the two pages, "The sun is so it can be a great day"; the afterword, "A book is to look at," to crawl over, to doze on and have pleasant dreams.

Like the word-meanings, the drawings are observations—as distinct from formalized illustrations. Like the words, too, the figures seem to dance through the pages; Krauss had studied music as well as art, Sendak has often spoken of his indebtedness to it. But it is life and more than life that he is depicting. "Mashed potatoes are to give everybody enough" might have been set at the family dinner table where the idea was born; instead we have a steaming mountain of (meatless) mashed potatoes and around it, stamping and banging their spoons, children of all sizes: a mashed-potato pandemonium. "Dogs are to kiss people" is, in turn, a kiss-fest, with sixteen pairs of kids and pups looking like Central Park of a summer afternoon. Or take "A party is to say how do you do and shake hands"—and curtseying, bowing, scraping, squeezing, sniffing are big children and miniature children, baby children, boy children, dogs, a cat, oh so serious and comical in party hats. "A face is so you can make faces" asks, as it were, for a demonstration (503), "Rugs are so you don't get splinters in you" is wide open, a natural playground (505); but the others are fantasy-scenes of Sendak's making, a penchant, a vision, peculiarly his and, early and late, enormously fruitful.

He multiplies meaning everywhere,

whether by giving the line "The world is so you have something to stand on" to a lone boy and girl, arms entwined, or by adding to "Hands are to make things" and "Hands are to eat with," a small acrobat, evidence that hands are to stand on too. He amplifies, that is, and extends; but he is starting not with a story which has inherent implications, but with expressions, to which he gives meaning, a particular implication, or with ideas, to which he adds one or more of his own—at the last, to the idea that "A book is to look at" the idea of a book on the floor to burrow into and, finally, to fall asleep on.

Ruth Krauss, he testifies, "pointed out that I was giving the kids who would read the book middle-class attitudes toward their roles. I had the boys doing what boys were expected to do and girls doing what *they* were expected to do. God forbid a boy should be jumping rope! Of course, that isn't the way it is, and at the last minute I made some quick changes." At the party, to be sure, one of the boys is curtseying while his girl partner bows.

Without the reminder, however, one might not notice the avoidance of sex typing as such because there are so few sex *roles*, only boys and girls together jumping in the mud, rolling in the snow, doing dishes, dancing on their toes—the last two, granted, usually sex-typed but here as natural a common pursuit as the first. There are no families, that is one thing: it is a world of children, and a world of children acting spontaneously. There are no expectations, strictures, norms, hence no established order to violate. Back of the Noisy Books was, in part, Margaret Wise Brown's recognition that it was natural for kids to make noise. Back of *A Hole Is To Dig*, implicit in the attention to kids' definitions, is acceptance of the meanings they're liable to give to words, and that whether they're being pragmatic ("The sun is to tell you when it's every day") or projecting their feelings ("The sun is so it can be a great day") or—from either or both—flouting convention. "A face is so you can make faces," and, as a protesting librarian was reminded, children will whether we want them to or not; "Mud is to jump in and slide in and yell doodleedoodleedoo"—not, mind you, to make niggardly mud pies. There's as much pensiveness, though, as acting crazy—more; more kisses, certainly, than snubs or taunts. There is, in fact, almost everything except conventional behavior; the book is absolutely without hypocrisy.

The time, again, was 1952. In the 1950s and early 1960s the prevailing assumptions of psychology and sociology, that man was plastic—pliant, pliable—and that society was in equilibrium, were joined, as Kenneth Keniston has written, "in the theory of socialization and acculturation. Malleable man was said to be related to stable society through a series of special socializing institutions like the family and the education system, whose primary function was to 'integrate' the individual into society. Specifically, families' and schools' chief job was to teach children the social roles and cultural values necessary for adult life in that society."[10] When Keniston himself studied alienated students at Harvard in the late Fifties and early Sixties, he found in them a focus on "sentience, awareness, expression, and feeling,"[11] and, corollary, a desire for a kind of experience—unstructured and unconstrained—"which is above all characteristic of early childhood."[12] By 1968–69, the disaffected have become the dissidents, and Keniston is writing not of deviant behavior but of a revolution of consciousness: "a special personal and psychological openness, flexibility and unfinishedness";[13] "the stress on the expressive, the aesthetic, and the creative; the emphasis on imagination, direct perception, and fantasy"; "a revolt against uniformity, equalization, standardization, and homogenization";[14] and so on.

All children had come to look like Sendak children, Ursula Nordstrom (and others) remarked in the early Seventies. To an extent, this is the way art recasts nature: after Grant Wood, we see Grant Wood farmers; after Renoir, Renoir women. It is true too that there always were such shaggy, dumpy little boys—as against the strapping towheaded all-American tyke; and that picturing them is, on Sendak's part, just so much more individual-

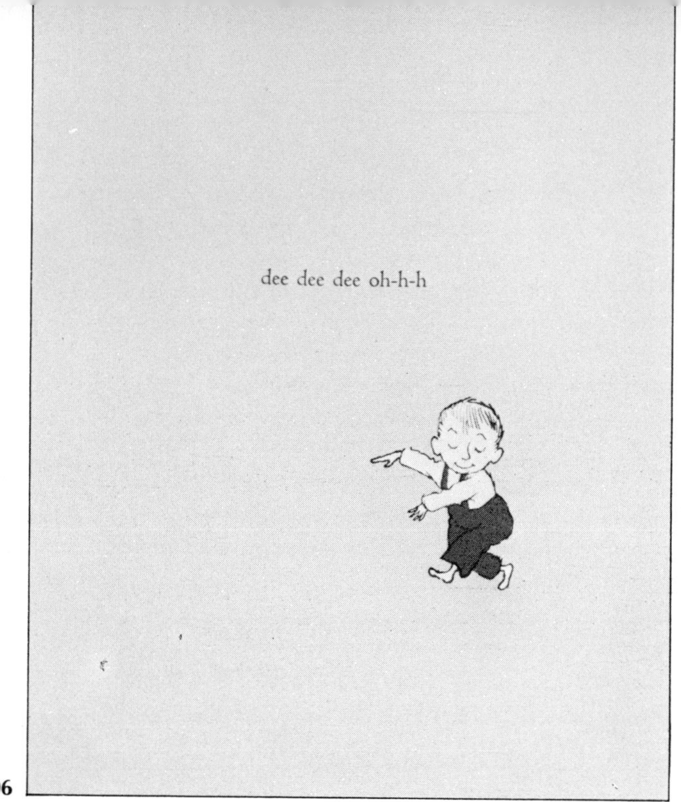

506

506–509. *A Very Special House,* text by Ruth Krauss, pictures by Maurice Sendak. Harper, 1953. 8 x 10.

ism. Still, at the start longer hair on boys and unkempt looks in general represented individuality as well—the right to be different, to be imperfect, the wish to be valued for oneself rather than for one's resemblance to an Ivy League or Jaycee model. Children came to look like Sendak children physically in the aftermath of young people's taking on much of the open, instinctual Krauss-Sendak spirit; and though we cannot call the books contributory in any measurable sense, where they were known they cannot but have been nurturants. At the very least they were prophetic.

A Very Special House is just what one of the youngsters in *A Hole Is To Dig* would have dreamed up; and there he is, doing his little dance, singing his little tune, not in advance of the title page, a herald or harbinger, but after, as a part of the book proper (506). A little boy in bright blue overalls, all alone, dancing—a revolutionary act; and then

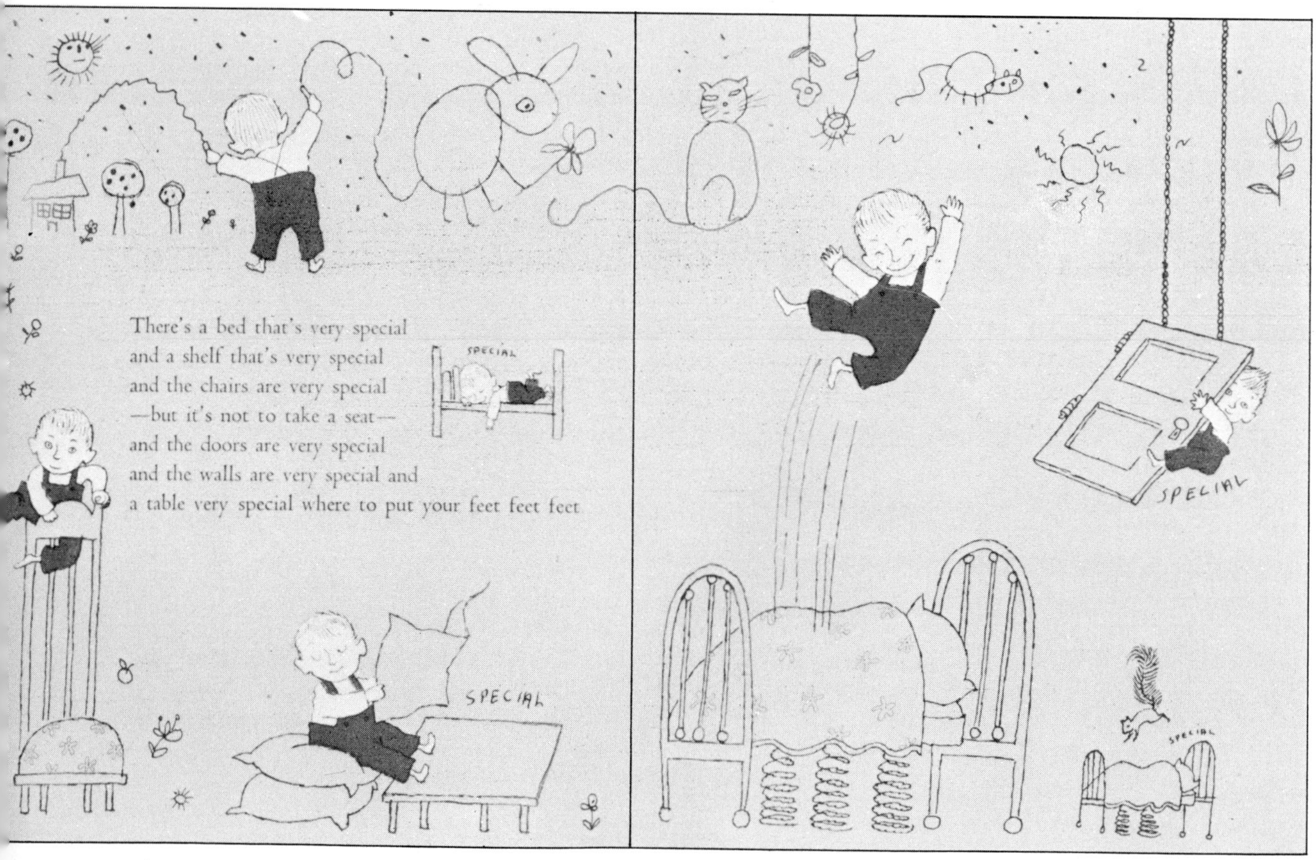

There's a bed that's very special
and a shelf that's very special
and the chairs are very special
—but it's not to take a seat—
and the doors are very special
and the walls are very special and
a table very special where to put your feet feet feet

SPECIAL

SPECIAL

SPECIAL

SPECIAL

507

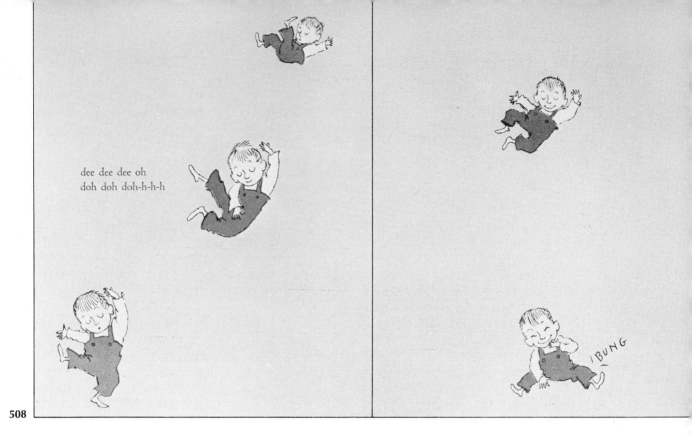

dee dee dee oh
doh doh doh-h-h-h

BUNG

508

skipping, bouncing, swinging through the pages, chanting, shouting, grinning, chortling, while the doodleeoo drawings, like the ones he crayons on his wall to begin with, bring the very special house to life (507). It's a life, he tells us, and a house, that's not anything, not anywhere, but "right in the middle" ("oh it's ret in the meedle—oh it's root in the moodle") "of my head head head." But neither is it expressly, antiseptically encased in a dream: bouncing, beaming even as he tells it, the little boy tumbles through the air (508) and straggles off (509). Are they so different—wishes, hopes, dreams?

A Hole Is To Dig was unique, and it was copied; *A Very Special House* is the extension, the implementation of much that is broached in *A Hole Is To Dig* and, less 'inspired,' more *formed*, it is by contrast assimilable. The relationship between *Hole* and *House* illustrates, as well, a salient feature of the Krauss-Sendak partnership, the way each built upon the work of the other, not in a single book only but book by book in the course of their collaboration.

The wonderful early Krauss books, the ones written to a child's measure, are constructed

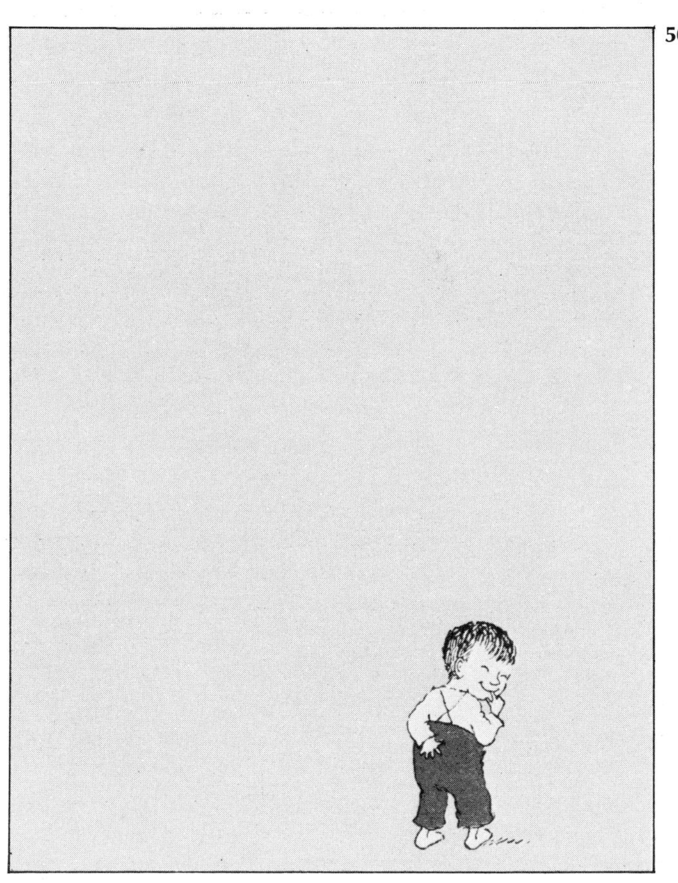

509

almost invariably on a one-to-one basis—one image or action per line per picture; and whether or not they grow (*Bears*, for instance, doesn't), they are sequential or, more properly, serial. A collection of definitions might have taken the form of a picture dictionary, the model of a one-to-one serial form, but it wouldn't have been in the least *A Hole Is To Dig*. By grouping the definitions and varying the groupings, an interplay of thoughts was set up, simultaneous and fluid; and Sendak, further, makes of the groupings now a tableau, now one-two-three 'frames,' now a kite trailing odd thoughts, now an arrow, a pointer —followed wordlessly by more more more. The stage was set for ripostes and asides, and for the baby's "boodlyboodlyboodly" (505); for changes of definition, new meanings, for a baby silently sucking his toes while, in the spotlight, "Toes are to dance on."

"Dee dee dee oh-h-h" dances the *Very Special House*'s little boy, and once inside he's all over the place, climbing and drawing, snoozing and swinging at once; and so, soon, are the turtle and the rabbit and the giant he brings home ". . . and I'm hopping and I'm skipping and I'm/jumping and I'm bumping and Everywhere is music—and/the giant spilled his drinking and it went all down the floor/and the rabbit ate a piece out of my very best door/and Everybody's telling for more More MORE." It runs on, it erupts, it runs together—like a dream, daydream or night-dream or play-dream; and the disarray, the flux, the indeterminacy were essential to the personal and private fancies that were to chiefly occupy Ruth Krauss thereafter.

Then and later, directly or through intermediaries, artists took up the pictorial ideas that Sendak himself returns to repeatedly and develops. He isolates the single child, making of his imagining a more immediate and individual experience; and so, for story-telling emphasis, does Blair Lent (p. 457). Sendak uses silence, or virtual silence, for free movement and a final fillip (after having, in effect, created silence by free movement in *A Hole Is To Dig*); and Mary Chalmers uses silence, and a last look, to specific dramatic effect (p. 491). Put *A Hole Is To Dig* and *A Very Special House* together and you have the makings of *Rain Makes Applesauce*—exploding all over the page, carrying a feedback-refrain (p. 479); but only the makings, the impetus. They were ideas—and not formulas —that allowed of varied original application.

The wellhead that *A Very Special House* was for artists, *I'll Be You and You Be Me* was for authors. It is the book in which the talk of small children is transmuted into a style that is Ruth Krauss's too, the embodiment of the thought of small children. *I'll Be You and You Be Me*: it fits.

What it says bears thinking. This book, the jacket tells us, is about love and friendship, but it "is also about something beyond love and friendship—a feeling of togetherness that it is impossible for an adult to describe but which children will recognize." Recognize is the proper word, for they won't be told, mostly, they'll be shown (510–512). The dream-giver makes his rounds, and each child marches off with a best-of-all dream (512); a little girl stands alone under a vast sky—"she is waiting for her friend, waiting and waiting"; a wedding party is a maypole dance, a game of tag, a bowl of chicken soup (510). A little boy making a poem makes a dream (without words) of a magic bird that flies him to the sun, to the moon, over seas and towns, and home to his mother—who is waiting. (There is good waiting, and not so good.) But they are not meant to be described either, these light-fantastic pages, where the pictures say things that can't be put in words, and the words say things that can't be put another way; and a poem is a poem ("dopey") and a play is a play (with an audience) and a story is a story ("and now listen") and one story is a mystery; and there's a "Dance For a Horse" and, opposite, "a new holiday and a good song /if you have a monkey for a friend friend friend." (The holiday, naturally, is Monkey Day, and you sing "Happy Monkey Day, dear Monkey . . .")

Within the book is enough for a dozen books (there was, later, a *Monkey Day*); it is like a notebook-sketchbook that Krauss and

love is when you send postcards
more than to other people—
love is they could push you down in the grass
and it doesn't even hurt—
love is the same as like
only you spell them different—
only more of the same, sort of—
Love has more stuff in it!
love is you give them
a leg off your gingerbread man.
No, two legs.
And the head!

510, 511. *I'll Be You and You Be Me,* text by Ruth Krauss, pictures by Maurice Sendak. Harper, 1954. 7½ x 9.

wo little houses
nd their smokes are joining
the monkey is in the beauty-parlor
getting his toes blacked
dopey
You are dopey
I am not
You are dopey
I am not
dopey dopey dopey dopey
You are dopey dopey dopey
You could even
have a dopey
for a friend.
sit on my cold feet and
I'll sit on your cold feet and
You sit on my cold feet and

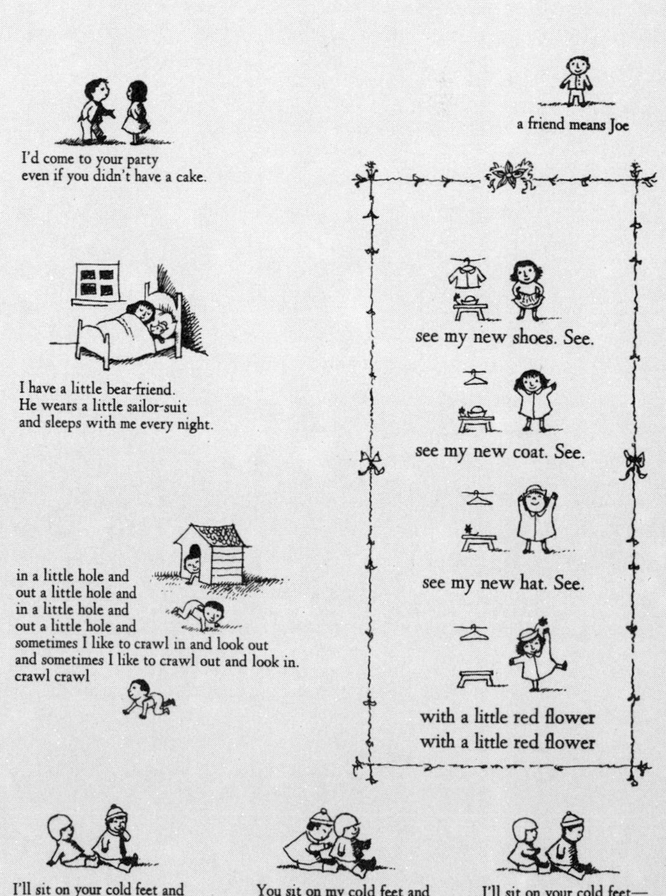

I'd come to your party
even if you didn't have a cake.
a friend means Joe
I have a little bear-friend.
He wears a little sailor-suit
and sleeps with me every night.
see my new shoes. See.
see my new coat. See.
see my new hat. See.
with a little red flower
with a little red flower
in a little hole and
out a little hole and
in a little hole and
out a little hole and
sometimes I like to crawl in and look out
and sometimes I like to crawl out and look in.
crawl crawl
I'll sit on your cold feet and
You sit on my cold feet and
I'll sit on your cold feet—

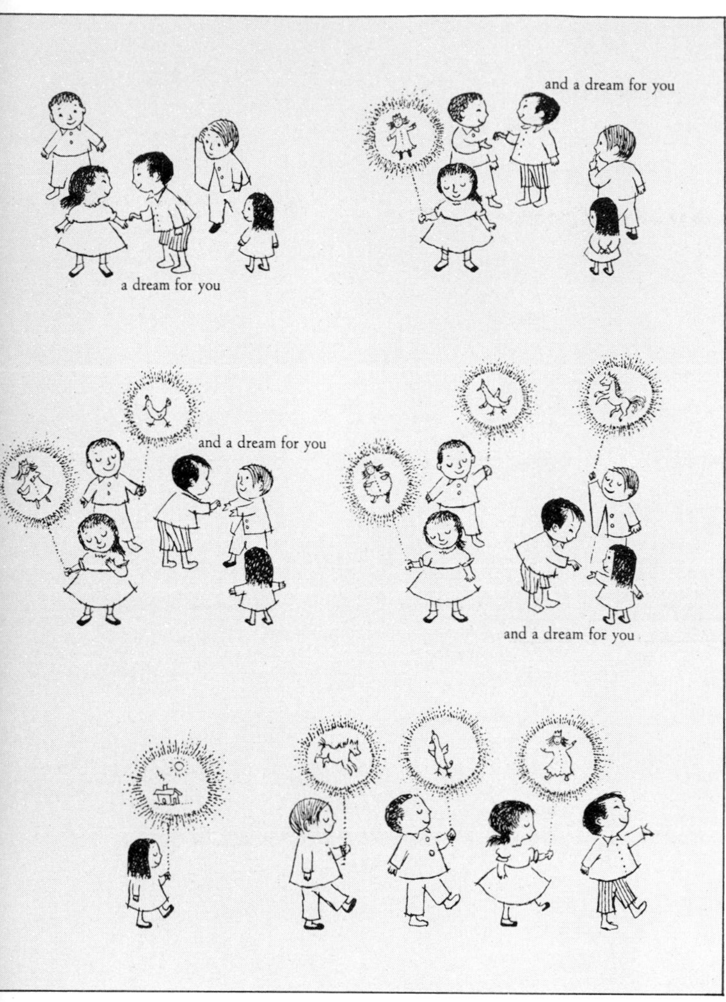
and a dream for you
a dream for you
and a dream for you
and a dream for you

512. *I'll Be You and You Be Me,* text by Ruth Krauss, pictures by Maurice Sendak. Harper, 1954. 7½ x 9.

Sendak made together, a scrapbook of her images and his, now complementary (510), more often conjoined (511, 512): I'll write for you and you draw for me. And because he could draw fantasy sequences, she wrote a poem for a little boy that ends with the words "a dream I made," after which comes the dream of the magic bird. But because the words "she is waiting for her friend, waiting and waiting," expand even in the saying, he pictures the little girl holding a bunch of flowers in an empty, endless meadow.

Because, too, the wedding party is so engagingly, unaffectedly comical, the definition of love, opposite, has less the waxen aspect of any attempt to say that love is this or that. It is difficult if not impossible to read it now without also reading in it what-came-after: Love Is a Special Way of Feeling, Happiness Is a Warm Puppy, et al. One can say easily enough that Love Is a Special Way of Feeling is slop, that Happiness Is a Warm Puppy is a pet-store slogan, the one everything and nothing, the other a sometime thing; and then perhaps see what is different about Ruth Krauss's terms of definition—that for one thing they're not categorical but actual: the word defined 'in terms of use' (Gesell) as per *A Hole Is To Dig.*

But out of them came, by abstraction and ascription, the others—looking alike, passing as child thoughts; and entered the language. The words defined in *A Hole Is To Dig* are concrete nouns, objects—a dream is the nearest to an intangible. But the definitions are invested with feeling, which *I'll Be You and You Be Me* took as its province, spinning out little stories, variations on fellow-feeling; and suddenly feelings were a subject—and an object. All kinds of feelings, for neither is *I'll Be You and You Be Me* a repository of only kindly thoughts: the kids who made faces in *A Hole Is To Dig* are acting out their aggressions now. "There are six friends and they all put on each other's coats. It is winter and they run in the snow. Then they begin to fight. Then they are unfriends. Then they yell at each other 'You give me back my coat!' It is winter—right in the middle—and they are running in the snow."

That's "A Story," and books were made afterward of little more (entitled *Let's Be Enemies*, for one); and little stories were made that, like the poets and dreamers in *I'll Be You and You Be Me*, children might tell to themselves.

First by Ruth Krauss. "This is the story of Charlotte and Milky Way, her horse," Charlotte begins, and were there not quotation marks we would still know it was she, so gravely does she tell it, and dramatically and ingenuously, in a mingling of Biblical phrases, matter-of-fact observations, and pathos. The pathos arises in the threat to sell her beloved Milky Way:

Then a big man comes, who is her father,
 and says,
he won't make a good race horse so we will
 sell him.
Then Nathan can go to college when he is grown.
—That's the little brother.
Now just sorrow is coming in
Now just sorrow is coming in

And when Daddy accedes to her pleas, "the flowers appear on the earth," the "multitude" rejoice.

In the gloom, Charlotte and her father are washed out, almost colorless; happiness restores the rose to her dress, and body to the scene. Alone in early morning and at evening, she and Milky Way are ethereal, sharers in a dream (513); but overleaf, the moonlight brighter, Charlotte waving good-by, "horses eat all night when they're not sleeping."

Somewhat evanescent and tenuous though it may be, *Charlotte and the White Horse* is not precious and it is not solemn; it is, in fact, a nice complement to Crockett Johnson's little-boy's-dream *Harold and the Purple Crayon* (p. 437), which appeared at the same time. Both have, in their own way, their heads in the clouds and their feet on the ground.

Subsequent Krauss-Sendak books are, for various reasons, less successful. In *I Want to Paint My Bathroom Blue* (Harper, 1956), Sendak's dreamer never does touch base, that is part of the trouble. *Somebody Else's Nut Tree* (Harper, 1958) is subtitled "and other Tales *from* Children" which suggests, per the stress added, both its strength—freshness of vision—and its major weakness—many of the stories are truly ephemeral. Opposite each, printed in toto, is an animated sequence which attempts to put it into pictures, an effort foredoomed insofar as few—"The Little Queen" made commoner is a notable exception—consist of concrete images or invoke direct experience.

A late little Krauss book says it; *I Write It* (Harper, 1970), it says, "On a piece of paper I write it . . ."

On my finger nails small skies
On pitchers of milk
I write it
On carousels
On park benches
On shells . . .

On you, waves
I write it
I write my name

The brimming pictures are by Mary Chalmers, the names are yours and mine and everyone's, the signature is unmistakably Ruth Krauss.

513. *Charlotte and the White Horse,* text by Ruth Krauss, pictures by Maurice Sendak. Harper, 1955. 5 x 6⅜.

she tucked him in and said goodnight.
And she always remembered—she never forgot—
to Leave him water to drink
and some hay and some oats because

CROCKETT JOHNSON

Barnaby Baxter, age maybe five, his cigar-wielding Fairy Godfather Mr. O'Malley and his prosaic by-the-psychology-book parents made their appearance in *PM*, the thinking man's tabloid, early in 1942 (514); two years later thirty-one papers carried the unorthodox comic strip and two books, *Barnaby* and *Barnaby and Mr. O'Malley*, preserved selected episodes for posterity. Some comments: "Barnaby is the most important addition to American arts and letters in Lord knows how many years" (Dorothy Parker, *PM*); "as right as the perfect nonsense of a Lewis Carroll or a James Stephens" (*The Los Angeles Times*); "A series of comic strips which, laid end to end, reach from here to wherever you want to go just once before you die" (Isabelle Mallet, *The New York Times*).[1]

Came 1946 (fifty-two papers, circ. 5,590,-000), and Crockett Johnson quietly quit; a self-styled loafer—"I'd like to do strips that were syndicated only in quarterlies"[2]—he had already illustrated *The Carrot Seed* (p. 419), and other books for children would come in time. By design, "Barnaby" had not been for children and Johnson expressed surprise that they read it: "The reason, he guesses, is that children like to side with Barnaby Baxter against Mr. and Mrs. Baxter, archetypical pragmatists against whose earthbound minds the Barnaby strip is directed."[3] In *A History of the Comic Strip*, Maurice Horn, extolling "Barnaby" for combining "the fantasy of 'Little Nemo' with the humor and poetry of 'Krazy Kat,' "[4] suggests further reason.

Whatever his intent, Johnson had inherently a child's point of view. It's a rare child who, learning that the world is round, doesn't puzzle over those inverted beings Down Under: how come they don't fall off? Nonsense, says Johnson, *Who's Upside Down?* (515) That mother kangaroo was hopping

514. "Barnaby," by Crockett Johnson. *PM,* Sept. 18, 1942.

The little kangaroo hopped to the ground, stepped back, and looked at the big kangaroo.

"You look all right to me, ma."

"That's because you're upside down too!" sobbed the big kangaroo, holding out the book. "Everything around here is upside down! See?"

"Everything?" The little kangaroo, who couldn't read either, stood frowning at the picture, tipping the book to one side or the other. "Then the book is upside down too, isn't it?"

"Everything," said the big kangaroo. "*Everything* is upside down! And we can't do a thing about it."

515. *Who's Upside Down?* by Crockett Johnson. Scott, 1952. 7⅞ x 9½.

along, feeling "on top of the world," when she found the geography book and inside a picture of the world, "like a big ball," with 'you' standing on top and, halfway round, she herself, upside down. Never mind that on the next page is a perfectly sensible explanation—"People and animals who have their feet on the ground any place in the world are not upside down. . . . *Down* is down to earth, the way things go when they slip out of your hand. . . . *Up* is up the other way"; the kangaroo can't read and, believing herself upside down, she feels upside down. Nothing to do about it? "At least we can turn the book around," says the little kangaroo; and once more she's on top of the world (though she feels a bit sad, now and then, for she thinks "ՈOʎ are upside down").

So much for up and down, top and bottom, the heights and the depths: just a matter of how you look at things. Or, in *Merry Go Round*, Johnson's fling with round and round, a matter of where you sit. In a heavy-paper spiral-bound volume hinged at the top, a little boy rides around and around "past the lake, past the swans and ducks past the woman reading a very long book . . . past the statue of a horse and a general past his mother and father who waited 'Isn't it ever going to stop?' " (516–518) It needn't: as long as the pages are turned over (and over and over), the merry go round will spin round, the scenery will flash past, the little boy will ride on, his helpless parents will wait. ('Your youngster may be able to enjoy this all night,' a reviewer observed.) One immobile figure in perpetual motion, one young rider with an open ticket: it is too simple, too apt, to be passed off as clever. A book without start or finish is genius.

Besides *The Carrot Seed*, Johnson and Krauss did others together, books different from the ones they did apart. *Is This You?* (Scott, 1954) is an invitation, by indirection —"Do you live in a mailbox?"—to draw your own life story; *How To Make an Earthquake* (Harper, 1954) tells, in addition, how to have Fun at the Post Office (look through the slots)

516

517

516-518. *Merry Go Round,* by Crockett Johnson. Harper, 1958. 7 x 9.

"ISN'T IT EVER GOING TO STOP?" THEY SIGHED

518

and A Good Way to Entertain Telephone Callers (depending on your special talent). How to make an earthquake? "First, you sit in some sand. . . ." After *A Very Special House*, how to stir up yours (and, recalls Johnson, some libraries classified the book as a manual of instruction).

Otherwise Johnson illustrated, apart from his own writing, only *Mickey's Magnet* (p. 399) and Bernadine Cook's classic nursery fish story *The Little Fish that Got Away* (Scott, 1956) about—"and you will never, no never, believe it"—a GREAT GREAT big fish that finally takes the bait, and a GREAT big fish and a BIG fish that bite, and a LITTLE fish that, sure enough, gets away. ("And the little boy LAUGHED, right out loud. Yes, he did.") The story turns on waiting, on suspense, and Johnson is the artist who can make of no motion much action; just let his little fish and little boy eye one another and the run-around begins.

The reviewer of *Merry Go Round* said, to be precise, "Your Harold may be able to enjoy this all night,"[5] referring to the small individualist who, after Barnaby, is Johnson's prime creation. Harold and the purple crayon, that is, whereby Harold, plying it as a child might along the walls of his room (or Klee 'going for a walk with a line'), draws for himself a wonderful moonlight adventure (519–520). The dragon was to guard the apples until they were ripe but once invoked, it takes on another aspect; and the moon that Harold draws because "he needed a moon for a walk in the moonlight" stays with him, as the moon will. When he is ready to return home—"He was tired and he felt he ought to be getting to bed"—and neither climbing a mountain to look out nor drawing buildings full of windows, brings him his own bedroom window, "He remembered where [it] was, when there was a moon." Crayon poised—"It was always right around the moon. And then Harold made his bed. He got in it and he drew up the covers." Finally, "The purple crayon dropped on the floor. And Harold dropped off to sleep." The language, too, is literal/figurative, either/or, as befits a waking dream.

Harold, a Rover Boy in sleepers, had others —"Further Adventures . . . ," "More Adventures with the Purple Crayon." In *Harold's Fairy Tale* (Harper, 1956) it takes him, overreaching, to a big castle where he feels very tiny—"So Harold used his purple crayon again. He made sure he was as tall as four and a half steps of stairs, his usual height." There is other mis-magic: an enchanted garden where nothing grows; a (mute) king who couldn't say "if the trouble was due to a witch or a giant"; a steeple, intended as an escape route, that becomes a witch's pointed hat, the hat of the GIANT witch who is trampling the enchanted garden—whom Harold routs with a swarm of mosquitoes which in turn rout him. Even the rug he wishes (thanks to a flower turned fairy) into a magic carpet runs away: whatever Harold dreams up takes on something, at least, of the aspect of a nightmare, where in the first his plights are only momentary reverses. It is a more intricate plot besides, or rather it is a plot—*Harold's Fairy Tale*—not, per the crayon line (*Harold and the Purple Crayon*), just what-happens-next.

Harold's Trip to the Sky (Harper, 1957) actually takes place in the dark, most of it—after Harold, getting up one night, "made sure there was a moon so he wouldn't see things in the dark." (Facing a totally dark page is Harold, drawing.) But there is nothing to see at all, he is in the desert; and very little to do. "Then he remembered how the government has fun in the desert. It shoots off rockets." Harold's rocket, aimed at the moon, misses—goes up and up, into the dark; what he needs to see by is another moon, what he gets is a flying saucer: "Harold had heard about flying saucers. People saw them in the dark. And nobody knew who was inside, flying them." He decides to land on a strange planet, discovers (a signpost) that the planet is Mars; decides—"the flying saucer out there," "the things people see in the dark"—that he needs a Martian for company, draws, to his horror, "a thing people see in the dark. And it was sitting in a flying saucer."

The crayon, cast as his subconscious, has gotten away from him. Instead of spontaneous invention we have foreboding, and fear materializing: specifically, night fears, explicitly, fears of the Fifties. Johnson, who in 1943 elected Barnaby's Fairy Godfather to Congress as 'the silent candidate,' is aiming his humor at the United States space program (then, prior to space flight, testing ballistic missiles—'the government's fun in the desert') and taking account of the flying saucers that appeared with it. To Jung and others the widespread sighting of UFO's at the time stemmed from fear of nuclear destruction, and the whole of *Harold's Trip to the Sky* can be seen as an expression of the anxieties that children absorbed and transformed, identifying flying saucers with things people see in the dark. In any case Harold has had enough of rockets; better, for going home, a climb, "slow and sure," down the stars.

Harold's crayon recovers its magic in *Harold at the North Pole* (521) where, besides drawing the reindeer and sled that can't make it up Santa's chimney—they're trapped by all that snow—he has room "for a sizeable bag of toys" (and not quite enough time 'to look to

519

519, 520. *Harold and the Purple Crayon,* by Crockett Johnson. Harper, 1955. 4½ x 5⅝.

520
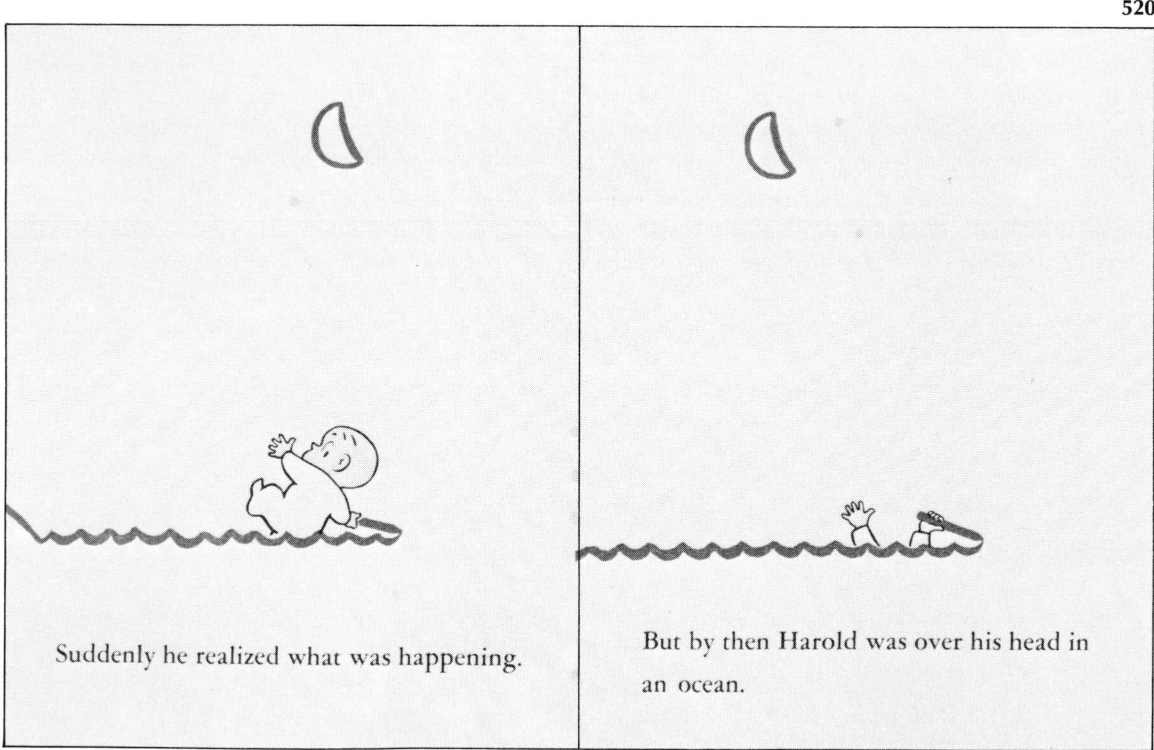

But this couldn't be really the North Pole, he told himself, because he knew that Santa Claus's workshop is at the North Pole.
And here all Harold could see was snow.

521. *Harold at the North Pole,* by Crockett Johnson. Harper, 1958. 4½ x 5⅝.

522. *Harold's Circus,* by Crockett Johnson. Harper, 1959. 4½ x 5⅝.

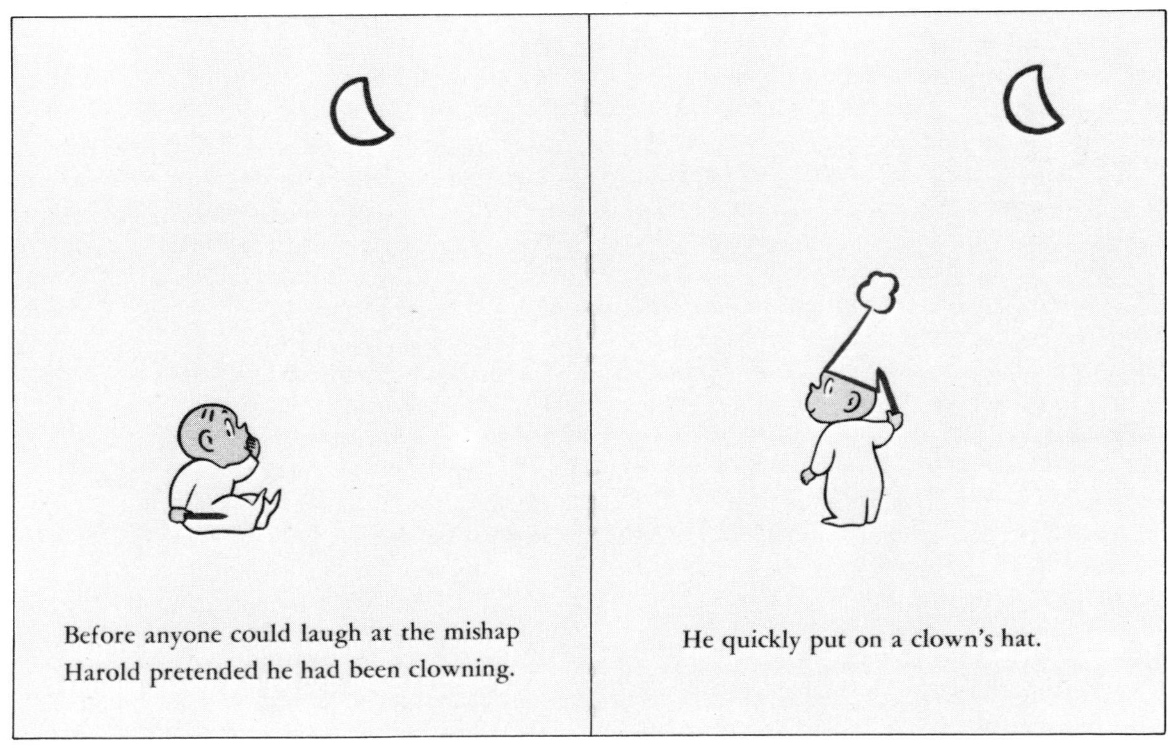

Before anyone could laugh at the mishap Harold pretended he had been clowning.
He quickly put on a clown's hat.

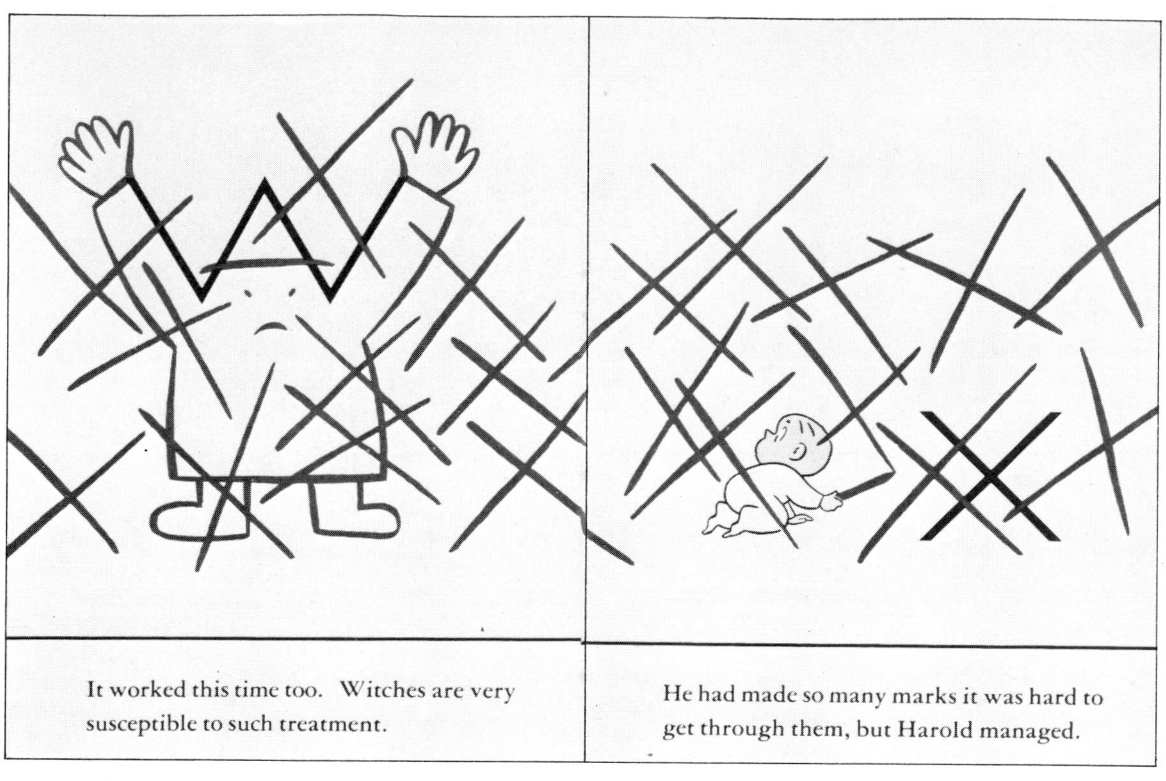

It worked this time too. Witches are very susceptible to such treatment.
He had made so many marks it was hard to get through them, but Harold managed.

523. *Harold's ABC,* by Crockett Johnson. Harper, 1963. 4½ x 5⅝.

see which were his'). In *Harold's Circus* he's a tightrope walker—"mainly to prove to himself he could do it"—and a bareback rider and, taking a tumble, *caramba!* a clown (522). "This . . . was probably the best circus he had ever seen in his life," and after caging a loose lion and, like "the bravest of lion tamers," putting his head in the lion's mouth, Harold takes a bow—having drawn for himself a happy audience. *Harold's ABC* is anything but an inert alphabet as, on his way from A to Z, one thing leads to another—Cake to Drink (and Dipper), Jet to Kite to Lightning (to Mountain to Nobody)—until at last, Xxxing-Out a Witch (523), he finds himself in his own Yard with only one letter left. "In his bedroom, as he dozed off, he made up a word. Z is for Zzzl, or little snore."

They are not dramatic epics, these last, but they exactly suit the small children whom the original wonder-working Harold suits best: all those marvelous things happening and the marvelous ways they happen. In the I Can Read companion to the series, however, *A Picture for Harold's Room* (Harper, 1960), there are the major turns of events—Harold giant in a small picture, then drawing larger, dwarfed—and with them the emotional shifts called for if a book is to satisfy a six-year-old (as well as drawings that, in keeping with the larger vertical format, take shape from above—notably the railroad tracks that, growing in size as Harold advances, ultimately dwarf him).

Johnson's work is so cerebral that one can easily overlook its extraordinary simplicity and clarity—a statement that, like much else to be said about his work, reads equally well, is equally true, in the reverse. The how is the what, the what the how, and both are utterly economical. In *Terrible Terrifying Toby* a pup out to see the world scares a squirrel, a frog and a sparrow; 'attacks' an approaching milk truck and watches it speed past (524):

"What a terrible terrifying thing I am!" But upstairs the dog in the mirror jumps back at him—until, cowering under the bed, he sees his frightened reflection: "I scared a terrible terrifying thing like ME!" ("WHAT A TERRIBLE TERRIFYING THING I AM!")

Toby is a pup; big as he is, and fearsome to squirrel and frog and sparrow, he has the unmistakable lineaments and demeanor of a puppy. Barnaby is never assigned an age in the comic strip, yet one after another commentator refers to him as five; and without thinking, one would call Harold three, and comparing Mickey of the magnet (471) with them, decide that he's four—which in each case follows. They are prototypical child figures, and Crockett Johnson figures at that; and they are at the same time—given more or less neck and waist, by other slight changes—persons of a certain age and condition. Someone spoke wonderingly of Johnson's characters in "Barnaby" as mitten people; and it helps to think of them as mittens, mobile, in contrast to gloves, molded. They are immanent, not achieved; they can look, by some alchemy, like everybody and like somebody. Barnaby is not only an archetypal five, he is Barnaby Baxter, an individual; and a character, that sine qua non of cartooning.

Someone also said about "Barnaby" (Johnson inspires comment) that it was not only art, it was literature, which is more to be remarked at in a comic strip than in a picturebook: it was both art and literature, hence Johnson's aptitude for picturebooks. Sometimes he wrote at length and drew less: *Time*

524. *Terrible Terrifying Toby,* by Crockett Johnson. Harper, 1957. 7 x 9½.

MILK
With a scowl and a growl, Toby jumped at it fearlessly. The milk truck sped away.
"I scared a terrible terrifying thing like him," said Toby. And then he barked out loud—

for Spring (Harper, 1957) *tells*, chiefly, of a little girl who is as sorry to lose her behind-hand snowman as she is glad to see the spring. *Ellen's Lion,* in turn, comprises "Twelve Stories by Crockett Johnson" and we could leave it aside; but I can't.

Ellen and the lion start talking, that's how it starts (525); and from the first, he's the realist. "You talked!" gasps Ellen. "You said something!" "It wasn't anything that important," says the lion. When she mimics him, and apologizes: "I'm nothing but a stuffed animal. I have no feelings." When she proposes to grow up into a tiger: "Your mother wouldn't like it. Neither would I." And when, stung by his answer, she says, "You're being silly": "Humorous," says the lion. "After all, this can hardly be called a serious conversation, can it?"

But they are, of course, for Ellen is very much in earnest: though the lion has observed —defensively, inferentially—"I think my voice sounds remarkably like yours," he is to her a second pair of eyes ("Mine are buttons," notwithstanding) to look out for the frightening things that follow behind in the dark; a trussed-up patient and, the next instant—"Pirates! Rustlers! Gangsters!"—a potential savior (but, still bandaged, "I have to take things easy"). If it suits him, however, he can be the soul of tact: when Ellen, costumed as a five-pointed star for the nursery school play, is forbidden by her mother to carry him on stage, he acquiesces gracefully with "one argument your mother didn't think of": "If you held me in one of your arms you'd only have four points." ("That's right. . . . Nobody would know I was a star." Yes, "And everybody would miss the point of the play.")

Johnson's dialogue is as quotable in its way as Shaw's; as quotable, too, as his pictures—visual puns and jests, many of them—are showable. But for all its witty sparkle his work is no more without meaning than the lion, whatever his protestations, is without feeling. Let Ellen bring in her new birthday squirrel, with a music box in its stomach, and he's grumpy—jealous, says Ellen: "You haven't got a music box in your stomach." "Neither have you," says the lion. "I don't think it is a matter to give either of us any great cause for envy." Which, one way or other, starts them reminiscing—while the squirrel, set away in a corner, tinkles to a stop.

Says Barnaby once to his Fairy Godfather, "But like Pop says, Seeing is Believing, huh, Mr. O'Malley?" "Or vice versa . . . Believing is Seeing is the way I put it."

525. *Ellen's Lion,* by Crockett Johnson. Harper, 1959. Detail.

THE JAPANESE ADVENT

AND BLAIR LENT

The nationality, the culture least represented before the Second World War, by artists or in books, is the one most in evidence thereafter, the Japanese. As there was no precedent for the American occupation of Japan, "so satisfactory to the victors and so tolerable to the vanquished" (Edwin Reischauer[1]), so was there, stemming from it, a sudden general fascination with things Japanese that few if any previous foreign encounters had engendered. Zen, origami and haiku entered the language along with sayonara.

Japanese art was of particular and immediate interest. "So many ex-servicemen, even those not bringing in Japanese objects for identification . . . [asked] the Boston Museum about its unsurpassed collections of Japanese art, dismantled in wartime, that the circumstances demanded the exhibition of the finest group of Japanese objects outside Japan," *Art News* reported in February 1948.[2] Some of the finest painting and sculpture in Japan, much of which had not hitherto left the country, was sent over by the Japanese government in 1953; and at the Metropolitan Museum Velma Varner, then the juvenile editor at Putnam, saw the twelfth-century "Scroll of Animal Caricatures" by Toba Sojo and arranged to photograph it—to reproduce it, with a brief text added, as a picturebook.

"Here was all the simplicity, vigor, humor, artistry and story appeal that we dream of finding in books for children," she writes. "Here was a great work of art that had never before been seen in this country and in another few months would again be tucked away in the Temple of Kozanji in Kyoto, Japan. It needed to be made available to children—and their parents, too." Miss Varner, sophisticate that she was, and venturesome editor, had been a librarian.

The photographing and reproduction arranged for, the text remained a problem: "in doing our research on Toba Sojo and his work, we soon discovered that there were almost as many interpretations of the scroll as there were scholars who had studied it. We felt strongly that our text should simply carry the continuity of the drawings, making no attempt to reflect the allegorical overtones that many people see in the scroll, but we did want it to reflect the spirit of the original. It was a stroke of luck that I happened to meet Mr. Taro Yashima, who had loved Toba Sojo's drawings as a child in Japan, and through him was introduced to one of his friends who is probably the only collector in the country who owns reproductions of all four of Toba Sojo's major works. By looking at them, by reading, and by listening to the painstaking criticism of the many friends who believed in the project we"—the editorial 'we'—"finally achieved the simple text of *The Animal Frolic.*"[3] (526)

In spirit, in form and manner, *Frogs Merry* (423) is the heir to *The Animal Frolic*, scroll or book; but the influence of Japanese art was widely and variously felt, as we'll see further. Velma Varner, in turn, was particularly active—subsequently, at World—in soliciting and publishing Japanese-oriented work. She was not alone, however. On the Harcourt list appeared, in 1949, *The Dancing*

"The frog is stronger! The frog will win!"
The frogs danced gleefully.

526. *The Animal Frolic,* by Toba Sojo [Kakuyu]. Text supplied by Velma Varner. Putnam, 1954. 8¾ x 7½.

Kettle, a collection of folk tales by a young Japanese-American, Yoshiko Uchida, and a Ford Foundation grant enabled Uchida to spend the year in Japan that was the basis for a second collection, *The Magic Listening Cap*, in 1955—together the books chiefly responsible for reintroducing Japanese folklore. And there was Taro Yashima, whom Velma Varner did not need to identify to *Horn Book* readers the year after *The Village Tree* appeared.

Taro Yashima had been in the United States since 1939, and not unnoticed; reads the jacket of *The New Sun*, 1943:

"Taro Yashima, although a native of Japan, is now one of America's foremost young artists. An anti-fascist all his life, he fought against internal suppression and military aggression in Japan as long as he could and finally escaped with his wife and son to this country where, with this book, he is now carrying on the same fight.

"He was born in Kagoshima in 1908. . . . After high school, he attended the Japanese Imperial Art Academy, from which he was expelled for refusing to attend military drill. [Earlier, 527] During his youth he used to wonder what the farmers in his native village muttered about students 'who didn't even know the price of rice,' and about how the farmers and laborers lived when their children died for want of medical attention. He found out when he saw these people lose all their possessions, even the land they had owned, and he realized that an artist searching for reality must represent these people instead of the decayed or undeveloped theories of the classroom.

"Taro Yashima married another young artist with a similar ambition and for a while he lived in the city among the factory workers and unemployed, while his wife lived among the farmers. He had already had several exhibitions of cartoons and oil paintings, and had written numerous magazine articles, but he sacrificed his recognized standing in order to denounce openly with his various works the fascistic tendencies which he saw throughout Japan. He joined a progressive movement and later an underground movement, traveled through the country, made a living by illustrating cheap magazines, and when even that became impossible he continued to fight for what he believed by working on an underground newspaper. He was jailed ten times, his wife was seized too, and before he left Japan they had lost two sons."

The New Sun is a searing picture-story—blunt Van Gogh landscapes, German Expressionist irony, agony—of the years of awakening, struggle and imprisonment. *Horizon Is Calling*, which followed after Yashima's wartime service in the Pacific, "begins with the winter of 1935, when for the first time all the family were out of jail. In his pictures Yashima manages to convey the slow awareness of people coming back to life after long confinement [528]. There is spontaneity and a true, deep joy in these pictures."

Yashima's son Mako was drawing too, and we see some of his pictures; one, of an ambulance, carries the explanation: "He comforts

An army officer, our instructor in military drill, once hit me in the face with a book which I had been carrying in my pocket.
125

527

In the northern country early green shoots which looked as if they had just sprung from the earth-bottom, made us catch our breath.
北國の初夏のみどりは、あたかも地の底からおどりあがつたもののやうに私たちの胸をゆさぶつた。
14

528

527. *The New Sun,* by Taro Yashima. Holt, 1943. 5¼ x 7¾.

528, 529. *Horizon Is Calling,* by Taro Yashima. Holt, 1947. 5¼ x 7¾.

529

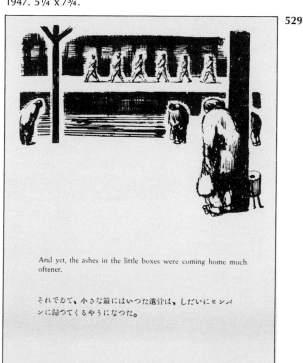

And yet, the ashes in the little boxes were coming home much oftener.
それでゐて、小さな箱にはいつた遺骨は、しだいにヒンパンに歸つてくるやうになつた。

wounded soldiers, who are coming home in heart-rending condition, by painting a pot of flowers on his picture." The Japanese invasion of China was under way (529), and Yashima closes the book with interpretive portraits of the artists whose work guided him and influenced his decision to leave. "The crows which beckoned Van Gogh to the hill where he killed himself, seemed also to beckon me." "But one day, coming from the eleventh century, Toba Sojo said to me: 'All my works, you know, were done after I was seventy-five years old. Young man, pessimism is the worst thing in the world.'" *Horizon Is Calling*, you'll notice, is printed in Japanese and English; and for a new daughter, Momo, born in the United States, Yashima pictured the village of his childhood in *The Village Tree*, and in *Plenty to Watch*, its successor, the work of the village, and the workers.

The Village Tree (Viking, 1953) has no story, no peg; and no young Taro. It is a chronicle in captioned pictures—cartoon sketches in tiers, sprawling landscapes, a still-life—as if Yashima had assembled some pages from *The New Sun* and *Horizon Is Calling* and some of the corresponding paintings of those years: an art-memoir. The same is true of *Plenty to Watch* (with Mitsu Yashima, Viking, 1954). Because the village is Japanese, we learn about a Japanese village, but one could in principle do likewise for Centreville or River Junction—or Bay Ridge, Brooklyn. What is personal to Yashima, and peculiar to his circumstance, is the intensity of vision.

The book that, on the same terms, became a picture-story is *Crow Boy*. The boy nicknamed Chibi, 'tiny boy' ("None of us knew him"), is found on the first day of school hiding under the schoolhouse, and remains odd and apart (530). In defense he withdraws, draws inward; and how he feels, what he sees and what engrosses him, Yashima depicts (531, 532). Like the first, the pictures are vividly, vibrantly colored—Chibi's 'egg,' his nest, is red-orange-yellow—but the weight of the images is as evident in black and white, and the shimmer of the ceiling, the texture of the desk top: still-lifes of the searching eye. And it is all the more remarkable in that contours as such hardly exist; Yashima draws, like Cézanne, from the interior outward. By chance, or perhaps not, a metaphor for his subject.

Chibi comes to school every day nonetheless; and in the sixth grade, the last in the school, the children have a new teacher. Mr. Isobe takes the class outdoors and admires Chibi's knowledge; he likes his drawings and tacks them on the wall with samples of his handwriting "which no one but Chibi could read." "And he often spent time talking with Chibi when no one was around." In the talent show of that year, to the children's amazement, Chibi appears on stage; he is going to imitate the voice of crows. We have then two pages of "The Voices of Crows," represented by Chibi, eyes shut, intent, and the crows themselves: "He showed how crows cry early in the morning. He showed how crows cry when the village people have some unhappy accident. He showed how crows cry when they are happy and gay." At the last, "to imitate a crow on an old tree, Chibi made very special sounds deep down in his throat, 'KAUUWWATT! KAUUWWATT!' Now everybody could imagine exactly the far and lonely place where Chibi lived with his family." Mr. Isobe explains (533).

Thenceforward Chibi, coming to town to sell charcoal, will be Crow Boy, to his evident pleasure; and when he heads for home, "from around the turn of the mountain road would come a crow call—the happy one." The artist showing to us Chibi bowing, Mr. Isobe's regardful stance, and the life of Chibi—the person, concern for him, the reason for that concern—and, opposite, the children's reaction, makes us see the story, within and without, as one experienced.

Crow Boy was also—'also' because his interests are somewhat different—Nicolas Mordvinoff's "Artist's Choice":

"A great many picture books are published each year. Among them are some good ones, but only a few that are excellent. One of the most striking published recently is *Crow Boy* by Taro Yashima. It does not belong in a class with painstakingly realistic representation or with sweet stereotyped stylizations. Neither could it be placed among the tasteful sophistications of the currently [1956] fashionable styles. It is therefore not altogether surprising that it did not attract more considerable attention.

"The design is unusual. This large book seems ever bigger than it is, yet not big enough for the colorful compositions that make the space surrounding them gleam magically more white than white. The sweeping rhythm of the pictures carries one through endless surprises. . . . The bold expressionism with a touch of humor, tempered by an oriental delicacy, blends in a rare poetic mood and carries through from the first to the last—not to ignore the end papers, which are among the most beautiful designs.

"Those who know the intricacies of the color separation technique for direct contact offset reproduction will be surprised by the ease with which Taro Yashima has mastered the medium. . . . With no more than three basic colors, not counting the black, he fills his pictures with all the colors of the prism, combining the bright light of the Impressionists with a refined elegance reminiscent of Japanese paintings. The exuberance of his imagination held within the restraining limits of the technique is the mark of a draughtsman expressing himself with freedom and spontaneity and of an artist with a quality I praise above all—sincerity."[4]

530. *Crow Boy*, by Taro Yashima. Viking, 1955. 8⅞ x 12.

サ
サクラ
This strange boy was afraid of our teacher and could not learn a thing.
6

He was afraid of the children and could not make friends with them at all.
7

Soon Chibi began to make his eyes cross-eyed,

so that he was able not to see whatever he did not want to see.

531

531-533. *Crow Boy*, by Taro Yashima. Viking, 1955. 8⅞ x 12.

532

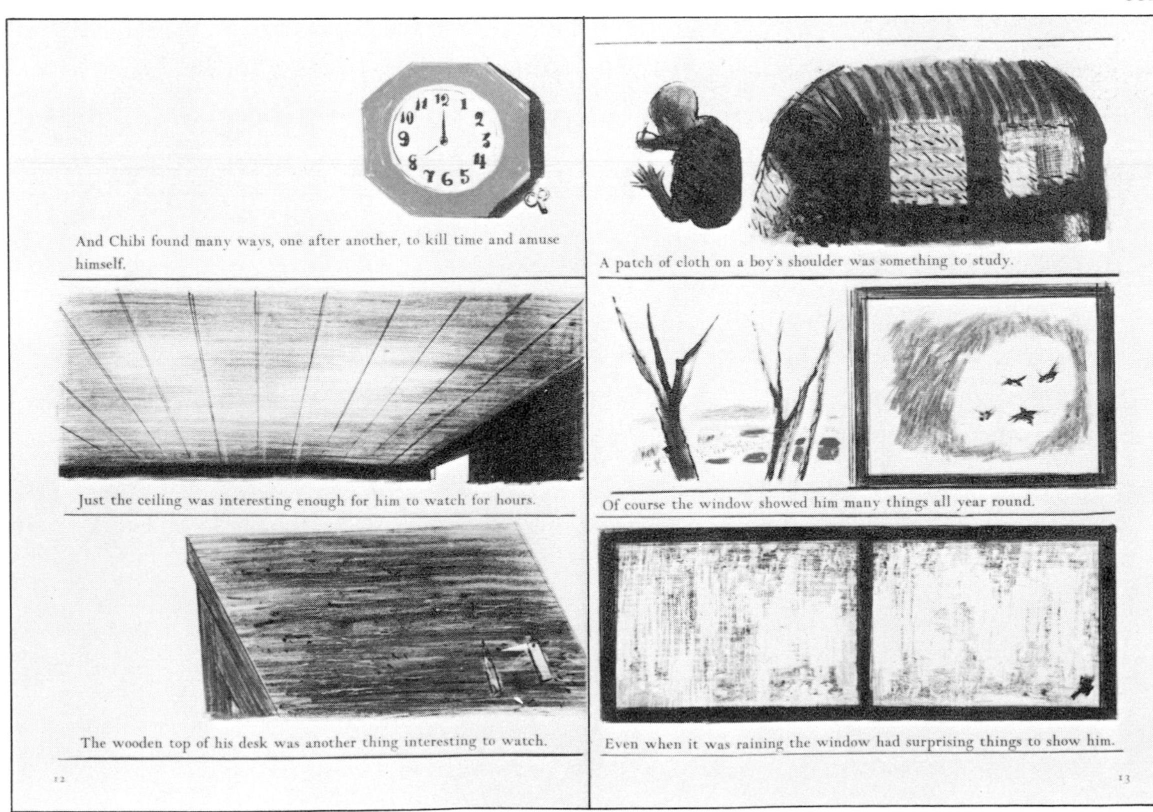

And Chibi found many ways, one after another, to kill time and amuse himself.
A patch of cloth on a boy's shoulder was something to study.
Just the ceiling was interesting enough for him to watch for hours.
Of course the window showed him many things all year round.
The wooden top of his desk was another thing interesting to watch.
Even when it was raining the window had surprising things to show him.

Then Mr. Isobe explained how Chibi had learned those calls — leaving his home for school at dawn,
and arriving home at sunset,
every day for six long years.
Every one of us cried, thinking how much we had been wrong to Chibi all those long years.

533

("Artist's Choice," a *Horn Book* feature of the Fifties, prompted also Maurice Sendak's remarks on *Two Little Trains* and Marcia Brown's on *Little Boy Brown*; when a discerning and articulate artist was called upon, it furnished criticism of unusual value.)

For Momo, then eight, came *Umbrella*, the story of Momo at three. A Japanese sign, *Haru (Spring)*; opposite, a tabletop and on it a few sprigs of blossoming peach and a glowing fruit: "Momo is the name of a little girl/who was born in New York./The word *Momo* means 'the peach' in Japan/where her father and mother used to live." The serene sureness of that opening, the confidence it places in the small listener and looker, give the lie to all claims that children have to be cajoled or assaulted, as anyone who has read *Umbrella* to a rapt group can attest.

"On her third birthday Momo was given two presents—red rubber boots and an umbrella! . . . Unfortunately, it was still Indian summer, and the sun was bright. Every morning Momo asked her mother, who used to take her to the nearby nursery school, 'Why the rain doesn't fall?' The answer was always the same: 'Wait, wait; it will come.' " The story is best presented verbatim because there is no simpler, more direct or succinct way of putting it: the narrative is an exact telling. We do have Momo's various expedients: on a sunny day—"I need my umbrella. The sunshine bothers my eyes!" and on a windy one—"I certainly need my umbrella today! The wind must bother my eyes!" (One must know a child to write 'must.')

"It was many, many days later that finally the rain fell . . . Momo did not stop to wash her face. She even pulled the boots onto her bare feet—she was so excited." I will not repeat the rest—the trip to nursery school (534) and, again, from nursery school, with the same grown-up pride, the same raindrop patter. "Does she remember or not," says

On the umbrella,
raindrops made a wonderful music
she never had heard before—
Bon polo
bon polo
ponpolo ponpolo
ponpolo ponpolo
bolo bolo ponpolo
bolo bolo ponpolo
boto boto ponpolo
boto boto ponpolo
20

534. *Umbrella,* by Taro Yashima. Viking, 1958. 9 x 8.

Yashima of Momo, to Momo, "it was not only the first day in her life that she used her umbrella, it was also the first day in her life that she walked alone, without holding either her mother's or her father's hand." Like the umbrella, like the memory of the day, it is also a book to possess, to keep.

There is much misplaced sentimentalism about books done for or about artists' children; but Yashima has in his books—others besides—pictured his life, and his children's as an extension of it, with the same clear-eyed regard, as if to preserve were to commemorate, which it is.

The occupation-stimulated interest in Japan brought forth not only work of Japanese origin but also the work of Americans of Japanese ancestry; wanted equally was Japanese work, reflective of the life, the art and thought, and work about Japan, authenticated by its authorship. Thus the impetus to Yoshiko Uchida—B.A. University of California (1942, "in absentia"), M.Ed. Smith College—to write, apart from Japanese folk tales, many many contemporary stories; and, among picture-books, the publication of Hawaiian-born Sanae Kawaguchi's *Taro's Festival Day* and *The Insect Concert* (both Little, Brown, 1957 and 1958). Thus, too, the initial opportunity for another Hawaiian of Japanese ancestry, Mamoru Funai (Sara Cone Bryant's old *The Burning Ricefields,* Holt, 1963), and for Marianne Yamaguchi, 'Japanese' by marriage (her husband Tohr's *The Golden Crane,* Holt, 1963).

Meanwhile Betty Jean Lifton, living in Japan, found, for Japanese stories—*Joji and the Dragon, Kap the Kappa* (Morrow, 1957 and 1960)—a Japanese illustrator, Eiichi Mitsui; and for a second, subsequent group—*The Dwarf Pine Tree, The Cock and the Ghost Cat* (Atheneum, 1963 and 1965)—another, Fuku Akino. It was possible now too for Japanese to come to the United States to study, as Kazue Mizumura did in 1955 on an art scholarship from Pratt Institute, and as Masako Matsuno did to go to the Columbia University Library School. Mizumura married and remained, and for some years she was as closely identified with the illustration of Japanese and Japanese-American themes as Kurt Wiese had once been with Chinese themes or Charlot, more recently, with Latin American; between 1959 and 1966 no less than fourteen such books bear her name. Matsuno, who returned to Japan, wrote a first picturebook before she left, and then others; the first was also Mizumura's first picturebook, *A Pair of Red Clogs.*

Japanese or not, Kazue Mizumura stands forth as that rarety, a natural illustrator. For her husband Claus Stamm's *The Very Special Badgers*, contemporaneous with *Clogs*, and after it *Three Strong Women*, another sneaky-funny Japanese tale, she extracts the nub of the story and sweeps it, fizzing and bubbling, through the pages—drawing Forever-Mountain, the famous wrestler, now head-on and, from ground level, page-high, now creeping up on the round merry little girl to tickle her, now caught, pinioned under her arm, straining with all his might, while "she couldn't have paid him less attention if he had been a puppy—a small one."

She is the first and least of the Three Strong Women: Mother is met bringing the cow back from the field, on her shoulder; Grandmother, uprooting an oak. Forever-Mountain has quietly fainted, so Grandmother, wizened, stooped, carries him into the house. Overleaf, training him for the wrestling matches in the capital, she is tossing him high in the air. The training is successful (535); the drawing—the visages, the very contours—is infectious.

"Masako Matsuno's first book for children," reads the flap copy for *A Pair of Red Clogs*, "grew out of her wish to capture the sound of wooden clogs on a stone road in the 'beautiful rhythm of the English language.'" And she is quoted further: "I shall be happy if this story

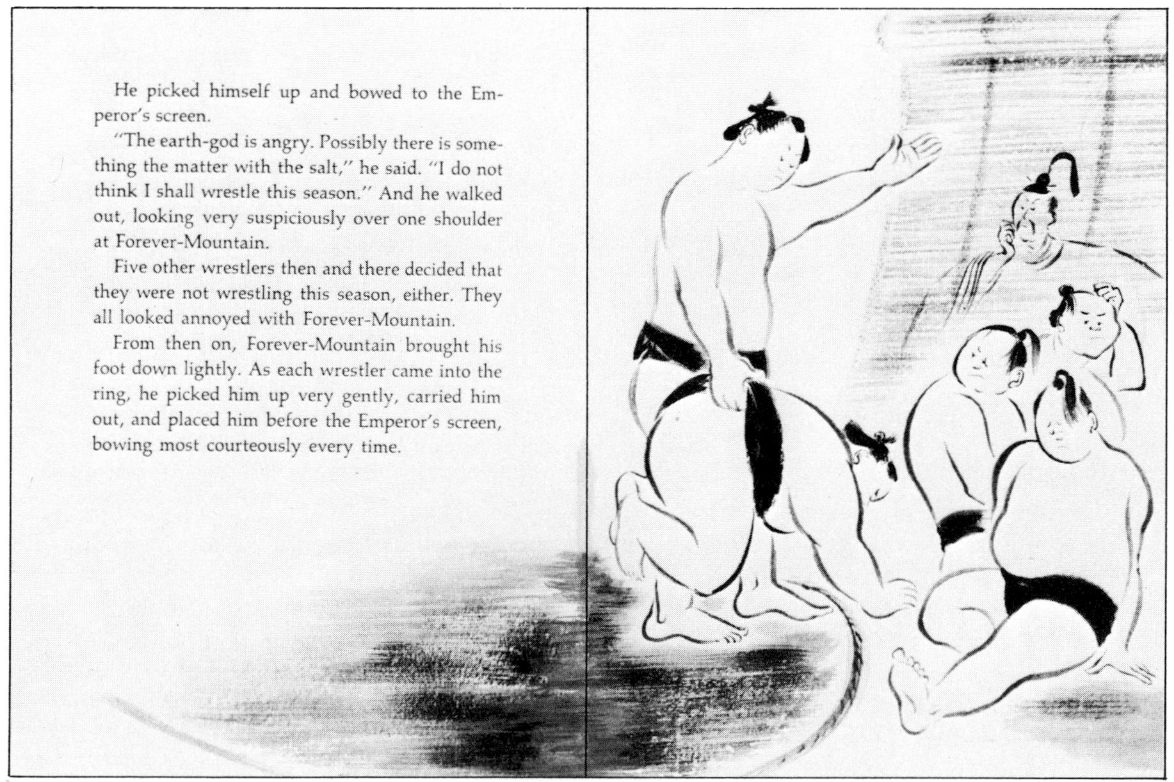

He picked himself up and bowed to the Emperor's screen.

"The earth-god is angry. Possibly there is something the matter with the salt," he said. "I do not think I shall wrestle this season." And he walked out, looking very suspiciously over one shoulder at Forever-Mountain.

Five other wrestlers then and there decided that they were not wrestling this season, either. They all looked annoyed with Forever-Mountain.

From then on, Forever-Mountain brought his foot down lightly. As each wrestler came into the ring, he picked him up very gently, carried him out, and placed him before the Emperor's screen, bowing most courteously every time.

535. *Three Strong Women,* by Claus Stamm, illus. by Kazue Mizumura. Viking, 1962. 6⅜ x 8⅝.

gives American children 'something Japanese' in sound as well as in spirit."

She was modest. "One evening, when I was as young as my granddaughter is now," begins this young woman, "I went shopping with my mother." She is going to buy clogs, a new pair "to wear to school starting the next day"; and after much thinking, she decides on red ones with a thong of red and black on each. It is almost dark when they leave: "Polished apples looked as if they were painted. Fresh bluish fishes looked almost alive on blocks of shining ice, and roses were still wearing dew on their dark red petals. . . . But my new clogs were the most beautiful of all!"

She is proud of her new clogs—full-cheeked, haughty, she might be one of William Steig's small fry showing off; and, carefree, she kicks her clogs into the air with her friends, playing the weather-telling game. If the clogs land upright, "it will be a fine day tomorrow"; on their side, "there will be snow"; upside down, rain. "And that is how I made a crack in my new clogs." (536) Perhaps . . . perhaps if they got dirty "Mother could not help buying a new pair, because she wouldn't like me to look dirty among the others."

> But while I was walking along,
> scuffing the dirty clogs,
> I began to get uneasy. I began to be afraid that
> my mother would know
> that I had made the clogs dirty on purpose
> BETA, BETA, BETA BETA,
> the muddy pair seemed to murmur,
> as if they were saying,
> "You are a liar; you are telling a lie."

Slowly she comes into the house, hears her mother say, "in her usual soft voice," to wash the clogs quickly; "And I remembered that you should try to clean a thing first before you decide to buy a new one. It was the way we always did." The dirt comes off, the black has run, the clogs are still cracked: there are two pages of Mako in utter misery. At dinner, praised for washing the clogs, asked what she played, Mako sits silent, ashamed. "Maybe I will buy you a new pair before long," says Mother. "The crack makes too much noise when you run. But don't play the weather-telling game on the stone road, and be sure not to get wooden clogs wet too often. All right, Mako?" She nods; "I wanted to say something to her . . . but I couldn't. I just knew that I would never try to trick my mother again."

Overleaf, the narrator is packing a new pair of clogs for her granddaughter: "Will she play the weather-telling game with this pair of clogs? . . . Will she get them wet? Yes, I think so, don't you?"

Modern picturebooks seldom pose a moral dilemma, and what little bad behavior occurs is explained, usually even before it occurs, by sibling or peer rivalry—or, latterly, by parental deficiencies, by natural resentments; so it isn't really wrong. Put otherwise, there is psychological but not moral stress. One has to go back to the generation of Helen Sewell (b. 1896) to find in *Ming and Mehitable* a youngster who mends her ways; and to Clare Newberry (b. 1903) for—in *April's Kittens*, in *Barkis*—an agonizing decision.

Mako's mother, guessing something at least of what happened, understands how she feels; she does not reprove her nor does she excuse her, she expects well of her. And Mako, as a grandmother remembering, recognizes that to be a child is to be tempted. That sympathy between an older and a younger generation adds a dimension also; and after remorse, another small gay picture, a 'today' picture.

It is an uncommonly interesting text, colloquial and literate at once, with a thoughtful, precise use of the language; and one of those texts, set with proper irregularity, that runs on rhythms and phrasing and key utterances. To top it off are the several sounds of the shoes, a touch like the 'bon polo' of the rain in *Umbrella*. That, words and pictures, the book was the work of two virtual novices is all the more noteworthy.

Matsuno and Mizumura collaborated again on *Taro and the Tōfu* and *Chie and the Sports Day* (World, 1962 and 1965), active contemporary stories; and for Yoshiko Uchida's longer *Sumi's Prize* (Scribner, 1964) and its successors Mizumura created another locale and another genuine child. But *Fireflies in the Night* (qq. v. p. 405) had given her the opportunity to illustrate something besides Japanese stories and, moreover, to do something besides narrative illustration. Further Let's-Read-and-Find-Outs followed, in the softer, less linear style of *Fireflies*, and with *I See the Winds* (Crowell, 1966) she began to do her own picturebooks. Of later, poster-like work—*If I Were a Mother*, *The Way of an Ant* (both Crowell, 1968 and 1970)—it can be said that it is impossible to recognize the artist of the Claus Stamm stories or *A Pair of Red Clogs*. Since many can compose and few can illustrate, many evoke and few beget, the change must be seen, on balance, as something of a loss.

For her part Masako Matsuno, continuing to write in Japan, wrote Japanese books too, and one of these, *Taro and the Bamboo Shoot*, published here in translation by Pantheon in 1964, served to introduce the superlative Yasuo Segawa and, in fact, the contemporary Japanese picturebook. (Not, it appears, since Little, Brown offered a series of crepe-paper fairy tales "printed and bound at the city of Tokio" in 1888 had there been a major import.) For reasons both economic and artistic, importation accelerated in the later Sixties under a variety of arrangements, and additional color printing was done in Japan, but this is a continuing development, one that awaits future summary.

Japan apart, American picturebooks felt the effect of Japanese art; and were one to cast about one might net Clement Hurd's woodblock and wash innovations for *The Day the Sun Danced* (Harper, 1965) or, on the other hand, Uri Shulevitz's Hokusai wave in *Rain Rain Rivers* (Farrar, Straus, 1969)—for two examples that have nothing to do with Japan. What happened besides was the illustration of Japanese tales (in common with others of the non-Western world), and those in a Japanese manner.

Blair Lent, painter, printmaker, did first an original doodad, *Pistachio* (Atlantic-Little, Brown, 1964), and then, immediately, *The Wave*. The story is Sara Cone Bryant's "The Burning of the Rice Fields" illustrated the year before by Mamoru Funai (a sign of the times), adapted now from the more authentic Lafcadio Hearn version: "Although Lafcadio Hearn did not record the story with children in mind . . . Margaret Hodges, children's librarian and noted storyteller, found that the tale had all the elements to keep children on the edge of their chairs. She has told the story many times and in the best oral tradition has made certain adaptations in the course of the retellings. The present version, therefore, though it maintains the spirit, and even much of Lafcadio Hearn's language, has been shaped by the responses of many young audiences."

Should one illustrate the wave surging across the title spread, the copyright page and dedication—the tidal wave that old Ojiisan knows is coming? The opening vignette of squat village houses and, before them, the sometimes angry sea, boats tossing, children bobbing? The great cloud-ringed mountain behind the village, Ojiisan's house perched high on its side? The house, foursquare, staunch, with Ojiisan and his grandson Tada looking out from the veranda or, above, from the balcony? Each one bears equally, variously, the imprint of the artist and a segment, no more nor less important than the next, of the story. It is a temptation to show the least of them, the string of village houses tilted this way and that by the earthquake's tremor, skeletons of houses, little seals, stamps, rocking across the bottom of the page.

Blair Lent made cardboard cuts: "Cardboard is less resistant than wood or linoleum. It is an ideal material for illustration because my ideas are realized much sooner. Large sections of cardboard that are not to be printed can be cut around and removed with a single motion. There is flexibility in working this way; I can cut up several cardboard cuts and reassemble them. Several textures of cardboard may be combined in one print. The natural pattern of wood grain is missing, but I have found several varieties of cardboard with their own interesting surfaces. . . .

536

536. *A Pair of Red Clogs,* text by Masako Matsuno, pictures by Kazue Mizumura. World, 1960. 9⅛ x 7⅞.

537. *The Wave,* adaptation by Margaret Hodges, pictures by Blair Lent. Boston, Houghton Mifflin, 1964. 9¼ x 9.

"After a cardboard cut is finished, I shellac it. The shellac protects the cardboard; otherwise it would deteriorate from the ink that I will apply.

"I brush block-printing ink onto the raised surfaces of the cardboard. I do not use a roller because I want the brush marks to show. I also like to control the amount of ink applied to each part of the design. Sometimes I brush the cardboard cut with ink that is almost dry. . . . I also vary the paper that I print on; one variety may absorb the ink, another may repel it. I use a small sixteen-by-twenty hand-pressure press, and may make as many as twenty-five impressions from one cardboard cut.

"I study the assortment of prints for each illustration and then scissor the most interesting parts from them. For a typical illustration in *The Wave*, the sea was taken from a blotty print. The village on the shore, on the same page, was chosen from a print that had been printed with a drier ink [e.g. 537]. This step would have been impossible for the early illustrator; his woodcuts were printed when the book went to press, and his illustrations were uniformly inked."[5]

Ojiisan, foreseeing the tidal wave—from the earthquake, the receding sea—has set fire to his precious rice fields to draw the people out of the village. They come with buckets but the fields are gone: "The old man is mad. He will destroy *our* fields next!" But "Look!" Overleaf is the advancing wave, "And then all shrieks and all sounds and all power to hear sounds were ended by a shock heavier than any thunder, as the great wave struck the shore with a weight that sent a shudder through the hills." The next opening is wordless, the wave catching up, carrying off houses, temple, boats; and we see a wasteland: "The village was no longer there, only broken bamboo poles and thatch scattered along the shore. Then the voice of Ojiisan was heard again, saying gently, 'That is why I set fire to the rice.' "

It is an ambitious book artistically and a fossil bed, an aggregate; a printmaker's book, as Walter Lorraine has observed, without a key drawing, a commanding structure—delimitation or definition; and it works. For six-year-olds and "All ages."

The next year Lent illustrated *Oasis of the Stars*, an Arabian story (by Olga Economakis, Coward-McCann, 1965), with an intricate design cut in the cardboard "to print as an Oriental rug." ("The cut made a pattern . . . that reminded me of the printing blocks made in India for decorating fabrics.") And then—an incomplete list—Franklyn Branley's *The Christmas Sky* (Crowell, 1966), where the information of a Hayden Planetarium Christmas show is incorporated into agreeably 'medieval' miniatures; *Baba Yaga*, the story of the terrible-tempered Russian witch (retold by Ernest Small, Houghton Mifflin 1966), fitted out with elaborate carvings and giant flowers and a burst of onion domes; *From King Boggen's Hall to Nothing-at-all* (Atlantic-Little, Brown, 1967), an album of odd dwellings ("There was an old man who when little/Fell casually into a kettle") and daffy, disarming drawings.

In 1968 there came the Nigerian *Why the Sun and the Moon Live in the Sky* (Houghton Mifflin), the Chinese *Tikki Tikki Tembo*, and Andersen's *Little Match Girl*.

I am partial to *The Little Match Girl*, forbidding as it is (538). Forbidding as it is, it represents—embodies and symbolizes—the situation of the solitary child shut out of the huddled houses, the crouching, soaring town, on a bitter cold New Year's Eve. Absent from Andersen, the town is Lent's creation, where from entrance gate to cathedral base the story takes shape—moving upward, fittingly, to the transcendent close. Lent has a special feeling for architecture; his buildings are everywhere presences, figures in a landscape.

It is customary to speak of his colors as 'muted,' not in every instance but often, in the late Sixties characteristically. In *The Little Match Girl* the reserve is the saving grace of Andersen's ecstatic conclusion, and throughout

537

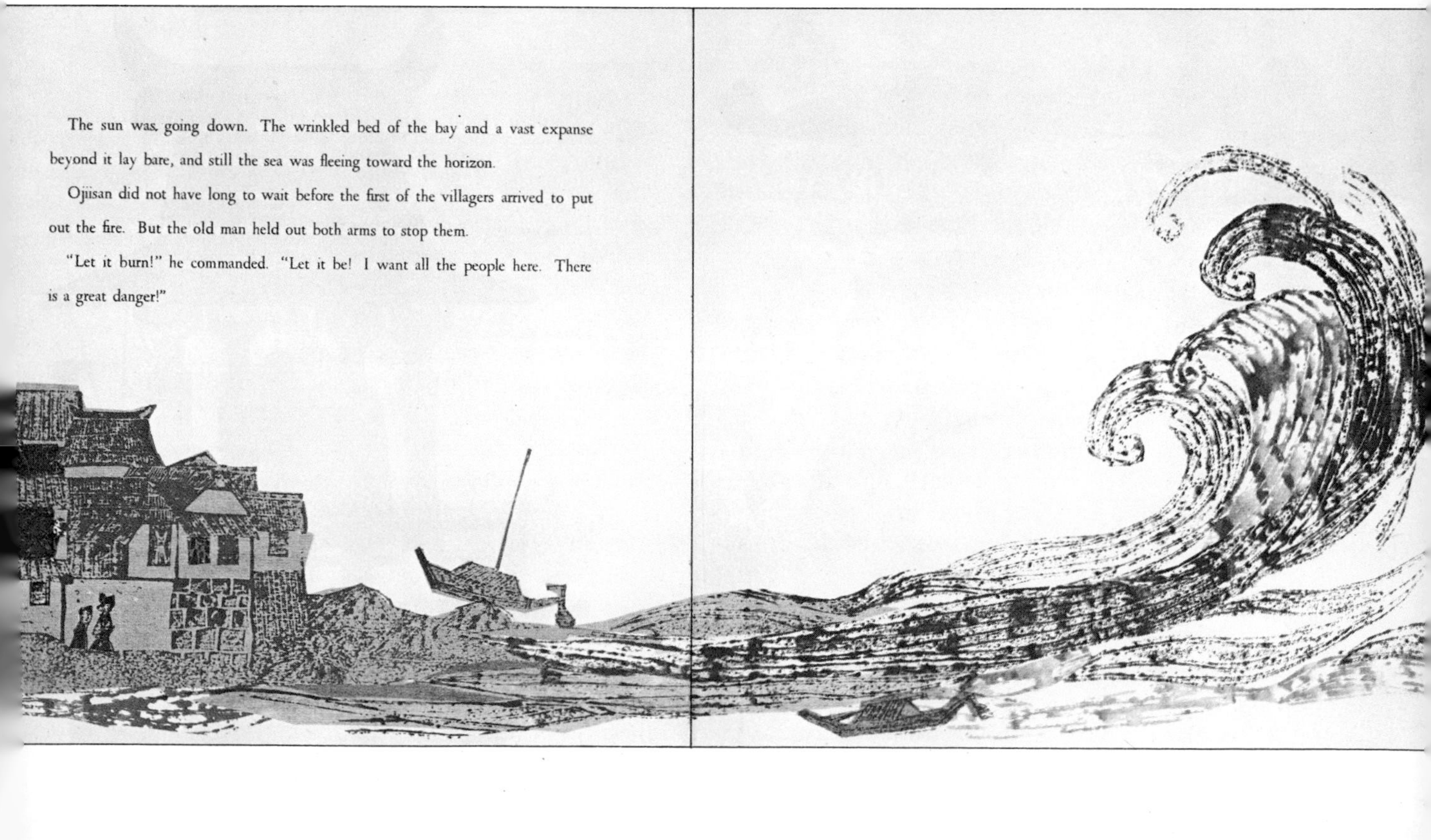

The sun was going down. The wrinkled bed of the bay and a vast expanse beyond it lay bare, and still the sea was fleeing toward the horizon.

Ojiisan did not have long to wait before the first of the villagers arrived to put out the fire. But the old man held out both arms to stop them.

"Let it burn!" he commanded. "Let it be! I want all the people here. There is a great danger!"

538. *The Little Match Girl,* text by Hans Christian Andersen, pictures by Blair Lent. Boston, Houghton Mifflin, 1968. 8¼ x 10⅜.

the sobriety tempers what would, in pastels, be bathos, in vivid hues, melodrama. The awkward little figures, as well, resist sentimentalizing. To elect to picture the sorrows and redemption of the little match girl in this skeptical, cynical age was an act of daring; and on its own terms it too works.

Why, hardly colored, not plain-as-plain or ingratiating, the books should succeed as they do, and with children, what Lent had to say about *Tikki Tikki Tembo* goes far to explain:

"What first interested me in Arlene Mosel's *Tikki Tikki Tembo* was that long name: Tikki tikki tembo-no sa rembo-chari bari ruchi-pip peri pembo. What fun to say it aloud! But why should an illustrator be drawn to a text by a phrase which he knows there is no possibility of illustrating?

"I have always considered the picture book a very special art form; and the sound of the words is just as important to me as the possibilities for pictures. I like to think about how the words and the pictures develop together throughout the book. The words themselves are part of the design; sometimes they can do things the illustrations can't do, and vice versa.

"I will have to go back a bit to explain how this works in *Tikki Tikki Tembo.* I once designed for television, working with a large pad of paper called a story board. A story board is divided into squares, each representing a development in the design of the film. The squares switch from close-ups to long-distance shots, to views from different angles, and so on. Now I begin to work on a picture book in the same way, considering how each page relates to the others. *Tikki Tikki Tembo* begins with a long-distance view of the village, the setting for the story. Within the village there are three important locations: the children's house, the well, and the Old Man With the Ladder's hill. Because of the first illustration, each time I focus on one of these major locations it is clear where we are in relation to the rest of the village. A kite hovers over the village in the first illustration and the early pages of the book, and then reappears at the end. Throughout the book there are other small toys and events: a festival, paper birds and streamers. All of these things serve to separate the main events of the story as well as to establish an over-all continuity. Very few of them are described with words, which makes their appearance in the pictures all the more effective. And just as the illustrations add details that the words need not describe, there are words in the text, such as the long name, which are not represented in pictures."

The orientation, the positioning, we spoke of first in connection with Marjorie Flack, the story board apropos of those other storytellers Burton, Gramatky et al; and Lent, for all his technical and artistic baggage and his constraint, is being a storyteller. Perhaps, with a story paced and pointed in the telling (Arlene Mosel is also a librarian), a better storyteller. Though he cannot illustrate the long name, not literally, he can illustrate how long it

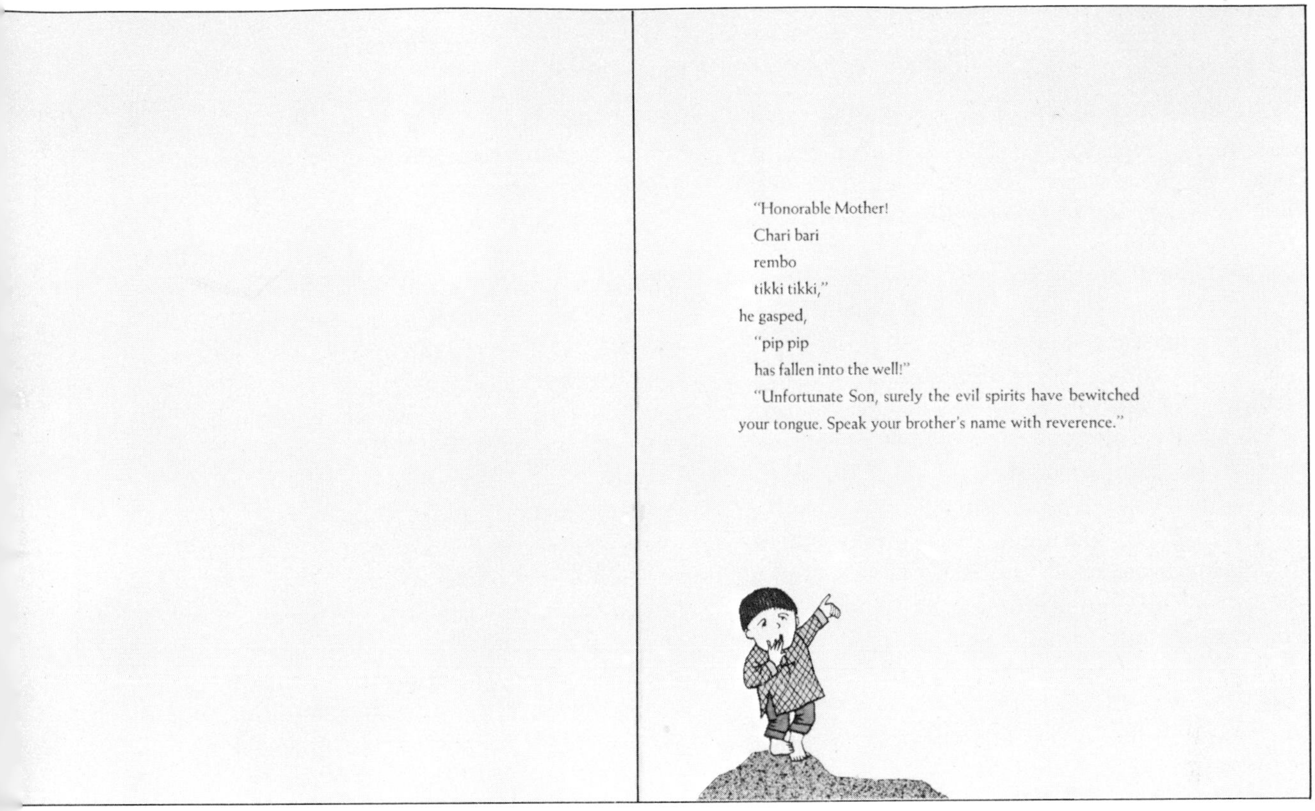

"Honorable Mother!
Chari bari
rembo
tikki tikki,"
he gasped,
"pip pip
has fallen into the well!"
"Unfortunate Son, surely the evil spirits have bewitched your tongue. Speak your brother's name with reverence."

539

539, 540. *Tikki Tikki Tembo,* adaptation by Arlene Mosel, pictures by Blair Lent. Holt, 1968. 8⅜ x 10.

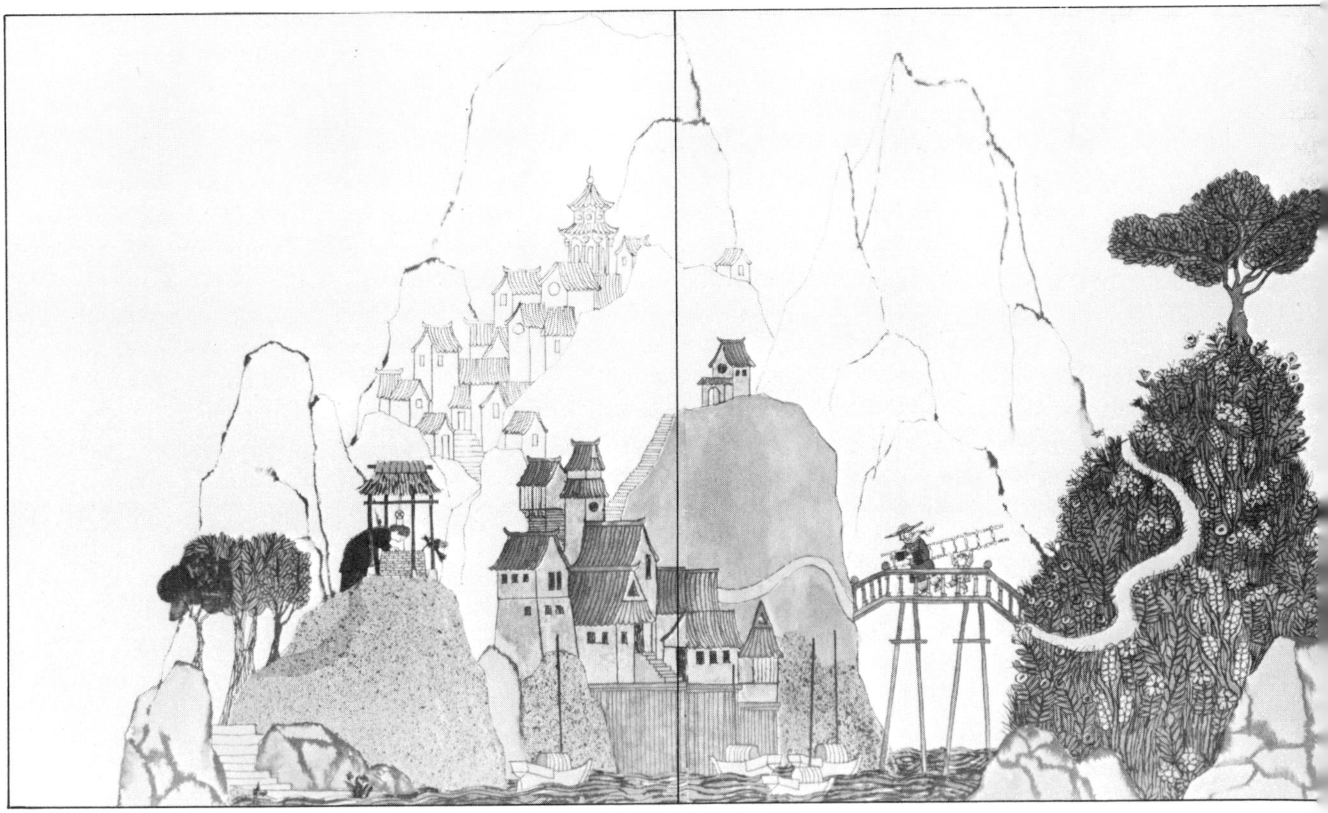

540

takes, how difficult it is, to say it (539). He can, as he remarks, "emphasize or exaggerate what the words say." So, too, when Chang finally makes himself understood and has to fetch the Old Man With the Ladder, "the illustrations heighten the tension by making the distance far too long to be possible in real life"—both there and back (540). The old man, meanwhile, is lost in a dreamlike gaze, a vision, his attitude itself "an exaggeration of a frequently-found motif in Chinese painting —the old man lost in thought or contemplating nature."

"And," Lent continues, "this brings me to another reason for my interest in this story: its setting in China. I sometimes wonder if I should illustrate books about places I haven't seen, but I can never resist the vicarious journey it always involves. And when the book is a fantasy I feel I am allowed to take some liberties anyway. Although the old man in the book has been suggested by Chinese water colors, I have in no way attempted to imitate Chinese painting. These illustrations are interpretations by a Westerner of a fabled land."[6]

The village, he says, "is based on Chinese architectural motifs," the costumes on "what little I could find of peasant clothing in old pictures as well as contemporary photographs." They had to be adapted to the exigencies of the story. Another reference to its being a fantasy follows—to be re-created "as colorfully and imaginatively as possible"; and another: it was de rigeur, on principle, for realistic stories to be authentically illustrated. But the old tales from the newly emerging nations and nations of new interest—from India, Japan, Nigeria, the Near East, North Africa alike—did not fall under this stricture. Nor was the traditional art, appropriate for a traditional tale, realistic in the Western sense. Librarians and teachers wanted the stories and scores were exhumed, artists were drawn to the aesthetics, the devices and motifs; and illusionism lost further ground.

This is not to endorse instant Mughal miniatures or appliqué African: apart from imitation and approximation—intended, as it happens, to convey (or confer) authenticity—there was, with Lent and others, creative adaptation, all the more so because the modes they drew upon were themselves symbolic, objectified, abstracted. *Why the Sun and the Moon Live in the Sky*, a reviewer wrote, "posits a previous sharing of earth by sun, moon and water until water visits the house of the sun . . . Mr. Lent's precise contours contain the abstraction by suggesting a dramatic reenactment, admirably represent[ing] generalized African motifs. An original approach to traditional belief. . . ."[7]

The non-Western modes, 'unreal' as they were, gave a boost to imaginative, dramatic storytelling in general, and to picturebooks provided a stimulus akin to that of graphic design the decade before. Particularly apparent is the change, actually an accrual, in coloration—descriptive on the whole in the Forties and before, or otherwise conventionalized; the primaries in the Fifties and high-key 'decorator' colors—pure, bright colors; and in the Sixties earth colors, mood colors—intimations and inflections.

In tapping other, coexistent cultures artists were, moreover, following the example of their predecessors who had drawn upon the past; Lent, in that respect, can be likened to Low. He can be likened to Low too, and to Frasconi, in his graphic experimentation; and even when as in *Tikki Tikki Tembo* he ceased to work in cardboard cuts, little Chang alone at the bottom of the page, stuck in every sense of the word, recalls the separate little house-shapes rocked by the earthquake in *The Wave*. Indeed, as Lent has moved further from his graphic origins and into full-color painting—in *The Angry Moon* (retold by William Sleator, Atlantic-Little, Brown, 1970) and *The Funny Little Woman* (Dutton, 1972)—his work has seemed to me less convincing; and this although *The Funny Little Woman*, his Caldecott winner, is another good story—another good Japanese story, retold by Arlene Mosel, cunningly set forth. Lent is less a draftsman or a painter than an artisan, one whose work expresses his will, and every part of the picture does not speak, as before, with the same force.

FEELINGS EXTENDED

CHARLOTTE ZOLOTOW, GENE ZION AND MARGARET BLOY GRAHAM, *A TREE IS NICE*, RUSSELL HOBAN AND LILLIAN HOBAN, *RAIN MAKES APPLESAUCE*, BERNARD WABER

...AND A FEW ENDEARMENTS

ALL KINDS OF TIME, MARY CHALMERS, PALMER BROWN

Books had long been regarded as an instrument for shaping character, "especially in the young," Josette Frank wrote in the winter of 1948–49, but in recent years they had begun to be looked to for "the promotion of mental health," and as a result there was being created "a new kind of book for children, purposefully slanted toward mental hygiene."[1]

We spoke of many such on the Scott list but lightly, in less clinical terms; they deal more in concepts than in situations and for the most part eschew prescription. But there had also arisen, as Mrs. Frank remarks, a plethora of little lessons "about everything from negativism to bathroom manners." There was, however, "a notable divergence in most of them from the *Struwwelpeter* tradition of crime and punishment. These recent books put their faith in the rewards of social sanction and approval: how pleasant it is to go to nursery school, how good you feel when you share your toys, etc." It was, she adds, "the sanction and approval not only of society but of the parent who reads to them."[2]

How exactly this accords with Kenneth Keniston's assessment of the period need only be mentioned. Continues Mrs. Frank: "Attempts to forestall sibling jealousies, too, may be seen in a number of stories at different age levels about the arrival of the new baby in the family. They usually include the pre-natal preparations for the baby's care, the departure of mother to the hospital, and her return with the new member of the family. One of these, *Round Robin*, for five-to-six-year-olds, brings the baby to its first birthday, almost to the playmate stage. *Peter and His New Brother* is a reassuringly simple photographic record of the baby's place in the family. *The Chosen Baby* tells the equivalent story for the adopted child, helpfully suggesting to adoptive parents a way to tell him his own story."[3]

"We have, as yet, no measure of the success of such stories. Will a three-year-old be cured of his negativism by a realistic picture-story of a little boy, like himself, who keeps on saying 'no' to everything until he happily learns to say 'yes'? Will wetting be overcome by a little boy whose mother daily reads to him a book (complete with pictures) about a little boy who learned to use the toilet and keep his pants dry? [Or, she says elsewhere, will tensions increase?] . . . Will a child's new experiences in nursery school or kindergarten be eased by a story about other children having these same experiences? These are questions to which answers still need to be sought by students of child behavior."[4]

The books wax and wane but the questions persist. Though the literature on what was called for some years 'bibliotherapy' has grown —it continued to grow through the mid-Sixties —Richard Darling, reviewing it in 1957, found no more concrete evidence than Josette Frank, and little appears to have been developed since, particularly as regards young children. Not however because it could not be. As Mrs. Frank observes, the belief is widespread among parents, librarians—everyone concerned—"that books do reach the emotions"; and, self-evidently, this book is written in that belief. What is lacking is systematic study, the one "significant experiment" mentioned by Mrs. Frank, that by Martha Wolfenstein in the Forties, being, so far as I know, the only one of its kind. But to say that books 'reach the emotions' is not to say that all books have that potential; if they have no emotional content, if, like those cited, they are chiefly role-models, all that can be asked is whether or not, in particular situations, they influence behavior, and it is in that, indeed, that Mrs. Frank's questions consist. The books that matter in themselves, and have come to matter to children, are otherwise—as emerges implicitly, along with a great deal else, from Martha Wolfenstein's study.

Specifically, it was an investigation of the reactions of mothers and children to a children's story, written to order, about the birth of a second child. As viewed by Dr. Wolfenstein—then staff psychologist at the Walden School, subsequently a professor of psychology at Albert Einstein College of Medicine—the problem was as follows:

"If the child in the story expresses some resentment towards the mother and the new baby, this may be supposed to affect the child reader in one of two ways. Either the story acts as a catharsis, helping to release and to reduce the child's own hostilities, and giving him reassurance that he is not the only one who has such feelings; or it acts as an example, a suggestion or incitement to the child, evoking or aggravating the feelings it depicts. If the mother accepts the story as a catharsis, she encourages the child towards the sublimation of impulses which he cannot carry through in reality. If the mother assumes a censorious attitude towards the story—fearing that it may provide an undesirable precedent for the expression of feelings which she thinks it dangerous to let out in any form—she favors repression. . . .

"Literary communication to children of non-reading age is roundabout. . . . The story as the child gets it has been subjected to the continual commentary of the reactions of [in this case] the mother as expressed in her tone of voice, her tenseness at certain points, her relaxedness at others, etc. The mother adds various emphases by elaborating on some passages, by discouraging the child's questions about others. What factors affect the mother's transmission of the story? . . .

"What does the child get from the mother's reading? To what extent may he react in his own way to things in the story which his mother has passed over without interest; to what extent may his interpretations differ from hers? The child brings to the story the emotional residues of his own related experiences and imaginings. His feelings about the birth of a new baby in the family are different from his mother's, and may vary more or less from what his mother wishes them to be."[5]

Apropos of the test story, it must be remembered that what was coming into existence was of the exemplary nature Josette Frank has described:

"A panel of child psychologists formulated a 'prescription' for the story. It was to deal with a subject hitherto scarcely treated in children's stories, the experience of the first child during the time when the second child is expected, ending with the birth and homecoming of the new baby. It was to be shown that the older child already experiences a sense of deprivation during the mother's pregnancy, as the mother becomes less able to lift the child, etc.; and that the child has very mixed feelings towards the coming baby, often wishing it were not there. It was also suggested that various devices by which the mother can help the child through this experience be introduced, such as letting the child help with the preparations for the baby, etc. It was intended that the story be one that mothers could read to their children, particularly under circumstances corresponding to those of the story, as an aid to working out the feelings involved.

"Starting from the suggestions of the psychologists a professional writer (Leo Rosten) produced the story, SALLY AND THE BABY AND THE RAMPATAN. . . . The major artistic ('art' is here defined as purposeful communication of imaginative experience) problem involved in the treatment of the given theme was to find means of expression for the child's ambivalence which would not arouse undue guilt. The author solved this problem in two ways. He had the child in the story develop a fantasy in which her feelings were expressed in a disguised form. And he provided the child in the story with a series of abrupt, concise verbal retorts (Ohs, Uh-huhs, and I knows) which expressed ambivalence acceptably because they were also funny.

"The fantasy which the child in the story develops is of special interest. After her parents have told her about the coming baby, she goes to bed and puzzles about how they don't know whether it will be a boy or girl. When she grows up she will manage things better. She'll have just what she wants. Suddenly the image of a strange new animal comes into her mind, an animal that is part duck, and part bunny, and part pussy-cat, an animal that she can make anything she likes, and that is equipped with a wonderful name —'Rampatan.' The little girl thinks how funny it would be if Mother had a Rampatan instead of a baby, and no one but her would know what it was. Next morning she teases her mother telling her that she has thought of a Rampatan, but refusing to tell what it is.

"The Rampatan fantasy expresses with the ingenious condensation of a dream image the wishes of the child in the given situation: the wish to create something as the parents have created something, the wish to determine what the baby will be, the wish to outdo the Mother, to destroy the Mother's baby and at the same time to make restitution, to substitute her own baby for the Mother's baby, to have a secret from the parents as they have secrets from her, and to take an active role in relation to happenings which she has suffered passively. The Rampatan fantasy may be taken as a focus for our analysis of the reactions of mothers and children to the story. It is the attempt of the child to find an outlet for wishes unrealizable in reality by means of imaginative creation."

About the procedure: "The main subjects were ten four-year-old children (five girls and five boys) and their mothers. Two of the boys and four of the girls already had younger siblings. All the mothers had college education and were taking special courses in child training. The setting of the study was an institute where mothers and children from various parts of the country came to live for a month in the summer. . . ."[6]

The children were observed in individual play sessions—family dolls and baby dolls provided—and given play interviews. "The mothers then read the story to their children and reported on their own and their children's reactions both individually and in a group discussion. . . ." The children's reactions were explored in further play interviews. "The day after the mother's reading of the story, the child was brought to the experimental play room, where the test book now appeared on the table. The child might avoid the book, or pick it up, retell the story or ask to have it read. His related play activities were observed. Comparison with earlier play interviews indicated any new themes which the story occasioned. The story was also reread to the children in a group."[7] Supplementary studies were made also, the most significant being that of the reactions of eight fathers.

Much of the story, printed in toto, Dr. Wolfenstein has covered. What she has not indicated is what occurs when Sally, who has known that her mother will be going to the hospital any day, awakens and discovers—her grandmother. Late in a day made worse by Grandmother's ineptitude, Sally's father calls to say that the baby has been born ("I *know*," says Sally), that it's a boy ("I *know*"); and, no, Sally can't talk to him ("He wouldn't understand") nor to her mother ("She's sleeping . . . Because she's tired and has to rest").

> And suddenly Sally said, "Daddy . . . the baby's *real* now, isn't it?"
> "Of course it's real."
> "It's all born, and everything, isn't it?"
> "Yes, darling."
> "Daddy . . . it isn't a Rampatan, is it?"
> "A *what*, Sally? I didn't hear you. What did you say?"
> Sally sighed and said, "I'll let you talk to Grandma."

The balance is Daddy's coming home ("That was fun—having Daddy all to herself"), the fuss of phone calls and visitors ("Was there all this fuss when I was born?"); and Mother's arrival with the baby, handled with utmost tact and ending—'Maybe, when he could understand things, she would tell him about the Rampatan! Maybe she would make up a special Rampatan, just for *him*'—in Sally's general acceptance.[8]

In sum, Dr. Wolfenstein found: "SALLY AND THE BABY AND THE RAMPATAN was much more of a success with the children than with the mothers. The children showed more comprehension and more positive, as well as more intensely positive affect. With reference to the Rampatan theme, there was much greater readiness in the children to grasp the connection between the Rampatan and the baby story (although the mother's tendency to dissociate the two sometimes delayed, or even prevented this understanding).

"Children of the four-year group, to whom the story was being reread by the experimenter, shouted when the mother in the story said she was going to have a baby, 'The baby's going to be a Rampatan!' They also expressed their feeling for the interchangeability of Rampatan and baby, and the common relation of both to the child's hostility, by slapping in an identical manner the picture of the Rampatan and the picture of the baby. One boy, when asked by the experimenter whether Sally's mother should have asked Sally if she should have a baby, replied, 'She would have wanted a Rampatan instead.' A little girl who was embodying her fantasies in clay while the story was being reread to her said, 'I'm making a baby. It's a Rampatan in bed, a Rampatan baby.' This child interpreted the Rampatan as the little child's hostility toward the baby projected and turned back against herself. Thus when asked how Sally felt about the baby, she said jokingly, 'It's a big bad wolf.'

"The value of the Rampatan as the child's secret was generally appreciated. The mother's puzzlement when Sally tells her the name 'Rampatan' but refuses to explain what it is generally evoked laughter. Children tended to take up the idea of the secret. Thus one boy, when asked by the experimenter what a Rampatan was, replied, 'It's a guess. I won't tell you!' A little girl remarked apropos of the Rampatan, 'The little girl knew what it was,' and proceeded to act out the idea of the little girl's secret by telling the experimenter to close her eyes so as not to see what she was making out of clay.

"The passage in the telephone conversation where Sally asks her father whether the baby is a Rampatan was generally a high point for the children. This was the turning point of the Rampatan fantasy, where its dangerousness is negated by reality. This passage usually evoked hearty laughter from the children."[9]

In addition, eight fathers, who were not the fathers of the test children, were asked to read the story to themselves (as a manuscript being prepared for publication): "Fathers' reactions to SALLY corresponded much more closely to children's reactions than did the mothers'. Our study of mothers' reactions showed that they tended almost entirely to identify with the mother in the story rather than with the child. Fathers tended more to put themselves in the child's place.

"Several fathers commented sympathetically on how the child feels left out of things. . . ." They also "showed greater facility than the mothers in interpreting the Rampatan symbol," and "duly noted the value of the Rampatan as Sally's secret or exclusive possession. . . . Less often the fathers spoke of the Rampatan as an escape. This interpretation, more favored by the mothers, involves a generalized conception of fantasy which may serve as a defense against recognizing the special meanings of a given fantasy. It is noteworthy that the fathers who used this interpretation also added some more specific observation. . . .[10]

"Although the fathers showed more comprehension of the significance of the Rampatan than did the mothers, they nevertheless expressed the feeling that the Rampatan is not connected with the rest of the story. Half of the fathers expressed this feeling spontaneously. How are we to reconcile their ability to interpret the Rampatan fantasy with their tendency to dissociate it from its context?

"A possible explanation seems to be this: that the adult in our society seems to have little ability for cathecting fantasy. [Cathexis: a concentration of mental energy or libido in a certain direction: e.g. toward some object or person] As we saw from a comparison of the reactions of mothers and children to this story, the mothers tended to prefer repression and reaction-formation as defenses against family ambivalence. Children of four were still able to sublimate such emotions into play and enjoyment of stories, although some were already severely impeded by their mothers' preference for other defense mechanisms. With the adult we see that the long term training in devaluation of fantasy has taken effect. The fathers, though better able to identify with the children than the mothers, tend to interpret the child's fantasy mainly in the sense of establishing an intellectual connection. Half of them are unable to feel that the fantasy is an emotional outlet capable of providing rich satisfactions."[11]

Apropos of the fathers' ability to identify with the children, Dr. Wolfenstein concludes: "It is interesting to recall that the creator of the Rampatan is a man, as is the creator of Stuart Little, a somewhat analogous fantasy. Both these fantasies, created by men, seem to appeal very much to children while arousing considerable antagonism in women."[12]

The nub of the report, as of the study, is the reaction of the children and mothers; in order to make it more comprehensible, excerpted as it is, I rearranged it somewhat. But the terminus is not inappropriate. The individuals whose work is included in this section were selected on their merits and grouped on the basis of the affinity among them, an affinity to which the section-title, 'Feelings Extended,' refers. When I had finished writing about the books I realized that the authors were for the most part men, and that it might not be accidental; but I decided to withhold comment. It was only then that I read the Wolfenstein report. In extenuation two points, raised in the report, might be made: that in the particular story the father's position in relation to the pregnant mother somewhat resembles the child's and there is, altogether, no father-child tension; that the mother's reaction is determined in part by circumstantial factors—her own upbringing, the stories she knew as a child, her present ideas about child training—that are susceptible, individually and en masse, of modification.

Having read the report I might also have incorporated references to it insofar as aspects of the story itself, the psychologists' thinking in formulating it, and the findings of the study are, all unknowingly, reflected in the various books or bear upon them; but this I think will be apparent, and as regards not only these particular books but others past and to come. For all that it was 'concocted,' *Sally and the Baby and the Rampatan* stands in considerable opposition to the books described by Josette Frank that fit so well into Keniston's picture of a socializing, acculturating society. Not only is *Sally* about a little girl's feelings—and not about the coming of a new baby—but it is not manipulative: it does not try, by representing all as well, to make all well or rather, by repressing the child, to make all appear well. What it proffers—on the basis of sublimation being the realistic solution—is the fantasy, 'an emotional outlet capable of providing rich satisfactions.'

As Beatrice Creighton recalls, Charlotte Zolotow wrote to say that she was busy with her small daughter Ellen, and what she told of long slow walks suggested *One Step, Two.* A toddler in a red coat and hat crosses the Spring-blue cover holding a yellow tulip—one of Duvoisin's simplest, most vibrant designs—and, on the fly-leaf, bends to examine a blossom (541).

541. *One Step, Two,* text by Charlotte Zolotow, pictures by Roger Duvoisin. Lothrop, 1955. Detail.

Mother and little girl come down the steps of their house and start "to walk to the corner." Why is unsaid, unneeded, for the mother is not taking the child but, in essence, the child is taking the mother for a walk. "See that!" says the little girl, spotting a crocus; "What?" and then she sees. 'One step, two steps, three steps more' and they stop for a prowling cat . . . a circling bluebird . . . a pebble . . . the milkman's horse. At the end of the block a school bus whishes by; "Truck," says the little girl; "Lunchtime," says the mother. And so, slowly, slower . . . "One, two, three, four, five, six, seven, eight, nine, ten e l-e-v-e-n, t-w-e-l-v-e . . ." home. "Up," says the little girl at the front steps, raising her arms. "Her mother gathered her up and hugged her close. 'What a lovely walk, and what a lot of things we saw. Thank you little girl for showing me—' " and she enumerates, recapitulates. "But the little girl didn't hear. She was fast asleep."

In 1951, analyzing changes in the *Infant Care* bulletin of the United States Government Children's Bureau—with respect to "the ideas about child training of the last forty years"[13] —Martha Wolfenstein (the same) remarked on the recent "characterization of parenthood in terms of fun and enjoyment,"[14] in contrast with the sterner, regulatory ethos of an earlier period. It would be quite possible, beginning with *The Little Family* (or, by probing, before), to trace parallel changes in picturebooks, remembering, however, that they are directed chiefly at the child—that what they reveal is incidental to their own image of themselves, to what they intend to convey. We have observed that it is not until the later Forties, in *Wait Till the Moon Is Full,* that parent-child conflict appears, not to be thrashed out for some years more; from this we can infer not that conflict was nonexistent but that, overall, it was not perceived as a likely topic for picturebooks. I have avoided saying 'not regarded as suitable' deliberately, for what is involved is not suppression but orientation: little by little, as the child-rearing strictures of the Thirties gave way (Dr. Spock's first advice in 1946 was to 'relax'), the open airing of conflict became more acceptable—more prevalent and familiar—at least in the psychologically aware circles where picturebooks for the most part originate. And when they owed their inception, now, to the writers' own children, they were not only for them—as, earlier, *The Little Family* "was made for S.C. age 3"—they were also about them. They came from enjoyment of a child's ways, and appreciation of his individuality.

Whether *One Step, Two* and its mates *The Quiet Mother and the Noisy Little Boy* (Lothrop, 1953) and *Not a Little Monkey* (Lothrop, 1957)—two titles that tell the tale —are not also directed as much at parents as at their children is another question; and, related, whether the truth-to-life of the little girl's lagging steps, her upraised arms, her

542. *The Storm Book,* text by Charlotte Zolotow, pictures by Margaret Bloy Graham. Harper, 1952. 7⅛ x 10.

dropping off to sleep are as satisfying—to a child—as a skip and a jump to lunch (and maybe a nap after). It is true that *One Step, Two* is for twos and threes, when the sense of dependence is stronger, still, than the quest for mastery; it is also true that even at two and three the child fantasizes himself somehow triumphant, that at any age his interest in something lies, in Ortega y Gasset's words, "in its desirability rather than in the fact that it is real."[15] It may be real and desirable, but it is not of interest on the basis of its reality alone.

The larger part of *One Step, Two*, nonetheless, casts the child in the lead, and in that respect it sets an example to children as well as to parents: whether or not their own mothers would be inclined to thank them for lingering, there is, they're told, a bluebird waiting to be discovered, and on somebody's windowsill a pot of geraniums, as well as, perhaps (in 1955), a milkman's horse. This is very much in the Zolotow vein but equally true of childhood, of "the child's leisure for 'the weave of the porch screen and the openings and closings of those doors.'"[16]

We have spoken of it before in connection with *The Park Book*, Zolotow's first, and in reference to *The Storm Book*. In *The Storm Book* are description, explanation—two facing pages of text—and then at the alternate openings, a single picture; and so compelling is the text, so convincing are the pictures, that this out-of-joint book, which requires a child to listen without seeing, and look without hearing, is a steady favorite. The storm begins, for the onlooker, in the country, where "the hazy sky begins to shift, and the yellow heat turns gray . . . something is astir, something soundless and still for which the little boy waits." Dark clouds form, a cool wind bends the grass. "Then it happens! Shooting through the sky like a streak of starlight comes a flash so beautiful, so fast, that the little boy barely has time to see the flowers straining into the storm wind. 'Oh, Mother,' he calls, '*what was that?*'" And we turn the page to see.

The storm is crashing around the house, the little boy and his mother are watching from upstairs . . . and "Miles away in the storm-darkened city, a young man closes his book and gets up to look out of the window." Below him on the street are this and that, the tops of the buildings look thus and so, the trees strain at their roots, "the wind whips the leaves from their branches. The automobile tires make a swish-swishing sound as they pass." And we turn the page to see (542). So with the rain at the seashore, where a fisherman is beaching a boat and a sandpiper skids across the sand ("on his way home"); in the mountains, where, while "a young husband herds his sheep to shelter," his wife looks out of the window, their baby sleeping in her arms; and back again at the farm, quiet now and light—glistening, sparkling.

The little boy is standing in the doorway watching and suddenly he yells. His mother comes "and looks through the yellow light to a great curving misty arch of color that, coming from farther than they can see, bends across the sky, over the city; over the yellow storm-whipped sand; over the clean-smelling, bird-singing mountains; over the hill toward the little boy's door." And, one last time, we turn the page to see.

Not such a bad way to make a book, really, if you know how; one that allows for the words to be absorbed, and anticipation aroused, whether the turn of the page yields a first glimpse of lightning or the sight of a sandpiper 'skidding home.' One that allows, too, for as long a look as you like and gives you, to look at, not just stormy weather but the myriad details you might notice were you there. Margaret Bloy Graham had an observing eye too.

Weather and places and seasons; and people, siblings particularly, and offspring—generations: these, separately and together, are the basis for many many Zolotow books, accelerating after she returned to Harper's as an editor. There is much creative absorption. Ruth Krauss might have had a child say, apropos of a movie, "I'll remember the song and sing it to you"; or, "Do you know what I'll do when I wake up? I'll remember my dreams and tell them to you." But it would be Charlotte Zolotow who'd have a little girl uttering both as pledges to a baby brother—in *Do You Know What I'll Do?* (Harper, 1958)—along with, naturally, "I'll make you a snowman" (a great spectral Garth Williams picture) and, at the last, straight Zolotow, "Do you know what I'll do when I grow up and am married? I'll bring you my baby to hug. Like this."

With her husband Gene Zion, Margaret Bloy Graham had already done *All Falling Down* (Harper, 1951). The thread that runs through *All Falling Down* is the things that do: petals onto a table, water into a pool; apples and sand castles and leaves. "Snow falls down on the hills . . . Boys and girls fall down in the snow. It's soft, it's fun. They fall on the ice. It's smooth, it's slippery." Rain falls down, shadows fall, and some stars. "Grandma's ball of wool falls down. It's round, it's rolling. The book falls down when Daddy's head begins to nod. Jimmy's house of blocks falls down and Mother says, 'It's time for bed.' He slowly puts his toys away then dreams until the morning when . . . Daddy lifts him up and tosses him in the air. He doesn't fall . . . Daddy catches him."

The idea is as simple, almost, as that behind Grace Skaar's *Nothing But Cats* but it hasn't the same abstract logic nor does its development. What *All Falling Down* has is child logic, the logic of appearances, and rootedness in an early fascination that is also an early fear. Observations are lined up in terms that are not equivalents—of the snow, "It's soft, it's fun," of the ball of wool, "It's round, it's rolling"—except, again, as a child makes them. There are children, alluded to or not, in all the pictures, and dogs usually, and other animals, other people: it is characteristic of Graham's work—as, say, of Rey's—that animals and people, old and young are drawn with the same lively interest, that together they constitute a populace. We are living in a world of kids, dog-walkers, mamas and babies, and so we come upon Jimmy's house, visible through oversized windows, where Grandma is knitting, Daddy is nodding, Mother is bustling—and Jimmy's blocks fall down. It is not a book about Jimmy but now, without a ripple, it is Jimmy's story, the better to identify with.

The pictures, similar in their softness and lightness and general wispiness to those in

The Storm Book, are of a species that shows up poorly in a reduced size at a glance. The composition is spacious, loose, airy, even empty; points of interest are scattered. The image is of a big world spotted with small figures which, however casual as design, is effective, empathic picturebook illustration.

Even more subjective in its logic, its free and easy association, is *Hide and Seek Day* (Harper, 1954). "Early one morning Jimmy's puppy hides a shoe. Mother can't look for it until she finds her glasses. [They're pushed up on her head.] Daddy is looking for his collar-button . . . Jimmy says, 'Let's play hide and seek all day!'" Thereupon we see Jimmy watching a train disappear in a tunnel, emerge, and 'hide' again around a hill; and, Jimmy gone, a turtle pulling his head in his shell, a fox hiding from hunters, a grasshopper and some beetles hiding from the rain (under a toadstool), people hiding too (under awnings, in doorways); a dog and a bone, another and a dog-catcher, boats in the fog, buildings in the mist . . . "Outside Jimmy's window, the moon and stars seem to look for each other as they play hide and seek behind the clouds. Jimmy's Mother and Daddy don't have to look for him. They know he's safe in his bed asleep." In the morning, for real (but to a child, no realer), "Everyone's playing Hide and Seek."

It was a prelude to *Really Spring*, the book that begins to look like a cartoon book—bold flat simplified drawing, genial-funny faces—

543. *Really Spring,* text by Gene Zion, pictures by Margaret Bloy Graham. Harper, 1956. 8⅜ x 12.

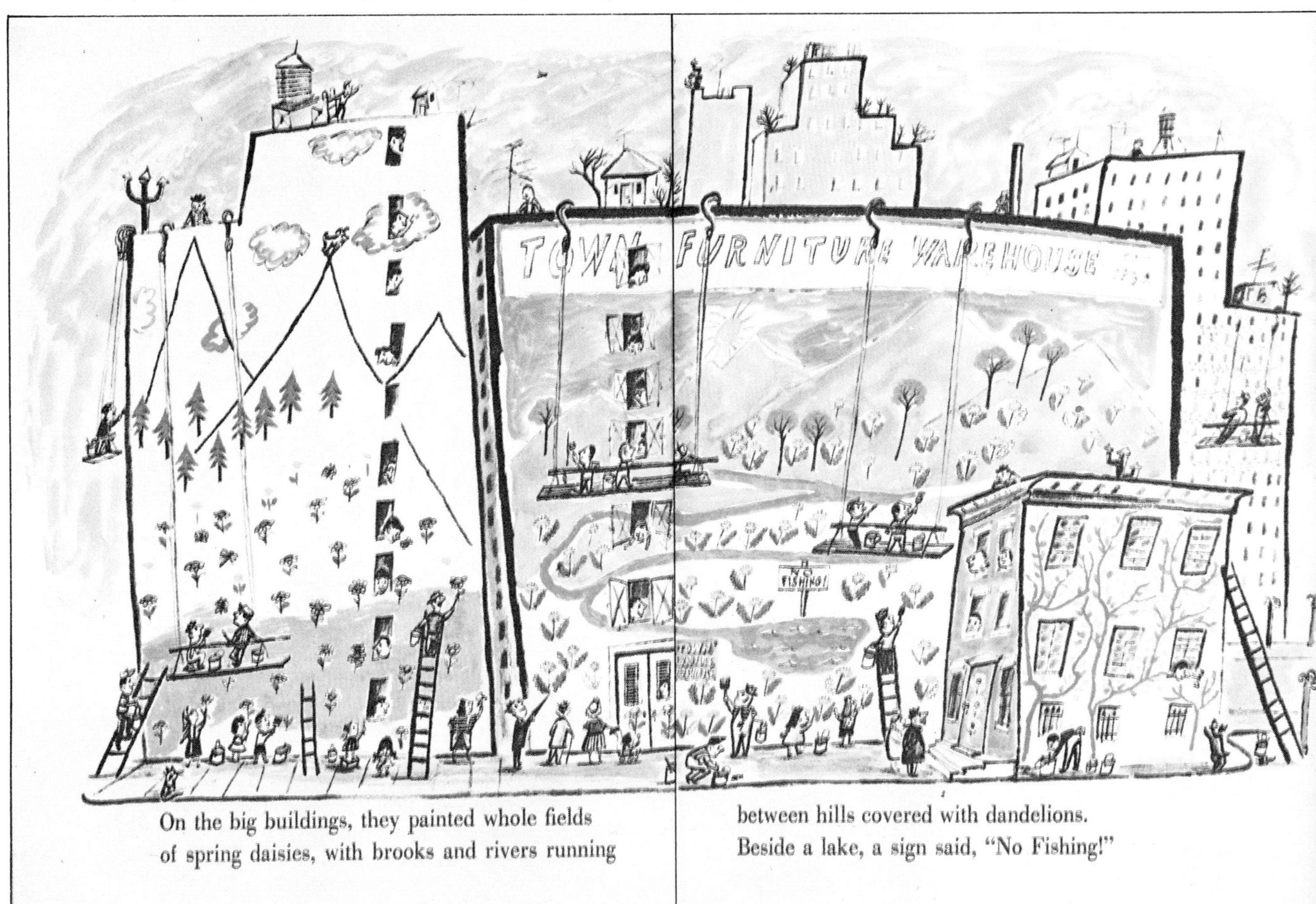
TOWN FURNITURE WAREHOUSE
FISHING!
On the big buildings, they painted whole fields of spring daisies, with brooks and rivers running
between hills covered with dandelions. Beside a lake, a sign said, "No Fishing!"

and *almost* makes an imaginative projection stick (543). Spring is in the air but there are no green signs of it, no grass and flowers; so, proposes a little boy, Let's change everything ourselves. It's unabashed child magic, this painting of buildings, bridges, barges, for an age that still finds it reasonable, plausible; and exuberant, an extravaganza—*I Want to Paint My Bathroom Blue* turned out of doors, externalized. Then, inevitably, the rain comes (at five, one knows that too) and washes away the paint; but it brings, as certainly, new growth—real vines, real buds and blossoms. "The boys and girls who had waited so long oiled their skates and polished their bicycles. Everything was awake and stirring as they looked all around them in the city . . . it was *really* Spring!"

To paraphrase Ernestine Evans, the growth is more abundant, the aspect cheerier, than my own impression of the city; but it is another, like *The Park Book*, that feels the city as an organism, and now—along with Burton's Popperville, McCloskey's Alto, Ohio—as a civic entity, a community of purpose, marshaled by none other than the mayor. I have alluded to ages, in this case peculiarly relevant: three-year-olds are inclined to regret the frogs and ponds washed away, the magic effaced, fives to welcome the roller skates and bicycles, real signs of spring—a shift that is not only a change in interests but in thinking, "I" the magician giving way, as Selma Fraiberg has put it, to "I" the reasoner.

A similar sense of being at home in the city pervades *Dear Garbage Man* (544), and paired with the cartoon style is recognition, now overt, that real people, grownups, are as important to children as other children—paired because it is a cartoon trait not to distinguish, to treat adults and kids (and—remember Frost—dogs and dignitaries) with

544. *Dear Garbage Man,* text by Gene Zion, pictures by Margaret Bloy Graham. Harper, 1957. 8 x 10¾.

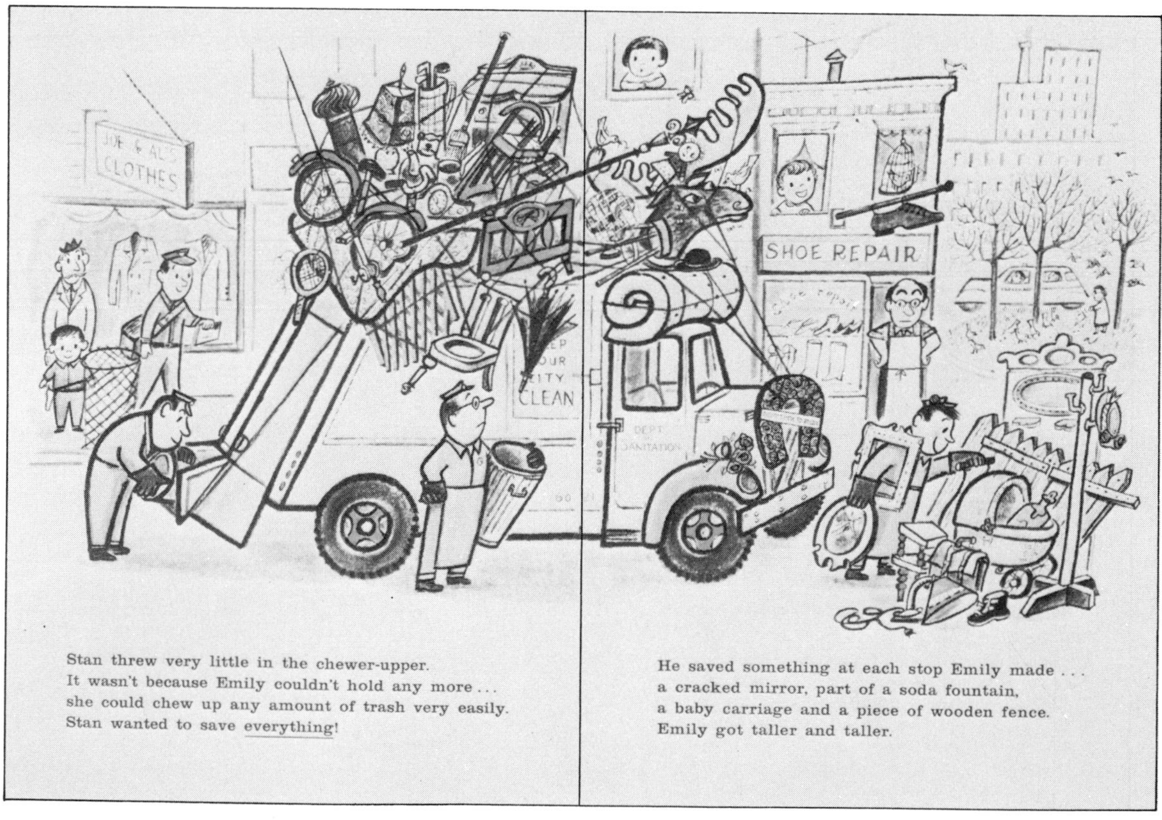
CLOTHES
SHOE REPAIR
CLEAN
Stan threw very little in the chewer-upper.
It wasn't because Emily couldn't hold any more . . .
she could chew up any amount of trash very easily.
Stan wanted to save everything!
He saved something at each stop Emily made . . .
a cracked mirror, part of a soda fountain,
a baby carriage and a piece of wooden fence.
Emily got taller and taller.

the same irreverence, and equal sympathy. *Dear Garbage Man*: a twice-blessed title.

Whether more or less inspired, all the books devolve upon child-ideas. Indeed, I can think of no one except, in his own way, Duvoisin, who has Zion's knack of spinning a realistic tale from an imagined situation, usually one that has no adult antecedent or equivalent. They are simply and vividly named too, for *children*—the way *Curious George* is, or *The Christmas Whale*—so that one could commit the folly of asking, 'Would you like me to read . . . ?' and not get no for an answer. But the youngster who spots the tiny snowman in a patch of flowers—*The Summer Snowman* (Harper, 1955)—will do the asking himself; it might even have occurred to him, as it does to Henry, to put a snowman away in the freezer for safekeeping. *The Plant Sitter* (Harper, 1959), on the other hand, is a Zion brainstorm, a way for Tommy to keep busy and earn money during the summer; and it begins, as do the later Zion-Graham books generally, on the half-title page, where Tommy is straining to reach a doorbell. (Not to look at a picturebook from the very beginning is to risk missing the opening curtain.)

Business is brisk, the house fills with plants and the plants, flourishing, fill the house—breakfast in the kitchen is "just like having a picnic in the woods," taking a bath is "like swimming in a little lake." To the point where Tommy dreams that the plants occupy all the space, push out the walls—and wakes up. He takes countermeasures, but somehow I always remember the book as ending with the monster topiary house triumphant. They were good pictorial ideas too.

And then there is Harry the personality dog. Harry the white dog with black spots who "liked everything except . . . getting a bath." Who buries the scrubbing brush in the backyard, runs away from home, plays where the street is being repaired (workmen aghast, children grinning), at the railroad yard, an excavation; slides down a coal chute and gets "the dirtiest of all. In fact, he changed from a white dog with black spots to a black dog with white spots." There's more to do, lots, but

and he flop-flipped.
He rolled over and played dead.

545. *Harry the Dirty Dog,* text by Gene Zion, pictures by Margaret Bloy Graham. Harper, 1956. 7⅞ x 10¾.

suppose his family thinks he's *really* run away; so Harry goes home—where no one recognizes him. He does his old tricks (545), to no avail: "it couldn't be Harry." Eyes cast down, tail drooping, Harry heads for the gate; and then, inspiration! the scrubbing brush (546).

> It was wonderful to be home.
> After dinner, Harry fell asleep
> in his favorite place, happily dreaming
> of how much fun it had been getting dirty.
> He slept so soundly,
> he didn't even feel the scrubbing brush
> he'd hidden under his pillow.

In *No Roses for Harry* (Harper, 1958), the adversary is the flowered sweater Grandma knits him—that once, twice, three times lost is found until Harry discovers a loose thread, a bird discovers the end of the loose thread, and "before Harry could even blink," the sweater begins to disappear, row by row, right in front

He jumped into the bathtub and sat up begging,
with the scrubbing brush in his mouth,
a trick he certainly had never done before.
"This little doggie wants a bath!"
cried the little girl, and her father said,
"Why don't you and your brother give him one?"

546. *Harry the Dirty Dog,* text by Gene Zion, pictures by Margaret Bloy Graham. Harper, 1956. 7⅞ x 10¾.

of his eyes. When Grandma comes for a visit, no one can produce the sweater—except Harry: high up in a tree in the park is a rose-patterned wool nest: "Harry gave his sweater to a bird!"

Unwanted bath or unwanted sweater, it could happen to anyone; and along with the glory of getting very dirty, the wondering and worry—have they missed me? will they think I've really run away? But Harry, as dog, can live through worse—non-recognition, rejection—and without being endangered a child can share in his relief as in his satisfaction and final, funny defiance. Or, unthreatened—in the case of the silly sweater—relish his twice-over reprieve.

Ludicrous yet logical, said a reviewer of the wind-up of *No Roses.* The imagination that could see in a falling leaf a child falling had no trouble in fashioning from a raveled sweater a bird's rosy nest. But in actuality both are visual likenesses that defy logic (give a bird whatever wool you will, she won't weave cabbage roses). When he wasn't writing Gene Zion was an artist and designer, and it is the seeing in this case that has us as well as children believing.

"Apples fall down," period, *plunk*, reads *All Falling Down*; but "Children pick up the apples and put them in baskets." And other things fall, in a steady, active progression. "Trees are very nice. They fill up the sky." *Trees are very nice They fill up the sky*!?!! An eminent Harper author, filling in as a manuscript reader, hooted; and *A Tree Is Nice* was almost stillborn.

Trees are nice for many reasons. "Trees make the woods. They make everything beautiful." "Even if you have just one tree, it is nice too. A tree is nice because it has leaves. The leaves whisper in the breeze all summer long." Trees are nice for reasons that have to do with children (547), and reasons that don't. "Cats can get away from dogs by going up the tree." Lastly, "A tree is nice for a house to be near. The tree shades the house and keeps it cool." "The tree holds off the wind and keeps the wind from blowing the roof off the house sometimes."

A tree is nice to plant. You dig the biggest
hole you can and put the little tree in.
Then you pour in lots of water and then the dirt.
You hang the shovel back in the garage.

Every day for years and YEARS
you watch the little tree grow.
You say to people, "I planted that tree."

They wish they had one so they
go home and plant a tree too.

[The End]

Margaret Wise Brown wrote of certain of her books that she 'merely dared to be very simple.' Janice Udry dares to set forth bare thoughts, singly or in a small cluster, in a sequence more tonal than conceptual: were they scrambled, one could reassemble them by ear, perhaps, but not by analysis. The last pair only is a pair; is, at two openings, reiterative and therefore weighted. The coda is as unconventional: a set of instructions, a personal confidence. The whole exists on a terrain between factual observation and fantasy, figuration—where wonder exists.

The pictures are nice, too, in the sense of the text. It is a weak word, *nice*, to an adult, a banality, but to a child the all-purpose term of approval, encompassing looks and feelings, description and ascription. They are good pictures for the book because, freely executed, fresh and lively, they don't impose a response (as, for instance, Symeon Shimin often does), they elicit it. The trees 'fill up the sky' with a canopy, a tunnel of greenery—for the viewer and for the boy lying, knees crossed, underneath; and you're not admiring the picture or

547. *A Tree Is Nice,* text by Janice May Udry, pictures by Marc Simont. Harper, 1956. 6⅜ x 11.

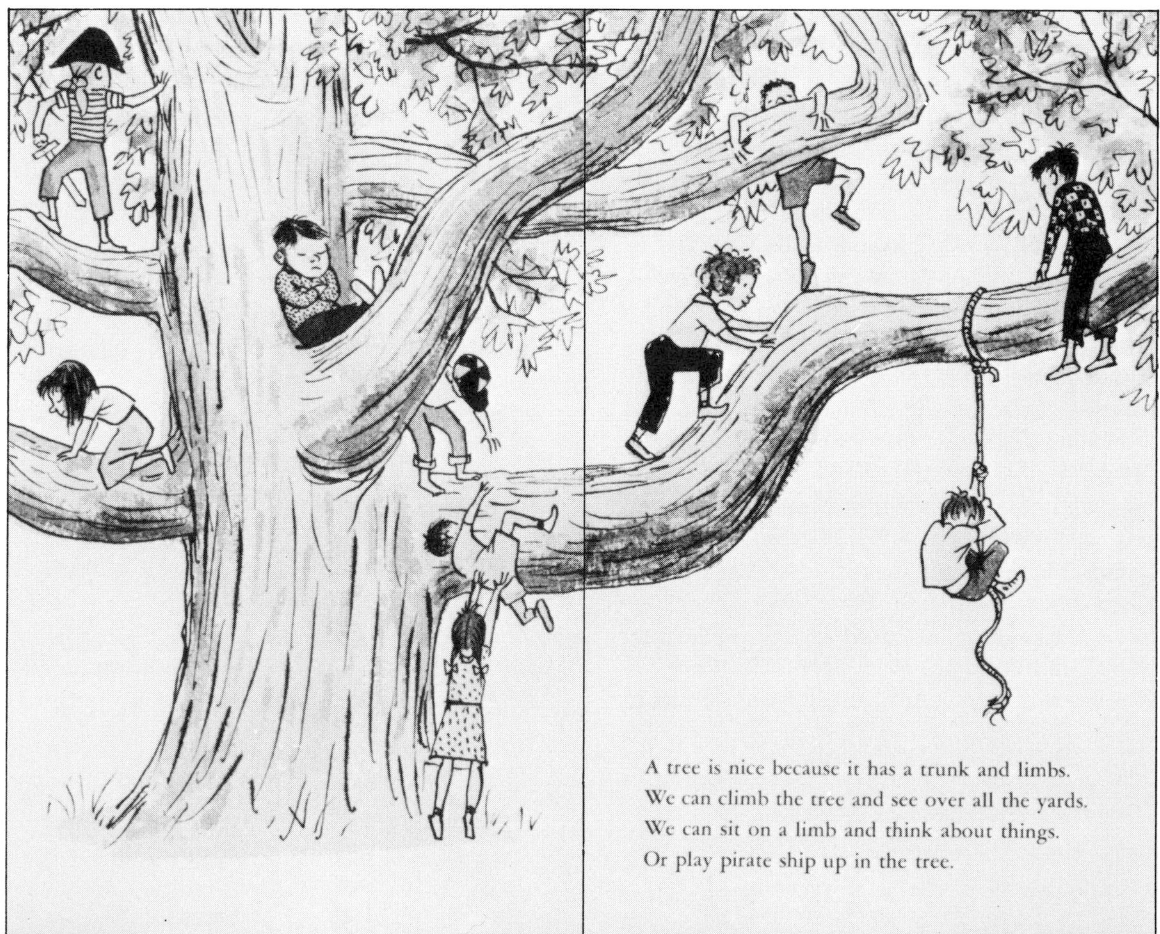
A tree is nice because it has a trunk and limbs.
We can climb the tree and see over all the yards.
We can sit on a limb and think about things.
Or play pirate ship up in the tree.

the trees, thinking 'lyrical' or 'majestic,' you're wishing—as with the kids climbing—that you were there too.

The pictures were sufficiently admired, however, to win for Simont the Caldecott; and this, not uncommonly, for work less distinctive, less creative than *The Happy Day*. But since it also brought the prize, and the attention and sales that accompany it, to one of the few simple, direct books—free of cultural or historic association—in the more than three decades of the award, it is difficult to take exception.

Other Udry books are, as it were, about the children Simont, in the spirit of the text, put in the trees and underneath—dreamy sometimes (*The Moon Jumpers*, p. 498), more likely ornery (*Let's Be Enemies*, *Glenda*, Harper, 1961 and 1969)—kids of whom it's said that they have a mind of their own. One could hardly say otherwise about live-alone-and-like-it Theodore who, on the advice of his new schoolmates—"For one thing, who is going to sign your report card?"—advertises for parents and interviews scores of prospects before settling on the congenial Firesides. Others are deemed too grouchy or too sweet, too curious or not curious enough: a boy has to be careful about parents.

Spoof that it is, *Theodore's Parents* (Lothrop, 1957) is, publicly, "a tall tale that will be especially fascinating to over-protected children and perfect to read to parents at bedtime." Family life was fair game, and of those who pursued it none were more successful than the Hobans.

Bedtime for Frances was the start, and Frances, to look at, is a badger. "Obviously, human children will feel far superior to Frances, and know that only a little animal could possibly act this way. And when their bedtime comes, they will be ready to get into bed and stay there, sleeping as soundly as Frances finally did." It is the language of the blurb for *Spotty*, and there will always be some truth in it; but even less than the raccoons in *Wait Till the Moon Is Full* are Frances and her sorely tested parents distinguishable from you and me. More intriguing, though, and funnier, the way it's funnier at any time—in Ylla or Garth Williams—to see ourselves in animal guise.

If it's bedtime there must be resistance, and Frances asks first for a glass of milk, a piggyback ride, another kiss; and then, lights out, she starts to sing a song of the alphabet. "'S is for sailboat, T is for Tiger, U is for underwear, down in the drier . . .' Frances stopped because 'drier' did not sound like 'tiger.' She started to think about tigers. She thought about big tigers and little tigers, baby tigers and mother and father tigers, sister tigers and brother tigers, aunt tigers and uncle tigers. 'I wonder if there are any tigers around here.'"

The tiger disposed of—if he didn't bite her or scratch her, "Then he is a friendly tiger"—Frances sees something big and dark (her bathrobe on a chair) that might be, must be, a giant. Assuaged with a piece of cake, she goes back to confront it—and in bed again, discovers a crack in the ceiling that something might come out of . . . "Maybe something with a lot of skinny legs in the dark."

You can't help but feel, about now, the way Frances's father is feeling; and when she comes to him in bed with her latest find, something moving the curtains, It's the wind's job to blow the curtains, he says . . . (548). And his job to go to the office every morning at nine o'clock, and her job to go to sleep so she can be wide awake for school.

> Frances said, "I know, but . . ."
> Father said, "I have not finished.
> If the wind does not blow the curtains,
> he will be out of a job.
> If I do not go to the office,
> I will be out of a job.
> And if you do not go to sleep now,
> do you know what will happen to you?"
> "I will be out of a job?" said Frances.
> "No," said Father.
> "I will get a spanking?" said Frances.
> "Right!" said Father.

A bump at the window, and she thinks about telling, and thinks again; and looks—only to find a moth. The bump and thump, whack and smack, make her think of a spanking: "And all of a sudden she was tired . . . 'That is just a moth, and he is only doing his job, the same as the wind. His job is bumping and thumping, and my job is to sleep.'" So she does.

A charmer, warm, snappy, full of 'humors and reflections'; and withal—but withal?—a cautionary/salutary tale.

Herman the Loser followed, the first that the two Hobans did together, and a book about a boy (modeled after their son Abrom) —a duffer of sorts with an ordinary 'dumb' name. "Everybody is a good finder but me," Herman remarks after his mother has found his cowboy hat (under his sweater, his jacket, his gun belt), his father has found his mitten (on the hall floor—while Herman looks behind the hi-fi), his big sister Sophie has found his cowboy boot: "How come I am just a loser and not a finder?" "We look in the places where we think things will be," his father tells him. "Where do *you* look?" "Different places," says Herman.

548. *Bedtime for Frances,* text by Russell Hoban, pictures by Garth Williams. Harper, 1960. 7⅞ x 10.

"How can the wind have a job?" said Frances.

He is going out—"I am going to fight with Timothy, and then I am going to play at Richard's." So that he'll know when to come back, Father lends him a watch, not his *good* watch but a pretty good watch, "so don't lose it." When he's gone: "Herman will lose the watch," says Mother; "Herman loses everything," says Sophie. "Herman will not lose the watch," says Father. "He will be careful because he feels bad about being a loser."

Herman does lose it, and with Father and Sophie along to help, we see him look—up at the telephone poles ("the little shiny things on top of the poles") and all around, finding a piece of green glass, a string, a round stone. We pass the place where he fought with Timothy (Timothy was on the bottom, "but he said he was winning. Was he winning?"), where he walked right and left and hopped five steps; and when we come to a red pail ("I had a red pail last year, didn't I?"), Herman finds the watch.

At dinner he says to his father, "I thought you would spank me when I lost the watch." "I don't think Father would spank you for that," says Mother. "No," says Father, "I would not." (549)

We can see the wheels turning, ever so gently: it is an 'enlightened,' constructive treatment of childhood, careful to value Herman's independent proclivities, equally careful to inculcate in him reasonable responsibility and demonstrate how to use it. Implicitly, parents are not to be arbitrary, neither are children to be left undirected, the one productive of fear, the other of guilt; and both destructive of the child's individual personality. The last is critical: behavior-model that it is, for parents and their offspring (who "will rejoice with Herman in his new role of finder

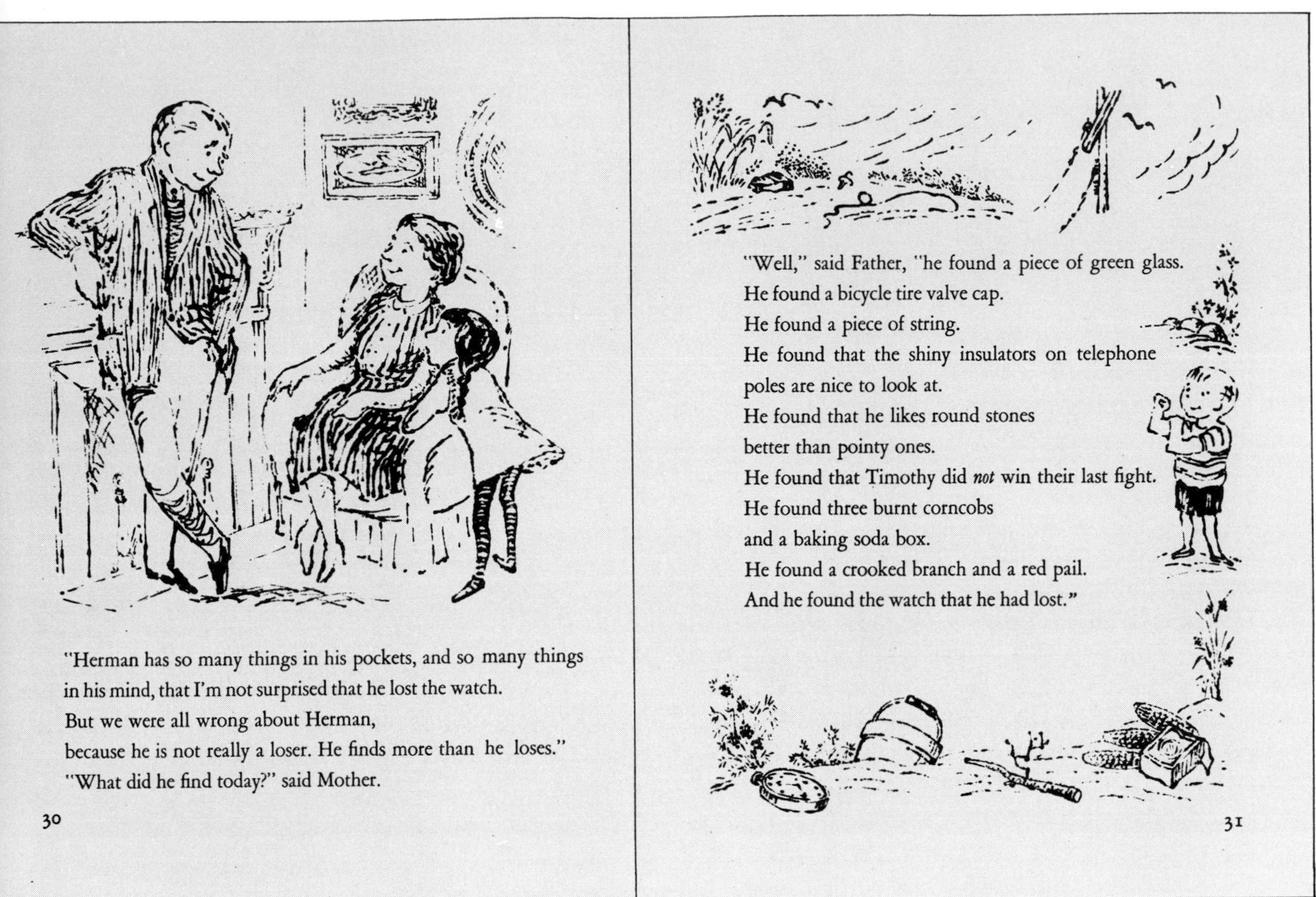

"Herman has so many things in his pockets, and so many things
in his mind, that I'm not surprised that he lost the watch.
But we were all wrong about Herman,
because he is not really a loser. He finds more than he loses."
"What did he find today?" said Mother.
30
"Well," said Father, "he found a piece of green glass.
He found a bicycle tire valve cap.
He found a piece of string.
He found that the shiny insulators on telephone
poles are nice to look at.
He found that he likes round stones
better than pointy ones.
He found that Timothy did not win their last fight.
He found three burnt corncobs
and a baking soda box.
He found a crooked branch and a red pail.
And he found the watch that he had lost."
31

549. *Herman the Loser,* text by Russell Hoban, pictures by Lillian Hoban. Harper, 1961. 7⅝ x 9⅞.

and . . . want to become finders too"), it is not, finally, mechanical—any more than are the psychological profiles of an Eriksen or a Fraiberg, or what one sees in the raw in a sandbox. The nub and, caught and held, the special pleasure, is Herman's personality. Loser or finder, he is a serious looker—per a typical Hoban throwaway line, "Different places."

One of the things he examines and considers is the ubiquitous baking soda box; a piece of green glass, a string, a round stone—"Which do you like better, Father, round stones or pointy ones?"—and a baking soda box, Arm and Hammer brand: "Did that box have little arms and hammers inside it when it was full?" From *Bedtime for Frances* onward, Russell Hoban situates his families in the material world—as natural to a child as grass and trees—where not to get to work on time means not to have a job (a mouthful more than 'Daddy goes to work in the morning'), where a trademark is a byword and (in *A Birthday for Frances*) a Chompo Bar is candy covered with glory.

Other child books followed fast (repeatedly, in picturebooks, one sees a creative burst), including *Nothing to Do* and *The Sorely Trying Day* (both Harper, 1964), which speak for themselves; and the same year Frances reappeared, now drawn also by Lillian Hoban, now faced with a real and lasting problem, a baby sister.

As the curtain opens ("It was a quiet evening"), Father is reading the paper, Mother is feeding Gloria, the new baby, Frances is sitting under the sink, singing a Frances-song; and when she stops, no one says anything. She puts some gravel in an empty coffee can and marches in rattling and singing; "Please don't do that, Frances," says Father. Acquiescing, she goes back under the sink. But Frances, if down, is not out: the question is how much allowance Gloria gets, and to Father's "Only big girls like you get allowances. Isn't it nice to be a big sister?"—another question, whether she may have a penny more "now that I am a big sister."

In the morning, her blue dress isn't ready and there are bananas instead of raisins on the oatmeal, understandable but to Frances inexcusable: "Well, things are not very good around here anymore . . . I think maybe I'll run away." Tonight, "after dinner," she announces to her mother, kissing her good-by and leaving for school.

That night, knapsack packed—special blanket, alligator doll, savings, provisions—and good-bys carefully said, Frances decamps to a cozy, handy spot under the dining room table; and a charade commences, a game of wits, between her parents—feeding each other lines, recalling snatches of her songs—and the attentive Frances (550), in the course of which she "convinces herself [in the winning words of the jacket] that she has convinced her parents of her very distinct importance." A timely wish "to hear from Frances" brings a phone call from the dining room, and then Frances herself, singing "a little traveling song":

Big sisters really have to stay
At home, not travel far away,
Because everybody misses them
And wants to hug-and-kisses them.

Gloria apart, and the songs momentarily aside, it is a different book than *Bedtime*, one that makes Frances less the object, more the subject; and less to be laughed at, more to be laughed at-with.

Frances, said a review of *Bread and Jam for Frances*, "is rapidly becoming the kindergartner's Everyman."[17] She is also the kindergartner's Russell Baker (or pick your favorite dry humorist) for, in a turn of the tables, it is now Father who is the straight man and Frances, the sharpie, who delivers the quips. Everyone has a soft-boiled egg for breakfast;

550. *A Baby Sister for Frances,* text by Russell Hoban, pictures by Lillian Hoban. Harper, 1964. 7⅞ x 10.

Frances ate three of the sandwich cookies
and put the other two aside for later.
She began to sing:
I am poor and hungry here, eating prunes and rice.
Living all alone is not really very nice.
She had no rice, but chocolate sandwich cookies
did not sound right for the song.
"I can almost hear her now," said Father,
humming the tune that Frances had just sung.
"She has a charming voice."
"It is just not a *family* without Frances," said Mother.
"Babies are very nice. Goodness knows I *like* babies,
but a baby is not a family."
"Isn't that a fact!" said Father.
"A family is *everybody all together.*"

Frances, looking askance at hers, is eating bread and jam: for one thing, "it does not slide off your spoon in a funny way."

"Well, of course," said Father,
not everyone is fond of soft-boiled eggs for
breakfast.
But there are other kinds of eggs.
There are sunny-side-up and sunny-side-down
eggs."
"Yes," said Frances. "But sunny-side-up eggs
lie on the plate and look up at you in a funny way.
And sunny-side-down eggs just lie on their
stomachs and *wait*."
"What about scrambled eggs?" said Father.
"Scrambled eggs fall off the fork
and roll under the table."

It is time for Frances "to go to school now"; but at dinner, over veal cutlets, the battle is rejoined. How will she know what she likes, asks Father, if she won't try anything new? "Well, there are many different things to eat, and they taste different ways. But when I have bread and jam I always know what I am getting, and I am always pleased." At lunchtime, it seems, she traded her chicken-salad sandwich to Albert—for bread and jam.

The cure, plainly, is a surfeit (551). At lunchtime Albert has a cream cheese-cucumber-and-tomato sandwich on rye bread, "And a pickle to go with it. And a hardboiled egg and a little cardboard shaker of salt to go with that. And a thermos bottle of milk. And a bunch of grapes and a tangerine. And a cup custard and a spoon to eat it with." What Frances has, you know; Albert isn't interested in trading. For a snack there is bread and jam ("Aren't you worried that maybe I will get

551. *Bread and Jam for Frances,* text by Russell Hoban, pictures by Lillian Hoban. Harper, 1964. 7⅞ x 10.

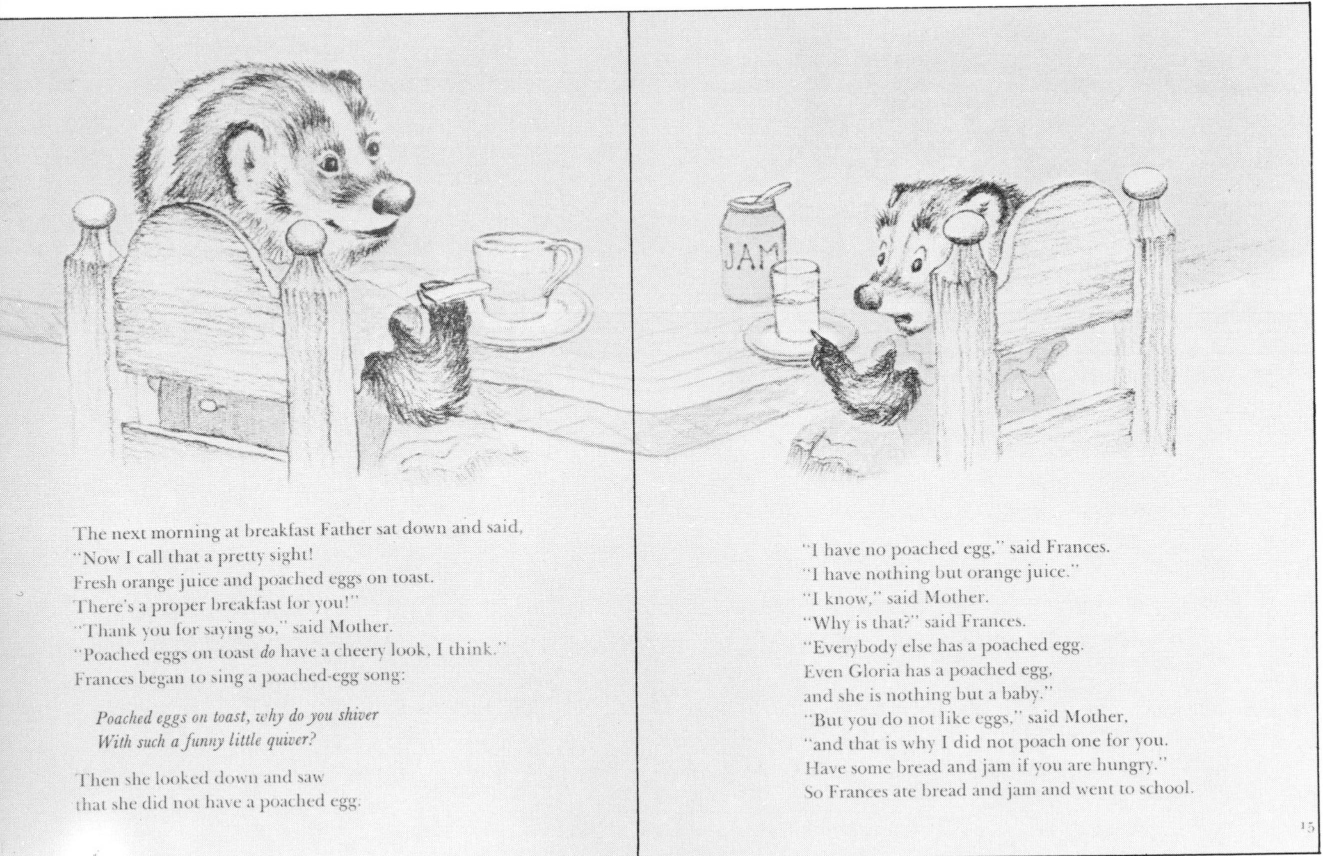

The next morning at breakfast Father sat down and said,
"Now I call that a pretty sight!
Fresh orange juice and poached eggs on toast.
There's a proper breakfast for you!"
"Thank you for saying so," said Mother.
"Poached eggs on toast *do* have a cheery look, I think."
Frances began to sing a poached-egg song:

Poached eggs on toast, why do you shiver
With such a funny little quiver?

Then she looked down and saw
that she did not have a poached egg.

"I have no poached egg," said Frances.
"I have nothing but orange juice."
"I know," said Mother.
"Why is that?" said Frances.
"Everybody else has a poached egg.
Even Gloria has a poached egg,
and she is nothing but a baby."
"But you do not like eggs," said Mother,
"and that is why I did not poach one for you.
Have some bread and jam if you are hungry."
So Frances ate bread and jam and went to school.

15

sick and all my teeth will fall out . . . ?"), for dinner, in place of spaghetti and meatballs, bread and jam again. Tears falling, Frances sings softly: "*What I am/Is tired of jam.*"

The next day, at lunchtime, Frances arranges on her doily "a thermos bottle with cream of tomato soup . . . And vanilla pudding with chocolate sprinkles and a spoon to eat it with"; and like Albert the day before, she makes everything come out even.

If only for the wrap-up, the story would be worth telling; but bright as it is, *Bread and Jam for Frances* marks also the emergence of the songs, either sotto voce or in solitude, unheard, as the still small voice of Frances speaking out (where before they were occasional ditties, pastimes or performances). In picturebooks there is little place for the omniscient narrator, reader of minds, hence the customary *He thought,* followed by quotes, for what is not actually said but might as well be, a kind of talking to oneself. The other kind of talking to oneself is of course the first-person voice when it is—in *A Tree Is Nice* as in *Play With Me*—more reverie than recital. Russell Hoban is preeminently a dramatist but he is also a poet, and his solution, an original one, is the songs, Frances's private thoughts manifest.

Altogether the action, dramatic and emotional, is in the words. Let us acknowledge that Lillian Hoban, who can draw people as states of being, is no badger-master; it is a measure of the text that the illustrations need only position the characters for the message to carry. Little things, internal things, help: concrete nouns, active verbs, and—for emphasis, for fun—repetition. As for instance (551) "she did not have a poached egg," " 'I have no poached egg,' " " 'Everyone else has a poached egg,' " " 'Even Gloria has a poached egg.' " (" 'But you do not like eggs,' said Mother, 'and that is why I did not poach one for you.' ")

In *A Birthday for Frances* it is, uh-ohh, the day before Gloria's birthday, and Frances is in the broom closet singing cryptically, "*Happy Thursday to you . . . Happy Thursday, dear Alice, Happy Thursday to you.*" Alice, it seems, "is someone that nobody can see . . . And that is why she does not have a birthday. So I am singing Happy Thursday to her." Frances's defenses, more complex, have set up a buffer, another non-birthday girl; but, Mother tells her, "Even if nobody can see her, Alice has one birthday every year, and so do you. Your birthday is two months from now. Then you will be the birthday girl." Reason does not much prevail; but at the last Gloria does—by innocently appealing to Frances's better nature and, simultaneously, to her power to grant and withhold favor.

A Birthday for Frances was published in 1968, and the flap copy speaks, lightly, of Frances's struggle "to set mind over matter" —meaning will she or will she not give Gloria the Chompo Bar she bought for her. It is the post-enlightenment era, for picturebooks and for the Hobans (the year before brought Russell Hoban's philosophic fantasy *A Mouse and His Child*), and the central issue is not adjustment but right action: whatever her resentments, Frances should not use them as an excuse for keeping the Chompo Bar. Put another way, when Frances is sitting under the sink, in *A Baby Sister for Frances,* or in the broom closet, she is all psyche—which is to say also all-vulnerable, all-malleable; and in *A Baby Sister for Frances,* that is chiefly what she is. In *A Birthday,* once past the pitiable Alice, Frances is engaged in a struggle *with herself,* quite another matter—one that allows, within a psychologically valid setting, for ethical choice.

She is perhaps also older; and Albert, hardly more than present in *Bread and Jam,* is a true friend—he has a little sister too.

'A new literature for the nursery,' William Scott called the work of Margaret Wise Brown, Grace Skaar and (as of 1951) the early Ruth Krauss. What ensued we might call a new literature for the kindergarten—or, in educational parlance, k-2, kindergarten to second grade: a literature of character and situation. The "area of direct communication to children's feelings"—Scott's characterization[18] —expanded to embrace the transmission, in fictional form, *of* children's feelings; such is the direction of the Krauss-Sendak output from *A Hole Is To Dig* to *Charlotte and the White Horse*, continued by Sendak's own work (p. 504). So, too, does the work of others develop, from the general to the particular, the communal to the individual. The observation of individual children entered in—with Zolotow and the Hobans, their own, openly; and so, it would appear, did the emergence beginning in 1957 of the easy reader as a literary form and specifically of the Harper I Can Reads.

The I Can Reads, which we will take up shortly, are dramatically structured narratives in the main; for first and second graders, novels in miniature. Character and situation are natural to them, as are the real lives of real children—or, in the case of *Little Bear*, the first, credible surrogate children; they are not about prototype figures or abstractions. (To command the attention of six- and seven-year-olds, they cannot be.) If one joins to the appreciation of small children's individuality the fictional impulse, one has the Hoban books and others in which the small child is a fully formed character, at one with the fictional adolescent, the stripling Tom Brown or Tom Sawyer, the delighting, despairing schoolgirl.

So much, at present, for the writing; now picture this:

> Elbows grow on a tickle tree
> . . . and rain makes applesauce.

True as it is that no picturebook would be the same in the hands of a different illustrator, *Rain Makes Applesauce* is hardly to be imagined without Marvin Bileck—without such an artist as Marvin Bileck.

It was the tiny line drawings in Alfred Kazin's 1951 memoir *A Walker in the City*, free, precise notations of the passing scene, that first brought Bileck to attention. The very appearance of any sort of illustration in a serious new book was noteworthy, and commenting on the 'development' (in 1970) Diana Klemin wrote: "Why didn't the art director have Bileck work on a larger scale? Why wasn't Bileck given more assignments along these lines so that he could develop his style? Fortunately, his whimsy and fantasy have been discovered for children's books."[19]

There were routine assignments and, interspersed, opportunities, albeit with insubstantial texts. Johanna Johnston's *Sugarplum* (Knopf, 1955) is just another pocket-doll story—if only she had a dress, the big dolls couldn't treat her as a trinket—that Bileck animates in toto, words and pictures, and with the intensity due an Andersen tale. Anne Colver's *Nobody's Birthday* (Knopf, 1961) is about a birthday on the loose, and if anybody could make such a fey whimsy convincing (nobody can), it would be Bileck, with his intricate tracery, his thousand-and-one surprises. Bileck, in fact, worked small naturally; given a larger format, he is a miniaturist on a grand scale.

Given scope, he whistles up worlds within worlds: a phantasmagoria.

It needn't have been so, not with the silly talk, the cheerful nonsense, that Julian Scheer and his three youngsters bandied about, that Scheer sifted and shaped and set down. There is, inescapably, something of Ruth Krauss in the doing, as there is something of *A Hole Is To Dig* and *A Very Special House* in the structure—the ripostes and the refrain. But *Rain Makes Applesauce* has a presence of its own, extravagant, bizarre, even weird, the projection of Bileck as an artist (552–553).

He is a visionary; a master penman with the festering imagination of a Rodolphe Bresdin, and something of his obsessive intricacy. Bileck's colors, too, faded, fabled, have the look of being plucked from a scrap-bag even when he is not patching, as often he is. But the picture materializing before one's eyes as it were, the close-knit interwoven movement, the animation, impartially, of the whole picture surface, suggest an affinity as well with Action Painting (Pollock, Hofmann). The appearance is of a conjunction between hazard and inspiration; and the pictures are to be searched out, explored, but no more than the visions they embody, plotted or explained.

552

552, 553. *Rain Makes Applesauce,* text by Julian Scheer, pictures by Marvin Bileck. Holiday House, 1964. 7¼ x 10½. [552, detail.]

553

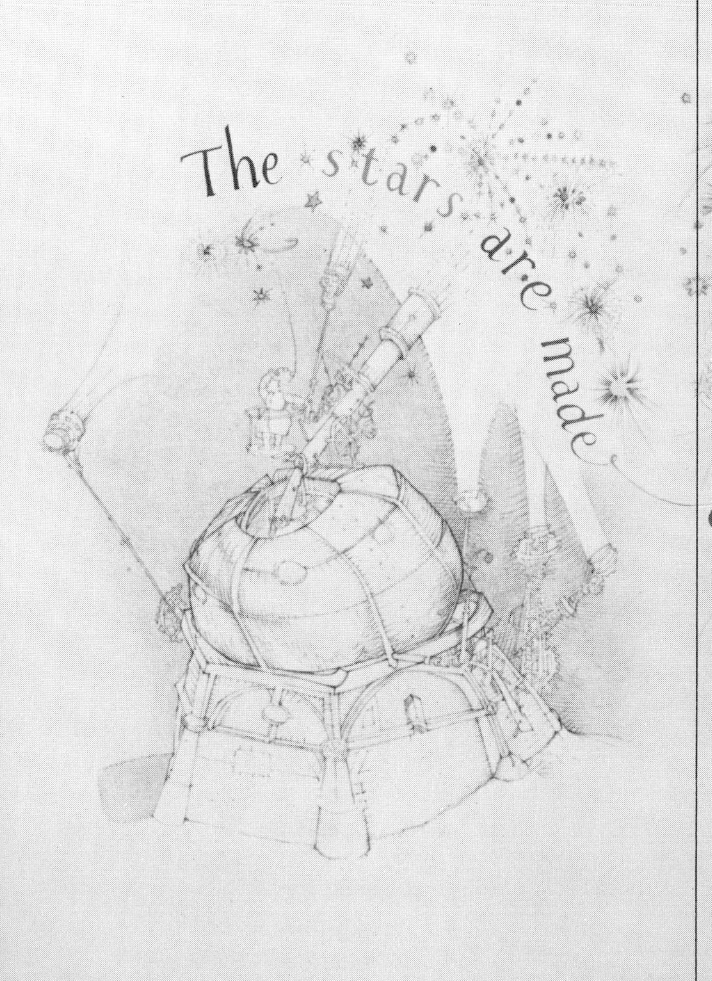

Perhaps that is why *Penny* (Viking, 1966), a tiny book about a second Thumbelina, which might have been—may have been—made to order for Bileck, amounts to very little at great length. *Rain Makes Applesauce* is another instance of less said, more to be seen.

"What impressed me most about children's books," Bernard Waber has written, "was the unlimited, unrestricted opportunity for creativity and originality."[20] As witness the first decade (plus one) of Waber picturebooks:

1961: *Lorenzo*
One little fish with a red spot doesn't swim with the crowd.

1962: *The House on East 88th Street*
When the Primms move in, there's a crocodile in the bathtub; and, says a note delivered at the door, "P.S. He will eat only Turkish caviar. P.P.S. His name is Lyle."

1963: *How To Go About Laying an Egg*
Need you know more?
Rich Cat, Poor Cat
Some cats have everything—ticked off; Scat hasn't so much as a hope.

1964: *Just Like Abraham Lincoln*
Mr. Potts, next door, looks just like Abraham Lincoln. Everyone says so. "Everyone says Mr. Potts has the biggest ears, the biggest hands, the biggest feet and the kindest heart . . . just like Abraham Lincoln."

1965: *Lyle, Lyle Crocodile*
See Lyle skate, bake cookies and languish at the zoo; see Lyle buss Loretta, the crocophobic cat.

1966: *"You Look Ridiculous" Said the Rhinoceros to the Hippopotamus*
But, like Donkey-donkey before him, the hippopotamus decides that Mother Nature knows best.
Lyle and the Birthday Party
Joshua Primm's party leaves Lyle out of sorts, morose; and speechless as he is, he can't explain why. (See Lyle carried downstairs on a stretcher.)

1967: *Cheese*
Ask a mouse to say "Cheese," and *click*! "Grrr."
An Anteater Named Arthur
Episodes in the life of Arthur (and his mother), or a study in slow confoundment.

1968: *A Rose for Mr. Bloom*
"It started with a tickling in his left ear that bothered him all the way to the city"; and blossomed.

1969: *Lovable Lyle*
Thinks Lyle, standing at the window, despondent: "Somebody out there hates me."

1970: *A Firefly Named Torchy*
Lights, color, action and reaction: Torchy's twinkle, alas, is a floodlight, and in firefly country that's not comme il faut.

1971: *Nobody Is Perfick*
Just kids, yakking; just sketches, captioned.

Waber is a storyteller with the imagination of a fabulist whose subject, fundamentally, is feelings. Especially, he pictures feelings: whatever Lyle is up to (554–556) or Arthur (558-560) or Lorenzo or Scat or Torchy, what we see first is how they feel about it, and second, how others feel. Limned with a felt-tipped pen or in fact a Magic Marker: it takes not a delicate touch but a sure one.

However unlike otherwise, many of his characters are outcasts wanting in—who feels more keenly?—and even lovable Lyle has to save his detractors from near death to win their acceptance. Torchy has a brief blaze of glory—he comes upon the city and outshines the city lights—before, heading happily home, he begins to twinkle like any other firefly. "Happiness is twinkling," didn't he say, "especially for fireflies." It's a near call to Tootle, the little engine who found happiness in staying on the track; but there is in Waber an ambivalence, wholely characteristic of children's books, which prompts him also to exalt the extraordinary. Mr. Bloom, typical husband, commuter, wage earner, really does to his

554

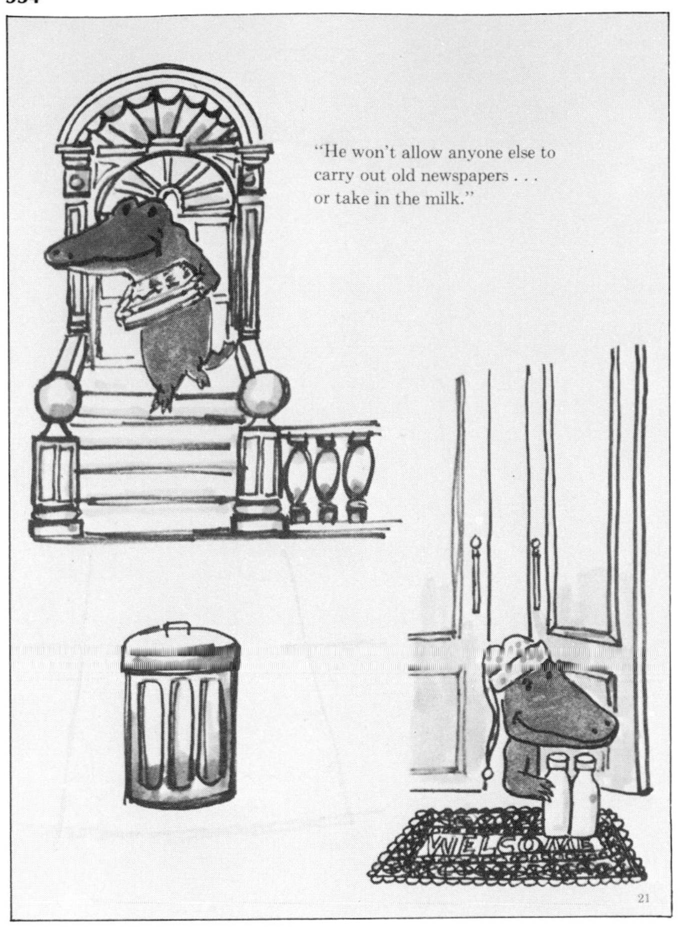

"He won't allow anyone else to
carry out old newspapers . . .
or take in the milk."

556

And it was more than he could bear
to watch Joshua unwrap his gifts.
Oh, how Lyle wished they were his
to unwrap!

554, 555. *The House on East 88th Street,* by Bernard Waber. Boston, Houghton Mifflin, 1962. 7⅞ x 10½.

556. *Lyle and the Birthday Party,* by Bernard Waber. Boston, Houghton Mifflin, 1966. 7⅞ x 10½.

555

"You can't have Lyle," cried Mrs. Primm,
"he is very happy living here, and we
love him dearly."
"Lyle must be returned to me,"
insisted Signor Valenti.
"Was it not I who raised him from
young crocodilehood?
Was it not I who taught him
his bag of tricks?
We have appeared together on
stages the world over."
"But why then did you leave him
alone in a strange house?" asked Mrs. Primm.
"Because," answered Signor Valenti,
"I could no longer afford to pay for
his Turkish caviar. But now
Lyle is famous and we shall be very rich."
Mrs. Primm was saddened, but she
knew Lyle properly belonged to
Signor Valenti and she had
to let him go.
36

It was a tearful parting for everyone.

Mr. Potts was willing.
"You could wear your stovepipe
and frock coat," I said.
Mr. Potts tried on the hat and coat.
He looked so much like Lincoln I couldn't
help saying, "If only you had a beard."
"Do you know," said Mr. Potts,
"I've always wanted a good reason
for growing a beard."

557. *Just Like Abraham Lincoln,* by Bernard Waber. Boston, Houghton Mifflin, 1964. 7⅞ x 10½.

delight sprout a rose in one ear, and far from being ostracized, he's admired. (In these environs, only, could it happen.)

Just Like Abraham Lincoln, for its part, might well be the unlikeliest picturebook since *Pet of the Met*. There's Mr. Potts, walking around looking like Lincoln, acting like Lincoln, reading and talking about Lincoln; and not being an embarrassment or a bore—being himself, a gentle lanky man who's good with animals and children, and evoking the popular image of Lincoln, barefoot boy and firelight scholar. As Lincoln's birthday approaches, Miss Robin, "our teacher," raises the subject of an assembly program; and what better prospect than Mr. Potts (557). "Now people look even more surprised when they see him"—Lincoln to the life, pushing a cart in the supermarket.

It is Waber's playing with the dual identity that makes it tolerable; even as, when the figure of Lincoln appears on stage to deliver the Gettysburg Address, cries of "It's Abraham Lincoln" are joined by shouts of "It's Mr. Potts."

"Now Mr. Potts has moved away," to Washington, D.C. "Mr. Potts is a lawyer . . . just like Abraham Lincoln." Before going he presents his young neighbor, "a fellow Lincolnphile," with his stovepipe hat, a symbolic transference and a crackerjack picture (for the cover too). That could have been the end of it, a small boy with a legacy to grow into; but no—"Someone new is moving in. Someone named Mr. Pettigrew. I wonder what he's like." From the glimpse we get, just like George Washington—a good joke, one that Lincoln would have appreciated, but at the expense of Mr. Potts's Lincolnphilia and of the child, the young child in particular, who takes it to heart.

An Anteater Named Arthur sounds like the next thing to a crocodile called Lyle but odd specimen that he is, and unlovely, Arthur is Waber's Frances or Little Bear, boy-child not incongruity. Except for the extra edge of lunacy and the stretch of sympathy that comes of putting an apron and a mobcap on an anteater and giving her the maternal presence of a Mother Badger or Mother Bear.

She's telling us, Our Town—or better, Molly Goldberg—fashion, about her son Arthur, who is, most of the time, "a kind, helpful, understanding, well-behaved, sensible, orderly, responsible, loving, loveable, altogether wonderful son." BUT sometimes (reasonably, stubbornly) Arthur doesn't understand why anteaters are called by what they eat—"the cat is not called a fisheater, the bird is not called a wormeater, and the cow is not called a grasseater"; sometimes (perversely) "Arthur has nothing to do." Funniest, a near match for Frances and the unsavory eggs, "Sometimes Arthur is choosy." Arthur, however, says hardly a word; and by keeping mum, he has the last word (558).

The finale, "Sometimes Arthur forgets," is, like the episodic structure itself, especially Little Bearish, a mix of the hopeless and huggable. Going to school, Arthur is soon back,

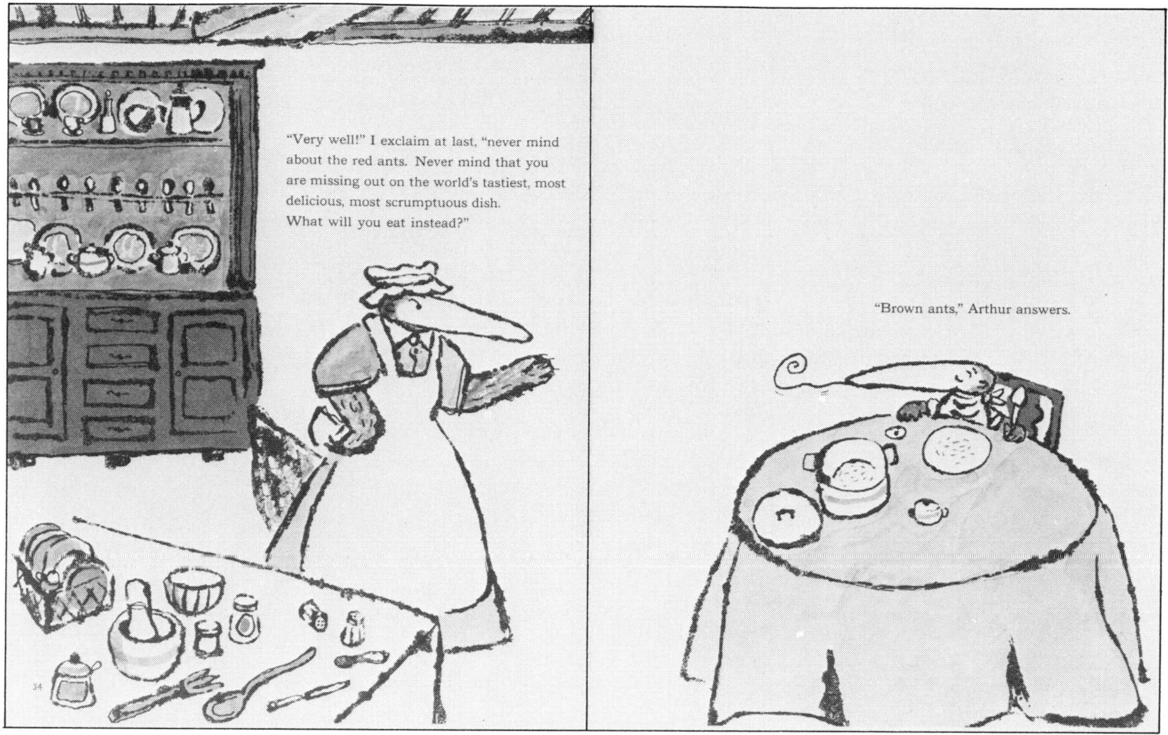

"Very well!" I exclaim at last, "never mind about the red ants. Never mind that you are missing out on the world's tastiest, most delicious, most scrumptuous dish. What will you eat instead?"
"Brown ants," Arthur answers.

558. *An Anteater Named Arthur,* by Bernard Waber. Boston, Houghton Mifflin, 1967. 8¼ x 9¾.

now for his spelling book (559), now for his sneakers, his pencil case, a good-by kiss (560). What it says about Waber, beyond his command of the idiom, is his mastery of pictorial movement, evident equally in the design of the spreads, the visual and dramatic flow, and in the ordering of the sequence, the pauses and pickups and anticipation. (There are, as the folios indicate, a dozen pages of coming and going, all different.) The door closes finally with a pregnant period, a cropped, incomplete image; and the page waits to be turned. "See what I mean about Arthur," says Mama Anteater, back at her neighborly open window.

A host of interesting and enlivening picture-book developments rebound in Waber's work, and while he is too good to be called typical, he is broadly representative.

He's funny; and so are Gene Zion and Margaret Bloy Graham in the Harry books and after, and Russell Hoban, regularly; and Crockett Johnson and Ruth Krauss. That humor suits children hardly needs belaboring; but there is (thank goodness) humor and humor.

Desmond McCarthy credits Lear, and Thurber after him, with creating humor out of lines and forms, independent of words; and Thurber and Peter Arno, "via *The New Yorker*," with conveying it to his British countrymen, still wedded to captions.[21] Our glowering dog at the very start is an unequivocal Thurber canine, and the small fry hero just after is of course by William Steig, another in the *New Yorker* van. *The New Yorker* is very much with us, like—and unlike—Disney, in that the Disney faculty for projecting emotion graphically has its counterpart in the *New Yorker* knack for embodying in a look, a physical attitude, a state of mind. The one begins with a story, which the characters act out; the other with characters whose aspect or actions, 'read,' constitute a story in themselves. (Margaret Wise Brown, you may recall, had

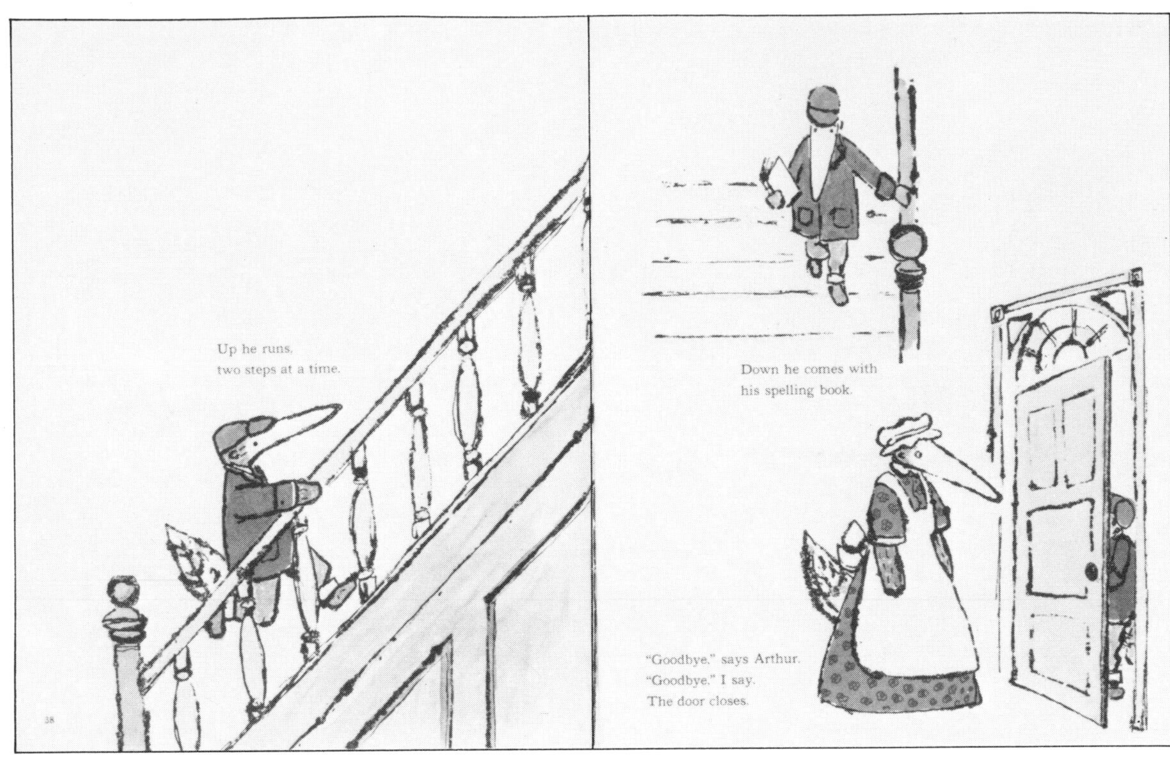

559

559, 560. *An Anteater Named Arthur,* by Bernard Waber. Boston, Houghton Mifflin, 1967. 8¼ x 9¾.

560

the idea of using Thurber drawings, plain, for this purpose.) An art that is funny independent of words is an art that children can see the point of for themselves, a very great boon indeed.

There is this too about humor, that "it aims at making us realise," as the British cartoonist Fougasse has written, "that the message is addressed to us personally, by its implied assumption that we are all really alike in this matter—that we are all of us very liable to act foolishly or thoughtlessly . . . And that's why it can successfully bring home to us the things that need overhauling in ourselves."[22] Fougasse—Kenneth Bird, later the editor of *Punch*—had in mind his wartime "Careless Talk Costs Lives" posters but whether the aim is a specific response or a more general awareness, the observation holds. On a different level, humor, in Desmond McCarthy's words, "is one way of coming to terms with what is painful or humiliating . . . a way of honestly facing facts without being overwhelmed by them."[23]

In the Thirties, William Steig's "Small Fry" in *The New Yorker* had their embarrassing moments—a boy caught by his buddies picking posies—and their dreams of glory: the little Napoleon at the start is from the series of that name. In the rain, they stalked the gutter in "New Boots"; the week before Christmas, they argued "Santa Claus—Man or Myth?" It was a wry, comprehending, sympathetic view of childhood at variance with the sentimental gloss then predominant in children's books, and what it may have contributed, ultimately, to turning the tide is unassayable; with the Fifties and Sixties and what they wrought, with the coming into the field of any number of *New Yorker* artists—Robert Kraus, Syd Hoff, A. Birnbaum, Warren Miller (texts), Mischa Richter, Edward Frascino, James Stevenson—it became, if not the dominant view in turn, at least a common one. In a 1972 cartoon of Syd Hoff's a small hedgehog? boar?— anyhow uncomely—is saying to a big one, "Mother, am I pretty?" It could be a page from a new picturebook, or from the Hobans' 1969 *Ugly Bird*.

. . . AND A FEW ENDEARMENTS

Theodore Roethke is quoted as saying, "On small poems: a thing may be small but it need not be a cameo; it may be a cinder in the shoe or the mind's eye or a pain in the neck."[24] Equally, a small book may be *Let's Be Enemies* (or another *Hole Is To Dig* redone). But to work small always, and authentically, is not to choose a format but to have, native to one, a mode of address; to confide and, almost of necessity, to cherish.

ALL KINDS OF TIME

He knew somehow as a child, Harry Behn wrote, why Blake spelled tiger as he did. "A tiger in a jungle is one of nature's most beautiful and dangerous creations. In a zoo he is hardly a tiger at all, not a complete tiger. But Blake's Tyger burning bright in a dark forest is forever magically all the most glorious tigers that ever were."[25] And as there were many ways of looking at a tiger, there were, there are, *All Kinds of Time*.

It was Behn's second small book of verse for children, following upon *The Little Hill* (Harcourt, 1949). Poems reminiscent of Walter de la Mare, many of them, make up *The Little Hill*, and small spruce decorations confer upon it a character of its own. In *All Kinds of Time* the pictures are partners with the verse and, disposed freely throughout, give a semblance of oneness, of wholeness, to the many and manifold observations.

To a poet's idea of all kinds of time—objective and subjective, figurative, immeasurable —are added a child's particular constructions, and in the central passage especially, the images of a child's experience:

> Sometimes there seems
> to be no time at all.
> Then sometimes
> there's all kinds of time,
> from second to forever.

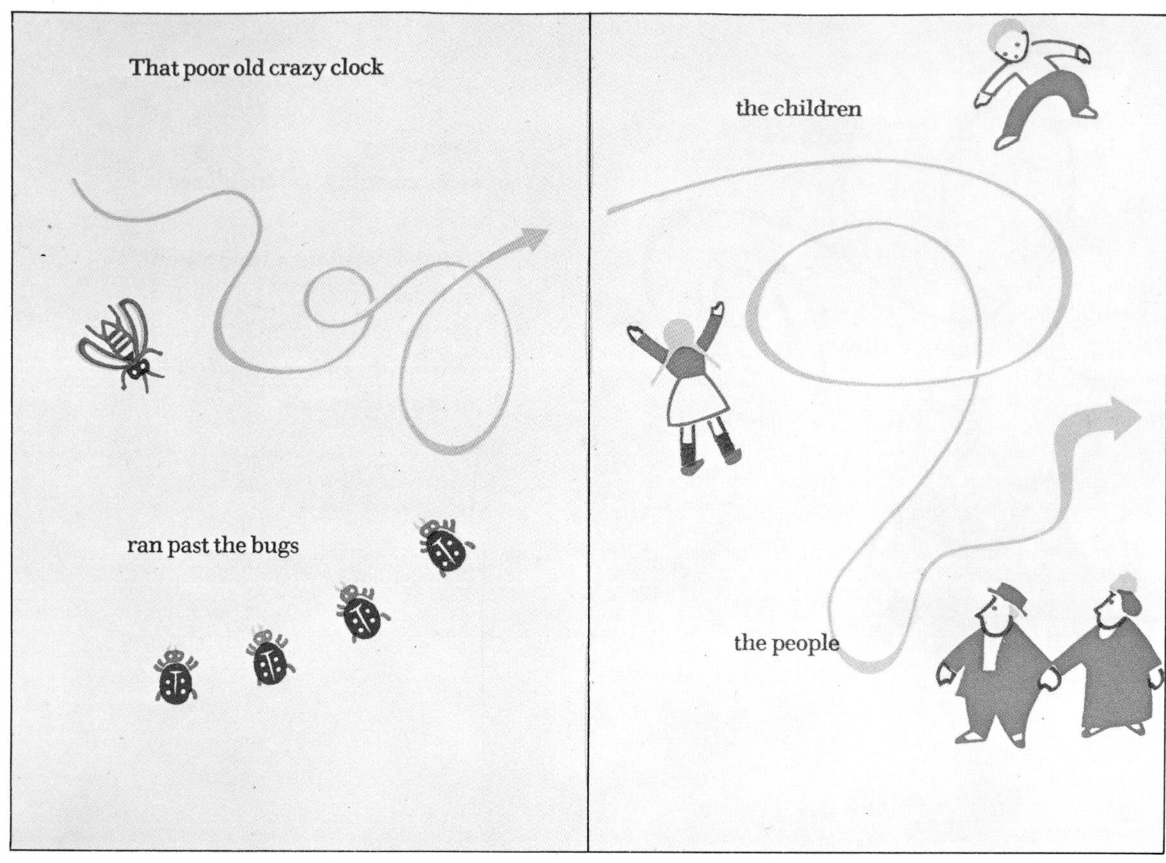

That poor old crazy clock
ran past the bugs
the children
the people

561. *All Kinds of Time,* by Harry Behn. Harcourt, 1950. 4¾ x 7¼.

Pictured, "Seconds are bugs . . . minutes are children . . . hours are people . . . days are postmen . . . weeks are Sunday School . . . ," and, most felicitous, "years are Santa Claus . . . centuries are George Washington . . . and forever is God."

My birthday is a fence post
where I sit all alone
and watch the sun move
like the hand of a clock.

But there is a time, before Spring, when "There's a great big space that's not anything"; to find it, one time, "I took a clock apart"; and put together again, "It ran away/as if something had frightened it." Cued in, we watch it run (561); see it shoot through a double-page outer space paroxysm, past Santa Claus and George Washington "and entirely past forever!" to a final collapse. There is fear in the image of a runaway clock: "I was glad when . . . it stopped."

Active and reflective, varied in mood and tempo, the sequence is an interweave, too, of sign, symbol, phrase, placement, spacing—together giving expression to the physical page. The all-important design—yet who would call it a designer's book?—was by Behn and Peter Beilenson, proprietor (with his wife Edna Beilenson) of the Peter Pauper Press, where the book was printed. The slender slip-cased volumes of the Peter Pauper Press, handsomely turned out and inexpensive, represent en masse an unusual success story and an institution, the seal, once, of friendship and courtship. Peripheral as the books are in the main to juvenile publishing, the Peter Pauper look—intimate and comely, a best-butter look—is unmistakable in the Behn books, and intrinsic to the pleasure of *All Kinds of Time*.

By design—by intent and execution—the whole is greater than the sum of its parts, "as if Now is also perhaps Forever."

MARY CHALMERS

Mary Chalmers's work is always soft, rounded, gentle; and not soft-minded, spineless, mushy. She looks you in the eye and smiles.

"This is a story about a little girl named Susan," *Come for a Walk with Me* begins. "She lived with her mother in a little white house beside a twisty road, and up the twisty road a little bit lived Mrs. Horseyfeather. She had a little white house too." There is no indication that anything of the least importance will happen, and it doesn't; to be there with Susan and her friend Will Rabbit—who lives, Winnie-the-Pooh fashion, behind a proper beamed door in a tree—is adventure enough.

Susan is going to borrow a cup of molasses from Mrs. Horseyfeather, and Will Rabbit is going with her (562). On the way they pick a bouquet of flowers for Mrs. Horseyfeather, disturb Harry Hop Toad and excuse themselves, clutch each other at the sound of "Grrrrrrrrrowwwwwwwl"—and laugh with Tommy Cat at the success of his joke; race down a grassy hill, row out into a pond for iris ("Don't fall out of the boat, please," says Will Rabbit, rowing), look for lilies of the valley in the woods—and, when they are almost there: "Here is a map to show where Susan and Will Rabbit went on their walk."

Mrs. Horseyfeather is delighted with her bouquet; Susan remembers "that she should remember something"—to ask for the molasses; and Susan and Will Rabbit have a piece of Mrs. Horseyfeather's huckleberry pie. The pie is so good and the walk was so lovely and they are so happy that they do a little dance. "And then they took the cup of molasses for Susan's mother and went home. Susan went along the twisty road to her little white house and Will Rabbit went along the twisty road to his little house in the big old elm tree. And that"—Susan and Will Rabbit waving—"is the end of the story."

Were it not so matter of fact, and so unfeigned in its pleasure, it would be insupportable; but there is a propriety about it, a modest punctiliousness, that keeps it within the child's make-believe world which whimsy, coy or clever (or both), commonly lacks.

It has no position, as it were; and there is little systematization, whether of persons or events: against all reason, except hers, Susan takes Will Rabbit's arm—"You be the papa and I'll be the mama." In *A Hat for Amy Jean* (Harper, 1956) there is less: no categorical order of beings exists, no fixed roles or differentiation, and no causal relation of events. "Tomorrow is Amy Jean's birthday and, you know, if you are lucky, someone might give you a present. . . . Billy, her brother, wants to buy Amy Jean a present and Amy Jean wants "A straw hat with roses and bluebells and ribbons on, please," "Well, where do you buy a hat like that? In the big city, of course."

Of course. So Billy enlists Michael (the dog) and Georgiana (the cat), and Tommy,

562. *Come for a Walk with Me*, by Mary Chalmers. Harper, 1955. 5¼ x 6.

"We could play house along the way," said Susan. "You be the papa and I'll be the mama." She took his arm and off they went through the daisy field.

his little brother, follows along behind; and when they stop in the woods to have lunch (providentially, *four* peanut butter sandwiches) and Tommy wanders off and gets lost, a deer asks him why he's crying; and when the deer, and Tommy on his back, see an airplane crash into a lake, they paddle in to rescue the pilot who, "much to their surprise," (!) is a cat.

Well, "just then Billy and Michael and Georgiana and the five rabbits [from the woods] come running up, with the three birds [ditto] flying overhead . . . They decide to go to the airport and take a helicopter the rest of the way into town." They land in a busy street ("How all of the people stare!"), hurry into a department store, and "What do you suppose! A lady is sitting at a little table with three mirrors and she is trying on a big straw hat with roses and bluebells and ribbons on." To the saleslady's "It looks lovely on you madam," Tommy adds ("in a rather loud voice"), "I think it would look good on Amy Jean. That is our hat that we came to buy for Amy Jean's birthday present."

The lady buys it for them—"and then you will all be able to buy something for yourselves too"; on the way home, "a long way," they meet a man with a wheelbarrow, who gives it to them; and, arriving, present Amy Jean with her hat—without ever, as it were, waking up. It is Wonderland without the rabbit hole; a wonderland given or, if you will, taken for granted.

George Appleton is a dragon; but that is to get way ahead of the story. "There was once a gray and white cat named Trilby. He lived with a little boy named Bobby and Bobby's mother and father." And there he is, licking his paws, a pet among toys; and, overleaf, in his room (563). And under the car, and on his way (564). "Run, run, run, run, run, run run run. All over the place," all over the page; and pouf! (565). He wonders what he'll see in the Deep Woods: "Maybe a little fox? (pictured) "Or a little opossum?" (ditto) "Or a rabbit? Or a raccoon? Or maybe a chipmunk?"

What he sees, what answers when he calls, is a very strange forlorn animal: a dragon, the animal tells Trilby, and will Trilby play with

563-565. *George Appleton*, by Mary Chalmers. Harper, 1957. 5¼ x 6.

One morning, Trilby woke up, blinked at the sunlight on his blanket and decided that this was going to be an especially nice day.
6
He jumped out of bed, did his morning exercises: one, two, one two; and ran to the kitchen, where he smelled bacon frying.
7

563

Trilby went and sat under the car. He always sat there when he wanted to think. He thought hard for a while and then decided that he would go to the Deep Woods.

10

Trilby had never been to the Deep Woods and he was very happy that he had thought of going. He hopped and skipped and kicked a little white stone. He ran and ran, just because it was fun to run.

11

564

Where did he go?
14
Peek!
15

565

him? They play and play, until it's time for Trilby to go home to his supper. "Trilby," says Bobby, stroking his head, "where have you been?" And Trilby tells him . . . "And tomorrow I will go to the Deep Woods and play with George Appleton again." It is as if nothing were predetermined, as if it were occurring spontaneously, directed by some inner force or intuitive impulse. *A Hat for Amy Jean* reads like a child's run-on add-on yarn; *George Appleton* doesn't so much read as—"run run run . . . Peek!"—it happens. And that because Mary Chalmers is letting the observer into the story to complete it, and linking his impulse with Trilby's.

As much as any others I know of, these small books duplicate in themselves, intentionally or not, the way the young child has been found to think, how he imagines, which is meritorious not per se but because the result, however irregular by ordinary standards, is also dramatically satisfying. Children haven't the ability that Mary Chalmers has to give form to formlessness. But there is a benefit insofar as Trilby's waking and doing his exercises; eating his morning fish and milk and, ungratefully, licking Bobby's mother's chocolate whipped cream pie; running and playing peek-a-boo; wondering what animal he'll find and finding a dragon are engrossing one by one or rather two by two, without reference to what precedes or what follows. The interesting everyday, the everyday-imaginative, the imaginative-fantastical coexist, coequal.

A Christmas Story (Harper, 1956) is a tiny board-covered book—out of the Holiday House *Night Before Christmas* by *Little Fur Family*—that, were I Santa Claus, would be in every three-year-old's holiday stocking. Elizabeth (girl) and Harry Dog and Hilary Cat and Alice Rabbit are trimming their Christmas tree—"a big job . . . it isn't every little girl and dog and cat and rabbit who can do it;" and they haven't a star for the top. So Elizabeth goes out in the snow, footprints trailing, to get one. A lady hasn't a star but she has a ginger cookie for her, a blue jay doesn't have a star but he shows her the way, five sleepy owls haven't a star and they're not interested; and then, "By very good luck Elizabeth meets the Santa Claus for Rabbits and Other Small Animals," and he has a star in his bag. Page of Elizabeth returning, star held high; and overleaf, tree complete, "There." Exactly.

Ursula Nordstrom was at an ALA convention and wrote to tell Mary Chalmers how much librarians were praising her "ferny pictures," and she received in reply a card, "Throw a Kiss to Ursula, Harry," that became *Throw a Kiss, Harry* and inaugurated a new Chalmers line, more pictures than words—the transient incident. A gesture, in effect, caught and fixed.

Harry is Trilby as a child-animal, in time between Margaret Wise Brown's progeny, just beginning to speak up, and the highly articulate Frances. Harry's voice, however, is the look about him as his mother takes him away from a turtle, and the flower he's picked for it; and as she stops to talk to a friend . . . (566). In another minute he's on top of the roof, at the next opening a fireman is carrying him down. His mother scolds him and starts to take him home; "But Harry had had a lovely time being rescued. He did not want to go home. He waved to the fireman and the fireman waved back." Suggests his mother to Harry, still waving, Why don't you throw a kiss? and there begins a mute performance that Chaplin could be proud of (567–572).

In the few years since the floppy, button-faced artlessness of *Come for a Walk with Me*, Mary Chalmers had acquired the skill to convey, by a tilt of the head, a glance, a particular gesture or gait, the play of emotions—which is not the physical pantomime that many of her successors were confined to. Like Helen Sewell, whom she resembles in this respect (cf. Sewell's pekingese, 112 and 113), Chalmers does not do away with words, she gives to each, words and pictures, that which is theirs. In her case the dialogue, mother-talk down pat, counterpoints Harry's silent contrariness, as it does in life, and it is lifelike

566-572. *Throw a Kiss, Harry,* by Mary Chalmers. Harper, 1958. 3¾ x 5¾.

566

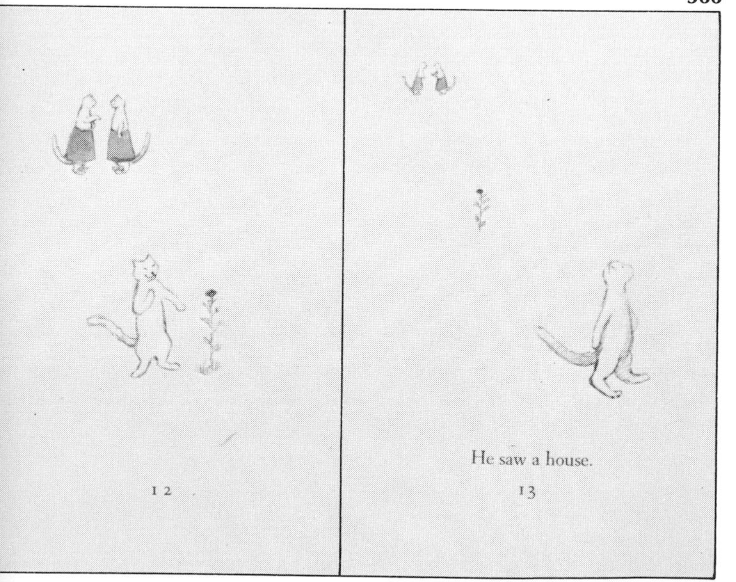

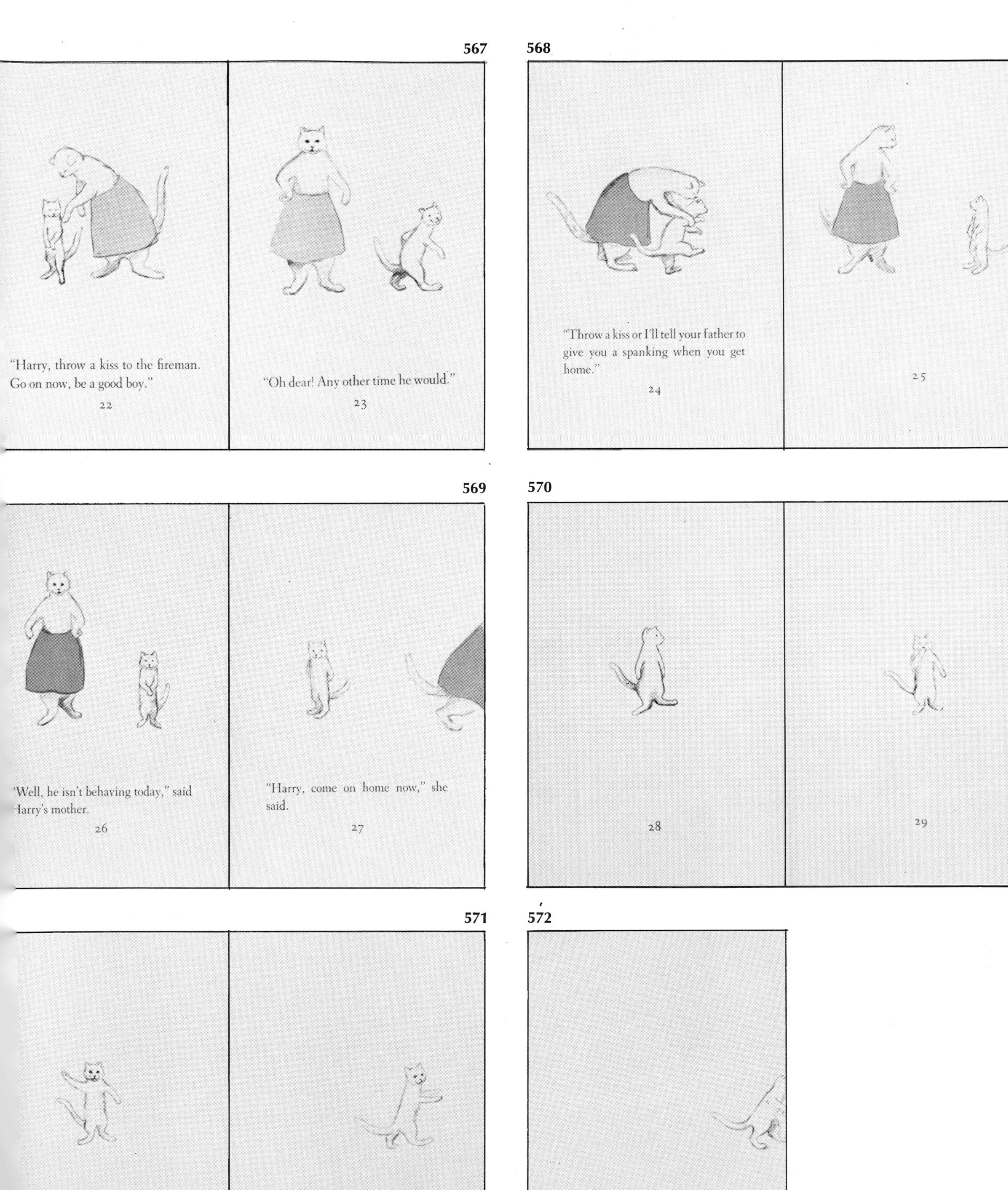
567
"Harry, throw a kiss to the fireman. Go on now, be a good boy."
22
"Oh dear! Any other time he would."
23
568
"Throw a kiss or I'll tell your father to give you a spanking when you get home."
24
25
569
'Well, he isn't behaving today," said Harry's mother.
26
"Harry, come on home now," she said.
27
570
28
29
571
30
31
572
32

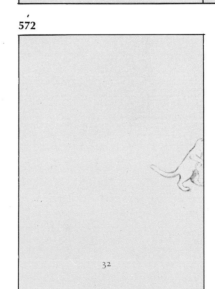

too, and naturally funny, for him to take action when she stops talking.

Besides her ear for speech patterns, Chalmers has a way of speaking her stories—as, in fact, they were spoken in the early Thirties. "It certainly looks as if it is going to snow," she says in *A Christmas Story*; and "You see? Here is the snow." The little white teddy bear has forgotten to put on his mittens, Dorothy Sherrill tells us (p. 74); and "See—he has no mittens on." Chalmers, heir to a generation of image-making, capitalizes on it: "It certainly looks as if it is going to snow" is a bare darkening landscape, "Here is the snow," a snowfall screen; and, unerringly, she places the star atop the tree with a contented and final, "There." In *Throw a Kiss, Harry* she puts into words also what, though we could guess it from the pictures—"Harry had had a lovely time being rescued"—expands and reverberates in the particular saying.

Beguiling books but, repeat, anything but trifles.

PALMER BROWN

Not long ago I met a woman at a rare book dealer's looking for something by Palmer Brown which she thought of, understandably, as English and antique; and naturally out of print. One imagines Palmer Brown writing to please himself, and drawing with infinite care the pictures he likes to go with his stories. And because others, children and adults, will always have a hankering for crystal violets and sunbeams and secret wishes, he pleases them too. His books are treats.

There are four only, the two stories of Anna Lavinia's magic journeys, *Beyond the Pawpaw Trees* and *The Silver Nutmeg* (Harper, 1954 and 1956), and the two small mouse books, otherwise quite different—*Cheerful* and *Something for Christmas*.

In *Cheerful* is the sober merriment of Beatrix Potter, and a most un-Potterish wistfulness; but Potter's fictions were not usually fairy tales. Cheerful, the youngest of four mice raised in a church, is the one who takes after his mother, a country mouse with impractical white feet; and listening to her sing of the woods and fields she came from, he too wants to go "to that land, where spring was a sudden sweetness on the air, and winter a warm tunnel beneath the snow, where white feet never grew grey with city soot."

That is the crux of it; the heart is incident. Cheerful and his sisters and brother playing tag in the rainbow shadows from the stained glass windows, and Cheerful, on his own patch of green shadow, his goal, singing, "Matthew, Mark, Luke, and John,/Guard the ground I stand upon!" His sister Faith growing up to marry a bakery mouse and growing fat on the crumbs of cakes and cookies "and cream-filled almond meringues"; his sister Hope marrying a delicatessen mouse and growing fat, in turn, on sausages and cheese; and his brother Solemnity, who resembles their father, deciding to become a church mouse too: "He no longer played games, but took to nibbling the parson's licorice lozenges, which were kept in a little box behind the pulpit and tasted very solemn."

For Cheerful, left alone, dreaming, an open window beckons; and a pushcart stands below. "Hide among the grapes," his mother calls. "They cost more and should take you to a better home than those string beans." But, good home that it is, with a grandmother who does not believe in putting everything away, Cheerful is not really happy. "He longed for a place where spring was more than just a potted cineraria on the window sill, and winter more than just a rattling in the radiator pipes."

The grandmother is wrapping presents to send to her granddaughter at Easter, and Cheerful, coming upon a candy egg and peering inside, thinks his dream has come true (573). He tugs off a sugar rose and slips in, only to discover that the lambs and meadow are candy too; and he sits on a marzipan mushroom and weeps. ("The tears were very sticky underfoot.") With Cheerful still inside, the egg is wrapped and mailed; "Matthew, Mark, Luke, and John . . . ," he sings and then, comforted, falls asleep. He awakens, be assured, in the country, and at the first oppor-

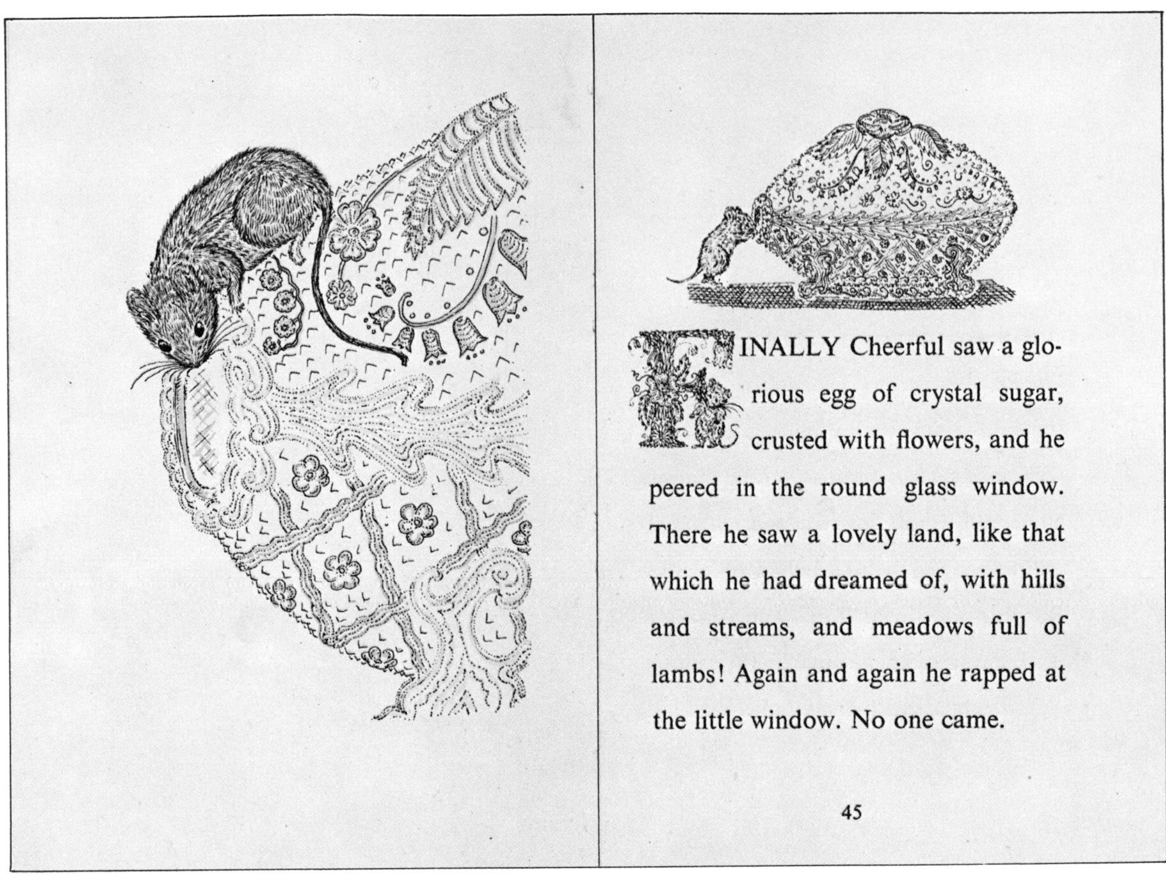

FINALLY Cheerful saw a glorious egg of crystal sugar, crusted with flowers, and he peered in the round glass window. There he saw a lovely land, like that which he had dreamed of, with hills and streams, and meadows full of lambs! Again and again he rapped at the little window. No one came.

45

573. *Cheerful,* by Palmer Brown. Harper, 1957. 3⅞ x 5¾.

tunity he is out and away, and the wet grass is washing his feet clean. A dozen breezes tell him "This is the land," and when a white-faced woodmouse asks him his name, he can answer, in truth, "I am Cheerful."

"How was it possible to put so much into such a little book?" Louise Bechtel remarked of *Beyond the Pawpaw Trees.*[26] *Cheerful*, far littler, is big too for its size, with words and thoughts to turn over, and in the thistle-pictures a small precise world to return to—a world equally of peppermint pastilles and glass-green, grass-green shadows.

Something for Christmas, by contrast, is a playlet, complete in the time it takes for mother and child mouse to speak their lines—an exchange reminiscent of others but in itself perfectly formed. It is throughout as you see it near the close (574), with mother mouse drawing from her child first his Christmas Eve worry—"I am wondering what to give-someone-for-Christmas"—and then, with Socratic persistence, pursuing the possibilities. The answer is in sight behind the wing chair: "Oh? And have you thought of giving her your love?" A hug, a snuggle, and "Now"—reciprocally—"let us see what we can find for a little mouse I love very much too."

It is not less a Palmer Brown book for being, through and through, a Harper book.

There is, or was, such a thing as certainly as there once existed Venetian painting or Irish theater: a fusion of form and spirit.

Ursula Nordstrom was its patron—not in the sense of the Renaissance princes, proposing and disposing, but of their predecessor Abbot Suger, builder of St. Denis, "A man who," in Erwin Panofsky's words, "takes his carpenters into the woods in quest of beams and personally picks the right trees." And who, against the monastic Puritanism of his time, upheld physical brightness—the new soaring windows—as a source of spiritual illumination; who opposed subjection and asceticism in any guise. Continues Panofsky: "Did Suger realize that his concentration of artists 'from all parts of the kingdom' inaugurated . . . that great selective synthesis of French regional styles which we call Gothic? Did he suspect that the rose window in his west façade . . . was one of the great innovations in architectural history . . . ?"[27] There is more—about thinking, philosophy; innovations come in aggregates.

So, too, in less exalted realms. In one representative year, 1956, Harper published *Three Little Animals, I Want to Paint My Bathroom Blue, A Hat for Amy Jean, Really Spring, The Little Elephant, A Tree Is Nice, Harry the Dirty Dog, A Christmas Story, Harold's Fairy Tale, Roar and More* and *Kenny's Window,* the first book of Maurice Sendak's authorship. We have had reason—reasons—to take notice of all of them, or will. The next year brought more Krauss (2) and Sendak (3), Crockett Johnson (2), Mary Chalmers (2), Zion and Graham; a second Kuskin, a new Charlotte Zolotow-Garth Williams, *Cheerful,* the first of Tomi Ungerer; and, to begin the I Can Reads, *Little Bear.* A list of luminaries, it speaks also of collective inspiration and purpose, and extraordinary fruitfulness.

Between 1939, when Ursula Nordstrom took charge of the juvenile department at Harper's, and her retirement from its administration in 1973, the firm published, by my rough reckoning, some four hundred picturebooks. Not nearly all of them are notable but few, through the mid-Sixties especially, are without some point of interest. Harper picturebooks do not necessarily stay in print, they go in and out of print; they have not so much authority as vitality.

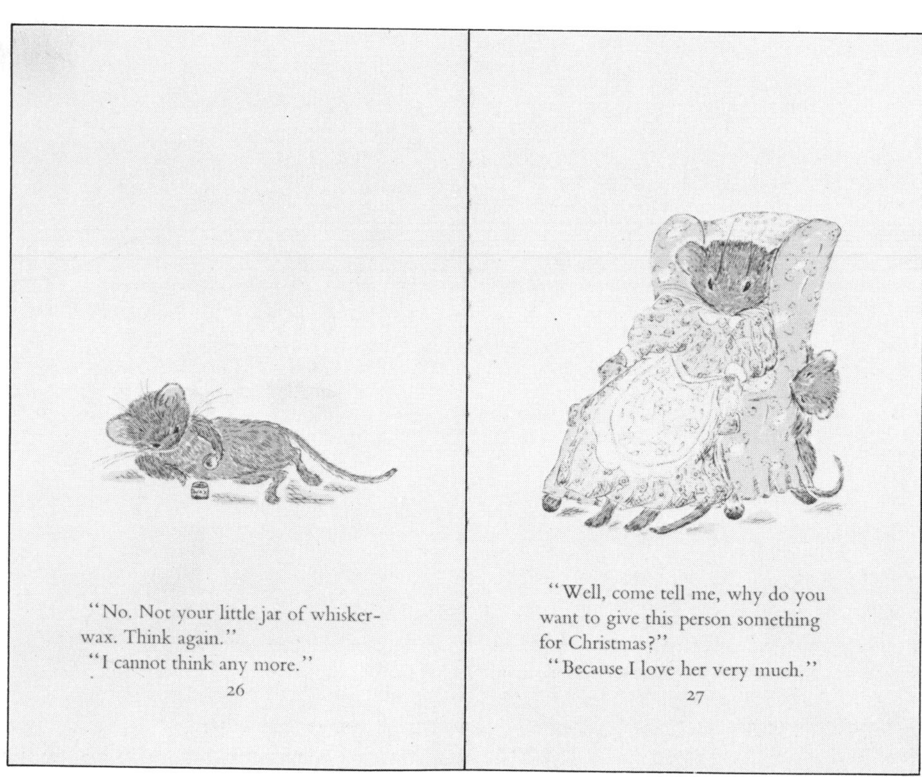

"No. Not your little jar of whisker-wax. Think again."
"I cannot think any more."
26
"Well, come tell me, why do you want to give this person something for Christmas?"
"Because I love her very much."
27

574. *Something for Christmas,* by Palmer Brown. Harper, 1958. 4 x 6⅝.

MAURICE SENDAK

The success of the illustrations for Marcel Aymé's animal frolic *The Wonderful Farm* (1951) and, following upon it, of *A Hole Is To Dig* (1952) and *A Very Special House* (1953), was for Sendak a threshold, on the one hand to more illustration, on the other to further picturebooks.

It was, propitiously, the period of Meindert DeJong's consort with the angels, and *Shadrach* and *Hurry Home, Candy* (both 1953), *The Wheel on the School* (1954), *The Little Cow and the Turtle* (1955), *The House of Sixty Fathers* (1956)—to stop there—provided Sendak with strong, poignant subjects. They are strange books, DeJong's, with their long arm of fate and their clasp of each instant; painfully sad and profoundly joyous; involved with life, really, with a seriousness quite beyond most latter-day writing for children. Today some of them would not be illustrated; but then today there are fewer illustrators and more picture-makers.

"The good illustrator," Edward Ardizzone has observed, "does more than just make a pictorial comment on the written word. He produces a visual counterpart which adds a third dimension to the book, making more vivid and more understandable the author's intention."[1] In Ardizzone's picturebooks, specifically in the stories of Little Tim, the words are his but the pictures have no less a full, rich life. Writes Helen Stone exuberantly of *Tim to the Rescue*: "As to depicting *types*, this artist tosses them off in a gust of sounds, tastes and smells. Their sea dog speech caught in waggish balloons, but not too often; their secret vanities (see Third Mate's cabin); the grousing and heady mixtures (in mess and galley); Tim the Scribe (see letters home); their common weakness, the common cat (see everywhere)—all are keenly observed. And where, oh where, is a sight so hilarious as Ginger, the barber's nemesis, transfixed under his bramble of hair, except in some of the good examples of genre illustration of the eighteenth and nineteenth centuries, including Cruikshank?"[2]

Speaking of graphic design we had occasion to note that 'books came to be more designed, less illustrated,' giving it a positive connotation; but one could say also, with a change of phrasing and emphasis, that as books came to be more designed, they were less illustrated. Accordingly a picturebook artist had less need to be an illustrator—to go the route, that is, of the Petershams from textbooks and stories, or of Helen Sewell from more literary works. And as picturebooks themselves increased in number, he had less reason to illustrate, less incentive; as they became more lucrative and prestigious, he had less inclination.

There is no absolute connection between picturebooks and illustration as it is generally understood—one reason, indeed, for their development as an independent form. Wanda Gág was not to begin with an illustrator; and from Esphyr Slobodkina and Clement Hurd, who were painters, to the upcoming Leo Lionni and Remy Charlip, designers, much of the most creative picturebook work cannot be construed—in the reductive Artzybasheff sense or the enlarging sense of Ardizzone—as illustration. The other side of the coin we glimpsed when we observed that among the moderns only Garth Williams, the illustrator of E. B. White, and Sendak, the illustrator of DeJong and Randall Jarrell, are able to invest real animals with individual personality.

Similarly, one can look back over several decades of picturebooks and find only a few children who stand out as individuals—Helen Sewell's Mehitable and Jemima, Kazue Mizumura's Mako of the cracked clogs, perhaps Lentil (foreshadowing McCloskey's *Homer Price*); and from the cartoonist-illustrators, Bemelmans's Madeline, Crockett Johnson's Harold. A special case, and all the more indicative, is Ezra Jack Keats's Peter who with his friend Archie, the clown, has survived gross overpainting because Keats, once a deft illustrator (Danny Dunn, for one), has still a way with kids. If Sendak's children in turn—the children of *A Hole Is To Dig* and the DeJong books—have any counterpart, it is Ardizzone's (575); were he not able to bring them to life there could hardly have been, later, Rosie and Pierre and Max and Mickey.

Among the picturebooks prompted by the Krauss-Sendak example were those for Sendak in particular—for what, demonstrably, he could do. *The Giant Story* (by Beatrice Schenk de Regniers, Harper, 1953) turns the

575. *The Little Bookroom,* by Eleanor Farjeon, illus. by Edward Ardizzone. Oxford, 1955. Detail.

576. *What Can You Do With a Shoe?* text by Beatrice Schenk de Regniers, pictures by Maurice Sendak. Harper, 1955. 10¾ x 5½.

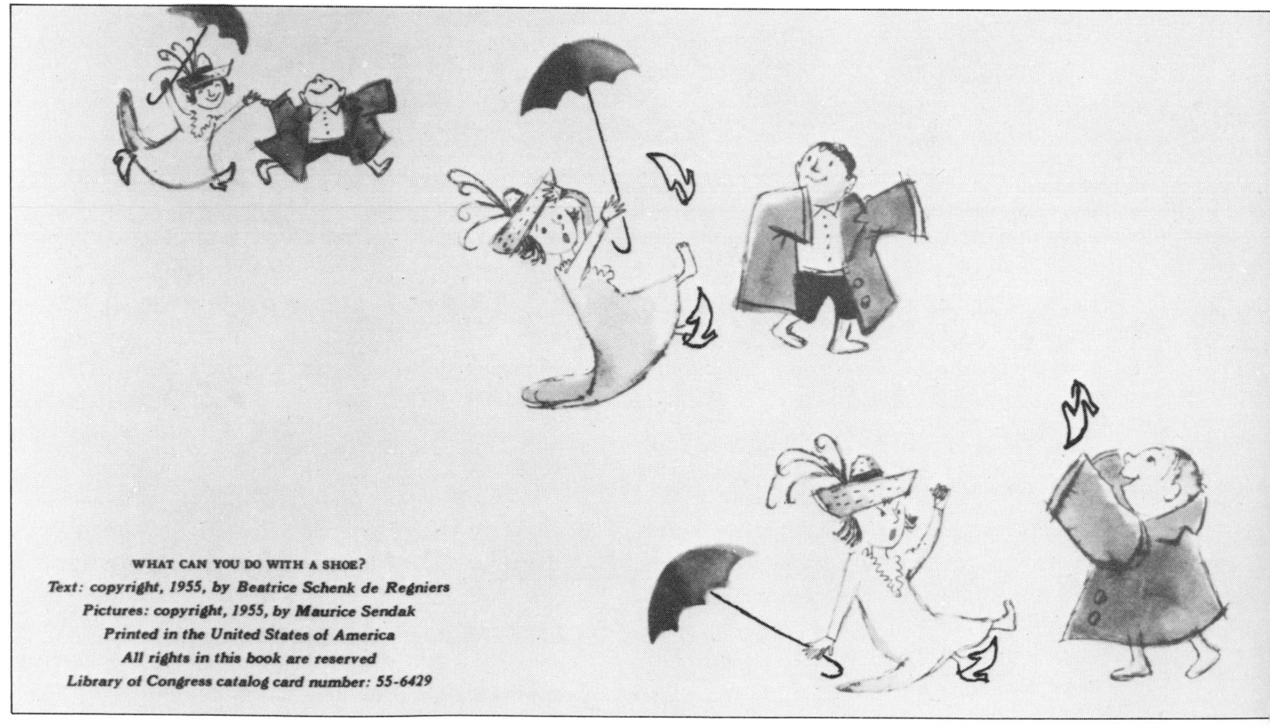

little boy of *A Very Special House* into a giant himself—until dark—and it is awkward, forced, as if Sendak were defeated by the very literalness of the construct. *What Can You Do With a Shoe?*, on the other hand, offers him some glorious pictorial possibilities as, beginning on the title spread, continuing over the copyright and dedication (576), he demonstrates "What can you do What can you do What can you do with a shoe?" The animated sequences are a howl—"What can you do . . . with a cup? You can gobble it up! Gobble gobble gobble gubble gubble gubble Crunch! Yummy! What a lunch!" But one after another shoes, cup, chair, broom resume their proper functions when the little girl—for it is typically she—has had enough of this nonsense; and I am left wishing that, just once, he'd trip her up. 'What you *really* do with shoes'—put them on your feet—smacks suspiciously of Mother-knows-best; or Chukovsky smiling at his daughter's little joke but insisting, by God, that dogs go bow-wow.

Why then does *What Do You Say, Dear?* (by Sesyle Joslin, Scott, 1958) not offend? It is, after all, subtitled "A Handbook of Etiquette for Young Ladies and Gentlemen. . . ." But listen further: "You are a cowboy riding around the range. Suddenly Bad-Nose Bill comes up behind you with a gun. He says, 'Would you like me to shoot a hole in your head?' " *What* do you say, dear? You say, "No, thank you," galloping off on your horse; and it's so ludicrous that you're laughing at the answer just as you laughed, to start with, at the sight of Bad-Nose Bill holding his six-shooter to the head of a diminutive, distinctly uncomfortable Sendak boy. *What Do You Say, Dear?* and its successor *What Do You Do, Dear?* (Scott, 1961) remain imaginary and remain nonsense where others, Krauss-Sendak in form but not in spirit, hedge and turn tail. Says *A Little House of Your Own*, between grassy nook and dining-cloth tent, "Of course you live in a house with your mother and father"; and several refuges later, "Of course you don't always want to be in your own little house all by yourself. Not even most of the time." (You're normal, of course, not some oddball or freak.)

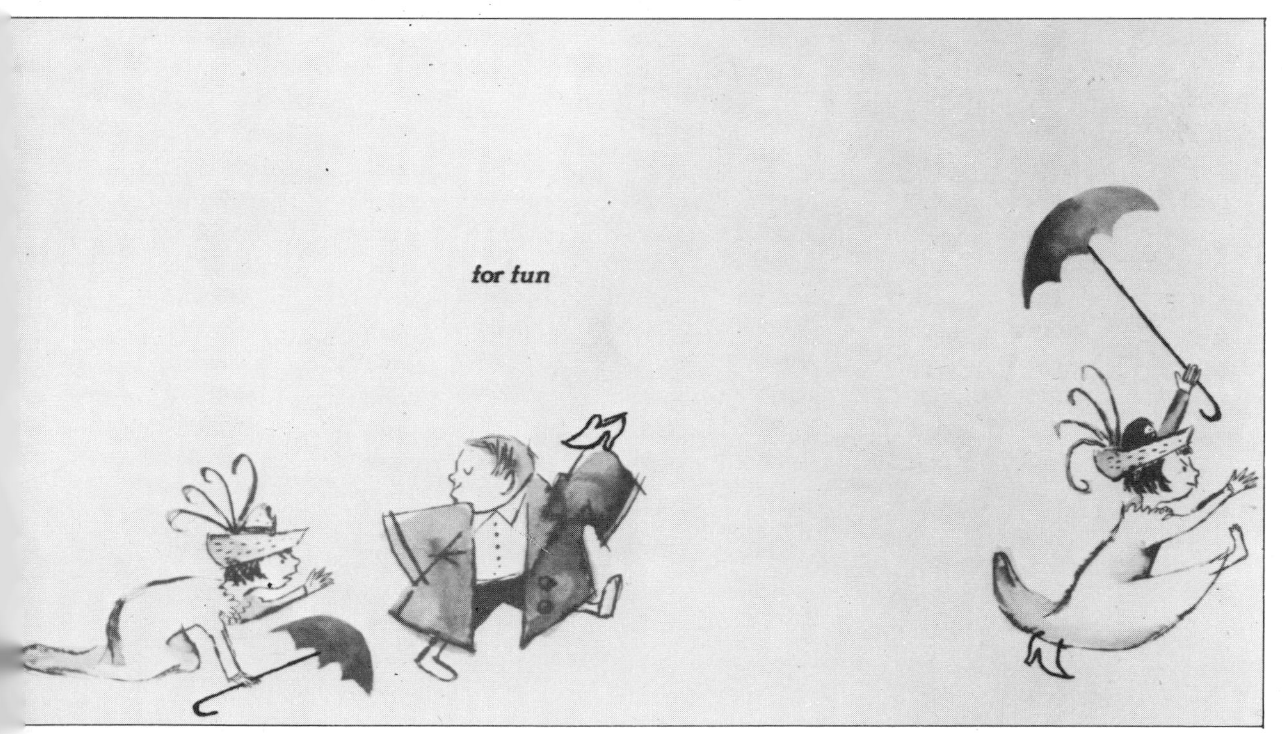

Quite apart—though it could, innocently, be a rebuttal to the last—is *The Tin Fiddle* (Oxford, 1954), the story of a small boy who wants desperately to find someone who likes his (awful) music. Explained author Edward Tripp, himself a musician: "Somewhere in one of Mr. Sendak's old sketchbooks is a pen drawing of a little boy playing a fiddle in the center of a ring of attentive animals. *The Tin Fiddle* grew out of a casual attempt to set this picture to words." Gentle, amusing, wistful, it is of a piece with the DeJong books and with the dreamers in *A Hole Is To Dig*. It is also, as they are, very much in pen and ink.

With *Charlotte and the White Horse*, however, Sendak had begun to use color—that is, to paint; and the color that is in *Charlotte* expressive, that illuminates a scene, literally and figuratively, much as a sensitive lighting designer illuminates a stage, becomes in *I Want to Paint My Bathroom Blue* virtually the whole show—there is almost no drawing—and we have with it the first of his leaping soaring boys, as vaporous as the color washes.

It is not to the point here to attempt to trace the permutations of Sendak's style—if, with so eclectic an artist, it ever is—or to conscientiously identify his sources. A flyer issued to introduce the film *Maurice Sendak* suggests that there be exhibited with it works by 'Antoine Watteau, William Blake, Wilhelm Busch, I. J. Grandville, Francisco Goya, Marc Chagall, Pablo Picasso, Henri Matisse'; and one could extract from Sendak's various written comments the names of perhaps a dozen others whose work he admires and has, in many cases, drawn upon. He is a frank and enthusiastic scavenger, a bent that Ardizzone identifies with the born illustrator; and the example of others, not only their style and technique, has given his work a range it could not have had otherwise.

So let us just say, lightly, that Sendak entered upon his Impressionist and Post-Impressionist period—at the same time drawing with nineteenth-century decorousness for the Else Minarik books, with breadth and dash for the Sesyle Joslin books, with surrealist particularity for his brother Jack's *Circus Girl* (Harper, 1957), and so forth. There is this to be said too, that when an artist attains a certain degree of prominence it is expected—by him and usually by others—that he will work in full color, more 'important' in itself. Presumably his books can be printed in a sufficiently large edition to absorb the extra cost, and he, the recognized artist, can spread himself as well as being spared the drudgery of doing separations. The last applies less to Sendak than to most, for insofar as he did separations, they were simple ones, color serving to supplement line, for definition and contrast. He did not compose in color and he is not naturally a colorist.

It is no disgrace; Picasso, for one, was not a colorist and, like Sendak, he was more effective as a draftsman and a modeler—using tone, light and shade—than as a painter. In *The Moon Jumpers* we have, by chance, vaguely Picassoid children (less vaguely close-up) prancing about in a landscape that is more or less Seurat, a painted setting for their ballet (577). The text is lyrical blather, much of it—"The sun is tired. It goes down the sky into the drowsy hills"—where that for *A Tree Is Nice* is notably not; and the book, with responsiveness its subject and object, begins and ends by striking attitudes.

Charlotte Zolotow's *Mr. Rabbit and the Lovely Present*, on the other hand, is a pleasantly matter-of-fact colloquy between a little girl seeking a birthday present for her mother and a rabbit who'd like to be helpful, and sometimes is. She has an earnest, hopeful look about her and he has the right cogitating air and ostensibly they move about the countryside discovering—because the mother likes red, yellow, green and blue—something red, something yellow, something green and something blue to give her. In actuality (578), they turn up in this dappled painting and that—deep woods, meadow, rocks and trees—without there being any sense of their going from here to there, without our having any sense, in fact, of where they are or where they're going; except when they find red apples, yellow bananas and the like, the pictures could as well be interchanged. The bananas are the remains of a half-eaten picnic they come upon; where the picnickers went, why they left their cloth spread, a cake half eaten, we haven't a clue. And when the rabbit suggests, "Well, there are yellow taxicabs," I wonder how in this never-never world, this pastoral no-place, he knows.

More seriously, the explanation may lie in an extension of Ardizzone's observation that the confirmed illustrator will model his work on that of other artists in preference to modeling it on nature. The version of the world that Sendak selected for *Mr. Rabbit*, the Impressionist, is of all possible models perhaps the least 'illustrational,' and as regards the text, inapplicable; he could successfully have recourse to Blake for *Charlotte and the White Horse* because the text has the mystical, impalpable quality of Blake's writing and painting, and Blake, the artist, illustrated—whether his own poetry, Milton or the Bible. To the extent that *Mr. Rabbit* has a particular spirit, it is closest to that of Mary Chalmers; but more in keeping, in any case, with Sendak's own Little Bear than with Monet's waterlilies (the light-flecked endpapers) or with Winslow Homer's watercolors (the scene illustrated, Homer's "Flock of Sheep, Houghton Farm"). In recording appearances, the Impressionists turned their back on content, however differently we may see their work today; in reproducing their record of appearances, Sendak at once disregarded his own content and gave us, to look at, reproduced paintings. And that in a double sense, for he was painting for reproduction. Impressionism is not a graphic mode—any more than, for instance, the Baroque of Rubens or Greco—but seeing such painterly painting endlessly reproduced has habituated us to it. In that sense *Mr. Rabbit* is the product of color reproduction besides: of the opportunity, working in full color, to work like a painter, a kind of vicious circle that has entrapped others as it did not, finally, entrap Sendak.

"Doubtless the most controversial book of 1955, Rudolph Flesch's *Why Johnny Can't Read* is still the subject of articles in popular and professional media," *PW* reported in January 1956.[3] Coming after John Hersey's 1954 attack on 'pallid primers' in *Life*, the spur to Dr. Seuss, *Why Johnny Can't Read* intensified the search for a better start than Dick and Jane.

Virginia Haviland, then at the Boston Public Library, had remarked to Ursula Nordstrom that the library stocked readers, deficient as they were, because children liked to show their parents, Look, I can read; and Harper's, with an idea to go on and a custom-made name, sought suitable material from its regular writers. What was found ultimately was, as so often, unsought: Else Minarik walked in with the manuscript, in picturebook form, of *Little Bear.*

The Random House Beginner Books, initiated by *The Cat in the Hat* and edited throughout by Geisel, were presented as supplementary readers with a controlled vocabulary—"ONLY with words which young children are learning to read in the First Grade at school";[4] they'd be easy, reinforcing and fun, and so they proved to be. The Harper I Can Reads, which appeared later the same year, set their sights at a slightly more advanced reader, typically one who had just finished first grade, and did not have a controlled vocabulary; but beyond the mechanical differences—and the practical difference that children can, customarily, read Beginner Books first—there was the underlying difference that I Can Reads were meant less as supplementary readers than as early reading: younger books. In the course of time they have been many things and not all of them have aspired to, no less attained, the status of a new basic literature; but some of them have—and there is always *Little Bear* to shoot at.

Little Bear is the story, as well, of Mother Bear—of Little Bear's wanting and seeking and Mother Bear's gentle, wise providing. In the first of the four episodes, Little Bear wants something to put on (579); and whatever Mother Bear makes for him—after the cap, a coat, after the coat, snow pants—he is still cold. "Do you want a fur coat, too?" asks Mother Bear; and divested of his new outer-

577. *The Moon Jumpers,* text by Janice May Udry, pictures by Maurice Sendak. Harper, 1959. $7\frac{1}{8}$ x $9\frac{7}{8}$.

578. *Mr. Rabbit and the Lovely Present,* text by Charlotte Zolotow, pictures by Maurice Sendak. Harper, 1962. $7\frac{7}{8}$ x $6\frac{5}{8}$.

wear, he is not cold: "What do you think of that?" "Birthday Soup" is Little Bear's substitute—"All my friends like soup"—for the cake he thinks his mother has forgotten; but when Hen and Duck and Cat ("Can you really cook?") are gathered around the table, in comes Mother Bear with a big cake—"a surprise for you. I never did forget your birthday, and I never will."

She understands, and he retains his dignity. To go to the moon, Little Bear jumps from the top of a little tree (580); and comes down with a big plop: "My, my . . . Here I am on the moon." The trees look familiar, and the birds and the house; and on the table is something that "looks like a good lunch for a little bear." Her little bear, Mother Bear says, flew to Earth, "So I guess you can have his lunch." Then, enveloped in her arms, in her voluminous skirts—"Mother Bear, stop fooling"; and she agrees, yes, "you are my Little Bear, and I know it." In feeling and expression, it takes us back to *The Runaway Bunny*, and sings its own song.

Talking about the Petershams, we remarked on the importance of the illustrations as an attractant in readers. In primers, in easy readers, they have the further function of making the meaning plain. Ideally, everything in the pictures is implicit in the text, and the child, understanding what's happening, can anticipate the words. The premium is on simplicity, economy, clarity, and on expressiveness—attitudes and feelings made manifest. In Sendak's illustrations, the suppression of detail and background is apparent in *Little Bear* and continues generally through *Little Bear's Friend*. Nor was it usually his way to call into play the roll of the eye, the lift of the head, the motion of the arms—to *project* personality and attitude, that is, to the extent that he does here. In that sense, and in the sense

579, 580. *Little Bear,* text by Else Holmelund Minarik, pictures by Maurice Sendak. Harper, 1957. 5¾ x 8⅜.

Here is Little Bear.
"Oh," said Mother Bear,
"do you want something?"
"I am cold," said Little Bear.
"I want something to put on."
So Mother Bear made something
for Little Bear.
14

579

Little Bear climbed to the top of a little hill,
and climbed to the top of a little tree,
a very little tree on the little hill,
and shut his eyes and jumped.
41

580

581. Mickey Mouse, from Robert D. Feild, *The Art of Walt Disney,* Macmillan, 1942. Detail.

that Little Bear is a character, he is not unlike the early winsome Mickey Mouse (581). But in his absolute bliss thinking of his new friend Emily, he is altogether human (584), as Mickey Mouse, confined to action and reaction—and denied reflection—cannot be.

No Fighting, No Biting (Harper, 1958) followed, a book that—through the stories cousin Joan tells to ructious Willy and Rosa—did much to make bad behavior an acceptable, approachable topic; and then, imperatively, *Father Bear Comes Home.* He is not to be seen in *Little Bear* and we soon learn, as if in explanation as well as anticipation, that "He is fishing on the ocean." Then he is expected and, says Little Bear, Maybe he saw a mermaid, "And maybe she could come home with him." First Hen, then Duck, then Cat fall in, Henny-Penny fashion, but Father Bear, waiting at the door, has no mermaid. *No little mermaid*!?!! "But I said maybe," says Little Bear, "I did say maybe."

As much as Mother Bear is the embodiment of sustaining motherhood, Father Bear is the exemplar of bluff, shrewd fatherhood. It is written in and depicted. Little Bear has the hiccups and not Owl's wisdom, not Duck and Hen's surprise appearance cure him; but, without any notice being taken, Father Bear does (582). In *Little Bear's Visit* the focus is on Grandmother and Grandfather and what they mean to Little Bear: Grandmother Bear's good cooking and Grandfather Bear's stories —postponed when Grandfather Bear ("I am never tired!") falls asleep and Grandmother Bear tells him, instead, a story of Mother Bear when she was little. Then Grandfather Bear wakes up; and they both laugh (583). It is a sneaky, spooky, scary goblin story he tells, but nothing beats the look between them, or Little Bear's skip, Grandfather's glow, when it's over.

Father and Mother Bear come to retrieve Little Bear at the close (only to find him, they think, fast asleep—listening) and then one can see distinctly how each is both bear and prototype: in truth, mother, father, grandmother, grandfather and little *bear.* Most difficult and most striking is Mother Bear as a girl; not a little girl but a young pensive girl, the heroine as a young bear.

Perhaps, however, one should reserve the palm for the hazardous undertaking that *Little Bear's Friend* represents, the injection of a human character. Climbing down from a tree—from which he saw not only his own home but something of the world (a town, a shepherd on the road)—Little Bear meets a little girl, Emily, who is just enough bigger to be little-girl size next to a little bear, and not too big to be not only Little Bear's friend but tacitly, delicately, Little Bear's girl-friend. Though the separate episodes have not quite the snap of their predecessors, the book comes off beautifully—and beautifully is the word, for there is a new romantic, poetic aura about the proceedings. Effectually and emotionally, Little Bear looking out from among the branches sets the scene for what is to follow.

We will not have occasion, in looking at Sendak's picturebooks, to speak of his illustration, in 1964, of Randall Jarrell's *Bat-Poet,* in 1965 of Jarrell's *Animal Family.* The poetic vision and the comfortable mingling of creatures are anticipated at least in *Little Bear's Friend;* but it is still very much Little Bear's story, as his sublime happiness suggests.

Coming after several years, *A Kiss for Little Bear* isn't. The book consists, this time, of one lengthy episode, the transmission of a kiss, intended for Little Bear—in thanks for the picture he sent her (585)—from Grand-

582

Father Bear roared—

"There is too much noise here.

Who is making all that noise?"

He looked at Owl, Cat, Hen and Duck.

"How can I read with all that noise?"

he asked.

And he looked at Little Bear.

"Noise?" said Little Bear.

"I was only hiccuping."

Grandfather looked at Little Bear.

Little Bear looked at Grandfather.

They both laughed.

"How about a goblin story?"

asked Little Bear.

39

583

582. *Father Bear Comes Home,* text by Else Holmelund Minarik, pictures by Maurice Sendak. Harper, 1959. 5¾ x 8⅜.

583. *Little Bear's Visit,* text by Else Holmelund Minarik, pictures by Maurice Sendak. Harper, 1961. 5¾ x 8⅜.

584. *Little Bear's Friend,* text by Else Holmelund Minarik, pictures by Maurice Sendak. Harper, 1960. Detail.

Grandmother was happy.
"This kiss is for Little Bear," she said.
8

585. *A Kiss for Little Bear,* by Else Holmelund Minarik, pictures by Maurice Sendak. Harper, 1968. 5¾ x 8⅜.

mother to Hen to Frog to Cat (who has to go into the pond—"Oogh!"—to get it) to Little Skunk who instead gives it to another little skunk, who gives it back. . . . And back and forth it goes, while Little Bear, eyes popping, watches, until Hen says, "Too much kissing," retrieves the kiss, gives it to Little Bear, the skunks get married, and Little Bear, the best man, kisses the bride.

Whatever was intended, what emerges in Sendak's pictures is mighty queer; he was illustrating George MacDonald by then (*The Golden Key* appeared the year previous) and there are similar ambiguous, prickling overtones. That there are overtones at all, that accompanying the lines "Grandmother was happy. 'This kiss is for Little Bear,' she said," are a monster picture, a dotty furbelowed granny—Whistler's grandmother—and a bristling hen, is an inversion of the Little Bear spirit of loving trust and, at the same time, a visual overload for an easy reader. Everything in the pictures is by no means implicit in the text; they are pictures to dwell on, set line by line to a text that is not only briefer than usual but says less than usual. Sendak, in effect, fills the void, as in actuality he filled out a book—not an I Can Read-in-comfort but a brooding picturebook which, for all their emotional weight, his own are not.

The year that *A Hole Is To Dig* came out, there appeared Dorothy Baruch's story of Kenneth, *One Little Boy.* "This book was written," she begins, "for those who want to know what children are like underneath the usually-spoken thoughts. . . . It could be about any child."

"The thoughts and feelings of childhood are deep and dark. If they creep out inadvertently and we meet them with the shock of believing them abnormal, we do one kind of thing to a child. If we meet them with the embracing sympathy born of having already encountered them and seen them as natural, we do another."

In the years since we encountered her congratulating the publishers of the Père Castor *Picture Play Book*, Dorothy Baruch, then a nursery-school leader, had had long experience as a child psychotherapist; she had also, in the late Twenties and the Thirties, written much for young children, and she wrote simply and feelingly. *One Little Boy*, in essence the story of Kenneth's therapy and hardly different from the briefer case histories of Erikson and others, was widely read and responded to. It seemed to touch a chord and it does still, when what it has to say is more familiar; with hindsight it seems also to have been written for Maurice Sendak, who drew from it the idea for his first book.

Kenny's Window is not Kenneth's story told and pictured for children, and indeed there is no direct parallel between Kenneth, the apathetic son of emotionally crippled parents, and Kenny, alone with his teddy bear and his dog and his lead soldiers in his room. But even in saying this much, and recognizing that apathy is a shelter from fear, we are coming upon Kenny throwing down his chalk and shouting at Bucky, the teddy bear, "I don't CARE!" when Bucky forbids him to draw a picture. "Can you draw a picture on the blackboard when somebody doesn't want you to?" is the question, the first of seven assigned Kenny by the four-legged rooster he meets in the garden of his dreams. If I find the answers, asks Kenny, "may I come and live in the garden?" But before the rooster can answer, the dream ends.

What we can say is that the seven episodes that answer the questions for Kenny deal figuratively with yearnings or fears that Kenneth confronts and comes to terms with in the course of his therapy; that when they are completed Kenny no longer wants to live in the magic garden, as Kenneth, no longer fearful of himself or of others, need not take refuge in asthma, failure or being a baby again; that both have the trust to look ahead, to put confidence in wishes and hopes. A wish, says the rooster, "is halfway to wherever you want to go" (586). This, however, is to read *Kenny's Window* in the light of *One Little Boy*. A more valid reaction is Ellen Buell's upon its appearance: "I must admit," she writes, "that the exact meaning of certain of Kenny's experiences eludes me. Children, however, have a way of picking up meaning and mood by osmosis. . . ."[5]

The shape is I think unintelligible because Kenny is indistinct. We have clues, but no clear sense of his condition at start or at close, and until near the close, little sense that his

586. *Kenny's Window,* by Maurice Sendak. Harper, 1956. 7½ x 8⅞.

"I thought I wanted to live in the garden with the moon on one side and the sun on the other, but I really don't."
"You've answered all the questions," the rooster shouted, "and you can have whatever you want."
"I wish," Kenny said slowly, "—I wish I had a horse, and a ship with an extra room for a friend."
"You can have them," said the rooster.
"When?" cried Kenny. "Where are they?"
"There," said the rooster, pointing out the window.
Kenny pressed his nose against the glass.
"Across the street?" he asked.
"Further than that," said the rooster.
Kenny stood on tip-toe.
"I can't see any further than that," he shouted.
The rooster hopped on Kenny's shoulder.
"I see them," he whispered, "past the houses, over the bridge, near a mountain on the edge of the ocean."
"That's too far," said Kenny and he looked away.
"But you're halfway there," the rooster said.
In the dark, Kenny's eyes grew big. "How did I get so far?" he asked.
"You made a wish," said the rooster, "and a wish is halfway to wherever you want to go."
Kenny leaned his head against the window frame and

thought about a horse, black and shiny, and a ship painted white.
"It's almost morning," said the rooster, "and I have to go."
He spread his wings and flew up into the sky.
"Goodby, Kenny."
Kenny watched the rooster fade slowly into the singing lights of the city.
"Goodby," he whispered.

condition is changing. What we have are the separate episodes or experiences and the extent to which they speak to us. The answer to the question "Can you draw a picture on the blackboard when somebody doesn't want you to?" which arises after Bucky has been left under the bed all night, is "Yes, if you write them a very nice poem," which is translatable as Yes, if you mollify them or, more positively, if you make amends, prove that you still care; but read it as one will, it's a long way round. However, Baby, the dog's fantasy of being an elephant, which gives us the answer to "What is a very narrow escape?" is, like the answer itself—"When somebody almost stops loving you"—touchingly on target: thinks Baby, "Kenny has lots of love for a little dog, but does he have enough for an elephant?"

Brightest, briskest (and my favorite) is "What is an only goat?" which takes Kenny out of the room, to Switzerland, up on a little mountain train, down to a village "that had only four houses and a great deal of mud," and ("My goat could not live here") into the presence of a goat that nibbles at his bouquet of flowers but declines, when all is said, to come to America to be his 'only goat.' From what Kenny has told him—confinement, no mud—"An only goat is a lonely goat."

The illustration—brown washes and gray over the pen-and-ink—is for the most part thinner and more pallid than was Sendak's wont, and the drawing is weaker, a reflection, perhaps, of Kenny's frailty physically and emotionally, but perhaps not: I may be reading Kenneth in overmuch. In any case the design, whether in the pictures or the spreads, is the more expressive element. The book as a whole hovers.

On firmer ground, *Very Far Away* begins the line of little boys whose names begin with M—Martin, Max, Mickey—who are Sendak stand-ins. We have seen authors writing reminiscence (Helen Sewell's *A Head for Happy*, Leo Politi's *Little Leo*); we have seen them writing for, and apropos of, a particular child; more recently we saw in Charlotte Zolotow and Russell Hoban (pre- and post-Sendak) authors writing percipiently about their own children. But to write about how one felt as a child was something new—as if Kenneth, grown to understand himself, were writing about Kenny. It is also of course the way all substantial writing about childhood is done, whether by a DeJong writing for children or a Proust writing for adults. But in fact of the picturebooks that dealt with children's emotions almost none had been about individual children. Margaret Wise Brown, we noted, almost never wrote about children; and the many eating-problem, sleeping-problem, sibling-problem children of the Forties are ciphers named Susie or John. In large measure it is with *A Hole Is To Dig* that real children enter in, with *Charlotte and the White Horse* (and *Harold and the Purple Crayon*) that individuals appear, with *Kenny's Window*, metaphorically, and *Very Far Away*, more directly, that we have individual problems and individual solutions.

Here then is Martin, asking his mother a question, "but she was busy washing the baby and didn't even hear him"; so, like Frances after him, he decides to go away, "Somewhere even very far away where somebody will answer my questions." (But because it is an artist's book and not a writer's, we get in one picture mother's preoccupation with baby and Martin's left-out-ness, in the next Martin, miffed, packing.) "Then he put on a cowboy suit and a false mustache—so no one would recognize him—and went looking for very far away" (587).

The old horse at the end of the street and the English sparrow he's talking to have their own griefs, and a cat that comes along adds hers, and soon the four are setting out for a place the cat knows "very far away"—"Many times around the block and two cellar windows from the corner." There Martin asks his questions "and everybody had time to answer"; the sparrow tells about the place where she was born, "How refined the people were"; the horse has the dream he wanted to dream, of lying in the deep blue grass; and the cat sings a song, many songs, and no one tells her to *hush*. "They lived together very happily for

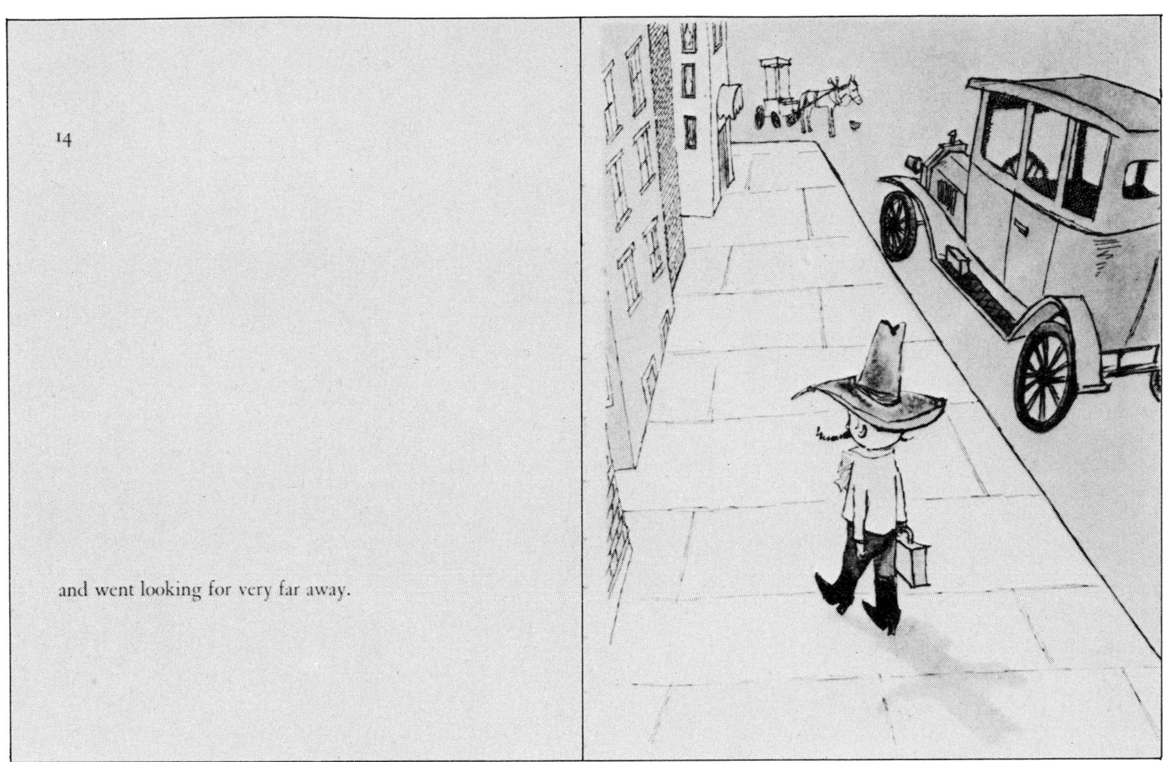

14
and went looking for very far away.

587. *Very Far Away,* by Maurice Sendak. Harper, 1957. 6 x 7⅞.

an hour and a half." Then the cat complains about Martin's questions ("I can't hear myself sing"), the horse tells them to stop disturbing his sleep, the sparrow remarks that it's not refined to raise your voice; and in a huff cat, horse and sparrow depart: this is not their idea of 'very far away.'

Left alone, Martin decides "Maybe the baby's all washed . . . But if Mama's *still* not finished I'll sit on the steps and count automobiles while I wait . . . And then Mama will tell me what refined means and why horses dream and why cats ever sing when they don't know how." Whereupon he runs home.

"Martin is not the first little boy who has decided to run 'very far away' because people are not paying enough attention to him," one review begins;[6] but, to splice quotations, "Maurice Sendak has produced a diverting fantasy illustrating the theme that the disgruntled runaway won't find the perfection he seeks outside of his own circle."[7] Several things are happening here. There's a new baby and Martin feels neglected; we might have had a solution for that particular problem, one that demonstrated to Martin and his fellow-sufferers that they were still valued; but insofar as there is a solution, it's that Martin has to wait his turn. His resentment is directed, in fact, not at the baby but at not being listened to, an ordinary (safe?) gripe; and in company with the refined English sparrow (!), the somnolent old horse and the caterwauling cat, he discovers that nobody wants to take turns, everyone places his own interests first. What was a problem has devolved into a fable, larger in scope. And just as Martin moves naturally from talking to his mother to talking to himself to talking to the horse and back, the story advances steadily on character and situation and resolves on those terms.

To call it a fantasy is to say merely that horses don't talk; but by now talking horses, rabbits, monkeys have become our familiars. The designation was prompted, in all likeli-

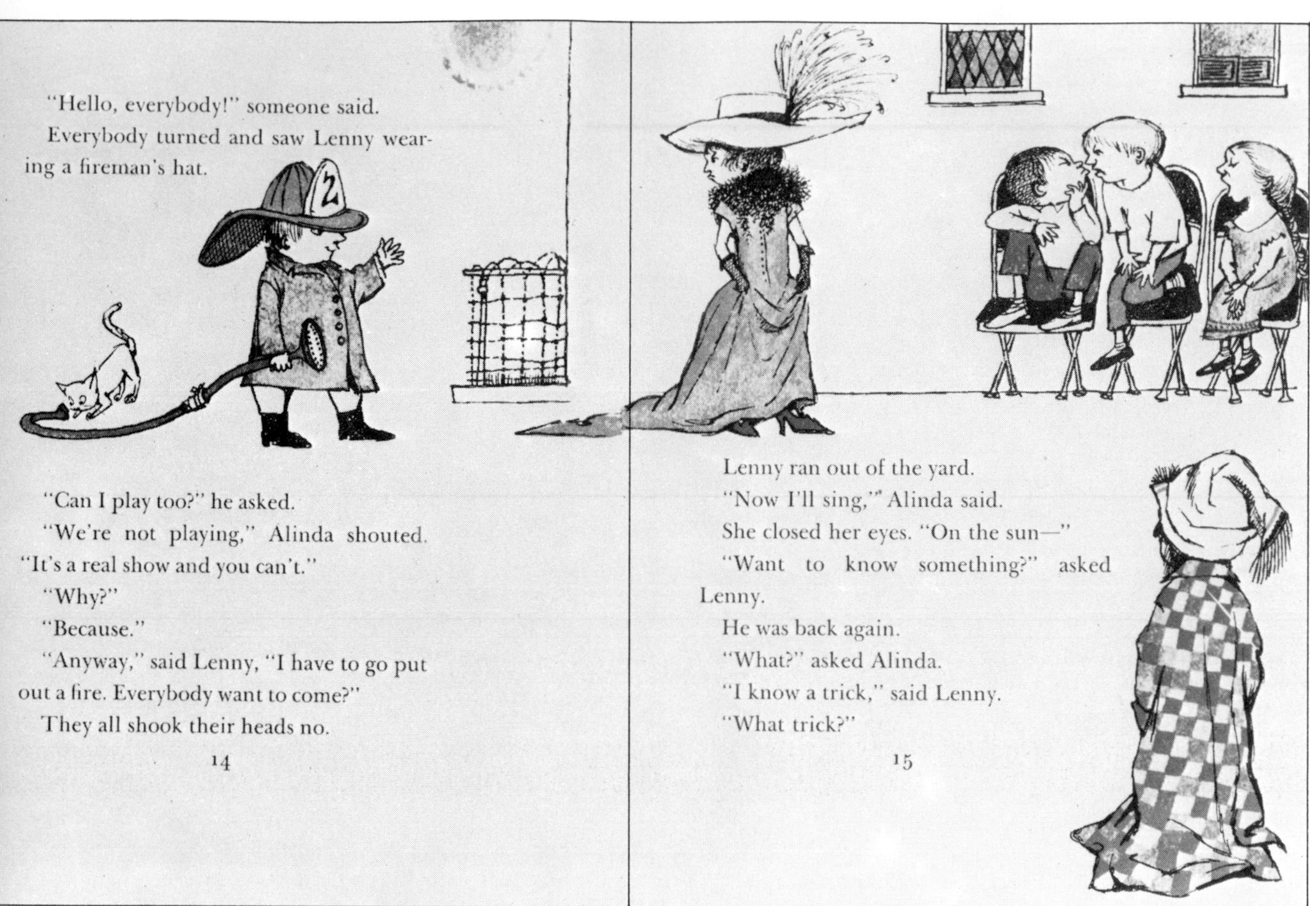

"Hello, everybody!" someone said.
Everybody turned and saw Lenny wearing a fireman's hat.

"Can I play too?" he asked.
"We're not playing," Alinda shouted. "It's a real show and you can't."
"Why?"
"Because."
"Anyway," said Lenny, "I have to go put out a fire. Everybody want to come?"
They all shook their heads no.

14

Lenny ran out of the yard.
"Now I'll sing," Alinda said.
She closed her eyes. "On the sun—"
"Want to know something?" asked Lenny.
He was back again.
"What?" asked Alinda.
"I know a trick," said Lenny.
"What trick?"

15

588, 589. *The Sign on Rosie's Door,* by Maurice Sendak. Harper, 1960. 6½ x 8½. **588**

hood, by Sendak's recourse to 'fantasy' to handle a distinctly human situation. With many benefits. It wouldn't be realistic, for instance, for four children to fall out over their very different bents. It wouldn't be Martin's story to the same degree—the animals serve as a foil; and it wouldn't be nearly as diverting as it surely is. In *Very Far Away*, the problem story takes its cue from the old storytellers, masters of quick, good-natured enlightenment.

The book that is not fantasy is *The Sign on Rosie's Door*, though to look at Rosie you wouldn't always know it (588). She's being Alinda the lovely lady singer, and Kathy, with the towel, is Cha-Charoo, the Arabian dancing girl, and even though fireman Lenny steals the audience, it was, they agree, "a wonderful show." Alone now, Rosie climbs on a chair, introduces Alinda, and sings "On the Sunny Side of the Street," uninterrupted, "all the way to the end." We see her from behind, a small Lautrec chanteuse whose back says all there is to say.

The explosiveness and the quiet are constants. In Chapters Two and Three the children have nothing to do, actively nothing to do; they sit with Alinda the lost girl (shrouded in a blanket—"I lost myself") waiting for Magic Man to find her and tell her what to do; and when it gets late—"I guess Magic Man isn't coming today," says Kathy—they separate, contented . . . (589). Then, Chapter Four, it's the Fourth of July, Rosie's mother won't be wheedled or cajoled into firecrackers, and Magic Man comes (eyes closed all around) and tells Rosie that she can be a big red firecracker. "And he told me . . . that all of you could be little silver firecrackers!" *Boom-te-de-boom-boom* . . . BOOMM!

I didn't say no fantasy. For Sendak as for Rosie and the other kids—"Did he wear a cowboy hat?" "And a mask?" "And wings?" (*Then it really was Magic Man!*)—fantasy is a fact, Brooklyn street or no. At the last Rosie and her cat Buttermilk come in tired—"We had a big Fourth of July day"—and go to sleep, Buttermilk tucked in bed, Rosie curled up on the rug; and to her mother's whispered "Good night," she answers "Meow."

The Sign on Rosie's Door is Sendak's closest approach to domestic or situation comedy and, in a book of his own, to genre illustration; his high-spirited kids have a home ground, with the substance we remarked on earlier—a richly sociable and naturally theatrical real-life. It is not one of the significant Sendak books but it is a nourishing one.

He likes books—of all kinds—and if you did, and could, you'd want to make once a set of little boxed books of your own, like the Nutshell Library (590). Proper library that it is, it has an alphabet and a counting book and a book of months and a cautionary tale. And, raffishly, they are *Alligators All Around*, an alphabet of alligators disporting themselves in the manner of *Bears* (591); *One Was Johnny*, who counted up his callers (592), and counted them down and o-u-t; *Chicken Soup with Rice* (593), which ends—*all together now*—"I told you once/I told you twice/all seasons/of the year/are nice/for eating/chicken soup/with rice!" Plus the cautionary tale *Pierre*, *Strüwwelpeter* post-Freud.

589

"Maybe he will come tomorrow," said Sal.

"Maybe," said Alinda. "Maybe not."

"Can we come and wait with you again tomorrow?" Dolly asked.

"I suppose so," said Alinda.

"We'll come earlier tomorrow," said Kathy. "Then we can wait longer."

"Let's all meet at twelve o'clock on Rosie's cellar door," said Pudgy.

"Twelve o'clock sharp!" said Sal.

"Sharp!" they all agreed.

And then they went home.

That evening, when their mothers asked them what they had done all afternoon, they said they had done so much there wasn't even enough time to do it in and they were going to do it all over again tomorrow.

"Good!" all their mothers said.

30

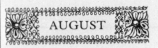

590. The Nutshell Library box. 1⅝ x 2¾ x 4.

591. *Alligators All Around,* by Maurice Sendak. Harper, 1962. 2⅜ x 3⅜.

592. *One Was Johnny,* by Maurice Sendak. Harper, 1962. 2⅜ x 3⅜.

593. *Chicken Soup with Rice,* by Maurice Sendak. Harper, 1962. 2⅜ x 3⅜.

594, 595. *Pierre,* by Maurice Sendak. Harper, 1962. 2⅜ x 3⅜.

591

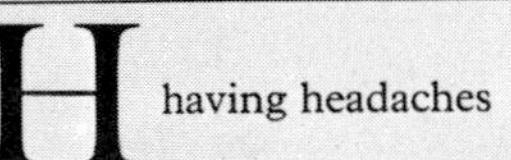

592

AUGUST

In August
it will be so hot
I will become
a cooking pot
cooking soup of course.
Why not?
Cooking once
cooking twice
cooking chicken soup
with rice.

20

593

His father said,
"Get off your head
or I will march you
up to bed!"
Pierre said,
"I don't care!"
"I would think
that you could see—"
"I don't care!"
"Your head is where
your feet should be!"
"I don't care!"

20

594

His father asked,
"Are you all right?"
Pierre said,
"I am feeling fine,
please take me home,
it's half past nine."
The lion said,
"If you would care
to climb on me,
I'll take you there."
Then everyone
looked at Pierre
who shouted,
"Yes, indeed I care!!"

46

595

No matter what (594), Pierre doesn't care. And doesn't care. "So his parents/left him there./They didn't take him/anywhere." A lion comes, threatens to eat him (*"I don't care"*), insists that he can (*"I don't care"*), asks if he may (*"I don't care"*), and does. His parents are distraught: "Where is Pierre?" From the lion, sick abed, "I don't care." Pierre's in there!

The lion upended, Pierre falls out, caring but not the least contrite (595); and a hero. In sum, a little nonsense library, all in rhyme, and except for *Alligators*, all about a little boy being himself.

Which brings us to *Where the Wild Things Are*, to

The night Max wore his wolf suit and made
mischief of one kind

and another

his mother called him "WILD THING!"
and Max said "I'LL EAT YOU UP!"
so he was sent to bed without eating anything.

That very night in Max's room a forest grew (596)

and grew—

and grew until his ceiling hung with vines
and the walls became the world all around (597)

and the ocean tumbled by with a private boat
for Max
and he sailed off through night and day

and in and out of weeks
and almost over a year
to where the wild things are.

In two sentences we have traversed eight openings and reached the midpoint and heart of the book; and returned, via Ruth Krauss's picture-sequences perhaps ("There are six friends/and they all put on each other's coats. It is winter . . ."), to Nicholson's riveting run-on texts: "One evening on the sands/ Mary found/the Pirate Twins—so . . . ."(77) As a form of storytelling, it had virtually disappeared. But the opening, you'll notice, is not the storyteller's customary 'One night,' it is the ubiquitous, exact 'The night'; and it pitches us straightaway, as the other (and an additional 'and') wouldn't, to the climax of the sentence, the clash between Max and his mother. The second has another familiar aspect, in effect a condensation of Harry Behn's child-image of time and the runaway clock (p. 486); but Max, in his boat, sails *in and out of* weeks and *almost over a* year, as one would sail in and out of bays, islands, seas, and almost over the globe—or almost more (maybe more, maybe less) than a year. Had there been any doubt that Sendak was going to be a writer, the text for *Where the Wild Things Are* would have been decisive. Try 'tumbled' for sound and for sense; or try to do without it.

Where the wild things are is where the pictures take over. From growing larger as Max's imaginings grow and the room grows to become the boundless page, they invade the second page, spread until they stretch across the double-spread and press downward until they crowd out the words; and for three openings have the field to themselves (598). "Now stop!" says Max, thinking of home; and the pictures contract, the wild things are left behind, and Max sails back "over a year and in and out of weeks and through a day . . ." (599). His room, his own room, is as large now as the envisaged world he set out from.

So exact a metaphor is it for his resentful rebellion, his release and his return, enhanced, to reality, that it needs no comment; and as exact an expression of fantasy as the visually present, the pictured or envisioned. Robert Coles writes of Erik Erikson as a young artist teaching the children of Freud's circle and in analysis with Anna Freud, the start, usually, of psychoanalytic training: "He remembers telling Anna Freud in one session that no matter how much he had learned about himself, psychoanalysis as a profession was not for him. He had been an artist, and he would be one again. He also remembers Anna Freud's reply, that psychoanalysis may need people who could make others *see*. That simple reminder," Coles continues, "was hard for him to forget—in fact, to this day he can recall her words. When I asked him how he began to build a bridge between art and

596

597

596–599. *Where the Wild Things Are*, by Maurice Sendak. Harper, 1963. 9¾ x 9.

598

psychoanalysis he said: 'I began to perceive how important visual configurations were, how they actually preceded words and formulations: certainly dreams are visual data, and so is children's play, not to speak of 'free associations' which are often a series of images—only later put into words.' "[8]

Words, in Max's world, are detonations: "WILD THING!" and "I'LL EAT YOU UP!" and to the wild things, to the wild thing in himself, "Now stop!" Instruments of control, of potential mastery; and unlike dreams, axiomatic.

The sureness of the pictorial metaphor means, too, that there is no disjunction between the reality and the fantasy—no possibility, as there was with *Sally and the Baby and the Rampatan*, of dissociating the fantasy from its context. It is not a possible catharsis, it is the story of a catharsis; and itself a myth. *Pierre*, directly antecedent, is couched still in terms of a cautionary tale, which gives it a kind of disguise or protective shield, and it is ostensible nonsense. When Johnny, in *One Was Johnny*, says to his unwelcome callers, "I'll eat all of you," he is talking to a blackbird and a robber. Max is threatening—and revenging himself upon—his mother, the mother of us all, and he's not fooling. She, however, is never seen; Max's quarrel is as much with discretionary authority, or the child-Fates.

No more than we see Max's mother do we, in reality, see Max's house or a little boy's room. It is in fact an impossible room, an abruptly foreshortened cell dominated by a huge bed; a stage setting. The miniaturists did likewise, and the early woodcut artists (600). The difference is that between the Ardizzone drawing, in appearance quick, spontaneous, replete with the movement, atmosphere, minutiae of life (575), and the woodcut—contained, concentrated, schematized, emblematic. The traditional popular mode of pictorial storytelling.

Only when the dream world opens up do we break into open space in a scene reminiscent of *The Moon Jumpers* (597, 577). Regardless, it is Max's creation and he comes capering out, a demon in what is appropriately an imaginary world. The wild things, in turn, are to regale ourselves with, much as Max does; and they are wholly upon us, on the shallow frontal plane, in a frieze that fills the eyes as it fills the pages.

599

At the last, wolf hood pushed back, Max finds his supper waiting for him; and overleaf, unpicturable, "it was still warm."

Where the Wild Things Are won the Caldecott, and made Sendak a celebrity and a culture hero. It won the Caldecott despite widespread misgivings, voiced as fear that children would be frightened; and that it did—the same year that the Newbery went to Emily Neville's *It's Like This, Cat*, one of the first of the new 'tough' teenage novels—was more than any other single event a sign that the old order passeth, that the dominion of the tasteful and discreet was at an end. (One orthodoxy is only succeeded by another, but that is to overstep our bounds.)

On the surface, the controversy it aroused resembles the long-dormant argument between the critics and supporters of fairy tales. But it found dissenting librarians on the side opposite the traditional library position of

600

600. *The Cologne Bible*, 1478.

601. *Dwarf Long-Nose*, by Wilhelm Hauff, trans. by Doris Orgel, illus. by Maurice Sendak. Random House, 1960. 7¼ x 9.

support for fairy tales as imaginative literature, and it found most, though not all, of the child-development forces, the original denouncers of fairy tales, ranged in the book's defense. What had happened was twofold. With the insights that psychology afforded, fairy tales, myths, legends had come to be seen as other than simple straightforward stories (however little agreement there was as to what, exactly, they represented); and children had come to be seen as rather less simple creatures too, and possessed of dark visions of their own. "The thoughts and feelings of childhood are deep and dark," we have quoted Dorothy Baruch as writing in 1952; approaching "This Question of Fairy Tales" in 1932, the same Dorothy Baruch wrote, "Little children need a sense of peace and tranquility," the start of a wide-ranging attack on 'fanciful stories.'[9] In the interim she had become a psychotherapist.

If we regard a myth as a metaphorical statement of the truth, *Where the Wild Things Are* is a myth; in everyday parlance it's a fairy tale—a full-blooded fairy tale where most picturebook fantasy is in the nature of fable. But it was, I imagine, consciousness of the first that caused unease, just as it was recognition of it—appreciative recognition—that catapulted Sendak to prominence as a prime mover, a vital force. He not only had talent, his work had meaning—interest to adults and power over children.

It is quite possible that working in a more generalized and pointed, less naturalistic manner came to Sendak in the course of illustrating old stories, a second (or third or fourth) career. The Andersen *Seven Tales* (translated by Eva Le Gallienne, Harper, 1959) is late medieval in style and setting and, I think, congealed (the major illustrations are also painted); but Wilhelm Hauff, the nineteenth-century German storyteller, and afterward Frank Stockton, provided more robust fare which, in different ways, Sendak's illustrations play up to. In Hauff's *Dwarf Long-Nose*, the comic and the pathetic are seldom far apart and Sendak, drawing with economy and vigor and real relish, gives us, up front, a cast of nincompoops and toadies the equal in their way of his devil-may-care children, and not far distant from the sublime foolishness of the wild things (601).

The wild things are not frightening, any youngster will tell you, they're funny. Sendak was looking at Rowlandson—the Stockton *Bee-Man of Orn* (Holt, 1964) is, as it were, after Rowlandson—and he knew Cruikshank, next in the English line of spirited, peppery draftsmen. In "England and Caricature," G. K. Chesterton contrasts the Continental ridicule of peculiarities with the English penchant for 'humane caricature': "The French prince called William [of Normandy] fat because he had had too much of him. But Dickens made Pickwick fat because you cannot have too much of a good thing. In this matter, however, the pictures of Pickwick are even more important than the letterpress. And, indeed, it will often be found that the English love of clear comicality for its own sake will be seen better in the old, clear, comic illustrations by 'Phiz' and Cruikshank than in any other place. Close your eyes and call up before your mind, say, an old English illustration of an angry admiral with a wooden leg. The wooden leg is insisted on, but not with contempt, and yet, again, not with commiseration. It is insisted on with gusto, as if the Admiral had grown his wooden leg by the sheer energy of his character. In any ordinary satire, in any ordinary sentimentality, the point would be that the Admiral had lost a leg. Here it is rather the point that he has gained a wooden leg."[10] The wild things are the gainers too, and—another Chesterton phrase—genial grotesques precisely.

Sendak had, besides, a standing admiration for Caldecott, successor to the tradition. His acceptance speech for the award given in Caldecott's name is the one in the long series that calls attention to Caldecott's particular qualities, and especially to one largely overlooked, in this country at least, Caldecott's way of enlarging upon a given text. Caldecott worked with nursery rhymes, and who does not know how a nursery rhyme goes? But, as Sendak points out, Caldecott's *Hey Diddle Diddle* does not end, happily, when "the dish ran away with the spoon," but overleaf where, without a word, the dish falls, shatters—and

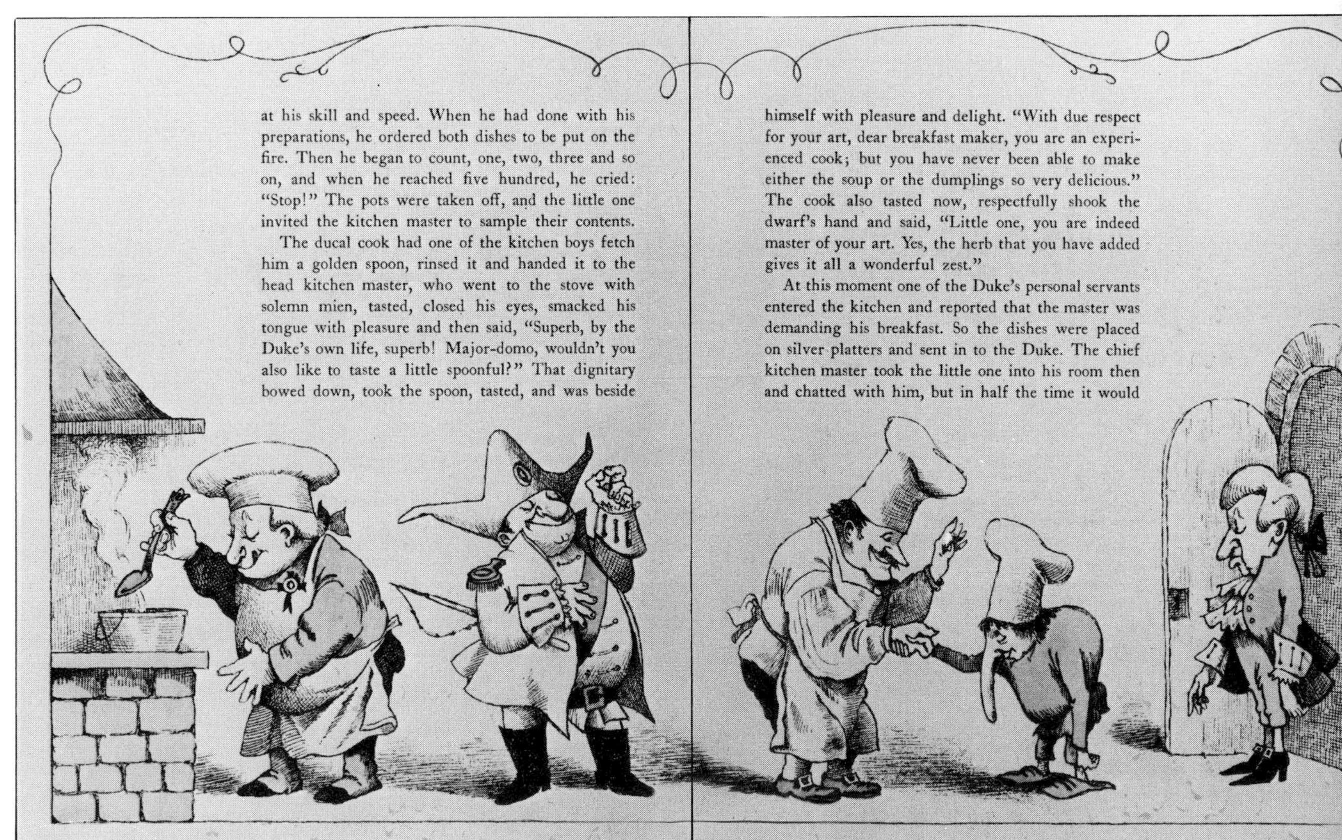

at his skill and speed. When he had done with his preparations, he ordered both dishes to be put on the fire. Then he began to count, one, two, three and so on, and when he reached five hundred, he cried: "Stop!" The pots were taken off, and the little one invited the kitchen master to sample their contents.

The ducal cook had one of the kitchen boys fetch him a golden spoon, rinsed it and handed it to the head kitchen master, who went to the stove with solemn mien, tasted, closed his eyes, smacked his tongue with pleasure and then said, "Superb, by the Duke's own life, superb! Major-domo, wouldn't you also like to taste a little spoonful?" That dignitary bowed down, took the spoon, tasted, and was beside himself with pleasure and delight. "With due respect for your art, dear breakfast maker, you are an experienced cook; but you have never been able to make either the soup or the dumplings so very delicious." The cook also tasted now, respectfully shook the dwarf's hand and said, "Little one, you are indeed master of your art. Yes, the herb that you have added gives it all a wonderful zest."

At this moment one of the Duke's personal servants entered the kitchen and reported that the master was demanding his breakfast. So the dishes were placed on silver platters and sent in to the Duke. The chief kitchen master took the little one into his room then and chatted with him, but in half the time it would

601

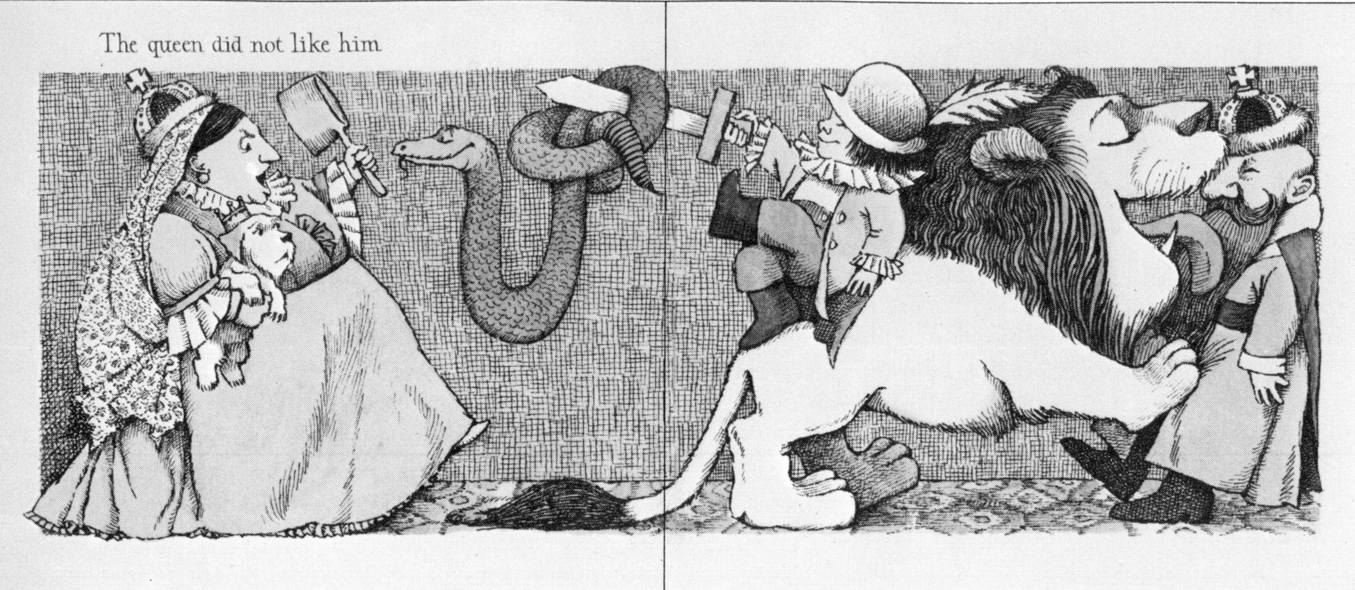
The queen did not like him

602

the spoon is marched off by her disapproving parents, a knife and a fork. "A last sorrowful touch," Sendak calls it;[11] and there are other such expansions, some more comical than sorrowful, within the rhymes as well.

Should anyone have missed the point, there appeared the next year *Hector Protector and As I Went Over the Water*, "Two Nursery Rhymes with Pictures"—animated sequences —by Maurice Sendak. As traditionally known, "Hector Protector" is plot without purpose:

Hector Protector was dressed all in green.
Hector Protector was sent to the queen.
The queen did not like him,
No more did the king
So Hector Protector was sent back again.

NO!
HECTOR'S ROOM
HO!

NO!

603

A school rhyme or street chant is identified by the Opies as a possible descendant; but whatever "Hector Protector" was to start with, it is an epic tale only in embryo—which is to say, for one thing, little known and less pictured; and all the more eligible for development.

Hector Protector was dressed all in green
  [over his adamant protests and those of the
  kibitzing bird.]
Hector Protector was sent to the queen
  [glowering,]
with a box of cake "For Her Highness."
  [Enroute, he smites a roaring lion, chokes
  a hissing snake;
  and riding the lion, brandishing the snake
  (and forgetting the cake),
  he breaks in upon Her Majesty—
  Victoria Regina, if ever, reading Mother Goose.]
The queen did not like him (602),
No more did the king
So Hector Protector was sent back again.
  [Good-bye to sad lion, sad snake,
  Hello to Mother, who has found the cake . . .]
  (603–604).

What Sendak has done, besides giving the king and queen cause to look askance at Hector Protector, is to give him the presence of a Max or a Pierre: Hector Protector he is, with helmet and sword—the scourge of wild beasts. And in so doing he gave children a story to figure out for themselves.

It was the beginning, the second beginning, of the wordless book, which we'll arrive at shortly; and the progenitor of many and many a wordless sequence; and the impetus, in other cases, for playing the pictures against a straight-faced text. Arresting as it was to see three openings of nothing but wild things, they constitute a kind of dance macabre, complete unto itself, whereas in *Hector Protector* —and the lesser *As I Went Over the Water*— the sequences where nothing is said (but maybe "No!") are, with the few words, what the story is made of. Caldecott, expanding upon this rhyme or that, gave it an interpretation of his own; Sendak, for all that he speaks of 'dimension,' has made something of his own out of the most cursory notes. In essence it is what he did in the Ruth Krauss books carried over into another area.

The animated sequences, too, of which the book consists with or without words, are founded in the fantasy sequences of *I'll Be*

602–604. *Hector Protector and As I Went Over the Water*, pictures by Maurice Sendak. Harper, 1965. 8¼ x 7.

604

You and You Be Me—which Sendak pursued independently—with the important addition of comic-strip framing, continuity, composition (for which see "Barnaby," 514). All this drawn, crosshatched and watercolored in fine 1800 fashion, as befits a time-honored rhyme. Verily, a classic comic.

Something of a classic in his own right is the blackbird who falls heir to the whole cake and suffers for it; harder hit, he is Steinlen's Bazouge (13) and before him Busch's *Hans Huchebein*, also done in by alcohol. Much in the way he expands the story, Sendak expands the role of the scurvy bird (who has *nothing* good to say for himself). Queen Victoria meets Max and Moritz is the size of it.

And this from the five uncommunicative lines set down at the start. However, had someone other than Sendak proposed, then, making a book of "Hector Protector" and "As I Went Over the Water," he would have been told by his publisher, Why don't you do "Old Mother Hubbard" and "Jack and Jill" (and "Mary Had a Little Lamb" and "Hey Diddle Diddle")? Nursery rhymes that people knew and wanted were illustrated and, except for the mass-market series, only in batches. The influence of its form aside, *Hector Protector* appears to have opened the floodgates to the independent illustration of rhymes—in part because of the possibilities for elaboration it suggested—and also to the disinterring of obscure and/or unlikely material, often for unusual treatment. The first might have come in any case, so general was the search beginning in the Sixties for additional picturebook fodder (about which more anent folklore); but the second development, of which the Emberleys' *Drummer Hoff* is a good example, seems clearly to be traceable, directly or indirectly, to *Hector Protector*.

What interested Sendak, he was able to undertake; apart from the merit his work was likely to have, it could be sold. For a considerable audience, indeed, his very interest in something lent interest to it. Thus, the collection of Alec Wilder songs, *Lullabies and Night Songs* (Harper, 1965), the one among Sendak's Old English books that is an out-and-out charmer; the auspicious launching of Isaac Singer's first collection for children, *Zlateh the Goat* (Harper, 1966), with its intense, introspective illustrations; new editions of George MacDonald's *The Golden Key* and *The Light Princess* (Farrar, Straus, 1967 and 1969), hushed and haunted. But he wasn't writing picturebooks, he was writing *Higglety Pigglety Pop!* (Harper, 1967), which insofar as it relates to his other work, relates at least equally to the foregoing. And apart from the wayward *Kiss for Little Bear*, he wasn't illustrating picturebooks.

When in 1970 *In the Night Kitchen* appeared, as much awaited as any picturebook has been, it was, as touted, unlike anything Sendak had done before; but more like *Hector Protector* than anything he had done since. No mists or quavers, just a *thump, dump, clump* and Mickey waking up and shouting "**QUIET DOWN THERE!**"

And he "fell through the dark (OH), out of his clothes (AAH) past the moon (OOH) & his mama and papa sleeping tight (MAMA! PAPA!) into the light of the night kitchen? Where the bakers who bake till the dawn so we can have bread in the morn mixed Mickey in the batter chanting: 'Milk in the batter! Milk in the batter! Stir it! Scrape it! Make it! Bake it' [605] and they put that batter up to bake a delicious Mickey-cake.

"But right in the middle of the steaming and the making and the smelling and the baking Mickey poked through and said: 'I'm not the milk and the milk's not me! I'm Mickey!' . . . [606] . . . till it looked okay. Then Mickey in dough was just on his way when the bakers ran up with a measuring cup, howling 'Milk!' 'Milk!' 'Milk for the morning cake!' 'What's all the fuss? I'm Mickey the pilot! I get milk the Mickey way!' And he grabbed the cup as he flew up and up and up over the top of the Milky Way in the night kitchen." (607)

Until Mickey is aloft, it's not to be stopped; until the words stop, that is, and we are once again, as with the wild things, all eyes. But the text prints effectively in paragraph form, you'll notice, as that for *Where the Wild*

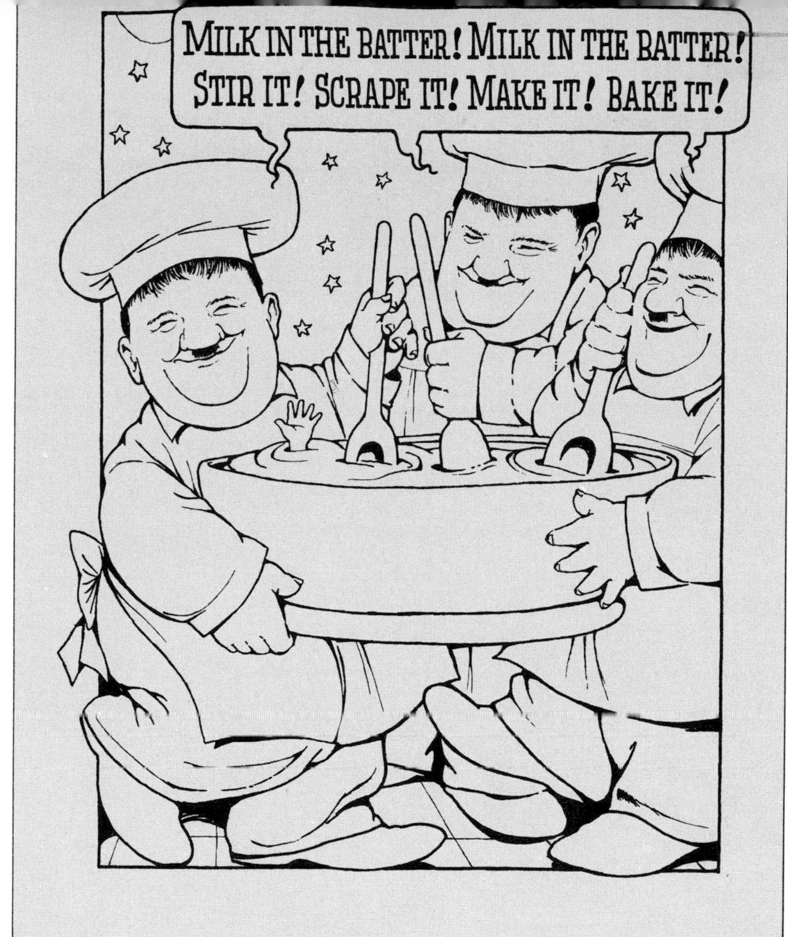

605, 606. *In the Night Kitchen,* by Maurice Sendak. Harper, 1970. 8½ x 10⅞.

605

606

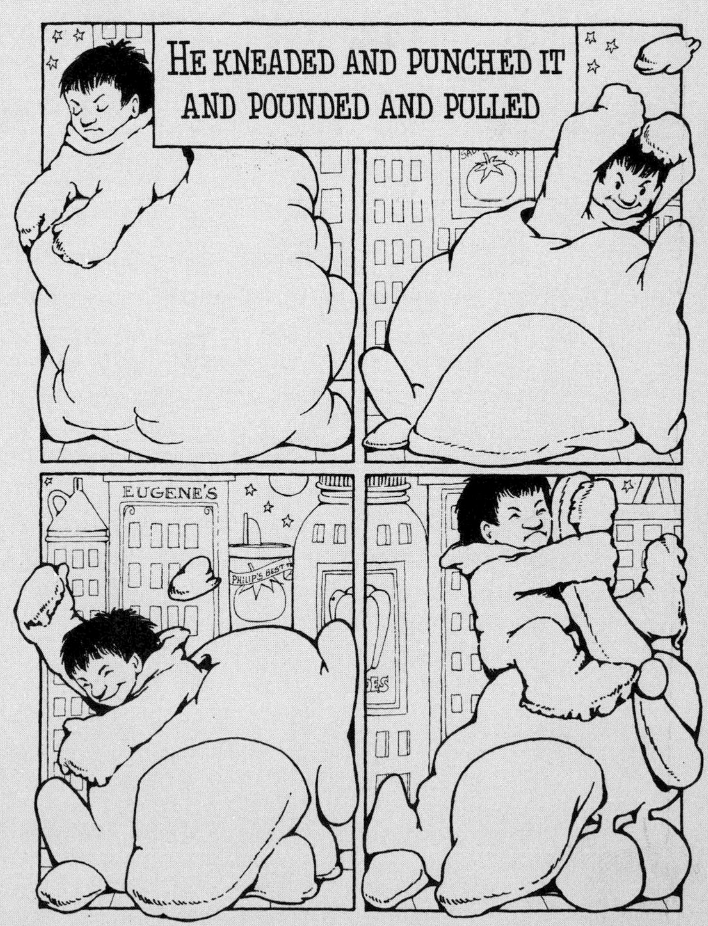

607. *In the Night Kitchen,* by Maurice Sendak. Harper, 1970. 8½ x 10⅞.

Things Are wouldn't; and yet it is composed, piece by piece, of captions in panels and talk enclosed in speech balloons.

In making his comic book Sendak has combined the two modes of comic-strip 'narration,' the caption and the balloon, exposition and dialogue, where one or the other was usually chosen; and in combining them he has integrated them into a continuous text that we could reproduce by enclosing the spoken words in quotation marks—a continuous rhythmic text, moreover, borne along by internal rhyme and near rhyme: a text designed to be read aloud, as a comic-strip text isn't.

Captions and balloons are one because both are bounded by the same heavy even line and the balloons, far from floating, are squared off, while the captions, rather than being appendages, are part of the total picture too. So, indeed, is the handsome lettering, like in weight, variable in size. It is a matter, now, of visual design, of treating the page as a unit in the manner of an illuminated manuscript; and Sendak, further, plays with his pictures as the illuminators did, letting them burst out of frames that in comic strips are usually sacrosanct. His model, notoriously, was Winsor McKay's "Little Nemo" (608); but the divergences are hardly less interesting than the resemblances.

July 26, 1908

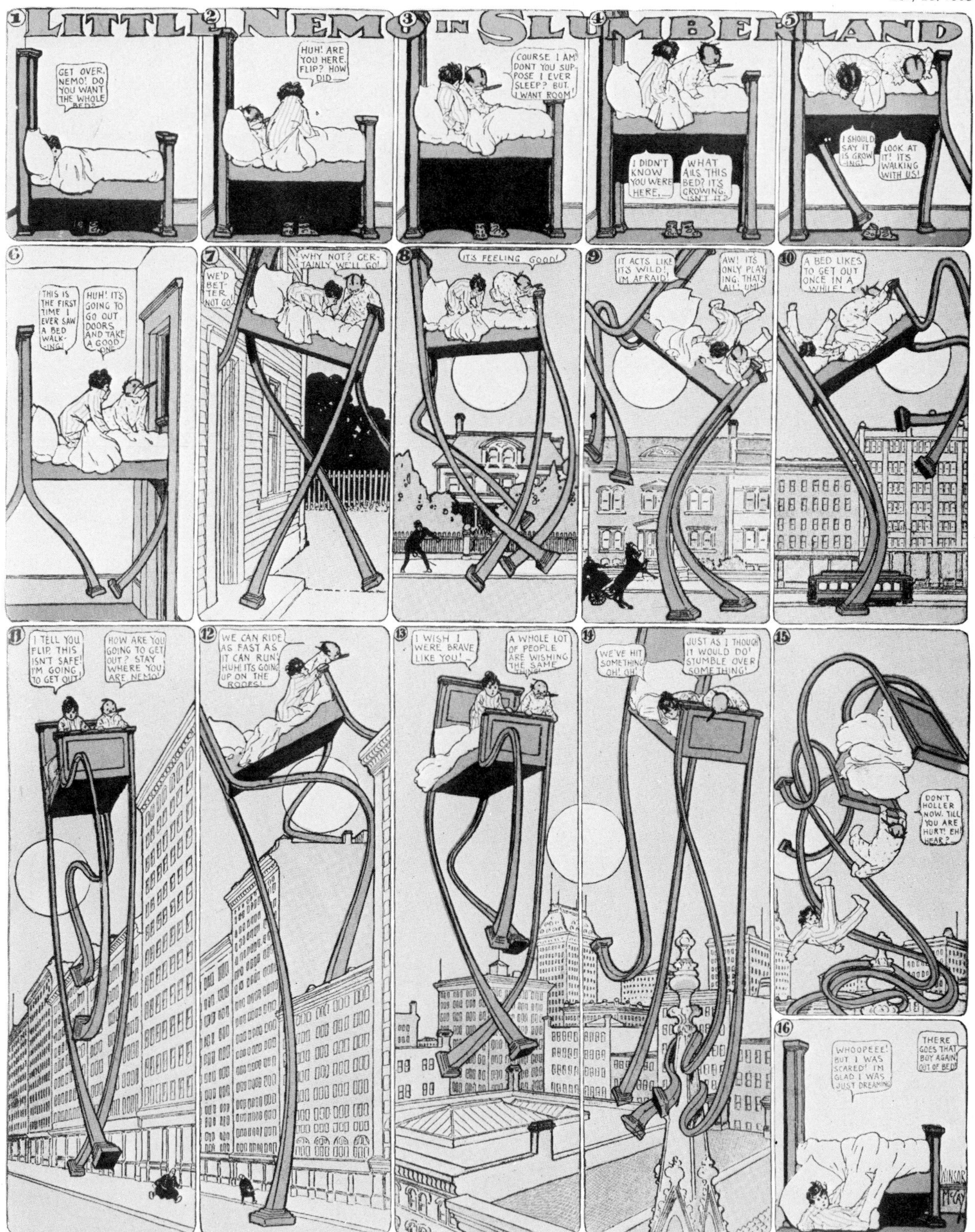

608. "Little Nemo in Slumberland," by Winsor McKay.

What Sendak did with "Little Nemo" is comparable in scope if not in kind to what McKay himself did with the means at his disposal. When "Little Nemo" started in 1905, comic strips consisted of rectangular frames—in effect, the separate pictures of *Max and Moritz* enclosed and brought closer (609). (In his picture sheets Busch made pages of them similar to Frost's infamous episode of the cat.) McKay extended his frames in length and width as the situation required, he altered their size to suit the dramatic needs of his story; and within this flexible framework he pursued (for one thing) accelerated narration, the decomposition of action such as we saw, in one form, in Caran d'Ache's strip silhouettes (260), in another in René d'Harnoncourt's *Hole in the Wall* (93).

It will not have escaped anyone's attention that the dramatic structure of *In the Night Kitchen*—out of bed, adventure and back—is that of "Little Nemo in Slumberland" as much as the pictorial structure; and that the central episode, Mickey as a dough-boy, is prefigured by the Sixth Trick of *Max and Moritz.* But so does *A Very Special House* anticipate the bounces and spills (508), and *I'll Be You and You Be Me* the magic transformations. The example of "Little Nemo," the specific motif of Busch, are catalysts: in the first and more important instance structuring—simplifying and fortifying—what had appeared as a spontaneous flow of invention.

As he made a picturebook text of comic-strip narration, so Sendak makes a volume

609. *Max and Moritz,* by Wilhelm Busch. Munich, Braun & Schneider, n.d. (first German edition, 1872). 5¼ x 8⅛.

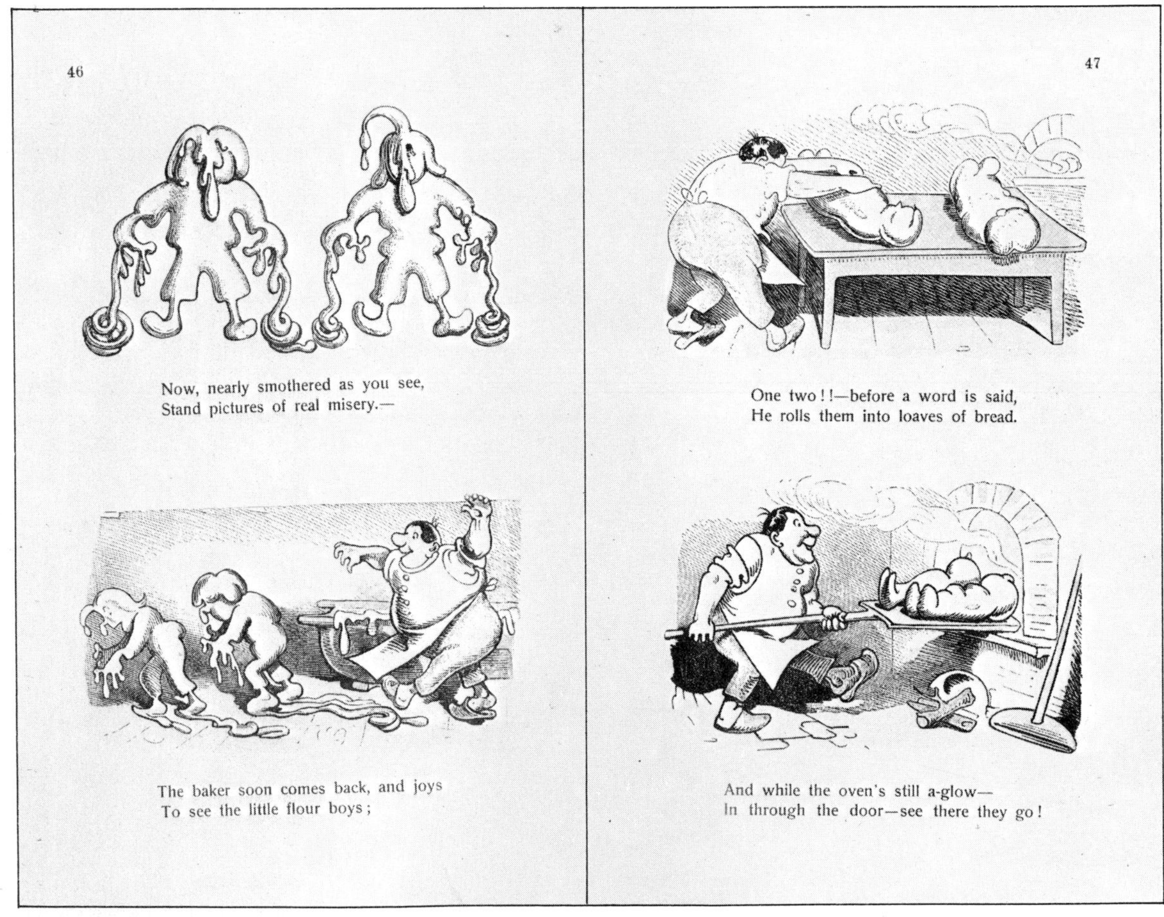
46
Now, nearly smothered as you see,
Stand pictures of real misery.—
The baker soon comes back, and joys
To see the little flour boys;
47
One two ! !—before a word is said,
He rolls them into loaves of bread.
And while the oven's still a-glow—
In through the door—see there they go !

that is a picturebook, not a comic book, in design; that translates McKay's structural flexibility into picturebook terms. Thus we have great full-page, page-filling pictures of the Oliver Hardy cooks (605); and overleaf a double-spread of the batter borne ceremoniously to the oven, with the grocery-built city looming behind. We have Mickey skipping one, two, three out of the oven (606), the separate panels breaking his fall even as they mark his descent; but though McKay continues his setting from one frame to the next (608, lower right), Sendak, doing him one better—and undoing the very idea of comic-strip sequence—backs his batter up from the last frame to the first.

On the right-hand page comes (1) the kneading and (2) the punching and (3) the pounding and (4) the pulling; and the looking and the wondering and the guessing . . . "till [overleaf] it looked okay." Wordlessly, below, Mickey spins the propeller; and when he's finally up and away, the book disappears, as it were, and what took on the aspect of a frieze in *Where the Wild Things Are* becomes a full-screen trick scene from a Thirties movie spectacle (607).

McKay, a prophet not without honor hitherto, has been referred to as a 'poet of the urban world.'[12] His cityscapes, drawn when cities had just come to look as he drew them, have, even in their meticulous rendering, a visionary quality, and he drew visionary cities as well. Sendak's fantasy makes of McKay's city, and Hollywood's, the kitchen-cabinet assemblage that we see, where egg beaters top one building and a shaker is the dome of another. A grown-up child's magic make-believe city, with lights shining from a bread-loaf el train.

There, "over the top of the Milky Way," Mickey is about to dive into the giant bottle (not part of the city proper but impossible without it); and, leaving his plane, losing his bread-batter suit, to swim about, bare as he was without his pajamas, singing: "I'm in the milk and the milk's in me, God Bless Milk and God Bless Me!" The cake finally baked, Mickey, with a "COCK-A-DOODLE DOO!" slides down the side of the bottle "straight into bed carefree and dried."

Mickey unclothed offended sensibilities, and a naked Mickey lolling in the milk and, after, crowing 'Cock-a-doodle doo,' was suggestive, period. There is much sensual pleasure, real and potential, in the Night Kitchen; or one could say that *In the Night Kitchen* is where sensual pleasure takes precedence, and stop there. But Mickey in clothes would be a mess in the batter and a drowning fly in the milk: we need him unclothed to avoid incongruity, we need him out of his everyday self —just as painters needed their nude Athenas and Psyches—so that he can be a figurative figure. Martin, you'll recall, put on a cowboy suit and a mustache 'for a disguise' and Max, of course, had his wolf suit. Dressed in a T-shirt, Max would be a tourist in Disneyland.

More even than the *Wild Things*, however, *In the Night Kitchen* has to be *seen*. Max's story can be summarized, sensibly, in a sentence; to put the *Night Kitchen* into a sentence or two—a little boy falls out of bed into the 'night kitchen' where three bakers mix him in a cake, etc—is to render it meaningless, not to say ridiculous. Similarly, the *Wild Things*, recorded, makes good listening with or without the book (noises do nicely for the beasts) while the *Night Kitchen*, heard and not seen, is literally unimaginable. Smooth-flowing as the text is, a narrative poem in effect, the pictures are the essential counterpoint; and, as in a piece of music, the two develop together.

We could expand on this, we could look further into the book: of all of Sendak's picturebooks, it is what one would call the most interesting. And to my mind, he has never drawn better. The reason for using, for the black and white illustrations here, the *Night Kitchen* coloring book rather than the picturebook itself is to show the drawing plain, the armature to which, in the picturebook, color was added. It is vital, forcible drawing, broad and clear and bold and yet quick with life. The marvelous dusky shades, meanwhile, take us back and away; this is stage coloring, an aura, almost an aroma of color. As a creation, the book could hardly be more successful.

It falters, I think, as a story. In Slumberland, Little Nemo has adventures, exciting, frightening adventures; Max, within and without, has an adventure too: in his own way he goes forth, to borrow Dorothy White's definition, "from security to insecurity and back to port."[13] Mickey's pleasant dream—enough said?—is an escapade. He is popped into the oven, true, but not as a consequence of anything he's done (Max and Moritz) or a wish to do anything to him (Hansel and Gretel). It's a case of mistaken identity—"I'm not the milk and the milk's not me! I'm Mickey!"—and as innocent, as harmless as the kind of Marx Brothers routine that is back of it. Otherwise Mickey's wishes are fulfilled with no more struggle than the effort to shape the plane; and even to speak of tension is to speak another language.

On the last page is a picture of Mickey, his arm around a bottle of milk, in a sunbeam aureole, and around it the legend: "And that's why, thanks to Mickey, we have cake every morning." Intimations of a trademark, that's obvious (of the Fisk Rubber baby with candle and tire, perhaps); and Sendak's little joke, but otherwise?

He has spoken often about his work and what it means to him; usually what it means to him is what it says to us, in the yield is the intent. But as a child he had, it seems, not only the common yearning to be part of the nighttime world, he had a specific beef against the Sunshine Bakers, "We Bake While You Sleep": "It seemed to me the most sadistic thing in the world, because all I wanted to do was stay up and watch. And it seemed so absurdly cruel and arbitrary for them to do it while I slept. And also for them to think I would think that was terrific stuff on their part, you know, and would eat their product on top of that. It bothered me a good deal, and I remember I used to save the coupons showing the three fat little Sunshine bakers going off to this magic place, wherever it was, at night to have their fun, while I had to go to bed."[14]

'And that's why, thanks to Mickey, we have cake every morning.'

Well, I had forgotten the Sunshine Bakers though I remember well the Fisk baby (whose significance to me was not what the ad intended either), which is not to say that the book depends on a recollection which, in any case, children can't have, but that the particular form that Mickey's—and Sendak's—wanting to stay up at night takes does not communicate the intensity of the experience. The meaning of the book to others falls short of its meaning to him.

But from it he made a coloring book: from this very personal, painstakingly wrought and expensively produced volume he made a sow's ear. It isn't only that kids could color it any which way, they could, if they wanted, try to color it his way; and either way—anyway—we've heard for years that coloring books are bad for children, that they stifle the imagination, impede creativity. Paper-doll books might pass muster, but coloring books, never. To children, though, coloring is more like lacing—or the cutting out of paper dolls—than it is like drawing or painting; an objective accomplishment, that is, over a subjective expression. Operative also perhaps is the impulse to fill a vacuum: old books will almost invariably be found with the outline drawings colored in. But theory apart, coloring books were generally dismissed—since those early efforts of Françoise's that we saw—as intrinsically unworthy, déclassé, dime-store rubbish.

If it was characteristic for Sendak to produce a coloring book because kids enjoy them and he makes books the way, indeed, bakers bake—now a macaroon, now a napoleon, now a tart—it was no less characteristic of him to make something plebeian. Beyond the manifold influence of his work, it has served to bring together the 'popular' and the 'artistic' strains that we spoke of as diverging upon the appearance of the aesthetic book. And in reconciling he creates anew: whatever its antecedents, *In the Night Kitchen* is not Tolstoy sweating alongside the peasants nor is it Pop art.

AWAY FROM WORDS

LEO LIONNI, REMY CHARLIP, *NOTHING EVER HAPPENS ON MY BLOCK*, WORDLESS BOOKS

Not to waste words: from design, graphic communication; from Sendak and circumstance, silent animation.

LEO LIONNI

On the record, it would have been logical to proceed directly from Paul Rand, firebrand of the Forties, to Leo Lionni, lion of the Fifties. In mid-1955 a "partial list" of the honors Lionni had garnered "during the past year" filled almost a column in *Print* and included his designation, by his peers, as Art Director of the Year. "All this," *Print* goes on, "plus being head of the Graphic Design Department at Parsons School; lecturer at Yale University; Design Director of the Olivetti Corporation of America; Art Director of *Fortune*; and, of course, Co-Editor of *Print*."[1] Where, not least, he contributed a monthly review of 'visual miscellanea,' old and new, celebrated and anonymous. A drawing by André François carries this caption: "André François, who like Steinberg, Osborn and too few others makes funny drawings that are both funny and drawings, sent us this invitation to his latest Paris show. We first met François a few years ago in *Little Boy Brown*, a sweet little children's book for children, parents, and poets. We still consult it as often as we do the *World Almanac*."[2]

To his "astonishingly varied activities" (*American Artist*[3]) Lionni added, in 1959, the making of picturebooks of his own; or, better put, a picturebook: *Little Blue and Little Yellow*. "The idea came to [him] when he was telling a story to his grandchildren. He picked up a few sheets of colored paper and created the characters of this book. The children were fascinated," continues the jacket copy, "and in retrospect, so was Lionni. He believes that abstract figures can not only communicate, but can be highly suggestive to a child's creative sense." For our purposes Lionni does not belong among the designers because he uses the devices and techniques of design, and its insights, for other outlying ends. He takes colored paper and makes a story.

"This is little blue," *Little Blue and Little Yellow* begins, showing us a true-blue blob. "Here he is at home with papa and mama blue. Little blue has many friends, but his best friend is little yellow who lives across the street." At the second opening we understand (610); it is a new language, and we have the vocabulary and the key; just as one can, given a particular child, his family and his friends Jane and Tim and Mark, devise a multiplicity of plots, so one could, with sufficient imagination, carry on with the life of little blue. But children are enthralled from the words "This is little blue" much as they are from the opening of *Umbrella*: "Momo is the name of a little girl who was born in New York . . ." accompanied by a picture of a peach and peach blossoms.

Lionni of course has in mind a plot intrinsic to his form—to his language of form and color. After pages of playing hide-and-seek (black streaks separate the patches one from another) and Ring-a-Ring o' Roses (the patches in a circle), of going to school ("in neat rows" in a black rectangle) and letting loose after school (just imagine), little blue, left alone one day—and told to "stay home"—goes looking for little yellow; but "Alas! The house across the street was empty." He looks here (on a white page) and there (on a black page) "and everywhere . . . until suddenly [the page is red], around a corner"—turn quickly—"there was little yellow!" They hug each other and hug each other "until they were green": one solid light green.

(611) Such a good time they have until, tired (the patch inert at the foot of the page), they go home. "You are not our little blue," say mama and papa blue; "You are not our little yellow," say mama and papa yellow. Little blue and little yellow cry, they cry big blue and yellow tears "until they were *all* tears"; and when they have "pulled themselves together" ("Will they believe us now?"), they are welcomed by mama and papa blue, and amid the general hugging, *they* turn green! It only remains to spread the news . . . "They all hugged each other with joy and the children played until suppertime."

The fascination in seeing *how* all these marvelous things happen—not only how little blue and little yellow become green but how they play in the park, run through a tunnel (611)—is akin to that of seeing how Crockett Johnson's Harold, frightened, his pencil-hand shaking, falls into the ocean. It is tangible but not literal: the sense, the feel of the experience—and isolated in Lionni's case, more immediate, more acute than the reality: the experience symbolized.

So, too, does the story have symbolic meaning—as individual or as general as one chooses. He was not writing about racial seg-

610, 611. *Little Blue and Little Yellow,* by Leo Lionni. Obolensky, 1959. 8 x 8.

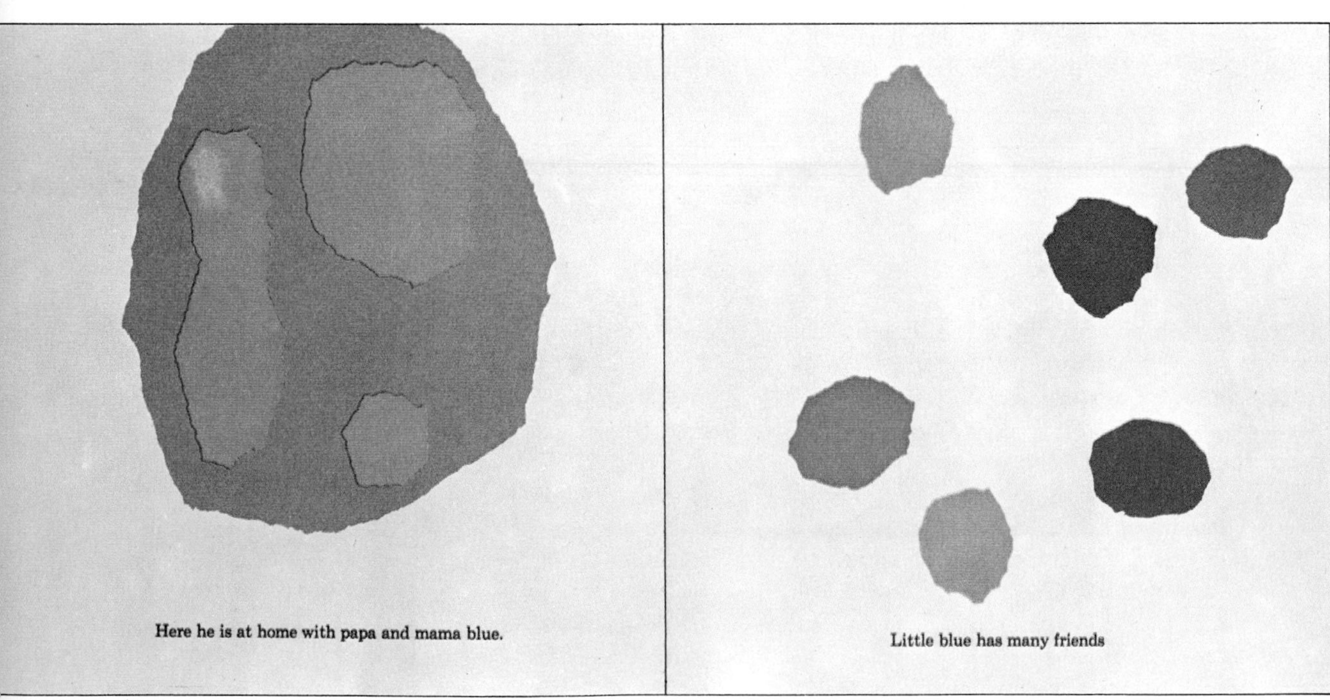
Here he is at home with papa and mama blue.
Little blue has many friends

610

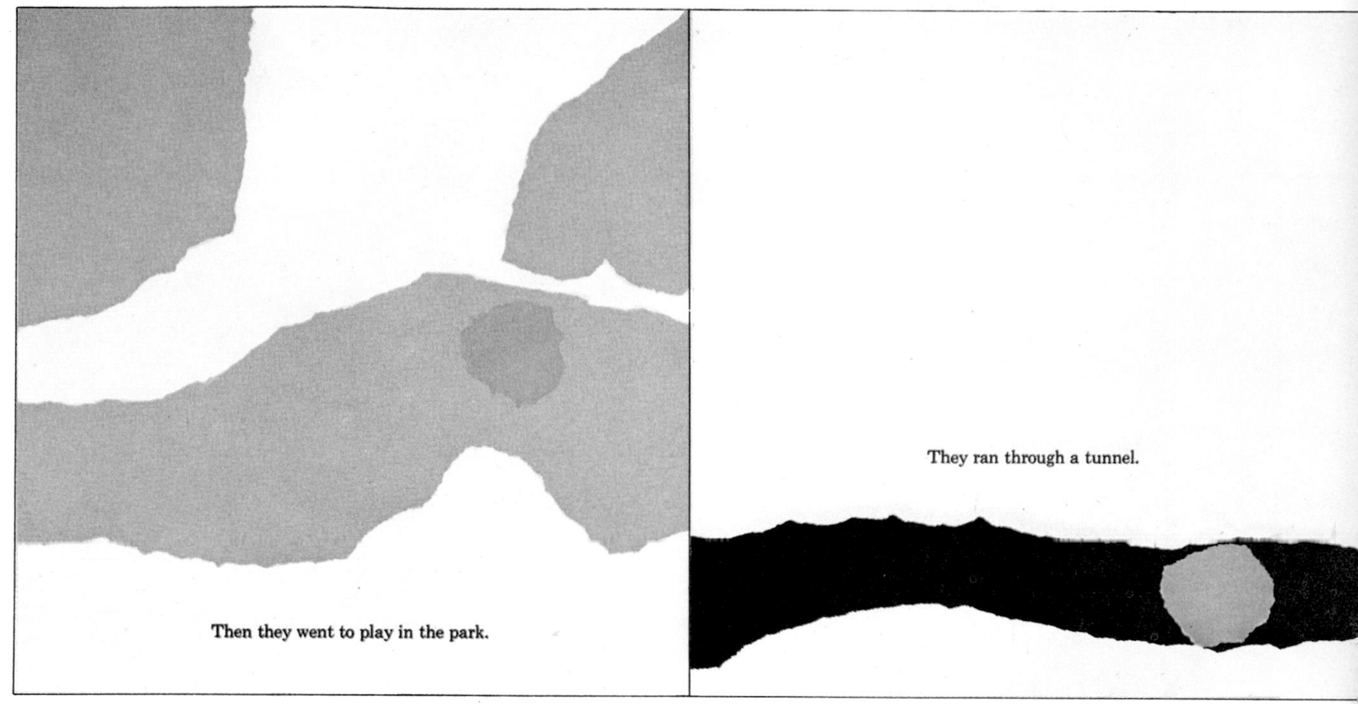

Then they went to play in the park.
They ran through a tunnel.

611

regation, Lionni has said; but, quite evidently, it was as natural for him to be thinking about it then as for the question to be raised. In allegorical form, he portrayed human problems and human situations: "It is easier to isolate situations, to bring them to a clean, uncluttered, symbolic pitch *outside* of ourselves." Speaking of a later book, the story of a little fish who discovers how to make the ocean safe for his kind, Lionni continues: "What a ponderous, complex story *Swimmy* could have been if some cruel dictator had slaughtered a whole village and only a little boy had been able to escape. One would have had to describe a plausible historical background and justify the characters in all the intricacies of human terms. Of course one can write such stories. Tolstoy could, Hemingway could. But I am not a novelist. To tell and illustrate such an epic in 30 pages for small children would be an absurd task."[4]

Nor would the conclusions, thinking particularly of *Little Blue and Little Yellow,* be as inescapable or, on the other hand, as admissible: to introduce circumstance is immediately to allow of exception, whether in the story or in oneself. We are at one with little blue and little yellow—as we were at one with Spotty—because we feel for them, but the significance of their plight is not forced upon us: it is because we feel it as a plight, see its source and understand its irrationality, that we can grasp its significance. And to the extent that the behavior in *Spotty* is indeed silly, it may be easier to dissociate ourselves from it than from the purely visual analogy that *Little Blue and Little Yellow* presents. "This is little blue"; and by the power we possess to abstract and identify, it is you and me.

To find spreads the equal of these in sheer visual force we have to go back to Charles Shaw, to *It Looked Like Spilt Milk* (322, 323), another that is in its own way 'suggestive to a child's visual sense.' Of further picturebooks that, on the other hand, engage us with abstract universals I can think offhand of only one, and that not for children, Norton Juster's tongue-in-cheek romance of *The Dot and the Line.* Lionni isn't joking but *Little*

612

612, 613. *Inch by Inch,* by Leo Lionni. Obolensky, 1960. 9 x 11.

Blue and Little Yellow is inherently funny: it *is* funny, an order of Nonsense, for a blue blob and a yellow blob to be best friends, for them to merge into a patch of green, for the green to emit blue and yellow tears. Lear would have appreciated it; he who could, with his own logical illogic, cast tragedy upon the Quangle Wangle and the Yonghy-Bonghy-Bò and the Pobble Who Has No Toes. Except for want of a better word, one has in actuality no business calling little blue a blob; he is no more to be considered nondescript than a Charles Shaw cloud, the one that is "just a Cloud in the Sky." Ultimately it is the artist in both Lionni and Shaw that gives their books character, and Lionni's art that gives his conviction.

"Floating shapes of color transform the flat confine of the page into an airy space—three-dimensional in feeling," Lionni wrote on another, earlier occasion; and, "Shapes with a spontaneous, undesigned look have the vivacity of a handmade object."[5] As we know, he was working in torn paper in *Little Blue and Little Yellow*; in the larger sense, in collage. For his next book, *Inch by Inch*, he used collage in the more particular sense of pre-printed or otherwise prepared paper—paper which by its own nature contributes to the image—and for equally evident reason.

Inch by Inch is the story of an inchworm who, to prove to a hungry robin that he is not dispensable—"I measure things"—proceeds to measure the robin's tail; and, set to measuring other birds, in whole or in part, takes the order to measure the nightingale's song ("or I'll eat you for breakfast") as an opportunity to measure and measure "Inch by Inch . . . [613] until he inched out of sight."

As an imaginative construct, it has the simplicity and inevitability of a poem; and with its sharply quizzical, block-patterned robin, its brilliantly crayoned head of a toucan, its sinuous neck of a flamingo, its elegantly elongated heron (612)—all silhouetted against stark white paper—it is a breathtaking thing to look at. I tend to think of it as Lionni's Italian book and to associate it with Bruno Munari, whose picturebooks had been appearing in Italy since 1945 (and more recently in the United States). It is not just that Munari too is fond of flamingos, it is the cleanness and sharpness of the white page, and the vivid clarity of the forms.

But what was seen was less the composure than the textured and patterned paper; and with collage in the air (following Matisse's *papiers découpés*, Rand's bits and pieces) and full-color reproduction, requisite for full collage, becoming more feasible, it directed artists into paper jungles that are with us still. Lionni's grasses, silhouetted cut-paper forms, exist to be measured by the inchworm; stretching across the spread, they form a clear-cut yardstick by which, as he measures away, to gauge his progress. At the same time they have the interest, across an expanse, of independent and related visual forms; and, pictorially, they evoke what they represent. Where collage has appeared since, it has seldom appeared to such advantage.

Swimmy (Pantheon, 1963) is a more questionable quantity altogether; the situation, too, has not the tight rightness of *Little Blue and Little Yellow* or *Inch by Inch.* One little fish in a red school, inexplicably black and faster than the others, escapes being swallowed by a predatory tuna; and, "scared, lonely and very sad," regains his accustomed *joie de vivre* in swimming "from marvel to marvel"—"a medusa made of rainbow jelly," a "forest of seaweeds growing from sugar-

candy rocks," "sea anemones who looked like palm trees swaying in the wind"—before finding another school of little fish just like his own. The way to be safe and SEE things, Swimmy concludes, is for the little fish to swim close together in the shape of a giant fish, and he will be the eye.

Objections can be raised on every hand. For a lone little fish-child, happiness is not 'a medusa made of rainbow jelly,' nor would a sea anemone look to him like 'palm trees swaying in the wind.' In union there may be strength, sometimes, but the composite fish remains a lot of little fishes: the visual illusion is visibly illusory (as, for instance, the nest woven of Harry's rose-strewn sweater is not). But if *Swimmy* does not cohere, if we are conscious, always, of Lionni pulling the strings, it is ravishing to look at in turn—a wet-wash wonderland that set up waves of its own.

It is impossible to see—at all—and not recognize the beauty of Lionni's books; or, indeed, to feel and not acknowledge the sincerity of his purpose. But of subsequent titles *The Biggest House in the World* (Pantheon, 1968) seems to me to most nearly come together—the pictures to be most closely expressive of the parable, and that a pictorial one. A small snail says to his father, "When I grow up I want to have the biggest house in the world"; and his father tells him a story of a little snail, *"just like you,"* who made his house grow and grow . . . until it was as big as a melon . . . sprouted pointed bulges . . . acquired beautiful bright designs . . . and was taken by a swarm of butterflies for a cathedral (or a circus). But, unable to move on for more food, the little snail *"slowly faded away"*; and in time his house too crumbled *"until nothing remained at all."* The small listener has learned his lesson—as, from the vision of Rome-in-ruins, have we all; and he goes off happily through a wordless spread of giant ferns and budding stems, cracked, weather-worn bark, stones of all shapes and sizes, flowers, grasses, moss—as wonderful and, enlarged, as amazing as the enormous shell. One stone is as brilliantly spotted.

REMY CHARLIP

We met Remy Charlip having fun in *Dress Up and Let's Have a Party* (424); and left him in the course of asking *Where Is Everybody?* (425) but before the imminent downpour that, moving across the spread, sends the bird diving into the tree, the man and boy into the house, the deer into the woods and, loosing a curtain of rain, obliterates one and all (614). Picture-language, graphic drama; and a reminder that Charlip was a designer and a choreographer.

As a creator he was also, as needn't follow, a peculiarly creative illustrator. Margaret Wise Brown had left some odds and ends that at a glance one would take as unlikely candidates for illustration. One was "The Dead Bird," a story Brown had written for her first collection, *The Fish with the Deep Sea Smile*, that is complete and self-sustaining as it is (p. 253). But *The Fish with the Deep Sea Smile* had long been out of print, the subject was one that the Fifties would be glad to see aired, and Charlip, drawing with a naive simplicity neither literal nor sentimental, could picture the story in the tenor of the text.

That he might was to be known from *David's Little Indian* (Scott, 1956). A little boy finds in the woods a tiny Indian, "no bigger than an ear of corn," but real; his first sound is *"Ugh!"* Asked what day it is, just what he's been pondering, he replies, *"Day of the dark bright light."* "And the little boy looked up and saw the dark bright light of that late summer day." Told that the little boy's name is David, he gives his as *"Carpe Diem,"* and explains: *"Carpe Diem means in your language 'Seize-The-Day.' It is a Latin name meaning 'Wo No So' in Indian. What does David mean?"* David doesn't know, but, grunts the little Indian, *"David must mean something."*

What the friendship between David and Carpe Diem means is in truth seize-the-day—the day of the bright green tree, of the little blue dish, of the yellow leaves falling, of the birds flying away; each of which Charlip represents by a sign, a color-field, a detail or just so. It is elusive but firm—like the friend-

A rain cloud floats by in the sky.

614. *Where Is Everybody?* by Remy Charlip. Scott, 1957. 9¼ x 7¼.

ship, which is sealed by the mingling of blood. Carpe Diem, I might add, is easily to be taken for a little wooden Indian.

Queer enough; but what as a picturebook would you make of this?

Oh, he walked around the world
on his four fur feet,
his four fur feet,
his four fur feet.
And he walked around the world
on his four fur feet
and never made a sound—O.

It came, a note at the back of *Four Fur Feet* tells us, from a collection of unpublished MWB poems. "Remy Charlip wanted to do this poem as a picture book when he first saw the collection. But it was not until his third working dummy that he conceived the present brilliant solution for the book."

Charlip's solution for walking around the world and staying on your feet—keeping up, up and down, down—is a book designed to be turned around too; and for the globe-circling animal, four giant fur feet (615). When he's gone around once—"along the river," "by the railroad," "into the country"—he folds up his four fur feet

and lies down; and dreams a dream that the world is round; "And"—another upright picture—"he walked around the world/on his four fur feet,/his four fur feet. . . ." It might go on, like the *Merry Go Round*, forever.

Thoughts of Crockett Johnson are not inappropriate. One of the two texts that Johnson undertook to illustrate (apart from his own and Ruth Krauss's) was, you may remember, Bernadine Cook's *The Little Fish That Got Away*. Bernadine Cook, a meteor in the Scott firmament, wrote another almost its equal, *The Curious Little Kitten* (1956), that Charlip illustrated with a like feeling for the least movement. Across a groundline that is a line (of grass) move a cautious turtle and a curious kitten, the first away from his pool (left), the second away from the fence that stands for home (right); and when the turtle, slapped, pulls in his head and then his feet, the kitten goes round behind him; and when the turtle pokes his head out and turns round, the kitten starts to step backward. "And the turtle took a step. And the kitten took a step." And another, and another, "Until the

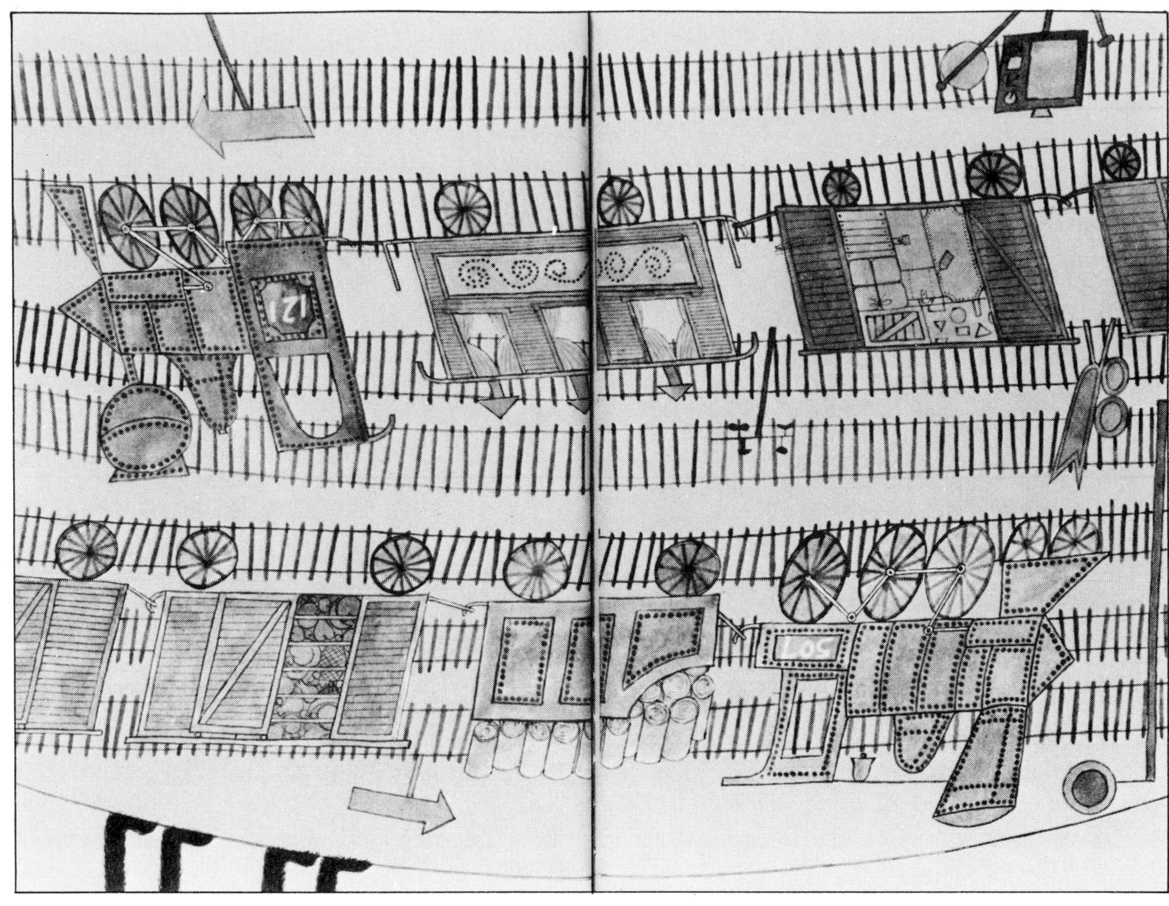

615. *Four Fur Feet,* text by Margaret Wise Brown, pictures by Remy Charlip. Scott, 1961. 6⅝ x 9⅞.

pool was right exactly behind him . . . Then the turtle took one more step. And the kitten took one more step. And, oh, my!" With the scene never changing, position is paramount; and with the pool always there, you can see danger looming and—*watch out*—see the SPLASH! coming.

Meanwhile Charlip was active with the Paper Bag Players, the group that, anticipated by *Dress Up*, put on plays for children using simple improvised materials; and first *The Tree Angel* (616), then *Jumping Beans* (617) came of that association. As evident even in black and white, the dialogue is color- and picture-keyed to the players—it's a picture-play or, for the reader, a talking-book. At the end, along with production tips, is a photograph—in the case of *Jumping Beans*—of Charlip, the bean-seller, Judith Martin, the vexed housekeeper, and a group of mocking children, the beans of course, on stage. Good showmanship all around.

Strictly on picturebook terms, so is *Fortunately*. Charlip is the man who appreciates 'the drama of the turning of the page,' and the words *fortunately*—and *unfortunately*—make of the turning, spread by spread, the Perils of Pauline (or Harold Lloyd) speeded up (618–621). The alternating black-and-white and full-color scheme is an expression of the structure, and when it serves to darken the cave and light up the tunnel, a great visual ploy. But Charlip's books, seen, are self-explanatory, a self-evident reason for their success.

Take *Mother Mother I Feel Sick Send for the Doctor Quick Quick Quick*; and take a breath: it's a jump-rope rhyme turned into a shadow play—in living color—of outrageous overindulgence remedied by a man of medicine who is also patently a magician (622). Charlip testifies that he made it old-fashioned "to remove it from present reality,"[6] a smart move that also makes it better vaudeville. For all its designs and devices, it's indelicate, tantamount to saying that kids eat it up.

Arm in Arm, on the other hand—another hand—is "a collection of connections, endless tales, reiterations, and other echolalia." Officially, echolalia is 1. the uncontrollable and immediate repetition of words spoken by another person; 2. the imitation by a baby of the vocal sounds produced by others, occurring as a natural phase of childhood development. It is also, or consequently, natural child nonsense, as Ruth Krauss realized; and Charlip had been working with Krauss on theater pieces and on books. As regards the concept and its embodiment—in plays, pic-

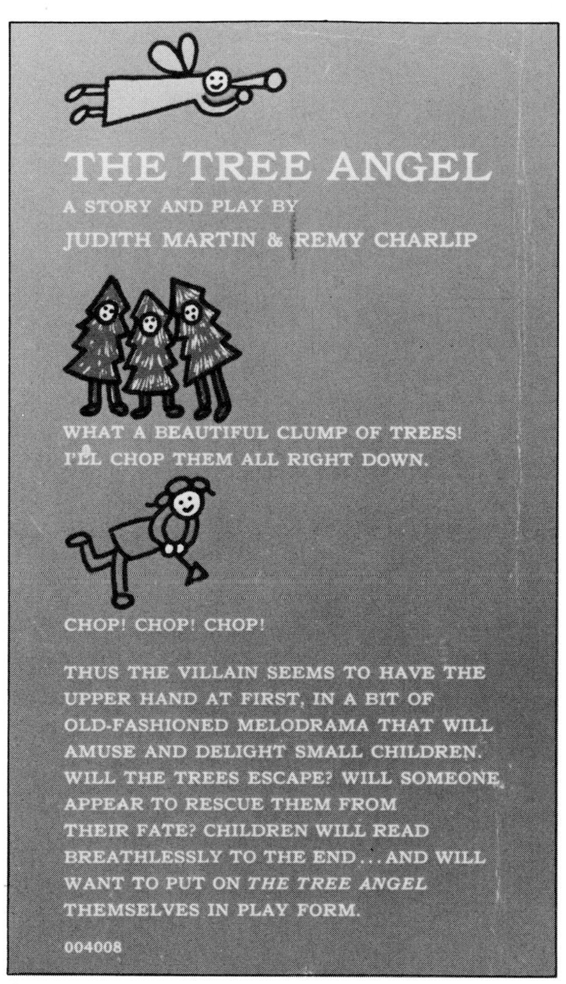

616

616. *The Tree Angel,* text by Judith Martin and Remy Charlip, pictures by Remy Charlip. Knopf, 1962. Jacket flap.

617. *Jumping Beans,* text by Judith Martin, pictures by Remy Charlip. Knopf, 1963. 5¾ x 6.

617

Unfortunately
he ran into a deep dark cave.

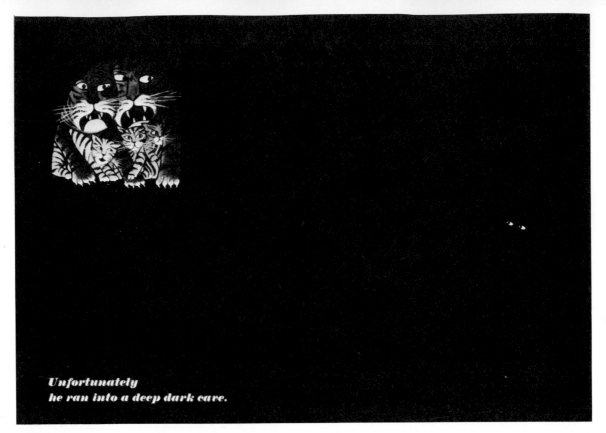

618-621. *Fortunately*, by Remy Charlip. Parents', 1964. 7 x 9⅞.

618

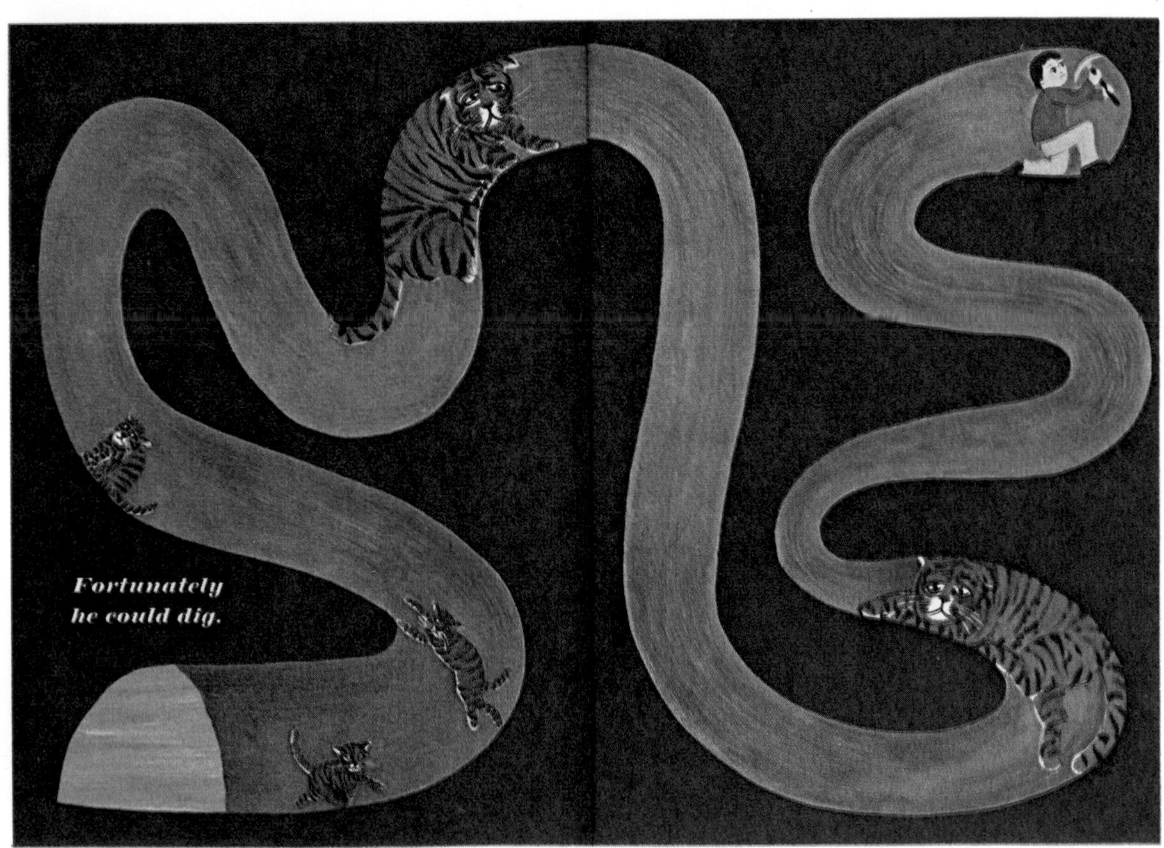
Fortunately
he could dig.

619

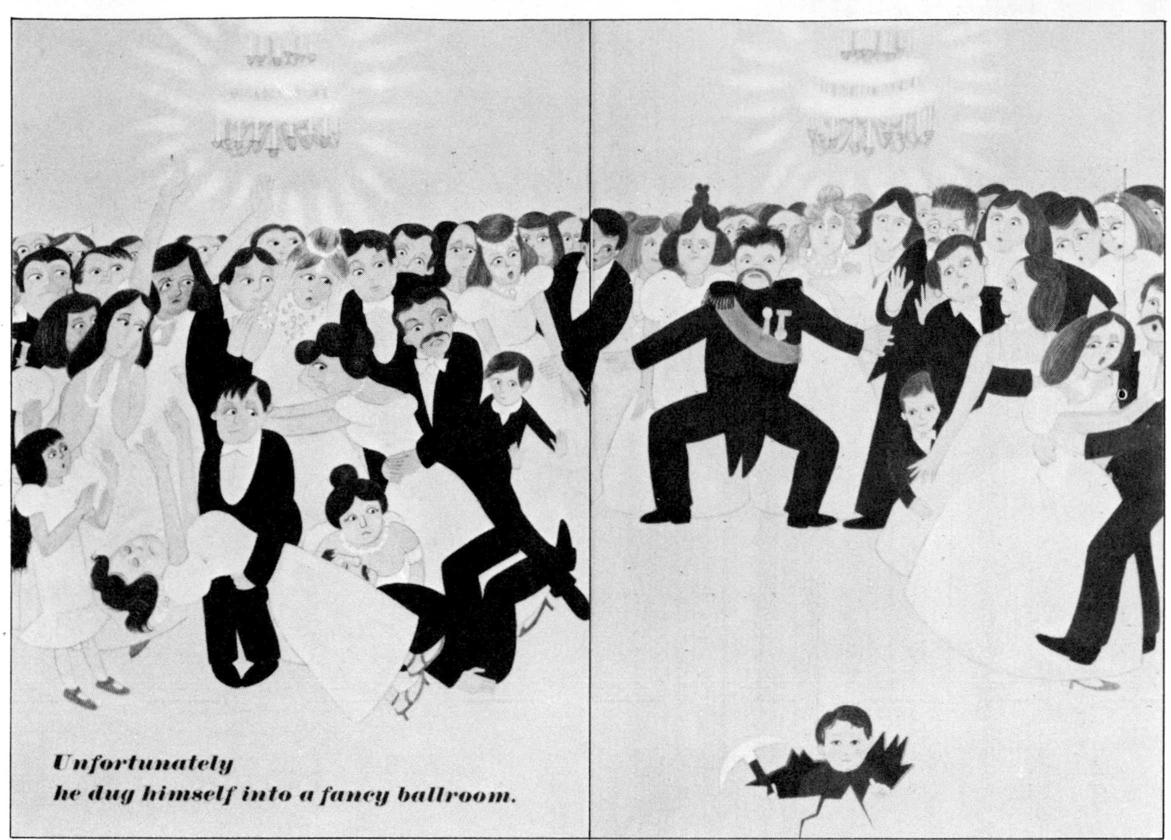
Unfortunately
he dug himself into a fancy ballroom.

620

Fortunately
there was a surprise party going on.
And fortunately
the party was for him,
because fortunately
it was his birthday!

621

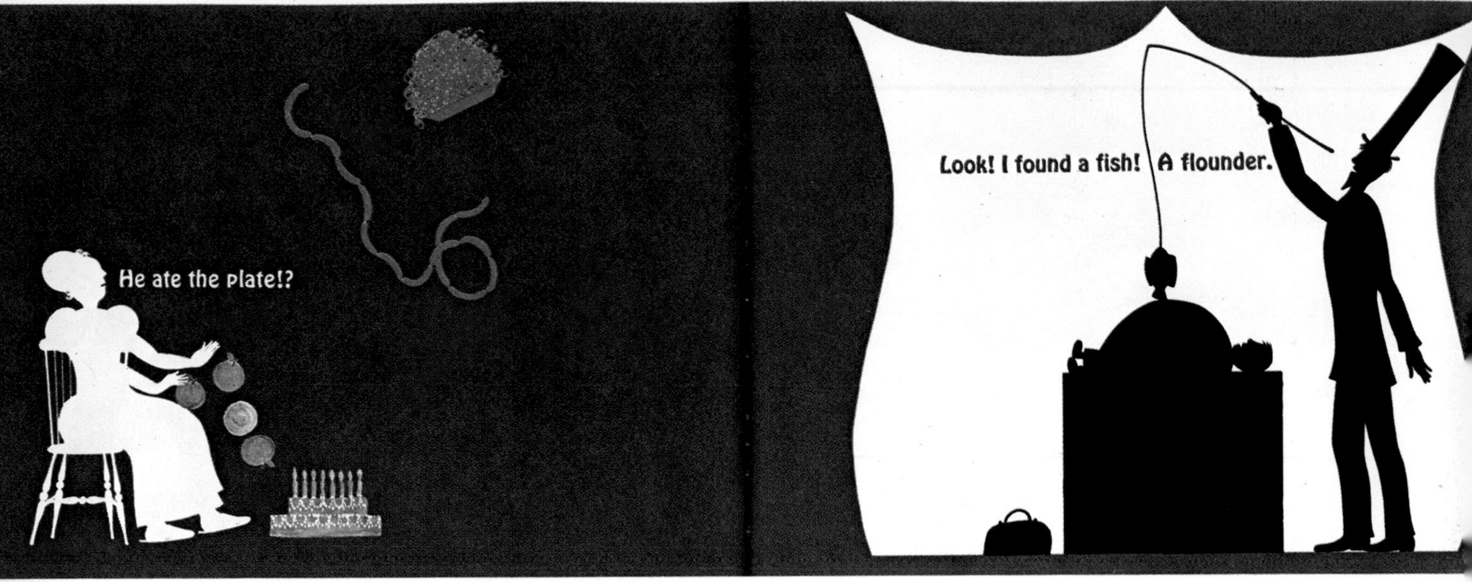

He ate the plate!?
Look! I found a fish! A flounder.

622

623

ture-sequences, spot comments—the beginnings of *Arm in Arm* are clearly to be seen in *I'll Be You and You Be Me.* Charlip, as clearly, has his own purposes: entertainment.

"Two octopuses got married and walked down the aisle arm in arm in arm in arm in arm in arm in arm in arm in arm in arm in arm in arm in arm in arm in arm in arm"—is how it starts; where it goes you can best see for yourself (623-625). Elsewhere, the theme elaborated (or simplified), a chicken says to an egg, "Who was first, me or you?" to which the egg replies, "Don't question it. Be grateful we have one another"; "WHAT IS WRITTEN ON THE OTHER SIDE OF THIS PAGE IS WRONG" is written on both sides of a page; an octopuss—striped eight colors—stands in a corner; "My Sister's Mother's Husband's Father's Grandchild Is Me," says a little boy, the last in line. ("DO NOT READ THIS SIGN," reads a sign.) To the extent that comparisons illumine, *Arm in Arm* is jokier than *I'll Be You* and more thoroughly visual—whether surreal and enigmatic (625, left), sometime-Steinberg (624) or streamlined Caran d'Ache (623).

Charlip it was, though, who once made a perfect book of perfectly blank pages, *It Looks Like Snow.*

622. *Mother Mother I Feel Sick Send for the Doctor Quick Quick Quick,* text by Remy Charlip and Burton Supree, pictures by Remy Charlip. Parents', 1966. 9¾ x 7¼.

623-625. *Arm in Arm,* by Remy Charlip. Parents', 1969. 7⅛ x 10.

624

625

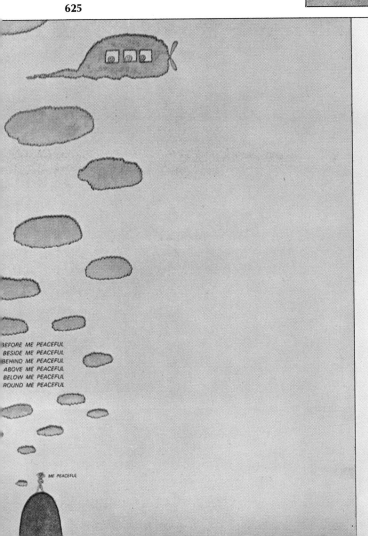

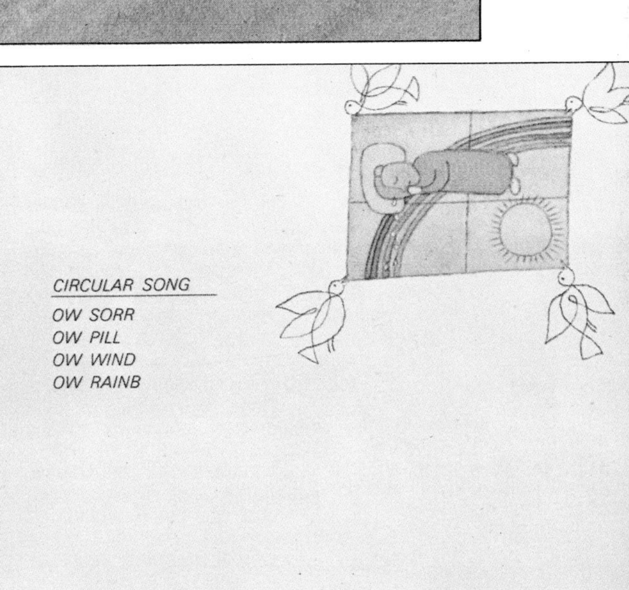

NOTHING EVER HAPPENS ON MY BLOCK

Before she did a picturebook independently, Ellen Raskin was the artist of a thousand jackets and the illustrator of Dylan Thomas, Ruth Krauss, Edgar Allan Poe; the year that *Nothing Ever Happens On My Block* came out, she illustrated Blake's *Songs of Innocence.* But with the appearance of Chester Filbert she was a cartoonist with a spirit-world of her own (626).

So to Chester sitting on the curb; sitting on the curb complaining, "Some places have marching bands or haunted houses, courageous hunters hunting ferocious lions and tigers . . ." while behind him, bit by bit, all hell breaks loose (627). At the first house the window-washer has been moving from window to window; at the second the children have twice rung the doorbell and hidden (when the postman rings, he'll suffer for it); in front of the third the man digging a hole has pulled up first a boot, now a chest; at the last a workman is repairing the ravages of a fire that destroyed the top story before the fire engine arrived. (It passed right in front of the unseeing Chester.) Still to come are a paddy wagon to take the thief away, a parachutist shouting "GERONIMO!", assorted accidents, a rainstorm, and a flurry of greenbacks —but Chester, all unawares, concludes "nothing ever happens on my block. When I grow up I'm going to move."

The great fun of seeing what Chester doesn't is a little like finding what the frantic husband is searching for in *A Good Man and His Good Wife*; and the story playing itself out in contraposition to the text is incipient in *Hector Protector.* What Raskin does—and this is not to suggest that she had either in mind—is to pit visual hijinks against a deadpan text and the effect, by itself, is comic opera. No more than the doings of little blue, moreover, or Charlip's quick saves, does *Nothing Ever Happens*, once seen, call for explanation; but it must be seen in color, as they must: getting away from words meant that color, as well, would have something to say.

Subsequent Raskin books are talkier, trickier, more complex, very complex. She is good

626, 627. *Nothing Ever Happens On My Block,* by Ellen Raskin. Atheneum, 1966. 6¾ x 5½.

626

My name is Chester Filbert.

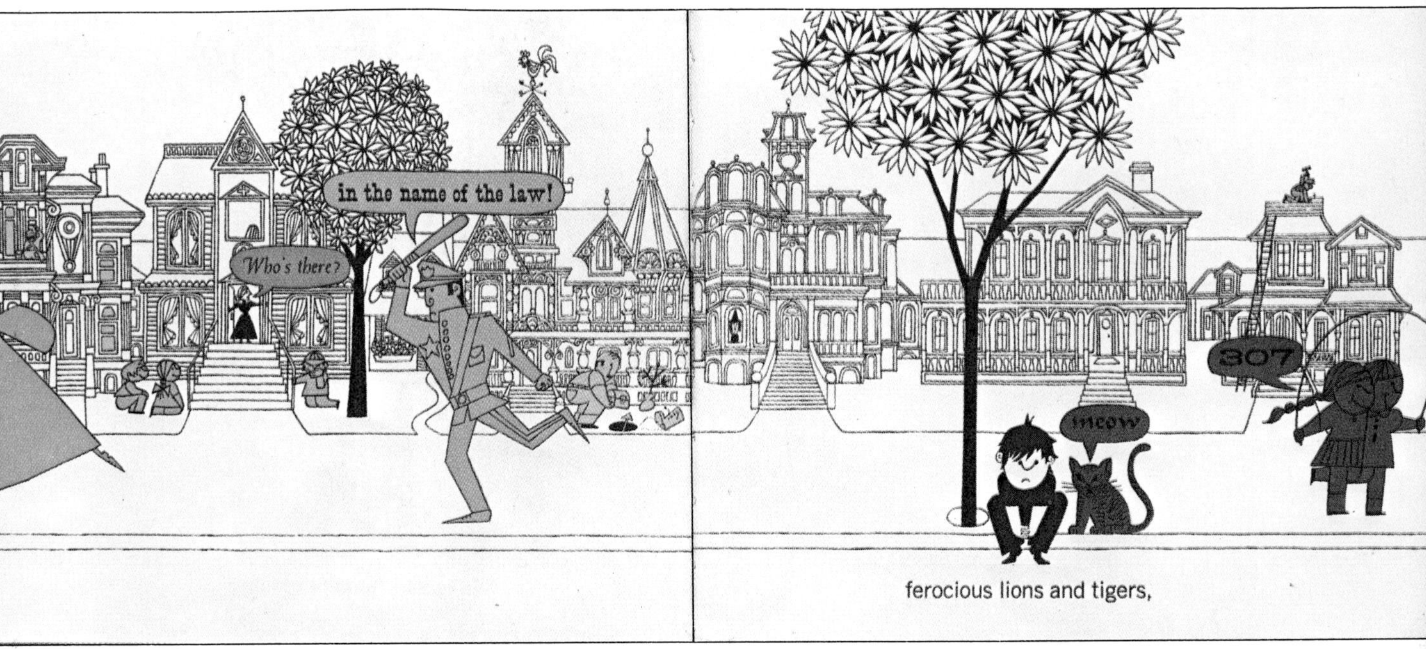

in the name of the law!
Who's there?
307
meow
ferocious lions and tigers,

627

enough to be simple. At house number five a witch appears now at one window, now at another, and suddenly there is a witch at every window; during the rainstorm the weathercock flies from house number four to house number two. Robbers and parachutists and firemen spell excitement, adventure; but a migrating weathervane is a discovery and a marvel.

The leitmotif is see for yourself—plus. As the new ways of design made art a more active experience, they came also to create experience—the free play of a blue and a yellow form, the circumambulating of the globe; to organize form and color into new nonverbal entities. They are experiences that the viewer receives and interprets directly, 'translates' in his head. The first wave, from Rand onward, brought the viewer into the picture; the second brought him boldly into the story.

It is indicative too that we have been finding a multiplicity of antecedents, within picturebooks and without, and will henceforth. That scouring ground of modernist art called by Malraux the Museum Without Walls was at the service of illustrators for their own purposes, and picturebooks had themselves developed resources, even traditions, to draw upon.

WORDLESS BOOKS

Appearances aside, the book without words is something else—narrative illustration for the most part—and its roots are quite different. Neither is it a new phenomenon in picturebooks. *A Head for Happy* is a story in pictures to the extent that the words serve primarily for emphasis (109–112): they are what the characters would say at a critical moment. As we noted, the wordless picturebook was imminent around 1930, and existent in the form of the wordless novel; the latter disappeared, the former died aborning (both, possibly, stifled by talking films) but not before the appearance of a certified "Story Without Words," *What Whiskers Did.*

What the black Scotty does—break away from his boy to follow rabbit tracks (628), flee from a wolf down a rabbit hole, bid the friendly rabbits farewell and return home—is related in pictures with the aid only of an occasional symbolic device: a question mark

628. *What Whiskers Did,* by Ruth Carroll. Macmillan, 1932. 7⅛ x 9¼.

for curiosity, tears for regret. In essence, though, the book is no different from the animated sequences of Frost (11) and other comic artists at the turn of the century. What is novel is the development of such a narrative especially for the newly prominent preschooler.

Redone, *What Whiskers Did* was brought out again in 1965, a sign of the times, for with the emphasis on cognitive learning and on 'reading' pictures in preparation for reading words (and funds available to back it up), a spate of picturebooks wholly or partially without words began to appear. The ground had been laid unwittingly by Sendak's picture sequences—dramatically in *Hector Protector,* implicitly before—but it was the conjunction of artistic thrust with felt need that produced the burgeoning of the form.

Most of the wordless books are more or less agile variations on the formula of self-contained, immediately apprehensible action—action that is comprehensible just because it matches expectations or directly confounds them. One of the first, Mercer Mayer's *A Boy, a Dog and a Frog* (Dial, 1967), is a convenient example. Slapstick and melodrama, scaled and toned down, are as natural to them as to the old comic sequences (or, for that matter, to silent films) and hardly less so is cumulative action: the Mounting Disaster. Quasi-realistic, they substitute for the story-in-words; and in most cases they are slight, with nothing to convey that extends beyond their covers.

An exception is the work of Fernando Krahn, the Chilean cartoonist active in New York in the Sixties. *Journeys of Sebastian,* Krahn's first independent effort, takes place entirely in Sebastian's head; or rather as fancy takes him, so he goes (629, 630). There was a bee buzzing around his head to start with; and at the close, after flying off with the mum-

mum-men (or whatever you like) to a giant garden and falling from a cut flower, he is on the floor holding the flower in his hand. What do you think of that! The second journey moves through mirrors; and the third finds him finding a string hanging from a hole . . . that, pulled, becomes the tail of a rubbery monster . . . that takes Sebastian, along with the mum-mums (mounted on like monsters), on a steeple-chase over rivers and rooftops to victory, and a victor's cup . . . that the monster slides into, until only the end of his tail hangs over the edge. Inexplicable? ask a child.

There's a little of Edward Gorey in *Journeys of Sebastian*, and a little of Dr. Seuss: Krahn is an original who can make the oddest twain meet. A natural mimic besides. *Gustavus and Stop* (Dutton, 1969) is broad old-time cartooning (pre-*Night Kitchen*) set up with brief captions—worded like silent film titles—to tell, mostly in pictures, about a little boy, Gustavus, and his dog, Stop, and their efforts to become circus clowns. Dog beats boy, that's the story; but the interest is, one by one, in the sobersides comedy of the cartoon frames.

With or without words, the books make something individual of their particular form. The least venturesome but, not surprisingly, the one with the widest appeal is *How Santa Claus Had a Long and Difficult Journey Delivering His Presents.* Krahn uses color emblematically too, and economically. *How Santa Claus* . . . looks as if it belongs under the tree by virtue of vivid red endpapers, just-as-green sheets opposite the illustrations and—when a bell-ringing bear wakes Santa and helps him dress—a red, naturally, Santa Claus suit. A merry Christmas book of drawings (631).

What happened was that the traces snapped and the reindeer flew off without the sled; and the toy airplanes tried and couldn't get it off the ground; and the dolls and animals marched out of the sack and picked Santa up; and the sled, righted, ran into a snowbank; *and what shall we do now*? The answer is angels but there's no hurry about finding it: each of the drawings, displayed

629, 630. *Journeys of Sebastian*, by Fernando Krahn. Seymour Lawrence/Delacorte, 1968. 6⅝ x 6.

629

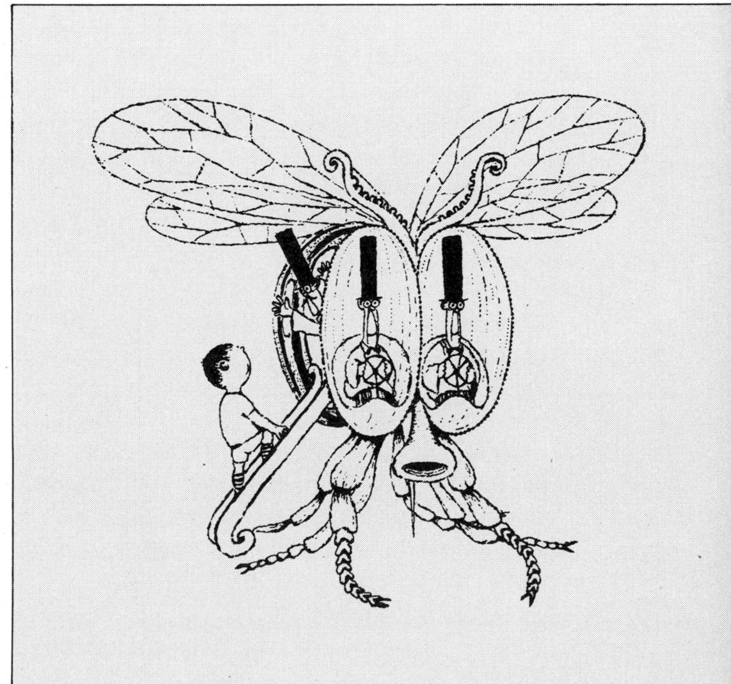

630

631

singly, is to look at and laugh at and look over: to 'read,' in other words, not like a road sign but like a book.

Another talent, another direction. Pat Hutchins made a grand entrance with *Rosie's Walk*, a book of thirty-two pages and thirty-three words—in one sentence. Rosie the hen has only to set out with her beak in the air for us to know what she doesn't, that a fox is stalking her; and for us to see what she never sees either, that disaster awaits him at every other turn of the page (632). The fox's patterned pelt, the ranked pears on the tree, all the flat stylizations borrowed from peasant art say that this is funny make-believe; and the cheerful conventionalized colors, particularly the absence of blue, suggest that reality will remain at bay. But the text, at alternate openings, supplies rhythm and emphasis to a story that would be comprehensible without words. The text, in fact, makes it a story, for Rosie, on the last page, "got back in time for dinner." To be precise, she "went . . . through the fence/under the beehives/and got back in time for dinner." Through the telling, Rosie's walk becomes more than the titular subject and the downfall of the fox takes second place to her providential return.

Changes, Changes, for its part, is all pantomime, fluid and in flux, and appropriately silent (633). Given are the wooden couple, their multicolored blocks, and one after another emergency; it's up to the observer to see —and if he wishes, to tell—what the resourceful pair are up to as they transform their burning house into a pumper, the flooded pumper into a ship, the beached ship into a truck, and so on and on. But he'll have to look sharp: would you know on the left-hand page what was coming on the right? *Changes, Changes* doesn't just happen, it builds; and on the last page it builds a new house for the couple just like the one that caught fire at the start. Manner, design and format are integral; the book is what block-building is about. And, like *Little Blue and Little Yellow*, its humor is inherent—or, equally, built in.

Who needs words? It depends.

632. *Rosie's Walk,* by Pat Hutchins. Macmillan, 1968. 9⅝ x 8.

631. *How Santa Claus Had a Long and Difficult Journey Delivering His Presents,* by Fernando Krahn. Seymour Lawrence/Delacorte, 1970. 10⅝ x 8¾.

633. *Changes, Changes,* by Pat Hutchins. Macmillan, 1971. 9⅝ x 8.

THE FABULISTS

TOMI UNGERER, EDWARD GOREY, HARRIET PINCUS, WILLIAM STEIG, MARGOT ZEMACH

If we were to set side by side an Ungerer octopus or hellion, a Gorey dilettante, a Pincus mädchen, a Steig donkey, a Zemach rustic, we would have not only five distinct, unmistakable styles and five types, we would have in the conjunction of style and type five apparitions: five ways of looking at life. The fabulists are storytellers, but subjective; fantasists, but in effect philosophers. In their figures is an attitude, a point of view; one has no need of a story to know something about them. In their very style is a posture, whether they are working with new material or old, the original or the given.

TOMI UNGERER

Tomi Ungerer is devilishly clever: the expression could have been coined for him. When he first came to the United States from his native France, his work was rejected by *The New Yorker*, reputedly, as looking too much like Saul Steinberg's. So Harper's got him, and his wiry line made its first appearance in *The Mellops Go Flying*; and children got, beginning with the Mellops, a succession of animals as civilized as the sainted Babar who inspired them.

To turn the pages of *The Mellops Go Flying* is to admire and wonder; to wonder, indeed, what it is about Mr. Mellops, "gentle pig and kind father," and his four sons Casimir, Isidor, Felix and Ferdinand constructing a plane that is so utterly absorbing—even before they take their first trip, run out of gas, and slide down a mountain to a sudden painful stop (634). The brief artless present-tense telling, largely absent since the Thirties; the very gentleness and kindliness, the industry and resourcefulness; the interesting, varying design and the movement it engenders, Ungerer strengths from the start; the small surprises (the sun downcast when the plane falls) and consistencies (Felix always rear-first): these are sufficient reason, perhaps, but there remain the individual figures—Mother Mellops majestically bearing in a tea tray, Casimir the miserable captive (635). In the intervening four pages, the Mellops, gasless, have built a distiller to make alcohol (for fuel) out of grass, and while they are filling their tank, Casimir, out hunting, falls prey to an Indian. A perilous air-borne rescue, a souvenir—the totem pole Casimir was tied to—and the adventure concludes.

Another followed immediately, *The Mellops Go Diving for Treasure* (Harper, 1957), a considerably more involved story with some hilariously pictured happenings (including a meeting with a menacing, music-prone octopus); and, over the years, three more. Meanwhile, however, there appeared Crictor the companionable boa constrictor, or the improbabilities of Babar extended (636). Crictor comes in a box, O-shaped, a birthday present from Madame Bodot's son in Africa, and once assured of his harmlessness, she does her best to make him feel at home (see Crictor stretched out in his long-drawn bed under a potted palm). Crictor reciprocates according to his kind: stiff, he's a slide for little boys; limp, a jump rope for little girls; and, cleverly,

Father's arm is cut.
Felix's head is hurt.
Ferdinand has a black eye.
And the poor dog has bad cuts too.

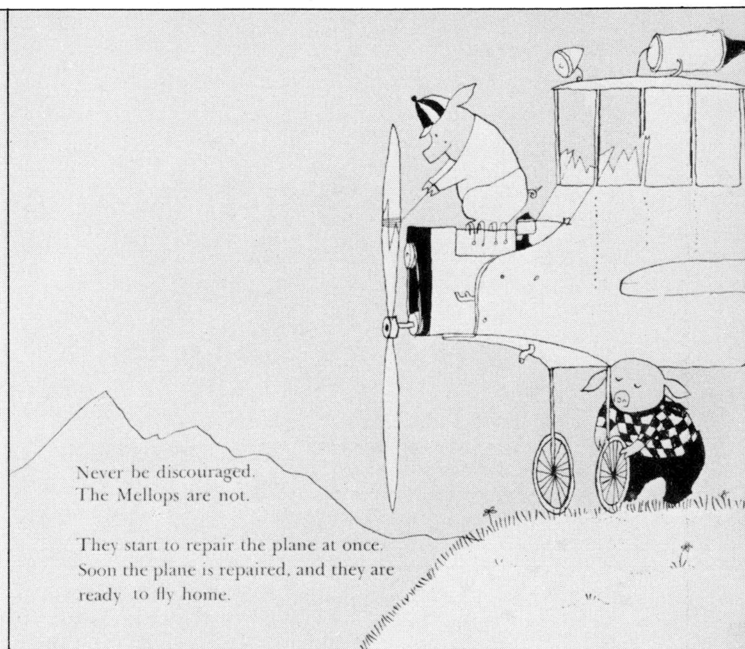

Never be discouraged.
The Mellops are not.
They start to repair the plane at once.
Soon the plane is repaired, and they are
ready to fly home.

634

636

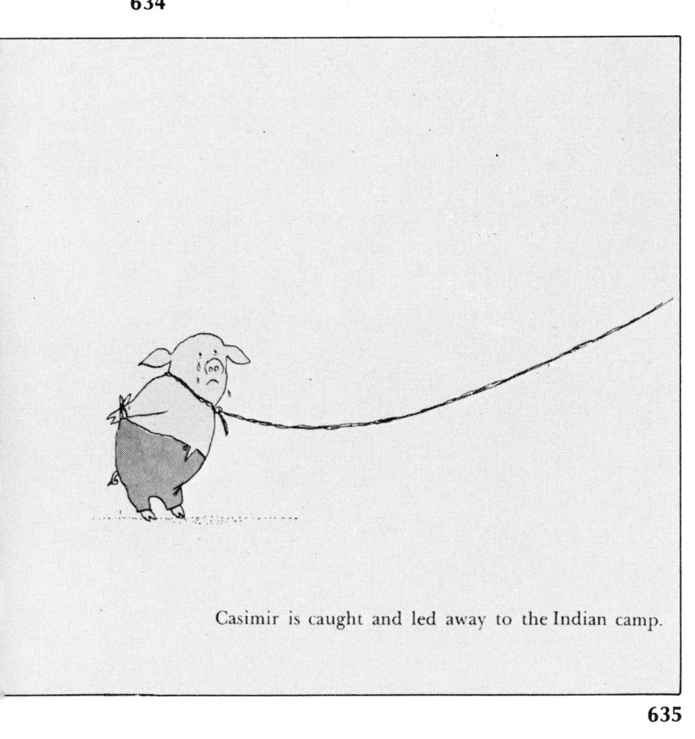

Casimir is caught and led away to the Indian camp.

635

16 In the winter it was fun for Crictor to wriggle in the snow.

634, 635. *The Mellops Go Flying,* by Tomi Ungerer. Harper, 1957. 9 x 7⅝.

636. *Crictor,* by Tomi Ungerer. Harper, 1958. 7⅞ x 10⅝.

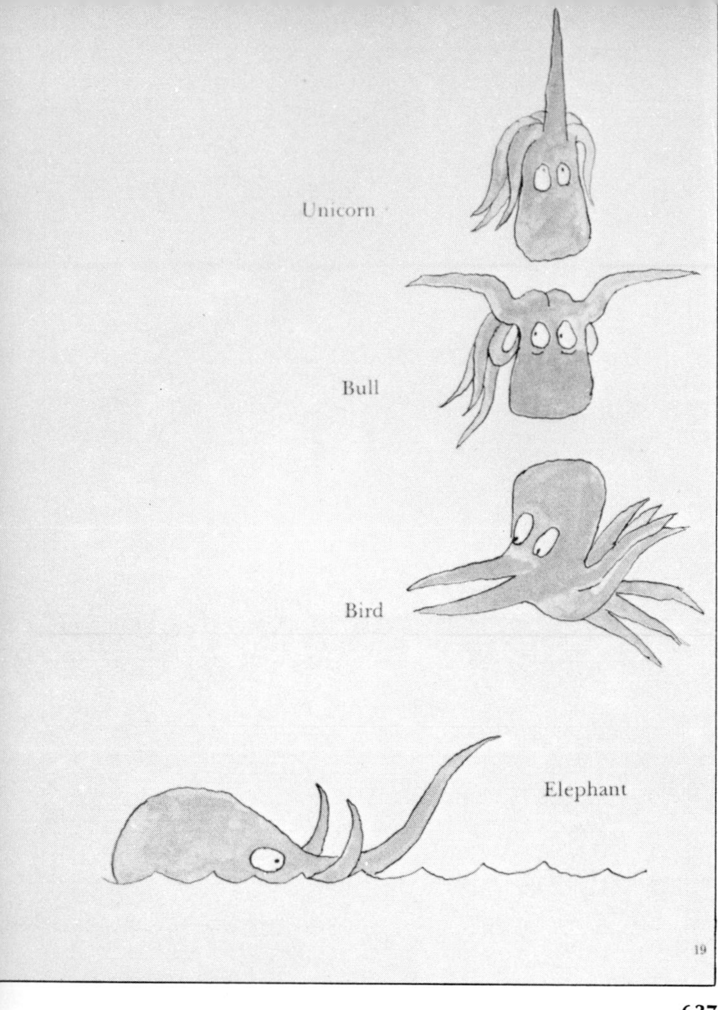

637

he forms the letters of the alphabet when Madame Bodot, a teacher, takes him to school. Comes a burglar and Crictor apprehends him (see the laurel-wreathed statue in his honor) but it takes no prodigious feats to justify his existence. Ungerer is a comic artist of delicate ease and Crictor is—snake and book—an exquisite creation.

Emile, though, is the nonpareil performer (637–640). An octopus—who would have thought it?—is a natural clown, and it's in the nature of the beast to be doing. From the moment he saves Captain Samofar, famous deep-sea diver, from a shark (by throwing a stone in the fish's mouth) and goes home with him, Emile is into one thing or another. He's a gifted musician, it turns out—a duo (at least) on the piano, an eight-armed one-man band. But, missing the sea, he gets a job as a lifeguard—teaches the children to swim, rescues the far-gone (sometimes four at a time), mimes at odd moments (637); and on his day off, winds up as the hero of a mad cops-and-robbers chase (638,639). Enough: the quiet life of the sea calls, and after a farewell fête

638

On his day off, Emile swam along next to the police launch on which Captain Samofar worked. One afternoon they stopped a suspicious-looking boat.

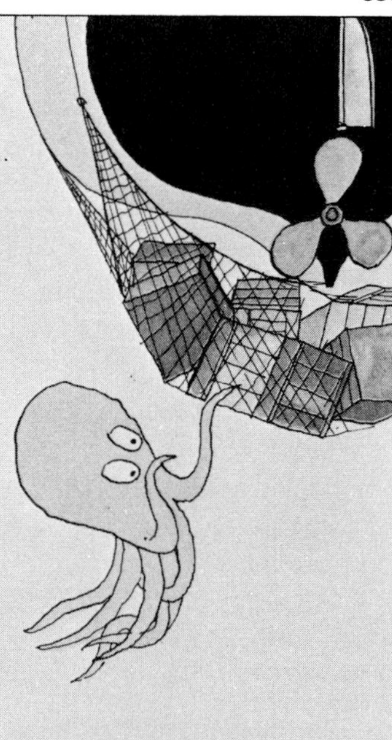

Emile noticed there were boxes hidden in a net under the water.

21

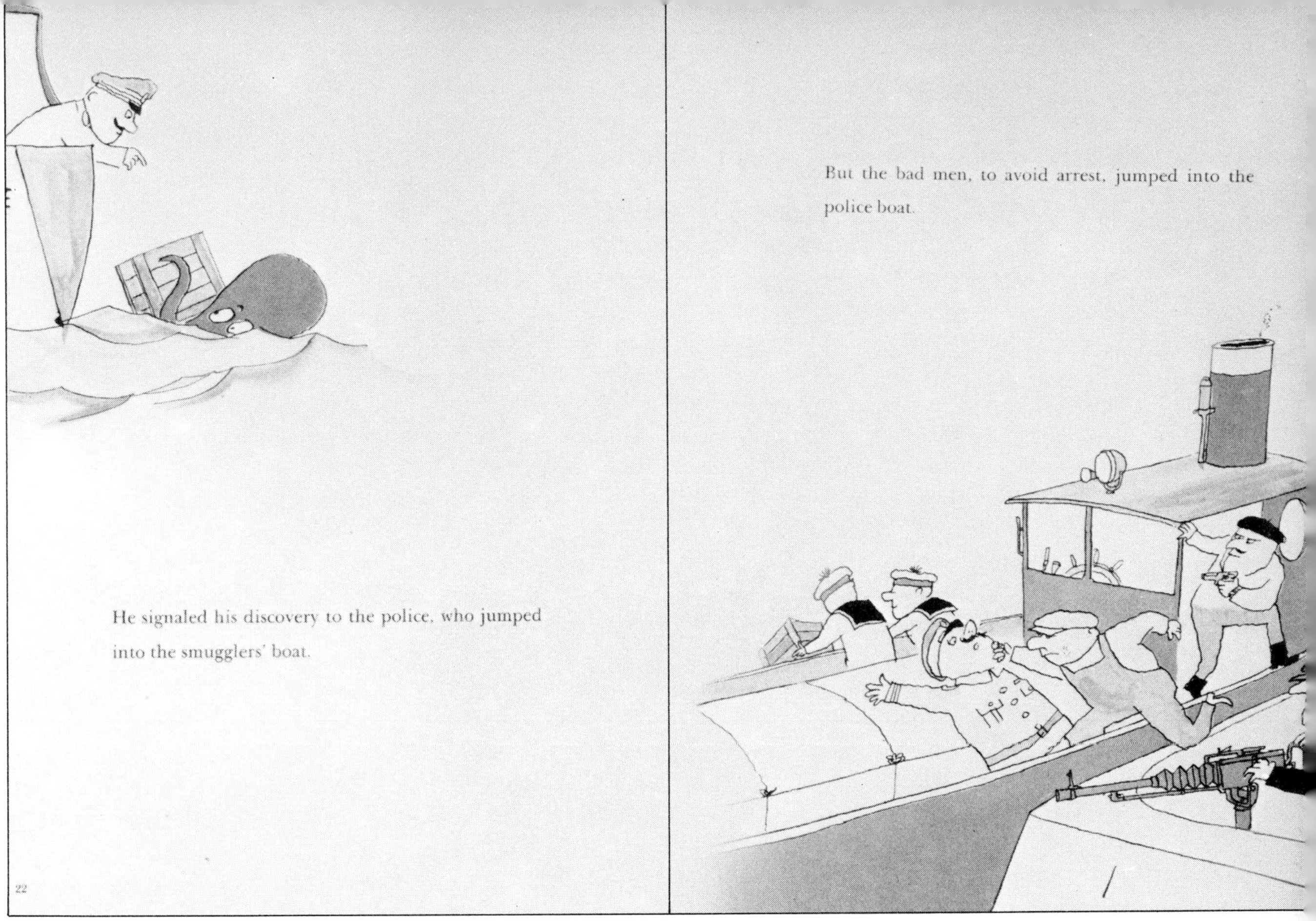

He signaled his discovery to the police, who jumped into the smugglers' boat.

22

But the bad men, to avoid arrest, jumped into the police boat.

639

637–640. *Emile*, by Tomi Ungerer. Harper, 1960. 7⅞ x 10⅝.

640

(see Emile, head swimming, holding eight glasses of champagne), he is off . . . (640).

As was said of Babar in French, it would be comprehensible and entertaining even if one didn't know the language. Indeed Ungerer, more the artist, charms us not only by what he shows us but how (the snowbank that throws Crictor's curves in relief, the seaweed that curls up as if to enclose Emile); and by the wit of his transpositions from the human norm (the seaweed potted, the fish caged), the peculiar aptness of his particular animal's adaptations (Emile the mass imbiber, Crictor the practice knot). It is incongruity elevated, an improvement on life.

He is also of course much more the designer—in this case, the animator. From the small scene-setting vignette of the two boats (638, left), indicatively light and dark, the eye moves quickly across the void to the green-toned page and the close-up of Emile finding the boxes—a natural movement from small to large, from less to more developed, from

Whenever Captain Samofar wanted to see his old friend he put on his diving suit and went down to visit him. No sea could be deep enough to separate the diver and the eight-legged hero.
32

lighter to heavier weight; and a dramatic demonstration of eye movement as spatial and temporal movement, something that Ungerer has utilized as much as or more than anyone. We exit as we entered, at page-edge (cf. Waber, 559,560, Sendak, 576), and find ourselves at the same pictorial level with the illusion—the lightening, the weight lifted—of having risen (639, left); and cast our eyes across and down to where, pictorially and actually, the action takes place and, with another upthrust, promises to continue. But not before a burst of back and forth movement.

The design, setting a fast pace, establishing large free rhythms, expresses the story, *tells* the story, a rampaging adventure, even as it guides us to and isolates the particulars. In Waber's different story (559,560), a deliberate, repetitive one, the pace is by comparison slow, the rhythm relatively fixed: a metaphor, in turn, for climbing steps and, in narrative terms, small, steady advance. The Sendak (576) is continuously active, loose, melodic—melodic in the sense of being a succession of single 'notes'—or chords (discords)—that together comprise an air. In the dream-giver's passage, it's another air (511). In either case, the appropriateness is apparent.

Ungerer has the further distinction of extreme mobility: he moves around things like a film director. We have spoken of the effect of films as regards perspective and scale, and alluded, in discussing *Emile*, to those changes of perspective and scale that set up movement. But the mobility is an expressive as well as a dynamic force, a matter of shifting his point of view (and ours) in effect as in fact—just as it is for a film maker. One has, indeed, only to compare the Ungerer sequence, and other recent work, with the differently structured sequences of Sewell (111,112) and Daugherty (203–208), each effective in its own right, to perceive the confluence of the design influence and the film influence in the later narrative treatments. Where we have not Ungerer's mobility, we have nonetheless a new fluidity; in the aggregate, new, freely expressive forms of *picturebook* movement.

But *Emile* is composed of pictures, and it is a book. To represent the picturebook as an entity and a medium, we have elected to write the term as one word; the medium, however, remains a vehicle, capable (McLuhan notwithstanding) of diverse messages in diverse forms. So we have Emile miming in a set of drawings that are sheer drawing, as amusing in themselves as Harry the dirty dog doing his tricks (545) or Lyle the crocodile doing his chores (554); and less essential—inessential—to the story. And to bring it to a close we have a last page that is quiet, in equilibrium, bounded, contained; our eye swings around to the center of weight, the checkerboard pattern, and can go no further (640).

With *The Three Robbers* (Atheneum, 1962), Ungerer shifted to a big, bright, bold style, painting instead of drawing and filling the page with arresting forms and intense, dramatic color. There was never such an electric blue, an assertive red or, in a picturebook, so much black. The tale, fittingly, is a melodrama, the story of a poor little rich girl, Tiffany by name, who to her delight is carried off by robbers on her way to live with a wicked aunt; and its content, as well as its look, was a challenge to placid pastel juvenalia. It has, however, chiefly cliffhanger interest—there is no internal development, no struggle or comeback; and the pictures themselves are best seen, emblematically, as posters.

To the extent that *The Three Robbers* is a spoof, even a parody, of villainy, it brought into the open a strain that the depiction of the smugglers in *Emile* hints at—the satire of evil and, in time, of society's evils: gluttony, for instance, and avarice, pomposity, callousness. Ungerer's acute line resembled George Grosz's and his caricature in turn was Grosz for kiddies (641); and a great many adults didn't—and don't—like it. There is real badness in Ungerer's new world and unvarnished stupidity; as there was once in the purview of Hoffmann and Busch.

The object of the chase, the alarm—though

POLICE

ICE CREAM

*

The noise brought hundreds of people from a nearby town.

12

Soldiers sped to defend the earth. Firemen hastened to quench the flaming light.

**The ice cream man hurried to set up his stand for the spectators.*

641

641, 642. *Moon Man,* by Tomi Ungerer. Harper, 1967. 9 x 13⅜.

no one knows it yet—is Moon Man who, envious of the people dancing on earth, catches hold of a shooting star and crash-lands. But officialdom, no better than it's shown to be, throws the 'invader' in jail; and Moon Man, crushed, languishes until—in a brilliant visual stratagem—the waning moon gives him a way out (642). When he returns to his full size he has a fling at dancing—at a costume party where, naturally, everyone takes him for 'the man in the moon'—before a complaint about the noise brings the police. Pursued, Moon Man flees to a remote castle where an ancient sage has just perfected a spaceship; and we last see him, curiosity forever satisfied, "curled up in his shimmering seat in space."

'Make the earth safe for Moon Man' might be the motto, and one is reminded more than once of Kurt Joos's antimilitarist ballet, "The

642

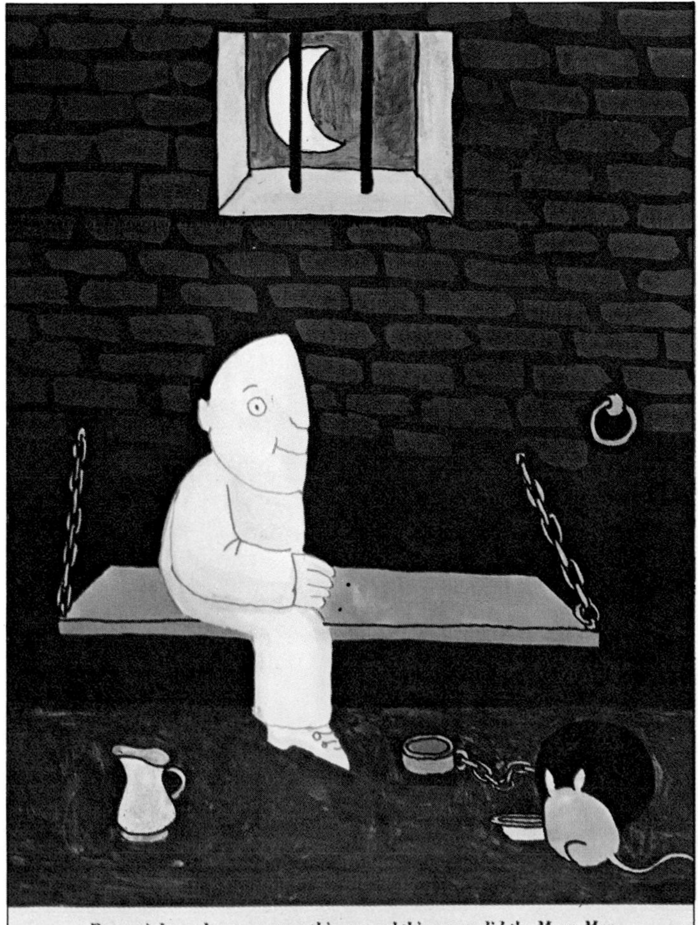

Every night as the moon grew thinner and thinner so did the Moon Man, until at last he was able to squeeze through the bars of his window.

21

Green Table" (1932). Actually the book is a more generalized comment—or condemnation—and it has, as satire hasn't, a true hero: a gentle soul (in transport over a rose) to suffer and hope for, and an avowal that wickedness isn't quite universal.

The next blockbuster is *The Beast of Monsieur Racine*, the book that, after *Moon Man*, is as grandly conceived as executed. Ungerer is amusing doing very little (*One, Two, Where's My Shoe?*) but a slight story inflated, even if it happens to be his (*The Hat*), is no match for the combination of passion and panache that distinguishes his work today.

Strong words, but not unwarranted (643, 644); and those are unexceptional moments. We're not looking at Monsieur Racine and his new pet, the pear thief, tenderly picnicking in the moonlight or its direct opposite, the sensation of the strange beast's arrival in Paris. Monsieur Racine, contented as he thought himself, wanted, needed, a friend: "Good night, gentle thing," he says to the beast that first evening. "Come back tomorrow. . . ."

It spends the days with him, vanishing at night; enjoys ice cream—vats are delivered from the city—and listening to music, riding in the trailer behind his motorcycle and sliding, swinging, playing games. Meanwhile Monsieur Racine studies it to find a clue to its origin. "Zero. This beast was unheard of." The Academy of Sciences, alerted, invites him to Paris to present his find. Reporters and photographers gather, the Mayor himself welcomes "the new French wonder." Fortunes are

643, 644. *The Beast of Monsieur Racine,* by Tomi Ungerer. Farrar, Straus, 1971. 9⅛ x 11⅞.

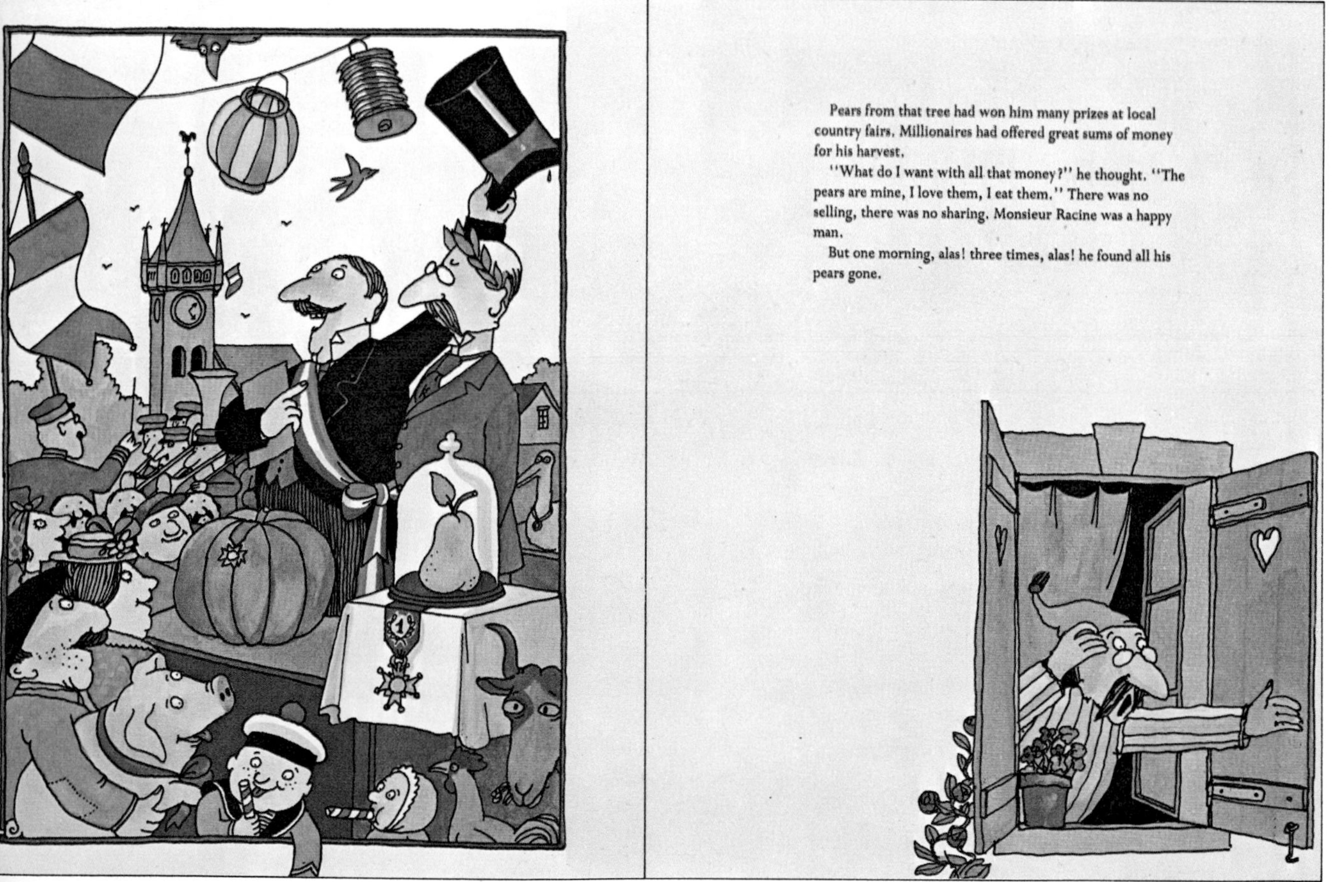

Pears from that tree had won him many prizes at local country fairs. Millionaires had offered great sums of money for his harvest.
"What do I want with all that money?" he thought. "The pears are mine, I love them, I eat them." There was no selling, there was no sharing. Monsieur Racine was a happy man.
But one morning, alas! three times, alas! he found all his pears gone.

643

The animal was playful and Monsieur Racine built a whole playground for its rompings.
Some sight it was when the old man and his pet frolicked all over the place.

644

offered for it; but "The beast is my friend, and friends are not for sale."

The members of the Academy assembled, Monsieur Racine mounts the platform, "fittingly dressed in a dark suit and followed by the beast." Ohs and ahs come from the audience, and unanimous applause; Monsieur Racine starts to speak . . . "THEN something incredible happened." The beast, heretofore silent, breaks into giggles; "Shaking, rolling on its side, it ripped and tore itself open. Out of a pile of skins and rags emerged two children." Uproar, pandemonium, outrage; outside, a riot—"Buses were overturned. Unspeakable acts were performed." But Monsieur Racine, "who had a sense of humor," congratulates the children, takes them on a tour of the capital and returns them to their parents. "Monsieur Racine soon had a new crop of pears, which he happily shared with his two young friends." On the last page we see, mounted, the head of the beast, snout dripping, and below Monsieur Racine, sedate as always, with his arms around a boy and a girl the like of whom adorn William Cole's *Beastly Boys and Ghastly Girls*.

Marvelous hoax that it is, a king of hoaxes, it is at least as good the second time round when like the kids inside, you *know*; when, seeing the vats of ice cream appear, the motorcycle tearing down the road, you know to whose benefit. And look as one will, there is always more to discover: after the medal for Monsieur Racine's pear, the blue-ribbon pumpkin, after the boy hanging over the picture (643) and the swing from the frame (644), the tear falling from the cut tree. In illuminated manuscripts a bird perches on a border, a painted dragonfly settles on a painted border flower; in the nineteenth century a pictured bee casts a shadow on a pictured page curled at the edges—which, through a hole, reveals the outdoors: trompe l'oeil and visual byplay are an old game. Ungerer doesn't play only with the borders, he plays with all creation; not only, that is, with the conventional dividing line between pictured scene and book page, but with pictorial convention and pictured scene alike—the one becoming as real, and unreal, as the other.

Thus, the border becomes a piece of flexible tubing, part of Monsieur Racine's equipment for studying the beast; and inside the elaborate frames on Monsieur Racine's parlor walls is nothing, a blank, the white of the paper. It is as if Ungerer were saying that that which he is showing us and that which we hold in our hands are equally illusory; and, to children especially, no less equally existent. It is a joke but not in itself a hoax.

M. Racine and his affection for the beast are genuine, that is the crux of it; and a cut tree, one feels, would cry if it could. (Small children, imputing their own emotions to plants will, seeing sap, assume just that.) The mysterious 'beast' is a child's joke—of larger dimension—not, uncovered, a joke on the child audience: not a figment of the imagination or some sorcerer's plaything. And just as the deception is not an unkind one, so, properly, the children are not punished—Monsieur Racine, for that matter, congratulates them "for their cleverness and endurance." It is here that Ungerer breaks with Busch who, like any good nineteenth-century moralist, would have had Max and Moritz paddled, at least, for their effrontery. But Busch did not conceive of a prank that was not in some way malicious; and it falls to Ungerer, a thorough twentieth-century man, to portray children's mischief—and mischievous children—as not, by definition, bad.

All pearly, sherberty watercolor, *The Beast of Monsieur Racine* is a lovely book, without the clangor of *Moon Man* and some of its contemporaries. More subtly colored, it is also more subtly imagined and composed—per the window flung wide, the serpentine slide, the framed swing, the trace of game. Still, there are those idiot people and, later, their 'unspeakable acts'; and there is the beast, which some took as itself something unspeakable.

> Take a dentist's drill, a meat grinder, a cartrack scraper, take buses and pleasure cars, bicycles, tandems and their tires, also wartime ersatz tires and deform them. Take lights and deform them as brutally as you can. Make locomotives crash into one another, curtains and portieres make threads of spider webs dance with window frames and break whimpering glass. Explode steam boilers to make railroad mist. Take petticoats and other kindred articles, shoes and false hair, also ice skates and throw them into place where they belong, and always at the right time. For all I care, take man-traps, automatic pistols, infernal machines, the tinfish and the funnel, all of course in an artistically deformed condition. Inner tubes are highly recommended. Take, in short, everything from the hair-net of the high class lady to the propellor of the S.S. *Leviathan*, always bearing in mind the dimensions required by the work.
>
> Even people can be used.
>
> People can even be tied to backdrops.
>
> People can even appear actively, even in their everyday position, they can speak on two legs, even in sensible sentences.[1]

That is Kurt Schwitters's description of his dadaist Merz stage; like *The Beast of Monsieur Racine*, total theater.

EDWARD GOREY

"There have been a group of Anchor book covers"—Henry Green, the Transcendentalists, Kafka, Colette—"that have a quality all their own. *Print* has discovered that these are the work of one man, Edward Gorey," the design journal announced in early 1958. "Gorey designs the covers, letters the titles and very often the rest of the cover. He also does the final illustrations. This versatility has resulted in a unity of feeling . . . a quality that is highly distinctive." In so competitive a field as paperback books, *Print* pointed out, "this is an important element."[2]

The following year when Jason Epstein left Anchor to found (for one) the Looking Glass Library, taking "his idea of quality reprints" and adapting it "to the juvenile field,"[3] the first Looking Glass list included, along with such eminent Victoriana as *The Princess and the Goblin* and Lear's *Book of Nonsense*, *The Haunted Looking Glass*, an anthology of ghost stories selected and, expectably, illustrated by Edward Gorey. It was the first thing Gorey did expressly for children and the kind of company that, in spirit, he'd continue to keep.

It was not, however, his first book. "I find that I cannot remember to have seen a single printed word about the books of Edward Gorey," Edmund Wilson wrote in *The New Yorker* in December 1959, "but it is not, I suppose, surprising that his work should have received no attention. It so far consists of four small volumes—never running to much over sixty pages—of drawings accompanied by captions." Noting that Gorey had (as yet) done little commissioned illustration, Wilson remarked: "He has been working quite perversely to please himself, and has created a whole little personal world, equally amusing and somber, nostalgic and claustrophobic, at the same time poetic and poisoned."[4]

The little books—*The Unstrung Harp* (1953), *The Listing Attic* (1954), *The Doubtful Guest* (1957) and, more ominous still, *The Object Lesson* (1958)—we would call picturebooks, and in appearance they are indistinguishable from those he did shortly after for children.

Or were his books for children? "I suppose I know a few tots who would like my books," he is quoted as remarking some years later—"and then, diffident but more assertive . . . 'I would have loved them as a child.'"[5] Curiously enough, to one accustomed to children's books, new and old, they appear far less 'unnatural' or 'sinister,' many of them, and rather funnier, than they do to others. The Doubtful Guest, for instance, is first seen peering in the window of a bleak mansion, a

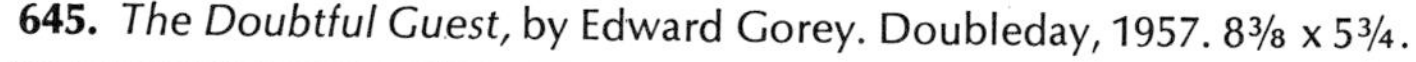
645. *The Doubtful Guest,* by Edward Gorey. Doubleday, 1957. 8⅜ x 5¾.

It eats umbrellas, gunny sacks,
Brass doorknobs, mud, and carpet tacks.

646. *The Wuggly Ump,* by Edward Gorey. Lippincott, 1963. 5⅞ x 4⅞.

penguin-like figure in a long striped muffler and basketball sneakers. Once inside it stands "with its nose to the wall," and thereafter it is not to be banished or swayed.

It wrenched off the horn from the new
gramophone,
And could not be persuaded to leave it alone. . . .

At times it would tear out whole chapters from
books,
Or put roomfuls of pictures askew on their hooks.
. . . (645)

It would carry off objects of which it grew fond,
And protect them by dropping them into the
pond.

It sounds like a child, it looks like a child; and it gets a certain serious pleasure from its misdoings, but, as Wilson observes, it is not happy. Could one not say, then, that it is a child: the Awful Nuisance. At the close it is sitting on a hassock, back turned: "It came seventeen years ago—and to this day/It has shown no intention of going away." A child can take satisfaction, if not comfort, from its stolid perseverance.

The Doubtful Guest is populated by common Gorey types—chill Edwardian gentlemen with flat sloping heads, rustling ladies of little ease—assembled, wordlessly, as a family: the father, feet apart, beard jutting; the mother, hands clasped submissively, shadowed by her mother; the grandfather, looking elsewhere; and the little boy, on the floor at their feet. Odd species that they are, there's no mistaking who they are. Seventeen years later, reassembled, father is hardly less feeble —and futile—than grandfather; mother and daughter are locked in silent contest; and the son, now a bearded young man, regards them with his father's erstwhile composure. Without expression, Gorey people express themselves.

Meant for children or not, many of the books are about children, or mock-children's books, or both. Thus, *The Hapless Child* (Obolensky, 1961) is the Victorian orphan's ordeal, literary version, carried to its logical end: an angelic, adored little girl, her father killed in Africa, her mother borne away by grief, her uncle struck down "by a piece of masonry," is sent by the family lawyer to a cruel boarding school whence she escapes into the hands of a "drunken brute" who puts her to work making artificial flowers until, her eyesight, her health, her looks gone, she runs into the street only to be struck down by the motorcar of her father, "not dead after all," and at that very moment searching for her. Most affronting to sentiment, "She was so changed, he did not recognize her."

In another vein, Gorey speaks of "the miseries of childhood"; and elsewhere writes discriminately: "The Baby, lying meek and quiet /Upon the customary rug/Has dreams about rampage and riot,/And will grow up to be a thug." The sorrow and savagery of childhood are as present to him as the complacency of youth or the futility of old age.

More lightly, *The Wuggly Ump*, the first to appear on a regular juvenile list, might be taken as the monster story where, finally, the worst comes to pass. Three children are frolicking in a flowery meadow: "Sing tirraloo, sing tirralay,/The Wuggly Ump lives far away" (646). But even as "We pass our happy childhood hours/In weaving endless chains of flowers"—"Across the hills the Wuggly Ump/ Is hurtling on, kerbash, kerblump!" Until under the window, at the doorstep: "It's making an unholy fuss;/Why has it come to visit us?" And one, two, three pages later, "Sing glogalimp, sing glugalump,/From deep inside the Wuggly Ump."

The three, unmussed, are floating feet up in the belly of the Wuggly Ump who, flashing his Cheshire cat grin, is no more to be taken seriously (who's afraid of a Wuggly Ump?) than the 'endless chains of flowers.' The name of the game is spoof and double-spoof: if monsters are to be believed, they must *sometime* claim a victim.

When Gorey spoke, 'diffidently,' of children liking his books he had in mind his own equivocal creations; by chance, or not, the books that come after—after *The Wuggly Ump* and the start of his illustrating children's books—are, with the exception of the Leary nonsense alphabet *The Utter Zoo* (Meredith, 1967), more distinctly not for children, and to date he has done no further children's books of his own.

What he has illustrated has been—to equivocate—broader, the same and different. Among the picturebooks are several volumes of John Ciardi poems including *The Monster Den* (Lippincott, 1966) where the children,

647. *Why We Have Day and Night,* text by Peter F. Neumeyer, pictures by Edward Gorey. Scott, 1970. 8 x 6⅜.

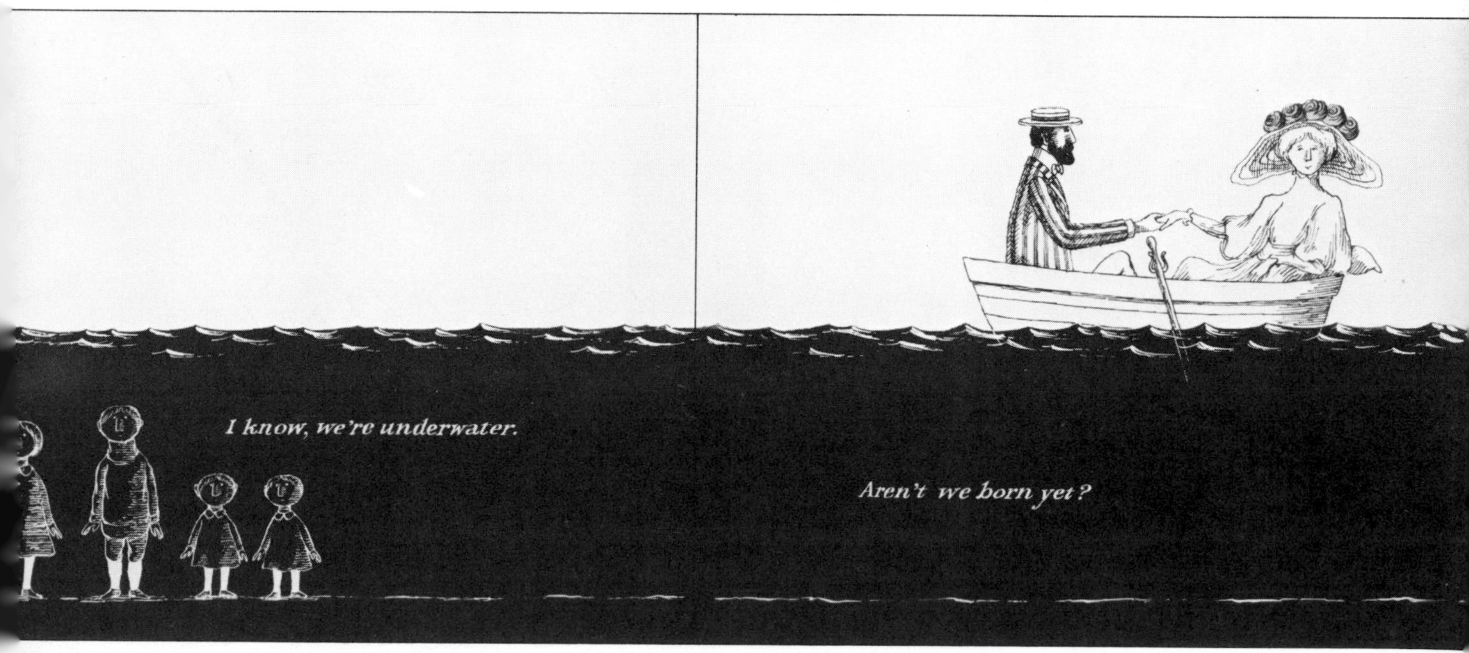

I know, we're underwater.
Aren't we born yet?

the monsters, are what the baby dreaming 'of rampage and riot' promises to become. The two volumes of Brer Rabbit stories retold in verse by Ennis Rees, *Brer Rabbit and His Tricks* and *More of Brer Rabbit's Tricks* (Scott, 1967 and 1968), sly-boots American primitive, as well as Rees's Aesop, *Lions and Lobsters and Foxes and Frogs* (Scott, 1971). Three collaborations with Peter Neumeyer, most notably *Why We Have Day and Night*, which makes nonsense of the usual science demonstration as the hypothetical bug on the spinning-earth orange gets hungrier and hungrier until he crawls deep inside and it is all, all . . . *dark*; or, to begin at the beginning, "What happened to the light? . . . Could a squirrel have chewed a wire? Did the ink spill? . . . Are we snails? Are we bats? . . ." (647) A man to watch with a concept is Mr. Gorey.

Then there was, ineluctably, Edward Lear. First, "The Jumblies."

They went to sea in a Sieve, they did,
  In a Sieve they went to sea:
In spite of all their friends could say,
On a winter's morn, on a stormy day,
  In a Sieve they went to sea!
And when the Sieve turned round and round,
And every one cried, 'You'll all be drowned!'
They called aloud, 'Our Sieve ain't big,
But we don't care a button! we don't care a fig!
  In a Sieve we'll go to sea!'
    Far and few, far and few,
      Are the lands where the Jumblies live;
    Their heads are green, and their hands
      are blue,
      And they went to sea in a Sieve.

Thus the first of six stanzas, all of them ending in the refrain "Far and few," most of

648. *The Jumblies,* text by Edward Lear, pictures by Edward Gorey. Scott, 1968. 8¾ x 6.

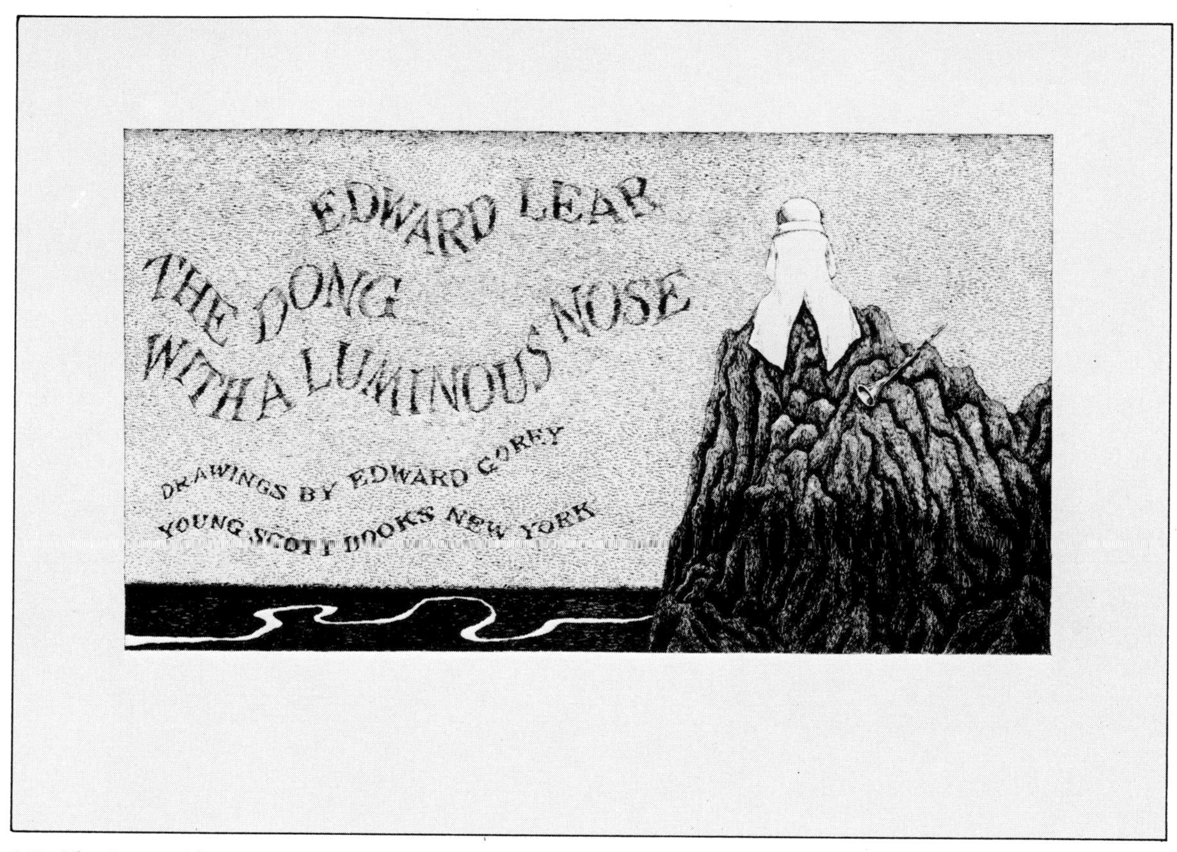

649. *The Dong with a Luminous Nose,* text by Edward Lear, pictures by Edward Gorey. Scott. 1969. 8¾ x 6.

them consisting of variations on the starting theme: a poem that Lear issued with only a headpiece drawing of the Sieve underway. We are showing the title-page not simply for the pleasure of Gorey's design—a constant pleasure—but also to better present the Jumblies, the party of high-English travelers that (Gorey in looks, Lear in proportions) entertain themselves, and us, en route (648). It is they who make the long journey successful, even feasible in pictures; and who, at each recurrence of the refrain, dispose themselves in one or another choreographic pattern, now in a casual line along the shore, now before a parapet as a human pyramid, now as a concert audience, circling dancers, statuettes. At the close, after the Jumblies' triumphal return, we hear the refrain once more and see in the last rays of evening the Sieve pulled up on shore, its sail trailing limply in the water.

Gorey's way with landscape is critical in *The Dong with a Luminous Nose*, that late sad song that begins

> When awful darkness and silence reign
> Over the great Gromboolian plain . . .

The Jumblies reappear, but only to bring a Jumbly Girl—who flies into the Dong's outstretched hands and his heart—and take her away again, leaving the Dong, now with "A Nose as strange as a Nose could be," forever wandering, searching, sounding his plaintive pipe. Except for the headpiece drawing of the Dong himself, Lear didn't illustrate this either; and it is as much an artist-poet's as an artist-illustrator's undertaking: the waves curling against the rocks like ghostly fingers, the beams of the luminous Nose shooting through a broad bare-armed tree—while nearby

650

650, 651. *The Shrinking of Treehorn,* text by Florence Parry Heide, pictures by Edward Gorey. Holiday House, 1971.

stands, from summer, from happier days, a single rattan chair. Or the title-page illustration which tells, like the ideal epigraph, everything except the story (649). For *The Jumblies* Gorey designed a divertissement, light, playful, impulsive; for *The Dong* he provides a threnody—a great furrowed mass, a ribbon of light, a pendent sky, one bright lost figure. The unspoken words are comedy and tragedy.

The break is a substitute for a transition that would have been artificial and a small tribute to Gorey's Lears, which stand alone, and to *The Shrinking of Treehorn*, which does also.

Though not of his writing, *The Shrinking of Treehorn* is peculiarly a Gorey story: the hapless child of today. Treehorn notices that he's shrinking little by little but he can't get his parents to take notice (650); or when they do, to take heed. Too small now to reach the mailbox ("You're *always* doing stupid things," says his friend Moshie, "but that's the *stupidest*") or to get on the school bus (651), unrecognized by his friend the bus driver (though he might be "Treehorn's kid brother"), directed to nursery school by his teacher (who, apprised, expects improvement tomorrow), Treehorn winds up in the principal's office for trying to jump up to the water fountain. The secretary gives him a printed form and the principal gives him, euphemistically speaking, a line of clichés and platitudes that poses as guidance. He, Treehorn, might as well not be there at all.

Salvation comes in the form of a game he sent away for from a cereal box—a continual preoccupation—called THE BIG GAME FOR KIDS TO GROW ON; and when he is his normal size his mother tells him, blankly, not to put his elbows on the table. That night, watching TV, he sees that he has turned green. "Treehorn sighed. 'I don't think I'll tell anyone,' he thought to himself. 'If I don't say anything, they won't notice.'" The end is a ha-ha, worthy of TV but unworthy of Treehorn; and the text is talky where, sometimes, silence would speak louder. But to set it off there are Gorey's spare, vacant pictures, graphic state-

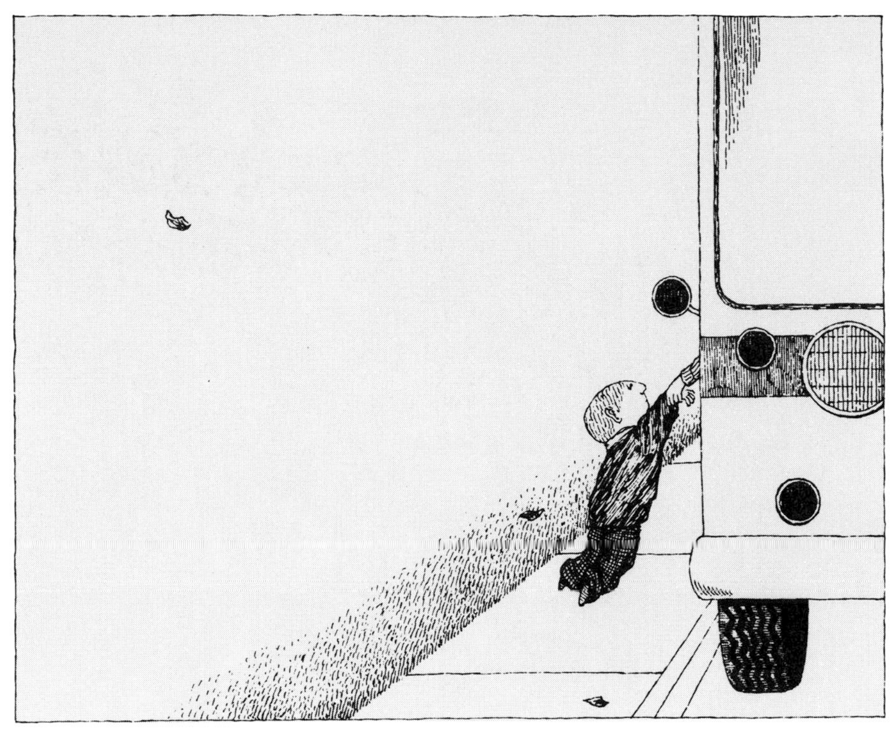
651

ments of the emptiness and hollowness of Treehorn's existence.

The sharpness and control evident in his later work generally—compare the brilliant *Dong* with the murky *Doubtful Guest*—assume a frigid, antiseptic aspect, at once ironic (Treehorn's mother is always cleaning), psychological and material. He has, indeed, as keen an eye for modern furnishings and dress as, elsewhere, for smoking jackets and heavy drapes. The kitchen he draws as a stringent pattern of closed cupboards; on the secretary's wall he puts a small abstraction of one squiggle, on the principal's a huge abstraction of two like squiggles. Gorey, be it said (as can't always), is an ironist with humor.

Early and late, he has an almost uncanny sense of mass and void, balance and contrast. Treehorn is being hoisted onto the bus, and we see the herringbone of the tire, the grid of the headlight, the solid rectangularity of the bus itself; and, opposite, a single flying leaf. On a dark night it would be a pinpoint moon.

It is perhaps his very precision that makes his work as a whole uncanny.

HARRIET PINCUS

It even sounded funny, Sandburg and Pincus, the prairie-American and the shtetl-Jewish; and Carl Sandburg's *Rootabaga Stories*, from which *The Wedding Procession of the Rag Doll and the Broom Handle and Who Was In It*—swallow that—was taken, is one of those very occasional works accorded the status of instant folklore. For Harriet Pincus, however, the story is in the words and she draws what she imagines (652).

In terms of illustration, any illustration, *The Wedding Procession* is a potential poison apple. On the one hand it is highly descriptive, a catalog of the friends of the Rag Doll and the members of the procession—the Spoon Lickers, the Tin Pan Bangers, the Dirty Bibs, the Clean Ears, the Easy Ticklers and the rest; but insofar as each is pictured in words, to illustrate them would appear redundant, even counteractive. One cannot, moreover, literally and specifically illustrate, for one, "they tickled themselves and laughed and looked around and tickled themselves again," or, without being tedious, confine one-

The Rag Doll had many friends. The Whisk Broom, the Furnace Shovel, the Coffee Pot, they all liked the Rag Doll very much.

652, 653. *The Wedding Procession of the Rag Doll and the Broom Handle and Who Was in It,* text by Carl Sandburg, pictures by Harriet Pincus. Harcourt, 1967. 9¾ x 7¾.

self to "they banged their pans and looked around and banged again" (653). Pincus's procession, in response, is less a march, for the most part, than a dance or suite of dances, a scene-by-scene performance; and the Easy Ticklers and the Tin Pan Bangers et al are, like the Whisk Broom and the Coffee Pot before them, personifications who can as well ride a turtle (backward) or wear jester's bells as otherwise. Taking a cue from Sandburg (and Sendak), Pincus opens up the account to all manner of marvels.

They are of course children, Tin Pan Bangers have to be, but the least childlike children conceivable—the farthest, in particular, from the image of childhood as unformed and unknowing. These are ancient children, wise children, and of all the celebrators—celebrants—only the Easy Ticklers are laughing. But in the seriousness is the humor, and in the two, the poignance. "But when the Rag Doll married," Sandburg tells us overleaf from 652, "it was the Broom Handle she picked because the Broom Handle fixed her eyes." In the picture, for me the most memorable, the two are on a swing, enrapt, and the unsuccessful suitors gravely serenade them. The overtones with which Pincus invests that scene she brings to the book as a whole.

She was young and untried; and she had absorbed much from Sendak; and the book is strikingly hers. One could say of Pincus as of Low that she has an individual color sense, meaning that her odd and oddly assorted colors are not to be mistaken. But it is her way of using them, as well, that is individual: her manner of applying them, solid or striated or hatched—and only selectively—to black and white drawings that have, and retain, the substance and aura of old engravings. Color does not merge with line, does not record form, it too retains its curious identity; and the effect is all the more strange in that reality is served—the appearance of reality maintained—even as it is contradicted. We are kept off-balance as, given the content, we might well be.

The hatched and cross-hatched surfaces are an obvious and insignificant Sendak carry-over; more vital is the example of *Hector Protector* in treating an old text not as a hallowed legacy but as raw material. Unlike Sendak, Pincus does not expand *The Wedding Procession* internally; but neither does she give it the period reference that he does, or any specific setting. She adds sequence by sequence, and what she adds is in the form of imagery: a mingled, envisioned presence. In part it is incontrovertibly Jewish, and not the pathos-Jewish of dark eyes and peaked faces: love-me-as-I-am Jewish, one might call it, looking at that last witch-child in her dainty dress. Sendak, distinctively, did not turn his back on his Jewishness; she embraces hers and melds it with bent wedding lilies and bespectacled turtles.

Lore Segal's *Tell Me a Mitzi* is intrinsically Jewish—the three stories are stories of Jewish family life; but that's just where we come in. "*Tell me a story,*" says Martha, and her mother, holding her baby brother, says "Once upon a time there was a Mitzi. She had a mother and a father and a brother who was a baby. His name was Jacob." A *real* once-upon-a-time story: it's enough to make a child squirm with pleasure.

The first is about the morning Mitzi and Jacob are up early and decide to go to Grandpa and Grandma's house and Mitzi makes Jacob's bottle and changes his diapers and dresses him—and almost forgets to dress herself—and takes him down in the elevator in his stroller and pushes it to the corner and calls "TAXI" and gets in; and doesn't know the address. "So the driver got out and came around to the other side and took the stroller from the front seat and unfolded it on the sidewalk and took Jacob out and put him in the stroller and walked around to his side and got in and drove away." Then . . . (654)

This is really storytelling too, a wonderful litany of who, what, how; and a recital of everyday deeds that, ordinarily, Mitzi wouldn't be doing. Mitzi in bed, her mother comes in to say Good morning; Jacob, a Solomon just before, utters his usual "Dadada"; and Mitzi's mother asks, "Mitzi, today can you be a *really big* girl and take off your *own* pajamas *all* by yourself?" But Mitzi is 'exhausted': "Mommy! Where do Grandma and Grandpa live?"

For an illustrator there was if anything too much to go on. But the richness of the story, the rootedness and roundedness, is matched, jointly and independently, by the pictures:

653

Next came the Tin Pan Bangers. Some had dishpans, some had frying pans, some had potato peeling pans. All the pans were tin with tight tin bottoms. And the Tin Pan Bangers banged with knives and forks and iron and wooden

bangers on the bottoms of the tin pans. And as they marched in the wedding procession of the Rag Doll and the Broom Handle, they banged their pans and looked around and banged again.

Mitzi pushed Jacob back to the house.
The doorman helped her get the stroller up the stairs and he pushed the elevator button for them. They got out on their floor and went in their front door and into their room. Mitzi took Jacob out of the stroller and untied his hat and took off his mittens. She took off his snowsuit and his right shoe and his left shoe and his socks and his overalls and his shirt and put on his pajamas and lifted him into his crib. Then she undressed herself and put her pajamas on and got back into bed and covered herself up and then the alarm clock rang in her mother and father's room.
1938

654. *Tell Me a Mitzi,* text by Lore Segal, pictures by Harriet Pincus. Farrar, Straus, 1970. 10¼ x 8⅞.

the doorman bending over to pat Jacob's lion, a most doorman-like gesture, and in the nursery the girlish rabbit (painted, too, on the parents' footboards), the ungainly rocking horse, the rag doll reposing under Mitzi's bed. On the endpapers—Pincus's are a feast, dream-wallpaper—the bunny is holding Jacob's bottle or pirouetting on the horse; Mitzi is kissing, dragging, fondling the doll, or lifting Jacob, carrying him, holding him; the doll is giving the horse the bottle: it is all—what else?—one big happy family.

This is to stray; but it is also a reason why, the longer one lives with the book, the more the first story stands out; good as the others are—the second the account of the cold that everybody gets, that Grandma conquers and catches too, the third of "Mitzi [and Jacob] and the President"—they aren't on the same intimate terms with maybe and make-believe. (The last, indeed, approaches social satire.)

Another reason is the animated sequences, picture-strips, serial pictures that, in the first, tell the story along with the text. Not slavishly, not always; and certainly not without variation. But it is as funny—and for a child, as fascinating—to see Mitzi changing Jacob's diaper and dressing him, step by step, as it is to hear about it; and moving as well—Ardizzone's extra dimension—to see his trepidation as she climbs into his crib at upper left, and his crowing triumph when, fully dressed, he sits on her shoulders at lower right. It is this last, the grasp of pictorial movement, that enables Pincus to carry off the difficult progressive pictures (654, right). In the spread, the action begins on the sidewalk, with a little of the doorway visible to the right; moves to the doorway, banded at the level of the picture just left; proceeds upstairs, where Mitzi enters as if from an upper hall; and swings around, as if approaching, to a spot closest, psychologically, to the viewer. This is accomplished without any obvious change in proportion; without any deviation, on the right-hand page particularly, from the present tense. It is simultaneous and progressive, altogether clear and completely convincing.

In Mitzi and Jacob, moreover, we have not automatons, we have living beings; and it is they, ultimately, that we believe in. When I think of Harriet Pincus I think, without thinking, of Grünewald's puckered-face weeping angels. Her children could cry.

WILLIAM STEIG

Listing a number of *New Yorker* artists who brought sidewalk comedy to picturebooks in recent years, we omitted the name of William Steig. When the father-confessor of Small Fry began to do books for children, he chose to follow what emerges in retrospect as a second *New Yorker* tradition. Writing in those pages in December 1945, Katharine White remarked that among the year's children's books were not only good collections of traditional fairy tales but "a number of pleasant modern stories about a world in which the fanciful happening is the natural one. Four of these, by some strange wizardry, seem to have been written by writers closely associated with this magazine."[6] One was her husband E. B. White's *Stuart Little*; and to it might be added, much later, *Sylvester and the Magic Pebble*.

Exact and effortless and timelessly true, *Sylvester* is the rare book that merits the accolade 'a born classic.'

"Sylvester Duncan lived with his mother and father at Acorn Road in Oatsdale. One of his hobbies was collecting pebbles of unusual shape and color." Overleaf—and who would not want to see where this penchant leads?—Sylvester, one rainy day, finds "a quite extraordinary one . . . flaming red, shiny, and perfectly round, like a marble." Wet, cold, he wishes out loud that the rain would stop—and it does. "It didn't stop gradually as rains usually do. It CEASED. The drops vanished on the way down, the clouds disappeared, everything was dry, and the sun was shining as if rain had never existed." Even the ducks look up in amazement.

In those three pages Steig's magic is established as firmly as the pebble's. Sylvester, for his part, is leaving nothing to chance: putting the pebble on the ground, he wishes for rain again, to no avail; holding it in his hand, he wishes once more, and his wish is granted. " 'What a lucky day this is!' thought Sylvester. 'From now on I can have anything I want. My father and mother can have anything they want. My relatives, my friends, and anybody at all can have everything anybody wants!' " It is a kind of storytelling all but nonexistent: the idealism, the faith (without the excrescences) of a *Country Bunny and the Little Gold Shoes*: a story to care about.

You do, intensely. Sylvester, starting home, meets a lion. "If he hadn't been so frightened, he could have made the lion disappear, or he could have wished himself safe at home with his father and mother. He could have wished the lion would turn into a butterfly or a daisy or a gnat. He could have wished many things, but he panicked and couldn't think carefully. 'I wish I were a rock,' he said, and he became a rock."

The situation is a perfect standoff: there is Sylvester, a rock on the hill, and next to him the magic pebble, he unable to pick it up, the chance of someone finding it and wishing that a rock were a donkey "one in a billion at best." His parents, frantic, inquire of the neighbors, the children, the police (pigs, at a time when the police were so-taunted, hence protests); and when Sylvester is not to be found, they are desolate, thinking they will never see him again—though as Steig reminds us parenthetically, "he was less than a mile away."

Comes the fall and Sylvester, resigning himself to being a rock forever, goes into an endless sleep; in the winter, in the snow, 'a wolf sits on the rock that is Sylvester and howls and howls because he is hungry.' In the spring, when the leaves and flowers reappear, Mr. Duncan insists on a cheering picnic; and there begins the excruciating wait for something to somehow bring rock and pebble together (655).

It is also a great picturebook—in the sense that one says of a movie (or used to) that it is also a great film. Not that the use of the medium is novel or ingenious or, in an obvious way, audacious; but *Sylvester* has, besides

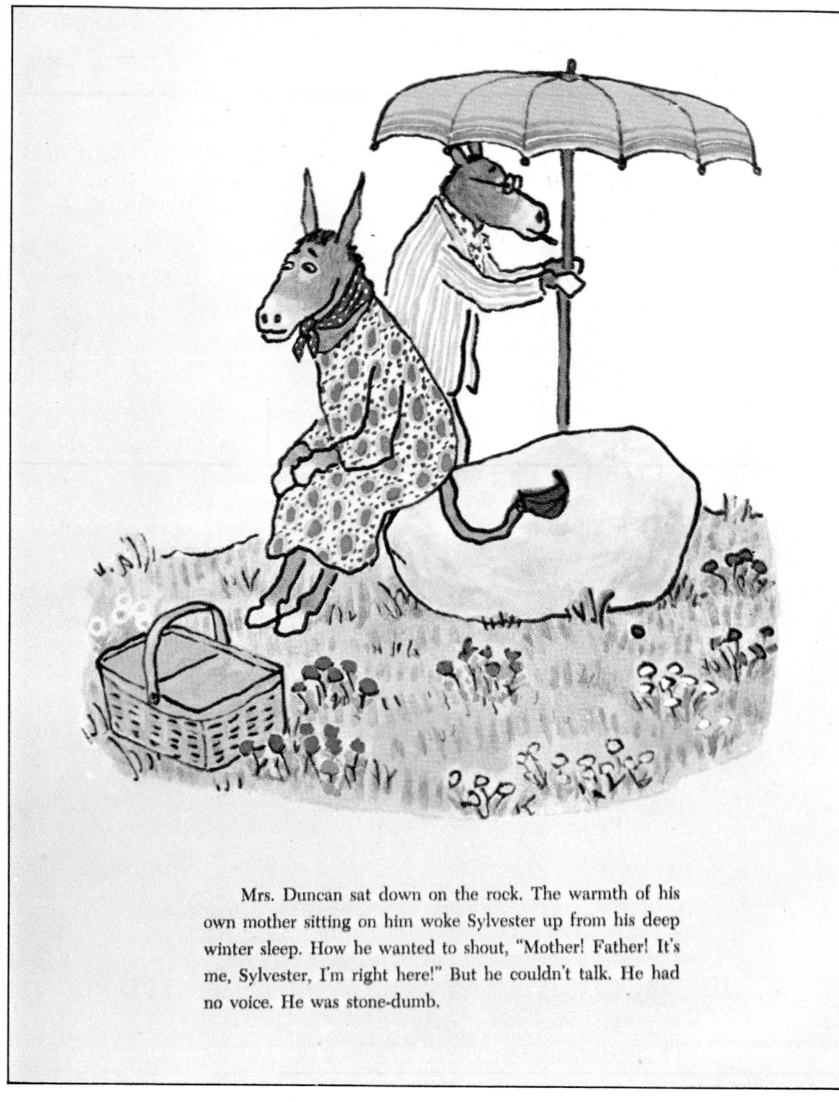

Mrs. Duncan sat down on the rock. The warmth of his own mother sitting on him woke Sylvester up from his deep winter sleep. How he wanted to shout, "Mother! Father! It's me, Sylvester, I'm right here!" But he couldn't talk. He had no voice. He was stone-dumb.

655. *Sylvester and the Magic Pebble,* by William Steig. Windmill/Simon & Schuster, 1969. 8⅞ x 11⅞.

an inherently visual idea, great visual moments. There is Sylvester, the first starry night, a rock alongside the pebble, and the same scene as green turns gold and the leaves fall, as snow blankets the earth and a wolf howls, as the spring sun warms the earth and everything buds: lyrical and touching, and the subject a rock. And there is Sylvester, suddenly, joyously himself but no proper picnic table, with jars and plates and sandwiches tumbling off his back. Above and beyond is the drawing —the fidelity of the characterizations, the sparkle of the execution. To the credit of that erratic award, *Sylvester* was a Caldecott winner.

Amos & Boris (an inspired pairing) has not the pictorial range nor the stature as a story; but in the friendship of a mouse and a whale —a seafaring mouse to begin with (656)—is a lift for the spirit and balm for the soul. One trusts that Steig, having embarked on books for older children, will not abandon picture-stories. Amos, sailing up and down as we see him, is described as "full of wonder, full of enterprise, and full of love for life": good words, beautifully pictured.

MARGOT ZEMACH

As an artist, Margot Zemach pictures children and animals only incidentally, and make-believe, as such, doesn't suit her at all. What is left is the great big field of folklore, which opened up shortly after she and her writer-husband Harve appeared on the scene. To review her work is also to survey the field and to touch upon the reasons why she, in particular, merits attention.

A rundown of the Zemach books alone is a reflection of the times. After a first original modern story, *Small Boy Is Listening* (Houghton, 1959), there appeared, usually but not invariably adapted by Harve Zemach, the ubiquitous-English *Three Sillies* (Holt, 1963); the Swedish *Nail*—otherwise the French *Stone*—*Soup* (Follett, 1964); the Russian *Salt* (Follett, 1965); Joseph Jacobs's "Teeny-Tiny" yclept *The Little Tiny Woman* (Bobbs-Merrill, 1965); a piece of original folk-spoofery, *The Tricks of Master Dabble* (Holt, 1965); *The Speckled Hen* (Holt, 1966), from a Russian nursery rhyme; *Mommy, Buy Me a China Doll* (Follett, 1966), from an Ozark children's song; the Grimm *Fisherman and His Wife* (Norton, 1966); the Italian *Too Much Nose* (Holt, 1967); and in addition various folk-type tales by Jay Williams, Jack Sendak and Isaac Singer.

Some of the stories were well known to librarians—which, if anything, enhanced their prospects—and were, furthermore, widely available in collections, which did not harm their prospects either: because "The Three Sillies" was in Jacobs's *English Fairy Tales*, owned by every library, and in Flora Steel's collection of the same name; in de la Mare's *Tales Told Again*, Johnson's *Anthology of Children's Literature* (the Jacobs version), Smith's *Laughing Matter* (ditto), all in print, did not mean that it would reach the eyes and ears of children. For one thing, children of an age to be able to read a collection like Jacobs's weren't—not as, it was felt, they once had; hence the utility of Virginia Haviland's simplified *Favorite Fairy Tales Told in . . .* series, which began in 1959 with retellings from Jacobs himself, Perrault ("and other French storytellers") and the Brothers Grimm. Listening, for another thing, had lost out to looking and listening, and not only among children raised on television; and both reading aloud and oral storytelling were in decline. If chil-

656. *Amos & Boris,* by William Steig. Farrar, Straus, 1971. Detail.

dren were to get to know the tales at all, the thinking went, it would be from pictured versions.

That they should has been a cardinal library principle. Bertha Mahony put it in terms of wonder and imagination and put it beautifully, quoting de la Mare quoting Coleridge, for one. Latterly, we hear less about wonder, more about 'satisfaction of needs' and 'cultural identity'; we hear specifically that "Folklore is sometimes called the 'mirror of a people.' It reveals their characteristic efforts to explain and deal with the strange phenomena of nature; to understand and interpret the ways of human beings with each other; and to give expression to deep universal emotions. . . ."[7] That is May Hill Arbuthnot, and it is at once one of the more restrained and less pedantic assessments; but it has the effect nonetheless of sanctifying folklore and endowing all that is 'folk' with intrinsic merit and potential power. A folktale is ipso facto 'a good thing.'

They are good stories, a great many of them; and there are a great many of them; and they are in the public domain. Add up the parts of that sentence, add them to the foregoing, add in the consideration that an artist of established reputation need not share the royalties with an author, that a folktale he illustrates will sell on its identity and his name, and you have, in an expanding market like that of the Sixties—supported by federal funds generally (qq. v. p. 372), by the growth of school libraries in particular—an ever-increasing, never-ending supply.

But even as they appear they give the lie to one of the justifications for their existence, their supposed reflection of the customs and beliefs of a particular people. "The Three Sillies" was known by Jacobs to be a variant of the Grimms' "Clever Elsie," and to be "spread throughout the world."[8] In the same way "Lazy Jack" (Jacobs) and "Prudent Hans" (Grimm), as we've had occasion to remark—and "What Should I Have Said?" (Afanasiev)—are variants of "What Should I Have Done?" which, Stith Thompson observes, "seems to go back to a Chinese Buddhistic source. . . . It has been collected not only all over Europe . . . but also in Indonesia, Japan, and all parts of Africa."[9] To pretend otherwise, to regard each version as native-born, is to do, in effect, what anthropologists do and folklorists decry: to "depict folk narratives collected from their society as a reflector of cultural traits and tensions in that society, unaware that the same tales are told at the other end of the world."[10]

"The Three Sillies" remains nonetheless a good story—Jacobs's good story, revised only slightly from its appearance in the *Folk-Lore Journal* of 1884, where it is set down as told, ostensibly, by the recorder's nursemaid in 1862. Jacobs's English stories have character and flavor, and they are tight and cannily told; oral storytellers are commonly advised not to tamper with them. The same, of course, would be true of "Teeny-Tiny." Taken together, they bring us to two further considerations: the relationship of the picturebook text to the original and the suitability of the story itself for picturing.

Margot Zemach's *The Three Sillies* is called simply "a folk tale illustrated by Margot Zemach"; even a few years later, such was the stress on sources, it would probably have been identified as an adaptation from Jacobs. As originally written, the story would fill more than three columns in this book, and it is shorter by only a few lines in the Zemach version—for a bona fide picturebook, considerable text. The tale devolves upon a girl who, sent to the cellar to get beer to serve her suitor, sees an axe stuck in the ceiling and starts to weep at the prospect of marrying the suitor and having a child who might come down just as the axe fell. This is Jacobs: "It must have been there a long, long time, but somehow or other she had never noticed it before, and she began a-thinking. And she thought it was very dangerous to have that mallet there, for she said to herself: 'Suppose him and me was to be married, and we was to have a son, and he was to grow up to be a man, and come down into the cellar to draw the beer, like as I'm doing now, and the mallet was to fall on his head and kill him, what a dreadful thing it would be!"

657. *The Three Sillies,* pictures by Margot Zemach. Holt, 1963. 8⅝ x 5¾.

And, hardly different, Zemach: "It must have been there a long time, but somehow or other she had never noticed it before; and it set her thinking.

"She thought it was very dangerous to have that axe there, and she said to herself, 'Suppose he and I were to be married, and we had a son, and he grew up to be a man, and came down into the cellar to draw the beer, and the axe were to fall on his head, what a dreadful thing it would be!" Whereupon, in either version, first her mother, then her father, then the suitor comes down and to each she repeats her plaint.

The strange 'mallet' has become the familiar 'axe,' an expedient I adopted too; the grammar has been corrected, although the original is more graphic and closer to common speech; certain storytelling devices—the reiterated 'many,' the initial 'And'—have been eliminated, and paragraphing has been inserted, stemming the flow; the unborn son has been saved from certain death—though not, presumably, from having his head split open. (Just as, later, a cow is left hanging by the neck, not "strangled.") The changes, whatever their relative merit, are intended in the aggregate to accommodate the story to young children—or perhaps their parents—because it is being made into a picturebook.

To what effect (657)? One may laugh at the sight of the silly girl, one will laugh certainly when her mother joins her on the floor, the beer oozes round them, and the father comes down the ladder in turn; but it is they who, as pictured, are ludicrous, not the situation. And to the extent that a child, looking, concentrates less on the text—one reason for shortening and simplifying it—he is missing just that much more of the substance and flavor of a story whose humor, essentially, is in the extended telling.

"Teeny-Tiny," on the other hand, is brief and quick, and a *ghost* story. "Its charm for children lies, first, in the constant repetition of 'teeny-tiny,' and then, if well read, in the explosive ending. . . ."[11] Viz: "Once upon a time there was a teeny-tiny woman who lived in a teeny-tiny house in a teeny-tiny village." She goes into a teeny-tiny churchyard, finds a teeny-tiny bone on a teeny-tiny grave, and takes it home "to make some teeny-tiny soup for my teeny-tiny supper"; but when she gets home she is "a teeny-tiny bit tired," so she goes up to her teeny-tiny bed and puts the bone into a teeny-tiny cupboard. "And when this teeny-tiny woman had been to sleep a teeny-tiny time, she was awakened by a teeny-tiny voice from the teeny-tiny cupboard, which said, *'Give me my bone.'*" Again and again, a little louder each time . . . until the teeny-tiny woman "put her teeny-tiny head out of the teeny-tiny [bed] clothes and said in her loudest teeny-tiny voice, 'TAKE IT!'" A little tiny woman in a little tiny book is a tin echo.

When picturebooks first began to appear in quantity, there were those who felt they would restrict children's imagination; and when they became omnipresent, felt that they did. The argument has merit when the pictures, by nature or circumstance, diminish rather than augment the words.

The Zemachs are not here, however, to serve as a bad example. Their adaptations are more sensitive than many; Margot Zemach's illustrations have more life than most; and within a few years their choice of material became surer. The Afanasiev *Salt* is a draw—altered to make it more palatable (e.g. happiness speaks rashly, not strong drink), pictured to make it more tempting; but the Russian rhyme *The Speckled Hen* is one of those wild pile-ups that—"Wonder of wonders!"—grows funnier at every opening, and *Mommy, Buy Me a China Doll*, the Ozark children's song, and *Too Much Nose*, the Italian tale, are in their very different ways splendid *books.*

Mommy, Buy Me a China Doll cumulates also (658); and with each amusing, appealing addition to the rhyme comes an amusing, appealing picture, for however much Daddy and horsey and Sister and baby might be discomfitted by Eliza Lou's plan, she imagines them (in Margot Zemach's mind) to be as little upset as she is by the piggies. So we see Daddy sound asleep in the horsey's stall, keeping the horsey up, and Grandma patiently darning in the piggies' pen—but "where would our horsey sleep," "where would our piggies go, Eliza Lou?" In each proposal is the need for the next, and Eliza Lou keeps improvising, and the pages as good as turn themselves. These are wonderful big strong pictures too (ill-matched by the type-face), in rusty reds and tawny pinks predominantly, with an inner strength that comes from the faces. It could have been silly, it could have been played for laughs, and it isn't.

The dopey grin, or droop, that represents the gamut of expression in the early Zemach books is gone, and the lumpy, clunky people.

658. *Mommy, Buy Me a China Doll,* adaptation by Harve Zemach, pictures by Margot Zemach. Follett, 1966. 9¾ x 8.

We could let them stay in my own bed,
Do, Mommy, do!
Trade our Daddy's featherbed,
Daddy in the horsey's bed,
Horsey in our Sister's bed,
Sister in the baby's bed,
Baby in the kittens' bed,
Kittens in the chicken coop,
Chickens on the rocking chair,
Granny in the piggy pen,
Piggies in Eliza's bed—
Then where would Eliza sleep, Eliza Lou?

Robust energy and abounding good spirits redeemed them—to the point that Zemach's style seemed the embodiment of those very qualities, and others illustrating earthy folktales began to draw as she did. But without losing the physical vitality, she was acquiring a new vitality of expression and the means of getting inside a story, as *Too Much Nose* might have been chosen to demonstrate.

The text of *Mommy, Buy Me a China Doll* —the Ozark children's song—is a find, exactly suited to picturebook presentation; the story on which *Too Much Nose* is based, the Italian tale "Twelve Feet of Nose," is a find too, because although the titular motif—the nose made to grow by eating this, to shrink by eating that—is a familiar one (the basis of *Dwarf Long-Nose* also), the characters and situations have a rich particularity, an interest and intimations of their own. If you happened to come across it, you'd enjoy the reading; but in the unlikely event you did find it (in an 1874 collection Harve Zemach identifies), you would enjoy it less than you do with Margot Zemach's pictures to point it up.

A poor old man has sent his three sons out into the world with, respectively, an old broken hat that makes its wearer invisible, a ragged coin purse that is never empty, and a rusty horn that, blown, brings Someone to answer any request. The second son (for once), passing below the windows of a palace, is summoned to play at cards with the queen (659); and when he loses, insists that, yes, he can pay, and produces the magic purse. Snatching it from him, the queen has him turned out and beaten; so he goes to his elder brother to borrow the magic hat. Wearing it, he steals dish after dish of the queen's dinner, threatening to torment her until she returns his purse; but she insists on seeing him, and as soon as she learns the secret, the hat is on her head and he is on the pavement. So with the third gift, the magic horn: he assaults the palace, she, feigning compliance, prizes the secret from him and out he goes.

Now you might say that this is one gullible fellow, and the original recorder does; you might even say, if you hadn't the picture, that

659

659, 660. *Too Much Nose,* adaptation by Harve Zemach, pictures by Margot Zemach. Holt, 1967. 7½ x 9.

660

he was a fool. Harve Zemach, though, tells it without comment; and Margot Zemach tells us that, however much duped, he isn't a fool.

Ashamed to face his brothers, he wanders in the countryside and coming upon a fig tree, eats one and then another—until he notices that his nose has grown to a terrible size; he will have to wander forever, it seems. But shortly he finds a cherry tree, and with each fruit that he eats his nose grows smaller: "Now I know what to do!"

With a basketful of figs and a bottle of cherry juice he is back at the palace; the queen's servants buy the figs, and the queen, "of course," eats more than anyone else (660). "Well, it happened to them, just the way it had happened to the second son"; and when nothing avails, he returns in the guise of a foreign doctor with special medicine for healing noses—all right for common folk, but "terribly strong stuff to give to a queen." Seeing that the medicine works, she is jealous, still, of the boast: he is not the only one who can work wonders, "I've got even greater wonders than yours." And to prove it she produces the hat, the purse and the horn. The second son flips the hat on his head, snatches up the purse and the horn, and is gone forever —leaving the queen "forever with TOO MUCH NOSE!" At the last, looking down her long protuberance, she is playing solitaire.

In the initial card game between the unwary youth and the pouncing, glinting queen is the crux of the story and its future course (659). The emotional undertones take us all the way back to Walter Crane's Bluebeard and wife (1); and elsewhere, for Zemach more than Crane is in the tradition of the artist who comments on life in the act of picturing it. How variously the victim's revenge shows plain (660). Where the one is a flash of insight, the other is to be read part by part: the servants tucking away the figs down below, the queen feasting above, and the youth outside, containing his pleasure. In *The Three Sillies* the cut-away dwelling, a Zemach stand-by, positions the characters graphically; in *Too Much Nose* it sets up the separate, convergent strands of the story and, enlarging each, positions the characters psychologically. Even the feet, under card table or kitchen table, have their part to play; Zemach is the master of the eloquent foot.

It is what she brings to a story altogether and brings out in it that distinguishes her folklore transcriptions from the many proficient renderings that proceed from analysis and follow fashions in illustration, that rest upon design and style; and in which the means, once mastered, becomes a manner.

The big step was beyond folklore—beyond re-creating one or another Russian or Italian or regional rhyme or tale—and into entertainment: into creating, out of old materials and modes, something new and intrinsically pictorial.

Thus *The Judge*, "an untrue tale" in rollicking rhyme and silent pictures. "This is prisoner number one,/Let justice be done!" . . . (661). "The man has told an untrue tale./Throw him in jail!" And so with number two, who adds to the story, and numbers four and five:

> Please let me go, Judge.
> I didn't know, Judge.
> That what I said was against the law.
> I just said what I saw.
>
> A horrible thing is coming this way,
> Creeping closer day by day.
> Its eyes are scary
> Its tail is hairy
> Its paws have claws
> It snaps its jaws
> It growls, it groans
> It chews up stones
> It spreads its wings
> And does bad things
> It belches flame
> It has no name
> I tell you, Judge, we all better pray!

By this time we know it by heart, and we know what the Judge will say. Do we know that we're in for a surprise, that the horrible thing is in fact coming his way . . . (662)? Will come in the door, swallow him down, let justice be done and the prisoners go free.

Prisoner number one, please observe, is only

661

Please let me go, Judge.
I didn't know, Judge,
That what I did was against the law.
I just said what I saw.

A horrible thing is coming this way,
Creeping closer day by day.
  Its eyes are scary
  Its tail is hairy
I tell you, Judge, we all better pray!

662

661, 662. *The Judge,* text by Harve Zemach, pictures by Margot Zemach. Farrar, Straus, 1969. 10¾ x 7¾.

shamming a wooden leg; a suspect witness at best; and the other prisoners, no less than the Judge, are a very dubious lot. The problem of the audience is the problem of a judge: what to believe, whom to credit? So we look to the figures and that, in any case, is where the interest lies: in the irascible Judge and the assortment of frenzied, abject, flighty souls who come before him, characters every one. (The question, then, is who'll be next?) This is comic portraiture of a high order, and the text plays to it as much as it aims at the wordless climax.

In its externals—the style, the monster, the animated sequence—*The Judge* is out of Rowlandson via Sendak. But it is also a separate, analogous return to Rowlandson: a Rowlandson subject viewed as he did, with rue and appreciative amusement.

Margot Zemach followed Sendak as the natural illustrator of Isaac Singer, and not because of any surface resemblance: drawing like herself, she has the requisite emotional range. If *The Judge* is grand and uproarious, ginger and mustard, *A Penny a Look,* billed simply as "An Old Story" and something of a music-hall turn too, is a tinkling piano and lemon fizz. It takes two brothers, the one a go-getter, the other a laggard, by road and river and balloon on the trail of a one-eyed man who, says the promoter, will make their fortune—while his battered companion worries more and more that "Maybe it's not right to do this to a poor, helpless one-eyed man." But when the first one-eyed man appears (663), neither brother has, ever after, anything to say.

That one-eyed man is like Chesterton's admiral with a wooden leg, the better for it (and, so goes the story, in the land of the one-eyed, a two-eyed man is a freak). He is also, with his one eye, as exactly poised between attack and flight, fierceness and terror and, for the beholder, a laugh and a gasp, as a figure could be; as if having only one central eye had, in itself, made him equivocal. "The brothers ran to catch him," reads the text. Anything can happen.

663. *A Penny a Look,* adaptation by Harve Zemach, pictures by Margot Zemach. Farrar, Straus, 1971. Detail.

To conclude, then, is not to bring the subject to a close. Given the dependence of picturebooks on art and commerce, on thinking and technology, today's outlook may alter without warning the day after tomorrow. What has been established is the picturebook itself, in William Scott's view "the simplest, subtlest, most communicative, most elusive, most challenging book form of them all."[12] And regardless of what occurs elsewhere, a single individual with creative vision—an editor, a writer, an artist—can make the critical difference.

NOTES

STARTING POINTS

1. Norman Hapgood, "A Painter of Children: Boutet de Monvel," *McClure's Magazine*, X (January 1898), 201.
2. Marie L. Van Viorst, "The Painter de Monvel," *Century*, LVII (February 1899), 577.
3. Subsequently there appeared *Susanna's Auction* (New York, Macmillan, 1923) and *Brother of the Birds: A Little History of Saint Francis of Assisi* (Philadelphia, McKay, 1929) with a new English text by Louisa Meigs Green.
4. H. T. Park, "The New Child and its Picture Books," *Bookman*, IV (December 1896), 306. Paraphrased.
5. Annie Carroll Moore, "*A List of Books Recommended for a Children's Library*" (Iowa Library Commission, 1905?), 4.
6. Josiah Titzell, "Rachel Field, 1894–1942," *Horn Book*, XVIII (July 1942), 218.
7. Mary Hazeltine, quoted in "Books and Libraries for Children," *Review of Reviews*, XXX (July 1904), 107.
8. Lucy E. Fay and Anne T. Eaton, *Instruction in the Use of Books and Libraries* (Boston, The Boston Globe Company, 1915), 315.
9. Quoted in M. H. Spielmann and G. S. Layard, *Kate Greenaway* (London, A. and C. Black, 1905), 281.
10. Quoted in Henry M. Reed, *The A. B. Frost Book*, 36.
11. F. Hopkinson Smith, *American Illustrators*, 19.
12. Gleeson White, *Children's Books and their Illustrators*, 47.
13. Anne Carroll Moore, *New Roads to Childhood*, 59. Further references: *The Three Owls* (first book), 70; *Horn Book*, XXX (August 1954), 241.
14. Charles Dana Gibson, "A. B. Frost—A Personal Tribute," *Scribner's Magazine*, LXXXIV (November 1928), 552.
15. New York *Sun*, quoted in Reed, *The A. B. Frost Book*, 110.
16. James Daugherty, "Children's Books in a Democracy," in *Newbery Medal Books, 1922–1955*, 190.

E. BOYD SMITH

1. "Literary Note," unidentified newspaper tearsheet [1903], Houghton Mifflin archive.
2. "Boston Notes," *New York Times*, August 5, 1905.
3. Elizabeth Seelye and Edward Eggleston, *Pocahontas* (New York, Dodd, Mead, 1879), 47.
4. Several of the original illustrations for *Santa Claus and All About Him* were given by Stokes to the New York Public Library and have been kept at the Hudson Park Branch.
5. Houghton Mifflin catalog, Christmas 1910–New Year's 1911.
6. Quoted in *Illustrators of Children's Books, 1744–1945*, 218.
7. Clara Whitehill Hunt, "Picture Books for Children," *Outlook*, XCVI (November 26, 1910), 744–745. Slightly condensed.
8. Alice Dalgliesh, *First Experiences with Literature*, 36.
9. David Bland, *A History of Book Illustration*, 329.

THE ERRATIC, ECLECTIC TWENTIES

1. Anne Carroll Moore, *New Roads to Childhood*, 173.
2. *Ibid.*, 193.
3. Mary Liddell, "Little Machinery Reviews," *Horn Book*, X (January 1934), 25.
4. Peggy Bacon, letter to the author, April 2, 1972.
5. Ernestine Evans, "The Red Horse Trots Again," *Four Star Final—Juvenile Supplement* (New York, Coward-McCann, Fall 1944), 5.

WANDA GÁG

1. "A Hotbed of Feminists," *Nation*, CXXIV (June 22, 1927), 691.
2. *Ibid.*, 693.
3. Ernestine Evans, "Wanda Gág as Writer," *Horn Book*, XI (November 1935), 184.
4. Wanda Gág, letter to Harold and Doris Larrabee, June 26, 1928. Copy in Wanda Gág archive, Philadelphia Museum of Art.
5. Ernestine Evans, "Wanda Gág as Writer," 184.
6. Anne Carroll Moore, New York *Herald Tribune Books*, September 9, 1928. Reprinted in *The Three Owls, Third Book*, 110.
7. Elizabeth Coatsworth, *Saturday Review of Literature*, V (September 22, 1928), 149.
8. Quoted in "Prints by Wanda Gág," *Bulletin of the Minneapolis Institute of Arts*, XXV (December 7, 1946), 157–158.

FOREIGN BACKGROUNDS

1. Karl Kup, "An International Exhibition of Juvenile Books in Germany," *Publishers' Weekly*, CXX (August 29, 1931), 828.
2. Florence Eilau Bamberger, "The Effect of the Physical Make-up of a Book upon Children's

Selection," *Johns Hopkins University Studies in Education*, No. 4 (Baltimore, Johns Hopkins Press, 1922).
3. Helen Martin, "Children's Preferences in Book Illustration," *Western Reserve University Bulletin*, No. 10 (Cleveland, 1931).
4. Neither did this list nor any other standard guide include two of their greatest popular successes, Olive Beaupré Miller's *Nursery Friends from France* and *Tales Told in Holland* (Chicago, The Book House for Children, 1925 and 1926).
5. Maud Petersham, "Illustrating Books for Children," *Elementary English Review*, II (March 1925), 86.
6. Helen Hammett Owen, in *The Three Owls, Third Book*, 441.
7. "Books by Lithography," *Publishers' Weekly*, CXVII (February 1, 1930), 617.
8. Lesley Newton, "Modern Trends in Book Illustration for Children," *Elementary English Review*, IX (March 1932), 94.
9. Ingri Parin d'Aulaire, letter to author, May 28, 1972.
10. Lewis Gannett, "Books and Things," New York *Herald Tribune*, November 18, 1936.
11. Henry C. Pitz, "Ludwig Bemelmans," *American Artist*, XV (May 1951), 49.
12. Ludwig Bemelmans, "And So Madeline Was Born," in *Caldecott Medal Books, 1938–1957*, 257.
13. "Unusual Cut-outs and Painting Books," *Horn Book*, V (November 1929), 43.

THE DYNAMICS AND FUN OF THE FORM

1. Dorothy White, *Books Before Five*, 23.
2. Lucile Morrison, "Sixes and Sevens," *Horn Book*, VI (November 1930), 312.
3. Viking catalog, 1936.

THE SMALL CHILD'S WORLD

1. Arnold Gesell, foreword to *The Child's First Books*.
2. Lois Hayden Meek, "The Preschool Movement," *Progressive Education*, VI (January–February–March 1929), 3.
3. Lois Hayden Meek, "Child Study in the Preschool Field," *Progressive Education*, III (January–February–March 1926), 39. Paraphrased.
4. May Lamberton Becker, *First Adventures in Reading*, 28.
5. Helen Hammett Owen, New York *Herald Tribune Books*, July 3, 1932.

HELEN SEWELL

1. Thomas Mann, introduction to Franz Masereel, *Passionate Journey* (New York, Lear, 1948), 14.
2. Louise Seaman Bechtel, "About Helen Sewell," *Horn Book*, X (July 1934), 244.
3. Lewis Gannett, "Books and Things," New York *Herald Tribune*, November 18, 1936.

INFORMATION

1. *New York Times Book Review and Magazine*, September 25, 1921.
2. Ernestine Evans, "Russian Children and Their Books," *Asia*, XXXI (November 1931), 689.
3. Hellmut Lehmann-Haupt, "Books About Bookmaking," *Publishers' Weekly*, CXXII (August 6, 1932), 432.
4. Dorothy Waugh to author, February 8, 1972.
5. Lucy Sprague Mitchell, *Two Lives*, 409.
6. Quoted in *Contemporary Illustrators of Children's Books*, 68.

PHOTOGRAPHIC BOOKS

1. Thomas Wood Stevens, "The Man at the Window," *Inland Printer*, XXXII (January 1904), 537.
2. Sougez, *Alphabet* (Paris, Éditions Antoine Roche, 1932).
3. Elisabeth Irwin, "Beginning to Meet the World," *Survey*, LXV (December 15, 1930), 340.
4. "A First Picture Book," Chicago *Post*, November 14, 1930.
5. Mary Steichen Martin, preface, *The First Picture Book*.
6. "The Ten-Cent Juvenile," *Publishers' Weekly*, CXXVI (November 10, 1934), 174–175.
7. Bettina Hürlimann, *Three Centuries of Children's Books*, 147.
8. *Life*, XXIV (May 24, 1948), 126.

IMPORTED FROM FRANCE

1. E. M. Forster, "Happiness!" originally "L'Expérience du Bonheur," *Atheneum*, XXIII (January 1920), 122–123. Reprinted in *Abinger Harvest* (New York, Harcourt, 1936), 35–37.
2. Douglas Percy Bliss, "The Picture Books of Edy Legrand," *Artwork*, V, No. 18 (1929), 130.
3. John Lewis, *The Twentieth Century Book*, 194.
4. *Ibid.*, 195.
5. Henry C. Pitz, "Edy Legrand, Famous French Artist who has influenced American Illustrators," *American Artist*, XVII (November 1953), 35.
6. Esther Averill, "Avant-Gardes and Traditions in France," in *Contemporary Illustrators of Children's Books*, 90.
7. *The Observer*, December 3, 1932.
8. Anne Carroll Moore, *Atlantic Monthly*, CL (December 1932), 22.
9. R.-L. Dupuy, "Fedor Rojankovsky," *Gebrauchsgraphik*, IX, No. 12 (1932), 41.
10. Esther Averill, "Fedor Rojankovsky and 'Les Peaux-Rouges,'" *Horn Book*, VIII (February 1932), 28.
11. *Ibid.*, 32.
12. *Ibid.*, 30.
13. Esther Averill, " A Publisher's Odyssey III," *Horn Book*, XV (January 1932), 22.
14. *Ibid.*, 23.
15. Esther Averill, quoted in Harper & Row biographical profile, n.d.
16. Isabelle Jan, "French Children's Classics: Tradition in a Non-Traditional Age," *Wilson Library Bulletin*, XLVII (October 1972), 167.
17. Benois's remarks appeared in a Russian journal published in Paris; Esther Averill gives the gist of them in "Feodor Rojankovsky, Illustrator," *Horn Book*, XIX (May 1943), 152.
18. "Ten-Cent Store Line," *Publishers' Weekly*, CXXIX (February 22, 1936), 898.

ROGER DUVOISIN

1. *Bookbinding and Book Production,* XXV (March 1937), 60.
2. Marguerite Mitchell, "Artists and Picture Books," *Horn Book,* XII (May–June 1937), 140.
3. There was also a later edition at $1.49.
4. Dorothy Waugh, "Roger Duvoisin as Illustrator for Children," in *Caldecott Medal Books, 1938–1957,* 178.
5. *Horn Book,* XXVII (January 1951), 28.
6. Quoted on the jacket of *The Rain Puddle.*

THE AMERICAN LINE

1. David Bland, *A History of Book Illustration,* 304.
2. Oliver Larkin, *Art and Life in America,* 481.
3. Alice Dalgliesh, "Improvement in Juvenile Books During the Last Ten Years," *Publishers' Weekly,* CXVIII (October 25, 1930), 1971.
4. Robert Lawson, "Howard Pyle and His Times," in *Illustrators of Children's Books, 1744–1945,* 105.
5. J. S. Coleman, Jr., Asheville *Citizen-Times,* February 25, 1946.
6. May Lamberton Becker, New York *Herald Tribune Books,* September 16, 1934. Partly paraphrased.
7. Robert Lawson, "Howard Pyle and His Times," 112.
8. *New York Times,* October 23, 1938.
9. Quoted in Helen Dean Fish, "Robert Lawson, Artist for Children," *Publishers' Weekly,* CXXXIX (June 21, 1941), 2466.
10. Norman Kent, "James Daugherty, Buckskin Illustrator," *American Artist,* IX (March 1945), 16.
11. Josiah Titzell, "James Daugherty, American," *Publishers' Weekly,* CXVI (October 26, 1929), 2073.
12. Hilton Kramer, "Paintings by Daugherty Recall an Era," *New York Times,* December 25, 1971.
13. James Daugherty, "Illustrating for Children," *Bulletin of the New York Public Library,* LX (November 1956), 571. Reprinted in Frances L. Spain, ed., *Reading Without Boundaries.*
14. Louise Seaman Bechtel, "Books on the Ladder of Time," a speech given in 1960 at the New York Public Library. Reprinted in Bechtel, *Books in Search of Children,* 249.
15. Lynd Ward, "James Daugherty," in *Newbery Medal Books, 1922–1955,* 183.
16. Anne Thaxter Eaton, *Treasure for the Taking* (New York, Viking, 1946), 121.
17. James Daugherty, *Horn Book,* XIX (November 1943), 425.

OF THE AMERICAN INDIAN

1. Frederic H. Douglas and René d'Harnoncourt, *Indian Art of the United States,* 44.
2. Mary Austin, "Indian Arts for Indians," *Survey,* LX (July 1, 1926), 381.
3. W. Carson, Jr., and Rose Brandt, "Indian Education Today," *Progressive Education,* IX (February 1932), 84.
4. *Time, XXVII* (February 10, 1936), 36.
5. *Indians at Work,* VII (March 1940), 15.
6. *Ibid.,* 15.
7. *Indian Education,* IV (November 1, 1940), 3.
8. Willard W. Beatty, "Bilingual Readers," in *Little Herder in Autumn,* 89.
9. *Ibid.,* 90.
10. Harry Behn, *Chrysalis: Concerning Children and Poetry* (New York, Harcourt, Brace, 1968), 12.
11. *Indians at Work,* VII (March 1940), 15.
12. Jacket of *In My Mother's House.*
13. Louise Seaman Bechtel, New York *Herald Tribune Books,* November 14, 1954.

TWO MASTERS: MARIE HALL ETS AND WILLIAM PÈNE DU BOIS

1. Marie Hall Ets, "Batik Illustration," *Horn Book,* XXX (October 1954), 346.
2. Marcia Brown, "Distinction in Picture Books," *Horn Book,* XXV (September 1949), 392–393.
3. William M. Ivins, Jr., *Prints and Books,* 241.
4. Yvonne Pène du Bois, "William Pène du Bois, Boy and Artist," *Newbery Medal Books, 1922–1955,* 307.
5. William Pène du Bois, Acceptance Paper, *Newbery Medal Books, 1922–1955,* 316–317.
6. William Pène du Bois, "Animal History Will Bear This Out," *Bulletin of the New York Public Library* (April 1957). Reprinted in Frances L. Spain, ed., *The Contents of the Basket,* 35–39 excerpted.
7. William Pène du Bois, Acceptance Paper, *Newbery Medal Books, 1922–1955,* 309–310.

SUI GENERIS:
SEVEN SIMEONS AND *BUTTONS*

1. Macmillan catalog, 1925.
2. Séan Jennett, *The Making of Books,* 404–405.
3. Lynd Ward, "Modern Picture Books," in *The Three Owls, Third Book,* 398. Slightly abridged.
4. Barbara Cooney, "The Artist at Work: Scratchboard Illustration," *Horn Book,* XL (April 1964), 163–164.
5. Ernest W. Watson, "The Art of Boris Artzybasheff," *American Artist,* V (December 1941), 15.
6. John Fairleigh, *Graven Image* (New York, Macmillan, 1940), 212.
7. Watson, "The Art of Boris Artzybasheff," 15.
8. "Seven Simeons Wins Clinic Honors," *Publishers' Weekly,* CXXXI (June 5, 1937), 2329.
9. Bruce Lockwood, "Boris Artzybasheff," *Creative Art,* XII (January 1933), 16.
10. Paul Standard, 'A Layman's Choice," *Publishers' Weekly,* CXXXI (June 5, 1937), 2332.
11. "Seven Simeons Wins Clinic Honors," *ibid.,* 2329.
12. Jacket of the original edition of *Lentil.*
13. *Ibid.*
14. Edward Alden Jewell, quoted in *Art Digest,* XIII (April 15, 1939), 34.
15. The Doves Press was one of several private presses that arose in the wake of William Morris's Kelmscott Press, and the five-volume Bible—500 copies, all told—appeared in 1903–05.
16. Arthur Thompson, "The Fifty for 1941," *Publishers' Weekly,* CXXXIX (February 1, 1941), 653. Slightly condensed.

THE STORYTELLERS

1. L. Felix Ranlett, "Books and Two Small Boys," *Horn Book,* XVIII (November 1942), 412.

2. Virginia Lee Burton, "Virginia Lee Burton," Houghton Mifflin brochure, n.d.
3. *Ibid.*
4. *Ibid.*
5. Robert Feild, *The Art of Walt Disney*, 142
6. *Ibid.*, 139.
7. Don Freeman, letter to author, April 14, 1972. Slightly condensed.
8. Morris Colman, "Some Tcehnical Notes on Book Illustration," Part II, *American Artist*, XVII (January 1953), 49.
9. Quoted in Bob Thomas, *The Art of Animation*, 38.
10. *Ibid.*, 22
11. Lillian Gerhardt, *Virginia Kirkus Bulletin* (June 22, 1965), 622.

DESIGNED FOR CHILDREN

1. Evelyn Harter, "Full Trim: A Bias on Current Bookmaking," *Publishers' Weekly*, CXXVII (January 5, 1935), 91.
2. Lucy Sprague Mitchell, foreword to *Another Here and Now Story Book*, xvi.
3. Evelyn Harter, *ibid.*, 93.
4. Vernon Ives, "Holiday House: The Formative Years, 1935–1965," unpublished history [February, 1972].
5. Helen Gentry, "Fine Books for Children, Too," *Horn Book*, XI (July 1935), 212.
6. Vernon Ives, "Making Books Is Fun," *Story Parade*, III (May 1938), 41.
7. William Scott, "New Editorial Techniques," *Library Journal*, LXVI (October 15, 1941), 854.
8. Margaret Wise Brown, "Writing for Five-Year-Olds," typescript, n.d.
9. Margaret Wise Brown, from "Books for Young Children," transcript of broadcast, "The Baby Institute" radio program, WJZ, November 19, 1943.
10. Margaret Wise Brown, "Why Gertrude Stein for Children," typescript, n.d.
11. William Gass, "Gertrude Stein, Geographer: I," *New York Review of Books*, XX (May 3, 1973), 8.
12. Louise Seaman Bechtel, "Gertrude Stein for Children," *Horn Book*, XV (September 1939). Reprinted in Bechtel, *Books in Search of Children*, 86.
13. *Ibid.*, 87.
14. Quoted in Bechtel, "Gertrude Stein for Children," and Scott 1940 catalog.
15. Margaret Wise Brown, "Comments on *The World Is Round*," typescript, n.d.
16. Margaret Wise Brown, "Leonard Weisgard Wins the Caldecott Medal," *Publishers' Weekly*, CLII (July 5, 1947), 41.
17. *Ibid.*
18. Aldous Huxley, foreword to *Posters by E. McKnight Kauffer* (New York, Museum of Modern Art, 1937).
19. Stuart Davis, in Diane Kelder, ed., *Stuart Davis* (New York, Praeger, 1971), 23, 26.
20. Margaret Wise Brown, from "Books for Young Children," transcript of broadcast, "The Baby Institute" radio program, WJZ, November 19, 1943.
21. Margaret Wise Brown, "Leonard Weisgard Wins the Caldecott Medal," *Publishers' Weekly*, CLII (July 5, 1947), 40.
22. Scott 1941–1942 catalog.
23. *Ibid.*
24. Scott 1946 catalog.
25. *Ibid.*
26. *Ibid.*
27. *Ibid.*
28. Scott Fall 1947 catalog.
29. Scott 1945 catalog.
30. William R. Scott, "A New Literature for the Nursery," *AIGA Journal*, III, No. 3, 6.
31. A slight rearrangement of the original.
32. William R. Scott, "Some Notes on Communication in Picture Books," *Elementary English*, XXIV (February 1957), 67–68.
33. Scott Fall 1949 catalog.
34. The book was originally done in seven colors; then the plates were lost, and it was redone in a less expensive form.
35. F. J. Harvey Darton, *Children's Books in England* (Cambridge [Eng.] University Press, 1932), 221.
36. *Publishers' Weekly*, CXVIII (August 30, 1930), 810.
37. *Publishers' Weekly*, CXXXVI (August 26, 1939), 689.
38. Vernon Ives, letter to author, February 23, 1972.
39. Louise Fargo Brown, "Eleska," *Horn Book*, XXI (September 1945), 343.
40. May Lamberton Becker, New York *Herald Tribune Books*, November 10, 1940.
41. Ad in *Publishers' Weekly*, CXLII (November 28, 1942), 2184.
42. *Publishers' Weekly*, CXLII (August 1, 1942), 293.
43. *Life*, XV (December 27, 1943), 87.
44. *Publishers' Weekly*, CXLII (November 28, 1942), 2184.
45. Ellen Lewis Buell, *New York Times Book Review*, May 28, 1944.
46. Alice Dalgliesh, *Parents' Magazine*, XIX (July 1944), 28.
47. *Publishers' Weekly*, CLI (March 22, 1947), 1709.
48. *Publishers' Weekly*, CLII (April 26, 1947), 2189.

THE EMOTIONAL ELEMENT

1. *Horn Book*, VIII (February 1932), 58.
2. Quoted in *Illustrators of Children's Books, 1744–1945*, 341. Paraphrased.
3. Anne Thaxter Eaton, *New York Times Book Review*, November 15, 1936.
4. Evelyn Harter, "An Exhibition of Books Made for Children," *Horn Book*, XVIII (March 1942), 96.
5. Valenti Angelo, "Five Years of Books Made for Children," *Publishers' Weekly*, CXL (November 1, 1941), 1766. Paraphrased.
6. Ursula Nordstrom to author, January 12, 1972.
7. Louise Seaman Bechtel, New York *Herald Tribune Books*, April 27, 1952.
8. Janet Adam Smith, *Children's Illustrated Books*, 38.
9. Margaret Wise Brown, notes for an unidentified talk, n.d.
10. Clement Hurd, "Excerpts from a talk on Margaret Wise Brown to the California School Li-

brarians, October 1956," typescript on deposit in the MWB Westerly achive.
11. Ursula Nordstrom to author, January 12, 1972.
12. Margaret Wise Brown, "Creative Writing for Very Young Children," 1951 *Book of Knowledge Annual*, 81.
13. Margaret Wise Brown, "Writing for Five-Year-Olds," typescript, n.d.
14. Bruce Bliven, Jr., "Child's Best Seller," *Life* XXI (December 2, 1946), 62.
15. Margaret Wise Brown, notes for a talk at the Mills School, n.d.
16. Margaret Wise Brown, "Leonard Weisgard Wins the Caldecott Medal," *Publishers' Weekly*, CLII (July 5, 1947), 42.
17. Ursula Nordstrom to author, January 12, 1972.
18. Margaret Wise Brown, "Creative Writing for Very Young Children," 1951. *Book of Knowledge Annual*, 81.
19. Margaret Wise Brown, "Writing for Five-Year-Olds," typescript, n.d.
20. Margaret Wise Brown, "Creative Writing for Very Young Children," 1951 *Book of Knowledge Annual*, 81.
21. Margaret Wise Brown, "Writing for Children," *Hollins Alumnae Magazine*, XXII (Winter 1949), 1.
22. Margaret Wise Brown, notes for a talk given in Richmond, Virginia, in 1949.
23. Dorothy White, *Books Before Five*, 71.
24. *Ibid.*, 73
25. Quoted in Sue Dickinson, "Former Virginia College Student Leads in Children's Book Writing," Richmond *News-Leader*, April 1, 1952.
26. Margaret Wise Brown, "Creative Writing for Very Young Children,' 1951 *Book of Knowledge Annual*, 80. Paraphrased.
27. Margaret Wise Brown, "Stories to be Sung and Songs to be Told," 1952 *Book of Knowledge Annual*, 170.

JEAN CHARLOT
1. Paul Sachs, *Modern Prints and Drawings* (New York, Knopf, 1954), 195.
2. Jean Charlot, *The Mexican Mural Renaissance, 1920–1925*, 9–10.
3. *Ibid.*, 178
4. *Ibid.*, 179.
5. *Ibid.*
6. Anita Brenner, *Idols Behind Altars*, 249.
7. *Ibid.*, 259.
8. Jean Charlot, *Art-Making from Mexico ta China*, 44.
9. Jean Charlot, *The Mexican Mural Renaissance. 1920–1925*, 12.
10. *Ibid.*, 6.
11. Jean Charlot, *Art-Making from Mexico to China*, 274.
12. Margaret Wise Brown, "Creative Writing for Very Young Children," 1951 *Book of Knowledge Annual*, 81.
13. Maurice Sendak, "Artist's Choice: *Two Little Trains*," *Horn Book*, XXI (August 1955), 296–297.
14. Louise Seaman Bechtel, New York *Herald Tribune Books*, May 17, 1953.
15. Jean Charlot, *Art-Making from Mexico to China*, 222.

GOLDEN BOOKS
1. *Publishers' Weekly*, CXLIV (July 31, 1943), 330.
2. *Publishers' Weekly*, CXLV (February 26, 1944), 951.
3. *Publishers' Weekly*, CXLVIII (October 27, 1945), 1972.
4. Albert R. Leventhal, "The Children's Book in the Mass Market," *Publishers' Weekly*, CLXIV (November 21, 1953), 2106.
5. Anne T. Eaton, *New York Times Book Review*, February 14, 1943.
6. Anne T. Eaton, *New York Times Book Review*, November 17, 1940.
7. Dorothy White, *Books Before Five*, 49–50.
8. Margaret Wise Brown, copy of letter to "Dorothy" [Bennett], n.d.
9. Margaret Wise Brown, "Leonard Weisgard Wins the Caldecott Medal," *Publishers' Weekly*, CLII (July 5, 1947), 42.
10. Iona and Peter Opie, eds., *The Oxford Dictionary of Nursery Rhymes* (London, Oxford University Press, 1951), 38.
11. Annual report of the Central Children's Room, New York Public Library, 1936.
12. Melville Cane, *Making a Poem* (1953; enlarged reprint, Harvest-Harcourt, 1962), 100.

DR. SEUSS
1. Janice Dohm, "The Curious Case of Dr. Seuss," *Top of the News*, XXI (January 1965), 151.
2. Anne Carroll Moore, *My Roads*, 339.
3. Quoted in E. J. Kahn, Jr., "Children's Friend," *New Yorker*, XXXVI (December 17, 1960), 64.
4. John J. Bailey, Jr., "Three Decades of Dr. Seuss," *Elementary English*, XXXXII (January 1965), 7.
5. Selma G. Lanes, *Down the Rabbit Hole* (New York, Atheneum, 1971), 81.
6. Clifton Fadiman, "Professionals and Confessionals: Dr. Seuss and Kenneth Grahame," in Sheila Egoff, ed., *Only Connect: Readings on Children's Literature* (Toronto, Oxford University Press, 1969), 320.
7. E. J. Kahn, Jr., "Children's Friend," *New Yorker*, XXXVI (December 17, 1960), 82.
8. Helen P. Geisel, "Dr. Seuss Was Born an Artist," *Young Wings* (January 1948), 8.
9. John Hersey, "Why Do Students Bog Down on First R?" *Life*, XXXVI (May 24, 1954), 148.
10. Quoted in Anne Carroll Moore, "The Three Owls," *Horn Book*, XIV (January 1938), 32.

MARCIA BROWN
1. Anne Carroll Moore, "Work with Children," in New York Public Library, *Report of the Director* for the Year Ending December 31, 1911.
2. Maria Cimino, "Report of Exhibitions for 1935 in the Central Children's Room," typescript.
3. Quoted in Maria Cimino, "Report of Exhibitions for 1940 in the Central Children's Room."
4. Marcia Brown, "Storytelling at the Library My Best Fun," *Young Wings* (February 1948), 7.
5. Marcia Brown, "Integrity and Intuition," in *Caldecott Medal Books, 1938–1957*, 276.

6. *Ibid.*, 277.
7. *Ibid.*, 276.
8. Marcia Brown, "Distinction in Picture Books," *Horn Book*, XXV (September 1949), caption, 382.
9. Marcia Brown, "Integrity and Intuition," in *Caldecott Medal Books, 1938–1957*, 275.
10. *Ibid.*, 272.
11. Marcia Brown, "Big and Little," in *Newbery and Caldecott Medal Books, 1956–1965*, 226.
12. Marcia Brown, "My Goals as an Illustrator," *Horn Book*, XLIII (June 1967), 312, 313.
13. Marcia Brown, "Big and Little," in *Newbery and Caldecott Medal Books, 1956–1965*, 231.

EXPANDING POSSIBILITIES

1. Frederic G. Melcher, editorial, *Publishers' Weekly*, CXLVII (March 3, 1949), 997.
2. Dorothy V. Knibb, "Reading Trends Stir Book Trade," *Domestic Commerce*, XXXIII (November 1945), 25.
3. Russell Reynolds, letter to the editor, *Publishers' Weekly*, CLII (September 27, 1947), 1503.
4. Marian Herr, article so-titled, *Library Journal*, LXXII (November 1, 1947), 1527.
5. Quoted in "Convention Panel on Children's Books," *Publishers' Weekly*, CLIII (June 12, 1948), 2463.
6. "Booksellers are overstocked in juvenile department," *Publishers' Weekly*, CLII (April 26, 1947), 2189.
7. Adrienne Adams, "The Artist at Work: Color separation," *Horn Book*, XLI (April 1965), 153–155.
8. *Horn Book*, XXIV (June 1958), 190.
9. *Booklist*, XLI (January 15, 1945), 156.

NEW LOOKS

1. Lynd Ward, "The Book Artist," in *Illustrators of Children's Books, 1946–1956*, 33.
2. Fritz Eichenberg, "Artist's Choice: *The Two Reds*." *Horn Book*, XXVII (July 1951), 239.
3. Louise Seaman Bechtel, New York *Herald Tribune Books*, September 10, 1950.
4. Catalog, Children's Book Show, 1945–1950 (New York, American Institute of Graphic Arts, 1950).
5. William S. Lieberman, "Antonio Frasconi: Woodcutter," *Print*, IX (July–August 1955), 52.
6. Manuel Gasser, "Antonio Frasconi: *A Book of Many Suns*," *Graphis*, 100 (March–April 1962), 208.
7. "Frasconi's Brio with a Book," *Horizon*, III (March 1961), 122–123.
8. Margaret McElderry, in "Top Drawer," *Print*, IX (July–August 1955), 3.
9. *Saturday Review of Literature*, XXX (November 15, 1947), 62.
10. Frank J. Lieberman, "My Introduction to Joseph Low," *Print*, VI (Winter, 1950–51), 3–5.
11. Henry Pitz, "Joseph Low," *American Artist, XV* (October 1951), 31–32.
12. *Ibid.*, 32.
13. David Bland, *A History of Book Illustration*, 401.
14. Leo Lionni, "The Lion's Tale," *Print*, IX (May–June 1955), 63.
15. Quoted in *Illustrators of Children's Books, 1946–1956*, 139.
16. Alfred H. Barr, Jr., *Matisse: His Art and His Public* (New York, Museum of Modern Art, 1951), 274.
17. Patricia Sloane, *Color: basic principles and new directions* (London, Studio Vista, 1968), 9.
18. Séan Jennett, *The Making of Books*, 239.
19. Herbert Bayer, "Typographie und Werbsachengestaltung," *Bauhaus Magazin*, 1928, I, 10; quoted, in translation, in Alexander Dorner, *The Way Beyond "Art": The Work of Herbert Bayer* (New York, Wittenborn, 1947), 195.
20. Jan Tschichold, *Asymmetric Typography*, 46.
21. L. Moholy Nagy, *Vision in Motion*, 306.
22. Sol Cantor, "The Composing Room, Inc.," *PM*, I (February 1935), 14.
23. "The Composing Room: 25 Years of Typographic Service," *Publishers' Weekly*, CLXII (November 1, 1952), 1900.
24. Quoted in *Illustrators of Children's Books, 1957–1966*, 194.
25. Quoted in Peter Selz, *The Work of Jean Dubuffet* (New York, Museum of Modern Art, 1962), 64.
26. Marcia Brown, "Artist's Choice: *Little Boy Brown*," *Horn Book*, XXVI (January 1950), 28–29.

SOCIAL CHANGE

1. Ernestine Evans, "1947 Childrens Books," *Commonweal*, XLVII (November 21, 1947), 151. Slightly condensed.
2. Jonathan Daniels, "A Native at Large," *Nation*, CL (October 19, 1940), 366.
3. Julia L. Sauer, "Making the World Safe for the Janey Larkins," *Library Journal*, LXVI (January 15, 1941), 51.
4. Josette Frank, quoted in Helen Hoke et al, "The Problem Book," *Publishers' Weekly*, CXL (October 18, 1941), 1553.
5. Claire Nolte, *Library Journal*, LXXV (September 15, 1950), 1514.
6. "Books for Brotherhood," 1952.
7. Lewis Gannett, "Books and Things," New York *Herald Tribune*, November 20, 1930.
8. Josette Frank, quoted in Helen Hoke et al, "The Problem Book," *Publishers' Weekly*, CXL (October 18, 1941), 1554.
9. Biographical note, second edition, *Childhood and Society*.
10. Charles S. Carleton, "Head Start or False Start?" *American Education*, II (September 1966), 20.
11. *Booklist*, LXVI (September 1969), 58.

NEGRO IDENTIFICATION, BLACK IDENTITY

1. Helen Trager, "Intercultural Books for Children," *Childhood Education*, (November 1945), 138.
2. Ruth Theobald, "Library Service for Negro Children," *Children's Library Yearbook*, No. 4 (Chicago, American Library Association, 1932), 116.
3. Marjorie Hill Allee, "Books Negro Children Like," *Horn Book*, XIV (March 1938), 85.
4. Eva Knox Evans, "The Negro in Children's Fiction," *Publishers' Weekly*, CXL (August 30, 1941), 651.
5. "Negro Dialect in Children's Books," *Publishers' Weekly*, CXL (October 18, 1941), 1555.

6. Letter to the editor, *Publishers' Weekly*, CXLI (January 10, 1942), 105.
7. Anne Carroll Moore, quoted in Stokes ad, *Horn Book*, XII (November 1936), 397.
8. "Report of the Central Children's Room, 1940," New York Public Library.
9. Anne Thaxter Eaton, *Treasure for the Taking* (New York, Viking, 1946), 15.
10. Julia L. Sauer, "Making the World Safe for the Janey Larkins," *Library Journal*, LXVI (January 15, 1941), 49.
11. Stella Gentry Sharpe, quoted on the jacket of *Tobe*.
12. Eslanda Goode Robeson ("Mrs. Paul Robeson"), Hartford *Courant Magazine*, February 4, 1945.
13. Harold Rosenberg, "The Philosophy of Put-Togethers," *New Yorker*, XLVIII (March 11, 1972), 117.
14. Aline Saarinen, quoted in Grace Glueck, "New show at the Terry Dintenfass Gallery," *Art in America*, LVIII (January 1968), 113.
15. Jacob Lawrence, quoted in Elizabeth McCausland, "Jacob Lawrence," *Magazine of Art*, XXXVIII (November 1945), 253.
16. Aline B. Loucheim (Saarinen), "An Artist Reports on the Troubled Mind," *New York Times Magazine* (October 15, 1950), 36.
17. Jacob Lawrence, quoted in Elizabeth McCausland, "Jacob Lawrence," *Magazine of Art*, XXXVIII (November 1945), 253.
18. *Ibid.*, 251.

MORE INFORMATION

1. Dorothy Waugh to author, February 8, 1972.
2. Jacket of *Travelers All.*
3. James Newman, "Children's Books; a special review of those about science for groping parents at Christmastime," *Scientific American*, CLXXXI (December 1949), 55
4. Ernestine Evans, "1947 Children's Books," *Commonweal*, XLVII (November 21, 1947), 148.
5. James Newman, "Children's Books . . . ," *Scientific American*, CLXXXI (December 1949), 54.
6. Herbert S. Zim, "Modern Kids Want Facts," *Publishers' Weekly*, CXLII (August 29, 1942), 673.
7. "Herbert S. Zim's Science Books," *Publishers' Weekly*, CLXII (July 26, 1942), 360.
8. Louise Seaman Bechtel, New York *Herald Tribune Books*, November 16, 1952.
9. Scott Fall 1949 catalog.
10. *Ibid.*
11. Miriam Lindstrom, *Children's Art*, 28.
12. "Elizabeth Riley of Crowell," *Publishers' Weekly*, CLIX (March 10, 1951), 1263.
13. Crowell 1954 catalog.
14. Crowell 1956 catalog.
15. Crowell 1960 catalog.
16. Elizabeth Riley to author, November 24, 1972.
17. Jerome Bruner, *The Process of Education* (Cambridge, Harvard University Press, 1960), 33.
18. *Indian Education*, III (January 15, 1940), 3.
19. James Newman, "Children's Books . . . ," *Scientific American*, CLXXXI (December 1949), 56.
20. Lynd Ward, "The Book Artist," in *Illustrators of Children's Books, 1946–1956,* 21.
21. Louise Seaman Bechtel, New York *Herald Tribune Books*, November 13, 1949.
22. Louise Seaman Bechtel, New York *Herald Tribune Books*, November 11, 1951.

RUTH KRAUSS:
RUTH KRAUSS AND MAURICE SENDAK

1. Kornei Chukovsky, *From Two to Five*, xx.
2. Stith Thompson, *The Folktale* (New York, Holt, 1946), 194.
3. *Ibid.*, 195.
4. Kornei Chukovsky, *From Two to Five*, 20.
5. *Ibid.*, 97–98.
6. *Ibid.*, 103.
7. Arnold Gesell and Frances L. Ilg, *Infant and Child in the Culture of Today* (New York, Harper, 1943), 26.
8. Quoted in Saul Braun, "Sendak Raises the Shades on Childhood," *New York Times Magazine*, June 7, 1970, 49.
9. Marshall Lee, *Publishers' Weekly*, CLXII (November 1, 1952), 1908.
10. Kenneth Keniston, *Youth and Dissent: The Rise of a New Opposition* (New York, Harcourt, 1971), 372.
11. Kenneth Keniston, *The Uncommitted: Alienated Youth in American Society* (New York, Harcourt, 1965), 71.
12. *Ibid.*, 183.
13. Kenneth Keniston, *Youth and Dissent,* 289.
14. *Ibid.*, 314.

CROCKETT JOHNSON

1. Jacket of *Barnaby and Mr. O'Malley* (New York, Holt, 1944).
2. Quoted in *Current Biography, 1943*, 346.
3. *Time*, XLIV (September 18, 1944), 50.
4. Maurice Horn, "The Crisis of the Forties," in Pierre Couperie and Maurice Horn, eds., *A History of the Comic Strip*, 87.
5. New York *Herald Tribune Books*, May 11, 1958.

THE JAPANESE ADVENT

1. Edwin O. Reischauer, *Japan: The Story of a Nation* (New York, Knopf, 1970), 219.
2. As recapitulated in *Art News Annual*, XVIII (1948), 142.
3. Velma Varner, in "The Hunt Breakfast," *Horn Book*, XXX (April 1954), 70, 75.
4. Nicolas Mordvinoff, "Artist's Choice: *Crow Boy*," *Horn Book*, XXXII (December 1956), 429–430.
5. Blair Lent, "The Artist at Work: Cardboard Cuts," *Horn Book*, XLI (August 1965), 408–409, 411–412.
6. Blair Lent, "On Illustrating *Tikki Tikki Tembo*," *Owlet Among the Colophons* III (November 1968), 1, 3.
7. Nancy Klein, *Kirkus Reviews* (April 1, 1968), j 385.

FEELINGS EXTENDED

1. Josette Frank, "Books and Children's Emotions," *Child Study*, XXVI (Winter 1948–49), 5.
2. *Ibid.*
3. *Ibid.*, 6.
4. *Ibid.*

5. Martha Wolfenstein, "The Impact of a Children's Story on Mothers and Children," *Monographs of the Society for Research in Child Development*, No. 42 (Washington, Society for Research in Child Development, 1947), 3–4.
6. *Ibid.*, 4.
7. *Ibid.*, 4–5.
8. *Ibid.*, 8.
9. *Ibid.*, 31.
10. *Ibid.*, 27.
11. *Ibid.*, 28.
12. *Ibid.*, 30.
13. Martha Wolfenstein, "Fun Morality: An Analysis of Recent American Child-training Literature," in Margaret Mead and Martha Wolfenstein, eds., *Childhood in Contemporary Cultures* (Chicago, University of Chicago Press–Phoenix, 1955), 168. "A slightly revised version of the article which appeared originally in *The Journal of Social Issues*, VII, No. 4 (1951), 15–25."
14. *Ibid.*, 173.
15. José Ortega y Gasset, "The Magic Wand," trans. by Tony Talbot, in Tony Talbot, ed., *The World of the Child* (Garden City, Doubleday-Anchor, 1967), 53.
16. Emmet Gowin, quoted in A. D. Coleman, "His Spirit Is Gravely Innocent," *New York Times*, March 12, 1972.
17. *Bulletin of the Center for Children's Books*, XVIII (November 1964), 36.
18. William R. Scott, "A New Literature for the Nursery,"*AIGA Journal*, III, No. 3, 6.
19. Diana Klemin, *The Art of Art for Children's Books*, 27.
20. Bernard Waber, quoted in *Illustrators of Children's Books, 1957–1966*, 187.
21. Desmond McCarthy, *Memories* (New York, Oxford University Press, 1953), 160.
22. Fougasse, *. . . and the gatepost* (London, Chatto & Windus, 1940), viii–ix.
23. Desmond McCarthy, *Memories*, 158.
24. Quoted by William Cole in "One Line Poems and Longer, but Not Much," *New York Times Book Review*, December 2, 1973.
25. Harry Behn, *Chrysalis: Concerning Children and Poetry* (New York, Harcourt, 1968), 58.
26. Louise Seaman Bechtel, New York *Herald Tribune Books*, November 14, 1954.
27. Erwin Panofsky, Introduction to *Abbot Suger on the Abbey Church of St.-Denis* (Princeton, Princeton University Press, 1946). Reprinted in Erwin Panofsky, *Meaning in the Visual Arts* (Garden City, N.Y., Anchor-Doubleday, 1955), 143–144.

MAURICE SENDAK

1. Edward Ardizzone, "The Born Illustrator," *Motif*, No. 1 (November 1958), 38.
2. Helen Stone, "Artist's Choice: *Tim to the Rescue*," *Horn Book*, XXVI (May 1950), 211.
3. *Publishers' Weekly*, CLXIX (January 21, 1956), 195.
4. Random House 1960 catalog.
5. Ellen Lewis Buell, *New York Times Book Review*, January 24, 1956.
6. *Horn Book*, XXXIII (June 1957), 216.
7. George A. Woods, *New York Times Book Review*, July 7, 1957.
8. Robert Coles, *Erik Erikson*, 22–23.
9. Dorothy W. Baruch, "This Question of Fairy Tales," *Progressive Education*, IX (May 1932), 364.
10. G. K. Chesterton, "England and Caricature" (1908), reprintel in *Lunacy and Letters* (New York, Sheed & Ward, 1958), 141.
11. Maurice Sendak, Caldecott Award acceptance, in *Newbery and Caldecott Medal Books, 1956–1965*, 249.
12. Pierre Couperie, "The World of the Comic Strip," in Pierre Couperie and Maurice C. Horn, eds., *A History of the Comic Strip*, 155.
13. Dorothy White, *Books Before Five*, 119.
14. Quoted in "Questions to an Artist Who Is Also an Author," *Quarterly Journal of the Library of Congress*, XVIII (October 1971), 270.

AWAY FROM WORDS

1. *Print*, IX (July–August 1955), 6.
2. Leo Lionni, "The Lion's Tale," *Print*, IX (July–August 1955), 69.
3. Eugene M. Ettenberg, "Leo Lionni," *American Artist*, XVII (April 1953), 30.
4. Leo Lionni, "My Books for Children," *Wilson Library Bulletin*, XXXIX (October 1964), 144.
5. Leo Lionni, "Designs for the Printed Page," *Fortune* brochure, n.d.
6. Quoted in Martha Monigle, "Remy Charlip's Children's Books," *Print*, XX (July–August 1966), 44.

THE FABULISTS

1. Kurt Schwitters, from an article in *Sturm-Bühne*, No. 8 (October 1919), trans. by Ralph Manheim in Robert Motherwell, ed., *The Dada Painters and Poets* (New York, Wittenborn, 1951), 63.
2. *Print*, XI (January–February 1958), 44.
3. *Newsweek*, LIV (September 7, 1959), 81.
4. Edmund Wilson, "The Albums of Edward Gorey," *New Yorker*, XXXV (December 26, 1959). Reprinted in *The Bit Between My Teeth: A Literary Chronicle of 1950–1965*, 479.
5. Quoted in *Newsweek*, LXII (August 26, 1963), 79.
6. Katherine White, *New Yorker*, XXI (December 8, 1945), 120.
7. May Hill Arbuthnot, *Children and Books*, 252.
8. Joseph Jacobs, *English Fairy Tales*, 3rd ed. rev. (New York, Putnam, n.d.), 268.
9. Stith Thompson, *The Folktale* (New York, Holt, 1946), 195.
10. Richard Dorson, *Folklore: Selected Essays* (Bloomington, Indiana University Press, 1972), 19.
11. Edna Johnson, et al, *Anthology of Children's Literature*, 4th ed. (Boston, Houghton, 1970), 188–189.
12. William R. Scott, "Some Notes on Communication in Picture Books," *Elementary English*, XXXIV (February 1957), 72.

BIBLIOGRAPHY

I. GENERAL

A. Book Illustration

Bland, David. *A History of Book Illustration.* Second edition. London, Faber & Faber, 1969.

Gill, Bob and Lewis, John. *Illustration: Aspects and Directions.* New York, Reinhold, 1964.

Hogarth, Paul. *The Artist as Reporter.* London, Studio Vista; New York, Reinhold, 1967.

Ivins, William M., Jr. *Prints and Books.* Cambridge, Harvard University Press, 1927.

——. *Prints and Visual Communication.* Cambridge, M.I.T. Press, 1953.

Klemin, Diana. *The Illustrated Book.* New York, Clarkson N. Potter, 1970.

Lewis, John. *The Twentieth Century Book, Its Illustration and Design.* London, Studio Vista; New York, Reinhold, 1967.

Pennell, Joseph. *Pen Drawing and Pen Draughtsmen.* New York, Macmillan, 1889.

B. Book Design and Production

Bookbinding Magazine. 1925–1950.

Curwen, Harold. *Processes of Graphic Reproduction in Printing.* New York, Oxford University Press, 1934.

Fern, Alan. "Graphic Design," in *Art Nouveau,* ed. by Peter Selz and Mildred Constantine. New York, Museum of Modern Art, 1959.

Horn Book. "The Artist at Work" series. 1963–1966.

Inland Printer. 1895–1935.

Jeannett, Séan. *The Making of Books.* Fourth edition. New York, Praeger, 1967.

Lewis, John. *Typography: Basic Principles.* New York, Reinhold, 1963.

PM; an intimate journal for advertising production managers, art directors and their associates. New York. 1934–1942. (known as *A–D,* 1940–1942).

Print. 1940 to date.

Publishers' Weekly. 1895 to date.

C. Comic Strips and Animated Cartoons

Briggs, Clare. *How To Draw Cartoons.* Foreword by John T. McCutcheon. New York, Harper, 1926.

Couperie, Pierre and Horn, Maurice C., Eds. *A History of the Comic Strip.* Trans. by Eileen B. Hennessy. New York, Crown, 1968.

Feild, Robert. *The Art of Walt Disney.* New York, Macmillan, 1942.

Gaines, M. C. "Narrative Illustration: The Story of the Comics." *Print,* III, No. 2 (Summer 1942), 25–38.

——. "Good Triumphs Over Evil:—More About the Comics." *Print,* III, No. 3 (1942), 18–24.

Thomas, Bob. *The Art of Animation.* New York, Simon & Schuster, 1938.

D. Children's Books

Arbuthnot, May Hill. *Children and Books.* Third Edition. Chicago, Scott, Foresman, 1964.

Bechtel, Louise Seaman. *Books in Search of Children.* Selected and with an introduction by Virginia Haviland. New York, Macmillan, 1969.

Becker, May Lamberton. *First Adventures in Reading.* New York, Stokes, 1936.

Children's Catalog. First–tenth edition. New York, H. W. Wilson, 1909–1961.

Current Biography. 1940 to date.

Dalgliesh, Alice. *First Experiences with Literature.* New York, Scribner, 1932.

De Montreville, Doris and Hill, Donna, Eds. *Third Book of Junior Authors.* New York, H. W. Wilson, 1972.

Fuller, Muriel, Ed. *More Junior Authors.* New York, H. W. Wilson, 1963.

Horn Book. 1924 to date.

Hürlimann, Bettina. *Three Centuries of Children's Books in Europe.* Trans. and ed. by Brian W. Alderson. Cleveland, World, 1968.

Kingman, Lee, Ed. *Newbery and Caldecott Medal Books, 1956–1963.* Boston, Horn Book, 1965.

Kunitz, Stanley J. and Haycraft, Howard. *Junior Book of Authors.* Second edition, revised. New York, H. W. Wilson, 1951.

Mahony, Bertha E. and Whitney, Elinor. *Realms of Gold in Children's Books.* Garden City, N.Y., Doubleday, 1929.

——. *Five Years of Children's Books.* Garden City, N.Y., Doubleday, 1936. A supplement to *Realms of Gold.*

Meigs, Cornelia L., Ed. *A Critical History of Children's Literature.* Second edition. New York, Macmillan, 1969.

Miller, Bertha (Mahony) and Field, Elinor W., Eds. *Caldecott Medal Books, 1938–1957.* Boston, Horn Book, 1957.

——. *Newbery Medal Books, 1922–1955.* Boston, Horn Book, 1955.

Moore, Anne Carroll. *My Roads to Childhood.* Boston, Horn Book, 1961. Incorporating *Roads to Childhood* (1920); *New Roads to Childhood* (1923); *Crossroads to Childhood* (1926). Expanded and updated, 1939, when published by Doubleday as *My Roads to Childhood.*

——. *The Three Owls: A Book About Children's Books.* New York, Macmillan, 1925.
——. *The Three Owls, Second Book.* New York, Coward-McCann, 1928.
——. *The Three Owls, Third Book.* New York, Coward-McCann, 1931.
Publishers' Weekly. 1895 to date.
U.S. Library of Congress. Children's Book Section. *Children's Literature: A Guide to Reference Sources.* Prepared under the direction of Virginia Haviland. Washington, D.C., Library of Congress, 1966.
——. ——. First supplement. Compiled by Virginia Haviland with the assistance of Margaret N. Coughlan. Washington, D.C. Library of Congress, 1972.
White, Dorothy. *Books Before Five.* New York, Oxford University Press, 1954.
Young Wings. 1929–1955. The Junior Literary Guild bulletin, containing brief autobiographical pieces by the authors and illustrators of JLG books.

E. Children's Book Illustration

American Institute of Graphic Arts. Catalogs of Children's Books Shows, under various titles. 1941 to date.
James, Philip. *Children's Books of Yesterday.* Ed. by C. Geoffrey Holme. London, The Studio; New York, The Studio Publications, 1933.
Klemin, Diana. *The Art of Art for Children's Books.* New York, Clarkson N. Potter, 1966.
Mahony, Bertha E. and Whitney, Elinor, Comps. *Contemporary Illustrators of Children's Books.* Boston, Bookshop for Boys and Girls, Women's Educational and Industrial Union, 1930.
Mahony, Bertha E.; Latimer, Louis Payson; and Folmsbee, Beulah, Comps. *Illustrators of Children's Books, 1744–1945.* Boston, Horn Book, 1947.
——. ——. Supplement, 1946–1956. Comp. by Ruth H. Viguers, Marcia Dalphin and Bertha M. Miller. Boston, Horn Book, 1958.
——. ——. Supplement, 1957–1966. Comp. by Lee Kingman, Joanna Foster and Ruth Giles Lontoft. Boston, Horn Book, 1968.
Smith, Janet Adam. *Children's Illustrated Books.* London, Collins, 1948.
White, Gleeson. *Children's Books and Their Illustrators.* The Special Winter Number of *International Studio,* 1897–98.

F. Child Development and Child Art

Chukovsky, Kornei. *From Two to Five.* Trans. and ed. by Miriam Morton. Berkeley, University of California Press, 1963.
Coles, Robert. *Erik Erikson: The Growth of His Work.* Boston, Atlantic Monthly Press–Little, Brown, 1970.
Eng, Helga. *The Psychology of Children's Drawings.* Second edition. London, Routledge, 1954.
Erikson, Erik. *Childhood and Society.* Second edition. New York, Norton, 1963.
Fraiberg, Selma H. *The Magic Years.* New York, Scribner, 1959.
Gesell, Arnold and Gesell, Beatrice C. *The Normal Child and Primary Education.* Boston, Ginn, 1912. This early work is more broadly suggestive than Gesell's well-known developmental studies of later years, though they too contain pertinent observations in specific areas.
Holt, John. *How Children Learn.* New York, Pitman, 1947.
Isaacs, Susan. *Intellectual Growth in Young Children.* London, Routledge, 1930.
——. *The Nursery Years.* London, Routledge, 1938.
Lindstrom, Miriam. *Children's Art.* Berkeley, University of California Press, 1957.
Millar, Susanna. *The Psychology of Play.* Harmondsworth, Eng.; Baltimore, Penguin, 1968.
Piaget, Jean. *The Language and Thought of the Child.* Trans. by Marjorie Gabain. Third edition. London, Routledge; New York, Humanities Press, 1959.
——. *Play, Dreams and Imitation in Childhood.* Trans. by C. Gattegno and F. M. Hodgson. New York, Norton, 1951.
Piers, Maria, Ed. *Play and Development.* New York, Norton, 1972.
Pitcher, Evelyn G. and Prelinger, Ernst. *Children Tell Stories: An Analysis of Fantasy.* New York, International Universities Press, 1963.
Richardson, Elwyn S. *In the Early World.* New York, Pantheon, 1964.
Viola, Wilhelm. *Child Art and Franz Cizek.* Vienna, Austrian Junior Red Cross; New York, John Day, 1937.

II. TOPICAL

The information on individual authors and illustrators is derived chiefly from the standard sources listed above under "Children's Books" and "Children's Book Illustration," supplemented by book jackets, catalogs and other publishers' ephemera. Reference to specific sources is made in the Notes.

Readers are reminded that the *National Union Catalog,* from the catalog of pre-1956 imprints onward, provides the most complete listing available of the works of illustrators as well as authors; that artists who win the Caldecott Medal are customarily written about extensively the year they win the award; that *Current Biography* carries authoritative articles, with references, on those artists and any others who have gained independent recognition (e.g. Jean Charlot, Crockett Johnson); that authors who are not illustrators, as well as illustrators who are also authors, are covered by the increasingly informative H. W. Wilson *Junior Authors* series, making these volumes complementary—as well as supplementary—to the Horn Book *Illustrators of Children's Books* series.

In sum, one may expect to find, for an author-illustrator of the period, an entry in each of the two last-named sources, and if he or she has won the Caldecott, an article that year in *Publishers' Weekly, Library Journal* and *Horn Book.* The latter is reprinted, along with the award-winner's acceptance speech, in *Caldecott Medal Books, 1938–1957* or subsequent volumes; and these writings together form the basis of the entry in *Current Biography.*

The writings about individuals listed below are those that fall outside this framework which the author drew upon for background or considers of particular interest to readers. Individuals apart, sources are given for each subject-area according to its nature. In some instances, that is, extensive recourse was had to printed sources; in others, comparatively little.

STARTING POINTS

English Illustrated Books

Hardie, Martin. *English Coloured Books.* London, Methuen, 1906.

McLean, Ruari. *Victorian Book Design and Colour Printing.* London, Faber, 1963.

Muir, Percy. *Victorian Illustrated Books.* New York, Praeger, 1971.

American Illustration

Smith, F. Hopkinson. *American Illustrators.* New York, Scribner, 1892.

Weitenkampf, Frank. "The American Illustrator." A scrapbook of clippings with a typescript text. New York Public Library, 1955.

——. *American Graphic Art.* Revised edition. New York, Macmillan, 1924. Less applicable than the above but useful for its bibliographies.

Children's Book Illustration

In addition to certain writings cited in the Notes, the following is highly representative of American thinking during this period:

Field, Walter Taylor. "Illustrating of Children's Books." *Dial,* XXXV (December 16, 1903), 457–460. Reprinted in Field, *Fingerposts to Children's Reading* (Chicago, McClurg, 1907), a popular book that went through several editions.

Maurice Boutet de Monvel

Some of the many contemporaneous articles referred to in the text are cited in the Notes, the others may be located through the appropriate periodical index. They span the period between 1894 and 1913, the year of the artist's death.

W. W. Denslow

Writing about Denslow falls into two periods: from about 1894 to 1905, when his best-known work was appearing; and from 1960 onward, when he caught the interest of book collectors. The fullest early treatment, championing Denslow's theory and practice, is:

Bowles, J. M. "Children's Books for Children." *Brush and Pencil,* XII (September 1903), 377–387.

More recently, Denslow may be approached through:

American Book Collector, Special Number, December 1964. Articles on Denslow and a checklist of his work.

Hearn, Michael Patrick. "W. W. Denslow: The Forgotten Illustrator." *American Artist,* XXXVII (May, 1973), 40–45, 71–73.

Further references are found in both.

A. B. Frost

Frost, of course, figures in all writing on the graphic art of the period, as the Notes suggest. The following are outstanding individual sources:

Bunner, H. C. "A. B. Frost." *Harper's Magazine,* LXXXV (October, 1892), 699–706.

Gibson, Charles Dana. "A. B. Frost—A Personal Tribute." *Scribner's Magazine,* LXXXIV (November 1928), 539–552.

Reed, Henry M. *The A. B. Frost Book.* Rutland, Vt., Charles E. Tuttle Co., 1967.

E. BOYD SMITH

As indicated, information about Smith is scant. The account of his activities is based chiefly on ephemeral material in various files at Houghton Mifflin and the Houghton Mifflin correspondence files on deposit at the Houghton Library, Harvard University. Solid assistance for anyone studying Smith's work is provided by:

Dykes, Jeff C. "Bibliographic Checklist of E[lmer] Boyd Smith." *American Book Collector,* XVIII (January 1967), 15–19. A descriptive bibliography of 72 items written and illustrated by Smith, or illustrated by him. (*The American Book Collector* contains both biographical and bibliographical information on a great many popular but not necessarily hallowed illustrators—per the reference to Denslow above also.)

Also, a nice appreciation of Smith's work for children appeared after his death:

Eaton, Anne Thaxter. "E. Boyd Smith." *Horn Book,* XX (April 1944), 94–96.

THE ERRATIC, ECLECTIC TWENTIES

Children's Book Illustration

New American picturebooks were few, but no period has left a fuller record of developments in children's book illustration—the consequence of prosperity, interest and growing activity. Thus we have Anne Carroll Moore's writings and those she engendered, gathered in the *Roads* books and the *Three Owls* series, and at the end of the decade the two landmark Mahony-Whitney volumes, *Realms of Gold* and *Contemporary Illustrators of Children's Books.*

Louise Seaman Bechtel and May Massee

Louise Seaman Bechtel is best met as an editor in the August 1929 issue of the *Horn Book* commemorating the tenth anniversary of the founding of the Macmillan children's book department. A collection of her critical writings—liberally quoted herein—appears in *Books in Search of Children,* listed above. The introduction by Virginia Haviland outlines her full career.

May Massee was the focus of the July 1936 issue of the *Horn Book.* She also wrote frequently about her books and authors, both in national and local publications. These materials are on file at the May Massee Memorial Collection of the William Allen White Library, Kansas State Teachers College, along with reminiscences by her authors, illustrators and colleagues. Among the articles is one that handsomely embodies her early picturebook enthusiasms: "Picture Book Parade," *Country Life,* LXVII (December 1934), 35–42.

And for a sense of the excitement of publishing and selling children's books at the time, see:

Seaman, Louise. "Some adventures of a Book Week Traveler." *Publishers' Weekly,* CXVI (December 7, 1929), 2660–2661.

C. B. Falls

Kent, Norman. "C. B. Falls, 1874–1960: A Career in Retrospect." *American Artist,* XXVI (February 1962), 24–41.

Berta and Elmer Hader

The Haders won the Caldecott Medal in 1949 (see bibliographic note, p. 582). Germane to their early books is also:

Seaman, Louise H. "'Berta and Elmer' and Their Picture Books." *Horn Book,* IV (August 1928), 52–57. Reprinted in Bechtel, *Books in Search of Children.*

WANDA GÁG

Wanda Gág's papers are on deposit at the Department of Prints, Drawings and Photographs, Philadelphia Museum of Art, and that archive in its totality—letters, clippings, catalogs—is the basis of the account. Her autobiography *Growing Pains* (New York, Coward McCann, 1940) contains diaries and drawings for the years 1908–1917; it ends when she leaves for New York. The biography by her early friend Alma Scott, *Wanda Gág: The Story of an Artist* (Minneapolis, University of Minnesota Press, 1940), reads like a juvenile biography and obscures as much as it reveals.

What she meant to children's books is conveyed by the Wanda Gág issue of the *Horn Book* (November 1935). Her personality comes across in "A Hotbed of Feminists," cited in the Notes. A comprehensive list (to 1937) of public collections where she is represented, exhibitions of her work, articles about her, and reproductions of her work appears in *Index of American Artists,* 1933–1937 (One-volume reprint. New York, Arno, 1970).

FOREIGN BACKGROUNDS

Maud and Miska Petersham

The Petershams won the Caldecott Medal in 1946 (see bibliographic note, p. 582). The following may also be of interest:

Massee, May. "The Petershams." *Publishers' Weekly,* CXXVI (October 20, 1934), 1467–1470.

Petersham, Maud. "Illustrating Books for Children." *Elementary English Review,* II (March 1925), 85–89.

Ingri and Edgar Parin d'Aulaire

The d'Aulaires won the Caldecott Medal in 1940 (see bibliographic note, p. 582). Earlier and later articles that add somewhat to the record are:

Massee, May. "Ingri and Edgar d'Aulaire." *Horn Book,* XI (September 1935), 265–270.

Sparrow, C. G. "Ingri and Edgar Parin d'Aulaire." *American Scandinavian Review,* XXX (May 1942) 49–53.

The Painted Pig and Other Latin Americana

The catalog *Mexican Arts* (American Federation of Arts, 1930) contains relevant commentary by René d'Harnoncourt, notably under "Contemporary Toys and Maquettes." The manifold activities of d'Harnoncourt himself are set forth in *Current Biography 1952* and related more intimately in *René d'Harnoncourt, 1901-1968: A Tribute* (New York, Museum of Modern Art, 1968).

Ludwig Bemelmans

Everything you ever wanted to know about Bemelmans has probably been recorded somewhere. There are his own autobiographical books; there is a long entry in *Current Biography 1941,* with nine periodical references; his later doings are reported in the weekly newsmagazines; and in 1954 he won the Caldecott Medal.

Best on his children's books of the Thirties is "The Humor of Ludwig Bemelmans," *Publishers' Weekly,* CXXXIV (October 22, 1938). For an appreciation by a fellow-illustrator, see:

Pitz, Henry. "Ludwig Bemelmans." *American Artist,* XV (May 1951), 1508–1510

Françoise

Biographical information from the Scribner files was helpful in preparing the account. The following is a bouquet from her editor:

Dalgliesh, Alice. "Françoise Speaks to Children." *Horn Book,* XXIX (December 1953), 442–446.

Books Out of Africa and Asia

Information about Erick Berry and Armstrong Sperry may be found in the standard reference works. The account of Evelyn Young and her books comes from the author-artist herself (b. 1911), who now lives in England and has not done further children's books.

Politi and the Persistence of Things Foreign

The name of Alice Dalgliesh recurs in these pages—as teacher, author, commentator, editor. Various facets of her career are touched upon by Louise Seaman Bechtel in "Alice Dalgliesh and Her Books," *Horn Book,* XXIII (March 1947), 126–134. Specifically about her work as an editor is:

Fuller, Muriel. "Alice Dalgliesh of Scribners." *Publishers' Weekly,* CLVI (July 30, 1949), 416–417. One of a series of 37 biographical pieces on children's book editors written by Muriel Fuller for *Publishers' Weekly* from 1935 to 1952.

Katherine Milhous and Leo Politi won the Caldecott Medal in 1951 and 1950 respectively (see bibliographic note, p. 582).

THE DYNAMICS AND FUN OF THE FORM

Apart from the standard reference sources, only the following is of consequence:

"Kurt Wiese, Busiest Illustrator, Has 14 Juveniles on Fall Lists." *Publishers' Weekly,* CLVIII (October 28, 1950), 1924–1925.

THE SMALL CHILD'S WORLD

The Preschool Movement and Books for Preschool Children

Alschuler, Rose H. *Two to Six: Suggestions for Parents and Teachers of Young Children.* Foreword by Carleton Washburne and Rose H. Alschuler. New York, Morrow, 1933. Includes a section "Books, Stories and Poetry" which, updated in successive editions (1937, 1947), constitutes a running record of books compatible with progressive preschool thinking, with the reasons why.

Bechtel, Louise Seaman. "Books Before Five." *Horn Book,* XVII (September 1941), 383–396. Reprinted in Bechtel, *Books in Search of Children.* (The list reflects chiefly developments covered under "Designed for Children" and "The Emotional Element.")

Child Study Association *The Child's First Books.* Prepared by Elsa H. Naumburg with a foreword by Arnold Gesell. New York, Child Study Association, 1925. The list of 400 titles includes inexpensive books and works in foreign languages—a remarkable gathering at that date. (This was catalogued by the Library of Congress and should therefore be available.)

Mitchell, Lucy Sprague. "Children's Experiments in Language." *Progressive Education,* V (Jan–Feb–Mar, 1928), 21–27.

——. *Here and Now Story Book.* New York, Dutton, 1921. The 72-page introduction is the basic text of experimental writing for young children.

——. ——. Revised edition. New York, Dutton, 1948. The introduction, "What Language Means to Young Children," is reprinted, preceded by a new foreword.

——. "Imagination in Realism." *Childhood Education,* VIII (November 1931), 129–131.

——. *Two Lives: The Story of Wesley Clair Mitchell and Myself.* New York, Simon & Schuster, 1953.

Phelps, Mary and Brown, Margaret Wise. "Lucy Sprague Mitchell." *Horn Book,* XIII (May 1937), 158–163.

Progressive Education, 1924–1940.

Lois Lenski

Lois Lenski won the Newbery Medal in 1946, and the biographical paper in *Newbery Medal Books, 1922–1955* covers her entire career to that date. The following pertains to her early work as an illustrator:

Titzell, Josiah. "Lois Lenski: A Serious Artist with a Sense of Humor." *Publishers' Weekly,* CXVIII (October 25, 1930), 1966–1969.

HELEN SEWELL

Allen, Grace. "Helen Sewell." *Publishers' Weekly,* CXXVII (April 20, 1935), 1579–1581.

Bechtel, Louise Seaman. "About Helen Sewell." *Horn Book,* X (July 1934), 243–247.

——. "Helen Sewell and Her Art for Children." *Horn Book,* XXII (March 1946), 147–155.

——. "Helen Sewell, 1896–1956, The Development of a Great Illustrator." *Horn Book,* XXXIII (October 1957), 368–388. Reprinted in Bechtel, *Books in Search of Children.*

Pitz, Henry C. "The Book Illustrations of Helen Sewell." *American Artist,* XXII (January 1958), 34–39.

Sewell, Helen. "Illustrator Meets the Comics." *Horn Book,* XXIV (March 1948), 136–140. About the genesis of *Three Tall Tales.*

INFORMATION

Russian Picturebooks

Aranowitsch, D. "The Modern Russian Children's Book." *Gebrauchsgraphik,* V (July 1828), 55–69. (Text in English and German.) A contemporary Russian appraisal, as distinct from the others.

Binder, Pearl. "Books for Children in Modern Russia." *London Studio,* No. 7 (June 1934), 309–313.

Deutsch, Babette. "Children's Books in Russia." *Creative Art,* IX (September 1931), 223–227.

Evans, Ernestine. "Russian Children and Their Books." *Asia,* XXXI (November 1931), 686–691, 736–737.

Mass-Market Picturebooks

The one big gap in the extensive coverage of children's books provided by the *Illustrators of Children's Books* series and the other standard reference works is the output of the mass-market publishers. Thus, for example, the long-lived *Little Engine That Could* (Platt & Munk, 1930) is not listed among the books illustrated by Lois Lenski, while illustrators whose only work chanced to be for mass-market houses, such as Naomi Averill, are overlooked altogether. The modern record of children's books, as generally available, is a record of trade publishing.

The account in this section draws upon information and leads provided by Lucille Ogle, as well as the publishing record. Sources for other aspects of the subject are identified under subsequent headings. (Naomi Averill appears under "Of the American Indian.")

PHOTOGRAPHIC BOOKS

At any level this is a relatively unexplored area, for no study of photographic books in general has yet appeared. But interest in the photographic book—as distinct from the album of photographs—was considerable in the Thirties, as represented by the following which pertain to both juvenile and adult books:

"Illustrated Books for Adult Illiterates." A list prepared by the American Library Association Committee on Institutional Libraries. *Library Journal,* LX (March 15, 1935), 261–263. Many though not all are photographic books and together they comprise, however inadvertently, the most extensive list of Thirties' photographic books, juvenile and adult, that I know of.

Lehmann-Haupt, Hellmut. "Photographs for Book Illustration." *Production Yearbook,* No. 6 (1940), 112–118.

Melcher, Frederic G. Editorial, "The New Era of the Photograph." *Publishers' Weekly,* CXXXI (May 29, 1937), 2149.

"Modern Photographic Illustration Discussed by Textbook Clinic." *Bookbinding Magazine,* XXVII (June 1938), 42. The remarks of the participants are summarized; they do not pertain only to textbooks.

"'Orbis Pictus.'" *Nation,* CXLI (October 16, 1935), 426. About the increasing number of picturebooks for adults.

Owen, Helen Hammett. "Photographic Picture Books." *Publishers' Weekly,* CXIX (October 24, 1931), 1923–1924. Specifically about books for children.

See also references to *Publishers' Weekly* in the text.

As regards specific works and individuals, the account of the *First* and *Second Picture Book* is based in part on the papers of Dr. Mary Steichen Calderone on deposit at the Schlesinger Library, Radcliffe College. Lewis Hine's career is treated in Beaumont Newhall's *History of Photography* (New York, Museum of Modern Art, 1964) and in greater detail by Judith Mara Gutman in *Lewis W. Hine and the American Social Conscience* (New York, Walker, 1967), which provides access to his published photographs and to writings about him. Information about Ylla and her books was supplied by her agent, Rapho Guillumette, and the legatee of her estate, Pryor Dodge. A substantive obituary appeared in the New York *Herald Tribune*, March 31, 1955.

Lastly, a general discussion of photography in children's books may be found in Hürlimann, *Three Centuries of Children's Books in Europe.*

IMPORTED FROM FRANCE

EDY LEGRAND

In addition to the articles cited in the Notes, the following may be of interest:

Feisenberger, Eleanor. "Edy LeGrand—Illustrator." *Print,* III, No. 3 (1948), 1–6. The artist's views are represented and a list of his illustrated books is appended.

THE DOMINO PRESS AND ROJANKOVSKY

Averill, Esther. "Fedor Rojankovsky and 'Les Peaux-Rouges.'" *Horn Book,* VIII (February 1932), 28.

——. "Feodor Rojankovsky, Illustrator." *Horn Book,* XIX (May 1943), 151–157.

——. "A Publisher's Odyssey." *Horn Book,* XIV (September 1938), 275–281; XIV (November 1938), 391–396; XV (January 1939), 20–23. Reprinted in *A Horn Book Sampler* (Boston, Horn Book, 1959).

——. "Unfinished Portrait of an Artist, Feodor Rojankovsky." *Horn Book,* XXXII (August 1956), 246–253. Reprinted in *Caldecott Medal Books, 1938–1957* and *Newbery and Caldecott Medal Books, 1956–1965.*

Eichenberg, Fritz, "Feodor Rojankovsky, Friend of Children." *American Artist,* XXI (January 1957), 28–35. Many independent drawings and paintings are illustrated but the text contains a number of factual errors.

"Rojankovsky and His Books for Children." *Publishers' Weekly,* CXLVI (October 28, 1944), 1741–1744.

Other writings (apart from Miss Averill's) appeared on the occasion of Rojankovsky's winning the Caldecott Medal in 1956.

THE ARTISTS AND WRITERS PRESS

Information on the Artists and Writers Press was provided by H. M. Benstead, H. M. Benstead, Jr., Lucille Ogle, Roger Duvoisin and others directly or indirectly connected with its operations. Also helpful for background was the Golden Anniversary Issue of Western Publishing Company's house organ, *The Westerner* (Jaunary 1966), devoted to the firm's "oldest and largest subsidiary," Whitman. Finally, the obituary of Samuel T. Lowe in *Publishers' Weekly* (CLXI, February 23, 1952) sets forth his contribution to mass-market publishing as a whole.

ROGER DUVOISIN

Roger Duvoisin won the Caldecott Medal in 1948 (see bibliographic note, p. 582). Also of interest are:

Duvoisin, Roger. "Design in Children's Books." Comments on the AIGA show, 1958–1960. *Horn Book,* XXXVII (August 1961), 367–371.

Pitz, Henry C. "Roger Duvoisin." *American Artist,* XIII (December 1949). 44–47, 76.

THE AMERICAN LINE

The general works listed above under "Starting Points, American Illustration" are applicable, and also:

Brown, Milton W. *American Painting from the Armory Show to the Depression.* Princeton, Princeton University Press, 1955.

Larkin, Oliver. *Art and Life in America.* New York, Rinehart, 1949.

ELLIS CREDLE

Information about Ellis Credle may be found in the standard reference works.

ROBERT LAWSON

Robert Lawson won the Caldecott Medal in 1941 and the Newbery Medal in 1945. On the first occasion the major articles about him were written by two of his three chief editors, May Massee (*Library Journal*) and Helen Dean Fish (*Horn Book, Publishers' Weekly*). The third, Helen L. Jones, subsequently presented a selection of his illustrations in *Robert Lawson, Illustrator* (Boston, Little, Brown, 1972), a volume which includes comment by Miss Jones, a list of his illustrated books and reference to other sources.

As anyone who has followed this bibliography will have noticed, it was customary until the mid-1950s for children's book editors to write about the personalities on their lists; and it is this engaging, knowledgeable writing that shaped the general conception, or image, of a number of individuals.

Lawson himself aside, the history of *Ferdinand* is recapitulated by Arthur Bell in *Publishers' Weekly,* August 22, 1966.

GLEN ROUNDS

Information about Glen Rounds may be found in the standard reference works. The following, in addition, anticipates *Once We Had a Horse* by thirty years:

"Here's Glen Rounds from His Homeland of Ranch and Prairie." *Young Wings,* XII (November 1941), 10–11.

JAMES DAUGHERTY

James Daugherty won the Newbery Medal in 1940. The biographical paper written by Lynd Ward on that occasion deals chiefly, however, with his illustration, as do the following:

Daugherty, James. "Illustrating for Children." *Bulletin of the New York Public Library,* LX (November 1956), 569–572. Reprinted in Spain, Frances L., Ed., *Reading Without Boundaries* (New York, New York Public Library, 1956).

Kent, Norman. "James Daugherty, Buckskin Illustrator." *American Artist,* IX (March 1945), 16–20,

Robert Schoelkopf Gallery, New York. *James H. Daugherty.* Catalog of an exhibition of Daugherty's paintings, 1915–1969, with an essay by William C. Agee and several illustrations. New York, Robert Schoelkopf Gallery, 1971.

Titzell, Josiah. "James Daugherty, American." *Publishers' Weekly,* CXVI (October 26, 1929), 2073–2076.

ROBERT MCCLOSKEY

Robert McCloskey won the Caldecott Medal in 1942 and 1958 (see bibliographic note, p. 582).

OF THE AMERICAN INDIAN

NAOMI AVERILL

Because Naomi Averill's books were all produced by the Artists and Writers Guild for Grosset & Dunlap, a mass-market publisher, she is not generally known. Therefore a biographical note seems in order.

Naomi Averill was born in Thomaston, Maine, in

1905. She studied art at Pratt Institute and worked with Roger Duvoisin at Mallinson's, the silk manufacturer (she is Naomi the hen of *Donkey-Donkey*). Through Duvoisin she began doing books for A & W —the six constituting *A Child's Story of the World* which she illustrated, and the two featured in this section, which she also wrote. Subsequently she returned to Thomaston and married, and lives there today. Though there is little record of her work elsewhere, *Whistling Two-Teeth* has the distinction of being the only American work illustrated in the catalog of the AIGA exhibition, *International Book Illustration, 1935–1945.*

Indian Art and the Indian Service Books

Austin, Mary. "Indian Arts for Indians." *The Survey,* LX (July 1926), 381–388.

Douglas, Frederic H. and d'Harnoncourt, René. *Indian Art of the United States.* New York, Museum of Modern Art, 1941.

Dunn, Dorothy. *American Indian Painting of the Southwest and Plains Areas.* Albuquerque, University of New Mexico Press, 1968.

——. "The Development of Modern American Indian Painting in the Southwest and Plains Areas." *El Palacio* (Santa Fe), LXVIII (November 1951), 331–353.

Indian Education. 1936–1944.

Indians at Work. 1933–1945.

Both these publications of the Bureau of Indian Affairs, Department of the Interior, are indexed in *Indian Index,* also published by the Department of the Interior, along with much other inaccessible material.

Rehnstrand, Jane. "Young Indians Revive Their Native Arts." *School Arts,* XXVI (November 1936), 137–144.

Information on individual Indian artists may also be located through *Indian Index.*

Ann Nolan Clark

Ann Nolan Clark's work for the Bureau of Indian Affairs can be traced through the publications cited above and others indexed in *Indian Index.* She discusses her teaching and her writing in *Journey to the People* (New York, Viking, 1969), which also contains the text of her Newbery and Regina Medal acceptance speeches. Additional articles appeared in 1953 in conjunction with her receipt of the Newbery.

TWO MASTERS, MARIE HALL ETS AND WILLIAM PENE DU BOIS

Marie Hall Ets won the Caldecott Medal in 1960, William Pène du Bois won the Newbery Medal in 1948. Apart from what appeared on those occasions (see bibliographic note, p. 582), the following are of interest:

Ets, Marie Hall. "Batik Illustration." *Horn Book,* XXX (October 1954), 346–347.

Du Bois, William Pène. "Animal History Will Bear This Out." *Bulletin of the New York Public Libray* (April 1957). Reprinted in Spain, Frances L., Ed., *The Contents of the Basket* (New York, New York Public Library, 1960).

Also comments by William Pène du Bois in *Young Wings* apropos of *The Great Geppy* (April 1940), *The Twenty-One Balloons* (June 1947), *Peter Graves* (February 1951) and *Bear Party* (April 1952).

SUI GENERIS: *SEVEN SIMEONS* AND *BUTTONS*

Boris Artzybasheff

Bechtel, Louise Seaman. "Boris Artzybasheff, 1899–1965." *Horn Book,* XLII (April 1966), 176–180. Reprinted in Bechtel, *Books in Search of Children.*

Current Biography 1945.

Lockwood, Bruce. "Boris Artzybasheff." *Creative Art,* XII (January 1933), 11–18.

New York Public Library. Art Division. Typescript chronology of Artzybasheff's activities to 1931, evidently prepared with his collaboration.

New York Times. Obituary, July 18, 1965.

Watson, Ernest W. "The Art of Boris Artzybasheff." *American Artist,* V (December 1941), 11–15.

Peggy Bacon

Index of Twentieth Century American Artists, 1933–1937. Reprint in one volume. New York, Arno, 1970. 258–261; 264–265; 268. A brief biography with a comprehensive list (to 1937) of public collections where she is represented, exhibitions of her work, books illustrated by her, articles about her, and reproductions of her work.

THE STORYTELLERS

Virginia Lee Burton won the Caldecott Medal in 1943 (See bibliographic note, p. 582). Also of interest are:

Burton, Virginia Lee. "Symphony in Comics." *Horn Book,* XVII (July 1941), 307–311.

Kingman, Lee. "Virginia Lee Burton's Dynamic Sense of Design." *Horn Book,* XLVI (October 1970), 449–460; XLVI (December 1970), 593–602.

"Virginia Lee Burton." Autobiographical brochure. Boston, Houghton Mifflin, n.d.

Information about Hardie Gramatky, H. A. Rey, Don Freeman and Bill Peet may be found in the standard reference works. Rey and Peet are also represented by Houghton Mifflin biographical brochures, and Freeman's autobiographical *Come One, Come All* (New York, Rinehart, 1949), "drawn from memory," will give pleasure to anyone who enjoys his work. The following are pertinent contributions by Hardie Gramatky:

"Little Toot's 25th Birthday." *Horn Book,* XL (October 1964), 518–519.

"Technique for Making Color Separations." *American Artist,* XXVI (May 1962), 43–47, 54–55. About *Little Toot* and a later book, *Bolivar.*

DESIGNED FOR CHILDREN

Holiday House

Fuller, Muriel. "Vernon Ives of Holiday House." *Publishers' Weekly,* CLII (April 26, 1947), 2206–2207.

Gentry, Helen. "Fine Books for Children, Too." *Horn Book,* XI (July 1935), 210–213.

"Helen Gentry of Holiday House, New York City." *Bookbinding Magazine* (November 1938), 54. One of a series of "Production Portraits" of designers, art directors and production heads that ran in *Bookbinding Magazine* from 1934 on. Grace Allen

Hogarth, Eunice Blake and others prominent in juvenile publishing are included.
Holiday House News. Twenty-fifth Anniversary Issue, March 1960.
Ives, Vernon. "Holiday House: The Formative Years, 1935–1965." Unpublished manuscript [1972].
——. "Making Books Is Fun." *Story Parade*, III (May 1938), 38–41.

WILLLIAM R. SCOTT, INC.

Insofar as the Scott publishing program constitutes an extension of the progressive preschool movement, the works listed above under "The Small Child's World, The Preschool Movement and Books for Preschool Children" are applicable, in particular those by or about Lucy Sprague Mitchell. Also basic is *Another Here and Now Story Book* (New York, Dutton, 1937), edited and with a foreword by Lucy Sprague Mitchell, to which many of those identified with Scott books contributed.

Like other contemporaneous editors, William Scott was himself an articulate exponent of his aims. The reader is reminded that, in addition to the following published writings, he and John McCullough wrote extensive notes for Scott catalogs.

Scott, William R. "New editorial technique: test readings with children." *Library Journal*, LXVI (October 15, 1941), 854.
——. "A New Literature for the Nursery." *AIGA Journal*, III, No. 3 [1951], 3–6.
——. "Some Notes on Communication in Picture Books." *Elementary English*, XXXIV (February 1957), 67–72.
Trager, Helen R. "Story of a Unique Publishing House." *Publishers' Weekly*, CLIII (April 24, 1948), 1796–1798. With "Ten Years of Studied Growth," directly following, a reprise of the first decade.

The account is based also on additional information supplied by William Scott and John McCullough.

MARGARET WISE BROWN

See under "The Emotional Element," below.

EDITH THACHER HURD AND CLEMENT HURD

More Junior Authors contains an extensive, uncommonly interesting autobiographical sketch by each of the Hurds. In addition, see:

"Clement Hurd: Children's Book Illustrator as Artist and Exhibitor." *Publishers' Weekly*, CLXXXIX (February 7, 1966), 106–108.

LEONARD WEISGARD

Leonard Weisgard won the Caldecott Medal in 1947, at which time there appeared solid articles about him by the Hurds and Margaret Wise Brown in particular. Articles by Weisgard include:

"Artist at Work: Influences and Applications." *Horn Book*, XL (August 1964), 409–414.
"Contemporary Art and Children's Book Illustration." *Horn Book*, XXXVI (April 1960), 155–158.

CLOTH BOOKS AND TOY BOOKS

The toy book flurry is recorded in the pages of *Publishers' Weekly* and the printing trades journals, and reflected in the following:

Hogarth, Grace Allen. "Toy, Play and Game Books for Indoor Days." *Horn Book*, XIX (January 1943), 21–26.

Specifically about Elena Eleska are:

Brown, Louise Fargo. "Eleska." *Horn Book*, XXI (September 1945), 337–343.
"Cloth Books by Eleska Studios." *Publishers' Weekly*, CXLV (April 29, 1944), 1696–1697.

THE EMOTIONAL ELEMENT

CLARE TURLAY NEWBERRY

Fuller, Muriel. "Cats and a Lion." *Horn Book*, XII (March 1936), 91–93.
Newberry, Clare Turlay. "Kittens Always!" *Young Wings* (January 1953), 8–9.

MARGARET WISE BROWN

The account of Margaret Wise Brown in this and other sections is based overall on the collection of her books and papers at the Westerly (R.I.) Public Library. Additional information was supplied by William Scott, Ursula Nordstrom, Edith Thacher Hurd, Clement Hurd and Louise Seaman Bechtel.

Following is a list of her published writing about children's books and of the writing about her. Reference to unpublished papers is made in the Notes. Comparison with the checklist of her children's books at the Westerly Library and my own compilation indicates that the listing in the *National Union Catalog Pre-1956 Imprints* and the succeeding volume is complete with the exception of *O Said the Squirrel*, cited in the text, which was published in England. She also contributed to *Good Housekeeping*, *Story Parade* and other magazines.

By Margaret Wise Brown:

"Creative Writing for Very Young Children." 1951 *Book of Knowledge Annual*, 77–81.
"Leonard Weisgard Wins the Caldecott Medal." *Publishers' Weekly*, CLII (July 5, 1947), 40–42.
"Stories to be Sung and Songs to be Told." 1952 *Book of Knowledge Annual*, 166–170.
"Writing for Children." *Hollins Alumnae Magazine*, XXII (Winter 1949), 1, 14.
Co-author, with Mary Phelps. "Lucy Sprague Mitchell." *Horn Book*, XIII (May 1937), 158–163.

About Margaret Wise Brown:

Bechtel, Louise Seaman. "Margaret Wise Brown, 'Laureate of the Nursery.'" *Horn Book*, XXXIV (June 1958), 172–186. Reprinted in Bechtel, *Books in Search of Children.*
Bliven, Bruce, Jr. "Child's Best Seller." *Life*, XXI (December 2, 1946), 59–66.
Mitchell, Lucy Sprague. "Margaret Wise Brown, 1910–1952." *Children Here and Now: Notes from 69 Bank Street.* I, No. 1 (1953), 18–20.

JEAN CHARLOT

Brenner, Anita. *Idols Behind Altars.* New York, Payson & Clarke, 1929.
Charlot, Jean. *Art from the Mayans to Disney.* New York, Sheed & Ward, 1939.
——. *Art-Making from Mexico to China.* New York, Sheed & Ward, 1950.
——. *The Mexican Mural Renaissance, 1920–1925.* New Haven, Yale University Press, 1963.
Current Biography 1945.
Merida, Carlos. *Modern Mexican Artists.* Mexico, Frances Toor Studios, 1937.

GOLDEN BOOKS

Apart from the reports in *Publishers' Weekly*, many of which are cited in the Notes, virtually nothing appears to have been written about this publishing phenomenon. The account also draws upon information supplied by Albert Leventhal, Lucille Ogle, H. M. Benstead, H. M. Benstead, Jr., Edith Thacher Hurd and Richard Eiger.

DR. SEUSS

Much has been written on Theodor Seuss Geisel, much of it repetitious; the entry in *Current Biography* 1968 is an effective summary. The following, however, fill in the background in various respects:

Dohm, Janice H. "The Curious Case of Dr. Seuss: A Minority Report from America." *Top of the News*, XXI (January 1965), 151–155. Reprinted from *Junior Bookshelf*, December 1963.

Jennings, Robert C. "Dr. Seuss: 'What am I doing here?'" *Saturday Evening Post*, CCXXXVIII (October 23, 1965), 105–109.

Kahn, E. J., Jr. "Profiles: Children's Friend." *New Yorker*, XXXVI (Decmeber 17, 1960), 47–93.

Silverman, Betsy Marden. "Doctor Seuss Talks to Parents." *Parents Magazine*, XXXV (November 1960), 44–45, 135–136. Subtitled: "About learning to read and what makes children want to do it."

"The 25th Anniversary of Dr. Seuss." *Publishers' Weekly*, CLXXXII (December 17, 1962), 11–14.

MARCIA BROWN

Marcia Brown won the Caldecott Medal in 1955 and 1962. In addition to the writing called forth on those occasions (see bibliographic note, p. 582), the following have particular interest and bearing:

Brown, Marcia. "Distinction in Picture Books." *Horn Book*, XXV (September, 1949), 382–395. Reprinted in *Illustrators of Children's Books, 1946–1956.*

——. "My Goals as an Illustrator." *Horn Book*, XLIII (June 1967), 304–316.

Kent, Norman. "Marcia Brown, Author & Illustrator." *American Artist*, XXVII (January 1963), 26–31.

EXPANDING POSSIBILITIES:
EASTER, FOR INSTANCE

Sources are indicated in the Notes.

NEW LOOKS

GENERAL WORKS

Kepes, Gyorgy. *Language of Vision.* With introductory essays by S. Giedion and S. I. Hayakawa. Chicago, Paul Theobald, 1944.

Moholy-Nagy, László. *The New Vision.* Fourth revised edition, with *Abstract of an Artist.* New York, Wittenborn, 1947.

——. *Vision in Motion.* Chicago, Paul Theobald, 1947.

Rand, Paul. *Thoughts on Design.* With an introduction by E. McKnight Kauffer. New York, Wittenborn, 1947.

Tschichold, Jan. *Asymmetric Typography.* Trans. by Ruari McLean from *Typographische Gestaltung*, Basle, 1935. Toronto, Cooper & Beatty; New York, Reinhold, 1967.

NICOLAS MORDVINOFF

Nicolas Mordvinoff won the Caldecott Medal in 1952 (see bibliographic note, p. 582).

PAUL RAND

Ettenberg, Eugene M. "The Paul Rand Legend." *American Artist*, XVII (October 1953), 36–41, 60–61.

Paul Rand: His Work from 1946 to 1958. Ed. by Yusaku Kamekura. Tokyo, Zokeisha; New York, Knopf, 1959.

ANTONIO FRASCONI

Frasconi: Against the Grain. The woodcuts of Antonio Frasconi, with an introduction by Nat Hentoff and an appreciation by Charles Parkhurst. New York, Macmillan, 1974.

"Frasconi's Brio with a Book." *Horizon*, III (March 1961), 122–128.

Gasser, Manuel. "Antonio Frasconi: *A Book of Many Suns.*" *Graphis*, No. 100 (March–April 1962), 208–217+.

Lieberman, William S. "Antonio Frasconi: Woodcutter." *Print*, IX (July–August 1955), 52–62.

JOSEPH LOW

Lieberman, Frank J. "My Introduction to Joseph Low." *Print*, VI (Winter 1950–1951), 3–10.

Low, Joseph. "Picture Books." *Horn Book*, XLIII (December 1967), 715–720.

Pitz, Henry C. "Joseph Low." *American Artist*, XV (October 1951), 28–32.

JULIET KEPES

Information on Juliet Kepes appears in the standard reference works. The following explains her method of preparing the art for *Lady Bird, Quickly*:

Kepes, Juliet. "Color Separation II: The Use of Photostats." *Horn Book*, XLI (December 1965), 651–654.

SOCIAL CHANGE

SOCIAL CONCERNS AND CHILDREN'S BOOKS

Bishop, Claire Huchet. "Children are Poor, Too." *Commonweal*, LXVI (May 24, 1957), 207–215.

Books for Brotherhood. Annual lists issued by the National Conference of Christians and Jews, 1950–51—1970–71.

Hoke, Helen et al. "The Problem Book." *Publishers' Weekly*, CXL (October 18, 1941), 1550–1555.

Sauer, Julia L. "Making the World Safe for the Janey Larkins." *Library Journal*, LXVI (January 15, 1941), 49–53.

Straus, Flora. "Let Them Face It: Today's World in Books for Boys and Girls." *Horn Book*, XXI (January 1945), 63–64.

SOCIAL ACTION PROGRAMS

American Education (Washington, D.C.) 1965–1970.

Levitan, Sar A. *The Great Society's Poor Law: A New Approach to Poverty.* Baltimore, The Johns Hopkins Press, 1969.

Public Library Service to the Disadvantaged. Proceedings of an Institute, December 7th and 8th, 1967. Atlanta, Emory University, 1969.

NEGRO IDENTIFICATION, BLACK IDENTITY

Allee, Marjorie H. "Books Negro Children Like." *Horn Book*, XIV (March 1938), 81–87.

Baker, Augusta. *Books About Negro Life for Children.* New York, Bureau for Intercultural Education, 1946.

—. —. Second edition. New York, New York Public Library, 1949. Subsequent editions appeared in 1957, 1961 and 1965; the 1971 edition is entitled *The Black Experience in Children's Books*.

—. "Books for Children: The Negro in Literature." *Child Study*, XXII (February 1945), 58+.

Breed, Clara E. "Books That Build Better Racial Attitudes." *Horn Book*, XXI (January 1945), 55–61.

Evans, Eva Knox. "The Negro in Children's Fiction." *Publishers' Weekly*, CXL (August 30, 1941), 650–653.

"Negro Dialect in Children's Books." *Publishers' Weekly*, CXL (October 18, 1941), 1555–1558. Also, "A Further Statement on Negro Dialect in Children's Books." *Publishers' Weekly*, CXLI (January 10, 1942), 104–105. Both follow upon the Eva Knox Evans article.

Nolen, Eleanor W. "The Colored Child in Contemporary Literature." *Horn Book*, XVIII (September 1942), 348–355.

Rollins, Charlemae. "Books about Negroes for Children." *ALA Bulletin*, LIII (April 1959), 306–308.

—. *We Build Together*. Chicago, National Council of Teachers of English [1941]. "A Reader's Guide to Negro Life and Literature for Elementary and High School Use," with an introductory discussion of criteria.

—. —. Second edition. Chicago, National Council of Teachers of English, 1948.

—. —. Third edition. Champagne, Ill., National Council of Teachers of English, 1967.

Theobald, Ruth. "Library Service for Negro Children." *Children's Library Yearbook*, No. 4. Chicago, American Library Association, 1932. 111–122.

Trager, Helen. "Intercultural Books for Children." *Childhood Education*, XXII (November 1945), 138–145.

EZRA JACK KEATS

Ezra Jack Keats won the Caldecott Medal in 1962 (see bibliographic note, p. 582). Of additional interest are:

"Ezra Jack Keats on Collage as an Illustration Medium." *Publishers' Weekly* (April 4, 1966), 94–95.

Perry, Erma. "The Gentle World of Ezra Jack Keats." *American Artist*, XXXV (September 1971), 48–53, 71–73.

JACOB LAWRENCE

Loucheim, Aline B. "An Artist Reports on the Troubled Mind." *New York Times Magazine*, October 15, 1950, 15+.

McCausland, Elizabeth. "Jacob Lawrence." *Magazine of Art*, XXXVIII (November 1945), 251–254.

JOHN STEPTOE

"*Stevie*: realism in a book about black children." *Life*, LXVII (August 29, 1969), 54–59.

MORE INFORMATION

Sources are indicated in the Notes. Background on the Let's-Read-and-Find-Out series was supplied by Elizabeth Riley; acknowledgment is made in the text to Matilda Welter for information on the books themselves.

RUTH KRAUSS;
RUTH KRAUSS AND MAURICE SENDAK

An autobiographical sketch by Ruth Krauss appears in *More Junior Authors*. References to Maurice Sendak are listed under "Maurice Sendak," below.

CROCKETT JOHNSON

Current Biography 1943 has a lengthy entry on Crockett Johnson, with references appended. An obituary appeared in the *New York Times*, July 13, 1975.

THE JAPANESE ADVENT

Sources are indicated in the Notes. For Taro Yashima, see also:

Yashima, Taro. "On Making a Book for a Child." *Horn Book*, XXXI (February 1955), 21–24. A lecture given at the New York Public Library, November 1954; reprinted in Spain, Frances L., Ed., *The Contents of the Basket* (New York, New York Public Library, 1960).

BLAIR LENT

Blair Lent won the Caldecott Medal in 1973 (see bibliographic note, p. 582). The following are also of interest:

Lent, Blair. "The Artist at Work: Cardboard Cuts." *Horn Book*, XLI (August 1965), 408–412.

—. "On Illustrating *Tikki Tikki Tembo*." *Owlet Among the Colophons*, III (November 1968), 1, 3.

FEELINGS EXTENDED

Darling, Richard. "Mental Hygiene and Books: Bibliotherapy as Used with Children and Adolescents." *Wilson Library Bulletin*, XXXII (December 1957), 293–296. A bibliographic survey.

Frank, Josette. "Books and Children's Emotions." *Child Study*, XXVI (Winter 1948–49), 5–6, 24–26.

Wolfenstein, Martha. "The Impact of a Children's Story on Mothers and Children." *Monographs of the Society for Research in Child Development*, No. 42, Washington, Society for Research in Child Development, 1947.

Information on the individual authors and illustrators may be found in the standard reference works.

MAURICE SENDAK

Writings by and about Maurice Sendak abound, and there is almost nothing in which he is quoted that is entirely without interest. Following are some of the more extensive or significant items, omitting those directly connected with Sendak's receipt of the Caldecott Medal in 1964 (for which see bibliographic note, p. 582).

Braun, Saul. "Sendak Raises the Shade on Childhood." *New York Times Magazine*, June 7, 1970, 34+.

Hentoff, Nat. "Profiles: Among the Wild Things." *New Yorker*, XLI (January 22, 1966), 39–73.

Lanes, Selma G. "The Art of Maurice Sendak: A diversity of influences inform an art for children." *Artforum*, IX (May 1971), 70–73.

Michel, Joan Hess. "Maurice Sendak, Illustrator of the Child's World." *American Artist*, XXVIII (September 1964), 44–49, 77.

"Questions to an Artist Who Is Also an Author." Transcript of an exchange between Virginia Haviland and Maurice Sendak. *Quarterly Journal of the Library of Congress,* XVIII (October 1971), 263–280.

Sendak, Maurice. "A Prize Is Won: how Maurice Sendak discovered where the wild things are." Text of the Hans Christian Andersen Illustrator's Medal acceptance speech. *Publishers' Weekly* (May 25, 1970), 30–31.

——. "The Shape of Music." New York *Herald Tribune Book Week,* November 1, 1964, 1, 4–5.

AWAY FROM WORDS

Leo Lionni

Agree, Rose. "Lionni's Artichokes: An Interview with Leo Lionni." *Wilson Library Bulletin,* XLIV (May 1970), 947–950.

Ettenberg, Eugene. "Leo Lionni." *American Artist,* XVII (April 1953), 30–35.

Lionni, Leo. "Mrs. Sanborn, I Love you." *Publishers' Weekly,* CLXXXIX (July 11, 1966), 134–135.

——. "My Books for Children." *Wilson Library Bulletin,* XXXIX (October 1964), 142–145.

Remy Charlip

Monigle, Martha. "Remy Charlip's Children's Books." *Print,* XX (July–August 1966), 42–47.

THE FABULISTS

Tomi Ungerer

Michel, Joan Hess. "A Visit with Tomi Ungerer." *American Artist,* XXXIII (May 1969), 40–45, 78–79.

Edward Gorey

McDade, Thomas. "Edward Gorey: An American Gothic." *American Book Collector,* XXI (May 1971), 12–17. A brief essay with a bibliography.

Wilson, Edmund. "The Albums of Edward Gorey." *New Yorker,* XXXV (December 26, 1959), 479–484. Reprinted in *The Bit Between My Teeth: A Literary Chronicle of 1950–1965.* (New York, Farrar, Straus, 1965).

William Steig

William Steig won the Caldecott Medal in 1970 (see bibliographic note, p. 582). His early career is summarized in *Current Biography* 1944.

Margot Zemach

Margot Zemach won the Caldecott Medal in 1974 (See bibliographic note, p. 582).

INDEX

Figures in **bold face** refer to principal references; figures in *italics* refer to illustrations.

A

A for the Ark **137–139,** *138*, 331
"A Was an Archer" 213, *213*
Abbott, Berenice 100, 106
ABC Book (Falls) 24–25, *24*
ABC Bunny 36, *37*
ABC for Every Day **81,** *81*, 86
Abe Lincoln Grows Up 151
Abeita, Louise 164–165
Abeyta, Narcisco 164
Abraham Lincoln (d'Aulaire) **45–46**
Across the Cotton Patch *142*, **143,** 375
Adams, Adrienne **327–329,** 402
Adams, Ansel 100
After They Came Out of the Ark 22
Akino, Fuku 450
Aladdin and the Wonderful Lamp (MacKinstry, illus.) 314
Alajalov, Constantin 195
Alay-Oop 365
Albers, Josef 332, 338, 361, 362
Alger, Joseph 103
Aliki (Aliki Brandenberg) 381, 400, **404–405, 407**
All Aboard! 271
All About Dogs, Dogs, Dogs 233
All About Eggs 387–388, **388**
All About Us 403–404
All Alone 299
All Around You 390, *390*
All Falling Down 466, 470
All Kinds of Babies and How They Grow 388
All Kinds of Time 356, 358, **485–487,** *486*
All My Shoes Come in Twos 397
Alland, Alexander 377–378
Alland, Alexandra 377-378
Allee, Marjorie Hill 373
Allen, Grace (Grace Allen Hogarth) 57
Alligator Case 183
Alligators All Around 509, *510*
Along the Coast 127
Alphabet (Nicholson) 24
Alphabet of Birds, Bugs and Beasts 98
Alphabet People 76
Alphonse That Bearded One 337, 338
Alston, Charles 382
America Builds Homes 59
America Travels 59
American Library Association 11, 12
Among the Leaves and Grasses **90–91,** *91*, 383
Amos & Boris 564, *565*
Anansi, the Spider Man (Sherlock-Brown) 316
And Now Miguel 365
And There Was America 134
And to Think That I Saw It on Mulberry Street **302–304,** *303*, 305, 308, 309, 312
Andersen, Hans Christian 29, 127, 212, 321, 456, 514
Andy and the Lion **151–154,** *152–153*, 175, 198, 221, 314
Angelo, Valenti 198, *213*, 245
Angry Moon 458
Angus and the Cat 62–63, *64*
Angus and the Ducks **61–62,** *61–63*, 355
Angus Lost 63
Animal Family 502
Animal Frolic 443, *444*
Animal Stories (Duplaix-Rojankovsky) 289
Animals Everywhere 222
Animals of Farmer Jones 279, **280–281,** *280*
Another Day 170
Another Here and Now Story Book 212, 221, 222, 252, 253
Anteater Named Arthur 482–483, *483–484*
Anybody at Home? 239
Anywhere in the World 385–387, *386*
Appolonia's Valentine 59
April's Kittens 242, **244,** *244*, 245, 355, 364, 452
Araminta 373–374
Arbuthnot, May Hill, quoted 566
Ardizzone, Edward 495, 496, 498, 499, 513
'Ariane' (Georges Duplaix) 278
Arm in Arm **533,** 536, *536–537*
Art Deco 90
Art Nouveau 187, 189
Artists and Writers Guild (and Artists and Writers Press) 95, 106, 108, **126–127,** 148, 158, **277–278,** 282, 285, 297, 411, 413
Art-Making from Mexico to China 266, *266*
Artzybasheff, Boris 25, 89, **187–196,** 197, 268, 495
Asch, Frank 369–370
Ask Mr. Bear **63, 75**
At Our House 231, 260, 371
Atwater, Richard and Florence 146
Aulaire, Ingri and Edgar Parin d'. *See* D'Aulaire, Ingri and Edgar Parin
Austin, Mary 14, 100, 160
Averill, Esther **118–123** *passim*, 290
Averill, Naomi 95, 158–160
Aymé, Marcel 424

Baba Yaga 455

B

Babar books 249, 278, 358, 544, 547
Babette 242, **243–244,** *243*, 364
Baby Sister for Frances **474–475,** *475*, 477
Backward Day **422,** *423*, 424
Bacon, Peggy 25–26, 196–198
Bad Little Duckhunter 217
Bahti, Tom 166
Baker, Augusta 373, 374, 378
Baldwin, Bird T. 73, 74
Ballad of Tangle Street **25–26,** *27*, 197
Ballantine, Bill 391, 393

Ballets-Russe 25, 30, 235, 354
Bandeira Duarte, Margarida Estrela 47
Bangs, John Kendrick 311
Bank Street Books (Little Golden Books) 279, 285
Bank Street Schools 214, 224, 254, 391
Barkis 242, **244**, 452
"Barnaby" **434**, *434*, 441
Bartholomew and the Oobleck 304–305
Baruch, Dorothy 126, 504, 514
Bat-Poet 502
Bauhaus 332, 354, 355, 361
Baumeister, Margaret 80
Bayer, Herbert 332, 355, 357
"Bazouge, The Sad Tale of" 11, *12*, 518
Beady Bear 208, *208*
Bear Circus 183–186, *183–186*
Bear Party **178**, 182
Beardsley, Aubrey 189, 196
Bears **419–420**, *420*, 509
Bears on Hemlock Mountain 86
Beast of Monsieur Racine 550–552, *550–551*
Beastly Boys and Ghastly Girls 551
Beasts and Nonsense 173, *174*
Beasts from a Brush 352
Beatty, Willard 161
Bechtel, Louise Seaman **23–26**, 74, 193, 221; quoted 135, 224, 388, 394, 414–415, 493
Becker, May Lamberton 75; quoted 216, 221, 238
Bedtime for Frances 260, **472–473**, *473*, 474
Bee-Man of Orn 514
Bees and Beelines 406–407, *407*
Before You Came This Way 166
Beginner Books 312, 499
Behind the Wheel 400
Behn, Harry 162, **485–487**, 511
Beilenson, Edna 486
Beilenson, Peter 486
Belinda the Mouse 85–86
Bell for Ursli 358
Bemelmans, Ludwig **47–51**, 52, 59, 198, 204, 248, 496
Ben and Me 146–147, *147*
Ben Day tints 27, 41, 134, 329, 337
Bendick, Jeanne **389–390**, 391
Benjamin Franklin (d'Aulaire) 45
Benjie 379
Bennett, Dorothy 278
Benny and His Penny 76
Benois, Alexander, quoted 124
Benton, Thomas Hart 140, 141
Berman, Sam 394
Berry, Erick **56**, 373, 374
Beskow, Elsa 30
Best, Herbert 56, 373
Beyond the Pawpaw Trees 492
Bianco, Margery 25, 143
'Bibliotherapy' 460
Big and Little 108
Big Book of Real Airplanes 415
Big Book of Real Trains 414–415, *415*
Big Brown Bear 278, **282**, *283*, 290
Big City 364
Big Cowboy Western 379
Big Dog Little Dog 217, 227
Big Fur Secret 255
Big Snow 29
Biggest Bear 424
Biggest House in the World 530
Bileck, Marvin 478–480
Bilibin, I. Y. 187, 193
Billy Boy 149
Binney, Ida 230
Bird, Beast and Fish 71
Birnbaum, A. 485
Birth of Sunset's Kittens 117
Birthday for Frances 474, **477**
Bishop, Claire Huchet **66–68**, 299, 313
Bits That Grow Big 387
Black, Irma Simonton 284
Black and White 255
Black Folk Tales 56
Black power movement 368, 381
Blacks, books about 108, 143, 364, 372, 373–382
Blair, Mary 286, 288
Blake, Eunice 57, 175, 324, 419
Blake, William 485, 498, 499
Bland, David, quoted 22, 140, 347
Blind Colt 148, 151
Bliss, Douglas, quoted 118
Bloch, Lucienne 114, **232**, 402
Blough, Glenn 390
Blue Barns 84
Blue Canyon Horse 166
Bluebeard (Crane, illus.) 3, *3*, 570
Blueberries for Sal 156–157, *156–157*
Bluebonnets for Lucinda 84
Boats on the River 65, 198
Bobri, Vladimir **329–331** *passim*, 402
Bock, George 89
Boll Weevil 149, *149*
Boners 302
Book of Christopher Columbus (Claudel-Charlot) 265
Book of Cowboys 411
Book of Indians 158, **410–411**, *411*
Book of Many Suns 343
Book of Moon Rockets for You 399, 400
Book of Satellites for You 399, 400
Books 408
"Books About Negro Life for Children" 373, 374
Bookselling, children's 23
Bookshop for Boys and Girls, Boston 11, 12, 23, 119, 313
Borten, Helen 358, **401–403** *passim*, 407
Bourke-White, Margaret 100, 112
Boutet de Monvel, Maurice. *See* Monvel, Maurice Boutel de
Box with Red Wheels **41–42**, *41*
Boy, a Dog and a Frog 540
Boy Who Could Do Anything **268–269**, 273
Bradley, Will 8
Brandt, Rose 161
Branley, Franklyn **399–403** *passim*, 455
Braque, Georges 341
Brave Mr. Buckingham 72
Bread and Jam for Frances **475–477**, *476*
Breed, Clara, quoted 374
Bremen Band (Dobias, illus.) 27–29, *28*
Brenner, Anita 266, 268, 273
Brer Rabbit and His Tricks 556
Bresdin, Rodolphe 478
Brett, George 23
Brewer, Warren & Putnam 241
Broadsides (Holiday House) 212–213, *213*
Brooke, L. Leslie 7, 24
Brown, Marcia 171, **313–322**, 362, 364
Brown, Margaret Wise 73, 109–111, 127, **215–229** *passim*, 231, 235, 239, 247, 248, 251, **252–264**, **269–270**, 273, 276, **285–288**, **289–292**, 302, 356, 391, 393, 427, 471, 484, 490, **530–531**
Brown, Palmer 492–493
Brownies 11
Bruner, Jerome, quoted 402
Bryant, Sara Cone 450, 453
Budney, Blossom 331
Buell, Ellen Lewis 279; quoted 505
Buffalo Bill (d'Aulaire) 45
Buford and the Little Bighorn 210, *211*
Building a House in Sweden 84
Building a Skyscraper 117
Bull Calf and Other Tales 10
Bulla, Clyde 400
Bumble Bug and Elephants **216–217**, *217*, 221, 222, 230, 254
Bundle Book 424
Bunyan, Paul 147, 311
Bureau for Intercultural Education 373, 374
Bureau of Educational Experiments 73, 215
Burgess, Gelett 11
"Burning of the Rice Fields" 453

Burning Ricefields (Funai, illus.) 450
Burton, Virginia Lee **199–203,** 456, 468
Busch, Wilhelm 8, 62, 70, 199, 498, 518, 522, 548, 552
Buttons **196–198,** *197*, 221, 365

C

Caldecott, Randolph **3,** 4, 6, 24, 280, 289, 515, 517
Caldecott Medal 12; winners 29, 41, 45, 57, 133, 147, 157, 173, 229, 301, 321, 326, 333, 379, 418, 458, 513, 564
Calderone, Mary 101
Calendrier des Enfants **124,** *125*, 127, 301
Calico, the Wonder Horse 202–203
Call It Courage 59
Call Me Bandicoot 183
Cane, Melville, quoted 299–300
Cantor, Sol 357
Caps for Sale 234–235, *234*
Capt. Kidd's Cat 146
Caran d'Ache (Emanuel Poiré) **203,** 522, 536
Cardboard cuts 453
Carigiet, Alois 358
Carlo **10–11,** *10–11*, 61
Carlson, Natalie Savage 133, 338
Carrot Seed *418*, **419,** 434, 435
Cartier Sails the Saint Lawrence 122. *See also Voyages of Jacques Cartier*
Cassandre, A. M. 332, 338
Castle Number Nine 50, *50*
Cat in the Hat 311–312, *312*
Catch a Cricket 114
Catfish 222
Cecily G. and the Nine Monkeys 205
Cendrars, Blaise 241
Centerburg Tales 157
Chagall, Marc 498
Chalmers, Mary 430, 433, **487–492,** 494, 499
Changes, Changes 542, *543*
Chansons de France 4
Charge of the Light Brigade (Provensen, illus.) 259
Charlip, Remy 253, **359,** 495, **530–536,** 538
Charlot, Jean 47, 53, 141, 231, **265–276,** 320, 353, 394, 451
Charlotte and the White Horse **432–433,** *433*, 478, 498, 506
Cheerful 330, **492–493,** *493*, 494
Cheese 480
Chekhov, Anton 252
Chermayeff, Ivan 361–362
Cherr, Pat 369
Chester the Worldly Pig 210, *210*
Chesterton, G. K., quoted 514–515, 572
Chicken Book 257, *257*
Chicken Little (cloth book) 236
Chicken Soup with Rice 509, *510*
Chicken World **20–22,** *21–22*, 61
Chie and the Sports Day 452
Child art 222, 397–398
Child Study Association 74
Childhood and Society 369
Children of the Northlights **44–45,** *45*
Children's Book Council 323
Children's Catalog 12
Children's preferences in book illustration, studies of 38
Children's Press 323
Children's Year 127
Child's Good Morning 273
Child's Good Night Book 231–232, **269–270,** *270–271*
Child's Story of the World **95,** 159
Chönz, Selina 358
Choochee 158–160, *159*
Choo-Me-Shoo the Eskimo 158
Choosing Book 79–80, *80*
Christ Child 41
Christmas in the Barn 264
Christmas Manger 87
Christmas Sky 455
Christmas Story **490,** 492, 494
Christmas Whale 469
Chukovsky, Kornei 415, 420, 422–424, 497
Ciardi, John 555
Cigalou **124,** *125*, 299
Cimino, Maria 313
Cinderella (Brown, illus.) 318, **320,** *320*
Cinderella (Sewell, illus.) 314
Cinderella (Weisgard, illus.) 226
Circus and All About It 18
Circus Baby **41–42,** *42*, 75
Circus Girl 498
City and Country School, New York 73, 214
City as a Community 372
City in the Summer **370,** 372
City in the Winter 370–372, *371*
Civil rights movement 368, 378
Civilité Puérile et Honnête 4
Clark, Ann Nolan 47, **161–163, 165–166,** 198
Clark, Margery 25
Claudel, Paul 265
Claws of the Thunderbird 158
Clean Brook 402
Clever Bill 31, 33, **60–61,** *60*
Cloth Book No. 1 237, *237*
Cloth books 52, 214, 230, **235–238**
Coatsworth, Elizabeth, quoted 34
Cock and the Ghost Cat 450
Cole, William 551
Coles, Robert 368, 369, 511
Collage 340–342 *passim*, 354, 379, 528, 529
Collier, John 161
Colman, Morris 198, 206
Cologne Bible (1478) *514*
Color Kittens 285
Coloring books 52, 524
Colum, Padraic 158, 187
Columbus (d'Aulaire) 45
Columbus Story (Dalgliesh-Politi) 59
Colver, Anne 478
Come for a Walk with Me **487,** *487*, 490
Composing Room, Inc. 357–358
Conquest of the Atlantic *44*, 45
Cook, Bernadine 436, 531–532
Cooney, Barbara 191, 264
Corcos, Loris 240
Cortez the Conqueror 122
Cottontails 221, **236,** *237*
Coucou 124
Country 221–222
Country Bunny and the Little Gold Shoes 65, **325–326,** *325*, 330, 563
Country Noisy Book 225
Covarrubias, Miguel 121, 332
Coward-McCann 31
Cowboy Small 79, *79*
Cox, Palmer 11
Crampton, Gertrude 283
Crane, Walter **3,** 4, 6, 24, 90, 280, 289, 314, 570
Credle, Ellis 141–143, 375
Creighton, Beatrice 331, 464
Cricket in a Thicket 299
Crictor **544–546,** *545*, 547
Crow Boy 198, **446–447,** *447-448*
Crowell 264, 349, 399–408 *passim*
Crowley, Maude 86
Cruikshank, George 495, 515
Crunch Crunch 399
Cubism 224–225, 342
Curious George **204–205,** *205*, 249, 324, 469
Curious George Goes to the Hospital 205
Curious Little Kitten 531–532
Curious Raccoons 112, *112*
Curry, John Steuart 140
Curtis, Nell C. 92

D

Dalgliesh, Alice 52, **58–59,** 74, **79–80,** 86, **87,** 148, 364
Dana, Mary Pepperell 220–221, 236
Dance of Death (Charlot) 276
Dancing Kettle 443–444

Dandelion 209, *209*
Daniel Boone (Averill-Rojankovsky) **118–120,** *121,* 122, 123, 124, 126, 291, 353
Daniel Boone (Daugherty-Daugherty) 154
Daniel Boone (White-Daugherty) 151
Dark Is Dark 231
Dark Wood of the Golden Birds 264
Darling, Richard 460
Darton, Harvey, quoted 235
Daugherty, James 11, 141, **151–154,** 198, 314, 548
D'Aulaire, Ingri and Edgar Parin **42–46,** 50, 59, 198, 222
Daumier, Honoré 196, 198
David's Little Indian 530–531
Davis, Stuart 224–225
Day the Sun Danced 453
Dead Bird **253,** 254, 530
Dear Garbage Man 368, **468–469,** *468*
Death at an Early Age 368
DeJong, Meindert 47, **495,** 496, 506
De la Mare, Walter 148, 485
Delivery Men **92–93,** *92,* 364
Deming, E. W. 158
Deming, Therese 158
Denetsosie, Hoke 162, 166
Denslow, W. W. **7–8,** 11, 296
De Regniers, Beatrice Schenk 496
Desert People 166
De Stijl 342
Dewey, John 97, 236, 362
DeWitt, Cornelius 121, 282, **411–414**
D'Harnoncourt, René **46–47, 68–71,** 161, 166, 522
Dick Whittington and His Cat 316–317, *317*
Digging in Yucatan 266
Discovering Design 331
Disney, Walt 37, 127, 146, 203, 204, 205, 209, 210, 282, 294, 312
Do You Know What I'll Do? 466
Do You See What I See? 358–359, 401
Dobias, Frank 27–29
Dr. Seuss (Theodor Seuss Geisel) **303–312,** 449, 541
Documentary films 377–378
Domino Press 118–123 *passim*
Dong with a Luminous Nose 557–558, *557*
Donkey-Donkey *128,* 129
Don't Frighten the Lion 239, 255
Dorey, Jacques 192
Dot and the Line 527
Doubleday 23–25 *passim,* 227–229 *passim*
Doubleday, Frank 10
Doubtful Guest **553–554,** *553,* 559
Down Down the Mountain 141–143, *142*
Down the River 127
Downer, Marion 331
Dream Keeper 84, 373
Dress Up and Let's Have a Party *358,* **359,** 530, 532
Du Bois, William Pène 50, 141, 167, **175–186,** 198, 251
Du Chaillu, Paul 56
Dulac, Edmund 187
Dumb Juan and the Bandits 273
Dumbo 203, 209, 210
Dunbar, Paul Laurence 373
Duncan, Preston 98
Dunn, Dorothy 160, 161
Duplaix, Georges **277–278,** 289
Duplaix, Lily 278
Dutton 253
Duvoisin, Roger **128–139,** 204, 221, 251, 271, 296, 326, 330, [illegible], [illegible], [illegible], **404,** 409
Dwarf Long-Nose 514, *515*
Dwarf Pine Tree 450

E

Early Life of Mr. Man Before Noah 22
Easter Bunny That Overslept **326–327,** *327–328,* 330–331
Easter Treat 326
Eaton, Anne Thaxter **278–279,** 280, 281, 374
Ebird 164
Economakis, Olga 455
Economic Opportunity Act (1964) 372
Egg to Chick 387
Egg Tree **59, 326,** *326,* 330
Eichenberg, Fritz 148, 333
Eisele, Ernest 312
Elementary and Secondary Education Act (1965) 372
Eleska, Elena 86, **237–238**
Elisabeth the Cow Ghost (1936) **175,** *176,* 176
Elisabeth the Cow Ghost (1964) 182–183
Elle Kari 108
Ellen's Lion 442, *442*
Elliott, Gertrude 279, 282, 287–288
Emberley, Ed 401, 404
Emile 546–548, *546–547*
En Famille 123
Enchanted Eve 317
Epic of Kings 89
Erikson, Erik 369, 504, 511–513 *passim*
Ernst, Margaret S. 103
Eskimos, books about 158–160
Ethical Culture School, New York 103, 391
Ets, Marie Hall **167–174,** 198, 251, **377–378,** 406
Evans, Edmund 3
Evans, Ernestine **31,** 33, 34; quoted 88, 364, 387
Evans, Eva Knox 373–374
Evans, Walker 100, 112
Evers, Alf 86
Everybody Eats 230
Everybody Has a House 230
E-Yeh-Shure 164–165

F

Fable of a Proud Poppy 120
Fadiman, Clifton, quoted 303
Fairleigh, John, quoted 191
Fairy Shoemaker **189–190,** *190,* 191, 193
Fairy tales as basis of picturebooks 314
Falls, C. B. 24–25
Fanchette and Jeannot 52
Fantasia 203, 209
Farm Book **18–19,** *19,* 141, 247
"Farm Sale" *32–33,* 33
Farmer Sows His Wheat 104
Farther and Faster 399
Fast Is Not a Ladybug 359, 362, 394–396, *396*
Father Bear Comes Home 502, *503*
Fatio, Louise 139
Faucher, Paul 123
Favorite Fairy Tales Told in . . . series 565
Feats on the Fjord 187, 313
Federal funds for book purchase 372, 402
Feed the Animals 239
Feild, Robert, quoted 203
Felt, Sue 365
Ferdinand, The Story of **145–146,** *145,* 198
Ferrer, Melchor 268
Filles et Garçons 4, *5*
Finders Keepers 333
Fireflies in the Night **405–406,** *406,* 453
Firefly Named Torchy 480
First Bible 86
First Experiences with Literature 74
First Picture Book 80, **100–103,** *101,* 117, 358
First Story 264
Fischer, Hans 358
Fish, Helen Dean 146
Fish in the Air 57
Fish with the Deep Sea Smile **253–254,** 264, 530

Fisher, Dorothy Canfield 374
Fisherman and His Wife (Zemach, illus.) 565
Fitch, Florence Mary 331
Five Chinese Brothers 57, **66–68,** *68–69*
500 Hats of Bartholomew Cubbins **304,** *304,* 305
Five Little Firemen 217, **285–286,** *287,* 393
Five Little Monkeys **350–351,** *350–351,* 355
Five Years of Children's Books 12, 103
Flack, Marjorie **61–65,** 66, 153, 158, 456
Flanagan, Geraldine Lux 116
Flash 120
Flesch, Rudolph 499
Fliegende Blätter 8, 152
Flop-Eared Hound 375
Flying Carpet 320–321, *321*
Flying Locomotive 177–178
Folk Tales of a Savage 56
Folklore as the basis of picturebooks 349, 458, 518, 565–570 *passim*
Follow the Road **134,** *135,* 356
Forge in the Forest **187, 189,** *188–189,* 192, 313
Forster, E. M., quoted 118
Fortunately 532, *534–535*
Fortune magazine 100, 187, 195, 382, 415, 525
Fougasse (Kenneth Bird), quoted 485
Four and Twenty Blackbirds 146
Four Corners of the World 134
Four Fur Feet 531, 532
Fourth of July Story 59
Fox Eyes 273
Foxes in the Woodshed 111
Fraiberg, Selma, quoted 468
France, Anatole 4
Francis, J. G. 94
François, André 348, **362–363,** 525
Françoise (Françoise Seignobosc) **52–53,** 357
Frank, Josette 368, 459–460, 463
Frascino, Edward 485
Frasconi, Antonio **343–346,** 354, 358, 458
Frawg 373
Freeman, Don 198, **206–209**
Freeman, Lydia 206
Freeman, Mae and Ira 394
Freud, Anna, quoted 511
Freud, Sigmund 509, 511
Freund, Rudolph 279, 280, 282
Friedrich, Priscilla and Otto 330–331
Frog Went A-Courtin' 299, 301
Frogs Merry **352–353,** *353,* 443
From King Boggen's Hall to Nothing-at-all 455
"From Madrid to Moscow" *202*
From Two to Five 416
Frost, A. B. **8–11,** 13, 14, 62, 143, 149, 151, 152, 468, 522
Fun in the Radio World 22
Fun with Chemistry 394
Fun with Science 394
Funai, Mamoru 450
Funny Little Woman 458
Funny Thing 33, **34,** *36*

G

Gág, Howard 76
Gág,Wanda 31, **32–37,** 61, 141, 494
Galdone, Paul 399, 403
Gale, Leah 279, 280
Gannett, Lewis, quoted 45, 84, 366
Gans, Roma 400
Garelick, May 112–113
Garthwaite, Jimmy 236
Gass, William, quoted 223
Gasser, Manuel, quoted 343
Gaston and Josephine 278
Gaston and Josephine in America 278
Gauguin, Paul 343
Gay, Jan and Zhenya 47
Gay ABC 53
Gay Mother Goose 53
Gay Neck 187
Geisel, Theodor Seuss **302–312,** 499, 541
Gekiere, Madeleine 86
Gentry, Helen **212–214** *passim,* 299
George Appleton 488–490, *488–489*
George Washington (d'Aulaire) 45–46, *45*
George's Store 369
Gere, Frances Kent 94
Gergely, Tibor 282, 284, 287–288, 333
Gesell, Arnold 73, 424
Ghond the Hunter 187
Giant, The 178
Giant Otto 175, **176,** *177*
Giant Story 496
Gibson, Charles Dana, quoted 10
Gibson, Katharine 97
Gidal, Tim and Sonia 108
Glaser, William 50
Glenda 472
Glick, Milton 194, 198, 212
God's Man 83
Golden Basket 49–50, *49*
Golden Bible: The New Testament 294
Golden Bible: The Old Testament 289, 294
Golden Books 30, 87, 120, 127, 227, 240, 257, 263, **277–295,** 297, 298, 301, 314, 324
Golden Crane 450
Golden Dictionary 289
Golden Egg Book 227, 285, **289–292,** *290–291,* 330
Golden Encyclopedia 289
Golden Goose (Seaman, illus.) **29–31,** *30–31,* 353
Golden Key 504
Golden Nature Guides 294
Goldin, Augusta 404
Gone Is Gone 37, *37*
Good Man and His Good Wife **416–419,** *416–417,* 422, 538
Goodnight Moon 227, 256, **258–259,** *259,* 331, 353
Goops 11
Gorey, Edward 541, 544, **552–559**
Grabhorn Press 212
Graham, Margaret Bloy **466–470,** 483, 494
Gramatky, Hardie **203–204,** 456
Gravure 98, 245
Great Geppy **176–177,** *178,* 198, 314
Great Tradition 373
Green, Mary McBurney 113–114
"Green Table" (Joos ballet) 549–550
Greenaway, Kate **3–4,** 6, 24, 285, 289
Grimms' Tales (Sewell & Gekiere, illus.) 85, *86*
Gropper, William 365–368
Grosset & Dunlap 148
Grosz, George 548
Guard Mouse 208
Guertik, Hélène 125, 127
Guess Book 230, *231*
Gustavus and Stop 541

H

Hader, Berta and Elmer **27–29,** 31, 158, 364
Hamilton, Elisabeth 358
Handforth, Thomas 47, 57
Hans Huchebein 518
Hansi **47–49,** *48,* 154
Hapless Child 554–555
Happy Day **420–422,** *421,* 472
Happy Family 278
Happy Hour series 26–30, 92
Happy Lion 139, *139*
Harcourt, Brace 358, 443
Harold and the Purple Crayon 433, **437,** *438,* 506
Harold at the North Pole **437,** *439,* 440
Harold's ABC 440, *440*

Harold's Circus 439, 440
Harold's Fairy Tale **437**, 494
Harold's Trip to the Sky 437
Harper, 236, 245–264 *passim*, 278
424, 466, 493–494, 544
Harper's Magazine 140
Harriet and the Promised Land
380, 382
Harrington, Isis L. 163
Harry the Dirty Dog 356, 357,
368, **469**, *469–470*, 494
Harter, Evelyn, quoted 212, 245
Harter Publishing Co. 97, 106, 108
Hartman, Gertrude 92
Harvest of World Folk Tales 347
Hat, The 550
Hat for Amy Jean **487**, 489, 494
Hauff, Wilhelm 514
Haunted Looking Glass 553
Haviland, Virginia, 499, 565
Hawaii 408
Hawes, Judy 405–407
Hayakawa, S., quoted 332
Hayter, Stanley William 343
Head for Happy **81–84**, *82–83*,
506, 539
Head Start program 372, 381
Hear Your Heart 403
Hearn, Lafcadio 453
Heavy Is a Hippopotamus
396–397, *397*
Hector Protector and As I Went Over the Water **516–518**, *516–517*, 538, 540, 560
Hellé, André 30, 123
Henry-Fisherman 316, *316*
Herbert the Lion 241–242, *242*
Here and Now Story Book 73, 105,
212
Herford, Oliver 311
Herman the Loser, 473–474, *474*
Herndon, James 368
Hero by Mistake 272, 273
Herrera, Velino 162, **165–166**
Hersey, John 311, 499
Hess, Lilo 111-112
Hewins, Caroline 11
Hey Diddle Diddle (Caldecott, illus.) 515–516
Heyward, DuBose **325–326**, 330
Hezekiah Horton 377
Hiawatha Primer 14
Hide and Seek Day 467
Hide and Seek Fog 139
Higglety Pigglety Pop! 518
Hine, Lewis **102–104**, 106
History of Tom Thumb (Gentry ed.) 212–214 *passim*, *214*
Hoban, Lillian 473–477 *passim*,
478
Hoban, Russell **472–477**, 478, 483,
506
Hoban, Tana 117
Hoberman, Mary Ann and Len 397
Hodges, Margaret 453
Hoff, Syd 485
Hoffmann, Felix 358
Hoffmann, Heinrich 8, 548
Hofmann, Hans 478
Hogarth, Grace Allen. *See* Grace Allen
Hogben, Lancelot 88
Hogner, Dorothy Childs 111
Hogrogian, Nonny 401
Hole in the Wall **68–70**, *70*, 353,
522
Hole Is To Dig **424–428**, *425-426*,
429, 430, 432, 478, 485, 495,
498, 504, 506
Holiday House 147, **212–214**,
236–238
Holl, Adelaide 139
Holling, Holling C. 158, 410–411
Holt, John 368; quoted, 3
Homer, Winslow 499
Homer Price 157, 496
Honk: the Moose **66**
Horace Mann School, New York
59, 79, 364
Horizon Is Calling 445–446, *445*
Horn, Maurice, quoted 434
Horn Book 12, 74, 221, 449
Horses 254
Horton Hatches the Egg 305–306,
305
Horton Hears a Who! 307–308, *307*
Houghton Mifflin 13, 14, 18
House of a Hundred Windows 263
House of Sixty Fathers 495
House on East 88th Street 480, 481
House That Jack Built (Frasconi, illus.) *345*, 346
"House That Jack Built" (Gág story box) 33–34, *35*
Houser, Allan 164, 165, 166
How a Seed Grows 407
How Big Is Big? 394, *395*
How Do I Go? 397
How It All Began 92, **93**, 394
How Many Kisses Good Night 232,
232
How Santa Claus Had a Long and Difficult Journey Delivering His Presents 541–542, *542*
How the Derrick Works 89, *90*
How To Go About Laying an Egg
480
How To Make an Earthquake
435–436
Howe, Oscar 162
Hoytema, T. van 22
Hughes, Langston 84, 373
Humbo the Hippo and Little-Boy-Bumpo 56
Hunt, Clara 18–19, 141
Huntington, Harriet 97–98
Hurd, Clement **216**, 217, 221, **222**,
252, **256**, **258–259**, 453, 495
Hurd, Edith Thacher **220–222**,
285–288 *passim*, 391, 393, 400
Hurdy-Gurdy Man 143–145,
143-144
Hürlimann, Bettina, quoted 108
Hurry Home, Candy 495
Hurry Hurry 220–221, *220*
Hurston, Zora Neale 375
Hutchins, Pat 542–543
Huxley, Aldous, quoted 224

I

I Am a Pueblo Indian Girl 164-165,
164
I Can Fly 285, *286*
"I Can Read" books 221, 312, 440,
478, 494, **499**, 500–504 *passim*
I Count 238
I Discover Columbus 146
I Know a Lot of Things 330, **342**
I Know a Magic House 394
I Love 238
I Play 238
I Play at the Beach 299–301,
300–301
I Saw the Sea Come In 134
I See 237, 238
I See the Winds 543
I Want to Fly 399
I Want to Paint My Bathroom Blue
433, 468, 494, **498**
I Write It 433
Ice Cream for Two 242
Idols Behind Altars 268
If I Ran the Circus 308–309
If I Ran the Zoo 308, *308*
If I Were a Mother 453
If You Could See Inside 394
Iger, Martin 114, 117
Iliad (Golden) 294
I'll Be You and You Be Me
430–432, *431–432*, 517, 522, 536
I'll Show You How It Happens 394
Ilín, M. 88
Images à Colorier 52
Important Book 263
In My Mother's House **161**, 164,
165–166, *166*, 171
In the Forest **170–171**, *170-171*,
172, 174
In the Night Kitchen 518–524
passim, *519-520*
Inch by Inch 528–529, *528-529*
Indian Child Life 158
Indians, books about 16–17, 108,
158, 160–166, 372, 410–411
Indoor Noisy Book 225
Infant and Child in the Culture of Today 424
Infant Care 464
Insect Concert 450
Institute of Design, Chicago 332,
361

Interracial understanding. *See* Prejudice, books to combat
Iowa (University) Child Welfare Research Station 73
Ipcar, Dahlov 216
Iron Horse 103, 104
Irwin, Elisabeth 100, 103
Is It Hard? Is It Easy? 113–114, *115*
Is This You? 435
Isotype books 88, 394
It Looked Like Spilt Milk **250–251,** *250–251,* 527
It Looks Like Snow 536
It Looks Like This 394, *395*
It's About Time 397
It's Like This, Cat 513
Ives, Vernon **212, 214,** 238
Ivins, Barbara 393

J

Jack Horner's Pie 76
Jacobs, Joseph 565, 566
Jakobsen, Rena 113
Jan, Isabelle, quoted 123
Janie Belle 377
Jarrell, Randall 495, 502
Jazz 354
Jeanne d'Arc **4–6,** *5,* 16
Jeanne-Marie Counts Her Sheep **53,** *55,* 357
Jennett, Séan, quoted 188
Jersey City Printing Company 26–27, 40–41, 50
Jeux en Images 126
Jewell, Edward Alden, quoted 198
Jimmy and Jemima 85, *85*
Jingle Book 236
Job, pseud. 119, 123, 318
Joe Buys Nails 65
John Gilpin 4
Johnny Crow's Garden 6
Johnson, Crockett 70, 394, **399–401, 419,** 433, **434–442,** 483, 494, 496, 526, 531
Johnson, Theodore 212
Johnston, Johanna 478
Johnston, Otta Taggart 107
Joji and the Dragon 450
Jones, Virginia Lacy 374
Jones, Wilfred 89, 104
Joos, Kurt 549
Joslin, Sesyle 497, 498
Journeys of Sebastian 540–541, *541*
Joyous Aztecs 94
Judd, George Hubbard 97
Judge, The 570–572, *571*
Jumblies (Gorey, illus.) **556–557,** *556,* 558
Jumping Beans 532, 533
June, Larry 90, 103
Junket Is Nice **71,** *71,* 294
Just Like Abraham Lincoln 480, **482,** *482*
Just Like You—All Babies Have Mummies and Daddies 230, 231, 388
Just So Stories (Mordvinoff, illus.) 338
Juster, Norton 527

K

Kabotie, Fred 160, 163, 165
Kaleidoscope 346
Kane, Henry **98–99,** 108, 111
Kap the Kappa 450
Karoo the Kangaroo 65
Katzenjammer Kids 8
Kauffer, E. McKnight 224–225, 338
Kawaguchi, Sanae 450
Keats, Ezra Jack **368–369, 379,** 402, 408, 496
Kemble, E. W. 11
Keniston, Kenneth 427, 459, 463
Kenny's Window 494, **504–506,** *505,* 506
Kepes, Gyorgy 332, 350, 357
Kepes, Juliet 350–353
Kermit the Hermit 210, *210*
Kessler, Ethel 399
Kessler, Leonard 358, 359, **396–399,** 401
Key, Ellen 73
Kimo, the Whistling Boy 158
King, Martin Luther 368
Kiss for Little Bear **502–504,** *504,* 518
Kiss Is Round 331
Kittens, Cats and Babies 276
Klee, Paul 222, 337
Klemin, Diana, quoted 478
Knave of Hearts 126
Knickerbocker's History of New York 151
Knopf 38, 193
Knudsen process 41
Koch, Dorothy 299–301 *passim*
Kohl, Herbert 368
Kollwitz, Kaethe 196
Komoki of the Cliffs 163
Koren, Edward 400
Kozol, Jonathan 368, 369
Krahn, Fernando 540–542
Kramer, Hilton, quoted 151
Kraus, Robert 382, 485
Krauss, Ruth 285, 356, **416–428,** 435, 466, 477, 478, 483, 494, 496, 511, 533
Kredel, Fritz 411
Kuh, Charlotte 92
Kunhardt, Dorothy **71–72, 238–239, 292–294** *passim,* 358
Kuskin, Karla **359–361,** 494

L

Lady Bird, Quickly 353
La Farge, Oliver 161, 162, 164
Lahner, Emile 120
Lambert, Clara 105
Lambert's Bargain **245–246,** *245,* 251
Land of Little Rain 14, *14*
Language of Vision 332
Lanigan, George Thomas 311
Larkin, Oliver, quoted 140
Lasansky, Mauricio 343
Last One Home Is a Green Pig 222
Lauritzen, Jonreed 166
Lawrence, Gwen 382
Lawrence, Jacob 381–382
Lawson, Robert 141, **143–147,** 198
Lazy Tommy Pumpkinhead 183
Leaf, Munro **145–146, 248**
Lear, Edward 71, 310, 483, 528, **556–558**
Le Gallienne, Eva 514
Legend of the Palm Tree 47
Legend of the Willow Plate *349,* 350
Leger, Fernand 216, 332
Legrand, Edy **118,** 119, **317–318,** 320
Lehmann-Haupt, Hellmut, quoted 83, 88
Leif the Lucky 45–46
Lenski, Lois 31, **75–79,** 148, **236,** 260, 325, 357, 365
Lent, Blair 430, *453–458*
Lentil **154–155,** *154,* 197, 198, 362, 496
Lerner, Abe 198, 346
Leslie, Robert 357
Let's Be Enemies 432, 472, 485
Let's Find Out 387, **391,** *391,* 394
Let's Go Outdoors **97–98,** *98,* 99, 104, 325
Let's Go to the Seashore 98
Let's Look Inside Your House 393
Let's Look Under the City 393–394, *393*
Let's-Read-and-Find-Out series 349, **399–408,** 453
Leventhal, Albert 278, 279
Lewellen, John 399
Lewis, John, quoted 8
Lexau, Joan 379
Liang and Lo 50, 57, **65–66,** *66–67,* 355
Liberator 140
Library Services and Construction Act (1964) 372
Liddell, Mary 25
Lieberman, Frank, quoted 347
Life magazine 93, 111, 112, 168, 182, 187, 193, 198, 252, 311, 499
Life of a Wooden Doll 100
Lifton, Betty Jean 450

Light Princess (Sendak, illus.) 518
Lincoln School, New York 91, 92, 279
Linda 369–370, *370*
Lindstrom, Miriam 397
Lingnell, Lois 59
Linocuts 347
Lion **178–181,** *179–180,* 182, 198, 221
Lion-Hearted Kitten 25
Lionni, Leo 332, 348, 379, 495, **525–530**
Lions and Lobsters and Foxes and Frogs 556
Lipkind, William 333, 336–337
Lissitzky, El 355
Listen! Listen! 342
Listing Attic 553
Little Auto 77, *77*
Little Bear 478, 494, **499–501,** *501,* 502
Little Bear's Friend 501, **502,** 503
Little Big Bye and Bye 158
Little Black Sambo *373,* **374–375**
Little Black Stories for Little White Children 241
Little Blue and Little Yellow **525–528,** *526–527,* 542
Little Bookroom 496
Little Boy Brown *348,* **362–363,** *363,* 525
Little Boy Was Drawing 128, *128*
Little Boy with Three Names 161, 163
Little Brass Band 264
Little Carousel **315,** 316, 364
Little Chicken 227, 255
Little Cow and the Turtle 495
Little Cowboy 216
Little Elephant **111,** *111,* 494
Little Engine That Could 203
Little Family **75–77,** *76,* 260, 370, 371, 464
Little Farm 78, *79*
Little Farmer 216
Little Fir Tree 264
Little Fireman **215–219** *passim,* *218–219,* **235,** 254, 285, 353
Little Fish That Got Away 436, 532
Little Fisherman 216
Little Fur Family *217,* **256–257,** *257,* 260, 261, 262, 292, 490
Little Geography of the United States 411
Little Golden Sleepy Book 285
Little Green Cart 52
Little Herder in Autumn 162, *163*
Little Herder in Spring 161
Little Hill 485
Little History of the United States 411
Little House (Burton) **201–202,** *201,* 355–356
Little House books 87
Little House of Your Own 497
Little Island 229
Little Jeemes Henry 375, *375*
Little Leo **59,** *59,* 154, 506
Little Lost Lamb 229
Little Machinery 25, *26*
Little Match Girl 455–456, *456*
"Little Nemo in Slumberland" 434, **520–523** *passim,* *521*
Little Old Automobile **171–172,** *172,* 174, 203, 222
Little 1 342
Little Pancho 59
Little Pig's Picnic 285
Little Red Schoolhouse, New York 100
Little Sail Boat **77,** *78,* 175
Little Tailor **365–368,** *366–367,* 372
Little Tim books 495
Little Tiny Woman 565, 568
Little Toot 203–204, *204*
Little White Teddy Bear, The Story of a **74–75,** *75,* **492**
Little Wooden Farmer 79, *80*
Littlefield, William 329-331 *passim*
Lively Little Rabbit 278, 281
Log of a Cowboy 14
Log of Columbus' First Voyage to America 215, 221
Lonely Crowd 283
Look Again! *116–117,* 117
Looking Glass Library 553
Lord, Isabel Ely 103
Lorentz, Pare 271, 377
Lorenzo 480
Lorraine, Walter 355, 455
Lothrop 133, **331**
Lovable Lyle 480
Low, Joseph **346–350,** 354, 358, 401, **407–408,** 458, 560
Lowe, Sam 106, 124, 129, 277
Lowrey, Janette Sebring 281
Lucky Mrs. Ticklefeather 72
Lujan, Tonita 161
Lullabies and Night Songs 518
Lyle and the Birthday Party 480, *481*
Lyle, Lyle Crocodile 480

M

Macao et Cosmage 118
McCarthy, Desmond, quoted 483, 485
McCloskey, Robert 141, **154–157,** 198, 210, 468
McCullough, John C. 214, 383, 399
MacDonald, George 504, 518
MacDonald, Golden (pseud. for Margaret Wise Brown) 227–229
McElderry, Margaret 323, 338, 344, **358**
McElligot's Pool 308
McGraw-Hill 390
McKay, Winsor 520–523 *passim*
MacKinstry, Elizabeth 314
McLeod, Emily 352
McLoughlin Bros. 6, 7, 280, 289, 296, 314
Macmillan **23–30** *passim,* 193
McNeer, May 152, 414
Macrae, John 253
Madeline **50–51,** *51,* 496
Madeline's Rescue 51
Magic Listening Cap 444
Magic Rug 42, 44
Mahony, Bertha 12, 45, 566
Make Way for Ducklings **155–156,** *155,* 198, 324
Making a Poem 299-300
Malcolmson, Anne 157
Malraux, André 539
Mamba's Daughters 325
Man in the Manhole 285, **391–392**
Manhattan, Now and Long Ago 92
Mann, Thomas, quoted 83
March Wind 331
Maria Rosa: Everyday Fun and Carnival Frolic . . . 47
Mariana (Marian Curtis Foster) 330
Marshmallow 242
Martin, Judith 532, 533
Martin, Mary Steichen 80, 100–103
Martineau, Harriet 187
Martinez del Rio, Amelia 268
Masereel, Franz 83
Mason, Arthur 145
Massee, May **23–25,** 38, 39, 47, 50, 65, 175, **198,** 302, 377
Masses 140
Mass-market picturebooks 95–97, 106–168 *passim,* 124-127 *passim,* 240. *See also* Golden Books, McLoughlin Bros.
Matisse, Henri 354, 379, 408
Matsuno, Masako 450–453
Matulka, Mrs. Jan 313
Max and Moritz 8, *8,* 522, *522*
Mayer, Mercer 540
Meigs, Cornelia 29, 148
Mei Li 57
Melcher, Frederic, quoted 323
Mellops Go Diving for Treasure 544
Mellops Go Flying 544, *545*
Men at Work **102–104,** *102*
Menagerie 81
Mercy and the Mouse 25
Mérida, Carlos 266
Merrill-Palmer Nursery School, Detroit 73
Merry Chase 222
Merry Go Round **435,** *436,* 531
Merry Shipwreck 278
Mexican Folkways magazine 266
Meynell, Sir Francis 355
Mickey Mouse 203, 249, 502, *502*
Mickey's Magnet **399–401,** *400,* 436

Mike Mulligan and His Steam Shovel **199–201,** *200*, 355
Miki *31*, 38, **39–40,** *39*, 59, 154
Miki and Mary *40*, 41
Milhous, Katherine 59, 326
Miller, J. P. 282, 284, 288
Miller, Warren 485
Millions of Cats 31, 32, **33–37** *passim*, *34–35*, 76, 198, 324
Minarik, Else 498, **499–504** *passim*
Ming and Mehitable **84,** *84*, 452
Minn of the Mississippi 411
Miss Flora McFlimsey and the Baby New Year 411
Miss Flora McFlimsey's Christmas Eve 330
Miss Flora McFlimsey's Easter Bonnet 330
Mr. and Mrs. So and So 53, *54*
Mister Dog **262–263,** *263*, 285, **288,** 289
Mister Penny **167–168,** *168*, 171, 172, 174
Mister Penny's Circus 168
Mister Penny's Race Horse 168
Mr. Popper's Penguins 146
Mr. Rabbit and the Lovely Present 498-499, *500*
Mr. Revere and I 146
Mr. T. W. Anthony Woo 168
Mitchell, Lucy Sprague **73,** 74, 88, 92, 105, 106, 107, 212, **214–215,** 216, 254, 279, 283
Mitchell, Marguerite, quoted 45
Mitsui, Eiichi 450
Mittens 242–243, *243*
Mizimura, Kazue **406,** 407, **450–453,** 496
Moccasin Trail 365
Moholy-Nagy, László 332, 355, 356
Mom du Jos: The Story of a Little Black Doll 56
Mommy, Buy Me a China Doll 565, **568,** *568*
Mon Chat 126
Mondrian, Piet 342, 354
Monet, Claude 499
Monkey Day 430
Monrad, Jean 232
Monster Den 555
Monvel, Maurice Boutet de **4–6,** 16, 21, 61, 119
Moon Jumpers 472, **498,** *500*, 513
Moon Man **548–550,** *549*, 552
Moon Seems to Change 402–403, *402–403*
Moonlight and Rainbow 164
Moore, Anne Carroll **7,** 10, 11, 12, 25, 34, 37, 119, 149, 251, 302, 313, 374
Mop Top 208, *208*
Mordvinoff, Nicolas **333–338,** 424, 446
More Boners 302
More of Brer Rabbit's Tricks 556
Morris, Ann Axtell 266
Morrow, Elizabeth **46–47,** 71
Mosel, Arlene 456, 458
Mother Goose (Duvoisin, illus.) **129–130,** *129*, 291, 296
Mother Goose, illustration of 295–297
Mother Goose Riddle Rhymes 347–348
Mother Mother I Feel Sick . . . 532–533, *536*
Mouse and His Child 477
Mukerji, Dhan Gopal 187
Munari, Bruno 529
Munch, Edvard 343
Munthe, Gerhard 42
My Dog Is Lost! 368, *369*
My Dog Rinty 198, **377–378,** *378*, 379, 382
My First Geography of the Americas 411
My First Geography of the Pacific 411–412, *413*
My Happy Days, 376–377, *377*
My Painting Book 52
My Village 13, *13*
My Visit to the Dinosaurs 404–405, *405*
My World 258

N

N Is for Nursery School 331
Nail Soup 565
Nailor, Gerald 163, 165
Nathan, Adele Gutman 103
National Defense Education Act (1958) 400
Naumburg, Elsa H. 104
Navajo Boy 158
Neumeyer, Peter 556
Neurath, Marie 88, 394
Neurath, Otto 88
Neurath, Walter 88
Neville, Emily 513
New Masses *32–33*, 33, 140
New Sun **444–445,** *445*, 446
New York *Herald Tribune* 12, 75, 285
New York Public Library 7, 12, 66, **313–314,** 373, 374
New York Times 279
New Yorker magazine 130, 195, 257, **483–484,** 544, 563
Newberry, Clare **241–246,** 364, 452
Newbery Medal 140; winners 59, 147, 154, 514
Newell, Peter 11, 311
Newman, James, quoted 387, 412
"Newsstand" 206, *206*
Nibble Nibble 227
Nicholson, William **24–25,** 31, **60–61,** 241, 511
Nicolas (Nicolas Mordvinoff) **333–338,** 424, 446
'Nicole' (Georges Duplaix) 278
Night and Day 227, 255, 260
Night Before Christmas (Holiday House ed.) **213,** 490
Nightingale (Gentry ed.) 212
Nine Days to Christmas 173
No Fighting, No Biting 502
No Roses for Harry 469-470
Noah's Ark, The Story of 14–15, *15*
Nobody Is Perfick 480
Nobody's Birthday 478
Noisy Bird Book 225
Noisy Book 221, **224–226,** *226–227*, 227, 353
Noisy Books **224–226,** 227, 254, 259, 263, 264, 427
Noodle 248
Nordstrom, Ursula 239, 245, 246, **251,** 252, 278, 424, 427, 490, **493–494,** 499
Norman the Doorman 208
North America: The Land They Live in . . . 92
Nos Enfants 4
Not a Little Monkey 464
Not Only for Ducks 390
Nothing at All 37
Nothing But Cats, Cats, Cats **232–233,** 233, 419, 466
Nothing Ever Happens On My Block 538, *538–539*
Nothing to Do 474
Novel-in-pictures 83, 365
Now I Know 394
Now Open the Box **71–72,** 72, 294
Now Try This 387, **393,** 392
Nuit de la Saint Sylvain 317–318, *317*
Nursery schools 73, 221, 324
Nutshell Library 509–511, *510*

O

O Said the Squirrel 111
Oasis of the Stars 455
Object Lesson 553
Odd Pets 111
Odyssey (Golden) 294
Ogle, Lucille **97, 106,** 108, 277, 278, 279
Oh Lord, I Wish I Was a Buzzard **381,** 404
Ol' Paul, the Mighty Logger 147
Ola **42–43,** *43*, 45, 154
Ola and Blakken 44
Olcott, Frances Jenkins 11
Old Man Is Always Right 127
Oley the Sea Monster 171

Olfers, Sybille v. 30
On Beyond Zebra 309, *310–311*
On the Slain Collegians 346
On Top of the World 108, 158
Once a Mouse 321–322, *322*
Once Upon a Time in Egypt 94
Once We Had a Horse *150*, 151
One Day with Jambi 57
One Day with Manu 56–57, *57*
One Day with Tuktu 57, 158
One God 331
One Little Boy 504
One Morning in Maine **157,** 424
One Step, Two 464–465, *464*
One Thousand Christmas Beards 136–137, *137*
One, Two,Where's My Shoe? 550
One Was Johnny **509,** *510*, 513
Opie, Iona and Peter, quoted 297, 517
Orbis Pictus 104, 346
Ordeal of the Young Hunter 166
Orozco, José Clemente [illegible]
Ortega y Gasset, José, quoted 465
Otto and the Magic Potatoes 182
Otto at Sea (1936) 175, **176,** *177*
Otto at Sea (1958) 182
Otto in Africa *181*, 182
Otto in Texas 182
Otto of the Silver Hand 141
"Our Cat Eats Rat Poison" 9, *10*
Our Day 236, *237*
Our Neighbors *237*, 238
Our Planet the Earth 65
Overton, Jacqueline 313
Ovington, Mary White 373
Oxford Nursery Rhyme Book 297
Oxford University Press 57

P

Paddle-to-the-Sea 411, *412*
Painted Pig **46–47,** *47*, 70
Pair of Red Clogs 451–452, *454*
Palmer, Helen (Helen Palmer Geisel) 285
Panache l'Ecureuil 123–124, *124*
Pancho and His Burro 47
Pandora 242
Panofsky, Erwin, quoted 494
Panorama books 221–222
Paper, cut-and-pasted 215, 340–344 *passim*, 354, 379
Paper Bag Players 359, 532
Parain, Nathalie 123, 126, 127
Parish, Helen Rand 47
Park Book **246–248,** *247*, 379, 465, 468
Parkhurst, Helen 97
Parrish, Maxfield 126, 127
Passionate Journey 83
Pat the Bunny 72, **238–239,** *238*, 294
Paysans de France 52
Payson & Clarke 241
Peattie, Donald Culross 95
Pedro, the Angel of Olivera Street 59
Peet, Bill 209–211
Peggy and Peter 103
Peggy and the Pony 84–85, *85*
Pène du Bois, William. *See* Du Bois, William Pène
Penguin Books 88
Pennell, Joseph, quoted 140, 187
Penny 480
Penny a Look 572, *572*
Penny-Whistle 56, *56*
Pépé Was the Saddest Bird **333,** *333*, **336**
Pepper and Salt 141
Percy, Polly and Pete 242
Père Castor books 22, 88, 120, **123–124,** 126, 127, 278, 301, 358
Perrault, Charles [illegible] *passim*
Pet of the Met 206–208, *207*
Peter Graves 178
Peter Pauper Press 486
Peter Rabbit, The Tale of 6
Petersham, Maud and Miska 25, 31, **38–42,** 45, **93–95,** 198, 495, 501
Petit Élephant 111
Petit Lion 110–111, *110*
Petits et les Grands 123
Petunia *132–133*, **135–136,** 249, 318, 337, 356
Petunia's Christmas 136, *136*
Photo-composition 357
Photo-engraving 140, **187–189,** 192, 357
Photographic books 97–99, 100–117, 385–378
Photographic books for adults 104
Piaget, Jean 73
Picasso, Pablo 337, 341, 498
Pick the Vegetables *239*, 240
Picture Book (Charlot) 265
Picture Book of Animals 103
Picture Book of Children Around the World 108
Picture Book of Houses Around the World 107–108, *107*
Picture for Harold's Room 440
Picture Play Book 126–127, *126*
Pierre **509–511,** *510*, 513
Pilgrim's Progress (Lawson, illus.) 146
Pincus, Harriet 544, **559–563**
Pinsard, Pierre 241
Pirate Twins 31, **60–61,** *60*
Pistachio 453
Pittsburgh, Carnegie Library 11
Pitz, Henry, quoted 48, 347
Plain Girl 365
Plant Sitter 469
Play with Me **172–173,** *173*, 174, 198, 356, 357, 477
Play with Plants 387
Play with Trees 387
Pleasure Is Mutual 372
Plenty to Watch 446
Plink Plink 399
Plum to Plum Jam 93
Plus Vieille Histoire du Monde 52–53, *53*
PM (the newspaper) 434
Pocahontas and Captain John Smith, The Story of 16–17, *16–17*
Pogany, Willy 187
Poky Little Puppy 281–282, *281*
Polite Penguin 254–255
Politi, Leo **59,** 506
Pollock, Jackson 478
Poodle and the Sheep 227
Poor Cock Robin (McLoughlin Bros.) [illegible]
Poor Shaydullah 189, **190–191,** *190*, 192, 197
Poppy Seed Cakes 25, 38, 39
Porgy 325
Porko von Popbutton 183
Portinari, Candido 47
Posada, J. G. 266, 343
Potter, Beatrix 7, 24, 249, 250, 257, 258, 312, 492
Powder: The Story of a Colt . . . 120
Pre-binding 323
Prejudice, books to combat 248–250 *passim*, 364, 373, 375–378 *passim*, 391-392, 526–527
Preschool movement 73–74, 100, 126, 214–215, 221; post-World War II 323-324
Preschool story hours 74, 323
Pretty Pretty Peggy Moffitt 183
Pretzel 248, *248*
Prévert, Jacques 111
Princehorn, Bentz 59
Print magazine 344, 525, 552
Progressive Education magazine 92, 97, 161
Progressive schools 91–93, 97, 161, 215, 391
Proust, Marcel 506
Provensen, Alice and Martin 282, 294, 295
Pryor, Helen Sloman 108
Pryor, William Clayton 108
Puffin Picture Books 88
Punch & Judy 226–227, *228*
Push Kitty 84
Puss in Boots (Brown, Illus.) **317–320,** *318–319*, 320, 356
Putnam 443
Pyle, Howard 141, 312
Pyne, Mabel 411

Q

Queens Borough Public Library 372
"Quick, Henry! The Flit!" 302, *303*
Quiet Mother and the Noisy Little Boy 464
Quiet Noisy Book 225
Quipic le Hérisson 124, *125*

R

Rabbit Hill 146, 147
Rabbits in the Meadow 111
Race, The 222
Rackham, Arthur 25, 39, 187
Railroad Book 19–20, *20*
Rain Drop Splash **229–230,** *229*, 331
Rain Makes Applesauce 430, **478–480,** *479*
Rain Puddle 139
Rain Rain Rivers 453
Rainbow Dictionary 346, *346*
Rand, Paul 331, 332, **338–342,** 343, 355, 357, 358, 361, 379, 525
Rand McNally 106
Random House 499
Ranlett, Felix, quoted 199
Raskin, Ellen 408, **538–539**
Really Spring **467–468,** *467*, 494
Realms of Gold 12, 38
Red Folk and White Folk 158
Red Horse 30–31
Red Light Green Light 217, **227–229,** *228*, 248, 362
Reed, Mary 279
Rees, Ennis 556
Reinhardt, Ad 418–419
Reischauer, Edwin, quoted 443
Reisman, David 283
Reno, Esther 57, 240
Rey, H. A. 204–205, 239–240, 247–250, 333
Rey, Margret 248–250, 333
Rhoads, Dorothy 276
Rice, Inez 331
Rice to Rice Pudding 93
Rich Cat, Poor Cat 480
Richter, Mischa 485
Riis, Jacob 103, 377
Riley, Elizabeth 349, 399, 400
Rip Van Winkle (Gentry ed.) 212
Rivera, Diego 266
Riverside Press 13
Riwkin-Brick, Anna 108
Roar and More **359,** *360*, 494
Robertson, Keith 157
Robeson, Eslanda Goode 376–377
Robinson, Tom 187, 196
Roethke, Theodore, quoted 485
Rogers, Bruce 355
Rojankovsky, Feodor **118–124,** 127, 188, 189, 204, 257, 277, 278, 282, 294, **295–301,** 333
Rollins, Charlemae 374
Rooster Crows 41
Rootabaga Stories 559
Rosa-Too-Little **365,** *365*, 372, 382
Rose for Mr. Bloom 480
Rosenberg, Harold, quoted 379
Rosie's Walk 542, *543*
Rosten, Leo 461
Rouault, Georges 382
Rounds, Glen 141, **147–151,** 237
Rowand, Phyllis 420
Rowlandson, Thomas 514, 572
Rudge, The Printing House of William Edwin 212
Run, Run, Run 222
Runaway Bunny 253, *254–255*, **255–256,** 260, 501
Runaway Elephant 379
Rushmore, Arthur **244–245,** 355
Russian picturebooks **88–89,** 93, 123, 127
Rusty Rings a Bell 399, 403

S

Sachs, Paul, quoted 265
"Sad Tale of Bazouge" **11,** *12*, 518
Sage, Juniper (pseud. for Margaret Wise Brown and Edith Thacher Hurd) 391
Saggy Baggy Elephant 281
St. Nicholas magazine 140, 148
Sally and the Baby and the Rampatan **461–463,** 513
Salt 565, 568
Sambo and the Twins 374
Sandburg, Carl 599, 560
Sandpiper Press 278
Santa Claus and All About Him 17–18, *18*
Santa Fe Indian School 160–161, 165
Sargent, John F. 11
Saturday Flight 230
Saturday Ride 230
Saturday Walk 171, **230**
Sayers, Frances Clarke 84
Scarry, Richard 281, 282
Scheer, Julian 478
Schick, Eleanor 370–372 *passim*
Schlein, Miriam 271, **394, 396–397**
Schneider, Herman and Nina 391–394
Schwartz, Julius 394
Schwitters, Kurt 552
Scott, Ann Herbert 379
Scott, Ethel McC. 214, 236
Scott, Hilda 214
Scott, William R. 214, 215, 221, 223, 232, 387, 477
Scott, William R., Inc. 73, **112–113, 214–237,** *passim*, 280, 358, **383–398,** 459, 531
Scratchboard 191–192
Scribner 59–60
Scribner's Magazine 10, 140
"Scroll of Animal Caricatures" 443
Seabird 411
Seaman, Louise. *See* Bechtel, Louise Seaman
Seaman, Mary Lott 29–30
Seashore Book **19,** 247
Seashore Noisy Book 225
Second Picture Book **101–103,** 358
See Again, Say Again 346
See and Say *343*, **344–346,** *345*, 356
See How We Work 108
See the Circus 239
Seeing Stars 97, *97*
Segal, Lore 561
Segawa, Yasuo 453
Seignobosc, Françoise **52–53,** 357
Selsam, Millicent 117, **387–388**
Sendak, Jack 498, 565
Sendak, Maurice 141, 271, 356, 362, 365, **424–433,** 478, 494, **495–524,** 525, 540, 548, 560, 561, 572
Seurat, Georges 498
Seuss, Dr. (Theodor Seuss Geisel) **302–312,** 409, 541
Seven Little Postmen 217, **286,** 393
Seven Remarkable Bears 351–352, *352*
Seven Simeons **192–196,** *193–195*, 198, 314
Seven Stories about a Cat Named Sneakers 276. *See also* "Sneakers, That Rapscallion cat" 254
Seven Tales (Andersen) 514
Sewell, Helen **81–87,** 148, 314, 373, 452, 490, 495, 496, 506, 548
Shadow's Holiday 103
Shadrach 495
Shady Hill Play Book 91
Shady Hill School, Cambridge, Mass. 91
Shannon, Monica 276
Shapes 394
Shapes and Things *116*, 117
Sharpe, Stella Gentry 375–376
Shaw, Charles G. 226, **230, 250–251,** 527,528
Shaw, Spencer 378
Shepard, Ernest 258
Sherlock, Philip 316
Sherrill, Dorothy **74–75,** 76, 492
SHHhhhh . . . BANG 255

Shimin, Symeon 394–395, 471
Shimkin, Leon 277, 278
Showers, Paul 403–404
Shrimps 349, **407–408,** *408–409*
Shrinking of Treehorn 558–559, *558–559*
Shulevitz, Uri 452
Shy Little Kitten 281
Sign on Rosie's Door 365, **508–509,** *508–509*
Silver Nutmeg 492
Simon & Schuster 277–278, 295
Simont, Marc 264, 394, 418, **422, 472,**
Sing a Song of Sixpence (Lenski) 77, **236,** *236*
Singer, Isaac 518, 565, 572
Siqueiros, David 266
Six Who Were Left in a Shoe 158
Size One 240, *240*
Skaar, Grace **232–234,** 477
Skyscraper 104–106, *105–106*
Sleator, William 458
Sleepy ABC 235
Sleepy Book 331
Sleepy Little Lion 110–111, *110*
Sloan, John 140, 160, 206
Slobodkina, Esphyr **215–216, 234–235,** 248, 379, 495
Slocum, Rosalie 253
Small Boy Is Listening 565
Smalley, Janet 93
Smart Little Boy and His Smart Little Kitty 230, 233
Smiling Duke 348, *348*
Smith, E. Boyd 6, 12, **13–22,** 61, 108, 113, 222, 376
Smith, Janet Adam, quoted 249
Smith, Susan 47
Smudge 242
"Sneakers, That Rapscallion Cat" 254. *See also Seven Stories about a Cat Named Sneakers* 276
Snippy and Snappy 33, **34–36,** *36*
Snow, C. P. 387
Snow and the Sun 346
Snow Is Falling 401
Snow White and the Seven Dwarfs (Disney) 37, 127, 203, 282
Snow White and the Seven Dwarfs (Gág) 37
Snowy Day 379, *380*
So Long Ago 22
Sojo, Toba 443, 446
Sojo: The Story of Little Lazy-Bones 56
Sokol, Bill 401
Somebody Else's Nut Tree 433
Something for Christmas 492, **493,** *494*
Sondergard, Arensa 411
Song of Robin Hood *202*, 203
Sorely Trying Day 474
Sound of Things 359, *360*
Soviet picturebooks **88–89,** 93, 123, 127
Sparkle and Spin **338–342,** *339–342*, 362
Spaulding, William 312
Speckled Hen 565, 568
Sperry, Armstrong **59–60,** 158
Spock, Benjamin 464
Spotty **248–250,** *249*, 472, 527
Springfield Plan 377
Sputnik I 387, 400
Square Book of Animals 24, *24*
Stamm, Claus **451,** 453
Standing-Soldier, Andrew 162
Stanley, Lila 118
Stanton, Jessie 214, 284
Steadfast Tin Soldier 321
Steichen, Edward **100,** 101
Steig, William 452, 483, **485,** 544, **563–565**
Stein, Gertrude **222–224,** 259
Steinberg, Saul 536, 544
Steinlen, T. A. 8, 11, 123, 518
Steptoe, John 382
Stevens, Carla 114, 117
Stevens, Leonard 117
Stevenson, James 485
Stevie *381*, 382
Stieglitz, Alfred 100
'Stocking books' 212–214, 490
Stockton, Frank 514
Stolen Pony 151
Stone, Helen 401, 495
Stone, William 333
Stone Soup **314–315,** *315*, 316
Stop Tim! 152, 203
Storm Book 247, **465–466,** *465*, 467
Story about Ping 50, 57, 65, **66,** *67*, 198
Story Book of Earth's Treasures 94
Story Book of Foods from the Field 94
Story Book of Things We Use 93–94, *93–94*
Story Book of Things We Wear 94
Story Book of Wheels, Ships, Trains, Aircraft 94
Story of a Baby 168–170, *169*
Story of a Little White Teddy Bear **74–75,** *75*, 492
Story of Alaska 413
Story of America 95
Story of Ancient Civilization 95, *96*
Story of California *414*
Story of Chan Yuc 276
Story of Ferdinand **145–146,** *145*, 198
Story of Florida 414
Story of Johnny Appleseed 381
Story of Noah's Ark **14–15,** *15*, 22
Story of Our Country 22
Story of Pocahontas and Captain John Smith 16–17, *16–17*
Story of the First Men 95
Story of the Middle Ages 95, *96*
Story of the Mississippi 413
Story of the Modern Age 95, *95*
Story of the New Lands 95
Story of the Southwest 413
Story Parade magazine **147–148,** 175, 214, 252
Straight Hair, Curly Hair 404
Strand, Paul 100, 103
Strawberry Roan 149
Streamlined Pig 254
Stringer, Charles 26
Struwwelpeter 8, *8*, 509
Stryker, Roy 108
Stuart Little 250, 257, 463, 563
Stuff and Nonsense 10
Sugarplum 478
Suger, Abbot 493–494
Suki, the Siamese Pussy 226
Sullivan, Louis 356
Sumi's Prize 452
Summer Snowman 469
Sun: our nearest star 402
Sun, the Moon and a Rabbit *267*, 268
Sun Up 134
Surrealism 224, 342
Swimmy 527, 529–530
Sylvester and the Magic Pebble 563–564, *564*
Symonds, John 348

T

Tactile books 236, 238–239
Taktuk, an Arctic Boy 158
Tale of Peter Rabbit 6
Tale of Tai 57–58, *58*
Tale of the Bullfrog 99, *99*
Tale of the Whitefoot Mouse 99
Tales from Grimm (Gág) 37, *37*
Tales of Poindi 122
Tales of the Home Folk in Peace and War 13
Tales of the Pampas 130
Talking Cat 133
Talking Leaves **97,** 97, 107
Tall Book of Mother Goose 278, **295–297**
Tall Book of Nursery Tales 297
Tamarindo! 316
Taro and the Bamboo Shoot 453
Taro and the Tōfu 452
Taro's Festival Day 450
Tarry, Ellen **377–378,** 379
Tawny-Scrawny Lion 281
Tawnymore 276
Taxi That Hurried 283–285, *284*, 288
Taylor, Katharine 91
T-Bone, the Baby Sitter 242
Teachers College 59, 73, 400

"Teeny-Tiny" 565, 566, 567–568
Telephone Book 238
Tell Me a Mitzi 561–563, *562*
Tenggren, Gustaf 279, **281–283**, 290
Tenggren's Story Book 289
Terrible Terrifying Toby 440–441, *441*
Thacher, Edith. *See* Hurd, Edith Thacher
Thanksgiving Story 59, **86–87**, *87*, 353
Thank-you Book 53
Theodore's Parents 472
These United States: And How They Came To Be 92
They All Saw It **109–110**, *109–110*, 225, 255
They Put Out to Sea 134
They Were Strong and Good 146–147, *146*
Thidwick the Big-Hearted Moose 306, *306*
Things Around the House 389
Thinking Book 361–362, *361*
36 Children 368
This Is the Way the Animals Walk 230, 285
Thompson, Stith, quoted 416, 566
Three and the Moon *191*, **192**, 197
Three Bears (Rojankovsky, illus.) 297–298, *298*
Three Bears (Tolstoi-Vasnetzov) 297–298, *297*
Three Billy Goats Gruff (Brown, illus.) 321, *321*
Three Japanese Mice and Their Whiskers 59
Three Kings of Saba 86
Three Little Animals 217, **261–262**, *262*, 494
Three Little Kittens (Wiese, illus.) *28*, 29, 65
Three Little Pigs 203, 278
Three Policemen (1938) 175, **176**, *177*, 221
Three Policemen (1960) *181*, **182**, 183
Three Robbers 548
Three Sillies 565, **566–567**, *567*, 570
Three Sneezes 134
Three Strong Women 451, *451*
Three Tall Tales 86
Throw a Kiss, Harry 490–492, *490–491*
Thumbelina (Holiday House ed.) 214, *214*
Thurber, James 173, 252, 483, 485
Tico-Tico 111
Tikki Tikki Tembo 455, 456–458, *457*
Tim Tadpole and the Great Bullfrog 63, *64*
Tim to the Rescue 495
Time for Sleep 388
Time for Spring 441–442
Time magazine 187, 193
Time of Wonder 157
Timid Ghost 273, *276*
Timid Timothy 230
Timmy and the Tin-Can Telephone 403
Tin Fiddle 498
Tiny Animal Stories 292, 294
Tiny Nonsense Stories 72, **292–294**, *293–294*
Title I, Elementary and Secondary Education Act (1965) 372
Tito's Hats 268, *269*
Toba Sojo 443, 446
Tobe 375–376, *376*, 377
Tolmer 52, 118
Tom Thumb (Gentry-Holiday House ed.) 212–214 *passim*, *214*
Tommy Learns to Fly 399–400, *401*
Tommy's Wonderful Rides *284*, 285
Too Much Nose 565, 568, **569–570**, *569*
Tooky 158
Tootle 283, *283*
Topsy Turvy Circus 278, 279
Town 221–222, *221*
Townsend, Charles 375
Towsley, Lena 103
Toy books (books as toys) 238–240
Toy-books 3, 6, 8, 280
Trager, Helen, quoted 374
Train Book 108
Train Ride 382
Train to Timbuktoo 285
Tranquilina's Paradise 47
Travelers All 385
Travels of Ching 175
Travels with a Donkey 133
Treasure Trove of the Sun 299
Tree Angel 532, **533**
Tree in the Trail 411
Tree Is Nice **470–472**, *471*, 477, 494, 498
Treeless Plains 149, *149*
Tresselt, Alvin ***133–134***, 139, 229, 330, 390
Tricks of Master Dabble 565
Tripp, Edward 498
Tschichold, Jan 355, 356
Tsihnahjinnie, Van 162
Tsireh, Awa 160, 165
Tubman, Harriet 381, 382
Tucci, Niccolo 111
Twenty-One Balloons 170
Two Funny Clowns 29, *29*
Two Is a Team 404
Two Little Bears 111
Two Little Gardeners 286–288, *287*
Two Little Miners 217
Two Little Trains 217, **270–273**, *274–275*
Two Reds 333–337, *334–335*, 358, 364
Typography 354–359 *passim*

U

Uchida, Yoshika 44, 450, 452
Udry, Janice 471–472
Ugly Bird 485
Ugly Duckling (Hader, illus.) 29, *29*
Umbrella **449–450**, *450*, 452, 525
Uncle Remus collections 10, 252, 373
Uncle Tom's Cabin (Daugherty, illus.) 151
Under the Window 3–4, *4*
Ungerer, Tomi 494, **544–552**
University of North Carolina Press 376
Unstrung Harp 553
Up Above and Down Below 383–385, *384–385*
Up the Mountain 127
Updike, Daniel Berkeley 355
Uptown 382
Utter Zoo 555

V

Valens, E. D. 106
Van Gogh, Vincent 445, 446
Van Stockum, Hilda 47
Varner, Velma 443
Vaughan, Eleanor 399
Velveteen Rabbit 25, 60
Verotchka's Tales 187
Very Far Away 506–508, *507*
Very Little Dog 233–234, *233*
Very Special Badgers 451
Very Special House 356, 361, **428–430**, *428–429*, 436, 478, 495, 497
Vieilles Chancons et Rondes 4
Viking, 38, **198**
Village Tree 444, 446
Volland P. F. & Co. 158
Voyages et Glorieuses Découvertes . . . **118**, *119*, 120
Voyages of Jacques Cartier **120–122**, *122–123*, 188, 189

W

Waber, Bernard **480–483**, 548
Wait for the Sunshine 390
Wait for William 63

Wait Till the Moon Is Full **260–261,** *264,* 372, 464, 472
Wake-Up, City! 134
Wake-Up, Farm! 134
Walker, Dugald Stewart 158
Walker in the City 478
Walt Disney's Surprise Package 289
'War on Poverty' 368, 372
Ward, Lynd 83, 152, 424; quoted 189, 413
Warm Earth 91, **383,** *383–384*
Wartik, Herschel 389
Washburne, Carlton 97, 161
Watson, Aldren 402
Waugh, Dorothy **90–91,** 130, **383**
Wave, The **453–455,** *455,* 458
Way It Spozed to Be 368
Way of an Ant 453
Weaver, A. V. 373
Webber, Irma **383–387,** 390, **394**
Wedding Procession of the Rag Doll . . . 559–561, *560–561*
Wee Gillis 140
Wee Men of Ballywooden 145
Weed Is a Flower 381, 404
Weisgard, Leonard 217, **224–230, 237,** 239–240, 248, 255, 282, **290–292** *passim*
Wells, Carolyn 311
Welter, Matilda 405
Welty, Eudora, quoted 3
Wenz-Vietor, Else 30
Werneck, Paulo 47
Western Printing Co. 126, 127, 278, 295, 413
Weston, Edward 100
Wexler, Jerome 117
What Can You Do With a Shoe? 497, *497*
What Do You Do, Dear? 497
What Do You Say, Dear? 497
What Happens to a Hamburger 403
What Makes Day and Night 402
What Makes the Wheels Go Round 89, *90*
What the Moon Is Like 402
What Whiskers Did 539–540, *540*
What's In a Line? 358, **397,** *398*
What's Inside? **112–113,** *113–114,* 114
What's Inside of Animals? 389
What's Inside of Engines? 389
What's Inside of Me? 388–389, *389*
What's Inside of Plants? 388
What's Inside the Earth? 389
Wheel on the School 495
When Clay Sings 166
When the Wind Blew 252-253
When Will the World be Mine? 275–276, 394
Where Have You Been? 264, *264*
Where Is Everybody? 359, *359,* 530, *531*
Where the Wild Things Are **511–514,** *512–513,* 518, 523
Where's My Baby 239
While Susie Sleeps 231
Whiskers of Ho Ho 329–331 *passim,* *329*
Whistle for the Train 227
Whistling-Two-Teeth **160,** *160,* 353
White, Dorothy, quoted 63, 259, 280–281, 299, 524
White, E. B. 257, 495, 563
White, Gleeson, quoted 10
White, Katherine, quoted 563
White, Stewart Edward 151
White Snow, Bright Snow 133, 134, *324,* 331
Whitey Takes a Trip 148
Whitey's First Round-Up, 148, *148*
Whitman, Albert, & Co. 126
Whitman Publishing Co. 106, 126, 127
Who Wants To Be a Prairie Dog 161
Who's Upside Down? 394, **434–435,** *435*
Why Johnny Can't Read 499
Why the Sun and the Moon Live in the Sky 455, 458
Why We Have Day and Night 555, 556
Widget 242
Wiese, Kurt **27–29,** 31, 50, **57,** 61, **65–69, 93,** 99, 148, 198, 237, 451
Wild Horses of the Desert *150,* 151
Wilder, Alec 518
Wilkin, Eloise Burns 80, 282, **285**
Williams, Garth **257–258, 262–263,** 282, **288, 292–294** *passim,* 466, **472–473,** 494, 495
Williams, Jay 565
Wilson, Edmund, quoted 553, 554
Windmill Books 382
Window into an Egg 117
Wing on a Flea 401
Winnie-the-Pooh 249
Winter Noisy Book 225
Wolfenstein, Martha, quoted 460–463, 464
Wonder City 76
Wonder Clock 141
Wonder Smith and His Son 187
Wonderful Farm 424, 495
Wonderful Feast 235
Wonderful Locomotive 29, *29*
Wonderful Story Book 285, 289
Wondriska, William 359–361
Wood, Grant 140
Wood, Harrie 104
Woodcock, Louise 230, 285
Woodcuts 322, 343
Wordless picturebooks 83, 517, 539–543 *passim*
World in the Candy Egg 330
World Is Round 221, 222–224, *223,* 235
World Publishing Co. 346, 443
World We Live In 92
Wright, Wendell 346
Writers' Laboratory, Bank Street 215, 221, 222, 377, 416
Wu and Lu and Li 57–58, *58*
Wuggly Ump *551,* 555

Y

Yale School of Design 361
Yamaguchi, Marianne 450
Yamaguchi, Tohr 450
Yankee Doodle's Cousins 157
Yashima, Mitsu 446
Yashima, Taro 198, 443, **444–450**
Ylla (Ylla Koffler) **108–111,** 225, 255
"You Look Ridiculous" Said the Rhinocerous . . . 480
Young, Ella 187
Young, Evelyn 57–58
Your Skin and Mine 403–404, *404*

Z

Zaffo, George 414–415
Zemach, Harve 565–572 *passim*
Zemach, Margot, 544, **565–572**
Zim, Herbert **388–389,** 390, 391
Zion, Gene **466–470,** 483, 494
Zlateh the Goat 518
Zolotow, Charlotte **246–248,** 299, 331, **464–466,** 478, 494, **498–499,** 506

PERMISSION ACKNOWLEDGMENTS

ADDISON-WESLEY PUBLISHING CO.
149–151. *What's Inside?* by May Garelick, photos by Rena Jakobsen
152, 153. *Is It Hard?* by Mary McBurney Green, photos by Len Gittleman
282–285. *The Little Fireman* by Margaret Wise Brown, illustrated by Esphyr Slobodkina
289. *The World Is Round* by Gertrude Stein, illustrated by Clement Hurd
298. *Nothing but Cats, Cats, Cats* by Grace Skaar
299. *The Very Little Dog* by Grace Skaar
300. *Caps for Sale* by Esphyr Slobodkina
338, 339. *A Child's Good Night* by Margaret Wise Brown, illustrated by Jean Charlot
340–343. *Two Little Trains* by Margaret Wise Brown, illustrated by Jean Charlot
344, 345. *A Hero by Mistake* by Anita Brenner, illustrated by Jean Charlot
346. *The Timid Ghost* by Anita Brenner, illustrated by Jean Charlot
425. *Where Is Everybody?* by Remy Charlip
452–454. *Up Above & Down Below* by Irma E. Webber
457. *All About Eggs* by Millicent Selsam, illustrated by Helen Ludwig
460. *Let's Find Out* by Herman and Nina Schneider, illustrated by Jeanne Bendick
461, 462. *Now Try This to Move a Heavy Load* by Herman and Nina Schneider, illustrated by Bill Ballantine
463. *Let's Look Under the City* by Herman and Nina Schneider, illustrated by Bill Ballantine
464. *How Big Is Big?* by Herman and Nina Schneider, illustrated by Symeon Shimin
466, 467. *Fast Is Not a Ladybug* by Miriam Schlein, illustrated by Leonard Kessler
468. *Heavy Is a Hippopotamus* by Miriam Schlein, illustrated by Leonard Kessler
614. *Where Is Everybody?* by Remy Charlip
615. *Four Fur Feet* by Margaret Wise Brown, illustrated by Remy Charlip
647. *Why We Have Day and Night* by Peter F. Neumeyer, illustrated by Edward Gorey
648. *The Jumblies* by Edward Lear, illustrated by Edward Gorey
649. *The Dong with a Luminous Nose* by Edward Lear, illustrated by Edward Gorey

ARTS ET MÉTIERS GRAPHIQUES
146. *The Little Lion* by Jacques Prévert, photos by Ylla, published by Arts et Métiers Graphiques, Paris, by whose permission the text is reprinted

ASSOCIATION FOR THE STUDY OF NEGRO LIFE AND HISTORY, INC.
445. *My Happy Days* by Jane Dabney Shackleford, photos by Cecil Vinson, Copyrighted 1944 by The Associated Publishers, Inc.

ASTOR-HONOR, INC.
610, 611. *Little Blue and Little Yellow* by Leo Lionni
612, 613. *Inch by Inch* by Leo Lionni

ATHENEUM PUBLISHERS
626, 627. *Nothing Ever Happens On My Block*, Copyright © 1966 by Ellen Raskin

ESTHER AVERILL
161. *Daniel Boone* by Esther Averill and Lila Stanley, illustrated by Feodor Rojankovsky

PEGGY BACON
26. *The Ballad of Tangle Street* by Peggy Bacon

ERICK BERRY BEST
70. *Penny-Whistle* by Erick Berry

THE BODLEY HEAD
447. *The Snowy Day* by Ezra Jack Keats
544. *Dear Garbage Man* by Gene Zion, illustrated by Margaret Bloy Graham
545, 546. *Harry the Dirty Dog* by Gene Zion, illustrated by Margaret Bloy Graham
578. *Mr. Rabbit and the Lovely Present* by Charlotte Zolotow, illustrated by Maurice Sendak
588, 589. *The Sign on Rosie's Door* by Maurice Sendak
596–599. *Where the Wild Things Are* by Maurice Sendak
602–604. *Hector Protector and As I Went Over the Water*, illustrated by Maurice Sendak
605–607. *In the Night Kitchen* by Maurice Sendak
632. *Rosie's Walk* by Pat Hutchins
633. *Changes, Changes* by Pat Hutchins

THE CARDAVON PRESS, INC. AVON, CONN.
173. *Mother Goose* illustrated by Roger Duvoisin for the Heritage Press edition, Copyright © 1936, 1964

JEAN CHARLOT
336, 337. *Tito's Hats* by Melchor Ferrer, illustrated by Jean Charlot. Text Copyright 1940 by Melchor G. Ferrer; pictures Copyright 1940 by Jean Charlot

CHILDRENS PRESS
200. *The Boll Weevil* by Glen Rounds, published by Golden Gate Junior Books Department, Childrens Press, Chicago

WILLIAM COLLINS SONS & CO., LTD.
590. The Nutshell Library Box; 591, *Alligators All Around*; 592, *One Was Johnny*; 593, *Chicken Soup with Rice*—all by Maurice Sendak

COWARD, McCANN & GEOGHEGAN, INC.
36. *Millions of Cats* by Wanda Gág, Copyright 1928 by Coward, McCann, Inc.

38. *The Funny Thing* by Wanda Gág, Copyright 1929 by Coward, McCann, Inc.
39, 40. *Snippy and Snappy* by Wanda Gág, Copyright 1931 by Wanda Gág
41. *The ABC Bunny* by Wanda Gág, Copyright 1933 by Wanda Gág
42. *Gone Is Gone* by Wanda Gág, Copyright 1935 by Wanda Gág
43. *Tales from Grimm* by Wanda Gág, Copyright 1936 by Wanda Gág
87–92. *The Five Chinese Brothers* by Claire Huchet Bishop, illustrated by Kurt Wiese; text Copyright 1938 by Claire Huchet Bishop; illustrations Copyright 1938 by Kurt Wiese

THOMAS Y. CROWELL CO., INC.
332. *Where Have You Been?* by Margaret Wise Brown, illustrated by Barbara Cooney, illustrations Copyright © 1952 by Barbara Cooney
438. *My Dog Is Lost!* by Ezra Jack Keats and Pat Cherr, Copyright © 1960 by Thomas Y. Crowell Company, Inc.
471–473. *Mickey's Magnet* by Franklyn M. Branley and Eleanor K. Vaughan, illustrations Copyright © 1956 by Crockett Johnson
474, 475, *Tommy Learns to Fly* by John Lewellen, illustrated by Leonard Kessler, illustrations Copyright © 1956 by Leonard Kessler
476, 477. *The Moon Seems to Change* by Franklyn M. Branley, illustrated by Helen Borten, illustrations Copyright © 1960 by Helen Borten
478, 479. *Your Skin and Mine* by Paul Showers, illustrated by Paul Galdone, illustrations Copyright © 1965 by Paul Galdone
480. *My Visit to the Dinosaurs* by Aliki, Copyright © 1969 by Aliki Brandenberg
481. *Fireflies in the Night* by Judy Hawes, illustrated by Kazue Mizumura, illustrations Copyright © 1963 by Kazue Mizumura
482, 483. *Bees and Beelines* by Judy Hawes, illustrated by Aliki, illustrations Copyright © 1964 by Aliki Brandenberg
484–486. *Shrimps* by Judy Hawes, illustrated by Joseph Low, illustrations Copyright © 1966 by Joseph Low

SARAH D'HARNONCOURT
93. *The Hole in the Wall* by René d'Harnoncourt

DELACORTE PRESS
327. *The Chicken Book* by Garth Williams, Copyright © 1946, 1969 by Garth Williams
629, 630. *The Journeys of Sebastian* by Fernando Krahn, Copyright © 1968 by Fernando Krahn, published by Seymour Lawrence/Delacorte Press
631. *How Santa Claus Had a Long and Difficult Journey Delivering His Presents* by Fernando Krahn, Copyright © 1970 by Fernando Krahn, published by Seymour Lawrence/Delacorte Press

LUCIENNE BLOCH DIMITROFF
297. *How Many Kisses Good Night* by Jean Monrad, illustrated by Lucienne Bloch

WALT DISNEY PRODUCTIONS
581. *The Art of Walt Disney* by Robert D. Feild; © Walt Disney Productions

DOUBLEDAY & CO., INC.
12. *Carlo* by A. B. Frost, Copyright 1913 by Doubleday & Co., Inc.
24. *ABC Book* by C. B. Falls, Copyright 1923 by Doubleday & Company, Inc.
45. *Miki* by Maud and Miska Petersham, Copyright 1929 by Doubleday & Company, Inc.
50–52. *Ola* by Ingri and Edgar Parin d'Aulaire, Copyright 1936 by Doubleday & Company, Inc.
55. *George Washington* by Ingri and Edgar Parin d'Aulaire, Copyright 1936 by Doubleday & Company, Inc.
78–81. *Angus and the Ducks* by Marjorie Flack, Copyright 1930 by Marjorie Flack Larsson
82. *Angus and the Cat* by Marjorie Flack, Copyright 1931 by Marjorie Flack Larsson
83. *Tim Tadpole and the Great Bullfrog* by Marjorie Flack, Copyright 1934 by Marjorie Flack Larsson
84, 85. *Liang and Lo* by Kurt Wiese, Copyright 1930 by Kurt Wiese
98, 99. *The Little Family* by Lois Lenski, Copyright 1932 by Lois Lenski
132–134. *Let's Go Outdoors* by Harriet E. Huntington, photos by Preston Duncan, Copyright 1939 by Doubleday & Company, Inc.
293. *Red Light Green Light* by Margaret Wise Brown, illustrated by Leonard Weisgard, Copyright 1944 by Doubleday & Company, Inc.
434. *Rosa-Too-Little* by Sue Felt, Copyright 1950 by Sue Felt
645. *The Doubtful Guest* by Edward Gorey, Copyright © 1957 by Edward Gorey

ROGER DUVOISIN
171, 172. *Donkey-Donkey* by Roger Duvoisin

FABER AND FABER LTD.
224. *In the Forest* by Marie Hall Ets

FARRAR, STRAUS & GIROUX, INC.
76. *Clever Bill* by William Nicholson; all rights reserved
77. *The Pirate Twins* by William Nicholson; all rights reserved
643, 644. *The Beast of Monsieur Racine* by Tomi Ungerer, Copyright © 1971 by Tomi Ungerer
654. *Tell Me a Mitzi* by Lore Segal, illustrated by Harriet Pincus, Text Copyright © 1970 by Lore Segal, illustrations Copyright © 1970 by Harriet Pincus
656. *Amos & Boris* by William Steig, Copyright © 1971 by William Steig
661, 662. *The Judge* by Harve Zemach, illustrated by Margot Zemach, Text Copyright © 1969 by Harve Zemach, Pictures Copyright © 1969 by Margot Zemach
663. *A Penny a Look* adapted by Harve Zemach, illustrated by Margot Zemach, Text Copyright © 1971 by Harve Zemach, Pictures Copyright © 1971 by Margot Zemach

LIBRAIRIE ERNEST FLAMMARION
(PÈRE CASTOR-FLAMMARION, PARIS)
165. Panache l'Écureuil by Lida, illustrated by Feodor Rojankovsky
166. Quipic le Hérisson by Lida, illustrated by Feodor Rojankovsky

167. Calendrier des Enfants by Y. Lacôte, illustrated by Feodor Rojankovsky
168. *Cigalou* by Marie Colmont, illustrated by Feodor Rojankovsky
169. *The Picture Play Book* by Rose Celli, illustrated by Nathalie Parain

DON FREEMAN
267. *Newsstand* by Don Freeman (Volume II, No. 3, January, 1940)

ELAINE GREEN LTD.
62, 63, *Madeline*, Copyright 1939 by Ludwig Bemelmans, renewed © 1967 by Mrs. Madeleine Bemelmans and Mrs. Barbara Bemelmans Marciano

WILLIAM GROPPER
435–437. *The Little Tailor* by William Gropper

GROSSET & DUNLAP, INC.
493. *The Big Book of Real Trains* by George Zaffo, Copyright 1949 by George Zaffo

BERTA AND ELMER HADER
29. *Two Funny Clowns* by Berta and Elmer Hader

HAMISH HAMILTON LTD.
192, 193. *The Story of Ferdinand* by Munro Leaf, illustrated by Robert Lawson, Copyright 1936 by Munro Leaf and Robert Lawson, renewed © 1964 by Munro Leaf and John W. Boyd

HARCOURT BRACE JOVANOVICH, INC.
391. *The Three Billy Goats Gruff*, taken from the translation by G. W. Dasent, illustrations © 1957 by Marcia Brown
400–403. *The Two Reds* by Will and Nicolas, Copyright 1950 by William Lipkind and Nicolas Mordvinoff
404. *Alphonse, That Bearded One* by Natalie Savage Carlson, illustrated by Nicolas Mordvinoff, Copyright 1954 by Harcourt Brace Jovanovich, Inc.
405–409. *Sparkle and Spin* © 1957 by Ann and Paul Rand
410–412. *See and Say, A Picture Book in Four Languages*, Copyright © 1955 by Antonio Frasconi
413. *The House That Jack Built, A Picture Book in Two Languages*, illustrations © 1958 by Antonio Frasconi; French translation © 1958 by Harcourt Brace Jovanovich, Inc.
561. *All Kinds of Time*, Copyright 1950 by Harry Behn
652, 653. *The Wedding Procession of the Rag Doll and the Broom Handle and Who Was in It* by Carl Sandburg, illustrated by Harriet Pincus, text Copyright 1922 by Harcourt Brace Jovanovich, Inc.; Copyright 1950 by Carl Sandburg; illustrations Copyright © 1967 by Harriet Pincus

HARPER, & ROW, PUBLISHERS, INC.
142–144. *They All Saw It* by Margaret Wise Brown, text Copyright 1944 by Harper & Brothers
145. *The Sleepy Little Lion* by Margaret Wise Brown, photos by Ylla, Copyright 1947 by Harper & Brothers
162–164. *The Voyages of Jacques Cartier* by Esther Averill, illustrated by Feodor Rojankovsky, Copyright 1937 by Harper & Brothers
290, 291. *The Noisy Book* by Margaret Wise Brown, illustrated by Leonard Weisgard, Copyright 1939 by Harper & Brothers
319. *The Park Book* by Charlotte Zolotow, illustrated by H. A. Rey, Copyright 1944 by Harper & Brothers
320. *Pretzel* by Margret Rey, illustrated by H. A. Rey, text Copyright 1944 by Margret Rey, pictures Copyright 1944 by H. A. Rey
321. *Spotty* by Margret Rey, illustrated by H. A. Rey; text Copyright 1945 by Margret Rey, pictures Copyright 1945 by H. A. Rey
322, 323. *It Looked Like Spilt Milk* by Charles G. Shaw; Copyright 1947 by Charles G. Shaw
324, 325. *The Runaway Bunny* by Margaret Wise Brown, illustrated by Clement Hurd, Copyright 1942 by Harper & Brothers
326. *Little Fur Family* by Margaret Wise Brown, illustrated by Garth Williams; text Copyright 1946 by Margaret Wise Brown, pictures Copyright 1946 by Garth Williams
328. *Goodnight Moon* by Margaret Wise Brown, illustrated by Clement Hurd, Copyright 1947 by Harper & Brothers
329. *Wait Till the Moon Is Full* by Margaret Wise Brown, illustrated by Garth Williams, text Copyright 1948 by Margaret Wise Brown, pictures Copyright 1948 by Garth Williams
330. *Three Little Animals* by Margaret Wise Brown, illustrated by Garth Williams, pictures copyright © 1956 by Garth Williams
428–430. *Roar and More* by Karla Kuskin, Copyright 1956 by Karla Kuskin
449. *Stevie* by John Steptoe, Copyright © 1969 by John Steptoe
494–496. *A Good Man and His Good Wife* by Ruth Krauss, illustrated by Ad Reinhardt; Copyright 1944 by Harper & Brothers
497, 498. *The Carrot Seed* by Ruth Krauss, illustrated by Crockett Johnson, Copyright 1945 by Harper & Brothers
499. *Bears* by Ruth Krauss, illustrated by Phyllis Rowand, Copyright 1948 by Ruth Krauss
500, 501. *The Happy Day* by Ruth Krauss, illustrated by Marc Simont, text Copyright 1949 by Ruth Krauss, pictures Copyright 1949 by Marc Simont
502. *The Backward Day* by Ruth Krauss, illustrated by Marc Simont, text Copyirght 1950 by Ruth Krauss, pictures Copyright 1950 by Marc Simont
503–505. *A Hole Is To Dig* by Ruth Krauss, illustrated by Maurice Sendak, text Copyright 1952 by Ruth Krauss, pictures Copyright 1952 by Maurice Sendak
506–509. *A Very Special House* by Ruth Krauss, illustrated by Maurice Sendak, text Copyright 1953 by Ruth Krauss, pictures Copyright 1953 by Maurice Sendak
510–512. *I'll Be You and You Be Me* by Ruth Krauss, illustrated by Maurice Sendak, text Copyright 1954 by Ruth Krauss, pictures Copyright 1954 by Maurice Sendak
513. *Charlotte and the White Horse* by Ruth Krauss, illustrated by Maurice Sendak; text Copyright 1955 by Ruth Krauss, pictures Copyright 1955 by Maurice Sendak
519, 520. *Harold and the Purple Crayon* by Crockett Johnson, Copyright © 1955 by Crockett Johnson

542. *The Storm Book* by Charlotte Zolotow, illustrated by Margaret Bloy Graham, text Copyright 1952 by Charlotte Zolotow, pictures Copyright 1952 by Margaret Bloy Graham
543. *Really Spring,* by Gene Zion, illustrated by Margaret Bloy Graham, text Copyright © 1956 by Eugene Zion, pictures Copyright © 1956 by Margaret Bloy Graham
544. *Dear Garbage Man* by Gene Zion, illustrated by Margaret Bloy Graham, text Copyright © 1957 by Eugene Zion, pictures Copyright © 1957 by Margaret Bloy Graham
545, 546. *Harry the Dirty Dog* by Gene Zion, illustrated by Margaret Bloy Graham, text Copyright © 1956 by Eugene Zion, pictures Copyright © 1956 by Margaret Bloy Graham
547. *A Tree Is Nice* by Janice May Udry, illustrated by Marc Simont, Copyright © 1956 by Janice May Udry, pictures Copyright © 1956 by Marc Simont
548. *Bedtime for Frances* by Russell Hoban, illustrated by Garth Williams, text Copyright © 1960 by Russell Hoban, pictures Copyright © 1960 by Garth Williams
549. *Herman the Loser* by Russell Hoban, illustrated by Lillian Hoban, text Copyright © 1961 by Russell Hoban, pictures Copyright © 1961 by Lillian Hoban
550. *A Baby Sister for Frances* by Russell Hoban, illustrated by Lillian Hoban, text Copyright © 1964 by Russell Hoban, pictures Copyright © 1964 by Lillian Hoban
551. *Bread and Jam for Frances* by Russell Hoban, illustrated by Lillian Hoban, text Copyright © 1964 by Russell Hoban, pictures Copyright © 1964 by Lillian Hoban
562. *Come for a Walk with Me* by Mary Chalmers, Copyright © 1955 by Mary Chalmers
563–565. *George Appleton* by Mary Chalmers, Copyright © 1957 by Mary Chalmers
566–572. *Throw a Kiss, Harry* by Mary Chalmers, Copyright © 1958 by Mary Chalmers
573. *Cheerful* by Palmer Brown, Copyright © 1957 by Palmer Brown
574. *Something for Christmas* by Palmer Brown, Copyright © 1958 by Palmer Brown
576. *What Can You Do With a Shoe?* by Beatrice Schenk de Regniers, illustrated by Maurice Sendak, pictures Copyright © 1955 by Maurice Sendak
577. *The Moon Jumpers* by Janice May Udry, illustrated by Maurice Sendak, pictures Copyright © 1959 by Maurice Sendak
578. *Mr. Rabbit and the Lovely Present* by Charlotte Zolotow, illustrated by Maurice Sendak, pictures Copyright © 1962 by Maurice Sendak
579, 580. *Little Bear* by Else Holmelund Minarik, illustrated by Maurice Sendak, text Copyright © 1957 by Else Holmelund Minarik, pictures Copyright © 1957 by Maurice Sendak
582. *Father Bear Comes Home* by Else Holmelund Minarik, illustrated by Maurice Sendak, text Copyright © 1959 by Else Holmelund Minarik, pictures Copyright © 1959 by Maurice Sendak
583. *Little Bear's Visit* by Else Holmelund Minarik, illustrated by Maurice Sendak, text Copyright © 1961 by Else Holmelund Minarik, pictures Copyright © 1961 by Maurice Sendak
584. *Little Bear's Friend* by Else Holmelund Minarik, illustrated by Maurice Sendak, text Copyright © 1960 by Else Holmelund Minarik, illustrated by Maurice Sendak, pictures Copyright © 1960 by Maurice Sendak
585. *A Kiss for Little Bear* by Else Holmelund Minarik, illustrated by Maurice Sendak, text Copyright © 1968 by Else Holmelund Minarik, pictures Copyright © 1968 by Maurice Sendak
586. *Kenny's Window* by Maurice Sendak, Copyright © 1956 by Maurice Sendak
587. *Very Far Away* by Maurice Sendak, Copyright © 1956 by Maurice Sendak
588, 589. *The Sign on Rosie's Door* by Maurice Sendak, Copyright © 1960 by Maurice Sendak
590–595. The Nutshell Library—*Alligators All Around, One Was Johnny, Chicken Soup with Rice, Pierre*—all Copyright © 1962 by Maurice Sendak
596–599. *Where the Wild Things Are* by Maurice Sendak, Copyright © 1963 by Maurice Sendak
602–604. *Hector Protector* by Maurice Sendak, Copyright © 1965 by Maurice Sendak
605–607. *In the Night Kitchen* by Maurice Sendak, Copyright © 1970 by Maurice Sendak
634, 635. *The Mellops Go Flying* by Tomi Ungerer, Copyright © 1957 by Tomi Ungerer
636. *Crictor* by Tomi Ungerer, Copyright © 1958 by Tomi Ungerer
637–640. *Emile* by Tomi Ungerer, Copyright © 1960 by Tomi Ungerer
641, 642. *Moon Man* by Tomi Ungerer, Copyright © 1967 by Tomi Ungerer

A. M. HEATH & CO., LTD. AND THE ESTATE OF WILLIAM NICHOLSON
76. *Clever Bill* by William Nicholson
77. *The Pirate Twins* by William Nicholson

WILLIAM HEINEMANN LTD. AND THE ESTATE OF WILLIAM NICHOLSON
23. *The Square Book of Animals* by Arthur Waugh, illustrated by William Nicholson

PATRICIA C. HILL
107, 108. *ABC for Every Day* by Helen Sewell
109–112. *A Head for Happy* by Helen Sewell
113. *Ming and Mehitable* by Helen Sewell
115. *Jimmy and Jemima* by Helen Sewell

HOLIDAY HOUSE, INC.
196, 197. *Whitey's First Roundup* by Glen Rounds
198, 199, *The Treeless Plains* by Glen Rounds
201. *Wild Horses of the Red Desert* by Glen Rounds
202. *Once We Had a Horse* by Glen Rounds
279. "A Was an Archer" by Valenti Angelo
280. *The History of Tom Thumb,* illustrated by Hilda Scott
281. *Thumbelina* by Hans Christian Andersen, illustrated by Hilda Scott
304. *Cloth Book No. 1* by Leonard Weisgard
368–371. *I Play at the Beach* by Dorothy Koch, illustrated by Feodor Rojankovsky
552. 553. *Rain Makes Applesauce* by Julian Scheer, illustrated by Marvin Bileck
650, 651. *The Shrinking of Treehorn* by Florence Parry Heide, illustrated by Edward Gorey

HOLT, RINEHART AND WINSTON, INC.
71. *One Day with Manu* by Armstrong Sperry, Copyright 1933 by Armstrong Sperry
97. *The Story of a Little White Teddy Bear Who Didn't Want to Go to Bed,* Copyright 1931 © 1959 by Dorothy Sherrill
121, 122. *Among the Leaves and Grasses* by Dorothy Waugh. All rights reserved
527. *The New Sun* written and illustrated by Taro Yashima, Copyright 1943 by Holt, Rinehart and Winston, Inc., Copyright © 1971 by Taro Yashima
528, 529. *Horizon Is Calling* written and illustrated by Taro Yashima, Copyright 1947 by Holt, Rinehart and Winston, Inc.
539, 540. *Tikki Tikki Tembo* retold by Arlene Mosel, illustrated by Blair Lent, Copyright © 1968 by Arlene Mosel, Copright © 1968 by Blair Lent, Jr.
657. *The Three Sillies* written and illustrated by Margot Zemach, Copyright © 1963 by Margot Zemach
659, 660. *Too Much Nose* adapted by Harve Zemach, illustrated by Margot Zemach, Copyright © 1967 by Harve Zemach, Copyright © 1967 by Margot Zemach

HOUGHTON MIFFLIN CO.
15. *The Land of Little Rain* by Mary Austin, illustrated by E. Boyd Smith
16. *The Story of Noah's Ark* by E. Boyd Smith
17. *The Story of Pocahontas and Captain John Smith* by E. Boyd Smith
19. *The Farm Book* by E. Boyd Smith
20. *The Railroad Book* by E. Boyd Smith
256, 257. *Mike Mulligan and His Steam Shovel* by Virginia Lee Burton
258, 259. *The Little House* by Virginia Lee Burton
261. *Song of Robin Hood* edited by Anne Malcolmson, illustrated by Virginia Lee Burton
265, 266. *Curious George* by H. A. Rey
274. *Chester the Worldly Pig* by Bill Peet
275. *Kermit the Hermit* by Bill Peet
276–278. *Buford the Little Bighorn* by Bill Peet
393. *The Country Bunny and the Little Gold Shoes* by DuBose Heyward, illustrated by Marjorie Flack
416, 417. *Smiling Duke* by Joseph Low
420, 421. *Five Little Monkeys* by Juliet Kepes
422. *The Seven Remarkable Bears* by Emilie McLeod, illustrated by Juliet Kepes
489. *Paddle-to-the-Sea* by Holling Clancy Holling
537. *The Wave* adapted by Margaret Hodges, illustrated by Blair Lent
538. *The Little Match Girl* by Hans Christian Andersen, illustrated by Blair Lent
554, 555. *The House on East 88th Street* by Bernard Waber
556. *Lyle and the Birthday Party* by Bernard Waber
557. *Just Like Abraham Lincoln* by Bernard Waber
558–560. *An Anteater Named Arthur* by Bernard Waber

CLEMENT HURD
286. *Bumblebugs and Elephants* by Margaret Wise Brown, illustrated by Clement Hurd
288. *Town* by Clement Hurd

INTERNATIONAL FAMOUS AGENCY
61. *The Castle Number Nine* by Ludwig Bemelmans

CROCKETT JOHNSON
515. *Who's Upside Down?* Copyright © 1952 by Crockett Johnson; published 1969 by Albert Whitman & Co. as *Upside Down,* Copyright © 1969 by Crockett Johnson
516–518. *Merry Go Round,* Copyright © 1958 by Crockett Johnson
521. *Harold at the North Pole,* Copyright © 1958 by Crockett Johnson
522. *Harold's Circus,* Copyright © 1959 by Crockett Johnson
523. *Harold's ABC,* Copyright © 1963 by Crockett Johnson
524. *Terrible Terrifying Toby,* Copyright © 1957 by Crockett Johnson
525. *Ellen's Lion,* Copyright © 1959 by Crockett Johnson

LEONARD H. KESSLER
469, 470. *What's In a Line?* by Leonard Kessler

DOROTHY M. KUNHARDT
95, 96. *Now Open the Box* by Dorothy Kunhardt

LOIS LENSKI
301. *Sing a Song of Sixpence* by Lois Lenski

J. B. LIPPINCOTT CO.
18. *Santa Claus and All About Him,* Copyright 1908 by E. Boyd Smith; renewal 1936 by E. Boyd Smith
432, 433. *Little Boy Brown* by Isobel Harris, illustrated by André François, Copyright 1949 by Isobel Harris and André François
646. *The Wuggly Ump* by Edward Gorey, Copyright © 1963 by Edward Gorey

LITTLE BROWN & CO.
195. *Ben and Me* by Robert Lawson
431. *The Thinking Book* by Sandol Stoddard Warburg, illustrated by Ivan Chermayeff, Copyright © 1960

MACMILLAN PUBLISHING CO., INC.
27. *The Bremen Band* illustrated by Frank Dobias, Copyright 1927 by Macmillan Publishing Co., Inc.
28. *The Three Little Kittens* illustrated by Kurt Wiese, Copyright 1928 by Macmillan Publishing Co., Inc.
30. *The Ugly Duckling* illustrated by Berta and Elmer Hader, Copyright 1927 by Macmillan Publishing Co., Inc.
31. *The Wonderful Locomotive* by Cornelia Meigs, illustrated by Berta and Elmer Hader, Copyright 1928 by Macmillan Publishing Co., Inc.
32–34. *The Golden Goose* illustrated by Mary Lott Seaman, Copyright 1928 by Macmillan Publishing Co., Inc.
44. *In Animal Land* by Mabel Guinnip La Rue, illustrated by Maud and Miska Petersham, Copyright 1927 by Macmillan Publishing Co., Inc.
48. *The Box with Red Wheels* by Maud and Miska Petersham, Copyright 1949 by Macmillan Publishing Co., Inc.
49. *The Circus Baby* by Maud and Miska Petersham, Copyright 1950 by Macmillan Publishing Co., Inc.

104. *The Little Wooden Farmer* by Alice Dalgliesh, illustrated by Margaret Baumeister, Copyright 1930 by Macmillan Publishing Co., Inc.
105, 106. *The Choosing Book* by Alice Dalgliesh, illustrated by Eloise Burns Wilkin, Copyright 1932 by Macmillan Publishing Co., Inc.
123. *The Delivery Men* by Charlotte Kuh, illustrated by Kurt Wiese, Copyright 1929 by Macmillan Publishing Co., Inc.
154, 155. *Shapes and Things* by Tana Hoban, Copyright © 1970 by Tana Hoban
156–159. *Look Again!* by Tana Hoban, Copyright © 1971 by Tana Hoban
440, 441. *City in the Winter* by Eleanor Schick, Copyright © 1970 by Eleanor Schick.
632. *Rosie's Walk* by Pat Hutchins, Copyright © 1968 by Pat Hutchins
633. *Changes, Changes* by Pat Hutchins, Copyright © 1971 by Pat Hutchins

McGRAW HILL BOOK CO.
185. *The Happy Lion* by Louise Fatio, illustrated by Roger Duvoisin, pictures Copyright 1954 by Roger Duvoisin
439. *Linda* by Frank Asch, Copyright © 1969 by Frank Asch
459. *All Around You* by Jeanne Bendick, Copyright 1951 by Jeanne Bendick

McINTOSH & OTIS, INC.
311, 312. *Herbert the Lion,* Copyright © 1939 by Clare Turlay Newberry, Copyright renewed
313. *Mittens,* Copyright © 1936 by Clare Turlay Newberry, Copyright renewed
314. *Babette,* Copyright © 1937 by Clare Turlay Newberry, Copyright renewed
315. *April's Kittens,* Copyright © 1940 by Clare Turlay Newberry, Copyright renewed
316–318. *Lambert's Bargain,* Copyright © 1941 by Clare Turlay Newberry, Copyright renewed

WILLIAM MORROW & CO., INC.
124. *How It All Began* by Janet Smalley, Copyright 1932 by Janet Smalley
179. *Follow the Road* by Alvin Tresselt, illustrated by Roger Duvoisin, pictures Copyright 1953 by Roger Duvoisin
182–184. *A for the Ark* by Roger Duvoisin, Copyright 1952 by Roger Duvoisin
217. *I Am a Pueblo Indian Girl* by E-Yeh-Shuré (Louise Abeita), illustrated by Allan Houser, Tony Martinez, Gerald Nailor and Quincy Tahoma, Copyright 1939 by William Morrow & Co., Inc.
294. *Rain Drop Splash* by Alvin Tresselt, illustrated by Leonard Weisgard, pictures Copyright 1946 by Leonard Weisgard
308. *Pick the Vegetables* by Esther Reno, illustrated by Leonard Weisgard, pictures Copyright 1944 by William Morrow & Co., Inc.
309. *Size One* by Loris Corcos, Copyright 1945 by Loris Corcos
395, 396. *The Easter Bunny That Overslept* by Priscilla and Otto Friedrich, illustrated by Adrienne Adams, pictures Copyright © 1957 by Adrienne Adams
397, 398. *The Whiskers of Ho Ho,* by William Littlefield, illustrated by Vladimir Bobri, Copyright © 1958 by William Morrow & Co., Inc.
458. *What's Inside of Me?* by Herbert Zim, illustrated by Herschel Wartik, Copyright 1952 by Herbert S. Zim
541. *One Step, Two Step* by Charlotte Zolotow, illustrated by Roger Duvoisin, pictures Copyright 1955 by Roger Duvoisin

THOMAS NELSON INC.
186. *Down Down the Mountain* by Ellis Credle
187. *Across the Cotton Patch* by Ellis Credle
442. *Little Jeemes Henry* by Ellis Credle

THE NEW YORKER
174. Drawing by Roger Duvoisin; Copr. © 1945 The New Yorker Magazine, Inc.

NOSTALGIA PRESS
600. "Little Nemo" by Winsor McKay, July 26, 1908

HAROLD OBER ASSOCIATES, INC.
393. *The Country Bunny and the Little Gold Shoes* by DuBose Heyward, illustrated by Marjorie Flack

PARENTS' MAGAZINE PRESS
418, 419. *The Legend of the Willow Plate* by Alvin Tresselt and Nancy Cleaver, illustrated by Joseph Low
618–621. *Fortunately* by Remy Charlip, Copyright © 1964 by Remy Charlip
622. *Mother Mother I Feel Sick Send for the Doctor Quick* by Remy Charlip and Burton Supree, pictures Copyright © 1966 by Remy Charlip
623–625. *Arm in Arm* by Remy Charlip, Copyright © 1969 by Remy Charlip

MARJORIE REAGAN PETERSHAM
125, 126. *The Story Book of Things We Use* by Maud and Miska Petersham

PHILADELPHIA MUSEUM OF ART
37. "Happiwork Box," by Wanda Cág

G. P. PUTNAM'S SONS
21, 22. *Chicken World* by E. Boyd Smith, Copyright © 1910 by E. Boyd Smith; © renewed 1938 by E. Boyd Smith
262–264. *Little Toot* by Hardie Gramatky, Copyright © 1939 by Hardie Gramatky; © renewed 1967 by Hardie Gramatky
526. *The Animal Frolic* by Toba Sojo, text by Velma Varner, Copyright 1954 by Toba Sojo

QUESTOR EDUCATION PRODUCTS CO.
487, 488. *The Book of Indians* by Holling C. Holling, copyrighted © by Platt & Munk Publishers. Portions of this book were reprinted by special permission of the publisher.

RAND McNALLY & CO.
131. *Neighbors in Space* by W. B. White, illustrated by Ruth C. Willians, Copyright 1942 as *Seeing Stars* by Rand McNally & Co.

RANDOM HOUSE, INC., PANTHEON BOOKS/A DIVISION OF RANDOM HOUSE, INC. AND ALFRED A. KNOPF, INC.
56, 57. *The Painted Pig* by Elizabeth Morrow, illustrated by René d'Harnoncourt, Copyright 1930 by René d'Harnoncourt
135. *The Tale of the Bullfrog* by Henry B. Kane, Copyright 1941 by Henry B. Kane
176–178. *Petunia* by Roger Duvoisin, Copyright 1950 by Roger Duvoisin
180. *Petunia's Christmas* by Roger Duvoisin, Copyright 1952 by Roger Duvoisin
181. *One Thousand Christmas Beards* by Roger Duvoisin, Copyright 1955 by Roger Duvoisin
248. *Three and the Moon* by Jacques Dorey, illustrated by Boris Artzybasheff, Copyright 1929 by Alfred A. Knopf, Inc.
375. *Horton Hatches the Egg* by Dr. Seuss, Copyright 1940 by Theodore Geisel
376. *Thidwick the Big-Hearted Moose* by Dr. Seuss, Copyright 1948 by Theodore Geisel
377. *Horton Hears a Who!* by Dr. Seuss, Copyright 1954 by Theodore Geisel
378. *If I Ran the Zoo* by Dr. Seuss, Copyright 1950 by Theodore Geisel
379, 380. *On Beyond Zebra!* by Dr. Seuss, Copyright 1955 by Theodore Geisel
423. *Frogs Merry* by Juliet Kepes, Copyright 1961 by Juliet Kepes
601. *Dwarf Long-Nose* by Wilhelm Hauff, translated by Doris Orgel, illustrated by Maurice Sendak, text Copyright © 1960 by Doris Orgel, pictures Copyright © 1960 by Maurice Sendak
616. *The Tree Angel* by Judith Martin and Remy Charlip, Copyright © 1962 by Judith Martin and Remy Charlip
617. *Jumping Beans* by Judith Martin, illustrated by Remy Charlip, text Copyright © 1963 by Judith Martin, pictures Copyright © 1963 by Remy Charlip
Drawing by William Steig from *Dreams of Glory*, Copyright 1952 by William Steig

RAPHO GUILLUMETTE PICTURES
146. *Le Petit Lion,* photos by Ylla, text by Jacques Prévert
147. *The Little Elephant,* photos by Ylla, text by Arthur Gregor

SALADA FOODS LTD.
94. *Junket Is Nice* by Dorothy Kunhardt

ETHEL McCULLOUGH SCOTT
302. Cottontails by Ethel McCullough, illustrated by Sister Mary Veronica

CHARLES SCRIBNER'S SONS
68, 69. *Jeanne-Marie Counts Her Sheep* by Françoise, Copyright 1951 by Françoise
75. *Little Leo* by Leo Politi, Copyright 1951 by Charles Scribner's Sons
117. *The Thanksgiving Story* by Alice Dalgliesh, illustrated by Helen Sewell, pictures Copyright 1954 by Helen Sewell
148. *The Curious Raccoons* by Lilo Hess, Copyright © 1968 by Lilo Less
170. *A Little Boy Was Drawing* by Roger Duvoisin, Copyright 1932 by Roger Duvoisin
382. *Stone Soup* by Marcia Brown, Copyright 1947 by Marcia Brown
383. *Henry-Fisherman* by Marcia Brown, Copyright 1950 by Marcia Brown
384. *Dick Whittington and His Cat* by Marcia Brown, Copyright 1950 by Marcia Brown
386–388. *Puss in Boots* by Marcia Brown, Copyright 1952 by Marcia Brown
389. *Cinderella* by Marcia Brown, Copyright 1954 by Marcia Brown
390. *The Flying Carpet* by Marcia Brown, Copyright © 1956 by Marcia Brown
392. *Once a Mouse* by Marcia Brown, Copyright © 1961 by Marcia Brown
394. *The Egg Tree* by Katherine Milhous, Copyright 1950 by Katherine Milhous

CHARLES SHAW
295, 296. *The Guess Book* by Charles Shaw

SHEED AND WARD, INC.
333. *Art-Making from Mexico to China* by Jean Charlot, Copyright 1950 by Sheed & Ward, Inc., New York
334, 335. *The Sun, the Moon and a Rabbit* by Amelia Martinez del Rio, Copyright 1935 by Sheed & Ward, Inc., New York

MARY DANA SHIPMAN
287. *Hurry Hurry* by Edith Thacher, illustrated by Mary Dana

SIMON & SCHUSTER
448. *Harriet and the Promised Land* by Jacob Lawrence
655. *Sylvester and the Magic Pebble* by William Steig

JOANNA STEICHEN
136. *The First Picture Book* by Mary Steichen Martin, photos by Edward Steichen

HELEN THURBER
Drawing by James Thurber from *The Thurber Carnival*

UNIVERSITY OF NORTH CAROLINA PRESS
443, 444. *Tobe* by Stella Gentry Sharpe, photos by Charles Farrell

VANGUARD PRESS, INC.
373. *And to Think That I Saw It on Mulberry Street* by Dr. Seuss. Copyright 1937 by Dr. Seuss, Copyright renewed 1964
374. *The 500 Hats of Bartholomew Cubhins* by Dr. Seuss, Copyright 1938 by Dr. Seuss, Copyright renewed 1965

THE VIKING PRESS
46, 47. *Miki and Mary: Their Search for Treasure* by Maud and Miska Petersham, Copyright 1934, © 1962 by Maud and Miska Petersham
53. *The Conquest of the Atlantic* by Ingri and Edgar Parin d'Aulaire, Copyright 1933 by Ingri and Edgar Parin d'Aulaire

54. *Children of the Northlights* by Ingri and Edgar Parin d'Aulaire, Copyright 1935, © 1963 by Ingri and Edgar Parin d'Aulaire
58, 59. *Hansi* by Ludwig Bemelmans, Copyright 1934, © 1962 by Ludwig Bemelmans
60. *The Golden Basket* by Ludwig Bemelmans, Copyright 1936 by Ludwig Bemelmans, renewed © 1967 by Mrs. Madeleine Bemelmans and Mrs. Barbara Bemelmans Marciano
86. *The Story about Ping* by Marjorie Flack, illustrated by Kurt Wiese, Copyright 1933 by Marjorie Flack and Kurt Wiese, renewed © 1961 by Helma Barnum and Kurt Wiese
192, 193. *The Story of Ferdinand* by Munro Leaf, illustrated by Robert Lawson, Copyright 1936 by Munro Leaf and Robert Lawson, renewed © 1964 by Munro Leaf and John W. Boyd
194. *They Were Strong and Good* by Robert Lawson, Copyright 1940 by Robert Lawson, renewed © 1968 by John W. Boyd
203–208. *Andy and the Lion* by James Daugherty, Copyright © 1966 by James Daugherty
209. *Lentil* by Robert McCloskey, Copyright 1940, © 1968 by Robert McCloskey
210. *Make Way for Ducklings* by Robert McCloskey, Copyright 1941, © 1969 by Robert McCloskey
211, 212. *Blueberries for Sal* by Robert McCloskey, Copyright 1948 by Robert McCloskey
218. *In My Mother's House* by Ann Nolan Clark, illustrated by Velino Herrara, Copyright 1941, © 1969 by Ann Nolan Clark
219. *Mister Penny* by Marie Hall Ets, Copyright 1935, © 1963 by Marie Hall Ets
220–223. *The Story of a Baby* by Marie Hall Ets, Copyright 1939, © 1967 by Marie Hall Ets
224. *In the Forest* by Marie Hall Ets, Copyright 1944, © 1972 by Marie Hall Ets
225, 226. *Little Old Automobile* by Marie Hall Ets, Copyright 1948 by Marie Hall Ets
227. *Play with Me* by Marie Hall Ets, Copyright © 1955 by Marie Hall Ets
228, 229. *Beasts and Nonsense* by Marie Hall Ets, Copyright 1952 by Marie Hall Ets
230. *Elisabeth the Cow Ghost* by William Pène du Bois, Copyright 1936, © 1963, 1964 by William Pène du Bois
231. *Giant Otto & Otto at Sea* by William Pène du Bois, Copyright 1936, © 1964 by William Pène du Bois
232, 237. *Three Policemen* by William Pène du Bois, Copyright 1938, © 1960, 1966 by William Pène du Bois
233. *The Great Geppy* by William Pène du Bois, Copyright 1940, © 1968 by William Pène du Bois
234, 235. *Lion* by William Pène du Bois, Copyright 1955, © 1956 by William Pène du Bois
236. *Otto in Africa* by William Pène du Bois, Copyright © 1961 by William Pène du Bois
238–243. *Bear Circus* by William Pène du Bois, Copyright © 1971 by William Pène du Bois
250–253. *Seven Simeons* by Boris Artzybasheff, Copyright 1937, © 1965 by Boris Artzybasheff
254, 255. *Buttons* by Tom Robinson, illustrated by Peggy Bacon, Copyright 1938 by Tom Robinson and Peggy Bacon, renewed © 1966 by Peggy Bacon and Donald F., Jack F., and Lincoln F. Robinson
268, 269. *Pet of the Met* by Lydia and Don Freeman, Copyright 1953 by Lydia and Don Freeman
270. *Beady Bear* by Don Freeman, Copyright 1954 by Don Freeman
271. *Mop Top* by Don Freeman, Copyright 1955 by Don Freeman
272, 273. *Dandelion* by Don Freeman, Copyright © 1964 by Don Freeman
446. *My Dog Rinty* by Ellen Tarry Patton and Marie Hall Ets, Copyright 1946 by Marie Hall Ets and Ellen Tarry Patton
447. *The Snowy Day* by Ezra Jack Keats, Copyright © 1962 by Ezra Jack Keats. All rights reserved.
530–533. *Crow Boy* by Taro Yashima, Copyright © 1955 by Mitsu and Taro Yashima
534. *Umbrella* by Taro Yashima, Copyright © 1958 by Taro Yashima
535. *Three Strong Women* by Claus Stamm, illustrated by Kazue Mizumura, Copyright © 1962 by Claus Stamm and Kazue Mizumura

HENRY Z. WALCK, INC.
72, 73. *Wu and Lu and Li* by Evelyn Young, Copyright 1939 by Henry Z. Walck, Inc., Copyright © renewed 1967 by Evelyn Young
74. *The Tale of Tai* by Evelyn Young, Copyright 1940 by Oxford University Press, Copyright © renewed 1968 by Evelyn Young
100. *The Little Auto* by Lois Lenski, Copyright 1934 by Lois Lenski, Copyright © renewed 1962 by Lois Lenski
101. *The Little Sail Boat* by Lois Lenski, Copyright 1937 by Lois Lenski, Copyright © renewed 1965 by Lois Lenski
102. *The Little Farm* by Lois Lenski, Copyright 1954 by Lois Lenski, Copyright © renewed 1970 by Lois Lenski
103. *Cowboy Small* by Lois Lenski, Copyright 1949 by Lois Lenski
114. *Peggy and the Pony* by Helen Sewell, Copyright 1936 by Oxford University Press, Copyright © renewed 1964 by Allan F. Ayers, Jr.
116. *Grimm's Tales,* illustrated by Helen Sewell and Madeleine Gekiere, Copyright 1954 by Oxford University Press, Inc.
450, 451. *The Warm Earth* by Dorothy Waugh, Copyright 1943 by Dorothy Waugh, Copyright © renewed 1971 by Dorothy Waugh
575. *The Little Bookroom* by Eleanor Farjeon, illustrated by Edward Ardizzone, Copyright © 1955 by Oxford University Press, Inc.
628. *What Whiskers Did* by Ruth Carroll, Copyright 1932 by The Macmillan Company, Copyright © renewed 1960 by Ruth Carroll, Copyright © 1965 by Ruth Carroll

FREDERICK WARNE & CO., INC.
6. *Johnny Crow's Garden* by L. Leslie Brooke
7. *The Tale of Peter Rabbit* by Beatrix Potter

IRMA E. WEBBER
455, 456. *Anywhere in the World* by Irma E. Webber
465. *It Looks like This* by Irma E. Webber

MARY LIDDELL WEHLE
25. *Little Machinery* by Mary Liddell